P9-ARB-535

Homework, test-prep tutorials, and assessment—made easy to manage.

my**om**lab is a text-specific, powerful online homework and assessment tool that helps students practice operations management problems and improve their understanding of course concepts. In addition, it gives instructors feedback on their students' performance. This online product lets professors assign homework that is automatically graded and also serves as a valuable tutorial experience for students.

Powerful Homework and Test Manager

Choose from the hundreds of available exercises correlated to the textbook exercises to create and manage online homework assignments and tests. Select from assignment options including time limits, mastery levels, prerequisites, and maximum number of attempts allowed.

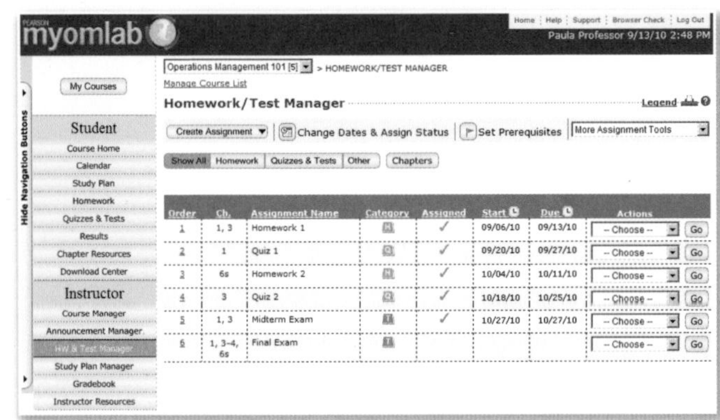

Comprehensive Gradebook

my**om**lab automatically tracks your students' results. The online gradebook provides a number of views of student data and allows for easy exporting to other gradebooks through Microsoft® Excel®.

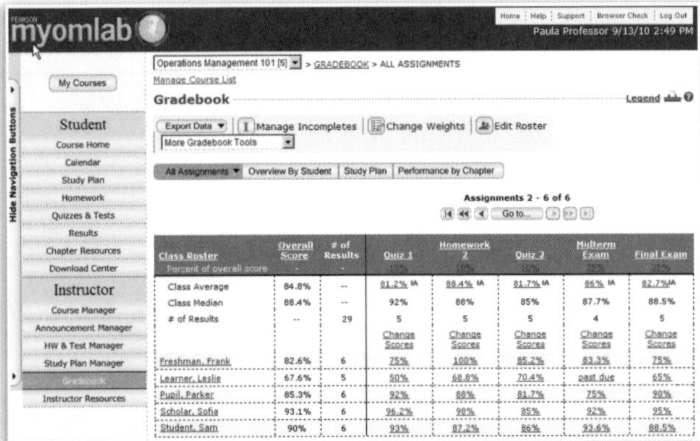

IMPROVED INSIGHT INTO LEARNING

Log in before class to see where students struggled on homework, then target instruction where it is needed.

Course Sharing Tools

You can re-apply course settings between semesters and let other instructors copy your settings, enabling you to maintain a standardized departmental syllabus. You can also easily add, remove, or modify existing course content to suit your needs.

Training and Support

Faculty training ranges from video support to live WebEx™ sessions to on-campus workshops. Toll-free tech support is available well into the evening hours.

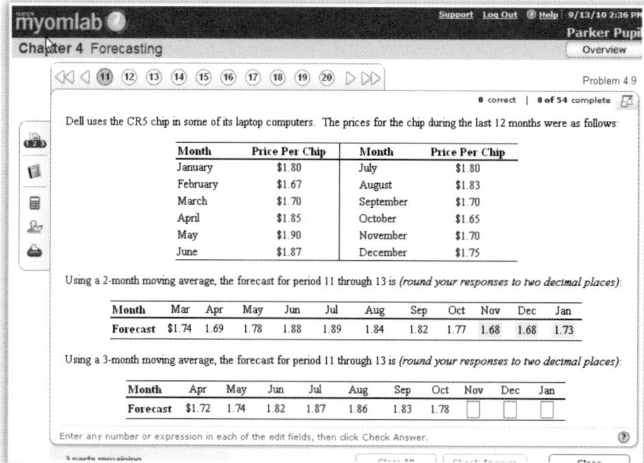

Built-in Student Help
The exercises correspond to the exercises in this textbook, and they regenerate algorithmically to give students unlimited opportunity for practice and mastery.

Student Learning Aids
Break the problem into steps for a more active learning process.

Review a problem similar to the one assigned.

Link to the section in the textbook where this problem is covered.

See an instructor explain this concept.

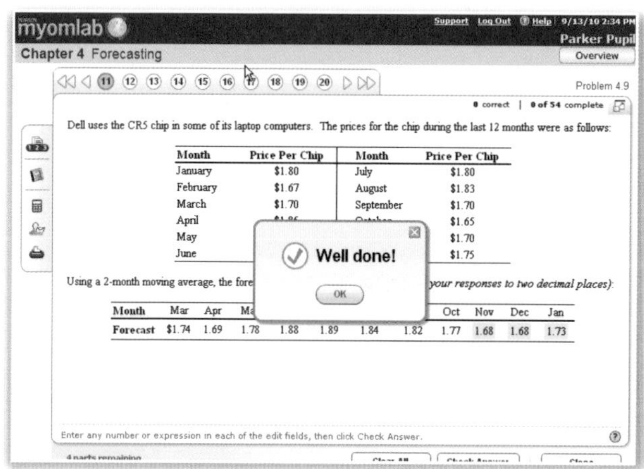

Study Plan for Self-paced Learning
my**om**lab generates a personalized Study Plan for each student based on his or her test results. The Study Plan links directly to interactive tutorial exercises for topics the student has not mastered.

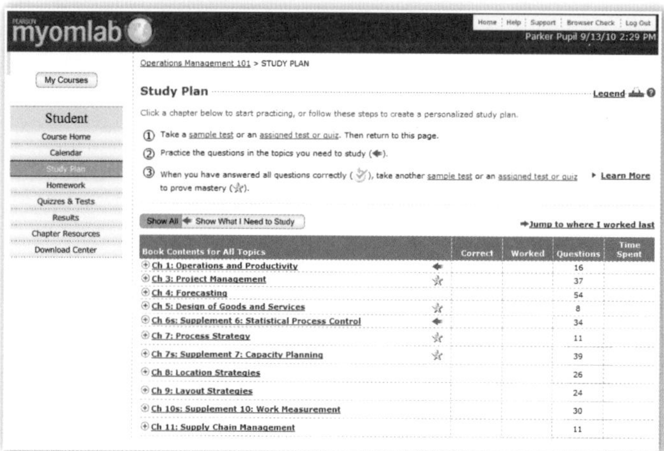

STUDENT PURCHASING OPTIONS

- Purchase an access kit bundled with a new textbook
- Purchase access online at **www.myomlab.com**

PRINCIPLES OF

OPERATIONS MANAGEMENT

EIGHTH EDITION

JAY HEIZER

Jesse H. Jones Professor of Business Administration
Texas Lutheran University

BARRY RENDER

Charles Harwood Professor of Operations Management
Crummer Graduate School of Business
Rollins College

Prentice Hall

Boston Columbus Indianapolis New York San Francisco Upper Saddle River
Amsterdam Cape Town Dubai London Madrid Milan Munich Paris Montreal Toronto
Delhi Mexico City Sao Paulo Sydney Hong Kong Seoul Singapore Taipei Tokyo

Editorial Director: Sally Yagan
Editor in Chief: Eric Svendsen
Senior Acquisitions Editor: Chuck Synovec
Editorial Project Manager: Mary Kate Murray
Editorial Assistant: Jason Calcano
Director of Marketing: Patrice Lumumba Jones
Marketing Manager: Anne Fahlgren
Marketing Assistant: Melinda Jones
Senior Managing Editor: Judy Leale
Project Manager: Becca Richter
Senior Operations Supervisor: Arnold Vila
Manager, Design Development: John Christiana
Interior and Cover Designer: Laura Gardner
Manager, Visual Research: Beth Brenzel
Manager, Rights and Permissions: Zina Arabia
Image Permission Coordinator: Annette Linder
Photo Researcher: Sheila Norman
Manager, Cover Visual Research & Permissions: Karen Sanatar
Cover Photo: Igor Dutina/iStockphoto.com
Permissions Project Manager: Shannon Barbe
Media Project Manager, Editorial: Allison Longley
Media Project Manager, Production: Lisa Rinaldi
Supplements Editor: Mary Kate Murray
Full-Service Project Management: GGS Higher Education Resources, a Division of PreMedia Global, Inc.
Composition: GGS Higher Education Resources, a Division of PreMedia Global, Inc.
Printer/Binder: Courier/Kendalville
Cover Printer: Lehigh-Phoenix Color/Hagerstown
Text Font: 10/12 Times

Credits and acknowledgments borrowed from other sources and reproduced, with permission, in this textbook appear on appropriate page within text (or on page P1–P2).

Library of Congress Cataloging-in-Publication Data

Heizer, Jay H.
Principles of operations management / Jay Heizer, Barry Render. — 8th ed.
p. cm.
ISBN-13: 978-0-13-61446-8
ISBN-10: 0-13-611446-6
1. Production management. I. Render, Barry. II. Title.
TS155.H3726 2010
658.5—dc22 2009034096

10 9 8 7 6 5 4 3 2

Prentice Hall
is an imprint of

www.pearsonhighered.com

ISBN 10: 0-13-611446-6
ISBN 13: 978-0-13-611446-8

To: Dorothy J. Bothe, thank you.

—JH

To: Donna, Charlie, and Jesse

—BR

About the Authors

Jay Heizer Professor Emeritus, the Jesse H. Jones Chair of Business Administration, Texas Lutheran University, Seguin, Texas. He received his B.B.A. and M.B.A. from the University of North Texas and his Ph.D. in Management and Statistics from Arizona State University. He was previously a member of the faculty at the University of Memphis, the University of Oklahoma, Virginia Commonwealth University, and the University of Richmond. He has also held visiting positions at Boston University, George Mason University, the Czech Management Center, and the Otto-Von-Guericka University, Magdeburg.

Dr. Heizer's industrial experience is extensive. He learned the practical side of operations management as a machinist apprentice at Foringer and Company, as a production planner for Westinghouse Airbrake, and at General Dynamics, where he worked in engineering administration. In addition, he has been actively involved in consulting in the OM and MIS areas for a variety of organizations, including Philip Morris, Firestone, Dixie Container Corporation, Columbia Industries, and Tenneco. He holds the CPIM certification from APICS—the Association for Operations Management.

Professor Heizer has co-authored 5 books and has published more than 30 articles on a variety of management topics. His papers have appeared in the *Academy of Management Journal*, *Journal of Purchasing*, *Personnel Psychology*, *Production & Inventory Control Management*, *APICS—The Performance Advantage*, *Journal of Management History*, *IIE Solutions,* and *Engineering Management*, among others. He has taught operations management courses in undergraduate, graduate, and executive programs.

Barry Render Professor Emeritus, the Charles Harwood Professor of Operations Management, Crummer Graduate School of Business, Rollins College, Winter Park, Florida. He received his B.S. in Mathematics and Physics at Roosevelt University, and his M.S. in Operations Research and Ph.D. in Quantitative Analysis at the University of Cincinnati. He previously taught at George Washington University, University of New Orleans, Boston University, and George Mason University, where he held the Mason Foundation Professorship in Decision Sciences and was Chair of the Decision Science Department. Dr. Render has also worked in the aerospace industry, for General Electric, McDonnell Douglas, and NASA.

Professor Render has co-authored 10 textbooks for Prentice Hall, including *Managerial Decision Modeling with Spreadsheets*, *Quantitative Analysis for Management*, *Service Management*, *Introduction to Management Science*, and *Cases and Readings in Management Science*. *Quantitative Analysis for Management,* now in its 10th edition, is a leading text in that discipline in the United States and globally. Dr. Render's more than 100 articles on a variety of management topics have appeared in *Decision Sciences*, *Production and Operations Management*, *Interfaces*, *Information and Management*, *Journal of Management Information Systems*, *Socio-Economic Planning Sciences*, *IIE Solutions*, and *Operations Management Review*, among others.

Dr. Render has been honored as an AACSB Fellow and was twice named a Senior Fulbright Scholar. He was Vice President of the Decision Science Institute Southeast Region and served as Software Review Editor for *Decision Line* for six years and as Editor of the *New York Times* Operations Management special issues for five years. From 1984 to 1993, Dr. Render was President of Management Service Associates of Virginia, Inc., whose technology clients included the FBI; the U.S. Navy; Fairfax County, Virginia; and C&P Telephone.

Dr. Render has taught operations management courses in Rollins College's MBA and Executive MBA programs. He has received that school's Welsh Award as leading Professor and was selected by Roosevelt University as the 1996 recipient of the St. Claire Drake Award for Outstanding Scholarship. In 2005, Dr. Render received the Rollins College MBA Student Award for Best Overall Course, and in 2009, was named Professor of the Year by full-time MBA students.

Brief Table of Contents

Table of Contents

12. Inventory Management 465

13. Aggregate Planning 509

14. Material Requirements Planning (MRP) and ERP 543

15. Short-Term Scheduling 581

Preface

Welcome to your operations management (OM) course. In this book, we present a state-of-the-art view of the activities of the operations function. Operations is an exciting area of management that has a profound effect on the productivity of both manufacturing and services. Indeed, few other activities have as much impact on the quality of our lives. The goal of this text is to present a broad introduction to the field of operations in a realistic, practical manner. OM includes a blend of topics from accounting, industrial engineering, management, management science, and statistics. Even if you are not planning on a career in the operations area, you will likely be working with people who are. Therefore, having a solid understanding of the role of operations in an organization is of substantial benefit to you. This book will also help you understand how OM affects society and your life. Certainly, you will better understand what goes on behind the scenes when you purchase a bag of Frito-Lay potato chips; buy a meal at an Olive Garden, a Red Lobster, or a Hard Rock Cafe; place an order through Amazon.com; buy a customized Dell computer over the Internet; or enter Arnold Palmer Hospital for medical care.

Although many of our readers are not OM majors, we know that marketing, finance, accounting, and MIS students across the globe will find the material both interesting and useful as we develop a fundamental working knowledge of the operations side of the firm. More than 600,000 readers of our earlier editions seem to have endorsed this premise. We welcome comments by email from our North American readers, from students using the EU edition, the Indian edition, and our editions in Portuguese, Spanish, Turkish, Indonesian, and Chinese. Our goal is to make this material useful and interesting to each of you.

NEW TO THIS EDITION

Manufacturing Integration with Video Case Studies on Frito-Lay In this edition, we take you behind the scenes at one of the most exciting manufacturers in North America, Frito-Lay, a subsidiary of PepsiCo. We provide five new *Video Case Studies*, photos, examples, problems, and a *Global Company Profile* (Chapter 13). This multi-billion-dollar snack food producer opened its doors so we could examine its use of statistical quality control (Supplement 6), green manufacturing and sustainability (Chapter 7), inventory management (Chapter 12), and maintenance (Chapter 17), as well as its overall OM strategy (Chapter 1) in a series of 8- to 14-minute videos.

Our prior editions focused on Darden Restaurants (Olive Garden/Red Lobster), Hard Rock Cafe, Arnold Palmer Hospital, Wheeled Coach Ambulances, and Regal Marine. These videos and cases appear in this edition as well, along with the five new ones for Frito-Lay.

► Green Manufacturing and Sustainability at Frito-Lay — Video Case

Frito-Lay, the multi-billion-dollar snack food giant, requires vast amounts of water, electricity, natural gas, and fuel to produce its 41 well-known brands. In keeping with growing environmental concerns, Frito-Lay has initiated ambitious plans to produce environmentally friendly snacks. But even environmentally friendly snacks require resources. Recognizing the environmental impact, the firm is an aggressive "green manufacturer," with major initiatives in resource reduction and sustainability.

For instance, the company's energy management program includes a variety of elements designed to engage employees in reducing energy consumption. These elements include scorecards and customized action plans that empower employees and recognize their achievements.

At Frito-Lay's factory in Casa Grande, Arizona, more than 500,000 pounds of potatoes arrive every day to be washed, sliced, fried, seasoned, and portioned into bags of Lay's and Ruffles chips. The process consumes enormous amounts of energy and creates vast amounts of wastewater, starch, and potato peelings. Frito-Lay plans to take the plant off the power grid and run it almost entirely on renewable fuels and recycled water. The managers at the Casa Grande plant have also installed skylights in conference rooms, offices, and a finished goods warehouse to reduce the need for artificial light. More fuel-efficient ovens recapture heat from exhaust stacks. Vacuum hoses that pull moisture from potato slices to recapture the water and to reduce the amount of heat needed to cook the potato chips are also being used.

Rapid Reviews In our never-ending quest to make this the most student-friendly text in our field, we now include a two-page Rapid Review at the end of each chapter, supplement, and module. This detailed yet concise summary of the main points and equations in the chapter helps students prepare for homework, exams, and lectures by capturing the essence of the material. Each Rapid Review also includes a self-test, with questions linked to the learning objectives in that chapter. Key terms introduced in the chapter are part of the Rapid Review.

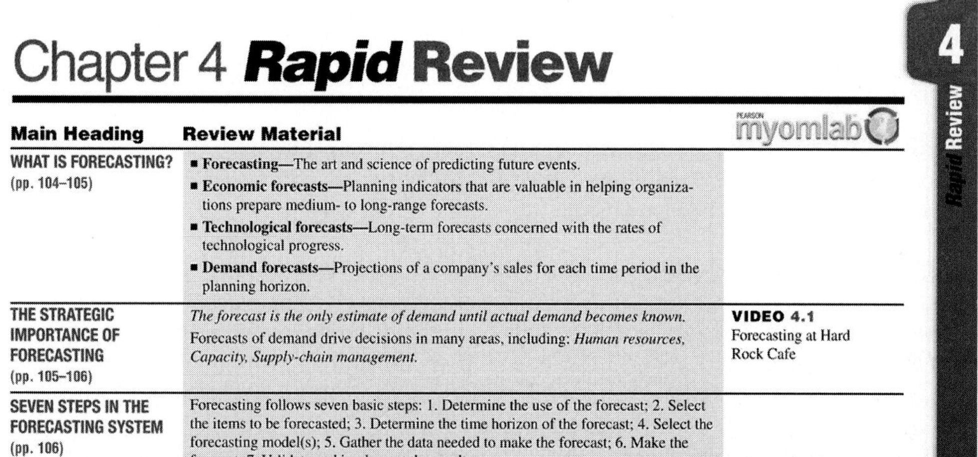

Chapter 4 **Rapid** Review

Main Heading	Review Material	myomlab
WHAT IS FORECASTING? (pp. 104–105)	▪ **Forecasting**—The art and science of predicting future events. ▪ **Economic forecasts**—Planning indicators that are valuable in helping organizations prepare medium- to long-range forecasts. ▪ **Technological forecasts**—Long-term forecasts concerned with the rates of technological progress. ▪ **Demand forecasts**—Projections of a company's sales for each time period in the planning horizon.	
THE STRATEGIC IMPORTANCE OF FORECASTING (pp. 105–106)	*The forecast is the only estimate of demand until actual demand becomes known.* Forecasts of demand drive decisions in many areas, including: *Human resources, Capacity, Supply-chain management.*	**VIDEO 4.1** Forecasting at Hard Rock Cafe
SEVEN STEPS IN THE FORECASTING SYSTEM (pp. 106)	Forecasting follows seven basic steps: 1. Determine the use of the forecast; 2. Select the items to be forecasted; 3. Determine the time horizon of the forecast; 4. Select the forecasting model(s); 5. Gather the data needed to make the forecast; 6. Make the forecast; 7. Validate and implement the results.	

myomlab and the Learning Process This powerful tool ties together all elements in our book into an innovative learning tool, an exam tool, a homework tool, and an assessment center. myomlab's new version 2.0 accompanies this edition of the text. By using myomlab, instructors can assign thousands of problems from the text and/or problems/questions from the Test Item File for their students to take online, in any time frame determined by the instructor. With many options for randomizing the sequence, timing, and scoring, myomlab makes giving and grading homework and exams easy. Most problems have also been converted to an algorithmic form, meaning that there are numerous versions of each problem, with different data for each student. Solutions to each problem and its data set are available, if instructors wish, to students immediately after they complete each assignment. The program records grades into the instructor's grade book. For help, students can click directly to the relevant text page, watch the text authors solve a similar problem, walk through other sample problems, or seek other useful forms of help. This new and innovative feature is truly a wonderful teaching and learning aid. Visit **www.myomlab.com** for more information.

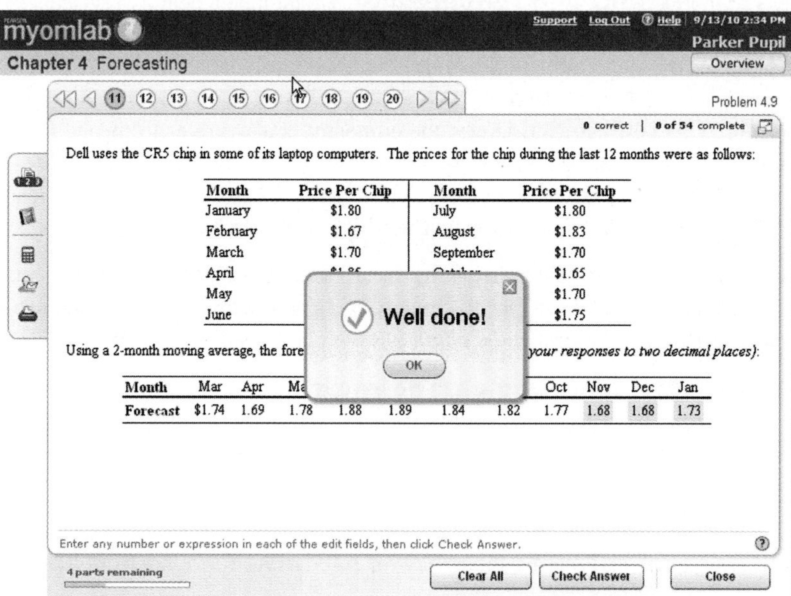

Integration of Ethics Throughout the Book With this revision, we provide broad coverage of ethics as an OM consideration. The topic is addressed in most chapters, and at the end of each chapter we present an *Ethical Dilemma* that can be used for classroom discussion or homework.

Expanded Treatment of the Theory of Constraints Supplement 7 now contains expanded treatment on the theory of constraints, including the material previously covered in Chapter 15. Theory of constraints and bottleneck analysis coverage includes examples, a solved problem, and seven new homework problems.

Sustainability as an OM Responsibility Sustainability is now highlighted in several chapters, especially Chapters 5 ("Design of Goods and Services") and 7 ("Process Strategy and Sustainability"). Chapter 7 also has two new case studies on the topic as it relates to Frito-Lay and to Walmart.

Author Comments You will notice a new feature throughout every chapter that we call Author Comments. Here we point out why a section, a figure, or a table is so important. The comments are intended to be motivational to students, as well as educational.

TECHNOLOGY IN SERVICES

Just as we have seen rapid advances in technology in the manufacturing sector, so we also find dramatic changes in the service sector. These range from electronic diagnostic equipment at auto repair shops, to blood- and urine-testing equipment in hospitals, to retinal security scanners at airports and high-security facilities. The hospitality industry provides other examples, as discussed in the *OM in Action* box "Technology Changes the Hotel Industry."

AUTHOR COMMENT
Although less dramatic than manufacturing, technology also improves quality and productivity in services.

Additional Homework Problems Our text already contains more homework problems than any other text in the discipline. We have also added hundreds more problems to our Web site for instructors who seek even more variety and freshness. These problems are available at **www.myomlab.com**. Solutions to these additional problems appear along with regular text problems in our *Instructor's Solution Manual,* which was created and proofed by the authors.

CHAPTER-BY-CHAPTER CHANGES

To highlight the extent of the revision from the eighth edition, here are a few of the changes, on a chapter-by-chapter basis. We have added new material on the subject of the theory of constraints (to Supplement 7); combined Chapter 10 and Supplement 10 into a new Chapter 10, called "Human Resources, Job Design, and Work Measurement"; and have added extensive new material on supply chains in Chapter 11 and Supplement 11. The Rapid Review section is new to each chapter. Active Models, which were illustrated with screen captures in most chapters, now appear in myomlab and the Companion Web site, **www.pearsonhighered.com/heizer**.

Chapter 1. Operations and Productivity We include a heavily revised section to help motivate students, called "Exciting New Trends in OM," with a new emphasis on the environment and ethics that runs throughout the book. Four homework problems have been expanded. And the chapter closes with the new *Video Case Study* "Frito-Lay: Operations Management in Manufacturing." This new case introduces the company that we refer to throughout this edition and makes an excellent teaching comparison to the other Chapter 1 *Video Case Study* "Hard Rock Cafe: Operations Management in Services." The Zychol Chemical Corporation case has been moved to the Companion Web site, **www.pearsonhighered.com/heizer**.

Chapter 2. Operations Strategy in a Global Environment This chapter has a new figure (Figure 2.4) that relates OM to strategy and a new section called "Issues in Operations Strategy," which includes Porter's *value chain analysis* and *five forces model.*

Chapter 3. Project Management We have revised our treatment of work breakdown structure with a more visual approach (Figure 3.3), added a new *OM in Action* box, "Prepping for the Miami Heat Game," and shortened coverage of Microsoft Project (from seven screen captures down to three).

Chapter 4. Forecasting We have revised the formula for tracking signals [see Equation (4.18) and Example 16] and moved the review of forecasting formulas from Table 4.1 into the Rapid Review section.

Chapter 5. Design of Goods and Services We have added a manufacturer, Cisco, to our discussion of new product yields (Figure 5.6) and created a major new section titled "Ethics, the Environment, and Sustainability."

Chapter 6. Managing Quality This chapter contains expanded coverage of ISO 14000, including a new *OM in Action* box, "Subaru's Clean, Green Set of Wheels with ISO 14001," and a discussion of ISO 24700. We have also added "A Hospital Benchmarks Against the Ferrari Racing Team" as another *OM in Action* box and have illustrated checklists as a way to improve quality. A new homework problem uses data from *The Economist*'s poll of air travel dislikes.

Supplement 6. Statistical Process Control Frito-Lay's use of SPC is featured in both photographs and a new *Video Case Study,* "Frito-Lay's Quality-Controlled Potato Chips." This video is not only an exploration of the firm's quality program but a tutorial on how a real firm creates control charts from scratch. There are seven expanded homework problems and one new one, which is based on the former Alabama Air case study.

Chapter 7. Process Strategy and Sustainability The chapter begins with a new *Global Company Profile* featuring Harley-Davidson's repetitive manufacturing. We have extensively revised our treatment of the four process strategies. It is shortened and concisely illustrated in Figure 7.2. There is a new *OM in Action* box, "Mass Customization for Straight Teeth." We have added a major new section on sustainability, where we introduce the four *R*s of sustainability. At the end of the chapter are two new cases: "Environmental Sustainability at Walmart" and the *Video Case Study,* "Green Manufacturing and Sustainability at Frito-Lay."

Supplement 7. Capacity and Constraint Management This supplement has been retitled and extensively revised to include coverage of constraint management and the theory of constraints. Material on the theory of constraints, formerly in Chapter 15, has been melded into this new treatment. A new section, "Bottleneck Analysis and Theory of Constraints," includes two examples (S3 and S4), a solved problem (S7.5), an *OM in Action* box on banking and the theory of constraints, and seven new homework problems (S7.9–S7.15). So as not to lengthen Supplement 7, we shortened our coverage of multi-product break-even analysis, replaced decision trees with an EMV approach to capacity decisions, and reduced our treatment of net present value analysis. Finally, the *Video Case Study,* "Capacity Planning at Arnold Palmer Hospital" has been updated.

Chapter 8. Location Strategies The homework problem selection has been expanded, and 11 problems have been revised to make them more challenging.

Chapter 9. Layout Strategies The main addition to this chapter is the new *OM in Action* box "Work Cells Increase Productivity at Canon."

Chapter 10. Human Resources, Job Design, and Work Measurement With this edition, we have merged Supplement 10 ("Work Measurement") into Chapter 10. This helps make the coverage of this material more concise, while bringing more quantitative material into the main chapter. Coverage of labor planning, job design, ergonomics, and the visual workplace has been edited for brevity. Examples S1–S6 from Supplement 10 remain, now as Examples 1–6. Solved Problems S10.1–S10.5 are now Solved Problems 10.2–10.6. There is a new *OM in Action* box, "Saving Seconds at Retail Boosts Productivity." The case study "The Fleet That Wanders" has been moved to our Web site.

Chapter 11. Supply-Chain Management In keeping with the growing importance of supply chains as an OM topic, we have rewritten this chapter (and Supplement 11) to keep readers current in this dynamic field. There is new treatment of supply-chain risks, a new section on ethics and sustainability, more coverage of joint ventures, a new section on CPFR, a revision of the material on e-procurement, and new material explaining the SCOR model.

Supplement 11. Outsourcing as a Supply-Chain Strategy The material here has been heavily edited to keep current with this important topic, including a new Table S11.1 on ranking of outsourcing countries, NASA's outsourcing shipments to the Space Station, and back-sourcing. We have deleted the section on break-even analysis, which is a model discussed in other chapters, and revised four of the homework problems to make them more challenging.

Chapter 12. Inventory Management The explanation of how to graph costs as a function of order quantity has been expanded to help students better understand the concept (Figure 12.4). We now cover the single-period model in Example 15 and in three new homework problems (12.36–12.38). Seven other homework problems have been revised and expanded. Finally, a new *Video Case Study* is called "Managing Inventory at Frito-Lay."

Chapter 13. Aggregate Planning The chapter begins with a new *Global Company Profile* illustrating aggregate planning at Frito-Lay. We have also revised Examples 2–4 to make them more current.

Chapter 14. Material Requirements Planning (MRP) and ERP MRP II and its example in Table 14.4 have been rewritten, the order splitting discussion (and its Example 7) has been revised, the ERP section has been shortened, and a new case study, "Hill's Automotive, Inc." replaces the Ikon case, which now appears on the Companion Web site, **www.pearsonhighered.com/heizer**.

Chapter 15. Short-Term Scheduling We have expanded and moved the treatment of the theory of constraints to Supplement 7 and rewritten Problem 15.17.

Chapter 16. Just-in-Time and Lean Operations The *Global Company Profile* on Toyota has been revised; Figure 16.3, explaining hidden problems, is new; there is a revised kanban figure (Figure 16.9); and kaizan is expanded both in the text and in the new *OM in Action* box "Kaizen at Ducati." There is also a new *OM in Action* box on TPS at the Los Angeles Police Department, and there is a new case study, "JIT After a Catastrophe."

Chapter 17. Maintenance and Reliability There are three new elements: a section covering autonomous maintenance, an *Ethical Dilemma* regarding the Space Shuttle, and a *Video Case Study* called "Maintenance Drives Profits at Frito-Lay."

STUDENT RESOURCES

To liven up the course and help students learn the content material, we have made available the following resources:

- ***Student Study Guide*** (ISBN: 0-13-510725-3) created by Michael Donovan of Cedar Crest College. The Study Guide is designed to help students understand the concepts and quantitative methods of operations management. Each chapter in the study guide consists nine basic components: Summary; Learning Objectives; Skills to Develop; Annotated Outline; Hints and Tips; Key Terms; Formulas; Self-test Questions; and Supplementary Materials.
- ***Thirty-one exciting video cases*** (Located on the Operations Management DVD Library, ISBN: 0-13-611981-6, and at **www.myomlab.com**.) These *Video Case Studies* feature real companies (Frito-Lay, Darden Restaurants, Regal Marine, Hard Rock Cafe, Ritz-Carlton, Wheeled Coach, and Arnold Palmer Hospital) and allow students to watch short videos, read about the key topics, and answer questions. These case studies can also be assigned without using class time to show the videos. Each of them was developed and written by the text authors to specifically supplement the book's content.
- ***DVD video clips*** (Located on the Operations Management DVD Library, ISBN: 0-13-611981-6, and at **www.myomlab.com**.) We have provided 37 one- to two-minute videos, clips to illustrate chapter-related topics with videos at Frito-Lay, Harley-Davidson, Ritz-Carlton, Hard Rock Cafe, Olive Garden, and other firms.
- ***Virtual tours*** (Located on the Companion Web site, **www.pearsonhighered.com/heizer**). These company tours provide direct links to companies—ranging from a hospital to an auto manufacturer—that practice key concepts. After touring each Web site, students are asked questions directly related to the concepts discussed in the chapter.
- ***Self-study quizzes*** (Located on the Companion Web site, **www.pearsonhighered.com/heizer**.) These quizzes allow students to test their understanding of each topic. These extensive quizzes contain a broad assortment of questions, 20–25 per chapter, including multiple-choice, true/false, and Internet essay questions. The quiz questions are graded and can be transmitted to the instructor for extra credit or serve as practice exams.
- ***Active Models*** The 24 Active Models appear in files at **www.myomlab.com** and the Companion Web site, **www.pearsonhighered.com/heizer**.
- ***Excel OM data files*** Examples in the text that can be solved with Excel OM appear on data files at **www.myomlab.com** and the Companion Web site, **www.pearsonhighered.com/heizer**. They are identified at the end of each example.
- ***POM for Windows software*** (Located at **www.myomlab.com** and the Companion Web site, **www.pearsonhighered.com/heizer**.) POM for Windows is a powerful tool for easily solving OM problems. Its 24 modules can be used to solve most of the homework problems in the text.
- ***Excel OM problem-solving software*** (Located at **www.myomlab.com** and the Companion Web site, **www.pearsonhighered.com/heizer**.) Excel OM is our exclusive user-friendly Excel add-in. Excel OM automatically creates worksheets to model and solve problems. Users select a topic from the pull-down menu and fill in the data, and then Excel will display and graph (where appropriate) the results. This software is great for student

homework, what-if analysis and classroom demonstrations. This edition includes a new version of Excel OM that's compatible with Microsoft Excel 2007 as well as earlier versions of Excel.

- ***Online Tutorial Chapters*** (Located at **www.myomlab.com** and the Companion Web site, **www.pearsonhighered.com/heizer**.) *Statistical Tools for Managers, Acceptance Sampling, The Simplex Method of Linear Programming, The MODI and VAM Methods of Solving Transportation Problems*, and *Vehicle Routing and Scheduling* are provided as additional material.
- ***Virtual office hours*** (Located at **www.myomlab.com**.) Professors Heizer and Render appear on myomlab, walking students through 72 Solved Problems.
- ***Additional practice problems*** (Located at **www.myomlab.com**.) These problems provide problem-solving experience. They supplement the examples and solved problems found in each chapter.
- ***Additional case studies*** (Located at **www.myomlab.com**.) These additional case studies supplement the ones in the text. Detailed solutions appear in the Solutions Manual.
- ***Microsoft Project 2007*** (ISBN: 0-13-145421-8.) Microsoft Project, the most popular and powerful project management package, is now available on an additional student CD-ROM. This full version, documented in Chapter 3, is activated to work for 60 days.

INSTRUCTOR RESOURCES

Register, Redeem, Log in At **www.pearsonhighered.com/irc**, instructors can register and access a variety of print, media, and presentation resources that are available with this text in downloadable digital format. For most texts, resources are also available for course management platforms such as Blackboard, WebCT, and Course Compass.

It Gets Better Once you register, you will not have additional forms to fill out or multiple usernames and passwords to remember to access new titles and/or editions. As a registered faculty member, you can log in directly to download resource files and receive immediate access and instructions for installing course management content to your campus server.

Need Help? Our dedicated technical support team is ready to answer instructors' questions about the media supplements that accompany this text. Visit **http://247.prenhall.com** for answers to frequently asked questions and toll-free user support phone numbers. The supplements are available to adopting instructors. Detailed descriptions are provided at the Instructor's Resource Center, **www.pearsonhighered.com/heizer**.

Instructor's Resource Manual The Instructor's Resource Manual, extensively updated by Professor Charles Munson of Washington State University, contains many useful resources for instructors—course outlines, video notes, learning techniques, Internet exercises and sample answers, case analysis ideas, additional teaching resources, and faculty notes. It also provides a snapshot of the PowerPoint lecture slides. Instructors can download the Instructor's Resource Manual from the Instructor's Resource Center, at **www.pearsonhighered.com/heizer**.

Instructor's Solutions Manual The Instructor's Solutions Manual, written by the authors (and extensively proofed by Professor Annie Puciloski), contains the answers to all of the discussion questions, *Ethical Dilemmas*, Active Models, and cases in the text, as well as worked-out solutions to all the end-of-chapter problems, Internet problems, and Internet cases. Instructors can download the Instructor's Solutions Manual from the Instructor's Resource Center, at **www.pearsonhighered.com/heizer**.

PowerPoint Presentations An extensive set of PowerPoint presentations, created by Professor Jeff Heyl of Lincoln University, is available for each chapter. Comprising well over 2,000 slides, this set has excellent color and clarity. These slides can also be downloaded from the Instructor's Resource Center, at **www.pearsonhighered.com/heizer**.

Test Item File The test item file, updated by Professor Greg Bier of University of Missouri–Columbia, contains a variety of true/false, multiple-choice, fill-in-the-blank, short-answer, and problem- and topic-integrating questions for each chapter. Instructors can download the test item file from the Instructor's Resource Center, at **www.pearsonhighered.com/heizer**.

TestGen The computerized TestGen package allows instructors to customize, save, and generate classroom tests. The test program permits instructors to edit, add, and delete questions from the test bank, edit existing graphics and create new graphics, analyze test results, and organize a database of test and student results. This software allows for extensive flexibility and ease of use. It provides many options for organizing and displaying tests, along with search and sort features. The software and the test banks can be downloaded from the Instructor's Resource Center, at **www.pearsonhighered.com/heizer**.

myomlab This powerful tool, noted on the inside front cover, ties together all elements in this book into an innovative learning tool, an exam tool, a homework tool, and an assessment center. By using myomlab, instructors can assign thousands of problems from the text and/or problems/questions from the test item file for their students to take online at any time, as determined by the instructor. Visit **www.myomlab.com** for more information.

Video Package Designed and created by the authors specifically for their Heizer/Render texts, the video package contains the following 31 videos:

- Frito-Lay: Operations Management in Manufacturing (Ch. 1)
- Operations Management at Hard Rock (Ch. 1)
- Regal Marine: Operations Strategy (Ch. 2)
- Hard Rock Cafe's Global Strategy (Ch. 2)
- Project Management at Arnold Palmer Hospital (Ch. 3)
- Managing Hard Rock's Rockfest (Ch. 3)
- Forecasting at Hard Rock Cafe (Ch. 4)
- Regal Marine: Product Design (Ch. 5)
- The Culture of Quality at Arnold Palmer Hospital (Ch. 6)
- Ritz-Carlton: Quality (Ch. 6)
- Frito-Lay's Quality-Controlled Potato Chips (Supp. 6)
- SPC and Quality at Darden Restaurants (Supp. 6)
- Green Manufacturing and Sustainability at Frito-Lay (Ch. 7)
- Wheeled Coach: Process Strategy (Ch. 7)
- Process Analysis at Arnold Palmer Hospital (Ch. 7)
- Capacity Planning at Arnold Palmer Hospital (Supp. 7)
- Locating the Next Red Lobster (Ch. 8)
- Where to Place the Hard Rock Cafe (Ch. 8)
- Wheeled Coach: Facility Layout (Ch. 9)
- Laying Out Arnold Palmer Hospital's New Facility (Ch. 9)
- Hard Rock Cafe's Human Resource Strategy (Ch. 10)
- Darden's Global Supply Chains (Ch. 11)
- Regal Marine: Supply-Chain Management (Ch. 11)
- Arnold Palmer Hospital's Supply Chain (Ch. 11)
- Darden's Global Outsourcing (Supp. 11)
- Managing Inventory at Frito-Lay (Ch. 12)
- Wheeled Coach: Inventory Control (Ch. 12)
- Wheeled Coach: Materials Requirements Planning (Ch. 14)
- Scheduling at Hard Rock Cafe (Ch. 15)
- JIT at Arnold Palmer Hospital (Ch. 16)
- Maintenance Drives Profits at Frito-Lay (Ch. 17)

ACKNOWLEDGMENTS

We thank the many individuals who were kind enough to assist us in this endeavor. The following professors provided insights that guided us in this edition (their names are in bold) and prior editions.

ALABAMA

Philip F. Musa
University of Alabama at Birmingham

Doug Turner
Auburn University

ALASKA

Paul Jordan
University of Alaska

ARIZONA

Susan K. Norman
Northern Arizona University

Scott Roberts
Northern Arizona University

Vicki L. Smith-Daniels
Arizona State University

CALIFORNIA

Jean-Pierre Amor
University of San Diego

Moshen Attaran
California State University–Bakersfield

Ali Behnezhad
California State University–Northridge

Joe Biggs
California Polytechnic State University

Lesley Buehler
Ohlone College

Richard Martin
California State University–Long Beach

Zinovy Radovilsky
California State University–Hayward

Robert J. Schlesinger
San Diego State University

V. Udayabhanu
San Francisco State University

Rick Wing
San Francisco State University

COLORADO

Peter Billington
Colorado State University–Pueblo

CONNECTICUT

David Cadden
Quinnipiac University

Larry A. Flick
Norwalk Community Technical College

FLORIDA

Rita Gibson
Embry-Riddle Aeronautical University

Jim Gilbert
Rollins College

Donald Hammond
University of South Florida

Ronald K. Satterfield
University of South Florida

Theresa A. Shotwell
Florida A&M University

GEORGIA

John H. Blackstone
University of Georgia

Johnny Ho
Columbus State University

John Hoft
Columbus State University

John Miller
Mercer University

Spyros Reveliotis
Georgia Institute of Technology

ILLINOIS

Suad Alwan
Chicago State University

Lori Cook
DePaul University

Zafar Malik
Governors State University

INDIANA

Barbara Flynn
Indiana University

B.P. Lingeraj
Indiana University

Frank Pianki
Anderson University

Stan Stockton
Indiana University

Jianghua Wu
Purdue University

Xin Zhai
Purdue University

IOWA

Kevin Watson
Iowa State University

Lifang Wu
University of Iowa

KANSAS

William Barnes
Emporia State University

George Heinrich
Wichita State University

Sue Helms
Wichita State University

Hugh Leach
Washburn University

M. J. Riley
Kansas State University

Teresita S. Salinas
Washburn University

Avanti P. Sethi
Wichita State University

KENTUCKY

Wade Ferguson
Western Kentucky University

Kambiz Tabibzadeh
Eastern Kentucky University

LOUISIANA

Roy Clinton
University of Louisiana at Monroe

L.Wayne Shell (retired)
Nicholls State University

MARYLAND

Eugene Hahn
Salisbury University

Samuel Y. Smith, Jr.
University of Baltimore

MASSACHUSETTS

Peter Ittig
University of Massachusetts

Jean Pierre Kuilboer
University of Massachusetts–Boston

Dave Lewis
University of Massachusetts–Lowell

Mike Maggard
Northeastern University

Peter Rourke
Wentworth Institute of Technology

Daniel Shimshak
University of Massachusetts–Boston

Ernest Silver
Curry College

MICHIGAN

Darlene Burk
Western Michigan University

Damodar Golhar
Western Michigan University

Dana Johnson
Michigan Technological University

Doug Moodie
Michigan Tech University

MINNESOTA

Rick Carlson
Metropolitan State University

John Nicolay
University of Minnesota

Michael Pesch
St. Cloud State University

MISSOURI

Shahid Ali
Rockhurst University

Stephen Allen
Truman State University

Sema Alptekin
University of Missouri–Rolla

Gregory L. Bier
University of Missouri–Columbia

James Campbell
University of Missouri–St. Louis

Wooseung Jang
University of Missouri–Columbia

Mary Marrs
University of Missouri–Columbia

A. Lawrence Summers
University of Missouri

NEBRASKA

Zialu Hug
University of Nebraska–Omaha

NEW JERSEY

Leon Bazil
Stevens Institute of Technology

Mark Berenson
Montclair State University

Joao Neves
The College of New Jersey

Leonard Presby
William Paterson University

NEW MEXICO

William Kime
University of New Mexico

NEW YORK

Theodore Boreki
Hofstra University

John Drabouski
DeVry University

Richard E. Dulski
Daemen College

Beate Klingenberg
Marist College

Donna Mosier
SUNY Potsdam

Elizabeth Perry
SUNY Binghamton

William Reisel
St. John's University

Kaushik Sengupta
Hofstra University

Girish Shambu
Canisius College

Rajendra Tibrewala
New York Institute of Technology

NORTH CAROLINA

Ray Walters
Fayetteville Technical Community College

OHIO

Victor Berardi
Kent State University

OKLAHOMA

Wen-Chyuan Chiang
University of Tulsa

OREGON

Anne Deidrich
Warner Pacific College

Gordon Miller
Portland State University

PENNSYLVANIA

Henry Crouch
Pittsburgh State University

Prafulla Oglekar
LaSalle University

David Pentico
Duquesne University

Stanford Rosenberg
LaRoche College

Edward Rosenthal
Temple University

Susan Sherer
Lehigh University

RHODE ISLAND

Laurie E. Macdonald
Bryant College

John Swearingen
Bryant College

Susan Sweeney
Providence College

SOUTH CAROLINA

Larry LaForge
Clemson University

Emma Jane Riddle
Winthrop University

TENNESSEE

Hugh Daniel
Lipscomb University

TEXAS

Warren W. Fisher
Stephen F. Austin State University

Garland Hunnicutt
Texas State University

Gregg Lattier
Lee College

Henry S. Maddux III
Sam Houston State University

Arunachalam Narayanan
Texas A&M University

Ranga V. Ramasesh
Texas Christian University

Victor Sower
Sam Houston State University

Cecelia Temponi
Texas State University

John Visich-Disc
University of Houston

Bruce M. Woodworth
University of Texas–El Paso

UTAH

William Christensen
Dixie State College of Utah

Shane J. Schvaneveldt
Weber State University

Madeline Thimmes (retired)
Utah State University

VIRGINIA

Andy Litteral
University of Richmond

Arthur C. Meiners, Jr.
Marymount University

Michael Plumb
Tidewater Community College

WASHINGTON

Mark McKay
University of Washington

Chuck Munson
Washington State University

Chris Sandvig
Western Washington University

John Stec
Oregon Institute of Technology

WASHINGTON, DC

Narendrea K. Rustagi
Howard University

WEST VIRGINIA

Charles Englehardt
Salem International University

Daesung Ha
Marshall University

John Harpell
West Virginia University

James S. Hawkes
University of Charleston

WISCONSIN

James R. Gross
University of Wisconsin–Oshkosh

Marilyn K. Hart (retired)
University of Wisconsin–Oshkosh

Niranjan Pati
University of Wisconsin–La Crosse

X. M. Safford
Milwaukee Area Technical College

Rao J. Taikonda
University of Wisconsin–Oshkosh

WYOMING

Cliff Asay
University of Wyoming

INTERNATIONAL

Ronald Lau
Hong Kong University of Science and Technology

In addition, we appreciate the wonderful people at Prentice Hall who provided both help and advice: Eric Svendsen, our editor-in-chief; Chuck Synovec, our decision sciences editor; Anne Fahlgren, our marketing manager; Jason Calcano, our editorial assistant; Allison Longley, our media project development manager; Douglas Ruby and Courtney Kamauf for their dedicated work on myomlab; Judy Leale, our senior managing editor; Becca Richter, our production project manager; Mary Kate Murray, our editorial project manager, and Heidi Allgair, our senior production editor at GGS Higher Education Resources. Reva Shader developed the exemplary subject indexes for this text. Donna Render and Kay Heizer provided the accurate typing and proofing so critical in a rigorous textbook. We are truly blessed to have such a fantastic team of experts directing, guiding, and assisting us.

In this edition we were thrilled to be able to include one of the country's premiere manufacturers, Frito-Lay, in our ongoing video case series. This was possible because of the wonderful efforts of Tom Rao, VP-Florida Operations and his superb management team, including Todd Ehinger, Jim Wentzel, Angela McCormack, and Rod Hof. We are also particularly grateful to Aurora Gonzalez in the Public Relations Department at Frito-Lay headquarters in Plano, Texas.

We also appreciate the efforts of colleagues who have helped to shape the entire learning package that accompanies this text. Professor Howard Weiss (Temple University) developed the Active Models, Excel OM, and POM for Windows microcomputer software; Professor Jeff Heyl (Lincoln University) created the PowerPoints. Professor Chuck Munson (Washington State University) created the Instructor's Resource Manual and did a major edit of Supplement 7; Professor Gregory L. Bier (University of Missouri–Columbia) prepared the Test Bank; Professor Geoff Willis (University of Central Oklahoma) created the online study guide and online virtual tours; Professor Michael Donovan (Cedar Crest College) prepared the study guide; Beverly Amer (Northern Arizona University) produced and directed the videos and DVD Video Case Study series; Professors Keith Willoughby (Bucknell University) and Ken Klassen (Brock University) contributed the two Excel-based simulation games; Professor Gary LaPoint (Syracuse University) developed the Microsoft Project crashing exercise and the dice game for SPC. Finally, thanks to our accuracy checkers, Annie Puciloski and Vijay Gupta, for their attention to detail. We have been fortunate to have been able to work with all these people.

We wish you a pleasant and productive introduction to operations management.

Barry Render
Graduate School of Business
Rollins College
Winter Park, FL 32789
Email: brender@rollins.edu

Jay Heizer
Texas Lutheran University
1000 W. Court Street
Seguin, TX 78155
Email: jheizer@tlu.edu

THREE VERSIONS ARE AVAILABLE

This text is available in the three versions: *Operations Management*, tenth edition, a hardcover; *Principles of Operations Management*, eighth edition, a paperback; and *Operations Management*, flexible edition, a package of a paperback text and the unique Student Lecture Guide. All three books include the identical core Chapters 1–17. However, *Operations Management*, tenth edition and flexible edition, also include six quantitative modules in Part IV.

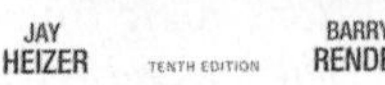

OPERATIONS MANAGEMENT, TENTH EDITION

ISBN: 0-13-611941-7

PRINCIPLES OF OPERATIONS MANAGEMENT, EIGHTH EDITION

ISBN: 0-13-611446-6

1 Operations and Productivity

PART ONE
Introduction to Operations Management
(Chapters 1–4)

Chapter Outline

10
OM Strategy Decisions

- Design of Goods and Services
- Managing Quality
- Process Strategy
- Location Strategies
- Layout Strategies
- Human Resources
- Supply-Chain Management
- Inventory Management
- Scheduling
- Maintenance

OPERATIONS MANAGEMENT AT HARD ROCK CAFE

Operations managers throughout the world are producing products every day to provide for the well-being of society. These products take on a multitude of forms. They may be washing machines at Whirlpool, motion pictures at Dreamworks, rides at Disney World, or food at Hard Rock Cafe. These firms produce thousands of complex products every day—to be delivered as the customer ordered them, when the customers wants them, and where the customer wants them. Hard Rock does this for over 35 million guests worldwide every year. This is a challenging task, and the operations manager's job,

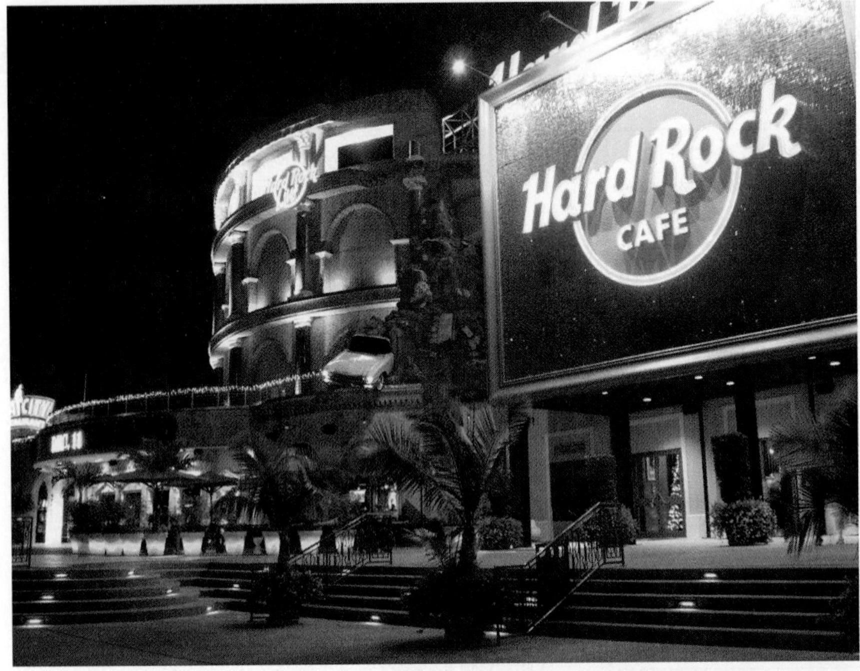

Hard Rock Cafe in Orlando, Florida, prepares over 3,500 meals each day. Seating more than 1,500 people, it is one of the largest restaurants in the world. But Hard Rock's operations managers serve the hot food hot and the cold food cold.

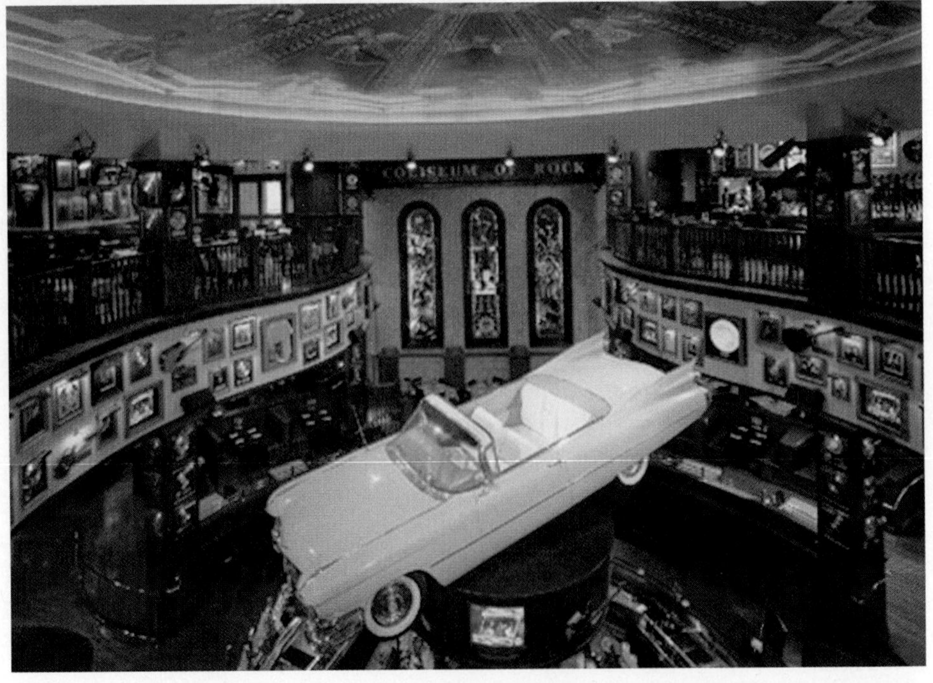

Operations managers are interested in the attractiveness of the layout, but they must be sure that the facility contributes to the efficient movement of people and material with the necessary controls to ensure that proper portions are served.

Lots of work goes into designing, testing, and costing meals. Then suppliers deliver quality products on time, every time, for well-trained cooks to prepare quality meals. But none of that matters unless an enthusiastic wait staff, such as the one shown here, is doing its job.

whether at Whirlpool, Dreamworks, Disney, or Hard Rock, is demanding.

Orlando-based Hard Rock Cafe opened its first restaurant in London in 1971, making it over 39 years old and the granddaddy of theme restaurants. Although other theme restaurants have come and gone, Hard Rock is still going strong, with 129 restaurants in more than 40 countries—and new restaurants opening each year. Hard Rock made its name with rock music memorabilia, having started when Eric Clapton, a regular customer, marked his favorite bar stool by hanging his guitar on the wall in the London cafe. Now Hard Rock has millions of dollars invested in memorabilia. To keep customers coming back time and again, Hard Rock creates value in the form of good food and entertainment.

The operations managers at Hard Rock Cafe at Universal Studios in Orlando provide more than 3,500 custom products, in this case meals, every day. These products are designed, tested, and then analyzed for cost of ingredients, labor requirements, and customer satisfaction. On approval, menu items are put into production—and then only if the ingredients are available from qualified suppliers. The production process, from receiving, to cold storage, to grilling or baking or frying, and a dozen other steps, is designed and maintained to yield a quality meal. Operations managers, using the best people they can recruit and train, also prepare effective employee schedules and design efficient layouts.

Efficient kitchen layouts, motivated personnel, tight schedules, and the right ingredients at the right place at the right time are required to delight the customer.

Managers who successfully design and deliver goods and services throughout the world understand operations. In this text, we look not only at how Hard Rock's managers create value but also how operations managers in other services, as well as in manufacturing, do so. Operations management is demanding, challenging, and exciting. It affects our lives every day. Ultimately, operations managers determine how well we live.

Chapter 1 **Learning Objectives**

AUTHOR COMMENT
Let's begin by defining what this course is about.

WHAT IS OPERATIONS MANAGEMENT?

LO1: Define operations management

Operations management (OM) is a discipline that applies to restaurants like Hard Rock Cafe as well as to factories like Ford and Whirlpool. The techniques of OM apply throughout the world to virtually all productive enterprises. It doesn't matter if the application is in an office, a hospital, a restaurant, a department store, or a factory—the production of goods and services requires operations management. And the *efficient* production of goods and services requires effective applications of the concepts, tools, and techniques of OM that we introduce in this book.

VIDEO 1.1
Operations Management at Hard Rock

VIDEO 1.2
Operations Management at Frito-Lay

As we progress through this text, we will discover how to manage operations in a changing global economy. An array of informative examples, charts, text discussions, and pictures illustrates concepts and provides information. We will see how operations managers create the goods and services that enrich our lives.

In this chapter, we first define *operations management*, explaining its heritage and exploring the exciting role operations managers play in a huge variety of organizations. Then we discuss production and productivity in both goods- and service-producing firms. This is followed by a discussion of operations in the service sector and the challenge of managing an effective and efficient production system.

Production
The creation of goods and services.

Operations management (OM)
Activities that relate to the creation of goods and services through the transformation of inputs to outputs.

Production is the creation of goods and services. **Operations management (OM)** is the set of activities that creates value in the form of goods and services by transforming inputs into outputs. Activities creating goods and services take place in all organizations. In manufacturing firms, the production activities that create goods are usually quite obvious. In them, we can see the creation of a tangible product such as a Sony TV or a Harley-Davidson motorcycle.

In an organization that does not create a tangible good or product, the production function may be less obvious. We often call these activities *services*. The services may be "hidden" from the public and even from the customer. The product may take such forms as the transfer of funds from a savings account to a checking account, the transplant of a liver, the filling of an empty seat on an airplane, or the education of a student. Regardless of whether the end product is a good or service, the production activities that go on in the organization are often referred to as operations, or *operations management*.

AUTHOR COMMENT
Operations is one of the three functions that every organization performs.

ORGANIZING TO PRODUCE GOODS AND SERVICES

To create goods and services, all organizations perform three functions (see Figure 1.1). These functions are the necessary ingredients not only for production but also for an organization's survival. They are:

1. *Marketing*, which generates the demand, or at least takes the order for a product or service (nothing happens until there is a sale).
2. *Production/operations*, which creates the product.
3. *Finance/accounting*, which tracks how well the organization is doing, pays the bills, and collects the money.

Universities, churches or synagogues, and businesses all perform these functions. Even a volunteer group such as the Boy Scouts of America is organized to perform these three basic functions. Figure 1.1 shows how a bank, an airline, and a manufacturing firm organize themselves to perform these functions. The blue-shaded areas of Figure 1.1 show the operations functions in these firms.

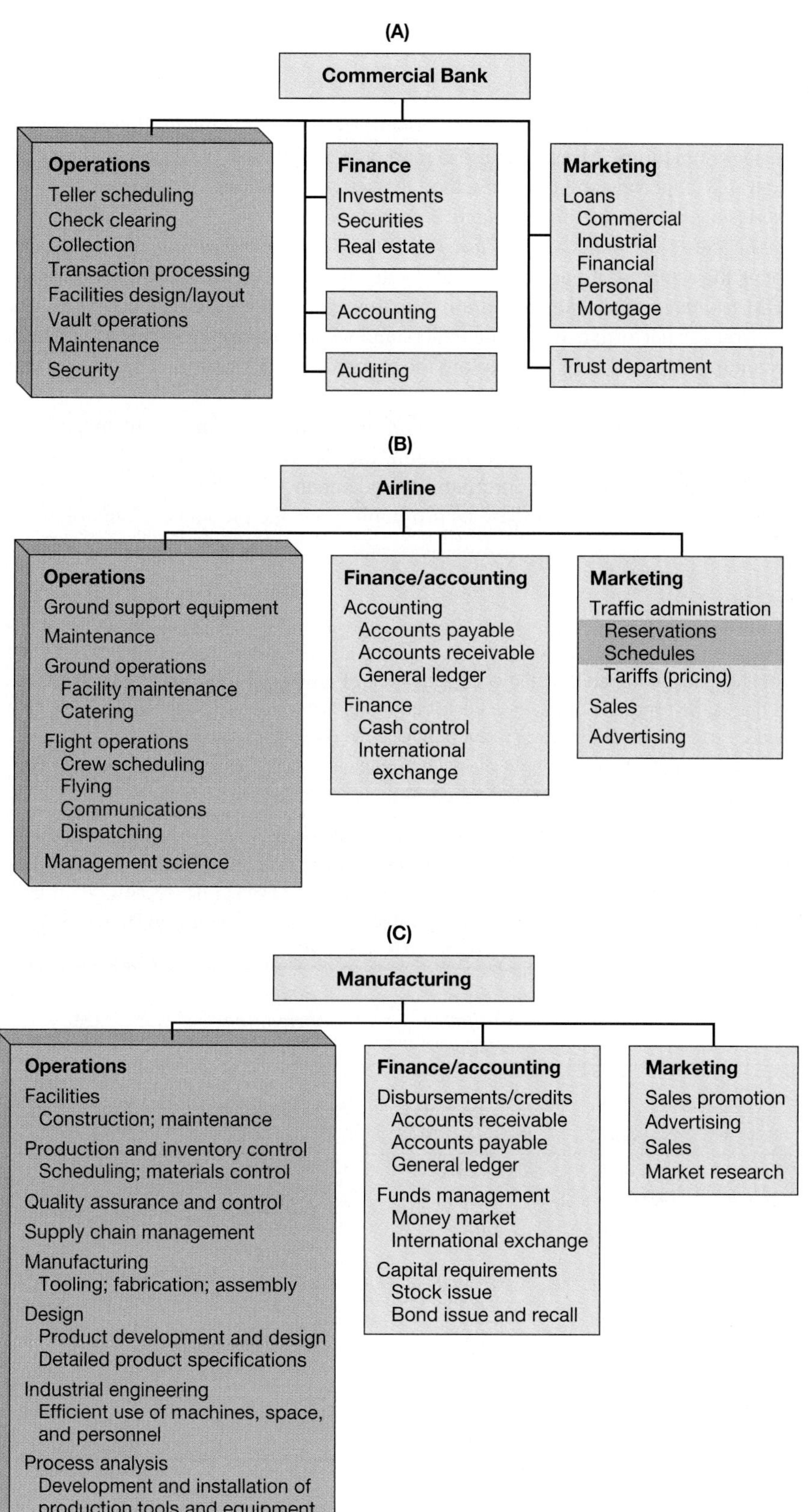

◀ **FIGURE 1.1**

Organization Charts for Two Service Organizations and One Manufacturing Organization

(A) A bank, (B) an airline, and (C) a manufacturing organization. The blue areas are OM activities.

AUTHOR COMMENT
The areas in blue indicate the significant role that OM plays in both manufacturing and service firms.

AUTHOR COMMENT
Good OM managers are scarce and, as a result, career opportunities and pay are excellent.

WHY STUDY OM?

We study OM for four reasons:

1. OM is one of the three major functions of any organization, and it is integrally related to all the other business functions. All organizations market (sell), finance (account), and produce (operate), and it is important to know how the OM activity functions. Therefore, we study *how people organize themselves for productive enterprise.*
2. We study OM because we want to know *how goods and services are produced.* The production function is the segment of our society that creates the products and services we use.
3. We study OM to *understand what operations managers do.* Regardless of your job in an organization, you can perform better if you understand what operation managers do. In addition, understanding OM will help you explore the numerous and lucrative career opportunities in the field.
4. We study OM *because it is such a costly part of an organization.* A large percentage of the revenue of most firms is spent in the OM function. Indeed, OM provides a major opportunity for an organization to improve its profitability and enhance its service to society. Example 1 considers how a firm might increase its profitability via the production function.

EXAMPLE 1 ▶

Examining the options for increasing contribution

Fisher Technologies is a small firm that must double its dollar contribution to fixed cost and profit in order to be profitable enough to purchase the next generation of production equipment. Management has determined that if the firm fails to increase contribution, its bank will not make the loan and the equipment cannot be purchased. If the firm cannot purchase the equipment, the limitations of the old equipment will force Fisher to go out of business and, in doing so, put its employees out of work and discontinue producing goods and services for its customers.

APPROACH ▶ Table 1.1 shows a simple profit-and-loss statement and three strategic options (marketing, finance/accounting, and operations) for the firm. The first option is a *marketing option,* where good marketing management may increase sales by 50%. By increasing sales by 50%, contribution will in turn increase 71%. But increasing sales 50% may be difficult; it may even be impossible.

▶ TABLE 1.1
Options for Increasing Contribution

		Marketing Option[a]	*Finance/Accounting Option*[b]	*OM Option*[c]
	Current	**Increase Sales Revenue 50%**	**Reduce Finance Costs 50%**	**Reduce Production Costs 20%**
Sales	$100,000	$150,000	$100,000	$100,000
Costs of goods	−80,000	−120,000	−80,000	−64,000
Gross margin	20,000	30,000	20,000	36,000
Finance costs	−6,000	−6,000	−3,000	−6,000
Subtotal	14,000	24,000	17,000	30,000
Taxes at 25%	−3,500	−6,000	−4,250	−7,500
Contribution[d]	$ 10,500	$ 18,000	$ 12,750	$ 22,500

[a]Increasing sales 50% increases contribution by $7,500, or 71% (7,500/10,500).
[b]Reducing finance costs 50% increases contribution by $2,250, or 21% (2,250/10,500).
[c]Reducing production costs 20% increases contribution by $12,000, or 114% (12,000/10,500).
[d]Contribution to fixed cost (excluding finance costs) and profit.

The second option is a *finance/accounting option,* where finance costs are cut in half through good financial management. But even a reduction of 50% is still inadequate for generating the necessary increase in contribution. Contribution is increased by only 21%.

The third option is an *OM option,* where management reduces production costs by 20% and increases contribution by 114%.

SOLUTION ▶ Given the conditions of our brief example, Fisher Technologies has increased contribution from $10,500 to $22,500. It may now have a bank willing to lend it additional funds.

INSIGHT ▶ The OM option not only yields the greatest improvement in contribution but also may be the only feasible option. Increasing sales by 50% and decreasing finance cost by 50% may both be virtually impossible. Reducing operations cost by 20% may be difficult but feasible.

LEARNING EXERCISE ▶ What is the impact of only a 15% decrease in costs in the OM option? [Answer: A $19,500 contribution; an 86% increase.]

Example 1 underscores the importance of an effective operations activity of a firm. Development of increasingly effective operations is the approach taken by many companies as they face growing global competition.

WHAT OPERATIONS MANAGERS DO

AUTHOR COMMENT An operations manager must successfully address the 10 decisions around which this text is organized.

All good managers perform the basic functions of the management process. The **management process** consists of *planning*, *organizing*, *staffing*, *leading*, and *controlling*. Operations managers apply this management process to the decisions they make in the OM function. The 10 major decisions of OM are shown in Table 1.2. Successfully addressing each of these decisions requires planning, organizing, staffing, leading, and controlling. Typical issues relevant to these decisions and the chapter where each is discussed are also shown.

Management process
The application of planning, organizing, staffing, leading, and controlling to the achievement of objectives.

Where Are the OM Jobs? How does one get started on a career in operations? The 10 OM decisions identified in Table 1.2 are made by individuals who work in the disciplines shown in the blue areas of Figure 1.1. Competent business students who know their accounting, statistics, finance, and OM have an opportunity to assume entry-level positions in all of these areas. As you read this text, identify disciplines that can assist you in making these decisions. Then take courses in those

◀ TABLE 1.2
Ten Critical Decisions of Operations Management

Ten Decision Areas	Issues	Chapter(s)
1. Design of goods and services	What good or service should we offer? How should we design these products?	5
2. Managing quality	How do we define the quality? Who is responsible for quality?	6, Supplement 6
3. Process and capacity design	What process and what capacity will these products require? What equipment and technology is necessary for these processes?	7, Supplement 7
4. Location strategy	Where should we put the facility? On what criteria should we base the location decision?	8
5. Layout strategy	How should we arrange the facility? How large must the facility be to meet our plan?	9
6. Human resources and job design	How do we provide a reasonable work environment? How much can we expect our employees to produce?	10
7. Supply-chain management	Should we make or buy this component? Who should be our suppliers and how can we integrate them into our strategy?	11, Supplement 11
8. Inventory, material requirements planning, and JIT (just-in-time)	How much inventory of each item should we have? When do we reorder?	12, 14, 16
9. Intermediate and short-term scheduling	Are we better off keeping people on the payroll during slowdowns? Which job do we perform next?	13, 15
10. Maintenance	How do we build reliability into our processes? Who is responsible for maintenance?	17

AUTHOR COMMENT Current OM emphasis on quality and supply chain has increased job opportunities in these 10 areas.

Operations Management Positions

SEARCH JOBS

Date	Job Title
1/15	**Plant Manager** Division of Fortune 1000 company seeks plant manager for plant located in the upper Hudson Valley area. This plant manufacturers loading dock equipment for commercial markets. The candidate must be experienced in plant management including expertise in production planning, purchasing, and inventory management. Good written and oral communication skills are a must, along with excellent application of skills in managing people.
2/23	**Operations Analyst** Expanding national coffee shop: top 10 "Best Places to Work" wants junior level systems analyst to join our excellent store improvement team. Business or I.E. degree, work methods, labor standards, ergonomics, cost accounting knowledge a plus. This is a hands-on job and excellent opportunity for a team player with good people skills. West coast location. Some travel required.
3/18	**Quality Manager** Several openings exist in our small package processing facilities in the Northeast, Florida, and Southern California for quality managers. These highly visible positions require extensive use of statistical tools to monitor all aspects of service, timeliness, and workload measurement. The work involves (1) a combination of hands-on applications and detailed analysis using databases and spreadsheets. (2) process audits to identify areas for improvement and (3) management of implementation of changes. Positions involve night hours and weekends. Send resume.
4/6	**Supply Chain Manager and Planner** Responsibilities entail negotiating contracts and establishing long-term relationships with suppliers. We will rely on the selected candidate to maintain accuracy in the purchasing system, invoices, and product returns. A bachelor's degree and up to 2 years related experience are required. Working knowledge of MRP, ability to use feedback to master scheduling and suppliers and consolidate orders for best price and delivery are necessary. Proficiency in all PC Windows applications, particularly Excel and Word, is essential. Knowledge of Oracle business systems I is a plus. Effective verbal and written communication skills are essential.
5/14	**Process Improvement Consultants** An expanding consulting firm is seeking consultants to design and implement lean production and cycle time reduction plans in both service and manufacturing processes. Our firm is currently working with an international bank to improve its back office operations, as well as with several manufacturing firms. A business degree required; APICS certification a plus.

▲ **FIGURE 1.2** **Many Opportunities Exist for Operations Managers**

areas. The more background an OM student has in accounting, statistics, information systems, and mathematics, the more job opportunities will be available. About 40% of *all* jobs are in OM.

The following professional organizations provide various certifications that may enhance your education and be of help in your career:

- APICS, the Association for Operations Management (**www.apics.org**)
- American Society for Quality (ASQ) (**www.asq.org**)
- Institute for Supply Management (ISM) (**www.ism.ws**)
- Project Management Institute (PMI) (**www.pmi.org**)
- Council of Supply Chain Management Professionals (**www.cscmp.org**)

Figure 1.2 shows some recent job opportunities.

THE HERITAGE OF OPERATIONS MANAGEMENT

The field of OM is relatively young, but its history is rich and interesting. Our lives and the OM discipline have been enhanced by the innovations and contributions of numerous individuals. We now introduce a few of these people, and we provide a summary of significant events in operations management in Figure 1.3.

Cost Focus		Quality Focus	Customization Focus
Early Concepts 1776–1880 Labor Specialization (Smith, Babbage) Standardized Parts (Whitney) **Scientific Management Era 1880–1910** Gantt Charts (Gantt) Motion & Time Studies (Gilbreth) Process Analysis (Taylor) Queuing Theory (Erlang)	**Mass Production Era 1910–1980** Moving Assembly Line (Ford/Sorensen) Statistical Sampling (Shewhart) Economic Order Quantity (Harris) Linear Programming PERT/CPM (DuPont) Material Requirements Planning (MRP)	**Lean Production Era 1980–1995** Just-in-Time (JIT) Computer-Aided Design (CAD) Electronic Data Interchange (EDI) Total Quality Management (TQM) Baldrige Award Empowerment Kanbans	**Mass Customization Era 1995–2015** Globalization Internet/E-Commerce Enterprise Resource Planning International Quality Standards (ISO) Finite Scheduling Supply-Chain Management Mass Customization Build-to-Order Sustainability

▲ **FIGURE 1.3 Significant Events in Operations Management**

Eli Whitney (1800) is credited for the early popularization of interchangeable parts, which was achieved through standardization and quality control. Through a contract he signed with the U.S. government for 10,000 muskets, he was able to command a premium price because of their interchangeable parts.

Frederick W. Taylor (1881), known as the father of scientific management, contributed to personnel selection, planning and scheduling, motion study, and the now popular field of ergonomics. One of his major contributions was his belief that management should be much more resourceful and aggressive in the improvement of work methods. Taylor and his colleagues, Henry L. Gantt and Frank and Lillian Gilbreth, were among the first to systematically seek the best way to produce.

Another of Taylor's contributions was the belief that management should assume more responsibility for:

1. Matching employees to the right job.
2. Providing the proper training.
3. Providing proper work methods and tools.
4. Establishing legitimate incentives for work to be accomplished.

By 1913, Henry Ford and Charles Sorensen combined what they knew about standardized parts with the quasi-assembly lines of the meatpacking and mail-order industries and added the revolutionary concept of the assembly line, where men stood still and material moved.

Quality control is another historically significant contribution to the field of OM. Walter Shewhart (1924) combined his knowledge of statistics with the need for quality control and provided the foundations for statistical sampling in quality control. W. Edwards Deming (1950) believed, as did Frederick Taylor, that management must do more to improve the work environment and processes so that quality can be improved.

Operations management will continue to progress with contributions from other disciplines, including *industrial engineering* and *management science*. These disciplines, along with statistics, management, and economics, contribute to improved models and decision making.

Innovations from the *physical sciences* (biology, anatomy, chemistry, physics) have also contributed to advances in OM. These innovations include new adhesives, faster integrated circuits, gamma rays to sanitize food products, and higher-quality glass for LCD and plasma TVs. Innovation in products and processes often depends on advances in the physical sciences.

Especially important contributions to OM have come from *information technology*, which we define as the systematic processing of data to yield information. Information technology—with wireless links, Internet, and e-commerce—is reducing costs and accelerating communication.

Decisions in operations management require individuals who are well versed in management science, in information technology, and often in one of the biological or physical sciences. In this textbook, we look at the diverse ways a student can prepare for a career in operations management.

AUTHOR COMMENT Services are especially important because almost 80% of all jobs are in service firms.

OPERATIONS IN THE SERVICE SECTOR

Manufacturers produce a tangible product, while service products are often intangible. But many products are a combination of a good and a service, which complicates the definition of a service. Even the U.S. government has trouble generating a consistent definition. Because definitions vary, much of the data and statistics generated about the service sector are inconsistent. However, we define **services** as including repair and maintenance, government, food and lodging, transportation, insurance, trade, financial, real estate, education, legal, medical, entertainment, and other professional occupations.[1]

Services
Economic activities that typically produce an intangible product (such as education, entertainment, lodging, government, financial, and health services).

Differences Between Goods and Services

Let's examine some of the differences between goods and services:

LO2: Explain the distinction between goods and services

- Services are usually *intangible* (for example, your purchase of a ride in an empty airline seat between two cities) as opposed to a tangible good.
- Services are often *produced and consumed simultaneously*; there is no stored inventory. For instance, the beauty salon produces a haircut that is "consumed" simultaneously, or the doctor produces an operation that is "consumed" as it is produced. We have not yet figured out how to inventory haircuts or appendectomies.
- Services are often *unique*. Your mix of financial coverage, such as investments and insurance policies, may not be the same as anyone else's, just as the medical procedure or a haircut produced for you is not exactly like anyone else's.
- Services have *high customer interaction*. Services are often difficult to standardize, automate, and make as efficient as we would like because customer interaction demands uniqueness. In fact, in many cases this uniqueness is what the customer is paying for; therefore, the operations manager must ensure that the product is designed (i.e., customized) so that it can be delivered in the required unique manner.
- Services have *inconsistent product definition*. Product definition may be rigorous, as in the case of an auto insurance policy, but inconsistent because policyholders change cars and mature.
- Services are often *knowledge based*, as in the case of educational, medical, and legal services, and therefore hard to automate.
- Services are frequently *dispersed*. Dispersion occurs because services are frequently brought to the client/customer via a local office, a retail outlet, or even a house call.

The activities of the operations function are often very similar for both goods and services. For instance, both goods and services must have quality standards established, and both must be designed and processed on a schedule in a facility where human resources are employed.

Having made the distinction between goods and services, we should point out that in many cases, the distinction is not clear-cut. In reality, almost all services and almost all goods are a mixture of a service and a tangible product. Even services such as consulting may require a tangible report. Similarly, the sale of most goods includes a service. For instance, many products

[1]This definition is similar to the categories used by the U.S. Bureau of Labor Statistics.

have the service components of financing and delivery (e.g., automobile sales). Many also require after-sale training and maintenance (e.g., office copiers and machinery). "Service" activities may also be an integral part of production. Human resource activities, logistics, accounting, training, field service, and repair are all service activities, but they take place within a manufacturing organization. Very few services are "pure," meaning they have no tangible component. Counseling may be one of the exceptions.

Growth of Services

Services constitute the largest economic sector in postindustrial societies. Until about 1900, most Americans were employed in agriculture. Increased agricultural productivity allowed people to leave the farm and seek employment in the city. Similarly, manufacturing employment has decreased in the past 30 years. The changes in manufacturing and service employment, in millions, are shown in Figure 1.4(a). Interestingly, as Figure 1.4(b) indicates, the number of people employed in manufacturing has decreased since 1950, but each person is now producing almost 20 times more than in 1950. Services became the dominant employer in the early 1920s, with manufacturing employment peaking at about 32% in 1950. The huge productivity increases in agriculture and manufacturing have allowed more of our economic resources to be devoted to services, as shown in Figure 1.4(c). Consequently, much of the world can now enjoy the pleasures of education, health services, entertainment, and myriad other things that we call services. Examples of firms and percentage of employment in the U.S. **service sector** are shown in Table 1.3. Table 1.3 also provides employment percentages for the nonservice sectors of manufacturing, construction, agriculture, and mining on the bottom four lines.

Service sector
The segment of the economy that includes trade, financial, lodging, education, legal, medical, and other professional occupations.

Service Pay

Although there is a common perception that service industries are low paying, in fact, many service jobs pay very well. Operations managers in the maintenance facility of an airline are very well paid, as are the operations managers who supervise computer services to the financial community. About 42% of all service workers receive wages above the national average. However, the service-sector average is driven down because 14 of the U.S. Department of Commerce categories of the 33 service industries do indeed pay below the all-private industry average. Of these, retail trade, which pays only 61% of the national private industry average, is large. But even considering the retail sector, the average wage of all service workers is about 96% of the average of all private industries.

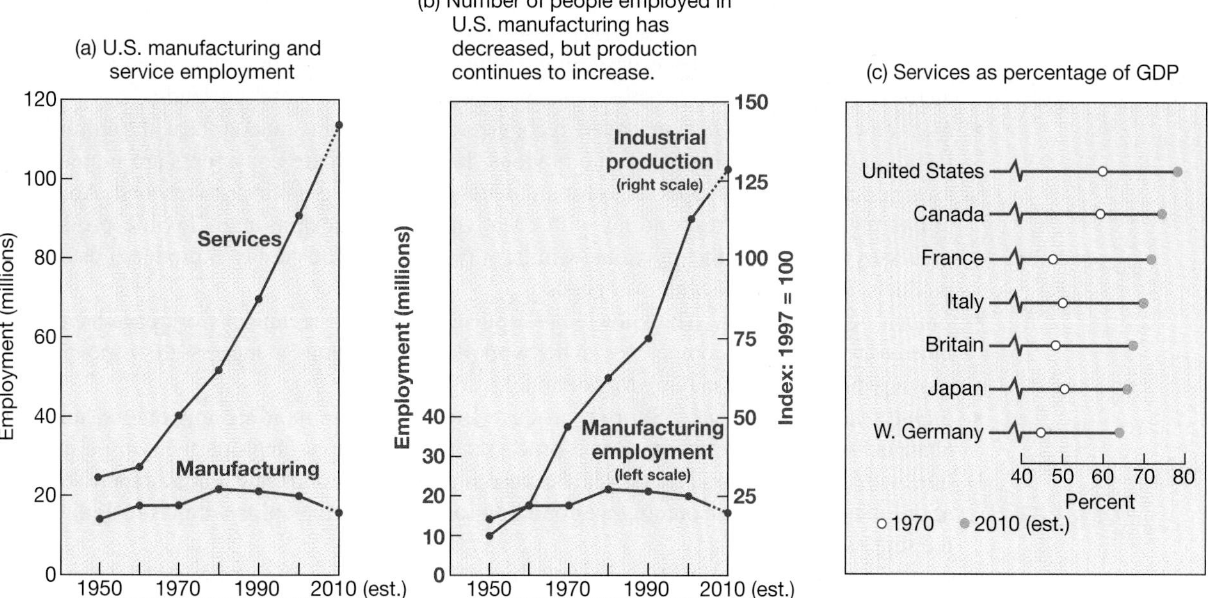

▲ **FIGURE 1.4 Development of the Service Economy and Manufacturing Productivity**

Sources: U.S. Bureau of Labor Statistics; Federal Reserve Board, Industrial Production and Capacity Utilization (2009); and Statistical Abstract of the United States (2008).

TABLE 1.3
Examples of Organizations in Each Sector

Sources: Statistical Abstract of the United States (2008), Table 600, and Bureau of Labor Statistics, 2008.

AUTHOR COMMENT
Service jobs with their operations component are growing as a percentage of all jobs.

Sector	Example	Percent of All Jobs	
Service Sector			
Education, Legal, Medical, Other	San Diego Zoo, Arnold Palmer Hospital	25.8	78.8
Trade (retail, wholesale)	Walgreen's, Wal-Mart, Nordstrom	14.4	
Utilities, Transportation	Pacific Gas & Electric, American Airlines	5.2	
Professional and Business Services	Snelling and Snelling, Waste Management, Inc.	10.7	
Finance, Information, Real Estate	Citicorp, American Express, Prudential, Aetna	9.6	
Food, Lodging, Entertainment	Olive Garden, Motel 6, Walt Disney	8.5	
Public Administration	U.S., State of Alabama, Cook County	4.6	
Manufacturing Sector	General Electric, Ford, U.S. Steel, Intel		11.2
Construction Sector	Bechtel, McDermott		8.1
Agriculture	King Ranch		1.4
Mining Sector	Homestake Mining		.5
Grand Total			100.0

AUTHOR COMMENT
One of the reasons OM is such an exciting discipline is that an operations manager is confronted with ever-changing issues, from technology to sustainability.

EXCITING NEW TRENDS IN OPERATIONS MANAGEMENT

OM managers operate in an exciting and dynamic environment. This environment is the result of a variety of challenging forces, from globalization of world trade to the transfer of ideas, products, and money at electronic speeds. The direction now being taken by OM—where it has been and where it is going—is shown in Figure 1.5. Let's look at some of these challenges:

- *Ethics:* Operations managers' roles of buying from suppliers, transforming resources into finished goods, and delivering to customers places them at critical junctures where they must frequently make ethical decisions.
- *Global focus:* The rapid decline in communication and transportation costs has made markets global. Similarly, resources in the form of capital, materials, talent, and labor are now also global. As a result, countries throughout the world are contributing to globalization as they vie for economic growth. Operations managers are rapidly responding with creative designs, efficient production, and quality goods.
- *Rapid product development:* Rapid international communication of news, entertainment, and lifestyles is dramatically chopping away at the life span of products. Operations managers are responding with management structures, technology, and alliances (partnerships) that are more responsive and effective.
- *Environmentally sensitive production:* Operation managers' continuing battle to improve productivity is increasingly concerned with designing products and processes that are ecologically sustainable. That means designing products and packaging that minimize resource use, are biodegradable, can be recycled, and are generally environmentally friendly.
- *Mass customization:* Once managers recognize the world as the marketplace, the cultural and individual differences become quite obvious. In a world where consumers are increasingly aware of innovation and options, substantial pressure is placed on firms to respond. And operations managers are responding with creative product designs and flexible production processes that cater to the individual whims of consumers. The goal is to produce customized products, whenever and wherever needed.
- *Empowered employees:* The knowledge explosion and more technical workplace have combined to require more competence in the workplace. Operations managers are responding by moving more decision making to individual workers.
- *Supply-chain partnering:* Shorter product life cycles, demanding customers, and fast changes in technology, material, and processes require supply-chain partners to be more in tune with the needs of end users. And because suppliers can contribute unique expertise, operations managers are outsourcing and building long-term partnerships with critical players in the supply chain.
- *Just-in-time performance:* Inventory requires financial resources and impedes response to rapid changes in the marketplace. These forces push operations managers to viciously cut inventories at every level, from raw materials to finished goods.

These trends are part of the exciting OM challenges that are discussed in this text.

Traditional Approach	Reasons for Change	Current Challenges
Ethics and regulation not at the forefront	*Public concern over pollution, corruption, child labor, etc.*	High ethical and social responsibility; increased legal and professional standards (all chapters)
Local, regional, national focus	*Growth of reliable, low-cost communication and transportation*	Global focus; international collaboration (Chapters 2, 11)
Lengthy product development	*Shorter life cycles; growth of global communication; CAD; Internet*	Rapid product development; design collaboration (Chapter 5)
Low-cost production, with little concern for environment; free resources (air, water) ignored	*Public sensitivity to environment; ISO 14000 standard; increasing disposal costs*	Environmentally sensitive production; green manufacturing; sustainability (Chapters 5, 7)
Low-cost standard products	*Rise of consumerism; increased affluence; individualism*	Mass customization (Chapters 5, 7)
Emphasis on specialized, often manual tasks	*Recognizing the importance of the employee's total contribution; knowledge society*	Empowered employees; enriched jobs (Chapter 10)
"In-house" production; low-bid purchasing	*Rapid technology change; increasing competitive forces*	Supply-chain partnering; joint ventures; alliances (Chapter 11, Supplement 11)
Large lot production	*Shorter product life; increasing need to reduce inventory*	Just-in-time performance; lean; continuous improvement (Chapter 16)

▲ **FIGURE 1.5 Changing Challenges for the Operations Manager**

THE PRODUCTIVITY CHALLENGE

AUTHOR COMMENT Why is productivity important? Because it determines our standard of living.

The creation of goods and services requires changing resources into goods and services. The more efficiently we make this change, the more productive we are and the more value is added to the good or service provided. **Productivity** is the ratio of outputs (goods and services) divided by the inputs (resources, such as labor and capital) (see Figure 1.6). The operations manager's job is to enhance (improve) this ratio of outputs to inputs. Improving productivity means improving efficiency.[2]

Productivity

The ratio of outputs (goods and services) divided by one or more inputs (such as labor, capital, or management).

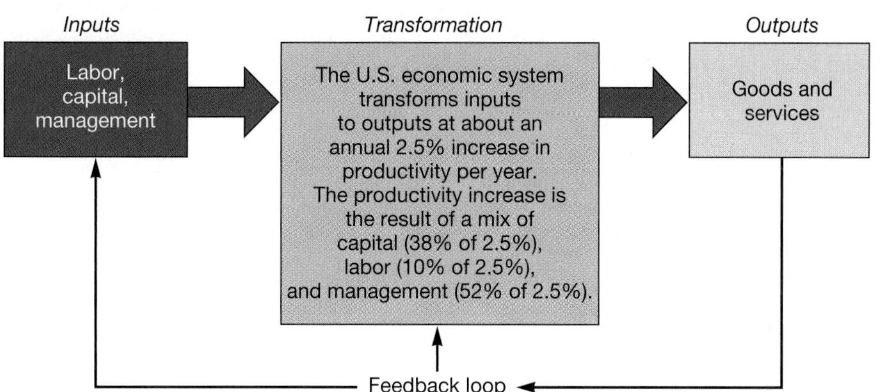
Inputs
Labor, capital, management
Transformation
The U.S. economic system transforms inputs to outputs at about an annual 2.5% increase in productivity per year. The productivity increase is the result of a mix of capital (38% of 2.5%), labor (10% of 2.5%), and management (52% of 2.5%).
Outputs
Goods and services
Feedback loop

◄ **FIGURE 1.6 The Economic System Adds Value by Transforming Inputs to Outputs**

An effective feedback loop evaluates performance against a strategy or standard. It also evaluates customer satisfaction and sends signals to managers controlling the inputs and transformation process.

[2]*Efficiency* means doing the job well—with a minimum of resources and waste. Note the distinction between being *efficient*, which implies doing the job well, and *effective*, which means doing the right thing. A job well done—say, by applying the 10 decisions of operations management—helps us be *efficient*; developing and using the correct strategy helps us be *effective*.

OM in Action ► Improving Productivity at Starbucks

"This is a game of seconds . . ." says Silva Peterson, whom Starbucks has put in charge of saving seconds. Her team of 10 analysts is constantly asking themselves: "How can we shave time off this?"

Peterson's analysis suggested that there were some obvious opportunities. First, stop requiring signatures on credit-card purchases under $25. This sliced 8 seconds off the transaction time at the cash register.

Then analysts noticed that Starbucks's largest cold beverage, the Venti size, required two bending and digging motions to scoop up enough ice. The scoop was too small. Redesign of the scoop provided the proper amount in one motion and cut 14 seconds off the average time of one minute.

Third were new espresso machines; with the push of a button, the machines grind coffee beans and brew. This allowed the server, called a "barista" in Starbucks's vocabulary, to do other things. The savings: about 12 seconds per espresso shot.

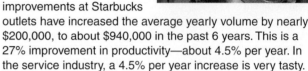

As a result, operations improvements at Starbucks outlets have increased the average yearly volume by nearly $200,000, to about $940,000 in the past 6 years. This is a 27% improvement in productivity—about 4.5% per year. In the service industry, a 4.5% per year increase is very tasty.

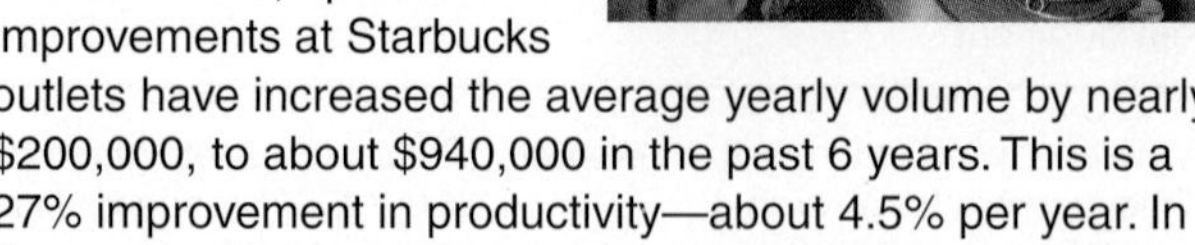

Sources: The Wall Street Journal (August 4, 2009): A1, A10 and (April 12, 2005): B2:B7; *Industrial Engineer* (January 2006): 66; and **www.finfacts.com**, October 6, 2005.

This improvement can be achieved in two ways: reducing inputs while keeping output constant or increasing output while keeping inputs constant. Both represent an improvement in productivity. In an economic sense, inputs are labor, capital, and management, which are integrated into a production system. Management creates this production system, which provides the conversion of inputs to outputs. Outputs are goods and services, including such diverse items as guns, butter, education, improved judicial systems, and ski resorts. *Production* is the making of goods and services. High production may imply only that more people are working and that employment levels are high (low unemployment), but it does not imply high *productivity*.

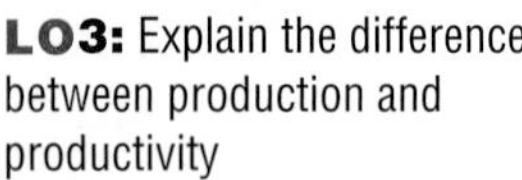

LO3: Explain the difference between production and productivity

Measurement of productivity is an excellent way to evaluate a country's ability to provide an improving standard of living for its people. *Only through increases in productivity can the standard of living improve.* Moreover, only through increases in productivity can labor, capital, and management receive additional payments. If returns to labor, capital, or management are increased without increased productivity, prices rise. On the other hand, downward pressure is placed on prices when productivity increases, because more is being produced with the same resources.

The benefits of increased productivity are illustrated in the *OM in Action* box "Improving Productivity at Starbucks."

For well over a century (from about 1869), the U.S. has been able to increase productivity at an average rate of almost 2.5% per year. Such growth has doubled U.S. wealth every 30 years. The manufacturing sector, although a decreasing portion of the U.S. economy, has recently seen annual productivity increases exceeding 4%, and the service sector, with increases of almost 1%, has also shown some improvement. The combination has moved U.S. annual productivity growth in this early part of the 21st century slightly above the 2.5% range for the economy as a whole.[3]

In this text, we examine how to improve productivity through operations management. Productivity is a significant issue for the world and one that the operations manager is uniquely qualified to address.

LO4: Compute single-factor productivity

Productivity Measurement

The measurement of productivity can be quite direct. Such is the case when productivity is measured by labor-hours per ton of a specific type of steel. Although labor-hours is a common measure of input, other measures such as capital (dollars invested), materials (tons of ore), or energy (kilowatts of electricity) can be used.[4] An example of this can be summarized in the following equation:

$$\text{Productivity} = \frac{\text{Units produced}}{\text{Input used}} \tag{1-1}$$

[3] U.S. Dept. of Labor, July 2009: www.bls.gov/ipc/prodybar.html

[4] The quality and time period are assumed to remain constant.

For example, if units produced = 1,000 and labor-hours used is 250, then:

$$\text{Productivity} = \frac{\text{Units produced}}{\text{Labor-hours used}} = \frac{1{,}000}{250} = 4 \text{ units per labor-hour}$$

Single-factor productivity
Indicates the ratio of one resource (input) to the goods and services produced (outputs).

The use of just one resource input to measure productivity, as shown in Equation (1-1), is known as **single-factor productivity**. However, a broader view of productivity is **multifactor productivity**, which includes all inputs (e.g., capital, labor, material, energy). Multifactor productivity is also known as *total factor productivity*. Multifactor productivity is calculated by combining the input units as shown here:

Multifactor productivity
Indicates the ratio of many or all resources (inputs) to the goods and services produced (outputs).

$$\text{Productivity} = \frac{\text{Output}}{\text{Labor} + \text{Material} + \text{Energy} + \text{Capital} + \text{Miscellaneous}} \qquad \text{(1-2)}$$

To aid in the computation of multifactor productivity, the individual inputs (the denominator) can be expressed in dollars and summed as shown in Example 2.

EXAMPLE 2

Computing single-factor and multifactor gains in productivity

Collins Title wants to evaluate its labor and multifactor productivity with a new computerized title-search system. The company has a staff of four, each working 8 hours per day (for a payroll cost of $640/day) and overhead expenses of $400 per day. Collins processes and closes on 8 titles each day. The new computerized title-search system will allow the processing of 14 titles per day. Although the staff, their work hours, and pay are the same, the overhead expenses are now $800 per day.

APPROACH ▶ Collins uses Equation (1-1) to compute labor productivity and Equation (1-2) to compute multifactor productivity.

SOLUTION: ▶

$$\text{Labor productivity with the old system: } \frac{8 \text{ titles per day}}{32 \text{ labor-hours}} = .25 \text{ titles per labor-hour}$$

$$\text{Labor productivity with the new system: } \frac{14 \text{ titles per day}}{32 \text{ labor-hours}} = .4375 \text{ titles per labor-hour}$$

$$\text{Multifactor productivity with the old system: } \frac{8 \text{ titles per day}}{\$640 + 400} = .0077 \text{ titles per dollar}$$

$$\text{Multifactor productivity with the new system: } \frac{14 \text{ titles per day}}{\$640 + 800} = .0097 \text{ titles per dollar}$$

Labor productivity has increased from .25 to .4375. The change is $(.4375 - .25)/.25 = 0.75$, or a 75% increase in labor productivity. Multifactor productivity has increased from .0077 to .0097. This change is $(.0097 - .0077)/.0077 = 0.26$, or a 26% increase in multifactor productivity.

LO5: Compute multifactor productivity

INSIGHT ▶ Both the labor (single-factor) and multifactor productivity measures show an increase in productivity. However, the multifactor measure provides a better picture of the increase because it includes all the costs connected with the increase in output.

LEARNING EXERCISE ▶ If the overhead goes to $960 (rather than $800), what is the multifactor productivity? [Answer: .00875.]

RELATED PROBLEMS ▶ 1.1, 1.2, 1.5, 1.6, 1.7, 1.8, 1.9, 1.11, 1.12, 1.14, 1.15

Use of productivity measures aids managers in determining how well they are doing. But results from the two measures can be expected to vary. If labor productivity growth is entirely the result of capital spending, measuring just labor distorts the results. Multifactor productivity is usually better, but more complicated. Labor productivity is the more popular measure. The multifactor-productivity measures provide better information about the trade-offs among factors, but substantial measurement problems remain. Some of these measurement problems are:

1. *Quality* may change while the quantity of inputs and outputs remains constant. Compare an HDTV of this decade with a black-and-white TV of the 1950s. Both are TVs, but few people would deny that the quality has improved. The unit of measure—a TV—is the same, but the quality has changed.
2. *External elements* may cause an increase or a decrease in productivity for which the system under study may not be directly responsible. A more reliable electric power service may

greatly improve production, thereby improving the firm's productivity because of this support system rather than because of managerial decisions made within the firm.

3. *Precise units of measure* may be lacking. Not all automobiles require the same inputs: Some cars are subcompacts, others are 911 Turbo Porsches.

Productivity measurement is particularly difficult in the service sector, where the end product can be hard to define. For example, economic statistics ignore the quality of your haircut, the outcome of a court case, or service at a retail store. In some cases, adjustments are made for the quality of the product sold but *not* the quality of the sales presentation or the advantage of a broader product selection. Productivity measurements require specific inputs and outputs, but a free economy is producing worth—what people want—which includes convenience, speed, and safety. Traditional measures of outputs may be a very poor measure of these other measures of worth. Note the quality-measurement problems in a law office, where each case is different, altering the accuracy of the measure "cases per labor-hour" or "cases per employee."

Productivity Variables

Productivity variables
The three factors critical to productivity improvement—labor, capital, and the art and science of management.

As we saw in Figure 1.6, productivity increases are dependent on three **productivity variables**:

1. *Labor*, which contributes about 10% of the annual increase.
2. *Capital*, which contributes about 38% of the annual increase.
3. *Management*, which contributes about 52% of the annual increase.

These three factors are critical to improved productivity. They represent the broad areas in which managers can take action to improve productivity.

LO6: Identify the critical variables in enhancing productivity

Labor Improvement in the contribution of labor to productivity is the result of a healthier, better-educated, and better-nourished labor force. Some increase may also be attributed to a shorter workweek. Historically, about 10% of the annual improvement in productivity is attributed to improvement in the quality of labor. Three key variables for improved labor productivity are:

1. Basic education appropriate for an effective labor force.
2. Diet of the labor force.
3. Social overhead that makes labor available, such as transportation and sanitation.

Illiteracy and poor diets are a major impediment to productivity, costing countries up to 20% of their productivity. Infrastructure that yields clean drinking water and sanitation is also an opportunity for improved productivity, as well as an opportunity for better health, in much of the world.

In developed nations, the challenge becomes *maintaining and enhancing the skills of labor* in the midst of rapidly expanding technology and knowledge. Recent data suggest that the average American 17-year-old knows significantly less mathematics than the average Japanese at the same age, and about half cannot answer the questions in Figure 1.7. Moreover, more than 38% of American job applicants tested for basic skills were deficient in reading, writing, or math.[5]

FIGURE 1.7 ▶
About Half of the 17-Year-Olds in the U.S. Cannot Correctly Answer Questions of This Type

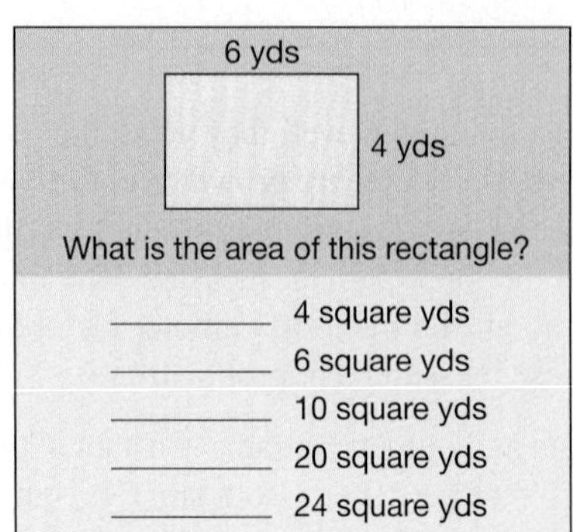

If $9y + 3 = 6y + 15$ then $y =$

_______ 1 _______ 4
_______ 2 _______ 6

Which of the following is true about 84% of 100?

_______ It is greater than 100
_______ It is less than 100
_______ It is equal to 100

AUTHOR COMMENT
Perhaps as many as 25% of U.S. workers lack the basic skills needed for their current job.

[5] "Can't Read, Can't Count," *Scientific American* (October 2001): 24; and "Economic Time Bomb: U.S. Teens Are among Worst at Math," *The Wall Street Journal* (December 7, 2004): B1.

Overcoming shortcomings in the quality of labor while other countries have a better labor force is a major challenge. Perhaps improvements can be found not only through increasing competence of labor but also via *better utilized labor with a stronger commitment*. Training, motivation, team building, and the human resource strategies discussed in Chapter 10, as well as improved education, may be among the many techniques that will contribute to increased labor productivity. Improvements in labor productivity are possible; however, they can be expected to be increasingly difficult and expensive.

Capital Human beings are tool-using animals. Capital investment provides those tools. Capital investment has increased in the U.S. every year except during a few very severe recession periods. Annual capital investment in the U.S. has increased at an annual rate of 1.5% after allowances for depreciation.

Inflation and taxes increase the cost of capital, making capital investment increasingly expensive. When the capital invested per employee drops, we can expect a drop in productivity. Using labor rather than capital may reduce unemployment in the short run, but it also makes economies less productive and therefore lowers wages in the long run. Capital investment is often a necessary, but seldom a sufficient ingredient in the battle for increased productivity.

The trade-off between capital and labor is continually in flux. The higher the cost of capital, the more projects requiring capital are "squeezed out": they are not pursued because the potential return on investment for a given risk has been reduced. Managers adjust their investment plans to changes in capital cost.

Management Management is a factor of production and an economic resource. Management is responsible for ensuring that labor and capital are effectively used to increase productivity. Management accounts for over half of the annual increase in productivity. This increase includes improvements made through the use of knowledge and the application of technology.

Using knowledge and technology is critical in postindustrial societies. Consequently, postindustrial societies are also known as knowledge societies. **Knowledge societies** are those in which much of the labor force has migrated from manual work to technical and information-processing tasks requiring ongoing education. The required education and training are important high-cost items that are the responsibility of operations managers as they build organizations and workforces. The expanding knowledge base of contemporary society requires that managers use *technology and knowledge effectively.*

Knowledge society
A society in which much of the labor force has migrated from manual work to work based on knowledge.

More effective use of capital also contributes to productivity. It falls to the operations manager, as a productivity catalyst, to select the best new capital investments as well as to improve the productivity of existing investments.

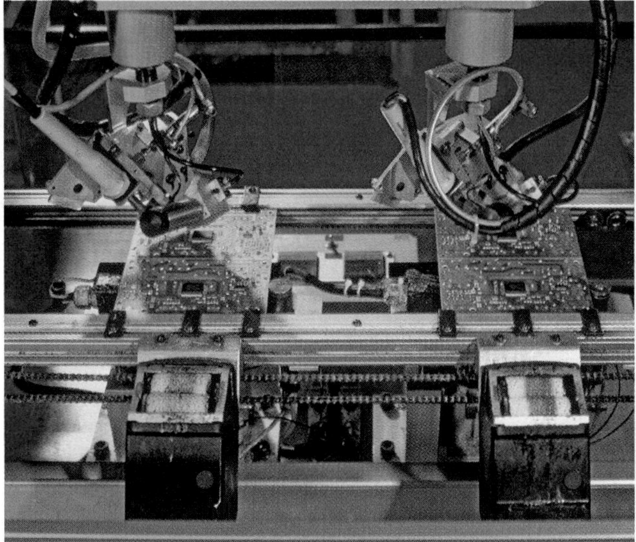

The effective use of capital often means finding the proper trade-off between investment in capital assets (automation, left) and human assets (a manual process, right). While there are risks connected with any investment, the cost of capital and physical investments is fairly clear-cut, but the cost of employees has many hidden costs including fringe benefits, social insurance, and legal constraints on hiring, employment, and termination.

Siemens, the multi-billion-dollar German conglomerate, has long been known for its apprentice programs in its home country. Because education is often the key to efficient operations in a technological society, Siemens has spread its apprentice-training programs to its U.S. plants. These programs are laying the foundation for the highly skilled workforce that is essential for global competitiveness.

The productivity challenge is difficult. A country cannot be a world-class competitor with second-class inputs. Poorly educated labor, inadequate capital, and dated technology are second-class inputs. High productivity and high-quality outputs require high-quality inputs, including good operations managers.

Productivity and the Service Sector

The service sector provides a special challenge to the accurate measurement of productivity and productivity improvement. The traditional analytical framework of economic theory is based primarily on goods-producing activities. Consequently, most published economic data relate to goods production. But the data do indicate that, as our contemporary service economy has increased in size, we have had slower growth in productivity.

Productivity of the service sector has proven difficult to improve because service-sector work is:

1. Typically labor intensive (for example, counseling, teaching).
2. Frequently focused on unique individual attributes or desires (for example, investment advice).
3. Often an intellectual task performed by professionals (for example, medical diagnosis).
4. Often difficult to mechanize and automate (for example, a haircut).
5. Often difficult to evaluate for quality (for example, performance of a law firm).

The more intellectual and personal the task, the more difficult it is to achieve increases in productivity. Low-productivity improvement in the service sector is also attributable to the growth of low-productivity activities in the service sector. These include activities not previously a part of the measured economy, such as child care, food preparation, house cleaning, and laundry service. These activities have moved out of the home and into the measured economy as more and more women have joined the workforce. Inclusion of these activities has probably resulted in lower measured productivity for the service sector, although, in fact, actual productivity has probably increased because these activities are now more efficiently produced than previously.

However, in spite of the difficulty of improving productivity in the service sector, improvements are being made. And this text presents a multitude of ways to make these improvements. Indeed, what can be done when management pays attention to how work actually gets done is astonishing!

Although the evidence indicates that all industrialized countries have the same problem with service productivity, the U.S. remains the world leader in overall productivity *and* service productivity. Retailing is twice as productive in the U.S. as in Japan, where laws protect shopkeepers from discount chains. The U.S. telephone industry is at least twice as productive as Germany's. The U.S. banking system is also 33% more efficient than Germany's banking oligopolies. However, because productivity is central to the operations manager's job and because the service sector is so large, we take special note in this text of how to improve productivity in the service sector. (See, for instance, the *OM in Action* box "Taco Bell Improves Productivity and Goes Green to Lower Costs.")

OM in Action ► Taco Bell Improves Productivity and Goes Green to Lower Costs

Founded in 1962 by Glenn Bell, Taco Bell seeks competitive advantage via low cost. Like many other services, Taco Bell relies on its operations management to improve productivity and reduce cost.

Its menu and meals are designed to be easy to prepare. Taco Bell has shifted a substantial portion of food preparation to suppliers who could perform food processing more efficiently than a stand-alone restaurant. Ground beef is precooked prior to arrival and then reheated, as are many dishes that arrive in plastic boil bags for easy sanitary reheating. Similarly, tortillas arrive already fried and onions prediced. Efficient layout and automation has cut to 8 seconds the time needed to prepare tacos and burritos and has cut time in the drive-thru lines by one minute. These advances have been combined with training and empowerment to increase the span of management from one supervisor for 5 restaurants to one supervisor for 30 or more.

Operations managers at Taco Bell believe they have cut in-store labor by 15 hours per day and reduced floor space by more than 50%. The result is a store that can handle twice the volume with half the labor.

In 2010, Taco Bell will have completed the rollout of its new Grill-to-Order kitchens by installing water- and energy-savings grills that conserve 300 million gallons of water and 200 million KwH of electricity each year. This "green"-inspired cooking method also saves the company's 5,600 restaurants $17 million per year.

Effective operations management has resulted in productivity increases that support Taco Bell's low-cost strategy. Taco Bell is now the fast-food low-cost leader with a 73% share of the Mexican fast-food market.

Sources: Energy Business Journal (May 12, 2008): 111; *Harvard Business Review* (July/August 2008): 118; and J. Hueter and W. Swart, *Interfaces* (January–February 1998): 75–91.

ETHICS AND SOCIAL RESPONSIBILITY

AUTHOR COMMENT Ethics must drive all of a manager's decisions.

Operations managers are subjected to constant changes and challenges. The systems they build to convert resources into goods and services are complex. The physical and social environment changes, as do laws and values. These changes present a variety of challenges that come from the conflicting perspectives of stakeholders such as customers, distributors, suppliers, owners, lenders, and employees. These stakeholders, as well as government agencies at various levels, require constant monitoring and thoughtful responses.

Identifying ethical and socially responsible responses while building productive systems is not always clear-cut. Among the many ethical challenges facing operations managers are:

- Efficiently developing and producing safe, quality products.
- Maintaining a sustainable environment.
- Providing a safe workplace.
- Honoring stakeholder commitments.

Managers must do all of this in an ethical and socially responsible way while meeting the demands of the marketplace. If operations managers have a *moral awareness and focus on increasing productivity* in a system where all stakeholders have a voice, then many of the ethical challenges will be successfully addressed. The organization will use fewer resources, the employees will be committed, the market will be satisfied, and the ethical climate will be enhanced. Throughout this text, we note ways in which operations managers can take ethical and socially responsible actions while successfully addressing these challenges of the market. We also conclude each chapter with an *Ethical Dilemma* exercise.

CHAPTER SUMMARY

Operations, marketing, and finance/accounting are the three functions basic to all organizations. The operations function creates goods and services. Much of the progress of operations management has been made in the twentieth century, but since the beginning of time, humankind has been attempting to improve its material well-being. Operations managers are key players in the battle to improve productivity.

As societies become increasingly affluent, more of their resources are devoted to services. In the U.S., more than three-quarters of the workforce is employed in the service sector. Productivity improvements are difficult to achieve, but operations managers are the primary vehicle for making improvements.

Key Terms

Production (p. 4)
Operations management (OM) (p. 4)
Management process (p. 7)
Services (p. 10)
Service sector (p. 11)
Productivity (p. 13)
Single-factor productivity (p. 15)
Multifactor productivity (p. 15)
Productivity variables (p. 16)
Knowledge society (p. 17)

Ethical Dilemma

Major corporations with overseas subcontractors (such as IKEA in Bangladesh, Unilever in India, and Nike in China) have been criticized, often with substantial negative publicity, when children as young as 10 have been found working in the subcontractor's facilities. The standard response is to perform an audit and then enhance controls so it does not happen again. In one such case, a 10-year-old was terminated. Shortly thereafter, the family, without the 10-year-old's contribution to the family income, lost its modest home, and the 10-year-old was left to scrounge in the local dump for scraps of metal. Was the decision to hire the 10-year-old ethical? Was the decision to terminate the 10-year-old ethical?

Discussion Questions

1. Why should one study operations management?
2. Identify four people who have contributed to the theory and techniques of operations management.
3. Briefly describe the contributions of the four individuals identified in the preceding question.
4. Figure 1.1 outlines the operations, finance/accounting, and marketing functions of three organizations. Prepare a chart similar to Figure 1.1 outlining the same functions for one of the following:
   a. a newspaper
   b. a drugstore
   c. a college library
   d. a summer camp
   e. a small costume-jewelry factory
5. Answer Question 4 for some other organization, perhaps an organization where you have worked.
6. What are the three basic functions of a firm?
7. Name the 10 decision areas of operations management.
8. Name four areas that are significant to improving labor productivity.
9. The U.S., and indeed much of the world, has been described as a "knowledge society." How does this affect productivity measurement and the comparison of productivity between the U.S. and other countries?
10. What are the measurement problems that occur when one attempts to measure productivity?
11. Mass customization and rapid product development were identified as current trends in modern manufacturing operations. What is the relationship, if any, between these trends? Can you cite any examples?
12. What are the five reasons productivity is difficult to improve in the service sector?
13. Describe some of the actions taken by Taco Bell to increase productivity that have resulted in Taco Bell's ability to serve "twice the volume with half the labor."

Solved Problems **Virtual Office Hours help is available at www.myomlab.com**

▼ SOLVED PROBLEM 1.1

Productivity can be measured in a variety of ways, such as by labor, capital, energy, material usage, and so on. At Modern Lumber, Inc., Art Binley, president and producer of apple crates sold to growers, has been able, with his current equipment, to produce 240 crates per 100 logs. He currently purchases 100 logs per day, and each log requires 3 labor-hours to process. He believes that he can hire a professional buyer who can buy a better-quality log at the same cost. If this is the case, he can increase his production to 260 crates per 100 logs. His labor-hours will increase by 8 hours per day.

What will be the impact on productivity (measured in crates per labor-hour) if the buyer is hired?

▼ SOLUTION

(a) $$\text{Current labor productivity} = \frac{240 \text{ crates}}{100 \text{ logs} \times 3 \text{ hours/log}} = \frac{240}{300} = .8 \text{ crates per labor-hour}$$

(b) $$\text{Labor productivity with buyer} = \frac{260 \text{ crates}}{(100 \text{ logs} \times 3 \text{ hours/log}) + 8 \text{ hours}} = \frac{260}{308} = .844 \text{ crates per labor-hour}$$

Using current productivity (.80 from [a]) as a base, the increase will be 5.5% (.844/.8 = 1.055, or a 5.5% increase).

▼ SOLVED PROBLEM 1.2

Art Binley has decided to look at his productivity from a multifactor (total factor productivity) perspective (refer to Solved Problem 1.1). To do so, he has determined his labor, capital, energy, and material usage and decided to use dollars as the common denominator. His total labor-hours are now 300 per day and will increase to 308 per day. His capital and energy costs will remain constant at $350 and $150 per day, respectively. Material costs for the 100 logs per day are $1,000 and will remain the same. Because he pays an average of $10 per hour (with fringes), Binley determines his productivity increase as follows:

▼ SOLUTION

	Current System		System with Professional Buyer	
Labor:	300 hrs. @10 =	3,000	308 hrs. @10 =	$3,080
Material:	100 logs/day	1,000		1,000
Capital:		350		350
Energy:		150		150
Total Cost:		$4,500		$4,580

Multifactor productivity of current system:
= 240 crates/4,500 = .0533 crates/dollar

Multifactor productivity of proposed system:
= 260 crates/4,580 = .0568 crates/dollar

Using current productivity (.0533) as a base, the increase will be .066. That is, .0568/.0533 = 1.066, or a 6.6% increase.

Problems*

• **1.1** John Lucy makes wooden boxes in which to ship motorcycles. John and his three employees invest a total of 40 hours per day making the 120 boxes.

a) What is their productivity?
b) John and his employees have discussed redesigning the process to improve efficiency. If they can increase the rate to 125 per day, what will be their new productivity?
c) What will be their unit *increase* in productivity per hour?
d) What will be their percentage change in productivity? PX

• **1.2** Riverside Metal Works produces cast bronze valves on a 10-person assembly line. On a recent day, 160 valves were produced during an 8-hour shift.

a) Calculate the labor productivity of the line.
b) The manager at Riverside changed the layout and was able to increase production to 180 units per 8-hour shift. What is the new labor productivity per labor-hour?
c) What is the percentage of productivity increase? PX

• **1.3** This year, Benson, Inc., will produce 57,600 hot water heaters at its plant in Yulee, Florida, in order to meet expected global demand. To accomplish this, each laborer at the Yulee plant will work 160 hours per month. If the labor productivity at the plant is 0.15 hot water heaters per labor-hour, how many laborers are employed at the plant?

• **1.4** As a library or Internet assignment, find the U.S. productivity rate (increase) last year for the (a) national economy, (b) manufacturing sector, and (c) service sector.

• **1.5** Lori produces "Final Exam Care Packages" for resale by her sorority. She is currently working a total of 5 hours per day to produce 100 care packages.

a) What is Lori's productivity?
b) Lori thinks that by redesigning the package, she can increase her total productivity to 133 care packages per day. What will be her new productivity?
c) What will be the percentage increase in productivity if Lori makes the change? PX

•• **1.6** Eric Johnson makes billiard balls in his New England plant. With recent increases in his costs, he has a newfound interest in efficiency. Eric is interested in determining the productivity of his organization. He would like to know if his organization is maintaining the manufacturing average of 3% increase in productivity. He has the following data representing a month from last year and an equivalent month this year:

	Last Year	Now
Units produced	1,000	1,000
Labor (hours)	300	275
Resin (pounds)	50	45
Capital invested ($)	10,000	11,000
Energy (BTU)	3,000	2,850

Show the productivity percentage change for each category and then determine the improvement for labor-hours, the typical standard for comparison. PX

•• **1.7** Eric Johnson (using data from Problem 1.6) determines his costs to be as follows:

- *Labor:* $10 per hour
- *Resin:* $5 per pound
- *Capital expense:* 1% per month of investment
- *Energy:* $.50 per BTU.

Show the percent change in productivity for one month last year versus one month this year, on a multifactor basis with dollars as the common denominator. PX

**Note:* PX means the problem may be solved with POM for Windows and/or Excel OM.

• **1.8** Kleen Karpet cleaned 65 rugs in October, consuming the following resources:

Labor:	520 hours at $13 per hour
Solvent:	100 gallons at $5 per gallon
Machine rental:	20 days at $50 per day

a) What is the labor productivity per dollar?
b) What is the multifactor productivity? PX

•• **1.9** David Upton is president of Upton Manufacturing, a producer of Go-Kart tires. Upton makes 1,000 tires per day with the following resources:

Labor:	400 hours per day @ $12.50 per hour
Raw material:	20,000 pounds per day @ $1 per pound
Energy:	$5,000 per day
Capital costs:	$10,000 per day

a) What is the labor productivity per labor-hour for these tires at Upton Manufacturing?
b) What is the multifactor productivity for these tires at Upton Manufacturing?
c) What is the percent change in multifactor productivity if Upton can reduce the energy bill by $1,000 per day without cutting production or changing any other inputs? PX

•• **1.10** Sawyer's, a local bakery, is worried about increased costs—particularly energy. Last year's records can provide a fairly good estimate of the parameters for this year. Judy Sawyer, the owner, does not believe things have changed much, but she did invest an additional $3,000 for modifications to the bakery's ovens to make them more energy efficient. The modifications were supposed to make the ovens at least 15% more efficient. Sawyer has asked you to check the energy savings of the new ovens and also to look over other measures of the bakery's productivity to see if the modifications were beneficial. You have the following data to work with:

	Last Year	Now
Production (dozen)	1,500	1,500
Labor (hours)	350	325
Capital investment ($)	15,000	18,000
Energy (BTU)	3,000	2,750

PX

•• **1.11** Cunningham Performance Auto, Inc., modifies 375 autos per year. The manager, Peter Cunningham, is interested in obtaining a measure of overall performance. He has asked you to provide him with a multifactor measure of last year's performance as a benchmark for future comparison. You have assembled the following data. Resource inputs were: labor, 10,000 hours; 500 suspension and engine modification kits; and energy, 100,000 kilowatt-hours. Average labor cost last year was $20 per hour, kits cost $1,000 each, and energy costs were $3 per kilowatt-hour. What do you tell Mr. Cunningham? PX

•• **1.12** Lake Charles Seafood makes 500 wooden packing boxes for fresh seafood per day, working in two 10-hour shifts. Due to increased demand, plant managers have decided to operate three 8-hour shifts instead. The plant is now able to produce 650 boxes per day.
a) Calculate the company's productivity before the change in work rules and after the change.
b) What is the percentage increase in productivity?
c) If production is increased to 700 boxes per day, what is the new productivity? PX

••• **1.13** Charles Lackey operates a bakery in Idaho Falls, Idaho. Because of its excellent product and excellent location, demand has increased by 25% in the last year. On far too many occasions, customers have not been able to purchase the bread of their choice. Because of the size of the store, no new ovens can be added. At a staff meeting, one employee suggested ways to load the ovens differently so that more loaves of bread can be baked at one time. This new process will require that the ovens be loaded by hand, requiring additional manpower. This is the only thing to be changed. If the bakery makes 1,500 loaves per month with a labor productivity of 2.344 loaves per labor-hour, how many workers will Lackey need to add? (*Hint:* Each worker works 160 hours per month.)

•• **1.14** Refer to Problem 1.13. The pay will be $8 per hour for employees. Charles Lackey can also improve the yield by purchasing a new blender. The new blender will mean an increase in his investment. This added investment has a cost of $100 per month, but he will achieve the same output (an increase to 1,875) as the change in labor-hours. Which is the better decision?
a) Show the productivity change, in loaves per dollar, with an increase in labor cost (from 640 to 800 hours).
b) Show the new productivity, in loaves per dollar, with only an increase in investment ($100 per month more).
c) Show the percent productivity change for labor and investment.

••• **1.15** Refer to Problems 1.13 and 1.14. If Charles Lackey's utility costs remain constant at $500 per month, labor at $8 per hour, and cost of ingredients at $0.35 per loaf, but Charles does not purchase the blender suggested in Problem 1.14, what will the productivity of the bakery be? What will be the percent increase or decrease?

•• **1.16** In December, General Motors produced 6,600 customized vans at its plant in Detroit. The labor productivity at this plant is known to have been 0.10 vans per labor-hour during that month. 300 laborers were employed at the plant that month.
a) How many hours did the average laborer work that month?
b) If productivity can be increased to 0.11 vans per hour, how many hours would the average laborer work that month?

•• **1.17** Natalie Attired runs a small job shop where garments are made. The job shop employs eight workers. Each worker is paid $10 per hour. During the first week of March, each worker worked 45 hours. Together, they produced a batch of 132 garments. Of these garments, 52 were "seconds" (meaning that they were flawed). The seconds were sold for $90 each at a factory outlet store. The remaining 80 garments were sold to retail outlets at a price of $198 per garment. What was the labor productivity, in dollars per labor-hour, at this job shop during the first week of March?

► **Refer to myomlab for these additional homework problems: 1.18–1.19**

Case Studies

► National Air Express

National Air is a competitive air-express firm with offices around the country. Frank Smith, the Chattanooga, Tennessee, station manager, is preparing his quarterly budget report, which will be presented at the Southeast regional meeting next week. He is very concerned about adding capital expense to the operation when business has not increased appreciably. This has been the worst first quarter he can remember: snowstorms, earthquakes, and bitter cold. He has asked Martha Lewis, field services supervisor, to help him review the available data and offer possible solutions.

Service Methods

National Air offers door-to-door overnight air-express delivery within the U.S. Smith and Lewis manage a fleet of 24 trucks to handle freight in the Chattanooga area. Routes are assigned by area, usually delineated by zip code boundaries, major streets, or key geographical features, such as the Tennessee River. Pickups are generally handled between 3:00 P.M. and 6:00 P.M., Monday through Friday. Driver routes are a combination of regularly scheduled daily stops and pickups that the customer calls in as needed. These call-in pickups are dispatched by radio to the driver. Most call-in customers want as late a pickup as possible, just before closing (usually at 5:00 P.M.).

When the driver arrives at each pickup location, he or she provides supplies as necessary (an envelope or box if requested) and must receive a completed air waybill for each package. Because the industry is extremely competitive, a professional, courteous driver is essential to retaining customers. Therefore, Smith has always been concerned that drivers not rush a customer to complete his or her package and paperwork.

Budget Considerations

Smith and Lewis have found that they have been unable to meet their customers' requests for a scheduled pickup on many occasions in the past quarter. Although, on average, drivers are not handling any more business, they are unable on some days to arrive at each location on time. Smith does not think he can justify increasing costs by $1,200 per week for additional trucks and drivers while productivity (measured in shipments per truck/day) has remained flat. The company has established itself as the low-cost operator in the industry but has at the same time committed itself to offering quality service and value for its customers.

Discussion Questions

1. Is the productivity measure of shipments per day per truck still useful? Are there alternatives that might be effective?
2. What, if anything, can be done to reduce the daily variability in pickup call-ins? Can the driver be expected to be at several locations at once at 5:00 P.M.?
3. How should package pickup performance be measured? Are standards useful in an environment that is affected by the weather, traffic, and other random variables? Are other companies having similar problems?

Source: Adapted from a case by Phil Pugliese under the supervision of Professor Marilyn M. Helms, University of Tennessee at Chattanooga. Reprinted by permission.

► Frito-Lay: Operations Management in Manufacturing

Video Case

Frito-Lay, the massive Dallas-based subsidiary of PepsiCo, has 38 plants and 48,000 employees in North America. Seven of Frito-Lay's 41 brands exceed $1 billion in sales: Fritos, Lay's Cheetos, Ruffles, Tostitos, Doritos, and Walker's Potato Chips. Operations is the focus of the firm—from designing products for new markets, to meeting changing consumer preferences, to adjusting to rising commodity costs, to subtle issues involving flavors and preservatives—OM is under constant cost, time, quality, and market pressure. Here is a look at how the 10 decisions of OM are applied at this food processor.

In the food industry, product development kitchens experiment with new products, submit them to focus groups, and perform test marketing. Once the product specifications have been set, processes capable of meeting those specifications, and the necessary quality standards are created. At Frito-Lay, quality begins at the farm, with onsite inspection of the potatoes used in Ruffles and the corn used in Fritos. Quality continues throughout the manufacturing process, with visual inspections and with statistical process control of product variables such as oil, moisture, seasoning, salt, thickness, and weight. Additional quality evaluations are conducted throughout shipment, receipt, production, packaging, and delivery.

The production process at Frito-Lay is designed for large volumes and small variety, using expensive special-purpose equipment, and with swift movement of material through the facility. Product-focused facilities, such as Frito-Lay's, typically have high capital costs, tight schedules, and rapid processing. Frito-Lay's facilities are located regionally to aid in the rapid delivery of products because freshness is a critical issue. Sanitary issues and necessarily fast processing of products put a premium on an efficient layout. Production lines are designed for balanced throughput and high utilization. Cross-trained workers, who handle a variety of production lines, have promotion paths identified for their particular skill set. The company rewards employees with medical, retirement, and education plans. Its turnover is very low.

The supply chain is integral to success in the food industry; vendors must be chosen with great care. Moreover, the finished food product is highly dependent on perishable raw materials. Consequently, the supply chain brings raw material (potatoes, corn, etc.) to the plant securely and rapidly to meet tight production schedules. For instance, from the time that potatoes are picked in St. Augustine, Florida, until they are unloaded at the Orlando plant, processed, packaged, and shipped from the plant is under 12 hours. The requirement for fresh product requires on-time, just-in-time deliveries combined with both low raw material and finished goods inventories. The continuous-flow nature of the specialized equipment in the production process permits little work-in-process inventory. The plants usually run 24/7. This means that there are four shifts of employees each week.

Tight scheduling to ensure the proper mix of fresh finished goods on automated equipment requires reliable systems and effective maintenance. Frito-Lay's workforce is trained to recognize problems early, and professional maintenance personnel are available on every shift. Downtime is very costly and can lead to late deliveries, making maintenance a high priority.

Discussion Questions*

1. From your knowledge of production processes and from the case and the video, identify how each of the 10 decisions of OM is applied at Frito-Lay.
2. How would you determine the productivity of the production process at Frito-Lay?
3. How are the 10 decisions of OM different when applied by the operations manager of a production process such as Frito-Lay versus a service organization such as Hard Rock Cafe (see the Hard Rock Cafe video case below)?

*You may wish to view the video that accompanies this case before addressing these questions.

Source: Professors Beverly Amer (Northern Arizona University), Barry Render (Rollins College), and Jay Heizer (Texas Lutheran University).

► Hard Rock Cafe: Operations Management in Services

Video Case

In its 39 years of existence, Hard Rock has grown from a modest London pub to a global power managing 129 cafes, 12 hotels/casinos, live music venues, and a huge annual Rockfest concert. This puts Hard Rock firmly in the service industry—a sector that employs over 75% of the people in the U.S. Hard Rock moved its world headquarters to Orlando, Florida, in 1988 and has expanded to more than 40 locations throughout the U.S., serving over 100,000 meals each day. Hard Rock chefs are modifying the menu from classic American—burgers and chicken wings—to include higher-end items such as stuffed veal chops and lobster tails. Just as taste in music changes over time, so does Hard Rock Cafe, with new menus, layouts, memorabilia, services, and strategies.

At Orlando's Universal Studios, a traditional tourist destination, Hard Rock Cafe serves over 3,500 meals each day. The cafe employs about 400 people. Most are employed in the restaurant, but some work in the retail shop. Retail is now a standard and increasingly prominent feature in Hard Rock Cafes (since close to 48% of revenue comes from this source). Cafe employees include kitchen and wait staff, hostesses, and bartenders. Hard Rock employees are not only competent in their job skills but are also passionate about music and have engaging personalities. Cafe staff is scheduled down to 15-minute intervals to meet seasonal and daily demand changes in the tourist environment of Orlando. Surveys are done on a regular basis to evaluate quality of food and service at the cafe. Scores are rated on a 1 to 7 scale, and if the score is not a 7, the food or service is a failure.

Hard Rock is adding a new emphasis on live music and is redesigning its restaurants to accommodate the changing tastes. Since Eric Clapton hung his guitar on the wall to mark his favorite bar stool, Hard Rock has become the world's leading collector and exhibitor of rock 'n' roll memorabilia, with changing exhibits at its cafes throughout the world. The collection includes 1,000's of pieces, valued at $40 million. In keeping with the times, Hard Rock also maintains a Web site, **www.hardrock.com**, which receives over 100,000 hits per week, and a weekly cable television program on VH-1. Hard Rock's brand recognition, at 92%, is one of the highest in the world.

Discussion Questions*

1. From your knowledge of restaurants, from the video, from the *Global Company Profile* that opens this chapter, and from the case itself, identify how each of the 10 decisions of operations management is applied at Hard Rock Cafe.
2. How would you determine the productivity of the kitchen staff and wait staff at Hard Rock?
3. How are the 10 decisions of OM different when applied to the operations manager of a service operation such as Hard Rock versus an automobile company such as Ford Motor Company?

*You may wish to view the video that accompanies this case before addressing these questions.

► **Additional Case Study:** Visit **www.myomlab.com** or **www.pearsonhighered.com/heizer** for this free case study:
Zychol Chemicals Corp.: The production manager must prepare a productivity report, which includes multifactor analysis.

Bibliography

Broedner, P., S. Kinkel, and G. Lay. "Productivity Effects of Outsourcing." *International Journal of Operations and Production Management* 29, no. 2 (2009): 127.

Hounshell, D. A. *From the American System to Mass Production 1800–1932: The Development of Manufacturing.* Baltimore: Johns Hopkins University Press, 1985.

Lewis, William W. *The Power of Productivity.* Chicago: University of Chicago Press, 2004.

Maroto, A., and L. Rubalcaba. "Services Productivity Revisited." *The Service Industries Journal* 28, no. 3 (April 2008): 337.

Sahay, B. S. "Multi-factor Productivity Measurement Model for Service Organization." *International Journal of Productivity and Performance Management* 54, no. 1–2 (2005): 7–23.

San, G., T. Huang, and L. Huang. "Does Labor Quality Matter on Productivity Growth?" *Total Quality Management and Business Excellence* 19, no. 10 (October 2008): 1043.

Sprague, Linda G. "Evolution of the Field of Operations Management," *Journal of Operations Management* 25, no. 2 (March 2007): 219–238.

Tangen, S. "Demystifying Productivity and Performance." *International Journal of Productivity and Performance Measurement* 54, no. 1–2 (2005): 34–47.

Taylor, F. W. *The Principles of Scientific Management.* New York: Harper & Brothers, 1911.

van Biema, Michael, and Bruce Greenwald. "Managing Our Way to Higher Service-Sector Productivity." *Harvard Business Review* 75, no. 4 (July–August 1997): 87–95.

Wren, Daniel A. *The Evolution of Management Thought,* New York: Wiley, 1994.

Chapter 1 *Rapid* Review

Main Heading	Review Material	myomlab
WHAT IS OPERATIONS MANAGEMENT? (p. 4)	▪ **Production**—The creation of goods and services. ▪ **Operations management (OM)**—Activities that relate to the creation of goods and services through the transformation of inputs to outputs.	**VIDEOS 1.1 and 1.2** OM at Hard Rock OM at Frito-Lay
ORGANIZING TO PRODUCE GOODS AND SERVICES (pp. 4–5)	All organizations perform three functions to create goods and services: 1. *Marketing*, which generates demand 2. *Production/operations,* which creates the product 3. *Finance/accounting,* which tracks how well the organization is doing, pays the bills, and collects the money	
WHY STUDY OM? (pp. 6–7)	We study OM for four reasons: 1. To learn how people organize themselves for productive enterprise 2. To learn how goods and services are produced 3. To understand what operations managers do 4. Because OM is a costly part of an organization	
WHAT OPERATIONS MANAGERS DO (pp. 7–8)	▪ **Management process**—The application of planning, organizing, staffing, leading, and controlling to achieve objectives. Ten major OM decisions are required of operations managers: 1. Design of goods and services 2. Managing quality 3. Process and capacity design 4. Location strategy 5. Layout strategy 6. Human resources, job design, and work measurement 7. Supply-chain management 8. Inventory, material requirements planning, and JIT (just-in-time) 9. Intermediate and short-term scheduling 10. Maintenance About 40% of *all* jobs are in OM. Operations managers possess job titles such as plant manager, quality manager, process improvement consultant, and operations analyst.	
THE HERITAGE OF OPERATIONS MANAGEMENT (pp. 8–10)	Significant events in modern OM can be classified into five eras: 1. Early concepts (1776–1880)—Labor specialization (Smith, Babbage), standardized parts (Whitney) 2. Scientific management (1880–1910)—Gantt charts (Gantt), motion and time studies (Gilbreth), process analysis (Taylor), queuing theory (Erlang) 3. Mass production (1910–1980)—Assembly line (Ford/Sorensen), statistical sampling (Shewhart), economic order quantity (Harris), linear programming (Dantzig), PERT/CPM (DuPont), material requirements planning 4. Lean production (1980–1995)—Just-in-time, computer-aided design, electronic data interchange, total quality management, Baldrige Award, empowerment, kanbans 5. Mass customization (1995–present)—Globalization, Internet/e-commerce, enterprise resource planning, international quality standards, finite scheduling, supply-chain management, mass customization, build-to-order, sustainability	
OPERATIONS IN THE SERVICE SECTOR (pp. 10–12)	▪ **Services**—Economic activities that typically produce an intangible product (such as education, entertainment, lodging, government, financial, and health services). Almost all services and almost all goods are a mixture of a service and a tangible product. ▪ **Service sector**—The segment of the economy that includes trade, financial, lodging, education, legal, medical, and other professional occupations. Services now constitute the largest economic sector in postindustrial societies. The huge productivity increases in agriculture and manufacturing have allowed more of our economic resources to be devoted to services. Many service jobs pay very well.	
EXCITING NEW TRENDS IN OPERATIONS MANAGEMENT (pp. 12–13)	Some of the current challenges for operations managers include: • High ethical and social responsibility; increased legal and professional standards • Global focus; international collaboration • Rapid product development; design collaboration • Environmentally sensitive production; green manufacturing; sustainability • Mass customization • Empowered employees; enriched jobs • Supply-chain partnering; joint ventures; alliances • Just-in-time performance; lean; continuous improvement	

Chapter 1 **Rapid Review** *continued*

Main Heading	Review Material	myomlab
THE PRODUCTIVITY CHALLENGE (pp. 13–19)	■ **Productivity**—The ratio of outputs (goods and services) divided by one or more inputs (such as labor, capital, or management). High production means producing many units, while high productivity means producing units efficiently. Only through increases in productivity can the standard of living of a country improve. U.S. productivity has averaged 2.5% per year for over a century. $$\text{Productivity} = \frac{\text{Units produced}}{\text{Input used}} \quad (1\text{-}1)$$ ■ **Single-factor productivity**—Indicates the ratio of one resource (input) to the goods and services produced (outputs). ■ **Multifactor productivity (total factor productivity)**—Indicates the ratio of many or all resources (inputs) to the goods and services produced (outputs). Multifactor Productivity $$= \frac{\text{Output}}{\text{Labor} + \text{Material} + \text{Energy} + \text{Capital} + \text{Miscellaneous}} \quad (1\text{-}2)$$ Measurement problems with productivity include: (1) the quality may change, (2) external elements may interfere, and (3) precise units of measure may be lacking. ■ **Productivity variables**—The three factors critical to productivity improvement are labor (10%), capital (38%), and management (52%). ■ **Knowledge society**—A society in which much of the labor force has migrated from manual work to work based on knowledge.	Problems: 1.1–1.17 Virtual Office Hours for Solved Problems: 1.1, 1.2
ETHICS AND SOCIAL RESPONSIBILITY (p. 19)	Among the many ethical challenges facing operations managers are (1) efficiently developing and producing safe, quality products; (2) maintaining a clean environment; (3) providing a safe workplace; and (4) honoring stakeholder commitments.	

Self **Test**

■ **Before taking the self-test,** refer to the learning objectives listed at the beginning of the chapter and the key terms listed at the end of the chapter.

LO1. Productivity increases when:
- **a)** inputs increase while outputs remain the same.
- **b)** inputs decrease while outputs remain the same.
- **c)** outputs decrease while inputs remain the same.
- **d)** inputs and outputs increase proportionately.
- **e)** inputs increase at the same rate as outputs.

LO2. Services often:
- **a)** are tangible. **b)** are standardized.
- **c)** are knowledge based. **d)** are low in customer interaction.
- **e)** have consistent product definition.

LO3. Productivity:
- **a)** can use many factors as the numerator.
- **b)** is the same thing as production.
- **c)** increases at about 0.5% per year.
- **d)** is dependent upon labor, management, and capital.
- **e)** is the same thing as effectiveness.

LO4. Single-factor productivity:
- **a)** remains constant. **b)** is never constant.
- **c)** usually uses labor as a factor. **d)** seldom uses labor as a factor.
- **e)** uses management as a factor.

LO5. Multi-factor productivity:
- **a)** remains constant.
- **b)** is never constant.
- **c)** usually uses substitutes as common variables for the factors of production.
- **d)** seldom uses labor as a factor.
- **e)** always uses management as a factor.

LO6. Productivity increases each year in the United States are a result of three factors:
- **a)** labor, capital, management
- **b)** engineering, labor, capital
- **c)** engineering, capital, quality control
- **d)** engineering, labor, data processing
- **e)** engineering, capital, data processing

Answers: **LO1.** b; **LO2.** c; **LO3.** d; **LO4.** c; **LO5.** c; **LO6.** a.

2 Operations Strategy in a Global Environment

Chapter Outline

10

OM Strategy Decisions

- Design of Goods and Services
- Managing Quality
- Process Strategy
- Location Strategies
- Layout Strategies
- Human Resources
- Supply Chain Management
- Inventory Management
- Scheduling
- Maintenance

BOEING'S GLOBAL STRATEGY YIELDS COMPETITIVE ADVANTAGE

Boeing's strategy for its 787 Dreamliner is unique from both an engineering and global perspective.

The Dreamliner incorporates the latest in a wide range of aerospace technologies, from airframe and engine design to superlightweight titanium graphite laminate, carbon fiber and epoxy, and composites. Another innovation is the electronic monitoring system that allows the airplane to report maintenance requirements to ground-based computer systems. Boeing has also worked with General Electric and Rolls-Royce to develop more efficient engines. The advances in engine technology contribute as much as 8% of the increased fuel/payload efficiency of the new airplane, representing a nearly two-generation jump in technology.

Some of the International Suppliers of Boeing 787 Components

Latecoere	France	Passenger doors
Labinel	France	Wiring
Dassault	France	Design and PLM software
Messier-Bugatti	France	Electric brakes
Thales	France	Electrical power conversion system and integrated standby flight display
Messier-Dowty	France	Landing gear structure
Diehl	Germany	Interior lighting
Cobham	UK	Fuel pumps and valves
Rolls-Royce	UK	Engines
Smiths Aerospace	UK	Central computer system
BAE Systems	UK	Electronics
Alenia Aeronautica	Italy	Upper center fuselage and horizontal stabilizer
Toray Industries	Japan	Carbon fiber for wing and tail units
Fuji Heavy Industries	Japan	Center wing box
Kawasaki Heavy Industries	Japan	Forward fuselage, fixed sections of wing, landing gear wheel well
Teijin Seiki	Japan	Hydraulic actuators
Mitsubishi Heavy Industries	Japan	Wing box
Chengdu Aircraft Group	China	Rudder
Hafei Aviation	China	Parts
Korean Airlines	South Korea	Wingtips
Saab	Sweden	Cargo and access doors

With the 787's state-of-the-art design, more spacious interior, and global suppliers, Boeing has garnered record sales worldwide.

This state-of-the-art Boeing 787 is also *global.* Led by Boeing at its Everett, Washington, facility, an international team of aerospace companies developed the airplane. New technologies, new design, new manufacturing processes, and committed international suppliers are helping Boeing and its partners achieve unprecedented levels of performance in design, manufacture, and operation.

The 787 is global not only because it has a range of 8,300 miles but also because it is built all over the world—with a huge financial risk of over $5 billion, Boeing needed partners. The global nature of both technology and the aircraft market meant finding exceptional developers and suppliers, wherever they might be. It also meant finding firms willing to step up to the risk associated with a very expensive new product. These partners not only spread the risk but also bring commitment to the table. Countries that have a stake in the 787 are more likely to buy from Boeing than from the European competitor Airbus Industries.

Boeing teamed with more than 20 international systems suppliers to develop technologies and design concepts for the 787. Boeing found its 787 partners in over a dozen countries; a few of them are shown in the table on the left.

Boeing's collaborative technology enables a "virtual workspace" that allows engineers on the 787, including partners in Australia, Japan, Italy, Canada and across the United States, to make concurrent design changes to the airplane in real time. Designing, building, and testing the 787 digitally before production reduced design errors and improved production efficiencies.

The Japanese companies Toray, Teijin Seiki, Fuji, Kawasaki, and Mitsubishi are producing over 35% of the project, providing whole composite fuselage sections. Italy's Alenia Aeronautica is building an additional 10% of the plane.

Many U.S. companies, including Crane Aerospace, Fairchild Controls, Goodrich, General Dynamics, Hamilton Sundstrand, Honeywell, Moog, Parker Hannifin, Rockwell Collins, and Triumph Group are also suppliers. Boeing has 70% to 80% of the Dreamliner built by other companies. And even some of the portion built by Boeing is produced at Boeing facilities outside the United States, in Australia and Canada.

The global Dreamliner is efficient, has a global range, and is made from components produced around the world. The result: a state-of-the-art airplane reflecting the global nature of business in the 21st century and one of the fastest-selling commercial jets in history.

State-of-the-art composite sections of the 787 are built around the world and shipped to Boeing for final assembly.

Components from Boeing's worldwide supply chain come together on an assembly line in Everett, Washington. Although components come from throughout the world, about 35% of the 787 structure comes from Japanese companies.

Chapter 2 **Learning Objectives**

AUTHOR COMMENT
As Prof. Thomas Sewell observed, "No great civilization has developed in isolation."

A GLOBAL VIEW OF OPERATIONS

Today's operations manager must have a global view of operations strategy. Since the early 1990s, nearly 3 billion people in developing countries have overcome the cultural, religious, ethnic, and political barriers that constrain productivity and are now players on the global economic stage. As these barriers disappear, simultaneous advances are being made in technology, reliable shipping, and cheap communication. The unsurprising result is the growth of world trade (see Figure 2.1), global capital markets, and the international movement of people; This means: increasing economic integration and interdependence of countries—in a word, globalization. In response, organizations are hastily extending their operations globally with innovative strategies. For instance:

- Boeing is competitive because both its sales and production are worldwide.
- Italy's Benetton moves inventory to stores around the world faster than its competition by building flexibility into design, production, and distribution.
- Sony purchases components from suppliers in Thailand, Malaysia, and elsewhere around the world for assembly in its electronic products.
- Volvo, considered a Swedish company, recently controlled by a U.S. company, Ford. But the current Volvo S40 is built in Belgium on a platform shared with the Mazda 3 (built in Japan) and the Ford Focus (built and sold in Europe.)
- China's Haier (pronounced "higher") is now producing compact refrigerators (it has one-third of the U.S. market) and refrigerated wine cabinets (it has half of the U.S. market) in South Carolina.

Globalization means that domestic production and exporting may no longer be a viable business model; local production and exporting no longer guarantee success or even survival. There are new standards of global competitiveness that impact quality, variety, customization, convenience, timeliness, and cost. The globalization of strategy contributes efficiency and adds value to products and services, but it also complicates the operations manager's job. Complexity, risk and competition are intensified; companies must carefully account for them.

▶ FIGURE 2.1
Growth of World Trade (world trade as a percentage of world GDP)

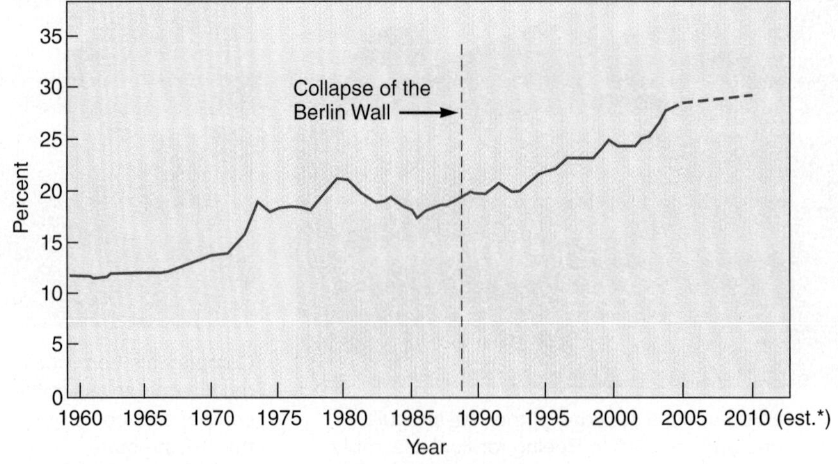

* Author estimate for 2010.

Source: Based on a speech by Mark A. Wynne, Federal Reserve Bank of Dallas, June 2009.

We have identified six reasons why domestic business operations decide to change to some form of international operation. They are:

1. Reduce costs (labor, taxes, tariffs, etc.).
2. Improve the supply chain.
3. Provide better goods and services.
4. Understand markets.
5. Learn to improve operations.
6. Attract and retain global talent.

Let us examine, in turn, each of the six reasons.

Reduce Costs Many international operations seek to take advantage of the tangible opportunities to reduce their costs. Foreign locations with lower wages can help lower both direct and indirect costs. (See the *OM in Action* box "U.S. Cartoon Production at Home in Manila.") Less stringent government regulations on a wide variety of operation practices (e.g., environmental control, health and safety, etc.) reduce costs. Opportunities to cut the cost of taxes and tariffs also encourage foreign operations. In Mexico, the creation of **maquiladoras** (free trade zones) allows manufacturers to cut their costs of taxation by paying only on the value added by Mexican workers. If a U.S. manufacturer, such as GM, brings a $500 engine to a maquiladora operation for assembly work costing $25, tariff duties will be charged only on the $25 of work performed in Mexico.

Maquiladoras
Mexican factories located along the U.S.–Mexico border that receive preferential tariff treatment.

Shifting low-skilled jobs to another country has several potential advantages. First, and most obviously, the firm may reduce costs. Second, moving the lower skilled jobs to a lower cost location frees higher cost workers for more valuable tasks. Third, reducing wage costs allows the savings to be invested in improved products and facilities (and the retraining of existing workers, if necessary) at the home location. The impact of this approach is shown in the *OM in Action* box "Going Global to Compete" on the next page.

World Trade Organization (WTO)
An international organization that promotes world trade by lowering barriers to the free flow of goods across borders.

Trade agreements have also helped reduce tariffs and thereby reduce the cost of operating facilities in foreign countries. The **World Trade Organization (WTO)** has helped reduce tariffs from 40% in 1940 to less than 3% today. Another important trade agreement is the **North American Free Trade Agreement (NAFTA)**. NAFTA seeks to phase out all trade and tariff barriers among Canada, Mexico, and the U.S. Other trade agreements that are accelerating global trade include APEC (the Pacific Rim countries), SEATO (Australia, New Zealand, Japan, Hong Kong, South Korea, New Guinea, and Chile), MERCOSUR (Argentina, Brazil, Paraguay, and Uruguay), and CAFTA (Central America, Dominican Republic, and United States).

NAFTA
A free trade agreement between Canada, Mexico, and the United States.

Another trading group is the **European Union (EU)**.[1] The European Union has reduced trade barriers among the participating European nations through standardization and a common

European Union (EU)
A European trade group that has 27 member states.

OM in Action ► U.S. Cartoon Production at Home in Manila

Fred Flintstone is not from Bedrock. He is actually from Manila, capital of the Philippines. So are Tom and Jerry, Aladdin, and Donald Duck. More than 90% of American television cartoons are produced in Asia and India, with the Philippines leading the way. With their natural advantage of English as an official language and a strong familiarity with U.S. culture, animation companies in Manila now employ more than 1,700 people. Filipinos understand Western culture, and "you need to have a group of artists that can understand the humor that goes with it," says Bill Dennis, a Hanna-Barbera executive.

Major studios like Disney, Marvel, Warner Brothers, and Hanna-Barbera send *storyboards*—cartoon action outlines—and voice tracks to the Philippines. Artists there draw, paint, and film about 20,000 sketches for a 30-minute episode. The cost of $130,000 to produce an episode in the Philippines compares with $160,000 in Korea and $500,000 in the United States.

Sources: Journal of Global Information Technology Management (2007): 1–6; *The New York Times* (February 26, 2004): A29; and *The Wall Street Journal* (August 9, 2005): D8.

[1]The 27 members of the European Union (EU) as of 2010 were Austria, Belgium, Bulgaria, Cyprus, Czech Republic, Denmark, Estonia, Finland, France, Germany, Greece, Hungary, Ireland, Italy, Latvia, Lithuania, Luxembourg, Malta, the Netherlands, Poland, Portugal, Romania, Slovakia, Slovenia, Spain, Sweden, United Kingdom. Not all have adopted the euro. In addition, Croatia, Macedonia, and Turkey are candidates for entry into the European Union.

currency, the euro. However, this major U.S. trading partner, with almost 500 million people, is also placing some of the world's most restrictive conditions on products sold in the EU. Everything from recycling standards to automobile bumpers to hormone-free farm products must meet EU standards, complicating international trade.

Improve the Supply Chain The supply chain can often be improved by locating facilities in countries where unique resources are available. These resources may be expertise, labor, or raw material. For example, auto-styling studios from throughout the world are migrating to the auto mecca of southern California to ensure the necessary expertise in contemporary auto design. Similarly, world athletic shoe production has migrated from South Korea to Guangzhou, China: this location takes advantage of the low-cost labor and production competence in a city where 40,000 people work making athletic shoes for the world. And a perfume essence manufacturer wants a presence in Grasse, France, where much of the world's perfume essences are prepared from the flowers of the Mediterranean.

Provide Better Goods and Services Although the characteristics of goods and services can be objective and measurable (e.g., number of on-time deliveries), they can also be subjective and less measurable (e.g., sensitivity to culture). We need an ever better understanding of differences in culture and of the way business is handled in different countries. Improved understanding as the result of a local presence permits firms to customize products and services to meet unique cultural needs in foreign markets.

Another reason to have international operations is to reduce response time to meet customers' changing product and service requirements. Customers who purchase goods and services from U.S. firms are increasingly located in foreign countries. Providing them with quick and adequate service is often improved by locating facilities in their home countries.

Understand Markets Because international operations require interaction with foreign customers, suppliers, and other competitive businesses, international firms inevitably learn about opportunities for new products and services. Europe led the way with cell phone innovations, and now the Japanese lead with the latest cell phone fads. Knowledge of these markets not only helps firms understand where the market is going but also helps firms diversify their customer base, add production flexibility, and smooth the business cycle.

Another reason to go into foreign markets is the opportunity to expand the *life cycle* (i.e., stages a product goes through; see Chapter 5) of an existing product. While some products in the U.S. are in a "mature" stage of their product life cycle, they may represent state-of-the-art products in less developed countries. For example, the U.S. market for personal computers could be characterized as "mature" but as in the "introductory" stage in many developing countries, such as Albania, Vietnam, and Myanmar (Burma).

OM in Action ► Going Global to Compete

Wachovia Corp, the giant subsidiary of Wells Fargo, has inked a $1.1 billion deal with India's Genpact to outsource finance and accounting jobs. Wachovia has also handed over administration of its human resources programs to Illinois-based Hewitt Associates. This is "what we need to do to become a great customer-relationship company," says Wachovia executive P. J. Sidebottom. The expected cost savings of $600 million to $1 billion over the next three years will be invested in the U.S. to boost the core banking business. These investments will be made in new ATMs, branches, and personnel.

Similarly, Dana Corp. of Toledo, Ohio, is also taking a global approach. Dana established a joint venture with Cardanes S.A. to produce truck transmissions in Queretaro, Mexico. Then Dana switched 288 U.S. employees in its Jonesboro, Arkansas, plant from producing truck transmissions at breakeven to axle production at a profit. Productivity is up in Jonesboro, and the Mexican joint venture is making money. Employees in both Jonesboro and Queretaro, as well as stockholders, came out ahead on the move. Dana is also moving operations to China, India, Eastern Europe, and South America.

Resourceful organizations like Wachovia and Dana use a global perspective to become more efficient, which allows them to develop new products, retrain employees, and invest in new plant and equipment.

Sources: Business Week (January 30, 2006): 50–64; *Forbes* (May 8, 2006): 58; and **www.dana.com/news/.**

A worldwide strategy places added burdens on operations management. Because of economic and lifestyle differences, designers must target products to each market. For instance, clothes washers sold in northern countries must spin-dry clothes much better than those in warmer climates, where consumers are likely to line-dry them. Similarly, as shown here, Whirlpool refrigerators sold in Bangkok are manufactured in bright colors because they are often put in living rooms.

Learn to Improve Operations Learning does not take place in isolation. Firms serve themselves and their customers well when they remain open to the free flow of ideas. For example, GM found that it could improve operations by jointly building and running, with the Japanese, an auto assembly plant in San Jose, California. This strategy allowed GM to contribute its capital and knowledge of U.S. labor and environmental laws while the Japanese contributed production and inventory ideas. Similarly, operations managers have improved equipment and layout by learning from the ergonomic competence of the Scandinavians.

Attract and Retain Global Talent Global organizations can attract and retain better employees by offering more employment opportunities. They need people in all functional areas and areas of expertise worldwide. Global firms can recruit and retain good employees because they provide both greater growth opportunities and insulation against unemployment during times of economic downturn. During economic downturns in one country or continent, a global firm has the means to relocate unneeded personnel to more prosperous locations.

So, to recap, successfully achieving a competitive advantage in our shrinking world means maximizing all of the possible opportunities, from tangible to intangible, that international operations can offer.

Cultural and Ethical Issues

AUTHOR COMMENT
As the owner of a Guatemala plant said, "The ethics of the world markets is very clear: Manufacturers will move wherever it is cheapest or most convenient to their interests."

While there are great forces driving firms toward globalization, many challenges remain. One of these challenges is reconciling differences in social and cultural behavior. With issues ranging from bribery, to child labor, to the environment, managers sometimes do not know how to respond when operating in a different culture. What one country's culture deems acceptable may be considered unacceptable or illegal in another. It is not by chance that there are fewer female managers in the Middle East than in India.

In the last decade, changes in international laws, agreements, and codes of conduct have been applied to define ethical behavior among managers around the world. The WTO, for example, helps to make uniform the protection of both governments and industries from foreign firms that engage in unethical conduct. Even on issues where significant differences between cultures exist, as in the area of bribery or the protection of intellectual property, global uniformity is slowly being accepted by most nations.

In spite of cultural and ethical differences, we live in a period of extraordinary mobility of capital, information, goods, and even people. We can expect this to continue. The financial sector, the telecommunications sector, and the logistics infrastructure of the world are healthy institutions that foster efficient and effective use of capital, information, and goods. Globalization, with all its opportunities and risks, is here and will continue. It must be embraced as managers develop their missions and strategies.

AUTHOR COMMENT
Getting an education and managing an organization both require a mission and strategy.

DEVELOPING MISSIONS AND STRATEGIES

An effective operations management effort must have a *mission* so it knows where it is going and a *strategy* so it knows how to get there. This is the case for a small domestic organization, as well as a large international organization.

Mission

Mission
The purpose or rationale for an organization's existence.

LO1: Define mission and strategy

Economic success, indeed survival, is the result of identifying missions to satisfy a customer's needs and wants. We define the organization's **mission** as its purpose—what it will contribute to society. Mission statements provide boundaries and focus for organizations and the concept around which the firm can rally. The mission states the rationale for the organization's existence. Developing a good strategy is difficult, but it is much easier if the mission has been well defined. Figure 2.2 provides examples of mission statements.

Once an organization's mission has been decided, each functional area within the firm determines its supporting mission. By *functional area* we mean the major disciplines required by the firm, such as marketing, finance/accounting, and production/operations. Missions for each function are developed to support the firm's overall mission. Then within that function lower-level supporting missions are established for the OM functions. Figure 2.3 provides such a hierarchy of sample missions.

Strategy

Strategy
How an organization expects to achieve its missions and goals.

With the mission established, strategy and its implementation can begin. **Strategy** is an organization's action plan to achieve the mission. Each functional area has a strategy for achieving its mission and for helping the organization reach the overall mission. These strategies exploit opportunities and strengths, neutralize threats, and avoid weaknesses. In the following sections, we will describe how strategies are developed and implemented.

LO2: Identify and explain three strategic approaches to competitive advantage

VIDEO 2.1
Operations Strategy at Regal Marine

Firms achieve missions in three conceptual ways: (1) differentiation, (2) cost leadership, and (3) response. This means operations managers are called on to deliver goods and services that are (1) *better*, or at least different, (2) *cheaper*, and (3) more *responsive*. Operations managers translate these *strategic concepts* into tangible tasks to be accomplished. Any one or combination of these three strategic concepts can generate a system that has a unique advantage over competitors. For example, Hunter Fan has differentiated itself as a premier maker of quality ceiling fans that lower heating and cooling costs for its customers. Nucor Steel, on the other hand, satisfies customers by being the lowest-cost steel producer in the world. And Dell achieves rapid response by building personal computers with each customer's requested software in a matter of hours.

Clearly, strategies differ. And each strategy puts different demands on operations management. Hunter Fan's strategy is one of *differentiating* itself via quality from others in the industry. Nucor focuses on value at *low cost*, and Dell's dominant strategy is quick, reliable *response*.

► FIGURE 2.2
Mission Statements for Three Organizations

Sources: Annual reports: courtesy of Merck, Hard Rock Cafe: *Employee Handbook*, Arnold Palmer Childrens' Care Team.

Merck
The mission of Merck is to provide society with superior products and services—innovations and solutions that improve the quality of life and satisfy customer needs—to provide employees with meaningful work and advancement opportunities and investors with a superior rate of return.
Hard Rock Cafe
Our Mission: To spread the spirit of Rock 'n' Roll by delivering an exceptional entertainment and dining experience. We are committed to being an important, contributing member of our community and offering the Hard Rock family a fun, healthy, and nurturing work environment while ensuring our long-term success.
Arnold Palmer Hospital
Arnold Palmer Hospital for Children provides state of the art, family-centered healthcare focused on restoring the joy of childhood in an environment of compassion, healing and hope.

Sample Company Mission	
To manufacture and service an innovative, growing, and profitable worldwide microwave communications business that exceeds our customers' expectations.	
Sample Operations Management Mission	
To produce products consistent with the company's mission as the worldwide low-cost manufacturer.	
Sample OM Department Missions	
Product design	To design and produce products and services with outstanding quality and inherent customer value.
Quality management	To attain the exceptional value that is consistent with our company mission and marketing objectives by close attention to design, procurement, production, and field service opportunities.
Process design	To determine, design, and produce the production process and equipment that will be compatible with low-cost product, high quality, and a good quality of work life at economical cost.
Location	To locate, design, and build efficient and economical facilities that will yield high value to the company, its employees, and the community.
Layout design	To achieve, through skill, imagination, and resourcefulness in layout and work methods, production effectiveness and efficiency while supporting a high quality of work life.
Human resources	To provide a good quality of work life, with well-designed, safe, rewarding jobs, stable employment, and equitable pay, in exchange for outstanding individual contribution from employees at all levels.
Supply-chain management	To collaborate with suppliers to develop innovative products from stable, effective, and efficient sources of supply.
Inventory	To achieve low investment in inventory consistent with high customer service levels and high facility utilization.
Scheduling	To achieve high levels of throughput and timely customer delivery through effective scheduling.
Maintenance	To achieve high utilization of facilities and equipment by effective preventive maintenance and prompt repair of facilities and equipment.

◀ **FIGURE 2.3**
Sample Missions for a Company, the Operations Function, and Major OM Departments

ACHIEVING COMPETITIVE ADVANTAGE THROUGH OPERATIONS

AUTHOR COMMENT
For many organizations, the operations function provides *the* competitive advantage.

Each of the three strategies provides an opportunity for operations managers to achieve competitive advantage. **Competitive advantage** implies the creation of a system that has a unique advantage over competitors. The idea is to create customer value in an efficient and sustainable way. Pure forms of these strategies may exist, but operations managers will more likely be called on to implement some combination of them. Let us briefly look at how managers achieve competitive advantage via *differentiation*, *low cost*, and *response*.

Competitive advantage
The creation of a unique advantage over competitors.

Competing on Differentiation

Safeskin Corporation is number one in latex exam gloves because it has differentiated itself and its products. It did so by producing gloves that were designed to prevent allergic reactions about which doctors were complaining. When other glove makers caught up, Safeskin developed hypoallergenic gloves. Then it added texture to its gloves. Then it developed a synthetic disposable glove for those allergic to latex—always staying ahead of the competition. Safeskin's strategy is to develop a reputation for designing and producing reliable state-of-the-art gloves, thereby differentiating itself.

Differentiation is concerned with providing *uniqueness*. A firm's opportunities for creating uniqueness are not located within a particular function or activity but can arise in virtually everything the firm does. Moreover, because most products include some service, and most services include some product, the opportunities for creating this uniqueness are limited only by imagination. Indeed, **differentiation** should be thought of as going beyond both physical characteristics and service attributes to encompass everything about the product or service that influences the value that the customers derive from it. Therefore, effective operations managers assist in defining everything about a product or service that will influence the potential value to the customer. This may be the convenience of a broad product line, product features, or a service related to the product. Such services can manifest themselves through convenience (location of distribution centers, stores, or branches), training, product delivery and installation, or repair and maintenance services.

Differentiation
Distinguishing the offerings of an organization in a way that the customer perceives as adding value.

In the service sector, one option for extending product differentiation is through an *experience*. Differentiation by experience in services is a manifestation of the growing "experience economy." The idea of **experience differentiation** is to engage the customer—to use people's five senses so they become immersed, or even an active participant, in the product. Disney does this with the Magic Kingdom. People no longer just go on a ride; they are immersed in the Magic Kingdom—surrounded by a dynamic visual and sound experience that complements the physical ride. Some rides further engage the customer by having them steer the ride or shoot targets or villains.

Experience differentiation
Engaging a customer with a product through imaginative use of the five senses, so the customer "experiences" the product.

VIDEO 2.2
Hard Rock's Global Strategy

Theme restaurants, such as Hard Rock Cafe, likewise differentiate themselves by providing an "experience." Hard Rock engages the customer with classic rock music, big-screen rock videos, memorabilia, and staff who can tell stories. In many instances, a full-time guide is available to explain the displays, and there is always a convenient retail store so the guest can take home a tangible part of the experience. The result is a "dining experience" rather than just a meal. In a less dramatic way, both Starbucks and your local supermarket deliver an experience when they provide music and the aroma of fresh coffee or freshly baked bread.

Competing on Cost

Southwest Airlines has been a consistent moneymaker while other U.S. airlines have lost billions. Southwest has done this by fulfilling a need for low-cost and short-hop flights. Its operations strategy has included use of secondary airports and terminals, first-come, first-served seating, few fare options, smaller crews flying more hours, snacks-only or no-meal flights, and no downtown ticket offices.

Additionally, and less obviously, Southwest has very effectively matched capacity to demand and effectively utilized this capacity. It has done this by designing a route structure that matches the capacity of its Boeing 737, the only plane in its fleet. Second, it achieves more air miles than other airlines through faster turnarounds—its planes are on the ground less.

One driver of a low-cost strategy is a facility that is effectively utilized. Southwest and others with low-cost strategies understand this and utilize resources effectively. Identifying the optimum size (and investment) allows firms to spread overhead costs, providing a cost advantage. For instance, Wal-Mart continues to pursue its low-cost strategy with superstores, open 24 hours a day. For 20 years, it has successfully grabbed market share. Wal-Mart has driven down store overhead costs, shrinkage, and distribution costs. Its rapid transportation of goods, reduced warehousing costs, and direct shipment from manufacturers have resulted in high inventory turnover and made it a low-cost leader. Franz Colruyt, as discussed in the *OM in Action* box, is also winning with a low-cost strategy.

Low-cost leadership entails achieving maximum *value* as defined by your customer. It requires examining each of the 10 OM decisions in a relentless effort to drive down costs while meeting customer expectations of value. A low-cost strategy does *not* imply low value or low quality.

Low-cost leadership
Achieving maximum value as perceived by the customer.

Competing on Response

The third strategy option is response. Response is often thought of as *flexible* response, but it also refers to *reliable* and *quick* response. Indeed, we define **response** as including the entire range of values related to timely product development and delivery, as well as reliable scheduling and flexible performance.

Response
A set of values related to rapid, flexible, and reliable performance.

OM in Action ► Low-Cost Strategy Wins at Franz Colruyt

Belgian discount food retailer Franz Colruyt NV is so obsessed with cutting costs that there are no shopping bags at its checkout counters, the lighting at its stores is dimmed to save money on electricity, and employees clock out when they go on 5-minute coffee breaks. And to keep costs down at the company's spartan headquarters on the outskirts of Brussels, employees don't have voice mail on their phones. Instead, two receptionists take messages for nearly 1,000 staffers. The messages are bellowed out every few minutes from loudspeakers peppered throughout the building.

This same approach is evident at all 160 of Colruyt's shopping outlets, which are converted factory warehouses, movie theaters, or garages, with black concrete floors, exposed electrical wires, metal shelves, and discarded boxes strewn about. There is no background music (estimated annual cost saving: €2 million, or $2.5 million), nor are there bags for packing groceries (estimated annual cost saving: €5 million). And all the store's freezers have doors, so the company can save about €3 million a year on electricity for refrigeration.

The company also employs a team of 30 "work simplifiers"—in Colruyt jargon—whose job is to come up with new ways to improve productivity. One recently discovered that 5 seconds could be shaved from every minute it takes customers to check out if they paid at a separate station from where groceries are scanned, so that when one customer steps away from the scanner, another can step up right away.

Chief Executive Rene De Wit says Colruyt's strategy is simple: cut costs at every turn and undersell your competitors. In an industry where margins of 1% to 2% are typical, Colruyt's cost cutting is so effective that a profit margin of 6.5% dwarfs those of rivals.

A low-cost strategy places significant demands on operations management, but Franz Colruyt, like Wal-Mart, makes it work.

Sources: The Wall Street Journal (January 5, 2005): 1 and (September 22, 2003): R3, R7.

Flexible response may be thought of as the ability to match changes in a marketplace where design innovations and volumes fluctuate substantially.

Hewlett-Packard is an exceptional example of a firm that has demonstrated flexibility in both design and volume changes in the volatile world of personal computers. HP's products often have a life cycle of months, and volume and cost changes during that brief life cycle are dramatic. However, HP has been successful at institutionalizing the ability to change products and volume to respond to dramatic changes in product design and costs—thus building a *sustainable competitive advantage*.

The second aspect of response is the *reliability* of scheduling. One way the German machine industry has maintained its competitiveness despite having the world's highest labor costs is through reliable response. This response manifests itself in reliable scheduling. German machine firms have meaningful schedules—and they perform to these schedules. Moreover, the results of

Response strategy wins orders at Super Fast Pizza. Using a wireless connection, orders are transmitted to $20,000 kitchens in vans. The driver, who works solo, receives a printed order, goes to the kitchen area, pulls premade pizzas from the cooler, and places them in the oven—it takes about 1 minute. The driver then delivers the pizza—sometimes even arriving before the pizza is ready.

OM in Action ▶ Response Strategy at Hong Kong's Johnson Electric

Patrick Wang, managing director of Johnson Electric Holdings, Ltd., walks through his Hong Kong headquarters with a micromotor in his hand. This tiny motor, about twice the size of his thumb, powers a Dodge Viper power door lock. Although most people have never heard of Johnson Electric, we all have several of its micromotors nearby. This is because Johnson is the world's leading producer of micromotors for cordless tools, household appliances (such as coffee grinders and food processors), personal care items (such as hair dryers and electric shavers), and cars. A luxury Mercedes, with its headlight wipers, power windows, power seat adjustments, and power side mirrors, may use 50 Johnson micromotors.

Like all truly global businesses, Johnson spends liberally on communications to tie together its global network of factories, R&D facilities, and design centers. For example, Johnson Electric installed a $20 million videoconferencing system that allows engineers in Cleveland, Ohio, and Stuttgart, Germany, to monitor trial production of their micromotors in China.

Johnson's first strength is speed in product development, speed in production, and speed in delivering—13 million motors a month, mostly assembled in China but delivered throughout the world. Its second strength is the ability to stay close to its customers. Johnson has design and technical centers scattered across the United States, Europe, and Japan. "The physical limitations of the past are gone" when it comes to deciding where to locate a new center, says Patrick Wang. "Customers talk to us where they feel most comfortable, but products are made where they are most competitive."

Sources: Hoover's Company Records (January 1, 2006): 58682; *Far Eastern Economic Review* (May 16, 2002): 44–45; and *Just Auto* (November 2008): 18–19.

these schedules are communicated to the customer and the customer can, in turn, rely on them. Consequently, the competitive advantage generated through reliable response has value to the end customer.

The third aspect of response is *quickness*. Johnson Electric, discussed in the *OM in Action* box, competes on speed—speed in design, production, and delivery. Whether it is a production system at Johnson Electric, a pizza delivered in 5 minutes by Pizza Hut, or customized phone products delivered in three days from Motorola, the operations manager who develops systems that respond quickly can have a competitive advantage.

In practice, differentiation, low cost, and response can increase productivity and generate a sustainable competitive advantage (see Figure 2.4). Proper implementation of the following decisions by operations managers will allow these advantages to be achieved.

AUTHOR COMMENT
These 10 decisions are used to implement a specific strategy and yield a competitive advantage.

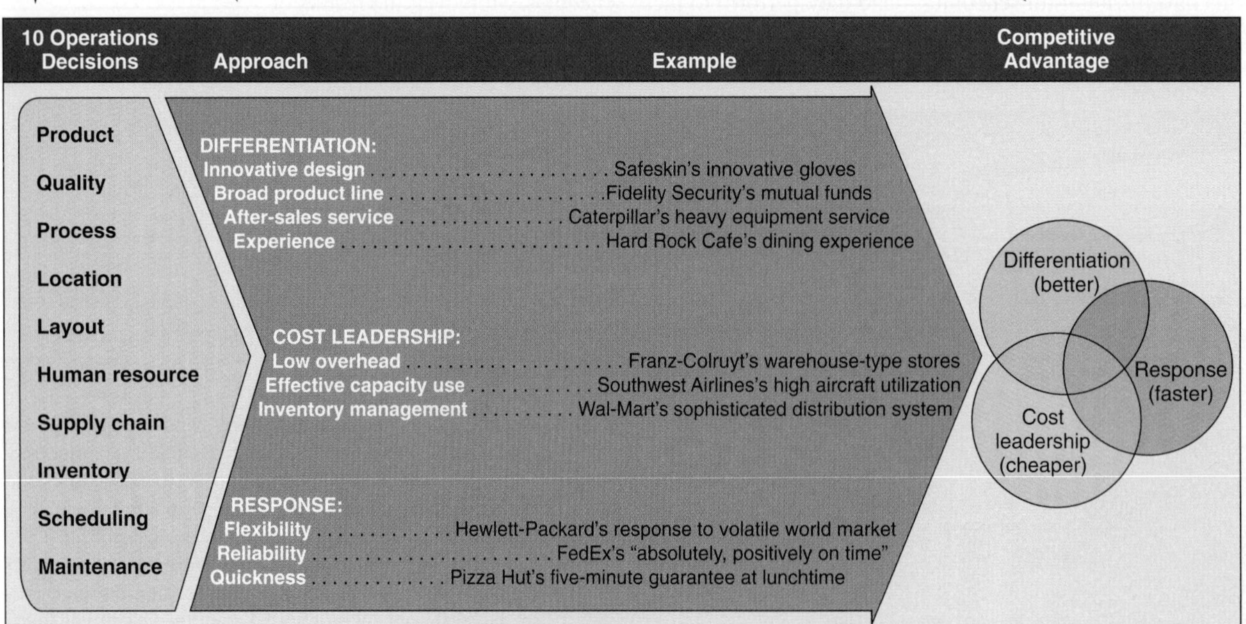

▲ **FIGURE 2.4 Achieving Competitive Advantage Through Operations**

TEN STRATEGIC OM DECISIONS

AUTHOR COMMENT
This text is structured around these 10 decisions.

Differentiation, low cost, and response can be achieved when managers make effective decisions in 10 areas of OM. These are collectively known as **operations decisions**. The 10 decisions of OM that support missions and implement strategies are:

Operations decisions
The strategic decisions of OM are goods and service design, quality, process design, location selection, layout design, human resources and job design, supply-chain management, inventory, scheduling, and maintenance.

1. *Goods and service design:* Designing goods and services defines much of the transformation process. Costs, quality, and human resource decisions are often determined by design decisions. Designs usually determine the lower limits of cost and the upper limits of quality.
2. *Quality:* The customer's quality expectations must be determined and policies and procedures established to identify and achieve that quality.
3. *Process and capacity design:* Process options are available for products and services. Process decisions commit management to specific technology, quality, human resource use, and maintenance. These expenses and capital commitments determine much of the firm's basic cost structure.
4. *Location selection:* Facility location decisions for both manufacturing and service organizations may determine the firm's ultimate success. Errors made at this juncture may overwhelm other efficiencies.
5. *Layout design:* Material flows, capacity needs, personnel levels, technology decisions, and inventory requirements influence layout.
6. *Human resources and job design:* People are an integral and expensive part of the total system design. Therefore, the quality of work life provided, the talent and skills required, and their costs must be determined.
7. *Supply-chain management:* These decisions determine what is to be made and what is to be purchased. Consideration is also given to quality, delivery, and innovation, all at a satisfactory price. Mutual trust between buyer and supplier is necessary for effective purchasing.
8. *Inventory:* Inventory decisions can be optimized only when customer satisfaction, suppliers, production schedules, and human resource planning are considered.
9. *Scheduling:* Feasible and efficient schedules of production must be developed; the demands on human resources and facilities must be determined and controlled.
10. *Maintenance:* Decisions must be made regarding desired levels of reliability and stability, and systems must be established to maintain that reliability and stability.

LO3: Identify and define the 10 decisions of operations management

Operations managers implement these 10 decisions by identifying key tasks and the staffing needed to achieve them. However, the implementation of decisions is influenced by a variety of issues, including a product's proportion of goods and services (see Table 2.1 on page 41). Few products are either all goods or all services. Although the 10 decisions remain the same for both goods and services, their relative importance and method of implementation depend on this ratio of goods and services. Throughout this text, we discuss how strategy is selected and implemented for both goods and services through these 10 operations management decisions.

Let's look at an example of strategy development through one of the 10 decisions.

EXAMPLE 1
Strategy development

Pierre Alexander has just completed culinary school and is ready to open his own restaurant. After examining both the external environment and his prospective strengths and weaknesses, he makes a decision on the mission for his restaurant, which he defines as "To provide outstanding French fine dining for the people of Chicago."

APPROACH ▶ Alexander's supporting operations strategy is to ignore the options of *cost leadership* and *quick response* and focus on *differentiation*. Consequently, his operations strategy requires him to evaluate product designs (menus and meals) and selection of process, layout, and location. He must also evaluate the human resources, suppliers, inventory, scheduling, and maintenance that will support his mission and a differentiation strategy.

SOLUTION ▶ Examining just one of these 10 decisions, *process design*, requires that Alexander consider the issues presented in the following figure.

(*Continued*)

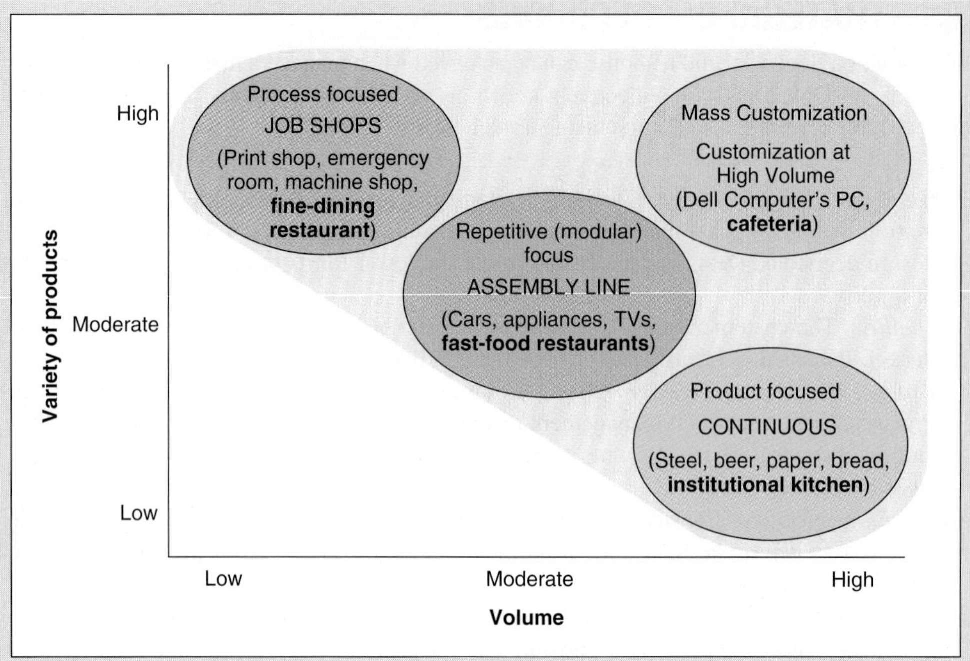

The first option is to operate in the lower right corner of the preceding figure, where he could produce high volumes of food with a limited variety, much as in an institutional kitchen. Such a process could produce large volumes of standard items such as baked goods and mashed potatoes prepared with state-of-the-art automated equipment. Alexander concludes that this is not an acceptable process option.

Alternatively, he can move to the middle of the figure, where he could produce more variety and lower volumes. Here he would have less automation and use prepared modular components for meals, much as a fast-food restaurant does. Again, he deems such process designs inappropriate for his mission.

Another option is to move to the upper right corner and produce a high volume of customized meals, but neither Alexander nor anyone else knows how to do this with gourmet meals.

Finally, Alexander can design a process that operates in the upper left corner of the figure, which requires little automation but lends itself to high variety. This process option suggests that he build an extremely flexible kitchen suitable for a wide variety of custom meals catering to the whims of each customer. With little automation, such a process would be suitable for a huge variety. This process strategy will support his mission and desired product differentiation. Only with a process such as this can he provide the fine French-style gourmet dining that he has in mind.

INSIGHT ▶ By considering the options inherent in each of the 10 OM decisions, managers—Alexander, in this case—can make decisions that support the mission.

LEARNING EXERCISE ▶ If Alexander's mission were to offer less expensive meals and reduce the variety offered but still do so with a French flair, what might his process strategy be? [Answer: Alexander might try a repetitive (modular) strategy and mimic the La Madeleine cafeteria-style restaurants.]

The 10 decisions of operations management are implemented in ways that provide competitive advantage, not just for fine-dining restaurants, but for all the goods and services that enrich our lives. How this might be done for two drug companies, one seeking a competitive advantage via differentiation, and the other via low cost, is shown in Table 2.2.

AUTHOR COMMENT
An effective strategy finds the optimum fit for the firm's resources in the dynamic environment.

ISSUES IN OPERATIONS STRATEGY

Resources view
A method managers use to evaluate the resources at their disposal and manage or alter them to achieve competitive advantage.

Whether the OM strategy is differentiation, cost, or response (as shown earlier in Figure 2.4), OM is a critical player. Therefore, prior to establishing and attempting to implement a strategy, some alternate perspectives may be helpful. One perspective is to take a **resources view**. This means thinking in terms of the financial, physical, human, and technological resources available and ensuring

▼ **TABLE 2.1**

The Differences between Goods and Services Influence How the 10 Operations Management Decisions Are Applied

Operations Decisions	Goods	Services
Goods and service design	Product is usually tangible (a computer).	Product is not tangible. A new range of product attributes (a smile).
Quality	Many objective quality standards (battery life).	Many subjective quality standards (nice color).
Process and capacity design	Customer is not involved in most of the process (auto assembly).	Customer may be directly involved in the process (a haircut). Capacity must match demand to avoid lost sales (customers often avoid waiting).
Location selection	May need to be near raw materials or labor force (steel plant near ore).	May need to be near customer (car rental).
Layout design	Layout can enhance production efficiency (assembly line).	Can enhance product as well as production (layout of a classroom or a fine-dining restaurant).
Human resources and job design	Workforce focused on technical skills (stone mason). Labor standards can be consistent (assembly line employee). Output-based wage system possible (garment sewing).	Direct workforce usually needs to be able to interact well with customer (bank teller); labor standards vary depending on customer requirements (legal cases).
Supply-chain management	Supply chain relationships critical to final product.	Supply chain relationships important but may not be critical
Inventory	Raw materials, work-in-process, and finished goods may be inventoried (beer).	Most services cannot be stored; so other ways must be found to accommodate fluctuations in demand (can't store haircuts, but even the barber shop has an inventory of supplies).
Scheduling	Ability to inventory may allow leveling of production rates (lawn mowers).	Often concerned with meeting the customer's immediate schedule with human resources.
Maintenance	Maintenance is often preventive and takes place at the production site.	Maintenance is often "repair" and takes place at the customer's site.

AUTHOR COMMENT
The production of both goods and services requires execution of the 10 OM decisions.

AUTHOR COMMENT
Notice how the 10 decisions are altered to build two distinct strategies in the same industry.

▼ **TABLE 2.2**

Operations Strategies of Two Drug Companies

	Brand Name Drugs, Inc.	**Generic Drug Corp.**
Competitive Advantage	**Product Differentiation**	**Low Cost**
Product Selection and Design	Heavy R&D investment; extensive labs; focus on development in a broad range of drug categories	Low R&D investment; focus on development of generic drugs
Quality	Quality is major priority, standards exceed regulatory requirements	Meets regulatory requirements on a country-by-country basis, as necessary
Process	Product and modular production process; tries to have long product runs in specialized facilities; builds capacity ahead of demand	Process focused; general production processes; "job shop" approach, short-run production; focus on high utilization
Location	Still located in city where it was founded	Recently moved to low-tax, low-labor-cost environment
Layout	Layout supports automated product-focused production	Layout supports process-focused "job shop" practices
Human Resources	Hire the best; nationwide searches	Very experienced top executives provide direction; other personnel paid below industry average
Supply Chain	Long-term supplier relationships	Tends to purchase competitively to find bargains
Inventory	Maintains high finished goods inventory primarily to ensure all demands are met	Process focus drives up work-in-process inventory; finished goods inventory tends to be low
Scheduling	Centralized production planning	Many short-run products complicate scheduling
Maintenance	Highly trained staff; extensive parts inventory	Highly trained staff to meet changing demands

Value-chain analysis
A way to identify those elements in the product/service chain that uniquely add value.

Five forces analysis
A method of analyzing the five forces in the competitive environment.

that the potential strategy is compatible with those resources. Another perspective is Porter's value-chain analysis.[2] **Value-chain analysis** is used to identify activities that represent strengths, or potential strengths, and may be opportunities for developing competitive advantage. These are areas where the firm adds its unique *value* through product research, design, human resources, supply-chain management, process innovation, or quality management. Porter also suggests analysis of competitors via what he calls his **five forces model**.[3] These potential competing forces are immediate rivals, potential entrants, customers, suppliers, and substitute products.

In addition to the competitive environment, the operations manager needs to understand that the firm is operating in a system with many other external factors. These factors range from political, to legal, to cultural. They influence strategy development and execution and require constant scanning of the environment.

The firm itself is also undergoing constant change. Everything from resources, to technology, to product life cycles is in flux. Consider the significant changes required within the firm as its products move from introduction, to growth, to maturity, and to decline (see Figure 2.5). These internal changes, combined with external changes, require strategies that are dynamic.

In this chapter's *Global Company Profile*, Boeing provides an example of how strategy must change as technology and the environment change. Boeing can now build planes from carbon

	Introduction	Growth	Maturity	Decline
Company Strategy / Issues	Best period to increase market share R&D engineering is critical	Practical to change price or quality image Strengthen niche	Poor time to change image, price, or quality Competitive costs become critical Defend market position	Cost control critical
Sales (products on the curve)	Twitter	Boeing 787 Avatars Xbox 360 iPods	LCD & plasma TVs Internet search engines Drive-thru restaurants	CD-ROMs Analog TVs
OM Strategy / Issues	Product design and development critical Frequent product and process design changes Short production runs High production costs Limited models Attention to quality	Forecasting critical Product and process reliability Competitive product improvements and options Increase capacity Shift toward product focus Enhance distribution	Standardization Fewer rapid product changes, more minor changes Optimum capacity Increasing stability of process Long production runs Product improvement and cost cutting	Little product differentiation Cost minimization Overcapacity in the industry Prune line to eliminate items not returning good margin Reduce capacity

▲ **FIGURE 2.5 Strategy and Issues During a Product's Life**

[2]M. E. Porter, *Competitive Advantage: Creating and Sustaining Superior Performance.* New York: The Free Press, 1985.

[3]Michael E. Porter, *Competitive Strategy: Techniques for Analyzing Industries and Competitors.* New York: The Free Press, 1980, 1998.

fiber, using a global supply chain. Like many other OM strategies, Boeing's strategy has changed with technology and globalization. Microsoft has also had to adapt quickly to a changing environment. Faster processors, new computer languages, changing customer preferences, increased security issues, the Internet, and Google have all driven changes at Microsoft. These forces have moved Microsoft's product strategy from operating systems to office products, to Internet service provider, and now to integrator of computers, cell phones, games, and television.

The more thorough the analysis and understanding of both the external and internal factors, the more likely that a firm can find the optimum use of its resources. Once a firm understands itself and the environment, a SWOT analysis, which we discuss next, is in order.

STRATEGY DEVELOPMENT AND IMPLEMENTATION

AUTHOR COMMENT
A SWOT analysis provides an excellent model for evaluating a strategy.

A **SWOT analysis** is a formal review of the internal Strengths and Weakness and the external Opportunity and Threats. Beginning with SWOT analyses, organizations position themselves, through their strategy, to have a competitive advantage. A firm may have excellent design skills or great talent at identifying outstanding locations. However, it may recognize limitations of its manufacturing process or in finding good suppliers. The idea is to maximize opportunities and minimize threats in the environment while maximizing the advantages of the organization's strengths and minimizing the weaknesses. Any preconceived ideas about mission are then reevaluated to ensure they are consistent with the SWOT analysis. Subsequently, a strategy for achieving the mission is developed. This strategy is continually evaluated against the value provided customers and competitive realities. The process is shown in Figure 2.6. From this process, key success factors are identified.

SWOT analysis
A method of determining internal strengths and weaknesses and external opportunities and threats.

Key Success Factors and Core Competencies

Because no firm does everything exceptionally well, a successful strategy requires determining the firm's critical success factors and core competencies. **Key success factors (KSFs)** are those activities that are necessary for a firm to achieve its goals. Key success factors can be so significant that a firm must get them right to survive in the industry. A KSF for McDonald's, for example, is layout. Without a play area, an effective drive-thru, and an efficient kitchen, McDonald's cannot be successful. KSFs are often necessary, but not sufficient for competitive advantage. On the other hand, **core competencies** are the set of unique skills, talents, and capabilities that a firm does at a world-class standard. They allow a firm to set itself apart and develop a competitive advantage. Organizations that prosper identify their core competencies and nurture them. While McDonald's KSFs may include layout, its core competency may be consistency and quality. Honda Motors's core competence is gas-powered engines—engines for automobiles, motorcycles, lawn mowers, generators, snow blowers, and more. The idea is to build KSFs and core competencies that provide a competitive advantage and support a successful strategy and mission. A core competence may be a subset of KSFs or a combination of KSFs. The operations manager begins this inquiry by asking:

Key success factors (KSFs)
Activities or factors that are *key* to achieving competitive advantage.

Core competencies
A set of skills, talents, and activities in which a firm is particularly strong.

- "What tasks must be done particularly well for a given strategy to succeed?"
- "Which activities will help the OM function provide a competitive advantage?"
- "Which elements contain the highest likelihood of failure, and which require additional commitment of managerial, monetary, technological, and human resources?"

LO4: Understand the significance of key success factors and core competencies

Analyze the Environment
Identify the strengths, weaknesses, opportunities, and threats.
Understand the environment, customers, industry, and competitors.

Determine the Corporate Mission
State the reason for the firm's existence and identify the value it wishes to create.

Form a Strategy
Build a competitive advantage, such as low price, design or volume flexibility, quality, quick delivery, dependability, after-sale services, or broad product lines.

◄ **FIGURE 2.6 Strategy Development Process**

Honda's core competence is the design and manufacture of gas-powered engines. This competence has allowed Honda to become a leader in the design and manufacture of a wide range of gas-powered products. Tens of millions of these products are produced and shipped around the world.

Only by identifying and strengthening key success factors and core competencies can an organization achieve sustainable competitive advantage.

In this text we focus on the 10 OM decisions that typically include the KSFs. Potential KSFs for marketing, finance, and operations are shown in Figure 2.7. The 10 OM decisions we develop in this text provide an excellent initial checklist for determining KSFs and identifying core competencies within the operations function. For instance, the 10 decisions, related KSFs, and core competencies can allow a firm to differentiate its product or service. That differentiation may be via a core competence of innovation and new products, where the KSFs are product design and speed to market, as is the case for 3M and Rubbermaid. Similarly, differentiation may be via quality, where the core competence is institutionalizing quality, as at Toyota. Differentiation may also be via maintenance, where the KSFs are product reliability and after-sale service, as is the case at IBM and Canon.

Activity map
A graphical link of competitive advantage, KSFs, and supporting activities.

Whatever the KSFs and core competences, they must be supported by the related activities. One approach to identifying the activities is an **activity map**, which links competitive advantage, KSFs, and supporting activities. For example, Figure 2.8 shows how Southwest Airlines, whose core competence is operations, built a set of integrated activities to support its low-cost competitive advantage. Notice how the KSFs support operations and in turn are supported by other activities. The activities fit together and reinforce each other. And the better they fit and reinforce each other, the more sustainable the competitive advantage. By focusing on enhancing its core

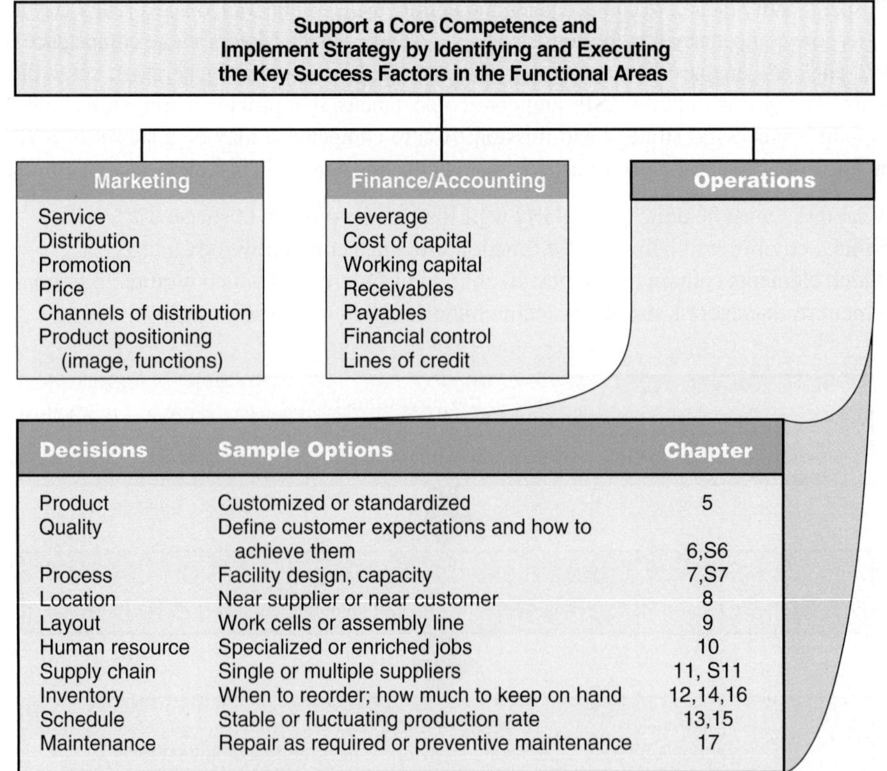

Decisions	Sample Options	Chapter
Product	Customized or standardized	5
Quality	Define customer expectations and how to achieve them	6,S6
Process	Facility design, capacity	7,S7
Location	Near supplier or near customer	8
Layout	Work cells or assembly line	9
Human resource	Specialized or enriched jobs	10
Supply chain	Single or multiple suppliers	11, S11
Inventory	When to reorder; how much to keep on hand	12,14,16
Schedule	Stable or fluctuating production rate	13,15
Maintenance	Repair as required or preventive maintenance	17

▶ **FIGURE 2.7**
Implement Strategy by Identifying and Executing Key Success Factors That Support Core Competences

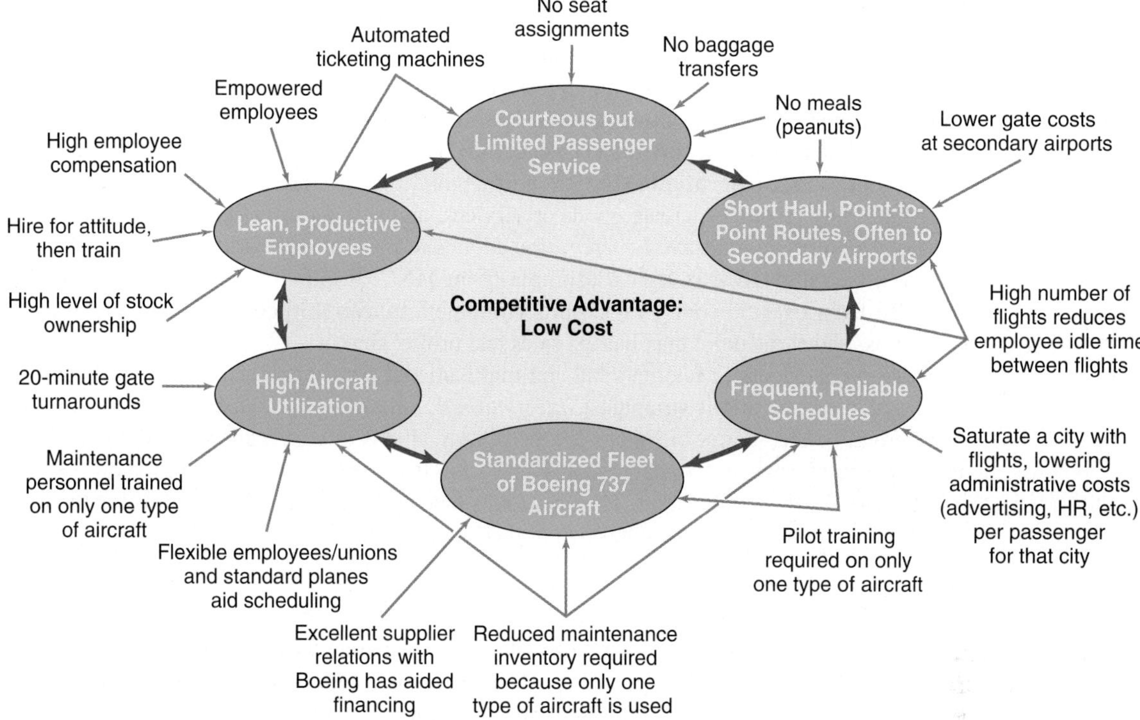

▲ **FIGURE 2.8 Activity Mapping of Southwest Airlines's Low-Cost Competitive Advantage**

To achieve a low-cost competitive advantage, Southwest has identified a number of key success factors (connected by red arrows) and support activities (shown by blue arrows). As this figure indicates, a low-cost advantage is highly dependent on a very well run operations function.

competence and KSFs with a supporting set of activities, Southwest Airlines has become one of the great airline success stories.

Build and Staff the Organization

The operations manager's job is a three-step process. Once a strategy and key success factors have been identified, the second step is to group the necessary activities into an organizational structure. The third step is to staff it with personnel who will get the job done. The manager works with subordinate managers to build plans, budgets, and programs that will successfully implement strategies that achieve missions. Firms tackle this organization of the operations function in a variety of ways. The organization charts shown in Chapter 1 (Figure 1.1) indicate the way some firms have organized to perform the required activities.

Integrate OM with Other Activities

The organization of the operations function and its relationship to other parts of the organization vary with the OM mission. Moreover, the operations function is most likely to be successful when the operations strategy is integrated with other functional areas of the firm, such as marketing, finance, information technology, and human resources. In this way, all of the areas support the company's objectives. For example, short-term scheduling in the airline industry is dominated by volatile customer travel patterns. Day-of-week preference, holidays, seasonality, college schedules, and so on, all play a role in changing flight schedules. Consequently, airline scheduling, although an OM activity, can be a part of marketing. Effective scheduling in the trucking industry is reflected in the amount of time trucks travel loaded. However, scheduling of trucks requires information from delivery and pickup points, drivers, and other parts of the organization. When the OM function results in effective scheduling in the air passenger and commercial trucking industries, a competitive advantage can exist.

The operations manager transforms inputs into outputs. The transformations may be in terms of storage, transportation, manufacturing, dissemination of information, and utility of the product or service. *The operations manager's job is to implement an OM strategy, provide competitive advantage, and increase productivity.*

AUTHOR COMMENT
Firms that ignore the global economy will not survive.

GLOBAL OPERATIONS STRATEGY OPTIONS

International business
A firm that engages in cross-border transactions.

Multinational corporation (MNC)
A firm that has extensive involvement in international business, owning or controlling facilities in more than one country.

As we suggested early in this chapter, many operations strategies now require an international dimension. We tend to call a firm with an international dimension an international business or a multinational corporation. An **international business** is any firm that engages in international trade or investment. This is a very broad category and is the opposite of a domestic, or local, firm.

A **multinational corporation (MNC)** is a firm with *extensive* international business involvement. MNCs buy resources, create goods or services, and sell goods or services in a variety of countries. The term *multinational corporation* applies to most of the world's large, well-known businesses. Certainly IBM is a good example of an MNC. It imports electronics components to the U.S. from over 50 countries, exports computers to over 130 countries, has facilities in 45 countries, and earns more than half its sales and profits abroad.

Operations managers of international and multinational firms approach global opportunities with one of four operations strategies: *international*, *multidomestic*, *global*, or *transnational* (see Figure 2.9). The matrix of Figure 2.9 has a vertical axis of cost reduction and a horizontal axis of local responsiveness. Local responsiveness implies quick response and/or the differentiation necessary for the local market. The operations manager must know how to position the firm in this matrix. Let us briefly examine each of the four strategies.

International Strategy

International strategy
A strategy in which global markets are penetrated using exports and licenses.

An **international strategy** uses exports and licenses to penetrate the global arena. As Figure 2.9 suggests, the international strategy is the least advantageous, with little local responsiveness and little cost advantage. There is little responsiveness because we are exporting or licensing goods from the home country. And the cost advantages may be few because we are using the existing production process at some distance from the new market. However, an international strategy is often the easiest, as exports can require little change in existing operations, and licensing agreements often leave much of the risk to the licensee.

LO5: Identify and explain four global operations strategy options

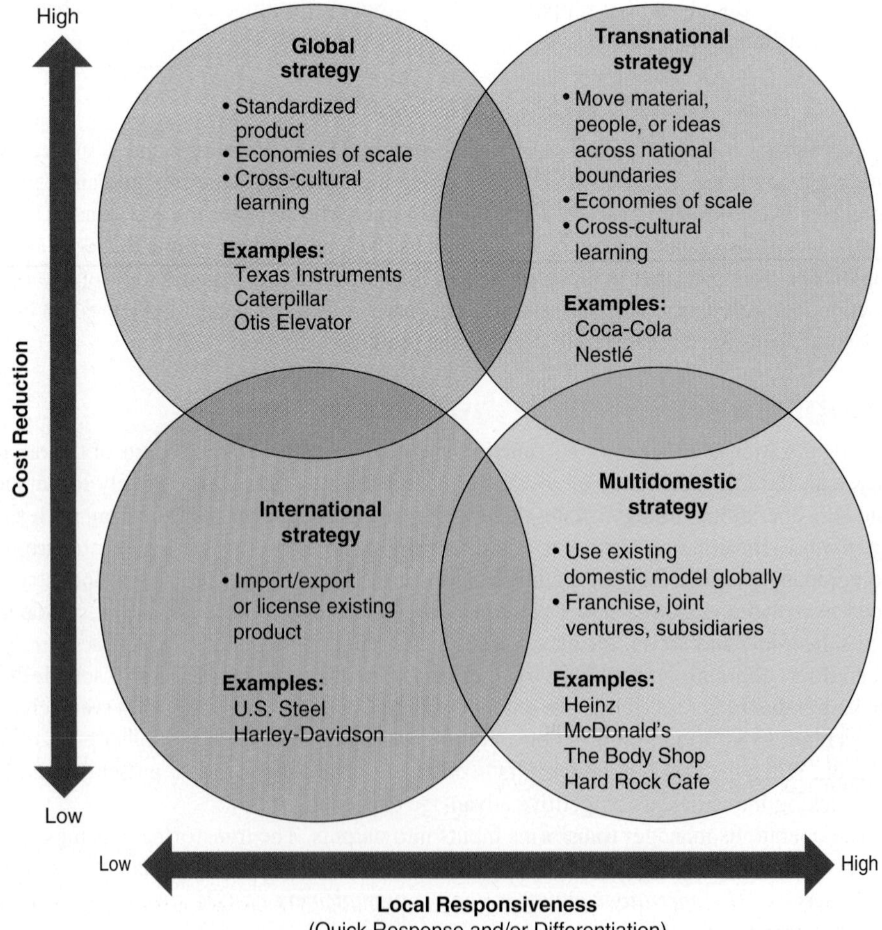

▶ FIGURE 2.9
Four International Operations Strategies

Sources: See a similar presentation in M. Hitt, R. D. Ireland, and R. E. Hoskisson, *Strategic Management, Competitiveness and Globalization,* 7th ed. (Cincinnati: Southwestern College Publishing, 2009).

Multidomestic Strategy

The **multidomestic strategy** has decentralized authority with substantial autonomy at each business. Organizationally these are typically subsidiaries, franchises, or joint ventures with substantial independence. The advantage of this strategy is maximizing a competitive response for the local market; however, the strategy has little or no cost advantage. Many food producers, such as Heinz, use a multidomestic strategy to accommodate local tastes because global integration of the production process is not critical. The concept is one of "we were successful in the home market; let's export the management talent and processes, not necessarily the product, to accommodate another market." McDonald's is operating primarily as a multidomestic, which gives it the local responsiveness needed to modify its menu country by country. McDonald's can then serve beer in Germany, wine in France, McHuevo (poached egg hamburger) in Uruguay, and hamburgers without beef in India. With over 2,000 restaurants in Japan and a presence for more than a generation, the average Japanese family thinks Japan invented McDonald's. Interestingly, McDonald's prefers to call itself *multilocal*.[4]

Multidomestic strategy
A strategy in which operating decisions are decentralized to each country to enhance local responsiveness.

Global Strategy

A **global strategy** has a high degree of centralization, with headquarters coordinating the organization to seek out standardization and learning between plants, thus generating economies of scale. This strategy is appropriate when the strategic focus is cost reduction but has little to recommend it when the demand for local responsiveness is high. Caterpillar, the world leader in earth-moving equipment, and Texas Instruments, a world leader in semiconductors, pursue global strategies. Caterpillar and Texas Instruments find this strategy advantageous because the end products are similar throughout the world. Earth-moving equipment is the same in Nigeria as in Iowa, which allows Caterpillar to have individual factories focus on a limited line of products to be shipped worldwide. This results in economies of scale and learning within each facility. A global strategy also allows Texas Instruments to build optimum-size plants with similar processes and to then maximize learning by aggressive communication between plants. The result is an effective cost reduction advantage for Texas Instruments.

Global strategy
A strategy in which operating decisions are centralized and headquarters coordinates the standardization and learning between facilities.

Transnational Strategy

A **transnational strategy** exploits the economies of scale and learning, as well as pressure for responsiveness, by recognizing that core competence does not reside in just the "home" country but can exist anywhere in the organization. *Transnational* describes a condition in which material, people, and ideas cross—or *transgress*—national boundaries. These firms have the potential to pursue all three operations strategies (i.e., differentiation, low cost, and response). Such firms can be

Transnational strategy
A strategy that combines the benefits of global-scale efficiencies with the benefits of local responsiveness.

In a continuing fierce worldwide battle, both Komatsu and Caterpillar seek global advantage in the heavy equipment market. As Komatsu (left) moved west to the UK, Caterpillar (right) moved east, with 13 facilities and joint ventures in China. Both firms are building equipment throughout the world as cost and logistics dictate. Their global strategies allow production to move as markets, risk, and exchange rates dictate.

[4]James L. Watson, ed., *Golden Arches East: McDonald's in East Asia* (Stanford University Press, 1997): 12. *Note:* McDonald's also operates with some of the advantages of a global organization. By using very similar product lines throughout the world, McDonald's obtains some of the standardization advantages of a global strategy. However, it manages to retain the advantages of a multidomestic strategy.

thought of as "world companies" whose country identity is not as important as its interdependent network of worldwide operations. Key activities in a transnational company are neither centralized in the parent company nor decentralized so that each subsidiary can carry out its own tasks on a local basis. Instead, the resources and activities are dispersed, but specialized, so as to be both efficient and flexible in an interdependent network. Nestlé is a good example of such a company. Although it is legally Swiss, 95% of its assets are held and 98% of its sales are made outside Switzerland. Fewer than 10% of its workers are Swiss. Similarly, service firms such as Asea Brown Boveri (an engineering firm that is Swedish but headquartered in Switzerland), Reuters (a news agency), Bertelsmann (a publisher), and Citicorp (a banking corporation) can be viewed as transnationals. We can expect the national identities of these transnationals to continue to fade.

CHAPTER SUMMARY

Global operations provide an increase in both the challenges and opportunities for operations managers. Although the task is challenging, operations managers can and do improve productivity. They can build and manage OM functions that contribute in a significant way to competitiveness. Organizations identify their strengths and weaknesses. They then develop effective missions and strategies that account for these strengths and weaknesses and complement the opportunities and threats in the environment. If this procedure is performed well, the organization can have competitive advantage through some combination of product differentiation, low cost, and response. This competitive advantage is often achieved via a move to international, multidomestic, global, or transnational strategies.

Effective use of resources, whether domestic or international, is the responsibility of the professional manager, and professional managers are among the few in our society who *can* achieve this performance. The challenge is great, and the rewards to the manager and to society substantial.

Key Terms

Maquiladoras (p. 31)
World Trade Organization (WTO) (p. 31)
North American Free Trade Agreement (NAFTA) (p. 31)
European Union (EU) (p. 31)
Mission (p. 34)
Strategy (p. 34)
Competitive advantage (p. 35)
Differentiation (p. 36)
Experience differentiation (p. 36)
Low-cost leadership (p. 36)
Response (p. 36)
Operations decisions (p. 39)
Resources view (p. 40)
Value-chain analysis (p. 42)
Five forces analysis (p. 42)
SWOT analysis (p. 43)
Key success factors (KSFs) (p. 43)
Core competencies (p. 43)
Activity map (p. 44)
International business (p. 46)
Multinational corporation (MNC) (p. 46)
International strategy (p. 46)
Multidomestic strategy (p. 47)
Global strategy (p. 47)
Transnational strategy (p. 47)

Ethical Dilemma

As a manufacturer of athletic shoes whose image, indeed performance, is widely regarded as socially responsible, you find your costs increasing. Traditionally, your athletic shoes have been made in Indonesia and South Korea. Although the ease of doing business in those countries has been improving, wage rates have also been increasing. The labor-cost differential between your present suppliers and a contractor who will get the shoes made in China now exceeds $1 per pair. Your sales next year are projected to be 10 million pairs, and your analysis suggests that this cost differential is not offset by any other tangible costs; you face only the political risk and potential damage to your commitment to social responsibility. Thus, this $1 per pair savings should flow directly to your bottom line. There is no doubt that the Chinese government engages in censorship, remains repressive, and is a long way from a democracy. Moreover, you will have little or no control over working conditions, sexual harassment, and pollution. What do you do and on what basis do you make your decision?

Discussion Questions

1. Based on the descriptions and analyses in this chapter, would Boeing be better described as a global firm or a transnational firm? Discuss.
2. List six reasons to internationalize operations.
3. Coca-Cola is called a global product. Does this mean that Coca-Cola is formulated in the same way throughout the world? Discuss.
4. Define *mission*.
5. Define *strategy*.
6. Describe how an organization's *mission* and *strategy* have different purposes.
7. Identify the mission and strategy of your automobile repair garage. What are the manifestations of the 10 OM decisions at the garage? That is, how is each of the 10 decisions accomplished?
8. As a library or Internet assignment, identify the mission of a firm and the strategy that supports that mission.
9. How does an OM strategy change during a product's life cycle?
10. There are three primary ways to achieve competitive advantage. Provide an example, not included in the text, of each. Support your choices.
11. Given the discussion of Southwest Airlines in the text, define an *operations* strategy for that firm.
12. How must an operations strategy integrate with marketing and accounting?

Solved Problem **Virtual Office Hours help is available at www.myomlab.com**

▼ SOLVED PROBLEM 2.1

The global tire industry continues to consolidate. Michelin buys Goodrich and Uniroyal and builds plants throughout the world. Bridgestone buys Firestone, expands its research budget, and focuses on world markets. Goodyear spends almost 4% of its sales revenue on research. These three aggressive firms have come to dominate the world tire market, with total market share approaching 60%. And the German tire maker Continental AG has strengthened its position as fourth in the world, with a dominant presence in Germany. Against this formidable array, the old-line Italian tire company Pirelli SpA found it difficult to respond effectively. Although Pirelli still had 5% of the market, it was losing millions a year while the competition was getting stronger. Tires are a tough, competitive business that rewards companies having strong market shares and long production runs. Pirelli has some strengths: an outstanding reputation for excellent high-performance tires and an innovative manufacturing function.

Use a SWOT analysis to establish a feasible strategy for Pirelli.

▼ SOLUTION

First, find an opportunity in the world tire market that avoids the threat of the mass-market onslaught by the big three tire makers. Second, utilize the internal marketing strength represented by Pirelli's strong brand name and history of winning World Rally Championships. Third, maximize the internal innovative capabilities of the operations function.

To achieve these goals, Pirelli made a strategic shift out of low-margin standard tires and into higher-margin performance tires. Pirelli established deals with luxury brands Jaguar, BMW, Maserati, Ferrari, Bentley, and Lotus Elise and established itself as a provider of a large share of tires on new Porsches, S-class Mercedes, and Saabs. As a result, more than 70% of the company's tire production is now high-performance tires. People are willing to pay a premium for Pirellis.

The operations function continued to focus its design efforts on performance tires and developing a system of modular tire manufacture that allows much faster switching between models. This modular system, combined with investments in new manufacturing flexibility, has driven batch sizes down to as small as 150 to 200, making small-lot performance tires economically feasible. Manufacturing innovations at Pirelli have streamlined the production process, moving it from a 14-step process to a 3-step process. A threat from the big three going after the performance market remains, but Pirelli has bypassed its weakness of having a small market share. The firm now has 24 plants in 12 countries and a presence in more than 160 countries, with sales exceeding $4.5 billion.

Sources: Just Auto (February 2009): 14–15 and (December 2008): 14–15; *Hoover's Company Records* (October 15, 2005): 41369; and *www.pirelli.com/web/investors.*

Problems

• **2.1** The text provides three primary ways-strategic approaches (differentiation, cost, and response)-for achieving competitive advantage. Provide an example of each not given in the text. Support your choices. (*Hint:* Note the examples provided in the text.)

• • **2.2** Within the food service industry (restaurants that serve meals to customers, but not just fast food), find examples of firms that have sustained competitive advantage by competing on the basis of (1) cost leadership, (2) response, and (3) differentiation. Cite one example in each category; provide a sentence or two in support of each choice. Do not use fast-food chains for all categories. (*Hint:* A "99¢ menu" is very easily copied and is not a good source of sustained advantage.)

• • **2.3** Browse through *The Wall Street Journal*, the financial section of a daily paper, or read business news online. Seek articles that constrain manufacturing innovation and productivity—workers aren't allowed to do this, workers are not or cannot be trained to do that, this technology is not allowed, this material cannot be handled by workers, and so forth. Be prepared to share your articles in class discussion.

•• **2.4** Match the product with the proper parent company and country in the table below:

Product	Parent Company	Country
Arrow Shirts	a. Volkswagen	1. France
Braun Household Appliances	b. Bidermann International	2. Great Britain
Lotus Autos	c. Bridgestone	3. Germany
Firestone Tires	d. Campbell Soup	4. Japan
Godiva Chocolate	e. Credit Lyonnais	5. U.S.
Häagen-Dazs Ice Cream (USA)	f. Tata	6. Switzerland
Jaguar Autos	g. Procter & Gamble	7. Malaysia
MGM Movies	h. Michelin	8. India
Lamborghini Autos	i. Nestlé	
Goodrich Tires	j. Proton	
Alpo Pet Foods		

••• **2.5** Identify how changes within an organization affect the OM strategy for a company. For instance, discuss what impact the following internal factors might have on OM strategy:

a) Maturing of a product.
b) Technology innovation in the manufacturing process.
c) Changes in laptop computer design that builds in wireless technology.

••• **2.6** Identify how changes in the external environment affect the OM strategy for a company. For instance, discuss what impact the following external factors might have on OM strategy:

a) Major increases in oil prices.
b) Water- and air-quality legislation.
c) Fewer young prospective employees entering the labor market.
d) Inflation versus stable prices.
e) Legislation moving health insurance from a pretax benefit to taxable income.

•• **2.7** Develop a ranking for corruption in the following countries: Mexico, Turkey, Denmark, the U.S., Taiwan, Brazil, and another country of your choice. (*Hint:* See sources such as *Transparency International*, *Asia Pacific Management News*, and *The Economist*.)

•• **2.8** Develop a ranking for competitiveness and/or business environment for Britain, Singapore, the U.S., Hong Kong, and Italy. (*Hint:* See the *Global Competitive Report*, *World Economic Forum*, Geneva, and *The Economist*.)

Case Studies

▶ Minit-Lube

A substantial market exists for automobile tune-ups, oil changes, and lubrication service for more than 200 million cars on U.S. roads. Some of this demand is filled by full-service auto dealerships, some by Sears and Firestone, and some by other tire/service dealers. However, Minit-Lube, Mobil-Lube, Jiffy-Lube and others have also developed strategies to accommodate this opportunity.

Minit-Lube stations perform oil changes, lubrication, and interior cleaning in a spotless environment. The buildings are clean, painted white, and often surrounded by neatly trimmed landscaping. To facilitate fast service, cars can be driven through three abreast. At Minit-Lube, the customer is greeted by service representatives who are graduates of Minit-Lube U. The Minit-Lube school is not unlike McDonald's Hamburger University near Chicago or Holiday Inn's training school in Memphis. The greeter takes the order, which typically includes fluid checks (oil, water, brake fluid, transmission fluid, differential grease) and the necessary lubrication, as well as filter changes for air and oil. Service personnel in neat uniforms then move into action. The standard three-person team has one person checking fluid levels under the hood, another assigned interior vacuuming and window cleaning, and the third in the garage pit, removing the oil filter, draining the oil, checking the differential and transmission, and lubricating as necessary. Precise task assignments and good training are designed to move the car into and out of the bay in 10 minutes. The idea is to charge no more, and hopefully less, than gas stations, automotive repair chains, and auto dealers, while providing better service.

Discussion Questions

1. What constitutes the mission of Minit-Lube?
2. How does the Minit-Lube operations strategy provide competitive advantage? (*Hint:* Evaluate how Minit-Lube's traditional competitors perform the 10 decisions of operations management vs. how Minit-Lube performs them.)
3. Is it likely that Minit-Lube has increased productivity over its more traditional competitors? Why? How would we measure productivity in this industry?

► Strategy at Regal Marine

Video Case

Regal Marine, one of the U.S.'s 10 largest power-boat manufacturers, achieves its mission—providing luxury performance boats to customers worldwide—using the strategy of differentiation. It differentiates its products through constant innovation, unique features, and high quality. Increasing sales at the Orlando, Florida, family-owned firm suggest that the strategy is working.

As a quality boat manufacturer, Regal Marine starts with continuous innovation, as reflected in computer-aided design (CAD), high-quality molds, and close tolerances that are controlled through both defect charts and rigorous visual inspection. In-house quality is not enough, however. Because a product is only as good as the parts put into it, Regal has established close ties with a large number of its suppliers to ensure both flexibility and perfect parts. With the help of these suppliers, Regal can profitably produce a product line of 22 boats, ranging from the \$14,000 19-foot boat to the \$500,000 44-foot Commodore yacht.

"We build boats," says VP Tim Kuck, "but we're really in the 'fun' business. Our competition includes not only 300 other boat, canoe, and yacht manufacturers in our \$17 billion industry, but home theaters, the Internet, and all kinds of alternative family entertainment." Fortunately Regal has been paying down debt and increasing market share.

Regal has also joined with scores of other independent boat makers in the American Boat Builders Association. Through economies of scale in procurement, Regal is able to navigate against billion-dollar competitor Brunswick (makers of the Sea Ray and Bayliner brands). The *Global Company Profile* featuring Regal Marine (which opens Chapter 5) provides further background on Regal and its strategy.

Discussion Questions*

1. State Regal Marine's mission in your own words.
2. Identify the strengths, weaknesses, opportunities, and threats that are relevant to the strategy of Regal Marine.
3. How would you define Regal's strategy?
4. How would each of the 10 operations management decisions apply to operations decision making at Regal Marine?

*You may wish to view the video that accompanies the case before addressing these questions.

► Hard Rock Cafe's Global Strategy

Video Case

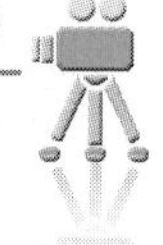

Hard Rock brings the concept of the "experience economy" to its cafe operation. The strategy incorporates a unique "experience" into its operations. This innovation is somewhat akin to mass customization in manufacturing. At Hard Rock, the experience concept is to provide not only a custom meal from the menu but a dining event that includes a unique visual and sound experience not duplicated anywhere else in the world. This strategy is succeeding. Other theme restaurants have come and gone while Hard Rock continues to grow. As Professor C. Markides of the London Business School says, "The trick is not to play the game better than the competition, but to develop and play an altogether different game."* At Hard Rock, the different game is the experience game.

From the opening of its first cafe in London in 1971, during the British rock music explosion, Hard Rock has been serving food and rock music with equal enthusiasm. Hard Rock Cafe has 40 U.S. locations, about a dozen in Europe, and the remainder scattered throughout the world, from Bangkok and Beijing to Beirut. New construction, leases, and investment in remodeling are long term; so a global strategy means special consideration of political risk, currency risk, and social norms in a context of a brand fit. Although Hard Rock is one of the most recognized brands in the world, this does not mean its cafe is a natural everywhere. Special consideration must be given to the supply chain for the restaurant and its accompanying retail store. About 48% of a typical cafe's sales are from merchandise.

The Hard Rock Cafe business model is well defined, but because of various risk factors and differences in business practices and employment law, Hard Rock elects to franchise about half of its cafes. Social norms and preferences often suggest some tweaking of menus for local taste. For instance, Hard Rock focuses less on hamburgers and beef and more on fish and lobster in its British cafes.

Because 70% of Hard Rock's guests are tourists, recent years have found it expanding to "destination" cities. While this has been a winning strategy for decades, allowing the firm to grow from 1 London cafe to 157 facilities in 57 countries, it has made Hard Rock susceptible to economic fluctuations that hit the tourist business hardest. So Hard Rock is signing a long-term lease for a new location in Nottingham, England, to join recently opened cafes in Manchester and Birmingham—cities that are not standard tourist destinations. At the same time, menus are being upgraded. Hopefully, repeat business from locals in these cities will smooth demand and make Hard Rock less dependent on tourists.

Discussion Questions†

1. Identify the strategy changes that have taken place at Hard Rock Cafe since its founding in 1971.
2. As Hard Rock Cafe has changed its strategy, how has its responses to some of the 10 decisions of OM changed?
3. Where does Hard Rock fit in the four international operations strategies outlined in Figure 2.9? Explain your answer.

*Constantinos Markides, "Strategic Innovation," *MIT Sloan Management Review* 38, no. 3 (spring 1997): 9.

†You may wish to view the video that accompanies this case before addressing these questions.

►**Additional Case Study:** Visit **www.myomlab.com** or **www.pearsonhighered.com/heizer** for this free case study:
Motorola's Global Strategy: Focuses on Motorola's international strategy.

Bibliography

Beckman, S. L., and D. B. Rosenfield. *Operations Strategy: Competing in the 21st Century*. New York: McGraw-Hill, 2008.

Crotts, J. C., D. R. Dickson, and R. C. Ford. "Aligning Organizational Processes with Mission." *Academy of Management Executive* 19, no. 3 (August 2005): 54–68.

Flynn, B. B., R. G. Schroeder, and E. J. Flynn. "World Class Manufacturing." *Journal of Operations Management* 17, no. 3 (March 1999): 249–269.

Friedman, Thomas. *The World Is Flat: A Brief History of the Twenty-first Century.* New York: Farrar, Straus, and Giroux, 2005.

Greenwald, Bruce, and Judd Kahn. "All Strategy Is Local." *Harvard Business Review*, 83, no. 9 (September 2005): 94–104.

Kaplan, Robert S., and David P. Norton. *Strategy Maps*. Boston: Harvard Business School Publishing, 2003.

Kathuria, R., M. P. Joshi, and S. Dellande. "International Growth Strategies of Service and Manufacturing Firms." *International Journal of Operations and Production Management* 28, no. 10 (2008): 968.

Porter, Michael, and Nicolaj Siggelkow. "Contextuality within Activity Systems and Sustainability of Competitive Advantage." *Academy of Management Perspectives* 22, no. 2 (May 2008): 34–36.

Rudberg, Martin, and B. M. West. "Global Operations Strategy." *Omega* 36, no. 1 (February 2008): 91.

Skinner, Wickham. "Manufacturing Strategy: The Story of Its Evolution." *Journal of Operations Management* 25, no. 2 (March 2007): 328–334.

Slack, Nigel, and Mike Lewis. *Operation Strategy*, 2nd ed. Upper Saddle River, NJ: Prentice Hall, 2008.

Wolf, Martin. *Why Globalization Works.* London: Yale University Press, 2004.

Zakaria, Fareed. *The Post American World.* New York: W.W. Norton, 2008.

Chapter 2 ***Rapid* Review**

Main Heading | **Review Material** | myomlab

A GLOBAL VIEW OF OPERATIONS (pp. 30–33)

Domestic business operations decide to change to some form of international operations for six main reasons:

1. Reduce costs (labor, taxes, tariffs, etc.)
2. Improve supply chain
3. Provide better goods and services
4. Understand markets
5. Learn to improve operations
6. Attract and retain global talent

- **Maquiladoras**—Mexican factories located along the U.S.–Mexico border that receive preferential tariff treatment.
- **World Trade Organization (WTO)**—An international organization that promotes world trade by lowering barriers to the free flow of goods across borders.
- **NAFTA**—A free trade agreement between Canada, Mexico, and the United States.
- **European Union (EU)**—A European trade group that has 27 member states.

Other trade agreements include APEC (the Pacific Rim countries), SEATO (Australia, New Zealand, Japan, Hong Kong, South Korea, New Guinea, and Chile), MERCOSUR (Argentina, Brazil, Paraguay, and Uruguay), and CAFTA (Central America, the Dominican Republic, and the United States).

The World Trade Organization helps to make uniform the protection of both governments and industries from foreign firms that engage in unethical conduct.

DEVELOPING MISSIONS AND STRATEGIES (pp. 34–35)

An effective operations management effort must have a *mission* so it knows where it is going and a *strategy* so it knows how to get there.

- **Mission**—The purpose or rationale for an organization's existence.
- **Strategy**—How an organization expects to achieve its missions and goals.

The three strategic approaches to competitive advantage are:

1. Differentiation
2. Cost leadership
3. Response

VIDEO 2.1
Operations Strategy at Regal Marine

ACHIEVING COMPETITIVE ADVANTAGE THROUGH OPERATIONS (pp. 35–38)

- **Competitive advantage**—The creation of a unique advantage over competitors.
- **Differentiation**—Distinguishing the offerings of an organization in a way that the customer perceives as adding value.
- **Experience differentiation**—Engaging the customer with a product through imaginative use of the five senses, so the customer "experiences" the product.
- **Low-cost leadership**—Achieving maximum value, as perceived by the customer.
- **Response**—A set of values related to rapid, flexible, and reliable performance.

Differentiation can be attained, for example, through innovative design, by providing a broad product line, by offering excellent after-sale service, or through adding a sensory experience to the product or service offering.

Cost leadership can be attained, for example, via low overhead, effective capacity use, or efficient inventory management.

Response can be attained, for example, by offering a flexible product line, reliable scheduling, or speedy delivery.

VIDEO 2.2
Hard Rock's Global Strategy

TEN STRATEGIC OM DECISIONS (pp. 39–40)

- **Operations decisions**—The strategic decisions of OM are goods and service design, quality, process and capacity design, location selection, layout design, human resources and job design, supply-chain management, inventory, scheduling, and maintenance.

ISSUES IN OPERATIONS STRATEGY (pp. 40–43)

- **Resources view**—A view in which managers evaluate the resources at their disposal and manage or alter them to achieve competitive advantage.
- **Value-chain analysis**—A way to identify the elements in the product/service chain that uniquely add value.
- **Five-forces analysis**—A way to analyze the five forces in the competitive environment.

The potential competing forces in Porter's five-forces model are (1) immediate rivals, (2) potential entrants, (3) customers, (4) suppliers, and (5) substitute products.

Different issues are emphasized during different stages of the product life cycle:

- **Introduction**—Company strategy: Best period to increase market share, R&D engineering is critical. OM strategy: Product design and development critical, frequent product and process design changes, short production runs, high production costs, limited models, attention to quality.
- **Growth**—Company strategy: Practical to change price or quality image, strengthen niche. OM strategy: Forecasting critical, product and process reliability, competi-

Main Heading	Review Material	myomlab
	tive product improvements and options, increase capacity, shift toward product focus, enhance distribution. • **Maturity**—Company strategy: Poor time to change image or price or quality, competitive costs become critical, defend market position. OM strategy: Standardization, less rapid product changes (more minor changes), optimum capacity, increasing stability of process, long production runs, product improvement and cost cutting. • **Decline**—Company strategy: Cost control critical. OM strategy: Little product differentiation, cost minimization, overcapacity in the industry, prune line to eliminate items not returning good margin, reduce capacity.	
STRATEGY DEVELOPMENT AND IMPLEMENTATION (pp. 43–45)	■ **SWOT analysis**—A method of determining internal strengths and weaknesses and external opportunities and threats. The strategy development process first involves performing environmental analysis, followed by determining the corporate mission, and finally forming a strategy. ■ **Key success factors (KSFs)**—Activities or factors that are key to achieving competitive advantage. ■ **Core competencies**—A set of skills, talents, and activities that a firm does particularly well. A core competence may be a subset of, or a combination of, KSFs. ■ **Activity map**—A graphical link of competitive advantage, KSFs, and supporting activities. An operations manager's job is to implement an OM strategy, provide competitive advantage, and increase productivity.	Virtual Office Hours for Solved Problem: 2.1
GLOBAL OPERATIONS STRATEGY OPTIONS (pp. 46–48)	■ **International business**—A firm that engages in cross-border transactions. ■ **Multinational corporation (MNC)**—A firm that has extensive involvement in international business, owning or controlling facilities in more than one country. ■ **International strategy**—A strategy in which global markets are penetrated using exports and licenses. ■ **Multidomestic strategy**—A strategy in which operating decisions are decentralized to each country to enhance local responsiveness. ■ **Global strategy**—A strategy in which operating decisions are centralized and headquarters coordinates the standardization and learning between facilities. ■ **Transnational strategy**—A strategy that combines the benefits of global-scale efficiencies with the benefits of local responsiveness. These firms transgress national boundaries. The four operations strategies for approaching global opportunities can be classified according to local responsiveness and cost reduction: 1. **International**—Little local responsiveness and little cost advantage 2. **Multidomestic**—Significant local responsiveness but little cost advantage 3. **Global**—Little local responsiveness but significant cost advantage 4. **Transnational**—Significant local responsiveness and significant cost advantage	

Self Test

■ **Before taking the self-test,** refer to the learning objectives listed at the beginning of the chapter and the key terms listed at the end of the chapter.

LO1. A mission statement is beneficial to an organization because it:
- **a)** is a statement of the organization's purpose.
- **b)** provides a basis for the organization's culture.
- **c)** identifies important constituencies.
- **d)** details specific income goals.
- **e)** ensures profitability.

LO2. The three strategic approaches to competitive advantage are _______, _______, and _______.

LO3. The 10 decisions of OM:
- **a)** are functional areas of the firm.
- **b)** apply to both service and manufacturing organizations.
- **c)** are the goals that are to be achieved.
- **d)** form an action plan to achieve a mission.
- **e)** are key success factors.

LO4. The relatively few activities that make a difference between a firm having and not having a competitive advantage are known as:
- **a)** activity maps.
- **b)** SWOT.
- **c)** key success factors.
- **d)** global profile.
- **e)** response strategy.

LO5. A company that is organized across international boundaries, with decentralized authority and substantial autonomy at each business via subsidiaries, franchises, or joint ventures has:
- **a)** a global strategy.
- **b)** a transnational strategy.
- **c)** an international strategy.
- **d)** a multidomestic strategy.
- **e)** a regional strategy.

Answers: LO1. a; LO2. differentiation, cost leadership, response; LO3. b; LO4. c; LO5. c.

3 Project Management

Chapter Outline

PROJECT MANAGEMENT PROVIDES A COMPETITIVE ADVANTAGE FOR BECHTEL

Now in its 112th year, the San Francisco–based Bechtel Group **(www.bechtel.com)** is the world's premier manager of massive construction and engineering projects. Known for billion-dollar projects, Bechtel is famous for its construction feats on the Hoover Dam, the Boston Central Artery/Tunnel project, and rebuilding of Kuwait's oil and gas infrastructure after the invasion by Iraq in 1990.

Conditions weren't what Bechtel expected when it won a series of billion-dollar contracts from the U.S. government to help reconstruct Iraq in 2003–2006.

Workers wrestle with a 1,500-ton boring machine, measuring 25 feet in diameter, that was used to dig the Eurotunnel between England and France in the early 1990s. With overruns that boosted the cost of the project to $13 billion, a Bechtel Group VP was brought in to head operations.

A massive dredge hired by Bechtel removes silt from Iraq's port at Umm Qasr. This paved the way for large-scale deliveries of U.S. food and the return of commercial shipping.

Saddam Hussein's defeat by Allied forces hadn't caused much war damage. Instead, what Bechtel found was a country that had been crumbling for years. None of the sewage plants in Baghdad worked. Power flicked on and off. Towns and cities in the anti-Hussein south had been left to decay as punishment. And to complicate matters even more, scavengers were stealing everything from museum artifacts to electric power lines. Bechtel's job was to oversee electric power, sewage, transportation, and airport repairs.

Bechtel's crews travelled under armed escort and slept in trailers surrounded by razor wire. But the company's efforts have paid off. Iraq's main seaport, Umm Qasr, was reopened when Bechtel dredged the water and repaired the grain elevators. Electrical generation was back to prewar levels in 10 months. Bechtel refurbished more than 1,200 schools.

With a global procurement program, Bechtel easily tapped the company's network of suppliers and buyers

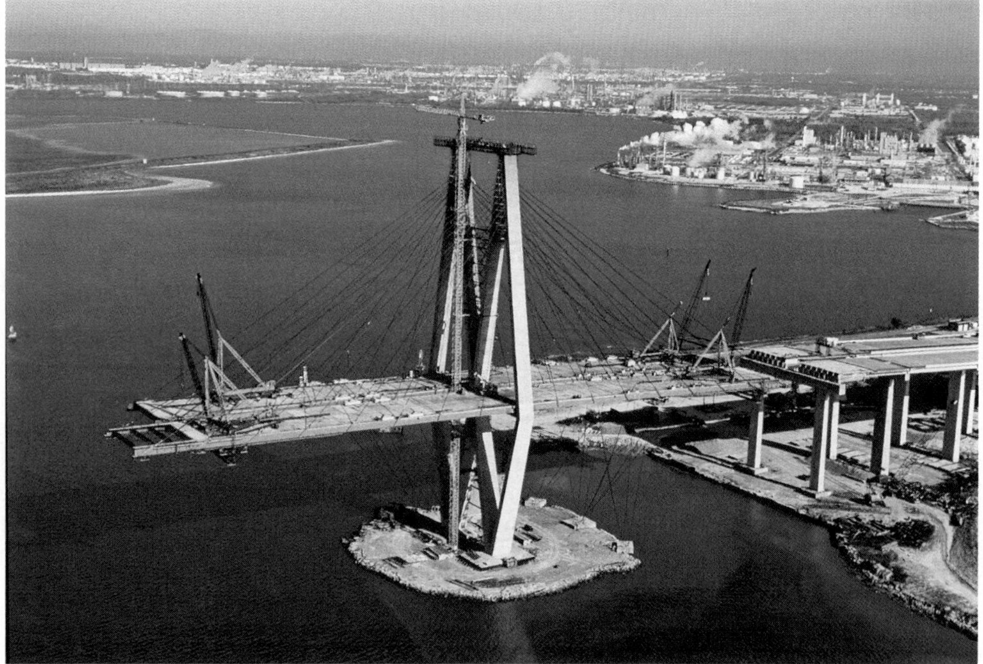

Managing massive construction projects such as this is the strength of Bechtel. With large penalties for late completion and incentives for early completion, a good project manager is worth his or her weight in gold.

worldwide to help rebuild Iraq's infrastructure. Other interesting recent Bechtel projects include:

- Building 26 massive distribution centers, in just 2 years, for the Internet company Webvan Group ($1 billion).
- Constructing 30 high-security data centers worldwide for Equinix, Inc. ($1.2 billion).
- Building and running a rail line between London and the Channel Tunnel ($4.6 billion).
- Developing an oil pipeline from the Caspian Sea region to Russia ($850 million).
- Expanding the Dubai Airport in the United Arab Emirates ($600 million) and the Miami International Airport ($2 billion).
- Building liquefied natural gas plants in Trinidad, West Indies ($1 billion).

Reconstructed terminal at Baghdad International Airport

- Building a new subway for Athens, Greece ($2.6 billion).
- Constructing a natural gas pipeline in Thailand ($700 million).
- Building 30 plants for iMotors.com, a company that sells refurbished autos online ($300 million).
- Building a highway to link the north and south of Croatia ($303 million).

When companies or countries seek out firms to manage massive projects, they go to Bechtel, which, again and again, through outstanding project management, has demonstrated its competitive advantage.

Bechtel was the construction contractor for the Hoover Dam. This dam, on the Colorado River, is the highest in the Western Hemisphere.

Chapter 3 **Learning Objectives**

AUTHOR COMMENT
Wherever your career takes you, one of the most useful tools you can have, as a manager, is the ability to manage a project.

THE IMPORTANCE OF PROJECT MANAGEMENT

When Bechtel, the subject of the opening Global Company Profile, entered Iraq after the 2003 war, it quickly had to mobilize an international force of manual workers, construction professionals, cooks, medical personnel, and security forces. Its project management team had to access millions of tons of supplies to rebuild ports, roads, schools, and electrical systems. Similarly, when Hard Rock Cafe sponsors Rockfest, hosting 100,000 plus fans at its annual concert, the project manager begins planning some 9 months earlier. Using the software package Microsoft Project, described in this chapter, each of the hundreds of details can be monitored and controlled. When a band can't reach the Rockfest site by bus because of massive traffic jams, Hard Rock's project manager is ready with a helicopter backup.

VIDEO 3.1
Project Management at Hard Rock's Rockfest

Bechtel and Hard Rock are just two examples of firms that face modern phenomena: growing project complexity and collapsing product/service life cycles. This change stems from awareness of the strategic value of time-based competition and a quality mandate for continuous improvement. Each new product/service introduction is a unique event—a project. In addition, projects are a common part of our everyday life. We may be planning a wedding or a surprise birthday party, remodeling a house, or preparing a semester-long class project.

Scheduling projects is a difficult challenge for operations managers. The stakes in project management are high. Cost overruns and unnecessary delays occur due to poor scheduling and poor controls.

Projects that take months or years to complete are usually developed outside the normal production system. Project organizations within the firm may be set up to handle such jobs and are often disbanded when the project is complete. On other occasions, managers find projects just a part of their job. The management of projects involves three phases (see Figure 3.1):

1. *Planning:* This phase includes goal setting, defining the project, and team organization.
2. *Scheduling:* This phase relates people, money, and supplies to specific activities and relates activities to each other.
3. *Controlling:* Here the firm monitors resources, costs, quality, and budgets. It also revises or changes plans and shifts resources to meet time and cost demands.

We begin this chapter with a brief overview of these functions. Three popular techniques to allow managers to plan, schedule, and control—Gantt charts, PERT, and CPM—are also described.

PROJECT PLANNING

Projects can be defined as a series of related tasks directed toward a major output. In some firms a **project organization** is developed to make sure existing programs continue to run smoothly on a day-to-day basis while new projects are successfully completed.

Project organization
An organization formed to ensure that programs (projects) receive the proper management and attention.

For companies with multiple large projects, such as a construction firm, a project organization is an effective way of assigning the people and physical resources needed. It is a temporary organization structure designed to achieve results by using specialists from throughout the firm. NASA and many other organizations use the project approach. You may recall Project Gemini and Project Apollo. These terms were used to describe teams that NASA organized to reach space exploration objectives.

The project organization works best when:

1. Work can be defined with a specific goal and deadline.
2. The job is unique or somewhat unfamiliar to the existing organization.
3. The work contains complex interrelated tasks requiring specialized skills.
4. The project is temporary but critical to the organization.
5. The project cuts across organizational lines.

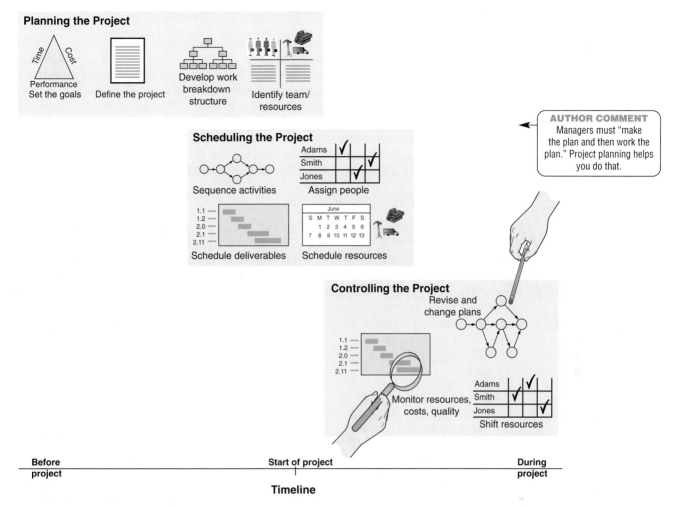

Planning the Project
Time Cost Performance
Set the goals
Define the project
Develop work breakdown structure
Identify team/ resources

Scheduling the Project
Sequence activities
Adams Smith Jones
Assign people
Schedule deliverables
Schedule resources

Controlling the Project
Revise and change plans
Monitor resources, costs, quality
Adams Smith Jones
Shift resources

Before project — Start of project — During project
Timeline

▲ **FIGURE 3.1** **Project Planning, Scheduling, and Controlling**

AUTHOR COMMENT
Managers must "make the plan and then work the plan." Project planning helps you do that.

The Project Manager

An example of a project organization is shown in Figure 3.2. Project team members are temporarily assigned to a project and report to the project manager. The manager heading the project coordinates activities with other departments and reports directly to top management. Project managers receive high visibility in a firm and are responsible for making sure that (1) all necessary activities are finished in proper sequence and on time; (2) the project comes in within budget; (3) the project meets its quality goals; and (4) the people assigned to the project receive the motivation, direction,

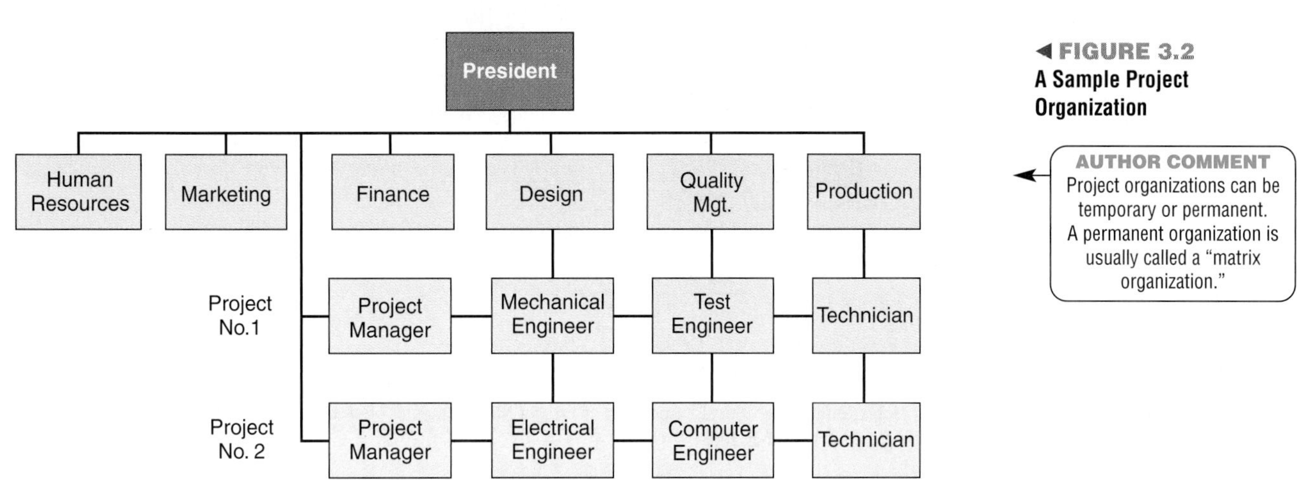

◀ **FIGURE 3.2** **A Sample Project Organization**

AUTHOR COMMENT
Project organizations can be temporary or permanent. A permanent organization is usually called a "matrix organization."

and information needed to do their jobs. This means that project managers should be good coaches and communicators, and be able to organize activities from a variety of disciplines.

Ethical Issues Faced in Project Management Project managers not only have high visibility but they also face ethical decisions on a daily basis. How they act establishes the code of conduct for the project. Project managers often deal with (1) offers of gifts from contractors, (2) pressure to alter status reports to mask the reality of delays, (3) false reports for charges of time and expenses, and (4) pressures to compromise quality to meet bonus or penalty schedules.

Using the Project Management Institute's **(www.pmi.org)** ethical codes is one means of trying to establish standards. Research has shown that without good leadership and a strong organizational culture, most people follow their own set of ethical standards and values.[1]

Work Breakdown Structure

The project management team begins its task well in advance of project execution so that a plan can be developed. One of its first steps is to carefully establish the project's objectives, then break the project down into manageable parts. This **work breakdown structure (WBS)** defines the project by dividing it into its major subcomponents (or tasks), which are then subdivided into more detailed components, and finally into a set of activities and their related costs. The division of the project into smaller and smaller tasks can be difficult, but is critical to managing the project and to scheduling success. Gross requirements for people, supplies, and equipment are also estimated in this planning phase.

Work breakdown structure (WBS)
A hierarchical description of a project into more and more detailed components.

The work breakdown structure typically decreases in size from top to bottom and is indented like this:

Level
1 Project
2 Major tasks in the project
3 Subtasks in major tasks
4 Activities (or "work packages") to be completed

This hierarchical framework can be illustrated with the development of Microsoft's operating system Windows 7. As we see in Figure 3.3, the project, creating a new operating system, is labeled 1.0. The first step is to identify the major tasks in the project (level 2). Three examples would be software design (1.1), project management (1.2), and system testing (1.3). Two major subtasks for 1.1 are development of graphical user interfaces (GUIs) (1.1.1) and creating compatibility with previous versions of Windows (1.1.2). The major subtasks for 1.1.2 are level-4 activities,

▶ **FIGURE 3.3**
Work Breakdown Structure

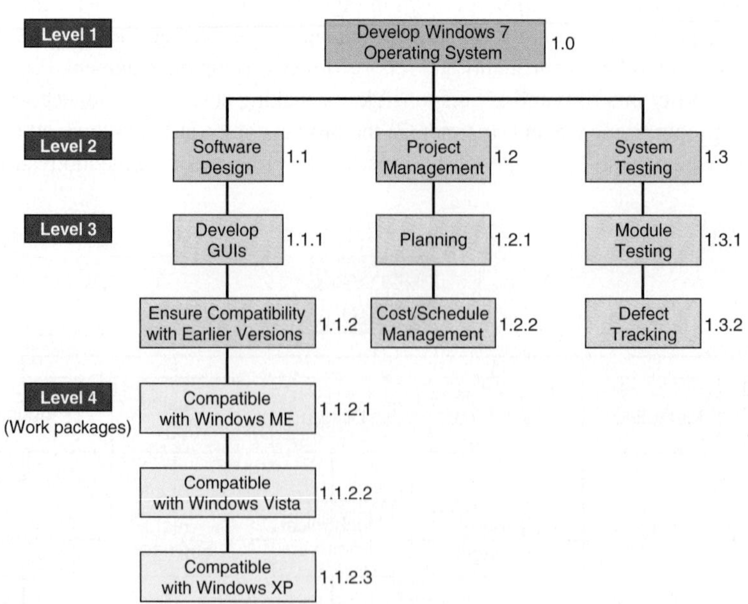

[1]See Hilder Helgadottir, "The Ethical Dimension of Project Management," *International Journal of Project Management* 26, no. 7 (October 2008): 743.

such as creating a team to handle compatibility with Windows ME (1.1.2.1), creating a team for Windows Vista (1.1.2.2), and creating a team for Windows XP (1.1.2.3). There are usually many level-4 activities.

PROJECT SCHEDULING

> **AUTHOR COMMENT** Gantt charts are simple and visual, making them widely used.

Project scheduling involves sequencing and allotting time to all project activities. At this stage, managers decide how long each activity will take and compute how many people and materials will be needed at each stage of production. Managers also chart separate schedules for personnel needs by type of skill (management, engineering, or pouring concrete, for example). Charts also can be developed for scheduling materials.

One popular project scheduling approach is the Gantt chart. **Gantt charts** are low-cost means of helping managers make sure that (1) activities are planned, (2) order of performance is documented, (3) activity time estimates are recorded, and (4) overall project time is developed. As Figure 3.4 shows, Gantt charts are easy to understand. Horizontal bars are drawn for each project activity along a time line. This illustration of a routine servicing of a Delta jetliner during a 40-minute layover shows that Gantt charts also can be used for scheduling repetitive operations. In this case, the chart helps point out potential delays. The *OM in Action* box on Delta provides additional insights. (A second illustration of a Gantt chart is also provided in Chapter 15, Figure 15.4.)

Gantt charts
Planning charts used to schedule resources and allocate time.

On simple projects, scheduling charts such as these permit managers to observe the progress of each activity and to spot and tackle problem areas. Gantt charts, though, do not adequately illustrate the interrelationships between the activities and the resources.

LO1: Use a Gantt chart for scheduling

PERT and CPM, the two widely used network techniques that we shall discuss shortly, *do* have the ability to consider precedence relationships and interdependency of activities. On complex projects, the scheduling of which is almost always computerized, PERT and CPM thus have an edge over the simpler Gantt charts. Even on huge projects, though, Gantt charts can be used as summaries of project status and may complement the other network approaches.

To summarize, whatever the approach taken by a project manager, project scheduling serves several purposes:

1. It shows the relationship of each activity to others and to the whole project.
2. It identifies the precedence relationships among activities.
3. It encourages the setting of realistic time and cost estimates for each activity.
4. It helps make better use of people, money, and material resources by identifying critical bottlenecks in the project.

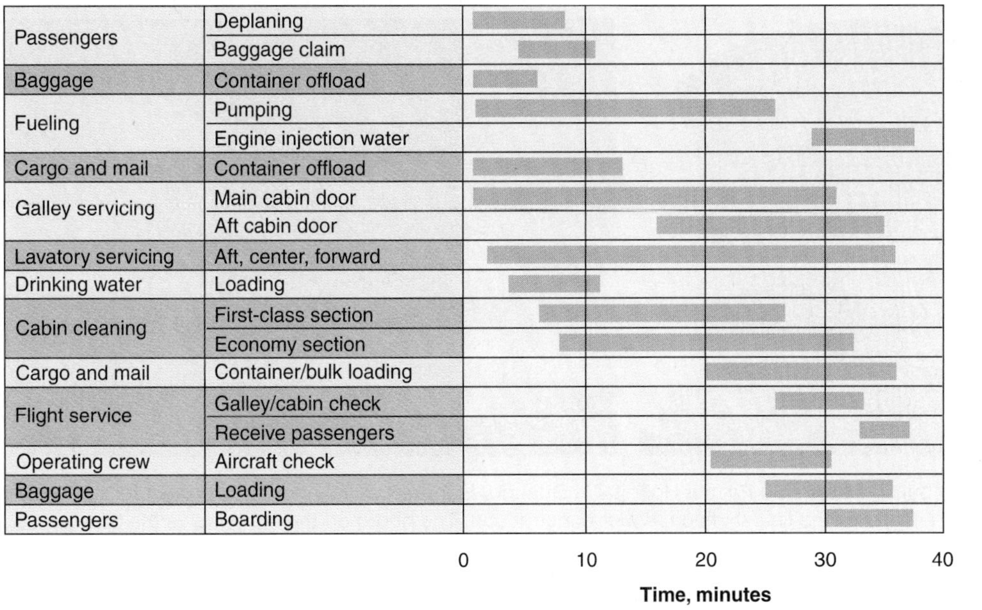

Passengers	Deplaning
	Baggage claim
Baggage	Container offload
Fueling	Pumping
	Engine injection water
Cargo and mail	Container offload
Galley servicing	Main cabin door
	Aft cabin door
Lavatory servicing	Aft, center, forward
Drinking water	Loading
Cabin cleaning	First-class section
	Economy section
Cargo and mail	Container/bulk loading
Flight service	Galley/cabin check
	Receive passengers
Operating crew	Aircraft check
Baggage	Loading
Passengers	Boarding

0 10 20 30 40
Time, minutes

◄ **FIGURE 3.4**
Gantt Chart of Service Activities for a Delta Jet during a 40-Minute Layover
Delta hopes to save $50 million a year with this turnaround time, which is a reduction from its traditional 60-minute routine.

OM in Action ▶ Delta's Ground Crew Orchestrates a Smooth Takeoff

Flight 574's engines screech its arrival as the jet lumbers down Richmond's taxiway with 140 passengers arriving from Atlanta. In 40 minutes, the plane is to be airborne again.

However, before this jet can depart, there is business to attend to: passengers, luggage, and cargo to unload and load; thousands of gallons of jet fuel and countless drinks to restock; cabin and restrooms to clean; toilet holding tanks to drain; and engines, wings, and landing gear to inspect.

The 10-person ground crew knows that a miscue anywhere—a broken cargo loader, lost baggage, misdirected passengers—can mean a late departure and trigger a chain reaction of headaches from Richmond to Atlanta to every destination of a connecting flight.

Carla Sutera, the operations manager for Delta's Richmond International Airport, views the turnaround operation like a pit boss awaiting a race car. Trained crews are in place for Flight 574 with baggage carts and tractors, hydraulic cargo loaders, a truck to load food and drinks, another to lift the cleanup crew, another to put fuel on, and a fourth to take water off. The "pit crew" usually performs so smoothly that most passengers never suspect the proportions of the effort. Gantt charts, such as the one in Figure 3.4, aid Delta and other airlines with the staffing and scheduling that are needed for this task.

Sources: Knight Ridder Tribune Business News (July 16, 2005): 1 and (November 21, 2002): 1.

AUTHOR COMMENT
Software has revolutionized project control.

PROJECT CONTROLLING

The control of projects, like the control of any management system, involves close monitoring of resources, costs, quality, and budgets. Control also means using a feedback loop to revise the project plan and having the ability to shift resources to where they are needed most. Computerized PERT/CPM reports and charts are widely available today on personal computers. Some of the more popular of these programs are Primavera (by Primavera Systems, Inc.), MacProject (by Apple Computer Corp.), Pertmaster (by Westminster Software, Inc.), VisiSchedule (by Paladin Software Corp.), Time Line (by Symantec Corp.), and Microsoft Project (by Microsoft Corp.), which we illustrate in this chapter.

VIDEO 3.2
Project Management at Arnold Palmer Hospital

These programs produce a broad variety of reports, including (1) detailed cost breakdowns for each task, (2) total program labor curves, (3) cost distribution tables, (4) functional cost and hour summaries, (5) raw material and expenditure forecasts, (6) variance reports, (7) time analysis reports, and (8) work status reports.

Construction of the new 11-story building at Arnold Palmer Hospital in Orlando, Florida, was an enormous project for the hospital administration. The photo on the left shows the first six floors under construction. The photo on the right shows the building as completed two years later. Prior to beginning actual construction, regulatory and funding issues added, as they do with most projects; substantial time to the overall project. Cities have zoning and parking issues; the EPA has drainage and waste issues; and regulatory authorities have their own requirements; as do issuers of bonds. The $100 million, 4-year project at Arnold Palmer Hospital is discussed in the Video Case Study at the end of this chapter.

PROJECT MANAGEMENT TECHNIQUES: PERT AND CPM

AUTHOR COMMENT
To use project management software, you first need to understand the next two sections in this chapter.

Program evaluation and review technique (PERT) and the **critical path method (CPM)** were both developed in the 1950s to help managers schedule, monitor, and control large and complex projects. CPM arrived first, in 1957, as a tool developed by J. E. Kelly of Remington Rand and M. R. Walker of duPont to assist in the building and maintenance of chemical plants at duPont. Independently, PERT was developed in 1958 by Booz, Allen, and Hamilton for the U.S. Navy.

Program evaluation and review technique (PERT)
A project management technique that employs three time estimates for each activity.

Critical path method (CPM)
A project management technique that uses only one time factor per activity.

Critical path
The computed *longest* time path(s) through a network.

The Framework of PERT and CPM

PERT and CPM both follow six basic steps:

1. Define the project and prepare the work breakdown structure.
2. Develop the relationships among the activities. Decide which activities must precede and which must follow others.
3. Draw the network connecting all the activities.
4. Assign time and/or cost estimates to each activity.
5. Compute the *longest* time path through the network. This is called the **critical path**.
6. Use the network to help plan, schedule, monitor, and control the project.

Step 5, finding the critical path, is a major part of controlling a project. The activities on the critical path represent tasks that will delay the entire project if they are not completed on time. Managers can gain the flexibility needed to complete critical tasks by identifying noncritical activities and replanning, rescheduling, and reallocating labor and financial resources.

Although PERT and CPM differ to some extent in terminology and in the construction of the network, their objectives are the same. Furthermore, the analysis used in both techniques is very similar. The major difference is that PERT employs three time estimates for each activity. These time estimates are used to compute expected values and standard deviations for the activity. CPM makes the assumption that activity times are known with certainty and hence requires only one time factor for each activity.

For purposes of illustration, the rest of this section concentrates on a discussion of PERT. Most of the comments and procedures described, however, apply just as well to CPM.

PERT and CPM are important because they can help answer questions such as the following about projects with thousands of activities:

1. When will the entire project be completed?
2. What are the critical activities or tasks in the project—that is, which activities will delay the entire project if they are late?
3. Which are the noncritical activities—the ones that can run late without delaying the whole project's completion?
4. What is the probability that the project will be completed by a specific date?
5. At any particular date, is the project on schedule, behind schedule, or ahead of schedule?
6. On any given date, is the money spent equal to, less than, or greater than the budgeted amount?
7. Are there enough resources available to finish the project on time?
8. If the project is to be finished in a shorter amount of time, what is the best way to accomplish this goal at the least cost?

Network Diagrams and Approaches

The first step in a PERT or CPM network is to divide the entire project into significant activities in accordance with the work breakdown structure. There are two approaches for drawing a project network: **activity on node (AON)** and **activity on arrow (AOA)**. Under the AON convention, *nodes* designate activities. Under AOA, *arrows* represent activities. Activities consume time and resources. The basic difference between AON and AOA is that the nodes in an AON diagram represent activities. In an AOA network, the nodes represent the starting and finishing times of an activity and are also called *events*. So nodes in AOA consume neither time nor resources.

Activity-on-node (AON)
A network diagram in which nodes designate activities.

Activity-on-arrow (AOA)
A network diagram in which arrows designate activities.

Figure 3.5 illustrates both conventions for a small portion of the airline turnaround Gantt chart (in Figure 3.4). The examples provide some background for understanding six common activity

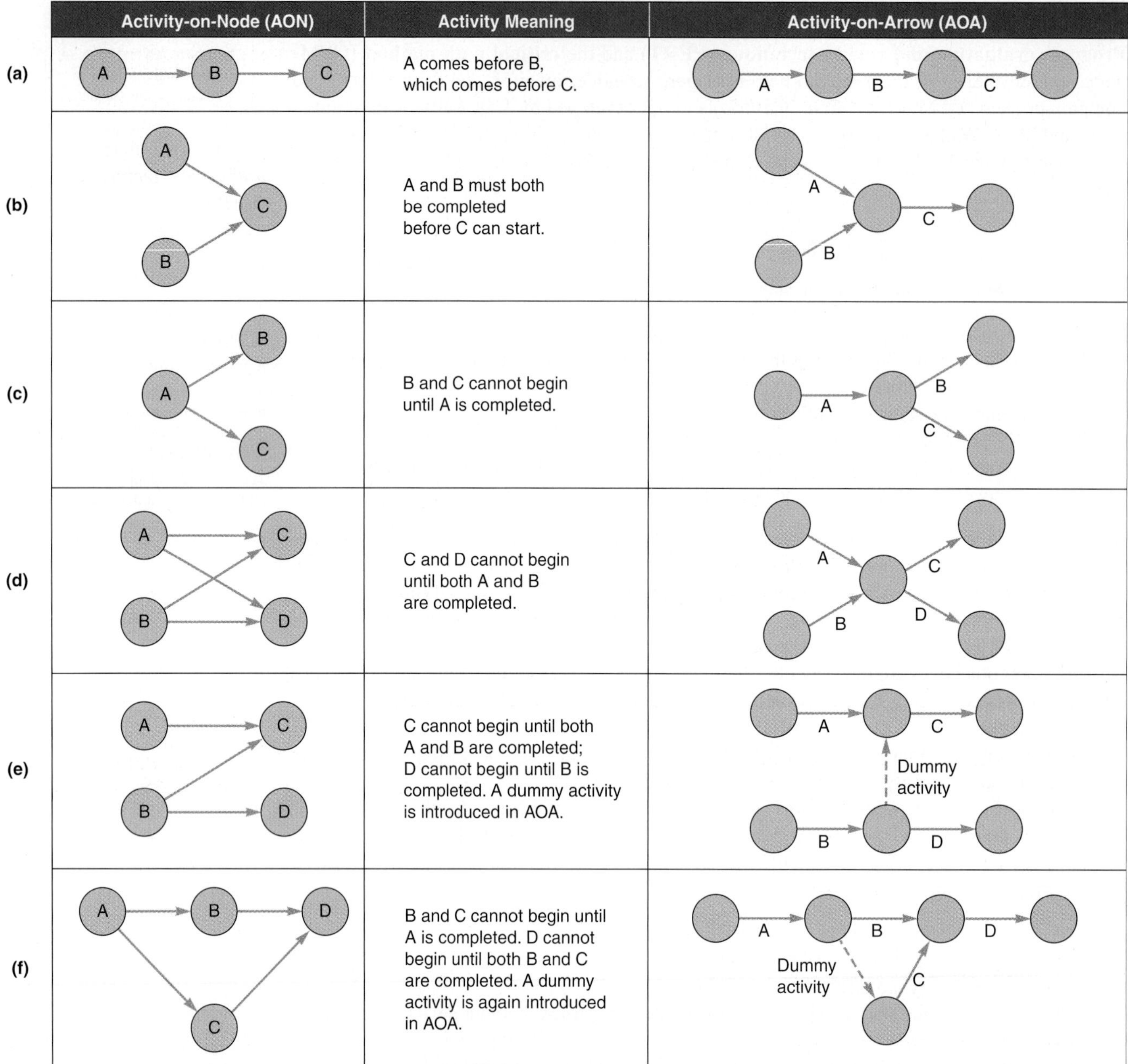

Activity-on-Node (AON)
Activity Meaning
Activity-on-Arrow (AOA)
(a)
A
B
C
A comes before B, which comes before C.
(b)
A and B must both be completed before C can start.
(c)
B and C cannot begin until A is completed.
(d)
D
C and D cannot begin until both A and B are completed.
(e)
C cannot begin until both A and B are completed; D cannot begin until B is completed. A dummy activity is introduced in AOA.
Dummy activity
(f)
B and C cannot begin until A is completed. D cannot begin until both B and C are completed. A dummy activity is again introduced in AOA.
Dummy activity

▲ **FIGURE 3.5 A Comparison of AON and AOA Network Conventions**

relationships in networks. In Figure 3.5(a), activity A must be finished before activity B is started, and B must, in turn, be completed before C begins. Activity A might represent "deplaning passengers," while B is "cabin cleaning," and C is "boarding new passengers."

Dummy activity
An activity having no time that is inserted into a network to maintain the logic of the network.

Figures 3.5(e) and 3.5(f) illustrate that the AOA approach sometimes needs the addition of a **dummy activity** to clarify relationships. A dummy activity consumes no time or resources, but is required when a network has two activities with identical starting and ending events, or when two or more follow some, but not all, "preceding" activities. The use of dummy activities is also important when computer software is employed to determine project completion time. A dummy activity has a completion time of zero and is shown graphically with a dashed line.

Although both AON and AOA are popular in practice, many of the project management software packages, including Microsoft Project, use AON networks. For this reason, although we illustrate both types of networks in the next examples, we focus on AON networks in subsequent discussions in this chapter.

Activity-on-Node Example

◄ EXAMPLE 1

Activity-on-node for EPA problem at Milwaukee Paper

Milwaukee Paper Manufacturing, Inc., located near downtown Milwaukee, has long been delaying the expense of installing air pollution control equipment in its facility. The Environmental Protection Agency (EPA) has recently given the manufacturer 16 weeks to install a complex air filter system. Milwaukee Paper has been warned that it may be forced to close the facility unless the device is installed in the allotted time. Joni Steinberg, the plant manager, wants to make sure that installation of the filtering system progresses smoothly and on time.

Given the following information, develop a table showing activity precedence relationships.

APPROACH ▶ Milwaukee Paper has identified the eight activities that need to be performed in order for the project to be completed. When the project begins, two activities can be simultaneously started: building the internal components for the device (activity A) and the modifications necessary for the floor and roof (activity B). The construction of the collection stack (activity C) can begin when the internal components are completed. Pouring the concrete floor and installation of the frame (activity D) can be started as soon as the internal components are completed and the roof and floor have been modified.

After the collection stack has been constructed, two activities can begin: building the high-temperature burner (activity E) and installing the pollution control system (activity F). The air pollution device can be installed (activity G) after the concrete floor has been poured, the frame has been installed, and the high-temperature burner has been built. Finally, after the control system and pollution device have been installed, the system can be inspected and tested (activity H).

LO2: Draw AOA and AON networks

SOLUTION ▶ Activities and precedence relationships may seem rather confusing when they are presented in this descriptive form. It is therefore convenient to list all the activity information in a table, as shown in Table 3.1. We see in the table that activity A is listed as an *immediate predecessor* of activity C. Likewise, both activities D and E must be performed prior to starting activity G.

◄ TABLE 3.1 Milwaukee Paper Manufacturing's Activities and Predecessors

Activity	Description	Immediate Predecessors
A	Build internal components	—
B	Modify roof and floor	—
C	Construct collection stack	A
D	Pour concrete and install frame	A, B
E	Build high-temperature burner	C
F	Install pollution control system	C
G	Install air pollution device	D, E
H	Inspect and test	F, G

INSIGHT ▶ To complete a network, all predecessors must be clearly defined.

LEARNING EXERCISE ▶ What is the impact on the sequence of activities if EPA approval is required after *Inspect and Test?* [Answer: The immediate predecessor for the new activity would be H, *Inspect and Test*, with *EPA approval* as the last activity.]

Note that in Example 1, it is enough to list just the *immediate predecessors* for each activity. For instance, in Table 3.1, since activity A precedes activity C, and activity C precedes activity E, the fact that activity A precedes activity E is *implicit*. This relationship need not be explicitly shown in the activity precedence relationships.

When there are many activities in a project with fairly complicated precedence relationships, it is difficult for an individual to comprehend the complexity of the project from just the tabular information. In such cases, a visual representation of the project, using a *project network*, is convenient and useful. A project network is a diagram of all the activities and the precedence relationships that exist between these activities in a project. Example 2 illustrates how to construct a project network for Milwaukee Paper Manufacturing.

OM in Action ▶ Prepping for the Miami Heat Game

Monday. It is time for John Nicely to make a grocery list. He's serving dinner on Saturday, so he'll need a few things . . . 150 pounds of steak and chicken, ingredients for 48 gallons of shrimp bisque, 400 sushi rolls, and 25 pounds of jambalaya. Plus a couple hundred pizzas and a couple thousand hot dogs—just enough to feed the Miami Heat basketball players and the 19,600 guests expected. You see, Nicely is the executive chef at American Airlines Arena in Miami, and on Saturday the Heat are hosting the L.A. Lakers.

How do you feed huge crowds good food in a short time? It takes good project management, combined with creativity and improvisation. With 250 facilities serving food and beverage, "The Arena," Nicely says, "is its own beast."

Tuesday. Shopping day.

Wednesday–Friday. The staff prepares whatever it can, chopping vegetables, marinating meats, mixing salad dressings—everything but cooking the food. Nicely also begins his shopping lists for next Monday's game against Toronto and for a Queen concert three days later.

Saturday. 3:55 P.M. Clutch time. Suddenly the kitchen is a joke-free zone. In five minutes, Nicely's first clients, 200 elite season ticket holders, expect their meals—from a unique menu created for each game.

5:00 P.M. As the Heat and Lakers start warming up, the chefs move their operation in a brisk procession of hot boxes and cold-food racks to the satellite kitchens.

6:00 P.M. Nicely and team face surprises at concession stands: a shortage of cashiers and a broken cash register.

Halftime. There is a run on roasted potatoes in the *Flagship* restaurant. But Nicely has thought ahead and anticipated. The backup potatoes arrive before customers even notice.

For John Nicely, successful project management means happy guests as the result of a thousand details that have been identified, planned, and executed. Just another night of delivering restaurant-quality meals and top-grade fast food to a sold-out stadium crowd in a span of a couple hours.

Sources: Fast Company (May, 2006): 52–57; and *Knight Ridder Tribune Business News* (March 9, 2006): 1.

EXAMPLE 2 ▶

AON graph for Milwaukee Paper

Draw the AON network for Milwaukee Paper, using the data in Example 1.

APPROACH ▶ In the AON approach, we denote each activity by a node. The lines, or arrows, represent the precedence relationships between the activities.

SOLUTION ▶ In this example, there are two activities (A and B) that do not have any predecessors. We draw separate nodes for each of these activities, as shown in Figure 3.6. Although not required, it is usually convenient to have a unique starting activity for a project. We have therefore included a *dummy activity* called *Start* in Figure 3.6. This dummy activity does not really exist and takes up zero time and resources. Activity *Start* is an immediate predecessor for both activities A and B, and serves as the unique starting activity for the entire project.

▶ **FIGURE 3.6**
Beginning AON Network for Milwaukee Paper

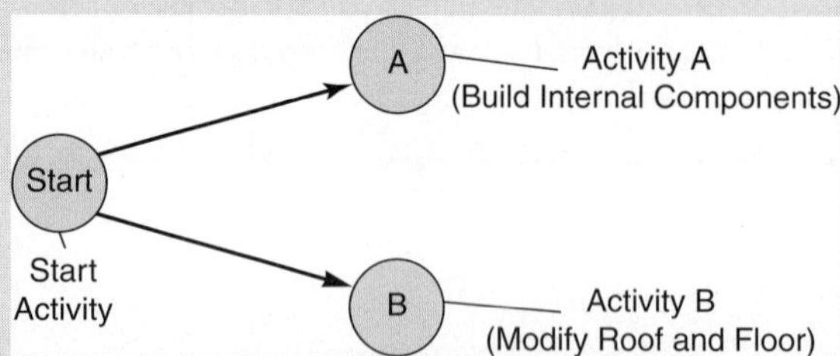

We now show the precedence relationships using lines with arrow symbols. For example, an arrow from activity Start to activity A indicates that Start is a predecessor for activity A. In a similar fashion, we draw an arrow from Start to B.

Next, we add a new node for activity C. Since activity A precedes activity C, we draw an arrow from node A to node C (see Figure 3.7). Likewise, we first draw a node to represent activity D. Then, since activities A and B both precede activity D, we draw arrows from A to D and from B to D (see Figure 3.7).

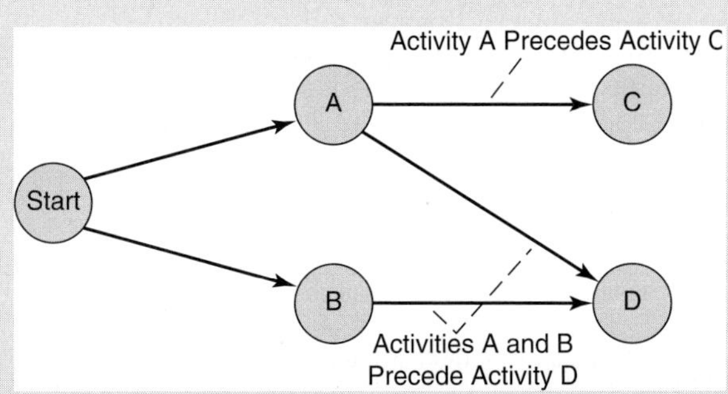

◀ **FIGURE 3.7**
Intermediate AON Network for Milwaukee Paper

We proceed in this fashion, adding a separate node for each activity and a separate line for each precedence relationship that exists. The complete AON project network for the Milwaukee Paper Manufacturing project is shown in Figure 3.8.

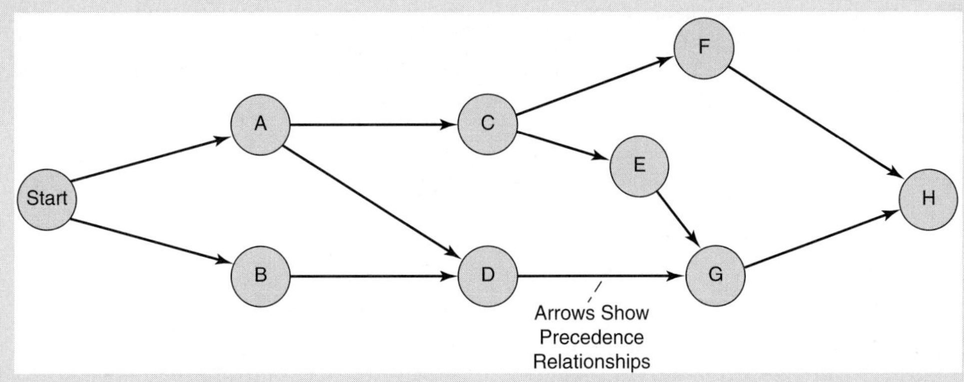

◀ **FIGURE 3.8**
Complete AON Network for Milwaukee Paper

INSIGHT ▶ Drawing a project network properly takes some time and experience. We would like the lines to be straight and arrows to move to the right when possible.

LEARNING EXERCISE ▶ If *EPA Approval* occurs after *Inspect and Test*, what is the impact on the graph? [Answer: A straight line is extended to the right beyond H to reflect the additional activity.]

RELATED PROBLEMS ▶ 3.3, 3.6, 3.7, 3.9a, 3.10, 3.12, 3.15a

When we first draw a project network, it is not unusual that we place our nodes (activities) in the network in such a fashion that the arrows (precedence relationships) are not straight lines. That is, the lines could be intersecting each other, and even facing in opposite directions. For example, if we had switched the location of the nodes for activities E and F in Figure 3.8, the lines from F to H and E to G would have intersected. Although such a project network is perfectly valid, it is good practice to have a well-drawn network. One rule that we especially recommend is to place the nodes in such a fashion that all arrows point in the same direction. To achieve this, we suggest that you first draw a rough draft of the network, making sure all the relationships are shown. Then you can redraw the network to make appropriate changes in the location of the nodes.

As with the unique starting node, it is convenient to have the project network finish with a unique ending node. In the Milwaukee Paper example, it turns out that a unique activity, H, is the last activity in the project. We therefore automatically have a unique ending node.

In situations in which a project has multiple ending activities, we include a "dummy" ending activity. This dummy activity has all the multiple ending activities in the project as immediate predecessors. We illustrate this type of situation in Solved Problem 3.2 at the end of this chapter.

Activity-on-Arrow Example

We saw earlier that in an AOA project network we can represent activities by arrows. A node represents an *event*, which marks the start or completion time of an activity. We usually identify an event (node) by a number.

EXAMPLE 3 ▶

Activity-on-arrow for Milwaukee Paper

Draw the complete AOA project network for Milwaukee Paper's problem.

APPROACH ▶ Using the data from Table 3.1 in Example 1, draw one activity at a time, starting with A.

SOLUTION ▶ We see that activity A starts at event 1 and ends at event 2. Likewise, activity B starts at event 1 and ends at event 3. Activity C, whose only immediate predecessor is activity A, starts at node 2 and ends at node 4. Activity D, however, has two predecessors (i.e., A and B). Hence, we need both activities A and B to end at event 3, so that activity D can start at that event. However, we cannot have multiple activities with common starting and ending nodes in an AOA network. To overcome this difficulty, in such cases, we may need to add a dummy line (activity) to enforce the precedence relationship. The dummy activity, shown in Figure 3.9 as a dashed line, is inserted between events 2 and 3 to make the diagram reflect the precedence between A and D. The remainder of the AOA project network for Milwaukee Paper's example is also shown.

▶ FIGURE 3.9
Complete AOA Network (with Dummy Activity) for Milwaukee Paper

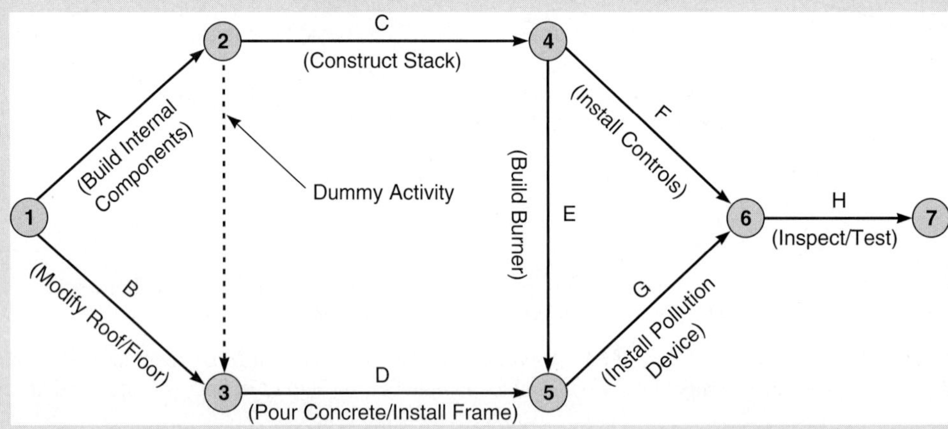

AUTHOR COMMENT The dummy activity consumes no time, but note how it changes precedence. Now activity D cannot begin until *both* B and the dummy are complete.

INSIGHT ▶ Dummy activities are common in AOA networks. They do not really exist in the project and take zero time.

LEARNING EXERCISE ▶ A new activity, *EPA Approval*, follows activity H. Add it to Figure 3.9. [Answer: Insert an arrowed line from node 7, which ends at a new node 8, and is labeled I (EPA Approval).]

RELATED PROBLEMS ▶ 3.4, 3.5, 3.9b

AUTHOR COMMENT We now add times to complete each activity. This lets us find the *critical path.*

DETERMINING THE PROJECT SCHEDULE

Look back at Figure 3.8 (in Example 2) for a moment to see Milwaukee Paper's completed AON project network. Once this project network has been drawn to show all the activities and their precedence relationships, the next step is to determine the project schedule. That is, we need to identify the planned starting and ending time for each activity.

Let us assume Milwaukee Paper estimates the time required for each activity, in weeks, as shown in Table 3.2. The table indicates that the total time for all eight of the company's activities is 25 weeks. However, since several activities can take place simultaneously, it is clear that the total project completion time may be less than 25 weeks. To find out just how long the project will take, we perform the **critical path analysis** for the network.

Critical path analysis
A process that helps determine a project schedule.

Activity	Description	Time (weeks)
A	Build internal components	2
B	Modify roof and floor	3
C	Construct collection stack	2
D	Pour concrete and install frame	4
E	Build high-temperature burner	4
F	Install pollution control system	3
G	Install air pollution device	5
H	Inspect and test	2
	Total time (weeks)	25

◀ **TABLE 3.2**
Time Estimates for Milwaukee Paper Manufacturing

AUTHOR COMMENT
Does this mean the project will take 25 weeks to complete? No. Don't forget that several of the activities are being performed at the same time. It would take 25 weeks if they were done sequentially.

As mentioned earlier, the critical path is the *longest* time path through the network. To find the critical path, we calculate two distinct starting and ending times for each activity. These are defined as follows:

Earliest start (ES) = earliest time at which an activity can start, assuming all predecessors have been completed
Earliest finish (EF) = earliest time at which an activity can be finished
Latest start (LS) = latest time at which an activity can start so as to not delay the completion time of the entire project
Latest finish (LF) = latest time by which an activity has to finish so as to not delay the completion time of the entire project

We use a two-pass process, consisting of a forward pass and a backward pass, to determine these time schedules for each activity. The early start and finish times (ES and EF) are determined during the **forward pass**. The late start and finish times (LS and LF) are determined during the backward pass.

Forward pass
A process that identifies all the early times.

Forward Pass

LO3: Complete forward and backward passes for a project

To clearly show the activity schedules on the project network, we use the notation shown in Figure 3.10. The ES of an activity is shown in the top left corner of the node denoting that activity. The EF is shown in the top right corner. The latest times, LS and LF, are shown in the bottom-left and bottom-right corners, respectively.

Earliest Start Time Rule Before an activity can start, *all* its immediate predecessors must be finished:

- If an activity has only a single immediate predecessor, its ES equals the EF of the predecessor.
- If an activity has multiple immediate predecessors, its ES is the maximum of all EF values of its predecessors. That is,

$$ES = \text{Max}\,\{\text{EF of all immediate predecessors}\} \quad (3\text{-}1)$$

AUTHOR COMMENT
All predecessor activities must be completed before an acitivity can begin.

Earliest Finish Rule The earliest finish time (EF) of an activity is the sum of its earliest start time (ES) and its activity time. That is,

$$EF = ES + \text{Activity time} \quad (3\text{-}2)$$

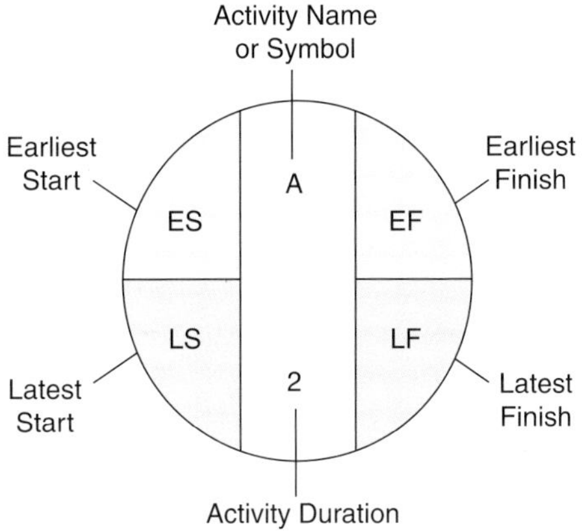

◀ **FIGURE 3.10**
Notation Used in Nodes for Forward and Backward Pass

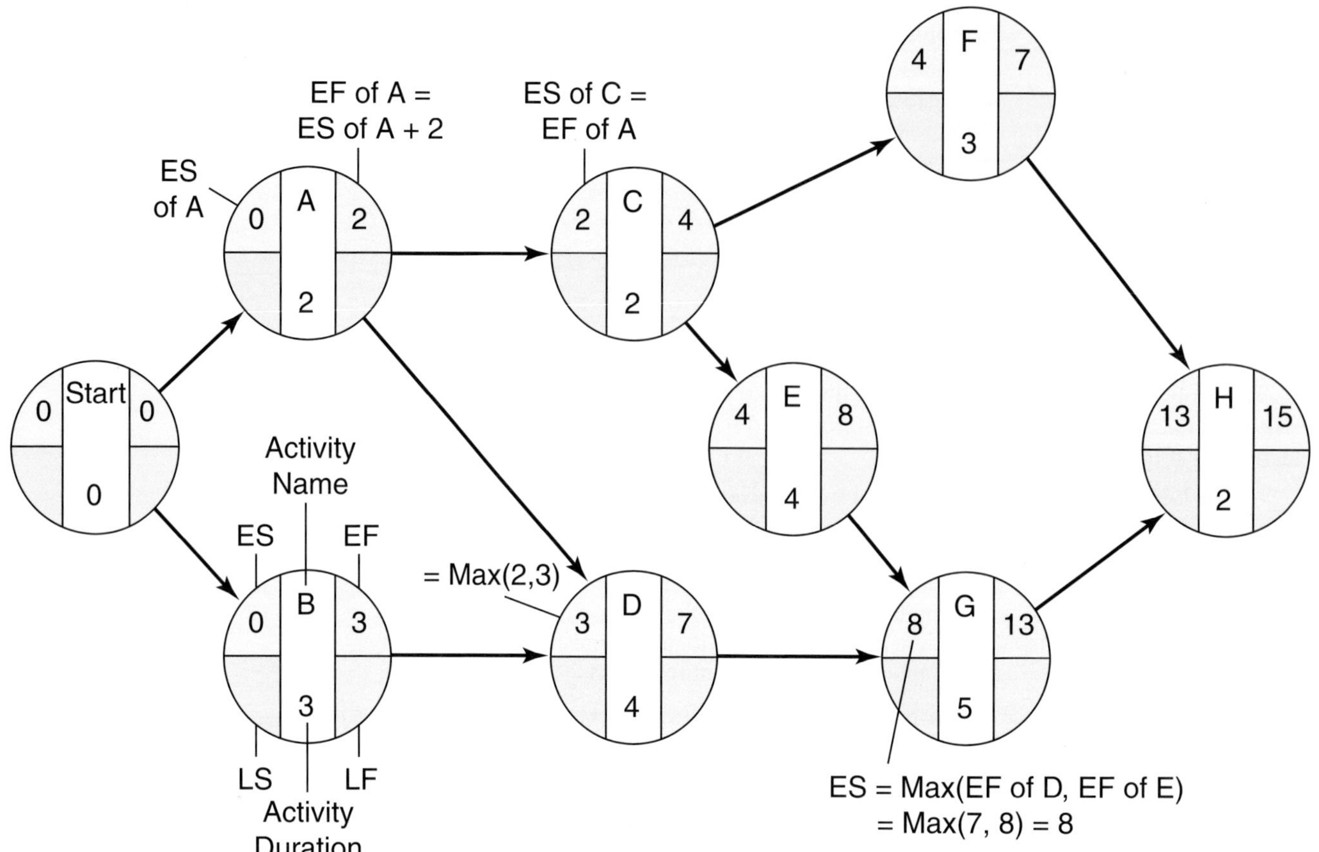

▲ **FIGURE 3.11 Earliest Start and Earliest Finish Times for Milwaukee Paper**

EXAMPLE 4 ▶

Computing earliest start and finish times for Milwaukee Paper

Calculate the earliest start and finish times for the activities in the Milwaukee Paper Manufacturing project.

APPROACH ▶ Use Table 3.2, which contains the activity times. Complete the project network for the company's project, along with the ES and EF values for all activities.

SOLUTION ▶ With the help of Figure 3.11, we describe how these values are calculated.

Since activity Start has no predecessors, we begin by setting its ES to 0. That is, activity Start can begin at time 0, which is the same as the beginning of week 1. If activity Start has an ES of 0, its EF is also 0, since its activity time is 0.

Next, we consider activities A and B, both of which have only Start as an immediate predecessor. Using the earliest start time rule, the ES for both activities A and B equals zero, which is the EF of activity Start. Now, using the earliest finish time rule, the EF for A is 2 (= 0 + 2), and the EF for B is 3 (= 0 + 3).

Since activity A precedes activity C, the ES of C equals the EF of A (= 2). The EF of C is therefore 4 (= 2 + 2).

We now come to activity D. Both activities A and B are immediate predecessors for B. Whereas A has an EF of 2, activity B has an EF of 3. Using the earliest start time rule, we compute the ES of activity D as follows:

$$\text{ES of D} = \text{Max(EF of A, EF of B)} = \text{Max}(2, 3) = 3$$

The EF of D equals 7 (= 3 + 4). Next, both activities E and F have activity C as their only immediate predecessor. Therefore, the ES for both E and F equals 4 (= EF of C). The EF of E is 8 (= 4 + 4), and the EF of F is 7 (= 4 + 3).

Activity G has both activities D and E as predecessors. Using the earliest start time rule, its ES is therefore the maximum of the EF of D and the EF of E. Hence, the ES of activity G equals 8 (= maximum of 7 and 8), and its EF equals 13 (= 8 + 5).

Finally, we come to activity H. Since it also has two predecessors, F and G, the ES of H is the maximum EF of these two activities. That is, the ES of H equals 13 (= maximum of 13 and 7). This implies that the EF of H is 15 (= 13 + 2). Since H is the last activity in the project, this also implies that the earliest time in which the entire project can be completed is 15 weeks.

INSIGHT ▶ The ES of an activity that has only one predecessor is simply the EF of that predecessor. For an activity with more than one predecessor, we must carefully examine the EFs of all immediate predecessors and choose the largest one.

LEARNING EXERCISE ▶ A new activity I, *EPA Approval*, takes 1 week. Its predecessor is activity H. What are I's ES and EF? [Answer: 15, 16]

RELATED PROBLEMS ▶ 3.11, 3.14c

EXCEL OM Data File **Ch03Ex4.xls** can be found at **www.pearsonhighered.com/heizer**.

Although the forward pass allows us to determine the earliest project completion time, it does not identify the critical path. To identify this path, we need to now conduct the backward pass to determine the LS and LF values for all activities.

Backward Pass

Just as the forward pass began with the first activity in the project, the **backward pass** begins with the last activity in the project. For each activity, we first determine its LF value, followed by its LS value. The following two rules are used in this process.

Backward pass
An activity that finds all the late start and late finish times.

Latest Finish Time Rule This rule is again based on the fact that before an activity can start, all its immediate predecessors must be finished:

- If an activity is an immediate predecessor for just a single activity, its LF equals the LS of the activity that immediately follows it.
- If an activity is an immediate predecessor to more than one activity, its LF is the minimum of all LS values of all activities that immediately follow it. That is:

$$\text{LF} = \text{Min}\{\text{LS of all immediate following activities}\} \tag{3-3}$$

Latest Start Time Rule The latest start time (LS) of an activity is the difference of its latest finish time (LF) and its activity time. That is:

$$\text{LS} = \text{LF} - \text{Activity time} \tag{3-4}$$

◀ **EXAMPLE 5**

Computing latest start and finish times for Milwaukee Paper

Calculate the latest start and finish times for each activity in Milwaukee Paper's pollution project.

APPROACH ▶ Use Figure 3.11 as a beginning point. Overlay 1 of Figure 3.11 shows the complete project network for Milwaukee Paper, along with LS and LF values for all activities. In what follows, we see how these values were calculated.

SOLUTION ▶ We begin by assigning an LF value of 15 weeks for activity H. That is, we specify that the latest finish time for the entire project is the same as its earliest finish time. Using the latest start time rule, the LS of activity H is equal to 13 (= 15 − 2).

Since activity H is the lone succeeding activity for both activities F and G, the LF for both F and G equals 13. This implies that the LS of G is 8 (= 13 − 5), and the LS of F is 10 (= 13 − 3).

Proceeding in this fashion, we see that the LF of E is 8 (= LS of G), and its LS is 4 (= 8 − 4). Likewise, the LF of D is 8 (= LS of G), and its LS is 4 (= 8 − 4).

We now consider activity C, which is an immediate predecessor to two activities: E and F. Using the latest finish time rule, we compute the LF of activity C as follows:

$$\text{LF of C} = \text{Min(LS of E, LS of F)} = \text{Min}(4, 10) = 4$$

The LS of C is computed as 2 (= 4 − 2). Next, we compute the LF of B as 4 (= LS of D), and its LS as 1 (= 4 − 3).

We now consider activity A. We compute its LF as 2 (= minimum of LS of C and LS of D). Hence, the LS of activity A is 0 (= 2 − 2). Finally, both the LF and LS of activity Start are equal to 0.

INSIGHT ▶ The LF of an activity that is the predecessor of only one activity is just the LS of that following activity. If the activity is the predecessor to more than one activity, its LF is the smallest LS value of all activities that follow immediately.

LEARNING EXERCISE ▶ A new activity I, *EPA Approval*, takes 1 week. Its predecessor is activity H. What are I's LS and LF? [Answer: 15, 16]

RELATED PROBLEMS ▶ 3.11, 3.14c.

Calculating Slack Time and Identifying the Critical Path(s)

Slack time
Free time for an activity.

After we have computed the earliest and latest times for all activities, it is a simple matter to find the amount of **slack time**[2] that each activity has. Slack is the length of time an activity can be delayed without delaying the entire project. Mathematically:

$$\text{Slack} = \text{LS} - \text{ES} \qquad \text{or} \qquad \text{Slack} = \text{LF} - \text{EF} \tag{3-5}$$

EXAMPLE 6 ▶

Calculating slack times for Milwaukee Paper

Calculate the slack for the activities in the Milwaukee Paper project.

APPROACH ▶ Start with the data in Overlay 1 of Figure 3.11 in Example 5 and develop Table 3.3 one line at a time.

SOLUTION ▶ Table 3.3 summarizes the ES, EF, LS, LF, and slack time for all of the firm's activities. Activity B, for example, has 1 week of slack time since its LS is 1 and its ES is 0 (alternatively, its LF is 4 and its EF is 3). This means that activity B can be delayed by up to 1 week, and the whole project can still be finished in 15 weeks.

▶ TABLE 3.3
Milwaukee Paper's Schedule and Slack Times

Activity	Earliest Start ES	Earliest Finish EF	Latest Start LS	Latest Finish LF	Slack LS – ES	On Critical Path
A	0	2	0	2	0	Yes
B	0	3	1	4	1	No
C	2	4	2	4	0	Yes
D	3	7	4	8	1	No
E	4	8	4	8	0	Yes
F	4	7	10	13	6	No
G	8	13	8	13	0	Yes
H	13	15	13	15	0	Yes

On the other hand, activities A, C, E, G, and H have *no* slack time. This means that none of them can be delayed without delaying the entire project. Conversely, if plant manager Joni Steinberg wants to reduce the total project times, she will have to reduce the length of one of these activities.

Overlay 2 of Figure 3.11 shows the slack computed for each activity.

INSIGHT ▶ Slack may be computed from either early/late starts or early/late finishes. The key is to find which activities have zero slack.

LEARNING EXERCISE ▶ A new activity I, *EPA Approval*, follows activity H and takes 1 week. Is it on the critical path? [Answer: Yes, it's LS – ES = 0]

RELATED PROBLEMS ▶ 3.6, 3.11, 3.27

ACTIVE MODEL 3.1 This example is further illustrated in Active Model 3.1 at **www.pearsonhighered.com/heizer**.

[2]Slack time may also be referred to as *free time, free float,* or *free slack.*

The activities with zero slack are called *critical activities* and are said to be on the critical path. The critical path is a continuous path through the project network that:

LO4: Determine a critical path

- Starts at the first activity in the project (Start in our example).
- Terminates at the last activity in the project (H in our example).
- Includes only critical activities (i.e., activities with no slack time).

EXAMPLE 7

Showing critical path with blue arrows

Show Milwaukee Paper's critical path and find the project completion time.

APPROACH ▶ We use Table 3.3 and Overlay 3 of Figure 3.11. Overlay 3 of Figure 3.11 indicates that the total project completion time of 15 weeks corresponds to the longest path in the network. That path is Start-A-C-E-G-H in network form. It is shown with thick blue arrows.

INSIGHT ▶ The critical path follows the activities with slack = 0. This is considered the longest path through the network.

LEARNING EXERCISE ▶ Why are activities B, D, and F not on the path with the thick blue line? [Answer: They are not critical and have slack values of 1, 1, and 6 weeks, respectively.]

RELATED PROBLEMS ▶ 3.3, 3.4, 3.5, 3.6, 3.7, 3.12, 3.14b, 3.15, 3.17, 3.20a, 3.22a, 3.23, 3.26

Total Slack Time Look again at the project network in Overlay 3 of Figure 3.11. Consider activities B and D, which have slack of 1 week each. Does it mean that we can delay *each* activity by 1 week, and still complete the project in 15 weeks? The answer is no.

Let's assume that activity B is delayed by 1 week. It has used up its slack of 1 week and now has an EF of 4. This implies that activity D now has an ES of 4 and an EF of 8. Note that these are also its LS and LF values, respectively. That is, activity D also has no slack time now. Essentially, the slack of 1 week that activities B and D had is, for that path, *shared* between them. Delaying either activity by 1 week causes not only that activity, but also the other activity, to lose its slack. This type of a slack time is referred to as **total slack**. Typically, when two or more noncritical activities appear successively in a path, they share total slack.

Total slack
Time shared among more than one activity.

VARIABILITY IN ACTIVITY TIMES

AUTHOR COMMENT PERT's ability to handle three time estimates for each activity enables us to compute the probability that we can complete the project by a target date.

In identifying all earliest and latest times so far, and the associated critical path(s), we have adopted the CPM approach of assuming that all activity times are known and fixed constants. That is, there is no variability in activity times. However, in practice, it is likely that activity completion times vary depending on various factors.

To plan, monitor, and control the huge number of details involved in sponsoring a rock festival attended by more than 100,000 fans, Hard Rock Cafe uses Microsoft Project and the tools discussed in this chapter. The *Video Case Study* "Managing Hard Rock's Rockfest," at the end of the chapter, provides more details of the management task.

For example, building internal components (activity A) for Milwaukee Paper Manufacturing is estimated to finish in 2 weeks. Clearly, factors such as late arrival of raw materials, absence of key personnel, and so on, could delay this activity. Suppose activity A actually ends up taking 3 weeks. Since A is on the critical path, the entire project will now be delayed by 1 week to 16 weeks. If we had anticipated completion of this project in 15 weeks, we would obviously miss our deadline.

Although some activities may be relatively less prone to delays, others could be extremely susceptible to delays. For example, activity B (modify roof and floor) could be heavily dependent on weather conditions. A spell of bad weather could significantly affect its completion time.

This means that we cannot ignore the impact of variability in activity times when deciding the schedule for a project. PERT addresses this issue.

Three Time Estimates in PERT

In PERT, we employ a probability distribution based on three time estimates for each activity, as follows:

Optimistic time
The "best" activity completion time that could be obtained in a PERT network.

Pessimistic time
The "worst" activity time that could be expected in a PERT network.

Most likely time
The most probable time to complete an activity in a PERT network.

Optimistic time (a) = time an activity will take if everything goes as planned. In estimating this value, there should be only a small probability (say, 1/100) that the activity time will be $< a$.

Pessimistic time (b) = time an activity will take assuming very unfavorable conditions. In estimating this value, there should also be only a small probability (also, 1/100) that the activity time will be $> b$.

Most likely time (m) = most realistic estimate of the time required to complete an activity.

When using PERT, we often assume that activity time estimates follow the beta probability distribution (see Figure 3.12). This continuous distribution is often appropriate for determining the expected value and variance for activity completion times.

To find the *expected activity time*, t, the beta distribution weights the three time estimates as follows:

$$t = (a + 4m + b)/6 \quad \text{(3-6)}$$

That is, the most likely time (m) is given four times the weight as the optimistic time (a) and pessimistic time (b). The time estimate t computed using Equation 3-6 for each activity is used in the project network to compute all earliest and latest times.

To compute the *dispersion* or *variance of activity completion time*, we use the formula[3]:

$$\text{Variance} = [(b - a)/6]^2 \quad \text{(3-7)}$$

▶ **FIGURE 3.12**
Beta Probability Distribution with Three Time Estimates

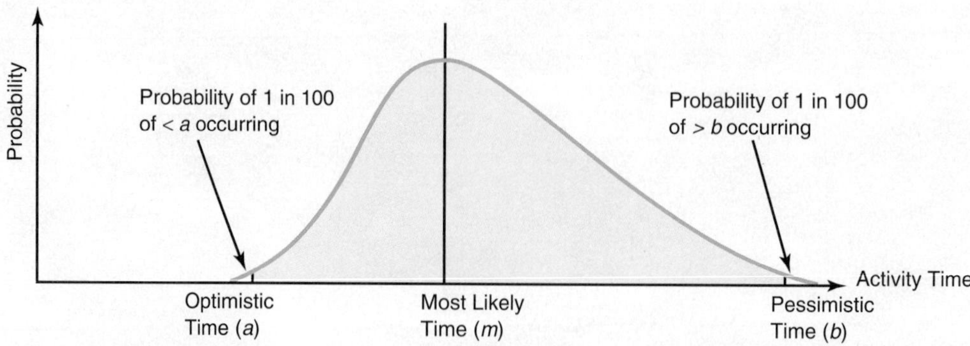

[3]This formula is based on the statistical concept that from one end of the beta distribution to the other is 6 standard deviations (±3 standard deviations from the mean). Since $(b - a)$ is 6 standard deviations, the variance is $[(b - a)/6]^2$.

EXAMPLE 8

Expected times and variances for Milwaukee Paper

Joni Steinberg and the project management team at Milwaukee Paper want an expected time and variance for Activity F (Installing the Pollution Control System) where:

$$a = 1 \text{ week}, m = 2 \text{ weeks}, b = 9 \text{ weeks}$$

APPROACH ▶ Use Equations 3-6 and 3-7 to compute the expected time and variance for F.

SOLUTION ▶ The expected time for Activity F is:

$$t = \frac{a + 4m + b}{6} = \frac{1 + 4(2) + 9}{6} = \frac{18}{6} = 3 \text{ weeks}$$

The variance for Activity F is:

$$\text{Variance} = \left[\frac{(b - a)}{6}\right]^2 = \left[\frac{(9 - 1)}{6}\right]^2 = \left(\frac{8}{6}\right)^2 = \frac{64}{36} = 1.78$$

INSIGHT ▶ Steinberg now has information that allows her to understand and manage Activity F. The expected time is, in fact, the activity time used in our earlier computation and identification of the critical path.

LO5: Calculate the variance of activity times

LEARNING EXERCISE ▶ Review the expected times and variances for all of the other activities in the project. These are shown in Table 3.4.

◀ TABLE 3.4
Time Estimates (in weeks) for Milwaukee Paper's Project

Activity	Optimistic a	Most Likely m	Pessimistic b	Expected Time $t = (a + 4m + b)/6$	Variance $[(b - a)/6]^2$
A	1	2	3	2	$[(3 - 1)/6]^2 = 4/36 = .11$
B	2	3	4	3	$[(4 - 2)/6]^2 = 4/36 = .11$
C	1	2	3	2	$[(3 - 1)/6]^2 = 4/36 = .11$
D	2	4	6	4	$[(6 - 2)/6]^2 = 16/36 = .44$
E	1	4	7	4	$[(7 - 1)/6]^2 = 36/36 = 1.00$
F	1	2	9	3	$[(9 - 1)/6]^2 = 64/36 = 1.78$
G	3	4	11	5	$[(11 - 3)/6]^2 = 64/36 = 1.78$
H	1	2	3	2	$[(3 - 1)/6]^2 = 4/36 = .11$

AUTHOR COMMENT Can you see why the variance is higher in some activities than in others? Note the spread between the optimistic and pessimistic times.

RELATED PROBLEMS ▶ 3.13, 3.14a, 3.17a,b, 3.21a

EXCEL OM Data File **Ch03Ex8.xls** can be found at **www.pearsonhighered.com/heizer**.

We see here a ship being built at the Hyundai shipyard, Asia's largest shipbuilder, in Korea. Managing this project uses the same techniques as managing the remodeling of a store or installing a new production line.

Probability of Project Completion

The critical path analysis helped us determine that Milwaukee Paper's expected project completion time is 15 weeks. Joni Steinberg knows, however, that there is significant variation in the time estimates for several activities. Variation in activities that are on the critical path can affect the overall project completion time—possibly delaying it. This is one occurrence that worries the plant manager considerably.

PERT uses the variance of critical path activities to help determine the variance of the overall project. Project variance is computed by summing variances of *critical* activities:

$$\sigma_p^2 = \text{Project variance} = \Sigma(\text{variances of activities on critical path}) \qquad \text{(3-8)}$$

EXAMPLE 9 ▶

Computing project variance and standard deviation for Milwaukee Paper

Milwaukee Paper's managers now wish to know the project's variance and standard deviation.

APPROACH ▶ Because the activities are independent, we can add the variances of the activities on the critical path and then take the square root to determine the project's standard deviation.

SOLUTION ▶ From Example 8 (Table 3.4), we have the variances of all of the activities on the critical path. Specifically, we know that the variance of activity A is 0.11, variance of activity C is 0.11, variance of activity E is 1.00, variance of activity G is 1.78, and variance of activity H is 0.11.

Compute the total project variance and project standard deviation:

$$\text{Project variance}\,(\sigma_p^2) = 0.11 + 0.11 + 1.00 + 1.78 + 0.11 = 3.11$$

which implies:

$$\text{Project standard deviation}\,(\sigma_p) = \sqrt{\text{Project variance}} = \sqrt{3.11} = 1.76 \text{ weeks}$$

INSIGHT ▶ Management now has an estimate not only of expected completion time for the project but also of the standard deviation of that estimate.

LEARNING EXERCISE ▶ If the variance for activity A is actually 0.30 (instead of 0.11), what is the new project standard deviation? [Answer: 1.817.]

RELATED PROBLEM ▶ 3.17e

How can this information be used to help answer questions regarding the probability of finishing the project on time? PERT makes two more assumptions: (1) total project completion times follow a normal probability distribution, and (2) activity times are statistically independent. With these assumptions, the bell-shaped normal curve shown in Figure 3.13 can be used to represent project completion dates. This normal curve implies that there is a 50% chance that the manufacturer's project completion time will be less than 15 weeks and a 50% chance that it will exceed 15 weeks.

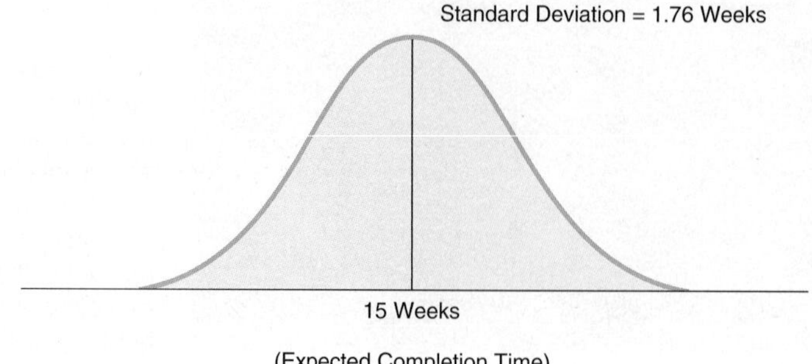

▶ FIGURE 3.13
Probability Distribution for Project Completion Times at Milwaukee Paper

◀ EXAMPLE 10

Probability of completing a project on time

Joni Steinberg would like to find the probability that her project will be finished on or before the 16-week EPA deadline.

APPROACH ▶ To do so, she needs to determine the appropriate area under the normal curve. This is the area to the left of the 16th week.

SOLUTION ▶ The standard normal equation can be applied as follows:

$$Z = (\text{Due date} - \text{Expected date of completion})/\sigma_p \quad (3\text{-}9)$$
$$= (16 \text{ weeks} - 15 \text{ weeks})/1.76 \text{ weeks} = 0.57$$

where Z is the number of standard deviations the due date or target date lies from the mean or expected date.

Referring to the Normal Table in Appendix I, we find a Z value of 0.57 to the right of the mean indicates a probability of 0.7157. Thus, there is a 71.57% chance that the pollution control equipment can be put in place in 16 weeks or less. This is shown in Figure 3.14.

AUTHOR COMMENT Here is a chance to review your statistical skills and use of a normal distribution table (Appendix I).

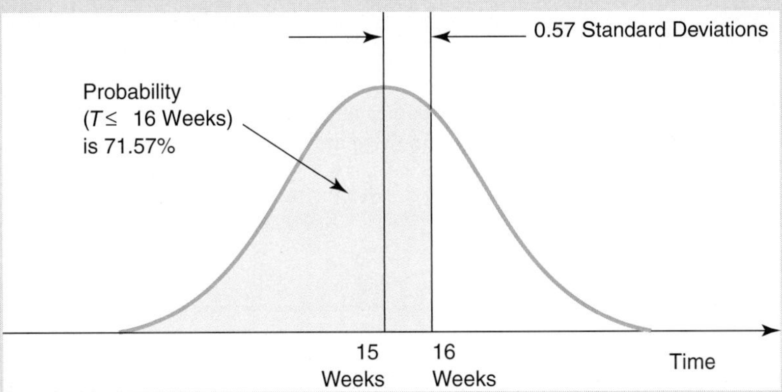

◀ FIGURE 3.14 Probability That Milwaukee Paper will Meet the 16-Week Deadline

INSIGHT ▶ The shaded area to the left of the 16th week (71.57%) represents the probability that the project will be completed in less than 16 weeks.

LEARNING EXERCISE ▶ What is the probability that the project will be completed on or before the 17th week? [Answer: About 87.2%.]

RELATED PROBLEMS ▶ 3.14d, 3.17f, 3.21d,e, 3.22b, 3.24

Determining Project Completion Time for a Given Confidence Level Let's say Joni Steinberg is worried that there is only a 71.57% chance that the pollution control equipment can be put in place in 16 weeks or less. She thinks that it may be possible to plead with the environmental group for more time. However, before she approaches the group, she wants to arm herself with sufficient information about the project. Specifically, she wants to find the deadline by which she has a 99% chance of completing the project. She hopes to use her analysis to convince the group to agree to this extended deadline.

Clearly, this due date would be greater than 16 weeks. However, what is the exact value of this new due date? To answer this question, we again use the assumption that Milwaukee Paper's project completion time follows a normal probability distribution with a mean of 15 weeks and a standard deviation of 1.76 weeks.

◀ EXAMPLE 11

Computing probability for any completion date

Joni Steinberg wants to find the due date that gives her company's project a 99% chance of *on-time* completion.

APPROACH ▶ She first needs to compute the Z-value corresponding to 99%, as shown in Figure 3.15. Mathematically, this is similar to Example 10, except the unknown is now Z rather than the due date.

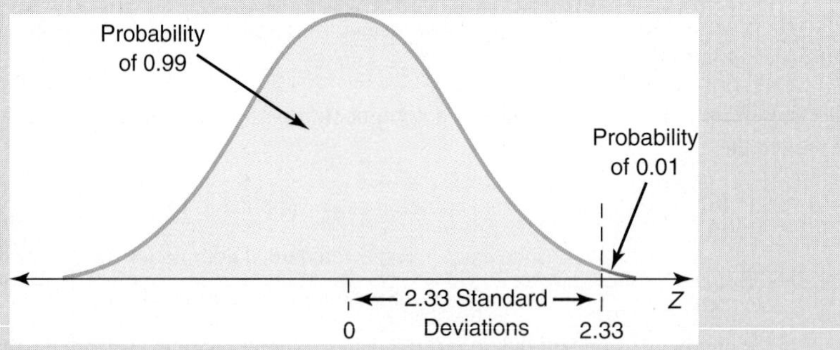

▶ **FIGURE 3.15**
***Z*-Value for 99% Probability of Project Completion at Milwaukee Paper**

SOLUTION ▶ Referring again to the Normal Table in Appendix I, we identify a Z-value of 2.33 as being closest to the probability of 0.99. That is, Joni Steinberg's due date should be 2.33 standard deviations above the mean project completion time. Starting with the standard normal equation (see Equation 3-9), we can solve for the due date and rewrite the equation as:

$$\text{Due date} = \text{Expected completion time} + (Z \times \sigma_p) \qquad \text{(3-10)}$$

$$= 15 + (2.33 \times 1.76) = 19.1 \text{ weeks}$$

INSIGHT ▶ If Steinberg can get the environmental group to agree to give her a new deadline of 19.1 weeks (or more), she can be 99% sure of finishing the project on time.

LEARNING EXERCISE ▶ What due date gives the project a 95% chance of on-time completion? [Answer: About 17.9 weeks.]

RELATED PROBLEMS ▶ 3.22c, 3.24e

Variability in Completion Time of Noncritical Paths In our discussion so far, we have focused exclusively on the variability in the completion times of activities on the critical path. This seems logical since these activities are, by definition, the more important activities in a project network. However, when there is variability in activity times, it is important that we also investigate the variability in the completion times of activities on *noncritical* paths.

Consider, for example, activity D in Milwaukee Paper's project. Recall from Overlay 3 in Figure 3.11 (in Example 7) that this is a noncritical activity, with a slack time of 1 week. We have therefore not considered the variability in D's time in computing the probabilities of project completion times. We observe, however, that D has a variance of 0.44 (see Table 3.4 in Example 8). In fact, the pessimistic completion time for D is 6 weeks. This means that if D ends up taking its pessimistic time to finish, the project will not finish in 15 weeks, even though D is not a critical activity.

For this reason, when we find probabilities of project completion times, it may be necessary for us to not focus only on the critical path(s). Indeed, some research has suggested that expending project resources to reduce the variability of activities not on the critical path can be an effective element in project management.[4] We may need also to compute these probabilities for noncritical paths, especially those that have relatively large variances. It is possible for a noncritical path to have a smaller probability of completion within a due date, when compared with the critical path. Determining the variance and probability of completion for a noncritical path is done in the same manner as Examples 9 and 10.

What Project Management Has Provided So Far Project management techniques have thus far been able to provide Joni Steinberg with several valuable pieces of management information:

1. The project's expected completion date is 15 weeks.
2. There is a 71.57% chance that the equipment will be in place within the 16-week deadline. PERT analysis can easily find the probability of finishing by any date Steinberg is interested in.

[4] F. M. Pokladnik, T. F. Anthony, R. R. Hill, G. Ulrich, "A Fresh Look at Estimated Project Duration: Noncritical Path Activity Contribution to Project Variance in PERT/CPM," *Proceedings of the 2003 Southwest Decision Science Conference*, Houston.

3. Five activities (A, C, E, G, and H) are on the critical path. If any one of these is delayed for any reason, the entire project will be delayed.
4. Three activities (B, D, F) are not critical and have some slack time built in. This means that Steinberg can borrow from their resources, and, if necessary, she may be able to speed up the whole project.
5. A detailed schedule of activity starting and ending dates, slack, and critical path activities has been made available (see Table 3.3 in Example 6).

COST–TIME TRADE-OFFS AND PROJECT CRASHING

AUTHOR COMMENT When a project needs to be shortened, we want to find the most economical way of "crashing" it.

While managing a project, it is not uncommon for a project manager to be faced with either (or both) of the following situations: (1) the project is behind schedule, and (2) the scheduled project completion time has been moved forward. In either situation, some or all of the remaining activities need to be speeded up (usually by adding resources) to finish the project by the desired due date. The process by which we shorten the duration of a project in the cheapest manner possible is called project **crashing**.

Crashing
Shortening activity time in a network to reduce time on the critical path so total completion time is reduced.

CPM is a technique in which each activity has a *normal* or *standard* time that we use in our computations. Associated with this normal time is the *normal* cost of the activity. However, another time in project management is the *crash time*, which is defined as the shortest duration required to complete an activity. Associated with this crash time is the *crash cost* of the activity. Usually, we can shorten an activity by adding extra resources (e.g., equipment, people) to it. Hence, it is logical for the crash cost of an activity to be higher than its normal cost.

The amount by which an activity can be shortened (i.e., the difference between its normal time and crash time) depends on the activity in question. We may not be able to shorten some activities at all. For example, if a casting needs to be heat-treated in the furnace for 48 hours, adding more resources does not help shorten the time. In contrast, we may be able to shorten some activities significantly (e.g., frame a house in 3 days instead of 10 days by using three times as many workers).

Likewise, the cost of crashing (or shortening) an activity depends on the nature of the activity. Managers are usually interested in speeding up a project at the least additional cost. Hence, when choosing which activities to crash, and by how much, we need to ensure the following:

- The amount by which an activity is crashed is, in fact, permissible
- Taken together, the shortened activity durations will enable us to finish the project by the due date
- The total cost of crashing is as small as possible

LO6: Crash a project

Crashing a project involves four steps:

STEP 1: Compute the crash cost per week (or other time period) for each activity in the network. If crash costs are linear over time, the following formula can be used:

$$\text{Crash cost per period} = \frac{(\text{Crash cost} - \text{Normal cost})}{(\text{Normal time} - \text{Crash time})} \tag{3-11}$$

STEP 2: Using the current activity times, find the critical path(s) in the project network. Identify the critical activities.

STEP 3: If there is only one critical path, then select the activity on this critical path that (a) can still be crashed and (b) has the smallest crash cost per period. Crash this activity by one period.

If there is more than one critical path, then select one activity from each critical path such that (a) each selected activity can still be crashed and (b) the total crash cost per period of *all* selected activities is the smallest. Crash each activity by one period. Note that the same activity may be common to more than one critical path.

STEP 4: Update all activity times. If the desired due date has been reached, stop. If not, return to Step 2.

We illustrate project crashing in Example 12.

EXAMPLE 12

Project crashing to meet a deadline at Milwaukee Paper

Suppose that Milwaukee Paper Manufacturing has been given only 13 weeks (instead of 16 weeks) to install the new pollution control equipment or face a court-ordered shutdown. As you recall, the length of Joni Steinberg's critical path was 15 weeks, but she must now complete the project in 13 weeks.

APPROACH ▶ Steinberg needs to determine which activities to crash, and by how much, to meet this 13-week due date. Naturally, Steinberg is interested in speeding up the project by 2 weeks, at the least additional cost.

SOLUTION ▶ The company's normal and crash times, and normal and crash costs, are shown in Table 3.5. Note, for example, that activity B's normal time is 3 weeks (the estimate used in computing the critical path), and its crash time is 1 week. This means that activity B can be shortened by up to 2 weeks if extra resources are provided. The cost of these additional resources is $4,000 (= difference between the crash cost of $34,000 and the normal cost of $30,000). If we assume that the crashing cost is linear over time (i.e., the cost is the same each week), activity B's crash cost per week is $2,000 (= $4,000/2).

▶ TABLE 3.5 Normal and Crash Data for Milwaukee Paper Manufacturing

	Time (Weeks)		*Cost ($)*			
Activity	**Normal**	**Crash**	**Normal**	**Crash**	**Crash Cost per Week ($)**	**Critical Path?**
A	2	1	22,000	22,750	750	Yes
B	3	1	30,000	34,000	2,000	No
C	2	1	26,000	27,000	1,000	Yes
D	4	3	48,000	49,000	1,000	No
E	4	2	56,000	58,000	1,000	Yes
F	3	2	30,000	30,500	500	No
G	5	2	80,000	84,500	1,500	Yes
H	2	1	16,000	19,000	3,000	Yes

This calculation for Activity B is shown in Figure 3.16. Crash costs for all other activities can be computed in a similar fashion.

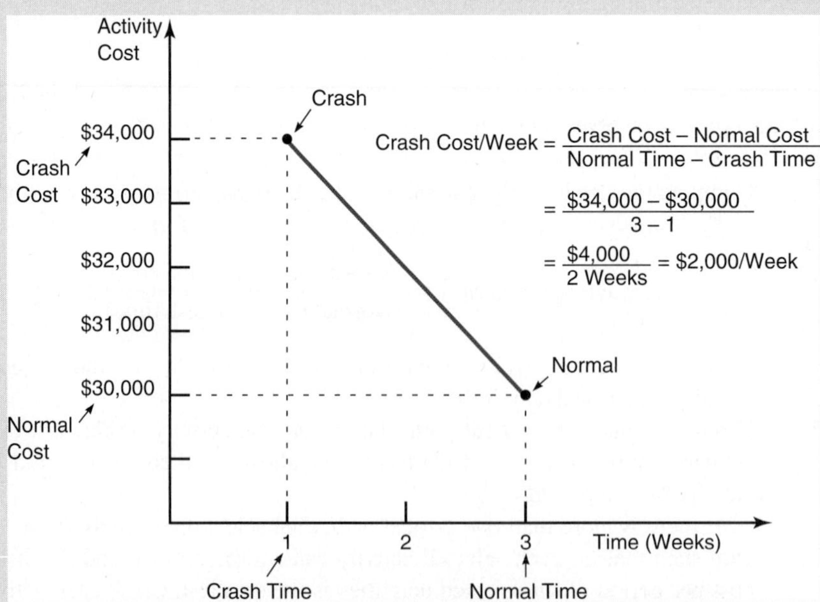

▶ FIGURE 3.16 Crash and Normal Times and Costs for Activity B

Steps 2, 3, and 4 can now be applied to reduce Milwaukee Paper's project completion time at a minimum cost. We show the project network for Milwaukee Paper again in Figure 3.17.

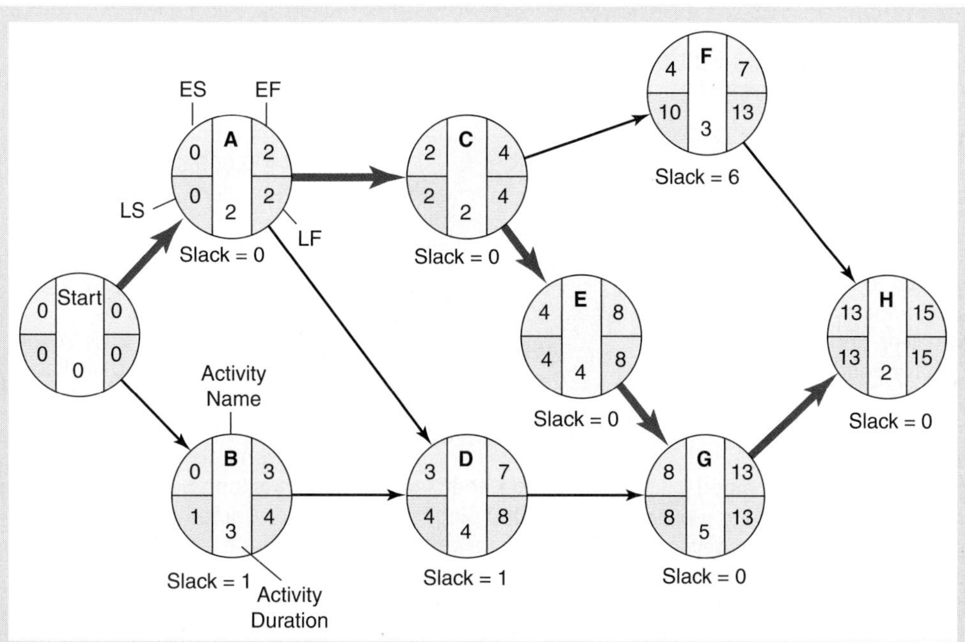

◀ **FIGURE 3.17**
Critical Path and Slack Times for Milwaukee Paper

The current critical path (using normal times) is Start-A-C-E-G-H, in which Start is just a dummy starting activity. Of these critical activities, activity A has the lowest crash cost per week of $750. Joni Steinberg should therefore crash activity A by 1 week to reduce the project completion time to 14 weeks. The cost is an additional $750. Note that activity A cannot be crashed any further, since it has reached its crash limit of 1 week.

At this stage, the original path Start-A-C-E-G-H remains critical with a completion time of 14 weeks. However, a new path Start-B-D-G-H is also critical now, with a completion time of 14 weeks. Hence, any further crashing must be done to both critical paths.

On each of these critical paths, we need to identify one activity that can still be crashed. We also want the total cost of crashing an activity on each path to be the smallest. We might be tempted to simply pick the activities with the smallest crash cost per period in each path. If we did this, we would select activity C from the first path and activity D from the second path. The total crash cost would then be $2,000 (= $1,000 + $1,000).

But we spot that activity G is common to both paths. That is, by crashing activity G, we will simultaneously reduce the completion time of both paths. Even though the $1,500 crash cost for activity G is higher than that for activities C and D, we would still prefer crashing G, since the total crashing cost will now be only $1,500 (compared with the $2,000 if we crash C and D).

INSIGHT ▶ To crash the project down to 13 weeks, Steinberg should crash activity A by 1 week, and activity G by 1 week. The total additional cost will be $2,250 (= $750 + $1,500). This is important because many contracts for projects include bonuses or penalties for early or late finishes.

LEARNING EXERCISE ▶ Say the crash cost for activity B is $31,000 instead of $34,000. How does this change the answer? [Answer: no change.]

RELATED PROBLEMS ▶ 3.16, 3.18, 3.19, 3.20, 3.25

A CRITIQUE OF PERT AND CPM

AUTHOR COMMENT Every technique has shortfalls as well as strengths. It is important to know both.

As a critique of our discussions of PERT, here are some of its features about which operations managers need to be aware:

Advantages

1. Especially useful when scheduling and controlling large projects.
2. Straightforward concept and not mathematically complex.
3. Graphical networks help highlight relationships among project activities.
4. Critical path and slack time analyses help pinpoint activities that need to be closely watched.
5. Project documentation and graphs point out who is responsible for various activities.
6. Applicable to a wide variety of projects.
7. Useful in monitoring not only schedules but costs as well.

OM in Action ► Rebuilding the Pentagon after 9/11

On September 11, 2001, American Airlines Flight 77 slammed into the Pentagon. The world was shocked by this and the other terrorist attacks on the Twin Towers in New York City. One hundred and twenty-five people died when a large portion of the Pentagon was severely damaged. Among the first to react were construction workers renovating another portion of the Pentagon. Their heroism saved lives and eased suffering. Within hours of the disaster, heavy equipment began arriving on the site, accompanied by hundreds of volunteer construction workers driven by patriotism and pride.

Just four days after the attack, Walker Evey, named program manager for "Project Phoenix," promised to rebuild the damaged portions of the Pentagon "faster than anyone has a right to expect . . . and to have people back in the damaged portion of the building, right where the plane hit, by September 11, 2002."

Preliminary construction reports estimated it would take 3 to 4 years and $3/4 billion to rebuild. By directing the project with teamwork, handshake contracts, creativity, and ingenuity—not to mention emotional 20-hour days 6 to 7 days a week—Evey's Project Phoenix met its psychological and physical goal. In less than 11 months, and for only $501 million, workers demolished and rebuilt the damaged sections—400,000 square feet of structure, 2 million square feet of offices, 50,000 tons of debris—using 1,000 construction workers from 80 companies. By September 9, 2002, over 600 military and civilian personnel were sitting at their desks in rebuilt Pentagon offices.

Outside, the blackened gash is long gone. Instead, some 4,000 pieces of limestone—mined from the same Indiana vein that the Pentagon's original stone came from 65 years ago—have been placed on the building's façade. For this impressive accomplishment, the Pentagon and Walker Evey were nominated for the Project Management Institute's 2003 Project of the Year Award.

Sources: Knight-Ridder Tribune Business News (February 1, 2004): 1; *ENR* (September 2, 2002): 6; *U.S. News & World Report* (September 16, 2002): 35.

Limitations

1. Project activities have to be clearly defined, independent, and stable in their relationships.
2. Precedence relationships must be specified and networked together.
3. Time estimates tend to be subjective and are subject to fudging by managers who fear the dangers of being overly optimistic or not pessimistic enough.
4. There is the inherent danger of placing too much emphasis on the longest, or critical, path. Near-critical paths need to be monitored closely as well.

AUTHOR COMMENT
Now that you understand the workings of PERT and CPM, you are ready to master this useful program. Knowing such software gives you an edge over others in the job market.

USING MICROSOFT PROJECT TO MANAGE PROJECTS

The approaches discussed so far are effective for managing small projects. However, for large or complex projects, specialized project management software is much preferred. In this section, we provide a brief introduction to the most popular example of such specialized software, Microsoft Project. A time-limited version of Microsoft Project may be requested with this text.

Microsoft Project is extremely useful in drawing project networks, identifying the project schedule, and managing project costs and other resources.

Milwaukee Paper Co.
Activities

Activity	Time (wks)	Predecessors
A	2	—
B	3	—
C	2	A
D	4	A, B
E	4	C
F	3	C
G	5	D, E
H	2	F, G

Entering Data Let us again consider the Milwaukee Paper Manufacturing project. Recall that this project has eight activities (repeated in the margin on page 83). The first step is to define the activities and their precedence relationships. To do so, we select File|New to open a blank project. We type the project start date (as July 1), then enter all activity information (see Program 3.1). For each activity (or task, as Microsoft Project calls it), we fill in the name and duration. The description of the activity is also placed in the *Task Name* column in Program 3.1. As we enter activities and durations, the software automatically inserts start and finish dates.

The next step is to define precedence relationships between these activities. To do so, we enter the relevant activity numbers (e.g., 1, 2) in the *Predecessors* column.

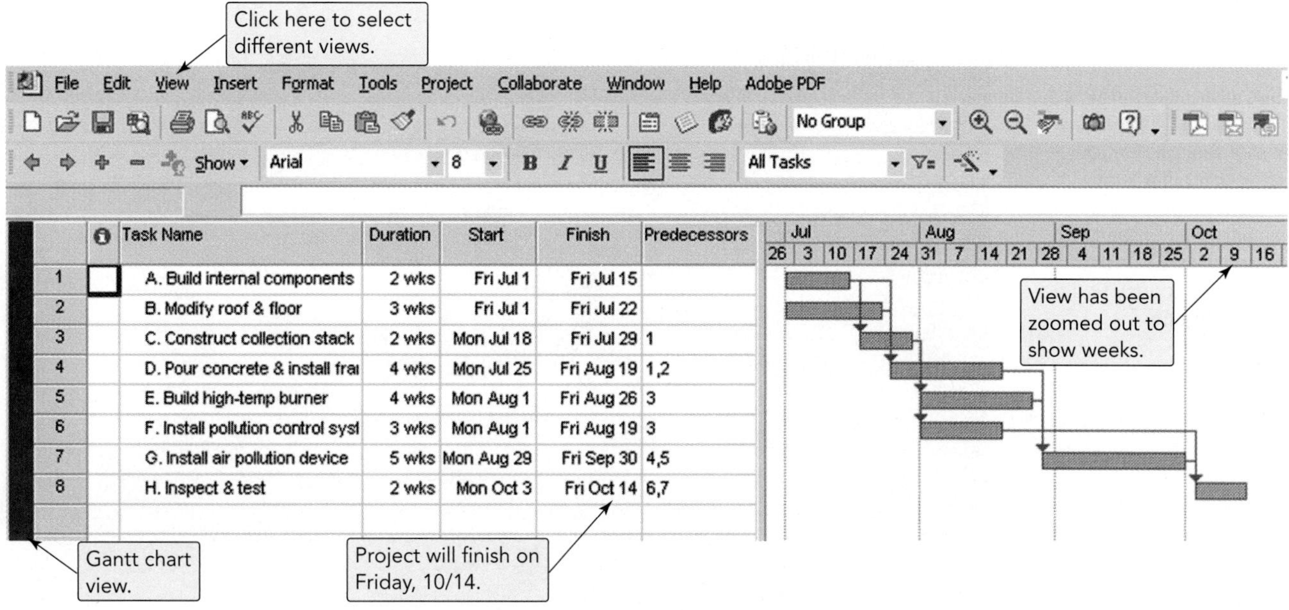

▲ **PROGRAM 3.1** **Gantt Chart in Microsoft Project for Milwaukee Paper Manufacturing**

Viewing the Project Schedule When all links have been defined, the complete project schedule can be viewed as a Gantt chart. We can also select **View|Network Diagram** to view the schedule as a project network (shown in Program 3.2). The critical path is shown in red on the screen in the network diagram. We can click on any of the activities in the project network to view details of the activities. Likewise, we can easily add or remove activities from the project network. Each time we do so, Microsoft Project automatically updates all start dates, finish dates, and the critical path(s). If desired, we can manually change the layout of the network (e.g., reposition activities) by changing the options in **Format|Layout**.

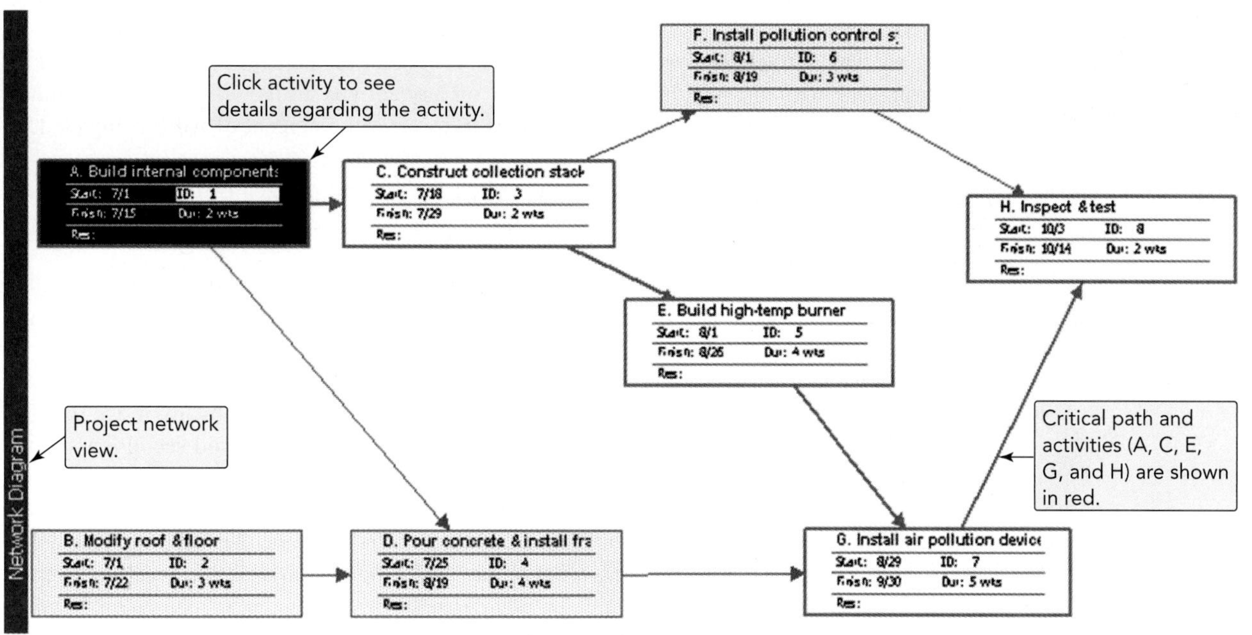

▲ **PROGRAM 3.2** **Project Network in Microsoft Project for Milwaukee Paper Manufacturing**

Using PERT/CPM, Taco Bell built and opened this fast-food restaurant in Compton, California, in just 2 days! Typically, 2 months are needed to accomplish such a task. Good project management means a faster revenue stream instead of money tied up in construction.

Programs 3.1 and 3.2 show that if Milwaukee Paper's project starts July 1, it can be finished on October 14. The start and finish dates for all activities are also clearly identified. Project management software, we see, can greatly simplify the scheduling procedures discussed earlier in this chapter.

PERT Analysis Microsoft Project does not perform the PERT probability calculations discussed in Examples 10 and 11. However, by clicking View|Toolbars|PERT Analysis, we can get Microsoft Project to allow us to enter optimistic, most likely, and pessimistic times for each activity. We can then choose to view Gantt charts based on any of these three times for each activity.

Tracking the Time Status of a Project Perhaps the biggest advantage of using software to manage projects is that it can track the progress of the project. In this regard, Microsoft Project has many features available to track individual activities in terms of time, cost, resource usage, and so on.

Pollution Project Percentage Completed on Aug. 12

Activity	Completed
A	100
B	100
C	100
D	10
E	20
F	20
G	0
H	0

An easy way to track the time progress of tasks is to enter the percent of work completed for each task. One way to do so is to double-click on any activity in the *Task Name* column in Program 3.1. A window is displayed that allows us to enter the percent of work completed for each task.

The table in the margin provides data regarding the percent of each of Milwaukee Paper's activities as of today. (Assume that today is Friday, August 12, i.e., the end of the sixth week of the project schedule.)

As shown in Program 3.3, the Gantt chart immediately reflects this updated information by drawing a thick line within each activity's bar. The length of this line is proportional to the percent of that activity's work that has been completed.

How do we know if we are on schedule? Notice that there is a vertical line shown on the Gantt chart corresponding to today's date. Microsoft Project will automatically move this line to correspond with the current date. If the project is on schedule, we should see all bars to the *left* of today's line indicate that they have been completed. For example, Program 3.3 shows that activities A, B, and C are on schedule. In contrast, activities D, E, and F appear to be behind schedule. These activities need to be investigated further to determine the reason for the delay. This type of easy *visual* information is what makes such software so useful in practice for project management.

We encourage you to load the copy of Microsoft Project that may be ordered with your text and to create a project network for work you are currently doing.

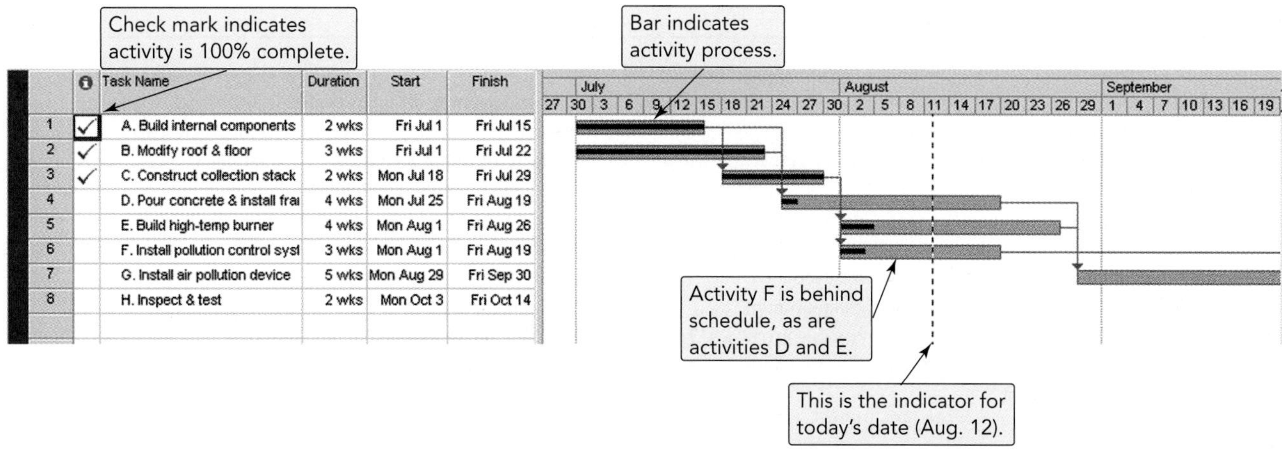

▲ **PROGRAM 3.3 Tracking Project Progress in Microsoft Project**

CHAPTER SUMMARY

PERT, CPM, and other scheduling techniques have proven to be valuable tools in controlling large and complex projects. With these tools, managers understand the status of each activity and know which activities are critical and which have slack; in addition, they know where crashing makes the most sense. Projects are segmented into discrete activities, and specific resources are identified. This allows project managers to respond aggressively to global competition. Effective project management also allows firms to create products and services for global markets. As with Microsoft Project illustrated in this chapter, a wide variety of software packages are available to help managers handle network modeling problems.

PERT and CPM do not, however, solve all the project scheduling and management problems. Good management practices, clear responsibilities for tasks, and straightforward and timely reporting systems are also needed. It is important to remember that the models we described in this chapter are only tools to help managers make better decisions.

Key Terms

Project organization (p. 58)
Work breakdown structure (WBS) (p. 60)
Gantt charts (p. 61)
Program evaluation and review technique (PERT) (p. 63)
Critical path method (CPM) (p. 63)
Critical path (p. 63)
Activity-on-node (AON) (p. 63)
Activity-on-arrow (AOA) (p. 63)
Dummy activity (p. 64)
Critical path analysis (p. 68)
Forward pass (p. 69)
Backward pass (p. 71)
Slack time (p. 72)
Total slack (p. 73)
Optimistic time (p. 74)
Pessimistic time (p. 74)
Most likely time (p. 74)
Crashing (p. 79)

Ethical Dilemma

Two examples of massively mismanaged projects are TAURUS and the "Big Dig." The first, formally called the London Stock Exchange Automation Project, cost $575 million before it was finally abandoned. Although most IT projects have a reputation for cost overruns, delays, and underperformance, TAURUS set a new standard.

But even TAURUS paled next to the biggest, most expensive public works project in U.S. history—Boston's 15-year-long Central Artery/Tunnel Project. Called the Big Dig, this was perhaps the poorest and most felonious case of project mismanagement in decades. From a starting $2 billion budget to a final price tag of $15 billion, the Big Dig cost more than the Panama Canal, Hoover Dam, or Interstate 95, the 1,919-mile highway between Maine and Florida.

Read about one of these two projects (or another of your choice) and explain why it faced such problems. How and why do project managers allow such massive endeavors to fall into such a state? What do you think are the causes?

Discussion Questions

1. Give an example of a situation in which project management is needed.
2. Explain the purpose of project organization.
3. What are the three phases involved in the management of a large project?
4. What are some of the questions that can be answered with PERT and CPM?
5. Define *work breakdown structure*. How is it used?
6. What is the use of Gantt charts in project management?
7. What is the difference between an activity-on-arrow (AOA) network and an activity-on-node (AON) network? Which is primarily used in this chapter?
8. What is the significance of the critical path?
9. What would a project manager have to do to crash an activity?
10. Describe how expected activity times and variances can be computed in a PERT network.
11. Define *early start*, *early finish*, *late finish*, and *late start* times.
12. Students are sometimes confused by the concept of critical path, and want to believe that it is the *shortest* path through a network. Convincingly explain why this is not so.
13. What are dummy activities? Why are they used in activity-on-arrow (AOA) project networks?
14. What are the three time estimates used with PERT?
15. Would a project manager ever consider crashing a noncritical activity in a project network? Explain convincingly.
16. How is the variance of the total project computed in PERT?
17. Describe the meaning of slack, and discuss how it can be determined.
18. How can we determine the probability that a project will be completed by a certain date? What assumptions are made in this computation?
19. Name some of the widely used project management software programs.

Using Software to Solve Project Management Problems

In addition to the Microsoft Project software just illustrated, both Excel OM and POM for Windows are available to readers of this text as project management tools.

Using Excel OM

Excel OM has a Project Scheduling module. Program 3.4 uses the data from the Milwaukee Paper Manufacturing example in this chapter (see Examples 4 and 5). The PERT/CPM analysis also handles activities with three time estimates.

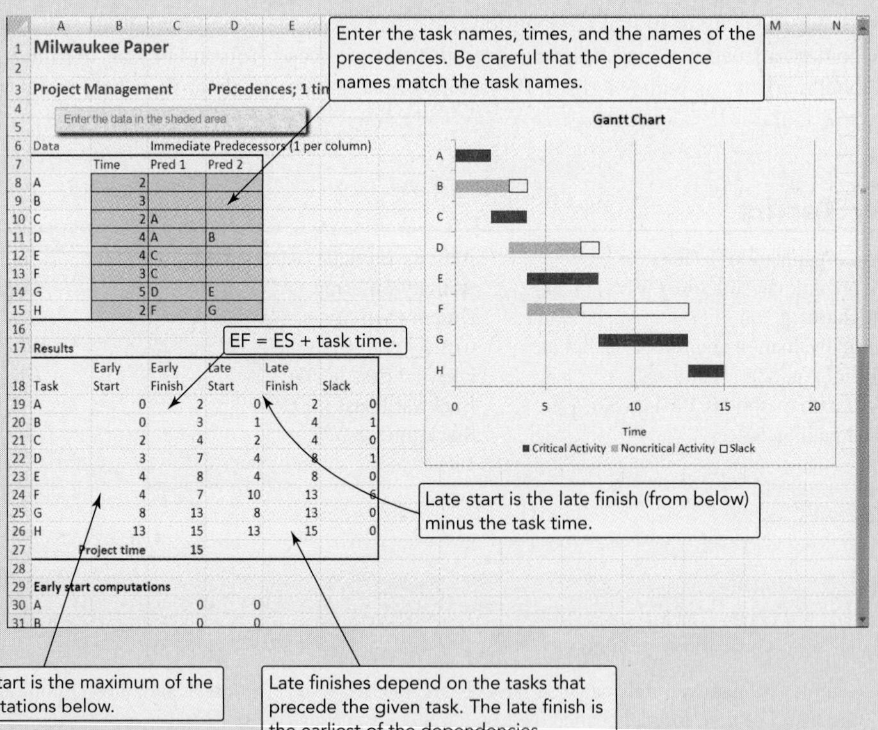

▶ **PROGRAM 3.4**
Excel OM's Use of Milwaukee Paper Manufacturing's Data from Examples 4 and 5

Using POM for Windows

POM for Window's Project Scheduling module can also find the expected project completion time for a CPM and PERT network with either one or three time estimates. POM for Windows also performs project crashing. For further details refer to Appendix IV.

Solved Problems Virtual Office Hours help is available at www.myomlab.com.

▼ SOLVED PROBLEM 3.1

Construct an AON network based on the following:

Activity	Immediate Predecessor(s)
A	—
B	—
C	—
D	A, B
E	C

▼ SOLUTION

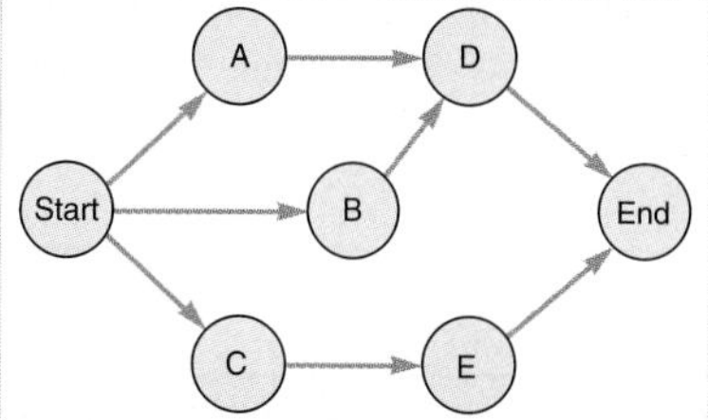

▼ SOLVED PROBLEM 3.2

Insert a dummy activity and event to correct the following AOA network:

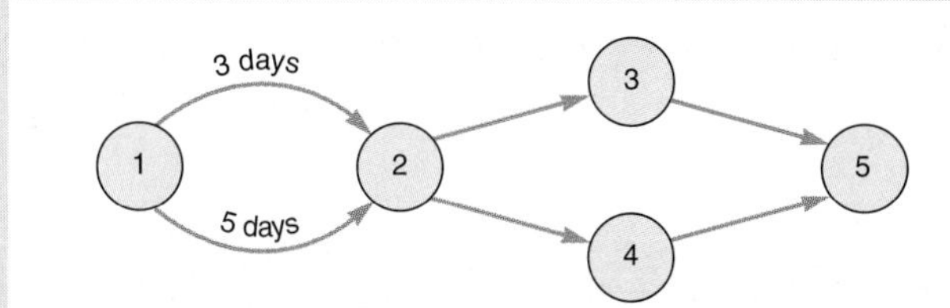

▼ SOLUTION

Since we cannot have two activities starting and ending at the same node, we add the following dummy activity and dummy event to obtain the correct AOA network:

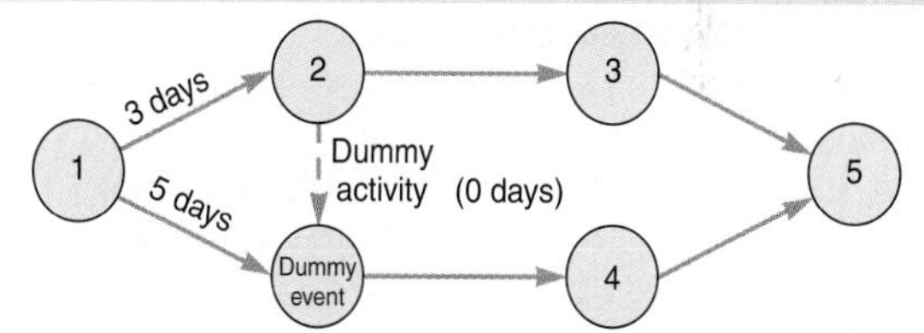

▼ SOLVED PROBLEM 3.3

Calculate the critical path, project completion time T, and project variance σ_p^2, based on the following AON network information:

Activity	Time	Variance	ES	EF	LS	LF	Slack
A	2	$\frac{2}{6}$	0	2	0	2	0
B	3	$\frac{2}{6}$	0	3	1	4	1
C	2	$\frac{4}{6}$	2	4	2	4	0
D	4	$\frac{4}{6}$	3	7	4	8	1
E	4	$\frac{2}{6}$	4	8	4	8	0
F	3	$\frac{1}{6}$	4	7	10	13	6
G	5	$\frac{1}{6}$	8	13	8	13	0

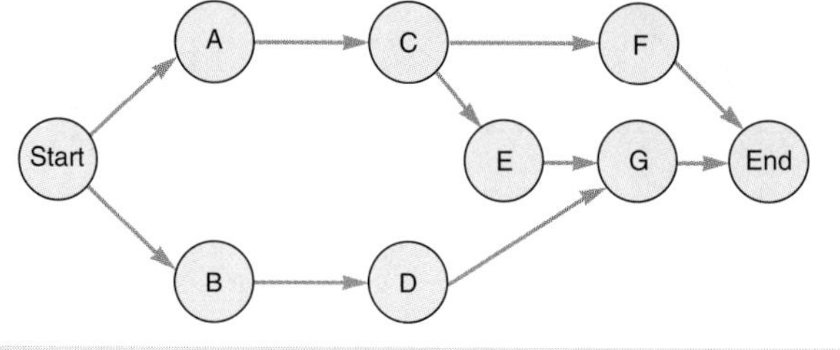

▼ SOLUTION

We conclude that the critical path is Start-A-C-E-G-End:

$$\text{Total project time} = T = 2 + 2 + 4 + 5 = 13$$

and

$$\sigma_p^2 = \Sigma \text{ Variances on the critical path} = \frac{2}{6} + \frac{4}{6} + \frac{2}{6} + \frac{1}{6} = \frac{9}{6} = 1.5$$

▼ SOLVED PROBLEM 3.4

To complete the wing assembly for an experimental aircraft, Jim Gilbert has laid out the seven major activities involved. These activities have been labeled A through G in the following table, which also shows their estimated completion times (in weeks) and immediate predecessors. Determine the expected time and variance for each activity:

Activity	*a*	*m*	*b*	Immediate Predecessors
A	1	2	3	—
B	2	3	4	—
C	4	5	6	A
D	8	9	10	B
E	2	5	8	C, D
F	4	5	6	D
G	1	2	3	E

▼ SOLUTION

Expected times and variances can be computed using Equations (3-6) and (3-7) presented on page 74 in this chapter. The results are summarized in the following table:

Activity	Expected Time (in weeks)	Variance
A	2	$\frac{1}{9}$
B	3	$\frac{1}{9}$
C	5	$\frac{1}{9}$
D	9	$\frac{1}{9}$
E	5	1
F	5	$\frac{1}{9}$
G	2	$\frac{1}{9}$

▼ SOLVED PROBLEM 3.5

Referring to Solved Problem 3.4, now Jim Gilbert would like to determine the critical path for the entire wing assembly project as well as the expected completion time for the total project. In addition, he would like to determine the earliest and latest start and finish times for all activities.

▼ SOLUTION

The AON network for Gilbert's project is shown in Figure 3.18. Note that this project has multiple activities (A and B) with no immediate predecessors, and multiple activities (F and G) with no successors. Hence, in addition to a unique starting activity (Start), we have included a unique finishing activity (End) for the project.

Figure 3.18 shows the earliest and latest times for all activities. The results are also summarized in the following table:

Activity	*Activity Time* ES	EF	LS	LF	Slack
A	0	2	5	7	5
B	0	3	0	3	0
C	2	7	7	12	5
D	3	12	3	12	0
E	12	17	12	17	0
F	12	17	14	19	2
G	17	19	17	19	0

Expected project length = 19 weeks

Variance of the critical path = 1.333

Standard deviation of the critical path = 1.155 weeks

The activities along the critical path are B, D, E, and G. These activities have zero slack as shown in the table.

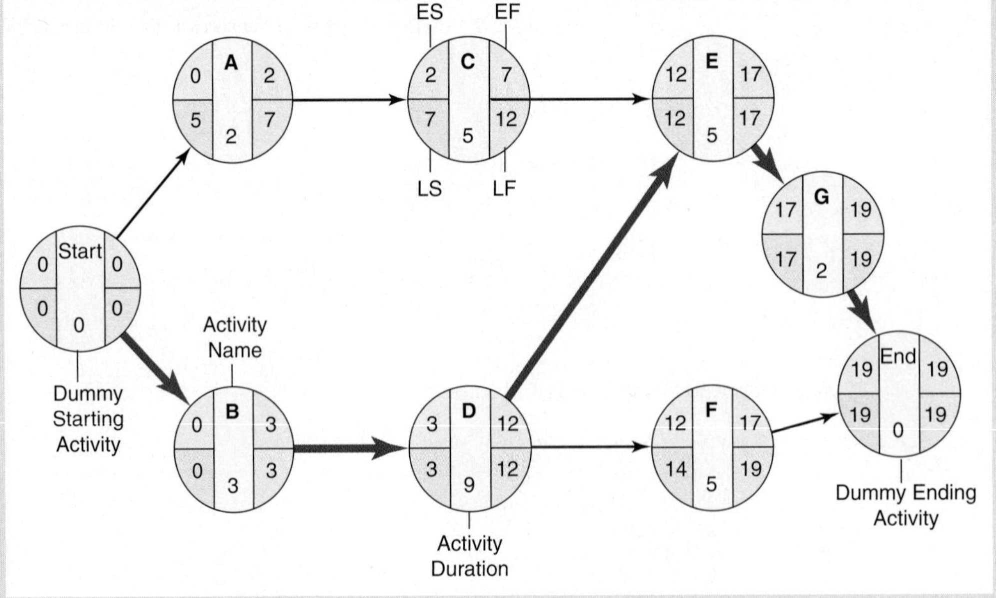

► FIGURE 3.18
Critical Path for Solved Problem 3.5

▼ SOLVED PROBLEM 3.6

The following information has been computed from a project:

$$\text{Expected total project time} = T = 62 \text{ weeks}$$

$$\text{Project variance } (\sigma_p^2) = 81$$

What is the probability that the project will be completed 18 weeks *before* its expected completion date?

▼ SOLUTION

The desired completion date is 18 weeks before the expected completion date, 62 weeks. The desired completion date is 44 (or 62 – 18) weeks:

$$\sigma_p = \sqrt{\text{Project variance}}$$

$$Z = \frac{\text{Due date} - \text{Expected completion date}}{\sigma_p}$$

$$= \frac{44 - 62}{9} = \frac{-18}{9} = -2.0$$

The normal curve appears as follows:

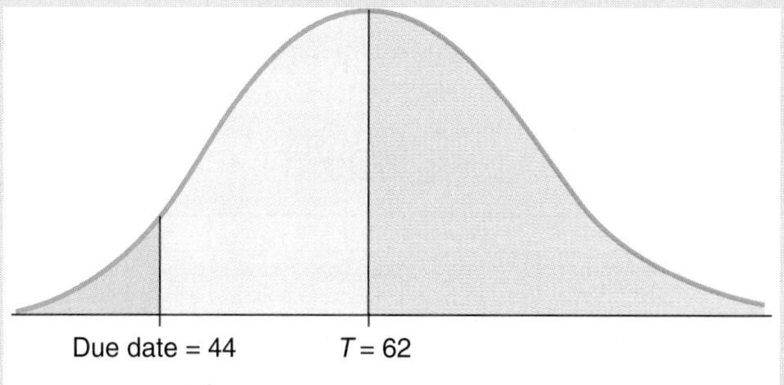

Because the normal curve is symmetrical and table values are calculated for positive values of Z, the area desired is equal to 1 – (table value). For Z = +2.0, the area from the table is .97725. Thus, the area corresponding to a Z value of –2.0 is .02275 (or 1 – .97725). Hence, the probability of completing the project 18 weeks before the expected completion date is approximately .023, or 2.3%.

▼ SOLVED PROBLEM 3.7

Determine the least cost of reducing the project completion date by 3 months based on the following information:

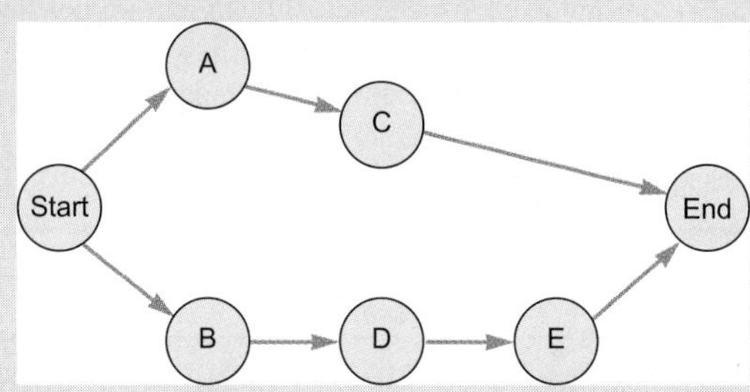

Activity	Normal Time (months)	Crash Time (months)	Normal Cost	Crash Cost
A	6	4	$2,000	$2,400
B	7	5	3,000	3,500
C	7	6	1,000	1,300
D	6	4	2,000	2,600
E	9	8	8,800	9,000

▼ SOLUTION

The first step in this problem is to compute ES, EF, LS, LF, and slack for each activity:

Activity	ES	EF	LS	LF	Slack
A	0	6	9	15	9
B	0	7	0	7	0
C	6	13	15	22	9
D	7	13	7	13	0
E	13	22	13	22	0

The critical path consists of activities B, D, and E.

Next, crash cost/month must be computed for each activity:

Activity	Normal Time – Crash Time	Crash Cost – Normal Cost	Crash Cost/ Month	Critical Path?
A	2	$400	$200/month	No
B	2	500	250/month	Yes
C	1	300	300/month	No
D	2	600	300/month	Yes
E	1	200	200/month	Yes

Finally, we will select that activity on the critical path with the smallest crash cost/month. This is activity E. Thus, we can reduce the total project completion date by 1 month for an additional cost of $200. We still need to reduce the project completion date by 2 more months. This reduction can be achieved at least cost along the critical path by reducing activity B by 2 months for an additional cost of $500. Neither reduction has an effect on noncritical activities. This solution is summarized in the following table:

Activity	Months Reduced	Cost
E	1	$200
B	2	500
		Total: $700

Problems*

• **3.1** The work breakdown structure for building a house (levels 1 and 2) is shown below:

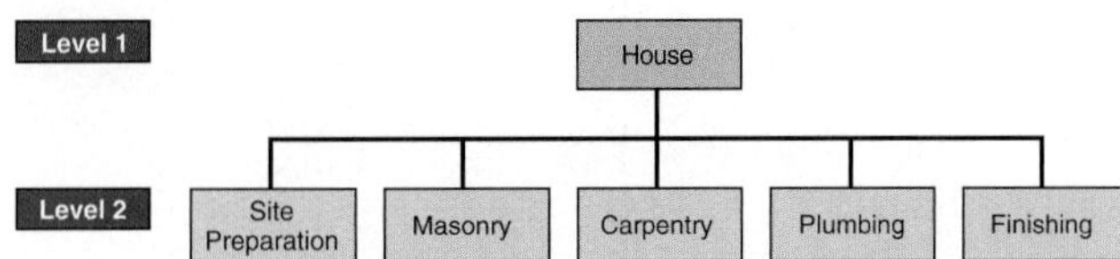

a) Add two level-3 activities to each of the level-2 activities to provide more detail to the WBS.
b) Select one of your level-3 activities and add two level-4 activities below it.

•• **3.2** Robert Mefford has decided to run for a seat as Congressman from the House of Representative district 34 in California. He views his 8-month campaign for office as a major project and wishes to create a work breakdown structure (WBS) to help control the detailed scheduling. So far, he has developed the following pieces of the WBS:

Level	Level ID No.	Activity
1	1.0	Develop political campaign
2	1.1	Fund-raising plan
3	1.11	______________
3	1.12	______________
3	1.13	______________
2	1.2	Develop a position on major issues
3	1.21	______________
3	1.22	______________
3	1.23	______________
2	1.3	Staffing for campaign
3	1.31	______________
3	1.32	______________
3	1.33	______________
3	1.34	______________
2	1.4	Paperwork compliance for candidacy
3	1.41	______________
3	1.42	______________
2	1.5	Ethical plan/issues
3	1.51	______________

Help Mr. Mefford by providing details where the blank lines appear. Are there any other major (level-2) activities to create? If so, add an ID no. 1.6 and insert them.

• **3.3** Draw the activity-on-node (AON) project network associated with the following activities for Dave Carhart's consulting company project. How long should it take Dave and his team to complete this project? What are the critical path activities?

Activity	Immediate Predecessor(s)	Time (days)
A	—	3
B	A	4
C	A	6
D	B	6
E	B	4
F	C	4
G	D	6
H	E, F	8

PX

*Note: PX means the problem may be solved with POM for Windows and/or Excel OM.

• **3.4** Given the activities whose sequence is described by the following table, draw the appropriate activity-on-arrow (AOA) network diagram.

a) Which activities are on the critical path?
b) What is the length of the critical path?

Activity	Immediate Predecessor(s)	Time (days)
A	—	5
B	A	2
C	A	4
D	B	5
E	B	5
F	C	5
G	E, F	2
H	D	3
I	G, H	5

PX

• **3.5** Using AOA, diagram the network described below for Sarah McComb's construction project. Calculate its critical path. How long is the minimum duration of this network?

Activity	Nodes	Time (weeks)	Activity	Nodes	Time (weeks)
J	1–2	10	N	3–4	2
K	1–3	8	O	4–5	7
L	2–4	6	P	3–5	5
M	2–3	3			

•• **3.6** Shirley Hopkins is developing a program in leadership training for middle-level managers. Shirley has listed a number of activities that must be completed before a training program of this nature could be conducted. The activities, immediate predecessors, and times appear in the accompanying table:

Activity	Immediate Predecessor(s)	Time (days)
A	—	2
B	—	5
C	—	1
D	B	10
E	A, D	3
F	C	6
G	E, F	8

a) Develop an AON network for this problem.
b) What is the critical path?
c) What is the total project completion time?
d) What is the slack time for each individual activity? PX

•• **3.7** Task time estimates for a production line setup project at Robert Klassen's Ontario factory are as follows:

Activity	Time (in hours)	Immediate Predecessors
A	6.0	—
B	7.2	—
C	5.0	A
D	6.0	B, C
E	4.5	B, C
F	7.7	D
G	4.0	E, F

Table for 3.8

Code	Activity	Description	Time (in hours)	Immediate Predecessor(s)
A	Planning	Find location; determine resource requirements	20	None
B	Purchasing	Requisition of lumber and sand	60	Planning
C	Excavation	Dig and grade	100	Planning
D	Sawing	Saw lumber into appropriate sizes	30	Purchasing
E	Placement	Position lumber in correct locations	20	Sawing, excavation
F	Assembly	Nail lumber together	10	Placement
G	Infill	Put sand in and under the equipment	20	Assembly
H	Outfill	Put dirt around the equipment	10	Assembly
I	Decoration	Put grass all over the garden, landscape, paint	30	Infill, outfill

Problem 3.7 (continued)

a) Draw the project network using AON.
b) Identify the critical path.
c) What is the expected project length?
d) Draw a Gantt chart for the project. PX

•• **3.8** The City Commission of Nashville has decided to build a botanical garden and picnic area in the heart of the city for the recreation of its citizens. The precedence table for all the activities required to construct this area successfully is given on the top of this page. Draw the Gantt chart for the whole construction activity.

•• **3.9** Refer to the table in Problem 3.8.

a) Draw the AON network for the construction activity.
b) Draw the AOA network for the construction activity.

• **3.10** The activities needed to build an experimental chemical contaminant tracking machine at Charlie Cook Corp. are listed in the following table. Construct an AON network for these activities.

Activity	Immediate Predecessor(s)	Activity	Immediate Predecessor(s)
A	—	E	B
B	—	F	B
C	A	G	C, E
D	A	H	D, F

• **3.11** Charlie Cook (see Problem 3.10) was able to determine the activity times for constructing his chemical contaminant tracking machine. Cook would like to determine ES, EF, LS, LF, and slack for each activity. The total project completion time and the critical path should also be determined. Here are the activity times:

Activity	Time (weeks)	Activity	Time (weeks)
A	6	E	4
B	7	F	6
C	3	G	10
D	2	H	7

PX

• **3.12** The activities described by the following table are given for the Duplaga Corporation:

Activity	Immediate Predecessor(s)	Time
A	—	9
B	A	7
C	A	3
D	B	6
E	B	9
F	C	4
G	E, F	6
H	D	5
I	G, H	3

a) Draw the appropriate AON PERT diagram for Ed Duplaga's management team.
b) Find the critical path.
c) What is the project completion time? PX

• **3.13** A small renovation of a Hard Rock Cafe gift shop has six activities (in hours). For the following estimates of *a*, *m*, and *b*, calculate the expected time and the standard deviation for each activity:

Activity	*a*	*m*	*b*
A	11	15	19
B	27	31	41
C	18	18	18
D	8	13	19
E	17	18	20
F	16	19	22

PX

•• **3.14** McGee Carpet and Trim installs carpet in commercial offices. Andrea McGee has been very concerned with the amount of time it took to complete several recent jobs. Some of her workers are very unreliable. A list of activities and their optimistic completion time, the most likely completion time, and the pessimistic completion time (all in days) for a new contract are given in the following table:

Activity	Time (days) *a*	*m*	*b*	Immediate Predecessor(s)
A	3	6	8	—
B	2	4	4	—
C	1	2	3	—
D	6	7	8	C
E	2	4	6	B, D
F	6	10	14	A, E
G	1	2	4	A, E
H	3	6	9	F
I	10	11	12	G
J	14	16	20	C
K	2	8	10	H, I

a) Determine the expected completion time and variance for each activity.
b) Determine the total project completion time and the critical path for the project.
c) Determine ES, EF, LS, LF, and slack for each activity.
d) What is the probability that McGee Carpet and Trim will finish the project in 40 days or less? PX

•• **3.15** The following is a table of activities associated with a project at Bill Figg Enterprises, their durations and what activities each must precede:

Activity	Duration (weeks)	Precedes
A (start)	1	B, C
B	1	E
C	4	F
E	2	F
F (end)	2	—

a) Draw an AON diagram of the project, including activity durations.
b) Define the critical path, listing all critical activities in chronological order.
c) What is the project duration (in weeks)?
d) What is the slack (in weeks) associated with any and all noncritical paths through the project?

•• **3.16** Assume that the activities in Problem 3.15 have the following costs to shorten: A, $300/week; B, $100/week; C, $200/week; E, $100/week; and F, $400/week. Assume also that you can crash an activity down to 0 weeks in duration and that every week you can shorten the project is worth $250 to you. What activities would you crash? What is the total crashing cost?

••• **3.17** Bill Fennema, president of Fennema Construction, has developed the tasks, durations, and predecessor relationships in the following table for building new motels. Draw the AON network and answer the questions that follow.

		Time Estimates (in weeks)		
Activity	Immediate Predecessor(s)	Optimistic	Most Likely	Pessimistic
A	—	4	8	10
B	A	2	8	24
C	A	8	12	16
D	A	4	6	10
E	B	1	2	3
F	E, C	6	8	20
G	E, C	2	3	4
H	F	2	2	2
I	F	6	6	6
J	D, G, H	4	6	12
K	I, J	2	2	3

a) What is the expected (estimated) time for activity C?
b) What is the variance for activity C?
c) Based on the calculation of estimated times, what is the critical path?
d) What is the estimated time of the critical path?
e) What is the activity variance along the critical path?
f) What is the probability of completion of the project before week 36? Px

••• **3.18** What is the minimum cost of crashing the following project that James Walters manages at Ball State University by 4 days?

Activity	Normal Time (days)	Crash Time (days)	Normal Cost	Crash Cost	Immediate Predecessor(s)
A	6	5	$ 900	$1,000	—
B	8	6	300	400	—
C	4	3	500	600	—
D	5	3	900	1,200	A
E	8	5	1,000	1,600	C

Px

•• **3.19** Three activities are candidates for crashing on a project network for a large computer installation (all are, of course, critical). Activity details are in the following table:

Activity	Predecessor	Normal Time	Normal Cost	Crash Time	Crash Cost
A	—	7 days	$6,000	6 days	$6,600
B	A	4 days	1,200	2 days	3,000
C	B	11 days	4,000	9 days	6,000

a) What action would you take to reduce the critical path by 1 day?
b) Assuming no other paths become critical, what action would you take to reduce the critical path one additional day?
c) What is the total cost of the 2-day reduction? Px

••• **3.20** Development of a new deluxe version of a particular software product is being considered by Ravi Behara's software house. The activities necessary for the completion of this project are listed in the following table:

Activity	Normal Time (weeks)	Crash Time (weeks)	Normal Cost	Crash Cost	Immediate Predecessor(s)
A	4	3	$2,000	$2,600	—
B	2	1	2,200	2,800	—
C	3	3	500	500	—
D	8	4	2,300	2,600	A
E	6	3	900	1,200	B
F	3	2	3,000	4,200	C
G	4	2	1,400	2,000	D, E

a) What is the project completion date?
b) What is the total cost required for completing this project on normal time?
c) If you wish to reduce the time required to complete this project by 1 week, which activity should be crashed, and how much will this increase the total cost?
d) What is the maximum time that can be crashed? How much would costs increase? Px

••• **3.21** The estimated times and immediate predecessors for the activities in a project at Caesar Douglas's retinal scanning company are given in the following table. Assume that the activity times are independent.

		Time (weeks)		
Activity	Immediate Predecessor	*a*	*m*	*b*
A	—	9	10	11
B	—	4	10	16
C	A	9	10	11
D	B	5	8	11

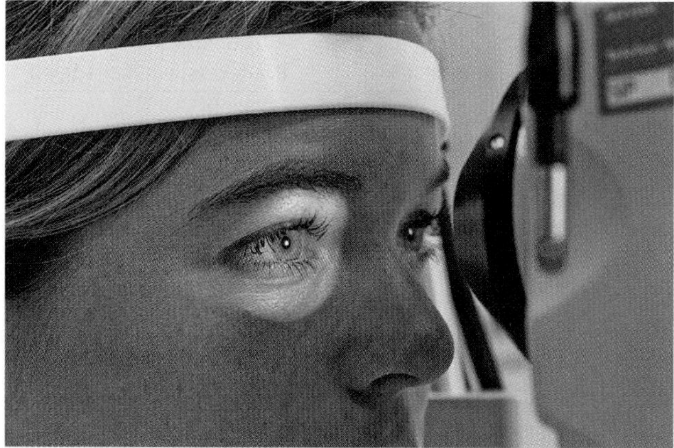

a) Calculate the expected time and variance for each activity.
b) What is the expected completion time of the critical path? What is the expected completion time of the other path in the network?
c) What is the variance of the critical path? What is the variance of the other path in the network?
d) If the time to complete path A–C is normally distributed, what is the probability that this path will be finished in 22 weeks or less?
e) If the time to complete path B–D is normally distributed, what is the probability that this path will be finished in 22 weeks or less?
f) Explain why the probability that the *critical path* will be finished in 22 weeks or less is not necessarily the probability that the *project* will be finished in 22 weeks or less. PX

••• **3.22** Jack Kanet Manufacturing produces custom-built pollution control devices for medium-size steel mills. The most recent project undertaken by Jack requires 14 different activities.
a) Jack's managers would like to determine the total project completion time (in days) and those activities that lie along the critical path. The appropriate data are shown in the following table.
b) What is the probability of being done in 53 days?
c) What date results in a 99% probability of completion?

Activity	Immediate Predecessor(s)	Optimistic Time	Most Likely Time	Pessimistic Time
A	—	4	6	7
B	—	1	2	3
C	A	6	6	6
D	A	5	8	11
E	B, C	1	9	18
F	D	2	3	6
G	D	1	7	8
H	E, F	4	4	6
I	G, H	1	6	8
J	I	2	5	7
K	I	8	9	11
L	J	2	4	6
M	K	1	2	3
N	L, M	6	8	10

PX

••• **3.23** Dream Team Productions, a firm hired to coordinate the release of the movie *Paycheck* (starring Uma Thurman and Ben Affleck), identified 16 activities to be completed before the release of the film.
a) How many weeks in advance of the film release should Dream Team have started its marketing campaign? What is the critical path? The tasks (in time units of weeks) are as follows:

Activity	Immediate Predecessors	Optimistic Time	Most Likely Time	Pessimistic Time
A	—	1	2	4
B	—	3	3.5	4
C	—	10	12	13
D	—	4	5	7
E	—	2	4	5
F	A	6	7	8
G	B	2	4	5.5
H	C	5	7.7	9
I	C	9.9	10	12
J	C	2	4	5
K	D	2	4	6
L	E	2	4	6
M	F, G, H	5	6	6.5
N	J, K, L	1	1.1	2
O	I, M	5	7	8
P	N	5	7	9

b) If activities I and J were not necessary, what impact would this have on the critical path and the number of weeks needed to complete the marketing campaign? PX

•• **3.24** Using PERT, Harold Benson was able to determine that the expected project completion time for the construction of a pleasure yacht is 21 months, and the project variance is 4.
a) What is the probability that the project will be completed in 17 months?
b) What is the probability that the project will be completed in 20 months?
c) What is the probability that the project will be completed in 23 months?
d) What is the probability that the project will be completed in 25 months?
e) What is the due date that yields a 95% chance of completion? PX

••• **3.25** Bolling Electronics manufactures DVD players for commercial use. W. Blaker Bolling, president of Bolling Electronics, is contemplating producing DVD players for home use. The activities necessary to build an experimental model and related data are given in the following table:

Activity	Normal Time (weeks)	Crash Time (weeks)	Normal Cost ($)	Crash Cost ($)	Immediate Predecessor(s)
A	3	2	1,000	1,600	—
B	2	1	2,000	2,700	—
C	1	1	300	300	—
D	7	3	1,300	1,600	A
E	6	3	850	1,000	B
F	2	1	4,000	5,000	C
G	4	2	1,500	2,000	D, E

a) What is the project completion date?
b) Crash this project to 10 weeks at the least cost.
c) Crash this project to 7 weeks (which is the maximum it can be crashed) at the least cost. Px

••• **3.26** The Maser is a new custom-designed sports car. An analysis of the task of building the Maser reveals the following list of relevant activities, their immediate predecessors, and their duration[6]:

Job Letter	Description	Immediate Predecessor(s)	Normal Time (days)
A	Start	—	0
B	Design	A	8
C	Order special accessories	B	0.1
D	Build frame	B	1
E	Build doors	B	1
F	Attach axles, wheels, gas tank	D	1
G	Build body shell	B	2
H	Build transmission and drivetrain	B	3
I	Fit doors to body shell	G, E	1
J	Build engine	B	4
K	Bench-test engine	J	2
L	Assemble chassis	F, H, K	1
M	Road-test chassis	L	0.5
N	Paint body	I	2
O	Install wiring	N	1
P	Install interior	N	1.5
Q	Accept delivery of special accessories	C	5
R	Mount body and accessories on chassis	M, O, P, Q	1
S	Road test car	R	0.5
T	Attach exterior trim	S	1
U	Finish	T	0

a) Draw a network diagram for the project.
b) Mark the critical path and state its length.
c) If the Maser had to be completed 2 days earlier, would it help to:
 i) Buy preassembled transmissions and drivetrains?
 ii) Install robots to halve engine-building time?
 iii) Speed delivery of special accessories by 3 days?
d) How might resources be borrowed from activities on the noncritical path to speed activities on the critical path? Px

[6]Source: James A. D. Stoner and Charles Wankel, *Management*, 3rd ed. (Upper Saddle River, NJ: Prentice Hall): 195.

► **Refer to myomlab for these additional homework problems: 3.27–3.33**

Case Studies

► Southwestern University: (A)*

Southwestern University (SWU), a large state college in Stephenville, Texas, 30 miles southwest of the Dallas/Fort Worth metroplex, enrolls close to 20,000 students. In a typical town–gown relationship, the school is a dominant force in the small city, with more students during fall and spring than permanent residents.

A longtime football powerhouse, SWU is a member of the Big Eleven conference and is usually in the top 20 in college football rankings. To bolster its chances of reaching the elusive and long-desired number-one ranking, in 2003, SWU hired the legendary Bo Pitterno as its head coach.

One of Pitterno's demands on joining SWU had been a new stadium. With attendance increasing, SWU administrators began to face the issue head-on. After 6 months of study, much political arm wrestling, and some serious financial analysis, Dr. Joel Wisner, president of Southwestern University, had reached a decision to expand the capacity at its on-campus stadium.

Adding thousands of seats, including dozens of luxury skyboxes, would not please everyone. The influential Pitterno had argued the need for a first-class stadium, one with built-in dormitory rooms for his players and a palatial office appropriate for the coach

* This integrated study runs throughout the text. Other issues facing Southwestern's football expansion include (B) forecasting game attendance (Chapter 4); (C) quality of facilities (Chapter 6); (D) break-even analysis for food services (Supplement 7 Web site); (E) location of the new stadium (Chapter 8 Web site); (F) inventory planning of football programs (Chapter 12 Web site); and (G) scheduling of campus security officers/staff for game days (Chapter 13).

▼ **TABLE 3.6 Southwestern University Project**

			Time Estimates (days)			
Activity	**Description**	**Predecessor(s)**	**Optimistic**	**Most Likely**	**Pessimistic**	**Crash Cost/Day**
A	Bonding, insurance, tax structuring	—	20	30	40	$1,500
B	Foundation, concrete footings for boxes	A	20	65	80	3,500
C	Upgrading skybox stadium seating	A	50	60	100	4,000
D	Upgrading walkways, stairwells, elevators	C	30	50	100	1,900
E	Interior wiring, lathes	B	25	30	35	9,500
F	Inspection approvals	E	0.1	0.1	0.1	0
G	Plumbing	D, F	25	30	35	2,500
H	Painting	G	10	20	30	2,000
I	Hardware/AC/metal workings	H	20	25	60	2,000
J	Tile/carpet/windows	H	8	10	12	6,000
K	Inspection	J	0.1	0.1	0.1	0
L	Final detail work/cleanup	I, K	20	25	60	4,500

of a future NCAA champion team. But the decision was made, and *everyone*, including the coach, would learn to live with it.

The job now was to get construction going immediately after the 2009 season ended. This would allow exactly 270 days until the 2010 season opening game. The contractor, Hill Construction (Bob Hill being an alumnus, of course), signed his contract. Bob Hill looked at the tasks his engineers had outlined and looked President Wisner in the eye. "I guarantee the team will be able to take the field on schedule next year," he said with a sense of confidence. "I sure hope so," replied Wisner. "The contract penalty of $10,000 per day for running late is nothing compared to what Coach Pitterno will do to you if our opening game with Penn State is delayed or canceled." Hill, sweating slightly, did not need to respond. In football-crazy Texas, Hill Construction would be *mud* if the 270-day target was missed.

Back in his office, Hill again reviewed the data (see Table 3.6) and noted that optimistic time estimates can be used as crash times. He then gathered his foremen. "Folks, if we're not 75% sure we'll finish this stadium in less than 270 days, I want this project crashed! Give me the cost figures for a target date of 250 days—also for 240 days. I want to be *early*, not just on time!"

Discussion Questions

1. Develop a network drawing for Hill Construction and determine the critical path. How long is the project expected to take?
2. What is the probability of finishing in 270 days?
3. If it is necessary to crash to 250 or 240 days, how would Hill do so, and at what costs? As noted in the case, assume that optimistic time estimates can be used as crash times.

▶ Project Management at Arnold Palmer Hospital — Video Case

The equivalent of a new kindergarten class is born every day at Orlando's Arnold Palmer Hospital. With more than 12,300 births in 2005 in a hospital that was designed in 1989 for a capacity of 6,500 births a year, the newborn intensive care unit was stretched to the limit. Moreover, with continuing strong population growth in central Florida, the hospital was often full. It was clear that new facilities were needed. After much analysis, forecasting, and discussion, the management team decided to build a new 273-bed building across the street from the existing hospital. But the facility had to be built in accordance with the hospital's Guiding Principles and its uniqueness as a health center dedicated to the specialized needs of women and infants. Those Guiding Principles are: *Family-centered focus, a healing environment where privacy and dignity are respected, sanctuary of caring that includes warm, serene surroundings with natural lighting, sincere and dedicated staff providing the highest quality care, and patient-centered flow and function.*

The vice president of business development, Karl Hodges, wanted a hospital that was designed from the inside out by the people who understood the Guiding Principles, who knew most about the current system, and who were going to use the new system, namely, the doctors and nurses. Hodges and his staff spent 13 months discussing expansion needs with this group, as well as with patients and the community before developing a proposal for the new facility on December 17, 2001. An administrative team created 35 user groups, which held over 1,000 planning meetings (lasting from 45 minutes to a whole day). They even created a "Supreme Court" to deal with conflicting views on the multifaceted issues facing the new hospital.

Funding and regulatory issues added substantial complexity to this major expansion, and Hodges was very concerned that the project stay on time and within budget. Tom Hyatt, director of facility development, was given the task of onsite manager of the $100 million project, in addition to overseeing ongoing renovations, expansions, and other projects. The activities in the multi-year project for the new building at Arnold Palmer are shown in Table 3.7.

▼ **TABLE 3.7 Expansion Planning and Arnold Palmer Hospital Construction Activities and Times**[a]

Activity	Scheduled Time	Precedence Activity(ies)
1. Proposal and review	1 month	—
2. Establish master schedule	2 weeks	1
3. Architect selection process	5 weeks	1
4. Survey whole campus and its needs	1 month	1
5. Conceptual architect's plans	6 weeks	3
6. Cost estimating	2 months	2, 4, 5
7. Deliver plans to board for consideration/decision	1 month	6
8. Surveys/regulatory review	6 weeks	6
9. Construction manager selection	9 weeks	6
10. State review of need for more hospital beds ("Certificate of Need")	3.5 months	7, 8
11. Design drawings	4 months	10
12. Construction documents	5 months	9, 11
13. Site preparation/demolish existing building	9 weeks	11
14. Construction start/building pad	2 months	12, 13
15. Relocate utilities	6 weeks	12
16. Deep foundations	2 months	14
17. Building structure in place	9 months	16
18. Exterior skin/roofing	4 months	17
19. Interior buildout	12 months	17
20. Building inspections	5 weeks	15, 19
21. Occupancy	1 month	20

[a]This list of activities is abbreviated for purposes of this case study. For simplification, assume each week = .25 months (i.e., 2 weeks = .5 month, 6 weeks = 1.5 months, etc.).

Discussion Questions*

1. Develop the network for planning and construction of the new hospital at Arnold Palmer.
2. What is the critical path and how long is the project expected to take?
3. Why is the construction of this 11-story building any more complex than construction of an equivalent office building?
4. What percent of the whole project duration was spent in planning that occurred prior to the proposal and reviews? Prior to the actual building construction? Why?

* You may wish to view the video accompanying this case before addressing these questions.

▶ Managing Hard Rock's Rockfest

Video Case

At the Hard Rock Cafe, like many organizations, project management is a key planning tool. With Hard Rock's constant growth in hotels and cafes, remodeling of existing cafes, scheduling for Hard Rock Live concert and event venues, and planning the annual Rockfest, managers rely on project management techniques and software to maintain schedule and budget performance.

"Without Microsoft Project," says Hard Rock Vice-President Chris Tomasso, "there is no way to keep so many people on the same page." Tomasso is in charge of the Rockfest event, which is attended by well over 100,000 enthusiastic fans. The challenge is pulling it off within a tight 9-month planning horizon. As the event approaches, Tomasso devotes greater energy to its activities. For the first 3 months, Tomasso updates his Microsoft Project charts monthly. Then at the 6-month mark, he updates his progress weekly. At the 9-month mark, he checks and corrects his schedule twice a week.

Early in the project management process, Tomasso identifies 10 major tasks (called level-2 activities in a work breakdown structure, or WBS)[†]: talent booking, ticketing, marketing/PR, online promotion, television, show production, travel, sponsorships, operations, and merchandising. Using a WBS, each of these is further divided into a series of subtasks. Table 3.8 identifies 26 of the major activities and subactivities, their immediate predecessors, and time estimates. Tomasso enters all these into the Microsoft Project software.[‡] Tomasso alters the Microsoft Project document and the time line as the project progresses. "It's okay to change it as long as you keep on track," he states.

The day of the rock concert itself is not the end of the project planning. "It's nothing but surprises. A band not being able to get to the venue because of traffic jams is a surprise, but an 'anticipated' surprise. We had a helicopter on stand-by ready to fly the band in," says Tomasso.

On completion of Rockfest in July, Tomasso and his team have a 3-month reprieve before starting the project planning process again.

Activity	Description	Predecessor(s)	Time (weeks)
A	Finalize site and building contracts	—	7
B	Select local promoter	A	3
C	Hire production manager	A	3
D	Design promotional Web site	B	5
E	Set TV deal	D	6
F	Hire director	E	4
G	Plan for TV camera placement	F	2
H	Target headline entertainers	B	4
I	Target support entertainers	H	4
J	Travel accommodations for talent	I	10
K	Set venue capacity	C	2
L	Ticketmaster contract	D, K	3
M	On-site ticketing	L	8
N	Sound and staging	C	6
O	Passes and stage credentials	G, R	7
P	Travel accommodations for staff	B	20
Q	Hire sponsor coordinator	B	4
R	Finalize sponsors	Q	4
S	Define/place signage for sponsors	R, X	3
T	Hire operations manager	A	4
U	Develop site plan	T	6
V	Hire security director	T	7
W	Set police/fire security plan	V	4
X	Power, plumbing, AC, toilet services	U	8
Y	Secure merchandise deals	B	6
Z	Online merchandise sales	Y	6

▶ **TABLE 3.8**
Some of the Major Activities and Subactivities in the Rockfest Plan

Discussion Questions[§]

1. Identify the critical path and its activities for Rockfest. How long does the project take?
2. Which activities have a slack time of 8 weeks or more?
3. Identify five major challenges a project manager faces in events such as this one.
4. Why is a work breakdown structure useful in a project such as this? Take the 26 activities and break them into what you think should be level-2, level-3, and level-4 tasks.

[†]The level-1 activity is the Rockfest concert itself.
[‡]There are actually 127 activities used by Tomasso; the list is abbreviated for this case study.

[§]You may wish to view the video accompanying this case before addressing these questions.

▶**Additional Case Study:** Visit **www.myomlab.com** or **www.pearsonhighered.com/heizer** for this free case study:
Shale Oil Company: This oil refinery must shut down for maintenance of a major piece of equipment.

Bibliography

Balakrishnan, R., B. Render, and R. M. Stair. *Managerial Decision Modeling with Spreadsheets*, 2nd ed. Upper Saddle River, NJ: Prentice Hall (2007).

Cleland, D. L., and L. R. Ireland. *Project Management*, 5th ed. New York: McGraw-Hill/Irwin (2007).

Gray, C. L., and E. W. Larson. *Project Management with MS Project.* New York: McGraw-Hill/Irwin (2008).

Helgadottir, Hilder. "The Ethical Dimension of Project Management." *International Journal of Project Management* 26, no. 7 (October 2008): 743.

Karlos, A., et al. "Foundations of Project Management." *International Journal of Project Management* 27, no. 1 (January 2009): 1.

Kerzner, H. *Project Management Case Studies*, 3rd ed. New York: Wiley (2009).

Kumar, P. P. "Effective Use of Gantt Chart for Managing Large-Scale Projects." *Cost Engineering* 47, no. 7 (July 2005): 14–21.

Ling, F. Y. Y., et al. "Key Project Management Practices Affecting Singaporean Firms' Project Performance in China."

International Journal of Project Management 27, no. 1 (January, 2009): 59.

Matta, N. F., and R. N. Ashkenas. "Why Good Projects Fail Anyways." *Harvard Business Review* (September 2003): 109–114.

Maylor, Harvey. *Project Management*, 4th ed. Upper Saddle River, NJ: Prentice Hall (2008).

Meredith, J. R., and S. Mantel. *Project Management*, 7th ed. New York: Wiley (2008).

Oates, David. "Understanding and Solving the Causes of Project Failure." *Knowledge Management Review* 9, no. 5 (May–June 2006): 5.

Render, B., R. M. Stair, and M. Hanna. *Quantitative Analysis for Management*, 10th ed. Upper Saddle River, NJ: Prentice Hall (2009).

Verzuh, Eric. *The Fast Forward MBA in Project Management.* New York: Wiley (2008).

Wysocki, R. K. *Effective Project Management,* 5th ed. New York: Wiley (2009).

Chapter 3 **Rapid Review**

Main Heading	Review Material	myomlab
THE IMPORTANCE OF PROJECT MANAGEMENT (p. 58)	The management of projects involves three phases: 1. **Planning**—This phase includes goal setting, defining the project, and team organization. 2. **Scheduling**—This phase relates people, money, and supplies to specific activities and relates activities to each other. 3. **Controlling**—Here the firm monitors resources, costs, quality, and budgets. It also revises or changes plans and shifts resources to meet time and cost demands.	**VIDEO 3.1** Project Management at Hard Rock's Rockfest
PROJECT PLANNING (pp. 58–61)	Projects can be defined as a series of related tasks directed toward a major output. ■ **Project organization**—An organization formed to ensure that programs (projects) receive the proper management and attention. ■ **Work breakdown structure (WBS)**—Defines a project by dividing it into more and more detailed components.	Problem 3.1
PROJECT SCHEDULING (pp. 61–62)	■ **Gantt charts**—Planning charts used to schedule resources and allocate time. Project scheduling serves several purposes: 1. It shows the relationship of each activity to others and to the whole project. 2. It identifies the precedence relationships among activities. 3. It encourages the setting of realistic time and cost estimates for each activity. 4. It helps make better use of people, money, and material resources by identifying critical bottlenecks in the project.	Problem 3.8
PROJECT CONTROLLING (pp. 62)	Computerized programs produce a broad variety of PERT/CPM reports, including (1) detailed cost breakdowns for each task, (2) total program labor curves, (3) cost distribution tables, (4) functional cost and hour summaries, (5) raw material and expenditure forecasts, (6) variance reports, (7) time analysis reports, and (8) work status reports.	**VIDEO 3.2** Project Management at Arnold Palmer Hospital
PROJECT MANAGEMENT TECHNIQUES: PERT AND CPM (pp. 63–68)	■ **Program evaluation and review technique (PERT)**—A project management technique that employs three time estimates for each activity. ■ **Critical path method (CPM)**—A project management technique that uses only one estimate per activity. ■ **Critical path**—The computed *longest* time path(s) through a network. PERT and CPM both follow six basic steps. The activities on the critical path will delay the entire project if they are not completed on time. ■ **Activity-on-node (AON)**—A network diagram in which nodes designate activities. ■ **Activity-on-arrow (AOA)**—A network diagram in which arrows designate activities. In an AOA network, the nodes represent the starting and finishing times of an activity and are also called *events*. ■ **Dummy activity**—An activity having no time that is inserted into a network to maintain the logic of the network. A dummy ending activity can be added to the end of an AON diagram for a project that has multiple ending activities.	Problems: 3.3–3.7, 3.9, 3.10, 3.12, 3.15 Virtual Office Hours for Solved Problems: 3.1, 3.2
DETERMINING THE PROJECT SCHEDULE (pp. 68–73)	■ **Critical path analysis**—A process that helps determine a project schedule. To find the critical path, we calculate two distinct starting and ending times for each activity: • *Earliest start (ES)* = Earliest time at which an activity can start, assuming that all predecessors have been completed • *Earliest finish (EF)* = Earliest time at which an activity can be finished • *Latest start (LS)* = Latest time at which an activity can start, without delaying the completion time of the entire project • *Latest finish (LF)* = Latest time by which an activity has to finish so as to not delay the completion time of the entire project ■ **Forward pass**—A process that identifies all the early start and early finish times. $ES = \text{Maximum } EF \text{ of all immediate predecessors}$ (3-1) $EF = ES + \text{Activity time}$ (3-2) ■ **Backward pass**—A process that identifies all the late start and late finish times. $LF = \text{Minimum } LS \text{ of all immediate following activities}$ (3-3) $LS = LF - \text{Activity time}$ (3-4) ■ **Slack time**—Free time for an activity. $\text{Slack} = LS - ES \quad \text{or} \quad \text{Slack} = LF - EF$ (3-5)	Problems: 3.11, 3.14, 3.15, 3.17, 3.20, 3.22, 3.23, 3.26

Main Heading	Review Material	PEARSON myomlab
	The activities with zero slack are called *critical activities* and are said to be on the critical path. The critical path is a continuous path through the project network that starts at the first activity in the project, terminates at the last activity in the project, and includes only critical activities.	Virtual Office Hours for Solved Problem: 3.3 **ACTIVE MODEL 3.1**
VARIABILITY IN ACTIVITY TIMES (pp. 73–79)	■ **Optimistic time** (a)—The "best" activity completion time that could be obtained in a PERT network. ■ **Pessimistic time** (b)—The "worst" activity time that could be expected in a PERT network. ■ **Most likely time** (m)—The most probable time to complete an activity in a PERT network. When using PERT, we often assume that activity time estimates follow the beta distribution. Expected activity time $t = (a + 4m + b)/6$ (3-6) Variance of Activity Completion Time $= [(b - a)/6]^2$ (3-7) σ_p^2 = Project variance = Σ(variances of activities on critical path) (3-8) Z = (Due date − expected date of completion)/σ_p (3-9) Due date = Expected completion time + $(Z \times \sigma_p)$ (3-10)	Problems: 3.13, 3.14. 3.21, 3.24 Virtual Office Hours for Solved Problems: 3.4, 3.5, 3.6
COST–TIME TRADE-OFFS AND PROJECT CRASHING (pp. 79–81)	■ **Crashing**—Shortening activity time in a network to reduce time on the critical path so total completion time is reduced. $\text{Crash cost per period} = \dfrac{(\text{Crash cost} - \text{Normal cost})}{(\text{Normal time} - \text{Crash time})}$ (3-11)	Problems: 3.16, 3.18, 3.19, 3.25 Virtual Office Hours for Solved Problem: 3.7
A CRITIQUE OF PERT AND CPM (pp. 81–82)	As with every technique for problem solving, PERT and CPM have a number of advantages as well as several limitations.	
USING MICROSOFT PROJECT TO MANAGE PROJECTS (pp. 82–85)	Microsoft Project, the most popular example of specialized project management software, is extremely useful in drawing project networks, identifying the project schedule, and managing project costs and other resources.	

Self Test

■ **Before taking the self-test,** refer to the learning objectives listed at the beginning of the chapter and the key terms listed at the end of the chapter.

LO1. Which of the following statements regarding Gantt charts is true?
- **a)** Gantt charts give a timeline and precedence relationships for each activity of a project.
- **b)** Gantt charts use the four standard spines: Methods, Materials, Manpower, and Machinery.
- **c)** Gantt charts are visual devices that show the duration of activities in a project.
- **d)** Gantt charts are expensive.
- **e)** All of the above are true.

LO2. Which of the following is true about AOA and AON networks?
- **a)** In AOA, arrows represent activities.
- **b)** In AON, nodes represent activities.
- **c)** Activities consume time and resources.
- **d)** Nodes are also called *events* in AOA.
- **e)** All of the above.

LO3. Slack time equals:
- **a)** ES + t.
- **b)** LS – ES.
- **c)** zero.
- **d)** EF – ES.

LO4. The critical path of a network is the:
- **a)** shortest-time path through the network.
- **b)** path with the fewest activities.
- **c)** path with the most activities.
- **d)** longest-time path through the network.

LO5. PERT analysis computes the variance of the total project completion time as:
- **a)** the sum of the variances of all activities in the project.
- **b)** the sum of the variances of all activities on the critical path.
- **c)** the sum of the variances of all activities not on the critical path.
- **d)** the variance of the final activity of the project.

LO6. The crash cost per period:
- **a)** is the difference in costs divided by the difference in times (crash and normal).
- **b)** is considered to be linear in the range between normal and crash.
- **c)** needs to be determined so that the smallest cost values on the critical path can be considered for time reduction first.
- **d)** all of the above.

Answers: LO1. c; LO2. e; LO3. b; LO4. d; LO5. b; LO6. d.

4 Forecasting

Chapter Outline

FORECASTING PROVIDES A COMPETITIVE ADVANTAGE FOR DISNEY

When it comes to the world's most respected global brands, Walt Disney Parks & Resorts is a visible leader. Although the monarch of this magic kingdom is no man but a mouse—Mickey Mouse—it's CEO Robert Iger who daily manages the entertainment giant.

Disney's global portfolio includes Hong Kong Disneyland (opened 2005), Disneyland Paris (1992), and Tokyo Disneyland (1983). But it is Walt Disney World Resort (in Florida) and Disneyland Resort (in California) that drive profits in this $43 billion corporation, which is ranked 54th in the *Fortune* 500 and 79th in the *Financial Times* Global 500.

Revenues at Disney are all about people—how many visit the parks and how they spend money while there. When Iger receives a daily report from his four theme parks near Orlando, the report contains only two numbers: the *forecast* of yesterday's attendance at the parks (Magic Kingdom, Epcot, Disney's Animal Kingdom, Disney-MGM Studios, Typhoon Lagoon, and Blizzard Beach) and the *actual* attendance. An error close to zero is expected. Iger takes his forecasts very seriously.

Mickey and Minnie Mouse, and other Disney characters, with Cinderella Castle in the background, provide the public image of Disney to the world. Forecasts drive the work schedules of 58,000 cast members working at Walt Disney World Resort near Orlando.

The giant sphere is the symbol of Epcot, one of Disney's four Orlando parks, for which forecasts of meals, lodging, entertainment, and transportation must be made. This Disney monorail moves guests among parks and the 20 hotels on the massive 47-square-mile property (about the size of San Francisco and twice the size of Manhattan).

▶ A daily forecast of attendance is made by adjusting Disney's annual operating plan for weather forecasts, the previous day's crowds, conventions, and seasonal variations. One of the two water parks at Walt Disney World Resort, Typhoon Lagoon, is shown here.

◀ Forecasts are critical to making sure rides are not overcrowded. Disney is good at "managing demand" with techniques such as adding more street activities to reduce long lines for rides.

▲ Disney uses characters such as Minnie Mouse to entertain guests when lines are forecast to be long. On slow days, Disney calls fewer cast members to work.

The forecasting team at Walt Disney World Resort doesn't just do a daily prediction, however, and Iger is not its only customer. The team also provides daily, weekly, monthly, annual, and 5-year forecasts to the labor management, maintenance, operations, finance, and park scheduling departments. Forecasters use judgmental models, econometric models, moving-average models, and regression analysis.

With 20% of Walt Disney World Resort's customers coming from outside the United States, its economic model includes such variables as gross domestic product (GDP), cross-exchange rates, and arrivals into the U.S. Disney also uses 35 analysts and 70 field people to survey 1 million people each year. The surveys, administered to guests at the parks and its 20 hotels, to employees, and to travel industry professionals, examine future travel plans and experiences at the parks. This helps forecast not only attendance but behavior at each ride (e.g., how long people will wait, how many times they will ride). Inputs to the monthly forecasting model include airline specials, speeches by the chair of the Federal Reserve, and Wall Street trends. Disney even monitors 3,000 school districts inside and outside the U.S. for holiday/vacation schedules. With this approach, Disney's 5-year attendance forecast yields just a 5% error on average. Its annual forecasts have a 0% to 3% error.

Attendance forecasts for the parks drive a whole slew of management decisions. For example, capacity on any day can be increased by opening at 8 A.M. instead of the usual 9 A.M., by opening more shows or rides, by adding more food/beverage carts (9 million hamburgers and 50 million Cokes are sold per year!), and by bringing in more employees (called "cast members"). Cast members are scheduled in 15-minute intervals throughout the parks for flexibility. Demand can be managed by limiting the number of guests admitted to the parks, with the "FAST PASS" reservation system, and by shifting crowds from rides to more street parades.

At Disney, forecasting is a key driver in the company's success and competitive advantage.

Chapter 4 **Learning Objectives**

AUTHOR COMMENT An increasingly complex world economy makes forecasting challenging.

WHAT IS FORECASTING?

Every day, managers like those at Disney make decisions without knowing what will happen in the future. They order inventory without knowing what sales will be, purchase new equipment despite uncertainty about demand for products, and make investments without knowing what profits will be. Managers are always trying to make better estimates of what will happen in the future in the face of uncertainty. Making good estimates is the main purpose of forecasting.

In this chapter, we examine different types of forecasts and present a variety of forecasting models. Our purpose is to show that there are many ways for managers to forecast. We also provide an overview of business sales forecasting and describe how to prepare, monitor, and judge the accuracy of a forecast. Good forecasts are an *essential* part of efficient service and manufacturing operations.

Forecasting
The art and science of predicting future events.

Forecasting is the art and science of predicting future events. Forecasting may involve taking historical data and projecting them into the future with some sort of mathematical model. It may be a subjective or intuitive prediction. Or it may involve a combination of these—that is, a mathematical model adjusted by a manager's good judgment.

As we introduce different forecasting techniques in this chapter, you will see that there is seldom one superior method. What works best in one firm under one set of conditions may be a complete disaster in another organization, or even in a different department of the same firm. In addition, you will see that there are limits as to what can be expected from forecasts. They are seldom, if ever, perfect. They are also costly and time-consuming to prepare and monitor.

Few businesses, however, can afford to avoid the process of forecasting by just waiting to see what happens and then taking their chances. Effective planning in both the short run and long run depends on a forecast of demand for the company's products.

Forecasting Time Horizons

LO1: Understand the three time horizons and which models apply for each

A forecast is usually classified by the *future time horizon* that it covers. Time horizons fall into three categories:

1. *Short-range forecast:* This forecast has a time span of up to 1 year but is generally less than 3 months. It is used for planning purchasing, job scheduling, workforce levels, job assignments, and production levels.
2. *Medium-range forecast:* A medium-range, or intermediate, forecast generally spans from 3 months to 3 years. It is useful in sales planning, production planning and budgeting, cash budgeting, and analysis of various operating plans.
3. *Long-range forecast:* Generally 3 years or more in time span, long-range forecasts are used in planning for new products, capital expenditures, facility location or expansion, and research and development.

Medium and long-range forecasts are distinguished from short-range forecasts by three features:

1. First, intermediate and long-run forecasts *deal with more comprehensive issues* and support management decisions regarding planning and products, plants, and processes. Implementing some facility decisions, such as GM's decision to open a new Brazilian manufacturing plant, can take 5 to 8 years from inception to completion.
2. Second, short-term forecasting usually *employs different methodologies* than longer-term forecasting. Mathematical techniques, such as moving averages, exponential smoothing,

and trend extrapolation (all of which we shall examine shortly), are common to short-run projections. Broader, *less* quantitative methods are useful in predicting such issues as whether a new product, like the optical disk recorder, should be introduced into a company's product line.

3. Finally, as you would expect, short-range forecasts *tend to be more accurate* than longer-range forecasts. Factors that influence demand change every day. Thus, as the time horizon lengthens, it is likely that forecast accuracy will diminish. It almost goes without saying, then, that sales forecasts must be updated regularly to maintain their value and integrity. After each sales period, forecasts should be reviewed and revised.

The Influence of Product Life Cycle

Another factor to consider when developing sales forecasts, especially longer ones, is product life cycle. Products, and even services, do not sell at a constant level throughout their lives. Most successful products pass through four stages: (1) introduction, (2) growth, (3) maturity, and (4) decline.

Products in the first two stages of the life cycle (such as virtual reality and the Boeing 787 Dreamliner) need longer forecasts than those in the maturity and decline stages (such as large SUVs and skateboards). Forecasts that reflect life cycle are useful in projecting different staffing levels, inventory levels, and factory capacity as the product passes from the first to the last stage. The challenge of introducing new products is treated in more detail in Chapter 5.

Types of Forecasts

Organizations use three major types of forecasts in planning future operations:

1. **Economic forecasts** address the business cycle by predicting inflation rates, money supplies, housing starts, and other planning indicators.
2. **Technological forecasts** are concerned with rates of technological progress, which can result in the birth of exciting new products, requiring new plants and equipment.
3. **Demand forecasts** are projections of demand for a company's products or services. These forecasts, also called *sales forecasts*, drive a company's production, capacity, and scheduling systems and serve as inputs to financial, marketing, and personnel planning.

Economic forecasts
Planning indicators that are valuable in helping organizations prepare medium- to long-range forecasts.

Technological forecasts
Long-term forecasts concerned with the rates of technological progress.

Demand forecasts
Projections of a company's sales for each time period in the planning horizon.

Economic and technological forecasting are specialized techniques that may fall outside the role of the operations manager. The emphasis in this book will therefore be on demand forecasting.

THE STRATEGIC IMPORTANCE OF FORECASTING

Good forecasts are of critical importance in all aspects of a business: *The forecast is the only estimate of demand until actual demand becomes known.* Forecasts of demand therefore drive decisions in many areas. Let's look at the impact of product demand forecast on three activities: (1) human resources, (2) capacity, and (3) supply-chain management.

Human Resources

VIDEO 4.1
Forecasting at Hard Rock Cafe

Hiring, training, and laying off workers all depend on anticipated demand. If the human resources department must hire additional workers without warning, the amount of training declines and the quality of the workforce suffers. A large Louisiana chemical firm almost lost its biggest customer when a quick expansion to around-the-clock shifts led to a total breakdown in quality control on the second and third shifts.

Capacity

When capacity is inadequate, the resulting shortages can lead to loss of customers and market share. This is exactly what happened to Nabisco when it underestimated the huge demand for its new low-fat Snackwell Devil's Food Cookies. Even with production lines working overtime, Nabisco could not keep up with demand, and it lost customers. As the photo on the next page shows, Amazon made the same error with its Kindle. On the other hand, when excess capacity exists, costs can skyrocket.

Even vaunted Amazon can make a major forecasting error, as it did in the case of its much-hyped Kindle e-book reader. With the holiday shopping season at hand, Amazon's Web page announced "Due to heavy customer demand, Kindle is sold out . . . ships in 11 to 13 weeks." Underforecasting demand for the product was the culprit, according to the Taiwanese manufacturer Prime View, which has since ramped up production.

Supply-Chain Management

Good supplier relations and the ensuing price advantages for materials and parts depend on accurate forecasts. In the global marketplace, where expensive components for Boeing 787 jets are manufactured in dozens of countries, coordination driven by forecasts is critical. Scheduling transportation to Seattle for final assembly at the lowest possible cost means no last-minute surprises that can harm already-low profit margins.

SEVEN STEPS IN THE FORECASTING SYSTEM

Forecasting follows seven basic steps. We use Disney World, the focus of this chapter's *Global Company Profile*, as an example of each step:

1. *Determine the use of the forecast:* Disney uses park attendance forecasts to drive decisions about staffing, opening times, ride availability, and food supplies.
2. *Select the items to be forecasted:* For Disney World, there are six main parks. A forecast of daily attendance at each is the main number that determines labor, maintenance, and scheduling.
3. *Determine the time horizon of the forecast:* Is it short, medium, or long term? Disney develops daily, weekly, monthly, annual, and 5-year forecasts.
4. *Select the forecasting model(s):* Disney uses a variety of statistical models that we shall discuss, including moving averages, econometrics, and regression analysis. It also employs judgmental, or nonquantitative, models.
5. *Gather the data needed to make the forecast:* Disney's forecasting team employs 35 analysts and 70 field personnel to survey 1 million people/businesses every year. Disney also uses a firm called Global Insights for travel industry forecasts and gathers data on exchange rates, arrivals into the U.S., airline specials, Wall Street trends, and school vacation schedules.
6. *Make the forecast.*
7. *Validate and implement the results:* At Disney, forecasts are reviewed daily at the highest levels to make sure that the model, assumptions, and data are valid. Error measures are applied; then the forecasts are used to schedule personnel down to 15-minute intervals.

These seven steps present a systematic way of initiating, designing, and implementing a forecasting system. When the system is to be used to generate forecasts regularly over time, data must be routinely collected. Then actual computations are usually made by computer.

Regardless of the system that firms like Disney use, each company faces several realities:

- Forecasts are seldom perfect. This means that outside factors that we cannot predict or control often impact the forecast. Companies need to allow for this reality.
- Most forecasting techniques assume that there is some underlying stability in the system. Consequently, some firms automate their predictions using computerized forecasting software, then closely monitor only the product items whose demand is erratic.
- Both product family and aggregated forecasts are more accurate than individual product forecasts. Disney, for example, aggregates daily attendance forecasts by park. This approach helps balance the over- and underpredictions of each of the six attractions.

FORECASTING APPROACHES

AUTHOR COMMENT
Forecasting is part science and part art.

There are two general approaches to forecasting, just as there are two ways to tackle all decision modeling. One is a quantitative analysis; the other is a qualitative approach. **Quantitative forecasts** use a variety of mathematical models that rely on historical data and/or associative variables to forecast demand. Subjective or **qualitative forecasts** incorporate such factors as the decision maker's intuition, emotions, personal experiences, and value system in reaching a forecast. Some firms use one approach and some use the other. In practice, a combination of the two is usually most effective.

Quantitative forecasts
Forecasts that employ mathematical modeling to forecast demand.

Qualitative forecasts
Forecasts that incorporate such factors as the decision maker's intuition, emotions, personal experiences, and value system.

Overview of Qualitative Methods

In this section, we consider four different *qualitative* forecasting techniques:

LO2: Explain when to use each of the four qualitative models

1. **Jury of executive opinion:** Under this method, the opinions of a group of high-level experts or managers, often in combination with statistical models, are pooled to arrive at a group estimate of demand. Bristol-Myers Squibb Company, for example, uses 220 well-known research scientists as its jury of executive opinion to get a grasp on future trends in the world of medical research.
2. **Delphi method:** There are three different types of participants in the Delphi method: decision makers, staff personnel, and respondents. Decision makers usually consist of a group of 5 to 10 experts who will be making the actual forecast. Staff personnel assist decision makers by preparing, distributing, collecting, and summarizing a series of questionnaires and survey results. The respondents are a group of people, often located in different places, whose judgments are valued. This group provides inputs to the decision makers before the forecast is made.

   The state of Alaska, for example, has used the Delphi method to develop its long-range economic forecast. An amazing 90% of the state's budget is derived from 1.5 million barrels of oil pumped daily through a pipeline at Prudhoe Bay. The large Delphi panel of experts had to represent all groups and opinions in the state and all geographic areas. Delphi was the perfect forecasting tool because panelist travel could be avoided. It also meant that leading Alaskans could participate because their schedules were not affected by meetings and distances.
3. **Sales force composite:** In this approach, each salesperson estimates what sales will be in his or her region. These forecasts are then reviewed to ensure that they are realistic. Then they are combined at the district and national levels to reach an overall forecast. A variation of this approach occurs at Lexus, where every quarter Lexus dealers have a "make meeting." At this meeting, they talk about what is selling, in what colors, and with what options, so the factory knows what to build.
4. **Consumer market survey:** This method solicits input from customers or potential customers regarding future purchasing plans. It can help not only in preparing a forecast but also in improving product design and planning for new products. The consumer market survey and sales force composite methods can, however, suffer from overly optimistic forecasts that arise from customer input. The 2001 crash of the telecommunication industry was the result of overexpansion to meet "explosive customer demand." Where did these data come from? Oplink Communications, a Nortel Networks supplier, says its "company forecasts over the last few years were based mainly on informal conversations with customers."[1]

Jury of executive opinion
A forecasting technique that uses the opinion of a small group of high-level managers to form a group estimate of demand.

Delphi method
A forecasting technique using a group process that allows experts to make forecasts.

Sales force composite
A forecasting technique based on salespersons' estimates of expected sales.

Consumer market survey
A forecasting method that solicits input from customers or potential customers regarding future purchasing plans.

Overview of Quantitative Methods

Five quantitative forecasting methods, all of which use historical data, are described in this chapter. They fall into two categories:

1. Naive approach 2. Moving averages 3. Exponential smoothing 4. Trend projection	**time-series models**
5. Linear regression	**associative model**

[1]"Lousy Sales Forecasts Helped Fuel the Telecom Mess," *The Wall Street Journal* (July 9, 2001): B1–B4.

Time series
A forecasting technique that uses a series of past data points to make a forecast.

Time-Series Models **Time-series** models predict on the assumption that the future is a function of the past. In other words, they look at what has happened over a period of time and use a series of past data to make a forecast. If we are predicting sales of lawn mowers, we use the past sales for lawn mowers to make the forecasts.

Associative Models Associative models, such as linear regression, incorporate the variables or factors that might influence the quantity being forecast. For example, an associative model for lawn mower sales might use factors such as new housing starts, advertising budget, and competitors' prices.

AUTHOR COMMENT
Here is the meat of this chapter. We now show you a wide variety of models that use time-series data.

TIME-SERIES FORECASTING

A time series is based on a sequence of evenly spaced (weekly, monthly, quarterly, and so on) data points. Examples include weekly sales of Nike Air Jordans, quarterly earnings reports of Microsoft stock, daily shipments of Coors beer, and annual consumer price indices. Forecasting time-series data implies that future values are predicted *only* from past values and that other variables, no matter how potentially valuable, may be ignored.

Decomposition of a Time Series

Analyzing time series means breaking down past data into components and then projecting them forward. A time series has four components:

1. *Trend* is the gradual upward or downward movement of the data over time. Changes in income, population, age distribution, or cultural views may account for movement in trend.
2. *Seasonality* is a data pattern that repeats itself after a period of days, weeks, months, or quarters. There are six common seasonality patterns:

AUTHOR COMMENT
The peak "seasons" for sales of Frito-Lay chips are the Super Bowl, Memorial Day, Labor Day, and the Fourth of July.

Period of Pattern	"Season" Length	Number of "Seasons" in Pattern
Week	Day	7
Month	Week	$4\text{–}4\frac{1}{2}$
Month	Day	28–31
Year	Quarter	4
Year	Month	12
Year	Week	52

   Restaurants and barber shops, for example, experience weekly seasons, with Saturday being the peak of business. See the *OM in Action* box "Forecasting at Olive Garden and Red Lobster." Beer distributors forecast yearly patterns, with monthly seasons. Three "seasons"—May, July, and September—each contain a big beer-drinking holiday.
3. *Cycles* are patterns in the data that occur every several years. They are usually tied into the business cycle and are of major importance in short-term business analysis and planning. Predicting business cycles is difficult because they may be affected by political events or by international turmoil.
4. *Random variations* are "blips" in the data caused by chance and unusual situations. They follow no discernible pattern, so they cannot be predicted.

Figure 4.1 illustrates a demand over a 4-year period. It shows the average, trend, seasonal components, and random variations around the demand curve. The average demand is the sum of the demand for each period divided by the number of data periods.

Naive Approach

Naive approach
A forecasting technique which assumes that demand in the next period is equal to demand in the most recent period.

The simplest way to forecast is to assume that demand in the next period will be equal to demand in the most recent period. In other words, if sales of a product—say, Nokia cell phones—were 68 units in January, we can forecast that February's sales will also be 68 phones. Does this make any sense? It turns out that for some product lines, this **naive approach** is the most cost-effective

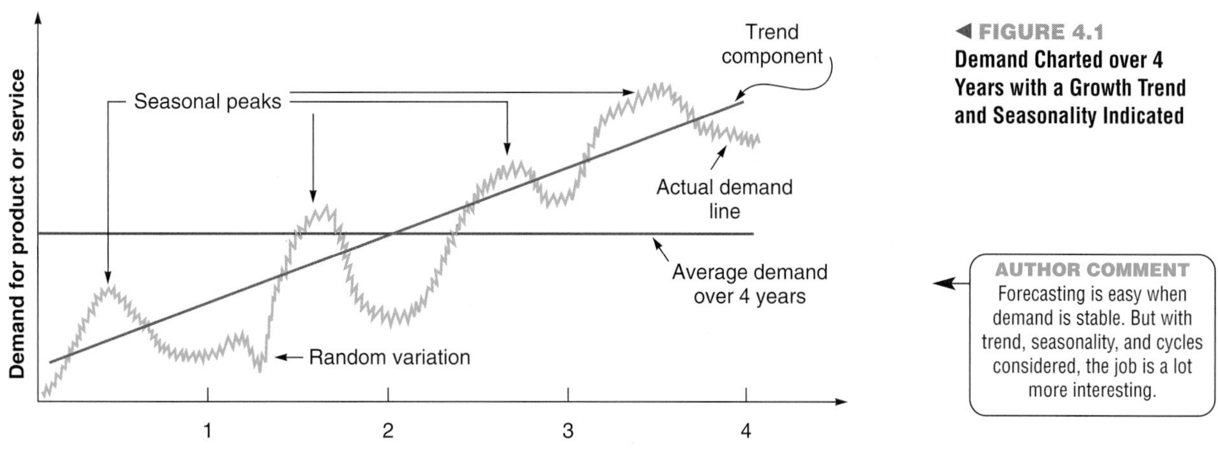

◀ **FIGURE 4.1**
Demand Charted over 4 Years with a Growth Trend and Seasonality Indicated

AUTHOR COMMENT
Forecasting is easy when demand is stable. But with trend, seasonality, and cycles considered, the job is a lot more interesting.

and efficient objective forecasting model. At least it provides a starting point against which more sophisticated models that follow can be compared.

Moving Averages

A **moving-average** forecast uses a number of historical actual data values to generate a forecast. Moving averages are useful *if we can assume that market demands will stay fairly steady over time*. A 4-month moving average is found by simply summing the demand during the past 4 months and dividing by 4. With each passing month, the most recent month's data are added to the sum of the previous 3 months' data, and the earliest month is dropped. This practice tends to smooth out short-term irregularities in the data series.

Moving averages
A forecasting method that uses an average of the *n* most recent periods of data to forecast the next period.

Mathematically, the simple moving average (which serves as an estimate of the next period's demand) is expressed as

$$\text{Moving average} = \frac{\Sigma \text{ demand in previous } n \text{ periods}}{n} \tag{4-1}$$

where n is the number of periods in the moving average—for example, 4, 5, or 6 months, respectively, for a 4-, 5-, or 6-period moving average.

OM in Action ► Forecasting at Olive Garden and Red Lobster

It's Friday night in the college town of Gainesville, Florida, and the local Olive Garden restaurant is humming. Customers may wait an average of 30 minutes for a table, but they can sample new wines and cheeses and admire scenic paintings of Italian villages on the Tuscan-style restaurant's walls. Then comes dinner with portions so huge that many people take home a doggie bag. The typical bill: under $15 per person.

Crowds flock to the Darden restaurant chain's Olive Garden, Red Lobster, Seasons 52, and Bahama Breeze for value and consistency—*and* they get it.

Every night, Darden's computers crank out forecasts that tell store managers what demand to anticipate the next day. The forecasting software generates a total meal forecast and breaks that down into specific menu items. The system tells a manager, for instance, that if 625 meals will be served the next day, "you will serve these items in these quantities. So before you go home, pull 25 pounds of shrimp and 30 pounds of crab out, and tell your operations people to prepare 42 portion packs of chicken, 75 scampi dishes, 8 stuffed flounders, and so on." Managers often fine tune the quantities based on local conditions, such as weather or a convention, but they know what their customers are going to order.

By relying on demand history, the forecasting system has cut millions of dollars of waste out of the system. The forecast also reduces labor costs by providing the necessary information for improved scheduling. Labor costs decreased almost a full percent in the first year, translating into additional millions in savings for the Darden chain. In the low-margin restaurant business, every dollar counts.

Source: Interviews with Darden executives.

Example 1 shows how moving averages are calculated.

EXAMPLE 1 ▶

Determining the moving average

Donna's Garden Supply wants a 3-month moving-average forecast, including a forecast for next January, for shed sales.

APPROACH ▶ Storage shed sales are shown in the middle column of the table below. A 3-month moving average appears on the right.

Month	Actual Shed Sales	3-Month Moving Average
January	10	
February	12	
March	13	
April	16	$(10 + 12 + 13)/3 = 11\frac{2}{3}$
May	19	$(12 + 13 + 16)/3 = 13\frac{2}{3}$
June	23	$(13 + 16 + 19)/3 = 16$
July	26	$(16 + 19 + 23)/3 = 19\frac{1}{3}$
August	30	$(19 + 23 + 26)/3 = 22\frac{2}{3}$
September	28	$(23 + 26 + 30)/3 = 26\frac{1}{3}$
October	18	$(26 + 30 + 28)/3 = 28$
November	16	$(30 + 28 + 18)/3 = 25\frac{1}{3}$
December	14	$(28 + 18 + 16)/3 = 20\frac{2}{3}$

SOLUTION ▶ The forecast for December is $20\frac{2}{3}$. To project the demand for sheds in the coming January, we sum the October, November, and December sales and divide by 3: January forecast $= (18 + 16 + 14)/3 = 16$.

INSIGHT ▶ Management now has a forecast that averages sales for the last 3 months. It is easy to use and understand.

LEARNING EXERCISE ▶ If actual sales in December were 18 (rather than 14), what is the new January forecast? [Answer: $17\frac{1}{3}$.]

RELATED PROBLEMS ▶ 4.1a, 4.2b, 4.5a, 4.6, 4.8a,b, 4.10a, 4.13b, 4.15, 4.47

EXCEL OM Data File **Ch04Ex1.xls** can be found at **www.pearsonhighered.com/heizer**.

ACTIVE MODEL 4.1 This example is further illustrated in Active Model 4.1 at **www.pearsonhighered.com/heizer.**

LO3: Apply the naive, moving-average, exponential smoothing, and trend methods

When a detectable trend or pattern is present, *weights* can be used to place more emphasis on recent values. This practice makes forecasting techniques more responsive to changes because more recent periods may be more heavily weighted. Choice of weights is somewhat arbitrary because there is no set formula to determine them. Therefore, deciding which weights to use requires some experience. For example, if the latest month or period is weighted too heavily, the forecast may reflect a large unusual change in the demand or sales pattern too quickly.

A weighted moving average may be expressed mathematically as:

$$\text{Weighted moving average} = \frac{\Sigma\,(\text{Weight for period } n)(\text{Demand in period } n)}{\Sigma\ \text{Weights}} \tag{4-2}$$

Example 2 shows how to calculate a weighted moving average.

EXAMPLE 2

Determining the weighted moving average

Donna's Garden Supply (see Example 1) wants to forecast storage shed sales by weighting the past 3 months, with more weight given to recent data to make them more significant.

APPROACH ▶ Assign more weight to recent data, as follows:

Weights Applied	Period
3	Last month
2	Two months ago
1	Three months ago
6	Sum of weights

Forecast for this month =

$$\frac{3 \times \text{Sales last mo.} + 2 \times \text{Sales 2 mos. ago} + 1 \times \text{Sales 3 mos. ago}}{\text{Sum of the weights}}$$

SOLUTION ▶ The results of this weighted-average forecast are as follows:

Month	Actual Shed Sales	3-Month Weighted Moving Average
January	10	
February	12	
March	13	
April	16	$[(3 \times 13) + (2 \times 12) + (10)]/6 = 12\frac{1}{6}$
May	19	$[(3 \times 16) + (2 \times 13) + (12)]/6 = 14\frac{1}{3}$
June	23	$[(3 \times 19) + (2 \times 16) + (13)]/6 = 17$
July	26	$[(3 \times 23) + (2 \times 19) + (16)]/6 = 20\frac{1}{2}$
August	30	$[(3 \times 26) + (2 \times 23) + (19)]/6 = 23\frac{5}{6}$
September	28	$[(3 \times 30) + (2 \times 26) + (23)]/6 = 27\frac{1}{2}$
October	18	$[(3 \times 28) + (2 \times 30) + (26)]/6 = 28\frac{1}{3}$
November	16	$[(3 \times 18) + (2 \times 28) + (30)]/6 = 23\frac{1}{3}$
December	14	$[(3 \times 16) + (2 \times 18) + (28)]/6 = 18\frac{2}{3}$

INSIGHT ▶ In this particular forecasting situation, you can see that more heavily weighting the latest month provides a much more accurate projection.

LEARNING EXERCISE ▶ If the assigned weights were 0.50, 0.33, and 0.17 (instead of 3, 2, and 1) what is the forecast for January's weighted moving average? Why? [Answer: There is no change. These are the same *relative* weights. Note that Σ weights = 1 now, so there is no need for a denominator. When the weights sum to 1, calculations tend to be simpler.

RELATED PROBLEMS ▶ 4.1b, 4.2c, 4.5c, 4.6, 4.7, 4.10b

EXCEL OM Data File **Ch04Ex2.xls** can be found at **www.pearsonhighered.com/heizer**.

Both simple and weighted moving averages are effective in smoothing out sudden fluctuations in the demand pattern to provide stable estimates. Moving averages do, however, present three problems:

1. Increasing the size of n (the number of periods averaged) does smooth out fluctuations better, but it makes the method less sensitive to *real* changes in the data.
2. Moving averages cannot pick up trends very well. Because they are averages, they will always stay within past levels and will not predict changes to either higher or lower levels. That is, they *lag* the actual values.
3. Moving averages require extensive records of past data.

Figure 4.2, a plot of the data in Examples 1 and 2, illustrates the lag effect of the moving-average models. Note that both the moving-average and weighted-moving-average lines lag the actual demand. The weighted moving average, however, usually reacts more quickly to demand

▶ **FIGURE 4.2**
Actual Demand vs. Moving-Average and Weighted-Moving-Average Methods for Donna's Garden Supply

AUTHOR COMMENT Moving average methods always lag behind when there is a trend present, as shown by the blue line (actual sales) for January through August.

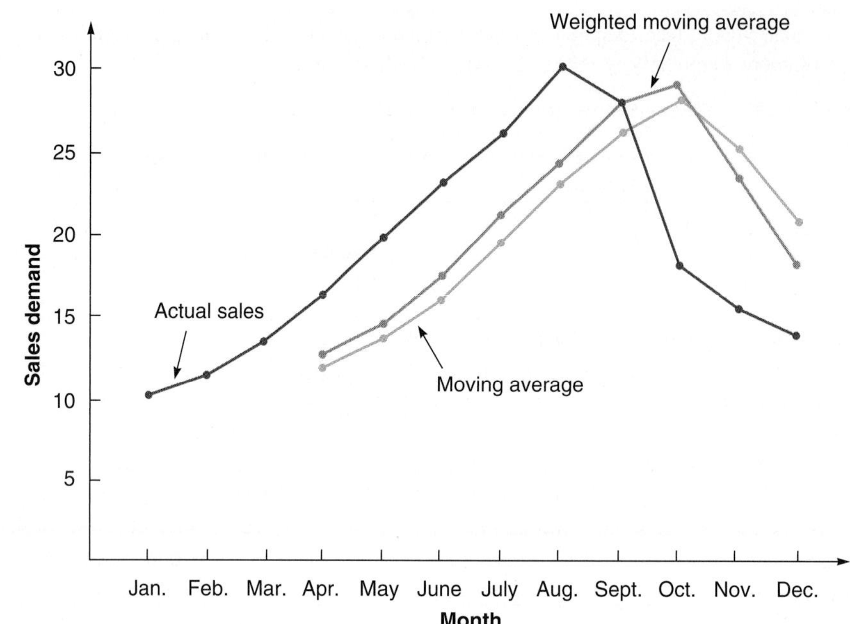

changes. Even in periods of downturn (see November and December), it more closely tracks the demand.

Exponential Smoothing

Exponential smoothing
A weighted-moving-average forecasting technique in which data points are weighted by an exponential function.

Exponential smoothing is a sophisticated weighted-moving-average forecasting method that is still fairly easy to use. It involves very *little* record keeping of past data. The basic exponential smoothing formula can be shown as follows:

$$\text{New forecast} = \text{Last period's forecast} + \alpha\,(\text{Last period's actual demand} - \text{Last period's forecast}) \quad (4\text{-}3)$$

Smoothing constant
The weighting factor used in an exponential smoothing forecast, a number between 0 and 1.

where α is a weight, or **smoothing constant**, chosen by the forecaster, that has a value between 0 and 1. Equation (4-3) can also be written mathematically as:

$$F_t = F_{t-1} + \alpha(A_{t-1} - F_{t-1}) \quad (4\text{-}4)$$

where F_t = new forecast
F_{t-1} = previous period's forecast
α = smoothing (or weighting) constant ($0 \le \alpha \le 1$)
A_{t-1} = previous period's actual demand

The concept is not complex. The latest estimate of demand is equal to the old estimate adjusted by a fraction of the difference between the last period's actual demand and the old estimate. Example 3 shows how to use exponential smoothing to derive a forecast.

EXAMPLE 3 ▶

Determining a forecast via exponential smoothing

In January, a car dealer predicted February demand for 142 Ford Mustangs. Actual February demand was 153 autos. Using a smoothing constant chosen by management of $\alpha = .20$, the dealer wants to forecast March demand using the exponential smoothing model.

APPROACH ▶ The exponential smoothing model in Equations (4-3) and (4-4) can be applied.

SOLUTION ▶ Substituting the sample data into the formula, we obtain:

$$\text{New forecast (for Marche demand)} = 142 + .2(153 - 142) = 142 + 2.2 = 144.2$$

Thus, the March demand forecast for Ford Mustangs is rounded to 144.

INSIGHT ▶ Using just two pieces of data, the forecast and the actual demand, plus a smoothing constant, we developed a forecast of 144 Ford Mustangs for March.

LEARNING EXERCISE ▶ If the smoothing constant is changed to .30, what is the new forecast? [Answer: 145.3]

RELATED PROBLEMS ▶ 4.1c, 4.3, 4.4, 4.5d, 4.6, 4.9d, 4.11, 4.12, 4.13a, 4.17, 4.18, 4.37, 4.43, 4.47, 4.49

The *smoothing constant*, α, is generally in the range from .05 to .50 for business applications. It can be changed to give more weight to recent data (when α is high) or more weight to past data (when α is low). When α reaches the extreme of 1.0, then in Equation (4-4), $F_t = 1.0A_{t-1}$. All the older values drop out, and the forecast becomes identical to the naive model mentioned earlier in this chapter. That is, the forecast for the next period is just the same as this period's demand.

The following table helps illustrate this concept. For example, when α = .5, we can see that the new forecast is based almost entirely on demand in the last three or four periods. When α = .1, the forecast places little weight on recent demand and takes many periods (about 19) of historical values into account.

	Weight Assigned to				
Smoothing Constant	**Most Recent Period (α)**	**2nd Most Recent Period α(1 – α)**	**3rd Most Recent Period $\alpha(1-\alpha)^2$**	**4th Most Recent Period $\alpha(1-\alpha)^3$**	**5th Most Recent Period $\alpha(1-\alpha)^4$**
α = .1	.1	.09	.081	.073	.066
α = .5	.5	.25	.125	.063	.031

Selecting the Smoothing Constant The exponential smoothing approach is easy to use, and it has been successfully applied in virtually every type of business. However, the appropriate value of the smoothing constant, α, can make the difference between an accurate forecast and an inaccurate forecast. High values of α are chosen when the underlying average is likely to change. Low values of α are used when the underlying average is fairly stable. In picking a value for the smoothing constant, the objective is to obtain the most accurate forecast.

Measuring Forecast Error

AUTHOR COMMENT
The forecast error tells us how well the model performed against itself using past data.

The overall accuracy of any forecasting model—moving average, exponential smoothing, or other—can be determined by comparing the forecasted values with the actual or observed values. If F_t denotes the forecast in period t, and A_t denotes the actual demand in period t, the *forecast error* (or deviation) is defined as:

$$\begin{aligned}\text{Forecast error} &= \text{Actual demand} - \text{Forecast value}\\ &= A_t - F_t\end{aligned}$$

LO4: Compute three measures of forecast accuracy

Several measures are used in practice to calculate the overall forecast error. These measures can be used to compare different forecasting models, as well as to monitor forecasts to ensure they are performing well. Three of the most popular measures are mean absolute deviation (MAD), mean squared error (MSE), and mean absolute percent error (MAPE). We now describe and give an example of each.

Mean Absolute Deviation The first measure of the overall forecast error for a model is the **mean absolute deviation (MAD)**. This value is computed by taking the sum of the absolute values of the individual forecast errors (deviations) and dividing by the number of periods of data (n):

Mean absolute deviation (MAD)
A measure of the overall forecast error for a model.

$$\text{MAD} = \frac{\Sigma|\text{Actual} - \text{Forecast}|}{n} \tag{4-5}$$

Example 4 applies MAD, as a measure of overall forecast error, by testing two values of α.

EXAMPLE 4

Determining the mean absolute deviation (MAD)

During the past 8 quarters, the Port of Baltimore has unloaded large quantities of grain from ships. The port's operations manager wants to test the use of exponential smoothing to see how well the technique works in predicting tonnage unloaded. He guesses that the forecast of grain unloaded in the first quarter was 175 tons. Two values of α are to be examined: $\alpha = .10$ and $\alpha = .50$.

APPROACH ▶ Compare the actual data with the data we forecast (using each of the two α values) and then find the absolute deviation and MADs.

SOLUTION ▶ The following table shows the *detailed* calculations for $\alpha = .10$ only:

Quarter	Actual Tonnage Unloaded	Forecast with α = .10	Forecast with α = .50
1	180	175	175
2	168	175.50 = 175.00 + .10(180 − 175)	177.50
3	159	174.75 = 175.50 + .10(168 − 175.50)	172.75
4	175	173.18 = 174.75 + .10(159 − 174.75)	165.88
5	190	173.36 = 173.18 + .10(175 − 173.18)	170.44
6	205	175.02 = 173.36 + .10(190 − 173.36)	180.22
7	180	178.02 = 175.02 + .10(205 − 175.02)	192.61
8	182	178.22 = 178.02 + .10(180 − 178.02)	186.30
9	?	178.59 = 178.22 + .10(182 − 178.22)	184.15

To evaluate the accuracy of each smoothing constant, we can compute forecast errors in terms of absolute deviations and MADs:

Quarter	Actual Tonnage Unloaded	Forecast with α = .10	Absolute Deviation for α = .10	Forecast with α = .50	Absolute Deviation for α = .50
1	180	175	5.00	175	5.00
2	168	175.50	7.50	177.50	9.50
3	159	174.75	15.75	172.75	13.75
4	175	173.18	1.82	165.88	9.12
5	190	173.36	16.64	170.44	19.56
6	205	175.02	29.98	180.22	24.78
7	180	178.02	1.98	192.61	12.61
8	182	178.22	3.78	186.30	4.30
Sum of absolute deviations:			82.45		98.62
$\text{MAD} = \frac{\Sigma\lvert\text{Deviations}\rvert}{n}$			10.31		12.33

INSIGHT ▶ On the basis of this comparison of the two MADs, a smoothing constant of $\alpha = .10$ is preferred to $\alpha = .50$ because its MAD is smaller.

LEARNING EXERCISE ▶ If the smoothing constant is changed from $\alpha = .10$ to $\alpha = .20$, what is the new MAD? [Answer: 10.21.]

RELATED PROBLEMS ▶ 4.5b, 4.8c, 4.9c, 4.14, 4.23, 4.37a

EXCEL OM Data File **Ch04Ex4a.xls** and **Ch04Ex4b.xls** can be found at **www.pearsonhighered.com/heizer**.

ACTIVE MODEL 4.2 This example is further illustrated in Active Model 4.2 at **www.pearsonhighered.com/heizer.**

Most computerized forecasting software includes a feature that automatically finds the smoothing constant with the lowest forecast error. Some software modifies the α value if errors become larger than acceptable.

Mean Squared Error The **mean squared error (MSE)** is a second way of measuring overall forecast error. MSE is the average of the squared differences between the forecasted and observed values. Its formula is:

Mean squared error (MSE)
The average of the squared differences between the forecasted and observed values.

$$\text{MSE} = \frac{\Sigma(\text{Forecast errors})^2}{n} \tag{4-6}$$

Example 5 finds the MSE for the Port of Baltimore introduced in Example 4.

EXAMPLE 5

Determining the mean squared error (MSE)

The operations manager for the Port of Baltimore now wants to compute MSE for α = .10.

APPROACH ▶ Use the same forecast data for α = .10 from Example 4, then compute the MSE using Equation (4-6).

SOLUTION ▶

Quarter	Actual Tonnage Unloaded	Forecast for α = .10	(Error)²
1	180	175	$5^2 = 25$
2	168	175.50	$(-7.5)^2 = 56.25$
3	159	174.75	$(-15.75)^2 = 248.06$
4	175	173.18	$(1.82)^2 = 3.33$
5	190	173.36	$(16.64)^2 = 276.89$
6	205	175.02	$(29.98)^2 = 898.70$
7	180	178.02	$(1.98)^2 = 3.92$
8	182	178.22	$(3.78)^2 = 14.31$
			Sum of errors squared = 1,526.46

$$\text{MSE} = \frac{\Sigma(\text{Forecast errors})^2}{n} = 1{,}526.54/8 = 190.8$$

INSIGHT ▶ Is this MSE = 190.8 good or bad? It all depends on the MSEs for other forecasting approaches. A low MSE is better because we want to minimize MSE. MSE exaggerates errors because it squares them.

LEARNING EXERCISE ▶ Find the MSE for α = .50. [Answer: MSE = 195.24. The result indicates that α = .10 is a better choice because we seek a lower MSE. Coincidentally, this is the same conclusion we reached using MAD in Example 4.]

RELATED PROBLEMS ▶ 4.8d, 4.14, 4.20

A drawback of using the MSE is that it tends to accentuate large deviations due to the squared term. For example, if the forecast error for period 1 is twice as large as the error for period 2, the squared error in period 1 is four times as large as that for period 2. Hence, using MSE as the measure of forecast error typically indicates that we prefer to have several smaller deviations rather than even one large deviation.

Mean Absolute Percent Error A problem with both the MAD and MSE is that their values depend on the magnitude of the item being forecast. If the forecast item is measured in thousands, the MAD and MSE values can be very large. To avoid this problem, we can use the **mean absolute percent error (MAPE)**. This is computed as the average of the absolute difference between the forecasted and actual values, expressed as a percentage of the actual values. That is, if we have forecasted and actual values for n periods, the MAPE is calculated as:

Mean absolute percent error (MAPE)
The average of the absolute differences between the forecast and actual values, expressed as a percent of actual values.

$$\text{MAPE} = \frac{\sum_{i=1}^{n} 100|\text{Actual}_i - \text{Forecast}_i|/\text{Actual}_i}{n} \tag{4-7}$$

Example 6 illustrates the calculations using the data from Examples 4 and 5.

EXAMPLE 6 ▶

Determining the mean absolute percent error (MAPE)

The Port of Baltimore wants to now calculate the MAPE when $\alpha = .10$.

APPROACH ▶ Equation (4-7) is applied to the forecast data computed in Example 4.

SOLUTION ▶

Quarter	Actual Tonnage Unloaded	Forecast for $\alpha = .10$	Absolute Percent Error 100 (|error|/actual)
1	180	175.00	100(5/180) = 2.78%
2	168	175.50	100(7.5/168) = 4.46%
3	159	174.75	100(15.75/159) = 9.90%
4	175	173.18	100(1.82/175) = 1.05%
5	190	173.36	100(16.64/190) = 8.76%
6	205	175.02	100(29.98/205) = 14.62%
7	180	178.02	100(1.98/180) = 1.10%
8	182	178.22	100(3.78/182) = 2.08%
			Sum of % errors = 44.75%

$$\text{MAPE} = \frac{\Sigma \text{ absolute percent errors}}{n} = \frac{44.75\%}{8} = 5.59\%$$

INSIGHT ▶ MAPE expresses the error as a percent of the actual values, undistorted by a single large value.

LEARNING EXERCISE ▶ What is MAPE when α is .50? [Answer: MAPE = 6.75%. As was the case with MAD and MSE, the $\alpha = .1$ was preferable for this series of data.]

RELATED PROBLEMS ▶ 4.8e, 4.33c

The MAPE is perhaps the easiest measure to interpret. For example, a result that the MAPE is 6% is a clear statement that is not dependent on issues such as the magnitude of the input data.

Exponential Smoothing with Trend Adjustment

Simple exponential smoothing, the technique we just illustrated in Examples 3 to 6, is like any other moving-average technique: It fails to respond to trends. Other forecasting techniques that can deal with trends are certainly available. However, because exponential smoothing is such a popular modeling approach in business, let us look at it in more detail.

Here is why exponential smoothing must be modified when a trend is present. Assume that demand for our product or service has been increasing by 100 units per month and that we have been forecasting with $\alpha = 0.4$ in our exponential smoothing model. The following table shows a severe lag in the 2nd, 3rd, 4th, and 5th months, even when our initial estimate for month 1 is perfect:

Month	Actual Demand	Forecast for Month $T(F_T)$
1	100	$F_1 = 100$ (given)
2	200	$F_2 = F_1 + \alpha(A_1 - F_1) = 100 + .4(100 - 100) = 100$
3	300	$F_3 = F_2 + \alpha(A_2 - F_2) = 100 + .4(200 - 100) = 140$
4	400	$F_4 = F_3 + \alpha(A_3 - F_3) = 140 + .4(300 - 140) = 204$
5	500	$F_5 = F_4 + \alpha(A_4 - F_4) = 204 + .4(400 - 204) = 282$

To improve our forecast, let us illustrate a more complex exponential smoothing model, one that adjusts for trend. The idea is to compute an exponentially smoothed average of the data and then adjust for positive or negative lag in trend. The new formula is:

$$\text{Forecast including trend}(FIT_t) = \text{Exponentially smoothed forecast}(F_t) + \text{Exponentially smoothed trend}(T_t) \qquad \text{(4-8)}$$

With trend-adjusted exponential smoothing, estimates for both the average and the trend are smoothed. This procedure requires two smoothing constants: α for the average and β for the trend. We then compute the average and trend each period:

$F_t = \alpha$(Actual demand last period) + $(1 - \alpha)$(Forecast last period + Trend estimate last period)

or:

$$F_t = \alpha(A_{t-1}) + (1 - \alpha)(F_{t-1} + T_{t-1}) \quad \text{(4-9)}$$

$T_t = \beta$(Forecast this period − Forecast last period) + $(1 - \beta)$(Trend estimate last period)

or:

$$T_t = \beta(F_t - F_{t-1}) + (1 - \beta)T_{t-1} \quad \text{(4-10)}$$

where F_t = exponentially smoothed forecast of the data series in period t
T_t = exponentially smoothed trend in period t
A_t = actual demand in period t
α = smoothing constant for the average $(0 \le \alpha \le 1)$
β = smoothing constant for the trend $(0 \le \beta \le 1)$

So the three steps to compute a trend-adjusted forecast are:

Step 1: Compute F_t, the exponentially smoothed forecast for period t, using Equation (4-9).
Step 2: Compute the smoothed trend, T_t, using Equation (4-10).
Step 3: Calculate the forecast including trend, FIT_t, by the formula $FIT_t = F_t + T_t$ (from Equation 4-8).

Example 7 shows how to use trend-adjusted exponential smoothing.

◄ EXAMPLE 7

Computing a trend-adjusted exponential smoothing forecast

A large Portland manufacturer wants to forecast demand for a piece of pollution-control equipment. A review of past sales, as shown below, indicates that an increasing trend is present:

Month (t)	Actual Demand (A_t)	Month (t)	Actual Demand (A_t)
1	12	6	21
2	17	7	31
3	20	8	28
4	19	9	36
5	24	10	?

Smoothing constants are assigned the values of $\alpha = .2$ and $\beta = .4$. The firm assumes the initial forecast for month 1 (F_1) was 11 units and the trend over that period (T_1) was 2 units.

APPROACH ► A trend-adjusted exponential smoothing model, using Equations (4-9), (4-10), and (4-8) and the three steps above, is employed.

SOLUTION ►

Step 1: Forecast for month 2:

$$F_2 = \alpha A_1 + (1 - \alpha)(F_1 + T_1)$$
$$F_2 = (.2)(12) + (1 - .2)(11 + 2)$$
$$= 2.4 + (.8)(13) = 2.4 + 10.4 = 12.8 \text{ units}$$

Step 2: Compute the trend in period 2:

$$T_2 = \beta(F_2 - F_1) + (1 - \beta)T_1$$
$$= .4(12.8 - 11) + (1 - .4)(2)$$
$$= (.4)(1.8) + (.6)(2) = .72 + 1.2 = 1.92$$

Step 3: Compute the forecast including trend (FIT_t):

$$FIT_2 = F_2 + T_2$$
$$= 12.8 + 1.92$$
$$= 14.72 \text{ units}$$

We will also do the same calculations for the third month:

Step 1: $F_3 = \alpha A_2 + (1 - \alpha)(F_2 + T_2) = (.2)(17) + (1 - .2)(12.8 + 1.92)$
$= 3.4 + (.8)(14.72) = 3.4 + 11.78 = 15.18$

Step 2: $T_3 = \beta(F_3 - F_2) + (1 - \beta)T_2 = (.4)(15.18 - 12.8) + (1 - .4)(1.92)$
$= (.4)(2.38) + (.6)(1.92) = .952 + 1.152 = 2.10$

Step 3: $FIT_3 = F_3 + T_3$
$= 15.18 + 2.10 = 17.28.$

Table 4.1 completes the forecasts for the 10-month period.

▶ TABLE 4.1
Forecast with $\alpha = .2$ and $\beta = .4$

Month	Actual Demand	Smoothed Forecast, F_t	Smoothed Trend, T_t	Forecast Including Trend, FIT_t
1	12	11	2	13.00
2	17	12.80	1.92	14.72
3	20	15.18	2.10	17.28
4	19	17.82	2.32	20.14
5	24	19.91	2.23	22.14
6	21	22.51	2.38	24.89
7	31	24.11	2.07	26.18
8	28	27.14	2.45	29.59
9	36	29.28	2.32	31.60
10	—	32.48	2.68	35.16

INSIGHT ▶ Figure 4.3 compares actual demand (A_t) to an exponential smoothing forecast that includes trend (FIT_t). *FIT* picks up the trend in actual demand. A simple exponential smoothing model (as we saw in Examples 3 and 4) trails far behind.

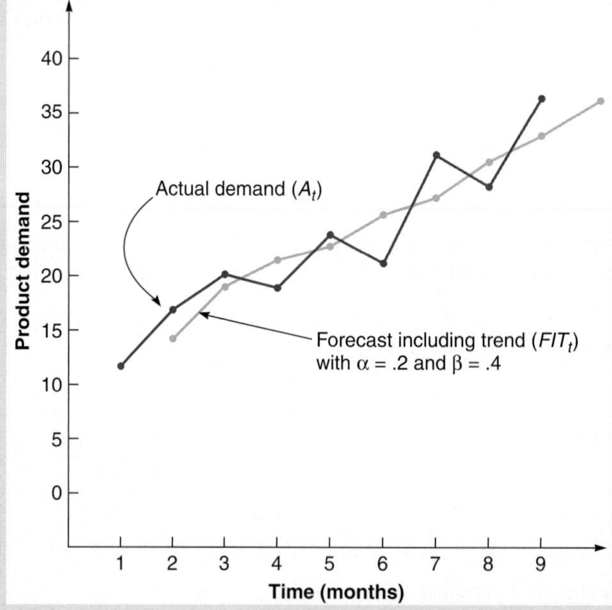

▶ FIGURE 4.3
Exponential Smoothing with Trend-Adjustment Forecasts Compared to Actual Demand Data

LEARNING EXERCISE ▶ Using the data for actual demand for the 9 months, compute the exponentially smoothed forecast *without* trend (using Equation (4-4) as we did earlier in Examples 3 and 4). Apply $\alpha = .2$ and assume an initial forecast for month 1 of 11 units. Then plot the months 2–10 forecast values on Figure 4.3. What do you notice? [Answer: Month 10 forecast = 24.65. All the points are below and lag the trend-adjusted forecast.]

RELATED PROBLEMS ▶ 4.19, 4.20, 4.21, 4.22, 4.44

ACTIVE MODEL 4.3 This example is further illustrated in Active Model 4.3 at **www.pearsonhighered.com/heizer**.

The value of the trend-smoothing constant, β, resembles the α constant because a high β is more responsive to recent changes in trend. A low β gives less weight to the most recent trends and tends to smooth out the present trend. Values of β can be found by the trial-and-error approach or by using sophisticated commercial forecasting software, with the MAD used as a measure of comparison.

Simple exponential smoothing is often referred to as *first-order smoothing*, and trend-adjusted smoothing is called *second-order*, or *double smoothing*. Other advanced exponential-smoothing models are also used, including seasonal-adjusted and triple smoothing, but these are beyond the scope of this book.[2]

Trend Projections

The last time-series forecasting method we will discuss is **trend projection**. This technique fits a trend line to a series of historical data points and then projects the line into the future for medium to long-range forecasts. Several mathematical trend equations can be developed (for example, exponential and quadratic), but in this section, we will look at *linear* (straight-line) trends only.

Trend projection
A time-series forecasting method that fits a trend line to a series of historical data points and then projects the line into the future for forecasts.

If we decide to develop a linear trend line by a precise statistical method, we can apply the *least-squares method*. This approach results in a straight line that minimizes the sum of the squares of the vertical differences or deviations from the line to each of the actual observations. Figure 4.4 illustrates the least-squares approach.

A least-squares line is described in terms of its y-intercept (the height at which it intercepts the y-axis) and its expected change (slope). If we can compute the y-intercept and slope, we can express the line with the following equation:

$$\hat{y} = a + bx \qquad \text{(4-11)}$$

where $\hat{y}$ (called "y hat") = computed value of the variable to be predicted (called the *dependent variable*)
a = y-axis intercept
b = slope of the regression line (or the rate of change in y for given changes in x)
x = the independent variable (which in this case is *time*)

Statisticians have developed equations that we can use to find the values of a and b for any regression line. The slope b is found by:

$$b = \frac{\Sigma xy - n\bar{x}\bar{y}}{\Sigma x^2 - n\bar{x}^2} \qquad \text{(4-12)}$$

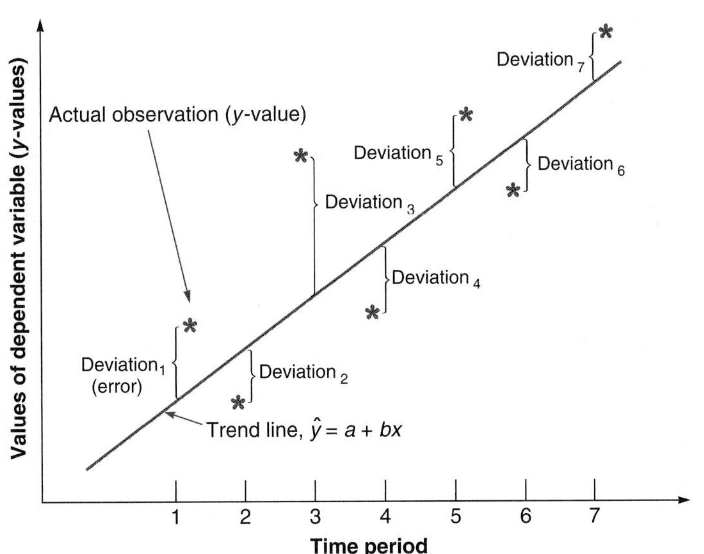

◄ **FIGURE 4.4**
The Least-Squares Method for Finding the Best-Fitting Straight Line, Where the Asterisks Are the Locations of the Seven Actual Observations or Data Points

[2]For more details, see D. Groebner, P. Shannon, P. Fry, and K. Smith, *Business Statistics*, 8th ed. (Upper Saddle River, NJ: Prentice Hall, 2011).

where b = slope of the regression line
Σ = summation sign
x = known values of the independent variable
y = known values of the dependent variable
$\bar{x}$ = average of the x-values
$\bar{y}$ = average of the y-values
n = number of data points or observations

We can compute the y-intercept a as follows:

$$a = \bar{y} - b\bar{x} \quad \text{(4-13)}$$

Example 8 shows how to apply these concepts.

EXAMPLE 8 ▶ Forecasting with least squares

The demand for electric power at N.Y. Edison over the period 2003 to 2009 is shown in the following table, in megawatts. The firm wants to forecast 2010 demand by fitting a straight-line trend to these data.

Year	Electrical Power Demand	Year	Electrical Power Demand
2003	74	2007	105
2004	79	2008	142
2005	80	2009	122
2006	90		

APPROACH ▶ With a series of data over time, we can minimize the computations by transforming the values of x (time) to simpler numbers. Thus, in this case, we can designate 2003 as year 1, 2004 as year 2, and so on. Then Equations (4-12) and (4-13) can be used to create the trend projection model.

SOLUTION ▶

Year	Time Period (x)	Electric Power Demand (y)	x^2	xy
2003	1	74	1	74
2004	2	79	4	158
2005	3	80	9	240
2006	4	90	16	360
2007	5	105	25	525
2008	6	142	36	852
2009	7	122	49	854
	$\Sigma x = 28$	$\Sigma y = 692$	$\Sigma x^2 = 140$	$\Sigma xy = 3{,}063$

$$\bar{x} = \frac{\Sigma x}{n} = \frac{28}{7} = 4 \qquad \bar{y} = \frac{\Sigma y}{n} = \frac{692}{7} = 98.86$$

$$b = \frac{\Sigma xy - n\bar{x}\bar{y}}{\Sigma x^2 - n\bar{x}^2} = \frac{3{,}063 - (7)(4)(98.86)}{140 - (7)(4^2)} = \frac{295}{28} = 10.54$$

$$a = \bar{y} - b\bar{x} = 98.86 - 10.54(4) = 56.70$$

Thus, the least squares trend equation is $\hat{y} = 56.70 + 10.54x$. To project demand in 2010, we first denote the year 2010 in our new coding system as $x = 8$:

$$\begin{aligned}\text{Demand in 2010} &= 56.70 + 10.54(8)\\ &= 141.02, \text{ or } 141 \text{ megawatts}\end{aligned}$$

INSIGHT ▶ To evaluate the model, we plot both the historical demand and the trend line in Figure 4.5. In this case, we may wish to be cautious and try to understand the 2008 to 2009 swing in demand.

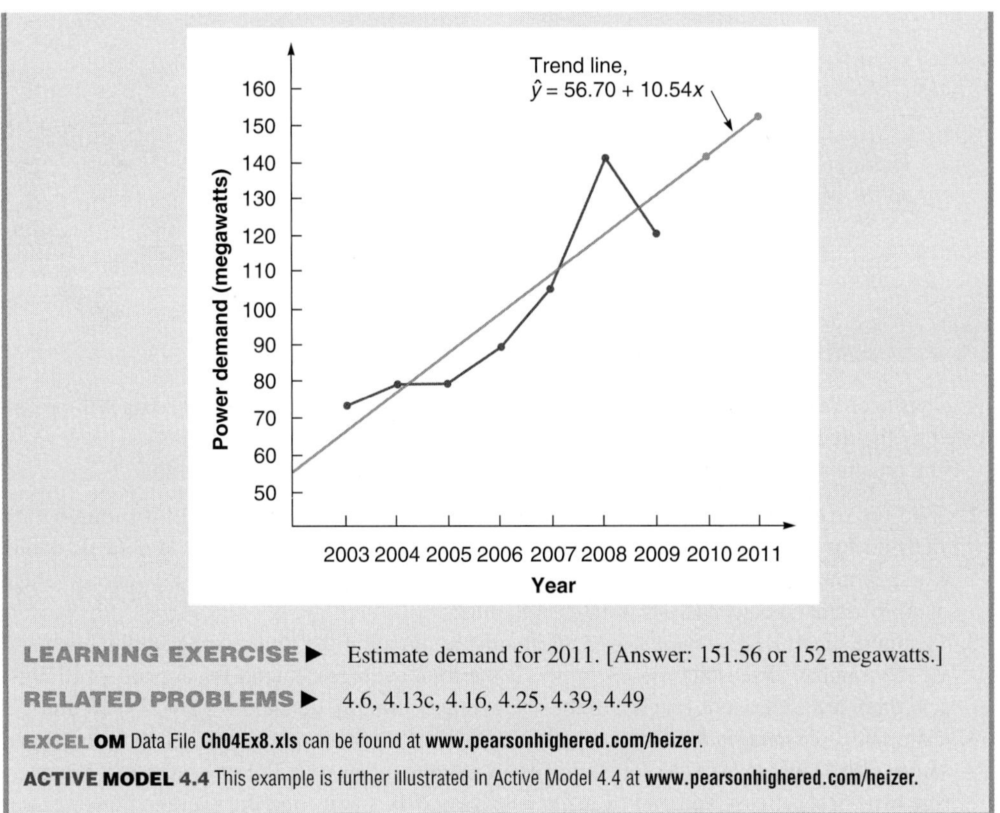

◀ **FIGURE 4.5**
Electrical Power and the Computed Trend Line

LEARNING EXERCISE ▶ Estimate demand for 2011. [Answer: 151.56 or 152 megawatts.]

RELATED PROBLEMS ▶ 4.6, 4.13c, 4.16, 4.25, 4.39, 4.49

EXCEL OM Data File **Ch04Ex8.xls** can be found at **www.pearsonhighered.com/heizer**.

ACTIVE MODEL 4.4 This example is further illustrated in Active Model 4.4 at **www.pearsonhighered.com/heizer.**

Notes on the Use of the Least-Squares Method Using the least-squares method implies that we have met three requirements:

1. We always plot the data because least-squares data assume a linear relationship. If a curve appears to be present, curvilinear analysis is probably needed.
2. We do not predict time periods far beyond our given database. For example, if we have 20 months' worth of average prices of Microsoft stock, we can forecast only 3 or 4 months into the future. Forecasts beyond that have little statistical validity. Thus, you cannot take 5 years' worth of sales data and project 10 years into the future. The world is too uncertain.
3. Deviations around the least-squares line (see Figure 4.4) are assumed to be random. They are normally distributed, with most observations close to the line and only a smaller number farther out.

Seasonal Variations in Data

AUTHOR COMMENT John Deere understands seasonal variations: It has been able to obtain 70% of its orders in advance of seasonal use so it can smooth production.

Seasonal variations in data are regular up-and-down movements in a time series that relate to recurring events such as weather or holidays. Demand for coal and fuel oil, for example, peaks during cold winter months. Demand for golf clubs or sunscreen may be highest in summer.

Seasonality may be applied to hourly, daily, weekly, monthly, or other recurring patterns. Fast-food restaurants experience *daily* surges at noon and again at 5 P.M. Movie theaters see higher demand on Friday and Saturday evenings. The post office, Toys "Я" Us, The Christmas Store, and Hallmark Card Shops also exhibit seasonal variation in customer traffic and sales.

Seasonal variations
Regular upward or downward movements in a time series that tie to recurring events.

Similarly, understanding seasonal variations is important for capacity planning in organizations that handle peak loads. These include electric power companies during extreme cold and warm periods, banks on Friday afternoons, and buses and subways during the morning and evening rush hours.

Time-series forecasts like those in Example 8 involve reviewing the trend of data over a series of time periods. The presence of seasonality makes adjustments in trend-line forecasts necessary. Seasonality is expressed in terms of the amount that actual values differ from average values in the time series. Analyzing data in monthly or quarterly terms usually makes it easy for a statistician to spot seasonal patterns. Seasonal indices can then be developed by several common methods.

In what is called a *multiplicative seasonal model*, seasonal factors are multiplied by an estimate of average demand to produce a seasonal forecast. Our assumption in this section is that

Demand for many products is seasonal. Yamaha, the manufacturer of these jet skis and snowmobiles, produces products with complementary demands to address seasonal fluctuations.

trend has been removed from the data. Otherwise, the magnitude of the seasonal data will be distorted by the trend.

Here are the steps we will follow for a company that has "seasons" of 1 month:

LO5: Develop seasonal indices

1. Find the *average historical demand each season* (or month in this case) by summing the demand for that month in each year and dividing by the number of years of data available. For example, if, in January, we have seen sales of 8, 6, and 10 over the past 3 years, average January demand equals (8 + 6 + 10)/3 = 8 units.
2. Compute the *average demand over all months* by dividing the total average annual demand by the number of seasons. For example, if the total average demand for a year is 120 units and there are 12 seasons (each month), the average monthly demand is 120/12 = 10 units.
3. Compute a *seasonal index* for each season by dividing that month's actual historical demand (from step 1) by the average demand over all months (from step 2). For example, if the average historical January demand over the past 3 years is 8 units and the average demand over all months is 10 units, the seasonal index for January is 8/10 = .80. Likewise, a seasonal index of 1.20 for February would mean that February's demand is 20% larger than the average demand over all months.
4. Estimate next year's total annual demand.
5. Divide this estimate of total annual demand by the number of seasons, then multiply it by the seasonal index for that month. This provides the *seasonal forecast*.

Example 9 illustrates this procedure as it computes seasonal indices from historical data.

EXAMPLE 9 ▶ Determining seasonal indices

A Des Moines distributor of Sony laptop computers wants to develop monthly indices for sales. Data from 2007–2009, by month, are available.

APPROACH ▶ Follow the five steps listed above.

SOLUTION ▶

Month	Demand 2007	Demand 2008	Demand 2009	Average 2007–2009 Demand	Average Monthly Demand[a]	Seasonal Index[b]
Jan.	80	85	105	90	94	.957 (= 90/94)
Feb.	70	85	85	80	94	.851 (= 80/94)
Mar.	80	93	82	85	94	.904 (= 85/94)
Apr.	90	95	115	100	94	1.064 (= 100/94)
May	113	125	131	123	94	1.309 (= 123/94)
June	110	115	120	115	94	1.223 (= 115/94)
July	100	102	113	105	94	1.117 (= 105/94)
Aug.	88	102	110	100	94	1.064 (= 100/94)
Sept.	85	90	95	90	94	.957 (= 90/94)
Oct.	77	78	85	80	94	.851 (= 80/94)
Nov.	75	82	83	80	94	.851 (= 80/94)
Dec.	82	78	80	80	94	.851 (= 80/94)
			Total average annual demand =	1,128		

[a] $\text{Average monthly demand} = \dfrac{1{,}128}{12 \text{ months}} = 94.$ [b] $\text{Seasonal index} = \dfrac{\text{Average 2007–2009 monthly demand}}{\text{Average monthly demand}}.$

If we expected the 2010 annual demand for computers to be 1,200 units, we would use these seasonal indices to forecast the monthly demand as follows:

Month	Demand	Month	Demand
Jan.	$\frac{1,200}{12} \times .957 = 96$	July	$\frac{1,200}{12} \times 1.117 = 112$
Feb.	$\frac{1,200}{12} \times .851 = 85$	Aug.	$\frac{1,200}{12} \times 1.064 = 106$
Mar.	$\frac{1,200}{12} \times .904 = 90$	Sept.	$\frac{1,200}{12} \times .957 = 96$
Apr.	$\frac{1,200}{12} \times 1.064 = 106$	Oct.	$\frac{1,200}{12} \times .851 = 85$
May	$\frac{1,200}{12} \times 1.309 = 131$	Nov.	$\frac{1,200}{12} \times .851 = 85$
June	$\frac{1,200}{12} \times 1.223 = 122$	Dec.	$\frac{1,200}{12} \times .851 = 85$

INSIGHT ▶ Think of these indices as percentages of average sales. The average sales (without seasonality) would be 94, but with seasonality, sales fluctuate from 85% to 131% of average.

LEARNING EXERCISE ▶ If 2010 annual demand is 1,150 laptops (instead of 1,200), what will the January, February, and March forecasts be? [Answer: 91.7, 81.5, and 86.6, which can be rounded to 92, 82, and 87]

RELATED PROBLEMS ▶ 4.27, 4.28

EXCEL OM Data File **Ch04Ex9.xls** can be found at **www.pearsonhighered.com/heizer**.

For simplicity, only 3 periods are used for each monthly index in the preceding example. Example 10 illustrates how indices that have already been prepared can be applied to adjust trend-line forecasts for seasonality.

◀ EXAMPLE 10

Applying both trend and seasonal indices

San Diego Hospital wants to improve its forecasting by applying both trend and seasonal indices to 66 months of data it has collected. It will then forecast "patient-days" over the coming year.

APPROACH ▶ A trend line is created; then monthly seasonal indices are computed. Finally, a multiplicative seasonal model is used to forecast months 67 to 78.

SOLUTION ▶ Using 66 months of adult inpatient hospital days, the following equation was computed:

$$\hat{y} = 8{,}090 + 21.5x$$

where $\hat{y}$ = patient days
x = time, in months

Based on this model, which reflects only trend data, the hospital forecasts patient days for the next month (period 67) to be:

$$\text{Patient days} = 8{,}090 + (21.5)(67) = 9{,}530 \text{ (trend only)}$$

While this model, as plotted in Figure 4.6, recognized the upward trend line in the demand for inpatient services, it ignored the seasonality that the administration knew to be present.

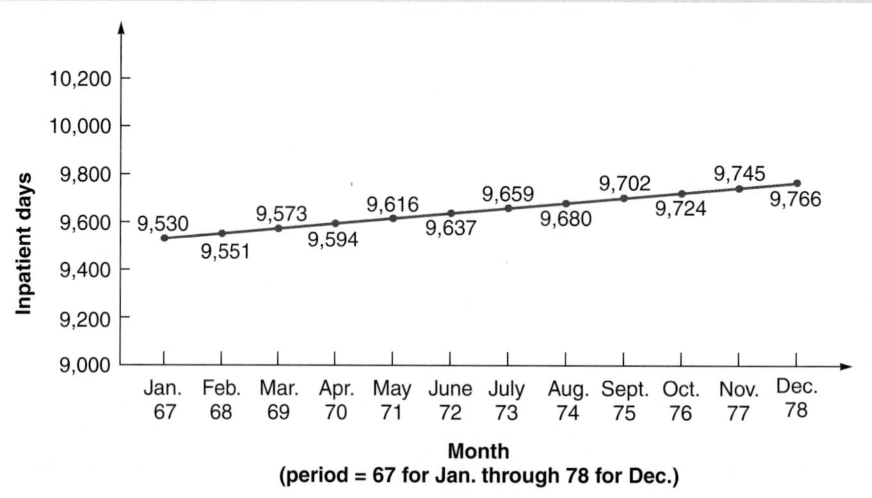

▶ **FIGURE 4.6**
Trend Data for San Diego Hospital

Source: From "Modern Methods Improve Hospital Forecasting" by W. E. Sterk and E. G. Shryock from *Healthcare Financial Management*, Vol. 41, no. 3, p. 97. Reprinted by permission of Healthcare Financial Management Association.

The following table provides seasonal indices based on the same 66 months. Such seasonal data, by the way, were found to be typical of hospitals nationwide.

Seasonality Indices for Adult Inpatient Days at San Diego Hospital

Month	Seasonality Index	Month	Seasonality Index
January	1.04	July	1.03
February	0.97	August	1.04
March	1.02	September	0.97
April	1.01	October	1.00
May	0.99	November	0.96
June	0.99	December	0.98

These seasonal indices are graphed in Figure 4.7. Note that January, March, July, and August seem to exhibit significantly higher patient days on average, while February, September, November, and December experience lower patient days.

However, neither the trend data nor the seasonal data alone provide a reasonable forecast for the hospital. Only when the hospital multiplied the trend-adjusted data times the appropriate seasonal index did it obtain good forecasts. Thus, for period 67 (January):

$$\text{Patient days} = (\text{Trend-adjusted forecast})\,(\text{Monthly seasonal index}) = (9{,}530)(1.04) = 9{,}911$$

The patient days for each month are:

Period	67	68	69	70	71	72	73	74	75	76	77	78
Month	Jan.	Feb.	March	April	May	June	July	Aug.	Sept.	Oct.	Nov.	Dec.
Forecast with Trend & Seasonality	9,911	9,265	9,764	9,691	9,520	9,542	9,949	10,068	9,411	9,724	9,355	9,572

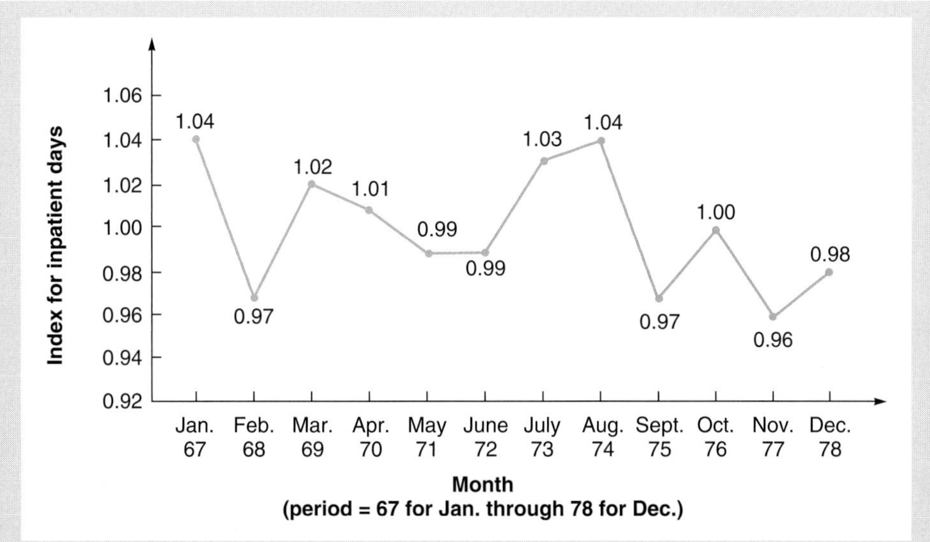

◀ **FIGURE 4.7**
Seasonal Index for San Diego Hospital

A graph showing the forecast that combines both trend and seasonality appears in Figure 4.8.

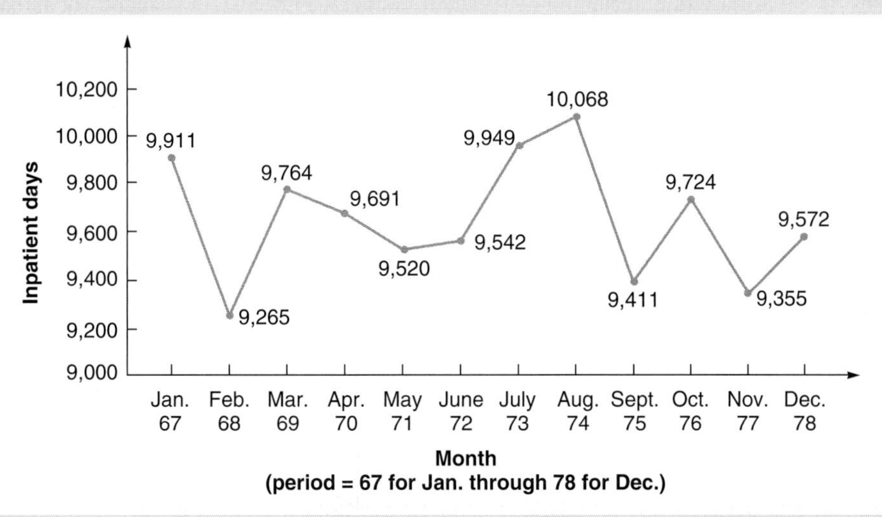

◀ **FIGURE 4.8**
Combined Trend and Seasonal Forecast

INSIGHT ▶ Notice that with trend only, the September forecast is 9,702, but with both trend and seasonal adjustments, the forecast is 9,411. By combining trend and seasonal data, the hospital was better able to forecast inpatient days and the related staffing and budgeting vital to effective operations.

LEARNING EXERCISE ▶ If the slope of the trend line for patient-days is 22.0 (rather than 21.5) and the index for December is .99 (instead of .98), what is the new forecast for December inpatient days? [Answer: 9,708.]

RELATED PROBLEMS ▶ 4.26, 4.29

Example 11 further illustrates seasonality for quarterly data at a department store.

◀ **EXAMPLE 11**

Adjusting trend data with seasonal indices

Management at Davis's Department Store has used time-series regression to forecast retail sales for the next 4 quarters. Sales estimates are \$100,000, \$120,000, \$140,000, and \$160,000 for the respective quarters. Seasonal indices for the 4 quarters have been found to be 1.30, .90, .70, and 1.10, respectively.

APPROACH ▶ To compute a seasonalized or adjusted sales forecast, we just multiply each seasonal index by the appropriate trend forecast:

$$\hat{y}_{\text{seasonal}} = \text{Index} \times \hat{y}_{\text{trend forecast}}$$

SOLUTION ▶

Quarter I: $\hat{y}_{I} = (1.30)(\$100{,}000) = \$130{,}000$
Quarter II: $\hat{y}_{II} = (.90)(\$120{,}000) = \$108{,}000$
Quarter III: $\hat{y}_{III} = (.70)(\$140{,}000) = \$98{,}000$
Quarter IV: $\hat{y}_{IV} = (1.10)(\$160{,}000) = \$176{,}000$

INSIGHT ▶ The straight-line trend forecast is now adjusted to reflect the seasonal changes.

LEARNING EXERCISE ▶ If the sales forecast for Quarter IV was 180,000 (rather than 160,000), what would be the seasonally adjusted forecast? [Answer: $198,000.]

RELATED PROBLEMS ▶ 4.26, 4.29

Cyclical Variations in Data

Cycles
Patterns in the data that occur every several years.

Cycles are like seasonal variations in data but occur every several *years*, not weeks, months, or quarters. Forecasting cyclical variations in a time series is difficult. This is because cycles include a wide variety of factors that cause the economy to go from recession to expansion to recession over a period of years. These factors include national or industrywide overexpansion in times of euphoria and contraction in times of concern. Forecasting demand for individual products can also be driven by product life cycles—the stages products go through from introduction through decline. Life cycles exist for virtually all products; striking examples include floppy disks, video recorders, and the original Game Boy. We leave cyclical analysis to forecasting texts.

Developing associative techniques of variables that affect one another is our next topic.

AUTHOR COMMENT
We now deal with the same mathematical model that we saw earlier, the least-squares method. But we use any potential "cause-and-effect" variable as *x*.

ASSOCIATIVE FORECASTING METHODS: REGRESSION AND CORRELATION ANALYSIS

Unlike time-series forecasting, *associative forecasting* models usually consider *several* variables that are related to the quantity being predicted. Once these related variables have been found, a statistical model is built and used to forecast the item of interest. This approach is more powerful than the time-series methods that use only the historical values for the forecasted variable.

Linear-regression analysis
A straight-line mathematical model to describe the functional relationships between independent and dependent variables.

Many factors can be considered in an associative analysis. For example, the sales of Dell PCs may be related to Dell's advertising budget, the company's prices, competitors' prices and promotional strategies, and even the nation's economy and unemployment rates. In this case, PC sales would be called the *dependent variable*, and the other variables would be called *independent variables*. The manager's job is to develop *the best statistical relationship between PC sales and the independent variables*. The most common quantitative associative forecasting model is **linear-regression analysis**.

Using Regression Analysis for Forecasting

We can use the same mathematical model that we employed in the least-squares method of trend projection to perform a linear-regression analysis. The dependent variables that we want to forecast will still be $\hat{y}$. But now the independent variable, x, need no longer be time. We use the equation:

$$\hat{y} = a + bx$$

LO6: Conduct a regression and correlation analysis

where
$\hat{y}$ = value of the dependent variable (in our example, sales)
a = y-axis intercept
b = slope of the regression line
x = independent variable

Example 12 shows how to use linear regression.

EXAMPLE 12

Computing a linear regression equation

Nodel Construction Company renovates old homes in West Bloomfield, Michigan. Over time, the company has found that its dollar volume of renovation work is dependent on the West Bloomfield area payroll. Management wants to establish a mathematical relationship to help predict sales.

APPROACH ▶ Nodel's VP of operations has prepared the following table, which lists company revenues and the amount of money earned by wage earners in West Bloomfield during the past 6 years:

Nodel's Sales (in \$ millions), *y*	Area Payroll (in \$ billions), *x*	Nodel's Sales (in \$ millions), *y*	Area Payroll (in \$ billions), *x*
2.0	1	2.0	2
3.0	3	2.0	1
2.5	4	3.5	7

The VP needs to determine whether there is a straight-line (linear) relationship between area payroll and sales. He plots the known data on a scatter diagram:

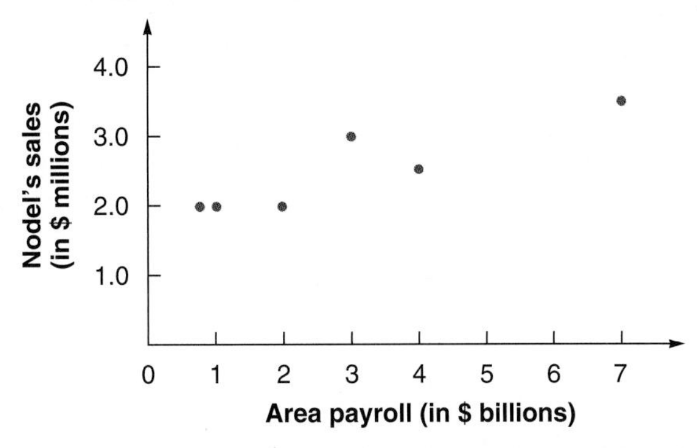

AUTHOR COMMENT
A scatter diagram is a powerful data analysis tool. It helps quickly size up the relationship between two variables.

From the six data points, there appears to be a slight positive relationship between the independent variable (payroll) and the dependent variable (sales): As payroll increases, Nodel's sales tend to be higher.

SOLUTION ▶ We can find a mathematical equation by using the least-squares regression approach:

Sales, *y*	Payroll, *x*	x^2	xy
2.0	1	1	2.0
3.0	3	9	9.0
2.5	4	16	10.0
2.0	2	4	4.0
2.0	1	1	2.0
3.5	7	49	24.5
$\Sigma y = 15.0$	$\Sigma x = 18$	$\Sigma x^2 = 80$	$\Sigma xy = 51.5$

$$\bar{x} = \frac{\Sigma x}{6} = \frac{18}{6} = 3$$

$$\bar{y} = \frac{\Sigma y}{6} = \frac{15}{6} = 2.5$$

$$b = \frac{\Sigma xy - n\bar{x}\bar{y}}{\Sigma x^2 - n\bar{x}^2} = \frac{51.5 - (6)(3)(2.5)}{80 - (6)(3^2)} = .25$$

$$a = \bar{y} - b\bar{x} = 2.5 - (.25)(3) = 1.75$$

The estimated regression equation, therefore, is:

$$\hat{y} = 1.75 + .25x$$

or:

$$\text{Sales} = 1.75 + .25\ (\text{payroll})$$

If the local chamber of commerce predicts that the West Bloomfield area payroll will be \$6 billion next year, we can estimate sales for Nodel with the regression equation:

$$\text{Sales (in \$ millions)} = 1.75 + .25(6) = 1.75 + 1.50 = 3.25$$

or:

$$\text{Sales} = \$3{,}250{,}000$$

INSIGHT ▶ Given our assumptions of a straight-line relationship between payroll and sales, we now have an indication of the slope of that relationship: on average, sales increase at the rate of a million dollars for every quarter billion dollars in the local area payroll. This is because $b = .25$.

LEARNING EXERCISE ▶ What are Nodel's sales when the local payroll is \$8 billion? [Answer: \$3.75 million.]

RELATED PROBLEMS ▶ 4.24, 4.30, 4.31, 4.32, 4.33, 4.35, 4.38, 4.40, 4.41, 4.46, 4.48, 4.49

EXCEL OM Data File **Ch04Ex12.xls** can be found at **www.pearsonhighered.com/heizer**.

The final part of Example 12 shows a central weakness of associative forecasting methods like regression. Even when we have computed a regression equation, we must provide a forecast of the independent variable *x*—in this case, payroll—before estimating the dependent variable *y* for the next time period. Although this is not a problem for all forecasts, you can imagine the difficulty of determining future values of *some* common independent variables (such as unemployment rates, gross national product, price indices, and so on).

Standard Error of the Estimate

The forecast of \$3,250,000 for Nodel's sales in Example 12 is called a *point estimate* of *y*. The point estimate is really the *mean*, or *expected value*, of a distribution of possible values of sales. Figure 4.9 illustrates this concept.

Standard error of the estimate
A measure of variability around the regression line—its standard deviation.

To measure the accuracy of the regression estimates, we must compute the **standard error of the estimate**, $S_{y,x}$. This computation is called the *standard deviation of the regression:* It measures the error from the dependent variable, *y*, to the regression line, rather than to the mean. Equation (4-14) is a similar expression to that found in most statistics books for computing the standard deviation of an arithmetic mean:

$$S_{y,x} = \sqrt{\frac{\Sigma(y - y_c)^2}{n - 2}} \qquad \textbf{(4-14)}$$

where y = y-value of each data point
y_c = computed value of the dependent variable, from the regression equation
n = number of data points

▶ **FIGURE 4.9**
Distribution about the Point Estimate of \$3.25 Million Sales

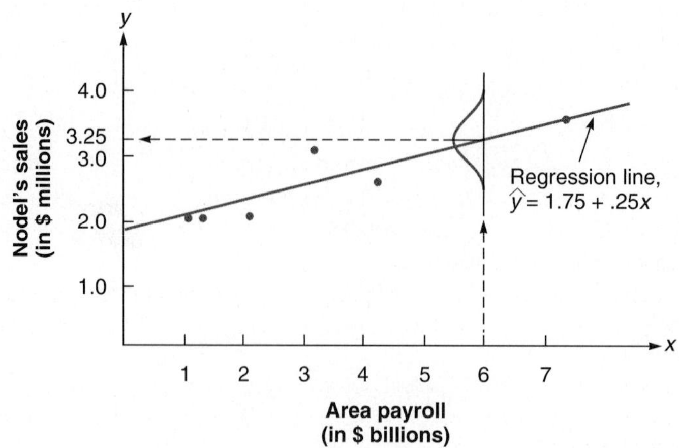

Glidden Paints' assembly lines fill thousands of cans per hour. To predict demand, the firm uses associative forecasting methods such as linear regression, with independent variables such as disposable personal income and GNP. Although housing starts would be a natural variable, Glidden found that it correlated poorly with past sales. It turns out that most Glidden paint is sold through retailers to customers who already own homes or businesses.

Equation (4-15) may look more complex, but it is actually an easier-to-use version of Equation (4-14). Both formulas provide the same answer and can be used in setting up prediction intervals around the point estimate[3]:

$$S_{y,x} = \sqrt{\frac{\Sigma y^2 - a\Sigma y - b\Sigma xy}{n - 2}} \tag{4-15}$$

Example 13 shows how we would calculate the standard error of the estimate in Example 12.

EXAMPLE 13

Computing the standard error of the estimate

Nodel's VP of operations now wants to know the error associated with the regression line computed in Example 12.

APPROACH ▶ Compute the standard error of the estimate, $S_{y,x}$, using Equation (4-15).

SOLUTION ▶ The only number we need that is not available to solve for $S_{y,x}$ is Σy^2. Some quick addition reveals $\Sigma y^2 = 39.5$. Therefore:

$$\begin{aligned} S_{y,x} &= \sqrt{\frac{\Sigma y^2 - a\Sigma y - b\Sigma xy}{n - 2}} \\ &= \sqrt{\frac{39.5 - 1.75(15.0) - .25(51.5)}{6 - 2}} \\ &= \sqrt{.09375} = .306 \text{ (in \$ millions)} \end{aligned}$$

The standard error of the estimate is then $306,000 in sales.

INSIGHT ▶ The interpretation of the standard error of the estimate is similar to the standard deviation; namely, ±1 standard deviation = .6827. So there is a 68.27% chance of sales being ±$306,000 from the point estimate of $3,250,000.

LEARNING EXERCISE ▶ What is the probability sales will exceed $3,556,000? [Answer: About 16%.]

RELATED PROBLEMS ▶ 4.41e, 4.48b

Correlation Coefficients for Regression Lines

The regression equation is one way of expressing the nature of the relationship between two variables. Regression lines are not "cause-and-effect" relationships. They merely describe the relationships among variables. The regression equation shows how one variable relates to the value and changes in another variable.

Another way to evaluate the relationship between two variables is to compute the **coefficient of correlation**. This measure expresses the degree or strength of the linear relationship. Usually

Coefficient of correlation
A measure of the strength of the relationship between two variables.

[3]When the sample size is large ($n > 30$), the prediction interval value of y can be computed using normal tables. When the number of observations is small, the t-distribution is appropriate. See D. Groebner et al., *Business Statistics*, 8th ed. (Upper Saddle River, NJ: Prentice Hall, 2011).

▶ **FIGURE 4.10**
Four Values of the Correlation Coefficient

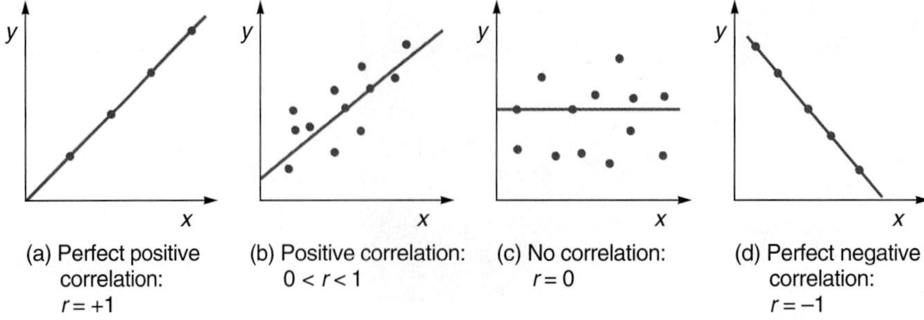

identified as r, the coefficient of correlation can be any number between +1 and −1. Figure 4.10 illustrates what different values of r might look like.

To compute r, we use much of the same data needed earlier to calculate a and b for the regression line. The rather lengthy equation for r is:

$$r = \frac{n\Sigma xy - \Sigma x\Sigma y}{\sqrt{[n\Sigma x^2 - (\Sigma x)^2][n\Sigma y^2 - (\Sigma y)^2]}} \quad \text{(4-16)}$$

Example 14 shows how to calculate the coefficient of correlation for the data given in Examples 12 and 13.

EXAMPLE 14 ▶ Determining the coefficient of correlation

In Example 12, we looked at the relationship between Nodel Construction Company's renovation sales and payroll in its hometown of West Bloomfield. The VP now wants to know the strength of the association between area payroll and sales.

APPROACH ▶ We compute the r value using Equation (4-16). We need to first add one more column of calculations—for y^2.

SOLUTION ▶ The data, including the column for y^2 and the calculations, are shown here:

y	x	x^2	xy	y^2
2.0	1	1	2.0	4.0
3.0	3	9	9.0	9.0
2.5	4	16	10.0	6.25
2.0	2	4	4.0	4.0
2.0	1	1	2.0	4.0
3.5	7	49	24.5	12.25
$\Sigma y = 15.0$	$\Sigma x = 18$	$\Sigma x^2 = 80$	$\Sigma xy = 51.5$	$\Sigma y^2 = 39.5$

$$r = \frac{(6)(51.5) - (18)(15.0)}{\sqrt{[(6)(80) - (18)^2][(6)(39.5) - (15.0)^2]}}$$

$$= \frac{309 - 270}{\sqrt{(156)(12)}} = \frac{39}{\sqrt{1{,}872}}$$

$$= \frac{39}{43.3} = .901$$

INSIGHT ▶ This r of .901 appears to be a significant correlation and helps confirm the closeness of the relationship between the two variables.

LEARNING EXERCISE ▶ If the coefficient of correlation was –.901 rather than +.901, what would this tell you? [Answer: The negative correlation would tell you that as payroll went up, Nodel's sales went down—a rather unlikely occurrence that would suggest you recheck your math.]

RELATED PROBLEMS ▶ 4.24d, 4.35d, 4.38c, 4.41f, 4.48b

Coefficient of determination
A measure of the amount of variation in the dependent variable about its mean that is explained by the regression equation.

Although the coefficient of correlation is the measure most commonly used to describe the relationship between two variables, another measure does exist. It is called the **coefficient of determination** and is simply the square of the coefficient of correlation—namely, r^2. The value of r^2 will always be a positive number in the range $0 \leq r^2 \leq 1$. The coefficient of determination is the percent of variation in the dependent variable (y) that is explained by the regression equation. In Nodel's case, the value of r^2 is .81, indicating that 81% of the total variation is explained by the regression equation.

Multiple-Regression Analysis

Multiple regression is a practical extension of the simple regression model we just explored. It allows us to build a model with several independent variables instead of just one variable. For example, if Nodel Construction wanted to include average annual interest rates in its model for forecasting renovation sales, the proper equation would be:

Multiple regression
An associative forecasting method with more than one independent variable.

$$\hat{y} = a + b_1x_1 + b_2x_2 \tag{4-17}$$

where $\hat{y}$ = dependent variable, sales
a = a constant, the y intercept
x_1 and x_2 = values of the two independent variables, area payroll and interest rates, respectively
b_1 and b_2 = coefficients for the two independent variables

The mathematics of multiple regression becomes quite complex (and is usually tackled by computer), so we leave the formulas for a, b_1, and b_2 to statistics textbooks. However, Example 15 shows how to interpret Equation (4-17) in forecasting Nodel's sales.

EXAMPLE 15
Using a multiple-regression equation

Nodel Construction wants to see the impact of a second independent variable, interest rates, on its sales.

APPROACH ▶ The new multiple-regression line for Nodel Construction, calculated by computer software, is:

$$\hat{y} = 1.80 + .30x_1 - 5.0x_2$$

We also find that the new coefficient of correlation is .96, implying the inclusion of the variable x_2, interest rates, adds even more strength to the linear relationship.

SOLUTION ▶ We can now estimate Nodel's sales if we substitute values for next year's payroll and interest rate. If West Bloomfield's payroll will be \$6 billion and the interest rate will be .12 (12%), sales will be forecast as:

$$\begin{aligned}\text{Sales(\$ millions)} &= 1.80 + .30(6) - 5.0(.12)\\ &= 1.8 + 1.8 - .6\\ &= 3.00\end{aligned}$$

or:

$$\text{Sales} = \$3{,}000{,}000$$

INSIGHT ▶ By using both variables, payroll and interest rates, Nodel now has a sales forecast of \$3 million and a higher coefficient of correlation. This suggests a stronger relationship between the two variables and a more accurate estimate of sales.

LEARNING EXERCISE ▶ If interest rates were only 6%, what would be the sales forecast? [Answer: 1.8 + 1.8 − 5.0(.06) = 3.3, or \$3,300,000.]

RELATED PROBLEMS ▶ 4.34, 4.36

MONITORING AND CONTROLLING FORECASTS

AUTHOR COMMENT
Using a tracking signal is a good way to make sure the forecasting system is continuing to do a good job.

Once a forecast has been completed, it should not be forgotten. No manager wants to be reminded that his or her forecast is horribly inaccurate, but a firm needs to determine why actual demand (or whatever variable is being examined) differed significantly from that projected. If the forecaster is accurate, that individual usually makes sure that everyone is aware of his or her talents. Very seldom does one read articles in *Fortune*, *Forbes*, or *The Wall Street Journal*, however, about money managers who are consistently off by 25% in their stock market forecasts.

Tracking signal
A measurement of how well a forecast is predicting actual values.

One way to monitor forecasts to ensure that they are performing well is to use a tracking signal. A **tracking signal** is a measurement of how well a forecast is predicting actual values. As forecasts are updated every week, month, or quarter, the newly available demand data are compared to the forecast values.

The tracking signal is computed as the cumulative error divided by the *mean absolute deviation (MAD)*:

$$\begin{aligned}(\text{Tracking signal}) &= \frac{\text{Cumulative error}}{\text{MAD}} \\ &= \frac{\Sigma(\text{Actual demand in period } i - \text{Forecast demand in period } i)}{\text{MAD}}\end{aligned} \qquad (4\text{-}18)$$

where $$(\text{MAD}) = \frac{\Sigma|\text{Actual} - \text{Forecast}|}{n}$$

as seen earlier, in Equation (4-5).

Positive tracking signals indicate that demand is *greater* than forecast. *Negative* signals mean that demand is *less* than forecast. A good tracking signal—that is, one with a low cumulative error—has about as much positive error as it has negative error. In other words, small deviations are okay, but positive and negative errors should balance one another so that the tracking signal centers closely around zero. A consistent tendency for forecasts to be greater or less than the actual values (that is, for a high absolute cumulative error) is called a **bias** error. Bias can occur if, for example, the wrong variables or trend line are used or if a seasonal index is misapplied.

Bias
A forecast that is consistently higher or consistently lower than actual values of a time series.

Once tracking signals are calculated, they are compared with predetermined control limits. When a tracking signal exceeds an upper or lower limit, there is a problem with the forecasting method, and management may want to reevaluate the way it forecasts demand. Figure 4.11 shows the graph of a tracking signal that is exceeding the range of acceptable variation. If the model being used is exponential smoothing, perhaps the smoothing constant needs to be readjusted.

LO7: Use a tracking signal

How do firms decide what the upper and lower tracking limits should be? There is no single answer, but they try to find reasonable values—in other words, limits not so low as to be triggered with every small forecast error and not so high as to allow bad forecasts to be regularly overlooked. One MAD is equivalent to approximately .8 standard deviation, ±2 MADs = ±1.6 standard deviations, ±3 MADs = ±2.4 standard deviations, and ±4 MADs = ±3.2 standard deviations. This fact suggests that for a forecast to be "in control," 89% of the errors are expected to fall within ±2 MADs, 98% within ±3 MADs, or 99.9% within ±4 MADs.[4]

Example 16 shows how the tracking signal and cumulative error can be computed.

▶ **FIGURE 4.11**
A Plot of Tracking Signals

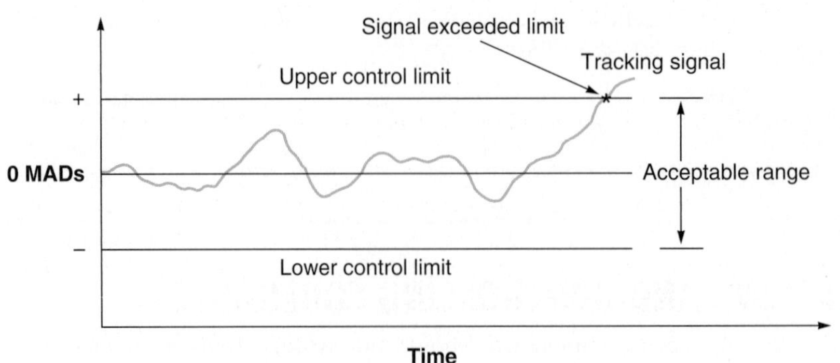

[4]To prove these three percentages to yourself, just set up a normal curve for ±1.6 standard deviations (z-values). Using the normal table in Appendix I, you find that the area under the curve is .89. This represents ±2 MADs. Likewise, ±3 MADs = ±2.4 standard deviations encompass 98% of the area, and so on for ±4 MADs.

EXAMPLE 16

Computing the tracking signal at Carlson's Bakery

Carlson's Bakery wants to evaluate performance of its croissant forecast.

APPROACH ▶ Develop a tracking signal for the forecast and see if it stays within acceptable limits, which we define as ±4 MADs.

SOLUTION ▶ Using the forecast and demand data for the past 6 quarters for croissant sales, we develop a tracking signal in the table below:

Quarter	Actual Demand	Forecast Demand	Error	Cumulative Error	Absolute Forecast Error	Cumulative Absolute Forecast Error	MAD	Tracking Signal (Cumulative Error/MAD)
1	90	100	−10	−10	10	10	10.0	−10/10 = −1
2	95	100	−5	−15	5	15	7.5	−15/7.5 = −2
3	115	100	+15	0	15	30	10.0	0/10 = 0
4	100	110	−10	−10	10	40	10.0	−10/10 = −1
5	125	110	+15	+5	15	55	11.0	+5/11 = +0.5
6	140	110	+30	+35	30	85	14.2	+35/14.2 = +2.5

$$\text{At the end of quarter 6, MAD} = \frac{\Sigma|\text{Forecast errors}|}{n} = \frac{85}{6} = 14.2$$

$$\text{and Tracking signal} = \frac{\text{Cumulative error}}{\text{MAD}} = \frac{35}{14.2} = 2.5 \text{ MADs}$$

INSIGHT ▶ Because the tracking signal drifted from −2 MAD to +2.5 MAD (between 1.6 and 2.0 standard deviations), we can conclude that it is within acceptable limits.

LEARNING EXERCISE ▶ If actual demand in quarter 6 was 130 (rather than 140), what would be the MAD and resulting tracking signal? [Answer: MAD for quarter 6 would be 12.5, and the tracking signal for period 6 would be 2 MADs.]

RELATED PROBLEMS ▶ 4.37, 4.45

Adaptive Smoothing

Adaptive forecasting refers to computer monitoring of tracking signals and self-adjustment if a signal passes a preset limit. For example, when applied to exponential smoothing, the α and β coefficients are first selected on the basis of values that minimize error forecasts and then adjusted accordingly whenever the computer notes an errant tracking signal. This process is called **adaptive smoothing**.

Adaptive smoothing
An approach to exponential smoothing forecasting in which the smoothing constant is automatically changed to keep errors to a minimum.

Focus Forecasting

Rather than adapt by choosing a smoothing constant, computers allow us to try a variety of forecasting models. Such an approach is called focus forecasting. **Focus forecasting** is based on two principles:

Focus forecasting
Forecasting that tries a variety of computer models and selects the best one for a particular application.

1. Sophisticated forecasting models are not always better than simple ones.
2. There is no single technique that should be used for all products or services.

Bernard Smith, inventory manager for American Hardware Supply, coined the term *focus forecasting*. Smith's job was to forecast quantities for 100,000 hardware products purchased by American's 21 buyers.[5] He found that buyers neither trusted nor understood the exponential smoothing model then in use. Instead, they used very simple approaches of their own. So Smith developed his new computerized system for selecting forecasting methods.

Smith chose to test seven forecasting methods. They ranged from the simple ones that buyers used (such as the naive approach) to statistical models. Every month, Smith applied the forecasts of all seven models to each item in stock. In these simulated trials, the forecast values were subtracted from the most recent actual demands, giving a simulated forecast error. The forecast

[5]Bernard T. Smith, *Focus Forecasting: Computer Techniques for Inventory Control* (Boston: CBI Publishing, 1978).

method yielding the least error is selected by the computer, which then uses it to make next month's forecast. Although buyers still have an override capability, American Hardware finds that focus forecasting provides excellent results.

AUTHOR COMMENT
Forecasting at McDonald's, FedEx, and Walmart is as important and complex as it is for manufacturers such as Toyota and Dell.

FORECASTING IN THE SERVICE SECTOR

Forecasting in the service sector presents some unusual challenges. A major technique in the retail sector is tracking demand by maintaining good short-term records. For instance, a barbershop catering to men expects peak flows on Fridays and Saturdays. Indeed, most barbershops are closed on Sunday and Monday, and many call in extra help on Friday and Saturday. A downtown restaurant, on the other hand, may need to track conventions and holidays for effective short-term forecasting. The *OM in Action* box "Forecasting at FedEx's Customer Service Centers" provides an example of a major service-sector industry, the call center.

Specialty Retail Shops Specialty retail facilities, such as flower shops, may have other unusual demand patterns, and those patterns will differ depending on the holiday. When Valentine's Day falls on a weekend, for example, flowers can't be delivered to offices, and those romantically inclined are likely to celebrate with outings rather than flowers. If a holiday falls on a Monday, some of the celebration may also take place on the weekend, reducing flower sales. However, when Valentine's Day falls in midweek, busy midweek schedules often make flowers the optimal way to celebrate. Because flowers for Mother's Day are to be delivered on Saturday or Sunday, this holiday forecast varies less. Due to special demand patterns, many service firms maintain records of sales, noting not only the day of the week but also unusual events, including the weather, so that patterns and correlations that influence demand can be developed.

Fast-Food Restaurants Fast-food restaurants are well aware not only of weekly, daily, and hourly but even 15-minute variations in demands that influence sales. Therefore, detailed forecasts of demand are needed. Figure 4.12(a) shows the hourly forecast for a typical fast-food restaurant. Note the lunchtime and dinnertime peaks. This contrasts to the mid-morning and mid-afternoon peaks at FedEx's call center in Figure 14.12(b).

Firms like Taco Bell now use point-of-sale computers that track sales every quarter hour. Taco Bell found that a 6-week moving average was the forecasting technique that minimized its mean squared error (MSE) of these quarter-hour forecasts. Building this forecasting methodology into each of Taco Bell's 6,500 stores' computers, the model makes weekly projections of customer

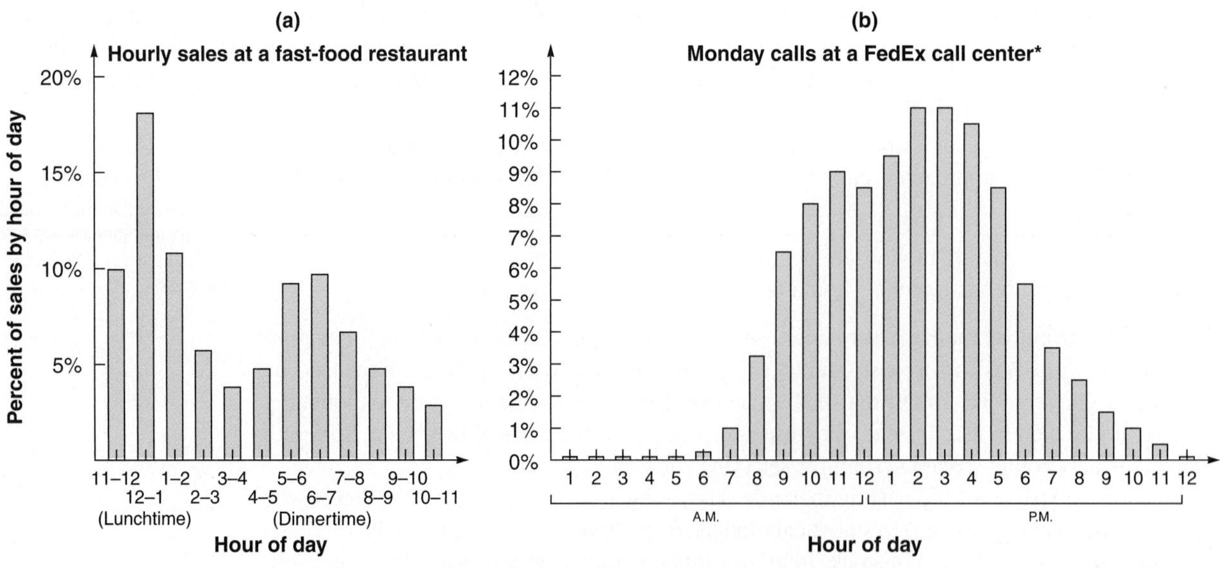

▲ **FIGURE 4.12 Forecasts Are Unique: Note the Variations between (a) Hourly Sales at a Fast-Food Restaurant and (b) Hourly Call Volume at FedEx**

*Based on historical data: see *Journal of Business Forecasting* (Winter 1999–2000): 6–11.

OM in Action ► Forecasting at FedEx's Customer Service Centers

The world's largest express shipping company, FedEx, generates $38 billion in revenues, using 675 planes, 44,000 trucks, and a workforce of 145,000 in 220 countries. To support this global network, the company has 51 customer service call centers, whose service goal is to answer 90% of all calls within 20 seconds. With a half-million daily calls just in the U.S., FedEx makes extensive use of forecasting models for staffing decisions and to ensure that customer satisfaction levels stay the highest in the industry.

FedEx's Forecasting & Modeling department makes several different forecasts. *One-year* and *five-year* models predict number of calls, average handle time, and staffing needs. They break forecasts into weekday, Saturday, and Sunday and then use the Delphi method and time-series analysis.

FedEx's *tactical forecasts* are monthly and use 8 years of historical daily data. This time-series model addresses

month, day of week, and day of month to predict caller volume. Finally, the *operational forecast* uses a weighted moving average and 6 weeks of data to project the number of calls on a half-hourly basis.

FedEx's forecasts are consistently accurate to within 1% to 2% of actual call volumes. This means coverage needs are met, service levels are maintained, and costs are controlled.

Sources: Hoover's Company Records (July 1, 2009): 10552; *Baseline* (January 2005): 54; and *Journal of Business Forecasting* (Winter 1999–2000): 7–11.

transactions. These in turn are used by store managers to schedule staff, who begin in 15-minute increments, not 1-hour blocks as in other industries. The forecasting model has been so successful that Taco Bell has increased customer service while documenting more than $50 million in labor cost savings in 4 years of use.[6]

CHAPTER SUMMARY

Forecasts are a critical part of the operations manager's function. Demand forecasts drive a firm's production, capacity, and scheduling systems and affect the financial, marketing, and personnel planning functions.

There are a variety of qualitative and quantitative forecasting techniques. Qualitative approaches employ judgment, experience, intuition, and a host of other factors that are difficult to quantify. Quantitative forecasting uses historical data and causal, or associative, relations to project future demands. The Rapid Review for this chapter summarizes the formulas we introduced in quantitative forecasting.

Forecast calculations are seldom performed by hand. Most operations managers turn to software packages such as Forecast PRO, SAP, AFS, SAS, SPSS, or Excel.

No forecasting method is perfect under all conditions. And even once management has found a satisfactory approach, it must still monitor and control forecasts to make sure errors do not get out of hand. Forecasting can often be a very challenging, but rewarding, part of managing.

Key Terms

Forecasting (p. 104)
Economic forecasts (p. 105)
Technological forecasts (p. 105)
Demand forecasts (p. 105)
Quantitative forecasts (p. 107)
Qualitative forecasts (p. 107)
Jury of executive opinion (p. 107)
Delphi method (p. 107)
Sales force composite (p. 107)
Consumer market survey (p. 107)
Time series (p. 108)
Naive approach (p. 108)
Moving averages (p. 109)
Exponential smoothing (p. 112)
Smoothing constant (p. 112)
Mean absolute deviation (MAD) (p. 113)
Mean squared error (MSE) (p. 115)
Mean absolute percent error (MAPE) (p. 115)
Trend projection (p. 119)
Seasonal variations (p. 121)
Cycles (p. 126)
Linear-regression analysis (p. 126)
Standard error of the estimate (p. 128)
Coefficient of correlation (p. 129)
Coefficient of determination (p. 130)
Multiple regression (p. 131)
Tracking signal (p. 132)
Bias (p. 132)
Adaptive smoothing (p. 133)
Focus forecasting (p. 133)

[6]J. Hueter and W. Swart, "An Integrated Labor Management System for Taco Bell," *Interfaces* 28, no. 1 (January–February 1998): 75–91.

Ethical Dilemma

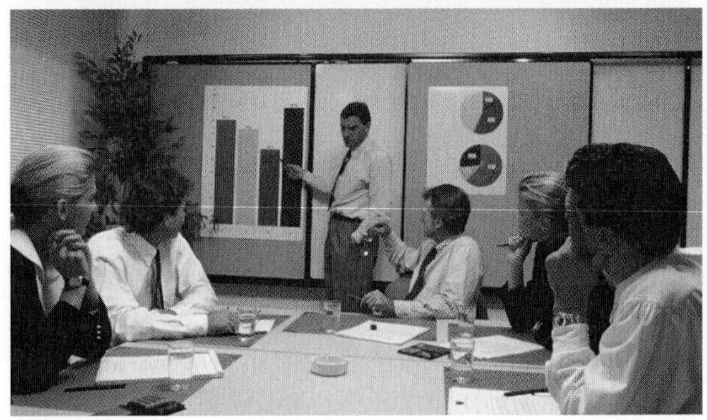

In 2009, the board of regents responsible for all public higher education funding in a large Midwestern state hired a consultant to develop a series of enrollment forecasting models, one for each college. These models used historical data and exponential smoothing to forecast the following year's enrollments. Based on the model, which included a smoothing constant (α) for each school, each college's budget was set by the board. The head of the board personally selected each smoothing constant based on what she called her "gut reactions and political acumen."

What do you think the advantages and disadvantages of this system are? Answer from the perspective of (a) the board of regents and (b) the president of each college. How can this model be abused and what can be done to remove any biases? How can a *regression model* be used to produce results that favor one forecast over another?

Discussion Questions

1. What is a qualitative forecasting model, and when is its use appropriate?
2. Identify and briefly describe the two general forecasting approaches.
3. Identify the three forecasting time horizons. State an approximate duration for each.
4. Briefly describe the steps that are used to develop a forecasting system.
5. A skeptical manager asks what medium-range forecasts can be used for. Give the manager three possible uses/purposes.
6. Explain why such forecasting devices as moving averages, weighted moving averages, and exponential smoothing are not well suited for data series that have trends.
7. What is the basic difference between a weighted moving average and exponential smoothing?
8. What three methods are used to determine the accuracy of any given forecasting method? How would you determine whether time-series regression or exponential smoothing is better in a specific application?
9. Research and briefly describe the Delphi technique. How would it be used by an employer you have worked for?
10. What is the primary difference between a time-series model and an associative model?
11. Define time series.
12. What effect does the value of the smoothing constant have on the weight given to the recent values?
13. Explain the value of seasonal indices in forecasting. How are seasonal patterns different from cyclical patterns?
14. Which forecasting technique can place the most emphasis on recent values? How does it do this?
15. In your own words, explain adaptive forecasting.
16. What is the purpose of a tracking signal?
17. Explain, in your own words, the meaning of the correlation coefficient. Discuss the meaning of a negative value of the correlation coefficient.
18. What is the difference between a dependent and an independent variable?
19. Give examples of industries that are affected by seasonality. Why would these businesses want to filter out seasonality?
20. Give examples of industries in which demand forecasting is dependent on the demand for other products.
21. What happens to the ability to forecast for periods farther into the future?

Using Software in Forecasting

This section presents three ways to solve forecasting problems with computer software. First, you can create your own Excel spreadsheets to develop forecasts. Second, you can use the Excel OM software that comes with the text and is found on our text web site. Third, POM for Windows is another program that is located on our web site at **www.pearsonhighered.com/heizer**.

Creating Your Own Excel Spreadsheets

Excel spreadsheets (and spreadsheets in general) are frequently used in forecasting. Exponential smoothing, trend analysis, and regression analysis (simple and multiple) are supported by built-in Excel functions.

Program 4.1 illustrates how to build an Excel forecast for the data in Example 8. The goal for N.Y. Edison is to create a trend analysis of the 2003–2009 data. Note that in cell D4 you can enter either = $B$16 + $B$17 * C4 *or* = TREND ($B$4: $B$10, $C$4: $C$10, C4).

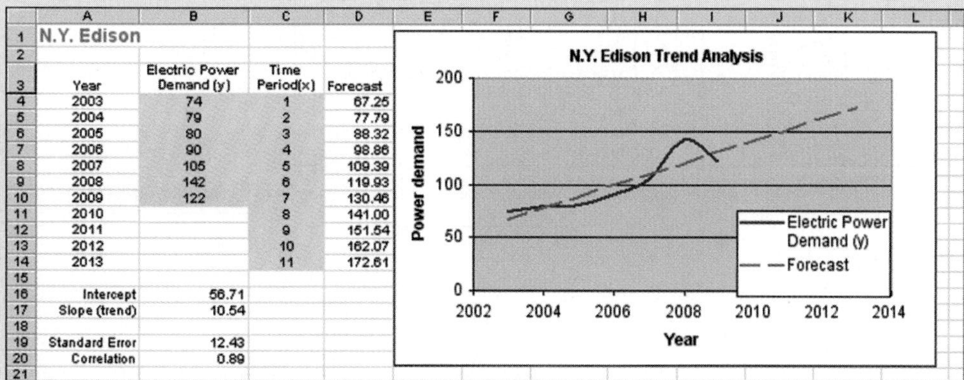

	A	B	C	D
1	N.Y. Edison			
2				
3	Year	Electric Power Demand (y)	Time Period(x)	Forecast
4	2003	74	1	67.25
5	2004	79	2	77.79
6	2005	80	3	88.32
7	2006	90	4	98.86
8	2007	105	5	109.39
9	2008	142	6	119.93
10	2009	122	7	130.46
11	2010		8	141.00
12	2011		9	151.54
13	2012		10	162.07
14	2013		11	172.61
15				
16	Intercept	56.71		
17	Slope (trend)	10.54		
18				
19	Standard Error	12.43		
20	Correlation	0.89		
21				

◀ **PROGRAM 4.1**
Using Excel to Develop Your Own Forecast, with Data from Example 8

Computations			
Value	**Cell**	**Excel Formula**	**Action**
Trend line column	D4	=$B$16+$B$17*C4 (or =TREND($B$4:$B$10,$C$4:$C$10,C4))	Copy to D5:D14
Intercept	B16	=INTERCEPT(B4:B10, C4:C10)	
Slope (trend)	B17	=SLOPE(B4:B10, C4:C10)	
Standard error	B19	=STEYX(B4:B10, C4:C10)	
Correlation	B20	=CORREL(B4:B10, C4:C10)	

As an alternative, you may want to experiment with Excel's built-in regression analysis. To do so, under the *Data* menu bar selection choose *Data Analysis*, then *Regression*. Enter your *Y* and *X* data into two columns (say B and C). When the regression window appears, enter the *Y* and *X* ranges, then select *OK*. Excel offers several plots and tables to those interested in more rigorous analysis of regression problems.

Using Excel OM

Excel OM's forecasting module has five components: (1) moving averages, (2) weighted moving averages, (3) exponential smoothing, (4) regression (with one variable only), and (5) decomposition. Excel OM's error analysis is much more complete than that available with the Excel add-in.

Program 4.2 illustrates Excel OM's input and output, using Example 2's weighted-moving-average data.

Using POM for Windows

POM for Windows can project moving averages (both simple and weighted), handle exponential smoothing (both simple and trend adjusted), forecast with least squares trend projection, and solve linear-regression (associative) models. A summary screen of error analysis and a graph of the data can also be generated. As a special example of exponential smoothing adaptive forecasting, when using an α of 0, POM for Windows will find the α value that yields the minimum MAD.

Appendix IV provides further details.

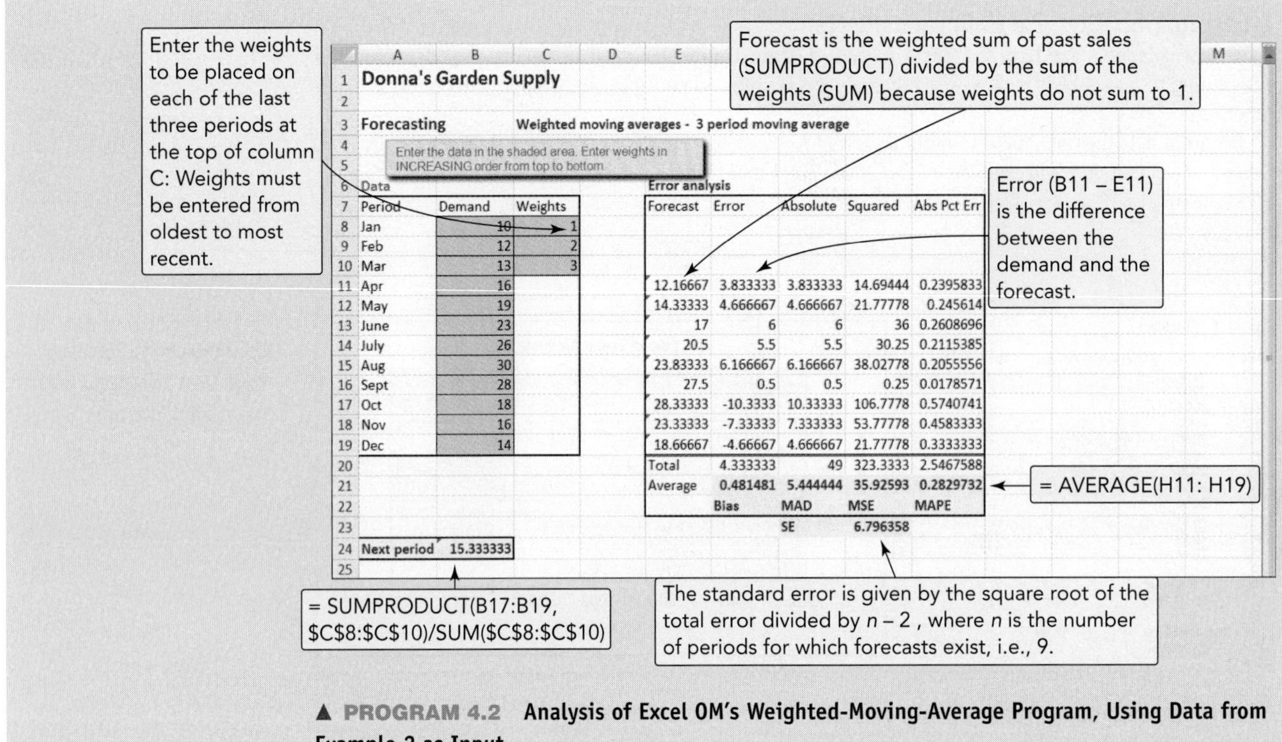

▲ **PROGRAM 4.2 Analysis of Excel OM's Weighted-Moving-Average Program, Using Data from Example 2 as Input**

Solved Problems

Virtual Office Hours help is available at www.myomlab.com.

▼ SOLVED PROBLEM 4.1

Sales of Volkswagen's popular Beetle have grown steadily at auto dealerships in Nevada during the past 5 years (see table below). The sales manager had predicted in 2004 that 2005 sales would be 410 VWs. Using exponential smoothing with a weight of $\alpha = .30$, develop forecasts for 2006 through 2010.

Year	Sales	Forecast
2005	450	410
2006	495	
2007	518	
2008	563	
2009	584	
2010	?	

▼ SOLUTION

Year	Forecast
2005	410.0
2006	422.0 = 410 + .3 (450 − 410)
2007	443.9 = 422 + .3 (495 − 422)
2008	466.1 = 443.9 + .3 (518 − 443.9)
2009	495.2 = 466.1 + .3 (563 − 466.1)
2010	521.8 = 495.2 + .3 (584 − 495.2)

▼ SOLVED PROBLEM 4.2

In Example 7, we applied trend-adjusted exponential smoothing to forecast demand for a piece of pollution-control equipment for months 2 and 3 (out of 9 months of data provided). Let us now continue this process for month 4. We want to confirm the forecast for month 4 shown in Table 4.1 (p. 118) and Figure 4.3 (p. 118).

For month 4, $A_4 = 19$, with $\alpha = .2$, and $\beta = .4$.

▼ SOLUTION

$$\begin{aligned}
F_4 &= \alpha A_3 + (1-\alpha)(F_3 + T_3) \\
&= (.2)(20) + (1 - .2)(15.18 + 2.10) \\
&= 4.0 + (.8)(17.28) \\
&= 4.0 + 13.82 \\
&= 17.82 \\
T_4 &= \beta(F_4 - F_3) + (1 - \beta)T_3 \\
&= (.4)(17.82 - 15.18) + (1 - .4)(2.10) \\
&= (.4)(2.64) + (.6)(2.10) \\
&= 1.056 + 1.26 \\
&= 2.32 \\
FIT_4 &= 17.82 + 2.32 \\
&= 20.14
\end{aligned}$$

▼ SOLVED PROBLEM 4.3

Room registrations in the Toronto Towers Plaza Hotel have been recorded for the past 9 years. To project future occupancy, management would like to determine the mathematical trend of guest registration. This estimate will help the hotel determine whether future expansion will be needed. Given the following time-series data, develop a regression equation relating registrations to time (e.g., a trend equation). Then forecast 2011 registrations. Room registrations are in the thousands:

2001: 17 2002: 16 2003: 16 2004: 21 2005: 20
2006: 20 2007: 23 2008: 25 2009: 24

▼ SOLUTION

Year	Transformed Year, x	Registrants, y (in thousands)	x^2	xy
2001	1	17	1	17
2002	2	16	4	32
2003	3	16	9	48
2004	4	21	16	84
2005	5	20	25	100
2006	6	20	36	120
2007	7	23	49	161
2008	8	25	64	200
2009	9	24	81	216
	$\Sigma x = 45$	$\Sigma y = 182$	$\Sigma x^2 = 285$	$\Sigma xy = 978$

$$b = \frac{\Sigma xy - n\bar{x}\bar{y}}{\Sigma x^2 - n\bar{x}^2} = \frac{978 - (9)(5)(20.22)}{285 - (9)(25)} = \frac{978 - 909.9}{285 - 225} = \frac{68.1}{60} = 1.135$$

$$a = \bar{y} - b\bar{x} = 20.22 - (1.135)(5) = 20.22 - 5.675 = 14.545$$

$$\hat{y}\text{ (registrations)} = 14.545 + 1.135x$$

The projection of registrations in the year 2011 (which is $x = 11$ in the coding system used) is:

$$\hat{y} = 14.545 + (1.135)(11) = 27.03$$

or 27,030 guests in 2011

▼ SOLVED PROBLEM 4.4

Quarterly demand for Ford F150 pickups at a New York auto dealer is forecast with the equation:

$$\hat{y} = 10 + 3x$$

where x = quarters, and:

Quarter I of 2008 = 0
Quarter II of 2008 = 1
Quarter III of 2008 = 2
Quarter IV of 2008 = 3
Quarter I of 2009 = 4
and so on

and:

$$\hat{y} = \text{quarterly demand}$$

The demand for trucks is seasonal, and the indices for Quarters I, II, III, and IV are 0.80, 1.00, 1.30, and 0.90, respectively. Forecast demand for each quarter of 2010. Then, seasonalize each forecast to adjust for quarterly variations.

▼ SOLUTION

Quarter II of 2009 is coded $x = 5$; Quarter III of 2009, $x = 6$; and Quarter IV of 2009, $x = 7$. Hence, Quarter I of 2010 is coded $x = 8$; Quarter II, $x = 9$; and so on.

$$\hat{y}(\text{2010 Quarter I}) = 10 + 3(8) = 34$$
$$\hat{y}(\text{2010 Quarter II}) = 10 + 3(9) = 37$$
$$\hat{y}(\text{2010 Quarter III}) = 10 + 3(10) = 40$$
$$\hat{y}(\text{2010 Quarter IV}) = 10 + 3(11) = 43$$

Adjusted forecast = (.80)(34) = 27.2
Adjusted forecast = (1.00)(37) = 37
Adjusted forecast = (1.30)(40) = 52
Adjusted forecast = (.90)(43) = 38.7

Problems*

• **4.1** The following gives the number of pints of type A blood used at Woodlawn Hospital in the past 6 weeks:

Week Of	Pints Used
August 31	360
September 7	389
September 14	410
September 21	381
September 28	368
October 5	374

a) Forecast the demand for the week of October 12 using a 3-week moving average.
b) Use a 3-week weighted moving average, with weights of .1, .3, and .6, using .6 for the most recent week. Forecast demand for the week of October 12.
c) Compute the forecast for the week of October 12 using exponential smoothing with a forecast for August 31 of 360 and $\alpha = .2$. PX

•• **4.2**

Year	1	2	3	4	5	6	7	8	9	10	11
Demand	7	9	5	9	13	8	12	13	9	11	7

a) Plot the above data on a graph. Do you observe any trend, cycles, or random variations?
b) Starting in year 4 and going to year 12, forecast demand using a 3-year moving average. Plot your forecast on the same graph as the original data.
c) Starting in year 4 and going to year 12, forecast demand using a 3-year moving average with weights of .1, .3, and .6, using .6 for the most recent year. Plot this forecast on the same graph.
d) As you compare forecasts with the original data, which seems to give the better results? PX

• **4.3** Refer to Problem 4.2. Develop a forecast for years 2 through 12 using exponential smoothing with $\alpha = .4$ and a forecast for year 1 of 6. Plot your new forecast on a graph with the actual data and the naive forecast. Based on a visual inspection, which forecast is better? PX

• **4.4** A check-processing center uses exponential smoothing to forecast the number of incoming checks each month. The number of checks received in June was 40 million, while the forecast was 42 million. A smoothing constant of .2 is used.
a) What is the forecast for July?
b) If the center received 45 million checks in July, what would be the forecast for August?
c) Why might this be an inappropriate forecasting method for this situation? PX

•• **4.5** The Carbondale Hospital is considering the purchase of a new ambulance. The decision will rest partly on the anticipated mileage to be driven next year. The miles driven during the past 5 years are as follows:

Year	Mileage
1	3,000
2	4,000
3	3,400
4	3,800
5	3,700

a) Forecast the mileage for next year using a 2-year moving average.
b) Find the MAD based on the 2-year moving average forecast in part (a). (*Hint:* You will have only 3 years of matched data.)
c) Use a weighted 2-year moving average with weights of .4 and .6 to forecast next year's mileage. (The weight of .6 is for the most recent year.) What MAD results from using this approach to forecasting? (*Hint:* You will have only 3 years of matched data.)
d) Compute the forecast for year 6 using exponential smoothing, an initial forecast for year 1 of 3,000 miles, and $\alpha = .5$. PX

•• **4.6** The monthly sales for Telco Batteries, Inc., were as follows:

Month	Sales
January	20
February	21
March	15
April	14
May	13
June	16
July	17
August	18
September	20
October	20
November	21
December	23

a) Plot the monthly sales data.
b) Forecast January sales using each of the following:
   i) Naive method.
   ii) A 3-month moving average.
   iii) A 6-month weighted average using .1, .1, .1, .2, .2, and .3, with the heaviest weights applied to the most recent months.
   iv) Exponential smoothing using an $\alpha = .3$ and a September forecast of 18.
   v) A trend projection.
c) With the data given, which method would allow you to forecast next March's sales? PX

•• **4.7** The actual demand for the patients at Omaha Emergency Medical Clinic for the first six weeks of this year follows:

Week	Actual No. of Patients
1	65
2	62
3	70
4	48
5	63
6	52

Clinic administrator Marc Schniederjans wants you to forecast patient demand at the clinic for week 7 by using this data. You decide to use a weighted moving average method to find this forecast. Your method uses four actual demand levels, with weights of 0.333 on the present period, 0.25 one period ago, 0.25 two periods ago, and 0.167 three periods ago.
a) What is the value of your forecast? PX
b) If instead the weights were 20, 15, 15, and 10, respectively, how would the forecast change? Explain why.
c) What if the weights were 0.40, 0.30, 0.20, and 0.10, respectively? Now what is the forecast for week 7?

**Note:* PX means the problem may be solved with POM for Windows and/or Excel OM.

• **4.8** Daily high temperatures in St. Louis for the last week were as follows: 93, 94, 93, 95, 96, 88, 90 (yesterday).

a) Forecast the high temperature today, using a 3-day moving average.
b) Forecast the high temperature today, using a 2-day moving average.
c) Calculate the mean absolute deviation based on a 2-day moving average.
d) Compute the mean squared error for the 2-day moving average.
e) Calculate the mean absolute percent error for the 2-day moving average. PX

••• **4.9** Dell uses the CR5 chip in some of its laptop computers. The prices for the chip during the past 12 months were as follows:

Month	Price per Chip	Month	Price per Chip
January	\$1.80	July	1.80
February	1.67	August	1.83
March	1.70	September	1.70
April	1.85	October	1.65
May	1.90	November	1.70
June	1.87	December	1.75

a) Use a 2-month moving average on all the data and plot the averages and the prices.
b) Use a 3-month moving average and add the 3-month plot to the graph created in part (a).
c) Which is better (using the mean absolute deviation): the 2-month average or the 3-month average?
d) Compute the forecasts for each month using exponential smoothing, with an initial forecast for January of \$1.80. Use $\alpha = .1$, then $\alpha = .3$, and finally $\alpha = .5$. Using MAD, which α is the best? PX

•• **4.10** Data collected on the yearly registrations for a Six Sigma seminar at the Quality College are shown in the following table:

Year	1	2	3	4	5	6	7	8	9	10	11
Registrations (000)	4	6	4	5	10	8	7	9	12	14	15

a) Develop a 3-year moving average to forecast registrations from year 4 to year 12.
b) Estimate demand again for years 4 to 12 with a 3-year weighted moving average in which registrations in the most recent year are given a weight of 2, and registrations in the other 2 years are each given a weight of 1.
c) Graph the original data and the two forecasts. Which of the two forecasting methods seems better? PX

• **4.11** a) Use exponential smoothing with a smoothing constant of 0.3 to forecast the registrations at the seminar given in Problem 4.10. To begin the procedure, assume that the forecast for year 1 was 5,000 people signing up.
b) What is the MAD? PX

•• **4.12** Consider the following actual and forecast demand levels for Big Mac hamburgers at a local McDonald's restaurant:

Day	Actual Demand	Forecast Demand
Monday	88	88
Tuesday	72	88
Wednesday	68	84
Thursday	48	80
Friday		

The forecast for Monday was derived by observing Monday's demand level and setting Monday's forecast level equal to this demand level. Subsequent forecasts were derived by using exponential smoothing with a smoothing constant of 0.25. Using this exponential smoothing method, what is the forecast for Big Mac demand for Friday? PX

••• **4.13** As you can see in the following table, demand for heart transplant surgery at Washington General Hospital has increased steadily in the past few years:

Year	1	2	3	4	5	6
Heart Transplants	45	50	52	56	58	?

The director of medical services predicted 6 years ago that demand in year 1 would be 41 surgeries.

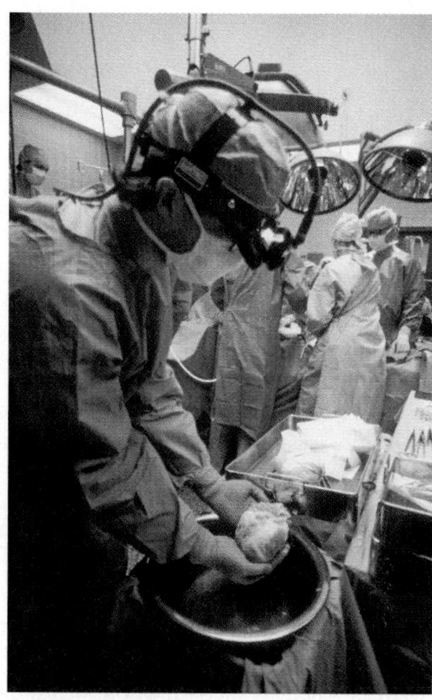

a) Use exponential smoothing, first with a smoothing constant of .6 and then with one of .9, to develop forecasts for years 2 through 6.
b) Use a 3-year moving average to forecast demand in years 4, 5, and 6.
c) Use the trend-projection method to forecast demand in years 1 through 6.
d) With MAD as the criterion, which of the four forecasting methods is best? PX

•• **4.14** Following are two weekly forecasts made by two different methods for the number of gallons of gasoline, in thousands, demanded at a local gasoline station. Also shown are actual demand levels, in thousands of gallons:

	Forecasts		
Week	Method 1	Method 2	Actual Demand
1	0.90	0.80	0.70
2	1.05	1.20	1.00
3	0.95	0.90	1.00
4	1.20	1.11	1.00

What are the MAD and MSE for each method?

• **4.15** Refer to Solved Problem 4.1 on page 138. Use a 3-year moving average to forecast the sales of Volkswagen Beetles in Nevada through 2010. What is the MAD? PX

• **4.16** Refer to Solved Problem 4.1. Using the trend projection method, develop a forecast for the sales of Volkswagen Beetles in Nevada through 2010. What is the MAD? PX

• **4.17** Refer to Solved Problem 4.1. Using smoothing constants of .6 and .9, develop forecasts for the sales of VW Beetles. What effect did the smoothing constant have on the forecast? Use MAD to determine which of the three smoothing constants (.3, .6, or .9) gives the most accurate forecast. PX

•••• **4.18** Consider the following actual (A_t) and forecast (F_t) demand levels for a product:

Time Period, t	Actual Demand, A_t	Forecast Demand, F_t
1	50	50
2	42	50
3	56	48
4	46	50
5		

The first forecast, F_1, was derived by observing A_1 and setting F_1 equal to A_1. Subsequent forecasts were derived by exponential smoothing. Using the exponential smoothing method, find the forecast for time period 5. (*Hint:* You need to first find the smoothing constant, α.)

••• **4.19** Income at the law firm Smith and Wesson for the period February to July was as follows:

Month	February	March	April	May	June	July
Income (in $ thousand)	70.0	68.5	64.8	71.7	71.3	72.8

Use trend-adjusted exponential smoothing to forecast the law firm's August income. Assume that the initial forecast for February is $65,000 and the initial trend adjustment is 0. The smoothing constants selected are $\alpha = .1$ and $\beta = .2$. PX

••• **4.20** Resolve Problem 4.19 with $\alpha = .1$ and $\beta = .8$. Using MSE, determine which smoothing constants provide a better forecast. PX

• **4.21** Refer to the trend-adjusted exponential smoothing illustration in Example 7 on pages 117–118. Using $\alpha = .2$ and $\beta = .4$, we forecast sales for 9 months, showing the detailed calculations for months 2 and 3. In Solved Problem 4.2, we continued the process for month 4.

In this problem, show your calculations for months 5 and 6 for F_t, T_t, and FIT_t. PX

• **4.22** Refer to Problem 4.21. Complete the trend-adjusted exponential-smoothing forecast computations for periods 7, 8, and 9. Confirm that your numbers for F_t, T_t, and FIT_t match those in Table 4.1 (p. 118). PX

•• **4.23** Sales of vegetable dehydrators at Bud Banis's discount department store in St. Louis over the past year are shown below. Management prepared a forecast using a combination of exponential smoothing and its collective judgment for the 4 months (March, April, May, and June of 2010):

Month	2009–2010 Unit Sales	Management's Forecast
July	100	
August	93	
September	96	
October	110	
November	124	
December	119	
January	92	
February	83	
March	101	120
April	96	114
May	89	110
June	108	108

a) Compute MAD and MAPE for management's technique.
b) Do management's results outperform (i.e., have smaller MAD and MAPE than) a naive forecast?
c) Which forecast do you recommend, based on lower forecast error?

•• **4.24** Howard Weiss, owner of a musical instrument distributorship, thinks that demand for bass drums may be related to the number of television appearances by the popular group Stone Temple Pilots during the previous month. Weiss has collected the data shown in the following table:

Demand for Bass Drums	3	6	7	5	10	7
Stone Temple Pilots' TV Appearances	3	4	7	6	8	5

a) Graph these data to see whether a linear equation might describe the relationship between the group's television shows and bass drum sales.
b) Use the least-squares regression method to derive a forecasting equation.
c) What is your estimate for bass drum sales if the Stone Temple Pilots performed on TV nine times last month?
d) What are the correlation coefficient (r) and the coefficient of determination (r^2) for this model, and what do they mean? PX

• **4.25** The following gives the number of accidents that occurred on Florida State Highway 101 during the past 4 months:

Month	Number of Accidents
January	30
February	40
March	60
April	90

Forecast the number of accidents that will occur in May, using least-squares regression to derive a trend equation. PX

• **4.26** In the past, Arup Mukherjee's tire dealership in Pensacola sold an average of 1,000 radials each year. In the past 2 years, 200 and 250, respectively, were sold in fall, 350 and 300 in winter, 150 and 165 in spring, and 300 and 285 in summer. With a major expansion planned, Mukherjee projects sales next year to increase to 1,200 radials. What will be the demand during each season?

•• **4.27** Mark Cotteleer owns a company that manufactures sailboats. Actual demand for Mark's sailboats during each season in 2006 through 2009 was as follows:

Season	Year 2006	2007	2008	2009
Winter	1,400	1,200	1,000	900
Spring	1,500	1,400	1,600	1,500
Summer	1,000	2,100	2,000	1,900
Fall	600	750	650	500

Mark has forecasted that annual demand for his sailboats in 2011 will equal 5,600 sailboats. Based on this data and the multiplicative seasonal model, what will the demand level be for Mark's sailboats in the spring of 2011?

•• **4.28** Attendance at Los Angeles's newest Disneylike attraction, Vacation World, has been as follows:

Quarter	Guests (in thousands)	Quarter	Guests (in thousands)
Winter '07	73	Summer '08	124
Spring '07	104	Fall '08	52
Summer '07	168	Winter '09	89
Fall '07	74	Spring '09	146
Winter '08	65	Summer '09	205
Spring '08	82	Fall '09	98

Compute seasonal indices using all of the data. PX

• **4.29** Central States Electric Company estimates its demand trend line (in millions of kilowatt hours) to be:

$$D = 77 + 0.43Q$$

where Q refers to the sequential quarter number and $Q = 1$ for winter 1986. In addition, the multiplicative seasonal factors are as follows:

Quarter	Factor (Index)
Winter	.8
Spring	1.1
Summer	1.4
Fall	.7

Forecast energy use for the four quarters of 2011, beginning with winter.

• **4.30** Brian Buckley has developed the following forecasting model:

$$\hat{y} = 36 + 4.3x$$

where $\hat{y}$ = demand for Aztec air conditioners and
x = the outside temperature (°F)

a) Forecast demand for the Aztec when the temperature is 70°F.
b) What is demand when the temperature is 80°F?
c) What is demand when the temperature is 90°F? PX

•• **4.31** Coffee Palace's manager, Joe Felan, suspects that demand for mocha latte coffees depends on the price being charged. Based on historical observations, Joe has gathered the following data, which show the numbers of these coffees sold over six different price values:

Price	Number Sold
$2.70	760
$3.50	510
$2.00	980
$4.20	250
$3.10	320
$4.05	480

Using these data, how many mocha latte coffees would be forecast to be sold according to simple linear regression if the price per cup were $2.80? PX

• **4.32** The following data relate the sales figures of the bar in Marty and Polly Starr's small bed-and-breakfast inn in Marathon, Florida, to the number of guests registered that week:

Week	Guests	Bar Sales
1	16	$330
2	12	270
3	18	380
4	14	300

a) Perform a linear regression that relates bar sales to guests (not to time).
b) If the forecast is for 20 guests next week, what are the sales expected to be? PX

• **4.33** The number of transistors (in millions) made at a plant in Japan during the past 5 years follows:

Year	Transistors
1	140
2	160
3	190
4	200
5	210

a) Forecast the number of transistors to be made next year, using linear regression.
b) Compute the mean squared error (MSE) when using linear regression.
c) Compute the mean absolute percent error (MAPE). PX

• **4.34** The number of auto accidents in a certain region is related to the regional number of registered automobiles in thousands (X_1), alcoholic beverage sales in $10,000s ($X_2$), and rainfall in inches (X_3). Furthermore, the regression formula has been calculated as:

$$Y = a + b_1X_1 + b_2X_2 + b_3X_3$$

where Y = number of automobile accidents
$a = 7.5$
$b_1 = 3.5$
$b_2 = 4.5$
$b_3 = 2.5$

Calculate the expected number of automobile accidents under conditions a, b, and c:

	X_1	X_2	X_3
(a)	2	3	0
(b)	3	5	1
(c)	4	7	2

PX

•• **4.35** John Howard, a Mobile, Alabama, real estate developer, has devised a regression model to help determine residential housing prices in South Alabama. The model was developed using recent sales in a particular neighborhood. The price (Y) of the house is based on the size (square footage = X) of the house. The model is:

$$Y = 13{,}473 + 37.65X$$

The coefficient of correlation for the model is 0.63.

a) Use the model to predict the selling price of a house that is 1,860 square feet.
b) An 1,860-square-foot house recently sold for $95,000. Explain why this is not what the model predicted.

c) If you were going to use multiple regression to develop such a model, what other quantitative variables might you include?
d) What is the value of the coefficient of determination in this problem? PX

• **4.36** Accountants at the firm Michael Vest, CPAs, believed that several traveling executives were submitting unusually high travel vouchers when they returned from business trips. First, they took a sample of 200 vouchers submitted from the past year. Then they developed the following multiple-regression equation relating expected travel cost to number of days on the road (x_1) and distance traveled (x_2) in miles:

$$\hat{y} = \$90.00 + \$48.50x_1 + \$.40x_2$$

The coefficient of correlation computed was .68.
a) If Wanda Fennell returns from a 300-mile trip that took her out of town for 5 days, what is the expected amount she should claim as expenses?
b) Fennell submitted a reimbursement request for $685. What should the accountant do?
c) Should any other variables be included? Which ones? Why? PX

•• **4.37** Sales of music stands at Johnny Ho's music store in Columbus, Ohio, over the past 10 weeks are shown in the table below.
a) Forecast demand for each week, including week 10, using exponential smoothing with $\alpha = .5$ (initial forecast = 20).

Week	Demand	Week	Demand
1	20	6	29
2	21	7	36
3	28	8	22
4	37	9	25
5	25	10	28

b) Compute the MAD.
c) Compute the tracking signal. PX

•• **4.38** City government has collected the following data on annual sales tax collections and new car registrations:

Annual Sales Tax Collections (in millions)	1.0	1.4	1.9	2.0	1.8	2.1	2.3
New Car Registrations (in thousands)	10	12	15	16	14	17	20

Determine the following:
a) The least-squares regression equation.
b) Using the results of part (a), find the estimated sales tax collections if new car registrations total 22,000.
c) The coefficients of correlation and determination. PX

•• **4.39** Dr. Susan Sweeney, a Providence, Rhode Island, psychologist, specializes in treating patients who are agoraphobic (i.e., afraid to leave their homes). The following table indicates how many patients Dr. Sweeney has seen each year for the past 10 years. It also indicates what the robbery rate was in Providence during the same year:

Year	1	2	3	4	5	6	7	8	9	10
Number of Patients	36	33	40	41	40	55	60	54	58	61
Robbery Rate per 1,000 Population	58.3	61.1	73.4	75.7	81.1	89.0	101.1	94.8	103.3	116.2

Using trend analysis, predict the number of patients Dr. Sweeney will see in years 11 and 12 as a function of time. How well does the model fit the data? PX

•• **4.40** Using the data in Problem 4.39, apply linear regression to study the relationship between the robbery rate and Dr. Sweeney's patient load. If the robbery rate increases to 131.2 in year 11, how many phobic patients will Dr. Sweeney treat? If the robbery rate drops to 90.6, what is the patient projection? PX

••• **4.41** Bus and subway ridership for the summer months in London, England, is believed to be tied heavily to the number of tourists visiting the city. During the past 12 years, the following data have been obtained:

Year (summer months)	Number of Tourists (in millions)	Ridership (in millions)
1	7	1.5
2	2	1.0
3	6	1.3
4	4	1.5
5	14	2.5
6	15	2.7
7	16	2.4
8	12	2.0
9	14	2.7
10	20	4.4
11	15	3.4
12	7	1.7

a) Plot these data and decide if a linear model is reasonable.
b) Develop a regression relationship.
c) What is expected ridership if 10 million tourists visit London in a year?
d) Explain the predicted ridership if there are no tourists at all.
e) What is the standard error of the estimate?
f) What is the model's correlation coefficient and coefficient of determination? PX

••• **4.42** Des Moines Power and Light has been collecting data on demand for electric power in its western subregion for only the past 2 years. Those data are shown in the table at the top of the next page.

To plan for expansion and to arrange to borrow power from neighboring utilities during peak periods, the utility needs to be able to forecast demand for each month next year. However, the standard

	Demand in Megawatts	
Month	**Last Year**	**This Year**
January	5	17
February	6	14
March	10	20
April	13	23
May	18	30
June	15	38
July	23	44
August	26	41
September	21	33
October	15	23
November	12	26
December	14	17

forecasting models discussed in this chapter will not fit the data observed for the 2 years.

a) What are the weaknesses of the standard forecasting techniques as applied to this set of data?
b) Because known models are not appropriate here, propose your own approach to forecasting. Although there is no perfect solution to tackling data such as these (in other words, there are no 100% right or wrong answers), justify your model.
c) Forecast demand for each month next year using the model you propose.

••• **4.43** Emergency calls to the 911 system of Gainesville, Florida, for the past 24 weeks are shown in the following table:

Week	1	2	3	4	5	6	7	8	9	10	11	12
Calls	50	35	25	40	45	35	20	30	35	20	15	40
Week	13	14	15	16	17	18	19	20	21	22	23	24
Calls	55	35	25	55	55	40	35	60	75	50	40	65

a) Compute the exponentially smoothed forecast of calls for each week. Assume an initial forecast of 50 calls in the first week, and use $\alpha = .2$. What is the forecast for week 25?
b) Reforecast each period using $\alpha = .6$.
c) Actual calls during week 25 were 85. Which smoothing constant provides a superior forecast? Explain and justify the measure of error you used. Px

••• **4.44** Using the 911 call data in Problem 4.43, forecast calls for weeks 2 through 25 with a trend-adjusted exponential smoothing model. Assume an initial forecast for 50 calls for week 1 and an initial trend of zero. Use smoothing constants of $\alpha = .3$ and $\beta = .2$. Is this model better than that of Problem 4.43? What adjustment might be useful for further improvement? (Again, assume that actual calls in week 25 were 85.) Px

••• **4.45** The following are monthly actual and forecast demand levels for May through December for units of a product manufactured by the N. Tamimi Pharmaceutical Company:

Month	**Actual Demand**	**Forecast Demand**
May	100	100
June	80	104
July	110	99
August	115	101
September	105	104
October	110	104
November	125	105
December	120	109

What is the value of the tracking signal as of the end of December?

•• **4.46** Thirteen students entered the business program at Hillcrest College 2 years ago. The following table indicates what each student scored on the high school SAT math exam and their grade-point averages (GPAs) after students were in the Hillcrest program for 2 years.

Student	A	B	C	D	E	F	G
SAT Score	421	377	585	690	608	390	415
GPA	2.90	2.93	3.00	3.45	3.66	2.88	2.15
Student	H	I	J	K	L	M	
SAT Score	481	729	501	613	709	366	
GPA	2.53	3.22	1.99	2.75	3.90	1.60	

a) Is there a meaningful relationship between SAT math scores and grades?
b) If a student scores a 350, what do you think his or her GPA will be?
c) What about a student who scores 800?

••• **4.47** City Cycles has just started selling the new Z-10 mountain bike, with monthly sales as shown in the table. First, co-owner Amit wants to forecast by exponential smoothing by initially setting February's forecast equal to January's sales with $\alpha = .1$. Co-owner Barbara wants to use a three-period moving average.

	Sales	**Amit**	**Barbara**	**Amit's Error**	**Barbara's Error**
January	400	—			
February	380	400			
March	410				
April	375				
May					

a) Is there a strong linear trend in sales over time?
b) Fill in the table with what Amit and Barbara each forecast for May and the earlier months, as relevant.
c) Assume that May's actual sales figure turns out to be 405. Complete the table's columns and then calculate the mean absolute deviation for both Amit's and Barbara's methods.
d) Based on these calculations, which method seems more accurate? Px

•• **4.48** Sundar Balakrishnan, the general manager of Precision Engineering Corporation (PEC), thinks that his firm's engineering services contracted to highway construction firms are directly related to the volume of highway construction business contracted with companies in his geographic area. He wonders if this is really so, and if it is, can this information help him plan his operations better by forecasting the quantity of his engineering services required by construction firms in each quarter of the year? The following table presents the sales of his services and total amounts of contracts for highway construction over the past 8 quarters:

Quarter	1	2	3	4	5	6	7	8
Sales of PEC Services (in \$ thousands)	8	10	15	9	12	13	12	16
Contracts Released (in \$ thousands)	153	172	197	178	185	199	205	226

a) Using this data, develop a regression equation for predicting the level of demand of Precision's services.
b) Determine the coefficient of correlation and the standard error of the estimate. PX

•••• **4.49** Salinas Savings and Loan is proud of its long tradition in Topeka, Kansas. Begun by Teresita Salinas 20 years after World War II, the S&L has bucked the trend of financial and liquidity problems that has repeatedly plagued the industry. Deposits have increased slowly but surely over the years, despite recessions in 1983, 1988, 1991, 2001, and 2008. Ms. Salinas believes it is necessary to have a long-range strategic plan for her firm, including a 1-year forecast and preferably even a 5-year forecast of deposits. She examines the past deposit data and also peruses Kansas's gross state product (GSP), over the same 44 years. (GSP is analogous to gross national product [GNP] but on the state level.) The resulting data are in the following table:

Year	Deposits[a]	GSP[b]	Year	Deposits[a]	GSP[b]
1966	.25	.4	1988	6.2	2.5
1967	.24	.4	1989	4.1	2.8
1968	.24	.5	1990	4.5	2.9
1969	.26	.7	1991	6.1	3.4
1970	.25	.9	1992	7.7	3.8
1971	.30	1.0	1993	10.1	4.1
1972	.31	1.4	1994	15.2	4.0
1973	.32	1.7	1995	18.1	4.0
1974	.24	1.3	1996	24.1	3.9
1975	.26	1.2	1997	25.6	3.8
1976	.25	1.1	1998	30.3	3.8
1977	.33	.9	1999	36.0	3.7
1978	.50	1.2	2000	31.1	4.1
1979	.95	1.2	2001	31.7	4.1
1980	1.70	1.2	2002	38.5	4.0
1981	2.3	1.6	2003	47.9	4.5
1982	2.8	1.5	2004	49.1	4.6
1983	2.8	1.6	2005	55.8	4.5
1984	2.7	1.7	2006	70.1	4.6
1985	3.9	1.9	2007	70.9	4.6
1986	4.9	1.9	2008	79.1	4.7
1987	5.3	2.3	2009	94.0	5.0

[a]In $ millions.
[b]In $ billions.

a) Using exponential smoothing, with $\alpha = .6$, then trend analysis, and finally linear regression, discuss which forecasting model fits best for Salinas's strategic plan. Justify the selection of one model over another.
b) Carefully examine the data. Can you make a case for excluding a portion of the information? Why? Would that change your choice of model? PX

▶ **Refer to myomlab for these additional homework problems: 4.50–4.62**

Case Studies

▶ Southwestern University: (B)*

Southwestern University (SWU), a large state college in Stephenville, Texas, enrolls close to 20,000 students. The school is a dominant force in the small city, with more students during fall and spring than permanent residents.

Always a football powerhouse, SWU is usually in the top 20 in college football rankings. Since the legendary Bo Pitterno was hired as its head coach in 2003 (in hopes of reaching the elusive number 1 ranking), attendance at the five Saturday home games each year increased. Prior to Pitterno's arrival, attendance generally averaged 25,000 to 29,000 per game. Season ticket sales bumped up by 10,000 just with the announcement of the new coach's arrival. Stephenville and SWU were ready to move to the big time!

The immediate issue facing SWU, however, was not NCAA ranking. It was capacity. The existing SWU stadium, built in 1953, has seating for 54,000 fans. The following table indicates attendance at each game for the past 6 years.

One of Pitterno's demands upon joining SWU had been a stadium expansion, or possibly even a new stadium. With attendance increasing, SWU administrators began to face the issue head-on. Pitterno had wanted dormitories solely for his athletes in the stadium as an additional feature of any expansion.

SWU's president, Dr. Joel Wisner, decided it was time for his vice president of development to forecast when the existing stadium would "max out." The expansion was, in his mind, a given. But Wisner needed to know how long he could wait. He also sought a revenue projection, assuming an average ticket price of $50 in 2010 and a 5% increase each year in future prices.

Discussion Questions

1. Develop a forecasting model, justifying its selection over other techniques, and project attendance through 2011.
2. What revenues are to be expected in 2010 and 2011?
3. Discuss the school's options.

* This integrated case study runs throughout the text. Other issues facing Southwestern's football stadium include (A) managing the stadium project (Chapter 3); (C) quality of facilities (Chapter 6); (D) break-even analysis of food services (Supplement 7 web site); (E) locating the new stadium (Chapter 8 web site); (F) inventory planning of football programs (Chapter 12 web site); and (G) scheduling of campus security officers/staff for game days (Chapter 13).

Southwestern University Football Game Attendance, 2004–2009

Game	2004 Attendees	2004 Opponent	2005 Attendees	2005 Opponent	2006 Attendees	2006 Opponent
1	34,200	Baylor	36,100	Oklahoma	35,900	TCU
2[a]	39,800	Texas	40,200	Nebraska	46,500	Texas Tech
3	38,200	LSU	39,100	UCLA	43,100	Alaska
4[b]	26,900	Arkansas	25,300	Nevada	27,900	Arizona
5	35,100	USC	36,200	Ohio State	39,200	Rice

Game	2007 Attendees	2007 Opponent	2008 Attendees	2008 Opponent	2009 Attendees	2009 Opponent
1	41,900	Arkansas	42,500	Indiana	46,900	LSU
2[a]	46,100	Missouri	48,200	North Texas	50,100	Texas
3	43,900	Florida	44,200	Texas A&M	45,900	Prairie View A&M
4[b]	30,100	Miami	33,900	Southern	36,300	Montana
5	40,500	Duke	47,800	Oklahoma	49,900	Arizona State

[a]Homecoming games.

[b]During the 4th week of each season, Stephenville hosted a hugely popular southwestern crafts festival. This event brought tens of thousands of tourists to the town, especially on weekends, and had an obvious negative impact on game attendance.

▶ Digital Cell Phone, Inc.

Paul Jordan has just been hired as a management analyst at Digital Cell Phone, Inc. Digital Cell manufactures a broad line of phones for the consumer market. Paul's boss, John Smithers, chief operations officer, has asked Paul to stop by his office this morning. After a brief exchange of pleasantries over a cup of coffee, he says he has a special assignment for Paul: "We've always just made an educated guess about how many phones we need to make each month. Usually we just look at how many we sold last month and plan to produce about the same number. This sometimes works fine. But most months we either have too many phones in inventory or we are out of stock. Neither situation is good."

Handing Paul the table shown here, Smithers continues, "Here are our actual orders entered for the past 36 months. There are 144 phones per case. I was hoping that since you graduated recently from the University of Alaska, you might have studied some techniques that would help us plan better. It's been awhile since I was in college—I think I forgot most of the details I learned then. I'd like you to analyze these data and give me an idea of what our business will look like over the next 6 to 12 months. Do you think you can handle this?"

"Of course," Paul replies, sounding more confident than he really is. "How much time do I have?"

"I need your report on the Monday before Thanksgiving—that would be November 20th. I plan to take it home with me and read it during the holiday. Since I'm sure you will not be around during the holiday, be sure that you explain things carefully so that I can understand your recommendation without having to ask you any more questions. Since you are new to the company, you should know that I like to see all the details and complete justification for recommendations from my staff."

With that, Paul was dismissed. Arriving back at his office, he began his analysis.

Orders Received, by Month

Month	Cases 2007	Cases 2008	Cases 2009
January	480	575	608
February	436	527	597
March	482	540	612
April	448	502	603
May	458	508	628
June	489	573	605
July	498	508	627
August	430	498	578
September	444	485	585
October	496	526	581
November	487	552	632
December	525	587	656

Discussion Question

1. Prepare Paul Jordan's report to John Smithers using regression analysis. Provide a summary of the cell phone industry outlook as part of Paul's response.
2. Adding seasonality into your model, how does the analysis change?

Source: Professor Victor E. Sower, Sam Houston State University.

▶ Forecasting at Hard Rock Cafe

Video Case

With the growth of Hard Rock Cafe—from one pub in London in 1971 to more than 129 restaurants in more than 40 countries today—came a corporatewide demand for better forecasting. Hard Rock uses long-range forecasting in setting a capacity plan and intermediate-term forecasting for locking in contracts for leather goods (used in jackets) and for such food items as beef, chicken, and pork. Its short-term sales forecasts are conducted each month, by cafe, and then aggregated for a headquarters view.

The heart of the sales forecasting system is the point-of-sale system (POS), which, in effect, captures transaction data on nearly every person who walks through a cafe's door. The sale of each entrée represents one customer; the entrée sales data are transmitted daily to the Orlando corporate headquarters' database. There, the financial team, headed by Todd Lindsey, begins the forecast process. Lindsey forecasts monthly guest counts, retail sales, banquet sales, and concert sales (if applicable) at each cafe. The general managers of individual cafes tap into the same database to prepare a daily forecast for their sites. A cafe manager pulls up prior years' sales for that day, adding information from the local Chamber of Commerce or Tourist Board on upcoming events such as a major convention, sporting event, or concert in the city where the cafe is located. The daily forecast is further broken into hourly sales, which drives employee scheduling. An hourly forecast of $5,500 in sales translates into 19 workstations, which are further broken down into a specific number of wait staff, hosts, bartenders, and kitchen staff. Computerized scheduling software plugs in people based on their availability. Variances between forecast and actual sales are then examined to see why errors occurred.

Hard Rock doesn't limit its use of forecasting tools to sales. To evaluate managers and set bonuses, a 3-year weighted moving average is applied to cafe sales. If cafe general managers exceed their targets, a bonus is computed. Todd Lindsey, at corporate headquarters, applies weights of 40% to the most recent year's sales, 40% to the year before, and 20% to sales 2 years ago in reaching his moving average.

An even more sophisticated application of statistics is found in Hard Rock's menu planning. Using multiple regression, managers can compute the impact on demand of other menu items if the price of one item is changed. For example, if the price of a cheeseburger increases from $7.99 to $8.99, Hard Rock can predict the effect this will have on sales of chicken sandwiches, pork sandwiches, and salads. Managers do the same analysis on menu placement, with the center section driving higher sales volumes. When an item such as a hamburger is moved off the center to one of the side flaps, the corresponding effect on related items, say french fries, is determined.

Hard Rock's Moscow Cafe[a]

Month	**1**	**2**	**3**	**4**	**5**	**6**	**7**	**8**	**9**	**10**
Guest count (in thousands)	21	24	27	32	29	37	43	43	54	66
Advertising (in $ thousand)	14	17	25	25	35	35	45	50	60	60

[a]These figures are used for purposes of this case study.

Discussion Questions*

1. Describe three different forecasting applications at Hard Rock. Name three other areas in which you think Hard Rock could use forecasting models.
2. What is the role of the POS system in forecasting at Hard Rock?
3. Justify the use of the weighting system used for evaluating managers for annual bonuses.
4. Name several variables besides those mentioned in the case that could be used as good predictors of daily sales in each cafe.
5. At Hard Rock's Moscow restaurant, the manager is trying to evaluate how a new advertising campaign affects guest counts. Using data for the past 10 months (see the table) develop a least squares regression relationship and then forecast the expected guest count when advertising is $65,000.

*You may wish to view the video that accompanies this case before answering these questions.

▶**Additional Case Study:** Visit **www.myomlab.com** or **www.pearsonhighered.com/heizer** for this free case study:
North-South Airlines: Reflects the merger of two airlines and addresses their maintenance costs.

Bibliography

Balakrishnan, R., B. Render, and R. M. Stair. *Managerial Decision Modeling with Spreadsheets*, 2nd ed. Upper Saddle River, NJ: Prentice Hall, 2007.

Berenson, Mark, Tim Krehbiel, and David Levine. *Basic Business Statistics*, 11th ed. Upper Saddle River, NJ: Prentice Hall, 2009.

Campbell, Omar. "Forecasting in Direct Selling Business: Tupperware's Experience." *The Journal of Business Forecasting* 27, no. 2 (Summer 2008): 18–19.

Diebold, F. X. *Elements of Forecasting*, 5th ed. Cincinnati: South-Western College Publishing, 2010.

Fildes, Robert, and Paul Goodwin. "Against Your Better Judgment? How Organizations Can Improve Their Use of Management Judgment in Forecasting." *Decision Sciences* 37, no. 6 (November–December 2007): 570–576.

Georgoff, D. M., and R. G. Murdick. "Manager's Guide to Forecasting." *Harvard Business Review* 64 (January–February 1986): 110–120.

Gilliland, M., and M. Leonard. "Forecasting Software—The Past and the Future." *The Journal of Business Forecasting* 25, no. 1 (Spring 2006): 33–36.

Hanke, J. E. and D. W. Wichern. *Business Forecasting*, 9th ed. Upper Saddle River, NJ: Prentice Hall, 2009.

Heizer, Jay. "Forecasting with Stagger Charts." *IIE Solutions* 34 (June 2002): 46–49.

Jain, Chaman L. "Benchmarking Forecasting Software and Systems." *The Journal of Business Forecasting* 26, no. 4 (Winter 2007/2008): 30–34.

Onkal, D., M. S. Gonul, and M. Lawrence. "Judgmental Adjustments of Previously Adjusted Forecasts." *Decision Sciences* 39, no. 2 (May 2008): 213–238.

Render, B., R. M. Stair, and M. Hanna. *Quantitative Analysis for Management*, 10th ed. Upper Saddle River, NJ: Prentice Hall, 2009.

Shah, Piyush. "Techniques to Support Better Forecasting." *APICS Magazine* (November/December 2008): 49–50.

Tabatabai, Bijan. "Improving Forecasting." *Financial Management* (October, 2008): 48–49.

Urs, Rajiv. "How to Use a Demand Planning System for Best Forecasting and Planning Results." *The Journal of Business Forecasting* 27, no. 2 (Summer 2008): 22–25.

Wilson, J. H., B. Keating, and J. Galt. *Business Forecasting,* 6th ed. New York: McGraw-Hill, 2009.

Yurklewicz, Jack. "Forecasting at Steady State." *Analytics* (Summer 2008): 42–45.

Chapter 4 ***Rapid* Review**

Main Heading	Review Material	PEARSON myomlab
WHAT IS FORECASTING? (pp. 104–105)	■ **Forecasting—**The art and science of predicting future events. ■ **Economic forecasts—**Planning indicators that are valuable in helping organizations prepare medium- to long-range forecasts. ■ **Technological forecasts—**Long-term forecasts concerned with the rates of technological progress. ■ **Demand forecasts—**Projections of a company's sales for each time period in the planning horizon.	
THE STRATEGIC IMPORTANCE OF FORECASTING (pp. 105–106)	*The forecast is the only estimate of demand until actual demand becomes known.* Forecasts of demand drive decisions in many areas, including: *Human resources, Capacity, Supply-chain management.*	**VIDEO 4.1** Forecasting at Hard Rock Cafe
SEVEN STEPS IN THE FORECASTING SYSTEM (p. 106)	Forecasting follows seven basic steps: 1. Determine the use of the forecast; 2. Select the items to be forecasted; 3. Determine the time horizon of the forecast; 4. Select the forecasting model(s); 5. Gather the data needed to make the forecast; 6. Make the forecast; 7. Validate and implement the results.	
FORECASTING APPROACHES (pp. 107–108)	■ **Quantitative forecasts**—Forecasts that employ mathematical modeling to forecast demand. ■ **Qualitative forecast**—Forecasts that incorporate such factors as the decision maker's intuition, emotions, personal experiences, and value system. ■ **Jury of executive opinion**—Takes the opinion of a small group of high-level managers and results in a group estimate of demand. ■ **Delphi method**—Uses an interactive group process that allows experts to make forecasts. ■ **Sales force composite**—Based on salespersons' estimates of expected sales. ■ **Consumer market survey**—Solicits input from customers or potential customers regarding future purchasing plans. ■ **Time series**—Uses a series of past data points to make a forecast.	
TIME-SERIES FORECASTING (pp. 108–126)	■ **Naïve approach**—Assumes that demand in the next period is equal to demand in the most recent period. ■ **Moving averages**—Uses an average of the n most recent periods of data to forecast the next period. $\text{Moving average} = \frac{\Sigma \text{Demand in previous } n \text{ periods}}{n}$ (4-1) $\text{Weighted moving average} = \frac{\Sigma(\text{Weight for period } n)\,(\text{Demand in period } n)}{\Sigma \text{ Weights}}$ (4-2) ■ **Exponential smoothing—**A weighted-moving-average forecasting technique in which data points are weighted by an exponential function. ■ **Smoothing constant—**The weighting factor, α, used in an exponential smoothing forecast, a number between 0 and 1. Exponential smoothing formula: $F_t = F_{t-1} + \alpha(A_{t-1} - F_{t-1})$ (4-4) ■ **Mean absolute deviation (MAD)—**A measure of the overall forecast error for a model. $MAD = \frac{\sum \lvert \text{Actual} - \text{Forecast} \rvert}{n}$ (4-5) ■ **Mean squared error (MSE)—**The average of the squared differences between the forecast and observed values. $\text{MSE} = \frac{\sum (\text{Forecast errors})^2}{n}$ (4-6) ■ **Mean absolute percent error (MAPE)—**The average of the absolute differences between the forecast and actual values, expressed as a percentage of actual values. $MAPE = \frac{\sum_{i=1}^{n} 100 \lvert \text{Actual}_t - \text{Forecast}_t \rvert / \text{Actual}_t}{n}$ (4-7)	Problems: 4.1, 4.2, 4.3, 4.4, 4.5, 4.6, 4.7, 4.8, 4.9, 4.10, 4.11-4.23, 4.25-4.29, 4.33, 4.37, 4.39, 4.43, 4.44, 4.47, 4.49 Virtual Office Hours for Solved Problems: 4.1–4.4 **ACTIVE MODELS: 4.1–4.4**

PEARSON myomlab

Main Heading	Review Material	
	Exponential Smoothing with Trend Adjustment Forecast including trend (FIT_t) = Exponentially smoothed forecast (F_t) + Exponentially smoothed trend (T_t) (4-8) ■ **Trend projection**—A time-series forecasting method that fits a trend line to a series of historical data points and then projects the line into the future for forecasts. Trend Projection and Regression Analysis $\hat{y} = a + bx$, where $b = \dfrac{\Sigma xy - n\bar{x}\bar{y}}{\Sigma x^2 - n\bar{x}^2}$, and $a = \bar{y} - b\bar{x}$ (4-11),(4-12),(4-13) ■ **Seasonal variations**—Regular upward or downward movements in a time series that tie to recurring events. ■ **Cycles**—Patterns in the data that occur every several years.	
ASSOCIATIVE FORECASTING METHODS: REGRESSION AND CORRELATION ANALYSIS (pp. 126–131)	■ **Linear-regression analysis**—A straight-line mathematical model to describe the functional relationships between independent and dependent variables. ■ **Standard error of the estimate**—A measure of variability around the regression line. ■ **Coefficient of correlation**—A measure of the strength of the relationship between two variables. ■ **Coefficient of determination**—A measure of the amount of variation in the dependent variable about its mean that is explained by the regression equation. ■ **Multiple regression**—An associative forecasting method with > 1 independent variable. Multiple regression forecast: $\hat{y} = a + b_1x_1 + b_2x_2$ (4-17)	Problems: 4.24, 4.30–4.32, 4.34–4.36, 4.38, 4.40, 4.41, 4.46, 4.48
MONITORING AND CONTROLLING FORECASTS (pp. 131–134)	■ **Tracking signal**—A measurement of how well the forecast is predicting actual values. $\text{Tracking signal} = \dfrac{\sum(\text{Actual demand in period } i - \text{Forecast demand in period } i)}{\text{MAD}}$ (4-18) ■ **Bias**—A forecast that is consistently higher or lower than actual values of a time series. ■ **Adaptive smoothing**—An approach to exponential smoothing forecasting in which the smoothing constant is automatically changed to keep errors to a minimum. ■ **Focus forecasting**—Forecasting that tries a variety of computer models and selects the best one for a particular application.	Problems: 4.37, 4.45
FORECASTING IN THE SERVICE SECTOR (pp. 134–135)	Service-sector forecasting may require good short-term demand records, even per 15-minute intervals. Demand during holidays or specific weather events may also need to be tracked.	

Self Test

■ **Before taking the self-test,** refer to the learning objectives listed at the beginning of the chapter and the key terms listed at the end of the chapter.

LO1. Forecasting time horizons include:
a) long range. **b)** medium range.
c) short range. **d)** all of the above.

LO2. Qualitative methods of forecasting include:
a) sales force composite. **b)** jury of executive opinion.
c) consumer market survey. **d)** exponential smoothing.
e) all except (d).

LO3. The difference between a *moving-average* model and an *exponential smoothing* model is that _________.

LO4. Three popular measures of forecast accuracy are:
a) total error, average error, and mean error.
b) average error, median error, and maximum error.
c) median error, minimum error, and maximum absolute error.
d) mean absolute deviation, mean squared error, and mean absolute percent error.

LO5. Average demand for iPods in the Rome, Italy, Apple store is 800 units per month. The May monthly index is 1.25. What is the seasonally adjusted sales forecast for May?
a) 640 units **b)** 798.75 units **c)** 800 units **d)** 1,000 units
e) cannot be calculated with the information given

LO6. The main difference between simple and multiple regression is _________.

LO7. The tracking signal is the:
a) standard error of the estimate.
b) cumulative error.
c) mean absolute deviation (MAD).
d) ratio of the cumulative error to MAD.
e) mean absolute percent error (MAPE).

Answers: LO1. d; LO2. e; LO3. exponential smoothing is a weighted moving-average model in which all prior values are weighted with a set of exponentially declining weights; LO4. d; LO5. d ; LO6. simple regression has only one independent variable ; LO7. d.

5 Design of Goods and Services

PART TWO
Designing Operations
(Chapters 5–10)

Chapter Outline

10 OM Strategy Decisions

- ► Design of Goods and Services
- ► Managing Quality
- ► Process Strategy
- ► Location Strategies
- ► Layout Strategies
- ► Human Resources
- ► Supply Chain Management
- ► Inventory Management
- ► Scheduling
- ► Maintenance

PRODUCT STRATEGY PROVIDES COMPETITIVE ADVANTAGE AT REGAL MARINE

Thirty years after its founding by potato farmer Paul Kuck, Regal Marine has become a powerful force on the waters of the world. The world's third-largest boat manufacturer (by global sales), Regal exports to 30 countries, including Russia and China. Almost one-third of its sales are overseas.

Product design is critical in the highly competitive pleasure boat business: "We keep in touch with our customers and we respond to the marketplace," says Kuck. "We're introducing six new models this year alone. I'd say we're definitely on the aggressive end of the spectrum."

CAD/CAM is used to design the hull of a new product. This process results in faster and more efficient design and production.

With changing consumer tastes, compounded by material changes and ever-improving marine engineering, the design function is under constant pressure. Added to these pressures is the constant issue of cost competitiveness combined with the need to provide good value for customers.

Consequently, Regal Marine is a frequent user of computer-aided design (CAD). New designs come to life via Regal's three-dimensional CAD system, borrowed from automotive technology. Regal's naval architects' goal is to continue to reduce the time from concept to prototype to production. The sophisticated CAD system not only has reduced product development time but also has reduced problems with tooling and production, resulting in a superior product.

All of Regal's products, from its $14,000 19-foot boat to the $500,000 44-foot Commodore yacht, follow a similar production process. Hulls and decks are separately hand-produced by spraying preformed molds with three to five layers of a fiberglass laminate. The hulls and decks harden and are

Once a hull has been pulled from the mold, it travels down a monorail assembly path. JIT inventory delivers engines, wiring, seats, flooring, and interiors when needed.

Larger boats, such as this luxurious Commodore 4260 Express, are water tested on a lake or ocean. Regal is one of the few boat builders in the world to earn the ISO 9001:2000 quality certification.

At the final stage, smaller boats, such as this one, are placed in this test tank, where a rain machine ensures watertight fits.

Here the deck, suspended from ceiling cranes, is being finished prior to being moved to join the hull.

removed to become the lower and upper structure of the boat. As they move to the assembly line, they are joined and components added at each workstation.

Wooden components, precut in-house by computer-driven routers, are delivered on a just-in-time basis for installation at one station. Engines—one of the few purchased components—are installed at another. Racks of electrical wiring harnesses, engineered and rigged in-house, are then installed. An in-house upholstery department delivers customized seats, beds, dashboards, or other cushioned components. Finally, chrome fixtures are put in place, and the boat is sent to Regal's test tank for watertight, gauge, and system inspection.

Chapter 5 **Learning Objectives**

AUTHOR COMMENT
Product strategy is critical to achieving competitive advantage.

GOODS AND SERVICES SELECTION

Global firms like Regal Marine know that the basis for an organization's existence is the good or service it provides society. Great products are the keys to success. Anything less than an excellent product strategy can be devastating to a firm. To maximize the potential for success, top companies focus on only a few products and then concentrate on those products. For instance, Honda's focus is engines. Virtually all of Honda's sales (autos, motorcycles, generators, lawn mowers) are based on its outstanding engine technology. Likewise, Intel's focus is on microprocessors, and Michelin's is on tires. However, because most products have a limited and even predictable life cycle, companies must constantly be looking for new products to design, develop, and take to market. Good operations managers insist on strong communication among customer, product, processes, and suppliers that results in a high success rate for their new products. 3M's goal is to produce 30% of its profit from products introduced in the last 4 years. Benchmarks, of course, vary by industry; Regal introduces six new boats a year, and Rubbermaid introduces a new product each day!

VIDEO 5.1
Product Strategy at Regal Marine

One product strategy is to build particular competence in customizing an established family of goods or services. This approach allows the customer to choose product variations while reinforcing the organization's strength. Dell Computer, for example, has built a huge market by delivering computers with the exact hardware and software desired by end users. And Dell does it fast—it understands that speed to market is imperative to gain a competitive edge.

Note that many service firms also refer to their offerings as products. For instance, when Allstate Insurance offers a new homeowner's policy, it is referred to as a new "product." Similarly, when Citicorp opens a mortgage department, it offers a number of new mortgage "products." Although the term *products* may often refer to tangible goods, it also refers to offerings by service organizations.

Product decision
The selection, definition, and design of products.

An effective product strategy links product decisions with investment, market share, and product life cycle, and defines the breadth of the product line. The *objective of the* **product decision** *is to develop and implement a product strategy that meets the demands of the marketplace with a competitive advantage.* As one of the 10 decisions of OM, product strategy may focus on developing a competitive advantage via differentiation, low cost, rapid response, or a combination of these.

Product Strategy Options Support Competitive Advantage

A world of options exists in the selection, definition, and design of products. Product selection is choosing the good or service to provide customers or clients. For instance, hospitals specialize in various types of patients and medical procedures. A hospital's management may decide to operate a general-purpose hospital or a maternity hospital or, as in the case of the Canadian hospital Shouldice, to specialize in hernias. Hospitals select their products when they decide what kind of hospital to be. Numerous other options exist for hospitals, just as they exist for Taco Bell and Toyota.

Service organizations like Shouldice Hospital *differentiate* themselves through their product. Shouldice differentiates itself by offering a distinctly unique and high-quality product. Its world-

Product Design Can Manifest Itself in Concepts, Technology, and Packaging. Whether it is a design focused on style at Nike (a), the application of technology at Michelin (b), or a new container at Sherwin-Williams (c), operations managers need to remind themselves that the creative process is ongoing with major implications for production.

(a) Concepts: Nike, in its creative way, has moved athletic shoes from utilitarian necessities into glamorous accessories and in the process is constantly reinventing all parts of the shoe, including the heel.

(b) Technology: Michelin's latest technology: radical new tires that don't go flat.

(c) Packaging: Sherwin Williams's Dutch Boy has revolutionized the paint industry with its square Twist & Pour paint container.

renowned specialization in hernia-repair service is so effective it allows patients to return to normal living in 8 days as opposed to the average 2 weeks—and with very few complications. The entire production system is designed for this one product. Local anesthetics are used; patients enter and leave the operating room on their own; rooms are spartan, and meals are served in a common dining room, encouraging patients to get out of bed for meals and join fellow patients in the lounge. As Shouldice has demonstrated, product selection affects the entire production system.

Taco Bell has developed and executed a *low-cost* strategy through product design. By designing a product (its menu) that can be produced with a minimum of labor in small kitchens, Taco Bell has developed a product line that is both low cost and high value. Successful product design has allowed Taco Bell to increase the food content of its products from 27¢ to 45¢ of each sales dollar.

Toyota's strategy is *rapid response* to changing consumer demand. By executing the fastest automobile design in the industry, Toyota has driven the speed of product development down to well under 2 years in an industry whose standard is still over 2 years. The shorter design time allows Toyota to get a car to market before consumer tastes change and to do so with the latest technology and innovations.

Product decisions are fundamental to an organization's strategy and have major implications throughout the operations function. For instance, GM's steering columns are a good example of the strong role product design plays in both quality and efficiency. The redesigned steering column has a simpler design, with about 30% fewer parts than its predecessor. The result: Assembly time is one-third that of the older column, and the new column's quality is about seven times higher. As an added bonus, machinery on the new line costs a third less than that on the old line.

Product Life Cycles

Products are born. They live and they die. They are cast aside by a changing society. It may be helpful to think of a product's life as divided into four phases. Those phases are introduction, growth, maturity, and decline.

LO1: Define product life cycle

Product life cycles may be a matter of a few hours (a newspaper), months (seasonal fashions and personal computers), years (video cassette tapes), or decades (Volkswagen Beetle). Regardless of the length of the cycle, the task for the operations manager is the same: to design a system that helps introduce new products successfully. If the operations function cannot perform

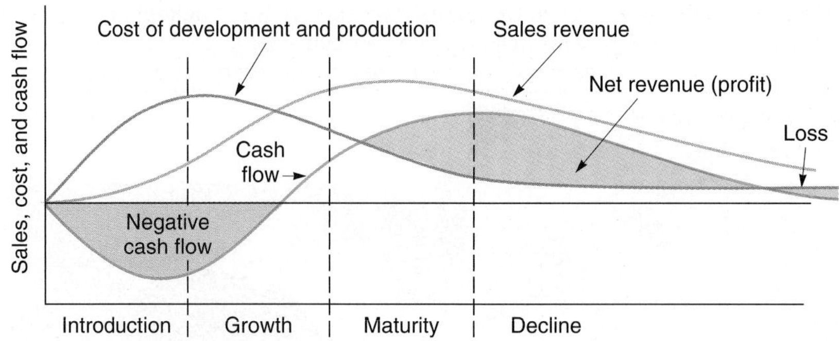

▶ **FIGURE 5.1 Product Life Cycle, Sales, Cost, and Profit**

effectively at this stage, the firm may be saddled with losers—products that cannot be produced efficiently and perhaps not at all.

Figure 5.1 shows the four life cycle stages and the relationship of product sales, cash flow, and profit over the life cycle of a product. Note that typically a firm has a negative cash flow while it develops a product. When the product is successful, those losses may be recovered. Eventually, the successful product may yield a profit prior to its decline. However, the profit is fleeting—hence, the constant demand for new products.

Life Cycle and Strategy

Just as operations managers must be prepared to develop new products, they must also be prepared to develop *strategies* for new and *existing* products. Periodic examination of products is appropriate because *strategies change as products move through their life cycle*. Successful product strategies require determining the best strategy for each product based on its position in its life cycle. A firm, therefore, identifies products or families of products and their position in the life cycle. Let us review some strategy options as products move through their life cycles.

Introductory Phase Because products in the introductory phase are still being "fine-tuned" for the market, as are their production techniques, they may warrant unusual expenditures for (1) research, (2) product development, (3) process modification and enhancement, and (4) supplier development. For example, when cellular phones were first introduced, the features desired by the public were still being determined. At the same time, operations managers were still groping for the best manufacturing techniques.

Growth Phase In the growth phase, product design has begun to stabilize, and effective forecasting of capacity requirements is necessary. Adding capacity or enhancing existing capacity to accommodate the increase in product demand may be necessary.

Maturity Phase By the time a product is mature, competitors are established. So high-volume, innovative production may be appropriate. Improved cost control, reduction in options, and a paring down of the product line may be effective or necessary for profitability and market share.

Decline Phase Management may need to be ruthless with those products whose life cycle is at an end. Dying products are typically poor products in which to invest resources and managerial talent. Unless dying products make some unique contribution to the firm's reputation or its product line or can be sold with an unusually high contribution, their production should be terminated.[1]

Product-by-Value Analysis

Product-by-value analysis
A list of products, in descending order of their individual dollar contribution to the firm, as well as the *total annual dollar contribution* of the product.

The effective operations manager selects items that show the greatest promise. This is the Pareto principle (i.e., focus on the critical few, not the trivial many) applied to product mix: Resources are to be invested in the critical few and not the trivial many. **Product-by-value analysis** lists products in descending order of their *individual dollar contribution* to the firm. It also lists the *total annual dollar contribution* of the product. Low contribution on a per-unit basis by a particular product may look substantially different if it represents a large portion of the company's sales.

A product-by-value report allows management to evaluate possible strategies for each product. These may include increasing cash flow (e.g., increasing contribution by raising selling price

[1]*Contribution* is defined as the difference between direct cost and selling price. Direct costs are labor and material that go into the product.

or lowering cost), increasing market penetration (improving quality and/or reducing cost or price), or reducing costs (improving the production process). The report may also tell management which product offerings should be eliminated and which fail to justify further investment in research and development or capital equipment. Product-by-value analysis focuses management's attention on the strategic direction for each product.

GENERATING NEW PRODUCTS

AUTHOR COMMENT Societies reward those who supply new products that reflect their needs.

Because products die; because products must be weeded out and replaced; because firms generate most of their revenue and profit from new products—product selection, definition, and design take place on a continuing basis. Consider recent product changes: TV to HDTV, radio to satellite radio, coffee shops to Starbucks lifestyle coffee, traveling circuses to Cirque du Soleil, land lines to cell phones, cell phone to Blackberry, Walkman to iPod, mops to Swiffers—and the list goes on. Knowing how to successfully find and develop new products is a requirement.

New Product Opportunities

Aggressive new product development requires that organizations build structures internally that have open communication with customers, innovative organizational cultures, aggressive R&D, strong leadership, formal incentives, and training. Only then can a firm profitably and energetically focus on specific opportunities such as the following:

1. *Understanding the customer* is the premier issue in new-product development. Many commercially important products are initially thought of and even prototyped by users rather than producers. Such products tend to be developed by "lead users"—companies, organizations, or individuals that are well ahead of market trends and have needs that go far beyond those of average users. The operations manager must be "tuned in" to the market and particularly these innovative lead users.
2. *Economic change* brings increasing levels of affluence in the long run but economic cycles and price changes in the short run. In the long run, for instance, more and more people can afford automobiles, but in the short run, a recession may weaken the demand for automobiles.
3. *Sociological and demographic change* may appear in such factors as decreasing family size. This trend alters the size preference for homes, apartments, and automobiles.
4. *Technological change* makes possible everything from cell phones to iPods to artificial hearts.
5. *Political/legal change* brings about new trade agreements, tariffs, and government requirements.
6. Other changes may be brought about through *market practice*, *professional standards*, *suppliers*, and *distributors*.

Operations managers must be aware of these dynamics and be able to anticipate changes in product opportunities, the products themselves, product volume, and product mix.

Importance of New Products

The importance of new products cannot be overestimated. As Figure 5.2(a) shows, leading companies generate a substantial portion of their sales from products less than 5 years old. Even Disney (Figure 5.2(b)) needs new theme parks to boost attendance. And giant Cisco Systems is expanding from its core business of making routers and switches into building its own computer servers (Figure 5.2(c)). The need for new products is why Gillette developed its multi-blade razors, in spite of continuing high sales of its phenomenally successful Sensor razor and why Disney innovates in spite of being the leading family entertainment company in the world.

Despite constant efforts to introduce viable new products, many new products do not succeed. Indeed, for General Mills to come up with a winner in the breakfast cereal market—defined as a cereal that gets a scant half of 1% of the market—isn't easy. Among the top 10 brands of cereal, the youngest, Honey Nut Cheerios, was created in 1979. DuPont estimates that it takes 250 ideas to yield one *marketable* product.[2]

[2]Rosabeth Kanter, John Kao, and Fred Wiersema, *Innovation Breakthrough Thinking at 3M, DuPont, GE, Pfizer, and Rubbermaid* (New York: HarperBusiness, 1997).

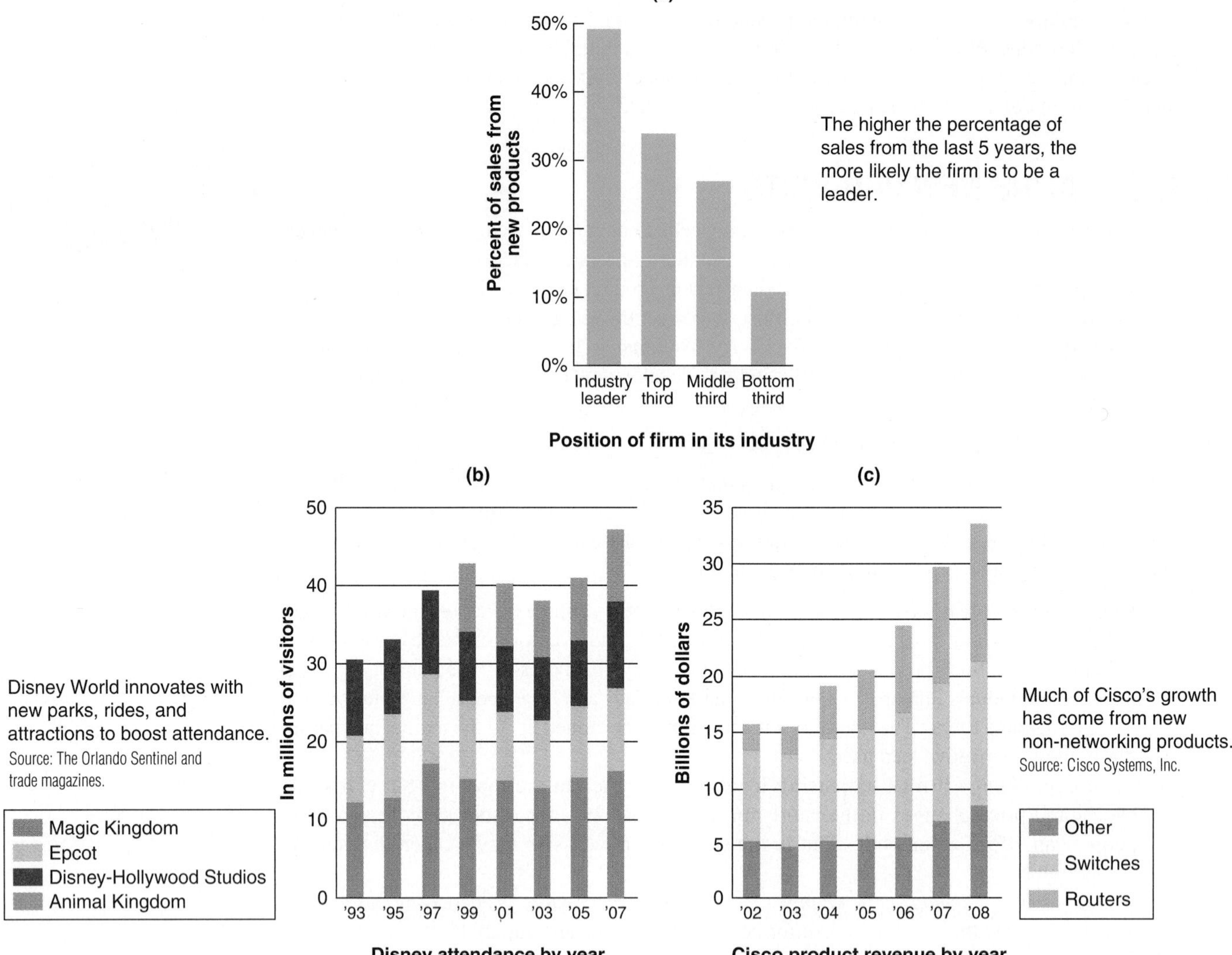

▲ **FIGURE 5.2 Innovation and New Products Yield Results for Both Manufacturing and Services**

As one can see, product selection, definition, and design occur frequently—perhaps hundreds of times for each financially successful product. Operations managers and their organizations must be able to accept risk and tolerate failure. They must accommodate a high volume of new product ideas while maintaining the activities to which they are already committed.

AUTHOR COMMENT Motorola went through 3,000 working models before it developed its first pocket cell phone.

PRODUCT DEVELOPMENT

Product Development System

An effective product strategy links product decisions with cash flow, market dynamics, product life cycle, and the organization's capabilities. A firm must have the cash for product development, understand the changes constantly taking place in the marketplace, and have the necessary talents and resources available. The product development system may well determine not only product success but also the firm's future. Figure 5.3 shows the stages of product development. In this system, product options go through a series of steps, each having its own screening and evaluation criteria, but providing a continuing flow of information to prior steps.

LO2: Describe a product development system

The screening process extends to the operations function. Optimum product development depends not only on support from other parts of the firm but also on the successful integration of all 10 of the OM decisions, from product design to maintenance. Identifying products that appear

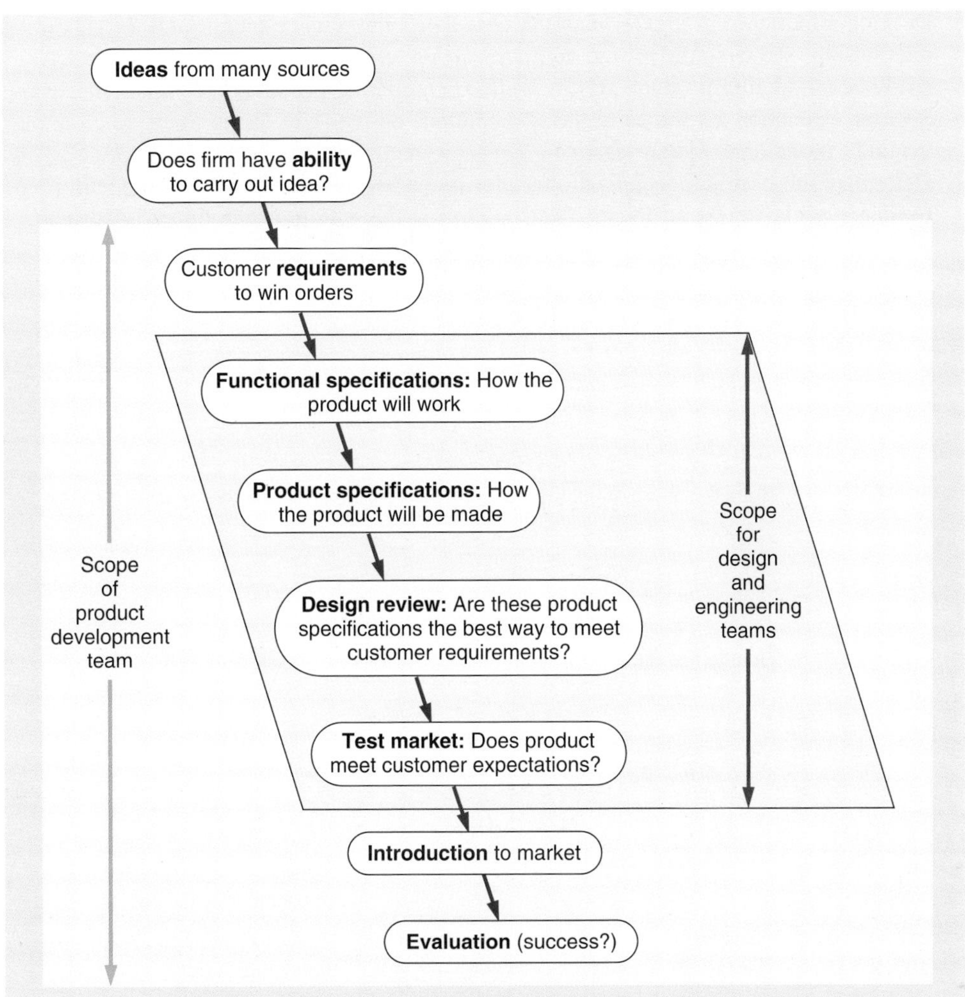

◀ **FIGURE 5.3**
Product Development Stages
Product concepts are developed from a variety of sources, both external and internal to the firm. Concepts that survive the product idea stage progress through various stages, with nearly constant review, feedback, and evaluation in a highly participative environment to minimize failure.

likely to capture market share, be cost effective, and profitable, but are in fact very difficult to produce, may lead to failure rather than success.

Quality Function Deployment (QFD)

Quality function deployment (QFD) refers to both (1) determining what will satisfy the customer and (2) translating those customer desires into the target design. The idea is to capture a rich understanding of customer wants and to identify alternative process solutions. This information is then integrated into the evolving product design. QFD is used early in the design process to help determine *what will satisfy the customer* and *where to deploy quality efforts*.

Quality function deployment (QFD)
A process for determining customer requirements (customer "wants") and translating them into the attributes (the "hows") that each functional area can understand and act on.

One of the tools of QFD is the house of quality. The **house of quality** is a graphic technique for defining the relationship between customer desires and product (or service). Only by defining this relationship in a rigorous way can operations managers design products and processes with features desired by customers. Defining this relationship is the first step in building a world-class production system. To build the house of quality, we perform seven basic steps:

House of quality
A part of the quality function deployment process that utilizes a planning matrix to relate customer "wants" to "how" the firm is going to meet those "wants."

1. Identify customer *wants*. (What do prospective customers want in this product?)
2. Identify *how* the good/service will satisfy customer wants. (Identify specific product characteristics, features, or attributes and show how they will satisfy customer *wants*.)
3. Relate customer *wants* to product *hows*. (Build a matrix, as in Example 1, that shows this relationship.)
4. Identify relationships between the firm's *hows*. (How do our *hows* tie together? For instance, in the following example, there is a high relationship between low electricity requirements and auto focus, auto exposure, and a paint pallet because they all require electricity. This relationship is shown in the "roof" of the house in Example 1.)

5. Develop importance ratings. (Using the *customer's* importance ratings and weights for the relationships shown in the matrix, compute *our* importance ratings, as in Example 1.)
6. Evaluate competing products. (How well do competing products meet customer wants? Such an evaluation, as shown in the two columns on the right of the figure in Example 1, would be based on market research.)
7. Determine the desirable technical attributes, your performance, and the competitor's performance against these attributes. (This is done at the bottom of the figure in Example 1).

LO3: Build a house of quality

The following series of overlays for Example 1 show how to construct a house of quality.

EXAMPLE 1 ▶

Constructing a house of quality

Great Cameras, Inc., wants a methodology that strengthens its ability to meet customer desires with its new digital camera.

APPROACH ▶ Use QFD's house of quality.

SOLUTION ▶ Build the house of quality for Great Cameras, Inc. We do so here using Overlays 1, 2, 3, and 4.

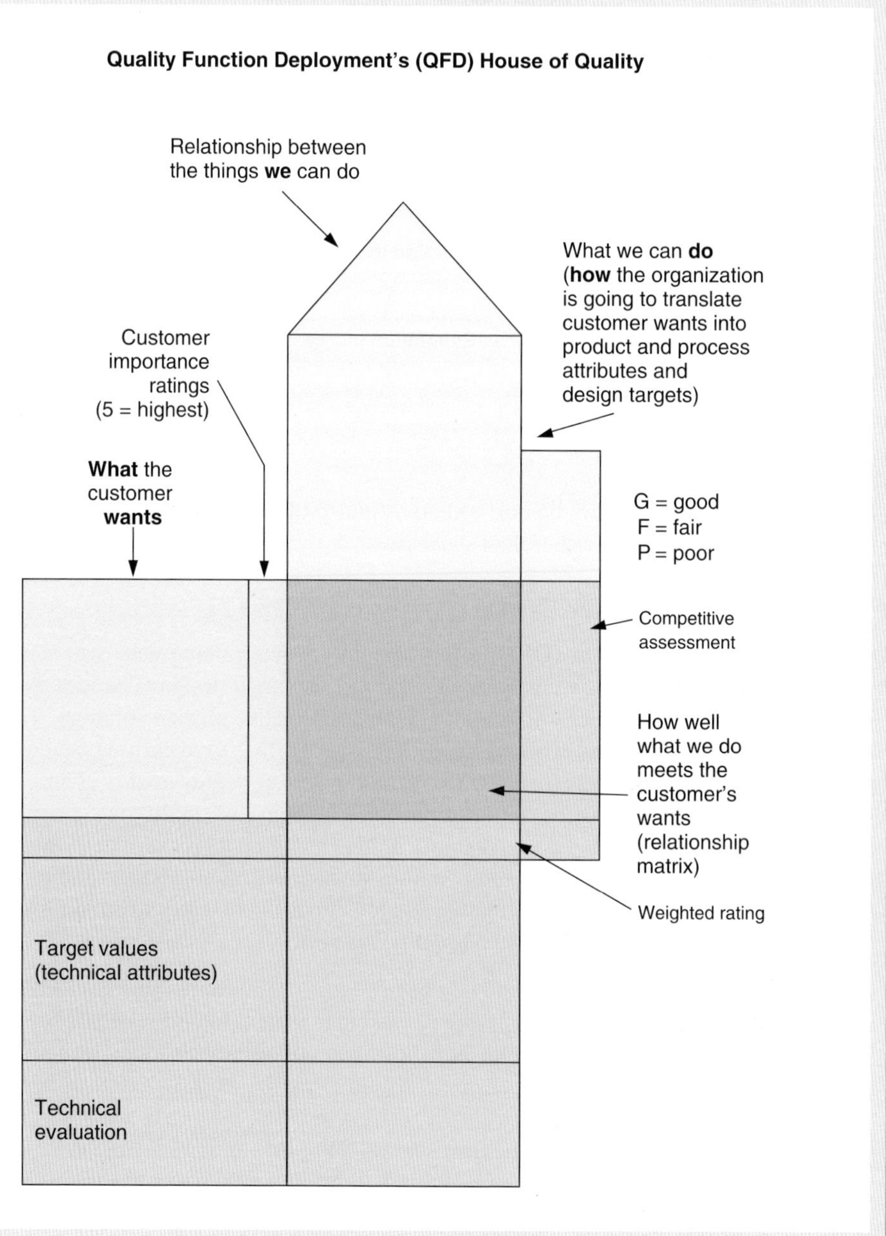

INSIGHT ▶ QFD provides an analytical tool that structures design features and technical issues, as well as providing importance rankings and competitor comparison.

LEARNING EXERCISE ▶ If the market research for another country indicates that "light-weight" has the most important customer ranking (5), and reliability a 3, what is the new total importance ranking for low electricity requirements, aluminum components, and ergonomic design? [Answer: 18, 15, 27, respectively.]

RELATED PROBLEMS ▶ 5.1, 5.2, 5.3, 5.4

Another use of quality function deployment (QFD) is to show how the quality effort will be *deployed*. As Figure 5.4 shows, *design characteristics* of House 1 become the inputs to House 2, which are satisfied by *specific components* of the product. Similarly, the concept is carried to House 3, where the specific components are to be satisfied through particular *production processes*. Once those production processes are defined, they become requirements of House 4 to be satisfied by a *quality plan* that will ensure conformance of those processes. The quality plan is a set of specific tolerances, procedures, methods, and sampling techniques that will ensure that the production process meets the customer requirements.

Much of the QFD effort is devoted to meeting customer requirements with design characteristics (House 1 in Figure 5.4), and its importance is not to be underestimated. However, the *sequence* of houses is a very effective way of identifying, communicating, and allocating resources throughout the system. The series of houses helps operations managers determine where to *deploy* quality resources. In this way we meet customer requirements, produce quality products, and win orders.

Organizing for Product Development

Let's look at four approaches to organizing for product development. *First*, the traditional U.S. approach to product development is an organization with distinct departments: a research and development department to do the necessary research; an engineering department to design the product; a manufacturing engineering department to design a product that can be produced; and a production department that produces the product. The distinct advantage of this approach is that fixed duties and responsibilities exist. The distinct disadvantage is lack of forward thinking: How will downstream departments in the process deal with the concepts, ideas, and designs presented to them, and ultimately what will the customer think of the product?

A *second* and popular approach is to assign a product manager to "champion" the product through the product development system and related organizations. However, a *third*, and perhaps the best, product development approach used in the U.S. seems to be the use of teams. Such teams are known variously as *product development teams, design for manufacturability teams*, and *value engineering teams*.

▼ FIGURE 5.4 House of Quality Sequence Indicates How to Deploy Resources to Achieve Customer Requirements

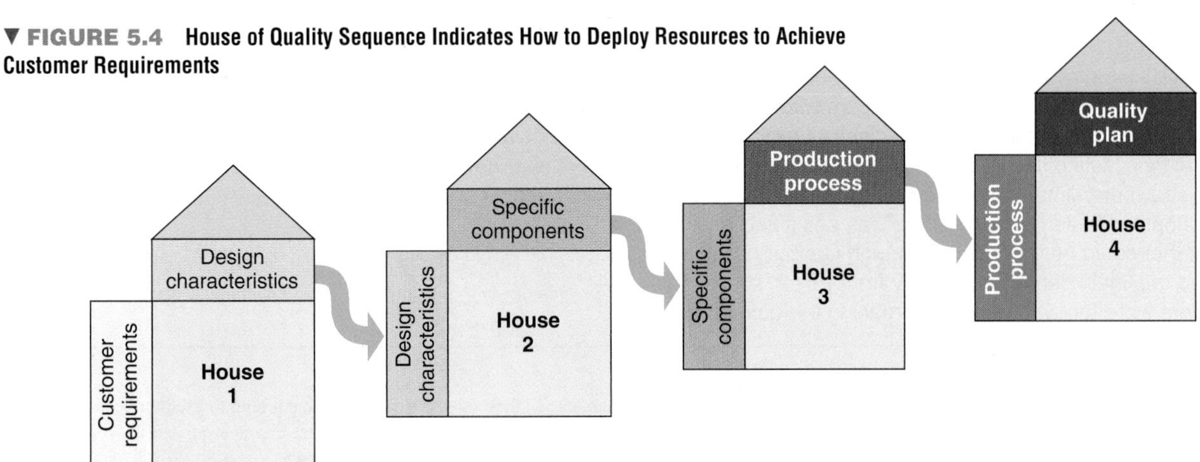

The Japanese use a *fourth* approach. They bypass the team issue by not subdividing organizations into research and development, engineering, production, and so forth. Consistent with the Japanese style of group effort and teamwork, these activities are all in one organization. Japanese culture and management style are more collegial and the organization less structured than in most Western countries. Therefore, the Japanese find it unnecessary to have "teams" provide the necessary communication and coordination. However, the typical Western style, and the conventional wisdom, is to use teams.

Product development teams
Teams charged with moving from market requirements for a product to achieving product success.

Product development teams are charged with the responsibility of moving from market requirements for a product to achieving a product success (refer to Figure 5.3 on page 159). Such teams often include representatives from marketing, manufacturing, purchasing, quality assurance, and field service personnel. Many teams also include representatives from vendors. Regardless of the formal nature of the product development effort, research suggests that success is more likely in an open, highly participative environment where those with potential contributions are allowed to make them. The objective of a product development team is to make the good or service a success. This includes marketability, manufacturability, and serviceability.

Concurrent engineering
Use of participating teams in design and engineering activities.

Use of such teams is also called **concurrent engineering** and implies a team representing all affected areas (known as a *cross-functional* team). Concurrent engineering also implies speedier product development through simultaneous performance of various aspects of product development.[3] The team approach is the dominant structure for product development by leading organizations in the U.S.

Manufacturability and Value Engineering

Manufacturability and value engineering
Activities that help improve a product's design, production, maintainability, and use.

Manufacturability and value engineering activities are concerned with improvement of design and specifications at the research, development, design, and production stages of product development. (See the *OM in Action* box "Design Challenges with Trident's Splash.") In addition to immediate, obvious cost reduction, design for manufacturability and value engineering may produce other benefits. These include:

1. Reduced complexity of the product.
2. Reduction of environmental impact.
3. Additional standardization of components.
4. Improvement of functional aspects of the product.

OM in Action ▶Design Challenges with Trident's Splash

Cadbury Schweppes PLC sells a lot of gum—Dentyne, Bubbaloo, and Trident—some $4.2 billion of a $15.4 billion market that is growing about 6% per year. However, Cadbury perceived a niche for a new gum that would be a low calorie substitute for unhealthy snacks. Cadbury wanted the new product to compete with the creamy or crunchy mouth experience one gets from snacks other than gum.

The R&D team eventually designed a unique three-layer pellet with a candy shell over sugarless gum with a liquid center. For the liquid center Cadbury scientists evaluated scores of long lasting flavors before settling on two unusual blends: strawberry-lime and peppermint-vanilla.

Development wasn't easy; neither was designing a product that could be produced. Although Cadbury acquired the liquid center technology from Pfizer, some of the flavors were too water-soluble—making the gum soft. Early formulations leaked during production. Others survived production only to fail when subjected to the punishment of transportation.

Adding to production problems was the lack of sugar in the gum. Sugar traditionally adds strength and bulk to aid the production process, but with artificial sweeteners, the centers were not strong enough for the application of the candy coating. The machinery crushed the weakened pellets and the liquid flavors oozed out. This in turn contributed to some messy production equipment.

It took two years and millions of dollars, but Cadbury's biggest ever new-product development effort, Trident Splash, is now on the market.

Sources: The Wall Street Journal (January 12, 2006): A1, A8; *Fortune* (April 3, 2006): 33

[3]Firms that have high technological or product change in their competitive environment tend to use more concurrent engineering practices. See X. Koufteros, M. Vonderembse, and W. Doll, "Concurrent Engineering and Its Consequences," *Journal of Operations Management* 19, no. 1 (January 2001): 97–115.

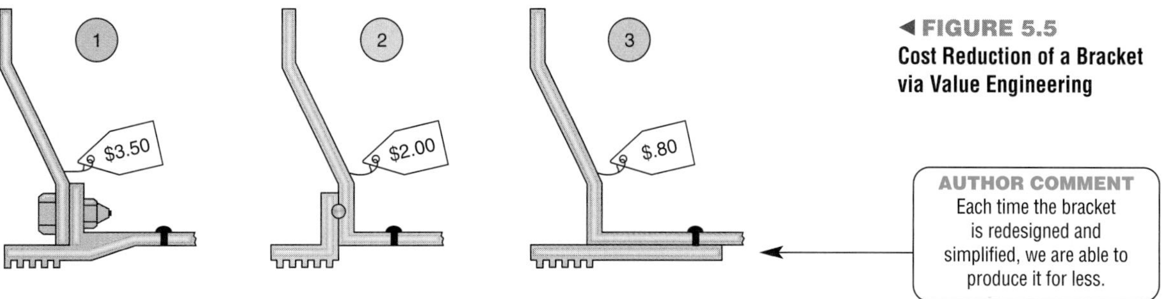

◀ **FIGURE 5.5**
Cost Reduction of a Bracket via Value Engineering

AUTHOR COMMENT
Each time the bracket is redesigned and simplified, we are able to produce it for less.

5. Improved job design and job safety.
6. Improved maintainability (serviceability) of the product.
7. Robust design.

Manufacturability and value engineering activities may be the best cost-avoidance technique available to operations management. They yield value improvement by focusing on achieving the functional specifications necessary to meet customer requirements in an optimal way. Value engineering programs, when effectively managed, typically reduce costs between 15% and 70% without reducing quality. Some studies have indicated that for every dollar spent on value engineering, $10 to $25 in savings can be realized.

Product design affects virtually all aspects of operating expense and sustainability. Consequently, the development process needs to ensure a thorough evaluation of design prior to a commitment to produce. The cost reduction achieved for a specific bracket via value engineering is shown in Figure 5.5

ISSUES FOR PRODUCT DESIGN

In addition to developing an effective system and organization structure for product development, several *techniques* are important to the design of a product. We will now review six of these: (1) robust design, (2) modular design, (3) computer-aided design (CAD), (4) computer-aided manufacturing (CAM), (5) virtual reality technology, and (6) value analysis.

Robust Design

Robust design means that the product is designed so that small variations in production or assembly do not adversely affect the product. For instance, Lucent developed an integrated circuit that could be used in many products to amplify voice signals. As originally designed, the circuit had to be manufactured very expensively to avoid variations in the strength of the signal. But after testing and analyzing the design, Lucent engineers realized that if the resistance of the circuit was reduced—a minor change with no associated costs—the circuit would be far less sensitive to manufacturing variations. The result was a 40% improvement in quality.

Robust design
A design that can be produced to requirements even with unfavorable conditions in the production process.

Modular Design

Products designed in easily segmented components are known as **modular designs**. Modular designs offer flexibility to both production and marketing. Operations managers find modularity helpful because it makes product development, production, and subsequent changes easier. Moreover, marketing may like modularity because it adds flexibility to the ways customers can be satisfied. For instance, virtually all premium high-fidelity sound systems are produced and sold this way. The customization provided by modularity allows customers to mix and match to their own taste. This is also the approach taken by Harley-Davidson, where relatively few different engines, chassis, gas tanks, and suspension systems are mixed to produce a huge variety of motorcycles. It has been estimated that many automobile manufacturers can, by mixing the available modules, never make two cars alike. This same concept of modularity is carried over to many industries, from airframe manufacturers to fast-food restaurants. Airbus uses the same wing modules on several planes, just as McDonald's and Burger King use relatively few modules (cheese, lettuce, buns, sauces, pickles, meat patties, french fries, etc.) to make a variety of meals.

Modular design
A design in which parts or components of a product are subdivided into modules that are easily interchanged or replaced.

Computer-Aided Design (CAD)

Computer-aided design (CAD)
Interactive use of a computer to develop and document a product.

Computer-aided design (CAD) is the use of computers to interactively design products and prepare engineering documentation. Use and variety of CAD software is extensive and is rapidly expanding. CAD software allows designers to use three-dimensional drawings to save time and money by shortening development cycles for virtually all products (see the 3-D design photos below). The speed and ease with which sophisticated designs can be manipulated, analyzed, and modified with CAD makes review of numerous options possible before final commitments are made. Faster development, better products, accurate flow of information to other departments—all contribute to a tremendous payoff for CAD. The payoff is particularly significant because most product costs are determined at the design stage.

Design for manufacture and assembly (DFMA)
Software that allows designers to look at the effect of design on manufacturing of the product.

One extension of CAD is **design for manufacture and assembly (DFMA)** software, which focuses on the effect of design on assembly. It allows designers to examine the integration of product designs before the product is manufactured. For instance, DFMA allows automobile designers to examine how a transmission will be placed in a car on the production line, even while both the transmission and the car are still in the design stage.

3-D object modeling
An extension of CAD that builds small prototypes.

A second CAD extension is **3-D object modeling**. The technology is particularly useful for small prototype development (as shown in the photo on page 165). 3-D object modeling rapidly builds up a model in very thin layers of synthetic materials for evaluation. This technology speeds development by avoiding a more lengthy and formal manufacturing process. 3-D printers, costing as little as $5,000, are also now available. Shoemaker Timberland, Inc., uses theirs to allow footwear designers to see their constructions overnight rather than waiting a week for model-makers to carve them.

Some CAD systems have moved to the Internet through e-commerce, where they link computerized design with purchasing, outsourcing, manufacturing, and long-term maintenance. This move supports rapid product change and the growing trend toward "mass customization." With CAD on the Internet, customers can enter a supplier's design libraries and make design changes. The supplier's software can then automatically generate the drawings, update the bill of material, and prepare instructions for the supplier's production process. The result is customized products produced faster and at less expense.

Standard for the exchange of product data (STEP)
A standard that provides a format allowing the electronic transmittal of three-dimensional data.

As product life cycles shorten and design becomes more complex, collaboration among departments, facilities and suppliers throughout the world becomes critical. The potential of such collaboration has proven so important that a standard for its exchange has been developed, known as the **standard for the exchange of product data (STEP)**. STEP permits manufacturers to express

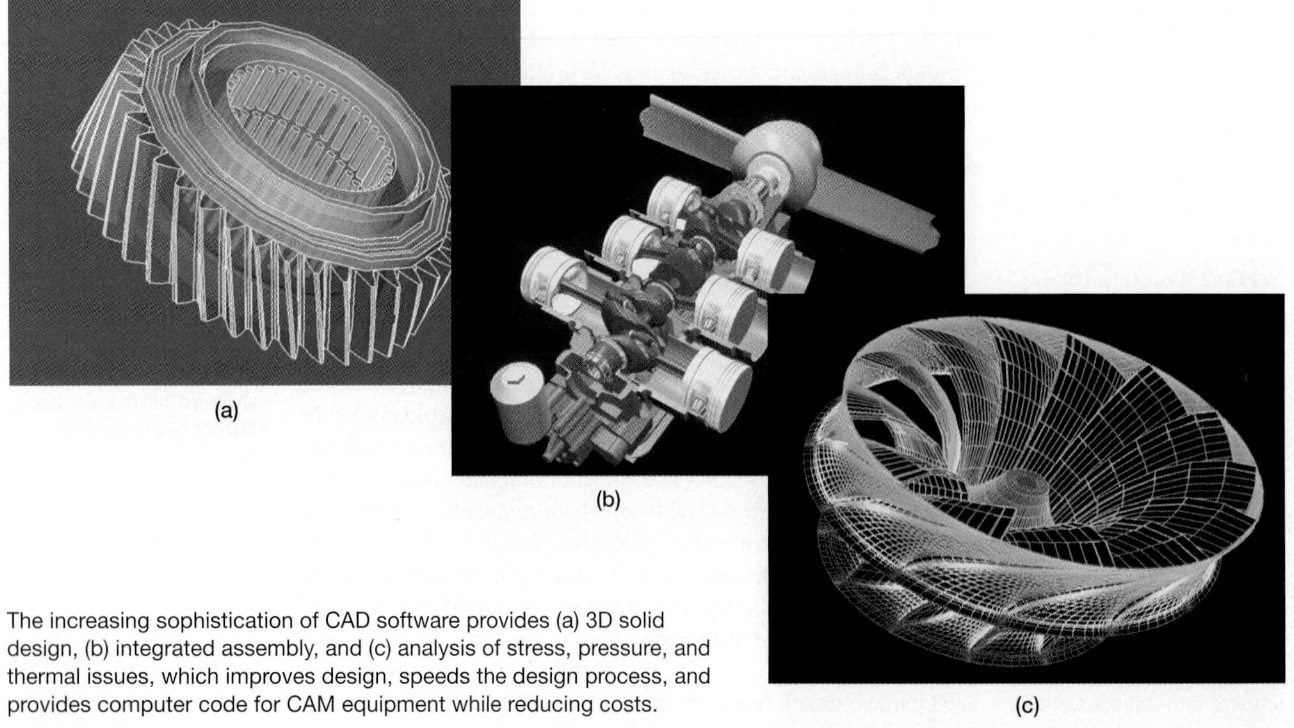

(a) (b) (c)

The increasing sophistication of CAD software provides (a) 3D solid design, (b) integrated assembly, and (c) analysis of stress, pressure, and thermal issues, which improves design, speeds the design process, and provides computer code for CAM equipment while reducing costs.

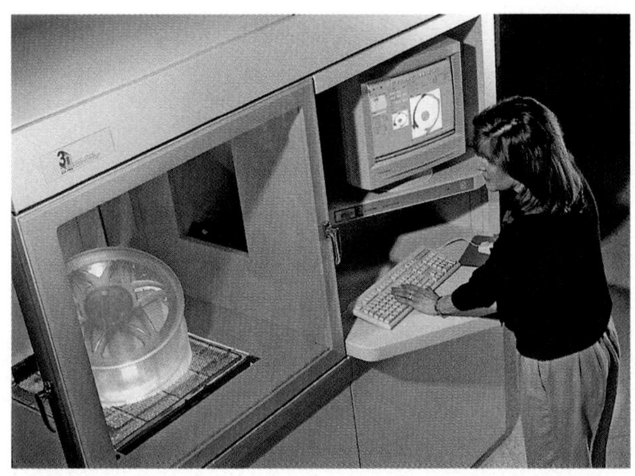

This prototype wheel for a tire (at the left of the photo) is being built using 3-D System's Stereolithography technology, a 3-D object modeling system. This technology uses data from CAD and builds structures layer by layer in .001-inch increments. The technique reduces the time it takes to create a sample from weeks to hours while also reducing costs. The technique is also known as rapid prototyping.

3-D product information in a standard format so it can be exchanged internationally, allowing geographically dispersed manufacturers to integrate design, manufacture, and support processes.[4]

Computer-Aided Manufacturing (CAM)

Computer-aided manufacturing (CAM) refers to the use of specialized computer programs to direct and control manufacturing equipment. When computer-aided design (CAD) information is translated into instructions for computer-aided manufacturing (CAM), the result of these two technologies is CAD/CAM.

Computer-aided manufacturing (CAM)
The use of information technology to control machinery.

The benefits of CAD and CAM include:

1. *Product quality:* CAD permits the designer to investigate more alternatives, potential problems, and dangers.
2. *Shorter design time:* A shorter design phase lowers cost and allows a more rapid response to the market.
3. *Production cost reductions:* Reduced inventory, more efficient use of personnel through improved scheduling, and faster implementation of design changes lower costs.
4. *Database availability:* Provides information for other manufacturing software and accurate product data so everyone is operating from the same information, resulting in dramatic cost reductions.
5. *New range of capabilities:* For instance, the abilities to rotate and depict objects in three-dimensional form, to check clearances, to relate parts and attachments, and to improve the use of numerically controlled machine tools—all provide new capability for manufacturing. CAD/CAM removes substantial detail work, allowing designers to concentrate on the conceptual and imaginative aspects of their task.

Virtual Reality Technology

Virtual reality is a visual form of communication in which images substitute for the real thing but still allow the user to respond interactively. The roots of virtual reality technology in operations are in computer-aided design. Once design information is in a CAD system, it is also in electronic digital form for other uses, such as developing 3-D layouts of everything from restaurants to amusement parks. Changes to mechanical design, restaurant layouts, or amusement park rides are much less expensive at the design stage than later.

Virtual reality
A visual form of communication in which images substitute for reality and typically allow the user to respond interactively.

Value Analysis

Although value engineering (discussed on page 162) focuses on *preproduction* design improvement, value analysis, a related technique, takes place *during* the production process, when it is clear that a new product is a success. **Value analysis** seeks improvements that lead to either a better product, or a product made more economically, or a product with less environmental impact. The techniques and advantages for value analysis are the same as for value engineering, although minor changes in implementation may be necessary because value analysis is taking place while the product is being produced.

Value analysis
A review of successful products that takes place during the production process.

[4]The STEP format is documented in the European Community's standard ISO 10303.

AUTHOR COMMENT
OM can do a lot to save our planet. Saving the planet is good business and good ethics.

ETHICS, ENVIRONMENTALLY-FRIENDLY DESIGNS, AND SUSTAINABILITY

Sustainability
A production system that supports conservation and renewal of resources.

An operations manager's task is to enhance productivity while delivering desired goods and services in an ethical, environmentally sound, and sustainable way. In an OM context, **sustainability** means ecological stability. This means operating a production system in a way that supports conservation and renewal of resources. The entire product life cycle—from design, to production, to final destruction or recycling—provides an opportunity to preserve resources. Planet Earth is finite; managers who squeeze more out of its resources are its heroes. The good news is that operations managers have tools that can drive down costs or improve margins while preserving resources. Here are examples of how firms do so:

- *At the design stage:* DuPont developed a polyester film stronger and thinner so it uses less material and costs less to make. Also, because the film performs better, customers are willing to pay more for it. Similarly, Nike's new Air Jordan shoe contains very little chemical-based glue and an outsole made of recycled material, yielding lower manufacturing cost and less impact on the environment.
- *At the production stage:* Bristol-Myers Squibb established an environmental and pollution prevention program designed to address environmental, health, and safety issues at all stages of the product life cycle. Ban Roll-On was one of the first products studied and an early success. Repackaging Ban in smaller cartons resulted in a reduction of 600 tons of recycled paperboard. The product then required 55% less shelf space for display. As a result, not only is pollution prevented but store operating costs are also reduced.
- *At the destruction stage:* The automobile industry has been very successful: The industry now recycles more than 84% of the material by weight of 13 million cars scrapped each year. Much of this success results from care at the design stage. For instance, BMW, with environmentally friendly designs, recycles most of a car, including many plastic components (see the photo).

These efforts are consistent with the environmental issues raised by the ISO 14000 standard, a topic we address in Chapter 6.

Systems and Life Cycle Perspectives

One way to accomplish programs like those at DuPont, Bristol-Myers Squibb, and BMW is to add an ethical and environmental charge to the job of operations managers and their value engineering/analysis teams. Team members from different functional areas working together can present a wide range of environmental perspectives and approaches. Managers and teams should consider two issues.

First, they need to view products from a "systems" perspective—that is, view a product in terms of its impact on sustainability—ecological stability. This means taking a comprehensive look at the inputs to the firm, the processes, and the outputs, recognizing that some of the resources, long considered free, are in fact not free. Particulates and sulfur in the air are pollution for someone else; similarly, bacteria and phosphates in the water going downstream become

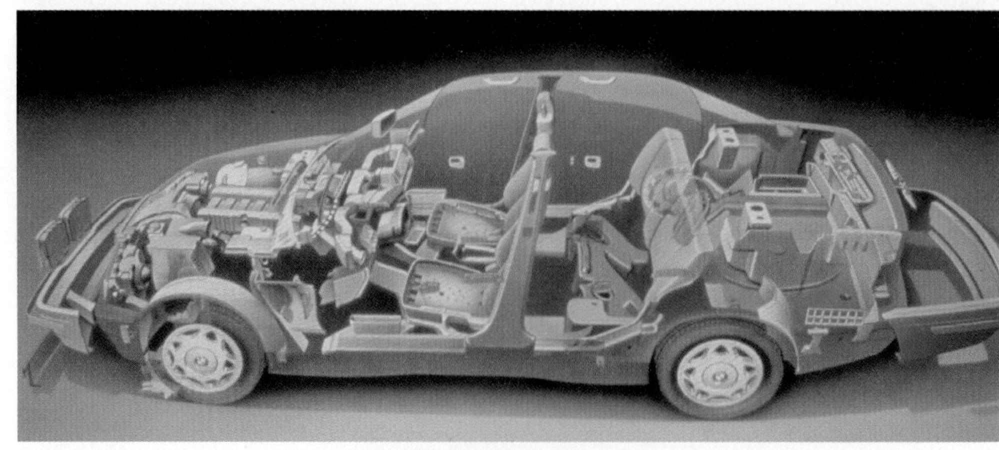

BMW uses parts made of recycled plastics (blue) and parts that can be recycled (green). "Green manufacturing" means companies can reuse, refurbish, or dispose of a product's components safely and reduce total life cycle product costs.

someone else's problem. In the case of the battle between styrofoam and paper containers, which one is really "better," and by what criteria? We may know which is more economical for the firm, but is that one also most economical for society?

Second, operations managers must consider the life cycle of the product, that is, from design, through production, to final disposition. This can be done via value engineering, as noted earlier, or as a part of a **life cycle assessment (LCA)** initiative. LCA is part of the ISO 14000 environmental management standard. The goal is to reduce the environmental impact of a product throughout its life—a challenging task.

Life cycle assessment (LCA)
Part of ISO 14000; assesses the environmental impact of a product, from material and energy inputs to disposal and environmental releases.

The likelihood that ethical decisions will be made is enhanced when managers maintain these two perspectives and maintain an open dialogue among all stakeholders.

Goals Consistent with the two issues above, goals for ethical, environment-friendly designs are:

1. Develop safe and more environmentally sound products.
2. Minimize waste of raw materials and energy.
3. Reduce environmental liabilities.
4. Increase cost-effectiveness of complying with environmental regulations.
5. Be recognized as a good corporate citizen.

Guidelines The following six guidelines may help operations managers achieve ethical and environmentally-friendly designs:

1. *Make products recyclable:* Many firms are doing this on their own, but the U.S. and the EU now have take-back laws that affect a variety of products, from automobiles and tires to computers. Not only is most of a car recycled but so are over half the aluminum cans and a large portion of paper, plastic, and glass. In some cases, as with tires, the manufacturer is responsible for 100% disposal.
2. *Use recycled materials:* Scotch-Brite soap pads at 3M are designed to use recycled plastics, as are the park benches and other products made by Plastic Recycling Corporation. Recycled plastics and old clothing are making their way into seat upholstery for the Ford Escape hybrid sport-utility. This application has added benefits: it's waterproof and it will save 600,000 gallons of water, 1.8 million pounds of carbon doxide, and more than 7 million kilowatt hours of electricity per year.[5]
3. *Use less harmful ingredients:* Standard Register, like most of the printing industry, has replaced environmentally dangerous inks with soy-based inks that reduce air and water pollution.
4. *Use lighter components:* The auto and truck industries continue to expand the use of aluminum and plastic components to reduce weight. Mercedes is even building car exteriors from a banana plant fiber that is both biodegradable and lightweight. Similarly, Boeing is using carbon fiber, epoxy composites, and titanium graphite laminate to reduce weight in its new 787 Dreamliner. These changes can be expensive, but they make autos, trucks, and aircraft more environmentally friendly by improving payload and fuel efficiency.
5. *Use less energy:* While the auto, truck, and airframe industries are redesigning to improve mileage, General Electric is designing a new generation of refrigerators that requires substantially less electricity during their lifetime. DuPont is so good at energy efficiency that it has turned its expertise into a consulting business.
6. *Use less material:* Organizations fight to drive down material use—in the plant and in the packaging. An employee team at a Sony semiconductor plant achieved a 50% reduction in the amount of chemicals used in the silicon wafer etching process. And Frito-Lay's U.S. plants have driven down water consumption over 31% in the past 10 years, with a goal of 75% reduction by 2017. These and similar successes reduce both production costs and environmental concerns. To conserve packaging, Boston's Park Plaza Hotel eliminated bars of soap and bottles of shampoo by installing pump dispensers in its bathrooms, saving the need for a million plastic containers a year.

Laws and Industry Standards Laws and industry standards can help operations managers make ethical and socially responsible decisions. In the last 100 years we have seen development of legal and industry standards to guide managers in product design, manufacture/assembly, and disassembly/disposal.

[5] "Vehicles That Use Recycled Material," *The Wall Street Journal* (January 25, 2007): D6.

With increasing restrictions on disposal of TVs, cell phones, computers, and other electronic waste, much of such waste (left) ends its life in Guangdong province on China's southern coast (right). Here, under less-than-ideal conditions, Chinese women strip old circuit boards to salvage the chips.

Design: On the legal side, U.S. laws and regulations such as those promulgated by the Food and Drug Administration, Consumer Product Safety Commission, National Highway Safety Administration, and Children's Product Safety Act provide guidance, if not explicit law, to aid decision making. Guidance is also provided by phrases in case law like "design for foreseeable misuse" and in regard to children's toys, "The concept of a prudent child is . . . a grotesque combination."

Manufacture/assembly: The manufacture and assembly of products has standards and guidelines from the Occupational Safety and Health Administration (OSHA), Environmental Protection Agency (EPA), professional ergonomic standards, and a wide range of state and federal laws that deal with employment standards, disabilities, discrimination, and the like.

Disassembly/disposal: Product disassembly and disposal in the U.S., Canada, and the EU are governed by increasingly rigid laws. In the U.S., the Vehicle Recycling Partnership, supported by the auto industry, provides *Design for Disassembly Standards* for auto disassembly and disposal. However, in the fragmented electronics industry, safe disposal of TVs, computers, and cell phones is much more difficult and dangerous (see the photo).

Ethical, socially responsible decisions can be difficult and complex—often with no easy answers—but such decisions are appreciated by the public, and they can save money, material, and the environment. These are the types of win–win situations that operations managers seek.

AUTHOR COMMENT
Fast communication, rapid technological change, and short product life cycles push product development.

TIME-BASED COMPETITION

As product life cycles shorten, the need for faster product development increases. Additionally, as technological sophistication of new products increases, so do the expense and risk. For instance, drug firms invest an average of 12 to 15 years and $600 million before receiving regulatory approval of each new drug. And even then, only 1 of 5 will actually be a success. Those operations managers who master this art of product development continually gain on slower product developers. To the swift goes the competitive advantage. This concept is called **time-based competition**.

Time-based competition
Competition based on time; rapidly developing products and moving them to market.

Often, the first company into production may have its product adopted for use in a variety of applications that will generate sales for years. It may become the "standard." Consequently, there is often more concern with getting the product to market than with optimum product design or process efficiency. Even so, rapid introduction to the market may be good management because until competition begins to introduce copies or improved versions, the product can sometimes be priced high enough to justify somewhat inefficient production design and methods. For example, when Kodak first introduced its Ektar film, it sold for 10% to 15% more than conventional film and Apple's innovative iPod and new versions have a 75% market share even after 5 years.

LO4: Describe how time-based competition is implemented by OM

Because time-based competition is so important, instead of developing new products from scratch (which has been the focus thus far in this chapter) a number of other strategies can be used. Figure 5.6 shows a continuum that goes from new, internally developed products (on the lower left) to "alliances." *Enhancements* and *migrations* use the organization's existing product strengths for innovation and therefore are typically faster while at the same time being less risky than developing entirely new products. Enhancements may be changes in color, size, weight, or features, such as are taking place in cellular phones (see *OM in Action* box "Chasing Fads in the Cell Phone Industry"), or even changes in commercial aircraft. Boeing's enhancements of the 737 since its introduction in 1967 has made the 737 the largest-selling commercial aircraft in

Product Development Continuum

External development strategies		
		Alliances
	Joint ventures	
Purchase technology or expertise by acquiring the developer		
Internal development strategies		
		Migrations of existing products
	Enhancements to existing products	
New internally developed products		
Internal ←	*Cost of product development*	→ **Shared**
Lengthy ←	*Speed of product development*	→ **Rapid and/or Existing**
High ←	*Risk of product development*	→ **Shared**

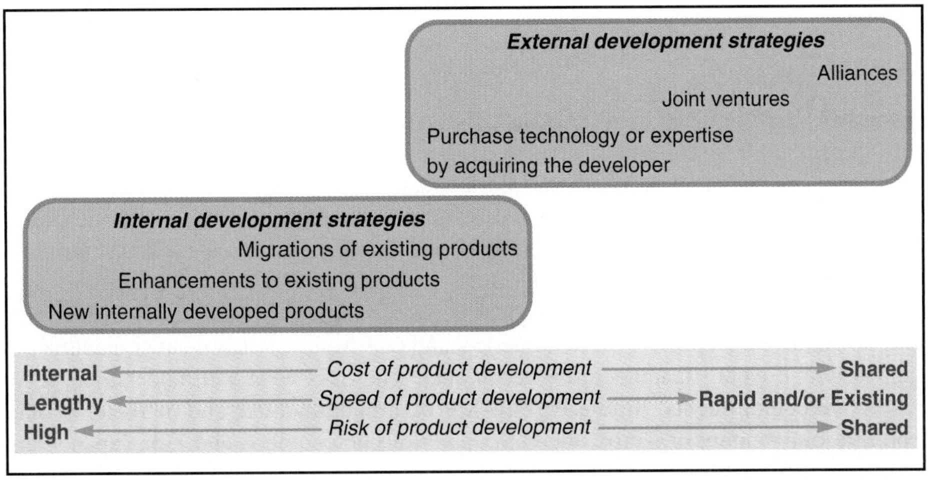

◄ **FIGURE 5.6 Product Development Continuum**

AUTHOR COMMENT
Managers seek a variety of approaches to obtain speed to market. The president of one U.S. firm says: "If I miss one product cycle, I'm dead."

history. Boeing also uses its engineering prowess in air frames to *migrate* from one model to the next. This allows Boeing to speed development while reducing both cost and risk for new designs. This approach is also referred to as building on *product platforms*. Black & Decker has used its "platform" expertise in hand-powered tools to build a leading position in that market. Similarly, Hewlett-Packard has done the same in the printer business. Enhancements and migrations are a way of building on existing expertise and extending a product's life cycle.

The product development strategies on the lower left of Figure 5.6 are *internal* development strategies, while the three approaches we now introduce can be thought of as *external* development strategies. Firms use both. The external strategies are (1) purchase the technology, (2) establish joint ventures, and (3) develop alliances.

Purchasing Technology by Acquiring a Firm

Microsoft and Cisco Systems are examples of companies on the cutting edge of technology that often speed development by *acquiring entrepreneurial firms* that have already developed the technology that fits their mission. The issue then becomes fitting the purchased organization, its

OM in Action ►Chasing Fads in the Cell Phone Industry

In the shrinking world marketplace, innovations that appeal to customers in one region rapidly become global trends. The process shakes up the structure of one industry after another, from computers to automobiles to consumer electronics.

Nowhere has this impact been greater in recent years than in the cell phone industry. The industry sells about 1.3 billion phones each year, but product life cycle is short. Competition is intense. Higher margins go to the innovator—and manufacturers that jump on an emerging trend early can reap substantial rewards. The swiftest Chinese manufacturers, such as Ningbo Bird and TCL, now replace some phone models after just 6 months. In the past, Motorola, Nokia, and other industry veterans enjoyed what are now considered long life cycles—2 years. New styles and technological advances in cell phones constantly appear somewhere in the world. Wired, well-traveled consumers seek the latest innovation; local retailers rush to offer it; and telecommunication providers order it.

Contemporary cell phones may be a curvy, boxy, or a clamshell fashion item; have a tiny keyboard for quick and easy typing or a more limited number pad for a phone; have a built-in radio or a digital music player; have a camera, Internet access, or TV clips; function on cellular or wireless (Wi-Fi) networks; or have games or personal organizers. Mattel and Nokia even have Barbie phones for preteen girls, complete with prepaid minutes, customized ringtones, and faceplates. The rapid changes in features and demand are forcing manufacturers into a frenzied race to keep up or simply to pull out.

"We got out of the handset business because we couldn't keep up with the cycle times," says Jeffrey Belk, Marketing V.P. for Qualcomm Inc., the San Diego company that now focuses on making handset chips.

Developing new products is always a challenge, but in the dynamic global market place of cell phones, product development takes on new technology and new markets at breakneck speed.

Sources: Supply Chain Management Review (October, 2007): 28; *The Wall Street Journal* (October 30, 2003): A1 and (Sept. 8, 2004): D5; and *International Business Times* (March 3,2009).

technology, its product lines, and its culture into the buying firm, rather than a product development issue.

Joint Ventures

Joint ventures
Firms establishing joint ownership to pursue new products or markets.

Joint ventures are combined ownership, usually between just two firms, to form a new entity. Ownership can be 50–50, or one owner can assume a larger portion to ensure tighter control. Joint ventures are often appropriate for exploiting specific product opportunities that may not be central to the firm's mission. Such ventures are more likely to work when the risks are known and can be equitably shared. For instance, GM and Toyota formed a joint venture to produce the GM Prism and the Toyota Corolla. Both companies saw a learning opportunity as well as a product they both needed in the North American market. Toyota wanted to learn about building and managing a plant in North America, and GM wanted to learn about manufacturing a small car with Toyota's manufacturing techniques. The risks were well understood, as were the respective commitments. Similarly, Fuji-Xerox, a manufacturer and marketer of photocopiers, is a joint venture of Xerox, the U.S. maker of photocopiers, and Fuji, Japan's largest manufacturer of film.

Alliances

Alliances
Cooperative agreements that allow firms to remain independent, but pursue strategies consistent with their individual missions.

Alliances are cooperative agreements that allow firms to remain independent but use complementing strengths to pursue strategies consistent with their individual missions. When new products are central to the mission, but substantial resources are required and sizable risk is present, then alliances may be a good strategy for product development. Alliances are particularly beneficial when the products to be developed also have technologies that are in ferment. For example, Microsoft is pursuing a number of alliances with a variety of companies to deal with the convergence of computing, the Internet, and television broadcasting. Alliances in this case are appropriate because the technological unknowns, capital demands, and risks are significant. Similarly, three firms, Mercedes Benz, Ford Motor, and Ballard Power Systems, have formed an alliance to develop "green" cars powered by fuel cells. However, alliances are much more difficult to achieve and maintain than joint ventures because of the ambiguities associated with them. It may be helpful to think of an alliance as an incomplete contract between the firms. The firms remain separate.

Enhancements, migration, acquisitions, joint ventures, and alliances are all strategies for speeding product development. Moreover, they typically reduce the risk associated with product development while enhancing the human and capital resources available.

AUTHOR COMMENT
Before anything can be produced, a product's functions and attributes must be defined.

DEFINING A PRODUCT

Once new goods or services are selected for introduction, they must be defined. First, a good or service is defined in terms of its *functions*—that is, what it is to *do*. The product is then designed, and the firm determines how the functions are to be achieved. Management typically has a variety of options as to how a product should achieve its functional purpose. For instance, when an alarm clock is produced, aspects of design such as the color, size, or location of buttons may make substantial differences in ease of manufacture, quality, and market acceptance.

LO5: Describe how products and services are defined by OM

Rigorous specifications of a product are necessary to assure efficient production. Equipment, layout, and human resources cannot be determined until the product is defined, designed, and documented. Therefore, every organization needs documents to define its products. This is true of everything from meat patties, to cheese, to computers, to a medical procedure. In the case of cheese, a written specification is typical. Indeed, written specifications or standard grades exist and provide the definition for many products. For instance, Monterey Jack cheese has a written description that specifies the characteristics necessary for each Department of Agriculture grade. A portion of the Department of Agriculture grade for Monterey Jack Grade AA is shown in Figure 5.7. Similarly, McDonald's Corp. has 60 specifications for potatoes that are to be made into french fries.

Engineering drawing
A drawing that shows the dimensions, tolerances, materials, and finishes of a component.

Bill of material (BOM)
A list of the components, their description, and the quantity of each required to make one unit of a product.

Most manufactured items as well as their components are defined by a drawing, usually referred to as an engineering drawing. An **engineering drawing** shows the dimensions, tolerances, materials, and finishes of a component. The engineering drawing will be an item on a bill of material. An engineering drawing is shown in Figure 5.8. The **bill of material (BOM)** lists the components, their description, and the quantity of each required to make one unit of a product.

§ 58.2469 Specifications for U.S. grades of Monterey (Monterey Jack) cheese

(a) *U.S. grade AA.* Monterey Cheese shall conform to the following requirements:

(1) *Flavor.* Is fine and highly pleasing, free from undesirable flavors and odors. May possess a very slight acid or feed flavor.

(2) *Body and texture.* A plug drawn from the cheese shall be reasonably firm. It shall have numerous small mechanical openings evenly distributed throughout the plug. It shall not possess sweet holes, yeast holes, or other gas holes.

(3) *Color.* Shall have a natural, uniform, bright, attractive appearance.

(4) *Finish and appearance—bandaged and paraffin-dipped.* The rind shall be sound, firm, and smooth, providing a good protection to the cheese.

Code of Federal Regulation, Parts 53 to 109, General Service Administration.

◄ **FIGURE 5.7**
Monterey Jack
A portion of the general requirements for the U.S. grades of Monterey cheese is shown here.

A bill of material for a manufactured item is shown in Figure 5.9(a). Note that subassemblies and components (lower-level items) are indented at each level to indicate their subordinate position. An engineering drawing shows how to make one item on the bill of material.

In the food-service industry, bills of material manifest themselves in *portion-control standards*. The portion-control standard for Hard Rock Cafe's hickory BBQ bacon cheeseburger is shown in Figure 5.9(b). In a more complex product, a bill of material is referenced on other bills of material of which they are a part. In this manner, subunits (subassemblies) are part of the next higher unit (their parent bill of material) that ultimately makes a final product. In addition to being defined by written specifications, portion-control documents, or bills of material, products can be defined in other ways. For example, products such as chemicals, paints, and petroleums may be defined by formulas or proportions that describe how they are to be made. Movies are defined by scripts, and insurance coverage by legal documents known as policies.

Make-or-Buy Decisions

For many components of products, firms have the option of producing the components themselves or purchasing them from outside sources. Choosing between these options is known as the make-or-buy decision. The **make-or-buy decision** distinguishes between what the firm wants to *produce* and what it wants to *purchase*. Because of variations in quality, cost, and delivery schedules, the make-or-buy decision is critical to product definition. Many items can be purchased as a "standard item" produced by someone else. Examples are the standard bolts listed on the bill of material shown in Figure 5.9(a), for which there will be SAE (Society of Automotive Engineers) specifications. Therefore, there typically is no need for the firm to duplicate this specification in another document. We discuss the make-or-buy decision in more detail in Chapter 11.

Make-or-buy decision
The choice between producing a component or a service and purchasing it from an outside source.

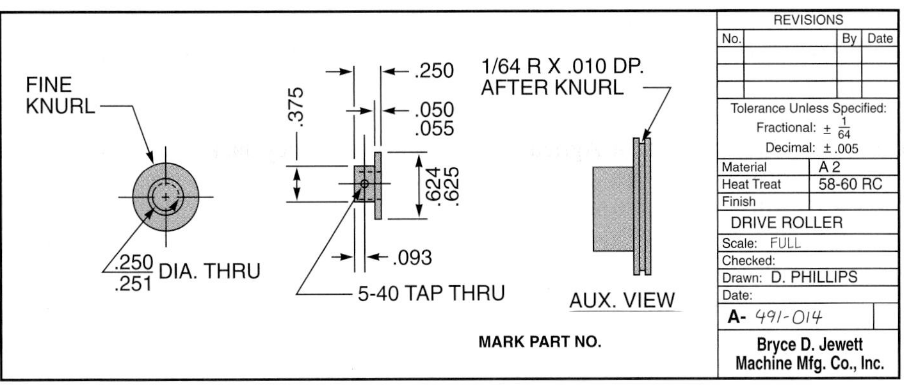

◄ **FIGURE 5.8**
Engineering Drawings Such as This One Show Dimensions, Tolerances, Materials, and Finishes

▶ **FIGURE 5.9 Bills of Material Take Different Forms in a (a) Manufacturing Plant and a (b) Restaurant, but in Both Cases, the Product Must Be Defined**

(a) **Bill of Material for a Panel Weldment**

NUMBER	DESCRIPTION	QTY
A 60-71	PANEL WELDM'T	1
A 60-7	LOWER ROLLER ASSM.	1
R 60-17	ROLLER	1
R 60-428	PIN	1
P 60-2	LOCKNUT	1
A 60-72	GUIDE ASSM. REAR	1
R 60-57-1	SUPPORT ANGLE	1
A 60-4	ROLLER ASSEM.	1
02-50-1150	BOLT	1
A 60-73	GUIDE ASSM. FRONT	1
A 60-74	SUPPORT WELDM'T	1
R 60-99	WEAR PLATE	1
02-50-1150	BOLT	1

(b) **Hard Rock Cafe's Hickory BBQ Bacon Cheeseburger**

DESCRIPTION	QTY
Bun	1
Hamburger patty	8 oz.
Cheddar cheese	2 slices
Bacon	2 strips
BBQ onions	1/2 cup
Hickory BBQ sauce	1 oz.
Burger set	
Lettuce	1 leaf
Tomato	1 slice
Red onion	4 rings
Pickle	1 slice
French fries	5 oz.
Seasoned salt	1 tsp.
11-inch plate	1
HRC flag	1

AUTHOR COMMENT Hard Rock's recipe here serves the same purpose as a bill of material in a factory: It defines the product for production.

Group Technology

Group technology
A product and component coding system that specifies the type of processing and the parameters of the processing; it allows similar products to be grouped.

Engineering drawings may also include codes to facilitate group technology. **Group technology** requires that components be identified by a coding scheme that specifies the type of processing (such as drilling) and the parameters of the processing (such as size). This facilitates standardization of materials, components, and processes as well as the identification of families of parts. As families of parts are identified, activities and machines can be grouped to minimize setups, routings, and material handling. An example of how families of parts may be grouped is shown in Figure 5.10. Group technology provides a systematic way to review a family of components to see if an existing component might suffice on a new project. Using existing or standard components eliminates all the costs connected with the design and development of the new part, which is a major cost reduction. For these reasons, successful implementation of group technology leads to the following advantages:

1. Improved design (because more design time can be devoted to fewer components).
2. Reduced raw material and purchases.
3. Simplified production planning and control.
4. Improved layout, routing, and machine loading.
5. Reduced tooling setup time, and work-in-process and production time.

The application of group technology helps the entire organization, as many costs are reduced.

AUTHOR COMMENT Production personnel need clear, specific documents to help them make the product.

DOCUMENTS FOR PRODUCTION

Once a product is selected, designed, and ready for production, production is assisted by a variety of documents. We will briefly review some of these.

Assembly drawing
An exploded view of the product.

An **assembly drawing** simply shows an exploded view of the product. An assembly drawing is usually a three-dimensional drawing, known as an *isometric drawing*; the relative locations of components are drawn in relation to each other to show how to assemble the unit (see Figure 5.11[a]).

Assembly chart
A graphic means of identifying how components flow into subassemblies and final products.

The **assembly chart** shows in schematic form how a product is assembled. Manufactured components, purchased components, or a combination of both may be shown on an assembly chart. The assembly chart identifies the point of production at which components flow into subassemblies and ultimately into a final product. An example of an assembly chart is shown in Figure 5.11(b).

Route sheet
A listing of the operations necessary to produce a component with the material specified in the bill of material.

The **route sheet** lists the operations necessary to produce the component with the material specified in the bill of material. The route sheet for an item will have one entry for each operation to be performed on the item. When route sheets include specific methods of operation and labor standards, they are often known as *process sheets*.

Work order
An instruction to make a given quantity of a particular item.

The **work order** is an instruction to make a given quantity of a particular item, usually to a given schedule. The ticket that a waiter writes in your favorite restaurant is a work order. In a hospital or factory, the work order is a more formal document that provides authorization to draw

(a) Ungrouped Parts	(b) Grouped Cylindrical Parts (families of parts)				
	Grooved	Slotted	Threaded	Drilled	Machined

◄ **FIGURE 5.10**
A Variety of Group Technology Coding Schemes Move Manufactured Components from (a) Ungrouped to (b) Grouped (families of parts)

various pharmaceuticals or items from inventory, to perform various functions, and to assign personnel to perform those functions.

Engineering change notices (ECNs) change some aspect of the product's definition or documentation, such as an engineering drawing or a bill of material. For a complex product that has a long manufacturing cycle, such as a Boeing 777, the changes may be so numerous that no two 777s are built exactly alike—which is indeed the case. Such dynamic design change has fostered the development of a discipline known as configuration management, which is concerned with product identification, control, and documentation. **Configuration management** is the system by which a product's planned and changing configurations are accurately identified and for which control and accountability of change are maintained.

Engineering change notice (ECN)
A correction or modification of an engineering drawing or bill of material.

Configuration management
A system by which a product's planned and changing components are accurately identified.

Product Life-Cycle Management (PLM)

Product life-cycle management (PLM) is an umbrella of software programs that attempts to bring together phases of product design and manufacture—including tying together many of the techniques discussed in the prior two sections, *Defining a Product* and *Documents for Production*. The idea behind PLM software is that product design and manufacture decisions can be performed more creatively, faster, and more economically when the data are integrated and consistent.

Product life-cycle management (PLM)
Software programs that tie together many phases of product design and manufacture.

Although there is not one standard, PLM products often start with product design (CAD/CAM); move on to design for manufacture and assembly (DFMA); and then into product

LO6: Describe the documents needed for production

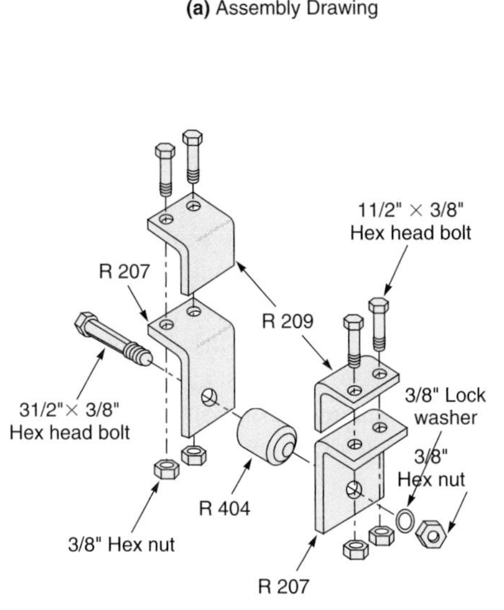

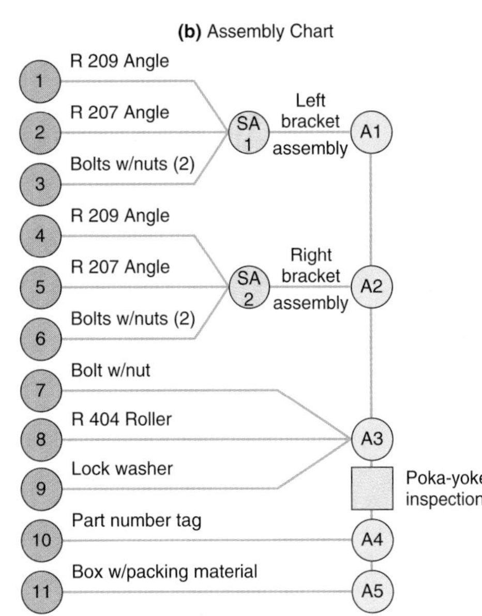

◄ **FIGURE 5.11**
Assembly Drawing and Assembly Chart

Each year the JR Simplot potato-processing facility in Caldwell, Idaho, produces billions of french fries for McDonald's (left photo). Sixty specifications (including a special blend of frying oil, a unique steaming process, and exact time and temperature for prefrying and drying) define how these potatoes become french fries. Further, 40% of all french fries must be 2 to 3 inches long, 40% must be over 3 inches long, and a few stubby ones constitute the final 20%. Quality control personnel use a micrometer to measure the fries (right photo).

routing, materials, layout, assembly, maintenance and even environmental issues.[6] Integration of these tasks makes sense because many of these decisions areas require overlapping pieces of data. PLM software is now a tool of many large organizations, including Lockheed Martin, GE, Procter & Gamble, Toyota, and Boeing. Boeing estimates that PLM will cut final assembly of its 787 jet from 2 weeks to 3 days. PLM is now finding its way into medium and small manufacture as well.

Shorter life cycles, more technologically challenging products, more regulations about materials and manufacturing processes, and more environmental issues all make PLM an appealing tool for operations managers.

AUTHOR COMMENT Services also need to be defined and documented.

SERVICE DESIGN

Much of our discussion so far has focused on what we can call tangible products, that is, goods. On the other side of the product coin are, of course, services. Service industries include banking, finance, insurance, transportation, and communications. The products offered by service firms range from a medical procedure that leaves only the tiniest scar after an appendectomy, to a shampoo and cut at a hair salon, to a great movie.

LO7: Describe customer participation in the design and production of services

Designing services is challenging because they often have unique characteristics. One reason productivity improvements in services are so low is because both the design and delivery of service products include customer interaction. When the customer participates in the design process, the service supplier may have a menu of services from which the customer selects options (see Figure 5.12a). At this point, the customer may even participate in the *design* of the service. Design specifications may take the form of a contract or a narrative description with photos (such as for cosmetic surgery or a hairstyle). Similarly, the customer may be involved in the *delivery* of a service (see Figure 5.12b) or in both *design and delivery*, a situation that maximizes the product design challenge (see Figure 5.12c).

However, as with goods, a large part of cost and quality of a service is defined at the design stage. Also as with goods, a number of techniques can both reduce costs and enhance the product. One technique is to design the product so that *customization is delayed* as late in the process as possible. This is the way a hair salon operates: Although shampoo and rinse are done in a standard way with lower-cost labor, the tint and styling (customizing) are done last. It is also the way most restaurants operate: How would you like that cooked? Which dressing would you prefer with your salad?

The second approach is to *modularize* the product so that customization takes the form of changing modules. This strategy allows modules to be designed as "fixed," standard entities. The modular approach to product design has applications in both manufacturing and service. Just as modular design allows you to buy a Harley-Davidson motorcycle or a high-fidelity sound system

[6]Some PLM vendors include supply chain elements such as sourcing, material management, and vendor evaluation in their packages, but in most instances, these are considered part of the ERP systems discussed along with MRP in Chapter 14. See, for instance, SAP PLM (**www.mySAP.com**), Parametric Technology Corp. (**www.ptc.com**), UGS Corp. (**www.ugs.com**), and Proplanner (**www.proplanner.com**).

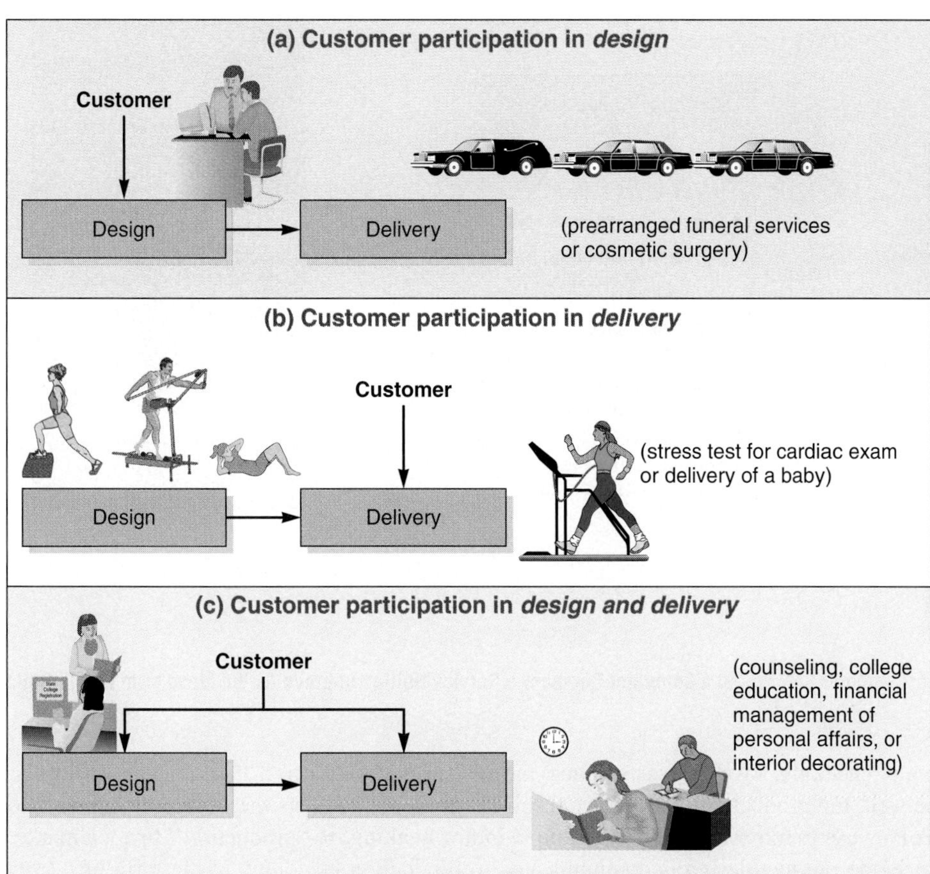

◀ **FIGURE 5.12**
Customer Participation in the Design of Services

with just the features you want, modular flexibility also lets you buy meals, clothes, and insurance on a mix-and-match (modular) basis. Similarly, investment portfolios are put together on a modular basis, as are college curricula. Both are examples of how the modular approach can be used to customize a service.

A third approach to the design of services is to divide the service into small parts and identify those parts that lend themselves to *automation* or *reduced customer interaction*. For instance, by isolating check-cashing activity via ATM machines, banks have been very effective at designing a product that both increases customer service and reduces costs. Similarly, airlines are moving to ticketless service. Because airlines spend $15 to $30 to produce a single ticket (including labor, printing, and travel agent's commission), ticketless systems save the industry a billion dollars a year. Reducing both costs and lines at airports—and thereby increasing customer satisfaction—provides a win–win "product" design.

Because of the high customer interaction in many service industries, a fourth technique is to focus design on the so-called moment of truth. Jan Carlzon, former president of Scandinavian Airways, believes that in the service industry there is a moment of truth when the relationship between the provider and the customer is crucial. At that moment, the customer's satisfaction with the service is defined. The *moment of truth* is the moment that exemplifies, enhances, or detracts from the customer's expectations. That moment may be as simple as a smile or having the checkout clerk focus on you rather than talking over his shoulder to the clerk at the next counter. Moments of truth can occur when you order at McDonald's, get a haircut, or register for college courses. Figure 5.13 shows a moment-of-truth analysis for a computer company's customer service hotline. The operations manager's task is to identify moments of truth and design operations that meet or exceed the customer's expectations.

Documents for Services

Because of the high customer interaction of most services, the documents for moving the product to production are different from those used in goods-producing operations. The documentation for a service will often take the form of explicit *job instructions* that specify what is to happen at the moment of truth. For instance, regardless of how good a bank's products may be in

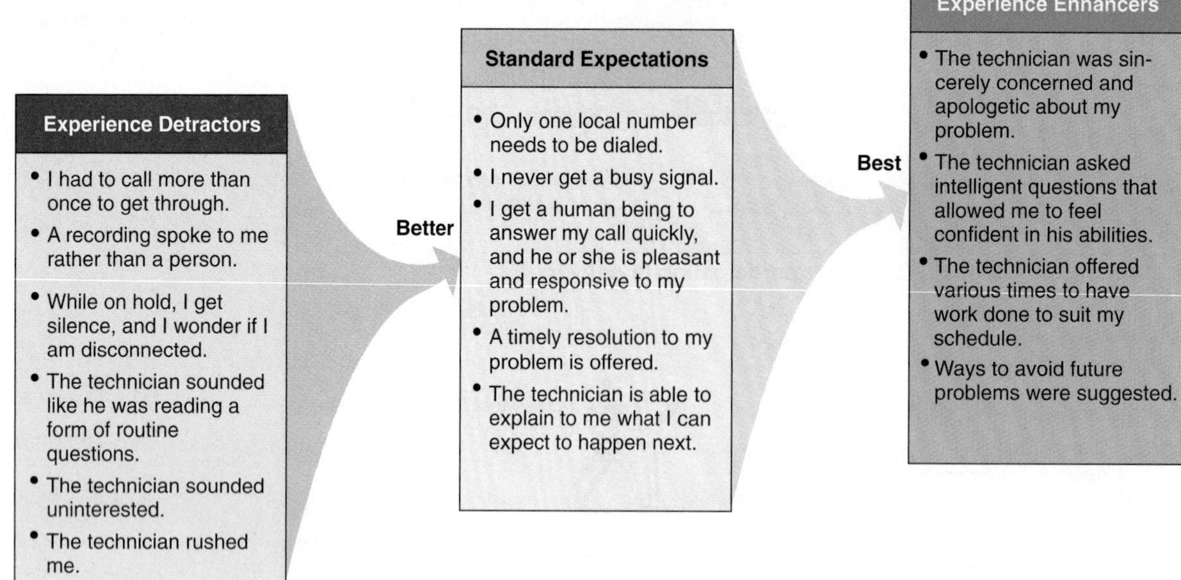

Experience Detractors
• I had to call more than once to get through.
• A recording spoke to me rather than a person.
• While on hold, I get silence, and I wonder if I am disconnected.
• The technician sounded like he was reading a form of routine questions.
• The technician sounded uninterested.
• The technician rushed me.
Better
Standard Expectations
• Only one local number needs to be dialed.
• I never get a busy signal.
• I get a human being to answer my call quickly, and he or she is pleasant and responsive to my problem.
• A timely resolution to my problem is offered.
• The technician is able to explain to me what I can expect to happen next.
Best
Experience Enhancers
• The technician was sincerely concerned and apologetic about my problem.
• The technician asked intelligent questions that allowed me to feel confident in his abilities.
• The technician offered various times to have work done to suit my schedule.
• Ways to avoid future problems were suggested.

▲ **FIGURE 5.13 Moment of Truth: Customer Contacts at a Computer Company's Service Hotline Improve As We Move from Left to Right.**

terms of checking, savings, trusts, loans, mortgages, and so forth, if the moment of truth is not done well, the product may be poorly received. Example 2 shows the kind of documentation a bank may use to move a product (drive-up window banking) to "production." In a telemarketing service, the product design is communicated to production personnel in the form of *telephone script*, while a *storyboard* is used for movie and TV production.

EXAMPLE 2 ▶

Service documentation for production

First Bank Corp. wants to ensure effective delivery of service to its drive-up customers.

APPROACH ▶ Develop a "production" document for the tellers at the drive-up window that provides the information necessary to do an effective job.

SOLUTION ▶

Documentation for Tellers at Drive-up Windows

Customers who use the drive-up teller windows rather than walk-in lobbies require a different customer relations technique. The distance and machinery between the teller and the customer raises communication barriers. Guidelines to ensure good customer relations at the drive-up window are:

- Be especially discreet when talking to the customer through the microphone.
- Provide written instructions for customers who must fill out forms you provide.
- Mark lines to be completed or attach a note with instructions.
- Always say "please" and "thank you" when speaking through the microphone.
- Establish eye contact with the customer if the distance allows it.
- If a transaction requires that the customer park the car and come into the lobby, apologize for the inconvenience.

Source: Adapted with permission from *Teller Operations* (Chicago, IL: The Institute of Financial Education, 1999): 32.

INSIGHT ▶ By providing documentation in the form of a script/guideline for tellers, the likelihood of effective communication and a good product/service is improved.

LEARNING EXERCISE: ▶ Modify the guidelines above to show how they would be different for a drive-through restaurant. [Answer: Written instructions, marking lines to be completed, or coming into the store are seldom necessary, but techniques for making change, and proper transfer of the order should be included.]

RELATED PROBLEM: ▶ 5.7

APPLICATION OF DECISION TREES TO PRODUCT DESIGN

AUTHOR COMMENT
A decision tree is a great tool for thinking through a problem.

Decision trees can be used for new-product decisions as well as for a wide variety of other management problems. They are particularly helpful when there are a series of decisions and various outcomes that lead to *subsequent* decisions followed by other outcomes. To form a decision tree, we use the following procedure:

LO8: Apply decision trees to product issues

1. Be sure that all possible alternatives and states of nature are included in the tree. This includes an alternative of "doing nothing."
2. Payoffs are entered at the end of the appropriate branch. This is the place to develop the payoff of achieving this branch.
3. The objective is to determine the expected value of each course of action. We accomplish this by starting at the end of the tree (the right-hand side) and working toward the beginning of the tree (the left), calculating values at each step and "pruning" alternatives that are not as good as others from the same node.

Example 3 shows the use of a decision tree applied to product design.

EXAMPLE 3

Decision tree applied to product design

Silicon, Inc., a semiconductor manufacturer, is investigating the possibility of producing and marketing a microprocessor. Undertaking this project will require either purchasing a sophisticated CAD system or hiring and training several additional engineers. The market for the product could be either favorable or unfavorable. Silicon, Inc., of course, has the option of not developing the new product at all.

With favorable acceptance by the market, sales would be 25,000 processors selling for $100 each. With unfavorable acceptance, sales would be only 8,000 processors selling for $100 each. The cost of CAD equipment is $500,000, but that of hiring and training three new engineers is only $375,000. However, manufacturing costs should drop from $50 each when manufacturing without CAD, to $40 each when manufacturing with CAD.

The probability of favorable acceptance of the new microprocessor is .40; the probability of unfavorable acceptance is .60.

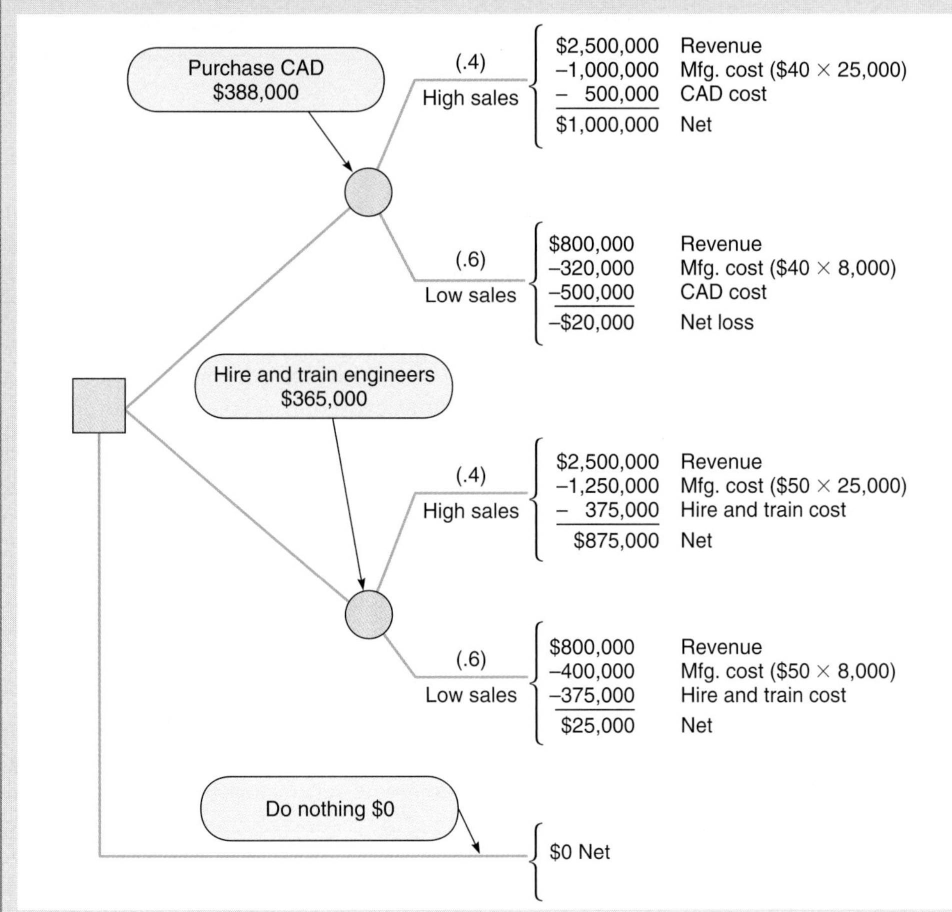

◄ **FIGURE 5.14**
Decision Tree for Development of a New Product

AUTHOR COMMENT
The manager's options are to purchase CAD, hire/train engineers, or do nothing. Purchasing CAD has the highest EMV.

APPROACH ▶ Use of a decision tree seems appropriate as Silicon, Inc., has the basic ingredients: a choice of decisions, probabilities, and payoffs.

SOLUTION ▶ In Figure 5.14 we draw a decision tree with a branch for each of the three decisions, assign the respective probabilities payoff for each branch, and then compute the respective EMVs. The expected monetary values (EMVs) have been circled at each step of the decision tree. For the top branch:

$$\text{EMV (purchase CAD syatem)} = (.4)(\$1{,}000{,}000) + (.6)(-\$20{,}000)$$
$$= \$388{,}000$$

This figure represents the results that will occur if Silicon, Inc., purchases CAD.

The expected value of hiring and training engineers is the second series of branches:

$$\text{EMV (Hire/train engineers)} = (.4)(\$875{,}000) + (.6)(\$25{,}000)$$
$$= \$365{,}000$$

The EMV of doing nothing is $0.

Because the top branch has the highest expected monetary value (an EMV of $388,000 vs. $365,000 vs. $0), it represents the best decision. Management should purchase the CAD system.

INSIGHT ▶ Use of the decision tree provides both objectivity and structure to our analysis of the Silicon, Inc., decision.

LEARNING EXERCISE ▶ If Silicon, Inc., thinks the probabilities of high sales and low sales may be equal, at .5 each, what is the best decision? [Answer: Purchase CAD remains the best decision, but with an EMV of $490,000.]

RELATED PROBLEMS ▶ 5.10, 5.11, 5.12, 5.13, 5.14, 5.15, 5.16, 5.18

ACTIVE MODEL 5.1 This example is further illustrated in Active Model 5.1 at **www.pearsonhighered.com/heizer.**

AUTHOR COMMENT One of the arts of management is knowing when a product should move from development to production.

TRANSITION TO PRODUCTION

Eventually, a product, whether a good or service, has been selected, designed, and defined. It has progressed from an idea to a functional definition, and then perhaps to a design. Now, management must make a decision as to further development and production or termination of the product idea. One of the arts of modern management is knowing when to move a product from development to production; this move is known as *transition to production*. The product development staff is always interested in making improvements in a product. Because this staff tends to see product development as evolutionary, they may never have a completed product, but as we noted earlier, the cost of late product introduction is high. Although these conflicting pressures exist, management must make a decision—more development or production.

Once this decision is made, there is usually a period of trial production to ensure that the design is indeed producible. This is the manufacturability test. This trial also gives the operations staff the opportunity to develop proper tooling, quality control procedures, and training of personnel to ensure that production can be initiated successfully. Finally, when the product is deemed both marketable and producible, line management will assume responsibility.

Some companies appoint a *project manager*; others use *product development teams* to ensure that the transition from development to production is successful. Both approaches allow a wide range of resources and talents to be brought to bear to ensure satisfactory production of a product that is still in flux. A third approach is *integration of the product development and manufacturing organizations*. This approach allows for easy shifting of resources between the two organizations as needs change. The operations manager's job is to make the transition from R&D to production seamless.

CHAPTER SUMMARY

Effective product strategy requires selecting, designing, and defining a product and then transitioning that product to production. Only when this strategy is carried out effectively can the production function contribute its maximum to the organization. The operations manager must build a product development system that has the ability to conceive, design, and produce products that will yield a competitive advantage for the firm. As products move through their life cycle (introduction, growth, maturity, and decline), the options that the operations manager should pursue change. Both manufactured and service products have a variety of techniques available to aid in performing this activity efficiently.

Written specifications, bills of material, and engineering drawings aid in defining products. Similarly, assembly drawings, assembly charts, route sheets, and work orders are often used to assist in the actual production of the product. Once a product is in production, value analysis is appropriate to ensure maximum product value. Engineering change notices and configuration management provide product documentation.

Key Terms

Product decision (p. 154)
Product-by-value analysis (p. 156)
Quality function deployment (QFD) (p. 159)
House of quality (p. 159)
Product development teams (p. 162)
Concurrent engineering (p. 162)
Manufacturability and value engineering (p. 162)
Robust design (p. 163)
Modular design (p. 163)
Computer-aided design (CAD) (p. 164)
Design for manufacture and assembly (DFMA) (p. 164)
3-D object modeling (p. 164)
Standard for the Exchange of Product Data (STEP) (p. 164)
Computer-aided manufacturing (CAM) (p. 165)
Virtual reality (p. 165)
Value analysis (p. 165)
Sustainability (p. 166)
Life cycle assessment (p. 167)
Time-based competition (p. 168)
Joint ventures (p. 170)
Alliances (p. 170)
Engineering drawing (p. 170)
Bill of material (BOM) (p. 170)
Make-or-buy decision (p. 171)
Group technology (p. 172)
Assembly drawing (p. 172)
Assembly chart (p. 172)
Route sheet (p. 172)
Work order (p. 172)
Engineering change notice (ECN) (p. 173)
Configuration management (p. 173)
Product life-cycle management (PLM) (p. 173)

Ethical Dilemma

John Edwards, president of Edwards Toy Company, Inc., in South Carolina, has just reviewed the design of a new pull-toy locomotive for 1- to 3-year-olds. John's design and marketing staff are very enthusiastic about the market for the product and the potential of follow-on circus train cars. The sales manager is looking forward to a very good reception at the annual toy show in Dallas next month. John, too, is delighted, as he is faced with a layoff if orders do not improve.

John's production people have worked out the manufacturing issues and produced a successful pilot run. However, the quality testing staff suggests that under certain conditions, a hook to attach cars to the locomotive and the crank for the bell can be broken off. This is an issue because children can choke on small parts such as these. In the quality test, 1- to 3-year-olds were unable to break off these parts; there were *no* failures. But when the test simulated the force of an adult tossing the locomotive into a toy box or a 5-year-old throwing it on the floor, there were failures. The estimate is that one of the two parts can be broken off 4 times out of 100,000 throws. Neither the design nor the material people know how to make the toy safer and still perform as designed. The failure rate is low and certainly normal for this type of toy, but not at the Six Sigma level that John's firm strives for. And, of course, someone, someday may sue. A child choking on the broken part is a serious matter. Also, John was recently reminded in a discussion with legal counsel that U.S. case law suggests that new products may not be produced if there is "actual or foreseeable knowledge of a problem" with the product.

The design of successful, ethically produced, new products, as suggested in this chapter, is a complex task. What should John do?

Discussion Questions

1. Why is it necessary to document a product explicitly?
2. What techniques do we use to define a product?
3. In what ways is product strategy linked to product decisions?
4. Once a product is defined, what documents are used to assist production personnel in its manufacture?
5. What is time-based competition?

6. Describe the differences between joint ventures and alliances.
7. Describe four organizational approaches to product development. Which of these is generally thought to be best?
8. Explain what is meant by robust design.
9. What are three specific ways in which computer-aided design (CAD) benefits the design engineer?
10. What information is contained in a bill of material?
11. What information is contained in an engineering drawing?
12. What information is contained in an assembly chart? In a process sheet?
13. Explain what is meant in service design by the "moment of truth."
14. Explain how the house of quality translates customer desires into product/service attributes.
15. What is meant by *sustainability* in the context of operations management?
16. What strategic advantages does computer-aided design provide?

Solved Problem

Virtual Office Hours help is available at www.myomlab.com.

▼ SOLVED PROBLEM 5.1

Sarah King, president of King Electronics, Inc., has two design options for her new line of high-resolution cathode-ray tubes (CRTs) for CAD workstations. The life cycle sales forecast for the CRT is 100,000 units.

Design option A has a .90 probability of yielding 59 good CRTs per 100 and a .10 probability of yielding 64 good CRTs per 100. This design will cost $1,000,000.

Design option B has a .80 probability of yielding 64 good units per 100 and a .20 probability of yielding 59 good units per 100. This design will cost $1,350,000.

Good or bad, each CRT will cost $75. Each good CRT will sell for $150. Bad CRTs are destroyed and have no salvage value. We ignore any disposal costs in this problem.

▼ SOLUTION

We draw the decision tree to reflect the two decisions and the probabilities associated with each decision. We then determine the payoff associated with each branch. The resulting tree is shown in Figure 5.15.

For design A:

$$\begin{aligned}\text{EMV(design A)} &= (.9)(\$350{,}000) + (.1)(\$1{,}100{,}000)\\ &= \$425{,}000\end{aligned}$$

For design B:

$$\begin{aligned}\text{EMV(design B)} &= (.8)(\$750{,}000) + (.2)(\$0)\\ &= \$600{,}000\end{aligned}$$

The highest payoff is design option B, at $600,000.

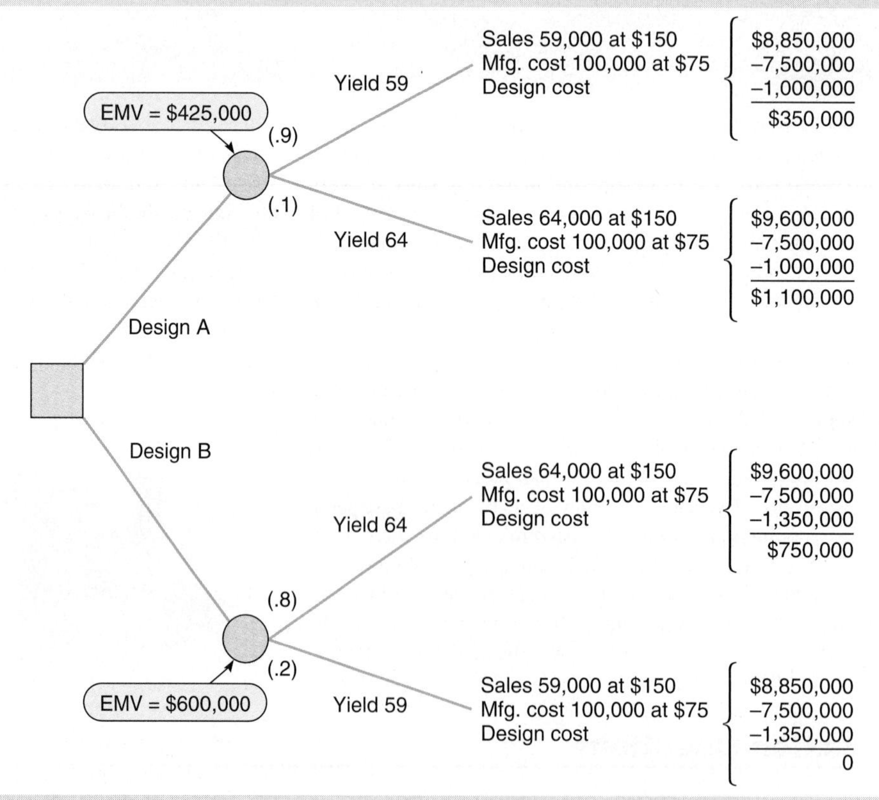

FIGURE 5.15 ▶ Decision Tree for Solved Problem 5.1

Problems*

•• **5.1** Construct a house of quality matrix for a wristwatch. Be sure to indicate specific customer wants that you think the general public desires. Then complete the matrix to show how an operations manager might identify specific attributes that can be measured and controlled to meet those customer desires.

•• **5.2** Using the house of quality, pick a real product (a good or service) and analyze how an existing organization satisfies customer requirements.

•• **5.3** Prepare a house of quality for a mousetrap.

•• **5.4** Conduct an interview with a prospective purchaser of a new bicycle and translate the customer's *wants* into the specific *hows* of the firm.

•• **5.5** Prepare a bill of material for (a) a pair of eyeglasses and its case or (b) a fast-food sandwich (visit a local sandwich shop like Subway, McDonald's, Blimpie, Quizno's; perhaps a clerk or the manager will provide you with details on the quantity or weight of various ingredients—otherwise, estimate the quantities).

•• **5.6** Draw an assembly chart for a pair of eyeglasses and its case.

•• **5.7** Prepare a script for telephone callers at the university's annual "phone-a-thon" fund raiser.

•• **5.8** Prepare an assembly chart for a table lamp.

••• **5.9** Prepare a product-by-value analysis for the following products, and given the position in its life cycle, identify the issues likely to confront the operations manager, and his or her possible actions. Product Alpha has annual sales of 1,000 units and a contribution of $2,500; it is in the introductory stage. Product Bravo has annual sales of 1,500 units and a contribution of $3,000; it is in the growth stage. Product Charlie has annual sales of 3,500 units and a contribution of $1,750; it is in the decline stage.

•• **5.10** Given the contribution made on each of the three products in the following table and their position in the life cycle, identify a reasonable operations strategy for each:

Product	Product Contribution (% of selling price)	Company Contribution (%: total annual contribution divided by total annual sales)	Position in Life Cycle
Kindle 2	30	40	Growth
Netbook computer	30	50	Introduction
Hand calculator	50	10	Decline

•• **5.11** The product design group of Flores Electric Supplies, Inc., has determined that it needs to design a new series of switches. It must decide on one of three design strategies. The market forecast is for 200,000 units. The better and more sophisticated the design strategy and the more time spent on value engineering, the less will be the variable cost. The chief of engineering design, Dr. W. L. Berry, has decided that the following costs are a good estimate of the initial and variable costs connected with each of the three strategies:

a) *Low-tech:* A low-technology, low-cost process consisting of hiring several new junior engineers. This option has a fixed cost of $45,000 and variable-cost probabilities of .3 for $.55 each, .4 for $.50, and .3 for $.45.
b) *Subcontract:* A medium-cost approach using a good outside design staff. This approach would have a fixed cost of $65,000 and variable-cost probabilities of .7 of $.45, .2 of $.40, and .1 of $.35.
c) *High-tech:* A high-technology approach using the very best of the inside staff and the latest computer-aided design technology. This approach has a fixed cost of $75,000 and variable-cost probabilities of .9 of $.40 and .1 of $.35.

What is the best decision based on an expected monetary value (EMV) criterion? (*Note:* We want the lowest EMV, as we are dealing with costs in this problem.) PX

•• **5.12** Clarkson Products, Inc., of Clarkson, New York, has the option of (a) proceeding immediately with production of a new top-of-the-line stereo TV that has just completed prototype testing or (b) having the value analysis team complete a study. If Ed Lusk, VP for operations, proceeds with the existing prototype (option a), the firm can expect sales to be 100,000 units at $550 each, with a probability of .6 and a .4 probability of 75,000 at $550. If, however, he uses the value analysis team (option b), the firm expects sales of 75,000 units at $750, with a probability of .7 and a .3 probability of 70,000 units at $750. Value analysis, at a cost of $100,000, is only used in option b. Which option has the highest expected monetary value (EMV)? PX

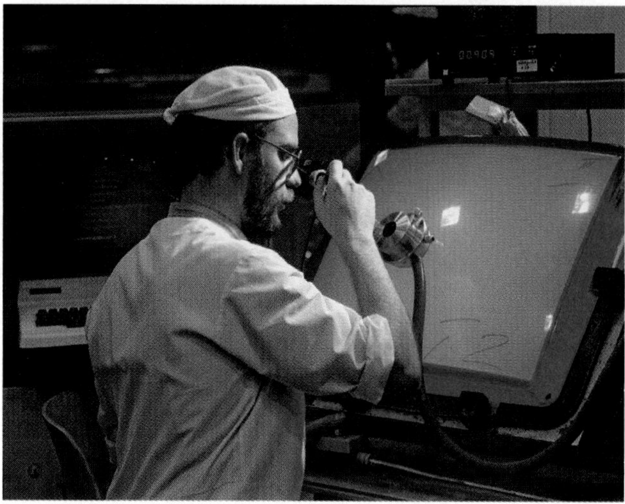

•• **5.13** Residents of Mill River have fond memories of ice skating at a local park. An artist has captured the experience in a drawing and is hoping to reproduce it and sell framed copies to current and former residents. He thinks that if the market is good he can sell 400 copies of the elegant version at $125 each. If the market is not good, he will sell only 300 at $90 each. He can make a deluxe version of the same drawing instead. He feels that if the market is good he can sell 500 copies of the deluxe version at $100

*Note: PX means the problem may be solved with POM for windows and/or Excel OM.

each. If the market is not good, he will sell only 400 copies at $70 each. In either case, production costs will be approximately $35,000. He can also choose to do nothing. If he believes there is a 50% probability of a good market, what should he do? Why? PX

•• **5.14** Ritz Products's materials manager, Bruce Elwell, must determine whether to make or buy a new semiconductor for the wrist TV that the firm is about to produce. One million units are expected to be produced over the life cycle. If the product is made, start-up and production costs of the *make* decision total $1 million, with a probability of .4 that the product will be satisfactory and a .6 probability that it will not. If the product is not satisfactory, the firm will have to reevaluate the decision. If the decision is reevaluated, the choice will be whether to spend another $1 million to redesign the semiconductor or to purchase. Likelihood of success the second time that the make decision is made is .9. If the second *make* decision also fails, the firm must purchase. Regardless of when the purchase takes place, Elwell's best judgment of cost is that Ritz will pay $.50 for each purchased semiconductor plus $1 million in vendor development cost.

a) Assuming that Ritz must have the semiconductor (stopping or doing without is not a viable option), what is the best decision?
b) What criteria did you use to make this decision?
c) What is the worst that can happen to Ritz as a result of this particular decision? What is the best that can happen? PX

•• **5.15** Page Engineering designs and constructs air conditioning and heating systems for hospitals and clinics. Currently the company's staff is overloaded with design work. There is a major design project due in 8 weeks. The penalty for completing the design late is $14,000 per week, since any delay will cause the facility to open later than anticipated, and cost the client significant revenue. If the company uses its inside engineers to complete the design, it will have to pay them overtime for all work. Page has estimated that it will cost $12,000 per week (wages and overhead), including late weeks, to have company engineers complete the design. Page is also considering having an outside engineering firm do the design. A bid of $92,000 has been received for the completed design. Yet another option for completing the design is to conduct a joint design by having a third engineering company complete all electromechanical components of the design at a cost of $56,000. Page would then complete the rest of the design and control systems at an estimated cost of $30,000.

Page has estimated the following probabilities of completing the project within various time frames when using each of the three options. Those estimates are shown in the following table:

	Probability of Completing the Design			
Option	**On Time**	**1 Week Late**	**2 Weeks Late**	**3 Weeks Late**
Internal Engineers	.4	.5	.1	—
External Engineers	.2	.4	.3	.1
Joint Design	.1	.3	.4	.2

What is the best decision based on an expected monetary value criterion? (*Note:* You want the lowest EMV because we are dealing with costs in this problem.) PX

••• **5.16** Use the data in Solved Problem 5.1 to examine what happens to the decision if Sarah King can increase yields from 59,000 to 64,000 by applying an expensive phosphorus to the screen at an added cost of $250,000. Prepare the modified decision tree. What are the payoffs, and which branch has the greatest EMV?

•••• **5.17** Using the house of quality sequence, as described in Figure 5.4 on page 161, determine how you might deploy resources to achieve the desired quality for a product or service whose production process you understand.

•••• **5.18** McBurger, Inc., wants to redesign its kitchens to improve productivity and quality. Three designs, called designs K1, K2, and K3, are under consideration. No matter which design is used, daily demand for sandwiches at a typical McBurger restaurant is for 500 sandwiches. A sandwich costs $1.30 to produce. Non-defective sandwiches sell, on the average, for $2.50 per sandwich. Defective sandwiches cannot be sold and are scrapped. The goal is to choose a design that maximizes the expected profit at a typical restaurant over a 300-day period. Designs K1, K2, and K3 cost $100,000, $130,000, and $180,000, respectively. Under design K1, there is a .80 chance that 90 out of each 100 sandwiches are non-defective and a .20 chance that 70 out of each 100 sandwiches are non-defective. Under design K2, there is a .85 chance that 90 out of each 100 sandwiches are non-defective and a .15 chance that 75 out of each 100 sandwiches are non-defective. Under design K3, there is a .90 chance that 95 out of each 100 sandwiches are non-defective and a .10 chance that 80 out of each 100 sandwiches are non-defective. What is the expected profit level of the design that achieves the maximum expected 300-day profit level?

▶ **Refer to myomlab for these additional homework problems: 5.19–5.25**

Case Studies

▶ De Mar's Product Strategy

De Mar, a plumbing, heating, and air-conditioning company located in Fresno, California, has a simple but powerful product strategy: *Solve the customer's problem no matter what, solve the problem when the customer needs it solved, and make sure the customer feels good when you leave*. De Mar offers guaranteed, same-day service for customers requiring it. The company provides 24-hour-a-day, 7-day-a-week service at no extra charge for customers whose air conditioning dies on a hot summer Sunday or whose toilet overflows at 2:30 A.M. As assistant service coordinator Janie Walter puts it: "We will be there to fix your A/C on the fourth of July, and it's not a penny extra. When our competitors won't get out of bed, we'll be there!"

De Mar guarantees the price of a job to the penny before the work begins. Whereas most competitors guarantee their work for 30 days, De Mar guarantees all parts and labor for one year. The company assesses no travel charge because "it's not fair to charge customers for driving out." Owner Larry Harmon says: "We are in an industry that doesn't have the best reputation. If we start making money our main goal, we are in trouble. So I stress customer satisfaction; money is the by-product."

De Mar uses selective hiring, ongoing training and education, performance measures and compensation that incorporate customer satisfaction, strong teamwork, peer pressure, empowerment, and aggressive promotion to implement its strategy. Says credit manager Anne Semrick: "The person who wants a nine-to-five job needs to go somewhere else."

De Mar is a premium pricer. Yet customers respond because De Mar delivers value—that is, benefits for costs. In 8 years, annual sales increased from about $200,000 to more than $3.3 million.

Discussion Questions

1. What is De Mar's product? Identify the tangible parts of this product and its service components.
2. How should other areas of De Mar (marketing, finance, personnel) support its product strategy?
3. Even though De Mar's product is primarily a service product, how should each of the 10 OM decisions in the text be managed to ensure that the product is successful?

Source: Reprinted with the permission of The Free Press, from *On Great Service: A Framework for Action* by Leonard L. Berry. Copyright © 1995 by Leonard L. Berry.

▶ Product Design at Regal Marine

Video Case

With hundreds of competitors in the boat business, Regal Marine must work to differentiate itself from the flock. As we saw in the *Global Company Profile* that opened this chapter, Regal continuously introduces innovative, high-quality new boats. Its differentiation strategy is reflected in a product line consisting of 22 models.

To maintain this stream of innovation, and with so many boats at varying stages of their life cycles, Regal constantly seeks design input from customers, dealers, and consultants. Design ideas rapidly find themselves in the styling studio, where they are placed onto CAD machines in order to speed the development process. Existing boat designs are always evolving as the company tries to stay stylish and competitive. Moreover, with life cycles as short as 3 years, a steady stream of new products is required. A few years ago, the new product was the three-passenger $11,000 Rush, a small but powerful boat capable of pulling a water-skier. This was followed with a 20-foot inboard–outboard performance boat with so many innovations that it won prize after prize in the industry. Another new boat is a redesigned 44-foot Commodore that sleeps six in luxury staterooms. With all these models and innovations, Regal designers and production personnel are under pressure to respond quickly.

By getting key suppliers on board early and urging them to participate at the design stage, Regal improves both innovations and quality while speeding product development. Regal finds that the sooner it brings suppliers on board, the faster it can bring new boats to the market. After a development stage that constitutes concept and styling, CAD designs yield product specifications. The first stage in actual production is the creation of the "plug," a foam-based carving used to make the molds for fiberglass hulls and decks. Specifications from the CAD system drive the carving process. Once the plug is carved, the permanent molds for each new hull and deck design are formed. Molds take about 4 to 8 weeks to make and are all handmade. Similar molds are made for many of the other features in Regal boats—from galley and stateroom components to lavatories and steps. Finished molds can be joined and used to make thousands of boats.

Discussion Questions*

1. How does the concept of product life cycle apply to Regal Marine products?
2. What strategy does Regal use to stay competitive?
3. What kind of engineering savings is Regal achieving by using CAD technology rather than traditional drafting techniques?
4. What are the likely benefits of the CAD design technology?

*You may wish to view the video that accompanies this case before addressing these questions.

Bibliography

Ambec, Stefan, and Paul Lanoie. "Does It Pay to Be Green? A Systematic Overview." *Academy of Management Perspectives* 22, no. 4 (November 2008): 13–20.

Brockman, Beverly K., and Robert M. Morgan. "The Role of Existing Knowledge in New Product Innovativeness and Performance." *Decision Sciences* 34, no. 2 (Spring 2003): 385–419.

Camevalli, J. A., and P. A. C. Miguel. "Review, Analysis, and Classification of the Literature on QFD." *International Journal of Production Economics* 114, no. 2 (August 2008): 737.

Ernst, David, and James Bamford. "Your Alliances Are Too Stable." *Harvard Business Review* 83, no. 5 (June 2005): 133–141.

Gerwin, Donald. "Coordinating New Product Development in Strategic Alliances." *The Academy of Management Review* 29, no. 2 (April 2004): 241–257.

Krishnan, V., and Karl T. Ulrich. "Product Development Decisions: A Review of the Literature." *Management Science* 47, no. 1 (January 2001): 1–21.

Loch, C. H., and C. Terwiesch. "Rush and Be Wrong or Wait and Be Late?" *Production and Operations Management* 14, no. 3 (Fall 2005): 331–343.

Miguel, P. A. C., and J. A. Camevalli. "Benchmarking Practices of Quality Function Deployment." *Benchmarking* 15, no. 6 (2008): 657.

Phyper, J. D., and D. MacLean. *Good to Green: Managers Business Risks and Opportunities in an Age of Environmental Awareness.* New York: Wiley, 2009.

Pisano, Gary P., and Roberto Verganti. "Which Kind of Collaboration Is Right for You?" *Harvard Business Review* 86, no. 12 (December 2008):78–86.

Saaksvuori, A., and A. Immonen. *Product Lifecycle Management.* Berlin: Springer-Verlag, 2004.

Seider, Warren D., et al. *Product and Process Design Principles.* 3rd. ed. New York: Wiley, 2008.

Ulrich, K., and S. Eppinger. *Product Design and Development*, 4th ed. New York: McGraw-Hill, 2008.

Chapter 5 ***Rapid*** **Review**

Main Heading	Review Material	PEARSON myomlab
GOODS AND SERVICES SELECTION (pp. 154–157)	Although the term *products* may often refer to tangible goods, it also refers to offerings by service organizations. *The objective of the product decision is to develop and implement a product strategy that meets the demands of the marketplace with a competitive advantage.* ▪ **Product decision**—The selection, definition, and design of products. The four phases of the product life cycle are introduction, growth, maturity, and decline. ▪ **Product-by-value analysis**—A list of products, in descending order of their individual dollar contribution to the firm, as well as the *total annual dollar* contribution of the product.	Problem: 5.9 **VIDEO 5.1** Product Strategy at Regal Marine
GENERATING NEW PRODUCTS (pp. 157–158)	Product selection, definition, and design take place on a continuing basis. Changes in product opportunities, the products themselves, product volume, and product mix may arise due to understanding the customer, economic change, sociological and demographic change, technological change, political/legal change, market practice, professional standards, suppliers, or distributors.	
PRODUCT DEVELOPMENT (pp. 158–163)	▪ **Quality function deployment (QFD)**—A process for determining customer requirements (customer "wants") and translating them into attributes (the "hows") that each functional area can understand and act on. ▪ **House of quality**—A part of the quality function deployment process that utilizes a planning matrix to relate customer wants to how the firm is going to meet those wants. ▪ **Product development teams**—Teams charged with moving from market requirements for a product to achieving product success. ▪ **Concurrent engineering**—Use of participating teams in design and engineering activities. ▪ **Manufacturability and value engineering**—Activities that help improve a product's design, production, maintainability, and use.	
ISSUES FOR PRODUCT DESIGN (pp. 163–165)	▪ **Robust design**—A design that can be produced to requirements even with unfavorable conditions in the production process. ▪ **Modular design**—A design in which parts or components of a product are subdivided into modules that are easily interchanged or replaced. ▪ **Computer-aided design (CAD)**—Interactive use of a computer to develop and document a product. ▪ **Design for manufacture and assembly (DFMA)**—Software that allows designers to look at the effect of design on manufacturing of a product. ▪ **3-D object modeling**—An extension of CAD that builds small prototypes. ▪ **Standard for the exchange of product data (STEP)**—A standard that provides a format allowing the electronic transmission of three-dimensional data. ▪ **Computer-aided manufacturing (CAM)**—The use of information technology to control machinery. ▪ **Virtual reality**—A visual form of communication in which images substitute for reality and typically allow the user to respond interactively. ▪ **Value analysis**—A review of successful products that takes place during the production process.	
ETHICS, ENVIRONMENTALLY-FRIENDLY DESIGNS, AND SUSTAINABILITY (pp. 166–168)	▪ **Sustainability**—A production system that supports conservation and renewal of resources. ▪ **Life Cycle Assessment (LCA)**—Part of ISO 14000; assesses the environmental impact of a product from material and energy inputs to disposal and environmental releases. Goals for ethical, environmentally friendly designs are (1) developing safe and environmentally sound products, (2) minimizing waste of resources, (3) reducing environmental liabilities, (4) increasing cost-effectiveness of complying with environmental regulations, and (5) being recognized as a good corporate citizen.	
TIME-BASED COMPETITION (pp. 168–170)	▪ **Time-based competition**—Competition based on time; rapidly developing products and moving them to market. *Internal development strategies* include (1) new internally developed products, (2) enhancements to existing products, and (3) migrations of existing products. *External development strategies* include (1) purchase the technology or expertise by acquiring the developer, (2) establish joint ventures, and (3) develop alliances. ▪ **Joint ventures**—Firms establishing joint ownership to pursue new products or markets. ▪ **Alliances**—Cooperative agreements that allow firms to remain independent but pursue strategies consistent with their individual missions.	

PEARSON myomlab

Main Heading	Review Material	
DEFINING A PRODUCT (pp. 170–172)	■ **Engineering drawing—**A drawing that shows the dimensions, tolerances, materials, and finishes of a component. ■ **Bill of material (BOM)—**A list of the components, their description, and the quantity of each required to make one unit of a product. ■ **Make-or-buy decision—**The choice between producing a component or a service and purchasing it from an outside source. ■ **Group technology—**A product and component coding system that specifies the type of processing and the parameters of the processing; it allows similar products to be grouped.	
DOCUMENTS FOR PRODUCTION (pp. 172–174)	■ **Assembly drawing—**An exploded view of a product. ■ **Assembly chart—**A graphic means of identifying how components flow into subassemblies and final products ■ **Route sheet—**A list of the operations necessary to produce a component with the material specified in the bill of material. ■ **Work order—**An instruction to make a given quantity of a particular item. ■ **Engineering change notice (ECN)—**A correction or modification of an engineering drawing or bill of material. ■ **Configuration management—**A system by which a product's planned and changing components are accurately identified. ■ **Product life cycle management (PLM)—**Software programs that tie together many phases of product design and manufacture.	
SERVICE DESIGN (pp. 174–176)	Techniques to reduce costs and enhance the service offering include (1) delaying customization, (2) modularizing, (3) automating, and (4) designing for the "moment of truth."	
APPLICATION OF DECISION TREES TO PRODUCT DESIGN (pp. 177–178)	To form a decision tree, (1) include all possible alternatives (including "do nothing") and states of nature; (2) enter payoffs at the end of the appropriate branch; and (3) determine the expected value of each course of action by starting at the end of the tree and working toward the beginning, calculating values at each step and "pruning" inferior alternatives.	Problems: 5.10–5.15, 5.18 Virtual Office Hours for Solved Problem: 5.1 **ACTIVE MODEL 5.1**
TRANSITION TO PRODUCTION (p. 178)	One of the arts of modern management is knowing when to move a product from development to production; this move is known as *transition to production*.	

Self Test

■ **Before taking the self-test,** refer to the learning objectives listed at the beginning of the chapter and the key terms listed at the end of the chapter.

LO1. A product's life cycle is divided into four stages, including:
- **a)** introduction.
- **b)** growth.
- **c)** maturity.
- **d)** all of the above.

LO2. Product development systems include:
- **a)** bills of material.
- **b)** routing charts.
- **c)** functional specifications.
- **d)** product-by-values analysis.
- **e)** configuration management.

LO3. A house of quality is:
- **a)** a matrix relating customer "wants" to the firm's "hows."
- **b)** a schematic showing how a product is put together.
- **c)** a list of the operations necessary to produce a component.
- **d)** an instruction to make a given quantity of a particular item.
- **e)** a set of detailed instructions about how to perform a task.

LO4. Time-based competition focuses on:
- **a)** moving new products to market more quickly.
- **b)** reducing the life cycle of a product.
- **c)** linking QFD to PLM.
- **d)** design database availability.
- **e)** value engineering.

LO5. Products are defined by:
- **a)** value analysis.
- **b)** value engineering.
- **c)** routing sheets.
- **d)** assembly charts.
- **e)** engineering drawings.

LO6. A route sheet:
- **a)** lists the operations necessary to produce a component.
- **b)** is an instruction to make a given quantity of a particular item.
- **c)** is a schematic showing how a product is assembled.
- **d)** is a document showing the flow of product components.
- **e)** all of the above.

LO7. Four techniques available when a service is designed are:
- **a)** recognize political or legal change, technological change, sociological demographic change, and economic change.
- **b)** understand product introduction, growth, maturity, and decline.
- **c)** recognize functional specifications, product specifications, design review, and test markets.
- **d)** ensure that customization is done as late in the process as possible, modularize the product, reduce customer interaction, and focus on the moment of truth.

LO8. Decision trees use:
- **a)** probabilities.
- **b)** payoffs.
- **c)** logic.
- **d)** options.
- **e)** all of the above.

Answers: LO1. d; LO2. c; LO3. a; LO4. a; LO5. e; LO6. a; LO7. d; LO8. e.

6 Managing Quality

Chapter Outline

10

OM Strategy Decisions

- ► Design of Goods and Services
- ► Managing Quality
- ► Process Strategy
- ► Location Strategies
- ► Layout Strategies
- ► Human Resources
- ► Supply-Chain Management
- ► Inventory Management
- ► Scheduling
- ► Maintenance

MANAGING QUALITY PROVIDES A COMPETITIVE ADVANTAGE AT ARNOLD PALMER HOSPITAL

Since 1989, the Arnold Palmer Hospital, named after its famous golfing benefactor, has touched the lives of over 7 million children and women and their families. Its patients come not only from its Orlando location but from all 50 states and around the world. More than 16,000 babies are delivered every year at Arnold Palmer, and its huge neonatal intensive care unit boasts one of the highest survival rates in the U.S.

Every hospital professes quality health care, but at Arnold Palmer quality is the mantra—practiced in a fashion like the Ritz-Carlton practices it in the hotel industry. The hospital typically scores in the top 10% of national benchmark studies in terms of patient satisfaction. And its managers follow patient questionnaire results daily. If anything is amiss, corrective action takes place immediately.

Virtually every quality management technique we present in this chapter is employed at Arnold Palmer Hospital:

- *Continuous improvement:* The hospital constantly seeks new ways to lower infection rates, readmission rates, deaths, costs, and hospital stay times.
- *Employee empowerment:* When employees see a problem, they are trained to take care of it; staff are empowered to give gifts to patients displeased with some aspect of service.
- *Benchmarking:* The hospital belongs to a 2,000-member organization that monitors standards in many areas and provides monthly feedback to the hospital.
- *Just-in-time:* Supplies are delivered to Arnold Palmer on a JIT basis. This keeps inventory costs low and keeps quality problems from hiding.

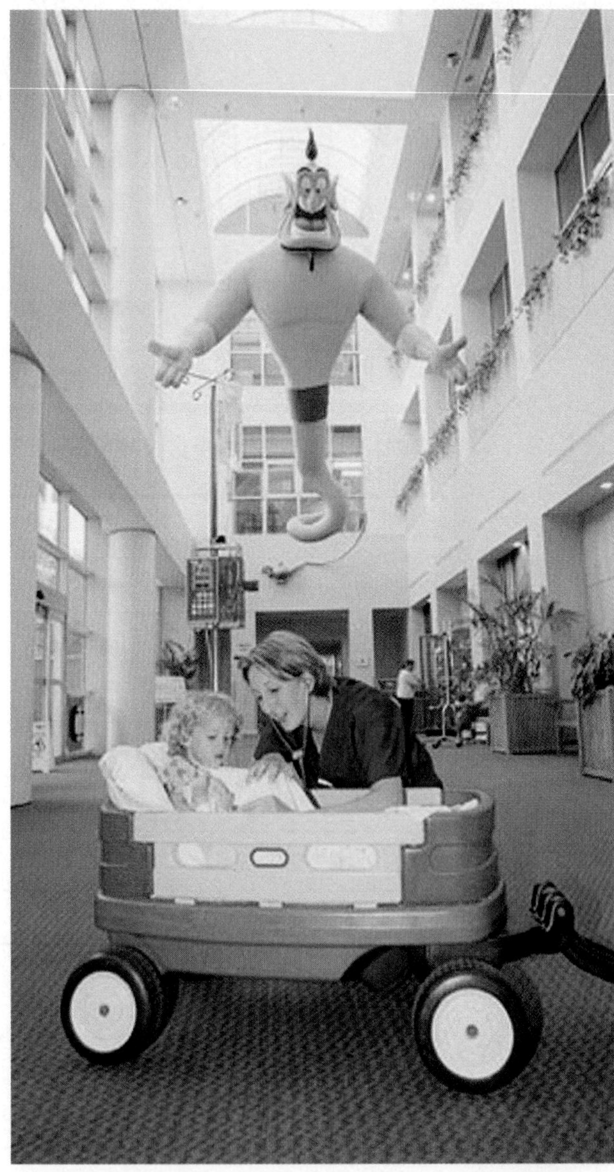

The lobby of Arnold Palmer Hospital, with its 20-foot-high Genie, is clearly intended as a warm and friendly place for children.

The Storkboard is a visible chart of the status of each baby about to be delivered, so all nurses and doctors are kept up-to-date at a glance.

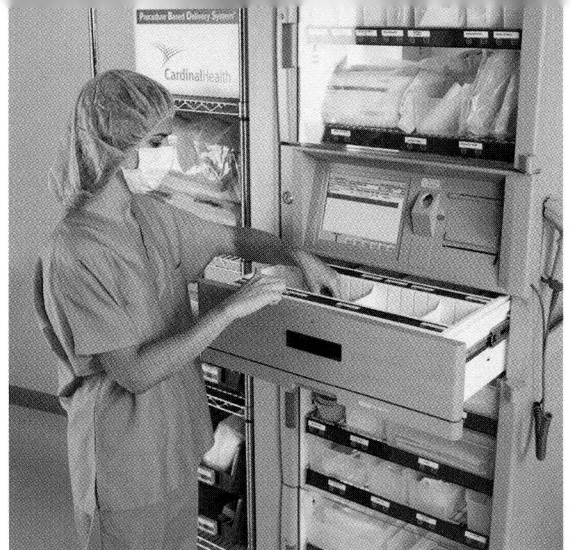

This PYXIS inventory station gives nurses quick access to medicines and supplies needed in their departments. When the nurse removes an item for patient use, the item is automatically billed to that account, and usage is noted at the main supply area.

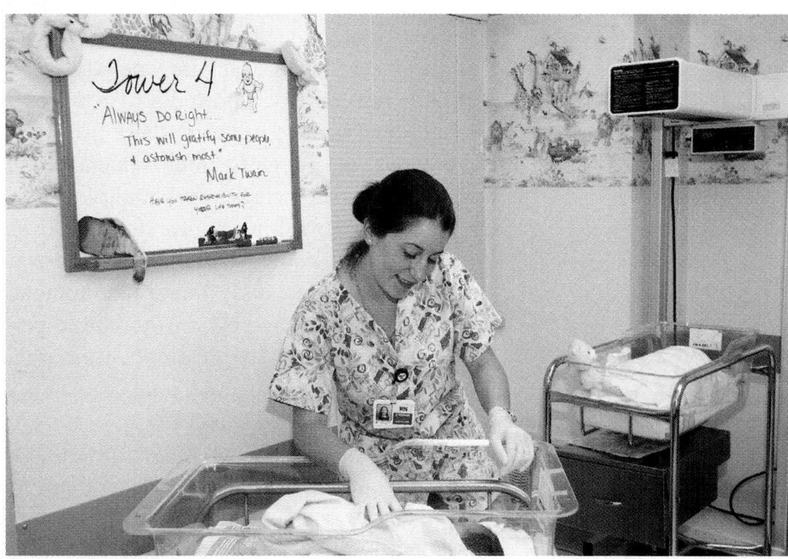

The Mark Twain quote on the board reads "Always Do Right. This will gratify some people and astonish most." The hospital has redesigned its neonatal rooms. In the old system, there were 16 neonatal beds in an often noisy and large room. The new rooms are semiprivate, with a quiet simulated-night atmosphere. These rooms have proven to help babies develop and improve more quickly.

When Arnold Palmer Hospital began planning for a new 11-story hospital across the street from its existing building, it decided on a circular pod design, creating a patient-centered environment. Rooms use warm colors, have pull-down Murphy beds for family members, 14-foot ceilings, and natural lighting with oversized windows. The pod concept also means there is a nursing station within a few feet of each 10-bed pod, saving much wasted walking time by nurses to reach the patient. The Video Case Study in Chapter 9 examines this layout in detail.

- *Tools such as Pareto charts and flowcharts:* These tools monitor processes and help the staff graphically spot problem areas and suggest ways they can be improved.

From their first day of orientation, employees from janitors to nurses learn that the patient comes first. Staff standing in hallways will never be heard discussing their personal lives or commenting on confidential issues of health care. This culture of quality at Arnold Palmer Hospital makes a hospital visit, often traumatic to children and their parents, a warmer and more comforting experience.

Chapter 6 **Learning Objectives**

AUTHOR COMMENT
Quality is an issue that affects an entire organization.

QUALITY AND STRATEGY

As Arnold Palmer Hospital and many other organizations have found, quality is a wonderful tonic for improving operations. Managing quality helps build successful strategies of *differentiation*, *low cost*, and *response*. For instance, defining customer quality expectations has helped Bose Corp. successfully *differentiate* its stereo speakers as among the best in the world. Nucor has learned to produce quality steel at *low cost* by developing efficient processes that produce consistent quality. And Dell Computers rapidly *responds* to customer orders because quality systems, with little rework, have allowed it to achieve rapid throughput in its plants. Indeed, quality may be the critical success factor for these firms just as it is at Arnold Palmer Hospital.

VIDEO 6.1
The Culture of Quality at Arnold Palmer Hospital

As Figure 6.1 suggests, improvements in quality help firms increase sales and reduce costs, both of which can increase profitability. Increases in sales often occur as firms speed response, increase or lower selling prices, and improve their reputation for quality products. Similarly, improved quality allows costs to drop as firms increase productivity and lower rework, scrap, and warranty costs. One study found that companies with the highest quality were five times as productive (as measured by units produced per labor-hour) as companies with the poorest quality. Indeed, when the implications of an organization's long-term costs and the potential for increased sales are considered, total costs may well be at a minimum when 100% of the goods or services are perfect and defect free.

Quality, or the lack of quality, affects the entire organization from supplier to customer and from product design to maintenance. Perhaps more importantly, *building* an organization that can achieve quality is a demanding task. Figure 6.2 lays out the flow of activities for an organization to use to achieve total quality management (TQM). A successful quality strategy begins with an organizational culture that fosters quality, followed by an understanding of the principles of quality, and then engaging employees in the necessary activities to implement quality. When these things are done well, the organization typically satisfies its customers and obtains a competitive advantage. The ultimate goal is to win customers. Because quality causes so many other good things to happen, it is a great place to start.

AUTHOR COMMENT
To create a quality good or service, operations managers need to know what the customer expects.

DEFINING QUALITY

An operations manager's objective is to build a total quality management system that identifies and satisfies customer needs. Total quality management takes care of the customer. Consequently, we accept the definition of **quality** as adopted by the American Society for Quality (ASQ, at **www.asq.org**): "The totality of features and characteristics of a product or service that bears on its ability to satisfy stated or implied needs."

Quality
The ability of a product or service to meet customer needs.

► **FIGURE 6.1**
Ways Quality Improves Profitability

AUTHOR COMMENT
High-quality products and services are the most profitable.

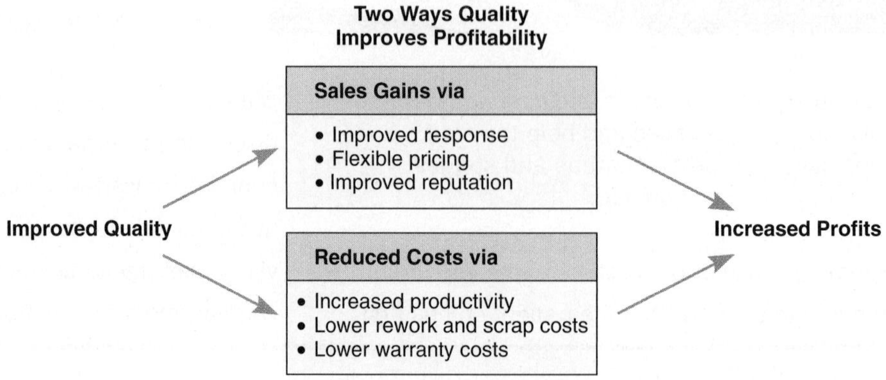

Two Ways Quality Improves Profitability

Improved Quality → Sales Gains via
- Improved response
- Flexible pricing
- Improved reputation

Improved Quality → Reduced Costs via
- Increased productivity
- Lower rework and scrap costs
- Lower warranty costs

→ Increased Profits

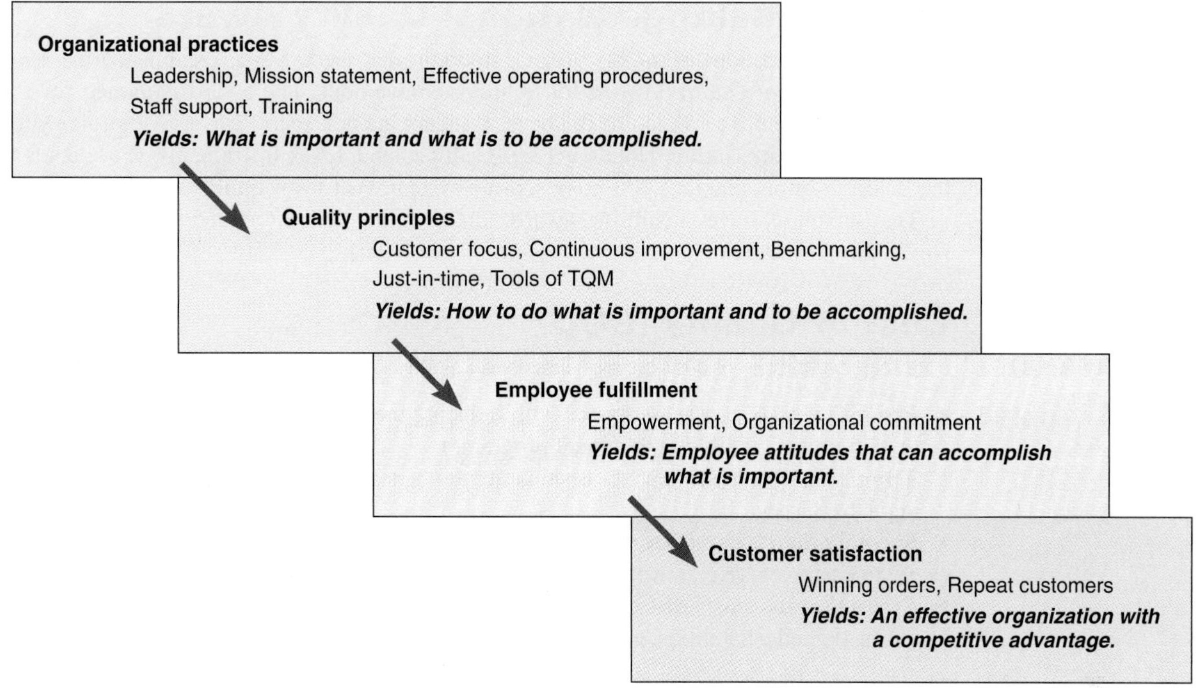

Organizational practices
Leadership, Mission statement, Effective operating procedures, Staff support, Training
Yields: What is important and what is to be accomplished.
Quality principles
Customer focus, Continuous improvement, Benchmarking, Just-in-time, Tools of TQM
Yields: How to do what is important and to be accomplished.
Employee fulfillment
Empowerment, Organizational commitment
Yields: Employee attitudes that can accomplish what is important.
Customer satisfaction
Winning orders, Repeat customers
Yields: An effective organization with a competitive advantage.

▲ **FIGURE 6.2 The Flow of Activities that Are Necessary to Achieve Total Quality Management**

LO1: Define quality and TQM

Others, however, believe that definitions of quality fall into several categories. Some definitions are *user based*. They propose that quality "lies in the eyes of the beholder." Marketing people like this approach and so do customers. To them, higher quality means better performance, nicer features, and other (sometimes costly) improvements. To production managers, quality is *manufacturing based*. They believe that quality means conforming to standards and "making it right the first time." Yet a third approach is *product based*, which views quality as a precise and measurable variable. In this view, for example, really good ice cream has high butterfat levels.

This text develops approaches and techniques to address all three categories of quality. The characteristics that connote quality must first be identified through research (a user-based approach to quality). These characteristics are then translated into specific product attributes (a product-based approach to quality). Then, the manufacturing process is organized to ensure that products are made precisely to specifications (a manufacturing-based approach to quality). A process that ignores any one of these steps will not result in a quality product.

Implications of Quality

In addition to being a critical element in operations, quality has other implications. Here are three other reasons why quality is important:

1. *Company reputation:* An organization can expect its reputation for quality—be it good or bad—to follow it. Quality will show up in perceptions about the firm's new products, employment practices, and supplier relations. Self-promotion is not a substitute for quality products.
2. *Product liability:* The courts increasingly hold organizations that design, produce, or distribute faulty products or services liable for damages or injuries resulting from their use. Legislation such as the Consumer Product Safety Act sets and enforces product standards by banning products that do not reach those standards. Impure foods that cause illness, nightgowns that burn, tires that fall apart, or auto fuel tanks that explode on impact can all lead to huge legal expenses, large settlements or losses, and terrible publicity.
3. *Global implications:* In this technological age, quality is an international, as well as OM, concern. For both a company and a country to compete effectively in the global economy, products must meet global quality, design, and price expectations. Inferior products harm a firm's profitability and a nation's balance of payments.

Malcolm Baldrige National Quality Award

The global implications of quality are so important that the U.S. has established the *Malcolm Baldrige National Quality Award* for quality achievement. The award is named for former Secretary of Commerce Malcolm Baldrige. Winners include such firms as Motorola, Milliken, Xerox, FedEx, Ritz-Carlton Hotels, AT&T, Cadillac, and Texas Instruments. (For details about the Baldrige Award and its 1,000-point scoring system, visit **www.quality.nist.gov**.)

The Japanese have a similar award, the Deming Prize, named after an American, Dr. W. Edwards Deming.

Cost of Quality (COQ)

Cost of quality (COQ)
The cost of doing things wrong—that is, the price of nonconformance.

Four major categories of costs are associated with quality. Called the **cost of quality (COQ)**, they are:

- *Prevention costs:* costs associated with reducing the potential for defective parts or services (e.g., training, quality improvement programs).
- *Appraisal costs:* costs related to evaluating products, processes, parts, and services (e.g., testing, labs, inspectors).
- *Internal failure:* costs that result from production of defective parts or services before delivery to customers (e.g., rework, scrap, downtime).
- *External costs:* costs that occur after delivery of defective parts or services (e.g., rework, returned goods, liabilities, lost goodwill, costs to society).

The first three costs can be reasonably estimated, but external costs are very hard to quantify. When GE had to recall 3.1 million dishwashers recently (because of a defective switch alleged to have started seven fires), the cost of repairs exceeded the value of all the machines. This leads to the belief by many experts that the cost of poor quality is consistently underestimated.

Takumi is a Japanese character that symbolizes a broader dimension than quality, a deeper process than education, and a more perfect method than persistence.

Observers of quality management believe that, on balance, the cost of quality products is only a fraction of the benefits. They think the real losers are organizations that fail to work aggressively at quality. For instance, Philip Crosby stated that quality is free. "What costs money are the unquality things—all the actions that involve not doing it right the first time."[1]

Leaders in Quality Besides Crosby there are several other giants in the field of quality management, including Deming, Feigenbaum, and Juran. Table 6.1 summarizes their philosophies and contributions.

Ethics and Quality Management

For operations managers, one of the most important jobs is to deliver healthy, safe, and quality products and services to customers. The development of poor-quality products, because of inadequate design and production processes, results not only in higher production costs but also leads to injuries, lawsuits, and increased government regulation.

If a firm believes that it has introduced a questionable product, ethical conduct must dictate the responsible action. This may be a worldwide recall, as conducted by both Johnson & Johnson (for Tylenol) and Perrier (for sparkling water), when each of these products was found to be contaminated. A manufacturer must accept responsibility for any poor-quality product released to the public. In recent years, Ford (the Explorer SUV maker) and Firestone (the radial tire maker) have been accused of failing to issue product recalls, of withholding damaging information, and of handling complaints on an individual basis.[2]

There are many stakeholders involved in the production and marketing of poor-quality products, including stockholders, employees, customers, suppliers, distributors, and creditors. As a matter of ethics, management must ask if any of these stakeholders are being wronged. Every company needs to develop core values that become day-to-day guidelines for everyone from the CEO to production-line employees.

[1]Philip B. Crosby, *Quality Is Free* (New York: McGraw-Hill, 1979). Further, J. M. Juran states, in his book *Juran on Quality by Design* (The Free Press 1992, p. 119), that costs of poor quality "are huge, but the amounts are not known with precision. In most companies the accounting system provides only a minority of the information needed to quantify this cost of poor quality. It takes a great deal of time and effort to extend the accounting system so as to provide full coverage."
[2]For further reading, see O. Fisscher and A. Nijhof, "Implications of Business Ethics for Quality Management," *TQM Magazine* 17 (2005): 150–161; and M. R. Nayebpour and D. Koehn, "The Ethics of Quality: Problems and Preconditions," *Journal of Business Ethics* 44 (April, 2003): 37–48.

▼ **TABLE 6.1 Leaders in the Field of Quality Management**

Leader	Philosophy/Contribution
W. Edwards Deming	Deming insisted management accept responsibility for building good systems. The employee cannot produce products that on average exceed the quality of what the process is capable of producing. His 14 points for implementing quality improvement are presented in this chapter.
Joseph M. Juran	A pioneer in teaching the Japanese how to improve quality, Juran believed strongly in top-management commitment, support, and involvement in the quality effort. He was also a believer in teams that continually seek to raise quality standards. Juran varies from Deming somewhat in focusing on the customer and defining quality as fitness for use, not necessarily the written specifications.
Armand Feigenbaum	His 1961 book, *Total Quality Control*, laid out 40 steps to quality improvement processes. He viewed quality not as a set of tools but as a total field that integrated the processes of a company. His work in how people learn from each other's successes led to the field of cross-functional teamwork.
Philip B. Crosby	*Quality is Free* was Crosby's attention-getting book published in 1979. Crosby believed that in the traditional trade-off between the cost of improving quality and the cost of poor quality, the cost of poor quality is understated. The cost of poor quality should include all of the things that are involved in not doing the job right the first time. Crosby coined the term *zero defects* and stated, "There is absolutely no reason for having errors or defects in any product or service."

INTERNATIONAL QUALITY STANDARDS

AUTHOR COMMENT
International quality standards grow in prominence every year. See **www.iso.ch** and **www.asq.org** to learn more about them.

ISO 9000

Quality is so important globally that the world is uniting around a single quality standard, **ISO 9000**. ISO 9000 is the only quality standard with international recognition. In 1987, 91 member nations (including the U.S.) published a series of quality assurance standards, known collectively as ISO 9000. The U.S., through the American National Standards Institute (ANSI), has adopted the ISO 9000 series as the ANSI/ASQ Q9000 series. The focus of the standards is to establish quality management procedures, through leadership, detailed documentation, work instructions, and recordkeeping. These procedures, we should note, say nothing about the actual quality of the product—they deal entirely with standards to be followed.

ISO 9000
A set of quality standards developed by the International Organization for Standardization (ISO).

To become ISO 9000 certified, organizations go through a 9- to 18-month process that involves documenting quality procedures, an on-site assessment, and an ongoing series of audits of their products or services. To do business globally being listed in the ISO directory is critical. As of 2009, there were over 1 million certifications awarded to firms in 175 countries. About 40,000 U.S. firms are ISO 9000 certified. Over 200,000 Chinese firms have received certificates.

ISO upgraded its standards in 2008 into more of a quality management system, which is detailed in its ISO 9001: 2008 component. Leadership by top management and customer requirements and satisfaction play a much larger role, while documented procedures receive less emphasis under ISO 9001: 2008.

LO2: Describe the ISO international quality standards

ISO 14000

The continuing internationalization of quality is evident with the development of **ISO 14000.** ISO 14000 is a series of environmental management standards that contain five core elements: (1) environmental management, (2) auditing, (3) performance evaluation, (4) labeling, and (5) life cycle assessment. The new standard could have several advantages:

- Positive public image and reduced exposure to liability.
- Good systematic approach to pollution prevention through the minimization of ecological impact of products and activities.
- Compliance with regulatory requirements and opportunities for competitive advantage.
- Reduction in need for multiple audits.

ISO 14000
A series of environmental management standards established by the International Organization for Standardization (ISO).

This standard is being accepted worldwide, with ISO 14001, which addresses environmental impacts of activities systematically, receiving great attention. The *OM in Action* box "Subaru's Clean, Green Set of Wheels with ISO 14001" illustrates the growing application of the ISO 14000 series.

As a follow-on to ISO 14000, ISO 24700 reflects the business world's current approach to reusing recovered components from many products. These components must be "qualified as

OM in Action ▶ Subaru's Clean, Green Set of Wheels with ISO 14001

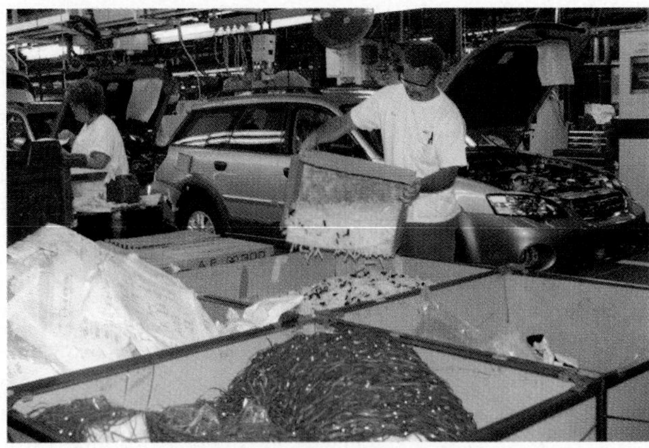

Going green had a humble beginning. First, it was newspapers, soda cans and bottles, and corrugated packaging—the things you typically throw into your own recycling bins. Similarly, at Subaru's Lafayette, Indiana, plant, the process of becoming the first completely waste-free auto plant in North America began with employees dropping these things in containers throughout the plant. Then came employee empowerment. "We had 268 suggestions for different things to improve our recycling efforts," said Denise Coogan, plant ISO 14001 environmental compliance leader.

Some ideas were easy to handle. "With plastic shrink wrap, we found some (recyclers) wouldn't take colored shrink wrap. So we went back to our vendors and asked for only clear shrink wrap," Coogan said. Some suggestions were a lot more dirty. "We went dumpster diving to see what we were throwing away and see what we could do with it."

The last load of waste generated by Subaru made its way to a landfill four years ago. Since then, everything that enters the plant eventually exits as a usable product. Coogan adds, "We didn't redefine 'zero.' Zero means zero. Nothing from our manufacturing process goes to the landfill."

Last year alone, the Subaru plant recycled 13,142 tons of steel, 1,448 tons of paper products, 194 tons of plastics, 10 tons of solvent-soaked rags, and 4 tons of light bulbs. It thereby conserved 29,200 trees, 670,000 gallons of oil, 34,700 gallons of gas, 10 million gallons of water, and 53,000 million watts of electricity.

Going green isn't easy, but it can be done!

Sources: The Wall Street Journal (March 23, 2009): R4; *Industry Week* (July 2008): 36–41; and *Industrial Engineer* (April 2006): 26–29.

good as new" and meet all safety and environmental criteria. Xerox was one of the companies that helped write ISO 24700 and an early applicant for certification.

AUTHOR COMMENT
The 7 concepts that make up TQM are part of the lexicon of business.

TOTAL QUALITY MANAGEMENT

Total quality management (TQM)
Management of an entire organization so that it excels in all aspects of products and services that are important to the customer.

Total quality management (TQM) refers to a quality emphasis that encompasses the entire organization, from supplier to customer. TQM stresses a commitment by management to have a continuing companywide drive toward excellence in all aspects of products and services that are important to the customer. Each of the 10 decisions made by operations managers deals with some aspect of identifying and meeting customer expectations. Meeting those expectations requires an emphasis on TQM if a firm is to compete as a leader in world markets.

Quality expert W. Edwards Deming used 14 points (see Table 6.2) to indicate how he implemented TQM. We develop these into seven concepts for an effective TQM program: (1) continuous improvement, (2) Six Sigma, (3) employee empowerment, (4) benchmarking, (5) just-in-time (JIT), (6) Taguchi concepts, and (7) knowledge of TQM tools.

▶ **TABLE 6.2**
Deming's 14 Points for Implementing Quality Improvement

1. Create consistency of purpose.
2. Lead to promote change.
3. Build quality into the product; stop depending on inspections to catch problems.
4. Build long-term relationships based on performance instead of awarding business on the basis of price.
5. Continuously improve product, quality, and service.
6. Start training.
7. Emphasize leadership.
8. Drive out fear.
9. Break down barriers between departments.
10. Stop haranguing workers.
11. Support, help, and improve.
12. Remove barriers to pride in work.
13. Institute a vigorous program of education and self-improvement.
14. Put everybody in the company to work on the transformation.

Source: Deming, W. Edwards. Out of the Crisis, pp. 23–24, © 2000 W. Edwards Deming Institute, published by The MIT Press. Reprinted by permission.

4. Act
Implement the plan, document.

1. Plan
Identify the problem and make a plan.

2. Do
Test the plan.

3. Check
Is the plan working?

◄ **FIGURE 6.3**
PDCA cycle

Continuous Improvement

Total quality management requires a never-ending process of continuous improvement that covers people, equipment, suppliers, materials, and procedures. The basis of the philosophy is that every aspect of an operation can be improved. The end goal is perfection, which is never achieved but always sought.

Plan-Do-Check-Act Walter Shewhart, another pioneer in quality management, developed a circular model known as **PDCA** (plan, do, check, act) as his version of continuous improvement. Deming later took this concept to Japan during his work there after World War II.[3] The PDCA cycle is shown in Figure 6.3 as a circle to stress the continuous nature of the improvement process.

PDCA
A continuous improvement model of plan, do, check. act.

The Japanese use the word *kaizen* to describe this ongoing process of unending improvement—the setting and achieving of ever-higher goals. In the U.S., *TQM* and *zero defects* are also used to describe continuous improvement efforts. But whether it's PDCA, kaizen, TQM, or zero defects, the operations manager is a key player in building a work culture that endorses continuous improvement.

Six Sigma

The term **Six Sigma**, popularized by Motorola, Honeywell, and General Electric, has two meanings in TQM. In a *statistical* sense, it describes a process, product, or service with an extremely high capability (99.9997% accuracy). For example, if 1 million passengers pass through the St. Louis Airport with checked baggage each month, a Six Sigma program for baggage handling will result in only 3.4 passengers with misplaced luggage. The more common *three-sigma* program (which we address in the supplement to this chapter) would result in 2,700 passengers with misplaced bags every month. See Figure 6.4.

Six Sigma
A program to save time, improve quality, and lower costs.

The second TQM definition of Six Sigma is a program designed to reduce defects to help lower costs, save time, and improve customer satisfaction. Six Sigma is a comprehensive system—a strategy, a discipline, and a set of tools—for achieving and sustaining business success:

LO3: Explain what Six Sigma is

- It is a *strategy* because it focuses on total customer satisfaction.
- It is a *discipline* because it follows the formal Six Sigma Improvement Model known as DMAIC. This five-step process improvement model (1) Defines the project's purpose, scope, and outputs and then identifies the required process information, keeping in mind the customer's

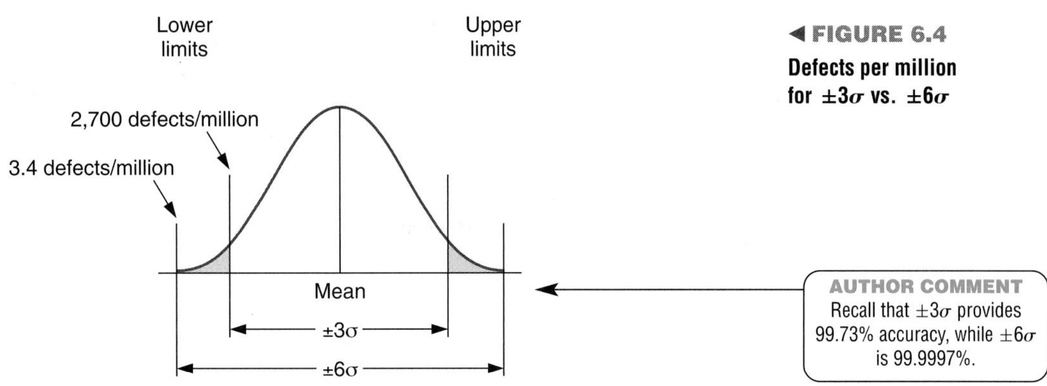

◄ **FIGURE 6.4**
Defects per million for $\pm 3\sigma$ vs. $\pm 6\sigma$

[3]As a result, the Japanese refer to the PDCA cycle as a Deming circle, while others call it a Shewhart circle.

definition of quality; (2) *Measures* the process and collects data; (3) Analyzes the data, ensuring repeatability (the results can be duplicated), and reproducibility (others get the same result); (4) *Improves*, by modifying or redesigning, existing processes and procedures; and (5) Controls the new process to make sure performance levels are maintained.

- It is a *set of seven tools* that we introduce shortly in this chapter: check sheets, scatter diagrams, cause-and-effect diagrams, Pareto charts, flowcharts, histograms, and statistical process control.

Motorola developed Six Sigma in the 1980s in response to customer complaints about its products, and to stiff competition. The company first set a goal of reducing defects by 90%. Within 1 year it had achieved such impressive results—through benchmarking competitors, soliciting new ideas from employees, changing reward plans, adding training, and revamping critical processes—that it documented the procedures into what it called Six Sigma. Although the concept was rooted in manufacturing, GE later expanded Six Sigma into services, including human resources, sales, customer services, and financial/credit services. The concept of wiping out defects turns out to be the same in both manufacturing and services.

Implementing Six Sigma Implementing Six Sigma "is a big commitment," says the head of that program at Praxair, a major industrial gas company. "We're asking our executives to spend upward of 15% of their time on Six Sigma. If you don't spend the time, you don't get the results." Indeed, successful Six Sigma programs in every firm, from GE to Motorola to DuPont to Texas Instruments require a major time commitment, especially from top management. These leaders have to formulate the plan, communicate their buy-in and the firm's objectives, and take a visible role in setting the example for others.

Successful Six Sigma projects are clearly related to the strategic direction of a company. It is a management-directed, team-based, and expert-led approach.[4]

Employee Empowerment

Employee empowerment
Enlarging employee jobs so that the added responsibility and authority is moved to the lowest level possible in the organization.

Employee empowerment means involving employees in every step of the production process. Consistently, business literature suggests that some 85% of quality problems have to do with materials and processes, not with employee performance. Therefore, the task is to design equipment and processes that produce the desired quality. This is best done with a high degree of involvement by those who understand the shortcomings of the system. Those dealing with the system on a daily basis understand it better than anyone else. One study indicated that TQM programs that delegate responsibility for quality to shop-floor employees tend to be twice as likely to succeed as those implemented with "top-down" directives.[5]

When nonconformance occurs, the worker is seldom wrong. Either the product was designed wrong, the system that makes the product was designed wrong, or the employee was improperly trained. Although the employee may be able to help solve the problem, the employee rarely causes it.

Techniques for building employee empowerment include (1) building communication networks that include employees; (2) developing open, supportive supervisors; (3) moving responsibility from both managers and staff to production employees; (4) building high-morale organizations; and (5) creating such formal organization structures as teams and quality circles.

Quality circle
A group of employees meeting regularly with a facilitator to solve work-related problems in their work area.

Teams can be built to address a variety of issues. One popular focus of teams is quality. Such teams are often known as quality circles. A **quality circle** is a group of employees who meet regularly to solve work-related problems. The members receive training in group planning, problem solving, and statistical quality control. They generally meet once a week (usually after work but sometimes on company time). Although the members are not rewarded financially, they do receive recognition from the firm. A specially trained team member, called the *facilitator*, usually helps train the members and keeps the meetings running smoothly. Teams with a quality focus have proven to be a cost-effective way to increase productivity as well as quality.

[4]To train employees in how to improve quality and its relationship to customers, there are three other key players in the Six Sigma program: Master Black Belts, Black Belts, and Green Belts. Master Black Belts are full-time teachers who have extensive training in statistics, quality tools, and leadership. They mentor Black Belts, who in turn are project team leaders, directing perhaps a half-dozen projects per year. Dow Chemical and DuPont have more than 1,000 Black Belts each in their global operations. DuPont also has 160 Master Black Belts and introduces over 2,000 Green Belts per year into its ranks.

[5]"The Straining of Quality," *The Economist* (January 14, 1995): 55. We also see that this is one of the strengths of Southwest Airlines, which offers bare-bones domestic service but whose friendly and humorous employees help it obtain number one ranking for quality. (See *Fortune* [March 6, 2006]: 65–69.)

Workers at this TRW airbag manufacturing plant in Marshall, Illinois, are their own inspectors. Empowerment is an essential part of TQM. This man is checking the quality of a crash sensor he built.

Benchmarking

Benchmarking is another ingredient in an organization's TQM program. **Benchmarking** involves selecting a demonstrated standard of products, services, costs, or practices that represent the very best performance for processes or activities very similar to your own. The idea is to develop a target at which to shoot and then to develop a standard or benchmark against which to compare your performance. The steps for developing benchmarks are:

Benchmarking
Selecting a demonstrated standard of performance that represents the very best performance for a process or an activity.

1. Determine what to benchmark.
2. Form a benchmark team.
3. Identify benchmarking partners.
4. Collect and analyze benchmarking information.
5. Take action to match or exceed the benchmark.

LO4: Explain how benchmarking is used in TQM

Typical performance measures used in benchmarking include percentage of defects, cost per unit or per order, processing time per unit, service response time, return on investment, customer satisfaction rates, and customer retention rates.

In the ideal situation, you find one or more similar organizations that are leaders in the particular areas you want to study. Then you compare yourself (benchmark yourself) against them. The company need not be in your industry. Indeed, to establish world-class standards, it may be best to look outside your industry. If one industry has learned how to compete via rapid product development while yours has not, it does no good to study your industry.

This is exactly what Xerox and Mercedes Benz did when they went to L.L. Bean for order-filling and warehousing benchmarks. Xerox noticed that L.L. Bean was able to "pick" orders three times as fast as it could. After benchmarking, it was immediately able to pare warehouse costs by 10%. Mercedes Benz observed that L.L. Bean warehouse employees used flowcharts to spot wasted motions. The auto giant followed suit and now relies more on problem solving at the worker level.

Benchmarks often take the form of "best practices" found in other firms or in other divisions. Table 6.3 illustrates best practices for resolving customer complaints.

Likewise, Britain's Great Ormond Street Hospital benchmarked the Ferrari Racing Team's pit stops to improve one aspect of medical care. (See the *OM in Action* box.)

Internal Benchmarking When an organization is large enough to have many divisions or business units, a natural approach is the internal benchmark. Data are usually much more accessible than from outside firms. Typically, one internal unit has superior performance worth learning from.

◄ **TABLE 6.3**
Best Practices for Resolving Customer Complaints

Best Practice	Justification
Make it easy for clients to complain.	It is free market research.
Respond quickly to complaints.	It adds customers and loyalty.
Resolve complaints on the first contact.	It reduces cost
Use computers to manage complaints.	Discover trends, share them, and align your services.
Recruit the best for customer service jobs.	It should be part of formal training and career advancement.

Source: Canadian Government Guide on Complaint Mechanism.

OM in Action ► A Hospital Benchmarks against the Ferrari Racing Team?

After surgeons successfully completed a 6-hour operation to fix a hole in a 3-year-old boy's heart, Dr. Angus McEwan supervised one of the most dangerous phases of the procedure: the boy's transfer from surgery to the intensive care unit.

Thousands of such "handoffs" occur in hospitals every day, and devastating mistakes can happen during them. In fact, at least 35% of preventable hospital mishaps take place because of handoff problems. Risks come from many sources: using temporary nursing staff, frequent shift changes for interns, surgeons working in larger teams, and an ever-growing tangle of wires and tubes connected to patients.

In one of the most unlikely benchmarks in modern medicine, Britain's largest children's hospital turned to Italy's Formula One Ferrari racing team for help in revamping patient handoff techniques. Armed with videos and slides, the racing team described how they analyze pit crew performance. It also explained how its system for recording errors stressed the small ones that go unnoticed in pit-stop handoffs.

To move forward, Ferrari invited a team of doctors to attend practice sessions at the British Grand Prix in order to get closer looks at pit stops. Ferrari's technical director, Nigel Stepney, then watched a video of a hospital handoff. Stepney was not impressed. "In fact, he was amazed at how clumsy, chaotic, and informal the process appeared," said one hospital official. At that meeting, Stepney described how each Ferrari crew member is required to do a specific job, in a specific sequence, and in silence. The hospital handoff, in contrast, had several conversations going on at once, while different members of its team disconnected or reconnected patient equipment, but in no particular order.

Results of the benchmarking process: handoff errors fell 42% to 49%, with a bonus of faster handoff time.

Sources: The Wall Street Journal (December 3, 2007): B11 and (November 14, 2006): A1, A8.

Xerox's almost religious belief in benchmarking has paid off not only by looking outward to L.L. Bean but by examining the operations of its various country divisions. For example, Xerox Europe, a $6 billion subsidiary of Xerox Corp., formed teams to see how better sales could result through internal benchmarking. Somehow, France sold five times as many color copiers as did other divisions in Europe. By copying France's approach, namely, better sales training and use of dealer channels to supplement direct sales, Norway increased sales by 152%, Holland by 300%, and Switzerland by 328%!

Benchmarks can and should be established in a variety of areas. Total quality management requires no less.[6]

Just-in-Time (JIT)

The philosophy behind just-in-time (JIT) is one of continuing improvement and enforced problem solving. JIT systems are designed to produce or deliver goods just as they are needed. JIT is related to quality in three ways:

- *JIT cuts the cost of quality:* This occurs because scrap, rework, inventory investment, and damage costs are directly related to inventory on hand. Because there is less inventory on hand with JIT, costs are lower. In addition, inventory hides bad quality, whereas JIT immediately *exposes* bad quality.
- *JIT improves quality:* As JIT shrinks lead time it keeps evidence of errors fresh and limits the number of potential sources of error. JIT creates, in effect, an early warning system for quality problems, both within the firm and with vendors.

[6]Note that benchmarking is good for evaluating how well you are doing the thing you are doing compared with the industry, but the more imaginative approach to process improvement is to ask, Should we be doing this at all? Comparing your warehousing operations to the marvelous job that L.L. Bean does is fine, but maybe you should be outsourcing the warehousing function (see Supplement 11).

- *Better quality means less inventory and a better, easier-to-employ JIT system:* Often the purpose of keeping inventory is to protect against poor production performance resulting from unreliable quality. If consistent quality exists, JIT allows firms to reduce all the costs associated with inventory.

Taguchi Concepts

Most quality problems are the result of poor product and process design. Genichi Taguchi has provided us with three concepts aimed at improving both product and process quality: *quality robustness*, *quality loss function*, and *target-oriented quality*.[7]

Quality robust products are products that can be produced uniformly and consistently in adverse manufacturing and environmental conditions. Taguchi's idea is to remove the *effects* of adverse conditions instead of removing the causes. Taguchi suggests that removing the effects is often cheaper than removing the causes and more effective in producing a robust product. In this way, small variations in materials and process do not destroy product quality.

Quality robust
Products that are consistently built to meet customer needs in spite of adverse conditions in the production process.

A **quality loss function (QLF)** identifies all costs connected with poor quality and shows how these costs increase as the product moves away from being exactly what the customer wants. These costs include not only customer dissatisfaction but also warranty and service costs; internal inspection, repair, and scrap costs; and costs that can best be described as costs to society. Notice that Figure 6.5(a) shows the quality loss function as a curve that increases at an increasing rate. It takes the general form of a simple quadratic formula:

Quality loss function (QLF)
A mathematical function that identifies all costs connected with poor quality and shows how these costs increase as product quality moves from what the customer wants.

$$L = D^2C$$

where L = loss to society
D^2 = square of the distance from the target value
C = cost of the deviation at the specification limit

All the losses to society due to poor performance are included in the loss function. The smaller the loss, the more desirable the product. The farther the product is from the target value, the more severe the loss.

LO5: Explain quality robust products and Taguchi concepts

Taguchi observed that traditional conformance-oriented specifications (i.e., the product is good as long as it falls within the tolerance limits) are too simplistic. As shown in Figure 6.5(b), conformance-oriented quality accepts all products that fall within the tolerance limits, producing more units farther from the target. Therefore, the loss (cost) is higher in terms of customer satisfaction and benefits to society. Target-oriented quality, on the other hand, strives to keep the product at the desired specification, producing more (and better) units near the target. **Target-oriented quality** is a philosophy of continuous improvement to bring the product exactly on target.

Target-oriented quality
A philosophy of continuous improvement to bring a product exactly on target.

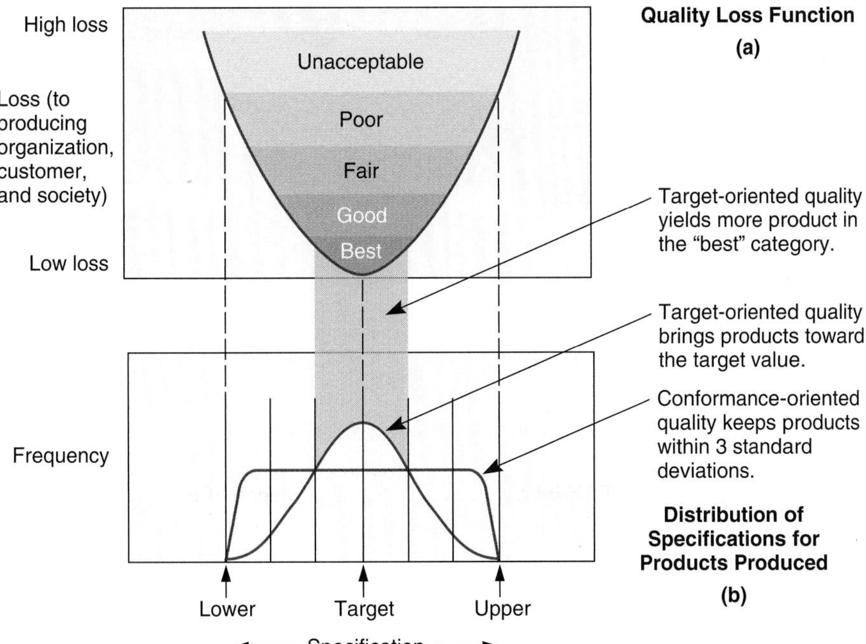

◀ **FIGURE 6.5**
(a) Quality Loss Function and (b) Distribution of Products Produced
Taguchi aims for the target because products produced near the upper and lower acceptable specifications result in higher quality loss function.

[7]G. Taguchi, S. Chowdhury, and Y. Wu, *Taguchi's Quality Engineering Handbook* (New York: Wiley, 2004).

Knowledge of TQM Tools

To empower employees and implement TQM as a continuing effort, everyone in the organization must be trained in the techniques of TQM. In the following section, we focus on some of the diverse and expanding tools that are used in the TQM crusade.

AUTHOR COMMENT
These 7 tools will prove useful in many of your courses and throughout your career.

TOOLS OF TQM

Seven tools that are particularly helpful in the TQM effort are shown in Figure 6.6. We will now introduce these tools.

Check Sheets

A check sheet is any kind of a form that is designed for recording data. In many cases, the recording is done so the patterns are easily seen while the data are being taken (see Figure 6.6[a]). Check sheets help analysts find the facts or patterns that may aid subsequent analysis. An

▼ **FIGURE 6.6 Seven Tools of TQM**

Tools for Generating Ideas

(a) *Check Sheet:* An organized method of recording data

	Hour							
Defect	1	2	3	4	5	6	7	8
A	///	/		/	/	/	///	/
B	//	/	/	/			//	///
C	/	//					//	////

(b) *Scatter Diagram:* A graph of the value of one variable vs. another variable

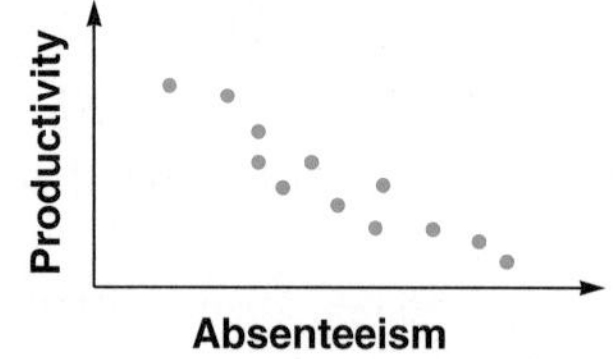

(c) *Cause-and-Effect Diagram:* A tool that identifies process elements (causes) that may affect an outcome

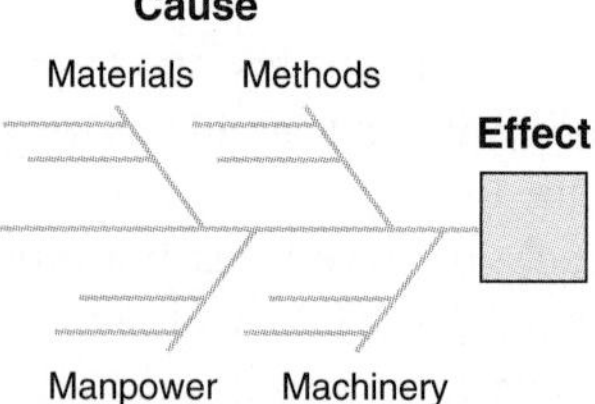

Tools for Organizing the Data

(d) *Pareto Chart:* A graph that identifies and plots problems or defects in descending order of frequency

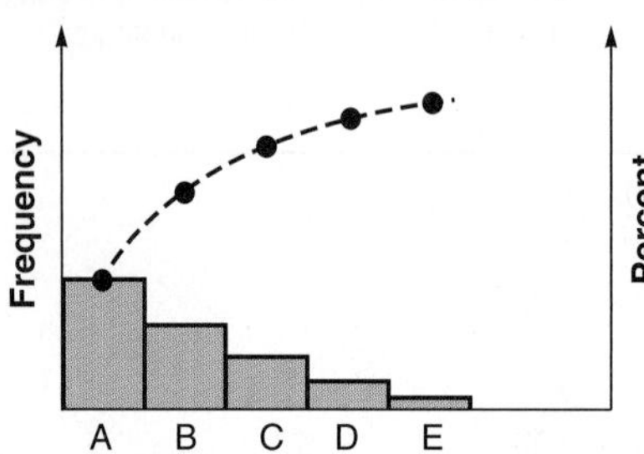

(e) *Flowchart (Process Diagram):* A chart that describes the steps in a process

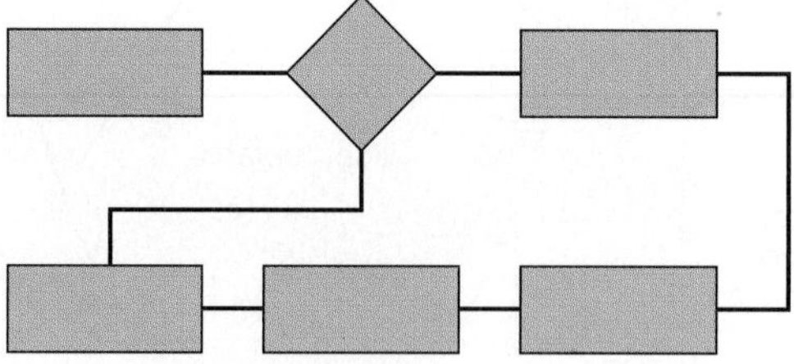

Tools for Identifying Problems

(f) *Histogram:* A distribution that shows the frequency of occurrences of a variable

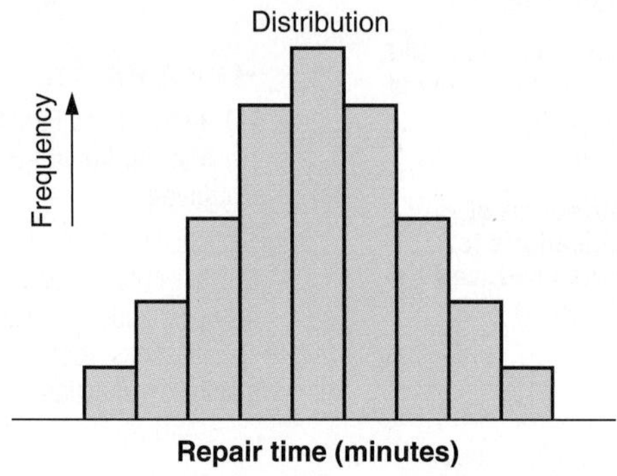

(g) *Statistical Process Control Chart:* A chart with time on the horizontal axis for plotting values of a statistic

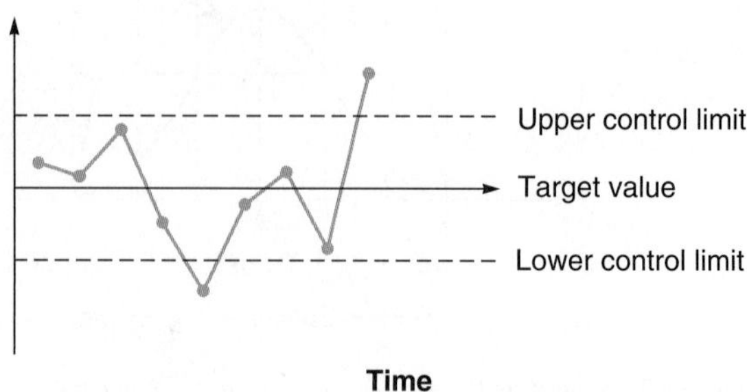

example might be a drawing that shows a tally of the areas where defects are occurring or a check sheet showing the type of customer complaints.

LO6: Use the seven tools of TQM

Scatter Diagrams

Scatter diagrams show the relationship between two measurements. An example is the positive relationship between length of a service call and the number of trips a repairperson makes back to the truck for parts. Another example might be a plot of productivity and absenteeism, as shown in Figure 6.6(b). If the two items are closely related, the data points will form a tight band. If a random pattern results, the items are unrelated.

Cause-and-Effect Diagrams

Another tool for identifying quality issues and inspection points is the **cause-and-effect diagram**, also known as an **Ishikawa diagram** or a **fish-bone chart**. Figure 6.7 illustrates a chart (note the shape resembling the bones of a fish) for a basketball quality control problem—missed free-throws. Each "bone" represents a possible source of error.

Cause-and-effect diagram
A schematic technique used to discover possible locations of quality problems.

The operations manager starts with four categories: material, machinery/equipment, manpower, and methods. These four *M*s are the "causes." They provide a good checklist for initial analysis. Individual causes associated with each category are tied in as separate bones along that branch, often through a brainstorming process. For example, the method branch in Figure 6.7 has problems caused by hand position, follow-through, aiming point, bent knees, and balance. When a fish-bone chart is systematically developed, possible quality problems and inspection points are highlighted.

Pareto Charts

Pareto charts are a method of organizing errors, problems, or defects to help focus on problem-solving efforts. They are based on the work of Vilfredo Pareto, a 19th-century economist. Joseph M. Juran popularized Pareto's work when he suggested that 80% of a firm's problems are a result of only 20% of the causes.

Pareto charts
Graphics that identify the few critical items as opposed to many less important ones.

Example 1 indicates that of the five types of complaints identified, the vast majority were of one type—poor room service.

▼ **FIGURE 6.7** Fish-Bone Chart (or Cause-and-Effect Diagram) for Problems with Missed Free-throws

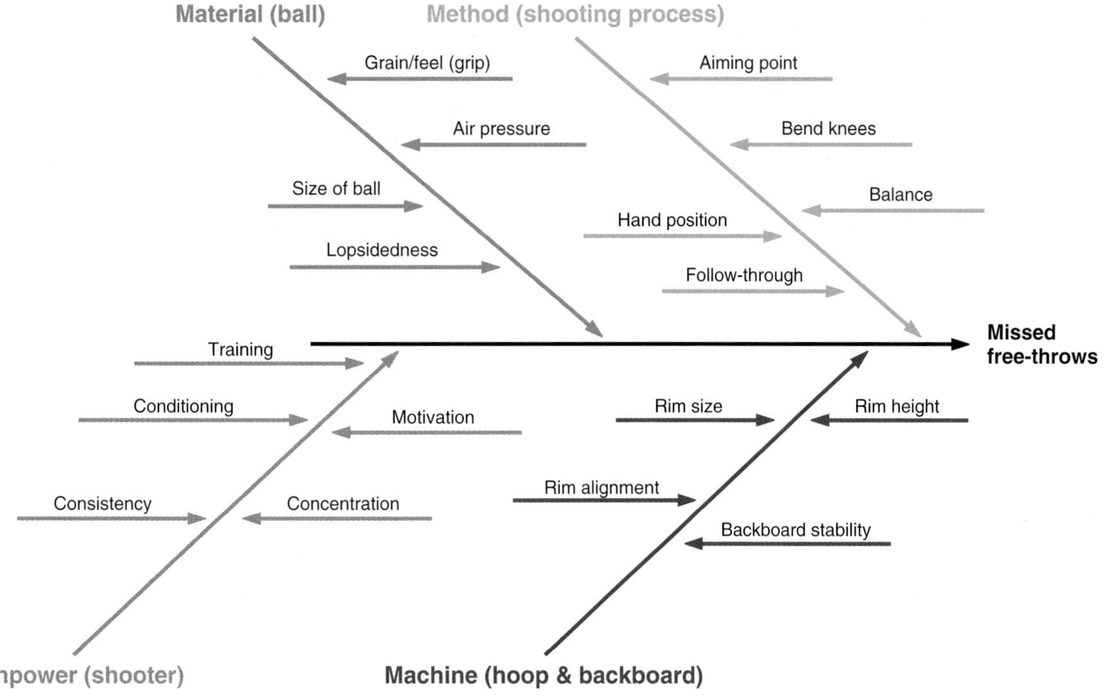

Source: Adapted from MoreSteam.com, 2007.

EXAMPLE 1 ▶

A Pareto chart at the Hard Rock Hotel

The Hard Rock Hotel in Bali has just collected the data from 75 complaint calls to the general manager during the month of October. The manager wants to prepare an analysis of the complaints. The data provided are room service, 54; check-in delays, 12; hours the pool is open, 4; minibar prices, 3; and miscellaneous, 2.

APPROACH ▶ A Pareto chart is an excellent choice for this analysis.

SOLUTION ▶ The Pareto chart shown below indicates that 72% of the calls were the result of one cause: room service. The majority of complaints will be eliminated when this one cause is corrected.

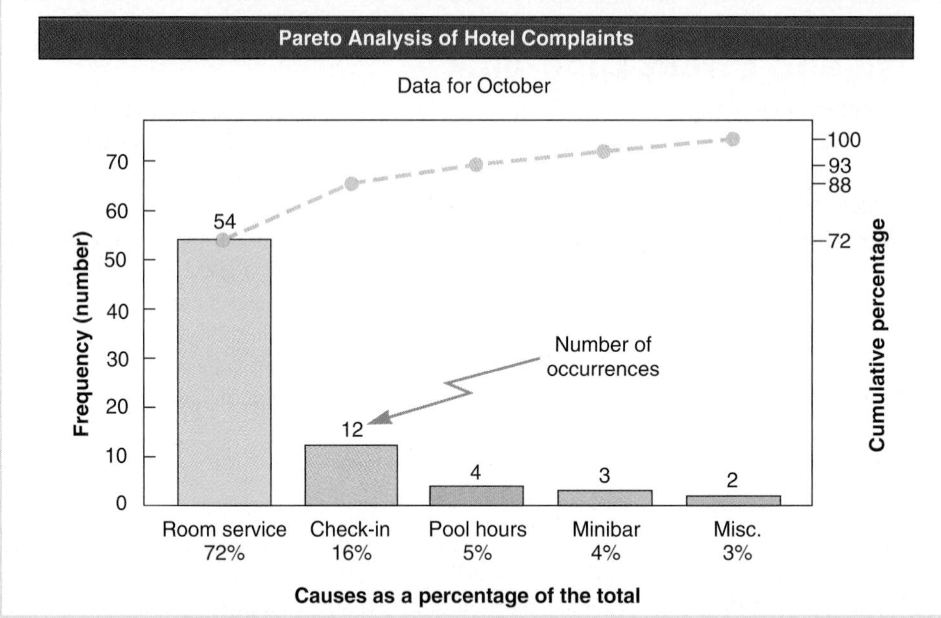

INSIGHT ▶ This visual means of summarizing data is very helpful—particularly with large amounts of data, as in the Southwestern University case study at the end of this chapter. We can immediately spot the top problems and prepare a plan to address them.

LEARNING EXERCISE ▶ Hard Rock's bar manager decides to do a similar analysis on complaints she has collected over the past year: too expensive, 22; weak drinks, 15; slow service, 65; short hours, 8; unfriendly bartender, 12. Prepare a Pareto chart. [Answer: slow service, 53%; expensive, 18%; drinks, 12%; bartender, 10%; hours, 7%.]

RELATED PROBLEMS ▶ 6.1, 6.3, 6.7b, 6.12, 6.13, 6.16c

ACTIVE MODEL 6.1 This example is further illustrated in Active Model 6.1 at **www.pearsonhighered.com/heizer.**

Pareto analysis indicates which problems may yield the greatest payoff. Pacific Bell discovered this when it tried to find a way to reduce damage to buried phone cable, the number-one cause of phone outages. Pareto analysis showed that 41% of cable damage was caused by construction work. Armed with this information, Pacific Bell was able to devise a plan to reduce cable cuts by 24% in one year, saving $6 million.

Likewise, Japan's Ricoh Corp., a copier maker, used the Pareto principle to tackle the "callback" problem. Callbacks meant the job was not done right the first time and that a second visit, at Ricoh's expense, was needed. Identifying and retraining only the 11% of the customer engineers with the most callbacks resulted in a 19% drop in return visits.

Flowcharts

Flowcharts
Block diagrams that graphically describe a process or system.

Flowcharts graphically present a process or system using annotated boxes and interconnected lines (see Figure 6.6[e]). They are a simple, but great tool for trying to make sense of a process or explain a process. Example 2 uses a flowchart to show the process of completing an MRI at a hospital.

EXAMPLE 2

A flowchart for hospital MRI service

Arnold Palmer Hospital has undertaken a series of process improvement initiatives. One of these is to make the MRI service efficient for patient, doctor, and hospital. The first step, the administrator believes, is to develop a flowchart for this process.

APPROACH ▶ A process improvement staffer observed a number of patients and followed them (and information flow) from start to end. Here are the 11 steps:

1. Physician schedules MRI after examining patient (START).
2. Patient taken to the MRI lab with test order and copy of medical records.
3. Patient signs in, completes required paperwork.
4. Patient is prepped by technician for scan.
5. Technician carries out the MRI scan.
6. Technician inspects film for clarity.
7. If MRI not satisfactory (20% of time), steps 5 and 6 are repeated.
8. Patient taken back to hospital room.
9. MRI is read by radiologist and report is prepared.
10. MRI and report are transferred electronically to physician.
11. Patient and physician discuss report (END).

SOLUTION ▶ Here is the flowchart:

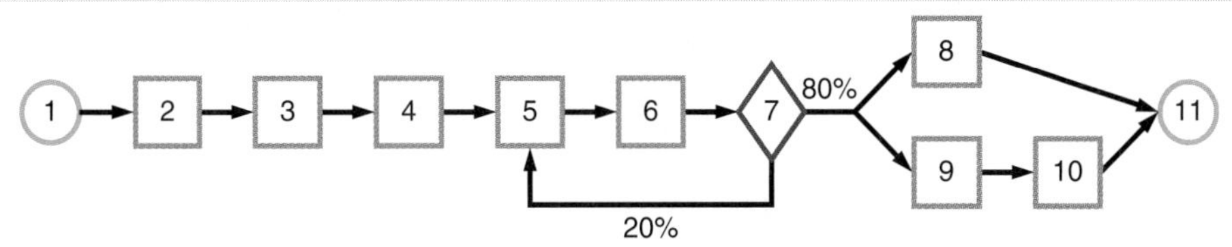

AUTHOR COMMENT
Flowcharting any process is an excellent way to understand and then try to improve that process.

INSIGHT ▶ With the flowchart in hand, the hospital can analyze each step and identify value-added activities and activities that can be improved or eliminated.

LEARNING EXERCISE ▶ If the patient's blood pressure is over 200/120 when being prepped for the MRI, she is taken back to her room for 2 hours and the process returns to Step 2. How does the flowchart change? Answer:

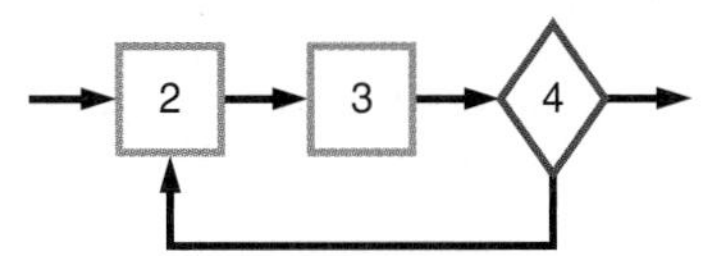

RELATED PROBLEMS ▶ 6.6, 6.15

Histograms

Histograms show the range of values of a measurement and the frequency with which each value occurs (see Figure 6.6[f]). They show the most frequently occurring readings as well as the variations in the measurements. Descriptive statistics, such as the average and standard deviation, may be calculated to describe the distribution. However, the data should always be plotted so the shape of the distribution can be "seen." A visual presentation of the distribution may also provide insight into the cause of the variation.

Statistical Process Control (SPC)

Statistical process control (SPC)
A process used to monitor standards, make measurements, and take corrective action as a product or service is being produced.

Statistical process control monitors standards, makes measurements, and takes corrective action as a product or service is being produced. Samples of process outputs are examined; if they are within acceptable limits, the process is permitted to continue. If they fall outside certain specific ranges, the process is stopped and, typically, the assignable cause located and removed.

Control charts
Graphic presentations of process data over time, with predetermined control limits.

Control charts are graphic presentations of data over time that show upper and lower limits for the process we want to control (see Figure 6.6[g]). Control charts are constructed in such a

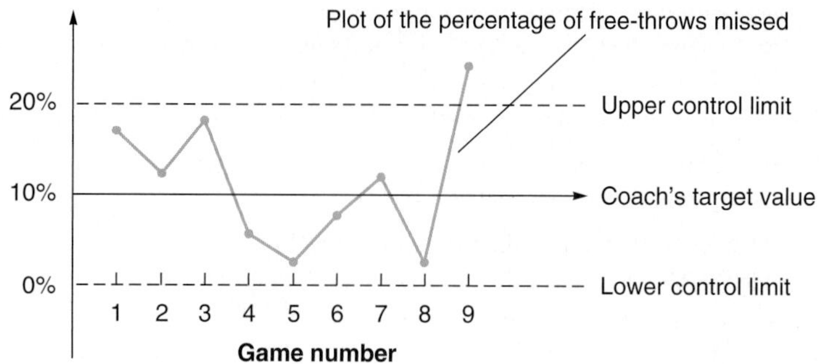

▶ **FIGURE 6.8**
Control Chart for Percentage of Free-throws Missed by the Chicago Bulls in Their First Nine Games of the New Season

way that new data can be quickly compared with past performance data. We take samples of the process output and plot the average of each of these samples on a chart that has the limits on it. The up-per and lower limits in a control chart can be in units of temperature, pressure, weight, length, and so on.

Figure 6.8 shows the plot of the average percentages of samples in a control chart. When the average of the samples falls within the upper and lower control limits and no discernible pattern is present, the process is said to be in control with only natural variation present. Otherwise, the process is out of control or out of adjustment.

The supplement to this chapter details how control charts of different types are developed. It also deals with the statistical foundation underlying the use of this important tool.

AUTHOR COMMENT
One of the themes of quality is that "quality cannot be inspected into a product."

THE ROLE OF INSPECTION

Inspection
A means of ensuring that an operation is producing at the quality level expected.

To make sure a system is producing at the expected quality level, control of the process is needed. The best processes have little variation from the standard expected. The operations manager's task is to build such systems and to verify, often by inspection, that they are performing to standard. This **inspection** can involve measurement, tasting, touching, weighing, or testing of the product (sometimes even destroying it when doing so). Its goal is to detect a bad process immediately. Inspection does not correct deficiencies in the system or defects in the products; nor does it change a product or increase its value. Inspection only finds deficiencies and defects. Moreover, inspections are expensive and do not add value to the product.

Inspection should be thought of as a vehicle for improving the system. Operations managers need to know critical points in the system: (1) *when to inspect* and (2) *where to inspect*.

When and Where to Inspect

Deciding when and where to inspect depends on the type of process and the value added at each stage. Inspections can take place at any of the following points:

1. At your supplier's plant while the supplier is producing.
2. At your facility upon receipt of goods from your supplier.
3. Before costly or irreversible processes.
4. During the step-by-step production process.
5. When production or service is complete.
6. Before delivery to your customer.
7. At the point of customer contact.

The seven tools of TQM discussed in the previous section aid in this "when and where to inspect" decision. However, inspection is not a substitute for a robust product produced by well-trained employees in a good process. In one well-known experiment conducted by an independent research firm, 100 defective pieces were added to a "perfect" lot of items and then subjected to 100% inspection.[8] The inspectors found only 68 of the defective pieces in their first inspection. It took another three passes by the inspectors to find the next 30 defects. The last two defects were never found. So the bottom line is that there is variability in the inspection process. Additionally, inspectors are only human: They become bored, they become tired, and

[8] *Statistical Quality Control* (Springfield, MA: Monsanto Chemical Company, n.d.): 19.

Good methods analysis and the proper tools can result in poka-yokes that improve both quality and speed. Here, two poka-yokes are demonstrated. First, the aluminum scoop automatically positions the french fries vertically, and second, the properly sized container ensures that the portion served is correct. McDonald's thrives by bringing rigor and consistency to the restaurant business.

the inspection equipment itself has variability. Even with 100% inspection, inspectors cannot guarantee perfection. Therefore, good processes, employee empowerment, and source control are a better solution than trying to find defects by inspection. You cannot inspect quality into the product.

For example, at Velcro Industries, as in many organizations, quality was viewed by machine operators as the job of "those quality people." Inspections were based on random sampling, and if a part showed up bad, it was thrown out. The company decided to pay more attention to the system (operators, machine repair and design, measurement methods, communications, and responsibilities), and to invest more money in training. Over time as defects declined, Velcro was able to pull half its quality control people out of the process.

Source Inspection

The best inspection can be thought of as no inspection at all; this "inspection" is always done at the source—it is just doing the job properly with the operator ensuring that this is so. This may be called **source inspection** (or source control) and is consistent with the concept of employee empowerment, where individual employees self-check their own work. The idea is that each supplier, process, and employee *treats the next step in the process as the customer*, ensuring perfect product to the next "customer." This inspection may be assisted by the use of checklists and controls such as a fail-safe device called a *poka-yoke*, a name borrowed from the Japanese.

Source inspection
Controlling or monitoring at the point of production or purchase—at the source.

A **poka-yoke** is a foolproof device or technique that ensures production of good units every time. These special devices avoid errors and provide quick feedback of problems. A simple example of a poka-yoke device is the diesel gas pump nozzle that will not fit into the "unleaded" gas tank opening on your car. In McDonald's, the french fry scoop and standard-size bag used to measure the correct quantity are poka-yokes. Similarly, in a hospital, the prepackaged surgical coverings that contain exactly the items needed for a medical procedure are poka-yokes. Checklists are another type of poka-yoke. The idea of source inspection and poka-yokes is to ensure that 100% good product or service is provided at each step in the process.

Poka-yoke
Literally translated, "foolproof"; it has come to mean a device or technique that ensures the production of a good unit every time.

Service Industry Inspection

In *service*-oriented organizations, inspection points can be assigned at a wide range of locations, as illustrated in Table 6.4. Again, the operations manager must decide where inspections are justified and may find the seven tools of TQM useful when making these judgments.

Attribute inspection
An inspection that classifies items as being either good or defective.

Inspection of Attributes versus Variables

When inspections take place, quality characteristics may be measured as either *attributes* or *variables*. **Attribute inspection** classifies items as being either good or defective. It does not address the *degree* of failure. For example, the lightbulb burns or it does not. **Variable inspection**

Variable inspection
Classifications of inspected items as falling on a continuum scale, such as dimension, or strength.

▶ **TABLE 6.4**
Examples of Inspection in Services

Organization	What Is Inspected	Standard
Jones Law Offices	Receptionist performance	Phone answered by the second ring
	Billing	Accurate, timely, and correct format
	Attorney	Promptness in returning calls
Hard Rock Hotel	Reception desk	Use customer's name
	Doorman	Greet guest in less than 30 seconds
	Room	All lights working, spotless bathroom
	Minibar	Restocked and charges accurately posted to bill
Arnold Palmer Hospital	Billing	Accurate, timely, and correct format
	Pharmacy	Prescription accuracy, inventory accuracy
	Lab	Audit for lab-test accuracy
	Nurses	Charts immediately updated
	Admissions	Data entered correctly and completely
Olive Garden Restaurant	Busboy	Serves water and bread within 1 minute
	Busboy	Clears all entrée items and crumbs prior to dessert
	Waiter	Knows and suggests specials, desserts
Nordstrom Department Store	Display areas	Attractive, well organized, stocked, good lighting
	Stockrooms	Rotation of goods, organized, clean
	Salesclerks	Neat, courteous, very knowledgeable

measures such dimensions as weight, speed, size, or strength to see if an item falls within an acceptable range. If a piece of electrical wire is supposed to be 0.01 inch in diameter, a micrometer can be used to see if the product is close enough to pass inspection.

Knowing whether attributes or variables are being inspected helps us decide which statistical quality control approach to take, as we will see in the supplement to this chapter.

AUTHOR COMMENT The personal component of a service can make quality measurement difficult.

TQM IN SERVICES

The personal component of services is more difficult to measure than the quality of the tangible component. Generally, the user of a service, like the user of a good, has features in mind that form a basis for comparison among alternatives. Lack of any one feature may eliminate the service from further consideration. Quality also may be perceived as a bundle of attributes in which many lesser characteristics are superior to those of competitors. This approach to product comparison differs little between goods and services. However, what is very different about the selection of services is the poor definition of the (1) *intangible differences between products* and (2) *the intangible expectations customers have of those products*. Indeed, the intangible attributes

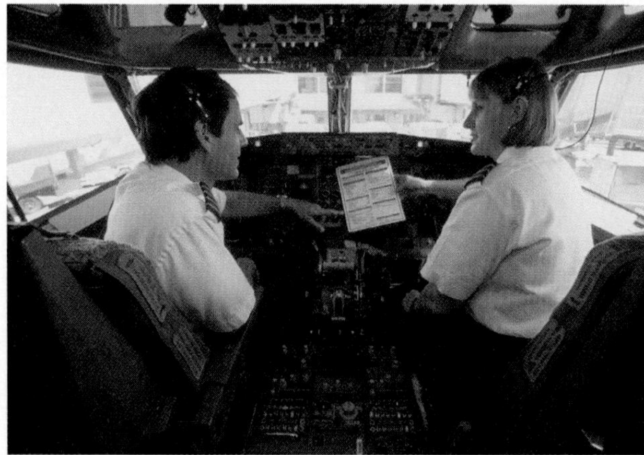

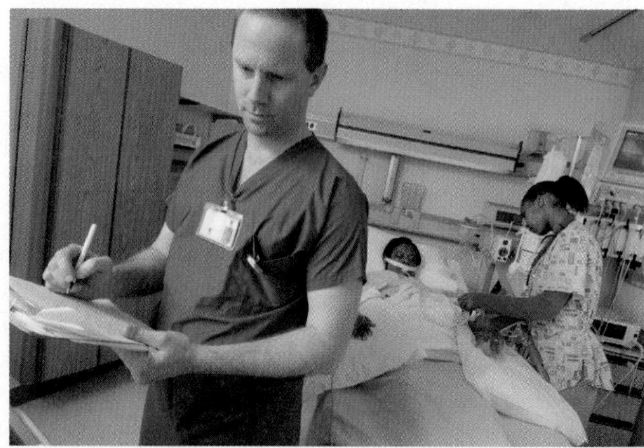

Using checklists, as simple as they are, is a powerful way to improve quality. Everyone from airline pilots to physicians use them. Johns Hopkins Hospital uses checklists to monitor patients, and the Michigan Health and Hospital Association is using them with great success to reduce infections.

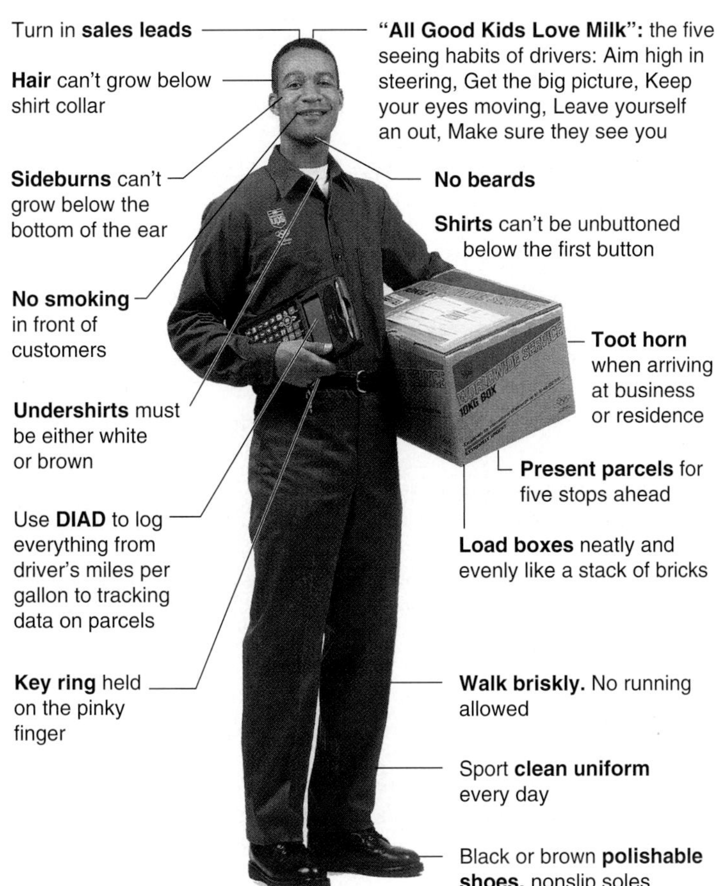
Turn in **sales leads**
Hair can't grow below shirt collar
Sideburns can't grow below the bottom of the ear
No smoking in front of customers
Undershirts must be either white or brown
Use **DIAD** to log everything from driver's miles per gallon to tracking data on parcels
Key ring held on the pinky finger
"All Good Kids Love Milk": the five seeing habits of drivers: Aim high in steering, Get the big picture, Keep your eyes moving, Leave yourself an out, Make sure they see you
No beards
Shirts can't be unbuttoned below the first button
Toot horn when arriving at business or residence
Present parcels for five stops ahead
Load boxes neatly and evenly like a stack of bricks
Walk briskly. No running allowed
Sport **clean uniform** every day
Black or brown **polishable shoes,** nonslip soles

UPS drivers are taught 340 precise methods of how to correctly deliver a package. Regimented? Absolutely. But UPS credits its uniformity and efficiency with laying the foundation for its high-quality service.

may not be defined at all. They are often unspoken images in the purchaser's mind. This is why all of those marketing issues such as advertising, image, and promotion can make a difference (see the photo of the UPS driver).

The operations manager plays a significant role in addressing several major aspects of service quality. First, the *tangible component of many services is important.* How well the service is designed and produced does make a difference. This might be how accurate, clear, and complete your checkout bill at the hotel is, how warm the food is at Taco Bell, or how well your car runs after you pick it up at the repair shop.

Second, another aspect of service and service quality is the process. Notice in Table 6.5 that 9 out of 10 of the determinants of service quality are related to *the service process.* Such things as reliability and courtesy are part of the process. An operations manager can *design processes (service products) that have these attributes* and can ensure their quality through the TQM techniques discussed in this chapter.

VIDEO 6.2
TQM at Ritz-Carlton Hotels

Third, the operations manager should realize that the customer's expectations are the standard against which the service is judged. Customers' perceptions of service quality result from a comparison of their before-service expectations with their actual-service experience. In other words, service quality is judged on the basis of whether it meets expectations. The *manager may be able to influence both the quality of the service and the expectation.* Don't promise more than you can deliver.

Fourth, the manager must expect exceptions. There is a standard quality level at which the regular service is delivered, such as the bank teller's handling of a transaction. However, there are "exceptions" or "problems" initiated by the customer or by less-than-optimal operating conditions (e.g., the computer "crashed"). This implies that the quality control system must recognize and *have a set of alternative plans for less-than-optimal operating conditions.*

Service recovery
Training and empowering frontline workers to solve a problem immediately.

Well-run companies have **service recovery** strategies. This means they train and empower frontline employees to immediately solve a problem. For instance, staff at Marriott Hotels are

▶ TABLE 6.5 Determinants of Service Quality

Reliability involves consistency of performance and dependability. It means that the firm performs the service right the first time and that the firm honors its promises.

Responsiveness concerns the willingness or readiness of employees to provide service. It involves timeliness of service.

Competence means possession of the required skills and knowledge to perform the service.

Access involves approachability and ease of contact.

Courtesy involves politeness, respect, consideration, and friendliness of contact personnel (including receptionists, telephone operators, etc.).

Communication means keeping customers informed in language they can understand and listening to them. It may mean that the company has to adjust its language for different consumers—increasing the level of sophistication with a well-educated customer and speaking simply and plainly with a novice.

Credibility involves trustworthiness, believability, and honesty. It involves having the customer's best interests at heart.

Security is the freedom from danger, risk, or doubt.

Understanding/knowing the customer involves making the effort to understand the customer's needs.

Tangibles include the physical evidence of the service.

Source: Adapted from A. Parasuranam, Valarie A. Zeithaml, and Leonard L. Berry, "A Conceptual Model of Service Quality and its Implications for Future Research," *Journal of Marketing* (Fall 1985): 44; *Journal of Marketing*, 58, no. 1 (January 1994): 111–125; *Journal of Retailing* 70 (Fall 1994): 201–230.

drilled in the LEARN routine—*L*isten, *E*mpathize, *A*pologize, *R*eact, *N*otify—with the final step ensuring that the complaint is fed back into the system. And at the Ritz-Carlton, staff members are trained not to say merely "sorry" but "please accept my apology." The Ritz gives them a budget for reimbursing upset guests.

Designing the product, managing the service process, matching customer expectations to the product, and preparing for the exceptions are keys to quality services. The *OM in Action* box "Richey International's Spies" provides another glimpse of how OM managers improve quality in services.

OM in Action ▶ Richey International's Spies

How do luxury hotels maintain quality? They inspect. But when the product is one-on-one service, largely dependent on personal behavior, how do you inspect? You hire spies!

Richey International is the spy. Preferred Hotels and Resorts Worldwide and Intercontinental Hotels have both hired Richey to do quality evaluations via spying. Richey employees posing as customers perform the inspections. However, even then management must have established what the customer expects and specific services that yield customer satisfaction. Only then do managers know where and how to inspect. Aggressive training and objective inspections reinforce behavior that will meet those customer expectations.

The hotels use Richey's undercover inspectors to ensure performance to exacting standards. The hotels do not know when the evaluators will arrive. Nor what aliases they will use. Over 50 different standards are evaluated before the inspectors even check in at a luxury hotel. Over the next 24 hours, using checklists, tape recordings, and photos, written reports are prepared. The reports include evaluation of standards such as:

- Does the doorman greet each guest in less than 30 seconds?
- Does the front-desk clerk use the guest's name during check-in?
- Is the bathroom tub and shower spotlessly clean?
- How many minutes does it take to get coffee after the guest sits down for breakfast?
- Did the waiter make eye contact?
- Were minibar charges posted correctly on the bill?

Established standards, aggressive training, and inspections are part of the TQM effort at these hotels. Quality does not happen by accident.

Sources: Hotel and Motel Management (August 2002): 128; *The Wall Street Journal* (May 12, 1999): B1, B12; and *Forbes* (October 5, 1998): 88–89.

CHAPTER SUMMARY

Quality is a term that means different things to different people. We define quality as "the totality of features and characteristics of a product or service that bears on its ability to satisfy stated or implied needs." Defining quality expectations is critical to effective and efficient operations.

Quality requires building a total quality management (TQM) environment because quality cannot be inspected into a product. The chapter also addresses seven TQM *concepts*: continuous improvement, Six Sigma, employee empowerment, benchmarking, just-in-time, Taguchi concepts, and knowledge of TQM tools. The seven TQM *tools* introduced in this chapter are check sheets, scatter diagrams, cause-and effect diagrams, Pareto charts, flowcharts, histograms, and statistical process control (SPC).

Key Terms

Quality (p. 190)
Cost of quality (COQ) (p. 192)
ISO 9000 (p. 193)
ISO 14000 (p. 193)
Total quality management (TQM) (p. 194)
PDCA (p. 195)
Six Sigma (p. 195)
Employee empowerment (p. 196)
Quality circle (p. 196)
Benchmarking (p. 197)
Quality robust (p. 199)
Quality loss function (QLF) (p. 199)
Target-oriented quality (p. 199)
Cause-and-effect diagram, Ishikawa diagram, or fish-bone chart (p. 201)
Pareto charts (p. 201)
Flowcharts (p. 202)
Statistical process control (SPC) (p. 203)
Control charts (p. 203)
Inspection (p. 204)
Source inspection (p. 205)
Poka-yoke (p. 205)
Attribute inspection (p. 205)
Variable inspection (p. 205)
Service recovery (p. 207)

Ethical Dilemma

A lawsuit a few years ago made headlines worldwide when a McDonald's drive-through customer spilled a cup of scalding hot coffee on herself. Claiming the coffee was too hot to be safely consumed in a car, the badly burned 80-year-old woman won \$2.9 million in court. (The judge later reduced the award to \$640,000.) McDonald's claimed the product was served to the correct specifications and was of proper quality. Further, the cup read "Caution—Contents May Be Hot." McDonald's coffee, at 180°, is substantially hotter (by corporate rule) than typical restaurant coffee, despite hundreds of coffee-scalding complaints in the past 10 years. Similar court cases, incidentally, resulted in smaller verdicts, but again in favor of the plaintiffs. For example, Motor City Bagel Shop was sued for a spilled cup of coffee by a drive-through patron, and Starbucks by a customer who spilled coffee on her own ankle.

Are McDonald's, Motor City, and Starbucks at fault in situations such as these? How do quality and ethics enter into these cases?

Discussion Questions

1. Explain how improving quality can lead to reduced costs.
2. As an Internet exercise, determine the Baldrige Award Criteria. See the Web site **www.quality.nist.gov.**
3. Which 3 of Deming's 14 points do you think are most critical to the success of a TQM program? Why?
4. List the seven concepts that are necessary for an effective TQM program. How are these related to Deming's 14 points?
5. Name three of the important people associated with the quality concepts of this chapter. In each case, write a short sentence about each one summarizing their primary contribution to the field of quality management.
6. What are seven tools of TQM?
7. How does fear in the workplace (and in the classroom) inhibit learning?
8. How can a university control the quality of its output (that is, its graduates)?
9. Philip Crosby said that quality is free. Why?
10. List the three concepts central to Taguchi's approach.
11. What is the purpose of using a Pareto chart for a given problem?
12. What are the four broad categories of "causes" to help initially structure an Ishikawa diagram or cause-and-effect diagram?
13. Of the several points where inspection may be necessary, which apply especially well to manufacturing?
14. What roles do operations managers play in addressing the major aspects of service quality?
15. Explain, in your own words, what is meant by *source inspection*.
16. What are 10 determinants of service quality?
17. Name several products that do not require high quality.
18. What does the formula $L = D^2C$ mean?
19. In this chapter, we have suggested that building quality into a process and its people is difficult. Inspections are also difficult. To indicate just how difficult inspections are, count the number of *E*s (both capital *E* and lowercase *e*) in the *OM in Action* box "Richey International's Spies" on page 208 (include the title but not the footnote). How many did you find? If each student does this individually, you are very likely to find a distribution rather than a single number!

Problems

• **6.1** An avant-garde clothing manufacturer runs a series of high-profile, risqué ads on a billboard on Highway 101 and regularly collects protest calls from people who are offended by them. The company has no idea how many people in total see the ad, but it has been collecting statistics on the number of phone calls from irate viewers:

Type	Description	Number of Complaints
R	Offensive racially/ethnically	10
M	Demeaning to men	4
W	Demeaning to women	14
I	Ad is Incomprehensible	6
O	Other	2

a) Depict this data with a Pareto chart. Also depict the cumulative complaint line.
b) What percent of the total complaints can be attributed to the most prevalent complaint?

• **6.2** Develop a scatter diagram for two variables of interest (say pages in the newspaper by day of the week; see example in Figure 6.6b).

• **6.3** Develop a Pareto chart of the following causes of poor grades on an exam:

Reason for Poor Grade	Frequency
Insufficient time to complete	15
Late arrival to exam	7
Difficulty understanding material	25
Insufficient preparation time	2
Studied wrong material	2
Distractions in exam room	9
Calculator batteries died during exam	1
Forgot exam was scheduled	3
Felt ill during exam	4

• **6.4** Develop a histogram of the time it took for you or your friends to receive six recent orders at a fast-food restaurant.

•• **6.5** Theresa Shotwell's restaurant in Tallahassee, Florida, has recorded the following data for eight recent customers:

Customer Number, i	Minutes from Time Food Ordered Until Food Arrived (y_i)	No. of Trips to Kitchen by Waitress (x_i)
1	10.50	4
2	12.75	5
3	9.25	3
4	8.00	2
5	9.75	3
6	11.00	4
7	14.00	6
8	10.75	5

a) Theresa wants you to graph the eight points (x_i, y_i), $i = 1, 2, \ldots 8$. She has been concerned because customers have been waiting too long for their food, and this graph is intended to help her find possible causes of the problem.
b) This is an example of what type of graph?

•• **6.6** Develop a flowchart (as in Figure 6.6[e] and Example 2) showing all the steps involved in planning a party.

•• **6.7** Consider the types of poor driving habits that might occur at a traffic light. Make a list of the 10 you consider most likely to happen. Add the category of "other" to that list.
a) Compose a check sheet (like that in Figure 6.6[a]) to collect the frequency of occurrence of these habits. Using your check sheet, visit a busy traffic light intersection at four different times of the day, with two of these times being during high-traffic periods (rush hour, lunch hour). For 15 to 20 minutes each visit, observe the frequency with which the habits you listed occurred.
b) Construct a Pareto chart showing the relative frequency of occurrence of each habit.

•• **6.8** Draw a fish-bone chart detailing reasons why an airline customer might be dissatisfied.

•• **6.9** Consider the everyday task of getting to work on time or arriving at your first class on time in the morning. Draw a fish-bone chart showing reasons why you might arrive late in the morning.

•• **6.10** Construct a cause-and-effect diagram to reflect "student dissatisfied with university registration process." Use the "four *Ms*" or create your own organizing scheme. Include at least 12 causes.

•• **6.11** Draw a fish-bone chart depicting the reasons that might give rise to an incorrect fee statement at the time you go to pay for your registration at school.

••• **6.12** Mary Beth Marrs, the manager of an apartment complex, feels overwhelmed by the number of complaints she is receiving. Below is the check sheet she has kept for the past 12 weeks. Develop a Pareto chart using this information. What recommendations would you make?

Week	Grounds	Parking/ Drives	Pool	Tenant Issues	Electrical/ Plumbing
1	✓✓✓	✓✓	✓	✓✓✓	
2	✓	✓✓✓	✓✓	✓✓	✓
3	✓✓✓	✓✓✓	✓✓	✓	
4	✓	✓✓✓✓	✓	✓	✓✓
5	✓✓	✓✓✓	✓✓✓✓	✓✓	
6	✓	✓✓✓✓	✓✓		
7		✓✓✓	✓✓	✓✓	
8	✓	✓✓✓✓	✓✓	✓✓✓	✓
9	✓	✓✓	✓		
10	✓	✓✓✓✓	✓✓	✓✓	
11		✓✓✓	✓✓	✓	
12	✓✓	✓✓✓	✓✓✓	✓	

• **6.13** Use Pareto analysis to investigate the following data collected on a printed-circuit-board assembly line:

Defect	Number of Defect Occurrences
Components not adhering	143
Excess adhesive	71
Misplaced transistors	601
Defective board dimension	146
Mounting holes improperly positioned	12
Circuitry problems on final test	90
Wrong component	212

a) Prepare a graph of the data.
b) What conclusions do you reach?

•• **6.14** A list of 16 issues that led to incorrect formulations in Richard Dulski's jam manufacturing unit is provided below:

List of Issues

1. Incorrect measurement	9. Variability
2. Antiquated scales	10. Equipment in disrepair
3. Lack of clear instructions	11. Technician calculation off
4. Damaged raw material	12. Jars mislabeled
5. Operator misreads display	13. Temperature controls off
6. Inadequate cleanup	14. Incorrect weights
7. Incorrect maintenance	15. Priority miscommunication
8. Inadequate flow controls	16. Inadequate instructions

Create a fish-bone diagram and categorize each of these issues correctly, using the "four *M*s" method.

•• **6.15** Develop a flowchart for one of the following:
a) Filling up with gasoline at a self-serve station.
b) Determining your account balance and making a withdrawal at an ATM.
c) Getting a cone of yogurt or ice cream from an ice cream store.

•••• **6.16** Boston Electric Generators has been getting many complaints from its major customer, Home Station, about the quality of its shipments of home generators. Daniel Shimshak, the plant manager, is alarmed that a customer is providing him with the only information the company has on shipment quality. He decides to collect information on defective shipments through a form he has asked his drivers to complete on arrival at customers' stores. The forms for the first 279 shipments have been turned in. They show the following over the past 8 weeks:

		No. of Ship- ments	*Reason for Defective Shipment*			
Week	**No. of Ship- ments**	**with Defects**	**Incorrect Bill of Lading**	**Incorrect Truck- load**	**Damaged Product**	**Trucks Late**
1	23	5	2	2	1	
2	31	8	1	4	1	2
3	28	6	2	3	1	
4	37	11	4	4	1	2
5	35	10	3	4	2	1
6	40	14	5	6	3	
7	41	12	3	5	3	1
8	44	15	4	7	2	2

Even though Daniel increased his capacity by adding more workers to his normal contingent of 30, he knew that for many weeks he exceeded his regular output of 30 shipments per week. A review of his turnover over the past 8 weeks shows the following:

Week	No. of New Hires	No. of Terminations	Total No. of Workers
1	1	0	30
2	2	1	31
3	3	2	32
4	2	0	34
5	2	2	34
6	2	4	32
7	4	1	35
8	3	2	36

a) Develop a scatter diagram using total number of shipments and number of defective shipments. Does there appear to be any relationship?
b) Develop a scatter diagram using the variable "turnover" (number of new hires plus number of terminations) and the number of defective shipments. Does the diagram depict a relationship between the two variables?
c) Develop a Pareto chart for the type of defects that have occurred.
d) Draw a fish-bone chart showing the possible causes of the defective shipments.

••• **6.17** A recent Gallup poll of 519 adults who flew in the past year (published in *The Economist*, June 16, 2007, p. 6) found the following their number 1 complaints about flying: cramped seats (45), cost (16), dislike or fear of flying (57), security measures (119), poor service (12), connecting flight problems (8), overcrowded planes (42), late planes/waits (57), food (7), lost luggage (7), and other (51).
a) What percentage of those surveyed found nothing they disliked?
b) Draw a Pareto chart summarizing these responses. Include the "no complaints" group.
c) Use the "four *M*s" method to create a fish-bone diagram for the 10 specific categories of dislikes (exclude "other" and "no complaints").
d) If you were managing an airline, what two or three specific issues would you tackle to improve customer service? Why?

► **Refer to myomlab for these additional homework problems: 6.18–6.21**

Case Studies

► Southwestern University: (C)*

The popularity of Southwestern University's football program under its new coach, Bo Pitterno, surged in each of the 5 years since his arrival at the Stephenville, Texas, college. (See Southwestern University: (A) in Chapter 3 and (B) in Chapter 4.) With a football stadium close to maxing out at 54,000 seats and a vocal coach pushing for a new stadium, SWU president Joel Wisner faced some difficult decisions. After a phenomenal upset victory over its archrival, the University of Texas, at the homecoming game in the fall, Dr. Wisner was not as happy as one would think. Instead of ecstatic alumni, students, and faculty, all Wisner heard were complaints. "The lines at the concession stands were too long"; "Parking was harder to find and farther away than in the old days" (that is, before the team won regularly); "Seats weren't comfortable"; "Traffic was backed up halfway to Dallas"; and on and on. "A college president just can't win," muttered Wisner to himself.

At his staff meeting the following Monday, Wisner turned to his VP of administration, Leslie Gardner. "I wish you would take care of these football complaints, Leslie," he said. "See what the *real* problems are and let me know how you've resolved them." Gardner wasn't surprised at the request. "I've already got a handle on it, Joel," she replied. "We've been randomly surveying 50 fans per game for the past year to see what's on their minds. It's all part of my campuswide TQM effort. Let me tally things up and I'll get back to you in a week."

When she returned to her office, Gardner pulled out the file her assistant had compiled (see Table 6.6). "There's a lot of information here," she thought.

▼ TABLE 6.6 Fan Satisfaction Survey Results (N = 250)

		Overall Grade				
		A	**B**	**C**	**D**	**E**
Game Day	A. Parking	90	105	45	5	5
	B. Traffic	50	85	48	52	15
	C. Seating	45	30	115	35	25
	D. Entertainment	160	35	26	10	19
	E. Printed Program	66	34	98	22	30
Tickets	A. Pricing	105	104	16	15	10
	B. Season Ticket Plans	75	80	54	41	0
Concessions	A. Prices	16	116	58	58	2
	B. Selection of Foods	155	60	24	11	0
	C. Speed of Service	35	45	46	48	76

Respondents	
Alumnus	113
Student	83
Faculty/Staff	16
None of the above	38

Open-Ended Comments on Survey Cards:

Parking a mess
Add a skybox
Get better cheerleaders
Double the parking attendants
Everything is okay
Too crowded
Seats too narrow
Great food
Joe P. for President!
I smelled drugs being smoked
Stadium is ancient
Seats are like rocks
Not enough cops for traffic
Game starts too late
Hire more traffic cops
Need new band
Great!
More hot dog stands
Seats are all metal
Need skyboxes
Seats stink
Go SWU!
Lines are awful
Seats are uncomfortable
I will pay more for better view
Get a new stadium
Student dress code needed
I want cushioned seats
Not enough police
Students too rowdy
Parking terrible
Toilets weren't clean
Not enough handicap spots in lot
Well done, SWU
Put in bigger seats
Friendly ushers
Need better seats
Expand parking lots
Hate the bleacher seats
Hot dogs cold
$3 for a coffee? No way!
Get some skyboxes
Love the new uniforms
Took an hour to park
Coach is terrific
More water fountains
Better seats
Seats not comfy
Bigger parking lot
I'm too old for bench seats
Cold coffee served at game
My company will buy a skybox—build it!
Programs overpriced
Want softer seats
Beat those Longhorns!
I'll pay for a skybox
Seats too small
Band was terrific
Love Pitterno
Everything is great
Build new stadium
Move games to Dallas
No complaints
Dirty bathroom

Discussion Questions

1. Using at least two different quality tools, analyze the data and present your conclusions.
2. How could the survey have been more useful?
3. What is the next step?

*This integrated case study runs throughout the text. Other issues facing Southwestern's football stadium include: (A) Managing the renovation project (Chapter 3); (B) Forecasting game attendance (Chapter 4); (D) Break-even analysis of food services (Supplement 7 Web site); (E) Locating the new stadium (Chapter 8 Web site); (F) Inventory planning of football programs (Chapter 12 Web site); and (G) Scheduling of campus security officers/staff for game days (Chapter 13).

► The Culture of Quality at Arnold Palmer Hospital

Video Case

Founded in 1989, Arnold Palmer Hospital is one of the largest hospitals for women and children in the U.S., with 431 beds in two facilities totaling 676,000 square feet. Located in downtown Orlando, Florida, and named after its famed golf benefactor, the hospital, with more than 2,000 employees serves an 18-county area in central Florida and is the only Level 1 trauma center for children in that region. Arnold Palmer Hospital provides a broad range of medical services including neonatal and pediatric intensive care, pediatric oncology and cardiology, care for high-risk pregnancies, and maternal intensive care.

The Issue of Assessing Quality Health Care

Quality health care is a goal all hospitals profess, but Arnold Palmer Hospital has actually developed comprehensive and scientific means of asking customers to judge the quality of care they receive. Participating in a national benchmark comparison against other hospitals, Arnold Palmer Hospital consistently scores in the top 10% in overall patient satisfaction. Executive Director Kathy Swanson states, "Hospitals in this area will be distinguished largely on the basis of their customer satisfaction. We must have accurate information about how our patients and their families judge the quality of our care, so I follow the questionnaire results daily. The in-depth survey helps me and others on my team to gain quick knowledge from patient feedback." Arnold Palmer Hospital employees are empowered to provide gifts in value up to $200 to patients who find reason to complain about any hospital service such as food, courtesy, responsiveness, or cleanliness.

Swanson doesn't focus just on the customer surveys, which are mailed to patients one week after discharge, but also on a variety of internal measures. These measures usually start at the grassroots level, where the staff sees a problem and develops ways to track performance. The hospital's longstanding philosophy supports the concept that each patient is important and respected as a person. That patient has the right to comprehensive, compassionate family-centered health care provided by a knowledgeable physician-directed team.

Some of the measures Swanson carefully monitors for continuous improvement are morbidity, infection rates, readmission rates, costs per case, and length of stays. The tools she uses daily include Pareto charts, flowcharts and process charts, in addition to benchmarking against hospitals both nationally and in the southeast region.

The result of all of these efforts has been a quality culture as manifested in Arnold Palmer's high ranking in patient satisfaction and one of the highest survival rates of critically ill babies.

Discussion Questions*

1. Why is it important for Arnold Palmer Hospital to get a patient's assessment of health care quality? Does the patient have the expertise to judge the health care she receives?
2. How would you build a culture of quality in an organization, such as Arnold Palmer Hospital?
3. What techniques does Arnold Palmer Hospital practice in its drive for quality and continuous improvement?
4. Develop a fish-bone diagram illustrating the quality variables for a patient who just gave birth at Arnold Palmer Hospital (or any other hospital).

*You may wish to view the video that accompanies this case before answering these questions.

► Quality at the Ritz-Carlton Hotel Company

Video Case

Ritz-Carlton. The name alone evokes images of luxury and quality. As the first hotel company to win the Malcolm Baldrige National Quality Award, the Ritz treats quality as if it is the heartbeat of the company. This means a daily commitment to meeting customer expectations and making sure that each hotel is free of any deficiency.

In the hotel industry, quality can be hard to quantify. Guests do not purchase a product when they stay at the Ritz: They buy an experience. Thus, creating the right combination of elements to make the experience stand out is the challenge and goal of every employee, from maintenance to management.

Before applying for the Baldrige Award, company management undertook a rigorous self-examination of its operations in an attempt to measure and quantify quality. Nineteen processes were studied, including room service delivery, guest reservation and registration, message delivery, and breakfast service. This period of self-study included statistical measurement of process work flows and cycle times for areas ranging from room service delivery times and reservations to valet parking and housekeeping efficiency. The results were used to develop performance benchmarks against which future activity could be measured.

With specific, quantifiable targets in place, Ritz-Carlton managers and employees now focus on continuous improvement. The goal is 100% customer satisfaction: If a guest's experience does not meet expectations, the Ritz-Carlton risks losing that guest to competition.

One way the company has put more meaning behind its quality efforts is to organize its employees into "self-directed" work teams. Employee teams determine work scheduling, what work needs to be done, and what to do about quality problems in their own areas. In order that they can see the relationship of their specific area to the overall goals, employees are also given the opportunity to take additional training in hotel operations. Ritz-Carlton believes that a more educated and informed employee is in a better position to make decisions in the best interest of the organization.

Discussion Questions*

1. In what ways could the Ritz-Carlton monitor its success in achieving quality?
2. Many companies say that their goal is to provide quality products or services. What actions might you expect from a company that intends quality to be more than a slogan or buzzword?
3. Why might it cost the Ritz-Carlton less to "do things right" the first time?
4. How could control charts, Pareto diagrams, and cause-and-effect diagrams be used to identify quality problems at a hotel?
5. What are some nonfinancial measures of customer satisfaction that might be used by the Ritz-Carlton?

*You may wish to view the video that accompanies this case before addressing these questions.

Source: Adapted from C. T. Horngren, S. M. Datar, and G. Foster, *Cost Accounting*, 13th ed. (Upper Saddle River, NJ: Prentice Hall, 2009).

Additional Case Study: Visit **www.myomlab.com** or **www.pearsonhighered.com/heizer** for this free case study:
Westover Electrical, Inc.: This electric motor manufacturer has a large log of defects in its wiring process.

Bibliography

Besterfield, Dale H. *Quality Control*, 8th ed. Upper Saddle River, NJ: Prentice Hall, 2009.

Brown, Mark G. *Baldrige Award Winning Quality*, 19th ed. University Park, IL: Productivity Press, 2010.

Crosby, P. B. *Quality Is Still Free*. New York: McGraw-Hill, 1996.

Evans, J. R., and W. M. Lindsay. *Managing for Quality and Performance Excellence*. 7th ed. Mason, OH: Thompson-Southwestern, 2008.

Feigenbaum, A. V. "Raising the Bar." *Quality Progress* 41, no. 7 (July 2008): 22–28.

Gitlow, Howard S. *A Guide to Lean Six Sigma Management Skills*. University Park, IL: Productivity Press, 2009.

Gonzalez-Benito, J., and O. Gonzalez-Benito. "Operations Management Practices Linked to the Adoption of ISO 14001." *International Journal of Production Economics* 113, no. 1 (May 2008): 60.

Gryna, F. M., R. C. H. Chua, and J. A. DeFeo. *Juran's Quality Planning and Analysis for Enterprise Quality*, 5th ed. New York: McGraw-Hill, 2007.

Harrington, D. R., M. Khanna, and G. Deltas. "Striving to Be Green: The Adoption of Total Quality Environmental Management." *Applied Economics* 40, no. 23 (December 2008): 2995.

Mitra, Amit. *Fundamentals of Quality Control and Improvement.* New York: Wiley, 2009.

Pande, P. S., R. P. Neuman, R. R. Cavanagh. *What Is Design for Six Sigma?* New York: McGraw-Hill, 2005.

Schroeder, Roger G., et al. "Six Sigma: Definition and Underlying Theory." *Journal of Operations Management* 26, no. 4 (2008): 536–554.

Soltani, E., P. Lai, and P. Phillips. "A New Look at Factors Influencing Total Quality Management Failure." *New Technology, Work, and Employment* 23, no. 1–2 (March 2008): 125.

Stewart, D. M. "Piecing Together Service Quality: A Framework for Robust Service." *Production and Operations Management* (Summer 2003): 246–265.

Summers, Donna. *Quality Management,* 2nd ed. Upper Saddle River, NJ: Prentice Hall, 2009.

Chapter 6 *Rapid* Review

Main Heading	Review Material	PEARSON myomlab
QUALITY AND STRATEGY (p. 190)	Managing quality helps build successful strategies of differentiation, low cost, and *response* Two ways that quality improves profitability are: • *Sales gains* via improved response, price flexibility, increased market share, and/or improved reputation • *Reduced costs* via increased productivity, lower rework and scrap costs, and/or lower warranty costs	**VIDEO 6.1** The Culture and Quality at Arnold Palmer Hospital
DEFINING QUALITY (pp. 190–193)	An operations manager's objective is to build a total quality management system that identifies and satisfies customer needs. ■ **Quality**—The ability of a product or service to meet customer needs. The American Society for Quality (ASQ) defines quality as "the totality of features and characteristics of a product or service that bears on its ability to satisfy stated or implied needs." The two most well-known quality awards are: • *U.S.*: Malcolm Baldrige National Quality Award, named after a former secretary of commerce • *Japan*: Deming Prize, named after an American, Dr. W. Edwards Deming ■ **Cost of quality (COQ)**—The cost of doing things wrong; that is, the price of non-conformance. The four major categories of costs associated with quality are: *Prevention costs, Appraisal costs, Internal failure*, and *External costs.* Four leaders in the field of quality management are W. Edwards Deming, Joseph M. Juran, Armand Feigenbaum, and Philip B. Crosby.	
INTERNATIONAL QUALITY STANDARDS (pp. 193–194)	■ **ISO 9000**—A set of quality standards developed by the International Organization for Standardization (ISO). ISO 9000 is the only quality standard with international recognition. To do business globally, being listed in the ISO directory is critical. ■ **ISO 14000**—A series of environmental management standards established by the ISO. ISO 14000 contains five core elements: (1) environmental management, (2) auditing, (3) performance evaluation, (4) labeling, and (5) life cycle assessment. As a follow-on to ISO 14000, ISO 24700 reflects the business world's current approach to reuse recovered components from many products.	Problem: 6.17
TOTAL QUALITY MANAGEMENT (pp. 194–200)	■ **Total quality management (TQM)**—Management of an entire organization so that it excels in all aspects of products and services that are important to the customer. Seven concepts for an effective TQM program are (1) continuous improvement, (2) Six Sigma, (3) employee empowerment, (4) benchmarking, (5) just-in-time (JIT), (6) Taguchi concepts, and (7) knowledge of TQM tools. ■ **PDCA**—A continuous improvement model that involves four stages: plan, do, check, and act. The Japanese use the word *kaizen* to describe the ongoing process of unending improvement—the setting and achieving of ever-higher goals. ■ **Six Sigma**—A program to save time, improve quality, and lower costs. In a statistical sense, Six Sigma describes a process, product, or service with an extremely high capability—99.9997% accuracy, or 3.4 defects per million. ■ **Employee empowerment**—Enlarging employee jobs so that the added responsibility and authority is moved to the lowest level possible in the organization. Business literature suggests that some 85% of quality problems have to do with materials and processes, not with employee performance. ■ **Quality circle**—A group of employees meeting regularly with a facilitator to solve work-related problems in their work area. ■ **Benchmarking**—Selecting a demonstrated standard of performance that represents the very best performance for a process or an activity. The philosophy behind just-in-time (JIT) involves continuing improvement and enforced problem solving. JIT systems are designed to produce or deliver goods just as they are needed. ■ **Quality robust**—Products that are consistently built to meet customer needs, in spite of adverse conditions in the production process.	Problems: 6.1, 6.3, 6.5, 6.13, 6.14, 6.16, and 6.17

Main Heading	Review Material	myomlab
	■ **Quality loss function (QLF)**—A mathematical function that identifies all costs connected with poor quality and shows how these costs increase as product quality moves from what the customer wants: $L = D^2C$. ■ **Target-oriented quality**—A philosophy of continuous improvement to bring the product exactly on target.	
TOOLS OF TQM (pp. 200–204)	TQM tools that generate ideas include the *check sheet* (organized method of recording data), *scatter diagram* (graph of the value of one variable vs. another variable), and *cause-and-effect diagram*. Tools for organizing the data are the *Pareto chart* and *flowchart*. Tools for identifying problems are the *histogram* (distribution showing the frequency of occurrences of a variable) and *statistical process control chart*. ■ **Cause-and-effect diagram**—A schematic technique used to discover possible locations of quality problems. (Also called an Ishikawa diagram or a fish-bone chart.) The 4 *Ms* (material, machinery/equipment, manpower, and methods) may be broad "causes." ■ **Pareto chart**—A graphic that identifies the few critical items as opposed to many less important ones. ■ **Flowchart**—A block diagram that graphically describes a process or system. ■ **Statistical process control (SPC)**—A process used to monitor standards, make measurements, and take corrective action as a product or service is being produced. ■ **Control chart**—A graphic presentation of process data over time, with predetermined control limits.	**ACTIVE MODEL 6.1**
THE ROLE OF INSPECTION (pp. 204–206)	■ **Inspection—**A means of ensuring that an operation is producing at the quality level expected. ■ **Source inspection—**Controlling or monitoring at the point of production or purchase: at the source. ■ **Poka-yoke—**Literally translated, "foolproof"; it has come to mean a device or technique that ensures the production of a good unit every time. ■ **Attribute inspection—**An inspection that classifies items as being either good or defective. ■ **Variable inspection—**Classifications of inspected items as falling on a continuum scale, such as dimension, size, or strength.	
TQM IN SERVICES (pp. 206–208)	Determinants of service quality: reliability, responsiveness, competence, access, courtesy, communication, credibility, security, understanding/knowing the customer, and tangibles. ■ **Service recovery—**Training and empowering frontline workers to solve a problem immediately.	**VIDEO 6.2** TQM at Ritz-Carlton Hotels

Self Test

■ **Before taking the self-test,** refer to the learning objectives listed at the beginning of the chapter and the key terms listed at the end of the chapter.

LO1. In this chapter, *quality* is defined as:
- **a)** the degree of excellence at an acceptable price and the control of variability at an acceptable cost.
- **b)** how well a product fits patterns of consumer preferences.
- **c)** the totality of features and characteristics of a product or service that bears on its ability to satisfy stated or implied needs.
- **d)** being impossible to define, but you know what it is.

LO2. ISO 14000 is an international standard that addresses _______.

LO3. If 1 million passengers pass through the Jacksonville Airport with checked baggage each year, a successful Six Sigma program for baggage handling would result in how many passengers with misplaced luggage?
- **a)** 3.4 **b)** 6.0
- **c)** 34 **d)** 2,700
- **e)** 6 times the monthly standard deviation of passengers

LO4. The process of identifying other organizations that are best at some facet of your operations and then modeling your organization after them is known as:
- **a)** continuous improvement. **b)** employee empowerment.
- **c)** benchmarking. **d)** copycatting.
- **e)** patent infringement.

LO5. The Taguchi method includes all except which of the following major concepts?
- **a)** Employee involvement
- **b)** Remove the effects of adverse conditions
- **c)** Quality loss function
- **d)** Target specifications

LO6. The seven tools of total quality management are _______, _______, _______, _______, _______, _______, and _______.

Answers: LO1. c; LO2. environmental management; LO3. a; LO4. c; LO5. a; LO6. check sheets, scatter diagrams, cause-and-effect diagrams, Pareto charts, flowcharts, histograms, SPC charts.

Statistical Process Control

Supplement Outline

BetzDearborn, A Division of Hercules Incorporated, is headquartered in Trevose, Pennsylvania. It is a global supplier of specialty chemicals for the treatment of industrial water, wastewater, and process systems. The company uses statistical process control to monitor the performance of treatment programs in a wide variety of industries throughout the world. BetzDearborn's quality assurance laboratory (shown here) also uses statistical sampling techniques to monitor manufacturing processes at all of the company's production plants.

Supplement 6 **Learning Objectives**

AUTHOR COMMENT
In this supplement we show you how to set up a control chart.

STATISTICAL PROCESS CONTROL (SPC)

Statistical process control (SPC)
A process used to monitor standards by taking measurements and corrective action as a product or service is being produced.

Control chart
A graphical presentation of process data over time.

In this supplement, we address statistical process control—the same techniques used at BetzDearborn, at IBM, at GE, and at Motorola to achieve quality standards. We also introduce acceptance sampling. **Statistical process control** is the application of statistical techniques to the control of processes. *Acceptance sampling* is used to determine acceptance or rejection of material evaluated by a sample.

Statistical process control (SPC) is a statistical technique that is widely used to ensure that processes meet standards. All processes are subject to a certain degree of variability. While studying process data in the 1920s, Walter Shewhart of Bell Laboratories made the distinction between the common and special causes of variation. Many people now refer to these variations as *natural* and *assignable* causes. He developed a simple but powerful tool to separate the two—the **control chart**.

We use statistical process control to measure performance of a process. A process is said to be operating *in statistical control* when the only source of variation is common (natural) causes. The process must first be brought into statistical control by detecting and eliminating special (assignable) causes of variation.[1] Then its performance is predictable, and its ability to meet customer expectations can be assessed. The *objective* of a process control system is to *provide a statistical signal when assignable causes of variation are present*. Such a signal can quicken appropriate action to eliminate assignable causes.

[1]Removing assignable causes is work. Quality expert W. Edwards Deming observed that a state of statistical control is not a natural state for a manufacturing process. Deming instead viewed it as an achievement, arrived at by elimination, one by one, by determined effort, of special causes of excessive variation. See J. R. Thompson and J. Koronacki, *Statistical Process Control, The Deming Paradigm and Beyond*. Boca Raton, FL: Chapman and Hall, 2002.

Natural Variations Natural variations affect almost every production process and are to be expected. **Natural variations** are the many sources of variation that occur within a process that is in statistical control. Natural variations behave like a constant system of chance causes. Although individual values are all different, as a group they form a pattern that can be described as a *distribution*. When these distributions are *normal*, they are characterized by two parameters:

Natural variations
Variability that affects every production process to some degree and is to be expected; also known as common cause.

- Mean, μ (the measure of central tendency—in this case, the average value)
- Standard deviation, σ (the measure of dispersion)

As long as the distribution (output measurements) remains within specified limits, the process is said to be "in control," and natural variations are tolerated.

Assignable Variations **Assignable variation** in a process can be traced to a specific reason. Factors such as machine wear, misadjusted equipment, fatigued or untrained workers, or new batches of raw material are all potential sources of assignable variations.

Assignable variation
Variation in a production process that can be traced to specific causes.

Natural and assignable variations distinguish two tasks for the operations manager. The first is to *ensure that the process is capable* of operating under control with only natural variation. The second is, of course, to *identify and eliminate assignable variations* so that the processes will remain under control.

Samples Because of natural and assignable variation, statistical process control uses averages of small samples (often of four to eight items) as opposed to data on individual parts. Individual pieces tend to be too erratic to make trends quickly visible.

Figure S6.1 provides a detailed look at the important steps in determining process variation. The horizontal scale can be weight (as in the number of ounces in boxes of cereal) or length (as in fence posts) or any physical measure. The vertical scale is frequency. The samples of five boxes of cereal in Figure S6.1 **(a)** are weighed; **(b)** form a distribution, and **(c)** can vary. The distributions formed in **(b)** and **(c)** will fall in a predictable pattern **(d)** if only natural variation is present. If assignable causes of variation are present, then we can expect either the mean to vary or the dispersion to vary, as is the case in **(e)**.

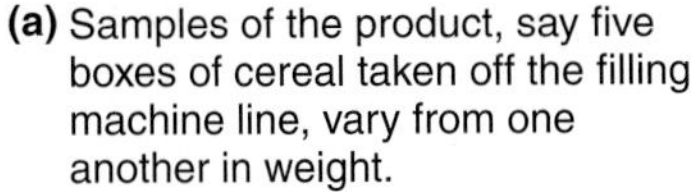

(a) Samples of the product, say five boxes of cereal taken off the filling machine line, vary from one another in weight.

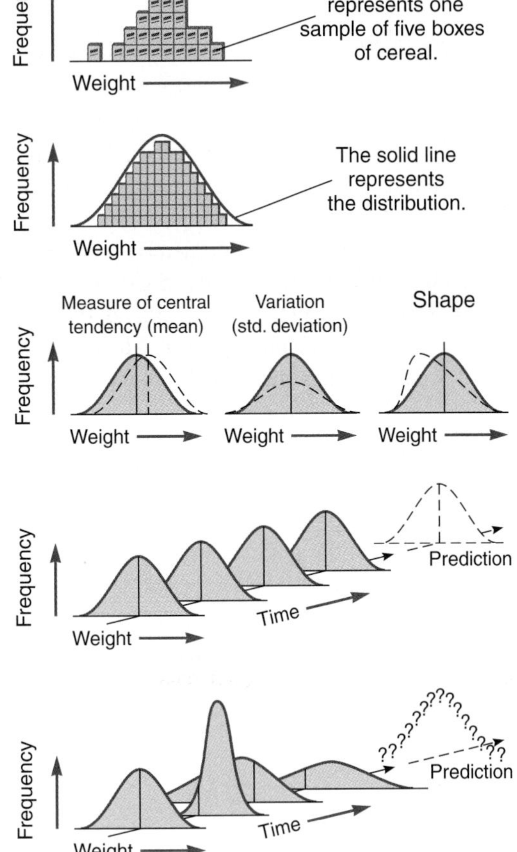

◄ **FIGURE S6.1 Natural and Assignable Variation**

▶ **FIGURE S6.2**
Process Control: Three Types of Process Outputs

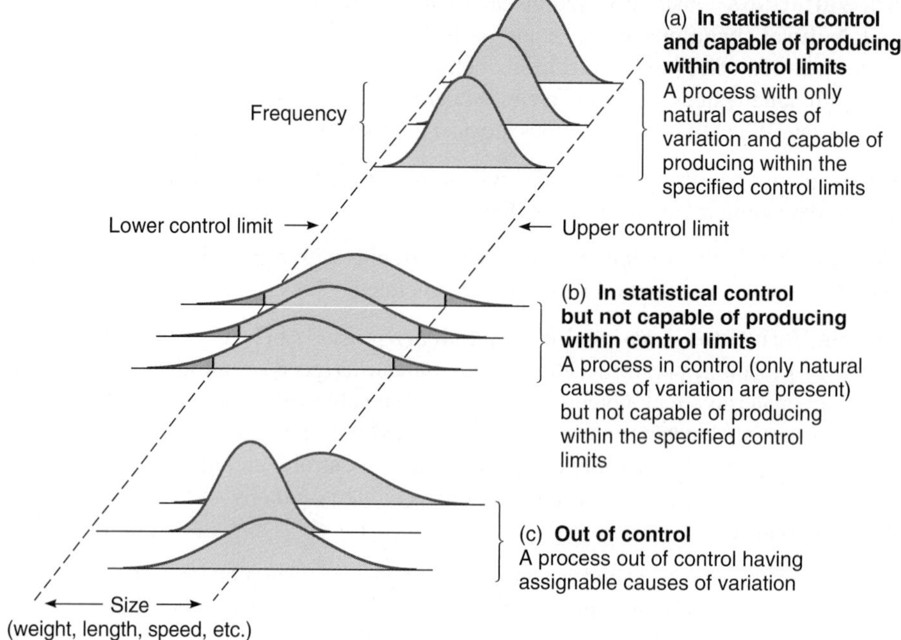
Frequency
(a) In statistical control and capable of producing within control limits
A process with only natural causes of variation and capable of producing within the specified control limits
Lower control limit
Upper control limit
(b) In statistical control but not capable of producing within control limits
A process in control (only natural causes of variation are present) but not capable of producing within the specified control limits
(c) Out of control
A process out of control having assignable causes of variation
Size
(weight, length, speed, etc.)

LO1: Explain the purpose of a control chart

Control Charts The process of building control charts is based on the concepts presented in Figure S6.2. This figure shows three distributions that are the result of outputs from three types of processes. We plot small samples and then examine characteristics of the resulting data to see if the process is within "control limits." The purpose of control charts is to help distinguish between natural variations and variations due to assignable causes. As seen in Figure S6.2, a process is **(a)** in control *and the process is capable of producing within established control limits*, **(b)** in control *but the process is not capable of producing within established limits*, or **(c)** out of control. We now look at ways to build control charts that help the operations manager keep a process under control.

Control Charts for Variables

$\bar{x}$-chart
A quality control chart for variables that indicates when changes occur in the central tendency of a production process.

***R*-chart**
A control chart that tracks the "range" within a sample; it indicates that a gain or loss in uniformity has occurred in dispersion of a production process.

The variables of interest here are those that have continuous dimensions. They have an infinite number of possibilities. Examples are weight, speed, length, or strength. Control charts for the mean, $\bar{x}$ or *x*-bar, and the range, R, are used to monitor processes that have continuous dimensions. The **$\bar{x}$-chart** tells us whether changes have occurred in the central tendency (the mean, in this case) of a process. These changes might be due to such factors as tool wear, a gradual increase in temperature, a different method used on the second shift, or new and stronger materials. The ***R*-chart** values indicate that a gain or loss in dispersion has occurred. Such a change may be due to worn bearings, a loose tool, an erratic flow of lubricants to a machine, or to sloppiness on the part of a machine operator. The two types of charts go hand in hand when monitoring variables because they measure the two critical parameters: central tendency and dispersion.

The Central Limit Theorem

Central limit theorem
The theoretical foundation for $\bar{x}$-charts, which states that regardless of the distribution of the population of all parts or services, the distribution of $\bar{x}$s tends to follow a normal curve as the number of samples increases.

The theoretical foundation for $\bar{x}$-charts is the **central limit theorem**. This theorem states that regardless of the distribution of the population, the distribution of $\bar{x}$s (each of which is a mean of a sample drawn from the population) will tend to follow a normal curve as the number of samples increases. Fortunately, even if the sample (n) is fairly small (say, 4 or 5), the distributions of the averages will still roughly follow a normal curve. The theorem also states that: (1) the mean of the distribution of the $\bar{x}$s (called $\bar{\bar{x}}$) will equal the mean of the overall population (called μ); and (2) the standard deviation of the *sampling distribution*, $\sigma_{\bar{x}}$, will be the *population standard deviation*, divided by the square root of the sample size, n. In other words:[2]

$$\bar{\bar{x}} = \mu \qquad \textbf{(S6-1)}$$

[2]The standard deviation is easily calculated as $\sigma = \sqrt{\frac{\sum_{i=1}^{n}(x_i - \bar{x})^2}{n-1}}$.

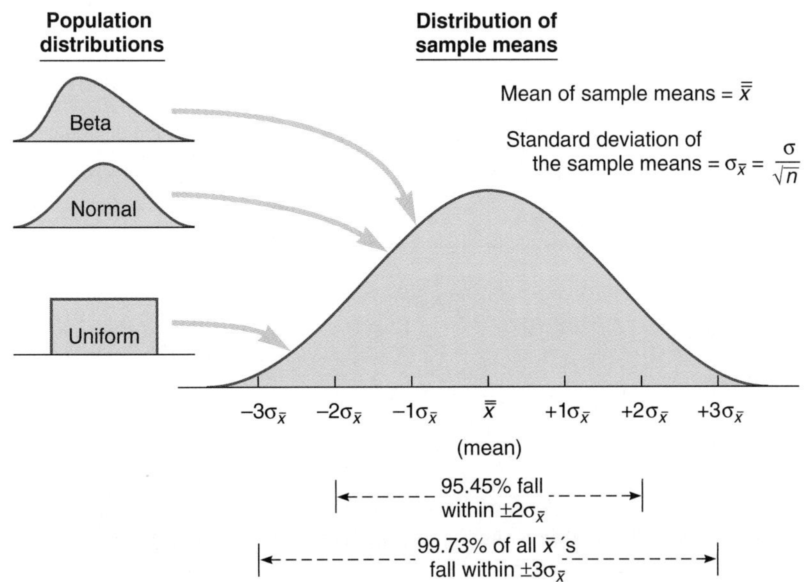

◀ **FIGURE S6.3**
The Relationship between Population and Sampling Distributions
Even though the population distributions will differ (e.g., normal, beta, uniform), each with its own mean (μ) and standard deviation (σ), the distribution of sample means always approaches a normal distribution.

and

$$\sigma_{\bar{x}} = \frac{\sigma}{\sqrt{n}} \quad \text{(S6-2)}$$

LO2: Explain the role of the central limit theorem in SPC

Figure S6.3 shows three possible population distributions, each with its own mean, μ, and standard deviation, σ. If a series of random samples ($\bar{x}_1$, $\bar{x}_2$, $\bar{x}_3$, $\bar{x}_4$, and so on), each of size n, is drawn from any population distribution (which could be normal, beta, uniform, and so on), the resulting distribution of $\bar{x}_i$s will appear as they do in Figure S6.3.

Moreover, the sampling distribution, as is shown in Figure S6.4, will have less variability than the process distribution. Because the sampling distribution is normal, we can state that:

- 95.45% of the time, the sample averages will fall within $\pm 2\sigma_{\bar{x}}$ if the process has only natural variations.
- 99.73% of the time, the sample averages will fall within $\pm 3\sigma_{\bar{x}}$ if the process has only natural variations.

If a point on the control chart falls outside of the $\pm 3\sigma_{\bar{x}}$ control limits, then we are 99.73% sure the process has changed. This is the theory behind control charts.

Setting Mean Chart Limits ($\bar{x}$-Charts)

If we know, through past data, the standard deviation of the process population, σ, we can set upper and lower control limits by using these formulas:

$$\text{Upper control limit (UCL)} = \bar{\bar{x}} + z\sigma_{\bar{x}} \quad \text{(S6-3)}$$

$$\text{Lower control limit (LCL)} = \bar{\bar{x}} - z\sigma_{\bar{x}} \quad \text{(S6-4)}$$

LO3: Build $\bar{x}$-charts and *R*-charts

where $\bar{\bar{x}}$ = mean of the sample means or a target value set for the process
z = number of normal standard deviations (2 for 95.45% confidence, 3 for 99.73%)
$\sigma_{\bar{x}}$ = standard deviation of the sample means $= \sigma/\sqrt{n}$
σ = population (process) standard deviation
n = sample size

Example S1 shows how to set control limits for sample means using standard deviations.

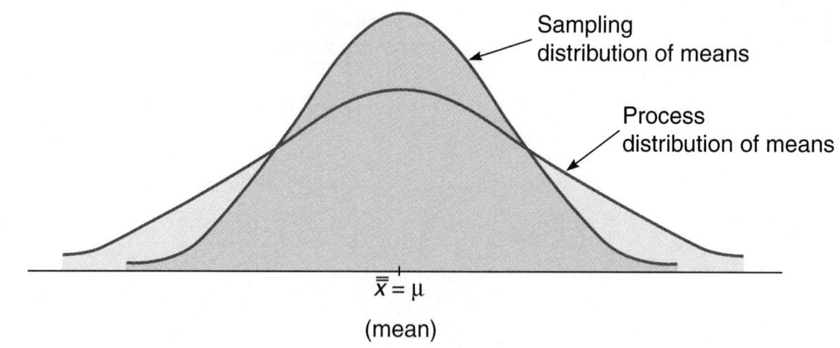

▶ FIGURE S6.4
The Sampling Distribution of Means Is Normal and Has Less Variability Than the Process Distribution

In this figure, the process distribution from which the sample was drawn was also normal, but it could have been any distribution.

EXAMPLE S1 ▶

Setting control limits using samples

The weights of boxes of Oat Flakes within a large production lot are sampled each hour. Managers want to set control limits that include 99.73% of the sample means.

APPROACH ▶ Randomly select and weigh nine ($n = 9$) boxes each hour. Then find the overall mean and use Equations (S6–3) and (S6–4) to compute the control limits. Here are the nine boxes chosen for Hour 1:

AUTHOR COMMENT If you want to see an example of such variability in your supermarket, go to the soft drink section and line up a few 2-liter bottles of Coke, Pepsi, or any other brand. Notice that the liquids are not the same measurement.

Oat Flakes 15 oz.
Oat Flakes 17 oz.
Oat Flakes 16 oz.

SOLUTION ▶

$$\text{The average weight in the first sample} = \frac{17 + 13 + 16 + 18 + 17 + 16 + 15 + 17 + 16}{9} = 16.1 \text{ ounces.}$$

Also, the *population* standard deviation (σ) is known to be 1 ounce. We do not show each of the boxes randomly selected in hours 2 through 12, but here are all 12 hourly samples:

	Weight of Sample		*Weight of Sample*		*Weight of Sample*
Hour	**(Avg. of 9 Boxes)**	**Hour**	**(Avg. of 9 Boxes)**	**Hour**	**(Avg. of 9 Boxes)**
1	16.1	5	16.5	9	16.3
2	16.8	6	16.4	10	14.8
3	15.5	7	15.2	11	14.2
4	16.5	8	16.4	12	17.3

The average mean of the 12 samples is calculated to be exactly 16 ounces. We therefore have $\bar{\bar{x}} = 16$ ounces, $\sigma = 1$ ounce, $n = 9$, and $z = 3$. The control limits are:

$$UCL_{\bar{x}} = \bar{\bar{x}} + z\sigma_{\bar{x}} = 16 + 3\left(\frac{1}{\sqrt{9}}\right) = 16 + 3\left(\frac{1}{3}\right) = 17 \text{ ounces}$$

$$LCL_{\bar{x}} = \bar{\bar{x}} - z\sigma_{\bar{x}} = 16 - 3\left(\frac{1}{\sqrt{9}}\right) = 16 - 3\left(\frac{1}{3}\right) = 15 \text{ ounces}$$

The 12 samples are then plotted on the following control chart:

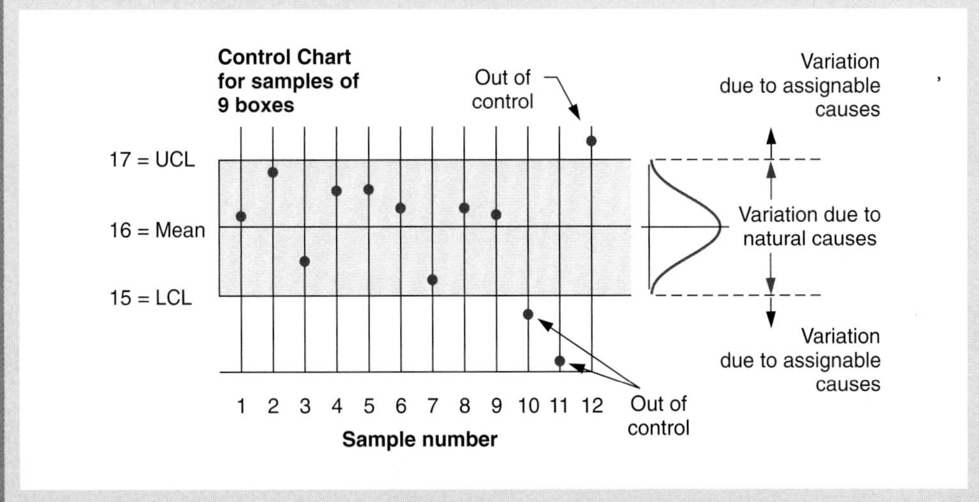

INSIGHT ▶ Because the means of recent sample averages fall outside the upper and lower control limits of 17 and 15, we can conclude that the process is becoming erratic and is *not* in control.

LEARNING EXERCISE ▶ If Oat Flakes's population standard deviation (σ) is 2 (instead of 1), what is your conclusion? [Answer: LCL = 14, UCL = 18; the process would be in control.]

RELATED PROBLEMS ▶ S6.1, S6.2, S6.4, S6.8, S6.10a,b

EXCEL OM Data File **Ch06SExS1.xls** can be found at **www.pearsonhighered.com/heizer**.

Because process standard deviations are either not available or difficult to compute, we usually calculate control limits based on the average *range* values rather than on standard deviations. Table S6.1 provides the necessary conversion for us to do so. The *range* is defined as the difference between the largest and smallest items in one sample. For example, the heaviest box of Oat Flakes in Hour 1 of Example S1 was 18 ounces and the lightest was 13 ounces, so the range for that hour is 5 ounces. We use Table S6.1 and the equations:

$$UCL_{\bar{x}} = \bar{\bar{x}} + A_2\bar{R} \quad \text{(S6-5)}$$

and:

$$LCL_{\bar{x}} = \bar{\bar{x}} - A_2\bar{R} \quad \text{(S6-6)}$$

where $\bar{R}$ = average range of the samples
A_2 = value found in Table S6.1
$\bar{\bar{x}}$ = mean of the sample means

Example S2 shows how to set control limits for sample means by using Table S6.1 and the average range.

◀ TABLE S6.1
Factors for Computing Control Chart Limits (3 sigma)

Sample Size, n	Mean Factor, A_2	Upper Range, D_4	Lower Range, D_3
2	1.880	3.268	0
3	1.023	2.574	0
4	.729	2.282	0
5	.577	2.115	0
6	.483	2.004	0
7	.419	1.924	0.076
8	.373	1.864	0.136
9	.337	1.816	0.184
10	.308	1.777	0.223
12	.266	1.716	0.284

Source: Reprinted by permission of American Society for Testing Materials. Copyright 1951. Taken from Special Technical Publication 15–C, "Quality Control of Materials," pp. 63 and 72. Copyright ASTM INTERNATIONAL. Reprinted with permission.

EXAMPLE S2 ▶

Setting mean limits using table values

Super Cola bottles soft drinks labeled "net weight 12 ounces." Indeed, an overall process average of 12 ounces has been found by taking many samples, in which each sample contained 5 bottles. The average range of the process is .25 ounce. The OM team wants to determine the upper and lower control limits for averages in this process.

APPROACH ▶ Super Cola applies Equations (S6-5) and (S6-6) and uses the A_2 column of Table S6.1.

SOLUTION ▶ Looking in Table S6.1 for a sample size of 5 in the mean factor A_2 column, we find the value .577. Thus, the upper and lower control chart limits are:

$$\begin{aligned} UCL_{\bar{x}} &= \bar{\bar{x}} + A_2\bar{R} \\ &= 12 + (.577)(.25) \\ &= 12 + .144 \\ &= 12.144 \text{ ounces} \\ LCL_{\bar{x}} &= \bar{\bar{x}} - A_2\bar{R} \\ &= 12 - .144 \\ &= 11.856 \text{ ounces} \end{aligned}$$

INSIGHT ▶ The advantage of using this range approach, instead of the standard deviation, is that it is easy to apply and may be less confusing.

LEARNING EXERCISE ▶ If the sample size was $n = 4$ and the average range = .20 ounces, what are the revised $UCL_{\bar{x}}$ and $LCL_{\bar{x}}$? [Answer: 12.146, 11.854.]

RELATED PROBLEMS ▶ S6.3a, S6.5, S6.6, S6.7, S6.9, S6.10b,c,d S6.11, S6.34

EXCEL OM Data File **Ch06SExS2.xls** can be found at **www.pearsonhighered.com/heizer**.

AUTHOR COMMENT Here the restaurant chain uses *weight* (11 oz) as a measure of SPC for salmon filets.

AUTHOR COMMENT The *range* here is the difference between the heaviest and the lightest salmon filets weighed in each sample. A range chart shows changes in *dispersion.*

VIDEO S6.1 Farm to Fork: Quality of Darden Restaurants

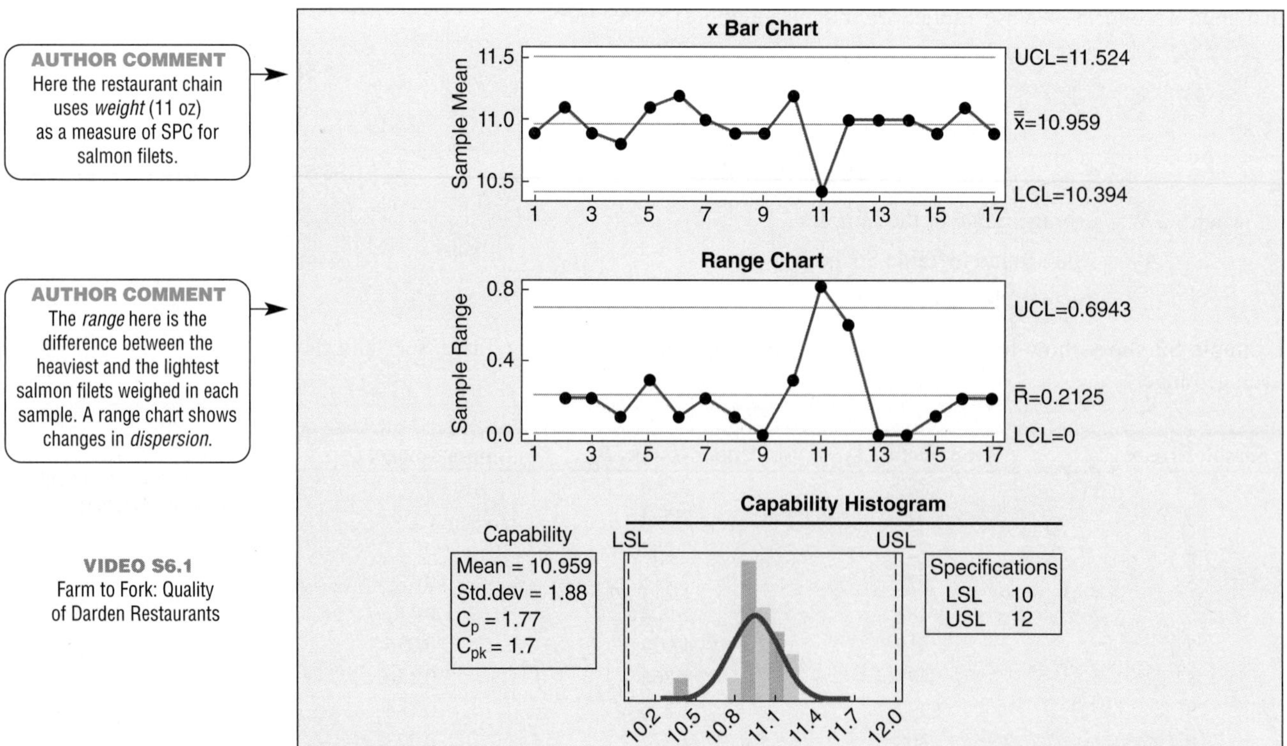

Salmon filets are monitored by Darden Restaurant's SPC software, which includes $\bar{x}$- and R-charts and a process capability histogram. The video case study "Farm to Fork," at the end of this supplement, asks you to interpret these figures.

Setting Range Chart Limits (*R*-Charts)

In Examples S1 and S2, we determined the upper and lower control limits for the process *average*. In addition to being concerned with the process average, operations managers are interested in the process *dispersion*, or *range*. Even though the process average is under control, the dispersion of the process may not be. For example, something may have worked itself loose in a piece of equipment that fills boxes of Oat Flakes. As a result, the average of the samples may remain the same, but the variation within the samples could be entirely too large. For this reason, operations managers use control charts for ranges to monitor the process variability, as well as control charts for averages, which monitor the process central tendency. The theory behind the control charts for ranges is the same as that for process average control charts. Limits are established that contain ±3 standard deviations of the distribution for the average range $\overline{R}$. We can use the following equations to set the upper and lower control limits for ranges:

$$\text{UCL}_R = D_4\overline{R} \quad \text{(S6-7)}$$

$$\text{LCL}_R = D_3\overline{R} \quad \text{(S6-8)}$$

where UCL_R = upper control chart limit for the range
LCL_R = lower control chart limit for the range
D_4 and D_3 = values from Table S6.1

Example S3 shows how to set control limits for sample ranges using Table S6.1 and the average range.

EXAMPLE S3

Setting range limits using table values

The average *range* of a product at Clinton Manufacturing is 5.3 pounds. With a sample size of 5, owner Roy Clinton wants to determine the upper and lower control chart limits.

APPROACH ▶ Looking in Table S6.1 for a sample size of 5, he finds that $D_4 = 2.115$ and $D_3 = 0$.

SOLUTION ▶ The range control limits are:

$$\text{UCL}_R = D_4\overline{R} = (2.115)(5.3 \text{ pounds}) = 11.2 \text{ pounds}$$

$$\text{LCL}_R = D_3\overline{R} = (0)(5.3 \text{ pounds}) = 0$$

INSIGHT ▶ Computing ranges with Table S6.1 is straightforward and an easy way to evaluate dispersion.

LEARNING EXERCISE ▶ Clinton decides to increase the sample size to $n = 7$. What are the new UCL_R and LCL_R values? [Answer: 10.197, 0.403]

RELATED PROBLEMS ▶ S6.3b, S6.5, S6.6, S6.7, S6.9, S6.10c, S6.11, S6.12, S6.34

Using Mean and Range Charts

The normal distribution is defined by two parameters, the *mean* and *standard deviation*. The $\overline{x}$ (mean)-chart and the *R*-chart mimic these two parameters. The $\overline{x}$-chart is sensitive to shifts in the process mean, whereas the *R*-chart is sensitive to shifts in the process standard deviation. Consequently, by using both charts we can track changes in the process distribution.

For instance, the samples and the resulting $\overline{x}$-chart in Figure S6.5(a) show the shift in the process mean, but because the dispersion is constant, no change is detected by the *R*-chart. Conversely, the samples and the $\overline{x}$-chart in Figure S6.5(b) detect no shift (because none is present), but the *R*-chart does detect the shift in the dispersion. Both charts are required to track the process accurately.

Steps to Follow When Using Control Charts There are five steps that are generally followed in using $\overline{x}$- and *R*-charts:

LO4: List the five steps involved in building control charts

1. Collect 20 to 25 samples, often of $n = 4$ or $n = 5$ observations each, from a stable process and compute the mean and range of each.
2. Compute the overall means ($\overline{\overline{x}}$ and $\overline{R}$), set appropriate control limits, usually at the 99.73% level, and calculate the preliminary upper and lower control limits. Refer to

▶ Figure S6.5

Mean and Range Charts Complement Each Other by Showing the Mean and Dispersion of the Normal Distribution

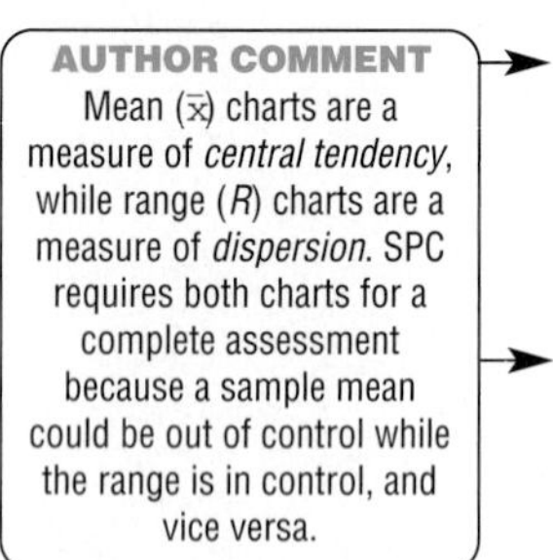

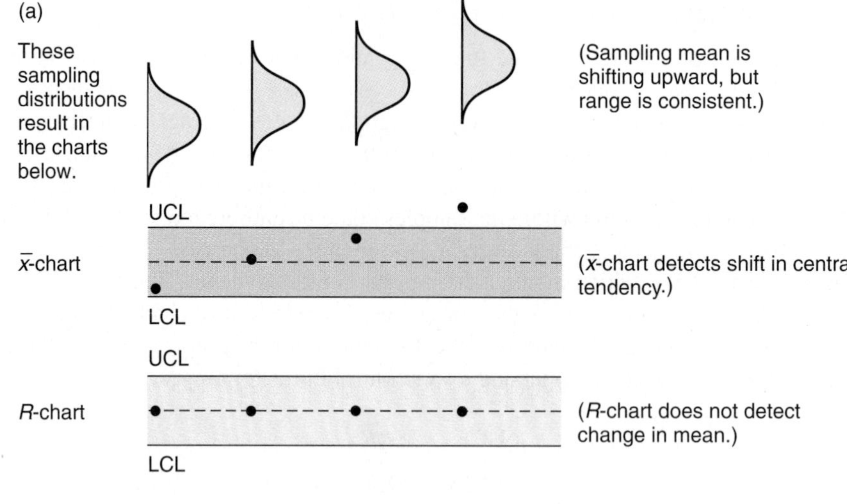

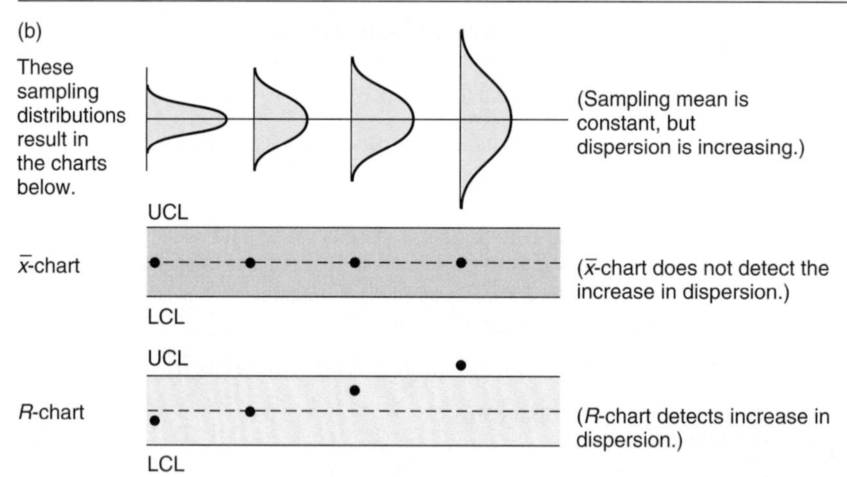

▼ TABLE S6.2
Common z Values

Desired Control Limit (%)	z-Value (standard deviation required for desired level of confidence)
90.0	1.65
95.0	1.96
95.45	2.00
99.0	2.58
99.73	3.00

Table S6.2 for other control limits. *If the process is not currently stable and in control*, use the desired mean, μ, instead of $\bar{\bar{x}}$ to calculate limits.

3. Graph the sample means and ranges on their respective control charts and determine whether they fall outside the acceptable limits.
4. Investigate points or patterns that indicate the process is out of control. Try to assign causes for the variation, address the causes, and then resume the process.
5. Collect additional samples and, if necessary, revalidate the control limits using the new data.

Control Charts for Attributes

LO5: Build p-charts and c-charts

Control charts for $\bar{x}$ and R do not apply when we are sampling *attributes*, which are typically classified as *defective* or *nondefective*. Measuring defectives involves counting them (for example, number of bad lightbulbs in a given lot, or number of letters or data entry records typed with errors), whereas *variables* are usually measured for length or weight. There are two kinds of attribute control charts: (1) those that measure the *percent* defective in a sample—called p-charts—and (2) those that count the *number* of defects—called c-charts.

p-chart
A quality control chart that is used to control attributes.

***p*-Charts** Using ***p*-charts** is the chief way to control attributes. Although attributes that are either good or bad follow the binomial distribution, the normal distribution can be used to calculate p-chart limits when sample sizes are large. The procedure resembles the $\bar{x}$-chart approach, which is also based on the central limit theorem.

The formulas for p-chart upper and lower control limits follow:

$$\text{UCL}_p = \bar{p} + z\sigma_{\hat{p}} \qquad \text{(S6-9)}$$

$$\text{LCL}_p = \bar{p} - z\sigma_{\hat{p}} \qquad \text{(S6-10)}$$

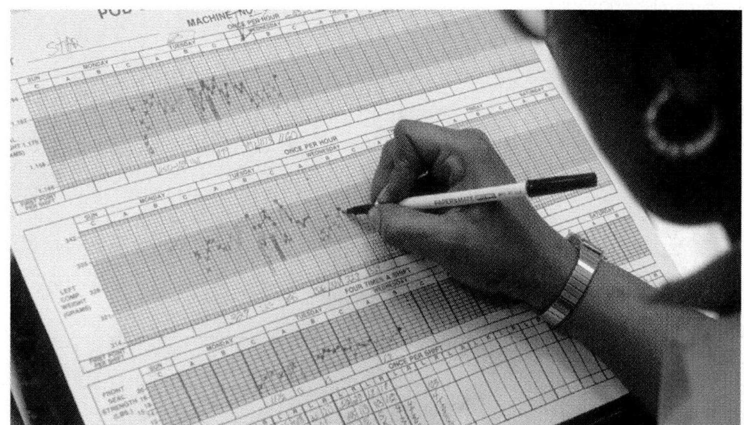

Frito-Lay uses $\bar{x}$ charts to control production quality at critical points in the process. Each half-hour, three batches of chips are taken from the conveyor (on the left) and analyzed electronically to get an average salt content which is plotted on an $\bar{x}$-chart (on the right). Points plotted in the green zone are "in control," while those in the yellow zone are "out of control." The SPC chart is displayed, where all production employees can monitor process stability.

where $\bar{p}$ = mean fraction defective in the samples
z = number of standard deviations ($z = 2$ for 95.45% limits; $z = 3$ for 99.73% limits)
$\sigma_{\hat{p}}$ = standard deviation of the sampling distribution

VIDEO S6.2
Frito-Lay's Quality-Controlled Potato Chips

$\sigma_{\hat{p}}$ is estimated by the formula:

$$\sigma_{\hat{p}} = \sqrt{\frac{\bar{p}(1 - \bar{p})}{n}} \qquad \text{(S6-11)}$$

where n = number of observations in *each* samples

Example S4 shows how to set control limits for p-charts for these standard deviations.

EXAMPLE S4

Setting control limits for percent defective

Clerks at Mosier Data Systems key in thousands of insurance records each day for a variety of client firms. CEO Donna Mosier wants to set control limits to include 99.73% of the random variation in the data entry process when it is in control.

APPROACH ▶ Samples of the work of 20 clerks are gathered (and shown in the table). Mosier carefully examines 100 records entered by each clerk and counts the number of errors. She also computes the fraction defective in each sample. Equations (S6-9), (S6-10), and (S6-11) are then used to set the control limits.

Sample Number	Number of Errors	Fraction Defective	Sample Number	Number of Errors	Fraction Defective
1	6	.06	11	6	.06
2	5	.05	12	1	.01
3	0	.00	13	8	.08
4	1	.01	14	7	.07
5	4	.04	15	5	.05
6	2	.02	16	4	.04
7	5	.05	17	11	.11
8	3	.03	18	3	.03
9	3	.03	19	0	.00
10	2	.02	20	4	.04
				80	

SOLUTION ▶

$$\bar{p} = \frac{\text{Total number of errors}}{\text{Total number of records examined}} = \frac{80}{(100)(20)} = .04$$

$$\sigma_{\hat{p}} = \sqrt{\frac{(.04)(1 - .04)}{100}} = .02 \text{ (rounded up from .0196)}$$

(*Note:* 100 is the size of *each* sample = n.)

$$UCL_p = \bar{p} + z\sigma_{\hat{p}} = .04 + 3(.02) = .10$$

$$LCL_p = \bar{p} - z\sigma_{\hat{p}} = .04 - 3(.02) = 0$$

(because we cannot have a negative percentage defective)

INSIGHT ▶ When we plot the control limits and the sample fraction defectives, we find that only one data-entry clerk (number 17) is out of control. The firm may wish to examine that individual's work a bit more closely to see if a serious problem exists (see Figure S6.6).

▶ **FIGURE S6.6**
***p*-Chart for Data Entry for Example S4**

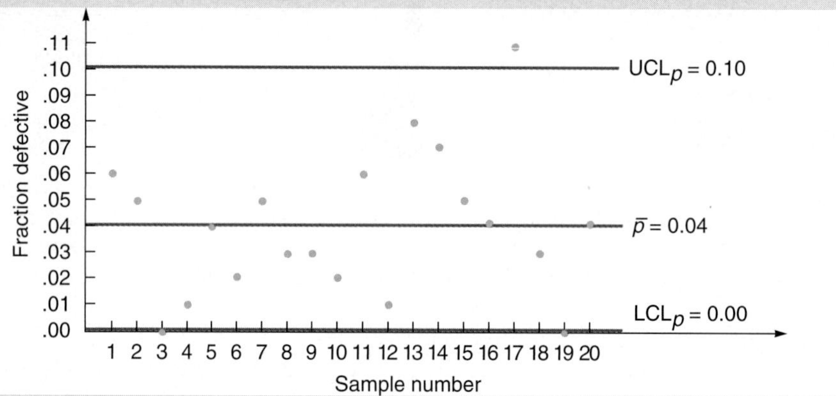

AUTHOR COMMENT
We are always pleased to be at zero or below the center line in a *p*-chart.

LEARNING EXERCISE ▶ Mosier decides to set control limits at 95.45% instead. What are the new UCL_p and LCL_p? [Answer: 0.08, 0]

RELATED PROBLEMS: ▶ S6.13, S6.14, S6.15, S6.16, S6.17, S6.18, S6.19, S6.20, S6.25, S6.35

EXCEL OM Data File **Ch06SExS4.xls** can be found at **www.pearsonhighered.com/heizer**.

ACTIVE MODEL S6.1 This example is further illustrated in Active Model S6.1 at **www.pearsonhighered.com/heizer**.

The *OM in Action* box "Unisys Corp.'s Costly Experiment in Health Care Services" provides a real-world follow-up to Example S4.

c-chart
A quality control chart used to control the number of defects per unit of output.

***c*-Charts** In Example S4, we counted the number of defective records entered. A defective record was one that was not exactly correct because it contained at least one defect. However, a bad record may contain more than one defect. We use **c-charts** to control the *number* of defects per unit of output (or per insurance record, in the preceding case).

OM in Action ▶ Unisys Corp.'s Costly Experiment in Health Care Services

When Unisys Corp. expanded into the computerized health care service business things looked rosy. It had just beat out Blue Cross/Blue Shield of Florida for an $86 million contract to serve Florida's state employee health-insurance services. Its job was to handle the 215,000 Florida employees' claims processing—a seemingly simple and lucrative growth area for an old-line computer company like Unisys.

But 1 year later the contract was not only torn up, Unisys was fined more than $500,000 for not meeting quality standards. Here are two of the measures of quality, both attributes (that is, either "defective" or "not defective") on which the firm was out of control:

1. *Percentage of claims processed with errors:* An audit over a 3-month period, by Coopers & Lybrand, found that Unisys made errors in 8.5% of claims processed. The industry standard is 3.5% "defectives."
2. *Percentage of claims processed within 30 days:* For this attribute measure, a "defect" is a processing time longer than the contract's time allowance. In one month's sample, 13% of the claims exceeded the 30-day limit, far above the 5% allowed by the state of Florida.

The Florida contract was a migraine for Unisys, which underestimated the labor-intensiveness of health claims. CEO James Unruh pulled the plug on future ambitions in health care. Meanwhile, the State of Florida's Ron Poppel says, "We really need somebody that's in the insurance business."

Sources: Knight Ridder Tribune Business News (October 20, 2004): 1 and (February 7, 2002): 1; and *BusinessWeek* (June 16, 1997): 6.

Sampling wine from these wooden barrels, to make sure it is aging properly, uses both SPC (for alcohol content and acidity) and subjective measures (for taste).

Control charts for defects are helpful for monitoring processes in which a large number of potential errors can occur, but the actual number that do occur is relatively small. Defects may be errors in newspaper words, bad circuits in a microchip, blemishes on a table, or missing pickles on a fast-food hamburger.

The Poisson probability distribution,[3] which has a variance equal to its mean, is the basis for *c*-charts. Because $\bar{c}$ is the mean number of defects per unit, the standard deviation is equal to $\sqrt{\bar{c}}$. To compute 99.73% control limits for $\bar{c}$, we use the formula:

$$\text{Control limits} = \bar{c} \pm 3\sqrt{\bar{c}} \quad \text{(S6-12)}$$

Example S5 shows how to set control limits for a $\bar{c}$-chart.

EXAMPLE S5

Setting control limits for number defective

Red Top Cab Company receives several complaints per day about the behavior of its drivers. Over a 9-day period (where days are the units of measure), the owner, Gordon Hoft, received the following numbers of calls from irate passengers: 3, 0, 8, 9, 6, 7, 4, 9, 8, for a total of 54 complaints. Hoft wants to compute 99.73% control limits.

APPROACH ▶ He applies Equation (S6–12).

SOLUTION ▶ $\bar{c} = \frac{54}{9} = 6$ complaints per day

Thus:

$$UCL_c = \bar{c} + 3\sqrt{\bar{c}} = 6 + 3\sqrt{6} = 6 + 3(2.45) = 13.35, \text{ or } 13$$

$$LCL_c = \bar{c} - 3\sqrt{\bar{c}} = 6 - 3\sqrt{6} = 6 - 3(2.45) = 0 \leftarrow \text{(since it cannot be negative)}$$

INSIGHT: ▶ After Hoft plotted a control chart summarizing these data and posted it prominently in the drivers' locker room, the number of calls received dropped to an average of three per day. Can you explain why this occurred?

LEARNING EXERCISE: ▶ Hoft collects 3 more days' worth of complaints (10, 12, and 8 complaints) and wants to combine them with the original 9 days to compute updated control limits. What are the revised UCL_c and LCL_c? [Answer: 14.94, 0.]

RELATED PROBLEMS: ▶ S6.21, S6.22, S6.23, S6.24

EXCEL OM Data File **Ch06SExS5.xls** can be found at **www.pearsonhighered.com/heizer**.

[3]A Poisson probability distribution is a discrete distribution commonly used when the items of interest (in this case, defects) are infrequent or occur in time and space.

TABLE S6.3
Helping You Decide Which Control Chart to Use

AUTHOR COMMENT
This is a really useful table. When you are not sure which control chart to use, turn here for clarification.

Variable Data
Using an $\bar{x}$-Chart and an R-Chart

1. Observations are *variables*, which are usually products measured for size or weight. Examples are the width or length of a wire being cut and the weight of a can of Campbell's soup.
2. Collect 20 to 25 samples, usually of $n = 4$, $n = 5$, or more, each from a stable process, and compute the means for an $\bar{x}$-chart and the ranges for an R-chart.
3. We track samples of n observations each, as in Example S1.

Attribute Data
Using a p-Chart

1. Observations are *attributes* that can be categorized as good or bad (or pass–fail, or functional–broken), that is, in two states.
2. We deal with fraction, proportion, or percent defectives.
3. There are several samples, with many observations in each. For example, 20 samples of $n = 100$ observations in each, as in Example S4.

Using a c-Chart

1. Observations are *attributes* whose defects per unit of output can be counted.
2. We deal with the number counted, which is a small part of the possible occurrences.
3. Defects may be: number of blemishes on a desk; complaints in a day; crimes in a year; broken seats in a stadium; typos in a chapter of this text; or flaws in a bolt of cloth, as is shown in Example S5.

Managerial Issues and Control Charts

In an ideal world, there is no need for control charts. Quality is uniform and so high that employees need not waste time and money sampling and monitoring variables and attributes. But because most processes have not reached perfection, managers must make three major decisions regarding control charts.

First, managers must select the points in their process that need SPC. They may ask "Which parts of the job are critical to success?" or "Which parts of the job have a tendency to become out of control?"

Second, managers need to decide if variable charts (i.e., $\bar{x}$ and R) or attribute charts (i.e., p and c) are appropriate. Variable charts monitor weights or dimensions. Attribute charts are more of a "yes–no" or "go–no go" gauge and tend to be less costly to implement. Table S6.3 can help you understand when to use each of these types of control charts.

Third, the company must set clear and specific SPC policies for employees to follow. For example, should the data-entry process be halted if a trend is appearing in percent defective records being keyed? Should an assembly line be stopped if the average length of five successive samples is above the centerline? Figure S6.7 illustrates some of the patterns to look for over time in a process.

AUTHOR COMMENT
Workers in companies such as Frito-Lay are trained to follow rules like these.

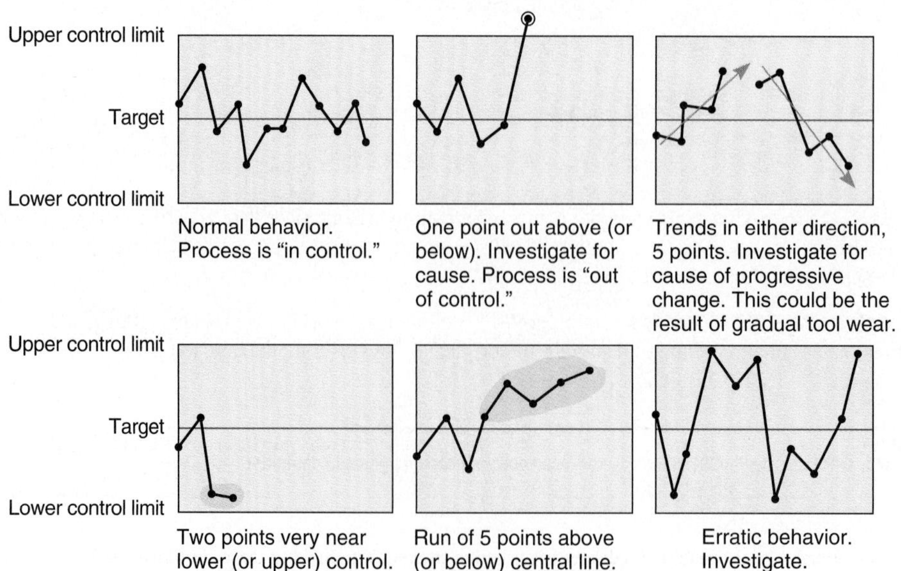

Upper control limit
Target
Lower control limit
Normal behavior. Process is "in control."
One point out above (or below). Investigate for cause. Process is "out of control."
Trends in either direction, 5 points. Investigate for cause of progressive change. This could be the result of gradual tool wear.
Upper control limit
Target
Lower control limit
Two points very near lower (or upper) control. Investigate for cause.
Run of 5 points above (or below) central line. Investigate for cause.
Erratic behavior. Investigate.

FIGURE S6.7
Patterns to Look for on Control Charts

Source: Adapted from Bertrand L. Hansen, *Quality Control: Theory and Applications* (1991): 65. Reprinted by permission of Prentice Hall, Upper Saddle River, New Jersey.

A tool called a **run test** is available to help identify the kind of abnormalities in a process that we see in Figure S6.7. In general, a run of 5 points above or below the target or centerline may suggest that an assignable, or nonrandom, variation is present. When this occurs, even though all the points may fall inside the control limits, a flag has been raised. This means the process may not be statistically in control. A variety of run tests are described in books on the subject of quality methods.[4]

Run test
A test used to examine the points in a control chart to see if nonrandom variation is present.

PROCESS CAPABILITY

AUTHOR COMMENT
Here we deal with whether a process meets the specification it was *designed* to yield.

Statistical process control means keeping a process in control. This means that the natural variation of the process must be stable. But a process that is in statistical control may not yield goods or services that meet their *design specifications* (tolerances). The ability of a process to meet design specifications, which are set by engineering design or customer requirements, is called **process capability**. Even though that process may be statistically in control (stable), the output of that process may not conform to specifications.

Process capability
The ability to meet design specifications.

For example, let's say the time a customer expects to wait for the completion of a lube job at Quik Lube is 12 minutes, with an acceptable tolerance of ±2 minutes. This tolerance gives an upper specification of 14 minutes and a lower specification of 10 minutes. The lube process has to be capable of operating within these design specifications—if not, some customers will not have their requirements met. As a manufacturing example, the tolerances for Harley-Davidson cam gears are extremely low, only 0.0005 inch—and a process must be designed that is capable of achieving this tolerance.

There are two popular measures for quantitatively determining if a process is capable: process capability ratio (C_p) and process capability index (C_{pk}).

LO6: Explain process capability and compute C_p and C_{pk}

Process Capability Ratio (C_p)

For a process to be capable, its values must fall within upper and lower specifications. This typically means the process capability is within ±3 standard deviations from the process mean. Since this range of values is 6 standard deviations, a capable process tolerance, which is the difference between the upper and lower specifications, must be greater than or equal to 6.

The process capability ratio, $\mathbf{C_p}$, is computed as:

C_p
A ratio for determining whether a process meets design specifications; a ratio of the specification to the process variation.

$$C_p = \frac{\text{Upper specification} - \text{Lower specification}}{6\sigma} \tag{S6-13}$$

Example S6 shows the computation of C_p.

EXAMPLE S6
Process capability ratio (C_p)

In a GE insurance claims process, $\bar{x} = 210.0$ minutes, and $\sigma = .516$ minutes.

The design specification to meet customer expectations is 210 ± 3 minutes. So the Upper Specification is 213 minutes and the lower specification is 207 minutes. The OM manager wants to compute the process capability ratio.

APPROACH ▶ GE applies Equation (S6-13).

SOLUTION ▶ $C_p = \frac{\text{Upper specification} - \text{Lower specification}}{6\sigma} = \frac{213 - 207}{6(.516)} = 1.938$

INSIGHT ▶ Since a ratio of 1.00 means that 99.73% of a process's outputs are within specifications, this ratio suggests a very capable process, with nonconformance of less than 4 claims per million.

LEARNING EXERCISE ▶ If $\sigma = .60$ (instead of .516), what is the new C_p? [Answer: 1.667, a very capable process still.]

RELATED PROBLEMS ▶ S6.26, S6.27

ACTIVE MODEL S6.2 This example is further illustrated in Active Model S6.2 at **www.pearsonhighered.com/heizer**.

A capable process has a C_p of at least 1.0. If the C_p is less than 1.0, the process yields products or services that are outside their allowable tolerance. With a C_p of 1.0, 2.7 parts in 1,000 can be

[4]See Gerald Smith, *Statistical Process Control and Process Improvement*, 7th ed. (Upper Saddle River, NJ: Prentice Hall, 2010).

expected to be "out of spec."[5] The higher the process capability ratio, the greater the likelihood the process will be within design specifications. Many firms have chosen a C_p of 1.33 (a 4-sigma standard) as a target for reducing process variability. This means that only 64 parts per million can be expected to be out of specification.

Recall that in Chapter 6 we mentioned the concept of *Six Sigma* quality, championed by GE and Motorola. This standard equates to a C_p of 2.0, with only 3.4 defective parts per million (very close to zero defects) instead of the 2.7 parts per 1,000 with 3-sigma limits.

Although C_p relates to the spread (dispersion) of the process output relative to its tolerance, it does not look at how well the process average is centered on the target value.

Process Capability Index (C_{pk})

The process capability index, $\mathbf{C_{pk}}$, measures the difference between the desired and actual dimensions of goods or services produced.

C_{pk}
A proportion of variation (3σ) between the center of the process and the nearest specification limit.

The formula for C_{pk} is:

$$C_{pk} = \text{Minimum of}\left[\frac{\text{Upper specification limit} - \overline{X}}{3\sigma}, \frac{\overline{X} - \text{Lower specification limit}}{3\sigma}\right] \quad \text{(S6-14)}$$

where $\overline{X}$ = process mean
σ = standard deviation of the process population

When the C_{pk} index for both the upper and lower specification limits equals 1.0, the process variation is centered and the process is capable of producing within ± 3 standard deviations (fewer than 2,700 defects per million). A C_{pk} of 2.0 means the process is capable of producing fewer than 3.4 defects per million. For C_{pk} to exceed 1, σ must be less than $\frac{1}{3}$ of the difference between the specification and the process mean ($\overline{X}$). Figure S6.8 shows the meaning of various measures of C_{pk}, and Example S7 shows an application of C_{pk}.

EXAMPLE S7

Process capability index (C_{pk})

You are the process improvement manager and have developed a new machine to cut insoles for the company's top-of-the-line running shoes. You are excited because the company's goal is no more than 3.4 defects per million and this machine may be the innovation you need. The insoles cannot be more than $\pm.001$ of an inch from the required thickness of .250″. You want to know if you should replace the existing machine, which has a C_{pk} of 1.0.

APPROACH ▶ You decide to determine the C_{pk}, using Equation (S6-14), for the new machine and make a decision on that basis.

SOLUTION ▶ Upper specification limit = .251 inch
Lower specification limit = .249 inch

Mean of the new process $\overline{X}$ = .250 inch.
Estimated standard deviation of the new process = σ = .0005 inch.

$$C_{pk} = \text{Minimum of}\left[\frac{\text{Upper specification limit} - \overline{X}}{3\sigma}, \frac{\overline{X} - \text{Lower specification limit}}{3\sigma}\right]$$

$$C_{pk} = \text{Minimum of}\left[\frac{(.251) - .250}{(3).0005}, \frac{.250 - (.249)}{(3).0005}\right]$$

Both calculations result in: $\frac{.001}{.0015} = .67.$

INSIGHT ▶ Because the new machine has a C_{pk} of only 0.67, the new machine should *not* replace the existing machine.

LEARNING EXERCISE ▶ If the insoles can be $\pm.002$″ (instead of .001″) from the required .250″, what is the new C_{pk}? [Answer: 1.33 and the new machine *should* replace the existing one.]

RELATED PROBLEMS ▶ S6.27, S6.28, S6.29, S6.30, S6.31

EXCEL OM Data File **Ch06SExS7.xls** can be found at **www.pearsonhighered.com/heizer**.

ACTIVE MODEL S6.2 This example is further illustrated in Active Model S6.3 at **www.pearsonhighered.com/heizer**.

[5]This is because a C_p of 1.0 has 99.73% of outputs within specifications. So 1.00 − .9973 = .0027; with 1,000 parts, there are .0027 × 1,000 = 2.7 defects.

For a C_p of 2.0, 99.99966% of outputs are "within spec." So 1.00 − .9999966 = .0000034; with 1 million parts, there are 3.4 defects.

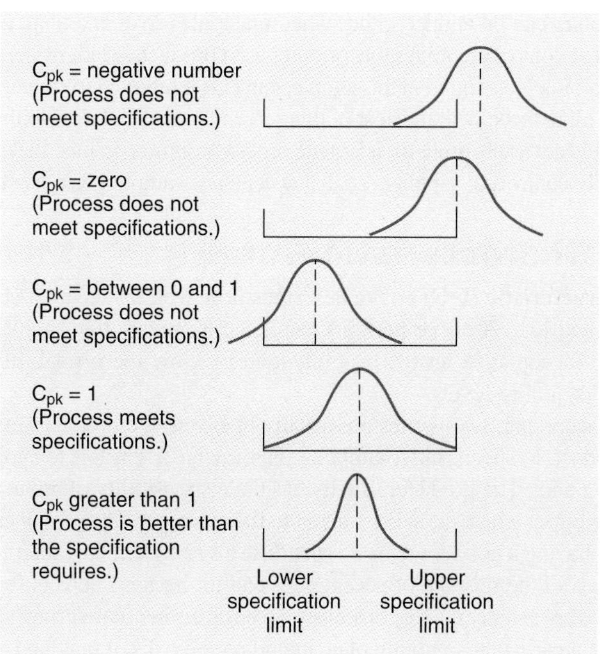

◀ **FIGURE S6.8**

Meanings of C_{pk} Measures

A C_{pk} index of 1.0 for both the upper and lower control limits indicates that the process variation is within the upper and lower control limits. As the C_{pk} index goes above 1.0, the process becomes increasingly target oriented, with fewer defects. If the C_{pk} is less than 1.0, the process will not produce within the specified tolerance. Because a process may not be centered, or may "drift," a C_{pk} above 1 is desired.

Note that C_p and C_{pk} will be the same when the process is centered. However, if the mean of the process is not centered on the desired (specified) mean, then the smaller numerator in Equation (S6-14) is used (the minimum of the difference between the upper specification limit and the mean or the lower specification limit and the mean). This application of C_{pk} is shown in Solved Problem S6.4. C_{pk} is the standard criterion used to express process performance.

ACCEPTANCE SAMPLING[6]

Acceptance sampling is a form of testing that involves taking random samples of "lots," or batches, of finished products and measuring them against predetermined standards. Sampling is more economical than 100% inspection. The quality of the sample is used to judge the quality of all items in the lot. Although both attributes and variables can be inspected by acceptance sampling, attribute inspection is more commonly used, as illustrated in this section.

Acceptance sampling
A method of measuring random samples of lots or batches of products against predetermined standards.

LO7: Explain acceptance sampling

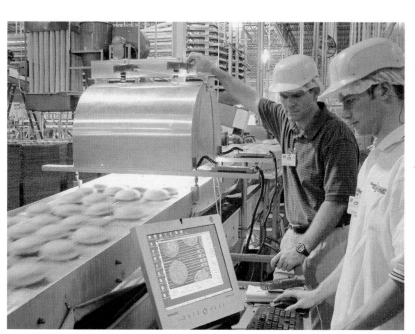

Flowers Bakery in Villa Rica, Georgia, uses a digital camera to inspect just-baked sandwich buns as they move along the production line. Items that don't measure up in terms of color, shape, seed distribution, or size are identified and removed automatically from the conveyor.

[6]Refer to Tutorial 2 on our free website **www.pearsonhighered.com/heizer** for an extended discussion of acceptance sampling.

Acceptance sampling can be applied either when materials arrive at a plant or at final inspection, but it is usually used to control incoming lots of purchased products. A lot of items rejected, based on an unacceptable level of defects found in the sample, can (1) be returned to the supplier or (2) be 100% inspected to cull out all defects, with the cost of this screening usually billed to the supplier. However, acceptance sampling is not a substitute for adequate process controls. In fact, the current approach is to build statistical quality controls at suppliers so that acceptance sampling can be eliminated.

Operating Characteristic Curve

Operating characteristic (OC) curve
A graph that describes how well an acceptance plan discriminates between good and bad lots.

Producer's risk
The mistake of having a producer's good lot rejected through sampling.

Consumer's risk
The mistake of a customer's acceptance of a bad lot overlooked through sampling.

Acceptable quality level (AQL)
The quality level of a lot considered good.

The **operating characteristic (OC) curve** describes how well an acceptance plan discriminates between good and bad lots. A curve pertains to a specific plan—that is, to a combination of n (sample size) and c (acceptance level). It is intended to show the probability that the plan will accept lots of various quality levels.

With acceptance sampling, two parties are usually involved: the producer of the product and the consumer of the product. In specifying a sampling plan, each party wants to avoid costly mistakes in accepting or rejecting a lot. The producer usually has the responsibility of replacing all defects in the rejected lot or of paying for a new lot to be shipped to the customer. The producer, therefore, wants to avoid the mistake of having a good lot rejected (**producer's risk**). On the other hand, the customer or consumer wants to avoid the mistake of accepting a bad lot because defects found in a lot that has already been accepted are usually the responsibility of the customer (**consumer's risk**). The OC curve shows the features of a particular sampling plan, including the risks of making a wrong decision.[7]

Figure S6.9 can be used to illustrate one sampling plan in more detail. Four concepts are illustrated in this figure.

The **acceptable quality level (AQL)** is the poorest level of quality that we are willing to accept. In other words, we wish to accept lots that have this or a better level of quality, but no lower. If an acceptable quality level is 20 defects in a lot of 1,000 items or parts, then AQL is $20/1{,}000 = 2\%$ defectives.

▶ FIGURE S6.9
An Operating Characteristic (OC) Curve Showing Producer's and Consumer's Risks
A good lot for this particular acceptance plan has less than or equal to 2% defectives. A bad lot has 7% or more defectives.

AUTHOR COMMENT
Figure S6.9 is further illustrated in Active Model S6.3 on our website, **www.pearsonhighered.com/heizer**

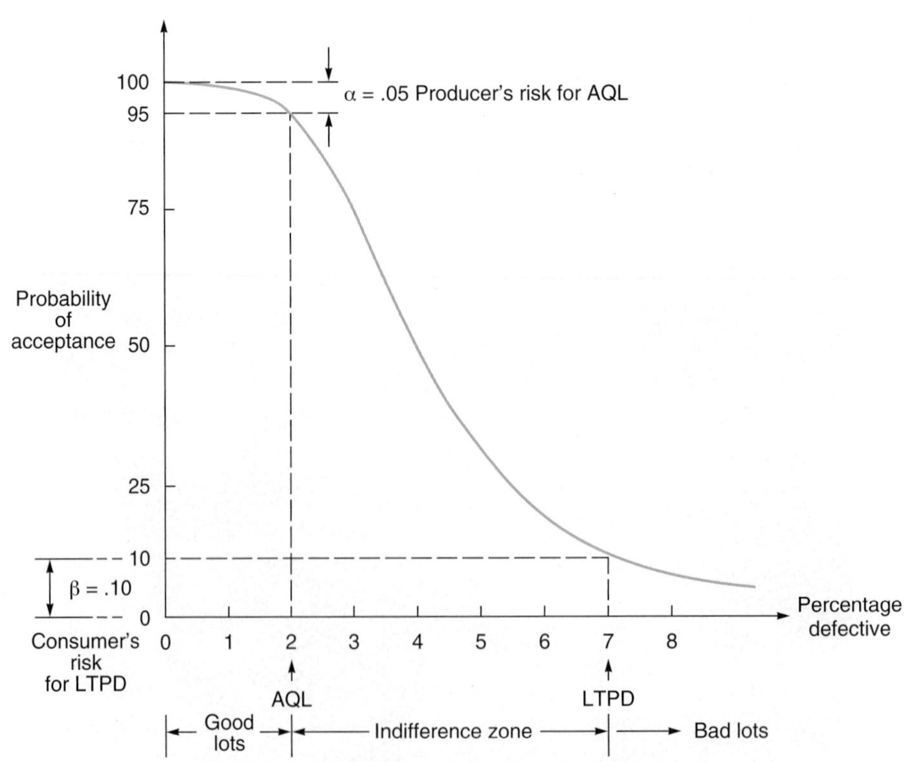

[7]Note that sampling always runs the danger of leading to an erroneous conclusion. Let us say in one company that the total population under scrutiny is a load of 1,000 computer chips, of which in reality only 30 (or 3%) are defective. This means that we would want to accept the shipment of chips, because for this particular firm 4% is the allowable defect rate. However, if a random sample of $n = 50$ chips was drawn, we could conceivably end up with 0 defects and accept that shipment (that is, it is okay), or we could find all 30 defects in the sample. If the latter happened, we could wrongly conclude that the whole population was 60% defective and reject them all.

This laser tracking device, by Faro Technologies, enables quality control personnel to measure and inspect parts and tools during production. The tracker can measure objects from 100 feet away and takes up to 1,000 readings per second.

The **lot tolerance percentage defective** (**LTPD**) is the quality level of a lot that we consider bad. We wish to reject lots that have this or a poorer level of quality. If it is agreed that an unacceptable quality level is 70 defects in a lot of 1,000, then the LTPD is $70/1{,}000 = 7\%$ defective.

Lot tolerance percentage defective (LTPD)
The quality level of a lot considered bad.

To derive a sampling plan, producer and consumer must define not only "good lots" and "bad lots" through the AQL and LTPD, but they must also specify risk levels.

Producer's risk (α) is the probability that a "good" lot will be rejected. This is the risk that a random sample might result in a much higher proportion of defects than the population of all items. A lot with an acceptable quality level of AQL still has an α chance of being rejected. Sampling plans are often designed to have the producer's risk set at $\alpha = .05$, or 5%.

Consumer's risk (β) is the probability that a "bad" lot will be accepted. This is the risk that a random sample may result in a lower proportion of defects than the overall population of items. A common value for consumer's risk in sampling plans is $\beta = .10$, or 10%.

The probability of rejecting a good lot is called a **type I error**. The probability of accepting a bad lot is a **type II error**.

Type I error
Statistically, the probability of rejecting a good lot.

Type II error
Statistically, the probability of accepting a bad lot.

Sampling plans and OC curves may be developed by computer (as seen in the software available with this text), by published tables, or by calculation, using binomial or Poisson distributions.

Average Outgoing Quality

In most sampling plans, when a lot is rejected, the entire lot is inspected and all defective items replaced. Use of this replacement technique improves the average outgoing quality in terms of percent defective. In fact, given (1) any sampling plan that replaces all defective items encountered and (2) the true incoming percent defective for the lot, it is possible to determine the **average outgoing quality (AOQ)** in percentage defective. The equation for AOQ is:

Average outgoing quality (AOQ)
The percentage defective in an average lot of goods inspected through acceptance sampling

$$\text{AOQ} = \frac{(P_d)(P_a)(N - n)}{N} \quad \text{(S6-15)}$$

where P_d = true percentage defective of the lot
P_a = probability of accepting the lot for a given sample size and quantity defective
N = number of items in the lot
n = number of items in the sample

The maximum value of AOQ corresponds to the highest average percentage defective or the lowest average quality for the sampling plan. It is called the *average outgoing quality limit (AOQL).*

Acceptance sampling is useful for screening incoming lots. When the defective parts are replaced with good parts, acceptance sampling helps to increase the quality of the lots by reducing the outgoing percent defective.

Figure S6.10 compares acceptance sampling, SPC, and C_{pk}. As Figure S6.10 shows, (a) acceptance sampling by definition accepts some bad units, (b) control charts try to keep the process in control, but (c) the C_{pk} index places the focus on improving the process. As operations managers, that is what we want to do—improve the process.

LO8: Compute the AOQ

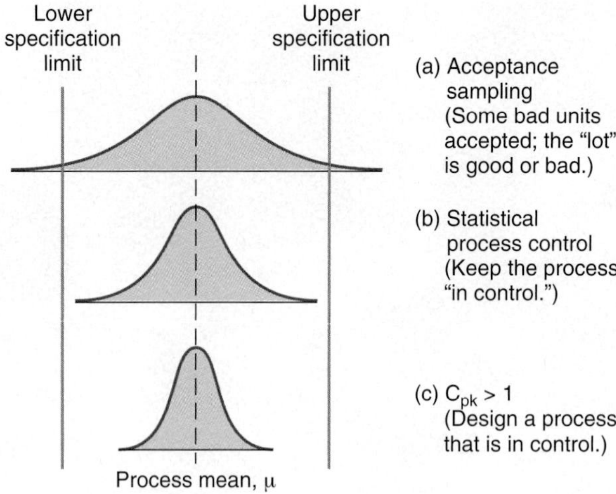

FIGURE S6.10 The Application of Statistical Process Techniques Contributes to the Identification and Systematic Reduction of Process Variability

SUPPLEMENT SUMMARY

Statistical process control is a major statistical tool of quality control. Control charts for SPC help operations managers distinguish between natural and assignable variations. The $\bar{x}$-chart and the *R*-chart are used for variable sampling, and the *p*-chart and the *c*-chart for attribute sampling. The C_{pk} index is a way to express process capability. Operating characteristic (OC) curves facilitate acceptance sampling and provide the manager with tools to evaluate the quality of a production run or shipment.

Key Terms

Statistical process control (SPC) (p. 218)
Control chart (p. 218)
Natural variations (p. 219)
Assignable variation (p. 219)
$\bar{x}$-chart (p. 220)
R-chart (p. 220)
Central limit theorem (p. 220)
p-chart (p. 226)
c-chart (p. 228)
Run test (p. 231)
Process capability (p. 231)
C_p (p. 231)
C_{pk} (p. 232)
Acceptance sampling (p. 233)
Operating characteristic (OC) curve (p. 234)
Producer's risk (p. 234)
Consumer's risk (p. 234)
Acceptable quality level (AQL) (p. 234)
Lot tolerance percentage defective (LTPD) (p. 235)
Type I error (p. 235)
Type II error (p. 235)
Average outgoing quality (AOQ) (p. 235)

Discussion Questions

1. List Shewhart's two types of variation. What are they also called?
2. Define "in statistical control."
3. Explain briefly what an $\bar{x}$-chart and an *R*-chart do.
4. What might cause a process to be out of control?
5. List five steps in developing and using $\bar{x}$-charts and *R*-charts.
6. List some possible causes of assignable variation.
7. Explain how a person using 2-sigma control charts will more easily find samples "out of bounds" than 3-sigma control charts. What are some possible consequences of this fact?
8. When is the desired mean, μ, used in establishing the centerline of a control chart instead of $\bar{\bar{x}}$?
9. Can a production process be labeled as "out of control" because it is too good? Explain.
10. In a control chart, what would be the effect on the control limits if the sample size varied from one sample to the next?
11. Define C_{pk} and explain what a C_{pk} of 1.0 means. What is C_p?
12. What does a run of 5 points above or below the centerline in a control chart imply?
13. What are the acceptable quality level (AQL) and the lot tolerance percentage defective (LTPD)? How are they used?
14. What is a run test and when is it used?
15. Discuss the managerial issues regarding the use of control charts.
16. What is an OC curve?
17. What is the purpose of acceptance sampling?
18. What two risks are present when acceptance sampling is used?
19. Is a *capable* process a *perfect* process? That is, does a capable process generate only output that meets specifications? Explain.

Using Software for SPC

Excel, Excel OM, and POM for Windows may be used to develop control charts for most of the problems in this chapter.

Creating Excel Spreadsheets to Determine Control Limits for a *c*-Chart

Excel and other spreadsheets are extensively used in industry to maintain control charts. Program S6.1 is an example of how to use Excel to determine the control limits for a *c*-chart. *c*-charts are used when the number of defects per unit of output is known. The data from Example S5 are used. In this example, 54 complaints occurred over 9 days. Excel also contains a built-in graphing ability with Chart Wizard.

PROGRAM S6.1 ▶ An Excel Spreadsheet for Creating a *c*-Chart for Example S5

	A	B	C	D	E	F	G	H
1	Red Top Cab Company							
2								
3	Number of samples	9						
4								
5		Complaints		Results				
6	Day 1	3		Total Defects	54			
7	Day 2	0		Defect rate, λ	6			
8	Day 3	8		Standard deviation	2.45			
9	Day 4	9		z value	3			99.73%
10	Day 5	6						
11	Day 6	7		Upper Control Limit	13.348469			
12	Day 7	4		Center Line	6			
13	Day 8	9		Lower Control Limit	0			
14	Day 9	8						

Value	Cell	Excel Formula
Total Defects	E6	=SUM(B6:B14)
Defect rate, λ	E7	=E6/B3
Standard deviation	E8	=SQRT(E7)
Upper Control Limit	E11	=E7+E9*E8
Center Line	E12	=E7
Lower Control Limit	E13	=IF(E7-E9*E8>0,E7-E9*E8,0)

Using Excel OM

Excel OM's Quality Control module has the ability to develop $\bar{x}$-charts, *p*-charts, and *c*-charts. It also handles OC curves, acceptance sampling, and process capability. Program S6.2 illustrates Excel OM's spreadsheet approach to computing the $\bar{x}$ control limits for the Oat Flakes company in Example S1.

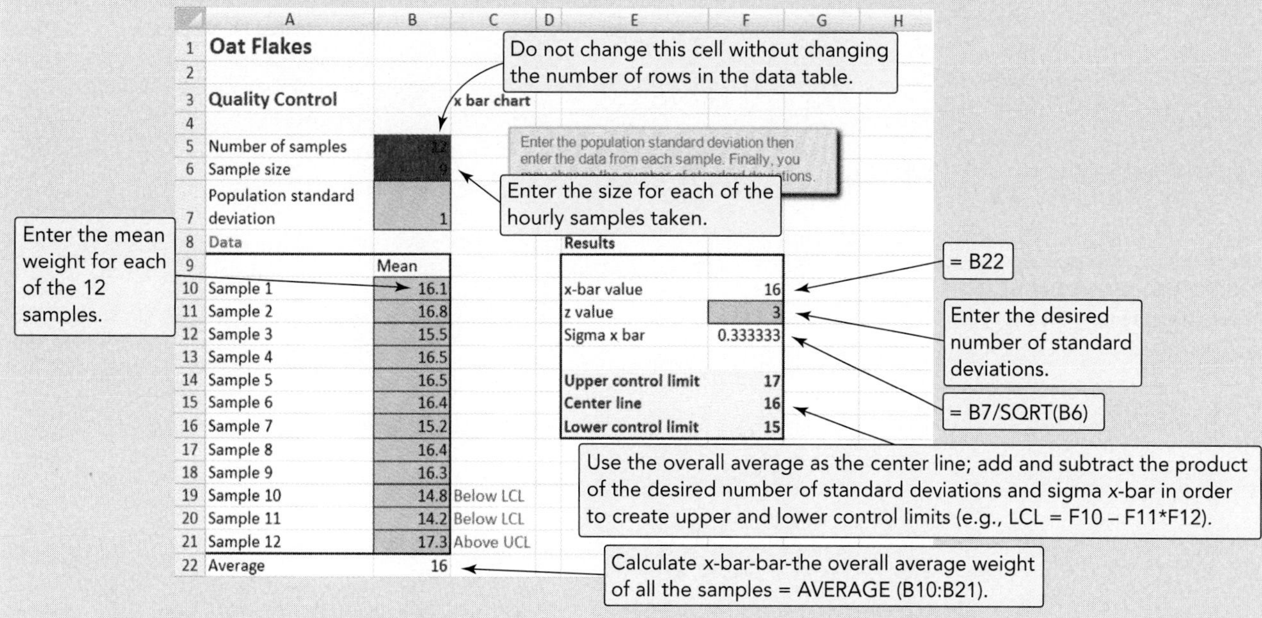

▲ PROGRAM S6.2
Excel OM Input and Selected Formulas for the Oat Flakes Example S1

Using POM for Windows

The POM for Windows Quality Control module has the ability to compute all the SPC control charts we introduced in this supplement, as well as OC curves, acceptance sampling, and process capability. See Appendix IV for further details.

Solved Problems

Virtual Office Hours help is available at www.myomlab.com.

▼ SOLVED PROBLEM S6.1

A manufacturer of precision machine parts produces round shafts for use in the construction of drill presses. The average diameter of a shaft is .56 inch. Inspection samples contain 6 shafts each. The average range of these samples is .006 inch. Determine the upper and lower $\bar{x}$ control chart limits.

▼ SOLUTION

The mean factor A_2 from Table S6.1 where the sample size is 6, is seen to be .483. With this factor, you can obtain the upper and lower control limits:

$$\begin{aligned} UCL_{\bar{x}} &= .56 + (.483)(.006) \\ &= .56 + .0029 \\ &= .5629 \text{ inch} \\ LCL_{\bar{x}} &= .56 - .0029 \\ &= .5571 \text{ inch} \end{aligned}$$

▼ SOLVED PROBLEM S6.2

Nocaf Drinks, Inc., a producer of decaffeinated coffee, bottles Nocaf. Each bottle should have a net weight of 4 ounces. The machine that fills the bottles with coffee is new, and the operations manager wants to make sure that it is properly adjusted. Bonnie Crutcher, the operations manager, randomly selects and weighs $n = 8$ bottles and records the average and range in ounces for each sample. The data for several samples is given in the following table. Note that every sample consists of 8 bottles.

Sample	Sample Range	Sample Average	Sample	Sample Range	Sample Average
A	.41	4.00	E	.56	4.17
B	.55	4.16	F	.62	3.93
C	.44	3.99	G	.54	3.98
D	.48	4.00	H	.44	4.01

Is the machine properly adjusted and in control?

▼ SOLUTION

We first find that $\bar{\bar{x}} = 4.03$ and $\bar{R} = .505$. Then, using Table S6.1, we find:

$$\begin{aligned} UCL_{\bar{x}} &= \bar{\bar{x}} + A_2\bar{R} = 4.03 + (.373)(.505) = 4.22 \\ LCL_{\bar{x}} &= \bar{\bar{x}} - A_2\bar{R} = 4.03 - (.373)(.505) = 3.84 \\ UCL_R &= D_4\bar{R} = (1.864)(.505) = .94 \\ LCL_R &= D_3\bar{R} = (.136)(.505) = .07 \end{aligned}$$

It appears that the process average and range are both in statistical control.

The operations manager needs to determine if a process with a mean (4.03) slightly above the desired mean of 4.00 is satisfactory; if it is not, the process will need to be changed.

▼ SOLVED PROBLEM S6.3

Altman Distributors, Inc., fills catalog orders. Samples of size $n = 100$ orders have been taken each day over the past six weeks. The average defect rate was .05. Determine the upper and lower limits for this process for 99.73% confidence.

▼ SOLUTION

$z = 3, \bar{p} = .05$. Using Equations (S6-9), (S6-10), and (S6-11),

$$\begin{aligned} UCL_p &= \bar{p} + 3\sqrt{\frac{\bar{p}(1-\bar{p})}{n}} = .05 + 3\sqrt{\frac{(.05)(1-.05)}{100}} \\ &= .05 + 3(0.0218) = .1154 \\ LCL_p &= \bar{p} - 3\sqrt{\frac{\bar{p}(1-\bar{p})}{n}} = .05 - 3(0.0218) \\ &= .05 - .0654 = 0 \text{ (because percentage defective cannot be negative)} \end{aligned}$$

▼ SOLVED PROBLEM S6.4

Ettlie Engineering has a new catalyst injection system for your countertop production line. Your process engineering department has conducted experiments and determined that the mean is 8.01 grams with a standard deviation of .03. Your specifications are:

$\mu = 8.0$ and $\sigma = .04$, which means an upper specification limit of 8.12 [$= 8.0 + 3(.04)$] and a lower specification limit of 7.88 [$= 8.0 - 3(.04)$].

What is the C_{pk} performance of the injection system?

▼ SOLUTION

Using Equation (S6-14):

$$C_{pk} = \text{Minimum of}\left[\frac{\text{Upper specification limit} - \overline{X}}{3\sigma}, \frac{\overline{X} - \text{Lower specification limit}}{3\sigma}\right]$$

where $\overline{X}$ = process mean

σ = standard deviation of the process population

$$C_{pk} = \text{minimum of}\left[\frac{8.12 - 8.01}{(3)(.03)}, \frac{8.01 - 7.88}{(3)(.03)}\right]$$

$$\left[\frac{.11}{.09} = 1.22, \frac{.13}{.09} = 1.44\right]$$

The minimum is 1.22, so the C_{pk} is within specifications and has an implied error rate of less than 2,700 defects per million.

Problems*

• **S6.1** Boxes of Organic Flakes are produced to contain 14 ounces, with a standard deviation of .1 ounce. Set up the 3-sigma $\bar{x}$-chart for a sample size of 36 boxes. PX

• **S6.2** The overall average on a process you are attempting to monitor is 50 units. The process standard deviation is 1.72. Determine the upper and lower control limits for a mean chart, if you choose to use a sample size of 5. PX
a) Set $z = 3$.
b) Now set $z = 2$. How do the control limits change?

• **S6.3** Thirty-five samples of size 7 each were taken from a fertilizer-bag-filling machine. The results were: Overall mean = 57.75 lb; Average range = 1.78 lb.
a) Determine the upper and lower control limits of the $\bar{x}$-chart, where $\sigma = 3$.
b) Determine the upper and lower control limits of the R-chart, where $\sigma = 3$. PX

• **S6.4** Pioneer Chicken advertises "lite" chicken with 30% fewer calories than standard chicken. When the process for "lite" chicken breast production is in control, the average chicken breast contains 420 calories, and the standard deviation in caloric content of the chicken breast population is 25 calories.

Pioneer wants to design an $\bar{x}$-chart to monitor the caloric content of chicken breasts, where 25 chicken breasts would be chosen at random to form each sample.
a) What are the lower and upper control limits for this chart if these limits are chosen to be *four* standard deviations from the target?
b) What are the limits with three standard deviations from the target? PX

• **S6.5** Cordelia Barrera is attempting to monitor a filling process that has an overall average of 705 cc. The average range is 6 cc. If you use a sample size of 10, what are the upper and lower control limits for the mean and range?

*Note: PX means the problem may be solved with POM for Windows and/or Excel OM/Excel.

•• **S6.6** Sampling 4 pieces of precision-cut wire (to be used in computer assembly) every hour for the past 24 hours has produced the following results:

Hour	$\bar{x}$	R	Hour	$\bar{x}$	R
1	3.25″	.71″	13	3.11″	.85″
2	3.10	1.18	14	2.83	1.31
3	3.22	1.43	15	3.12	1.06
4	3.39	1.26	16	2.84	.50
5	3.07	1.17	17	2.86	1.43
6	2.86	.32	18	2.74	1.29
7	3.05	.53	19	3.41	1.61
8	2.65	1.13	20	2.89	1.09
9	3.02	.71	21	2.65	1.08
10	2.85	1.33	22	3.28	.46
11	2.83	1.17	23	2.94	1.58
12	2.97	.40	24	2.64	.97

Develop appropriate control charts and determine whether there is any cause for concern in the cutting process. Plot the information and look for patterns. PX

•• **S6.7** Auto pistons at Yongpin Zhou's plant in Shanghai are produced in a forging process, and the diameter is a critical factor that must be controlled. From sample sizes of 10 pistons produced each day, the mean and the range of this diameter have been as follows:

Day	Mean (mm)	Range (mm)
1	156.9	4.2
2	153.2	4.6
3	153.6	4.1
4	155.5	5.0
5	156.6	4.5

a. What is the value of $\bar{\bar{x}}$?
b. What is the value of $\bar{R}$?
c. What are the $UCL_{\bar{x}}$ and $LCL_{\bar{x}}$ using 3σ?

d. What are the UCL_R and LCL_R using 3σ?
e. If the true diameter mean should be 155 mm and you want this as your center (nominal) line, what are the new $UCL_{\bar{x}}$ and $LCL_{\bar{x}}$? PX

•• **S6.8** Bill Kime's bowling ball factory makes bowling balls of adult size and weight only. The standard deviation in the weight of a bowling ball produced at the factory is known to be 0.12 pounds. Each day for 24 days, the average weight, in pounds, of nine of the bowling balls produced that day has been assessed as follows:

Day	Average (lb)	Day	Average (lb)
1	16.3	13	16.3
2	15.9	14	15.9
3	15.8	15	16.3
4	15.5	16	16.2
5	16.3	17	16.1
6	16.2	18	15.9
7	16.0	19	16.2
8	16.1	20	15.9
9	15.9	21	15.9
10	16.2	22	16.0
11	15.9	23	15.5
12	15.9	24	15.8

a) Establish a control chart for monitoring the average weights of the bowling balls in which the upper and lower control limits are each two standard deviations from the mean. What are the values of the control limits?
b) If three standard deviations are used in the chart, how do these values change? Why? PX

•• **S6.9** Whole Grains LLC uses statistical process control to ensure that its health-conscious, low-fat, multigrain sandwich loaves have the proper weight. Based on a previously stable and in-control process, the control limits of the $\bar{x}$- and R-charts are: $UCL_{\bar{x}} = 6.56$, $LCL_{\bar{x}} = 5.84$, $UCL_R = 1.141$, $LCL_R = 0$. Over the past few days, they have taken five random samples of four loaves each and have found the following:

	Net Weight			
Sample	Loaf #1	Loaf #2	Loaf #3	Loaf #4
1	6.3	6.0	5.9	5.9
2	6.0	6.0	6.3	5.9
3	6.3	4.8	5.6	5.2
4	6.2	6.0	6.2	5.9
5	6.5	6.6	6.5	6.9

Is the process still in control? Explain why or why not. PX

••• **S6.10** A process that is considered to be in control measures an ingredient in ounces. Below are the last 10 samples (each of size $n = 5$) taken. The population standard deviation is 1.36.

Samples									
1	2	3	4	5	6	7	8	9	10
10	9	13	10	12	10	10	13	8	10
9	9	9	10	10	10	11	10	8	12
10	11	10	11	9	8	10	8	12	9
9	11	10	10	11	12	8	10	12	8
12	10	9	10	10	9	9	8	9	12

a) What is the process standard deviation σ? What is $\sigma_{\bar{x}}$?
b) If $z = 3$, what are the control limits for the mean chart?
c) What are the control limits for the range chart?
d) Is the process in control? PX

••• **S6.11** Twelve samples, each containing five parts, were taken from a process that produces steel rods. The length of each rod in the samples was determined. The results were tabulated and sample means and ranges were computed. The results were:

Sample	Sample Mean (in.)	Range (in.)
1	10.002	0.011
2	10.002	0.014
3	9.991	0.007
4	10.006	0.022
5	9.997	0.013
6	9.999	0.012
7	10.001	0.008
8	10.005	0.013
9	9.995	0.004
10	10.001	0.011
11	10.001	0.014
12	10.006	0.009

a) Determine the upper and lower control limits and the overall means for $\bar{x}$-charts and R-charts.
b) Draw the charts and plot the values of the sample means and ranges.
c) Do the data indicate a process that is in control?
d) Why or why not? PX

•• **S6.12** Eagletrons are all-electric automobiles produced by Mogul Motors, Inc. One of the concerns of Mogul Motors is that the Eagletrons be capable of achieving appropriate maximum speeds. To monitor this, Mogul executives take samples of eight Eagletrons at a time. For each sample, they determine the average maximum speed and the range of the maximum speeds within the sample. They repeat this with 35 samples to obtain 35 sample means and 35 ranges. They find that the average sample mean is 88.50 miles per hour, and the average range is 3.25 miles per hour. Using these results, the executives decide to establish an R chart. They would like this chart to be established so that when it shows that the range of a sample is not within the control limits, there is only approximately a 0.0027 probability that this is due to natural variation. What will be the upper control limit (UCL) and the lower control limit (LCL) in this chart? PX

•• **S6.13** The defect rate for data entry of insurance claims has historically been about 1.5%.
a) What are the upper and lower control chart limits if you wish to use a sample size of 100 and 3-sigma limits?
b) What if the sample size used were 50, with 3σ?
c) What if the sample size used were 100, with 2σ?
d) What if the sample size used were 50, with 2σ?
e) What happens to $\sigma_{\hat{p}}$ when the sample size is larger?
f) Explain why the lower control limit cannot be less than 0. PX

•• **S6.14** You are attempting to develop a quality monitoring system for some parts purchased from Charles Sox Manufacturing Co. These parts are either good or defective. You have decided to take a sample of 100 units. Develop a table of the appropriate upper and lower control chart limits for various values of the average fraction defective in the samples taken. The values for $\bar{p}$ in this table should range from 0.02 to 0.10 in increments of 0.02. Develop the upper and lower control limits for a 99.73% confidence level.

n = 100		
$\bar{p}$	UCL	LCL
0.02		
0.04		
0.06		
0.08		
0.10		

PX

•• **S6.15** The results of inspection of DNA samples taken over the past 10 days are given below. Sample size is 100.

Day	1	2	3	4	5	6	7	8	9	10
Defectives	7	6	6	9	5	6	0	8	9	1

a) Construct a 3-sigma p-chart using this information.
b) If the number of defectives on the next three days are 12, 5, and 13, is the process in control? PX

• **S6.16** In the past, the defective rate for your product has been 1.5%. What are the upper and lower control chart limits if you wish to use a sample size of 500 and $z = 3$? PX

• **S6.17** Refer to Problem S6.16. If the defective rate was 3.5% instead of 1.5%, what would be the control limits ($z = 3$)? PX

•• **S6.18** Five data entry operators work at the data processing department of the Georgia Bank. Each day for 30 days, the number of defective records in a sample of 250 records typed by these operators has been noted, as follows:

Sample No.	No. Defective	Sample No.	No. Defective	Sample No.	No. Defective
1	7	11	18	21	17
2	5	12	5	22	12
3	19	13	16	23	6
4	10	14	4	24	7
5	11	15	11	25	13
6	8	16	8	26	10
7	12	17	12	27	4
8	9	18	4	28	6
9	6	19	6	29	12
10	13	20	16	30	3

a) Establish 3σ upper and lower control limits.
b) Why can the lower control limit not be a negative number?
c) The industry standards for the upper and lower control limits are 0.10 and 0.01, respectively. What does this imply about Georgia Bank's own standards? PX

•• **S6.19** Detroit Central Hospital is trying to improve its image by providing a positive experience for its patients and their relatives. Part of the "image" program involves providing tasty, inviting patient meals that are also healthful. A questionnaire accompanies each meal served, asking the patient, among other things, whether he or she is satisfied or unsatisfied with the meal. A 100-patient sample of the survey results over the past 7 days yielded the following data:

Day	No. of Unsatisfied Patients	Sample Size
1	24	100
2	22	100
3	8	100
4	15	100
5	10	100
6	26	100
7	17	100

Construct a p-chart that plots the percentage of patients unsatisfied with their meals. Set the control limits to include 99.73% of the random variation in meal satisfaction. Comment on your results. PX

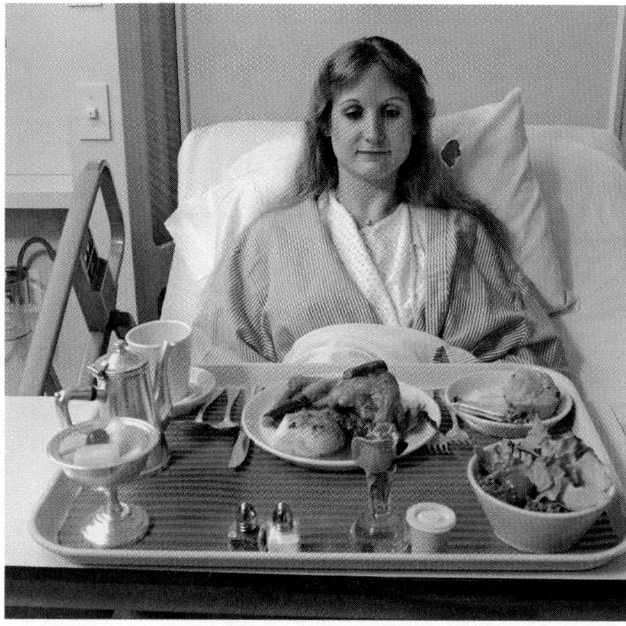

•• **S6.20** Chicago Supply Company manufactures paper clips and other office products. Although inexpensive, paper clips have provided the firm with a high margin of profitability. Sample size is 200. Results are given for the last 10 samples.

Sample	1	2	3	4	5	6	7	8	9	10
Defectives	5	7	4	4	6	3	5	6	2	8

a) Establish upper and lower control limits for the control chart and graph the data.
b) Is the process in control?
c) If the sample size were 100 instead, how would your limits and conclusions change? PX

• **S6.21** Peter Ittig's department store, Ittig Brothers, is Amherst's largest independent clothier. The store receives an average of six returns per day. Using $z = 3$, would nine returns in a day warrant action? PX

•• **S6.22** An ad agency tracks the complaints, by week received, about the billboards in its city:

Week	No. of Complaints
1	4
2	5
3	4
4	11
5	3
6	9

a. What type of control chart would you use to monitor this process and why?
b. What are the 3-sigma control limits for this process? Assume that the historical complaint rate is unknown.
c. Is the process mean in control, according to the control limits? Why or why not?
d. Assume now that the historical complaint rate has been four calls a week. What would the 3-sigma control limits for this process be now? Is the process in control according to the control limits? PX

•• **S6.23** The school board is trying to evaluate a new math program introduced to second-graders in five elementary schools across the county this year. A sample of the student scores on standardized math tests in each elementary school yielded the following data:

School	No. of Test Errors
A	52
B	27
C	35
D	44
E	55

Construct a *c*-chart for test errors, and set the control limits to contain 99.73% of the random variation in test scores. What does the chart tell you? Has the new math program been effective? PX

•• **S6.24** Telephone inquiries of 100 IRS "customers" are monitored daily at random. Incidents of incorrect information or other nonconformities (such as impoliteness to customers) are recorded. The data for last week follow:

Day	No. of Nonconformities
1	5
2	10
3	23
4	20
5	15

a) Construct a 3-standard deviation *c*-chart of nonconformities.
b) What does the control chart tell you about the IRS telephone operators? PX

••• **S6.25** The accounts receivable department at Rick Wing Manufacturing has been having difficulty getting customers to pay the full amount of their bills. Many customers complain that the bills are not correct and do not reflect the materials that arrived at their receiving docks. The department has decided to implement SPC in its billing process. To set up control charts, 10 samples of 50 bills each were taken over a month's time and the items on the bills checked against the bill of lading sent by the company's shipping department to determine the number of bills that were not correct. The results were:

Sample No.	No. of Incorrect Bills	Sample No.	No. of Incorrect Bills
1	6	6	5
2	5	7	3
3	11	8	4
4	4	9	7
5	0	10	2

a) Determine the value of *p*-bar, the mean fraction defective. Then determine the control limits for the *p*-chart using a 99.73% confidence level (3 standard deviations). Is this process in control? If not, which sample(s) were out of control?
b) How might you use the quality tools discussed in Chapter 6 to determine the source of the billing defects and where you might start your improvement efforts to eliminate the causes? PX

• **S6.26** The difference between the upper specification and the lower specification for a process is 0.6″. The standard deviation is 0.1″. What is the process capability ratio, C_p? Interpret this number. PX

•• **S6.27** Meena Chavan Corp.'s computer chip production process yields DRAM chips with an average life of 1,800 hours and $\sigma = 100$ hours. The tolerance upper and lower specification limits are 2,400 hours and 1,600 hours, respectively. Is this process capable of producing DRAM chips to specification? PX

•• **S6.28** Blackburn, Inc., an equipment manufacturer in Nashville, has submitted a sample cutoff valve to improve your manufacturing process. Your process engineering department has conducted experiments and found that the valve has a mean (μ) of 8.00 and a standard deviation (σ) of .04. Your desired performance is $\mu = 8.0$ and $\sigma = .045$. What is the C_{pk} of the Blackburn valve? PX

•• **S6.29** The specifications for a plastic liner for concrete highway projects calls for a thickness of 3.0 mm ±.1 mm. The standard deviation of the process is estimated to be .02 mm. What are the upper and lower specification limits for this product? The process is known to operate at a mean thickness of 3.0 mm. What is the C_{pk} for this process? About what percentage of all units of this liner will meet specifications? PX

•• **S6.30** The manager of a food processing plant desires a quality specification with a mean of 16 ounces, an upper specification limit of 16.5, and a lower specification limit of 15.5. The process has a mean of 16 ounces and a standard deviation of 1 ounce. Determine the C_{pk} of the process. PX

•• **S6.31** A process filling small bottles with baby formula has a target of 3 ounces ±0.150 ounce. Two hundred bottles from the process were sampled. The results showed the average amount of formula placed in the bottles to be 3.042 ounces. The standard deviation of the amounts was 0.034 ounce. Determine the value of C_{pk}. Roughly what proportion of bottles meet the specifications? PX

••• **S6.32** As the supervisor in charge of shipping and receiving, you need to determine *the average outgoing quality* in a plant where the known incoming lots from your assembly line have an average defective rate of 3%. Your plan is to sample 80 units of every 1,000 in a lot. The number of defects in the sample is not to exceed 3. Such a plan provides you with a probability of acceptance of each lot of .79 (79%). What is your average outgoing quality? PX

••• **S6.33** An acceptance sampling plan has lots of 500 pieces and a sample size of 60. The number of defects in the sample may not exceed 2. This plan, based on an OC curve, has a probability of .57 of accepting lots when the incoming lots have a defective rate of 4%, which is the historical average for this process. What do you tell your customer the average outgoing quality is? PX

••• **S6.34** West Battery Corp. has recently been receiving complaints from retailers that its 9-volt batteries are not lasting as long as other name brands. James West, head of the TQM program at West's Austin plant, believes there is no problem because his batteries have had an average life of 50 hours, about 10% longer than competitors' models. To raise the lifetime above this level would require a new level of technology not available to West. Nevertheless, he is concerned enough to set up hourly assembly line checks. Previously, after ensuring that the process was running properly, West took size $n = 5$ samples of 9-volt batteries for each of 25 hours to establish the standards for control chart limits. Those samples are shown in the following table:

West Battery Data—Battery Lifetimes (in hours)

	Sample						
Hour	1	2	3	4	5	$\bar{x}$	R
1	51	50	49	50	50	50.0	2
2	45	47	70	46	36	48.8	34
3	50	35	48	39	47	43.8	15

Hour	Sample 1	2	3	4	5	$\bar{x}$	R
4	55	70	50	30	51	51.2	40
5	49	38	64	36	47	46.8	28
6	59	62	40	54	64	55.8	24
7	36	33	49	48	56	44.4	23
8	50	67	53	43	40	50.6	27
9	44	52	46	47	44	46.6	8
10	70	45	50	47	41	50.6	29
11	57	54	62	45	36	50.8	26
12	56	54	47	42	62	52.2	20
13	40	70	58	45	44	51.4	30
14	52	58	40	52	46	49.6	18
15	57	42	52	58	59	53.6	17
16	62	49	42	33	55	48.2	29
17	40	39	49	59	48	47.0	20
18	64	50	42	57	50	52.6	22
19	58	53	52	48	50	52.2	10
20	60	50	41	41	50	48.4	19
21	52	47	48	58	40	49.0	18
22	55	40	56	49	45	49.0	16
23	47	48	50	50	48	48.6	3
24	50	50	49	51	51	50.2	2
25	51	50	51	51	62	53.0	12

With these limits established, West now takes 5 more hours of data, which are shown in the following table:

Hour	*Sample* 1	2	3	4	5
26	48	52	39	57	61
27	45	53	48	46	66
28	63	49	50	45	53
29	57	70	45	52	61
30	45	38	46	54	52

a. Determine means and the upper and lower control limits for $\bar{x}$ and R (using the first 25 hours only).
b. Is the manufacturing process in control?
c. Comment on the lifetimes observed. PX

•••• **S6.35** One of Alabama Air's top competitive priorities is on-time arrivals. Quality V.P. Mike Hanna decided to personally monitor Alabama Air's performance. Each week for the past 30 weeks, Hanna checked a random sample of 100 flight arrivals for on-time performance. The table that follows contains the number of flights that did not meet Alabama Air's definition of on time:

Sample (week)	Late Flights	Sample (week)	Late Flights
1	2	16	2
2	4	17	3
3	10	18	7
4	4	19	3
5	1	20	2
6	1	21	3
7	13	22	7
8	9	23	4
9	11	24	3
10	0	25	2
11	3	26	2
12	4	27	0
13	2	28	1
14	2	29	3
15	8	30	4

a. Using a 95% confidence level, plot the overall percentage of late flights ($\bar{p}$) and the upper and lower control limits on a control chart.
b. Assume that the airline industry's upper and lower control limits for flights that are not on time are .1000 and .0400, respectively. Draw them on your control chart.
c. Plot the percentage of late flights in each sample. Do all samples fall within Alabama Airlines's control limits? When one falls outside the control limits, what should be done?
d. What can Mike Hanna report about the quality of service? PX

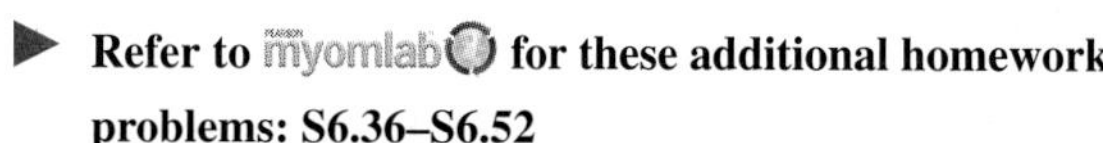

Refer to myomlab for these additional homework problems: S6.36–S6.52

Case Studies

▶ Bayfield Mud Company

In November 2009, John Wells, a customer service representative of Bayfield Mud Company, was summoned to the Houston warehouse of Wet-Land Drilling, Inc., to inspect three boxcars of mudtreating agents that Bayfield had shipped to the Houston firm. (Bayfield's corporate offices and its largest plant are located in Orange, Texas, which is just west of the Louisiana–Texas border.) Wet-Land had filed a complaint that the 50-pound bags of treating agents just received from Bayfield were short-weight by approximately 5%.

The short-weight bags were initially detected by one of Wet-Land's receiving clerks, who noticed that the railroad scale tickets indicated that net weights were significantly less on all three boxcars than those of identical shipments received on October 25, 2009. Bayfield's traffic department was called to determine if lighter-weight pallets were used on the shipments. (This might explain the lighter net weights.) Bayfield indicated, however, that no changes had been made in loading or palletizing procedures. Thus, Wet-Land engineers randomly checked 50 bags and discovered that the average net weight was 47.51 pounds. They noted from past shipments that the process yielded bag net weights averaging exactly 50.0 pounds, with an acceptable standard deviation σ of 1.2 pounds. Consequently, they concluded that the sample indicated a significant short-weight. (The reader may wish to verify this conclusion.)

Bayfield was then contacted, and Wells was sent to investigate the complaint. Upon arrival, Wells verified the complaint and issued a 5% credit to Wet-Land.

Wet-Land management, however, was not completely satisfied with the issuance of credit. The charts followed by their mud engineers on the drilling platforms were based on 50-pound bags of treating agents. Lighter-weight bags might result in poor chemical control during the drilling operation and thus adversely affect drilling efficiency. (Mud-treating agents are used to control the pH and other chemical properties of the core during drilling operation.) This defect could cause severe economic consequences because of the extremely high cost of oil and natural gas well-drilling operations. Consequently, special-use instructions had to accompany the delivery of these shipments to the drilling platforms. Moreover, the short-weight shipments had to be isolated in Wet-Land's warehouse, causing extra handling and poor space utilization. Thus, Wells was informed that Wet-Land might seek a new supplier of mud-treating agents if, in the future, it received bags that deviated significantly from 50 pounds.

The quality control department at Bayfield suspected that the lightweight bags might have resulted from "growing pains" at the Orange plant. Because of the earlier energy crisis, oil and natural gas exploration activity had greatly increased. In turn, this increased activity created increased demand for products produced by related industries, including drilling muds. Consequently, Bayfield had to expand from a one-shift (6:00 A.M. to 2:00 P.M.) to a two-shift (2:00 P.M. to 10:00 P.M.) operation in mid-2007, and finally to a three-shift operation (24 hours per day) in the fall of 2009.

The additional night-shift bagging crew was staffed entirely by new employees. The most experienced foremen were temporarily assigned to supervise the night-shift employees. Most emphasis was placed on increasing the output of bags to meet ever-increasing demand. It was suspected that only occasional reminders were made to double-check the bag weight-feeder. (A double-check is performed by systematically weighing a bag on a scale to determine if the proper weight is being loaded by the weight-feeder. If there is significant deviation from

Time	Average Weight (pounds)	*Range* Smallest	*Range* Largest	Time	Average Weight (pounds)	*Range* Smallest	*Range* Largest
6:00 A.M.	49.6	48.7	50.7	6:00	46.8	41.0	51.2
7:00	50.2	49.1	51.2	7:00	50.0	46.2	51.7
8:00	50.6	49.6	51.4	8:00	47.4	44.0	48.7
9:00	50.8	50.2	51.8	9:00	47.0	44.2	48.9
10:00	49.9	49.2	52.3	10:00	47.2	46.6	50.2
11:00	50.3	48.6	51.7	11:00	48.6	47.0	50.0
12 Noon	48.6	46.2	50.4	12 Midnight	49.8	48.2	50.4
1:00 P.M.	49.0	46.4	50.0	1:00 A.M.	49.6	48.4	51.7
2:00	49.0	46.0	50.6	2:00	50.0	49.0	52.2
3:00	49.8	48.2	50.8	3:00	50.0	49.2	50.0
4:00	50.3	49.2	52.7	4:00	47.2	46.3	50.5
5:00	51.4	50.0	55.3	5:00	47.0	44.1	49.7
6:00	51.6	49.2	54.7	6:00	48.4	45.0	49.0
7:00	51.8	50.0	55.6	7:00	48.8	44.8	49.7
8:00	51.0	48.6	53.2	8:00	49.6	48.0	51.8
9:00	50.5	49.4	52.4	9:00	50.0	48.1	52.7
10:00	49.2	46.1	50.7	10:00	51.0	48.1	55.2
11:00	49.0	46.3	50.8	11:00	50.4	49.5	54.1
12 Midnight	48.4	45.4	50.2	12 Noon	50.0	48.7	50.9
1:00 A.M.	47.6	44.3	49.7	1:00 P.M.	48.9	47.6	51.2
2:00	47.4	44.1	49.6	2:00	49.8	48.4	51.0
3:00	48.2	45.2	49.0	3:00	49.8	48.8	50.8
4:00	48.0	45.5	49.1	4:00	50.0	49.1	50.6
5:00	48.4	47.1	49.6	5:00	47.8	45.2	51.2
6:00	48.6	47.4	52.0	6:00	46.4	44.0	49.7
7:00	50.0	49.2	52.2	7:00	46.4	44.4	50.0
8:00	49.8	49.0	52.4	8:00	47.2	46.6	48.9
9:00	50.3	49.4	51.7	9:00	48.4	47.2	49.5
10:00	50.2	49.6	51.8	10:00	49.2	48.1	50.7
11:00	50.0	49.0	52.3	11:00	48.4	47.0	50.8
12 Noon	50.0	48.8	52.4	12 Midnight	47.2	46.4	49.2
1:00 P.M.	50.1	49.4	53.6	1:00 A.M.	47.4	46.8	49.0
2:00	49.7	48.6	51.0	2:00	48.8	47.2	51.4
3:00	48.4	47.2	51.7	3:00	49.6	49.0	50.6
4:00	47.2	45.3	50.9	4:00	51.0	50.5	51.5
5:00	46.8	44.1	49.0	5:00	50.5	50.0	51.9

50 pounds, corrective adjustments are made to the weight-release mechanism.)

To verify this expectation, the quality control staff randomly sampled the bag output and prepared the chart on the previous page. Six bags were sampled and weighed each hour.

Discussion Questions

1. What is your analysis of the bag-weight problem?
2. What procedures would you recommend to maintain proper quality control?

Source: Professor Jerry Kinard, Western Carolina University.

►Frito-Lay's Quality-Controlled Potato Chips

Video Case

Frito-Lay, the multi-billion-dollar snack food giant, produces billions of pounds of product every year at its dozens of U.S. and Canadian plants. From the farming of potatoes—in Florida, North Carolina, and Michigan—to factory and to retail stores, the ingredients and final product of Lay's chips, for example, are inspected at least 11 times: in the field, before unloading at the plant, after washing and peeling, at the sizing station, at the fryer, after seasoning, when bagged (for weight), at carton filling, in the warehouse, and as they are placed on the store shelf by Frito-Lay personnel. Similar inspections take place for its other famous products, including Cheetos, Fritos, Ruffles, and Tostitos.

In addition to these employee inspections, the firm uses proprietary vision systems to look for defective potato chips. Chips are pulled off the high-speed line and checked twice if the vision system senses them to be too brown.

The company follows the very strict standards of the American Institute of Baking (AIB), standards that are much tougher than those of the U.S. Food and Drug Administration. Two unannounced AIB site visits per year keep Frito-Lay's plants on their toes. Scores, consistently in the "excellent" range, are posted, and every employee knows exactly how the plant is doing.

There are two key metrics in Frito-Lay's continuous improvement quality program: (1) total customer complaints (measured on a complaints per million bag basis) and (2) hourly or daily statistical process control scores (for oil, moisture, seasoning, and salt content, for chip thickness, for fryer temperature, and for weight).

In the Florida plant, Angela McCormack, who holds engineering and MBA degrees, oversees a 15-member quality assurance staff. They watch all aspects of quality, including training employees on the factory floor, monitoring automated processing equipment, and developing and updating statistical process control (SPC) charts. The upper and lower control limits for one check point, salt content in Lay's chips, are 2.22% and 1.98%, respectively. To see exactly how these limits are created using SPC, watch the video that accompanies this case.

Discussion Questions*

1. Angela is now going to evaluate a new salt process delivery system and wants to know if the upper and lower control limits at 3 standard deviations for the new system will meet the upper and lower control specifications noted above.
   The data (in percents) from the initial trial samples are:
   Sample 1: 1.98, 2.11, 2.15, 2.06
   Sample 2: 1.99, 2.0, 2.08, 1.99
   Sample 3: 2.20, 2.10. 2.20, 2.05
   Sample 4: 2.18, 2.01, 2.23, 1.98
   Sample 5: 2.01, 2.08, 2.14, 2.16
   Provide the report to Angela.
2. What are the advantage and disadvantages of Frito-Lay drivers stocking their customers' shelves?
3. Why is quality a critical function at Frito-Lay?

Source: Professors Barry Render, Rollins College; Jay Heizer, Texas Lutheran University; and Beverly Amer, Northern Arizona University.

*You may wish to view the video that accompanies this case before answering these questions.

► Farm to Fork: Quality at Darden Restaurants

Video Case

Darden Restaurants, the \$5.2 billion owner of such popular brands as Olive Garden, Red Lobster, Seasons 52, and Bahama Breeze, serves more than 300 million meals annually in its 1,700 restaurants across the U.S. and Canada. Before any one of these meals is placed before a guest, the ingredients for each recipe must pass quality control inspections from the source, ranging from measurement and weighing, to tasting, touching, or lab testing. Darden has differentiated itself from its restaurant peers by developing the gold standard in continuous improvement.

To assure both customers and the company that quality expectations are met, Darden uses a rigorous inspection process, employing statistical process control (SPC) as part of its "Farm to Fork" program. More than 50 food scientists, microbiologists, and public health professionals report to Ana Hooper, vice president of quality assurance.

As part of Darden's Point Source program, Hooper's team, based in Southeast Asia (in China, Thailand, and Singapore) and Latin America (in Equador, Honduras, and Chile), approves and inspects—and works with Darden buyers to purchase—more than 50 million pounds of seafood each year for restaurant use. Darden used to build quality in at the end by inspecting shipments as they reached U.S. distribution centers. Now, thanks to coaching and partnering with vendors abroad, Darden needs but a few domestic inspection labs to verify compliance to its exacting standards. Food vendors in source countries know that when supplying Darden, they are subject to regular audits that are stricter than U.S. Food and Drug Administration (FDA) standards.

Two Quality Success Stories

Quality specialists' jobs include raising the bar and improving quality and safety at all plants in their geographic area. The Thai quality representative, for example, worked closely with several of Darden's largest shrimp vendors to convert them to a production-line-integrated quality assurance program. The vendors were able to improve the quality of shrimp supplied and reduce the percentage of defects by 19%.

Likewise, when the Darden quality teams visited fields of growers/shippers in Mexico recently, it identified challenges such as low employee hygiene standards, field food safety problems, lack of portable toilets, child labor, and poor working conditions. Darden addressed these concerns and hired third party independent food safety verification firms to ensure continued compliance to standards.

SPC Charts

SPC charts, such as the one shown on page 224 in this supplement, are particularly important. These charts document precooked food weights; meat, seafood and poultry temperatures; blemishes on produce; and bacteria counts on shrimp—just to name a few. Quality assurance is part of a much bigger process that is key to Darden's success—its supply chain (see Chapter 11 and Supplement 11 for discussion and case studies on this topic). That's because quality comes from the source and flows through distribution to the restaurant and guests.

Discussion Questions*

1. How does Darden build quality into the supply chain?
2. Select two potential problems—one in the Darden supply chain and one in a restaurant—that can be analyzed with a fish-bone chart. Draw a complete chart to deal with each problem.
3. Darden applies SPC in many product attributes. Identify where these are probably used.
4. The SPC chart on page 224 illustrates Darden's use of control charts to monitor the weight of salmon filets. Given these data, what conclusion do you, as a Darden quality control inspector, draw? What report do you issue to your supervisor? How do you respond to the salmon vendor?

*You might want to view the video that accompanies this case before answering these questions.

▶**Additional Case Study:** Visit **www.myomlab.com** or **www.pearsonhighered.com/heizer** *for this free case study*:
Green River Chemical Company: Involves a company that needs to set up a control chart to monitor sulfate content because of customer complaints.

Bibliography

Bakir, S. T. "A Quality Control Chart for Work Performance Appraisal." *Quality Engineering* 17, no. 3 (2005): 429.

Besterfield, Dale H. *Quality Control*, 8th ed. Upper Saddle River, NJ: Prentice Hall, 2009.

Elg, M., J. Olsson, and J. J. Dahlgaard. "Implementing Statistical Process Control." *The International Journal of Quality and Reliability Management* 25, no. 6 (2008): 545.

Goetsch, David L., and Stanley B. Davis. *Quality Management*, 5th ed. Upper Saddle River, NJ: Prentice Hall, 2006.

Gryna, F. M., R. C. H. Chua, and J. A. DeFeo. *Juran's Quality Planning and Analysis*, 5th ed. New York: McGraw-Hill, 2007.

Lin, H., and G. Sheen. "Practical Implementation of the Capability Index C_{pk} Based on Control Chart Data." *Quality Engineering* 17, no. 3 (2005): 371.

Matthes, N., et al. "Statistical Process Control for Hospitals." *Quality Management in Health Care* 16, no. 3 (July–September 2007): 205.

Mitra, Amit. *Fundamentals of Quality Control and Improvement*, 3rd ed. New York: Wiley, 2008.

Montgomery, D. C. *Introduction to Statistical Quality Control*, 6th ed. New York: Wiley, 2008.

Roth, H. P. "How SPC Can Help Cut Costs." *Journal of Corporate Accounting and Finance* 16, no. 3 (March–April 2005): 21–30.

Summers, Donna. *Quality Management*, 2nd ed. Upper Saddle River, NJ: Prentice Hall, 2009.

Supplement 6 *Rapid* Review

Main Heading	Review Material	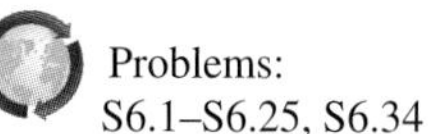
STATISTICAL PROCESS CONTROL (SPC) (pp. 218–231)	■ **Statistical process control (SPC)**—A process used to monitor standards by taking measurements and corrective action as a product or service is being produced.	Problems: S6.1–S6.25, S6.34

■ **Control chart**—A graphical presentation of process data over time.

A process is said to be operating *in statistical control* when the only source of variation is common (natural) causes. The process must first be brought into statistical control by detecting and eliminating special (assignable) causes of variation.
The objective of a process control system is to provide a statistical signal when assignable causes of variation are present.

■ **Natural variations**—The variability that affects every production process to some degree and is to be expected; also known as common cause.

When natural variations form a *normal distribution,* they are characterized by two parameters:

- Mean, μ (the measure of central tendency—in this case, the average value)
- Standard deviation, σ (the measure of dispersion)

As long as the distribution (output measurements) remains within specified limits, the process is said to be "in control," and natural variations are tolerated.

■ **Assignable variation**—Variation in a production process that can be traced to specific causes.

Control charts for the mean, $\bar{x}$, and the range, R, are used to monitor *variables* (outputs with continuous dimensions), such as weight, speed, length, or strength.

■ **$\bar{x}$-chart**—A quality control chart for variables that indicates when changes occur in the central tendency of a production process.

■ ***R*-chart**—A control chart that tracks the range within a sample; it indicates that a gain or loss in uniformity has occurred in dispersion of a production process.

■ **Central Limit Theorem**—The theoretical foundation for $\bar{x}$-charts, which states that regardless of the distribution of the population of all parts or services, the $\bar{x}$ distribution will tend to follow a normal curve as the number of samples increases:

$$\bar{\bar{x}} = \mu \quad \text{(S6-1)}$$

$$\sigma_{\bar{x}} = \frac{\sigma}{\sqrt{n}} \quad \text{(S6-2)}$$

The $\bar{x}$-chart limits, if we know the true standard deviation σ of the process population, are:

$$\text{Upper control limit (UCL)} = \bar{\bar{x}} + z\sigma_{\bar{x}} \quad \text{(S6-3)}$$

$$\text{Lower control limit (LCL)} = \bar{\bar{x}} + z\sigma_{\bar{x}} \quad \text{(S6-4)}$$

where z = the confidence level selected (e.g., $z = 3$ is 99.73% confidence)

The *range*, R, of a sample is defined as the difference between the largest and smallest items. If we do not know the true standard deviation, σ, of the population, the $\bar{x}$-chart limits are:

$$\text{UCL}_{\bar{x}} = \bar{\bar{x}} + A_2\bar{R} \quad \text{(S6-5)}$$

$$\text{LCL}_{\bar{x}} = \bar{\bar{x}} - A_2\bar{R} \quad \text{(S6-6)}$$

In addition to being concerned with the process average, operations managers are interested in the process dispersion, or range. The R-chart control limits for the range of a process are:

$$\text{UCL}_R = D_4\bar{R} \quad \text{(S6-7)}$$

$$\text{LCL}_R = D_3\bar{R} \quad \text{(S6-8)}$$

A*ttributes* are typically classified as *defective* or *nondefective*. The two attribute charts are (1) p-charts (which measure the *percent* defective in a sample, and (2) c-charts (which *count* the number of defects in a sample).

■ ***p*-chart—**A quality control chart that is used to control attributes:

$$\text{UCL}_p = \bar{p} + z\sigma_{\hat{p}} \quad \text{(S6-9)}$$

$$\text{LCL}_p = \bar{p} + z\sigma_{\hat{p}} \quad \text{(S6-10)}$$

$$\sigma_{\hat{p}} = \sqrt{\frac{\bar{p}(1-\bar{p})}{n}} \quad \text{(S6-11)}$$

VIDEO S6.1
Farm to Fork: Quality at Darden Restaurants

VIDEO S6.2
Frito-Lay's Quality-Controlled Potato Chips

Virtual Office Hours for Solved Problems: S6.1–S6.3

ACTIVE MODEL S6.1

Main Heading	Review Material	myomlab
	▪ ***c*-chart**—A quality control chart used to control the number of defects per unit of output. The Poisson distribution is the basis for *c*-charts, whose 99.73% limits are computed as: $$\text{Control limits} = \bar{c} \pm 3\sqrt{\bar{c}} \quad \text{(S6-12)}$$ ▪ **Run test**—A test used to examine the points in a control chart to determine whether nonrandom variation is present.	
PROCESS CAPABILITY (pp. 231–233)	▪ **Process capability**—The ability to meet design specifications. ▪ **C_p**—A ratio for determining whether a process meets design specifications. $$C_p = \frac{\text{(Upper specification} - \text{Lower specification)}}{6\sigma} \quad \text{(S6-13)}$$ ▪ **C_{pk}**—A proportion of variation (3σ) between the center of the process and the nearest specification limit: $$C_{pk} = \text{Minimum of}\left[\frac{\text{Upper spec limit} - \overline{X}}{3\sigma}, \frac{\overline{X} - \text{Lower spec limit}}{3\sigma}\right] \quad \text{(S6-14)}$$	Problems: S6.26–S6.31 Virtual Office Hours for Solved Problem: S6.4 **ACTIVE MODEL S6.2**
ACCEPTANCE SAMPLING (pp. 233–236)	▪ **Acceptance sampling**—A method of measuring random samples of lots or batches of products against predetermined standards. ▪ **Operating characteristic (OC) curve**—A graph that describes how well an acceptance plan discriminates between good and bad lots. ▪ **Producer's risk**—The mistake of having a producer's good lot rejected through sampling. ▪ **Consumer's risk**—The mistake of a customer's acceptance of a bad lot overlooked through sampling. ▪ **Acceptable quality level (AQL)**—The quality level of a lot considered good. ▪ **Lot tolerance percent defective (LTPD)**—The quality level of a lot considered bad. ▪ **Type I error**—Statistically, the probability of rejecting a good lot. ▪ **Type II error**—Statistically, the probability of accepting a bad lot. ▪ **Average outgoing quality (AOQ)**—The percent defective in an average lot of goods inspected through acceptance sampling: $$\text{AOQ} = \frac{(P_d)(P_a)(N - n)}{N} \quad \text{(S6-15)}$$	Problems: S6.32, S6.33 **ACTIVE MODEL S6.3**

Self Test

▪ **Before taking the self-test,** refer to the learning objectives listed at the beginning of the supplement and the key terms listed at the end of the supplement.

LO1. If the mean of a particular sample is within control limits and the range of that sample is not within control limits:
- **a)** the process is in control, with only assignable causes of variation.
- **b)** the process is not producing within the established control limits.
- **c)** the process is producing within the established control limits, with only natural causes of variation.
- **d)** the process has both natural and assignable causes of variation.

LO2. The Central Limit Theorem:
- **a)** is the theoretical foundation of the *c*-chart.
- **b)** states that the average of assignable variations is zero.
- **c)** allows managers to use the normal distribution as the basis for building some control charts.
- **d)** states that the average range can be used as a proxy for the standard deviation.
- **e)** controls the steepness of an operating characteristic curve.

LO3. The type of chart used to control the central tendency of variables with continuous dimensions is:
a) $\bar{x}$-chart. **b)** *R*-chart. **c)** *p*-chart.
d) *c*-chart. **e)** none of the above.

LO4. If parts in a sample are measured and the mean of the sample measurement is outside the tolerance limits:
- **a)** the process is out of control, and the cause should be established.
- **b)** the process is in control but not capable of producing within the established control limits.
- **c)** the process is within the established control limits, with only natural causes of variation.
- **d)** all of the above are true.

LO5. Control charts for attributes are:
a) *p*-charts. **b)** *c*-charts. **c)** *R*-charts.
d) $\bar{x}$-charts. **e)** both a and b.

LO6. The ability of a process to meet design specifications is called:
a) Taguchi. **b)** process capability.
c) capability index. **d)** acceptance sampling.
e) average outgoing quality.

LO7. The _____ risk is the probability that a lot will be rejected despite the quality level exceeding or meeting the _____.

LO8. In most acceptance sampling plans, when a lot is rejected, the entire lot is inspected, and all defective items are replaced. When using this technique, the AOQ:
- **a)** worsens (AOQ becomes a larger fraction).
- **b)** improves (AOQ becomes a smaller fraction).
- **c)** is not affected, but the AQL is improved.
- **d)** is not affected.
- **e)** falls to zero.

Answers: LO1. b; LO2. c; LO3. a; LO4. a; LO5. e; LO6. b; LO7. producer's risk, AQL; LO8. b.

7 Process Strategy and Sustainability

Chapter Outline

10

OM Strategy Decisions

- ► Design of Goods and Services
- ► Managing Quality
- ► **Process Strategy**
- ► Location Strategies
- ► Layout Strategies
- ► Human Resources
- ► Supply-Chain Management
- ► Inventory Management
- ► Scheduling
- ► Maintenance

REPETITIVE MANUFACTURING WORKS AT HARLEY-DAVIDSON

Since Harley-Davidson's founding in Milwaukee in 1903, it has competed with hundreds of manufacturers, foreign and domestic. The competition has been tough. Recent competitive battles have been with the Japanese, and earlier battles were with the German, English, and Italian manufacturers. But after over 100 years, Harley is the only major U.S. motorcycle company. The company now has five U.S. facilities and an assembly plant in Brazil. The Sportster powertrain is manufactured in Wauwatosa, Wisconsin, and the sidecars, saddlebags, windshields, and other specialty items are produced in Tomahawk, Wisconsin. The families of Touring and Softail bikes are assembled in York, Pennsylvania, while the Sportster models, Dyna models, and VRSC models of motorcycles are produced in Kansas City, Missouri.

As a part of management's lean manufacturing effort, Harley groups production of parts that require similar processes together. The result is work cells. Using the latest technology, work cells perform in one location all the operations necessary for production of a specific module. Raw materials are moved to the work cells and then the modules proceed to the assembly line. As a double check on quality, Harley has also installed "light curtain" technology which uses an infrared sensor to verify the bin from which an operator is taking parts. Materials go to the assembly line on a just-in-time basis, or as Harley calls it, using a Materials as Needed (MAN) system.

The 12.5-million-square-foot York facility includes manufacturing cells that perform tube bending, frame-building, machining, painting, and polishing. Innovative

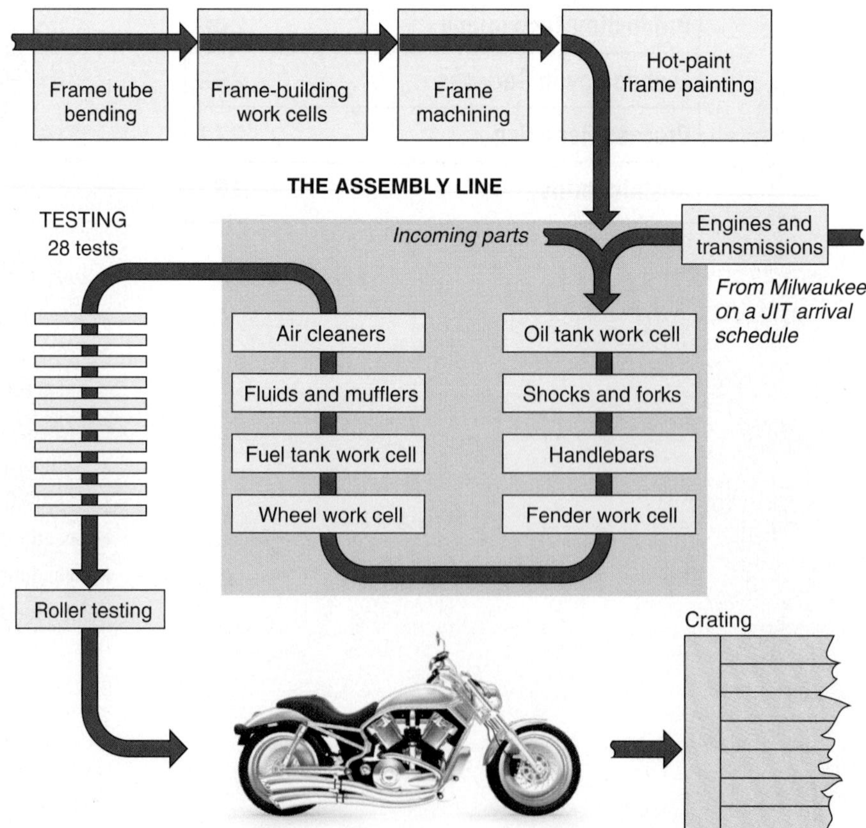

Flow Diagram Showing the Production Process at Harley-Davidson's York, Pennsylvania, Assembly Plant

manufacturing techniques use robots to load machines and highly automated production to reduce machining time. Automation and precision sensors play a key role in maintaining tolerances and producing a quality product. Each day the York facility produces up to 600 heavy-duty factory-custom motorcycles. Bikes are assembled with different engine displacements, multiple wheel options, colors, and accessories. The result is a huge number of variations in the motorcycles available which allows customers to individualize their purchase. The Harley-Davidson production system works because high-quality modules are brought together on a tightly scheduled repetitive production line.

Engines, having arrived just-in-time from the Milwaukee engine plant in their own protective shipping containers, are placed on an overhead conveyor for movement to the assembly line.

Wheel assembly modules are prepared in a work cell for JIT delivery to the assembly line.

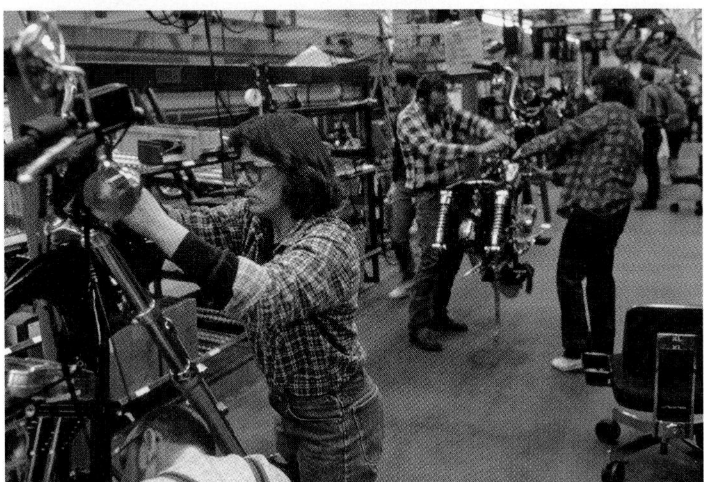

For manufacturers like Harley-Davidson, which produces a large number of end products from a relatively small number of options, modular bills of material provide an effective solution.

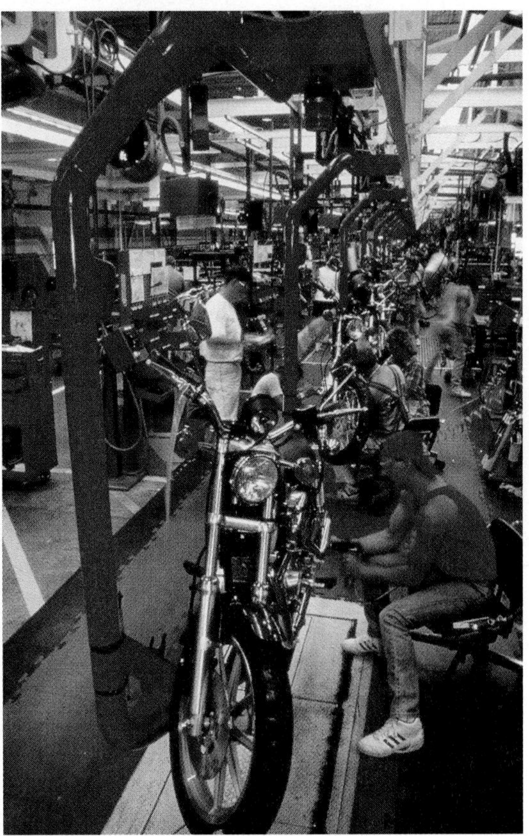

It all comes together on the line. Any employee who spots a problem has the authority to stop the line until the problem in corrected. The multicolored "andon" light above the motorcycle on the frame of the carrier signals the severity of the problem.

Chapter 7 **Learning Objectives**

AUTHOR COMMENT Production processes provide an excellent way to think about how we organize to produce goods and services.

FOUR PROCESS STRATEGIES

In Chapter 5, we examined the need for the selection, definition, and design of goods and services. Our purpose was to create environmentally-friendly designs that could be delivered in an ethical, sustainable manner. We now turn to their production. A major decision for an operations manager is finding the best way to produce so as not to waste our planet's resources. Let's look at ways to help managers design a process for achieving this goal.

Process strategy
An organization's approach to transforming resources into goods and services.

A **process** (or transformation) **strategy** is an organization's approach to transforming resources into goods and services. *The objective of a process strategy is to build a production process that meets customer requirements and product specifications within cost and other managerial constraints.* The process selected will have a long-term effect on efficiency and flexibility of production, as well as on cost and quality of the goods produced. Therefore, the limitations of a firm's operations strategy are determined at the time of the process decision.

LO1: Describe four production processes

Virtually every good or service is made by using some variation of one of four process strategies: (1) process focus, (2) repetitive focus, (3) product focus, and (4) mass customization. The relationship of these four strategies to volume and variety is shown in Figure 7.1. We examine *Arnold Palmer Hospital* as an example of a process-focused firm, *Harley-Davidson* as a repetitive producer, *Frito-Lay* as a product-focused operation, and *Dell* as a mass customizer.

Process Focus

Process focus
A production facility organized around processes to facilitate low-volume, high-variety production.

The vast majority of global production is devoted to making *low-volume, high-variety* products in places called "job shops." Such facilities are organized around specific activities or processes. In a factory, these processes might be departments devoted to welding, grinding, and painting. In an office, the processes might be accounts payable, sales, and payroll. In a restaurant, they might be bar, grill, and bakery. Such facilities are **process focused** in terms of equipment, layout, and supervision. They provide a high degree of product flexibility as products move between processes. Each process is designed to perform a wide variety of activities and handle frequent changes. Consequently, they are also called *intermittent processes.*

▶ **FIGURE 7.1 Process Selected Must fit with Volume and Variety**

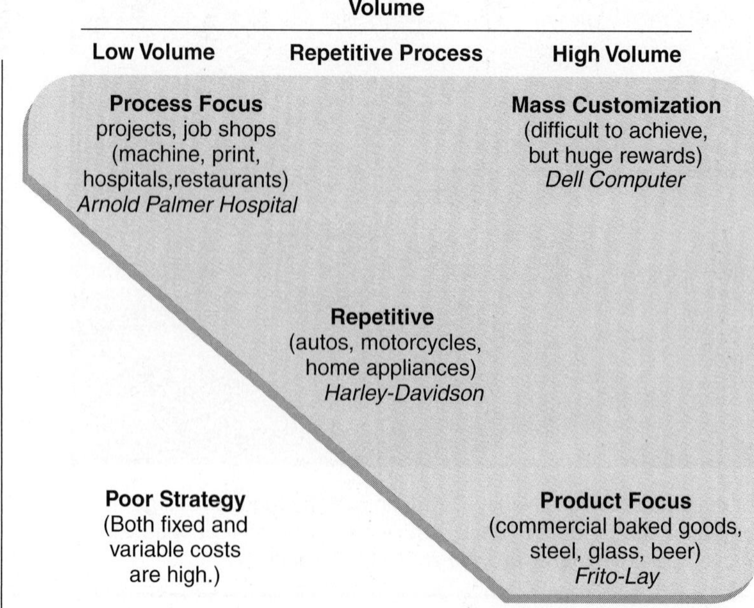

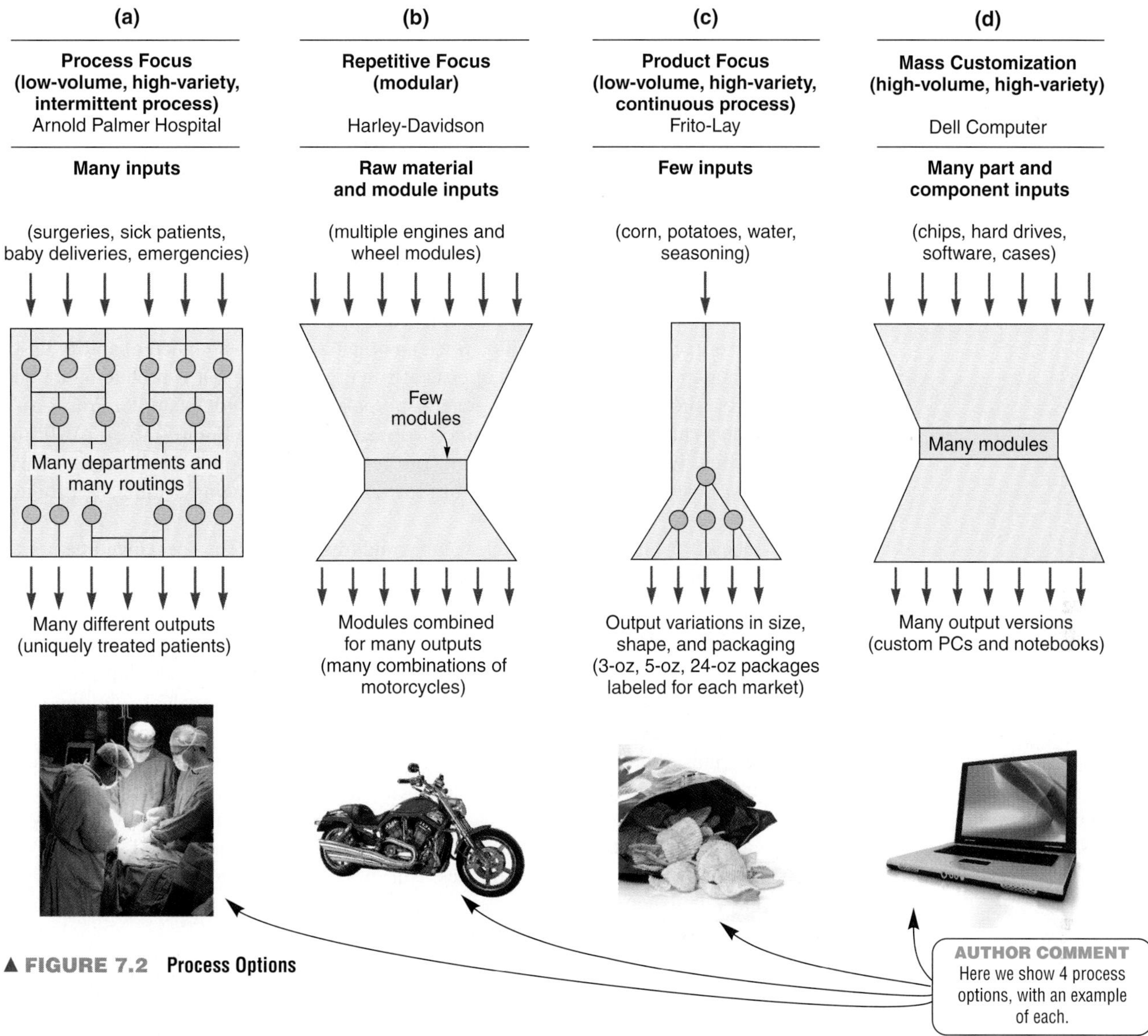

▲ **FIGURE 7.2 Process Options**

AUTHOR COMMENT Here we show 4 process options, with an example of each.

Referring to Figure 7.2(a), imagine a diverse group of patients entering Arnold Palmer Hospital, a process-focused facility, to be routed to specialized departments, treated in a distinct way, and then exiting as uniquely cared for individuals.

Process-focused facilities have high variable costs with extremely low utilization of facilities, as low as 5%. This is the case for many restaurants, hospitals, and machine shops. However, some facilities that lend themselves to electronic controls do somewhat better. With computer-controlled machines, it is possible to program machine tools, piece movement, tool changing, placement of the parts on the machine, and even the movement of materials between machines.

Repetitive Focus

A repetitive process falls between the product and process focuses seen in Figures 7.1 and 7.2(b). Repetitive processes, as we saw in the Global Company Profile on Harley-Davidson, use modules. Modules are parts or components previously prepared, often in a continuous process.

The **repetitive process** is the classic assembly line. Widely used in the assembly of virtually all automobiles and household appliances, it has more structure and consequently less flexibility than a process-focused facility.

Repetitive process
A product-oriented production process that uses modules.

Fast-food firms are another example of a repetitive process using **modules**. This type of production allows more customizing than a product-focused facility; modules (for example, meat, cheese, sauce, tomatoes, onions) are assembled to get a quasi-custom product, a cheeseburger. In this manner, the firm obtains both the economic advantages of the continuous model

Modules
Parts or components of a product previously prepared, often in a continuous process.

(where many of the modules are prepared) and the custom advantage of the low-volume, high-variety model.

Product Focus

Product focus
A facility organized around products; a product-oriented, high-volume, low-variety process.

High-volume, low-variety processes are **product focused**. The facilities are organized around *products*. They are also called *continuous processes*, because they have very long, continuous production runs. Products such as glass, paper, tin sheets, lightbulbs, beer, and potato chips are made via a continuous process. Some products, such as lightbulbs, are discrete; others, such as rolls of paper, are nondiscrete. Still others, such as repaired hernias at Shouldice Hospital, are services. It is only with standardization and effective quality control that firms have established product-focused facilities. An organization producing the same lightbulb or hot dog bun day after day can organize around a product. Such an organization has an inherent ability to set standards and maintain a given quality, as opposed to an organization that is producing unique products every day, such as a print shop or general-purpose hospital. For example, Frito-Lay's family of products is also produced in a product-focused facility (see Figure 7.2(c)). At Frito-Lay, corn, potatoes, water, and seasoning are the relatively few inputs, but outputs (like Cheetos, Ruffles, Tostitos, and Fritos) vary in seasoning and packaging within the product family.

A product-focused facility produces high volume and low variety. The specialized nature of the facility requires high fixed cost, but low variable costs reward high facility utilization.

Mass Customization Focus

Our increasingly wealthy and sophisticated world demands individualized goods and services. A peek at the rich variety of goods and services that operations managers are called on to supply is shown in Table 7.1. The explosion of variety has taken place in automobiles, movies, breakfast cereals, and thousands of other areas. In spite of this proliferation of products, operations managers have improved product quality while reducing costs. Consequently, the variety of products continues to grow. Operations managers use *mass customization* to produce this vast array of goods and services. **Mass customization** is the rapid, low-cost production of goods and services that fulfill increasingly unique customer desires. But mass customization (see the upper-right section of Figure 7.1) is not just about variety; it is about making precisely *what* the customer wants *when* the customer wants it economically.

Mass customization
Rapid, low-cost production that caters to constantly changing unique customer desires.

Mass customization brings us the variety of products traditionally provided by low-volume manufacture (a process focus) at the cost of standardized high-volume (product-focused) production. However, achieving mass customization is a challenge that requires sophisticated operational capabilities. Building agile processes that rapidly and inexpensively produce custom products requires imaginative and aggressive use of organizational resources. And the link between sales, design, production, supply chain, and logistics must be tight.

▶ TABLE 7.1
Mass Customization Provides More Choices Than Ever

Source: Various; however, many of the data are from the Federal Reserve Bank of Dallas.

	Number of Choices[a]	
Item	**1970s**	**21st Century**
Vehicle models	140	286
Vehicle styles	18	1,212
Bicycle types	8	211,000[c]
Software titles	0	400,000
Web sites	0	162,000,000[d]
Movie releases per year	267	765[e]
New book titles	40,530	300,000+
Houston TV channels	5	185
Breakfast cereals	160	340
Items (SKUs) in supermarkets	14,000[b]	150,000[f]
LCD TVs	0	102

[a]Variety available in America; worldwide the variety increases even more. [b]1989.
[c]Possible combinations for one manufacturer. [d]Royal Pingdom Estimate (2008).
[e]www.movieweb.com (2009). [f]SKUs managed by H. E. Butts grocery chain.

Dell Computer (see Figure 7.2(d)) has demonstrated that the payoff for mass customization can be substantial. More traditional manufacturers include Toyota, which recently announced delivery of custom-ordered cars in 5 days. Similarly, electronic controls allow designers in the textile industry to rapidly revamp their lines and respond to changes.

The service industry is also moving toward mass customization. For instance, not very many years ago, most people had the same telephone service. Now, not only is the phone service full of options, from caller ID to voice mail, but contemporary phones are hardly phones. They may also be part camera, computer, game player, GPS, and Web browser. Insurance companies are adding and tailoring new products with shortened development times to meet the unique needs of their customers. And firms like iTunes, Napster, and emusic maintain a music inventory on the Internet that allow customers to select a dozen songs of their choosing and have them made into a custom CD. Similarly, the number of new books and movies increases each year. Mass customization places new demands on operations managers who must build the processes that provide this expanding variety of goods and services.

One of the essential ingredients in mass customization is a reliance on modular design. In all the examples cited, as well as those in the *OM in Action* box "Mass Customization at Borders Books and at Smooth FM Radio," modular design is the key. However, as Figure 7.3 shows, very effective scheduling, personnel and facility flexibility, supportive supply chains, and rapid throughput are also required. These items influence all 10 of the OM decisions and therefore require excellent operations management.

Making Mass Customization Work Mass customization suggests a high-volume system in which products are built-to-order.[1] **Build-to-order** means producing to customer orders, not forecasts. Build-to-order can be a successful order-winning strategy when executed successfully. But high-volume build-to-order is difficult. Some major challenges are:

Build-to-order (BTO)
Produce to customer order rather than to a forecast.

- *Product design* must be imaginative and fast. Successful build-to-order designs often use modules. Ping Inc., the premier golf club manufacturer, uses different combinations of club heads, grips, shafts, and angles to make 20,000 variations of its golf clubs.
- *Process design* must be flexible and able to accommodate changes in both design and technology. For instance, **postponement** allows for customization late in the production process. Toyota installs unique interior modules very late in production for its popular Scion, a process also typical with customized vans. Postponement is further discussed in Chapter 11.

Postponement
The delay of any modifications or customization to a product as long as possible in the production process.

OM in Action ►Mass Customization at Borders Books and at Smooth FM Radio

So you want a hard-to-get, high-quality paperback book in 15 minutes? Borders can take care of you—even if you want a book that the store does not carry or have in stock. First, a Borders employee checks the digital database of titles that have been licensed from publishers. If the title is available, a digital file of the book is downloaded to two printers from a central server in Atlanta. One printer makes the book cover and the other the pages. Then the employee puts the two pieces together in a bookbinding machine. A separate machine cuts the book to size. And your book is ready. You get the book you want now, and Borders gets a sale. Books sold this way also avoid both inventory and incoming shipping cost, as well as the cost of returning books that do not sell.

Smooth FM provides a "customized" radio broadcast for Houston, Boston, Milwaukee, Albany, and Jacksonville from its midtown Manhattan station. Here is how it works. During Smooth FM's 40-minute music blocks, an announcer in Manhattan busily records 30-second blocks of local weather and traffic, commercials, promotions, and 5-second station IDs. Then the recorded material is transmitted to the affiliate stations. When the music block is over, the Manhattan announcer hits a button that signals computers at all the affiliates to simultaneously air the prerecorded "local" segments. Any "national" news or "national" ads can also be added from Manhattan. The result is the economy of mass production *and* a customized product for the local market. Radio people call it "local customization."

Sources: Hoover's Company Records (March 15, 2009): 101773; *The New York Times* (February 16, 2004): C3; *The Wall Street Journal* (June 1, 1999): B1, B4.

[1] Build-to-order (BTO) may be referred to and refined as engineer-to-order (ETO) and design-to-order (DTO), depending on the extent of the customization.

▶ **FIGURE 7.3**
Requirements to Achieve Mass Customization

AUTHOR COMMENT
OM must align a variety of factors to make mass customization work.

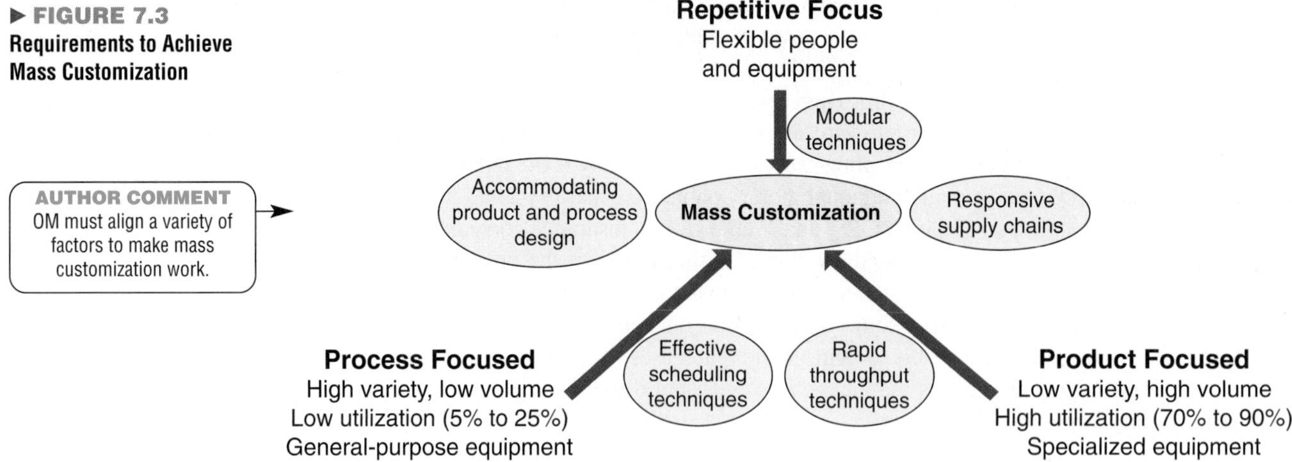

- *Inventory management* requires tight control. To be successful with build-to-order, a firm must avoid being stuck with unpopular or obsolete components. With virtually no raw material, Dell puts custom computers together in less than a day.
- *Tight schedules* that track orders and material from design through delivery are another requirement of mass customization. Align Technology, a well-known name in orthodontics, figured out how to achieve competitive advantage by delivering custom-made clear plastic aligners within three weeks of your first visit to the dentist's office.
- *Responsive partners* in the supply chain can yield effective collaboration. Forecasting, inventory management, and ordering for JCPenney shirts are all handled for the retailer by its supplier in Hong Kong.

Mass customization/build-to-order is difficult, but is the new imperative for operations. There are advantages to mass customization and building to order: first, by meeting the demands of the market place, firms win orders and stay in business; in addition, they trim costs (from personnel to inventory to facilities) that exist because of inaccurate sales forecasting. Mass customization and build-to-order can be done—and operations managers in leading organizations are accepting the challenge.

Comparison of Process Choices

The characteristics of the four processes are shown in Table 7.2 and Figure 7.2 (on page 253). Advantages exist across the continuum of processes, and firms may find strategic advantage in any process. Each of the processes, when properly matched to volume and variety, can produce a low-cost advantage. For instance, unit costs will be less in the continuous-process case when high volume (and high utilization) exists. However, we do not always use the continuous-process (that is, specialized equipment and facilities) because it is too expensive when volumes are low or flexibility is required. A low-volume, unique, highly differentiated good or service is more economical when produced under process focus; this is the way fine-dining restaurants and general-purpose hospitals are organized. Just as all four processes, when appropriately selected and well managed, can yield low cost, so too can all four be responsive and produce differentiated products.

Figure 7.3 indicated that equipment utilization in a process-focused facility is often in the range of 5% to 25%. When utilization goes above 15%, moving toward a repetitive or product focus, or even mass customization, may be advantageous. A cost advantage usually exists by improving utilization, provided the necessary flexibility is maintained. McDonald's started an entirely new industry by moving its limited menu from process focus to repetitive focus. McDonald's is now trying to add more variety and move toward mass customization.

Much of what is produced in the world is still produced in very small lots—often as small as one. This is true for most legal services, medical services, dental services, and restaurants. An X-ray machine in a dentist's office and much of the equipment in a fine-dining restaurant have low utilization. Hospitals, too, have low utilization, which suggests why their costs are considered high. Why such low utilization? In part because excess capacity for peak loads is desirable. Hospital administrators, as well as managers of other service facilities and their patients and customers, expect equipment to be available as needed. Another reason is poor scheduling (although

▼ **TABLE 7.2**

Comparison of the Characteristics of Four Types of Processes

Process Focus (low volume, high variety) (e.g., Arnold Palmer Hospital)	Repetitive Focus (modular) (e.g., Harley-Davidson)	Product Focus (high volume, low variety) (e.g., Frito-Lay)	Mass Customization (high volume, high variety) (e.g., Dell Computer)
1. Small quantity and large variety of products are produced.	1. Long runs, usually a standardized product with options, are produced from modules.	1. Large quantity and small variety of products are produced.	1. Large quantity and large variety of products are produced.
2. Equipment used is general purpose.	2. Special equipment aids in use of an assembly line.	2. Equipment used is special purpose.	2. Rapid changeover on flexible equipment.
3. Operators are broadly skilled.	3. Employees are modestly trained.	3. Operators are less broadly skilled.	3. Flexible operators are trained for the necessary customization.
4. There are many job instructions because each job changes.	4. Repetitive operations reduce training and changes in job instructions.	4. Work orders and job instructions are few because they are standardized.	4. Custom orders require many job instructions.
5. Raw-material inventories are high relative to the value of the product.	5. Just-in-time procurement techniques are used.	5. Raw material inventories are low relative to the value of the product.	5. Raw material inventories are low relative to the value of the product.
6. Work-in-process is high compared to output.	6. Just-in-time inventory techniques are used.	6. Work-in-process inventory is low compared to output.	6. Work-in-process inventory is driven down by JIT, kanban, lean production.
7. Units move slowly through the facility.	7. Assembly is measured in hours and days.	7. Swift movement of units through the facility is typical.	7. Goods move swiftly through the facility.
8. Finished goods are usually made to order and not stored.	8. Finished goods are made to frequent forecasts.	8. Finished goods are usually made to a forecast and stored.	8. Finished goods are often build-to-order (BTO).
9. Scheduling is complex and concerned with the trade-off between inventory availability, capacity, and customer service.	9. Scheduling is based on building various models from a variety of modules to forecasts.	9. Scheduling is relatively simple and concerned with establishing a rate of output sufficient to meet sales forecasts.	9. Sophisticated scheduling is required to accommodate custom orders.
10. Fixed costs tend to be low and variable costs high.	10. Fixed costs are dependent on flexibility of the facility.	10. Fixed costs tend to be high and variable costs low.	10. Fixed costs tend to be high, but variable costs must be low.

substantial efforts have been made to forecast demand in the service industry) and the resulting imbalance in the use of facilities.

Crossover Charts The comparison of processes can be further enhanced by looking at the point where the total cost of the processes changes. For instance, Figure 7.4 shows three alternative processes compared on a single chart. Such a chart is sometimes called a **crossover chart**. Process A has the lowest cost for volumes below V_1, process B has the lowest cost between V_1 and V_2, and process C has the lowest cost at volumes above V_2.

Crossover chart
A chart of costs at the possible volumes for more than one process.

Example 1 illustrates how to determine the exact volume where one process becomes more expensive than another.

◀ **EXAMPLE 1**
Crossover chart

Kleber Enterprises would like to evaluate three accounting software products (A, B, and C) to support changes in its internal accounting processes. The resulting processes will have cost structures similar to those shown in Figure 7.4. The costs of the software for these processes are:

	Total Fixed Cost	Dollars Required per Accounting Report
Software A	\$200,000	\$60
Software B	\$300,000	\$25
Software C	\$400,000	\$10

APPROACH ▶ Solve for the crossover point for software A and B and then the crossover point for software B and C.

SOLUTION ▶ Software A yields a process that is most economical up to V_1, but to exactly what number of reports (volume)? To determine the volume at V_1, we set the cost of software A equal to the cost of software B. V_1 is the unknown volume:

$$200{,}000 + (60)V_1 = 300{,}000 + (25)V_1$$
$$35V_1 = 100{,}000$$
$$V_1 = 2{,}857$$

This means that software A is most economical from 0 reports to 2,857 reports (V_1).

Similarly, to determine the crossover point for V_2, we set the cost of software B equal to the cost of software C:

$$300{,}000 + (25)V_2 = 400{,}000 + (10)V_2$$
$$15V_2 = 100{,}000$$
$$V_2 = 6{,}666$$

This means that software B is most economical if the number of reports is between 2,857 (V_1) and 6,666 (V_2) and that software C is most economical if reports exceed 6,666 (V_2).

INSIGHT ▶ As you can see, the software and related process chosen is highly dependent on the forecasted volume.

LEARNING EXERCISE ▶ If the vendor of software A reduces the fixed cost to \$150,000, what is the new crossover point between A and B? [Answer: 4,286.]

RELATED PROBLEMS ▶ 7.5, 7.6, 7.7, 7.8, 7.9, 7.10, 7.11, 7.12, 7.14

ACTIVE MODEL 7.1 This example is further illustrated in Active Model 7.1 at **www.pearsonhighered.com/heizer**.

▶ FIGURE 7.4
Crossover Charts

AUTHOR COMMENT Different processes can be expected to have different costs. However, at any given volume, only one will have the lowest cost.

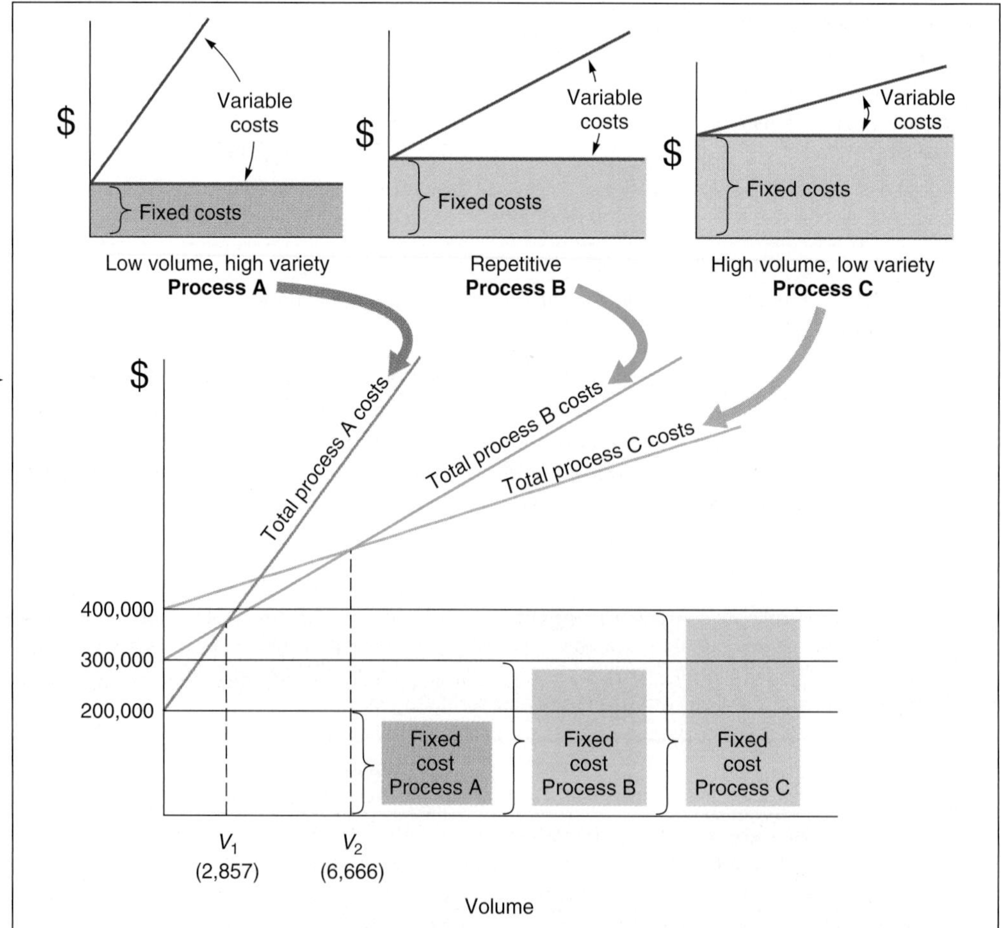

LO2: Compute crossover points for different processes

Focused Processes In an ongoing quest for efficiency, industrialized societies continue to move toward specialization. The focus that comes with specialization contributes to efficiency. Managers who focus on a limited number of activities, products, and technologies do better. As the variety of products in a facility increase, overhead costs increase even faster. Similarly, as the variety of products, customers, and technology increases, so does complexity. The resources necessary to cope with the complexity expand disproportionately. A focus on depth of product line as opposed to breadth is typical of outstanding firms, of which Intel, Motorola, L.M. Ericsson, Nokia, and Bosch are world-class examples. Specialization, simplification, concentration, and *focus* yield efficiency. They also contribute to building a core competence that yields market and financial success. The focus can be:

VIDEO 7.1
Process Strategy at Wheeled Coach Ambulance

- *Customers* (such as Winterhalter Gastronom, a German company that focuses on dishwashers for hotels and restaurants, for whom spotless glasses and dishes are critical)
- *Products* with similar attributes (such as Nucor Steel's Crawford, Ohio, plant, which processes only high-quality sheet steels, and Gallagher, a New Zealand company, which has 45% of the world market in electric fences)
- *Service* (such as Orlando's Arnold Palmer Hospital, with a focus on children and women; or Shouldice Hospital, in Canada, with a focus on hernia repair).
- *Technology* (such as Texas Instruments, with a focus on only certain specialized kinds of semiconductors; and SAP, which in spite of a world of opportunities, remains focused on software).

The key for the operations manager is to move continuously toward specialization, focusing on the products, technology, customers, processes, and talents necessary to excel in that specialty.

Changing Processes Changing the production system from one process model to another is difficult and expensive. In some cases, the change may mean starting over. Consider what would be required of a rather simple change—McDonald's adding the flexibility necessary to serve you a charbroiled hamburger. What appears to be rather straightforward would require changes in many of our 10 OM decisions. For instance, changes may be necessary in (1) purchasing (a different quality of meat, perhaps with more fat content, and supplies such as charcoal); (2) quality standards (how long and at what temperature the patty will cook); (3) equipment (the charbroiler); (4) layout (space for the new process and for new exhaust vents); and (5) training. So choosing where to operate on the process strategy continuum may determine the transformation strategy for an extended period. This critical decision must be done right the first time.

PROCESS ANALYSIS AND DESIGN

AUTHOR COMMENT
Here we look at 5 tools that help understand processes.

When analyzing and designing processes, we ask questions such as the following:

- Is the process designed to achieve competitive advantage in terms of differentiation, response, or low cost?
- Does the process eliminate steps that do not add value?
- Does the process maximize customer value as perceived by the customer?
- Will the process win orders?

LO3: Use the tools of process analysis

A number of tools help us understand the complexities of process design and redesign. They are simply ways of making sense of what happens or must happen in a process. Let's look at five of them: flowcharts, time-function mapping, value-stream mapping, process charts, and service blueprinting.

Flowchart

The first tool is the **flowchart**, which is a schematic or drawing of the movement of material, product, or people. For instance, the flowchart in the *Global Company Profile* for this chapter shows the assembly processes for Harley-Davidson. Such charts can help understanding, analysis, and communication of a process.

Flowchart
A drawing used to analyze movement of people or material.

Time-Function Mapping

A second tool for process analysis and design is a flowchart, but with time added on the horizontal axis. Such charts are sometimes called **time-function mapping**, or **process mapping**. With time-function mapping, nodes indicate the activities and the arrows indicate the flow direction, with time on the horizontal axis. This type of analysis allows users to identify and eliminate

Time-function mapping (or process mapping)
A flowchart with time added on the horizontal axis.

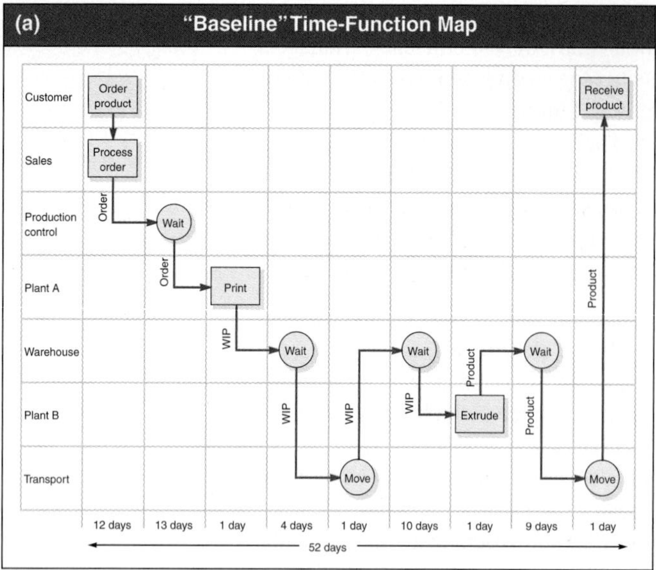

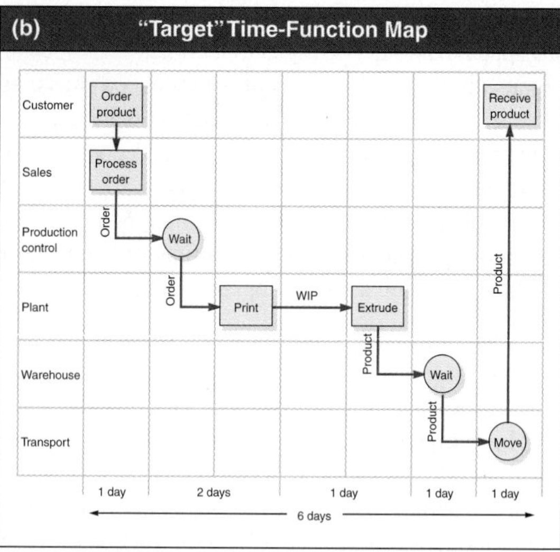

▲ **FIGURE 7.5 Time-Function Mapping (Process Mapping) for a Product Requiring Printing and Extruding Operations at American National Can Company**

This technique clearly shows that waiting and order processing contributed substantially to the 46 days that can be eliminated in this operation.

Source: Excerpted from Elaine J. Labach, "Faster, Better, and Cheaper," *Target* no. 5: 43 with permission of the Association for Manufacturing Excellence, 380 West Palatine Road, Wheeling, IL 60090-5863, 847/520-3282. **www.ame.org.** Reprinted with permission of Target Magazine.

waste such as extra steps, duplication, and delay. Figure 7.5 shows the use of process mapping before and after process improvement at American National Can Company. In this example, substantial reduction in waiting time and process improvement in order processing contributed to a savings of 46 days.

Value-stream mapping (VSM)
A process that helps managers understand how to add value in the flow of material and information through the entire production process.

Value-Stream Mapping

A variation of time-function mapping is **value-stream mapping (VSM)**; however, value-stream mapping takes an expanded look at where value is added (and not added) in the entire production process, including the supply chain. As with time-function mapping, the idea is to start with the customer and understand the production process, but value-stream mapping extends the analysis back to suppliers.

EXAMPLE 2 ▶

Value-stream mapping

Motorola has received an order for 11,000 cell phones per month and wants to understand how the order will be processed through manufacturing.

APPROACH ▶ To fully understand the process from customer to supplier, Motorola prepares a value-stream map.

SOLUTION ▶ Although value-stream maps appear complex, their construction is easy. Here are the steps needed to complete the value-stream map shown in Figure 7.6.

1. Begin with symbols for customer, supplier, and production to ensure the big picture.
2. Enter customer order requirements.
3. Calculate the daily production requirements.
4. Enter the outbound shipping requirements and delivery frequency.
5. Determine inbound shipping method and delivery frequency.
6. Add the process steps (i.e., machine, assemble) in sequence, left to right.
7. Add communication methods, add their frequency, and show the direction with arrows.
8. Add inventory quantities (shown with ⚠ I) between every step of the entire flow.
9. Determine total working time (value-added time) and delay (non-value-added time).

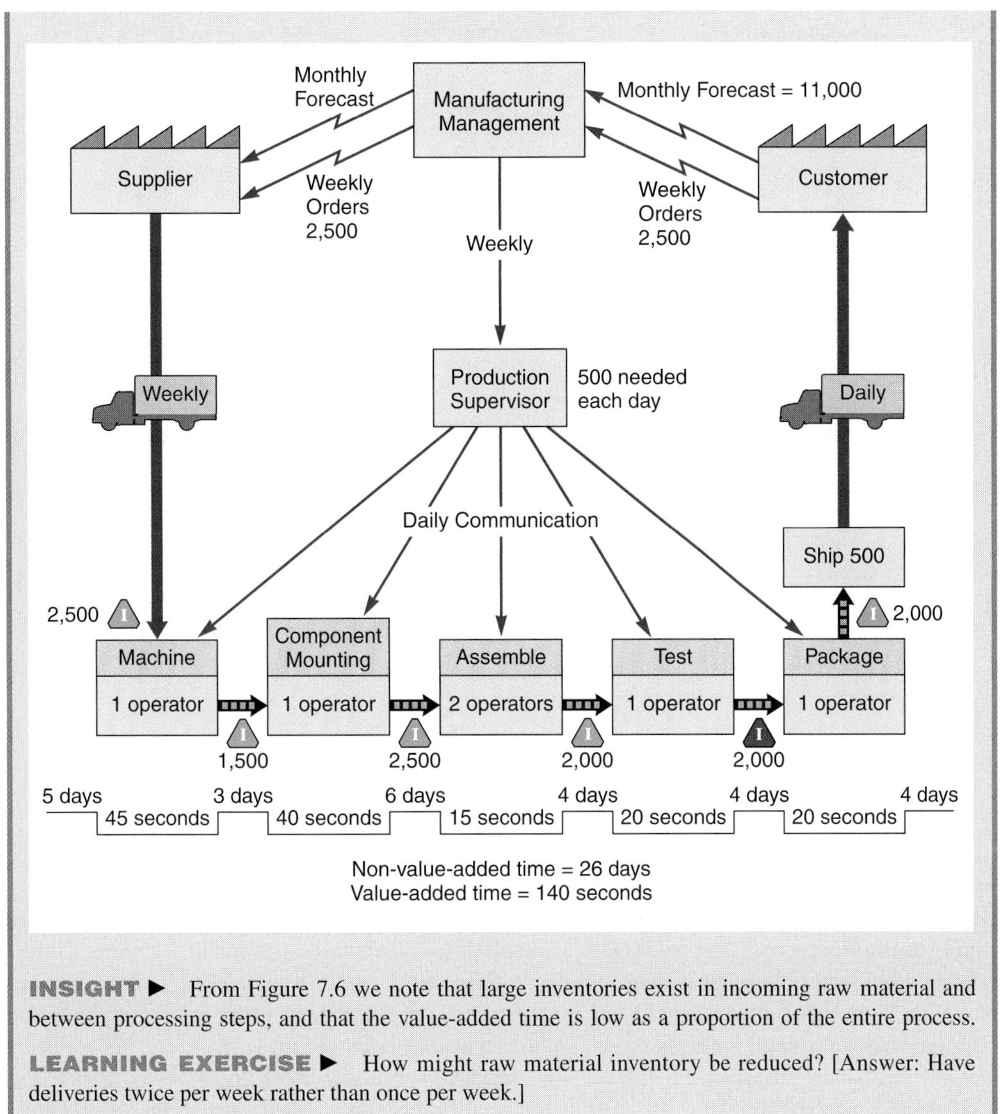

INSIGHT ▶ From Figure 7.6 we note that large inventories exist in incoming raw material and between processing steps, and that the value-added time is low as a proportion of the entire process.

LEARNING EXERCISE ▶ How might raw material inventory be reduced? [Answer: Have deliveries twice per week rather than once per week.]

RELATED PROBLEM ▶ 7.13

◀ **FIGURE 7.6**
Value-Stream Mapping (VSM)

Value-stream mapping takes into account not only the process but, as shown in Example 2, also the management decisions and information systems that support the process.

Process Charts

The fourth tool is the *process chart*. **Process charts** use symbols, time, and distance to provide an objective and structured way to analyze and record the activities that make up a process.[2] They allow us to focus on value-added activities. For instance, the process chart shown in Figure 7.7, which includes the present method of hamburger assembly at a fast-food restaurant, includes a value-added line to help us distinguish between value-added activities and waste. Identifying all value-added operations (as opposed to inspection, storage, delay, and transportation, which add no value) allows us to determine the percent of value added to total activities.[3] We can see from the computation at the bottom of Figure 7.7 that the value added in this case is 85.7%. The

Process charts
Charts that use symbols to analyze the movement of people or material.

[2]An additional example of a process chart is shown in Chapter 10.

[3]Waste includes *inspection* (if the task is done properly, then inspection is unnecessary); *transportation* (movement of material within a process may be a necessary evil, but it adds no value); *delay* (an asset sitting idle and taking up space is waste); *storage* (unless part of a "curing" process, storage is waste).

► **FIGURE 7.7**
Process Chart Showing a Hamburger Assembly Process at a Fast-Food Restaurant

Present Method [X] PROCESS CHART Proposed Method [ ]

SUBJECT CHARTED *Hamburger Assembly Process* DATE *8/1/10*

DEPARTMENT ______ CHART BY *KH* SHEET NO. *1* OF *1*

DIST. IN FEET	TIME IN MINS.	CHART SYMBOLS	PROCESS DESCRIPTION
	—	○ ⇨ □ D ▽	*Meat Patty in Storage*
1.5	*.05*	○ ⇨ □ D ▽	*Transfer to Broiler*
	2.50	○ ⇨ □ D ▽	*Broiler*
	.05	○ ⇨ □ D ▽	*Visual Inspection*
1.0	*.05*	○ ⇨ □ D ▽	*Transfer to Rack*
	.15	○ ⇨ □ D ▽	*Temporary Storage*
.5	*.10*	○ ⇨ □ D ▽	*Obtain Buns, Lettuce, etc.*
	.20	○ ⇨ □ D ▽	*Assemble Order*
.5	*.05*	○ ⇨ □ D ▽	*Place in Finish Rack*
		○ ⇨ □ D ▽	
3.5	*3.15*	*2 4 1 – 2*	TOTALS

Value-added time = Operation time/Total time = (2.50+.20)/3.15 = 85.7%

○ = operation; ⇨ = transportation; □ = inspection; D = delay; ▽ = storage.

operations manager's job is to reduce waste and increase the percent of value added. The non-value-added items are a waste; they are resources lost to the firm and to society forever.

Service Blueprinting

Service blueprinting
A process analysis technique that lends itself to a focus on the customer and the provider's interaction with the customer.

Products with a high service content may warrant use of yet a fifth process technique. **Service blueprinting** is a process analysis technique that focuses on the customer and the provider's interaction with the customer. For instance, the activities at level one of Figure 7.8 are under the control of the customer. In the second level are activities of the service provider interacting with the customer. The third level includes those activities that are performed away from, and not immediately visible to, the customer. Each level suggests different management issues. For instance, the top level may suggest educating the customer or modifying expectations, whereas the second level may require a focus on personnel selection and training. Finally, the third level lends itself to more typical process innovations. The service blueprint shown in Figure 7.8 also notes potential failure points and shows how poka-yoke techniques can be added to improve quality. The consequences of these failure points can be greatly reduced if identified at the design stage when modifications or appropriate poka-yokes can be included. A time dimension is included in Figure 7.8 to aid understanding, extend insight, and provide a focus on customer service.

Each of these five process analysis tools has its strengths and variations. Flowcharts are a quick way to view the big picture and try to make sense of the entire system. Time-function mapping adds some rigor and a time element to the macro analysis. Value-stream mapping extends beyond the immediate organization to customers and suppliers. Process charts are designed to provide a much more detailed view of the process, adding items such as value-added time, delay, distance, storage, and so forth. Service blueprinting, on the other hand, is designed to help us focus on the customer interaction part of the process. Because customer interaction is often an important variable in process design, we now examine some additional aspects of service process design.

AUTHOR COMMENT
Customer interaction with service processes increases the design challenge.

SPECIAL CONSIDERATIONS FOR SERVICE PROCESS DESIGN

Interaction with the customer often affects process performance adversely. But a service, by its very nature, implies that some interaction and customization is needed. Recognizing that the customer's unique desires tend to play havoc with a process, the more the manager designs the process to accommodate these special requirements, the more effective and efficient the process will be. Notice how well Align Technology has managed the interface

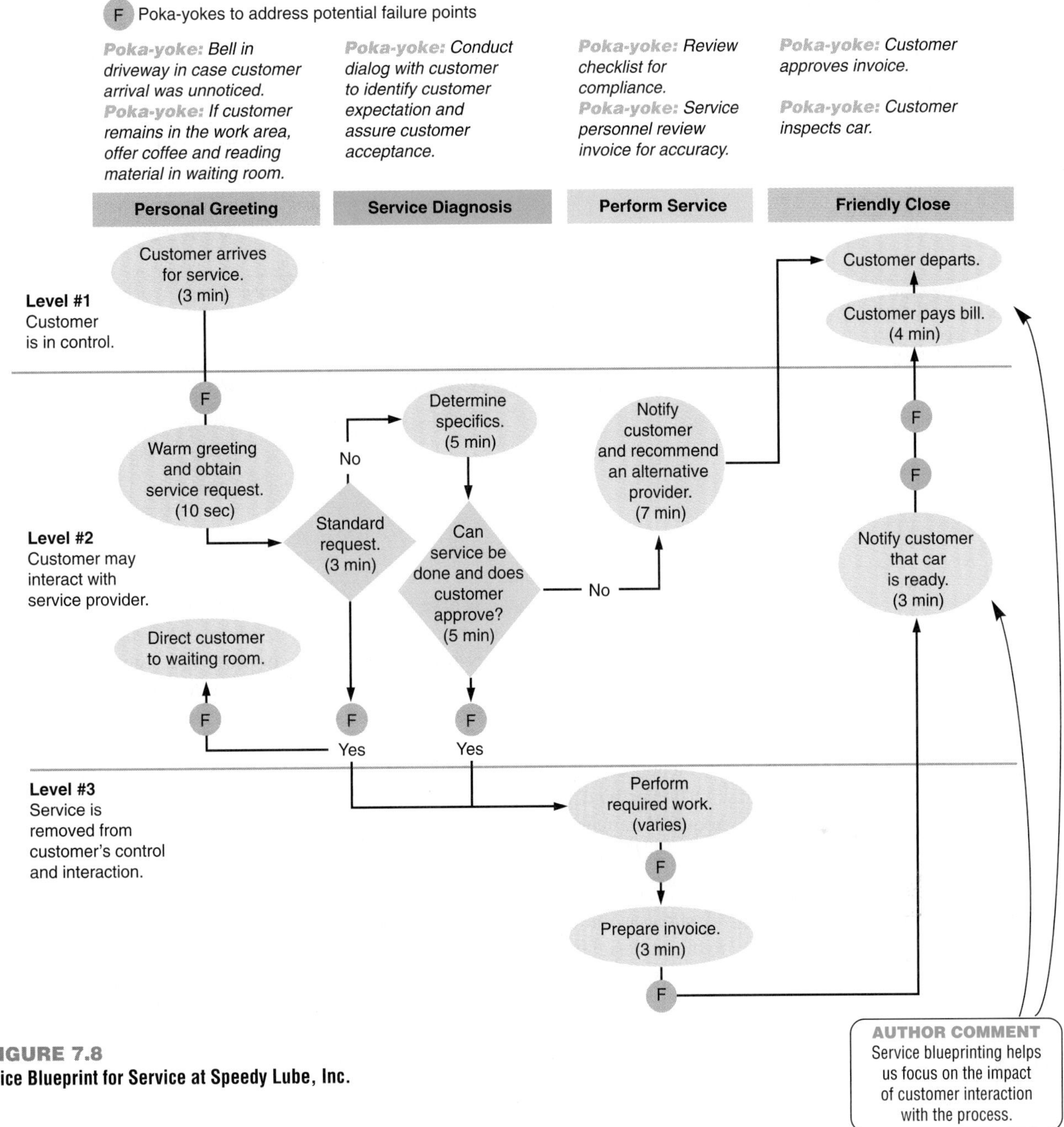

▲ **FIGURE 7.8**
Service Blueprint for Service at Speedy Lube, Inc.

between the customer and the process by using the Internet (see the *OM in Action* box "Mass Customization for Straight Teeth"). The trick is to find the right combination of cost and customer interaction.

Customer Interaction and Process Design

The four quadrants of Figure 7.9 provide additional insight on how operations managers design service processes to find the best level of specialization and focus while maintaining the necessary customer interaction and customization. The 10 operations decisions we introduced in Chapters 1 and 2 are used with a different emphasis in each quadrant. For instance:

LO4: Describe customer interaction in process design

- In the upper sections (quadrants) of *mass service* and *professional service*, where *labor content is high*, we expect the manager to focus extensively on human resources. This is often done with personalized services, requiring high labor involvement and therefore significant selection and training issues in the human resources area. This is particularly true in the professional service quadrant.

▶ **FIGURE 7.9**
Services Moving toward Specialization and Focus within the Service Process Matrix

Source: Adapted from work by Roger Schmenner, "Service Business and Productivity," *Decision Sciences* 35, no. 3 (Summer 2004): 333–347.

AUTHOR COMMENT
Notice how services find a competitive opportunity by moving from the rectangles to the ovals.

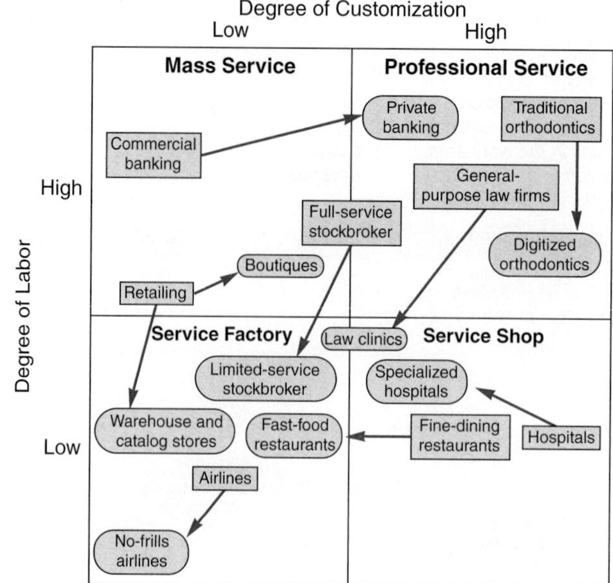

- The quadrants with *low customization* tend to (1) standardize or restrict some offerings, as do fast-food restaurants, (2) automate, as have airlines with ticket-vending machines, or (3) remove some services, such as seat assignments, as has Southwest Airlines. Offloading some aspect of the service through automation may require innovations in process design as well as capital investment. Such is the case with airline ticket vending and bank ATMs. This move to standardization and automation may require added capital expenditure, as well as putting operations managers under pressure to develop new skills for the purchase and maintenance of such equipment. A reduction in a customization capability will require added strength in other areas.
- Because customer feedback is lower in the quadrants with *low customization*, tight control may be required to maintain quality standards.
- Operations with *low labor intensity* may lend themselves particularly well to innovations in process technology and scheduling.

Table 7.3 shows some additional techniques for innovative process design in services. Managers focus on designing innovative processes that enhance the service. For instance, supermarket *self-service* reduces cost while it allows customers to check for the specific features they

OM in Action ▶ Mass Customization for Straight Teeth

Align Technology of Santa Clara, California, wants to straighten your teeth with a clear plastic removable aligner. The company is a mass customizer for orthodontic treatments. Each patient is *very* custom, requiring a truly unique product; no two patients are alike. Based on dental impressions, X-rays, and photos taken at the dentist's office and sent to Align headquarters, the firm builds a precise 3-D computer model and file of the patient's mouth. This digitized file is then sent to Costa Rica, where technicians develop a comprehensive treatment plan, which is then returned to the dentist for approval. After approval, data from the 3-D virtual models and treatment plan are used to program stereolithography equipment (see photo on page 165 in Chapter 5) to form molds. The molds are then shipped to Juarez, Mexico, where a series of customized teeth aligners—usually about 19 pairs—are made. The time required for this process: about 3 weeks from start to finish. The clear aligners take the place of the traditional "wire and brackets." Align calls the product "complex to make, easy to use." With good OM, mass customization works, even for a very complex, very individualized product, such as teeth aligners.

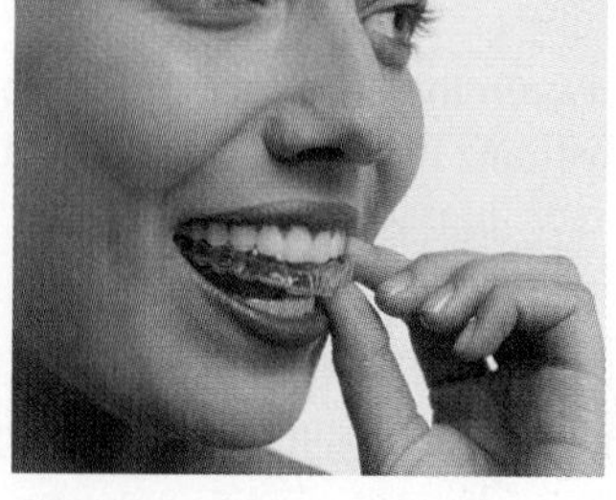

Sources: Laura Rock Kopezak and M. Eric Johnson, "Aligning the Supply Chain," Case #6-0024, Dartmouth College, 2006; and www.invisalign.com Annual Report, 2007.

Strategy	Technique	Example
Separation	*Structuring service* so customers must go where the service is offered	Bank customers go to a manager to open a new account, to loan officers for loans, and to tellers for deposits
Self-service	*Self-service* so customers examine, compare, and evaluate at their own pace	Supermarkets and department stores Internet ordering
Postponement	*Customizing at delivery*	Customizing vans at delivery rather than at production
Focus	*Restricting* the offerings	Limited-menu restaurant
Modules	*Modular* selection of service *Modular* production	Investment and insurance selection Prepackaged food modules in restaurants
Automation	*Separating services* that may lend themselves to some type of automation	Automatic teller machines
Scheduling	Precise personnel *scheduling*	Scheduling ticket counter personnel at 15-minute intervals at airlines
Training	*Clarifying the service* options *Explaining how to avoid problems*	Investment counselor, funeral directors After-sale maintenance personnel

◀ **TABLE 7.3**
Techniques for Improving Service Productivity

want, such as freshness or color. Dell Computer provides another version of self-service by allowing customers to design their own product on the Web. Customers seem to like this, and it is cheaper and faster for Dell.

More Opportunities to Improve Service Processes

Layout Layout design is an integral part of many service processes, particularly in retailing, dining, and banking. In retailing, layout can provide not only product exposure but also customer education and product enhancement. In restaurants, layout can enhance the dining experience as well as provide an effective flow between bar, kitchen, and dining area. In banks, layout provides security as well as work flow and personal comfort. Because layout is such an integral part of many services, it provides continuing opportunity for winning orders.

VIDEO 7.2
Process Analysis at Arnold Palmer Hospital

Human Resources Because so many services involve direct interaction with the customer (as the upper quadrants of Figure 7.9 suggest), the human resource issues of recruiting and training can be particularly important ingredients in service processes. Additionally, a committed workforce that exhibits flexibility when schedules are made and is cross-trained to fill in when the process requires less than a full-time person, can have a tremendous impact on overall process performance.

SELECTION OF EQUIPMENT AND TECHNOLOGY

AUTHOR COMMENT
A process that is going to win orders often depends on the selection of the proper equipment.

Ultimately, the decisions about a particular process require decisions about equipment and technology. Those decisions can be complex because alternative methods of production are present in virtually all operations functions, be they hospitals, restaurants, or manufacturing facilities. Picking the best equipment means understanding the specific industry and available processes and technology. That choice of equipment, be it an X-ray machine for a hospital, a computer-controlled lathe for a factory, or a new computer for an office, requires considering cost, quality, capacity, and flexibility. To make this decision, operations personnel develop documentation that indicates the capacity, size, and tolerances of each option, as well as its maintenance requirements. Any one of these attributes may be the deciding factor regarding selection.

The selection of equipment for a particular type of process can also provide competitive advantage. Many firms, for instance, develop unique machines or techniques within established processes that provide an advantage. This advantage may result in added flexibility in meeting customer requirements, lower cost, or higher quality. Innovations and equipment modification might also allow for a more stable production process requiring less adjustment, maintenance, and operator training. In any case, specialized equipment often provides a way to win orders.

Modern technology also allows operations managers to enlarge the scope of their processes. As a result, an important attribute to look for in new equipment and process selection is flexible equipment. **Flexibility** is the ability to respond with little penalty in time, cost, or customer value. This may mean modular, movable, even cheap equipment. Flexibility may also mean the development of sophisticated electronic equipment, which increasingly provides the rapid changes that mass customization demands. The technological advances that influence OM process strategy are substantial and are discussed next.

Flexibility
The ability to respond with little penalty in time, cost, or customer value.

AUTHOR COMMENT
Here are 9 technologies that can improve employee safety, product quality, and productivity.

LO5: Identify recent advances in production technology

PRODUCTION TECHNOLOGY

Advances in technology that enhance production and productivity have a wide range of applications in both manufacturing and services. In this section, we introduce nine areas of technology: (1) machine technology, (2) automatic identification systems (AIS), (3) process control, (4) vision systems, (5) robots, (6) automated storage and retrieval systems (ASRSs), (7) automated guided vehicles (AGVs), (8) flexible manufacturing systems (FMSs), and (9) computer-integrated manufacturing (CIM).

Machine Technology

Most of the world's machinery that performs operations such as cutting, drilling, boring, and milling is undergoing tremendous progress in both precision and control. New machinery turns out metal components that vary less than a micron—1/76 the width of a human hair. They can accelerate water to three times the speed of sound to cut titanium for surgical tools. Machinery of the 21st century is often five times more productive than that of previous generations while being smaller and using less power. And continuing advances in lubricants now allow the use of water-based lubricants rather than oil-based. Using water-based lubricants eliminates hazardous waste and allows shavings to be easily recovered and recycled.

The intelligence now available for the control of new machinery via computer chips allows more complex and precise items to be made faster. Electronic controls increase speed by reducing changeover time, reducing waste (because of fewer mistakes), and enhancing flexibility. Machinery with its own computer and memory is called **computer numerical control (CNC)** machinery.

Computer numerical control (CNC)
Machinery with its own computer and memory.

Advanced versions of such technology are used on Pratt and Whitney's turbine blade plant in Connecticut. The machinery has improved the loading and alignment task so much that Pratt has cut the total time for the grinding process of a turbine blade from 10 days to 2 hours. The new machinery has also contributed to process improvements that mean the blades now travel just 1,800 feet in the plant, down from 8,100 feet. The total throughput time for a turbine blade has been cut from 22 days to 7 days.

Automatic Identification Systems (AISs) and RFID

New equipment, from numerically controlled manufacturing machinery to ATM machines, is controlled by digital electronic signals. Electrons are a great vehicle for transmitting information, but they have a major limitation—most OM data does not start out in bits and bytes. Therefore, operations managers must get the data into an electronic form. Making data digital is done via computer keyboards, bar codes, radio frequencies, optical characters, and so forth. These **automatic identification systems (AISs)** help us move data into electronic form, where it is easily manipulated.

Automatic identification system (AIS)
A system for transforming data into electronic form, for example, bar codes.

Because of its decreasing cost and increasing pervasiveness, **radio frequency identification (RFID)** warrants special note. RFID is integrated circuitry with its own tiny antennas that use radio waves to send signals a limited range—usually a matter of yards. These RFID tags (sometimes called RFID circuits) provide unique identification that enables the tracking and monitoring of parts, pallets, people, and pets—virtually everything that moves. RFID requires no line of sight between tag and reader.

Radio frequency identification (RFID)
A wireless system in which integrated circuits with antennas send radio waves.

Innovative OM examples of AISs and RFID include:

With RFID, a cashier could scan the entire contents of a shopping cart in seconds.

- Nurses reduce errors in hospitals by matching bar codes on medication to ID bracelets on patients.
- RFID tags in agriculture monitor the temperature at which fruit is kept. They can also track what chemicals and fertilizers have been used on the fruit.
- Transponders attached to cars allow McDonald's to identify and bill customers who can now zip through the drive-through line without having to stop and pay. The transponders use the same technology that permits motorists to skip stops on some toll roads. McDonald's estimates that the change speeds up throughput time by 15 seconds.
- Stanford University School of Medicine doctors are using sponges embedded with RFID tags. Waving a detector over an incision can tell if a surgeon accidentally left a sponge in the patient.
- FedEx tags major airplane parts, which allows them to be scanned so maintenance data (e.g., part number, installation date, country of origin) can be tracked.

Process Control

Process control is the use of information technology to monitor and control a physical process. For instance, process control is used to measure the moisture content and thickness of paper as it travels over a paper machine at thousands of feet per minute. Process control is also used to determine and control temperatures, pressures, and quantities in petroleum refineries, petrochemical processes, cement plants, steel mills, nuclear reactors, and other product-focused facilities.

Process control
The use of information technology to control a physical process.

Process control systems operate in a number of ways, but the following is typical:

- Sensors collect data.
- Devices read data on some periodic basis, perhaps once a minute or once every second.
- Measurements are translated into digital signals, which are transmitted to a computer.
- Computer programs read the file (the digital data) and analyze the data.
- The resulting output may take numerous forms. These include messages on computer consoles or printers, signals to motors to change valve settings, warning lights or horns, or statistical process control charts.

Vision Systems

Vision systems combine video cameras and computer technology and are often used in inspection roles. Visual inspection is an important task in most food-processing and manufacturing organizations. Moreover, in many applications, visual inspection performed by humans is tedious, mind-numbing, and error prone. Thus vision systems are widely used when the items being inspected are very similar. For instance, vision systems are used to inspect Frito-Lay's potato chips so that imperfections can be identified as the chips proceed down the

Vision systems
Systems that use video cameras and computer technology in inspection roles.

In Anheuser-Busch's brewhouse control room, process control software monitors the process where wort is being fermented into beer.

production line. Vision systems are used to ensure that sealant is present and in the proper amount on Whirlpool's washing-machine transmissions, and to inspect switch assemblies at the Foster Plant in Des Plaines, Illinois. Vision systems are consistently accurate, do not become bored, and are of modest cost. These systems are vastly superior to individuals trying to perform these tasks.

Robots

Robot
A flexible machine with the ability to hold, move, or grab items. It functions through electronic impulses that activate motors and switches.

When a machine is flexible and has the ability to hold, move, and perhaps "grab" items, we tend to use the word *robot*. **Robots** are mechanical devices that use electronic impulses to activate motors and switches. Robots may be used effectively to perform tasks that are especially monotonous or dangerous or those that can be improved by the substitution of mechanical for human effort. Such is the case when consistency, accuracy, speed, strength, or power can be enhanced by the substitution of machines for people. Ford, for example, uses robots to do 98% of the welding and most of the painting on some automobiles.

Automated Storage and Retrieval Systems (ASRSs)

Automated storage and retrieval system (ASRS)
Computer-controlled warehouses that provide for the automatic placement of parts into and from designated places within a warehouse.

Because of the tremendous labor involved in error-prone warehousing, computer-controlled warehouses have been developed. These systems, known as **automated storage and retrieval systems (ASRSs)**, provide for the automatic placement and withdrawal of parts and products into and from designated places in a warehouse. Such systems are commonly used in distribution facilities of retailers such as Wal-Mart, Tupperware, and Benetton. These systems are also found in inventory and test areas of manufacturing firms.

Automated Guided Vehicles (AGVs)

Automated guided vehicle (AGV)
Electronically guided and controlled cart used to move materials.

Automated material handling can take the form of monorails, conveyors, robots, or automated guided vehicles. **Automated guided vehicles (AGVs)** are electronically guided and controlled carts used in manufacturing to move parts and equipment. They are also used in offices to move mail and in hospitals and in jails to deliver meals.

Flexible Manufacturing Systems (FMSs)

Flexible manufacturing system (FMS)
A system that uses an automated work cell controlled by electronic signals from a common centralized computer facility.

When a central computer provides instructions to each workstation *and* to the material-handling equipment (which moves material to that station), the system is known as an automated work cell or, more commonly, a **flexible manufacturing system (FMS)**. An FMS is flexible because both the material-handling devices and the machines themselves are controlled by easily changed electronic signals (computer programs). Operators simply load new programs, as necessary, to produce different products. The result is a system that can economically produce low volume but high variety. For example, the Lockheed Martin facility, near Dallas, efficiently builds one-of-a-kind spare parts for military aircraft. The costs associated with changeover and low utilization have been reduced substantially. FMSs bridge the gap between product-focused and process-focused facilities.

Computer-Integrated Manufacturing (CIM)

Computer-integrated manufacturing (CIM)
A manufacturing system in which CAD, FMS, inventory control, warehousing, and shipping are integrated.

Flexible manufacturing systems can be extended backward electronically into the engineering and inventory control departments and forward to the warehousing and shipping departments. In this way, computer-aided design (CAD) generates the necessary electronic instructions to run a numerically controlled machine. In a computer-integrated manufacturing environment, a design change initiated at a CAD terminal can result in that change being made in the part produced on the shop floor in a matter of minutes. When this capability is integrated with inventory control, warehousing, and shipping as a part of a flexible manufacturing system, the entire system is called **computer-integrated manufacturing (CIM)** (Figure 7.10).

Flexible manufacturing systems and computer-integrated manufacturing are reducing the distinction between low-volume/high-variety and high-volume/low-variety production. Information technology is allowing FMS and CIM to handle increasing variety while expanding to include a growing range of volumes.

TECHNOLOGY IN SERVICES

AUTHOR COMMENT
Although less dramatic than manufacturing, technology also improves quality and productivity in services.

Just as we have seen rapid advances in technology in the manufacturing sector, so we also find dramatic changes in the service sector. These range from electronic diagnostic equipment at auto repair shops, to blood- and urine-testing equipment in hospitals, to retinal security scanners at airports and high-security facilities. The hospitality industry provides other examples, as discussed in the *OM in Action* box "Technology Changes the Hotel Industry." The McDonald's approach is to use self-serve kiosks. The labor savings when ordering and speedier checkout service provide valuable productivity increases for both the restaurant and the customer.

Similarly, Andersen Windows, of Minnesota, has developed user-friendly computer software that enables customers to design their own window specifications. The customer calls up a product

▼ **FIGURE 7.10 Computer-Integrated Manufacturing (CIM)**

CIM includes computer-aided design (CAD), computer-aided manufacturing (CAM), flexible manufacturing systems (FMSs), automated storage and retrieval systems (ASRSs), automated guided vehicles (AGVs), and robots to provide an integrated and flexible manufacturing process.

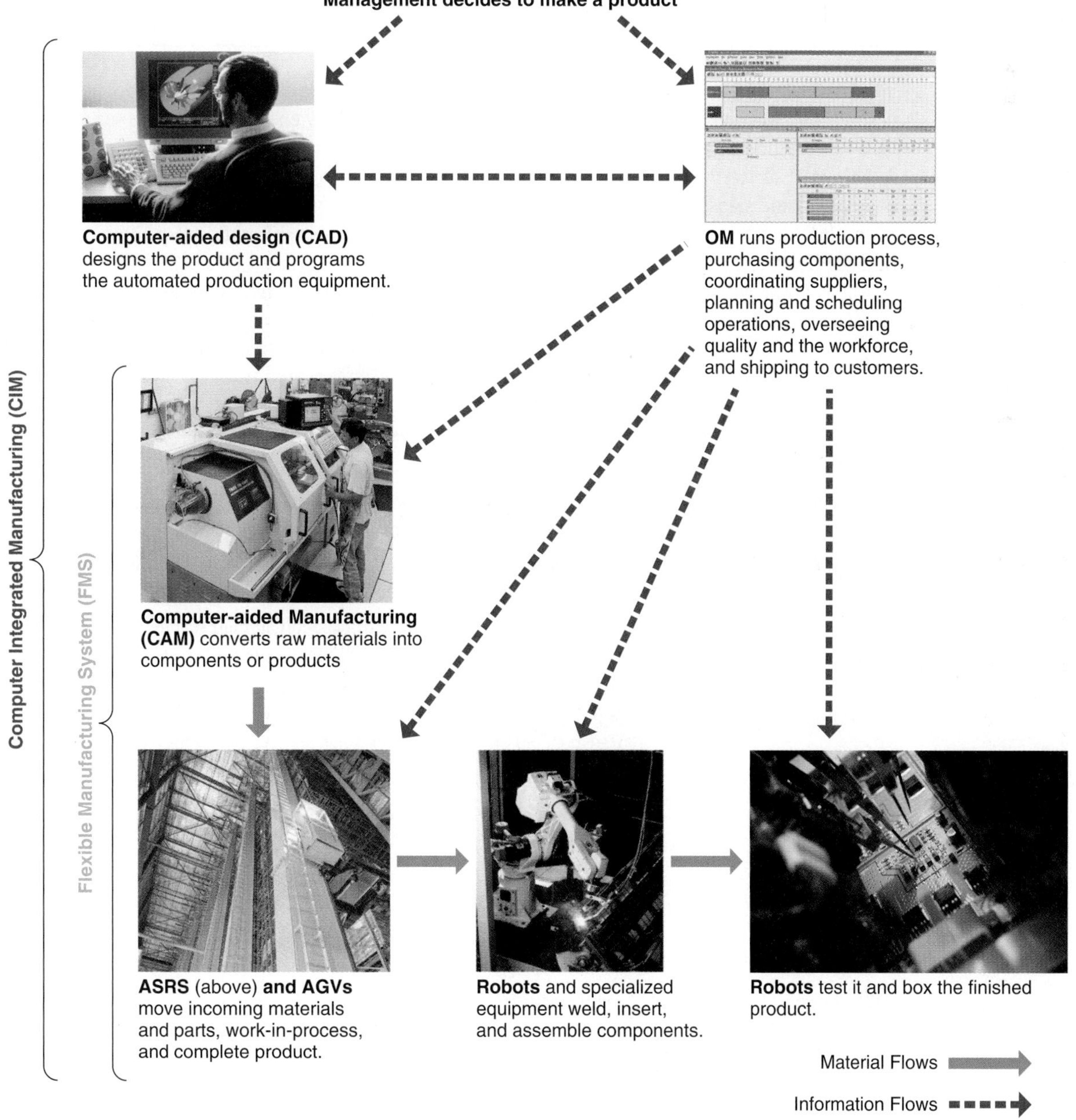
Management decides to make a product
Computer Integrated Manufacturing (CIM)
Flexible Manufacturing System (FMS)
Computer-aided design (CAD) designs the product and programs the automated production equipment.
OM runs production process, purchasing components, coordinating suppliers, planning and scheduling operations, overseeing quality and the workforce, and shipping to customers.
Computer-aided Manufacturing (CAM) converts raw materials into components or products
ASRS (above) **and AGVs** move incoming materials and parts, work-in-process, and complete product.
Robots and specialized equipment weld, insert, and assemble components.
Robots test it and box the finished product.
Material Flows
Information Flows

OM in Action ► Technology Changes the Hotel Industry

Technology is introducing "intelligent rooms" to the hotel industry. Hotel management can now precisely track a maid's time through the use of a security system. When a maid enters a room, a card is inserted that notifies the front-desk computer of the maid's location. "We can show her a printout of how long she takes to do a room," says one manager.

Security systems also enable guests to use their own credit cards as keys to unlock their doors. There are also other uses for the system. The computer can bar a guest's access to the room after checkout time and automatically control the air conditioning or heat, turning it on at check-in and off at checkout.

Minibars are now equipped with sensors that alert the central computer system at the hotel when an item is removed. Such items are immediately billed to the room. And now, with a handheld infrared unit, housekeeping staff can check, from the hallway, to see if a room is physically occupied. This both eliminates the embarrassment of having a hotel staffer walk in on a guest *and* improves security for housekeepers.

At Loew's Portofino Bay Hotel at Universal Studios, Orlando, guest smart cards act as credit cards in both the theme park and the hotel, and staff smart cards (programmed for different levels of security access) create an audit trail of employee movement. Starwood Hotels, which runs such properties as Sheraton and Westins, use Casio Pocket PCs to communicate with a hotel wireless network. Now guests can check in and out from any place on the property, such as at their restaurant table after breakfast or lunch.

Sources: Hotel and Motel Management (November 5, 2007): 16; *Hotels* (April 2004): 51–54; and *Newsweek* (international ed.) (September 27, 2004): 73.

information guide, promotion material, a gallery of designs, and a sketch pad to create the designs desired. The software also allows the customer to determine likely energy savings and see a graphic view of their home fitted with the new window.

In retail stores, POS terminals download prices quickly to reflect changing costs or market conditions, and sales are tracked in 15-minute segments to aid scheduling. Drug companies, such as Purdue Pharma LP, have begun tracking critical medications with radio frequency identification (RFID) tags to reduce counterfeiting and theft.

Table 7.4 provides a glimpse of the impact of technology on services. Operations managers in services, as in manufacturing, must be able to evaluate the impact of technology on their firm. This ability requires particular skill when evaluating reliability, investment analysis, human resource requirements, and maintenance/service.

►TABLE 7.4 Examples of Technology's Impact on Services

Service Industry	Example
Financial Services	Debit cards, electronic funds transfer, automatic teller machines, Internet stock trading, online banking via cell phone.
Education	Online newspapers, online journals, interactive assignments via Web CT, Blackboard, and smart phones.
Utilities and government	Automated one-man garbage trucks, optical mail scanners, flood-warning systems, meters allowing homeowners to control energy usage and costs.
Restaurants and foods	Wireless orders from waiters to the kitchen, robot butchering, transponders on cars that track sales at drive-throughs.
Communications	Interactive TV, ebooks via Kindle 2.
Hotels	Electronic check-in/checkout, electronic key/lock systems, mobile Web bookings.
Wholesale/retail trade	Point-of-sale (POS) terminals, e-commerce, electronic communication between store and supplier, bar-coded data, RFID
Transportation	Automatic toll booths, satellite-directed navigation systems, Wi-Fi in automobiles
Health care	Online patient-monitoring systems, online medical information systems, robotic surgery
Airlines	Ticketless travel, scheduling, Internet purchases, boarding passes downloaded as two-dimensional bar codes on smart phones

PROCESS REDESIGN

AUTHOR COMMENT
Most processes we design are existing processes, so the ability to redesign them is important.

Often a firm finds that the initial assumptions of its process are no longer valid. The world is a dynamic place, and customer desires, product technology, and product mix change. Consequently, processes are redesigned. **Process redesign** is the fundamental rethinking of business processes to bring about dramatic improvements in performance. Effective process redesign relies on reevaluating the purpose of the process and questioning both purpose and underlying assumptions. It works only if the basic process and its objectives are reexamined.

Process redesign
The fundamental rethinking of business processes to bring about dramatic improvements in performance.

Process redesign also focuses on those activities that cross functional lines. Because managers are often in charge of specific "functions" or specialized areas of responsibility, those activities (processes) that cross from one function or specialty to another may be neglected. Redesign casts aside all notions of how the process is currently being done and focuses on dramatic improvements in cost, time, and customer value. Any process is a candidate for radical redesign. The process can be a factory layout, a purchasing procedure, a new way of processing credit applications, or a new order-fulfillment process.

Shell Lubricants, for example, reinvented its order-fulfillment process by replacing a group of people who handled different parts of an order with one individual who does it all. As a result, Shell has cut the cycle time of turning an order into cash by 75%, reduced operating expenses by 45%, and boosted customer satisfaction 105%—all by introducing a new way of handling orders. Time, cost, and customer satisfaction—the dimension of performance shaped by operations—get major boosts from operational innovation.

SUSTAINABILITY

AUTHOR COMMENT
Process selection and management can support conservation and renewal of resources.

In Chapter 5 we discussed goods and services *design* and its potential impact on ethics, the environment, and sustainability. We now introduce the issue of sustainability in production *processes*.[4] Managers may find it helpful to think in terms of four *Rs* as they address sustainability. These are (1) the *resources* used by the production process, (2) the *recycling* of production materials and product components, (3) the *regulations* that apply, and (4) the firm's *reputation*. All four areas provide impetus for managers to perform well as they develop and refine production processes.

Resources

Operations is often the primary user of the firm's resources. This puts special pressure on using human, financial, and material resources in a sustainable way. Most firms are good at reducing resource use as it is a win–win situation: reducing resources lowers cost as well as being a positive force toward sustainability. Examples of sustainable use in production processes are actions taken by:

- Wal-Mart and Frito-Lay have both driven down their water and energy use. (These firms' efforts in sustainability are discussed in the video cases at the end of this chapter.)
- Subaru's Indiana plant has driven down energy use by 14% per car.
- Pepsi has reduced the weight of its plastic bottles for Aquafina by 20%. This reduces resource use and saves weight with the added advantage of cutting delivery cost.
- The Ritz-Carlton is doing laundry at night to reduce electricity costs.

VIDEO 7.3
Green Manufacturing and sustainability at Frito-Lay

Recycle

LO6: Discuss the four R's of sustainability

As managers seek sustainability, they should realize that there are only three things that can be done with waste: burn it, bury it, or reuse it. The first two have undesirable consequences. Burned waste pumps unwanted emissions into the atmosphere, and burying has the potential of releasing methane and ammonia, as well as creating fires, explosions, and water table issues. While recycling begins at design by specifying products and components that have recycle potential, managers must build processes that facilitate disassembly and reuse of those materials. Whether it is plastic, glass, or lead in an automobile or plastic bags and Styrofoam from the grocery store, recycling has a significant role in sustainability. Examples are:

- Anheuser-Busch saves over $30 million per year in energy and waste-treatment costs by using treated plant wastewater to generate the gas that powers its St. Louis brewery.
- Standard Register, a major manufacturer of multipart paper forms, produces considerable paper scrap—almost 20 tons of punch holes alone per month—which creates a significant

[4]We define *sustainable* in an OM context as a production system that supports conservation and renewal of resources.

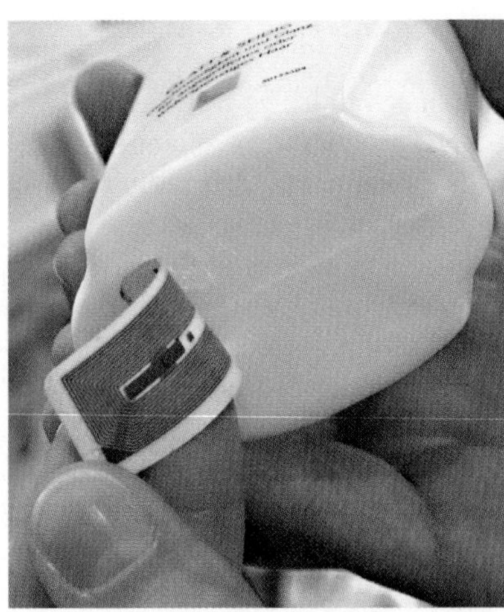

Pharmaceutical companies are counting on RFID to aid the tracking and tracing of drugs in the distribution system to reduce losses that total over $30 billion a year.

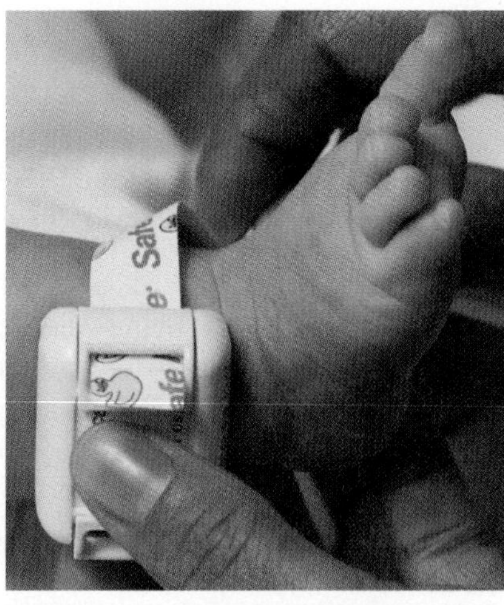

Hospitals use RFID sensors to track patients, staff, and equipment.

waste issue. But the company developed ways to recycle the paper scrap, as well as aluminum and silver from the plate-making process.

Regulations

Laws and regulations affecting transportation, waste, and noise are proliferating and can be as much of a challenge as reducing resource use. While the challenge can be difficult, firms must abide by the legal requirements of the host nation; society expects no less. The resources available from Planet Earth are finite and many by-products are undesirable. So organizations are increasingly under pressure from regulatory agencies to reduce by-products that yield greenhouse gasses and pollute the air and water. Greenhouse gasses (GHS) include carbon dioxide, methane, nitrous oxide, and fluorinated gasses that are believed to contribute to global warning. To meet regulatory requirements, firms design, redesign, and invest substantial human and financial resources. Some examples are:

- Home builders are required not just to manage water runoff but to have a pollution prevention plan for each site.
- Public drinking water systems must comply with the federal Safe Drinking Water Act's arsenic standard, even for existing facilities.
- Hospitals are required to meet the terms of the Resource Conservation and Recovery Act, which governs the storage and handling of hazardous material.
- Manufacturers, miners, dairies, refineries, and other firms that emit 25,000 metric tons or more per year of GHG emissions are required to submit annual reports to the EPA.

Carbon Footprint. Another sustainability issue is evaluating and reducing the *carbon footprint.* This is a measurement of greenhouse gasses for which international regulation is pending. A substantial portion of greenhouse gasses are released naturally by farming, cattle, and decaying forests, but also by manufacturing and services. Operations personnel are being asked to contribute to their reduction.

Industry leaders such as Frito-Lay have been able to break down the carbon emissions from various stages in the production process. For instance in potato chip production, a 34.5 gram (1.2 ounce) bag of chips is responsible for about twice its weight in emissions—75 grams per bag—with contributions coming from: (1) raw materials (potatoes, oil, seasonings), 44%; (2) manufacture (producing the chips in the factory), 30%; (3) packaging, 15%; (4) shipping, 9%; and (5) disposal by the customer of an empty bag, 2%. Frito-Lay has targeted its raw material suppliers and distributors to reduce the carbon footprint, which has already gone down by 7% in the past two years.

Reputation

The marketplace may reward leadership in sustainability. The free enterprise system operates on a voluntary basis: if employees, suppliers, distributors, providers of capital, and, of course, customers, do not want to do business with a firm, they are not required to do so. Those organizations that do not meet society's expectations can expect these voluntary relationships to be difficult to build and maintain. A bad reputation does have negative consequences. Our society is increasingly transparent, and both good news and bad news travel rapidly. But green processes can yield good news, a good reputation, and good results. Here are three examples:

- British cosmetic firm The Body Shop has successfully differentiated its products by stressing environmental sensitivity. It pursues a product design, development, and testing strategy that it believes to be ethical and socially responsible. This includes environment-friendly ingredients and elimination of animal testing.
- Ben & Jerry's pursues its socially responsible image (and saves $250,000 annually) just by using energy-efficient lighting.
- Frito-Lay has built a plant powered by solar energy in Modesto, California, and advertises the product as Sun Chips.

Imaginative, well-led firms are finding opportunities to build sustainable production processes that conserve resources, recycle, meet regulatory requirements, and foster a positive reputation.

CHAPTER SUMMARY

Effective operations managers understand how to use process strategy as a competitive weapon. They select a production process with the necessary quality, flexibility, and cost structure to meet product and volume requirements. They also seek creative ways to combine the low unit cost of high-volume, low-variety manufacturing with the customization available through low-volume, high-variety facilities. Managers use the techniques of lean production and employee participation to encourage the development of efficient equipment and processes. They design their equipment and processes to have capabilities beyond the tolerance required by their customers, while ensuring the flexibility needed for adjustments in technology, features, and volumes.

Key Terms

Process strategy (p. 252)
Process focus (p. 252)
Repetitive process (p. 253)
Modules (p. 253)
Product focus (p. 254)
Mass customization (p. 254)
Build-to-order (BTO) (p. 255)
Postponement (p. 255)
Crossover chart (p. 257)
Flowchart (p. 259)
Time-function mapping (or process mapping) (p. 259)
Value-stream mapping (VSM) (p. 260)
Process charts (p. 261)
Service blueprinting (p. 262)
Flexibility (p. 266)
Computer numerical control (CNC) (p. 266)
Automatic identification system (AIS) (p. 266)
Radio frequency identification (RFID) (p. 266)
Process control (p. 267)
Vision systems (p. 267)
Robot (p. 268)
Automated storage and retrieval system (ASRS) (p. 268)
Automated guided vehicle (AGV) (p. 268)
Flexible manufacturing system (FMS) (p. 268)
Computer-integrated manufacturing (CIM) (p. 268)
Process redesign (p. 271)

Ethical Dilemma

For the sake of efficiency and lower costs, Premium Standard Farms of Princeton, Missouri, has turned pig production into a standardized product-focused process. Slaughterhouses have done this for a hundred years—but after the animal was dead. Doing it while the animal is alive is a relatively recent innovation. Here is how it works.

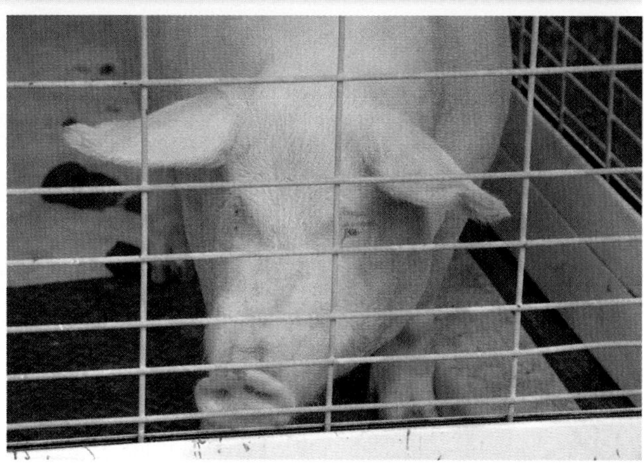

Impregnated female sows wait for 40 days in metal stalls so small that they cannot turn around. After an ultrasound test, they wait 67 days in a similar stall until they give birth. Two weeks after delivering 10 or 11 piglets, the sows are moved back to breeding rooms for another cycle. After 3 years, the sow is slaughtered. Animal-welfare advocates say such confinement drives pigs crazy. Premium Standard replies that its hogs are in fact comfortable, arguing that only 1% die before Premium Standard wants them to and that their system helps reduce the cost of pork products.

Discuss the productivity and ethical implications of this industry and these two divergent opinions.

Discussion Questions

1. What is process strategy?
2. What type of process is used for making each of the following products?
   (a) beer
   (b) wedding invitations
   (c) automobiles
   (d) paper
   (e) Big Macs
   (f) custom homes
   (g) motorcycles
3. What is service blueprinting?
4. What is process redesign?
5. What are the techniques for improving service productivity?
6. Name the four quadrants of the service process matrix. Discuss how the matrix is used to classify services into categories.
7. What is CIM?
8. What do we mean by a process-control system and what are the typical elements in such systems?
9. Identify *manufacturing* firms that compete on each of the four processes shown in Figure 7.1.
10. Identify the competitive advantage of each of the four firms identified in Discussion Question 9.
11. Identify *service* firms that compete on each of the four processes shown in Figure 7.1.
12. Identify the competitive advantage of each of the four firms identified in Discussion Question 11.
13. What are numerically controlled machines?
14. Describe briefly what an automatic identification system (AIS) is and how service organizations could use AIS to increase productivity and at the same time increase the variety of services offered.
15. Name some of the advances being made in technology that enhance production and productivity.
16. Explain what a flexible manufacturing system (FMS) is.
17. In what ways do CAD and FMS connect?
18. What are the four *R*s of sustainability?

Solved Problem

Virtual Office Hours help is available at www.myomlab.com.

▼ SOLVED PROBLEM 7.1

Bagot Copy Shop has a volume of 125,000 black-and-white copies per month. Two salesmen have made presentations to Gordon Bagot for machines of equal quality and reliability. The Print Shop 5 has a cost of $2,000 per month and a variable cost of $.03. The other machine (a Speed Copy 100) will cost only $1,500 per month but the toner is more expensive, driving the cost per copy up to $.035. If cost and volume are the only considerations, which machine should Bagot purchase?

▼ SOLUTION

$$2{,}000 + .03\,X = 1{,}500 + .035\,X$$
$$2{,}000 - 1{,}500 = .035\,X - .03\,X$$
$$500 = .005\,X$$
$$100{,}000 = X$$

Because Bagot expects his volume to exceed 100,000 units, he should choose the Print Shop 5.

Problems*

• **7.1** Prepare a flowchart for one of the following:
a) the registration process at a school
b) the process at the local car wash
c) a shoe shine
d) some other process with the approval of the instructor

• **7.2** Prepare a process chart for one of the activities in Problem 7.1.

•• **7.3** Prepare a time-function map for one of the activities in Problem 7.1.

•• **7.4** Prepare a service blueprint for one of the activities in Problem 7.1.

• **7.5** Meile Machine Shop, Inc., has a 1-year contract for the production of 200,000 gear housings for a new off-road vehicle. Owner Larry Meile hopes the contract will be extended and the volume increased next year. Meile has developed costs for three alternatives. They are general-purpose equipment (GPE), flexible manufacturing system (FMS), and expensive, but efficient, dedicated machine (DM). The cost data follow:

	General-Purpose Equipment (GPE)	Flexible Manufacturing System (FMS)	Dedicated Machine (DM)
Annual contracted units	200,000	200,000	200,000
Annual fixed cost	$100,000	$200,000	$500,000
Per unit variable cost	$ 15.00	$ 14.00	$ 13.00

Which process is best for this contract? PX

• **7.6** Using the data in Problem 7.5, determine the economical volume for each process. PX

• **7.7** Using the data in Problem 7.5, determine the best process for each of the following volumes: (1) 75,000, (2) 275,000, and (3) 375,000.

• **7.8** Refer to Problem 7.5. If a contract for the second and third years is pending, what are the implications for process selection?

•• **7.9** Stan Fawcett's company is considering producing a gear assembly that it now purchases from Salt Lake Supply, Inc. Salt Lake Supply charges $4 per unit with a minimum order of

*Note: PX means the problem may be solved with POM for Windows and/or Excel OM.

3,000 units. Stan estimates that it will cost $15,000 to set up the process and then $1.82 per unit for labor and materials.

a) Draw a graph illustrating the crossover (or indifference) point.
b) Determine the number of units where either choice has the same cost. Px

•• **7.10** Ski Boards, Inc., wants to enter the market quickly with a new finish on its ski boards. It has three choices: (a) refurbish the old equipment at a cost of $800, (b) make major modifications at the cost of $1,100, or (c) purchase new equipment at a net cost of $1,800. If the firm chooses to refurbish the equipment, materials and labor will be $1.10 per board. If it chooses to make modifications, materials and labor will be $0.70 per board. If it buys new equipment, variable costs are estimated to be $.40 per board.

a) Graph the three total cost lines on the same chart.
b) Which alternative should Ski Boards, Inc., choose if it thinks it can sell more than 3,000 boards?
c) Which alternative should the firm use if it thinks the market for boards will be between 1,000 and 2,000? Px

•• **7.11** Susan Meyer, owner/manager of Meyer's Motor Court in Key West, is considering outsourcing the daily room cleanup for her motel to Duffy's Maid Service. Susan rents an average of 50 rooms for each of 365 nights (365 × 50 equals the total rooms rented for the year). Susan's cost to clean a room is $12.50. The Duffy's Maid Service quote is $18.50 per room plus a fixed cost of $25,000 for sundry items such as uniforms with the motel's name. Susan's annual fixed cost for space, equipment, and supplies is $61,000. Which is the preferred process for Susan, and why? Px

•• **7.12** Keith Whittingham, as manager of Designs by Whittingham, is upgrading his CAD software. The high-performance (HP) software rents for $3,000 per month per workstation. The standard-performance (SP) software rents for $2,000 per month per workstation. The productivity figures that he has available suggest that the HP software is faster for his kind of design. Therefore, with the HP software he will need five engineers and with the SP software he will need six. This translates into a variable cost of $200 per drawing for the HP system and $240 per drawing for the SP system. At his projected volume of 80 drawings per month, which system should he rent? Px

•• **7.13** Using Figure 7.6 in the discussion of value-stream mapping as a starting point, analyze an opportunity for improvement in a process with which you are familiar and develop an improved process.

••• **7.14** Creative Cabinets, Inc., needs to choose a production method for its new office shelf, the Maxistand. To help accomplish this, the firm has gathered the following production cost data:

Process Type	**Annualized Fixed Cost of Plant & Equip.**	*Variable Costs (per unit) ($)* **Labor**	**Material**	**Energy**
Mass Customization	$1,260,000	30	18	12
Intermittent	$1,000,000	24	26	20
Repetitive	$1,625,000	28	15	12
Continuous	$1,960,000	25	15	10

Creative Cabinets projects an annual demand of 24,000 units for the Maxistand. The Maxistand will sell for $120 per unit.

a) Which process type will maximize the annual profit from producing the Maxistand?
b) What is the value of this annual profit? Px

Case Studies

► Rochester Manufacturing's Process Decision

Rochester Manufacturing Corporation (RMC) is considering moving some of its production from traditional numerically controlled machines to a flexible manufacturing system (FMS). Its computer numerical control machines have been operating in a high-variety, low-volume manner. Machine utilization, as near as it can determine, is hovering around 10%. The machine tool salespeople and a consulting firm want to put the machines together in an FMS. They believe that a $3 million expenditure on machinery and the transfer machines will handle about 30% of RMC's work. There will, of course, be transition and startup costs in addition to this.

The firm has not yet entered all its parts into a comprehensive group technology system, but believes that the 30% is a good estimate of products suitable for the FMS. This 30% should fit very nicely into a "family." A reduction, because of higher utilization, should take place in the number of pieces of machinery. The firm should be able to go from 15 to about 4 machines and personnel should go from 15 to perhaps as low as 3. Similarly, floor space reduction will go from 20,000 square feet to about 6,000. Throughput of orders should also improve with processing of this family of parts in 1 to 2 days rather than 7 to 10. Inventory reduction is estimated to yield a one-time $750,000 savings, and annual labor savings should be in the neighborhood of $300,000.

Although the projections all look very positive, an analysis of the project's return on investment showed it to be between 10% and 15% per year. The company has traditionally had an expectation that projects should yield well over 15% and have payback periods of substantially less than 5 years.

Discussion Questions

1. As a production manager for RMC, what do you recommend? Why?
2. Prepare a case by a conservative plant manager for maintaining the status quo until the returns are more obvious.
3. Prepare the case for an optimistic sales manager that you should move ahead with the FMS now.

▶ Environmental Sustainability at Walmart

Walmart views "environmental sustainability as one of the most important opportunities for both the future of our business, and the future of our world."* Its environmental vision is clear: ". . . to be supplied 100 percent by renewable energy; to create zero waste; and to sell products that sustain our natural resources and the environment." Its specific goals in the three areas are as follows:

- *Renewable energy:* existing stores are to be 20% more efficient in 7 years, new stores are to be 30% more efficient in 4 years, and the trucking fleet is to be 25% more efficient in 3 years and twice as efficient in 10 years.
- *Zero waste:* 25% reduction in solid waste in 3 years and improved brand packaging through right-sized packaging that uses reusable material.
- *Sustain resources and the environment:* 20% of its 61,000 suppliers will abide by the program within 3 years.

The three above goals make up what Walmart refers to as its Sustainable Value Network. Renewable energy includes global logistics, Greenhouse Gas (GHG) emissions, and sustainable buildings, in addition to alternative fuels. Waste refers to packaging, operations, and procurement.

Walmart has also launched various experiments and innovations, including the following:

- Building high-efficiency stores using recycled building material and lighting that conserves energy. These new facilities are 25% more energy efficient than the firm's 2005 baseline.
- Purchasing solar-powered equipment at a rate that could put it in the top 10 largest-ever solar-power purchasers in the U.S. Solar power is to be used at 22 locations in Hawaii and California.
- Reducing packaging. For example, changes to packaging for patio sets resulted in 400 fewer shipping containers. And the company used 230 fewer shipping containers to distribute toys.
- Selling reusable bags to reduce the use of disposable plastic bags; encouraging schools to collect plastic bags, for which the schools are paid.
- Adopting a series of aerodynamic innovations for its trucking fleet. It even developed a power unit to warm or cool drivers at night without turning on the truck's engine.

With these policies and initiatives, Walmart hopes to blunt criticism and as a major world wide employer lead the way in environmental sustainability. As one critic admitted begrudgingly, "Walmart has more green clout than anyone."

Discussion Questions

1. How is Walmart doing in terms of environmental sustainability?
2. Based on library and Internet research, report on other Walmart sustainability efforts.
3. Compare the firm's sustainability plan to those of Home Depot, Target, or other big-box retailers.
4. How much of Walmart's sustainability effort is (a) resource focused, (b) recycle focused, (c) regulation focused, and (d) reputation focused?

Source: Professor Asbjorn Osland, San Jose State University.

*(**http://walmartstores.com/sustainability**)

▶ Green Manufacturing and Sustainability at Frito-Lay — Video Case

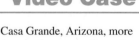

Frito-Lay, the multi-billion-dollar snack food giant, requires vast amounts of water, electricity, natural gas, and fuel to produce its 41 well-known brands. In keeping with growing environmental concerns, Frito-Lay has initiated ambitious plans to produce environmentally friendly snacks. But even environmentally friendly snacks require resources. Recognizing the environmental impact, the firm is an aggressive "green manufacturer," with major initiatives in resource reduction and sustainability.

For instance, the company's energy management program includes a variety of elements designed to engage employees in reducing energy consumption. These elements include scorecards and customized action plans that empower employees and recognize their achievements.

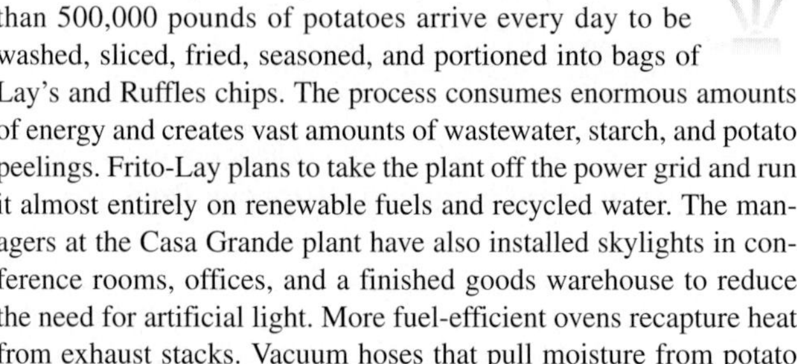

At Frito-Lay's factory in Casa Grande, Arizona, more than 500,000 pounds of potatoes arrive every day to be washed, sliced, fried, seasoned, and portioned into bags of Lay's and Ruffles chips. The process consumes enormous amounts of energy and creates vast amounts of wastewater, starch, and potato peelings. Frito-Lay plans to take the plant off the power grid and run it almost entirely on renewable fuels and recycled water. The managers at the Casa Grande plant have also installed skylights in conference rooms, offices, and a finished goods warehouse to reduce the need for artificial light. More fuel-efficient ovens recapture heat from exhaust stacks. Vacuum hoses that pull moisture from potato slices to recapture the water and to reduce the amount of heat needed to cook the potato chips are also being used.

Frito-Lay has also built over 50 acres of solar concentrators behind its Modesto, California, plant to generate solar power. The solar power is being converted into heat and used to cook Sun Chips. A biomass boiler, which will burn agricultural waste, is also planned to provide additional renewable fuel.

Frito-Lay is installing high-tech filters that recycle most of the water used to rinse and wash potatoes. It also recycles corn byproducts to make Doritos and other snacks; starch is reclaimed and sold, primarily as animal feed, and leftover sludge is burned to create methane gas to run the plant boiler.

There are benefits besides the potential energy savings. Like many other large corporations, Frito-Lay is striving to establish its green credentials as consumers become more focused on environmental issues. There are marketing opportunities, too. The company, for example, advertises that its popular Sun Chips snacks are made using solar energy.

At Frito-Lay's Florida plant, only 3½% of the waste goes to landfills, but that is still 1.5 million pounds annually. The goal is zero waste to landfills. The snack food maker earned its spot in the National Environmental Performance Track program by maintaining a sustained environmental compliance record and making new commitments to reduce, reuse, and recycle at this facility.

Substantial resource reductions have been made in the production process, with an energy reduction of 21% across Frito-Lay's 34 U.S. plants. But the continuing battle for resource reduction continues. The company is also moving toward biodegradable packaging and pursuing initiatives in areas such as office paper, packaging material, seasoning bags, and cans and bottles. While these multiyear initiatives are expensive, they have the backing at the highest levels of Frito-Lay as well as corporate executives at PepsiCo, the parent company.

Discussion Questions*

1. Using resources, regulation, and reputation as a basis, what are the sources of pressure on firms such as Frito-Lay to reduce their environmental footprint?
2. Identify the specific techniques that Frito-Lay is using to become a "green manufacturer."
3. Select another company and compare its green policies to those of Frito-Lay.

*You may wish to view the video that accompanies this case before addressing these questions.

Source: Professors Beverly Amer, Northern Arizona University; Barry Render, Rollins College; and Jay Heizer, Texas Lutheran University.

▶ Process Analysis at Arnold Palmer Hospital

Video Case

The Arnold Palmer Hospital (APH) in Orlando, Florida, is one of the busiest and most respected hospitals for the medical treatment of children and women in the U.S. Since its opening on golfing legend Arnold Palmer's birthday September 10, 1989, more than 1.6 million children and women have passed through its doors. It is the fourth busiest labor and delivery hospital in the U.S. and one of the largest neonatal intensive care units in the Southeast. APH ranks in the top 10% of hospitals nationwide in patient satisfaction.

"Part of the reason for APH's success," says Executive Director Kathy Swanson, "is our continuous improvement process. Our goal is 100% patient satisfaction. But getting there means constantly examining and reexamining everything we do, from patient flow, to cleanliness, to layout space, to a work-friendly environment, to speed of medication delivery from the pharmacy to a patient. Continuous improvement is a huge and never-ending task."

One of the tools the hospital uses consistently is the process flowchart (like those in Figure 7.1 to 7.3 in this chapter and Figure 6.6e in Chapter 6). Staffer Diane Bowles, who carries the title "clinical practice improvement consultant," charts scores of processes. Bowles's flowcharts help study ways to improve the turnaround of a vacated room (especially important in a hospital that has pushed capacity for years), speed up the admission process, and deliver warm meals warm.

Lately, APH has been examining the flow of maternity patients (and their paperwork) from the moment they enter the hospital until they are discharged, hopefully with their healthy baby a day or two later. The flow of maternity patients follows these steps:

1. Enter APH's Labor & Delivery (L&D) check-in desk entrance.
2. If the baby is born en route or if birth is imminent, the mother and baby are taken directly to Labor & Delivery on the second floor and registered and admitted directly at the bedside. If there are no complications, the mother and baby go to step 6.
3. If the baby is *not* yet born, the front desk asks if the mother is pre-registered. (Most do pre-register at the 28- to 30-week pregnancy mark). If she is not, she goes to the registration office on the first floor.
4. The pregnant woman is then taken to L&D Triage on the 8th floor for assessment. If she is in active labor, she is taken to an L&D room on the 2nd floor until the baby is born. If she is not ready, she goes to step 5.
5. Pregnant women not ready to deliver (i.e., no contractions or false alarm) are either sent home to return on a later date and reenter the system at that time, or if contractions are not yet close enough, they are sent to walk around the hospital grounds (to encourage progress) and then return to L&D Triage at a prescribed time.
6. When the baby is born, if there are no complications, after 2 hours the mother and baby are transferred to a "mother–baby care unit" room on floors 3, 4, or 5 for an average of 40–44 hours.
7. If there *are* complications with the mother, she goes to an operating room and/or intensive care unit. From there, she goes back to a mother–baby care room upon stabilization—or is discharged at another time if not stabilized. Complications for the baby may result in a stay in the neonatal intensive care unit (NICU) before transfer to the baby nursery near the mother's room. If the baby is not stable enough for discharge with the mother, the baby is discharged later.
8. Mother and/or baby, when ready, are discharged and taken by wheelchair to the discharge exit for pickup to travel home.

Discussion Questions*

1. As Diane's new assistant, you need to flowchart this process. Explain how the process might be improved once you have completed the chart.
2. If a mother is scheduled for a Caesarean-section birth (i.e., the baby is removed from the womb surgically), how would this flowchart change?
3. If *all* mothers were electronically (or manually) pre-registered, how would the flowchart change? Redraw the chart to show your changes.
4. Describe in detail a process that the hospital could analyze, besides the ones mentioned in this case.

*You may wish to view the video that accompanies this case before addressing these questions.

▶ Process Strategy at Wheeled Coach

Video Case

Wheeled Coach, based in Winter Park, Florida, is the world's largest manufacturer of ambulances. Working four 10-hour days each week, 350 employees make only custom-made ambulances: Virtually every vehicle is unique. Wheeled Coach accommodates the marketplace by providing a wide variety of options and an engineering staff accustomed to innovation and custom design. Continuing growth, which now requires that more than 20 ambulances roll off the assembly line each week, makes process design a continuing challenge. Wheeled Coach's response has been to build a focused factory: Wheeled Coach builds nothing but ambulances. Within the focused factory, Wheeled Coach established work cells for every major module feeding an assembly line, including aluminum bodies, electrical wiring harnesses, interior cabinets, windows, painting, and upholstery.

Labor standards drive the schedule so that every work cell feeds the assembly line on schedule, just-in-time for installations. The chassis, usually that of a Ford truck, moves to a station at which the aluminum body is mounted. Then the vehicle is moved to painting. Following a custom paint job, it moves to the assembly line, where it will spend 7 days. During each of these 7 workdays, each work cell delivers its respective module to the appropriate position on the assembly line. During the first day, electrical wiring is installed; on the second day, the unit moves forward to the station at which cabinetry is delivered and installed, then to a window and lighting station, on to upholstery, to fit and finish, to further customizing, and finally to inspection and road testing. The *Global Company Profile* featuring Wheeled Coach, which opens Chapter 14, provides further details about this process.

Discussion Questions*

1. Why do you think major auto manufacturers do not build ambulances?
2. What is an alternative process strategy to the assembly line that Wheeled Coach currently uses?
3. Why is it more efficient for the work cells to prepare "modules" and deliver them to the assembly line than it would be to produce the component (e.g., interior upholstery) on the line?
4. How does Wheeled Coach manage the tasks to be performed at each work station?

*You may wish to view the video that accompanies this case before addressing these questions.

▶**Additional Case Study:** Visit **www.myomlab.com** or **www.pearsonhighered.com/heizer** *for this free case study:*
Matthew Yachts, Inc.: Examines a possible process change as the market for yachts changes.

Bibliography

Davenport, T. H. "The Coming Commoditization of Processes." *Harvard Business Review* 83, no. 6 (June 2005): 101–108.

Debo, L. G., L. B. Toktay, and L. N. Van Wassenhove. "Market Segmentation and Product Technology Selection for Remanufacturable Products." *Management Science* 51, no. 8 (August 2005): 1193–1205.

Duray, R., P. T. Ward, G. W. Milligan, and W. L. Berry. "Approaches to Mass Customization: Configurations and Empirical Validation." *Journal of Operations Management* 18, no. 6 (November 2000): 605–625.

Duray, R. "Mass Customization Origins: Mass or Custom Manufacturing." *International Journal of Operations and Production Management* 22, no. 3 (2002): 314–328.

Gilmore, James H., and Joseph Pine II (eds.). *Markets of One: Creating Customer-Unique Value through Mass Customization.* Boston: Harvard Business Review Book, 2000.

Hall, Joseph M., and M. Eric Johnson. "When Should a Process Be Art, Not Science?" *Harvard Business Review* 87, no. 3 (March 2009): 58–65.

Hegde, V. G., et al. "Customization: Impact on Product and Process Performance." *Production and Operations Management* 14, no. 4 (Winter 2005): 388–399.

Inderfurth, Karl, I. M. Langella. "An Approach for Solving Disassembly-to-order Problems under Stochastic Yields." In *Logistik Management.* Heidelberg: Physica, 2004: 309–331.

Moeeni, F. "From Light Frequency Identification to Radio Frequency Identification in the Supply Chain," *Decision Line* 37, no. 3 (May 2006): 8–13.

Rugtusanatham, M. Johnny, and Fabrizio Salvador. "From Mass Production to Mass Customization." *Production and Operations Management* 17, no. 3 (May–June 2008): 385–396.

Su, J. C. P., Y. Chang, and M. Ferguson. "Evaluation of Postponement Structures to Accommodate Mass Customization." *Journal of Operations Management* 23, no. 3–4 (April 2005): 305–318.

Swamidass, Paul M. *Innovations in Competitive Manufacturing.* Dordrecht, NL: Kluwer, 2000.

Welborn, Cliff. "Mass Customization." *OR/MS Today* (December 2007): 38–42.

Zipkin, Paul. "The Limits of Mass Customization." *MIT Sloan Management Review* 40, no. 1 (Spring 2001): 81–88.

Chapter 7 **Rapid Review**

Main Heading	Review Material	PEARSON myomlab
FOUR PROCESS STRATEGIES (pp. 252–259)	■ **Process strategy**—An organization's approach to transforming resources into goods and services. *The objective of a process strategy is to build a production process that meets customer requirements and product specifications within cost and other managerial constraints.* Virtually every good or service is made by using some variation of one of four process strategies. **Process focus**—A facility organized around processes to facilitate low-volume, high-variety production. The vast majority of global production is devoted to making low-volume, high variety products in process focused facilities, also known as job shops or *intermittent process* facilities. Process focused facilities have high variable costs with extremely low utilization (5% to 25%) of facilities. ■ **Repetitive process**—A product-oriented production process that uses modules. ■ **Modules**—Parts or components of a product previously prepared, often in a continuous process. The repetitive process is the classic assembly line. It allows the firm to use modules and combine the economic advantages of the product-focused model with the customization advantages of the process-focus model. ■ **Product focus**—A facility organized around products; a product-oriented, high-volume, low-variety process. Product-focused facilities are also called *continuous processes,* because they have very long, continuous production runs. The specialized nature of a product-focused facility requires high fixed cost; however, low variable costs reward high facility utilization. ■ **Mass customization**—Rapid, low-cost production that caters to constantly changing unique customer desires. ■ **Build-to-order (BTO)**—Produce to customer order rather than to a forecast. Major challenges of a build-to-order system include: *Product design, Process design, Inventory management, Tight schedules* and *Responsive partners.* ■ **Postponement**—The delay of any modifications or customization to a product as long as possible in the production process. ■ **Crossover chart**—A chart of costs at the possible volumes for more than one process.	Problems: 7.5-7.14 **VIDEO 7.1** Process Strategy at Wheeled Coach Ambulance **ACTIVE MODEL 7.1** Virtual Office Hours for Solved Problem: 7.1
PROCESS ANALYSIS AND DESIGN (pp. 259–262)	Five tools of process analysis are (1) flowcharts, (2) time-function mapping, (3) value-stream mapping, (4) process charts, and (5) service blueprinting. ■ **Flowchart**—A drawing used to analyze movement of people or materials. ■ **Time-function mapping** (or **process mapping**)—A flowchart with time added on the horizontal axis. ■ **Value-stream mapping (VSM)**—A tool that helps managers understand how to add value in the flow of material and information through the entire production process. ■ **Process charts**—Charts that use symbols to analyze the movement of people or material. Process charts allow managers to focus on value-added activities and to compute the percentage of value-added time (= operation time/total time). ■ **Service blueprinting**—A process analysis technique that lends itself to a focus on the customer and the provider's interaction with the customer.	Problems: 7.2, 7.3
SPECIAL CONSIDERATIONS FOR SERVICE PROCESS DESIGN (pp. 262–265)	Services can be classified into one of four quadrants, based on relative degrees of labor and customization: 1. *Service factory* 2. *Service shop* 3. *Mass service* 4. *Professional service* Techniques for improving service productivity include: ■ *Separation*—Structuring service so customers must go where the service is offered ■ *Self-service*—Customers examining, comparing, and evaluating at their own pace ■ *Postponement*—Customizing at delivery ■ *Focus*—Restricting the offerings ■ *Modules*—Modular selection of service; modular production ■ *Automation*—Separating services that may lend themselves to a type of automation	**VIDEO 7.2** Process Analysis at Arnold Palmer Hospital

Main Heading	Review Material	myomlab
	■ *Scheduling*—Precise personnel scheduling ■ *Training*—Clarifying the service options; explaining how to avoid problems	
SELECTION OF EQUIPMENT AND TECHNOLOGY (pp. 265–266)	Picking the best equipment involves understanding the specific industry and available processes and technology. The choice requires considering cost, quality, capacity, and flexibility. ■ **Flexibility**—The ability to respond with little penalty in time, cost, or customer value.	
PRODUCTION TECHNOLOGY (pp. 266–268)	■ **Computer numerical control (CNC)**—Machinery with its own computer and memory. ■ **Automatic identification system (AIS)**—A system for transforming data into electronic form (e.g., bar codes). ■ **Radio frequency identification (RFID)**—A wireless system in which integrated circuits with antennas send radio waves. ■ **Process control**—The use of information technology to control a physical process. ■ **Vision systems**—Systems that use video cameras and computer technology in inspection roles. ■ **Robot**—A flexible machine with the ability to hold, move, or grab items. ■ **Automated storage and retrieval systems (ASRS)**—Computer-controlled warehouses that provide for the automatic placement of parts into and from designated places within a warehouse. ■ **Automated guided vehicle (AGV)**—Electronically guided and controlled cart used to move materials. ■ **Flexible manufacturing system (FMS)**—Automated work cell controlled by electronic signals from a common centralized computer facility. ■ **Computer-integrated manufacturing (CIM)**—A manufacturing system in which CAD, FMS, inventory control, warehousing, and shipping are integrated.	
TECHNOLOGY IN SERVICES (pp. 269–270)	Many rapid technological developments have occurred in the service sector. These range from POS terminals and RFID to online newspapers and ebooks.	
PROCESS REDESIGN (p. 271)	■ Process redesign—The fundamental rethinking of business processes to bring about dramatic improvements in performance. Process redesign often focuses on activities that cross functional lines.	
SUSTAINABILITY (pp. 271–273)	There are four *Rs* to consider when addressing sustainability: (1) the *resources* used by the production process, (2) the *recycling* of production materials and product components, (3) the *regulations* that apply, and (4) the firm's *reputation*.	**VIDEO 7.3** Frito-Lay's Green Manufacturing and Sustainability

Self Test

■ **Before taking the self-test,** refer to the learning objectives listed at the beginning of the chapter and the key terms listed at the end of the chapter.

LO1. Low-volume, high-variety processes are also known as:
- **a)** continuous processes.
- **b)** process focused.
- **c)** repetitive processes.
- **d)** product focused.

LO2. A crossover chart for process selection focuses on:
- **a)** labor costs.
- **b)** material cost.
- **c)** both labor and material costs.
- **d)** fixed and variable costs.
- **e)** fixed costs.

LO3. Tools for process analysis include all of the following except:
- **a)** flowchart.
- **b)** vision systems.
- **c)** service blueprinting.
- **d)** time-function mapping.
- **e)** value-stream mapping.

LO4. Customer feedback in process design is lower as:
- **a)** the degree of customization is increased.
- **b)** the degree of labor is increased.
- **c)** the degree of customization is lowered.
- **d)** both a and b.
- **e)** both b and c.

LO5. Computer-integrated manufacturing (CIM) includes manufacturing systems that have:
- **a)** computer-aided design, direct numerical control machines, and material handling equipment controlled by automation.
- **b)** transaction processing, a management information system, and decision support systems.
- **c)** automated guided vehicles, robots, and process control.
- **d)** robots, automated guided vehicles, and transfer equipment.

LO6. The four *R's* of sustainability are:
______, ______, ______, ______.

Answers: LO1. b; LO2. d; LO3. b; LO4. c; LO5. a; LO6: resources, recycling, regulations, reputation.

SUPPLEMENT 7 Capacity and Constraint Management

Supplement Outline

When designing a concert hall, management hopes that the forecasted capacity (the product mix—opera, symphony, and special events—and the technology needed for these events) is accurate and adequate for operation above the break-even point. However, in many concert halls, even when operating at full capacity, break-even is not achieved, and supplemental funding must be obtained.

Supplement 7 **Learning Objectives**

AUTHOR COMMENT Too little capacity loses customers and too much capacity is expensive. Like Goldilocks's porridge, capacity needs to be *just* right.

CAPACITY

What should be the seating capacity of a concert hall? How many customers per day should an Olive Garden or a Hard Rock Cafe be able to serve? How large should a Frito-Lay plant be to produce 75,000 bags of Ruffles in an 8-hour shift? In this supplement we look at tools that help a manager make these decisions.

Capacity
The "throughput," or number of units a facility can hold, receive, store, or produce in a period of time.

After selection of a production process (Chapter 7), managers need to determine capacity. **Capacity** is the "throughput," or the number of units a facility can hold, receive, store, or produce in a given time. Capacity decisions often determine capital requirements and therefore a large portion of fixed cost. Capacity also determines whether demand will be satisfied or whether facilities will be idle. If a facility is too large, portions of it will sit unused and add cost to existing production. If a facility is too small, customers—and perhaps entire markets—will be lost. Determining facility size, with an objective of achieving high levels of utilization and a high return on investment, is critical.

LO1: Define capacity

Capacity planning can be viewed in three time horizons. In Figure S7.1 we note that long-range capacity (greater than 1 year) is a function of adding facilities and equipment that have a long lead time. In the intermediate range (3 to 18 months), we can add equipment, personnel, and shifts; we can subcontract; and we can build or use inventory. This is the "aggregate planning" task. In the short run (usually up to 3 months), we are primarily concerned with scheduling jobs and people, as well as allocating machinery. Modifying capacity in the short run is difficult, as we are usually constrained by existing capacity.

Design and Effective Capacity

Design capacity
The theoretical maximum output of a system in a given period under ideal conditions.

Design capacity is the maximum theoretical output of a system in a given period under ideal conditions. It is normally expressed as a rate, such as the number of tons of steel that can be produced per week, per month, or per year. For many companies, measuring capacity can be

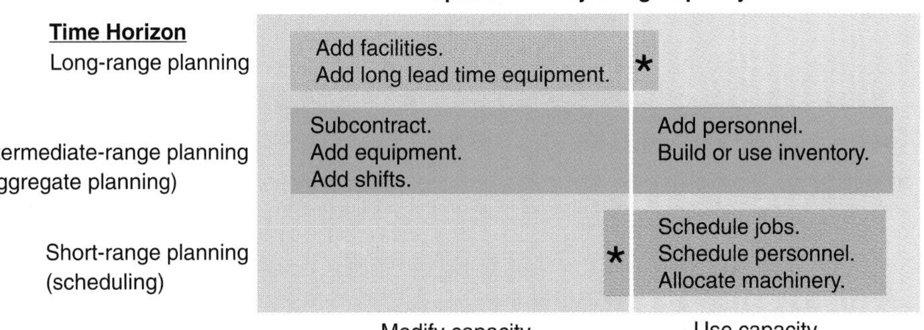

◀ **FIGURE S7.1**
Time Horizons and Capacity Options

straightforward: It is the maximum number of units the company is capable of producing in a specific time. However, for some organizations, determining capacity can be more difficult. Capacity can be measured in terms of beds (a hospital), active members (a church), or classroom size (a school). Other organizations use total work time available as a measure of overall capacity.

Most organizations operate their facilities at a rate less than the design capacity. They do so because they have found that they can operate more efficiently when their resources are not stretched to the limit. For example, Ian's Bistro has tables set with 2 or 4 chairs seating a total of 270 guests. But the tables are never filled that way. Some tables will have 1 or 3 guests; tables can be pulled together for parties of 6 or 8. There are always unused chairs. Design capacity is 270, but *effective capacity* is often closer to 220, which is 81% of design capacity.

Effective capacity is the capacity a firm *expects* to achieve given the current operating constraints. Effective capacity is often lower than design capacity because the facility may have been designed for an earlier version of the product or a different product mix than is currently being produced.

Effective capacity
The capacity a firm can expect to achieve, given its product mix, methods of scheduling, maintenance, and standards of quality.

Two measures of system performance are particularly useful: utilization and efficiency. **Utilization** is simply the percent of *design capacity* actually achieved. **Efficiency** is the percent of *effective capacity* actually achieved. Depending on how facilities are used and managed, it may be difficult or impossible to reach 100% efficiency. Operations managers tend to be evaluated on efficiency. The key to improving efficiency is often found in correcting quality problems and in effective scheduling, training, and maintenance. Utilization and efficiency are computed below:

Utilization
Actual output as a percent of design capacity.

Efficiency
Actual output as a percent of effective capacity.

$$\text{Utilization} = \text{Actual output/Design capacity} \quad \text{(S7-1)}$$

$$\text{Efficiency} = \text{Actual output/Effective capacity} \quad \text{(S7-2)}$$

In Example S1 we determine these values.

◀ **EXAMPLE S1**
Determining capacity utilization and efficiency

Sara James Bakery has a plant for processing *Deluxe* breakfast rolls and wants to better understand its capability. Determine the design capacity, utilization, and efficiency for this plant when producing this *Deluxe* roll.

APPROACH ▶ Last week the facility produced 148,000 rolls. The effective capacity is 175,000 rolls. The production line operates 7 days per week, with three 8-hour shifts per day. The line was designed to process the nut-filled, cinnamon-flavored *Deluxe* roll at a rate of 1,200 per hour. The firm first computes the design capacity and then uses Equation (S7-1) to determine utilization and Equation (S7-2) to determine efficiency.

SOLUTION ▶

$$\text{Design capacity} = (7 \text{ days} \times 3 \text{ shifts} \times 8 \text{ hours}) \times (1{,}200 \text{ rolls per hour}) = 201{,}600 \text{ rolls}$$

$$\text{Utilization} = \text{Actual output/Design capacity} = 148{,}000/201{,}600 = 73.4\%$$

$$\text{Efficiency} = \text{Actual output/Effective capacity} = 148{,}000/175{,}000 = 84.6\%$$

INSIGHT ▶ The bakery now has the information necessary to evaluate efficiency.

LEARNING EXERCISE ▶ If the actual output is 150,000, what is the efficiency? [Answer: 85.7%.]

RELATED PROBLEMS ▶ S7.1, S7.2, S7.4, S7.5, S7.7

ACTIVE MODEL S7.1 This example is further illustrated in Active Model S7.1 at **www.pearsonhighered.com/heizer**.

LO2: Determine design capacity, effective capacity, and utilization

Design capacity, utilization, and efficiency are all important measures for an operations manager. But managers often need to know the expected output of a facility or process. To do this, we solve for actual (or in this case, future or expected) output as shown in Equation (S7-3):

$$\text{Actual (or Expected) output} = (\text{Effective capacity})(\text{Efficiency}) \qquad \text{(S7-3)}$$

Expected output is sometimes referred to as *rated capacity*. With a knowledge of effective capacity and efficiency, a manager can find the expected output of a facility. We do so in Example S2.

EXAMPLE S2 ▶

Determining expected output

The manager of Sara James Bakery (see Example S1) now needs to increase production of the increasingly popular *Deluxe* roll. To meet this demand, she will be adding a second production line.

APPROACH ▶ The manager must determine the expected output of this second line for the sales department. Effective capacity on the second line is the same as on the first line, which is 175,000 *Deluxe* rolls. The first line is operating at an efficiency of 84.6%, as computed in Example S1. But output on the second line will be less than the first line because the crew will be primarily new hires; so the efficiency can be expected to be no more than 75%. What is the expected output?

SOLUTION ▶ Use Equation (S7-3) to determine the expected output:

$$\text{Expected output} = (\text{Effective capacity})(\text{Efficiency}) = (175{,}000)(.75) = 131{,}250 \text{ rolls}$$

INSIGHT ▶ The sales department can now be told the expected output is 131,250 *Deluxe* rolls.

LEARNING EXERCISE ▶ After 1 month of training, the crew on the second production line is expected to perform at 80% efficiency. What is the revised expected output of *Deluxe* rolls? [Answer: 140,000.]

RELATED PROBLEMS ▶ S7.3, S7.6, S7.8

If the expected output is inadequate, additional capacity may be needed. Much of the remainder of this supplement addresses how to effectively and efficiently add that capacity.

Capacity and Strategy

Sustained profits come from building competitive advantage, not just from a good financial return on a specific process. Capacity decisions must be integrated into the organization's mission and strategy. Investments are not to be made as isolated expenditures, but as part of a coordinated plan that will place the firm in an advantageous position. The questions to be asked are, "Will these investments eventually win profitable customers?" and "What competitive advantage (such as process flexibility, speed of delivery, improved quality, and so on) do we obtain?"

All 10 decisions of operations management we discuss in this text, as well as other organizational elements such as marketing and finance, are affected by changes in capacity. Change in capacity will have sales and cash flow implications, just as capacity changes have quality, supply chain, human resource, and maintenance implications. All must be considered.

Capacity Considerations

In addition to tight integration of strategy and investments, there are four special considerations for a good capacity decision:

1. *Forecast demand accurately:* An accurate forecast is paramount to the capacity decision. The new product may be Olive Garden's veal scampi, a dish that places added demands on the restaurant's food service, or the product may be a new maternity capability at Arnold Palmer Hospital, or the new hybrid Lexus. Whatever the new product, its prospects and the life cycle of existing products, must be determined. Management must know which products are being added and which are being dropped, as well as their expected volumes.
2. *Understand the technology and capacity increments:* The number of initial alternatives may be large, but once the volume is determined, technology decisions may be aided by analysis of cost, human resources required, quality, and reliability. Such a review often reduces the number of alternatives to a few. The technology may dictate the capacity increment. Meeting added demand with a few extra tables in an Olive Garden may not be difficult, but meeting increased demand for a new automobile by adding a new assembly line at BMW may be very difficult—and expensive. The operations manager is held responsible for the technology and the correct capacity increment.
3. *Find the optimum operating size (volume):* Technology and capacity increments often dictate an optimal size for a facility. A roadside motel may require 50 rooms to be viable. If smaller, the fixed cost is too burdensome; if larger, the facility becomes more than one manager can supervise. A hypothetical optimum for the motel is shown in Figure S7.2. This issue is known as *economies and diseconomies of scale*. As the Krispy Kreme photo suggests, most businesses have an optimal size—at least until someone comes along with a new business model. For decades, very large integrated steel mills were considered optimal. Then along came Nucor, CMC, and other minimills with a new process and a new business model that changed the optimum size of a steel mill.
4. *Build for change:* In our fast-paced world, change is inevitable. So operations managers build flexibility into the facility and equipment. They evaluate the sensitivity of the decision by testing several revenue projections on both the upside and downside for potential risks. Buildings can often be built in phases; and buildings and equipment can be designed with modifications in mind to accommodate future changes in product, product mix, and processes.

Rather than strategically manage capacity, managers may tactically manage demand.

Managing Demand

Even with good forecasting and facilities built to that forecast, there may be a poor match between the actual demand that occurs and available capacity. A poor match may mean demand exceeds capacity or capacity exceeds demand. However, in both cases, firms have options.

Demand Exceeds Capacity When *demand exceeds capacity*, the firm may be able to curtail demand simply by raising prices, scheduling long lead times (which may be inevitable), and discouraging marginally profitable business. However, because inadequate facilities reduce revenue

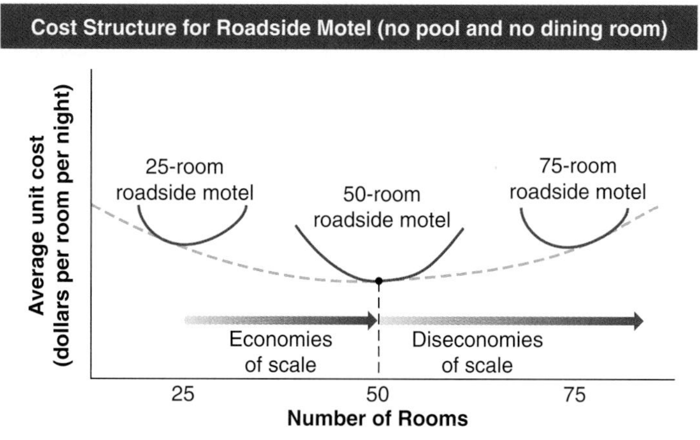

FIGURE S7.2 Economies and Diseconomies of Scale

AUTHOR COMMENT Each industry and technology has an optimum size.

Krispy Kreme originally had 8,000-square-foot stores but found them too large and too expensive for many markets. Then they tried tiny 1,300-square-foot stores, which required less investment, but such stores were too small to provide the mystique of seeing and smelling Krispy Kreme donuts being made. Krispy Kreme finally got it right with a 2,600-foot-store. This one includes a huge glass window to view doughnut production.

below what is possible, the long-term solution is usually to increase capacity (as we see in the *OM in Action* box "Too Little Capacity at Dalrymple Bay").

Capacity Exceeds Demand When *capacity exceeds demand*, the firm may want to stimulate demand through price reductions or aggressive marketing, or it may accommodate the market through product changes. When decreasing customer demand is combined with old and inflexible processes, layoffs and plant closings may be necessary to bring capacity in line with demand.

Adjusting to Seasonal Demands A seasonal or cyclical pattern of demand is another capacity challenge. In such cases, management may find it helpful to offer products with complementary demand patterns—that is, products for which the demand is high for one when low for the other. For example, in Figure S7.3 the firm is adding a line of snowmobile motors to its line of jet skis to smooth demand. With appropriate complementing of products, perhaps the utilization of facility, equipment, and personnel can be smoothed.

OM in Action ► Too Little Capacity at Dalrymple Bay

Nearly 20 ships were anchored in the Coral Sea on a recent morning. They were waiting to be loaded with coal to fuel Asia's voracious steel mills. Australia has some of the most prolific coal mines in the world, but its key port of Dalrymple Bay, just outside Queensland, isn't big enough to meet demand. So the ships sit idle for days. Capacity at the port is far below what is needed for the current worldwide demand. This makes Dalrymple Bay one of the key choke points.

The process is rather simple but expensive. Trains are loaded with coal at the mines, travel several hours to the port, and dump their coal into piles that are sprayed with water to prevent black coal dust from blowing onto homes and beaches. Eventually, the coal is loaded onto a conveyor belt that moves 2.5 miles out into the Coral Sea, to be loaded onto ships.

The current plan is to invest $610 million to expand port capacity to 85 million metric tons of coal in the next 3 years. But this is still less than the estimated demand requirement of 107 million metric tons needed. As a result, coal companies, even after the expansion is completed, may still find access to shipping rationed.

The demand must exist, the port must expand, and the mines must enlarge. Without that assurance, the risk remains high and the necessary ROI (return on investment) is not there. Managers are not going to put significant money into expanding port capacity until they are comfortable that both the demand and coal supply support a larger port. To justify investment in capacity, each phase of the chain must support that investment.

Sources: Railway Gazette International (December 2008): 947–951 and *The Wall Street Journal* (July 7, 2005): C1, C4.

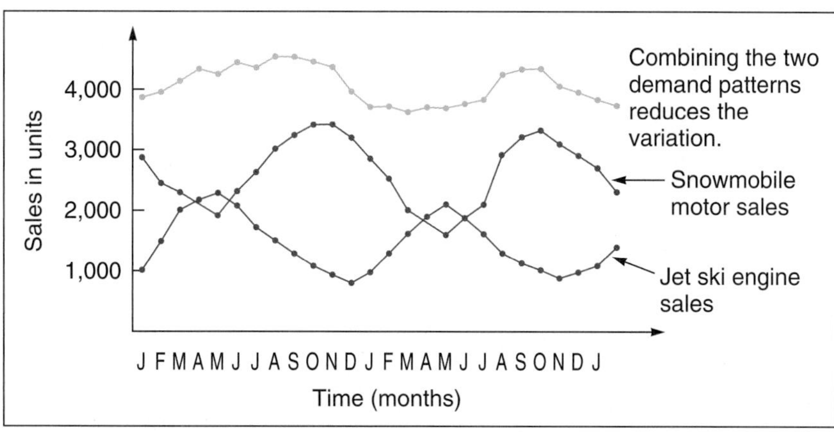

◀ **FIGURE S7.3**
By Combining Products That Have Complementary Seasonal Patterns, Capacity Can Be Better Utilized

AUTHOR COMMENT
A smoother sales demand contributes to improved scheduling and better human resource strategies.

Tactics for Matching Capacity to Demand Various tactics for matching capacity to demand exist. Options for adjusting capacity include:

1. Making staffing changes (increasing or decreasing the number of employees or shifts)
2. Adjusting equipment (purchasing additional machinery or selling or leasing out existing equipment)
3. Improving processes to increase throughput
4. Redesigning products to facilitate more throughput
5. Adding process flexibility to better meet changing product preferences
6. Closing facilities

The foregoing tactics can be used to adjust demand to existing facilities. The strategic issue is, of course, how to have a facility of the correct size.

Demand and Capacity Management in the Service Sector

In the service sector, scheduling customers is *demand management*, and scheduling the workforce is *capacity management*.

Demand Management When demand and capacity are fairly well matched, demand management can often be handled with appointments, reservations, or a first-come, first-served rule. In some businesses, such as doctors' and lawyers' offices, an *appointment system* is the schedule and is adequate. *Reservations systems* work well in rental car agencies, hotels, and some restaurants as a means of minimizing customer waiting time and avoiding disappointment over unfilled service.

Matching capacity and demand can be a challenge. When market share is declining the mismatch between demand and capacity means empty plants and laying off employees (left photo). On the other hand, when demand exceeds capacity, as at this opening of the Apple store on the outskirts of Rome, Italy, the mismatch may mean frustrated customers and lost revenue (right photo).

Many U.S. hospitals use services abroad to manage capacity for radiologists during night shifts. Night Hawk, an Idaho-based service with 50 radiologists in Zurich and Sydney, contracts with 900 facilities (20% of all U.S. hospitals). These trained experts, wide awake and alert in their daylight hours, usually return a diagnosis in 10 to 20 minutes, with a guarantee of 30 minutes.

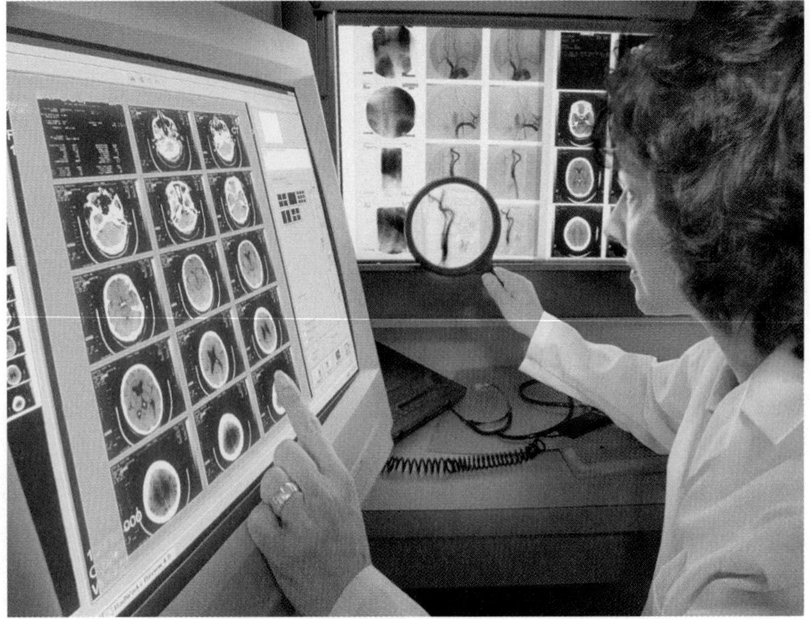

In retail shops, a post office, or a fast-food restaurant, a *first-come, first-served* rule for serving customers may suffice. Each industry develops its own approaches to matching demand and capacity. Other more aggressive approaches to demand management include many variations of discounts: "early bird" specials in restaurants, discounts for matinee performances or for seats at odd hours on an airline, and cheap weekend phone calls.

Capacity Management When managing demand is not feasible, then managing capacity through changes in full-time, temporary, or part-time staff may be an option. This is the approach in many services. For instance, hospitals may find capacity limited by a shortage of board-certified radiologists willing to cover the graveyard shifts. Getting fast and reliable radiology readings can be the difference between life and death for an emergency room patient. As the photo above illustrates, when an overnight reading is required (and 40% of CT scans are done between 8 P.M. and 8 A.M.), the image can be sent by e-mail to a doctor in Europe or Australia for immediate analysis.

AUTHOR COMMENT
There are always bottlenecks; a manager must identify and manage them.

BOTTLENECK ANALYSIS AND THE THEORY OF CONSTRAINTS

As managers seek to match capacity to demand, decisions must be made about the size of specific operations or work areas in the larger system. Each of the interdependent work areas can be expected to have its own unique capacity. **Capacity analysis** involves determining the throughput capacity of workstations in a system and ultimately the capacity of the entire system.

Capacity analysis
A means of determining throughput capacity of workstations or an entire production system.

A key concept in capacity analysis is the role of a constraint or bottleneck. A **bottleneck** is an operation that is the limiting factor or constraint. The term *bottleneck* refers to the literal neck of a bottle that constrains flow or, in the case of a production system, constrains throughput. A bottleneck has the lowest effective capacity of any operation in the system and thus limits the system's output. Bottlenecks occur in all facets of life—from job shops where a machine is constraining the work flow to highway traffic where two lanes converge into one inadequate lane, resulting in traffic congestion.

Bottleneck
The limiting factor or constraint in a system.

Arnold Palmer Hospital provides an example of managing a bottleneck. Its constraint for delivering more babies was hospital bed availability. The *long-term* solution to this bottleneck was to add capacity via a 4-year construction project. But the hospital staff sought an immediate way to increase capacity of the bottleneck. The solution: If a woman is ready for discharge and cannot be picked up prior to 5 P.M., staffers drive home the woman and her baby themselves. Not only does this free up a bed for the next patient, it also creates good will.

LO3: Perform bottleneck analysis

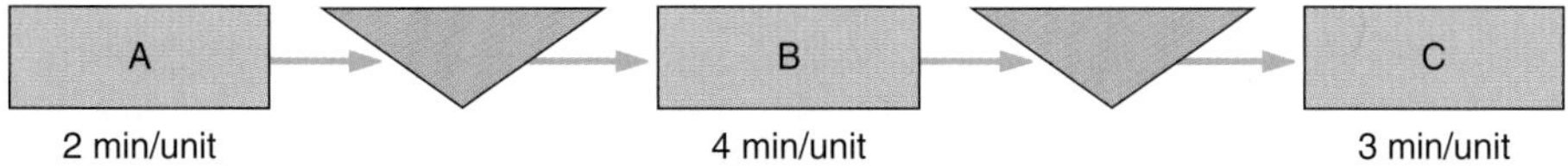

▲ **FIGURE S7.4 Three-Station Assembly Line**
A box represents an operation, a triangle represents inventory, and arrows represent precedence relationships

Process Times for Stations, Systems, and Cycles

Three metrics are important to help us analyze production system capacity. First, we define **process time of a station** as the time to produce a given number of units (or a batch of units) at that workstation. For example, if 60 windshields on a Ford assembly line can be installed in 30 minutes, then the process time is 0.5 minutes per windshield. (Process time is simply the inverse of capacity, which in this case is 60 minutes per hour/0.5 minutes per windshield = 120 windshields installed per hour.) **Process time of a system** is the time of the longest process (the slowest workstation) in the system, which is defined as the process time of the bottleneck. **Process cycle time**, on the other hand, is the time it takes for a unit of product, such as a car, to go through the entire empty system, from start to finish.[1]

Process time of a station
The time to produce units at a single workstation.

Process time of a system
The time of the longest (slowest) process; the bottleneck.

Process cycle time
The time it takes for a product to go through the production process with no waiting.

Process time of a system and *process cycle time* may be quite different. For example, a Ford assembly line may roll out a new car every minute (process time of the system, because this is the longest workstation), but it may take 30 hours to actually make a car from start to finish (process cycle time). This is because the assembly line has many workstations, with each station contributing to the completed car. Thus, the system's process time determines its capacity (one car per minute), while its process cycle time determines potential ability to build a product (30 hours).

Figure S7.4 displays a simple assembly line using a flowchart, with the individual *process station times* shown as 2, 4, and 3 minutes. The *process time for the system* is 4 minutes because station B is the slowest station, the bottleneck, with a 4-minute process time. Station A could work faster than that, but the result would be a pile of inventory continuously building in front of station B. Station C could also potentially work faster than 4 minutes per unit, but there is no way to tap into its excess capacity because station B will not be able to feed products to station C to work on any faster than one every 4 minutes. Thus, we see that the excess capacity at non-bottleneck stations cannot be used to somehow "make up for the bottleneck." Finally, the time to produce a new unit, *the process cycle time*, is 2 + 4 + 3 = 9 minutes.

The following two examples illustrate capacity analysis for slightly more complex systems. Example S3 introduces the concept of parallel processes, and Example S4 introduces the concept of simultaneous processing.

◄ **EXAMPLE S3**
Capacity analysis with parallel processes

Howard Kraye's sandwich shop provides healthy sandwiches for customers. Howard has two identical sandwich assembly lines. A customer first places and pays for an order, which takes approximately 30 seconds. The order is then sent to one of the two lines. Each assembly line has two workers and three major operations: (1) worker 1 retrieves and cuts the bread (15 seconds/sandwich), (2) worker 2 adds ingredients and places the sandwich onto the toaster conveyor belt (20 seconds/sandwich), and (3) the toaster heats the sandwich (40 seconds/sandwich). A wrapper then wraps heated sandwiches coming from both lines and provides final packaging for the customer (37.5 seconds/sandwich). A flowchart of the customer order is shown below.

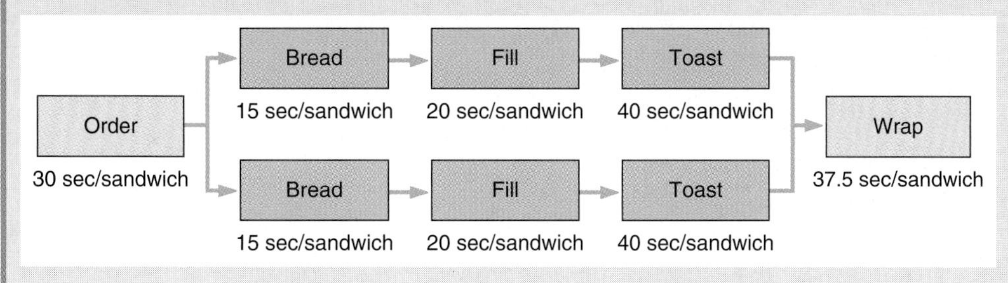

[1]The more general term is *manufacturing cycle time*, but we use *process cycle time* here to note that we are defining the time in an empty system. Cycle time varies, depending on the status of the system, from empty to substantial work-in-process.

APPROACH ▶ Clearly the toaster is the single slowest resource in the five-step process, but is it the bottleneck? Howard should first determine the process time of each assembly line, then the process time of the combined assembly lines, and finally the process time of the entire operation.

SOLUTION ▶ Because each of the three assembly-line operations uses a separate resource (worker or machine), separate partially completed sandwiches can be worked on simultaneously at each station. Thus, the process time of each assembly line is the longest process time of each of the three operations. In this case, the 40-second toasting time represents the process time of each assembly line. Next, the process time of the combined assembly-line operations is 40 seconds per two sandwiches, or 20 seconds per sandwich. Therefore, the wrapping and delivering operation becomes the bottleneck for the entire customer order operation, and the system process time is 37.5 seconds—the maximum of 30, 20, and 37.5. The capacity per hour equals 3,600 seconds per hour/37.5 seconds per sandwich = 96 sandwiches per hour. Finally, the process cycle time equals 30 + 15 + 20 + 40 + 37.5 = 142.5 seconds (or 2 minutes and 22.5 seconds), assuming no waiting in line to begin with.

INSIGHT ▶ If n parallel (redundant) operations are added, the process time of the combined operation will equal $1/n$ times the process time of the original.

LEARNING EXERCISE ▶ If Howard hires an additional wrapper, what will be the new hourly capacity? [Answer: The new bottleneck is the order-taking station: Capacity = 3,600 seconds per hour/30 seconds per sandwich = 120 sandwiches per hour]

RELATED PROBLEMS ▶ S7.9, S7.10, S7.11, S7.12, S7.13

In Example S3, how could we claim that the process time of the toaster was 20 seconds per sandwich when it takes 40 seconds to toast a sandwich? Because we had two toasters, two sandwiches could be toasted every 40 seconds, for an average of 1 sandwich every 20 seconds. And that time for a toaster can actually be achieved if the start times for the two are *staggered* (i.e., a new sandwich is placed in a toaster every 20 seconds). In that case, even though each sandwich will sit in the toaster for 40 seconds, a sandwich could emerge from one of the two toasters every 20 seconds. As we see, doubling the number of resources effectively cuts the process time in half, resulting in a doubling of the capacity of those resources.

EXAMPLE S4 ▶

Capacity analysis with simultaneous processes

Dr. Cynthia Knott's dentistry practice has been cleaning customers' teeth for decades. The process for a basic dental cleaning is relatively straightforward: (1) the customer checks in (2 minutes); (2) a lab assistant takes and develops four X-rays (2 and 4 minutes, respectively); (3) the dentist processes and examines the X-rays (5 minutes) *while* the hygienist cleans the teeth (24 minutes); (4) the dentist meets with the patient to poke at a few teeth, explain the X-ray results, and tell the patient to floss more often (8 minutes); and (5) the customer pays and books her next appointment (6 minutes). A flowchart of the customer visit is shown below.

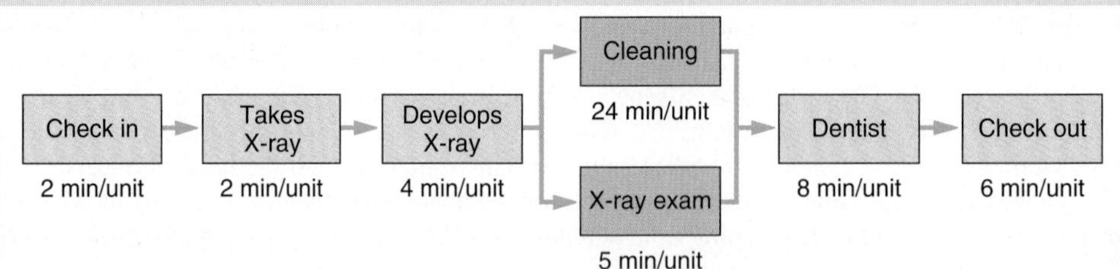

APPROACH ▶ With simultaneous processes, an order or a product is essentially *split* into different paths to be rejoined later on. To find the process time, each operation is treated separately, just as though all operations were on a sequential path. To find the process cycle time, the time over *all* paths must be computed, and it is the *longest* path.

SOLUTION ▶ The bottleneck in this system is the hygienist, at 24 minutes per patient, resulting in an hourly system capacity of 60 minutes/24 minutes per patient = 2.5 patients. The process cycle time is the maximum of the two paths through the system. The path through the X-ray exam is 2 + 2 + 4 + 5 + 8 + 6 = 27 minutes, while the path through the hygienist is 2 + 2 + 4 + 24 + 8 + 6 = 46 minutes. Thus a patient should be out the door after 46 minutes (i.e., the maximum of 27 and 46).

INSIGHT ▶ With simultaneous processing, all process times in the entire system are not simply added together to compute process cycle time, because some operations are occurring at the same time. Instead, the longest path through the system is deemed the process cycle time.

LEARNING EXERCISE ▶ Suppose that the same technician now has the hygienist start immediately after the X-rays are taken (allowing the hygienist to start 4 minutes sooner). The technician then processes the X-rays while the hygienist is cleaning teeth. The dentist still analyzes the X-rays while the teeth cleaning is occurring. What would be the new system capacity and process cycle time? [Answer: The X-ray development/processing operation is no longer on the initial path, reducing the total patient visit duration by 4 minutes, for a process cycle time of 42 minutes (the maximum of 27 and 42). However, the hygienist is still the bottleneck, so the capacity remains at 2.5 patients per hour.]

RELATED PROBLEMS ▶ S7.14, S7.15

To summarize: (1) the *system process time* is the process time of the bottleneck, which is the operation with the longest (slowest) process time, after dividing by the number of parallel (redundant) operations, (2) the *system capacity* is the inverse of the system process time, and (3) the *process cycle time* is the total time through the longest path in the system, assuming no waiting.

Theory of Constraints

The **theory of constraints (TOC)** has been popularized by the book *The Goal: A Process of Ongoing Improvement,* by Goldratt and Cox.[2] TOC is a body of knowledge that deals with anything that limits or constrains an organization's ability to achieve its goals. Constraints can be physical (e.g., process or personnel availability, raw materials, or supplies) or non-physical (e.g., procedures, morale, and training). Recognizing and managing these limitations through a five-step process is the basis of TOC.

Theory of constraints (TOC)
A body of knowledge that deals with anything that limits an organization's ability to achieve its goals.

Step 1: Identify the constraints.
Step 2: Develop a plan for overcoming the identified constraints.
Step 3: Focus resources on accomplishing Step 2.
Step 4: Reduce the effects of the constraints by offloading work or by expanding capability. Make sure that the constraints are recognized by all those who can have an impact on them.
Step 5: When one set of constraints is overcome, go back to Step 1 and identify new constraints.

The *OM in Action* box "Banking and the Theory of Constraints (TOC)" illustrates these five steps and shows that TOC is used in services as well as manufacturing.

Bottleneck Management

A crucial constraint in any system is the bottleneck, and managers must focus significant attention on it. We present four principles of bottleneck management:

1. *Release work orders to the system at the pace set by the bottleneck's capacity:* The theory of constraints utilizes the concept of *drum, buffer, rope* to aid in the implementation of bottleneck and non-bottleneck scheduling. In brief, the *drum* is the beat of the system. It provides the schedule—the pace of production. The *buffer* is the resource, usually inventory, which may be helpful to keep the bottleneck operating at the pace of the drum. Finally, the *rope* provides the synchronization or communication necessary to pull units through the system. The rope can be thought of as signals between workstations.
2. *Lost time at the bottleneck represents lost capacity for the whole system:* This principle implies that the bottleneck should always be kept busy with work. Well-trained and cross-trained employees and inspections prior to the bottleneck can reduce lost capacity at a bottleneck.
3. *Increasing the capacity of a non-bottleneck station is a mirage:* Increasing the capacity of *non-bottleneck* stations has no impact on the system's overall capacity. Working faster on a non-bottleneck station may just create extra inventory, with all of its adverse effects. This implies that non-bottlenecks should have planned idle time. Extra work or setups at non-bottleneck stations will not cause delay, which allows for smaller batch sizes and more frequent product changeovers at non-bottleneck stations.
4. *Increasing the capacity of the bottleneck increases capacity for the whole system:* Managers should focus improvement efforts on the bottleneck. Bottleneck capacity may be improved by

[2]See E. M. Goldratt and J. Cox, *The Goal: A Process of Ongoing Improvement*, 3rd rev. ed., Great Barrington, MA: North River Press, 2004).

OM in Action ▶ Banking and the Theory of Constraints (TOC)

When a Midwestern U.S. bank identified its weakest link as the mortgage department, with a home-loan processing time of over a month, it turned to the principles of TOC to reduce the average loan time. A cross-functional mortgage improvement team of eight people employed the five steps outlined in the text. Using flowcharting, the team discovered that it was taking too long to (1) conduct property appraisals and surveys and (2) verify applicant employment. So the first step of TOC was to identify these two constraints.

The second step in TOC was to develop a plan to reduce the time taken for employment verification and for conducting appraisals and surveys. The team learned that it could reduce employment verification to 2 weeks by having the loan officer request the last 2 years of W-2 forms and the last month's pay stub. It found similar solutions to reducing survey/appraisal time.

As a third step, it had personnel refocus their resources so the two constraints could be performed at a higher level of efficiency. The result was decreased operating expense and inventory (money, in this banking example) and increased throughput.

The fourth TOC step required that employees support the earlier steps by focusing on the two time constraints. The bank also placed a higher priority on verification so that constraint could be overcome.

Finally, the bank began to look for new constraints once the first ones were overcome. Like all continuing improvement efforts, the process starts over before complacency sets in.

Sources: Decision Support Systems (March 2001): 451–468; *The Banker's Magazine* (January–February 1997): 53–59; and *Bank Systems and Technology* (September 1999): S10.

various means, including offloading some of the bottleneck operations to another workstation (e.g., let the beer foam settle next to the tap at the bar, not under it, so the next beer can be poured), increasing capacity of the bottleneck (adding resources, working longer or working faster), subcontracting, developing alternative routings, and reducing setup times.

Even when managers have process and quality variability under control, changing technology, personnel, products, product mixes, and volumes can create multiple and shifting bottlenecks. Identifying and managing bottlenecks is a required operations task, but by definition, bottlenecks cannot be "eliminated." A system will always have at least one.

AUTHOR COMMENT
Failure to operate above break-even can be devastating.

BREAK-EVEN ANALYSIS

Break-even analysis
A means of finding the point, in dollars and units, at which costs equal revenues.

Break-even analysis is the critical tool for determining the capacity a facility must have to achieve profitability. The objective of **break-even analysis** is to find the point, in dollars and units, at which costs equal revenue. This point is the break-even point. Firms must operate above this level to achieve profitability. As shown in Figure S7.5, break-even analysis requires an estimation of fixed costs, variable costs, and revenue.

▶ **FIGURE S7.5**
Basic Break-even Point

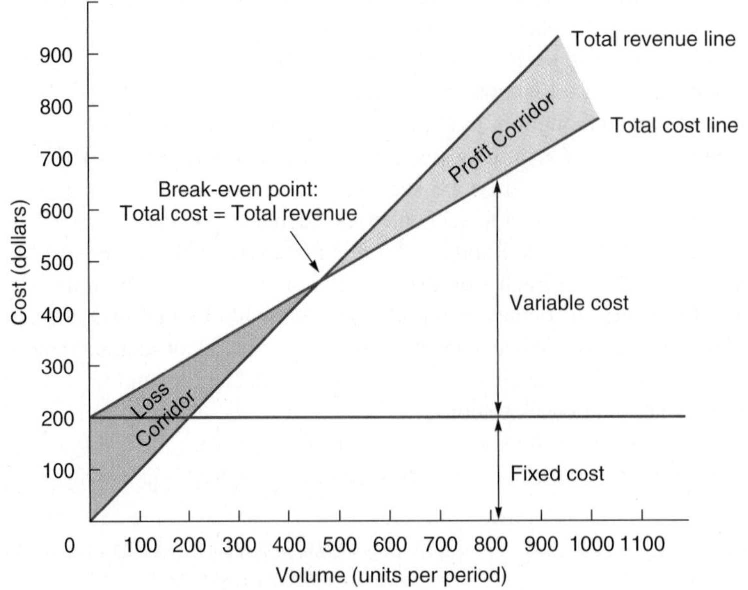

Fixed costs are costs that continue even if no units are produced. Examples include depreciation, taxes, debt, and mortgage payments. *Variable costs* are those that vary with the volume of units produced. The major components of variable costs are labor and materials. However, other costs, such as the portion of the utilities that varies with volume, are also variable costs. The difference between selling price and variable cost is *contribution*. Only when total contribution exceeds total fixed cost will there be profit.

Another element in break-even analysis is the *revenue function*. In Figure S7.5, revenue begins at the origin and proceeds upward to the right, increasing by the selling price of each unit. Where the revenue function crosses the total cost line (the sum of fixed and variable costs), is the break-even point, with a profit corridor to the right and a loss corridor to the left.

Assumptions A number of assumptions underlie the basic break-even model. Notably, costs and revenue are shown as straight lines. They are shown to increase linearly—that is, in direct proportion to the volume of units being produced. However, neither fixed costs nor variable costs (nor, for that matter, the revenue function) need be a straight line. For example, fixed costs change as more capital equipment or warehouse space is used; labor costs change with overtime or as marginally skilled workers are employed; the revenue function may change with such factors as volume discounts.

Graphic Approach The first step in the graphic approach to break-even analysis is to define those costs that are fixed and sum them. The fixed costs are drawn as a horizontal line beginning at that dollar amount on the vertical axis. The variable costs are then estimated by an analysis of labor, materials, and other costs connected with the production of each unit. The variable costs are shown as an incrementally increasing cost, originating at the intersection of the fixed cost on the vertical axis and increasing with each change in volume as we move to the right on the volume (or horizontal) axis.

LO4: Compute break-even

Algebraic Approach The formulas for the break-even point in units and dollars are shown below. Let:

BEP_x = break-even point in units
$BEP_\$$ = break-even point in dollars
P = price per unit (after all discounts)
x = number of units produced
TR = total revenue = Px
F = fixed costs
V = variable costs per unit
TC = total costs = $F + Vx$

The break-even point occurs where total revenue equals total costs. Therefore:

$$TR = TC \quad \text{or} \quad Px = F + Vx$$

Solving for x, we get

$$\text{Break-even point in units } (BEP_x) = \frac{F}{P - V}$$

and:

$$\text{Break-even point in dollars } (BEP_\$) = BEP_x P = \frac{F}{P - V}P = \frac{F}{(P - V)/P} = \frac{F}{1 - V/P}$$

$$\text{Profit} = TR - TC = Px - (F + Vx) = Px - F - Vx = (P - V)x - F$$

Using these equations, we can solve directly for break-even point and profitability. The two break-even formulas of particular interest are:

$$\text{Break-even in units} = \frac{\text{Total fixed cost}}{\text{Price} - \text{Variable cost}} \quad \text{(S7-4)}$$

$$\text{Break-even in dollars} = \frac{\text{Total fixed cost}}{1 - \dfrac{\text{Variable cost}}{\text{Selling price}}} \quad \text{(S7-5)}$$

Single-Product Case

In Example S5, we determine the break-even point in dollars and units for one product.

EXAMPLE S5
Single product break-even analysis

Stephens, Inc., wants to determine the minimum dollar volume and unit volume needed at its new facility to break even.

APPROACH ▶ The firm first determines that it has fixed costs of $10,000 this period. Direct labor is $1.50 per unit, and material is $.75 per unit. The selling price is $4.00 per unit.

SOLUTION ▶ The break-even point in dollars is computed as follows:

$$BEP_\$ = \frac{F}{1 - (V/P)} = \frac{\$10{,}000}{1 - [(1.50 + .75)/(4.00)]} = \frac{\$10{,}000}{.4375} = \$22{,}857.14$$

The break-even point in units is:

$$BEP_x = \frac{F}{P - V} = \frac{\$10{,}000}{4.00 - (1.50 + .75)} = 5{,}714$$

Note that we use total variable costs (that is, both labor and material).

INSIGHT ▶ The management of Stevens, Inc., now has an estimate in both units and dollars of the volume necessary for the new facility.

LEARNING EXERCISE ▶ If Stevens finds that fixed cost will increase to $12,000, what happens to the break-even in units and dollars? [Answer: The break-even in units increases to 6,857, and break-even in dollars increases to $27,428.57.]

RELATED PROBLEMS ▶ S7.16, S7.17, S7.18, S7.19, S7.20, S7.21, S7.22, S7.23, S7.24, S7.25

EXCEL OM Data File **Ch07SExS3.xls** can be found at **www.pearsonhighered.com/heizer**.

ACTIVE MODEL S7.2 This example is further illustrated in Active Model S7.2 at **www.pearsonhighered.com/heizer**.

Multiproduct Case

Most firms, from manufacturers to restaurants (even fast-food restaurants), have a variety of offerings. Each offering may have a different selling price and variable cost. Utilizing break-even analysis, we modify Equation (S7-5) to reflect the proportion of sales for each product.

Recessions (e.g., 2008–2010) and terrorist attacks (e.g., September 11, 2001) can make even the best capacity decision for an airline look bad. And excess capacity for an airline can be very expensive, with storage costs running as high as $60,000 per month per aircraft. Here, as a testimonial to excess capacity, aircraft sit idle in the Mojave Desert.

Paper machines such as the one shown here require a high capital investment. This investment results in a high fixed cost but allows production of paper at a very low variable cost. The production manager's job is to maintain utilization above the break-even point to achieve profitability.

We do this by "weighting" each product's contribution by its proportion of sales. The formula is then:

$$\text{Break-even point in dollars } (BEP_\$) = \frac{F}{\sum\left[\left(1 - \frac{V_i}{P_i}\right) \times (W_i)\right]} \tag{S7-6}$$

where V = variable cost per unit, P = price per unit, F = fixed cost, W = percent each product is of total dollar sales, i = each product

Example S6 shows how to determine the break-even point for the multiproduct case at the Le Bistro restaurant.

◀ EXAMPLE S6

Multiproduct break-even analysis

Le Bistro, like most other resturants, makes more than one product and would like to know its break-even point in dollars.

APPROACH ▶ Information for Le Bistro follows. Fixed costs are $3,000 per month.

Item	Price	Cost	Annual Forecasted Sales Units
Sandwich	$5.00	$3.00	9,000
Drinks	1.50	.50	9,000
Baked potato	2.00	1.00	7,000

With a variety of offerings, we proceed with break-even analysis just as in a single-product case, except that we weight each of the products by its proportion of total sales using Equation (S7.6).

SOLUTION ▶ Multiproduct Break-even: Determining Contribution

1	2	3	4	5	6	7	8
Item (i)	Selling Price (P)	Variable Cost (V)	(V/P)	1 − (V/P)	Annual Forecasted Sales $	% of Sales	Weighted Contribution (col. 5 × col. 7)
Sandwich	$5.00	$3.00	.60	.40	$45,000	.621	.248
Drinks	1.50	0.50	.33	.67	13,500	.186	.125
Baked potato	2.00	1.00	.50	.50	14,000	.193	.096
					$72,500	1.000	.469

Note: Revenue for sandwiches is \$45,000 (5.00 × 9,000), which is 62.1% of the total revenue of \$72,500. Therefore, the contribution for sandwiches is "weighted" by .621. The weighted contribution is .621 × .40 = .248. In this manner, its *relative* contribution is properly reflected.

Using this approach for each product, we find that the total weighted contribution is .469 for each dollar of sales, and the break-even point in dollars is \$76,759.

$$BEP_\$ = \frac{F}{\sum\left[\left(1 - \frac{V_i}{P_i}\right) \times (W_i)\right]} = \frac{\$3{,}000 \times 12}{.469} = \frac{\$36{,}000}{.469} = \$76{,}759.$$

The information given in this example implies total daily sales (52 weeks at 6 days each) of:

$$\frac{\$76{,}759}{312 \text{ days}} = \$246.02$$

INSIGHT ▶ The management of Le Bistro now knows that it must generate average sales of \$246.02 each day to break even. Management also knows that if the forecasted sales of \$72,500 are correct, Le Bistro will lose money, as break-even is \$76,759.

LEARNING EXERCISE ▶ If the manager of Le Bistro wants to make an additional \$1,000 per month in salary, and considers this a fixed cost, what is the new break-even point in average sales per day? [Answer: \$328.03.]

RELATED PROBLEMS ▶ S7.26, S7.27

Break-even figures by product provide the manager with added insight as to the realism of his or her sales forecast. They indicate exactly what must be sold each day, as we illustrate in Example S7.

EXAMPLE S7 ▶

Unit sales at break-even

Le Bistro also wants to know the break-even for the number of sandwiches that must be sold every day.

APPROACH ▶ Using the data in Example S6, we take the forecast sandwich sales of 62.1% times the daily break-even of \$246.02 divided by the selling price of each sandwich (\$5.00).

SOLUTION ▶ At break-even, sandwich sales must then be:

$$\frac{.621 \times \$246.02}{5.00} = \text{Number of sandwiches} = 30.6 \approx 31 \text{ sandwiches each day}$$

INSIGHT ▶ With knowledge of individual product sales, the manager has a basis for determining material and labor requirements.

LEARNING EXERCISE ▶ At a dollar break-even of \$328.03 per day, how many sandwiches must Le Bistro sell each day? [Answer: 40.]

RELATED PROBLEMS ▶ S7.26b, S7.27b

Once break-even analysis has been prepared, analyzed, and judged to be reasonable, decisions can be made about the type and capacity of equipment needed. Indeed, a better judgment of the likelihood of success of the enterprise can now be made.

AUTHOR COMMENT Capacity decisions require matching capacity to forecasts, which is always difficult.

REDUCING RISK WITH INCREMENTAL CHANGES

VIDEO S7.1 Capacity Planning at Arnold Palmer Hospital

When demand for goods and services can be forecast with a reasonable degree of precision, determining a break-even point and capacity requirements can be rather straightforward. But, more likely, determining the capacity and how to achieve it will be complicated, as many factors are difficult to measure and quantify. Factors such as technology, competitors, building restrictions, cost of capital, human resource options, and regulations make the decision interesting. To complicate matters further, demand growth is usually in small units, while capacity additions are

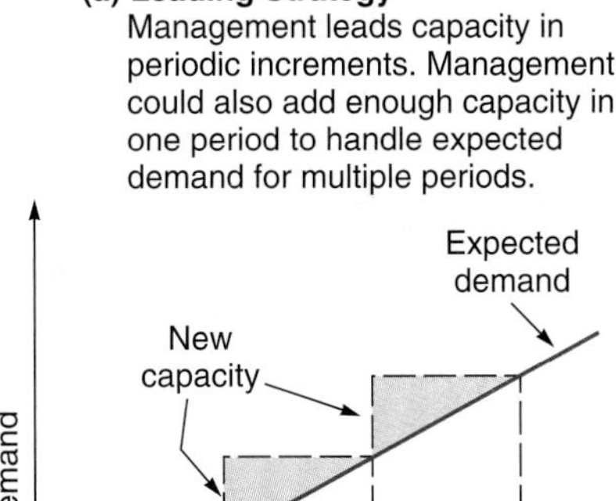
(a) Leading Strategy
Management leads capacity in periodic increments. Management could also add enough capacity in one period to handle expected demand for multiple periods.
Expected demand
New capacity
Demand
1
2
3
Time (periods)

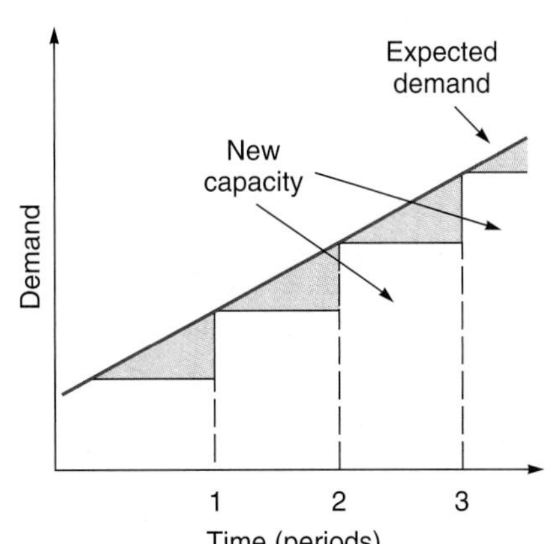
(b) Lag Strategy
Here management lags (chases) demand.
Expected demand
New capacity
Demand
1
2
3
Time (periods)

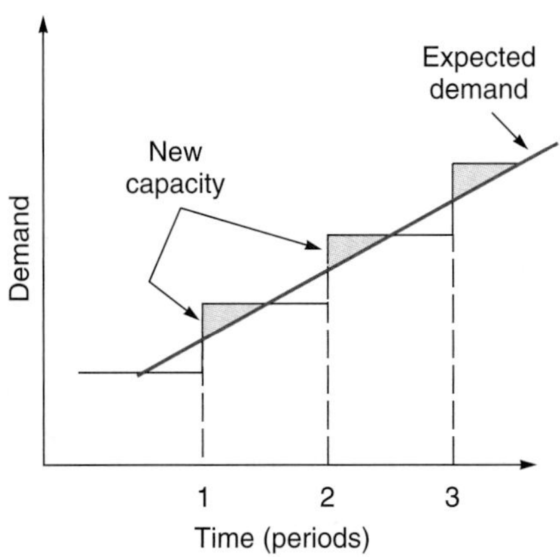
(c) Straddle Strategy
Here management uses average capacity increments to straddle demand.
Expected demand
New capacity
Demand
1
2
3
Time (periods)

FIGURE S7.6 Approaches to Capacity Expansion

likely to be both instantaneous and in large units. This contradiction adds to the capacity decision risk. To reduce risk, incremental changes that hedge demand forecasts may be a good option. Figure S7.6 illustrates three approaches to new capacity.

Alternative Figure S7.6(a) *leads* capacity—that is, acquires capacity to stay ahead of demand, with new capacity being acquired at the beginning of period 1. This capacity handles increased demand, until the beginning of period 2. At the beginning of period 2, new capacity is again acquired, which will allow the organization to stay ahead of demand until the beginning of period 3. This process can be continued indefinitely into the future. Here capacity is acquired *incrementally*—at the beginning of period 1 *and* at the beginning of period 2. But managers can also elect to make a larger increase at the beginning of period 1—an increase that may satisfy expected demand until the beginning of period 3.

Excess capacity gives operations managers flexibility. For instance, in the hotel industry, added (extra) capacity in the form of rooms can allow a wider variety of room options and perhaps flexibility in room cleanup schedules. In manufacturing, excess capacity can be used to do more setups, shorten production runs, and drive down inventory costs.

But Figure S7.6(b) shows an option that *lags* capacity, perhaps using overtime or subcontracting to accommodate excess demand. Figure S7.6(c) *straddles* demand by building capacity that is "average," sometimes lagging demand and sometimes leading it. Both the lag and straddle option have the advantage of delaying capital expenditure.

In cases where the business climate is stable, deciding between alternatives can be relatively easy. The total cost of each alternative can be computed, and the alternative with the least total cost can be selected. However, when capacity requirements are subject to significant unknowns, "probabilistic" models may be appropriate. One technique for making successful capacity planning decisions with an uncertain demand is decision theory, including the use of expected monetary value.

APPLYING EXPECTED MONETARY VALUE (EMV) TO CAPACITY DECISIONS

AUTHOR COMMENT Uncertainty in capacity decisions makes EMV a helpful tool.

Determining expected monetary value (EMV) requires specifying alternatives and various states of nature. For capacity planning situations, the state of nature usually is future demand or market favorability. By assigning probability values to the various states of nature, we can make decisions that maximize the expected value of the alternatives. Example S8 shows how to apply EMV to a capacity decision.

LO5: Determine expected monetary value of a capacity decision

EXAMPLE S8 ▶

EMV applied to capacity decision

Southern Hospital Supplies, a company that makes hospital gowns, is considering capacity expansion.

APPROACH: ▶ Southern's major alternatives are to do nothing, build a small plant, build a medium plant, or build a large plant. The new facility would produce a new type of gown, and currently the potential or marketability for this product is unknown. If a large plant is built and a favorable market exists, a profit of \$100,000 could be realized. An unfavorable market would yield a \$90,000 loss. However, a medium plant would earn a \$60,000 profit with a favorable market. A \$10,000 loss would result from an unfavorable market. A small plant, on the other hand, would return \$40,000 with favorable market conditions and lose only \$5,000 in an unfavorable market. Of course, there is always the option of doing nothing.

Recent market research indicates that there is a .4 probability of a favorable market, which means that there is also a .6 probability of an unfavorable market. With this information, the alternative that will result in the highest expected monetary value (EMV) can be selected.

SOLUTION ▶ Compute the EMV for each alternative:

$$\begin{aligned}
\text{EMV (large plant)} &= (.4)(\$100{,}000) + (.6)(-\$90{,}000) = -\$14{,}000 \\
\text{EMV (medium plant)} &= (.4)(\$60{,}000) + (.6)(-\$10{,}000) = +\$18{,}000 \\
\text{EMV (small plant)} &= (.4)(\$40{,}000) + (.6)(-\$5{,}000) = +\$13{,}000 \\
\text{EMV (do nothing)} &= \$0
\end{aligned}$$

Based on EMV criteria, Southern should build a medium plant.

INSIGHT ▶ If Southern makes many decisions like this, then determining the EMV for each alternative and selecting the highest EMV is a good decision criterion.

LEARNING EXERCISE ▶ If a new estimate of the loss from a medium plant in an unfavorable market increases to –\$20,000 what is the new EMV for this alternative? [Answer: \$12,000, which changes the decision because the small plant EMV is now higher.]

RELATED PROBLEMS ▶ S7.28, S7.29.

AUTHOR COMMENT An operations manager may be held responsible for return on investment (ROI).

APPLYING INVESTMENT ANALYSIS TO STRATEGY-DRIVEN INVESTMENTS

Once the strategy implications of potential investments have been considered, traditional investment analysis is appropriate. We introduce the investment aspects of capacity next.

Investment, Variable Cost, and Cash Flow

Because capacity and process alternatives exist, so do options regarding capital investment and variable cost. Managers must choose from among different financial options as well as capacity and process alternatives. Analysis should show the capital investment, variable cost, and cash flows as well as net present value for each alternative.

Net Present Value

Net present value
A means of determining the discounted value of a series of future cash receipts.

Determining the discount value of a series of future cash receipts is known as the **net present value** technique. By way of introduction, let us consider the time value of money. Say you invest \$100.00 in a bank at 5% for 1 year. Your investment will be worth \$100.00 + (\$100.00)(.05) = \$105.00. If you invest the \$105.00 for a second year, it will be worth \$105.00 + (\$105.00)(.05) = \$110.25 at the end of the second year. Of course, we could calculate the future value of \$100.00 at 5% for as many years as we wanted by simply extending this analysis. However, there is an easier way to express this relationship mathematically. For the first year:

$$\$105 = \$100(1 + .05)$$

For the second year:

$$\$110.25 = \$105(1 + .05) = \$100(1 + .05)^2$$

In general:

$$F = P(1 + i)^N \qquad \text{(S7-7)}$$

where F = future value (such as \$110.25 or \$105)
P = present value (such as \$100.00)
i = interest rate (such as .05)
N = number of years (such as 1 year or 2 years)

In most investment decisions, however, we are interested in calculating the present value of a series of future cash receipts. Solving for *P*, we get:

LO6: Compute net present value

$$P = \frac{F}{(1 + i)^N} \qquad \text{(S7-8)}$$

When the number of years is not too large, the preceding equation is effective. However, when the number of years, *N*, is large, the formula is cumbersome. For 20 years, you would have to compute $(1 + i)^{20}$. Without a sophisticated calculator, this computation would be difficult. Interest-rate tables, such as Table S7.1, alleviate this situation. First, let us restate the present value equation:

$$P = \frac{F}{(1 + i)^N} = FX \qquad \text{(S7-9)}$$

where X = a factor from Table S7.1 defined as $= 1/(1 + i)^N$ and F = future value

Thus, all we have to do is find the factor *X* and multiply it by *F* to calculate the present value, *P*. The factors, of course, are a function of the interest rate, *i*, and the number of years, *N*. Table S7.1 lists some of these factors.

Equations (S7-8) and (S7-9) are used to determine the present value of one future cash amount, but there are situations in which an investment generates a series of uniform and equal cash amounts. This type of investment is called an *annuity*. For example, an investment might yield \$300 per year for 3 years. Easy-to-use factors have been developed for the present value of annuities. These factors are shown in Table S7.2. The basic relationship is

$$S = RX$$

where X = factor from Table S7.2
S = present value of a series of uniform annual receipts
R = receipts that are received every year for the life of the investment (the annuity)

Year	6%	8%	10%	12%	14%
1	.943	.926	.909	.893	.877
2	.890	.857	.826	.797	.769
3	.840	.794	.751	.712	.675
4	.792	.735	.683	.636	.592
5	.747	.681	.621	.567	.519
6	.705	.630	.564	.507	.456
7	.665	.583	.513	.452	.400
8	.627	.540	.467	.404	.351
9	.592	.500	.424	.361	.308
10	.558	.463	.386	.322	.270
15	.417	.315	.239	.183	.140
20	.312	.215	.149	.104	.073

◄ **TABLE S7.1** Present Value of \$1

▶TABLE S7.2
Present Value of an Annuity of $1

Year	6%	8%	10%	12%	14%
1	.943	.926	.909	.893	.877
2	1.833	1.783	1.736	1.690	1.647
3	2.673	2.577	2.487	2.402	2.322
4	3.465	3.312	3.170	3.037	2.914
5	4.212	3.993	3.791	3.605	3.433
6	4.917	4.623	4.355	4.111	3.889
7	5.582	5.206	4.868	4.564	4.288
8	6.210	5.747	5.335	4.968	4.639
9	6.802	6.247	5.759	5.328	4.946
10	7.360	6.710	6.145	5.650	5.216
15	9.712	8.559	7.606	6.811	6.142
20	11.470	9.818	8.514	7.469	6.623

The present value of a uniform annual series of amounts is an extension of the present value of a single amount, and thus Table S7.2 can be directly developed from Table S7.1. The factors for any given interest rate in Table S7.2 are the cumulative sum of the values in Table S7.1. In Table S7.1, for example, .943, .890, and .840 are the factors for years 1, 2, and 3 when the interest rate is 6%. The cumulative sum of these factors is 2.673. Now look at the point in Table S7.2 where the interest rate is 6% and the number of years is 3. The factor for the present value of an annuity is 2.673, as you would expect.

Example S9 shows how to determine the present value of an annuity.

EXAMPLE S9 ▶

Determining net present value of future receipts of equal value

River Road Medical Clinic is thinking of investing in a sophisticated new piece of medical equipment. It will generate $7,000 per year in receipts for 5 years.

APPROACH ▶ Determine the present value of this cash flow; assume an interest rate of 6%.

SOLUTION ▶ The factor from Table S7.2 (4.212) is obtained by finding that value when the interest rate is 6% and the number of years is 5:

$$S = RX = \$7{,}000(4.212) = \$29{,}484$$

INSIGHT ▶ There is another way of looking at this example. If you went to a bank and took a loan for $29,484 today, your payments would be $7,000 per year for 5 years if the bank used an interest rate of 6% compounded yearly. Thus, $29,484 is the present value.

LEARNING EXERCISE ▶ If the interest rate is 8%, what is the present value? [Answer: $27,951.]

RELATED PROBLEMS ▶ S7.30, S7.31, S7.32, S7.33, S7.34, S7.35

The net present value method is straightforward: You simply compute the present value of all cash flows for each investment alternative. When deciding among investment alternatives, you pick the investment with the highest net present value. Similarly, when making several investments, those with higher net present values are preferable to investments with lower net present values.

Solved Problem S7.4 shows how to use the net present value to choose between investment alternatives.

Although net present value is one of the best approaches to evaluating investment alternatives, it does have its faults. Limitations of the net present value approach include the following:

1. Investments with the same net present value may have significantly different projected lives and different salvage values.
2. Investments with the same net present value may have different cash flows. Different cash flows may make substantial differences in the company's ability to pay its bills.

3. The assumption is that we know future interest rates, which we do not.
4. Payments are always made at the end of the period (week, month, or year), which is not always the case.

SUPPLEMENT SUMMARY

Managers tie equipment selection and capacity decisions to the organization's missions and strategy. Four additional considerations are critical: (1) accurately forecasting demand; (2) understanding the equipment, processes, and capacity increments; (3) finding the optimum operating size; and (4) ensuring the flexibility needed for adjustments in technology, product features and mix, and volumes.

Techniques that are particularly useful to operations managers when making capacity decisions include good forecasting, bottleneck analysis, break-even analysis, expected monetary value, cash flow, and net present value (NPV).

The single most important criterion for investment decisions is the contribution to the overall strategic plan and the winning of profitable orders. Successful firms select the correct process and capacity.

Key Terms

Capacity (p. 282)
Design capacity (p. 282)
Effective capacity (p. 283)
Utilization (p. 283)
Efficiency (p. 283)
Capacity analysis (p. 288)
Bottleneck (p. 288)
Process time of a station (p. 289)
Process time of a system (p. 289)
Process cycle time (p. 289)
Theory of constraints (TOC) (p. 291)
Break-even analysis (p. 292)
Net present value (p. 298)

Discussion Questions

1. Distinguish between design capacity and effective capacity.
2. What is effective capacity?
3. What is efficiency?
4. How is actual, or expected, output computed?
5. Explain why doubling the capacity of a bottleneck may not double the system capacity.
6. Distinguish between process time of a system and process cycle time.
7. What is the theory of constraints?
8. What are the assumptions of break-even analysis?
9. What keeps plotted revenue data from falling on a straight line in a break-even analysis?
10. Under what conditions would a firm want its capacity to lag demand? to lead demand?
11. Explain how net present value is an appropriate tool for comparing investments.
12. Describe the five-step process that serves as the basis of the theory of constraints.
13. What are the techniques available to operations managers to deal with a bottleneck operation? Which of these does not decrease process cycle time?

Using Software for Break-even Analysis

Excel, Excel OM, and POM for Windows all handle break-even and cost–volume analysis problems.

Using Excel

It is a straightforward task to develop the formulas to do a break-even analysis in Excel. Although we do not demonstrate the basics here, Active Model S7.2 provides a working example. You can see similar spreadsheet analysis in the Excel OM preprogrammed software that accompanies this text.

X Using Excel OM

Excel OM's Break-Even Analysis module provides the Excel formulas needed to compute the break-even points, and the solution and graphical output.

P Using POM for Windows

Similar to Excel OM, POM for Windows also contains a break-even/cost–volume analysis module.

Solved Problems

Virtual Office Hours help is available at www.myomlab.com.

▼ SOLVED PROBLEM S7.1

Sara James Bakery, described in Examples S1 and S2, has decided to increase its facilities by adding one additional process line. The firm will have two process lines, each working 7 days a week, 3 shifts per day, 8 hours per shift, with effective capacity of 300,000 rolls. This addition, however, will reduce overall system efficiency to 85%. Compute the expected production with this new effective capacity.

▼ SOLUTION

$$\begin{aligned}\text{Expected production} &= (\text{Effective capacity})(\text{Efficiency})\\ &= 300{,}000(.85)\\ &= 255{,}000 \text{ rolls per week}\end{aligned}$$

▼ SOLVED PROBLEM S7.2

Marty McDonald has a business packaging software in Wisconsin. His annual fixed cost is \$10,000, direct labor is \$3.50 per package, and material is \$4.50 per package. The selling price will be \$12.50 per package. What is the break-even point in dollars? What is break-even in units?

▼ SOLUTION

$$BEP_\$ = \frac{F}{1 - (V/P)} = \frac{\$10{,}000}{1 - (\$8.00/\$12.50)} = \frac{\$10{,}000}{.36} = \$27{,}777$$

$$BEP_x = \frac{F}{P - V} = \frac{\$10{,}000}{\$12.50 - \$8.00} = \frac{\$10{,}000}{\$4.50} = 2{,}222 \text{ units}$$

▼ SOLVED PROBLEM S7.3

John has been asked to determine whether the \$22.50 cost of tickets for the community dinner theater will allow the group to achieve break-even and whether the 175 seating capacity is adequate. The cost for each performance of a 10-performance run is \$2,500. The facility rental cost for the entire 10 performances is \$10,000. Drinks and parking are extra charges and have their own price and variable costs, as shown below:

1	2	3	4	5	6	7	8	9
	Selling Price (P)	Variable Cost (V)	Percent Variable Cost (V/P)	Contribution 1 − (V/P)	Estimated Quantity of Sales Units (sales)	Dollar Sales (Sales × P)	Percent of Sales	Contribution Weighted by Percent Sales (col. 5 × col. 8)
Tickets with Dinner	\$22.50	\$10.50	0.467	0.533	175	\$3,938	0.741	0.395
Drinks	\$ 5.00	\$ 1.75	0.350	0.650	175	\$ 875	0.165	0.107
Parking	\$ 5.00	\$ 2.00	0.400	0.600	100	\$ 500	0.094	0.056
					450	\$5,313	1.000	0.558

▼ SOLUTION

$$BEP_\$ = \frac{F}{\sum\left[\left(1 - \frac{V_i}{P_i}\right) \times (W_i)\right]} = \frac{\$(10 \times 2{,}500) + \$10{,}000}{0.558} = \frac{\$35{,}000}{0.558} = \$62{,}724$$

Revenue for each performance (from column 7) = \$5,313
Total forecasted revenue for the 10 performances = (10 × \$5,313) = \$53,130
Forecasted revenue with this mix of sales shows a break-even of \$62,724

Thus, given this mix of costs, sales, and capacity John determines that the theater will not break even.

▼ SOLVED PROBLEM S7.4

Your boss has told you to evaluate the cost of two machines. After some questioning, you are assured that they have the costs shown at the right. Assume:

a) The life of each machine is 3 years, and
b) The company thinks it knows how to make 14% on investments no riskier than this one.

Determine via the present value method which machine to purchase.

	Machine A	Machine B
Original cost	\$13,000	\$20,000
Labor cost per year	2,000	3,000
Floor space per year	500	600
Energy (electricity) per year	1,000	900
Maintenance per year	2,500	500
Total annual cost	\$ 6,000	\$ 5,000
Salvage value	\$ 2,000	\$ 7,000

▼ SOLUTION

		Machine A			Machine B		
		Column 1	Column 2	Column 3	Column 4	Column 5	Column 6
Now	Expense	1.000	$13,000	$13,000	1.000	$20,000	$20,000
1 yr.	Expense	.877	6,000	5,262	.877	5,000	4,385
2 yr.	Expense	.769	6,000	4,614	.769	5,000	3,845
3 yr.	Expense	.675	6,000	4,050	.675	5,000	3,375
				$26,926			$31,605
3 yr.	Salvage Revenue	.675	$ 2,000	−1,350	.675	$ 7,000	−4,725
				$25,576			$26,880

We use 1.0 for payments with no discount applied against them (that is, when payments are made now, there is no need for a discount). The other values in columns 1 and 4 are from the 14% column and the respective year in Table S7.1 (for example, the intersection of 14% and 1 year is .877, etc.). Columns 3 and 6 are the products of the present value figures times the combined costs. This computation is made for each year and for the salvage value.

The calculation for machine A for the first year is:

$$.877 \times (\$2{,}000 + \$500 + \$1{,}000 + \$2{,}500) = \$5{,}262$$

The salvage value of the product is *subtracted* from the summed costs, because it is a receipt of cash. Since the sum of the net costs for machine B is larger than the sum of the net costs for machine A, machine A is the low-cost purchase, and your boss should be so informed.

▼ SOLVED PROBLEM S7.5

T. Smunt Manufacturing Corp. has the process displayed below. The drilling operation occurs separately from and simultaneously with the sawing and sanding operations. The product only needs to go through one of the three assembly operations (the assembly operations are "parallel").

a. Which operation is the bottleneck?
b. What is the system's process time?
c. What is the process cycle time for the overall system?
d. If the firm operates 8 hours per day, 22 days per month, what is the monthly capacity of the manufacturing process?
e. Suppose that a second drilling machine is added, and it has the same process time as the original drilling machine. What is the new process time of the system?
f. Suppose that a second drilling machine is added, and it has the same process time as the original drilling machine. What is the new process cycle time?

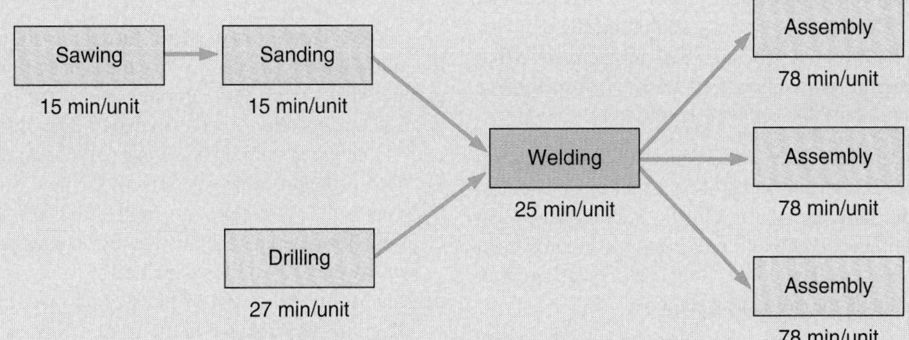

▼ SOLUTION

a. The process time of Assembly is 78 minutes/3 operators = 26 minutes per unit, so the station with the longest process time, hence the bottleneck, is Drilling, at 27 minutes.
b. The system's process time is 27 minutes per unit (the longest process, Drilling).
c. System process cycle time is the maximum of (15 + 15 + 25 + 78), (27 + 25 + 78) = maximum of (133, 130) = 133 minutes
d. Monthly capacity = (60 minutes)(8 hours)(22 days)/27 minutes per unit = 10,560 minutes per month /27 minutes per unit = 391.11 units/month.
e. The bottleneck shifts to assembly, with a process time of 26 minutes per unit.
f. Redundancy does not affect process cycle time. It is still 133 minutes.

Problems*

• **S7.1** If a plant was designed to produce 7,000 hammers per day but is limited to making 6,000 hammers per day because of the time needed to change equipment between styles of hammers, what is the utilization?

• **S7.2** For the past month, the plant in Problem S7.1, which has an effective capacity of 6,500, has made only 4,500 hammers per day because of material delay, employee absences, and other problems. What is its efficiency?

• **S7.3** If a plant has an effective capacity of 6,500 and an efficiency of 88%, what is the actual (planned) output?

• **S7.4** A plant has an effective capacity of 900 units per day and produces 800 units per day with its product mix; what is its efficiency?

• **S7.5** Material delays have routinely limited production of household sinks to 400 units per day. If the plant efficiency is 80%, what is the effective capacity?

• **S7.6** The effective capacity and efficiency for the next quarter at MMU Mfg. in Waco, Texas, for each of three departments are shown:

Department	Effective Capacity	Recent Efficiency
Design	93,600	.95
Fabrication	156,000	1.03
Finishing	62,400	1.05

Compute the expected production for next quarter for each department.

•• **S7.7** Southeastern Oklahoma State University's business program has the facilities and faculty to handle an enrollment of 2,000 new students per semester. However, in an effort to limit class sizes to a "reasonable" level (under 200, generally), Southeastern's dean, Tom Choi, placed a ceiling on enrollment of 1,500 new students. Although there was ample demand for business courses last semester, conflicting schedules allowed only 1,450 new students to take business courses. What are the utilization and efficiency of this system?

•• **S7.8** Under ideal conditions, a service bay at a Fast Lube can serve 6 cars per hour. The effective capacity and efficiency of a Fast Lube service bay are known to be 5.5 and 0.880, respectively. What is the minimum number of service bays Fast Lube needs to achieve an anticipated production of 200 cars per 8-hour day?

• **S7.9** A production line at V. J. Sugumaran's machine shop has three stations. The first station can process a unit in 10 minutes. The second station has two identical machines, each of which can process a unit in 12 minutes (each unit only needs to be processed on one of the two machines). The third station can process a unit in 8 minutes. Which station is the bottleneck station?

•• **S7.10** A work cell at Chris Ellis Commercial Laundry has a workstation with two machines, and each unit produced at the station needs to be processed by both of the machines. (The same unit cannot be worked on by both machines simultaneously.) Each machine has a production capacity of 4 units per hour. What is the process time of the work cell in minutes per unit?

•• **S7.11** The three-station work cell illustrated in Figure S7.7, has a product that must go through one of the two machines at station 1 (they are parallel) before proceeding to station 2.

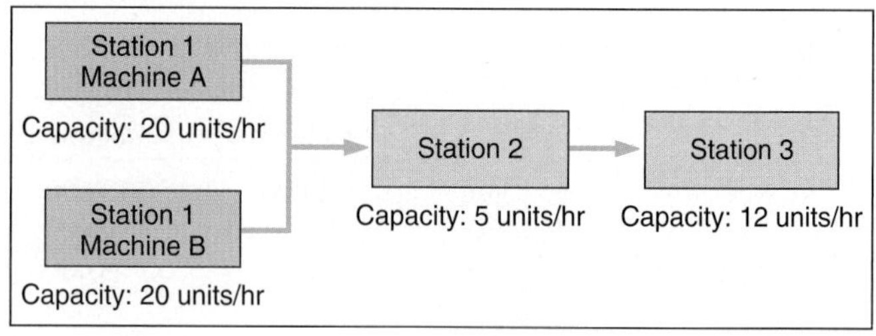

▲ **FIGURE S7.7**

a) What is the process time of the system?
b) What is the bottleneck time of this work cell?
c) What is the process cycle time?
d) If the firm operates 10 hours per day, 5 days per week, what is the weekly capacity of this work cell?

•• **S7.12** The three-station work cell at Pullman Mfg., Inc. is illustrated in Figure S7.8. It has two machines at station 1 in parallel (i.e., the product needs to go through only one of the two machines before proceeding to station 2).
a) What is the process cycle time of this work cell?
b) What is the system process time of this work cell?
c) If the firm operates 8 hours per day, 6 days per week, what is the weekly capacity of this work cell?

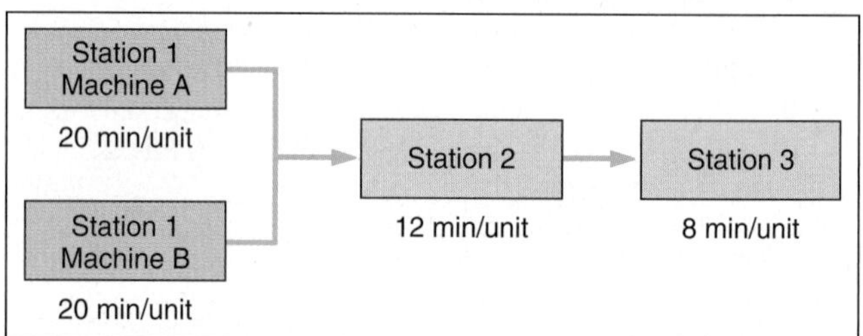

▲ **FIGURE S7.8**

•• **S7.13** The Pullman Mfg., Inc. three-station work cell illustrated in Figure S7.8 has two machines at station 1 in parallel. (The product needs to go through only one of the two machines before proceeding to station 2.) The manager, Ms. Hartley, has asked you to evaluate the system if she adds a parallel machine at station 2.
a) What is the process cycle time of the new work cell?
b) What is the system process time of the new work cell?
c) If the firm operates 8 hours per day, 6 days per week, what is the weekly capacity of this work cell?
d) How did the addition of the second machine at workstation 2 affect the performance of the work cell from Problem S7.12?

• **S7.14** Klassen Toy Company, Inc., assembles two parts (parts 1 and 2): Part 1 is first processed at workstation A for 15 minutes per unit and then processed at workstation B for 10 minutes per unit. Part 2 is simultaneously processed at workstation C for 20 minutes per unit. Work stations B and C feed the parts to an assembler at workstation D, where the two parts are assembled. The time at workstation D is 15 minutes.
a) What is the bottleneck of this process?
b) What is the hourly capacity of the process?

•• **S7.15** A production process at Kenneth Day Manufacturing is shown in Figure S7.9. The drilling operation occurs separately from, and simultaneously with, the sawing and sanding operations.

*Note: Px means the problem may be solved with POM for Windows and/or Excel OM.

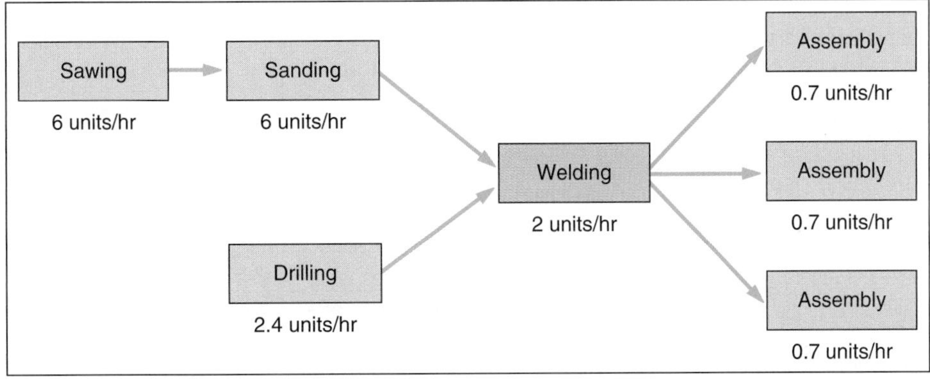

▲ **FIGURE S7.9**

A product needs to go through only one of the three assembly operations (the operations are in parallel).

a) Which operation is the bottleneck?
b) What is the process time of the overall system?
c) What is the process cycle time of the overall system?
d) If the firm operates 8 hours per day, 20 days per month, what is the monthly capacity of the manufacturing process?

• **S7.16** Smithson Cutting is opening a new line of scissors for supermarket distribution. It estimates its fixed cost to be $500.00 and its variable cost to be $0.50 per unit. Selling price is expected to average $0.75 per unit.

a) What is Smithson's break-even point in units?
b) What is the break-even point in dollars? PX

• **S7.17** Markland Manufacturing intends to increase capacity by overcoming a bottleneck operation by adding new equipment. Two vendors have presented proposals. The fixed costs for proposal A are $50,000, and for proposal B, $70,000. The variable cost for A is $12.00, and for B, $10.00. The revenue generated by each unit is $20.00.

a) What is the break-even point in units for proposal A?
b) What is the break-even point in units for proposal B? PX

• **S7.18** Using the data in Problem S7.17:

a) What is the break-even point in dollars for proposal A if you add $10,000 installation to the fixed cost?
b) What is the break-even point in dollars for proposal B if you add $10,000 installation to the fixed cost? PX

• **S7.19** Given the data in Problem S7.17, at what volume (units) of output would the two alternatives yield the same profit? PX

•• **S7.20** Janelle Heinke, the owner of Ha'Peppas!, is considering a new oven in which to bake the firm's signature dish, vegetarian pizza. Oven type A can handle 20 pizzas an hour. The fixed costs associated with oven A are $20,000 and the variable costs are $2.00 per pizza. Oven B is larger and can handle 40 pizzas an hour. The fixed costs associated with oven B are $30,000 and the variable costs are $1.25 per pizza. The pizzas sell for $14 each.

a) What is the break-even point for each oven?
b) If the owner expects to sell 9,000 pizzas, which oven should she purchase?
c) If the owner expects to sell 12,000 pizzas, which oven should she purchase?
d) At what volume should Janelle switch ovens? PX

• **S7.21** Given the following data, calculate: a) BEP_x; b) $BEP_\$$; and c) the profit at 100,000 units:

$$P = \$8/\text{unit} \quad V = \$4/\text{unit} \quad F = \$50{,}000$$ PX

•• **S7.22** You are considering opening a copy service in the student union. You estimate your fixed cost at $15,000 and the variable cost of each copy sold at $.01. You expect the selling price to average $.05.

a) What is the break-even point in dollars?
b) What is the break-even point in units? PX

•• **S7.23** An electronics firm is currently manufacturing an item that has a variable cost of $.50 per unit and a selling price of $1.00 per unit. Fixed costs are $14,000. Current volume is 30,000 units. The firm can substantially improve the product quality by adding a new piece of equipment at an additional fixed cost of $6,000. Variable cost would increase to $.60, but volume should jump to 50,000 units due to a higher-quality product. Should the company buy the new equipment? PX

•• **S7.24** The electronics firm in Problem S7.23 is now considering the new equipment and increasing the selling price to $1.10 per unit. With the higher-quality product, the new volume is expected to be 45,000 units. Under these circumstances, should the company purchase the new equipment and increase the selling price? PX

•••• **S7.25** Zan Azlett and Angela Zesiger have joined forces to start A&Z Lettuce Products, a processor of packaged shredded lettuce for institutional use. Zan has years of food processing experience, and Angela has extensive commercial food preparation experience. The process will consist of opening crates of lettuce and then sorting, washing, slicing, preserving, and finally packaging the prepared lettuce. Together, with help from vendors, they feel they can adequately estimate demand, fixed costs, revenues, and variable cost per 5-pound bag of lettuce. They think a largely manual process will have monthly fixed costs of $37,500 and variable costs of $1.75 per bag. A more mechanized process will have fixed costs of $75,000 per month with variable costs of $1.25 per 5-pound bag. They expect to sell the shredded lettuce for $2.50 per 5-pound bag.

a. What is the break-even quantity for the manual process?
b. What is the revenue at the break-even quantity for the manual process?
c. What is the break-even quantity for the mechanized process?
d. What is the revenue at the break-even quantity for the mechanized process?
e. What is the monthly profit or loss of the *manual* process if they expect to sell 60,000 bags of lettuce per month?
f. What is the monthly profit or loss of the *mechanized* process if they expect to sell 60,000 bags of lettuce per month?
g. At what quantity would Zan and Angela be indifferent to the process selected?
h. Over what range of demand would the *manual* process be preferred over the mechanized process? Over what range of demand would the *mechanized* process be preferred over the manual process? PX

•••• **S7.26** As a prospective owner of a club known as the Red Rose, you are interested in determining the volume of sales dollars necessary for the coming year to reach the break-even point. You have decided to break down the sales for the club into four categories, the first category being beer. Your estimate of the beer sales is that 30,000 drinks will be served. The selling price for each unit will average $1.50; the cost is $.75. The second major category is meals, which you expect to be 10,000 units with an average price of $10.00 and a cost of $5.00. The third major category is desserts and wine, of which you also expect to sell 10,000 units, but with an average price of $2.50 per unit sold and a cost of $1.00 per unit. The final category is lunches and inexpensive sandwiches, which you expect to total 20,000 units at an average price of $6.25 with a food cost of $3.25. Your fixed cost (that is, rent, utilities, and so on) is $1,800 per month plus $2,000 per month for entertainment.
a. What is your break-even point in dollars per month?
b. What is the expected number of meals each day if you are open 30 days a month?

••• **S7.27** As manager of the St. Cloud Theatre Company, you have decided that concession sales will support themselves. The following table provides the information you have been able to put together thus far:

Item	Selling Price	Variable Cost	% of Revenue
Soft drink	$1.00	$ .65	25
Wine	1.75	.95	25
Coffee	1.00	.30	30
Candy	1.00	.30	20

Last year's manager, Jim Freeland, has advised you to be sure to add 10% of variable cost as a waste allowance for all categories.

You estimate labor cost to be $250.00 (5 booths with 2 people each). Even if nothing is sold, your labor cost will be $250.00, so you decide to consider this a fixed cost. Booth rental, which is a contractual cost at $50.00 for *each* booth per night, is also a fixed cost.
a. What is break-even volume per evening performance?
b. How much wine would you expect to sell at the break-even point?

•• **S7.28** James Lawson's Bed and Breakfast, in a small historic Mississippi town, must decide how to subdivide (remodel) the large old home that will become its inn. There are three alternatives: Option A would modernize all baths and combine rooms, leaving the inn with four suites, each suitable for two to four adults. Option B would modernize only the second floor; the results would be six suites, four for two to four adults, two for two adults only. Option C (the status quo option) leaves all walls intact. In this case, there are eight rooms available, but only two are suitable for four adults, and four rooms will not have private baths. Below are the details of profit and demand patterns that will accompany each option:

	Annual Profit under Various Demand Patterns			
Alternatives	**High**	*p*	**Average**	*p*
A (modernize all)	$90,000	.5	$25,000	.5
B (modernize 2nd)	$80,000	.4	$70,000	.6
C (status quo)	$60,000	.3	$55,000	.7

Which option has the highest expected monetary value? PX

•••• **S7.29** As operations manager of Holz Furniture, you must make a decision about adding a line of rustic furniture. In discussing the possibilities with your sales manager, Steve Gilbert, you decide that there will definitely be a market and that your firm should enter that market. However, because rustic furniture has a different finish than your standard offering, you decide you need another process line. There is no doubt in your mind about the decision, and you are sure that you should have a second process. But you do question how large to make it. A large process line is going to cost $400,000; a small process line will cost $300,000. The question, therefore, is the demand for rustic furniture. After extensive discussion with Mr. Gilbert and Tim Ireland of Ireland Market Research, Inc., you determine that the best estimate you can make is that there is a two-out-of-three chance of profit from sales as large as $600,000 and a one-out-of-three chance as low as $300,000.

With a large process line, you could handle the high figure of $600,000. However, with a small process line you could not and would be forced to expand (at a cost of $150,000), after which time your profit from sales would be $500,000 rather than the $600,000 because of the lost time in expanding the process. If you do not expand the small process, your profit from sales would be held to $400,000. If you build a small process and the demand is low, you can handle all of the demand.

Should you open a large or small process line?

•• **S7.30** What is the net present value of an investment that costs $75,000 and has a salvage value of $45,000? The annual profit from the investment is $15,000 each year for 5 years. The cost of capital at this risk level is 12%. PX

• **S7.31** The initial cost of an investment is $65,000 and the cost of capital is 10%. The return is $16,000 per year for 8 years. What is the net present value? PX

• **S7.32** What is the present value of $5,600 when the interest rate is 8% and the return of $5,600 will not be received for 15 years? PX

•• **S7.33** Tim Smunt has been asked to evaluate two machines. After some investigation, he determines that they have the costs shown in the following table. He is told to assume that:
a) the life of each machine is 3 years, and
b) the company thinks it knows how to make 12% on investments no more risky than this one.

	Machine A	Machine B
Original cost	$10,000	$20,000
Labor per year	2,000	4,000
Maintenance per year	4,000	1,000
Salvage value	2,000	7,000

Determine, via the present value method, which machine Tim should recommend.

•••• **S7.34** Your boss has told you to evaluate two ovens for Tink-the-Tinkers, a gourmet sandwich shop. After some questioning of vendors and receipt of specifications, you are assured that the ovens have the attributes and costs shown in the following table. The following two assumptions are appropriate:

1. The life of each machine is 5 years.
2. The company thinks it knows how to make 14% on investments no more risky than this one.

	Three Small Ovens at $1,250 Each	Two Large Ovens at $2,500 Each
Original cost	$3,750	$5,000
Labor per year in excess of larger models	$ 750 (total)	
Cleaning/ maintenance	$ 750 ($250 each)	$ 400 ($200 each)
Salvage value	$ 750 ($250 each)	$1,000 ($500 each)

a. Determine via the present value method which machine to tell your boss to purchase.
b. What assumption are you making about the ovens?
c. What assumptions are you making in your methodology?

•••• **S7.35** Bold's Gym, a health club chain, is considering expanding into a new location: the initial investment would be $1 million in equipment, renovation, and a 6-year lease, and its annual upkeep and expenses would be $75,000. Its planning horizon is 6 years out, and at the end, it can sell the equipment for $50,000. Club capacity is 500 members who would pay an annual fee of $600. Bold's expects to have no problems filling membership slots. Assume that the interest rate is 10%. (See Table S7.1)

a. What is the present value profit/loss of the deal?
b. The club is considering offering a special deal to the members in the first year. For $3,000 upfront they get a full 6-year membership (i.e., 1 year free). Would it make financial sense to offer this deal?

► **Refer to myomlab for these additional homework problems: S7.36–S7.45**

Case Studies

► Capacity Planning at Arnold Palmer Hospital

Video Case

Since opening day, the Arnold Palmer Hospital has experienced an explosive growth in demand for its services. One of only six hospitals in the U.S. to specialize in health care for women and children, Arnold Palmer Hospital has cared for over 1,500,000 patients who came to the Orlando facility from all 50 states and more than 100 countries. With patient satisfaction scores in the top 10% of U.S. hospitals surveyed (over 95% of patients would recommend the hospital to others), one of Arnold Palmer Hospital's main focuses is delivery of babies. Originally built with 281 beds and a capacity for 6,500 births per year, the hospital steadily approached and then passed 10,000 births. Looking at Table S7.3, Executive Director Kathy Swanson knew an expansion was necessary.

With continuing population growth in its market area serving 18 central Florida counties, Arnold Palmer Hospital was delivering the equivalent of a kindergarten class of babies every day and still not meeting demand. Supported with substantial additional demographic analysis, the hospital was ready to move ahead with a capacity expansion plan and a new 11-story hospital building across the street from the existing facility.

Thirty-five planning teams were established to study such issues as (1) specific forecasts, (2) services that would transfer to the new facility, (3) services that would remain in the existing facility, (4) staffing needs, (5) capital equipment, (6) pro forma accounting data, and (7) regulatory requirements. Ultimately, Arnold Palmer Hospital was ready to move ahead with a budget of $100 million and a commitment to an additional 150 beds. But given the growth of the central Florida region, Swanson decided to expand the hospital in stages: the top two floors would be empty interiors ("shell") to be completed at a later date, and the fourth-floor operating room could be doubled in size when needed. "With the new facility in place, we are now able to handle up to 16,000 births per year," says Swanson.

▼**TABLE S7.3**
Births at Arnold Palmer Hospital

Year	Births
1995	6,144
1996	6,230
1997	6,432
1998	6,950
1999	7,377
2000	8,655
2001	9,536
2002	9,825
2003	10,253
2004	10,555
2005	12,316
2006	13,070
2007	14,028
2008	14,634

Discussion Questions*

1. Given the capacity planning discussion in the text (see Figure S7.6) what approach is being taken by Arnold Palmer Hospital toward matching capacity to demand?
2. What kind of major changes could take place in Arnold Palmer Hospital's demand forecast that would leave the hospital with an underutilized facility (namely, what are the risks connected with this capacity decision)?
3. Use regression analysis to forecast the point at which Swanson needs to "build out" the top two floors of the new building, namely, when demand will exceed 16,000 births.

*You may wish to view the video accompanying this case before addressing these questions.

►**Additional Case Study:** *Visit* **www.myomlab.com** or **www.pearsonhighered.com/heizer** *for this free case study:*
Southwestern University D: Requires the development of a multiproduct break-even solution.

Bibliography

Anupindi, Ravi, S. Deshmukh, and S. Chopra. *Managing Business Process Flows*, 2nd ed. Upper Saddle River, NJ: Prentice Hall (2007).

Atamturk, A., and D. S. Hochbaum. "Capacity Acquisition, Subcontracting, and Lot-Sizing." *Management Science* 47, no. 8 (August 2001): 1081–1100.

Bowers, John, et al. "Modeling Outpatient Capacity for a Diagnosis and Treatment Center." *Health Care Management Science* 8, no. 3 (August 2005): 205.

Brandl, Dennis. "Capacity and Constraints." *Control Engineering* (February 2008): 24.

Chambers, Chester, Eli M. Snir, and Asad Ata. "The Use of Flexible Manufacturing Capacity in Pharmaceutical Product Introductions." *Decision Sciences* 40, no. 2 (May 2009): 243–268.

Cheng, H. K., K. Dogan, and R. A. Einicki. "Pricing and Capacity Decisions for Non-Profit Internet Service Providers." *Information Technology and Management* 7, no. 2 (April 2006): 91.

Goldratt, Eliyaha. *The Choice*. Great Barrington, MA: North River Press (2009).

Goodale, John C., Rohit Verma, and Madeleine E. Pullman. "A Market Utility-Based Model for Capacity Scheduling in Mass Services." *Production and Operations Management* 12, no. 2 (Summer 2003): 165–185.

Gupta, M. C., and L. H. Boyd. "Theory of Constraints: A Theory for Operations Management." *International Journal of Operations Management* 28, no. 10 (2008): 991.

Jack, Eric P., and Amitabh S. Raturi. "Measuring and Comparing Volume Flexibility in the Capital Goods Industry." *Production and Operations Management* 12, no. 4 (Winter 2003): 480–501.

Jonsson, Patrik, and Stig-Arne Mattsson. "Use and Applicability of Capacity Planning Methods." *Production and Inventory Management Journal* (3rd/4th Quarter 2002): 89–95.

Kekre, Sunder, et al. "Reconfiguring a Remanufacturing Line at Visteon, Mexico." *Interfaces* 33, no. 6 (November–December 2003): 30–43.

Tibben-Lembke, Ronald S. "Theory of Constraints at UniCo." *International Journal of Production Research* 47, no. 7 (January 2009): 1815.

Watson, Kevin J., John H. Blackstone, and Stanley C. Gardiner. "The Evolution of a Management Philosophy: The Theory of Constraints." *Journal of Operations Management* 25, no. 2 (March 2007): 387–402.

Supplement 7 ***Rapid*** **Review**

Main Heading | **Review Material** | PEARSON myomlab

CAPACITY
(pp. 282–288)

- **Capacity**—The "throughput," or number of units a facility can hold, receive, store, or produce in a period of time.

Capacity decisions often determine capital requirements and therefore a large portion of fixed cost. Capacity also determines whether demand will be satisfied or whether facilities will be idle.

Determining facility size, with an objective of achieving high levels of utilization and a high return on investment, is critical.

Capacity planning can be viewed in three time horizons:

1. *Long-range* (> 1 year)—Adding facilities and long lead-time equipment
2. *Intermediate-range* (3–18 months)—"Aggregate planning" tasks, including adding equipment, personnel, and shifts; subcontracting; and building or using inventory
3. *Short-range* (< 3 months)—Scheduling jobs and people, and allocating machinery

- **Design capacity**—The theoretical maximum output of a system in a given period, under ideal conditions.

Most organizations operate their facilities at a rate less than the design capacity.

- **Effective capacity**—The capacity a firm can expect to achieve, given its product mix, methods of scheduling, maintenance, and standards of quality.
- **Utilization**—Actual output as a percent of design capacity.
- **Efficiency**—Actual output as a percent of effective capacity.

$$\text{Utilization} = \text{Actual output/Design capacity} \qquad \text{(S7-1)}$$

$$\text{Efficiency} = \text{Actual output/Effective capacity} \qquad \text{(S7-2)}$$

$$\text{Actual (or Expected) output} = \text{(Effective capacity)(Efficiency)} \qquad \text{(S7-3)}$$

Expected output is sometimes referred to as *rated capacity*.

When demand exceeds capacity, a firm may be able to curtail demand simply by raising prices, increasing lead times (which may be inevitable), and discouraging marginally profitable business.

When capacity exceeds demand, a firm may want to stimulate demand through price reductions or aggressive marketing, or it may accommodate the market via product changes.

In the service sector, scheduling customers is *demand management*, and scheduling the workforce is *capacity management.*

When demand and capacity are fairly well matched, demand management in services can often be handled with appointments, reservations, or a first-come, first-served rule. Otherwise, discounts based on time of day may be used (e.g., "early bird" specials, matinee pricing).

When managing demand in services is not feasible, managing capacity through changes in full-time, temporary, or part-time staff may be an option.

Problems: S7.1–S7.8

Virtual Office Hours for Solved Problems: S7.1

ACTIVE MODEL S7.1

BOTTLENECK ANALYSIS AND THEORY OF CONSTRAINTS
(pp. 288–292)

- **Capacity analysis**—Determining throughput capacity of workstations or an entire production system.
- **Bottleneck**—The limiting factor or constraint in a system.
- **Process time of a station**—The time to produce a given number of units at that single workstation.
- **Process time of a system**—The time of the longest (slowest) process, the bottleneck.
- **Process cycle time**—The time it takes for a product to go through the production process with no waiting: the longest path through the system.

A system's process time determines its capacity (e.g., one car per minute), while its process cycle time determines potential ability to build product (e.g., 30 hours).

If n parallel (redundant) operations are added, the process time of the combined operations will equal $1/n$ times the process time of the original.

With simultaneous processing, an order or product is essentially *split* into different paths to be rejoined later on. The longest path through the system is deemed the process cycle time.

- **Theory of constraints (TOC)**—A body of knowledge that deals with anything limiting an organization's ability to achieve its goals.

Problems: S7.9–S7.15

Main Heading	Review Material	myomlab
BREAK-EVEN ANALYSIS (pp. 292–296)	■ **Break-even analysis**—A means of finding the point, in dollars and units, at which costs equal revenues. *Fixed costs* are costs that exist even if no units are produced. Variable costs are those that vary with the volume of units produced. In the break-even model, costs and revenue are assumed to increase linearly. $$\text{Break-even in units} = \frac{\text{Total Fixed cost}}{\text{Price} - \text{Variable cost}} \quad \text{(S7-4)}$$ $$\text{Break-even in dollars} = \frac{\text{Total Fixed cost}}{1 - \dfrac{\text{Variable cost}}{\text{Selling price}}} \quad \text{(S7-5)}$$ $$\text{Multiproduct Break-even point in dollars} = BEP_\$ = \frac{F}{\sum\left[\left(1 - \dfrac{V_i}{P_i}\right) \times (W_i)\right]} \quad \text{(S7-6)}$$	Problems: S7.16–S7.27 Virtual Office Hours for Solved Problem: S7.3 **ACTIVE MODEL S7.2**
REDUCING RISK WITH INCREMENTAL CHANGES (pp. 296–297)	Demand growth is usually in small units, while capacity additions are likely to be both instantaneous and in large units. To reduce risk, incremental changes that hedge demand forecasts may be a good option. Three approaches to capacity expansion are (1) *leading* strategy, (2) *lag* strategy, and (3) *straddle* strategy. Both lag strategy and straddle strategy delay capital expenditure.	**VIDEO S7.1** Capacity Planning at Arnold Palmer Hospital
APPLYING EXPECTED MONETARY VALUE (pp. 297–298)	Determining expected monetary value requires specifying alternatives and various states of nature (e.g., demand or market favorability). By assigning probability values to the various states of nature, we can make decisions that maximize the expected value of the alternatives.	Problems: S7.28–S7.29
APPLYING INVESTMENT ANALYSIS TO STRATEGY-DRIVEN INVESTMENTS (pp. 298–301)	■ **Net present value**—A means of determining the discounted value of a series of future cash receipts. $$F = P(1 + i)^N \quad \text{(S7-7)}$$ $$P = \frac{F}{(1 + i)^N} \quad \text{(S7-8)}$$ $$P = \frac{F}{(1 + i)^N} = FX \quad \text{(S7-9)}$$ When making several investments, those with higher net present values are preferable to investments with lower net present values.	Problems: S7.30–S7.35 Virtual Office Hours for Solved Problem: S7.4

Self Test

■ **Before taking the self-test,** refer to the learning objectives listed at the beginning of the supplement and the key terms listed at the end of the supplement.

LO1. Capacity decisions should be made on the basis of:
- **a)** building sustained competitive advantage.
- **b)** good financial returns.
- **c)** a coordinated plan.
- **d)** integration into the company's strategy.
- **e)** all of the above.

LO2. Effective capacity is:
- **a)** the capacity a firm expects to achieve, given the current operating constraints.
- **b)** the percent of design capacity actually achieved.
- **c)** the percent of capacity actually achieved.
- **d)** actual output.
- **e)** efficiency.

LO3. System capacity is based on:
- **a)** process time of the bottleneck.
- **b)** throughput time.
- **c)** process time of the fastest station.
- **d)** throughput time plus waiting time.
- **e)** none of the above.

LO4. The break-even point is:
- **a)** adding processes to meet the point of changing product demands.
- **b)** improving processes to increase throughput.
- **c)** the point in dollars or units at which cost equals revenue.
- **d)** adding or removing capacity to meet demand.
- **e)** the total cost of a process alternative.

LO5. Expected monetary value is most appropriate:
- **a)** when the payoffs are equal.
- **b)** when the probability of each decision alternative is known.
- **c)** when probabilities are the same.
- **d)** when both revenue and cost are known.
- **e)** when probabilities of each state of nature are known.

LO6. Net present value (NPV):
- **a)** is greater if cash receipts occur later rather than earlier.
- **b)** is greater if cash receipts occur earlier rather than later.
- **c)** is revenue minus fixed cost.
- **d)** is preferred over breakeven analysis.
- **e)** is greater if $100 monthly payments are received in a lump sum ($1,200) at the end of the year.

Answers: LO1. e; LO2. a; LO3. a; LO4. c; LO5. b; LO6. b.

8 Location Strategies

Chapter Outline

10

OM Strategy Decisions

- Design of Goods and Services
- Managing Quality
- Process Strategy
- **Location Strategies**
- Layout Strategies
- Human Resources
- Supply-Chain Management
- Inventory Management
- Scheduling
- Maintenance

LOCATION PROVIDES COMPETITIVE ADVANTAGE FOR FEDEX

Overnight-delivery powerhouse FedEx has believed in the hub concept for its 40-year existence. Even though Fred Smith, founder and CEO, got a C on his college paper proposing a hub for small-package delivery, the idea has proven extremely successful. Starting with a hub in Memphis, Tennessee (now called its *superhub*), the $38 billion firm has added a European hub in Paris, an Asian hub in Guangzhou, China, a Latin American hub in Miami, and a Canadian hub in Toronto. FedEx's fleet of 672 planes flies into 375 airports worldwide, then delivers to the door with more than 80,000 vans and trucks.

Why was Memphis picked as FedEx's central location? (1) It is located in the middle of the U.S. (2) It has very few hours of bad weather closures, perhaps contributing to the firm's excellent flight-safety record.

Each night, except Sunday, FedEx brings to Memphis packages from throughout the world that are going to cities for which FedEx does not have direct flights. The central hub permits service to a far greater

At the FedEx hub in Memphis, Tennessee, approximately 100 FedEx aircraft converge each night around midnight with more than 5 million documents and packages.

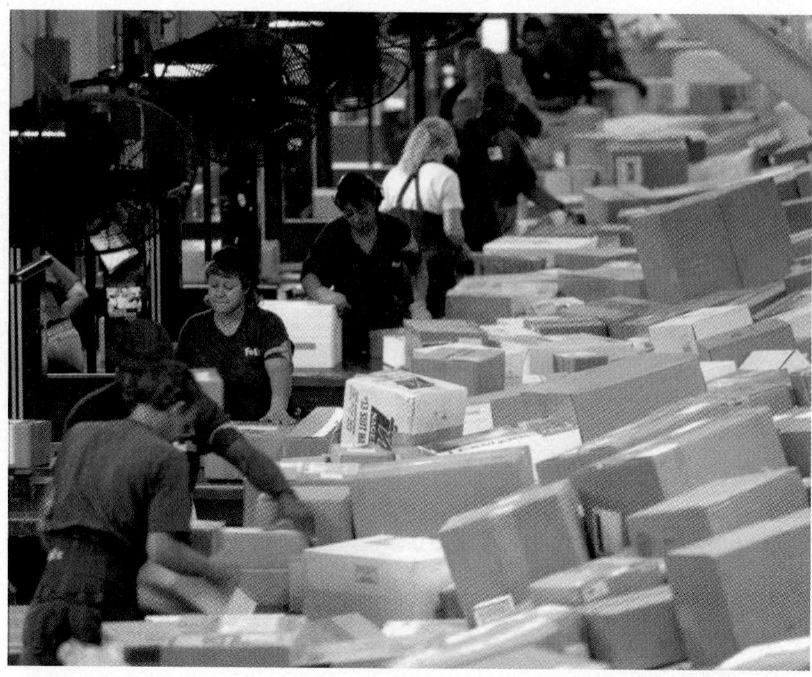

At the preliminary sorting area, packages and documents are sorted and sent to a secondary sorting area. The Memphis facility covers 1.5 million square feet; it is big enough to hold 33 football fields. Packages are sorted and exchanged until 4 A.M.

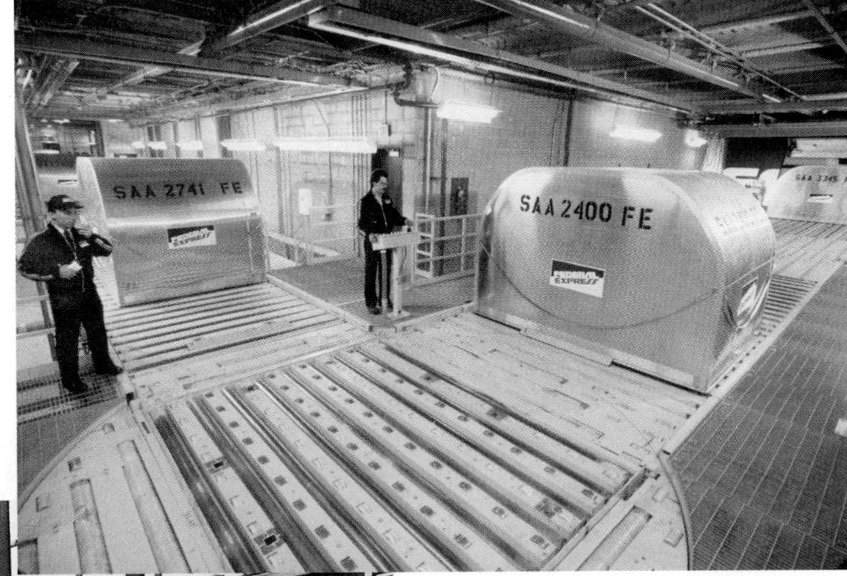

Packages and documents that have already gone through the primary and secondary sorts are checked by city, state, and zip code. They are then placed in containers that are loaded onto aircraft for delivery to their final destinations in 215 countries.

FedEx's fleet of 672 planes makes it the largest airline in the world. Over 80,000 trucks complete the delivery process.

The $150 million hub opened in Guangzhou in 2009 lies in the heart of one of China's fastest-growing manufacturing districts. FedEx controls 39% of the China-to-U.S. air express market.

number of points with fewer aircraft than the traditional City A–to–City B system. It also allows FedEx to match aircraft flights with package loads each night and to reroute flights when load volume requires it, a major cost savings. Moreover, FedEx also believes that the central hub system helps reduce mishandling and delay in transit because there is total control over the packages from pickup point through delivery.

Chapter 8 **Learning Objectives**

AUTHOR COMMENT
This chapter illustrates techniques organizations use to locate plants, warehouses, stores, or offices.

THE STRATEGIC IMPORTANCE OF LOCATION

World markets continue to expand, and the global nature of business is accelerating. Indeed, one of the most important strategic decisions made by many companies, including FedEx, Mercedes-Benz, and Hard Rock, is where to locate their operations. When FedEx opened its Asian hub in Guangzhou, China, in 2009, it set the stage for "round-the-world" flights linking its Paris and Memphis package hubs to Asia. When Mercedes-Benz announced its plans to build its first major overseas plant in Vance, Alabama, it completed a year of competition among 170 sites in 30 states and two countries. When Hard Rock Cafe opened in Moscow, it ended 3 years of advance preparation of a Russian food-supply chain. The strategic impact, cost, and international aspect of these decisions indicate how significant location decisions are.

VIDEO 8.1
Hard Rock's Location Selection

Firms throughout the world are using the concepts and techniques of this chapter to address the location decision because location greatly affects both fixed and variable costs. Location has a major impact on the overall risk and profit of the company. For instance, depending on the product and type of production or service taking place, transportation costs alone can total as much as 25% of the product's selling price. That is, one-fourth of a firm's total revenue may be needed just to cover freight expenses of the raw materials coming in and finished products going out. Other costs that may be influenced by location include taxes, wages, raw material costs, and rents. When all costs are considered, location may alter total operating expenses as much as 50%.

Companies make location decisions relatively infrequently, usually because demand has outgrown the current plant's capacity or because of changes in labor productivity, exchange rates, costs, or local attitudes. Companies may also relocate their manufacturing or service facilities because of shifts in demographics and customer demand.

Location options include (1) expanding an existing facility instead of moving, (2) maintaining current sites while adding another facility elsewhere, or (3) closing the existing facility and moving to another location.

The location decision often depends on the type of business. For industrial location decisions, the strategy is usually minimizing costs, although innovation and creativity may also be critical. For retail and professional service organizations, the strategy focuses on maximizing revenue. Warehouse location strategy, however, may be driven by a combination of cost and speed of delivery. *The objective of location strategy is to maximize the benefit of location to the firm.*

Location and Costs Because location is such a significant cost and revenue driver, location often has the power to make (or break) a company's business strategy. Key multinationals in every major industry, from automobiles to cellular phones, now have or are planning a presence in each of their major markets. Location decisions to support a low-cost strategy require particularly careful consideration.

Once management is committed to a specific location, many costs are firmly in place and difficult to reduce. For instance, if a new factory location is in a region with high energy costs, even good management with an outstanding energy strategy is starting at a disadvantage. Management is in a similar bind with its human resource strategy if labor in the selected location is expensive, ill-trained, or has a poor work ethic. Consequently, hard work to determine an optimal facility location is a good investment.

Location and Innovation When creativity, innovation, and research and development investments are critical to the operations strategy, the location criteria may change from a focus on costs. When innovation is the focus, four attributes seem to affect overall competitiveness as well as innovation:[1]

[1]See Michael E. Porter and Scott Stern, "Innovation: Location Matters," *MIT Sloan Management Review* 42, no. 4 (Summer 2001): 28–36.

- The presence of high-quality and specialized inputs such as scientific and technical talent
- An environment that encourages investment and intense local rivalry
- Pressure and insight gained from a sophisticated local market
- Local presence of related and supporting industries

Motorola and Intel are among those firms that have rejected low-cost locations when those locations could not support other important aspects of the strategy. In the case of Motorola, when analysis indicated that the infrastructure and education levels could not support specific production technologies, the locations were removed from consideration, even if they were low cost. And Intel opened its newest plant not in Asia but in the U.S. The $3 billion semiconductor facility, with 1,000 workers, ended up in Arizona in 2007 for four reasons: (1) the skilled labor requirements (for employees who understand statistics and scientific principles), (2) protection of intellectual property in the U.S., (3) tax breaks to help cover the cost of equipment, and (4) easy oversight from Intel's California headquarters.

FACTORS THAT AFFECT LOCATION DECISIONS

AUTHOR COMMENT
We now look at major location issues.

Selecting a facility location is becoming much more complex with the globalization of the workplace. As we saw in Chapter 2, globalization has taken place because of the development of (1) market economics; (2) better international communications; (3) more rapid, reliable travel and shipping; (4) ease of capital flow between countries; and (5) high differences in labor costs. Many firms now consider opening new offices, factories, retail stores, or banks outside their home country. Location decisions transcend national borders. In fact, as Figure 8.1 shows, the sequence of location decisions often begins with choosing a country in which to operate.

One approach to selecting a country is to identify what the parent organization believes are key success factors (KSFs) needed to achieve competitive advantage. Six possible country KSFs are listed at the top of Figure 8.1. Using such factors (including some negative ones, such as crime) the World Economic Forum biannually ranks the global competitiveness of 133 countries (see Table 8.1). Switzerland landed first, with the U.S. a close second, in 2009–2010 because of their high rates of saving and investment, openness to trade, quality education, and efficient governments.

Once a firm decides which country is best for its location, it focuses on a region of the chosen country and a community. The final step in the location decision process is choosing a specific

▼ **TABLE 8.1**
Competitiveness of 133 Selected Countries, Based on Annual Surveys of 13,000 Business Executives

Country	2009–2010 Ranking
Switzerland	1
U.S.	2
⋮	
Japan	8
Canada	9
⋮	
UK	13
⋮	
Israel	27
⋮	
China	29
⋮	
Italy	48
India	49
⋮	
Mexico	60
⋮	
Russia	63
⋮	
⋮	
Vietnam	75
⋮	
Zimbabwe	132
Burundi	133

Source: **www.weforum.org,** 2010. Used with permission of World Economic Forum.

Country Decision

Key Success Factors

1. Political risks, government rules, attitudes, incentives
2. Cultural and economic issues
3. Location of markets
4. Labor talent, attitudes, productivity, costs
5. Availability of supplies, communications, energy
6. Exchange rates and currency risk

Region/Community Decision

1. Corporate desires
2. Attractiveness of region (culture, taxes, climate, etc.)
3. Labor availability, costs, attitudes toward unions
4. Cost and availability of utilities
5. Environmental regulations of state and town
6. Government incentives and fiscal policies
7. Proximity to raw materials and customers
8. Land/construction costs

Site Decision

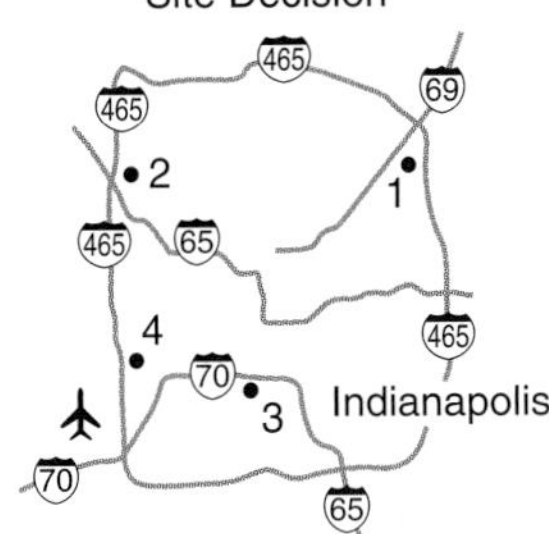

1. Site size and cost
2. Air, rail, highway, and waterway systems
3. Zoning restrictions
4. Proximity of services/supplies needed
5. Environmental impact issues

◀ **FIGURE 8.1**
Some Considerations and Factors That Affect Location Decisions

OM in Action ▶ Quality Coils Pulls the Plug on Mexico

Keith Gibson, president of Quality Coils, Inc., saw the savings of low Mexican wages and headed south. He shut down a factory in Connecticut and opened one in Juarez, where he could pay Mexicans one-third the wage rates he was paying Americans. "All the figures pointed out we should make a killing," says Gibson.

Instead, his company was nearly destroyed. The electromagnetic coil maker regularly lost money during 4 years in Mexico. High absenteeism, low productivity, and problems of long-distance management wore down Gibson until he finally pulled the plug on Juarez.

Moving back to the U.S. and rehiring some of his original workers, Gibson learned, "I can hire one person in Connecticut for what three were doing in Juarez."

When U.S. unions complain that they cannot compete against the low wages in other countries and when the teamster rallies chant "$4 a day/No way!" they overlook several factors. First, productivity in low-wage countries often erases a wage advantage that is not nearly as great as people believe. Second, a host of problems, from poor roads to corrupt governments, run up operating costs. Third, although labor costs in many underdeveloped countries are only one-third of those in the U.S., they may represent less than 10% of total manufacturing costs. Thus, the difference may not overcome other disadvantages. And most importantly, the cost of labor for most U.S. manufacturers is less important than such factors as the skill of the workforce, the quality of transportation, and access to technology.

Sources: Global Information Network (January 8, 2004): 1; and *The Wall Street Journal* (January 13, 2004): A12 and (September 15, 1993): A1.

site within a community. The company must pick the one location that is best suited for shipping and receiving, zoning, utilities, size, and cost. Again, Figure 8.1 summarizes this series of decisions and the factors that affect them.

LO1: Identify and explain seven major factors that affect location decisions

Besides globalization, a number of other factors affect the location decision. Among these are labor productivity, foreign exchange, culture, changing attitudes toward the industry, and proximity to markets, suppliers, and competitors.

Labor Productivity

When deciding on a location, management may be tempted by an area's low wage rates. However, wage rates cannot be considered by themselves, as Quality Coils, Inc., discovered when it opened its plant in Mexico (see the *OM in Action* box "Quality Coils Pulls the Plug on Mexico"). Management must also consider productivity.

As discussed in Chapter 1, differences exist in productivity in various countries. What management is really interested in is the combination of production and the wage rate. For example, if Quality Coils pays $70 per day with 60 units produced per day in Connecticut, it will spend less on labor than at a Mexican plant that pays $25 per day with production of 20 units per day:

$$\frac{\text{Labor cost per day}}{\text{Production (that is, units per day)}} = \text{Labor cost per unit}$$

Case 1: Connecticut plant:

$$\frac{\$70 \text{ Wages per day}}{60 \text{ Units produced per day}} = \frac{\$70}{60} = \$1.17 \text{ per unit}$$

AUTHOR COMMENT Final cost is the critical factor and low productivity can negate low cost.

Case 2: Juarez, Mexico, plant:

$$\frac{\$25 \text{ Wages per day}}{20 \text{ Units produced per day}} = \frac{\$25}{20} = \$1.25 \text{ per unit}$$

LO2: Compute labor productivity

Employees with poor training, poor education, or poor work habits may not be a good buy even at low wages. By the same token, employees who cannot or will not always reach their places of work are not much good to the organization, even at low wages. (Labor cost per unit is sometimes called the *labor content* of the product.)

Exchange Rates and Currency Risk

Although wage rates and productivity may make a country seem economical, unfavorable exchange rates may negate any savings. Sometimes, though, firms can take advantage of a particularly favorable exchange rate by relocating or exporting to a foreign country. However, the values of foreign currencies continually rise and fall in most countries. Such changes could well make what was a good location in 2010 a disastrous one in 2015.

Assembly plants operating along the Mexican side of the border, from Texas to California, are called maquiladoras. Some 3,000 firms and industrial giants such as Toyota, Panasonic, Zenith, Hitachi, and GE operate these plants, which employ over 1 million workers. Mexican wages are low, but at current exchange rates, companies also look to Asia.

Costs

We can divide location costs into two categories, tangible and intangible. **Tangible costs** are those costs that are readily identifiable and precisely measured. They include utilities, labor, material, taxes, depreciation, and other costs that the accounting department and management can identify. In addition, such costs as transportation of raw materials, transportation of finished goods, and site construction are all factored into the overall cost of a location. Government incentives, as we see in the *OM in Action* box "How Alabama Won the Auto Industry," certainly affect a location's cost.

Tangible costs
Readily identifiable costs that can be measured with some precision.

Intangible costs are less easily quantified. They include quality of education, public transportation facilities, community attitudes toward the industry and the company, and quality and attitude of prospective employees. They also include quality-of-life variables, such as climate and sports teams, that may influence personnel recruiting.

Intangible costs
A category of location costs that cannot be easily quantified, such as quality of life and government.

Ethical Issues Location decisions based on costs alone may create ethical situations such as the United Airlines case in Indianapolis (see the *Ethical Dilemma* at the end of this chapter). United accepted $320 million in incentives to open a facility in that location, only to renege a decade later, leaving residents and government holding the bag.[2]

OM in Action ▶ How Alabama Won the Auto Industry

Fifteen years ago, Alabama persuaded Mercedes-Benz to build its first U.S. auto plant in the town of Vance by offering the luxury carmaker $253 million worth of incentives—$169,000 for every job Mercedes promised the state.

Taxpayers considered the deal such a boondoggle that they voted Governor Jim Folsom out of office long before the first Mercedes SUV rolled off the new assembly line in 1997. Today, with 50,000 car-related jobs in Alabama, the deal looks a little more like a bargain—suggesting that the practice of paying millions of taxpayer dollars to lure big employers can *sometimes* have a big payoff.

Mercedes surpassed its pledge to create 1,500 jobs at the Vance plant and currently has a workforce of about 4,000.

In 2001, Honda opened a factory 70 miles east of the Mercedes plant, to build its Odyssey minivan. Toyota Motor Corp.'s plant near Huntsville started producing engines in 2002. Those two automakers also received incentives.

To cement Alabama's reputation as the South's busiest auto-making center, Hyundai Motor Co. of South Korea picked a site near Montgomery for its first U.S. assembly plant. The factory began production in 2005, employing 2,000 workers to make 300,000 sedans and SUVs a year.

Is the state giving away more than it gets in return? That's what many economists argue. Other former foes of incentives now argue that manufacturers' arrivals herald "Alabama's new day."

Sources: Automotive News (June 2, 2008): 30D and (March 10, 2008):16; and *The Wall Street Journal* (August 14, 2007): A6.

[2]So what's a city, county, or state to do? According to *Forbes* (June 19, 2006): 42, "Keep taxes low. Don't grant favors. Pursue non-discriminatory reforms like reining in debt and public spending. Remove barriers rather than trying to steer economic growth to this favored corporation or that one." While many inner cities have languished, Chicago has prospered by focusing on infrastructure and quality-of-life issues. Also see "Is There a Better Way to Court a Company?" *Business Week* (July 23, 2007): 55.

To what extent do companies owe long-term allegiance to a particular country or state or town if they are losing money—or if the firm can make greater profits elsewhere? Is it ethical for developed countries to locate plants in undeveloped countries where sweatshops and child labor are commonly used? Where low wages and poor working conditions are the norm? It has been said that the factory of the future will be a large ship, capable of moving from port to port as costs in one port become noncompetitive.

Political Risk, Values, and Culture

The political risk associated with national, state, and local governments' attitudes toward private and intellectual property, zoning, pollution, and employment stability may be in flux. Governmental positions at the time a location decision is made may not be lasting ones. However, management may find that these attitudes can be influenced by their own leadership.

Worker values may also differ from country to country, region to region, and small town to city. Worker views regarding turnover, unions, and absenteeism are all relevant factors. In turn, these values can affect a company's decision whether to make offers to current workers if the firm relocates to a new location. The case study at the end of this chapter, "Southern Recreational Vehicle Company," describes a St. Louis firm that actively chose *not to relocate* any of its workers when it moved to Mississippi.

One of the greatest challenges in a global operations decision is dealing with another country's culture. Cultural variations in punctuality by employees and suppliers make a marked difference in production and delivery schedules. Bribery likewise creates substantial economic inefficiency, as well as ethical and legal problems in the global arena. As a result, operations managers face significant challenges when building effective supply chains across cultures. Table 8.2 provides one ranking of corruption in countries around the world.

▼ TABLE 8.2 Ranking Corruption in Selected Countries (score of 10 represents a corruption-free country)

Rank	Score
1 Denmark, New Zealand, Sweden	9.3 (tie)
⋮	
9 Canada, Australia	8.7 (tie)
⋮	
18 Japan, U.S., Belgium	7.3 (tie)
⋮	
33 Israel, Dominica	6.0 (tie)
⋮	
80 Brazil, Thailand, Saudi Arabia	3.5 (tie)
⋮	
143 Iran, Yemen	2.3 (tie)
⋮	
177 Haiti	1.4
⋮	
180 Somalia	1.0

Source: Transparency International's 2008 survey, at **www.transparency.org.** Used with permission of Transparency International.

Proximity to Markets

For many firms, locating near customers is extremely important. Particularly, service organizations, like drugstores, restaurants, post offices, or barbers, find that proximity to market is *the* primary location factor. Manufacturing firms find it useful to be close to customers when transporting finished goods is expensive or difficult (perhaps because they are bulky, heavy, or fragile). Foreign-owned auto giants such as Mercedes, Honda, Toyota, and Hyundai are building millions of cars each year in the U.S.

In addition, with just-in-time production, suppliers want to locate near users. For a firm like Coca-Cola, whose product's primary ingredient is water, it makes sense to have bottling plants in many cities rather than shipping heavy (and sometimes fragile glass) containers cross country.

Proximity to Suppliers

Firms locate near their raw materials and suppliers because of (1) perishability, (2) transportation costs, or (3) bulk. Bakeries, dairy plants, and frozen seafood processors deal with *perishable* raw materials, so they often locate close to suppliers. Companies dependent on inputs of heavy or bulky raw materials (such as steel producers using coal and iron ore) face expensive inbound *transportation costs*, so transportation costs become a major factor. And goods for which there is a *reduction in bulk* during production (such as lumber mills locating in the Northwest near timber resources) typically need to be near the raw material.

Proximity to Competitors (Clustering)

Both manufacturing and service organizations also like to locate, somewhat surprisingly, near competitors. This tendency, called **clustering**, often occurs when a major resource is found in that region. Such resources include natural resources, information resources, venture capital resources, and talent resources. Table 8.3 presents nine examples of industries that exhibit clustering, and the reasons why.

Clustering
The location of competing companies near each other, often because of a critical mass of information, talent, venture capital, or natural resources.

Italy may be the true leader when it comes to clustering, however, with northern zones of that country holding world leadership in such specialties as ceramic tile (Modena), gold jewelry (Vicenza), machine tools (Busto Arsizio), cashmere and wool (Biella), designer eyeglasses (Belluma), and pasta machines (Parma).

▼ **TABLE 8.3 Clustering of Companies**

Industry	Locations	Reason for Clustering
Wine making	Napa Valley (U.S.), Bordeaux region (France)	Natural resources of land and climate
Software firms	Silicon Valley, Boston, Bangalore (India)	Talent resources of bright graduates in scientific/technical areas, venture capitalists nearby
Race car building	Huntington/North Hampton region (England)	Critical mass of talent and information
Theme parks (including Disney World, Universal Studios, and Sea World)	Orlando, Florida	A hot spot for entertainment, warm weather, tourists, and inexpensive labor
Electronics firms (such as Sony, IBM, HP, Motorola, and Panasonic)	Northern Mexico	NAFTA, duty-free export to U.S. (24% of all TVs are built here)
Computer hardware manufacturing	Singapore, Taiwan	High technological penetration rates and per capita GDP, skilled/educated workforce with large pool of engineers
Fast-food chains (such as Wendy's, McDonald's, Burger King, and Pizza Hut)	Sites within 1 mile of one another	Stimulate food sales, high traffic flows
General aviation aircraft (including Cessna, Learjet, Boeing, and Raytheon)	Wichita, Kansas	Mass of aviation skills (60–70% of world's small planes/jets built here)
Orthopedic device manufacturing	Warsaw, Indiana	Ready supply of skilled workers, strong U.S. market

METHODS OF EVALUATING LOCATION ALTERNATIVES

Four major methods are used for solving location problems: the factor-rating method, locational break-even analysis, the center-of-gravity method, and the transportation model. This section describes these approaches.

AUTHOR COMMENT
Here are four techniques that help in making good location decisions.

The Factor-Rating Method

There are many factors, both qualitative and quantitative, to consider in choosing a location. Some of these factors are more important than others, so managers can use weightings to make the decision process more objective. The **factor-rating method** is popular because a wide variety of factors, from education to recreation to labor skills, can be objectively included. Figure 8.1 listed a few of the many factors that affect location decisions.

Factor-rating method
A location method that instills objectivity into the process of identifying hard-to-evaluate costs.

The factor-rating method has six steps:

1. Develop a list of relevant factors called *key success factors* (such as those in Figure 8.1).
2. Assign a weight to each factor to reflect its relative importance in the company's objectives.
3. Develop a scale for each factor (for example, 1 to 10 or 1 to 100 points).
4. Have management score each location for each factor, using the scale in step 3.
5. Multiply the score by the weights for each factor and total the score for each location.
6. Make a recommendation based on the maximum point score, considering the results of other quantitative approaches as well.

◀ **EXAMPLE 1**
Factor-rating method for an expanding theme park

Five Flags over Florida, a U.S. chain of 10 family-oriented theme parks, has decided to expand overseas by opening its first park in Europe. It wishes to select between France and Denmark.

APPROACH ▶ The ratings sheet in Table 8.4 lists key success factors that management has decided are important; their weightings and their rating for two possible sites—Dijon, France, and Copenhagen, Denmark—are shown.

▶TABLE 8.4
Weights, Scores, and Solution

AUTHOR COMMENT
These weights do not need to be on a 0–1 scale or total to 1. We can use a 1–10 scale, 1–100 scale, or any other scale we prefer.

Key Success Factor	Weight	Scores (out of 100) France	Scores (out of 100) Denmark	Weighted Scores France	Weighted Scores Denmark
Labor availability and attitude	.25	70	60	(.25)(70) = 17.5	(.25)(60) = 15.0
People-to-car ratio	.05	50	60	(.05)(50) = 2.5	(.05)(60) = 3.0
Per capita income	.10	85	80	(.10)(85) = 8.5	(.10)(80) = 8.0
Tax structure	.39	75	70	(.39)(75) = 29.3	(.39)(70) = 27.3
Education and health	.21	60	70	(.21)(60) = 12.6	(.21)(70) = 14.7
Totals	1.00			70.4	68.0

LO3: Apply the factor-rating method

SOLUTION ▶ Table 8.4 uses weights and scores to evaluate alternative site locations. Given the option of 100 points assigned to each factor, the French location is preferable.

INSIGHT ▶ By changing the points or weights slightly for those factors about which there is some doubt, we can analyze the sensitivity of the decision. For instance, we can see that changing the scores for "labor availability and attitude" by 10 points can change the decision. The numbers used in factor weighting can be subjective and the model's results are not "exact" even though this is a quantitative approach.

LEARNING EXERCISE ▶ If the weight for "tax structure" drops to .20 and the weight for "education and health" increases to .40, what is the new result? [Answer: Denmark is now chosen, with a 68.0 vs. a 67.5 score for France.]

RELATED PROBLEMS ▶ 8.5, 8.6, 8.7, 8.8, 8.9, 8.10, 8.11, 8.12, 8.13, 8.14, 8.15, 8.24, 8.25

EXCEL OM Data File **Ch08Ex1.xls** can be found at **www.pearsonhighered.com/heizer**.

When a decision is sensitive to minor changes, further analysis of the weighting and the points assigned may be appropriate. Alternatively, management may conclude that these intangible factors are not the proper criteria on which to base a location decision. Managers therefore place primary weight on the more quantitative aspects of the decision.

Locational Break-Even Analysis

Locational break-even analysis
A cost–volume analysis to make an economic comparison of location alternatives.

Locational break-even analysis is the use of cost–volume analysis to make an economic comparison of location alternatives. By identifying fixed and variable costs and graphing them for each location, we can determine which one provides the lowest cost. Locational break-even analysis can be done mathematically or graphically. The graphic approach has the advantage of providing the range of volume over which each location is preferable.

The three steps to locational break-even analysis are as follows:

1. Determine the fixed and variable cost for each location.
2. Plot the costs for each location, with costs on the vertical axis of the graph and annual volume on the horizontal axis.
3. Select the location that has the lowest total cost for the expected production volume.

EXAMPLE 2 ▶
Locational break-even for a parts manufacturer

John Kros, owner of Carolina Ignitions Manufacturing, needs to expand his capacity. He is considering three locations—Akron, Bowling Green, and Chicago—for a new plant. The company wishes to find the most economical location for an expected volume of 2,000 units per year.

APPROACH ▶ Kros conducts locational break-even analysis. To do so, he determines that fixed costs per year at the sites are $30,000, $60,000, and $110,000, respectively; and variable costs are $75 per unit, $45 per unit, and $25 per unit, respectively. The expected selling price of each ignition system produced is $120.

SOLUTION: ▶ For each of the three locations, Kros can plot the fixed costs (those at a volume of zero units) and the total cost (fixed costs + variable costs) at the expected volume of output. These lines have been plotted in Figure 8.2.

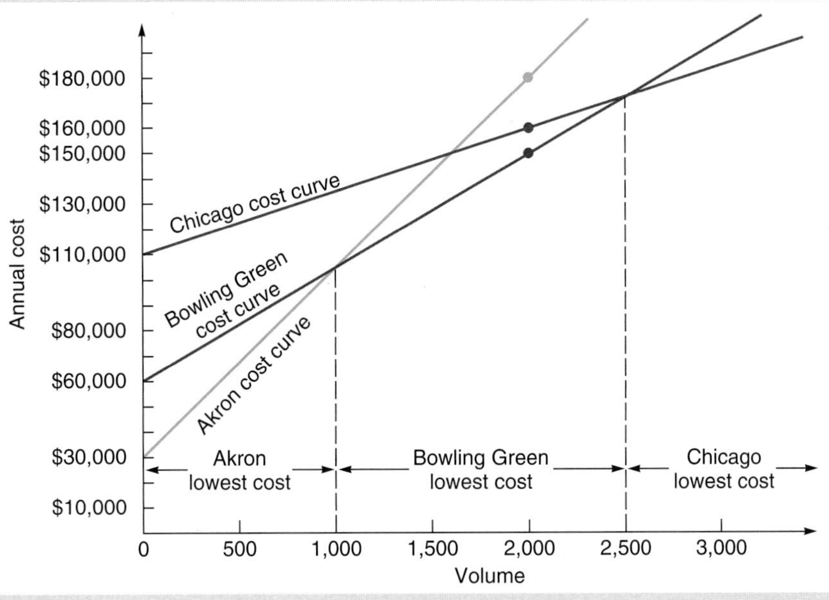

◀ **FIGURE 8.2 Crossover Chart for Locational Break-Even Analysis**

For Akron:

$$\text{Total cost} = \$30{,}000 + \$75(2{,}000) = \$180{,}000$$

For Bowling Green:

$$\text{Total cost} = \$60{,}000 + \$45(2{,}000) = \$150{,}000$$

For Chicago:

$$\text{Total cost} = \$110{,}000 + \$25(2{,}000) = \$160{,}000$$

LO4: Complete a locational break-even analysis graphically and mathematically

With an expected volume of 2,000 units per year, Bowling Green provides the lowest cost location. The expected profit is:

$$\text{Total revenue} - \text{Total cost} = \$120(2{,}000) - \$150{,}000 = \$90{,}000 \text{ per year}$$

The crossover point for Akron and Bowling Green is:

$$30{,}000 + 75(x) = 60{,}000 + 45(x)$$
$$30(x) = 30{,}000$$
$$x = 1{,}000$$

and the crossover point for Bowling Green and Chicago is:

$$60{,}000 + 45(x) = 110{,}000 + 25(x)$$
$$20(x) = 50{,}000$$
$$x = 2{,}500$$

INSIGHT ▶ As with every other OM model, locational break-even results can be sensitive to input data. For example, for a volume of less than 1,000, Akron would be preferred. For a volume greater than 2,500, Chicago would yield the greatest profit.

LEARNING EXERCISE ▶ The variable cost for Chicago is now expected to be $22 per unit. What is the new crossover point between Bowling Green and Chicago? [Answer: 2,174 units.]

RELATED PROBLEMS ▶ 8.16, 8.17, 8.18, 8.19

EXCEL OM Data File **Ch08Ex2.xls** can be found at **www.pearsonhighered.com/heizer**.

Center-of-Gravity Method

Center-of-gravity method
A mathematical technique used for finding the best location for a single distribution point that services several stores or areas.

The **center-of-gravity method** is a mathematical technique used for finding the location of a distribution center that will minimize distribution costs. The method takes into account the location of markets, the volume of goods shipped to those markets, and shipping costs in finding the best location for a distribution center.

The first step in the center-of-gravity method is to place the locations on a coordinate system. This will be illustrated in Example 3. The origin of the coordinate system and the scale used are arbitrary, just as long as the relative distances are correctly represented. This can be done easily by placing a grid over an ordinary map. The center of gravity is determined using Equations (8-1) and (8-2):

$$x\text{-coordinate of the center of gravity} = \frac{\sum_i d_{ix}Q_i}{\sum_i Q_i} \quad \text{(8-1)}$$

$$y\text{-coordinate of the center of gravity} = \frac{\sum_i d_{iy}Q_i}{\sum_i Q_i} \quad \text{(8-2)}$$

LO5: Use the center-of-gravity method

where d_{ix} = x-coordinate of location i
d_{iy} = y-coordinate of location i
Q_i = Quantity of goods moved to or from location i

Note that Equations (8-1) and (8-2) include the term Q_i, the quantity of supplies transferred to or from location i.

Since the number of containers shipped each month affects cost, distance alone should not be the principal criterion. The center-of-gravity method assumes that cost is directly proportional to both distance and volume shipped. The ideal location is that which minimizes the weighted distance between the warehouse and its retail outlets, where the distance is weighted by the number of containers shipped.[3]

EXAMPLE 3 ▶
Center of gravity

Quain's Discount Department Stores, a chain of four large Target-type outlets, has store locations in Chicago, Pittsburgh, New York, and Atlanta; they are currently being supplied out of an old and inadequate warehouse in Pittsburgh, the site of the chain's first store. The firm wants to find some "central" location in which to build a new warehouse.

APPROACH ▶ Quain will apply the center-of-gravity method. It gathers data on demand rates at each outlet (see Table 8.5).

▶TABLE 8.5
Demand for Quain's Discount Department Stores

Store Location	Number of Containers Shipped per Month
Chicago	2,000
Pittsburgh	1,000
New York	1,000
Atlanta	2,000

[3]Equations (8–1) and (8–2) compute a center of gravity (COG) under "squared Euclidean" distances and may actually result in transportation costs slightly (less than 2%) higher than an *optimal* COG computed using "Euclidean" (straight-line) distances. The latter, however, is a more complex and involved procedure mathematically, so the formulas we present are generally used as an attractive substitute. See C. Kuo and R. E. White, "A Note on the Treatment of the Center-of-Gravity Method in Operations Management Textbooks," *Decision Sciences Journal of Innovative Education* 2 (Fall 2004): 219–227.

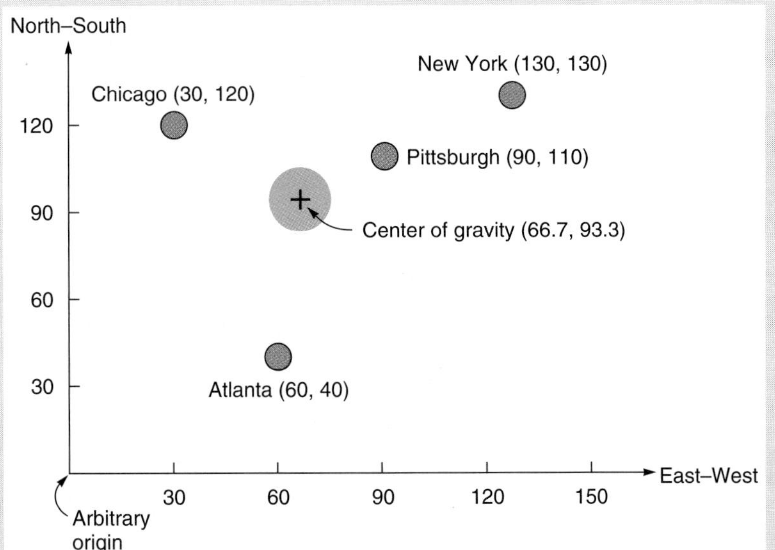

◀ **FIGURE 8.3**
Coordinate Locations of Four Quain's Department Stores and Center of Gravity

Its current store locations are shown in Figure 8.3. For example, location 1 is Chicago, and from Table 8.5 and Figure 8.3, we have:

$$d_{1x} = 30$$
$$d_{1y} = 120$$
$$Q_1 = 2{,}000$$

SOLUTION ▶ Using the data in Table 8.5 and Figure 8.3 for each of the other cities, and Equations (8–1) and (8–2) we find:

x-coordinate of the center of gravity:

$$= \frac{(30)(2000) + (90)(1000) + (130)(1000) + (60)(2000)}{2000 + 1000 + 1000 + 2000} = \frac{400{,}000}{6{,}000}$$

$$= 66.7$$

y-coordinate of the center of gravity:

$$= \frac{(120)(2000) + (110)(1000) + (130)(1000) + (40)(2000)}{2000 + 1000 + 1000 + 2000} = \frac{560{,}000}{6{,}000}$$

$$= 93.3$$

This location (66.7, 93.3) is shown by the crosshairs in Figure 8.3.

INSIGHT ▶ By overlaying a U.S. map on this exhibit, we find this location is near central Ohio. The firm may well wish to consider Columbus, Ohio, or a nearby city as an appropriate location. But it is important to have both North–South and East–West interstate highways near the city selected to make delivery times quicker.

LEARNING EXERCISE ▶ The number of containers shipped per month to Atlanta is expected to grow quickly to 3,000. How does this change the center of gravity, and where should the new warehouse be located? [Answer: (65.7, 85.7), which is closer to Cincinnati, Ohio.]

RELATED PROBLEMS ▶ 8.20, 8.21, 8.22, 8.23

EXCEL OM Data File Ch08Ex3.xls can be found at **www.pearsonhighered.com/heizer**

ACTIVE MODEL 8.1 This example is further illustrated in Active Model 8.1 at **www.pearsonhighered.com/heizer**.

Transportation Model

The objective of the **transportation model** is to determine the best pattern of shipments from several points of supply (sources) to several points of demand (destinations) so as to minimize total production and transportation costs. Every firm with a network of supply-and-demand points faces such a problem. The complex Volkswagen supply network (shown in Figure 8.4)

Transportation model
A technique for solving a class of linear programming problems.

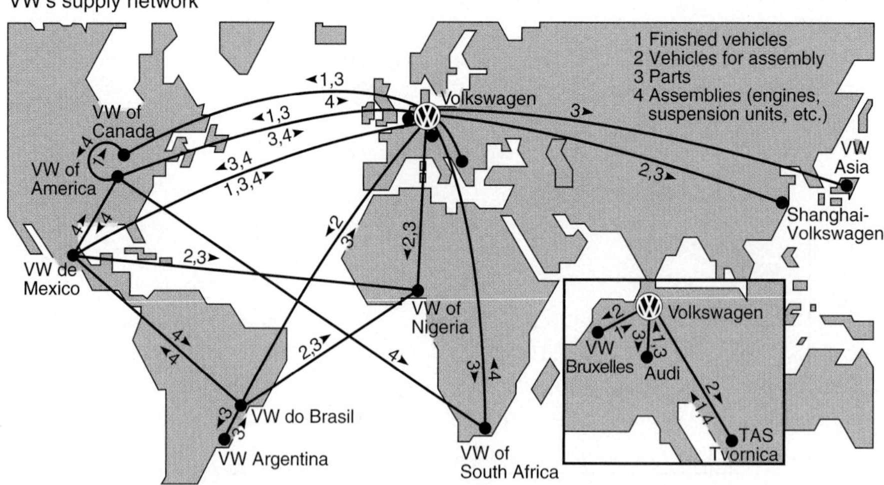

► **FIGURE 8.4**
Worldwide Distribution of Volkswagens and Parts
Source: The Economist, Ltd. Distributed by *The New York Times*/Special Edition.

provides one such illustration. We note in Figure 8.4, for example, that VW de Mexico ships vehicles for assembly and parts to VW of Nigeria, sends assemblies to VW do Brasil, and receives parts and assemblies from headquarters in Germany.

Although the linear programming (LP) technique can be used to solve this type of problem, more efficient, special-purpose algorithms have been developed for the transportation application. The transportation model finds an initial feasible solution and then makes step-by-step improvement until an optimal solution is reached.

AUTHOR COMMENT
Retail stores often attract more shoppers when competitors are close.

SERVICE LOCATION STRATEGY

While the focus in industrial-sector location analysis is on minimizing cost, the focus in the service sector is on maximizing revenue. This is because manufacturing firms find that costs tend to vary substantially among locations, while service firms find that location often has more impact on revenue than cost. Therefore, for the service firm, a specific location often influences revenue more than it does cost. This means that the location focus for service firms should be on determining the volume of business and revenue. See the *OM in Action* box "Location Analysis Tools Help Starbucks Brew Up New Cafes."

OM in Action ► Location Analysis Tools Help Starbucks Brew Up New Cafes

The secret to Starbucks Coffee's plan to open three new cafes around the world every day isn't in the coffee beans–it is in the location. The company's phenomenal growth has been fueled by site-selection software that strengthens the strategic decision-making process. The analysis is as follows: If a site's potential is not within a certain ROI parameter, the company doesn't waste its time.

Every site-acquisition decision evaluates geocoded demographic and consumer data. In the U.S., this is simple. Data from geographic information systems provides population, age, purchasing power, traffic counts, and competition on virtually every block in the country. Planners instantly see all the surrounding shops, proposed locations, and competing sites. When Starbucks entered Japan and China, the unavailability of these data was the biggest challenge.

"In the U.S., if you see a mall, it will probably still be there in two years," says Ernest Luk, VP for Starbucks Asia-Pacific. "A year passes by in a Chinese location, and you almost won't know your way around there anymore." So a team of "hot-spot" seekers traces the paths of where potential customers live, work, and play. Although Starbucks is a barely affordable luxury (at $2.65 for a medium latte where the average income is $143 per month in Shanghai), people don't go for just the coffee. "They go there to present themselves as modern Chinese in a public setting. Chinese are proudly conspicuous," says the North Asia director of the ad firm J. Walter Thompson.

With more than 500 stores in Japan and reaching saturation in key cities like Tokyo, Starbucks and its competition are finding more innovative locations. New cafes in a Nissan auto showroom, in office building lobbies, and in supermarkets remind us that it all boils down to location, location, location . . . determined by the latest site-selection technology.

Sources: The Wall Street Journal (April 3, 2007): B1, (September 1, 2006): A11–A12, and (July 29, 2005): C2; and *SinoCast China Business Daily News* (September 21, 2005): 1.

There are eight major determinants of volume and revenue for the service firm:

1. Purchasing power of the customer-drawing area
2. Service and image compatibility with demographics of the customer-drawing area
3. Competition in the area
4. Quality of the competition
5. Uniqueness of the firm's and competitors' locations
6. Physical qualities of facilities and neighboring businesses
7. Operating policies of the firm
8. Quality of management

Realistic analysis of these factors can provide a reasonable picture of the revenue expected. The techniques used in the service sector include correlation analysis, traffic counts, demographic analysis, purchasing power analysis, the factor-rating method, the center-of-gravity method, and geographic information systems. Table 8.6 provides a summary of location strategies for both service and goods-producing organizations.

How Hotel Chains Select Sites

One of the most important decisions in the hospitality industry is location. Hotel chains that pick good sites more accurately and quickly than competitors have a distinct strategic advantage. La Quinta Corporation is a moderately priced chain of 590 motels oriented toward frequent business travelers. To model motel-selection behavior and predict success of a site, La Quinta turned to statistical regression analysis.[4]

The hotel started by testing 35 independent variables, trying to find which of them would have the highest correlation with predicted profitability, the dependent variable. "Competitive" independent variables included the number of hotel rooms in the vicinity and average room rates. "Demand generator" variables were such local attractions as office buildings and hospitals that drew potential customers to a 4-mile-radius trade area. "Demographic" variables, such as local population and unemployment rate, can also affect the success of a hotel. "Market awareness" factors, such as the number of inns in a region, were a fourth category. Finally, "physical characteristics" of the site, such as ease of access or sign visibility, provided the last group of the 35 independent variables.

In the end, the regression model chosen, with a coefficient of determination (r^2) of 51%, included just four predictive variables. They are the *price of the inn*, *median income levels*, the

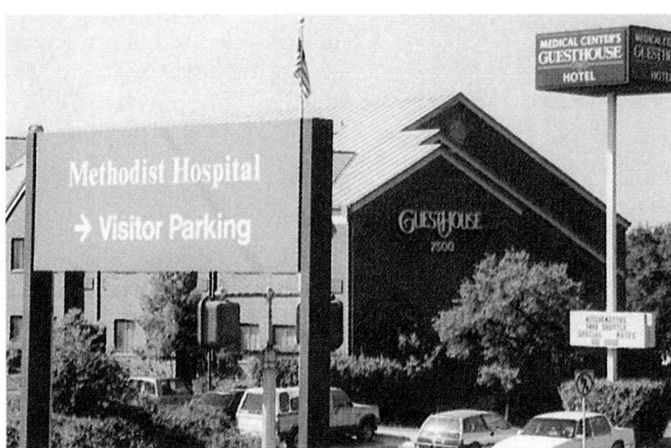

Picking good sites for service operations such as fast-food restaurants and hotels is increasingly difficult because of saturated markets. But opportunities still exist. Subway (on the left), with over 20,000 U.S. outlets (vs. 13,700 for McDonald's) has found success with "nontraditional" locations. True Bethel Baptist Church in Buffalo, New York, now houses a Subway. Similarly, a kosher Subway just opened in the Jewish Community Center of Cleveland. Good sites for hotels include those near hospitals and medical centers (right photo). Outpatient care, shorter hospital stays, and more diagnostic tests increase this need to house patients and their families.

[4]Sheryl Kimes and James Fitzsimmons, "Selecting Profitable Hotel Sites at La Quinta Motor Inns," *Interfaces* (March–April 1990): 12–20. Also see *The Wall Street Journal* (July 19, 1995): B1, B5, for a discussion of how Amerihost Inns makes its location decisions.

TABLE 8.6
Location Strategies—Service vs. Goods-Producing Organizations

AUTHOR COMMENT
This table helps differentiate between service- and manufacturing-sector decisions. Almost every aspect of the decision is different.

SERVICE/RETAIL/PROFESSIONAL	GOODS-PRODUCING
Revenue Focus	**Cost Focus**
Volume/revenue Drawing area; purchasing power Competition; advertising/pricing **Physical quality** Parking/access; security/lighting; appearance/image **Cost determinants** Rent Management caliber Operation policies (hours, wage rates)	**Tangible costs** Transportation cost of raw material Shipment cost of finished goods Energy and utility cost; labor; raw material; taxes, and so on **Intangible and future costs** Attitude toward union Quality of life Education expenditures by state Quality of state and local government
Techniques	**Techniques**
Regression models to determine importance of various factors Factor-rating method Traffic counts Demographic analysis of drawing area Purchasing power analysis of area Center-of-gravity method Geographic information systems	Transportation method Factor-rating method Locational break-even analysis Crossover charts
Assumptions	**Assumptions**
Location is a major determinant of revenue High customer-contact issues are critical Costs are relatively constant for a given area; therefore, the revenue function is critical	Location is a major determinant of cost Most major costs can be identified explicitly for each site Low customer contact allows focus on the identifiable costs Intangible costs can be evaluated

LO6: Understand the differences between service- and industrial-sector location analysis

state population per inn, and the *location of nearby colleges* (which serves as a proxy for other demand generators). La Quinta then used the regression model to predict profitability and developed a cutoff that gave the best results for predicting success or failure of a site. A spreadsheet is now used to implement the model, which applies the decision rule and suggests "build" or "don't build."

The Call Center Industry

Industries and office activities that require neither face-to-face contact with the customer nor movement of material broaden location options substantially. A case in point is the call center industry, in which the traditional variables are no longer relevant. Where inexpensive fiber-optic phone lines are available, the cost and availability of labor may drive the location decision.

A decade or so ago, big U.S. companies started hiring call center staff in low-wage countries like India to deal with customer contact jobs, such as product support, hotel reservations, and bill collection. India's highly educated, English-speaking workforce still attracts a large call center business. But the Philippines, Mexico, Canada, Ireland, and small-town U.S. are increasingly destinations of choice for matching employees and in-depth knowledge of American popular culture. The VP of Client-Logic, Inc., a firm that sets up call centers for companies such as DIRECTV, Sony, and TiVo, says "I'm looking for people who already know that Barbie's boyfriend is Ken." He increasingly likes Monterrey, Mexico, because the town's mall has an American-style 13-screen Cineplex, which shows almost all Hollywood films—meaning locals pick up U.S. slang, fashion trends, brands, and geography.[5]

How to use quantitative techniques to locate call centers is discussed in detail in Supplement 11.

[5]"Siting a Call Center? Check Out the Mall First." *The Wall Street Journal* (July 3, 2006): B1, B3.

Geographic Information Systems

Geographic information systems are an important tool to help firms make successful, analytical decisions with regard to location. A **geographic information system (GIS)** stores and displays information that can be linked to a geographical location. For instance, retailers, banks, food chains, gas stations, and print shop franchises can all use geographically coded files from a GIS to conduct demographic analyses. By combining population, age, income, traffic flow, and density figures with geography, a retailer can pinpoint the best location for a new store or restaurant.

Geographic information system (GIS)
A system that stores and displays information that can be linked to a geographic location.

Here are some of the geographic databases available in many GISs:

- Census data by block, tract, city, county, congressional district, metropolitan area, state, zip code
- Maps of every street, highway, bridge, and tunnel in the U.S.
- Utilities such as electrical, water, and gas lines
- All rivers, mountains, lakes, forests
- All major airports, colleges, hospitals

For example, airlines use GISs to identify airports where ground services are the most effective. This information is then used to help schedule and to decide where to purchase fuel, meals, and other services.

Commercial office building developers use GISs in the selection of cities for future construction. Building new office space takes several years so developers value the database approach that a GIS can offer. GIS is used to analyze factors that influence the location decisions by addressing five elements for each city: (1) residential areas, (2) retail shops, (3) cultural and entertainment centers, (4) crime incidence, and (5) transportation options. For example, one study of Tampa, Florida, showed that the city's central business district lacks the characteristics to sustain a viable high-demand office market, suggesting that builders should look elsewhere.

Here are five more examples of how location-scouting GIS software is turning commercial real estate into a science[6]:

- *Carvel Ice Cream:* This 73-year-old chain of ice cream shops uses GIS to create a demographic profile of what a typically successful neighborhood for a Carvel looks like—mostly in terms of income and ages.

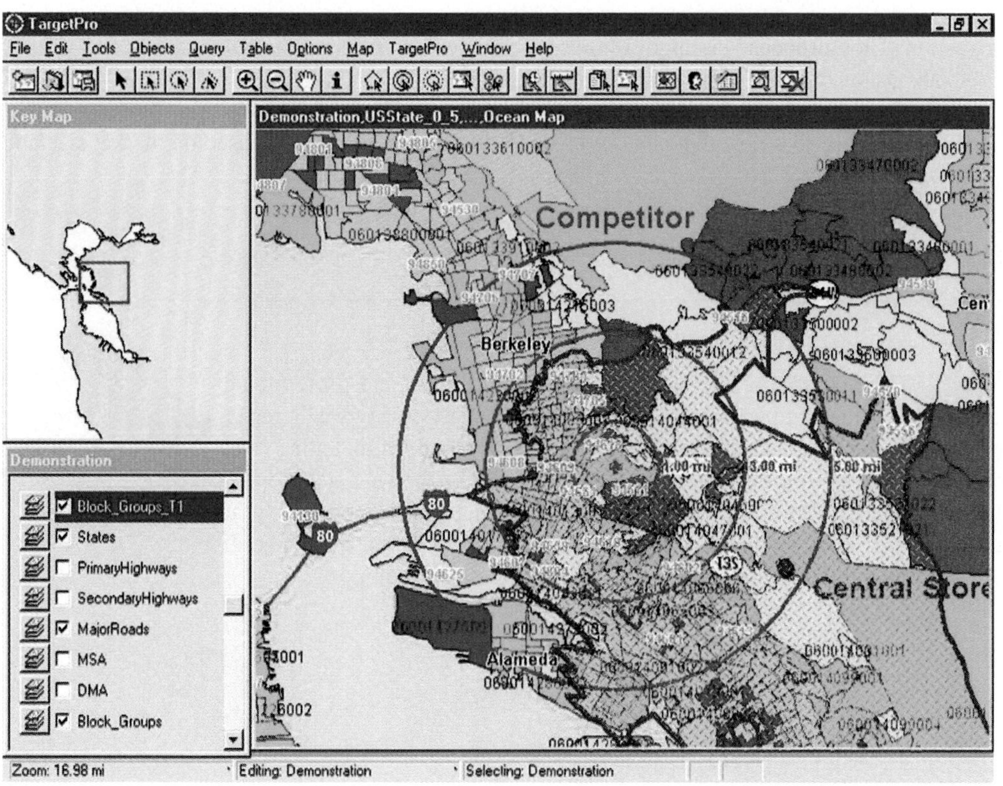

Geographic information systems (GISs) are used by a variety of firms, including Darden Restaurants, to identify target markets by income, ethnicity, product use, age, etc. Here, data from MapInfo helps with competitive analysis. Three concentric blue rings, each representing various mile radii, were drawn around the competitor's store. The heavy red line indicates the "drive" time to the firm's own central store (the red dot).

[6] *The Wall Street Journal* (July 3, 2007): B1 and (July 18, 2005): R-7; and *Business 2.0* (May 2004): 76–77.

- *Saber Roofing:* Rather than send workers out to estimate the costs for reroofing jobs, this Redwood City, California, firm pulls up aerial shots of the building via Google Earth. The owner can measure roofs, eyeball the conditions, and e-mail the client an estimate, saving hundreds of miles of driving daily. In one case, while on the phone, a potential client was told her roof was too steep for the company to tackle after the Saber employee quickly looked up the home on Google Earth.
- *Arby's:* As this fast-food chain learned, specific products can affect behavior. Using MapInfo, Arby's discovered that diners drove up to 20% farther for their roast beef sandwich (which they consider a "destination" product) than for its chicken sandwich.
- *Home Depot:* Wanting a store in New York City, even though Home Depot demographics are usually for customers who own big homes, the company opened in Queens when GIS software predicted it would do well. Although most people there live in apartments and very small homes, the store has become one of the chain's highest-volume outlets. Similarly, Home Depot thought it had saturated Atlanta two decades ago, but GIS analysis suggested expansion. There are now over 40 Home Depots in that area.
- *Jo-Ann Stores:* This fabric and craft retailer's 70 superstores were doing well a few years ago, but managers were afraid more big-box stores could not justify building expenses. So Jo-Ann used its GIS to create an ideal customer profile—female homeowners with families—and mapped it against demographics. The firm found it could build 700 superstores, which in turn increased the sales from $105 to $150 per square foot.

Other packages similar to MapInfo are Hemisphere Solutions (by Unisys Corp.), Atlas GIS (from Strategic Mapping, Inc.), Arc/Info (by ESRI), SAS/GIS (by SAS Institute, Inc.), Market Base (by National Decision Systems, Inc.), and MapPoint 2009 (by Microsoft).

To illustrate how extensive some of these GISs can be, consider Microsoft's MapPoint 2009, which includes a comprehensive set of map and demographic data. Its North American maps have more than 6.4 million miles of streets and 1.9 million points of interest to allow users to locate restaurants, airports, hotels, gas stations, ATMs, museums, campgrounds, and freeway exits. Demographic data includes statistics for population, age, income, education, and housing for 1980, 1990, 2000, and 2005. These data can be mapped by state, county, city, zip code, or census tract. MapPoint 2009 produces maps that identify business trends; pinpoint market graphics; locate clients, customers, and competitors; and visualize sales performance and product distribution. The European version of MapPoint includes 7.8 million kilometers of roads as well as 400,000 points of interest (see **www.mapapps.net**).

VIDEO 8.2
Locating the Next Red Lobster Restaurant

The *Video Case Study* "Locating the Next Red Lobster Restaurant" that appears at the end of this chapter describes how that chain uses its GIS to define trade areas based on market size and population density.

CHAPTER SUMMARY

Location may determine up to 50% of operating expense. Location is also a critical element in determining revenue for the service, retail, or professional firm. Industrial firms need to consider both tangible and intangible costs. Industrial location problems are typically addressed via a factor-rating method, locational break-even analysis, the center-of-gravity method, and the transportation method of linear programming.

For service, retail, and professional organizations, analysis is typically made of a variety of variables including purchasing power of a drawing area, competition, advertising and promotion, physical qualities of the location, and operating policies of the organization.

Key Terms

Tangible costs (p. 317)
Intangible costs (p. 317)
Clustering (p. 318)
Factor-rating method (p. 319)
Locational break-even analysis (p. 320)
Center-of-gravity method (p. 322)
Transportation model (p. 323)
Graphical information system (GIS) (p. 327)

Ethical Dilemma

In this chapter, we have discussed a number of location decisions. Consider another: United Air Lines announced its competition to select a town for a new billion-dollar aircraft-repair base. The bidding for the prize of 7,500 jobs paying at least $25 per hour was fast and furious, with Orlando offering $154 million in incentives and Denver more than twice that amount. Kentucky's governor angrily rescinded Louisville's offer of $300 million, likening the bidding to "squeezing every drop of blood out of a turnip."

When United finally selected from among the 93 cities bidding on the base, the winner was Indianapolis and its $320 million offer of taxpayers' money.

But in 2003, with United near bankruptcy, and having fulfilled its legal obligation, the company walked away from the massive center. This left the city and state governments out all that money, with no new tenant in sight. The city now even owns the tools, neatly arranged in each of the 12 elaborately equipped hangar bays. United outsourced its maintenance to mechanics at a Southern firm (which pays one-third of what United gave out in salary and benefits in Indianapolis).

What are the ethical, legal, and economic implications of such location bidding wars? Who pays for such giveaways? Are local citizens allowed to vote on offers made by their cities, counties, or states? Should there be limits on these incentives?

Discussion Questions

1. How is FedEx's location a competitive advantage? Discuss.
2. Why do so many U.S. firms build facilities in other countries?
3. Why do so many foreign companies build facilities in the U.S.?
4. What is clustering?
5. How does factor weighting incorporate personal preference in location choices?
6. What are the advantages and disadvantages of a qualitative (as opposed to a quantitative) approach to location decision making?
7. Provide two examples of clustering in the service sector.
8. What are the major factors that firms consider when choosing a country in which to locate?
9. What factors affect region/community location decisions?
10. Although most organizations may make the location decision infrequently, there are some organizations that make the decision quite regularly and often. Provide one or two examples. How might their approach to the location decision differ from the norm?
11. List factors, other than globalization, that affect the location decision.
12. Explain the assumptions behind the center-of-gravity method. How can the model be used in a service facility location?
13. What are the three steps to locational break-even analysis?
14. "Manufacturers locate near their resources, retailers locate near their customers." Discuss this statement, with reference to the proximity-to-markets arguments covered in the text. Can you think of a counterexample in each case? Support your choices.
15. Why shouldn't low wage rates alone be sufficient to select a location?
16. List the techniques used by service organizations to select locations.
17. Contrast the location of a food distributor and a supermarket. (The distributor sends truckloads of food, meat, produce, etc., to the supermarket.) Show the relevant considerations (factors) they share; show those where they differ.
18. Elmer's Fudge Factory is planning to open 10 retail outlets in Oregon over the next 2 years. Identify (and weight) those factors relevant to the decision. Provide this list of factors and weights.

Using Software to Solve Location Problems

This section presents three ways to solve location problems with computer software. First, you can create your own spreadsheets to compute factor ratings, the center of gravity, and break-even analysis. Second, Excel OM (free with your text and found at our website) is programmed to solve all three models. Third, POM for Windows is also found at **www.pearsonhighered.com/heizer** and can solve all problems labelled with a P.

Creating Your Own Excel Spreadsheets

Excel (and other spreadsheets) are easily developed to solve most of the problems in this chapter. We do not provide an example here, but you can see from Program 8.1 how the formulas are created.

Using Excel OM

Excel OM may be used to solve Example 1 (with the Factor Rating module), Example 2 (with the Break-Even Analysis module), and Example 3 (with the Center-of-Gravity module), as well as other location problems. To illustrate the factor-rating method, consider the case of Five Flags over Florida (Example 1), which wishes to expand its corporate presence to Europe. Program 8.1 provides the data inputs for five important factors, including their weights, and ratings on a 1–100 scale (where 100 is the highest rating) for each country. As we see, France is more highly rated, with a 70.4 score versus 68.0 for Denmark.

▶ PROGRAM 8.1
Excel OM's Factor Rating Module, Including Inputs, Selected Formulas, and Outputs Using Five Flags over Florida Data in Example 1

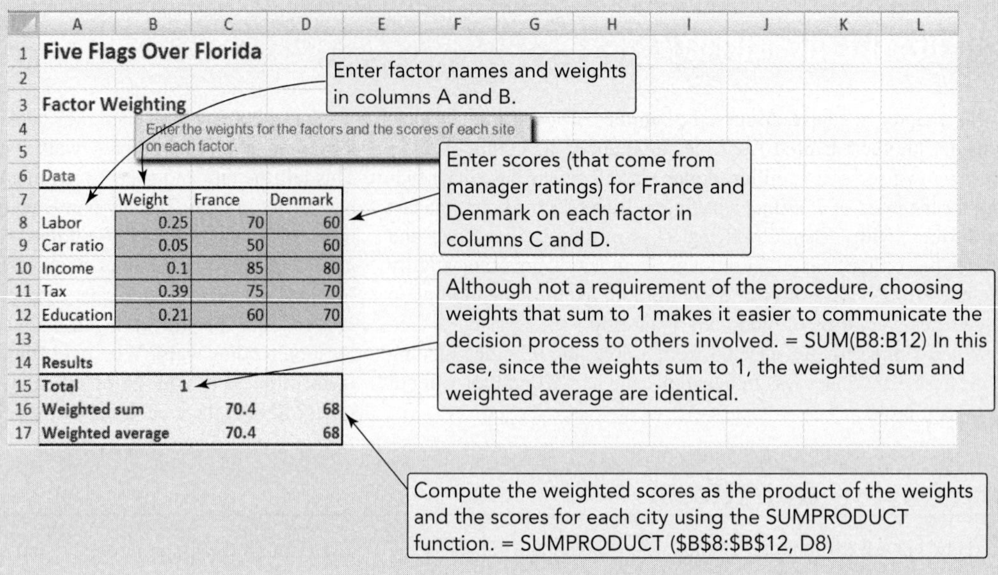

Five Flags Over Florida
Factor Weighting
Enter the weights for the factors and the scores of each site on each factor.
Data
Weight France Denmark
Labor 0.25 70 60
Car ratio 0.05 50 60
Income 0.1 85 80
Tax 0.39 75 70
Education 0.21 60 70
Results
Total 1
Weighted sum 70.4 68
Weighted average 70.4 68
Enter factor names and weights in columns A and B.
Enter scores (that come from manager ratings) for France and Denmark on each factor in columns C and D.
Although not a requirement of the procedure, choosing weights that sum to 1 makes it easier to communicate the decision process to others involved. = SUM(B8:B12) In this case, since the weights sum to 1, the weighted sum and weighted average are identical.
Compute the weighted scores as the product of the weights and the scores for each city using the SUMPRODUCT function. = SUMPRODUCT ($B$8:$B$12, D8)

Using POM for Windows

POM for Windows also includes three different facility location models: the factor-rating method, the center-of-gravity model, and locational break-even analysis. For details, refer to Appendix IV.

Solved Problems

Virtual Office Hours help is available at www.myomlab.com.

▼ SOLVED PROBLEM 8.1

Just as cities and communities can be compared for location selection by the weighted approach model, as we saw earlier in this chapter, so can actual site decisions within those cities. Table 8.7 illustrates four factors of importance to Washington, DC, and the health officials charged with opening that city's first public drug treatment clinic. Of primary concern (and given a weight of 5) was location of the clinic so it would be as accessible as possible to the largest number of patients. Due to a tight budget, the annual lease cost was also of some concern. A suite in the city hall, at 14th and U Streets, was highly rated because its rent would be free. An old office building near the downtown bus station received a much lower rating because of its cost. Equally important as lease cost was the need for confidentiality of patients and, therefore, for a relatively inconspicuous clinic. Finally, because so many of the staff at the clinic would be donating their time, the safety, parking, and accessibility of each site were of concern as well.

Using the factor-rating method, which site is preferred?

▼ SOLUTION

From the three rightmost columns in Table 8.7, the weighted scores are summed. The bus terminal area has a low score and can be excluded from further consideration. The other two sites are virtually identical in total score. The city may now want to consider other factors, including political ones, in selecting between the two remaining sites.

▼ TABLE 8.7 Potential Clinic Sites in Washington, DC

		Potential Locations[a]			*Weighted Scores*		
Factor	**Importance Weight**	**Homeless Shelter (2nd and D, SE)**	**City Hall (14th and U, NW)**	**Bus Terminal Area (7th and H, NW)**	**Homeless Shelter**	**City Hall**	**Bus Terminal Area**
Accessibility for addicts	5	9	7	7	45	35	35
Annual lease cost	3	6	10	3	18	30	9
Inconspicuous	3	5	2	7	15	6	21
Accessibility for health staff	2	3	6	2	6	12	4
				Total scores:	84	83	69

[a] All sites are rated on a 1 to 10 basis, with 10 as the highest score and 1 as the lowest.

Source: From *Service Management and Operations*, 2/e, by Haksever/Render/Russell/Murdick, p. 266. Copyright © 2000. Reprinted by permission of Prentice Hall, Inc., Upper Saddle River, NJ.

▼ SOLVED PROBLEM 8.2

Ching-Chang Kau is considering opening a new foundry in Denton, Texas; Edwardsville, Illinois; or Fayetteville, Arkansas, to produce high-quality rifle sights. He has assembled the following fixed-cost and variable-cost data:

		Per-Unit Costs		
Location	**Fixed Cost per Year**	**Material**	**Variable Labor**	**Overhead**
Denton	\$200,000	\$ .20	\$ .40	\$ .40
Edwardsville	\$180,000	\$ .25	\$ .75	\$ .75
Fayetteville	\$170,000	\$1.00	\$1.00	\$1.00

a) Graph the total cost lines.
b) Over what range of annual volume is each facility going to have a competitive advantage?
c) What is the volume at the intersection of the Edwardsville and Fayetteville cost lines?

▼ SOLUTION

(a) A graph of the total cost lines is shown in Figure 8.5.

(b) Below 8,000 units, the Fayetteville facility will have a competitive advantage (lowest cost); between 8,000 units and 26,666 units, Edwardsville has an advantage; and above 26,666, Denton has the advantage. (We have made the assumption in this problem that other costs—that is, delivery and intangible factors—are constant regardless of the decision.)

(c) From Figure 8.5, we see that the cost line for Fayetteville and the cost line for Edwardsville cross at about 8,000. We can also determine this point with a little algebra:

$$\$180{,}000 + 1.75Q = \$170{,}000 + 3.00Q$$
$$\$10{,}000 = 1.25Q$$
$$8{,}000 = Q$$

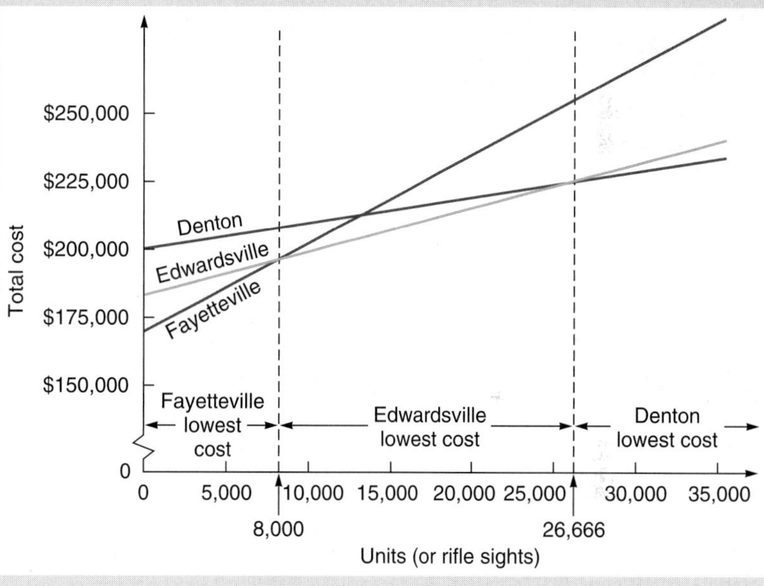

▶ **FIGURE 8.5**
Graph of Total Cost Lines for Ching-Chang Kau

Problems*

• **8.1** In Cambodia, 6 laborers, each making the equivalent of \$3 per day, can produce 40 units per day. In China, 10 laborers, each making the equivalent of \$2 per day, can produce 45 units. In Billings, Montana, two laborers, each making \$60 per day, can make 100 units. Based on labor costs only, which location would be most economical to produce the item?

• **8.2** Refer to Problem 8.1. Shipping cost from Cambodia to Denver, Colorado, the final destination, is \$1.50 per unit. Shipping cost from China to Denver is \$1 per unit, while the shipping cost from Billings to Denver is \$.25 per unit. Considering both labor and transportation costs, which is the most favorable production location?

•• **8.3** You have been asked to analyze the bids for 200 polished disks used in solar panels. These bids have been submitted by three suppliers: Thailand Polishing, India Shine, and Sacramento Glow. Thailand Polishing has submitted a bid of 2,000 baht. India Shine has submitted a bid of 2,000 rupee. Sacramento Glow has submitted a bid of \$200. You check with your local bank and find that \$1 = 10 baht and \$1 = 8 rupee. Which company should you choose?

• **8.4** Refer to Problem 8.3. If the final destination is New Delhi, India, and there is a 30% import tax, which firm should you choose?

•• **8.5** Subway, with more than 20,000 outlets in the U.S., is planning for a new restaurant in Buffalo, New York. Three locations are being considered. The following table gives the factors for each site.

Factor	Weight	Maitland	Baptist Church	Northside Mall
Space	.30	60	70	80
Costs	.25	40	80	30
Traffic density	.20	50	80	60
Neighborhood income	.15	50	70	40
Zoning laws	.10	80	20	90

a) At which site should Subway open the new restaurant?
b) If the weights for Space and Traffic density are reversed, how would this affect the decision? PX

*Note: PX means the problem may be solved with POM for Windows and/or Excel OM.

• **8.6** Gayla Delong owns the Oklahoma Warriors, a minor league baseball team in northwest Oklahoma. She wishes to move the Warriors east, to either Atlanta or Charlotte. The table below gives the factors that Gayla thinks are important, their weights, and the scores for Atlanta and Charlotte.

Factor	Weight	Atlanta	Charlotte
Incentive	.4	80	60
Player satisfaction	.3	20	50
Sports interest	.2	40	90
Size of city	.1	70	30

a) Which site should she select?
b) Charlotte just raised its incentive package, and the new score is 75. Why doesn't this impact your decision in part (a)? PX

•• **8.7** Insurance Company of Latin America (ILA) is considering opening an office in the U.S. The two cities under consideration are Philadelphia and New York. The factor ratings (higher scores are better) for the two cities are given in the following table. In which city should ILA locate?

Factor	Weight	Philadelphia	New York
Customer convenience	.25	70	80
Bank accessibility	.20	40	90
Computer support	.20	85	75
Rental costs	.15	90	55
Labor costs	.10	80	50
Taxes	.10	90	50

PX

•• **8.8** Marilyn Helm Retailers is attempting to decide on a location for a new retail outlet. At the moment, the firm has three alternatives—stay where it is but enlarge the facility; locate along the main street in nearby Newbury; or locate in a new shopping mall in Hyde Park. The company has selected the four factors listed in the following table as the basis for evaluation and has assigned weights as shown:

Factor	Factor Description	Weight
1	Average community income	.30
2	Community growth potential	.15
3	Availability of public transportation	.20
4	Labor availability, attitude, and cost	.35

Helm has rated each location for each factor, on a 100-point basis. These ratings are given below:

	Location		
Factor	Present Location	Newbury	Hyde Park
1	40	60	50
2	20	20	80
3	30	60	50
4	80	50	50

a) What should Helm do?
b) A new subway station is scheduled to open across the street from the present location in about a month, so its third factor score should be raised to 40. How does this change your answer? PX

•• **8.9** A location analysis for Temponi Controls, a small manufacturer of parts for high-technology cable systems, has been narrowed down to four locations. Temponi will need to train assemblers, testers, and robotics maintainers in local training centers. Cecilia Temponi, the president, has asked each potential site to offer training programs, tax breaks, and other industrial incentives. The critical factors, their weights, and the ratings for each location are shown in the following table. High scores represent favorable values.

		Location			
Factor	Weight	Akron, OH	Biloxi, MS	Carthage, TX	Denver, CO
Labor availability	.15	90	80	90	80
Technical school quality	.10	95	75	65	85
Operating cost	.30	80	85	95	85
Land and construction cost	.15	60	80	90	70
Industrial incentives	.20	90	75	85	60
Labor cost	.10	75	80	85	75

a) Compute the composite (weighted average) rating for each location.
b) Which site would you choose?
c) Would you reach the same conclusion if the weights for operating cost and labor cost were reversed? Recompute as necessary and explain. PX

••• **8.10** Consolidated Refineries, headquartered in Houston, must decide among three sites for the construction of a new oil-processing center. The firm has selected the six factors listed below as a basis for evaluation and has assigned rating weights from 1 to 5 on each factor:

Factor	Factor Name	Rating Weight
1	Proximity to port facilities	5
2	Power-source availability and cost	3
3	Workforce attitude and cost	4
4	Distance from Houston	2
5	Community desirability	2
6	Equipment suppliers in area	3

Management has rated each location for each factor on a 1- to 100-point basis.

Factor	Location A	Location B	Location C
1	100	80	80
2	80	70	100
3	30	60	70
4	10	80	60
5	90	60	80
6	50	60	90

a) Which site will be recommended based on *total* weighted scores?
b) If location B's score for Proximity to port facilities was reset at 90, how would the result change?
c) What score would location B need on Proximity to port facilities to change its ranking? PX

•• **8.11** A company is planning on expanding and building a new plant in one of three Southeast Asian countries. Chris Ellis, the manager charged with making the decision, has determined that five key success factors can be used to evaluate the prospective countries. Ellis used a rating system of 1 (least desirable country) to 5 (most desirable) to evaluate each factor.

Key Success Factors	Weight	*Candidate Country Ratings*		
		Taiwan	Thailand	Singapore
Technology	0.2	4	5	1
Level of education	0.1	4	1	5
Political and legal aspects	0.4	1	3	3
Social and cultural aspects	0.1	4	2	3
Economic factors	0.2	3	3	2

a) Which country should be selected for the new plant?
b) Political unrest in Thailand results in a lower score, 2, for Political and legal aspects. Does your conclusion change?
c) What if Thailand's score drops even further, to a 1, for Political and legal aspects? PX

• **8.12** Thomas Green College is contemplating opening a European campus where students from the main campus could go to take courses for 1 of the 4 college years. At the moment, it is considering five countries: Holland, Great Britain, Italy, Belgium, and Greece. The college wishes to consider eight factors in its decision. All the factors have equal weight. The following table illustrates its assessment of each factor for each country (5 is best).

Factor	Factor Description	Holland	Great Britain	Italy	Belgium	Greece
1	Stability of government	5	5	3	5	4
2	Degree to which the population can converse in English	4	5	3	4	3
3	Stability of the monetary system	5	4	3	4	3
4	Communications infrastructure	4	5	3	4	3
5	Transportation infrastructure	5	5	3	5	3
6	Availability of historic/ cultural sites	3	4	5	3	5
7	Import restrictions	4	4	3	4	4
8	Availability of suitable quarters	4	4	3	4	3

(Continued)

a) In which country should Thomas Green College choose to set up its European campus?
b) How would the decision change if the "degree to which the population can converse in English" was not an issue? PX

•• **8.13** Daniel Tracy, owner of Martin Manufacturing, must expand by building a new factory. The search for a location for this factory has been narrowed to four sites: A, B, C, or D. The following table shows the results thus far obtained by Tracy by using the factor-rating method to analyze the problem. The scale used for each factor scoring is 1 through 5.

Factor	Weight	*Site Scores*			
		A	B	C	D
Quality of labor	10	5	4	4	5
Construction cost	8	2	3	4	1
Transportation costs	8	3	4	3	2
Proximity to markets	7	5	3	4	4
Taxes	6	2	3	3	4
Weather	6	2	5	5	4
Energy costs	5	5	4	3	3

a) Which site should Tracy choose?
b) If site D's score for Energy costs increases from a 3 to a 5, do results change?
c) If site A's Weather score is adjusted to a 4, what is the impact? What should Tracy do at this point? PX

••• **8.14** An American consulting firm is planning to expand globally by opening a new office in one of four countries: Germany, Italy,

Key Success Factors	Weight	*Candidate Country Ratings*			
		Germany	Italy	Spain	Greece
Level of education					
Number of consultants	.05	5	5	5	2
National literacy rate	.05	4	2	1	1
Political aspects					
Stability of government	0.2	5	5	5	2
Product liability laws	0.2	5	2	3	5
Environmental regulations	0.2	1	4	1	3
Social and cultural Aspects					
Similarity in language	0.1	4	2	1	1
Acceptability of consultants	0.1	1	4	4	3
Economic factors					
Incentives	0.1	2	3	1	5

Spain, or Greece (see table on prior page). The chief partner entrusted with the decision, L. Wayne Shell, has identified eight key success factors that he views as essential for the success of any consultancy. He used a rating system of 1 (least desirable country) to 5 (most desirable) to evaluate each factor.

a) Which country should be selected for the new office?
b) If Spain's score were lowered in the Stability of government factor, to a 4, how would its overall score change? On this factor, at what score for Spain *would* the rankings change? PX

•• **8.15** A British hospital chain wishes to make its first entry into the U.S. market by building a medical facility in the Midwest, a region with which its director, Doug Moodie, is comfortable because he got his medical degree at Northwestern University. After a preliminary analysis, four cities are chosen for further consideration. They are rated and weighted according to the factors shown below:

		City			
Factor	**Weight**	**Chicago**	**Milwaukee**	**Madison**	**Detroit**
Costs	2.0	8	5	6	7
Need for a facility	1.5	4	9	8	4
Staff availability	1.0	7	6	4	7
Local incentives	0.5	8	6	5	9

a) Which city should Moodie select?
b) Assume a minimum score of 5 is now required for all factors. Which city should be chosen? PX

•• **8.16** The fixed and variable costs for three potential manufacturing plant sites for a rattan chair weaver are shown:

Site	Fixed Cost per Year	Variable Cost per Unit
1	$ 500	$11
2	1,000	7
3	1,700	4

a) Over what range of production is each location optimal?
b) For a production of 200 units, which site is best? PX

• **8.17** Peter Billington Stereo, Inc., supplies car radios to auto manufacturers and is going to open a new plant. The company is undecided between Detroit and Dallas as the site. The fixed costs in Dallas are lower due to cheaper land costs, but the variable costs in Dallas are higher because shipping distances would increase. Given the following costs:

	Dallas	Detroit
Fixed costs	$600,000	$800,000
Variable costs	$28/radio	$22/radio

a) Perform an analysis of the volume over which each location is preferable.
b) How does your answer change if Dallas's fixed costs increase by 10%? PX

••• **8.18** Audi Motors is considering three sites—A, B, and C—at which to locate a factory to build its new-model automobile, the Audi SUV XL500. The goal is to locate at a minimum-cost site, where cost is measured by the annual fixed plus variable costs of production. Audi Motors has gathered the following data:

Site	Annualized Fixed Cost	Variable Cost per Auto Produced
A	$10,000,000	$2,500
B	$20,000,000	$2,000
C	$25,000,000	$1,000

The firm knows it will produce between 0 and 60,000 SUV XL500s at the new plant each year, but, thus far, that is the extent of its knowledge about production plans.

a) For what values of volume, V, of production, if any, is site C a recommended site?
b) What volume indicates site A is optimal?
c) Over what range of volume is site B optimal? Why? PX

•• **8.19** Hugh Leach Corp., a producer of machine tools, wants to move to a larger site. Two alternative locations have been identified: Bonham and McKinney. Bonham would have fixed costs of $800,000 per year and variable costs of $14,000 per standard unit produced. McKinney would have annual fixed costs of $920,000 and variable costs of $13,000 per standard unit. The finished items sell for $29,000 each.

a) At what volume of output would the two locations have the same profit?
b) For what range of output would Bonham be superior (have higher profits)?
c) For what range would McKinney be superior?
d) What is the relevance of break-even points for these cities? PX

•• **8.20** The following table gives the map coordinates and the shipping loads for a set of cities that we wish to connect through a central hub.

City	Map Coordinate (x, y)	Shipping Load
A	(5, 10)	5
B	(6, 8)	10
C	(4, 9)	15
D	(9, 5)	5
E	(7, 9)	15
F	(3, 2)	10
G	(2, 6)	5

a) Near which map coordinates should the hub be located?
b) If the shipments from city A triple, how does this change the coordinates? PX

•• **8.21** A chain of home health care firms in Louisiana needs to locate a central office from which to conduct internal audits and other periodic reviews of its facilities. These facilities are scattered throughout the state, as detailed in the following table. Each site, except for Houma, will be visited three times each year by a team of workers, who will drive from the central office to the site. Houma will be visited five times a year. Which coordinates represent a good central location for this office? What other factors might influence the office location decision? Where would you place this office? Explain.

	Map Coordinates	
City	*X*	*Y*
Covington	9.2	3.5
Donaldsonville	7.3	2.5
Houma	7.8	1.4
Monroe	5.0	8.4
Natchitoches	2.8	6.5
New Iberia	5.5	2.4
Opelousas	5.0	3.6
Ruston	3.8	8.5

PX

•• **8.22** A small rural county has experienced unprecedented growth over the past 6 years, and as a result, the local school district built the new 500-student North Park Elementary School. The district has three older and smaller elementary schools: Washington,

Jefferson, and Lincoln. Now the growth pressure is being felt at the secondary level. The school district would like to build a centrally located middle school to accommodate students and reduce busing costs. The older middle school is adjacent to the high school and will become part of the high school campus.

a) What are the coordinates of the central location?

b) What other factors should be considered before building a school?

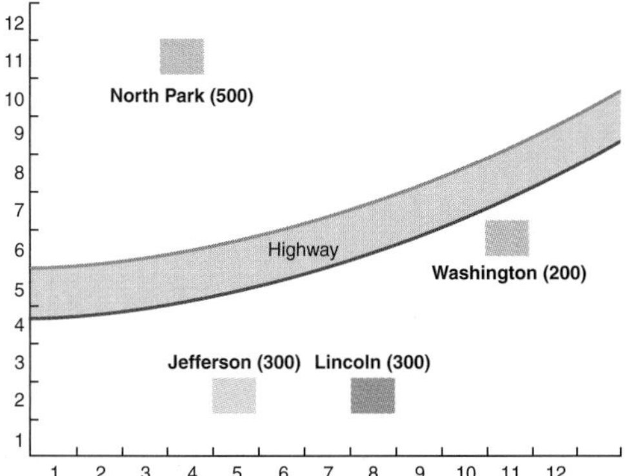

•• **8.23** Todd's Video, a major video rental and TV sales chain headquartered in New Orleans, is about to open its first outlet in Mobile, Alabama, and wants to select a site that will place the new outlet in the center of Mobile's population base. Todd examines the seven census tracts in Mobile, plots the coordinates of the center of each from a map, and looks up the population base in each to use as a weighting. The information gathered appears in the following table.

Census Tract	Population in Census Tract	*X*, *Y* Map Coordinates
101	2,000	(25, 45)
102	5,000	(25, 25)
103	10,000	(55, 45)
104	7,000	(50, 20)
105	10,000	(80, 50)
106	20,000	(70, 20)
107	14,000	(90, 25)

a) At what center-of-gravity coordinates should the new store be located?

b) Census tracts 103 and 105 are each projected to grow by 20% in the next year. How will this influence the new store's coordinates?

•••• **8.24** Eagle Electronics must expand by building a second facility. The search has been narrowed down to locating the new facility in one of four cities: Atlanta (A), Baltimore (B), Chicago (C), or Dallas (D). The factors, scores, and weights follow:

			Scores by Site			
i	Factor	Weight (W_i)	A	B	C	D
1	Labor quality	20	5	4	4	5
2	Quality of life	16	2	3	4	1
3	Transportation	16	3	4	3	2
4	Proximity to markets	14	5	3	4	4
5	Proximity to suppliers	12	2	3	3	4
6	Taxes	12	2	5	5	4
7	Energy supplies	10	5	4	3	3

a) Using the factor-rating method, what is the recommended site for Eagle Electronics's new facility?

b) For what range of values for the weight (currently $w_7 = 10$) does the site given as the answer to part (a) remain a recommended site?

•••• **8.25** The EU has made changes in airline regulation that dramatically affect major European carriers such as British International Air (BIA), KLM, Air France, Alitalia, and Swiss International Air.

Data for Problem 8.25		*Location*								
	Importance	*Italy*			*France*			*Germany*		
Factor	Weight	Milan	Rome	Genoa	Paris	Lyon	Nice	Munich	Bonn	Berlin
Financial incentives	85	8	8	8	7	7	7	7	7	7
Skilled labor pool	80	4	6	5	9	9	7	10	8	9
Existing facility	70	5	3	2	9	6	5	9	9	2
Wage rates	70	9	8	9	4	6	6	4	5	5
Competition for jobs	70	7	3	8	2	8	7	4	8	9
Ease of air traffic access	65	5	4	6	2	8	8	4	8	9
Real estate cost	40	6	4	7	4	6	6	3	4	5
Communication links	25	6	7	6	9	9	9	10	9	8
Attractiveness to relocating executives	15	4	8	3	9	6	6	2	3	3
Political considerations	10	6	6	6	8	8	8	8	8	8
Expansion possibilities	10	10	2	8	1	5	4	4	5	6
Union strength	10	1	1	1	5	5	5	6	6	6

With ambitious expansion plans, BIA has decided it needs a second service hub on the continent, to complement its large Heathrow (London) repair facility. The location selection is critical, and with the potential for 4,000 new skilled blue-collar jobs on the line, virtually every city in western Europe is actively bidding for BIA's business.

After initial investigations by Holmes Miller, head of the Operations Department, BIA has narrowed the list to 9 cities. Each is then rated on 12 factors, as shown in the table.

a) Help Miller rank the top three cities that BIA should consider as its new site for servicing aircraft.
b) After further investigation, Miller decides that an existing set of hangar facilities for repairs is not nearly as important as earlier thought. If he lowers the weight of that factor to 30, does the ranking change?
c) After Miller makes the change in part (b), Germany announces it has reconsidered its offer of financial incentives, with an additional 200-million-euro package to entice BIA. Accordingly, BIA has raised Germany's rating to 10 on that factor. Is there any change in top rankings in part (b)? Px

▶ **Refer to myomlab for these additional homework problems: 8.26–8.34**

Case Studies

▶ Southern Recreational Vehicle Company

In October 2010, top management of Southern Recreational Vehicle Company of St. Louis, Missouri, announced its plans to relocate its manufacturing and assembly operations to a new plant in Ridgecrest, Mississippi. The firm, a major producer of pickup campers and camper trailers, had experienced 5 consecutive years of declining profits as a result of spiraling production costs. The costs of labor and raw materials had increased alarmingly, utility costs had gone up sharply, and taxes and transportation expenses had steadily climbed upward. In spite of increased sales, the company suffered its first net loss since operations were begun in 1982.

When management initially considered relocation, it closely scrutinized several geographic areas. Of primary importance to the relocation decision were the availability of adequate transportation facilities, state and municipal tax structures, an adequate labor supply, positive community attitudes, reasonable site costs, and financial inducements. Although several communities offered essentially the same incentives, the management of Southern Recreational Vehicle Company was favorably impressed by the efforts of the Mississippi Power and Light Company to attract "clean, labor-intensive" industry and the enthusiasm exhibited by state and local officials, who actively sought to bolster the state's economy by enticing manufacturing firms to locate within its boundaries.

Two weeks prior to the announcement, management of Southern Recreational Vehicle Company finalized its relocation plans. An existing building in Ridgecrest's industrial park was selected (the physical facility had previously housed a mobile home manufacturer that had gone bankrupt due to inadequate financing and poor management); initial recruiting was begun through the state employment office; and efforts to lease or sell the St. Louis property were initiated. Among the inducements offered Southern Recreational Vehicle Company to locate in Ridgecrest were:

1. Exemption from county and municipal taxes for 5 years
2. Free water and sewage services
3. Construction of a second loading dock—free of cost—at the industrial site
4. An agreement to issue $500,000 in industrial bonds for future expansion
5. Public-financed training of workers in a local industrial trade school

In addition to these inducements, other factors weighed heavily in the decision to locate in the small Mississippi town. Labor costs would be significantly less than those incurred in St. Louis; organized labor was not expected to be as powerful (Mississippi is a right-to-work state); and utility costs and taxes would be moderate. All in all, management of Southern Recreational Vehicle Company felt that its decision was sound.

On October 15, the following announcement was attached to each employee's paycheck:

> To: Employees of Southern Recreational Vehicle Company
>
> From: Gerald O'Brian, President
>
> The Management of Southern Recreational Vehicle Company regretfully announces its plans to cease all manufacturing operations in St. Louis on December 31. Because of increased operating costs and the unreasonable demands forced upon the company by the union, it has become impossible to operate profitably. I sincerely appreciate the fine service that each of you has rendered to the company during the past years. If I can be of assistance in helping you find suitable employment with another firm, please let me know. Thank you again for your cooperation and past service.

Discussion Questions

1. Evaluate the inducements offered Southern Recreational Vehicle Company by community leaders in Ridgecrest, Mississippi.
2. What problems would a company experience in relocating its executives from a heavily populated industrialized area to a small rural town?
3. Evaluate the reasons cited by O'Brian for relocation. Are they justifiable?
4. What legal and ethical responsibilities does a firm have to its employees when a decision to cease operations is made?

Source: Reprinted by permission of Professor Jerry Kinard, Western Carolina University.

► Locating the Next Red Lobster Restaurant

Video Case

From its first Red Lobster in 1968, Darden Restaurants has grown the chain to 690 locations, with over $2.6 billion in U.S. sales annually. The casual dining market may be crowded, with competitors such as Chili's, Ruby Tuesday, Applebee's, TGI Friday's, and Outback, but Darden's continuing success means the chain thinks there is still plenty of room to grow. Robert Reiner, director of market development, is charged with identifying the sites that will maximize new store sales without cannibalizing sales at the existing Red Lobster locations.

Characteristics for identifying a good site have not changed in 40 years; they still include real estate prices, customer age, competition, ethnicity, income, family size, population density, nearby hotels, and buying behavior, to name just a few. What *has* changed is the powerful software that allows Reiner to analyze a new site in 5 minutes, as opposed to the 8 hours he spent just a few years ago.

Darden has partnered with MapInfo Corp., whose geographic information system (GIS) contains a powerful module for analyzing a trade area (see the discussion of GIS in the chapter). With the U.S. geo-coded down to the individual block, MapInfo allows Reiner to create a psychographic profile of existing and potential Red Lobster trade areas. "We can now target areas with greatest sales potential," says Reiner.

The U.S. is segmented into 72 "clusters" of customer profiles by MapInfo. If, for example, cluster #7, Equestrian Heights (see MapInfo description below), represents 1.7% of a household base within a Red Lobster trade area, but this segment also accounts for 2.4% of sales,

Cluster	PSYTE 2003	Snap Shot Description
7	Equestrian Heights	They may not have a stallion in the barn, but they likely pass a corral on the way home. These families with teens live in older, larger homes adjacent to, or between, suburbs but not usually tract housing. Most are married with teenagers, but 40% are empty nesters. They use their graduate and professional school education—56% are dual earners. Over 90% are white, non-Hispanic. Their mean family income is $99,000, and they live within commuting distance of central cities. They have white-collar jobs during the week but require a riding lawn mower to keep the place up on weekends.

Reiner computes that this segment is effectively spending 1.39 times more than average (Index = 2.4/1.7) and adjusts his analysis of a new site to reflect this added weight.

When Reiner maps the U.S., a state, or a region for a new site, he wants one that is at least 3 miles from the nearest Red Lobster and won't negatively impact its sales by more than 8%; MapInfo pinpoints the best spot. The software also recognizes the nearness of non-Darden competition and assigns a probability of success (as measured by reaching sales potential).

The specific spot selected depends on Darden's seven real estate brokers, whose list of considerations include proximity to a vibrant retail area, proximity to a freeway, road visibility, nearby hotels, and a corner location at a primary intersection.

"Picking a new Red Lobster location is one of the most critical functions we can do at Darden," says Reiner. "And the software we use serves as an independent voice in assessing the quality of an existing or proposed location."

Discussion Questions*

1. Visit the Web site for MapInfo (**www.mapinfo.com**). Describe the psychological profiling (PSYTE) clustering system. Select an industry, other than restaurants, and explain how the software can be used for that industry.
2. What are the major differences in site location for a restaurant vs. a retail store vs. a manufacturing plant?
3. Red Lobster also defines its trade areas based on market size and population density. Here are its seven density classes:

Density Class	Description	Households per Sq. Mile
1	Super Urban	8,000+
2	Urban	4,000–7,999
3	Light Urban	2,000–3,999
4	First Tier Suburban	1,000–1,999
5	Second Tier Suburban	600–999
6	Exurban/Small	100–599
7	Rural	0–99

Note: Density classes are based on the households and land area within 3 miles of the geography (e.g., census tract) using population-weighted centroids.

Ninety-two percent of the Red Lobster restaurants fall into three of these classes. Which three classes do you think the chain has the most restaurants in? Why?

*You may wish to view the video that accompanies this case before answering the questions.

► Where to Place the Hard Rock Cafe

Video Case

Some people would say that Oliver Munday, Hard Rock's vice president for cafe development, has the best job in the world. Travel the world to pick a country for Hard Rock's next cafe, select a city, and find the ideal site. It's true that selecting a site involves lots of incognito walking around, visiting nice restaurants, and drinking in bars. But that is not where Mr. Munday's work begins, nor where it ends. At the front end, selecting the country and city first involves a great deal of research. At the back end, Munday not only picks the final site and negotiates the deal but then works with architects and planners and stays with the project through the opening and first year's sales.

Munday is currently looking heavily into global expansion in Europe, Latin America, and Asia. "We've got to look at political risk, currency, and social norms—how does our brand fit into the country," he says. Once the country is selected, Munday focuses on the region and city. His research checklist is extensive:

Hard Rock's Standard Market Report (for offshore sites)

A. Demographics (local, city, region, SMSA), with trend analysis
   1. Population of area
   2. Economic indicators
B. Visitor market, with trend analysis
   1. Tourists/business visitors
   2. Hotels
   3. Convention center
   4. Entertainment
   5. Sports
   6. Retail
C. Transportation
   1. Airport ← subcategories include: (a) age of airport, (b) no. of passengers, (c) airlines, (d) direct flights, (e) hubs
   2. Rail
   3. Road
   4. Sea/river
D. Restaurants and nightclubs (a selection in key target market areas)
E. Political risk
F. Real estate market
G. Hard Rock Cafe comparable market analysis

Site location now tends to focus on the tremendous resurgence of "city centers," where nightlife tends to concentrate. That's what Munday selected in Moscow and Bogota, although in both locations he chose to find a local partner and franchise the operation. In these two political environments, "Hard Rock wouldn't dream of operating by ourselves," says Munday. The location decision also is at least a 10- to 15-year commitment by Hard Rock, which employs tools such as break-even analysis to help decide whether to purchase land and build, or to remodel an existing facility.

Currently, Munday is considering four European cities for Hard Rock's next expansion. Although he could not provide the names, for competitive reasons, the following is known:

Factor	*European City under Consideration* A	B	C	D	Importance of This Factor at This Time
A. Demographics	70	70	60	90	20
B. Visitor market	80	60	90	75	20
C. Transportation	100	50	75	90	20
D. Restaurants/ nightclubs	80	90	65	65	10
E. Low political risk	90	60	50	70	10
F. Real estate market	65	75	85	70	10
G. Comparable market analysis	70	60	65	80	10

Discussion Questions*

1. From Munday's Standard Market Report checklist, select any other four categories, such as population (A1), hotels (B2), or restaurants/nightclubs (D), and provide three subcategories that should be evaluated. (See item C1 (airport) for a guide.)
2. Which is the highest rated of the four European cities under consideration, using the table above?
3. Why does Hard Rock put such serious effort into its location analysis?
4. Under what conditions do you think Hard Rock prefers to franchise a cafe?

*You may wish to view the video case before answering the questions.

► **Additional Case Study:** Visit **www.myomlab.com** or **www.pearsonhighered.com/heizer** *for this free case study:*
Southwestern University (E): The university faces three choices where to locate its football stadium.

Bibliography

Ballou, Ronald H. *Business Logistics Management*, 5th ed. Upper Saddle River, NJ: Prentice Hall, 2004.

Bartness, A. D. "The Plant Location Puzzle." *Harvard Business Review* 72, no. 2 (March–April 1994).

Denton, B. "Decision Analysis, Location Models, and Scheduling Problems." *Interfaces* 30, no. 3 (May–June 2005): 262–263.

Drezner, Z. *Facility Location: Applications and Theory*. Berlin: Springer-Verlag, 2002.

Florida, R. *The Flight of the Creative Class: The New Global Competition for Talent.* New York: HarperCollins, 2005.

Klamroth, K. *Single Facility Location Problems.* Berlin: Springer-Verlag, 2002.

Kennedy, M. *Introducing Geographic Information Systems with ArcGIS.* New York: Wiley, 2006.

Mentzer, John T. "Seven Keys to Facility Location." *Supply Chain Management Review* 12, no. 5 (May 2008): 25.

Partovi, F. Y. "An Analytic Model for Locating Facilities Strategically." *Omega* 34, no. 1 (January 2006): 41.

Porter, Michael E., and Scott Stern. "Innovation: Location Matters." *MIT Sloan Management Review* (Summer 2001): 28–36.

Render, B., R. M. Stair, and M. Hanna. *Quantitative Analysis for Management*, 10th ed. Upper Saddle River, NJ: Prentice Hall, 2009.

Snyder, L. V. "Facility Location Under Uncertainty." *IIE Transactions* 38, no. 7 (July 2006): 547.

Tallman, Stephen, et al. "Knowledge, Clusters, and Competitive Advantage." *The Academy of Management Review* 29, no. 2 (April 2004): 258–271.

White, G. "Location, Location, Location." *Nation's Restaurant News* 42, no. 27 (July 14, 2008): S10–S11.

Chapter 8 *Rapid* Review

Main Heading	Review Material	PEARSON myomlab
THE STRATEGIC IMPORTANCE OF LOCATION (pp. 314–315)	Location has a major impact on the overall risk and profit of the company. Transportation costs alone can total as much as 25% of the product's selling price. When all costs are considered, location may alter total operating expenses as much as 50%. Companies make location decisions relatively infrequently, usually because demand has outgrown the current plant's capacity or because of changes in labor productivity, exchange rates, costs, or local attitudes. Companies may also relocate their manufacturing or service facilities because of shifts in demographics and customer demand. Location options include (1) expanding an existing facility instead of moving, (2) maintaining current sites while adding another facility elsewhere, and (3) closing the existing facility and moving to another location. For industrial location decisions, the location strategy is usually minimizing costs. For retail and professional service organizations, the strategy focuses on maximizing revenue. Warehouse location strategy may be driven by a combination of cost and speed of delivery. *The objective of location strategy is to maximize the benefit of location to the firm.* When innovation is the focus, overall competitiveness and innovation are affected by (1) the presence of high-quality and specialized inputs such as scientific and technical talent, (2) an environment that encourages investment and intense local rivalry, (3) pressure and insight gained from a sophisticated local market, and (4) local presence of related and supporting industries.	**VIDEO 8.1** Hard Rock's Location Selection
FACTORS THAT AFFECT LOCATION DECISIONS (pp. 315–319)	Globalization has taken place because of the development of (1) market economics; (2) better international communications; (3) more rapid, reliable travel and shipping; (4) ease of capital flow between countries; and (5) large differences in labor costs. Labor cost per unit is sometimes called the *labor content* of the product: Labor cost per unit = Labor cost per day ÷ Production (that is, units per day) Sometimes firms can take advantage of a particularly favorable exchange rate by relocating or exporting to (or importing from) a foreign country. ■ **Tangible costs**—Readily identifiable costs that can be measured with some precision. ■ **Intangible costs**—A category of location costs that cannot be easily quantified, such as quality of life and government. Many service organizations find that proximity to market is *the* primary location factor. Firms locate near their raw materials and suppliers because of (1) perishability, (2) transportation costs, or (3) bulk. ■ **Clustering**—Location of competing companies near each other, often because of a critical mass of information, talent, venture capital, or natural resources.	Problems: 8.1–8.4
METHODS OF EVALUATING LOCATION ALTERNATIVES (pp. 319–324)	■ **Factor-rating method**—A location method that instills objectivity into the process of identifying hard-to-evaluate costs. The six steps of the factor-rating method are: 1. Develop a list of relevant factors called *key success factors.* 2. Assign a weight to each factor to reflect its relative importance in the company's objectives. 3. Develop a scale for each factor (for example, 1 to 10 or 1 to 100 points). 4. Have management score each location for each factor, using the scale in step 3. 5. Multiply the score by the weight for each factor and total the score for each location. 6. Make a recommendation based on the maximum point score, considering the results of other quantitative approaches as well. ■ **Locational break-even analysis**—A cost–volume analysis used to make an economic comparison of location alternatives. The three steps to locational break-even analysis are: 1. Determine the fixed and variable cost for each location. 2. Plot the costs for each location, with costs on the vertical axis of the graph and annual volume on the horizontal axis. 3. Select the location that has the lowest total cost for the expected production volume.	Problems: 8.5–8.25 Virtual Office Hours for Solved Problems: 8.1, 8.2 **ACTIVE MODEL 8.1**

Main Heading	Review Material	
	■ **Center-of-gravity method**—A mathematical technique used for finding the best location for a single distribution point that services several stores or areas. The center-of-gravity method chooses the ideal location that minimizes the *weighted* distance between itself and the locations it serves, where the distance is weighted by the number of containers shipped Q_i: $$x\text{-coordinate of the center of gravity} = \sum_i d_{ix}Q_i \div \sum_i Q_i \quad (8\text{-}1)$$ $$y\text{-coordinate of the center of gravity} = \sum_i d_{iy}Q_i \div \sum_i Q_i \quad (8\text{-}2)$$ ■ **Transportation model**—A technique for solving a class of linear programming problems. The transportation model determines the best pattern of shipments from several points of supply to several points of demand in order to minimize total production and transportation costs.	
SERVICE LOCATION STRATEGY (pp. 324–328)	The eight major determinants of volume and revenue for the service firm are: 1. Purchasing power of the customer-drawing area 2. Service and image compatibility with demographics of the customer-drawing area 3. Competition in the area 4. Quality of the competition 5. Uniqueness of the firm's and competitors' locations 6. Physical qualities of facilities and neighboring businesses 7. Operating policies of the firm 8. Quality of management ■ **Geographic information system (GIS)**—A system that stores and displays information that can be linked to a geographic location. Some of the geographic databases available in many GISs include (1) census data by block, tract, city, county, congressional district, metropolitan area, state, and zip code; (2) maps of every street, highway, bridge, and tunnel in the United States; (3) utilities such as electrical, water, and gas lines; (4) all rivers, mountains, lakes, and forests; and (5) all major airports, colleges, and hospitals.	**VIDEO 8.2** Locating the Next Red Lobster Restaurant

Self Test

■ **Before taking the self-test,** refer to the learning objectives listed at the beginning of the chapter and the key terms listed at the end of the chapter.

LO1. The factors involved in location decisions include:
- **a)** foreign exchange.
- **b)** attitudes.
- **c)** labor productivity.
- **d)** all of the above.

LO2. If Fender Guitar pays $30 per day to a worker in its Ensenada, Mexico, plant, and the employee completes four instruments per 8-hour day, the labor cost/unit is:
- **a)** $30.00.
- **b)** $3.75.
- **c)** $7.50.
- **d)** $4.00.
- **e)** $8.00.

LO3. Evaluating location alternatives by comparing their composite (weighted-average) scores involves:
- **a)** factor-rating analysis.
- **b)** cost–volume analysis.
- **c)** transportation model analysis.
- **d)** linear regression analysis.
- **e)** crossover analysis.

LO4. On the crossover chart where the costs of two or more location alternatives have been plotted, the quantity at which two cost curves cross is the quantity at which:
- **a)** fixed costs are equal for two alternative locations.
- **b)** Variable costs are equal for two alternative locations.
- **c)** total costs are equal for all alternative locations.
- **d)** fixed costs equal variable costs for one location.
- **e)** total costs are equal for two alternative locations.

LO5. A regional bookstore chain is about to build a distribution center that is centrally located for its eight retail outlets. It will most likely employ which of the following tools of analysis?
- **a)** Assembly-line balancing
- **b)** Load–distance analysis
- **c)** Center-of-gravity model
- **d)** Linear programming
- **e)** All of the above

LO6. What is the major difference in focus between location decisions in the service sector and in the manufacturing sector?
- **a)** There is no difference in focus.
- **b)** The focus in manufacturing is revenue maximization, while the focus in service is cost minimization.
- **c)** The focus in service is revenue maximization, while the focus in manufacturing is cost minimization.
- **d)** The focus in manufacturing is on raw materials, while the focus in service is on labor.

Answers: LO1. d; LO2. c; LO3. a; LO4. e; LO5. c; LO6. c.

9 Layout Strategies

Chapter Outline

10

OM Strategy Decisions

- Design of Goods and Services
- Managing Quality
- Process Strategy
- Location Strategies
- **Layout Strategies**
- Human Resources
- Supply-Chain Management
- Inventory Management
- Scheduling
- Maintenance

McDONALD'S LOOKS FOR COMPETITIVE ADVANTAGE THROUGH LAYOUT

In its half-century of existence, McDonald's revolutionized the restaurant industry by inventing the limited-menu fast-food restaurant. It has also made seven major innovations. The first, the introduction of *indoor seating* (1950s), was a layout issue, as was the second, *drive-through windows* (1970s). The third, adding *breakfasts* to the menu (1980s), was a product strategy. The fourth, *adding play areas* (late 1980s), was again a layout decision.

In the 1990s, McDonald's completed its fifth innovation, a radically new *redesign of the kitchens* in its 14,000 North America outlets to facilitate a mass customization process. Dubbed the "Made by You" kitchen system, sandwiches were assembled to order with the revamped layout.

In 2004, the chain began the rollout of its sixth innovation, a new food ordering layout: the *self-service kiosk*. Self-service kiosks have been infiltrating the service sector since the introduction of ATMs in 1985 (there are over 1.5 million ATMs in banking). Alaska Airlines was the first airline to provide self-service airport check-in, in 1996. Most passengers of the major airlines now check themselves in for flights. Kiosks take up less space than an employee and reduce waiting line time.

Now, McDonald's is working on its seventh innovation, and not surprisingly, it also deals with restaurant layout. The company, on an unprecedented scale, is redesigning all 30,000 eateries around the globe to take on a *21st century look*. The dining area will be separated into three sections with distinct personalities: (1) the "linger" zone focuses on young adults and offers comfortable furniture and Wi-Fi connections; (2) the "grab and go" zone features tall counters, bar stools, and plasma TVs; and (3) the "flexible" zone has colorful family booths, flexible seating, and kid-oriented music. The cost per outlet: a whopping $300,000–$400,000 renovation fee.

As McDonald's has discovered, facility layout is indeed a source of competitive advantage.

McDonald's finds that kiosks reduce both space requirements and waiting; order taking is faster. An added benefit is that customers like them. Also, kiosks are reliable—they don't call in sick. And, most importantly, sales are up 10%–15% (an average of $1) when a customer orders from a kiosk, which consistently recommends the larger size and other extras.

▶ The redesigned kitchen of a McDonald's in Manhattan. The more efficient layout requires less labor, reduces waste, and provides faster service. A graphic of this "assembly line" is shown in Figure 9.12

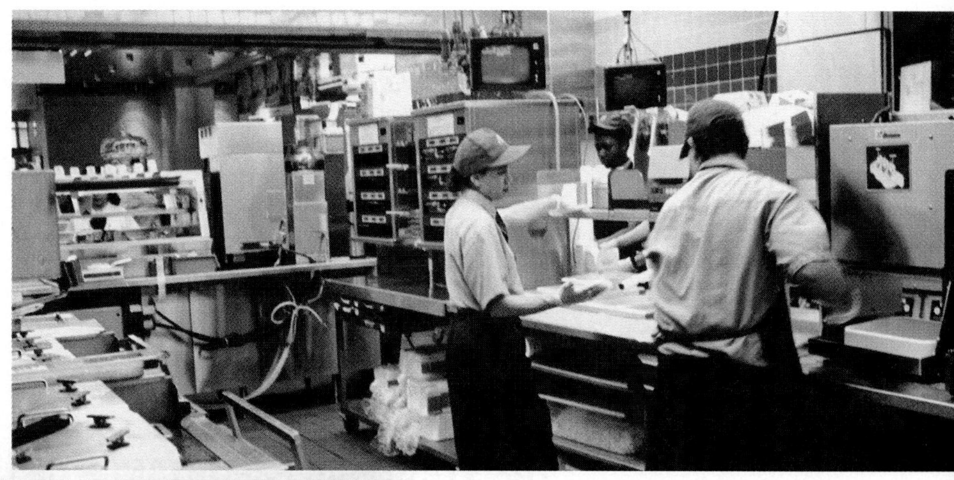

Linger Zone ▼
Cozy armchairs and sofas, plus Wi-Fi connections, make these areas attractive to those who want to hang out and socialize.

Grab & Go Zone ▼
This section has tall counters with bar stools for customers who eat alone. Plasma TVs keep them company.

Flexible Zone ▲
Booths with colorful fabric cushions make up the area geared to family and larger groups. Tables and chairs are movable.

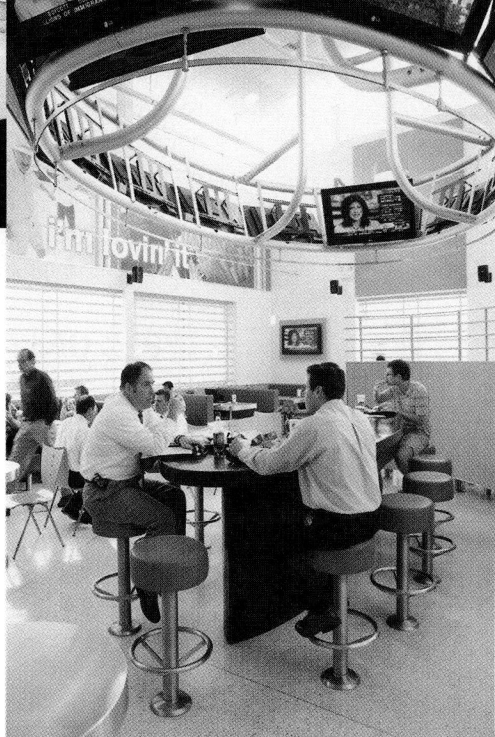

Chapter 9 **Learning Objectives**

THE STRATEGIC IMPORTANCE OF LAYOUT DECISIONS

Layout is one of the key decisions that determines the long-run efficiency of operations. Layout has numerous strategic implications because it establishes an organization's competitive priorities in regard to capacity, processes, flexibility, and cost, as well as quality of work life, customer contact, and image. An effective layout can help an organization achieve a strategy that supports differentiation, low cost, or response. Benetton, for example, supports a *differentiation* strategy by heavy investment in warehouse layouts that contribute to fast, accurate sorting and shipping to its 5,000 outlets. Wal-Mart store layouts support a strategy of *low cost*, as do its warehouse layouts. Hallmark's office layouts, where many professionals operate with open communication in work cells, support *rapid development* of greeting cards. *The objective of layout strategy is to develop an effective and efficient layout that will meet the firm's competitive requirements.*These firms have done so.

In all cases, layout design must consider how to achieve the following:

- Higher utilization of space, equipment, and people
- Improved flow of information, materials, or people
- Improved employee morale and safer working conditions
- Improved customer/client interaction
- Flexibility (whatever the layout is now, it will need to change).

In our increasingly short-life-cycle, mass-customized world, layout designs need to be viewed as dynamic.This means considering small, movable, and flexible equipment. Store displays need to be movable, office desks and partitions modular, and warehouse racks prefabricated. To make quick and easy changes in product models and in production rates, operations managers must design flexibility into layouts. To obtain flexibility in layout, managers cross train their workers, maintain equipment, keep investments low, place workstations close together, and use small, movable equipment. In some cases, equipment on wheels is appropriate, in anticipation of the next change in product, process, or volume.

TYPES OF LAYOUT

Layout decisions include the best placement of machines (in production settings), offices and desks (in office settings), or service centers (in settings such as hospitals or department stores). An effective layout facilitates the flow of materials, people, and information within and between areas. To achieve these objectives, a variety of approaches has been developed. We will discuss seven of them in this chapter:

1. *Office layout:* Positions workers, their equipment, and spaces/offices to provide for movement of information.
2. *Retail layout:* Allocates shelf space and responds to customer behavior.
3. *Warehouse layout:* Addresses trade-offs between space and material handling.
4. *Fixed-position layout:* Addresses the layout requirements of large, bulky projects such as ships and buildings.
5. *Process-oriented layout:* Deals with low-volume, high-variety production (also called "job shop," or intermittent production).

▼ **TABLE 9.1 Layout Strategies**

	Objectives	Examples
Office	Locate workers requiring frequent contact close to one another	Allstate Insurance Microsoft Corp.
Retail	Expose customer to high-margin items	Kroger's Supermarket Walgreen's Bloomingdale's
Warehouse (storage)	Balance low-cost storage with low cost material handling	Federal-Mogul's warehouse The Gap's distribution center
Project (fixed position)	Move material to the limited storage areas around the site	Ingall Ship Building Corp. Trump Plaza Pittsburgh Airport
Job Shop (process oriented)	Manage varied material flow for each product	Arnold Palmer Hospital Hard Rock Cafe Olive Garden
Work Cell (product families)	Identify a product family, build teams, cross train team members	Hallmark Cards Wheeled Coach Standard Aero
Repetitive/Continuous (product oriented)	Equalize the task time at each workstation	Sony's TV assembly line Toyota Scion

6. *Work-cell layout:* Arranges machinery and equipment to focus on production of a single product or group of related products.
7. *Product-oriented layout:* Seeks the best personnel and machine utilization in repetitive or continuous production.

Examples for each of these classes of layouts are noted in Table 9.1.

Because only a few of these seven classes can be modeled mathematically, layout and design of physical facilities are still something of an art. However, we do know that a good layout requires determining the following:

- *Material handling equipment:* Managers must decide about equipment to be used, including conveyors, cranes, automated storage and retrieval systems, and automatic carts to deliver and store material.
- *Capacity and space requirements:* Only when personnel, machines, and equipment requirements are known can managers proceed with layout and provide space for each component. In the case of office work, operations managers must make judgments about the space require-

This open office offers a large shared space that encourages employees to interact. Before Steelcase, the office furniture maker, went to an open office system, 80% of its office space was private; now it is just 20% private. The CEO even went from a private 700-square-foot office to a 48-square-foot enclosure in an open area. This dramatically increases unplanned and spontaneous communication between employees.

ments for each employee. It may be a 6 × 6-foot cubicle plus allowance for hallways, aisles, rest rooms, cafeterias, stairwells, elevators, and so forth, or it may be spacious executive offices and conference rooms. Management must also consider allowances for requirements that address safety, noise, dust, fumes, temperature, and space around equipment and machines.

- *Environment and aesthetics:* Layout concerns often require decisions about windows, planters, and height of partitions to facilitate air flow, reduce noise, provide privacy, and so forth.
- *Flows of information:* Communication is important to any organization and must be facilitated by the layout. This issue may require decisions about proximity as well as decisions about open spaces versus half-height dividers versus private offices.
- *Cost of moving between various work areas:* There may be unique considerations related to moving materials or to the importance of having certain areas next to each other. For example, moving molten steel is more difficult than moving cold steel.

OFFICE LAYOUT

Office layout
The grouping of workers, their equipment, and spaces/offices to provide for comfort, safety, and movement of information.

Office layouts require the grouping of workers, their equipment, and spaces to provide for comfort, safety, and movement of information. The main distinction of office layouts is the importance placed on the flow of information. Office layouts are in constant flux as the technological change sweeping society alters the way offices function.

Even though the movement of information is increasingly electronic, analysis of office layouts still requires a task-based approach. Paper correspondence, contracts, legal documents, confidential patient records, and hard-copy scripts, artwork, and designs still play a major role in many offices. Managers therefore examine both electronic and conventional communication patterns, separation needs, and other conditions affecting employee effectiveness. A useful tool for such an analysis is the *relationship chart* shown in Figure 9.1. This chart, prepared for an office of product designers, indicates that the chief marketing officer must be (1) near the designers' area, (2) less near the secretary and central files, and (3) not at all near the copy center or accounting department.

LO1: Discuss important issues in office layout

General office-area guidelines allot an average of about 100 square feet per person (including corridors). A major executive is allotted about 400 square feet, and a conference room area is based on 25 square feet per person.

On the other hand, some layout considerations are universal (many of which apply to factories as well as to offices). They have to do with working conditions, teamwork, authority, and status. Should offices be private or open cubicles, have low file cabinets to foster informal communication or high cabinets to reduce noise and contribute to privacy? (See the Steelcase photo on the previous page). Should all employees use the same entrance, rest rooms, lockers, and cafeteria? As mentioned earlier, layout decisions are part art and part science.

As a final comment on office layout, we note two major trends. First, technology, such as cell phones, iPods, faxes, the Internet, laptop computers, and PDAs, allows increasing layout flexibility by moving information electronically and allowing employees to work offsite. Second, modern firms create dynamic needs for space and services.

▶ FIGURE 9.1
Office Relationship Chart
Source: Adapted from Richard Muther, *Simplified Systematic Layout Planning*, 3rd ed. (Kansas City, Mgt. & Ind'l Research Publications). Used by permission of the publisher.

Value	CLOSENESS
A	Absolutely necessary
E	Especially important
I	Important
O	Ordinary OK
U	Unimportant
X	Not desirable

Here are two examples:[1]

- When Deloitte & Touche found that 30% to 40% of desks were empty at any given time, the firm developed its "hoteling programs." Consultants lost their permanent offices; anyone who plans to be in the building (rather than out with clients) books an office through a "concierge," who hangs that consultant's name on the door for the day and stocks the space with requested supplies.
- Cisco Systems cut rent and workplace service costs by 37% and saw productivity benefits of $2.4 billion per year by reducing square footage, reconfiguring space, creating movable, everything-on-wheels offices, and designing "get away from it all" innovation areas.

RETAIL LAYOUT

AUTHOR COMMENT
The goal in a retail layout is to maximize profit per square foot of store space.

Retail layouts are based on the idea that sales and profitability vary directly with customer exposure to products. Thus, most retail operations managers try to expose customers to as many products as possible. Studies do show that the greater the rate of exposure, the greater the sales and the higher the return on investment. The operations manager can change exposure with store arrangement and the allocation of space to various products within that arrangement.

Retail layout
An approach that addresses flow, allocates space, and responds to customer behavior

Five ideas are helpful for determining the overall arrangement of many stores:

1. Locate the high-draw items around the periphery of the store. Thus, we tend to find dairy products on one side of a supermarket and bread and bakery products on another. An example of this tactic is shown in Figure 9.2.
2. Use prominent locations for high-impulse and high-margin items. Best Buy puts fast-growing, high-margin digital goods—such as cameras and DVDs—in the front and center of its stores.
3. Distribute what are known in the trade as "power items"—items that may dominate a purchasing trip—to both sides of an aisle, and disperse them to increase the viewing of other items.
4. Use end-aisle locations because they have a very high exposure rate.
5. Convey the mission of the store by carefully selecting the position of the lead-off department. For instance, if prepared foods are part of a supermarket's mission, position the bakery and deli up front to appeal to convenience-oriented customers. Wal-Mart's push to increase sales of clothes means those departments are in broad view upon entering a store.

LO2: Define the objectives of retail layout

Once the overall layout of a retail store has been decided, products need to be arranged for sale. Many considerations go into this arrangement. However, the main *objective of retail layout is to maximize profitability per square foot of floor space* (or, in some stores, on linear foot of shelf space). Big-ticket, or expensive, items may yield greater dollar sales, but the profit per square foot may be lower. Computerized programs are available to assist managers in evaluating the profitability of various merchandising plans for hundreds of categories: this technique is known as category management.

An additional, and somewhat controversial, issue in retail layout is called slotting. **Slotting fees** are fees manufacturers pay to get their goods on the shelf in a retail store or supermarket

Slotting fees
Fees manufacturers pay to get shelf space for their products.

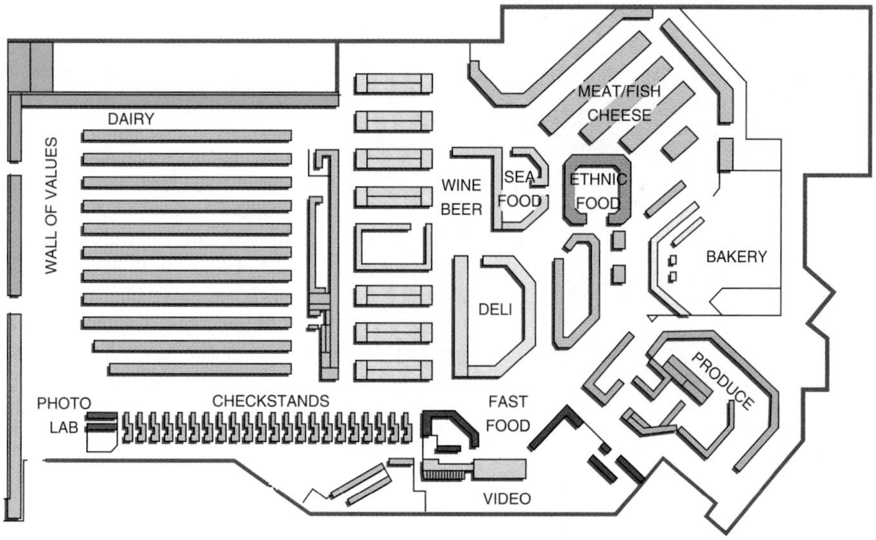

◀ **FIGURE 9.2**
Store Layout with Dairy and Bakery, High-Draw Items, in Different Areas of the Store

[1]"Square Feet. Oh, How Square!" *Business Week* (July 3, 2006): 100–101.

Trying to penetrate urban areas that have lofty land prices and strong antidevelopment movements, Wal-Mart is changing its layout to up, not out. A new generation of multi-level stores take only one-third the space of the traditional 25-acre swaths. Here, in the El Cajon, California, store, Wal-Mart trained workers to help shoppers confused by the device next to the escalator that carries shopping carts from one floor to another.

chain. The result of massive new-product introductions, retailers can now demand up to $25,000 to place an item in their chain. During the last decade, marketplace economics, consolidations, and technology have provided retailers with this leverage. The competition for shelf space is advanced by POS systems and scanner technology, which improve supply-chain management and inventory control. Many small firms question the legality and ethics of slotting fees, claiming the fees stifle new products, limit their ability to expand, and cost consumers money. Wal-Mart is one of the few major retailers that does not demand slotting fees. This removes the barrier to entry that small companies usually face. (See the *Ethical Dilemma* at the end of this chapter.)

Servicescapes

Servicescape
The physical surroundings in which a service takes place, and how they affect customers and employees.

Although the main objective of retail layout is to maximize profit through product exposure, there are other aspects of the service that managers consider. The term **servicescape** describes the physical surroundings in which the service is delivered and how the surroundings have a humanistic effect on customers and employees. To provide a good service layout, a firm considers three elements:

1. *Ambient conditions*, which are background characteristics such as lighting, sound, smell, and temperature. All these affect workers *and* customers and can affect how much is spent and how long a person stays in the building.
2. *Spatial layout and functionality*, which involve customer circulation path planning, aisle characteristics (such as width, direction, angle, and shelf spacing), and product grouping.
3. *Signs, symbols, and artifacts*, which are characteristics of building design that carry social significance (such as carpeted areas of a department store that encourage shoppers to slow down and browse).

A critical element contributing to the bottom line at Hard Rock Cafe is the layout of each cafe's retail shop space. The retail space, from 600 to 1,300 square feet in size, is laid out in conjunction with the restaurant area to create the maximum traffic flow before and after eating. The payoffs for cafes like this one in London are huge. Almost half of a cafe's annual sales are generated from these small shops, which have very high retail sales per square foot.

Examples of each of these three elements of servicescape are:

- *Ambient conditions:* Fine-dining restaurants with linen tablecloths and candlelit atmosphere; Mrs. Field's Cookie bakery smells permeating the shopping mall; leather chairs at Starbucks.
- *Layout/functionality:* Kroger's long aisles and high shelves; Best Buy's wide center aisle.
- *Signs, symbols, and artifacts:* Wal-Mart's greeter at the door; Hard Rock Cafe's wall of guitars; Disneyland's entrance looking like hometown heaven.

WAREHOUSING AND STORAGE LAYOUTS

AUTHOR COMMENT In warehouse layout, we want to maximize use of the whole building—from floor to ceiling.

The objective of **warehouse layout** *is to find the optimum trade-off between handling cost and costs associated with warehouse space.* Consequently, management's task is to maximize the utilization of the total "cube" of the warehouse—that is, utilize its full volume while maintaining low material handling costs. We define *material handling costs* as all the costs related to the transaction. This consists of incoming transport, storage, and outgoing transport of the materials to be warehoused. These costs include equipment, people, material, supervision, insurance, and depreciation. Effective warehouse layouts do, of course, also minimize the damage and spoilage of material within the warehouse.

Warehouse layout
A design that attempts to minimize total cost by addressing trade-offs between space and material handing.

Management minimizes the sum of the resources spent on finding and moving material plus the deterioration and damage to the material itself. The variety of items stored and the number of items "picked" has direct bearing on the optimum layout. A warehouse storing a few unique items lends itself to higher density than a warehouse storing a variety of items. Modern warehouse management is, in many instances, an automated procedure using *automated storage and retrieval systems* (ASRSs).

The Stop & Shop grocery chain, with 350 supermarkets in New England, has recently completed the largest ASRS in the world. The 1.3-million-square-foot distribution center in Freetown, Massachusetts, employs 77 rotating-fork automated storage and retrieval machines. These 77 cranes each access 11,500 pick slots on 90 aisles—a total of 64,000 pallets of food. The Wolfsburg, Germany parking garage photo (below) indicates that an ASRS can take many forms.

LO3: Discuss modern warehouse management and terms such as ASRS, cross-docking, and random stocking

An important component of warehouse layout is the relationship between the receiving/unloading area and the shipping/loading area. Facility design depends on the type of supplies unloaded, what they are unloaded from (trucks, rail cars, barges, and so on), and where they are unloaded. In some companies, the receiving and shipping facilities, or *docks*, as they are called, are even in the same area; sometimes they are receiving docks in the morning and shipping docks in the afternoon.

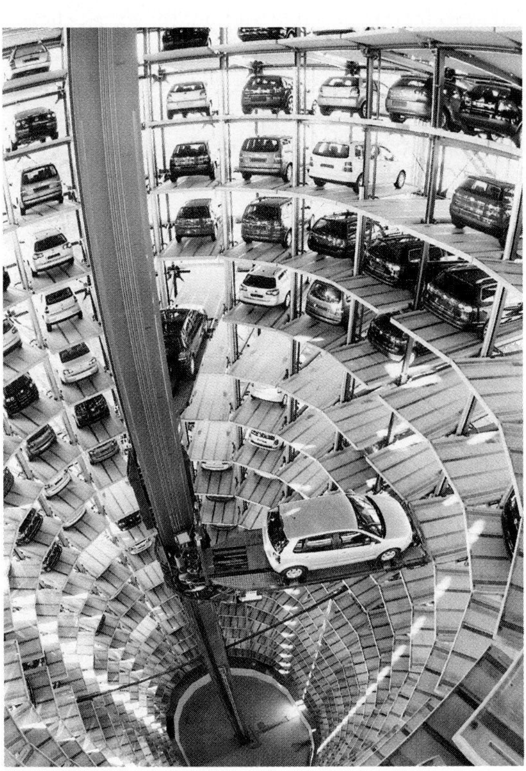

Automated storage and retrieval systems are not found only in traditional warehouses. This parking garage in Wolfsburg, Germany, occupies only 20% of the space of a traditionally designed garage. The ASRS "retrieves" autos in less time, without the potential of the cars being damaged by an attendant.

Cross-Docking

Cross-docking
Avoiding the placement of materials or supplies in storage by processing them as they are received for shipment.

Cross-docking means to avoid placing materials or supplies in storage by processing them as they are received. In a manufacturing facility, product is received directly to the assembly line. In a distribution center, labeled and presorted loads arrive at the shipping dock for immediate rerouting, thereby avoiding formal receiving, stocking/storing, and order-selection activities. Because these activities add no value to the product, their elimination is 100% cost savings. Wal-Mart, an early advocate of cross-docking, uses the technique as a major component of its continuing low-cost strategy. With cross-docking, Wal-Mart reduces distribution costs and speeds restocking of stores, thereby improving customer service. Although cross-docking reduces product handling, inventory, and facility costs, it requires both (1) tight scheduling and (2) accurate inbound product identification.

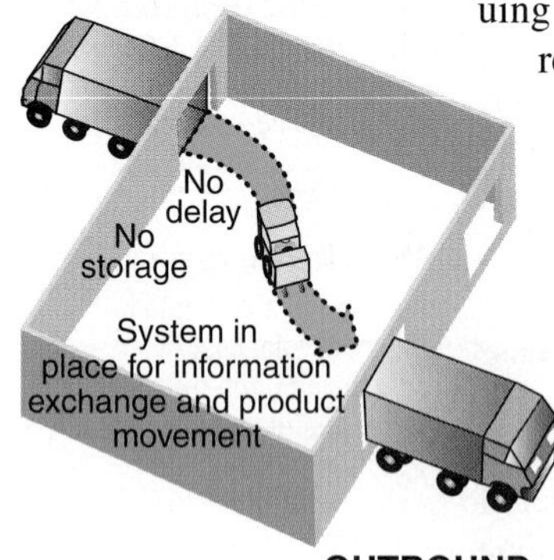

Random Stocking

Automatic identification systems (AISs), usually in the form of bar codes, allow accurate and rapid item identification. When automatic identification systems are combined with effective management information systems, operations managers know the quantity and location of every unit. This information can be used with human operators or with automatic storage and retrieval systems to load units anywhere in the warehouse—randomly. Accurate inventory quantities and locations mean the potential utilization of the whole facility because space does not need to be reserved for certain stock-keeping units (SKUs) or part families. Computerized **random stocking** systems often include the following tasks:

Random stocking
Used in warehousing to locate stock wherever there is an open location.

1. Maintaining a list of "open" locations
2. Maintaining accurate records of existing inventory and its locations
3. Sequencing items to minimize the travel time required to "pick" orders
4. Combining orders to reduce picking time
5. Assigning certain items or classes of items, such as high-usage items, to particular warehouse areas so that the total distance traveled within the warehouse is minimized

Random stocking systems can increase facility utilization and decrease labor cost, but they require accurate records.

Customizing

Although we expect warehouses to store as little product as possible and hold it for as short a time as possible, we are now asking warehouses to customize products. Warehouses can be places where value is added through **customizing**. Warehouse customization is a particularly useful way to generate competitive advantage in markets where products have multiple configurations. For instance, a warehouse can be a place where computer components are put together, software loaded, and repairs made. Warehouses may also provide customized labeling and packaging for retailers so items arrive ready for display.

Customizing
Using warehousing to add value to a product through component modification, repair, labeling, and packaging.

Increasingly, this type of work goes on adjacent to major airports, in facilities such as the FedEx terminal in Memphis. Adding value at warehouses adjacent to major airports also facilitates overnight delivery. For example, if your computer has failed, the replacement may be sent to you from such a warehouse for delivery the next morning. When your old machine arrives back at the warehouse, it is repaired and sent to someone else. These value-added activities at "quasi-warehouses" contribute to strategies of differentiation, low cost, and rapid response.

AUTHOR COMMENT
Fixed-position layout brings all the workers and materials to the project's site.

FIXED-POSITION LAYOUT

In a **fixed-position layout**, the project remains in one place and workers and equipment come to that one work area. Examples of this type of project are a ship, a highway, a bridge, a house, and an operating table in a hospital operating room.

Fixed-position layout
A system that addresses the layout requirements of stationary projects.

The techniques for addressing the fixed-position layout are complicated by three factors. First, there is limited space at virtually all sites. Second, at different stages of a project, different materials are needed; therefore, different items become critical as the project develops. Third, the volume of materials needed is dynamic. For example, the rate of use of steel panels for the hull of a ship changes as the project progresses.

Here are three versions of the fixed-position layout.

A house built via traditional fixed-position layout would be constructed onsite, with equipment, materials, and workers brought to the site. Then a "meeting of the trades" would assign space for various time periods. However, the home pictured here can be built at a much lower cost. The house is built in two movable modules in a factory. Scaffolding and hoists make the job easier, quicker, and cheaper, and the indoor work environment aids labor productivity.

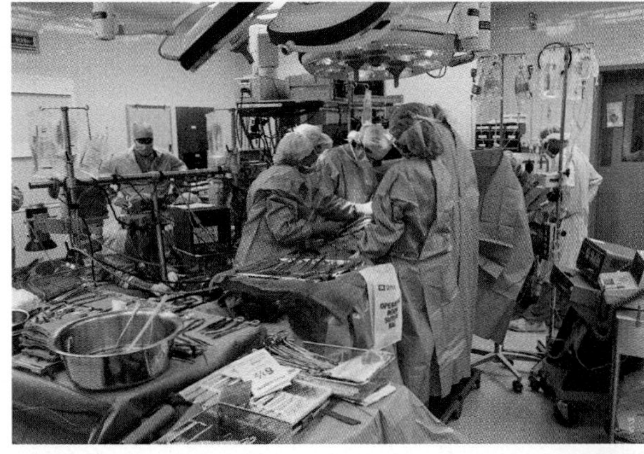

A service example of a fixed-position layout is an operating room; the patient remains stationary on the table, and medical personnel and equipment are brought to the site.

In shipbuilding, there is limited space next to the fixed-position layout. Shipyards call these loading areas platens, and they are assigned for various time periods to each contractor.

Because problems with fixed-position layouts are so difficult to solve well onsite, an alternative strategy is to complete as much of the project as possible offsite. This approach is used in the shipbuilding industry when standard units—say, pipe-holding brackets—are assembled on a nearby assembly line (a product-oriented facility). In an attempt to add efficiency to shipbuilding, Ingall Ship Building Corporation has moved toward product-oriented production when sections of a ship (modules) are similar or when it has a contract to build the same section of several similar ships. Also, as the top photo on the page shows, many home builders are moving from a fixed-position layout strategy to one that is more product oriented. About one-third of all new homes in the U.S. are built this way. In addition, many houses that are built onsite (fixed position) have the majority of components such as doors, windows, fixtures, trusses, stairs, and wallboard built as modules with more efficient offsite processes.

LO4: Identify when fixed-position layouts are appropriate

PROCESS-ORIENTED LAYOUT

A **process-oriented layout** can simultaneously handle a wide variety of products or services. This is the traditional way to support a product differentiation strategy. It is most efficient when making products with different requirements or when handling customers, patients, or clients with different

Process-oriented layout
A layout that deals with low-volume, high-variety production in which like machines and equipment are grouped together.

▶ **FIGURE 9.3**
An Emergency Room Process Layout Showing the Routing of Two Patients

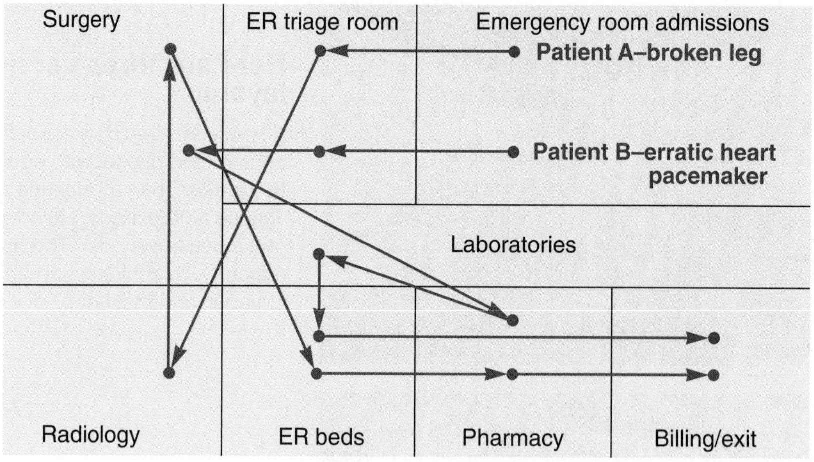

AUTHOR COMMENT
Patient A (broken leg) proceeds (blue arrow) to ER triage, to radiology, to surgery, to a bed, to pharmacy, to billing. Patient B (pacemaker problem) moves (red arrow) to ER triage, to surgery, to pharmacy, to lab, to a bed, to billing.

needs. A process-oriented layout is typically the low-volume, high-variety strategy discussed in Chapter 7. In this job-shop environment, each product or each small group of products undergoes a different sequence of operations. A product or small order is produced by moving it from one department to another in the sequence required for that product. A good example of the process-oriented layout is a hospital or clinic. Figure 9.3 illustrates the process for two patients, A and B, at an emergency clinic in Chicago. An inflow of patients, each with his or her own needs, requires routing through admissions, laboratories, operating rooms, radiology, pharmacies, nursing beds, and so on. Equipment, skills, and supervision are organized around these processes.

VIDEO 9.1
Layout at Arnold Palmer Hospital

A big advantage of process-oriented layout is its flexibility in equipment and labor assignments. The breakdown of one machine, for example, need not halt an entire process; work can be transferred to other machines in the department. Process-oriented layout is also especially good for handling the manufacture of parts in small batches, or **job lots**, and for the production of a wide variety of parts in different sizes or forms.

Job lots
Groups or batches of parts processed together.

The disadvantages of process-oriented layout come from the general-purpose use of the equipment. Orders take more time to move through the system because of difficult scheduling, changing setups, and unique material handling. In addition, general-purpose equipment requires high labor skills, and work-in-process inventories are higher because of imbalances in the production process. High labor-skill needs also increase the required level of training and experience, and high work-in-process levels increase capital investment.

LO5: Explain how to achieve a good process-oriented facility layout

When designing a process layout, the most common tactic is to arrange departments or work centers so as to minimize the costs of material handling. In other words, departments with large flows of parts or people between them should be placed next to one another. Material handling costs in this approach depend on (1) the number of loads (or people) to be moved between two departments during some period of time and (2) the distance-related costs of moving loads (or people) between departments. Cost is assumed to be a function of distance between departments. The objective can be expressed as follows:

$$\text{Minimize cost} = \sum_{i=1}^{n} \sum_{j=1}^{n} X_{ij} C_{ij} \qquad (9\text{-}1)$$

where n = total number of work centers or departments
i, j = individual departments
X_{ij} = number of loads moved from department i to department j
C_{ij} = cost to move a load between department i and department j

Process-oriented facilities (and fixed-position layouts as well) try to minimize loads, or trips, times distance-related costs. The term C_{ij} combines distance and other costs into one factor. We thereby assume not only that the difficulty of movement is equal but also that the pickup and setdown costs are constant. Although they are not always constant, for simplicity's sake we summarize these data (that is, distance, difficulty, and pickup and setdown costs) in this one variable, cost. The best way to understand the steps involved in designing a process layout is to look at an example.

◄ **EXAMPLE 1**

Designing a process layout

Walters Company management wants to arrange the six departments of its factory in a way that will minimize interdepartmental material handling costs. They make an initial assumption (to simplify the problem) that each department is 20 × 20 feet and that the building is 60 feet long and 40 feet wide.

APPROACH AND SOLUTION ▶ The process layout procedure that they follow involves six steps:

STEP 1: *Construct a "from–to matrix"* showing the flow of parts or materials from department to department (see Figure 9.4).

Number of loads per week

Department	Assembly (1)	Painting (2)	Machine Shop (3)	Receiving (4)	Shipping (5)	Testing (6)
Assembly (1)		50	100	0	0	20
Painting (2)			30	50	10	0
Machine Shop (3)				20	0	100
Receiving (4)					50	0
Shipping (5)						0
Testing (6)						

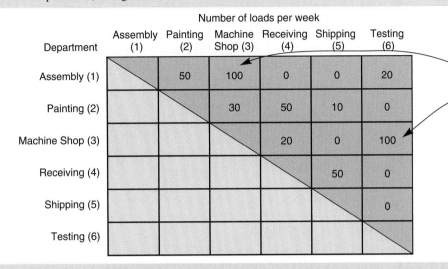

◄ **FIGURE 9.4**
Interdepartmental Flow of Parts

AUTHOR COMMENT The high flows between 1 and 3 and between 3 and 6 are immediately apparent. Departments 1, 3, and 6, therefore, should be close together.

STEP 2: *Determine the space requirements* for each department. (Figure 9.5 shows available plant space.)

Area A	Area B	Area C
Assembly Department (1)	Painting Department (2)	Machine Shop Department (3)
Receiving Department (4)	Shipping Department (5)	Testing Department (6)
Area D	Area E	Area F

40'
60'

◄ **FIGURE 9.5**
Building Dimensions and One Possible Department Layout

AUTHOR COMMENT Think of this as a starting, initial, layout. Our goal is to improve it, if possible.

STEP 3: *Develop an initial schematic diagram* showing the sequence of departments through which parts must move. Try to place departments with a heavy flow of materials or parts next to one another. (See Figure 9.6.)

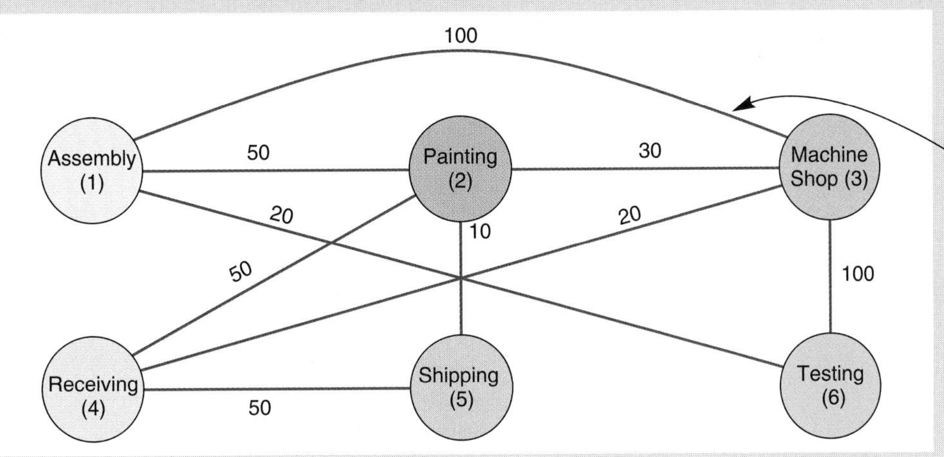

◄ **FIGURE 9.6**
Interdepartmental Flow Graph Showing Number of Weekly Loads

AUTHOR COMMENT This shows that 100 loads also move weekly between Assembly and the Machine Shop. We will probably want to move these two departments closer to one another to minimize the flow of parts through the factory.

STEP 4: *Determine the cost of this layout* by using the material-handling cost equation:

$$\text{Cost} = \sum_{i=1}^{n}\sum_{j=1}^{n} X_{ij}C_{ij}$$

For this problem, Walters Company assumes that a forklift carries all interdepartmental loads. The cost of moving one load between adjacent departments is estimated to be \$1. Moving a load between nonadjacent departments costs \$2. Looking at Figures 9.4 and 9.5, we thus see that the handling cost between departments 1 and 2 is \$50 (\$1 × 50 loads), \$200 between departments 1 and 3 (\$2 × 100 loads), \$40 between departments 1 and 6 (\$2 × 20 loads), and so on. Work areas that are diagonal to one another, such as 2 and 4, are treated as adjacent. The total cost for the layout shown in Figure 9.6 is:

$$\begin{aligned}\text{Cost} = &\ \underset{(1\text{ and }2)}{\$50} + \underset{(1\text{ and }3)}{\$200} + \underset{(1\text{ and }6)}{\$40} + \underset{(2\text{ and }3)}{\$30} + \underset{(2\text{ and }4)}{\$50}\\ &+ \underset{(2\text{ and }5)}{\$10} + \underset{(3\text{ and }4)}{\$40} + \underset{(3\text{ and }6)}{\$100} + \underset{(4\text{ and }5)}{\$50}\\ = &\ \$570\end{aligned}$$

STEP 5. By trial and error (or by a more sophisticated computer program approach that we discuss shortly), *try to improve the layout* pictured in Figure 9.5 to establish a better arrangement of departments.

By looking at both the flow graph (Figure 9.6) and the cost calculations, we see that placing departments 1 and 3 closer together appears desirable. They currently are nonadjacent, and the high volume of flow between them causes a large handling expense. Looking the situation over, we need to check the effect of shifting departments and possibly raising, instead of lowering, overall costs.

One possibility is to switch departments 1 and 2. This exchange produces a second departmental flow graph (Figure 9.7), which shows a reduction in cost to \$480, a savings in material handling of \$90:

$$\begin{aligned}\text{Cost} = &\ \underset{(1\text{ and }2)}{\$50} + \underset{(1\text{ and }3)}{\$100} + \underset{(1\text{ and }6)}{\$20} + \underset{(2\text{ and }3)}{\$60} + \underset{(2\text{ and }4)}{\$50}\\ &+ \underset{(2\text{ and }5)}{\$10} + \underset{(3\text{ and }4)}{\$40} + \underset{(3\text{ and }6)}{\$100} + \underset{(4\text{ and }5)}{\$50}\\ = &\ \$480\end{aligned}$$

▶ **FIGURE 9.7**
Second Interdepartmental Flow Graph

AUTHOR COMMENT
Notice how Assembly and Machine Shop are now adjacent. Testing stayed close to the Machine Shop also.

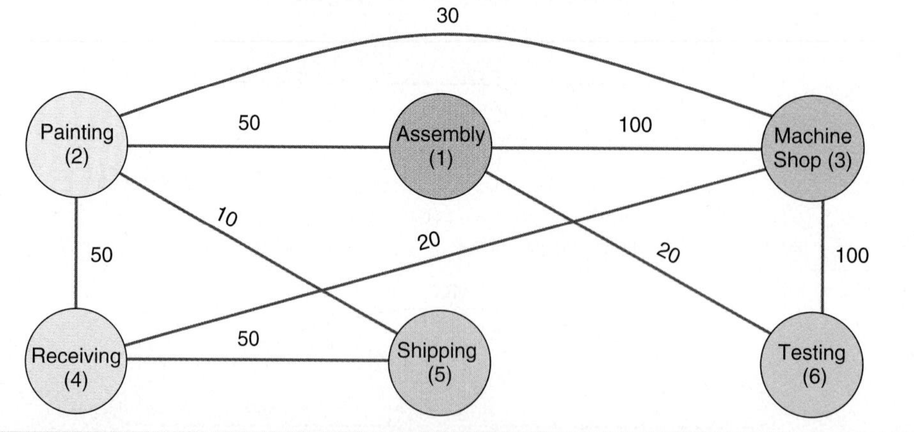

Suppose Walters Company is satisfied with the cost figure of \$480 and the flow graph of Figure 9.7. The problem may not be solved yet. Often, a sixth step is necessary:

STEP 6: *Prepare a detailed plan* arranging the departments to fit the shape of the building and its nonmovable areas (such as the loading dock, washrooms, and stairways). Often this step involves ensuring that the final plan can be accommodated by the electrical system, floor loads, aesthetics, and other factors.

In the case of Walters Company, space requirements are a simple matter (see Figure 9.8).

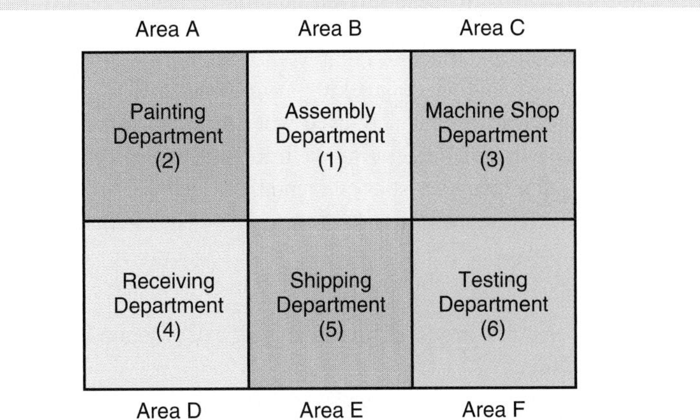

▶ **FIGURE 9.8**
A Feasible Layout for Walters Company

AUTHOR COMMENT Here we see the departments moved to areas A–F to try to improve the flow.

INSIGHT ▶ This switch of departments is only one of a large number of possible changes. For a six-department problem, there are actually 720 (or $6! = 6 \times 5 \times 4 \times 3 \times 2 \times 1$) potential arrangements! In layout problems, we may not find the optimal solution and may have to be satisfied with a "reasonable" one.

LEARNING EXERCISE ▶ Can you improve on the layout in Figures 9.7 and 9.8? [Answer: Yes, it can be lowered to $430 by placing Shipping in area A, Painting in area B, Assembly in area C, Receiving in area D (no change), Machine Shop in area E, and Testing in area F (no change).]

RELATED PROBLEMS ▶ 9.1, 9.2, 9.3, 9.4, 9.5, 9.6, 9.7, 9.8, 9.9

EXCEL OM Data File **Ch09Ex1.xls** can be found at **www.pearsonhighered.com/heizer**.

ACTIVE MODEL 9.1 Example 1 is further illustrated in Active Model 9.1 at **www.pearsonhighered.com/heizer**.

Computer Software for Process-Oriented Layouts

The graphic approach in Example 1 is fine for small problems. It does not, however, suffice for larger problems. When 20 departments are involved in a layout problem, more than 600 *trillion* different department configurations are possible. Fortunately, computer programs have been written to handle large layouts. These programs often add sophistication with flowcharts, multiple-story capability, storage and container placement, material volumes, time analysis, and cost comparisons. Such programs include **CRAFT** (Computerized Relative Allocation of Facilities Technique) (see Figure 9.9), Automated Layout Design program (ALDEP), Computerized Relationship Layout Planning (CORELAP), and Factory Flow. These programs tend to be interactive—that is, require participation by the user. And most only claim to provide "good," not "optimal," solutions.

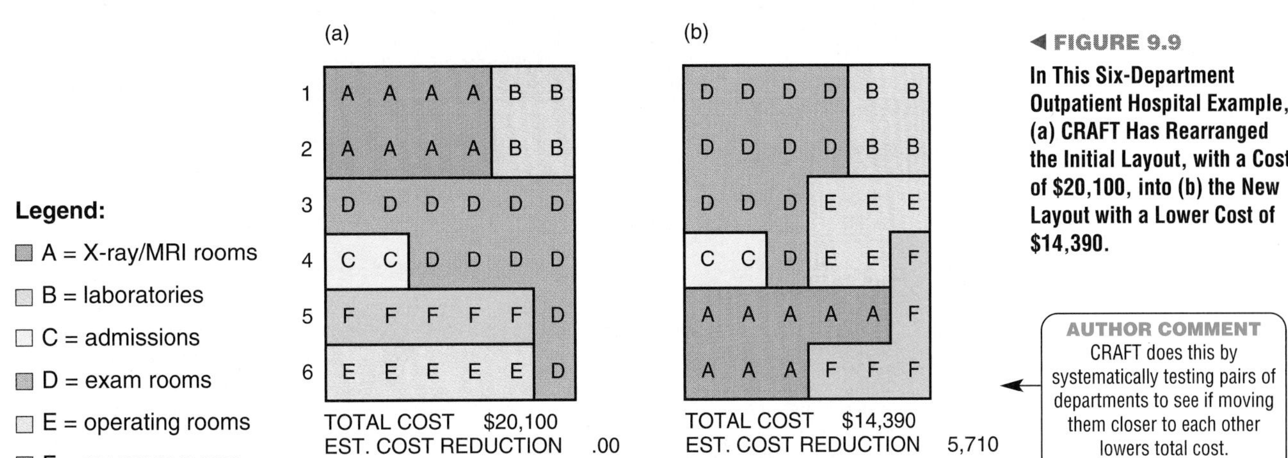

◀ **FIGURE 9.9**
In This Six-Department Outpatient Hospital Example, (a) CRAFT Has Rearranged the Initial Layout, with a Cost of $20,100, into (b) the New Layout with a Lower Cost of $14,390.

AUTHOR COMMENT CRAFT does this by systematically testing pairs of departments to see if moving them closer to each other lowers total cost.

AUTHOR COMMENT
Using work cells is a big step toward manufacturing efficiency. They can make jobs more interesting, save space, and cut inventory.

WORK CELLS

Work cell
An arrangement of machines and personnel that focuses on making a single product or family of related products.

A **work cell** reorganizes people and machines that would ordinarily be dispersed in various departments into a group so that they can focus on making a single product or a group of related products (Figure 9.10). Cellular work arrangements are used when volume warrants a special arrangement of machinery and equipment. In a manufacturing environment, *group technology* (Chapter 5) identifies products that have similar characteristics and lend themselves to being processed in a particular work cell. These work cells are reconfigured as product designs change or volume fluctuates. Although the idea of work cells was first presented by R. E. Flanders in 1925, only with the increasing use of group technology has the technique reasserted itself. The advantages of work cells are:

1. *Reduced work-in-process inventory* because the work cell is set up to provide one-piece flow from machine to machine.
2. *Less floor space* required because less space is needed between machines to accommodate work-in-process inventory.
3. *Reduced raw material and finished goods inventories* because less work-in-process allows more rapid movement of materials through the work cell.
4. *Reduced direct labor cost* because of improved communication among employees, better material flow, and improved scheduling.
5. *Heightened sense of employee participation* in the organization and the product: employees accept the added responsibility of product quality because it is directly associated with them and their work cell.
6. *Increased equipment and machinery utilization* because of better scheduling and faster material flow.
7. *Reduced investment in machinery and equipment* because good utilization reduces the number of machines and the amount of equipment and tooling.

LO6: Define work cell and the requirements of a work cell

Requirements of Work Cells

The requirements of cellular production include:

- Identification of families of products, often through the use of group technology codes or equivalents
- A high level of training, flexibility, and empowerment of employees
- Being self-contained, with its own equipment and resources.
- Test (poka-yoke) at each station in the cell

Work cells have at least five advantages over assembly lines and process facilities: (1) because tasks are grouped, inspection is often immediate; (2) fewer workers are needed; (3) workers can reach more of the work area; (4) the work area can be more efficiently

Contemporary software such as this from e-factory (UGS Corp.) allows operations managers to quickly place and connect symbols for factory equipment for a full three-dimensional view of the layout. Such presentations provide added insight into the issues of facility layout in terms of process, material handling, efficiency, and safety.

Note in both (a) and (b) that U-shaped work cells can reduce material and employee movement. The U shape may also reduce space requirements, enhance communication, cut the number of workers, and make inspection easier.

◀ **FIGURE 9.10**

Improving Layouts by Moving to the Work Cell Concept

(a)

Material

Current layout–workers in small closed areas.

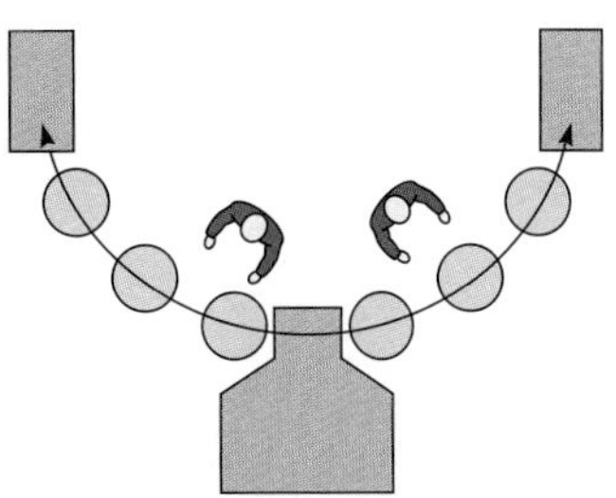

Improved layout—cross-trained workers can assist each other. May be able to add a third worker as added output is needed.

(b)

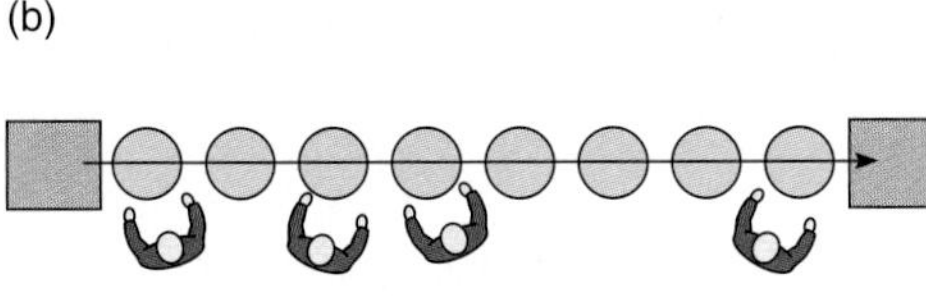

Current layout—straight lines make it hard to balance tasks because work may not be divided evenly.

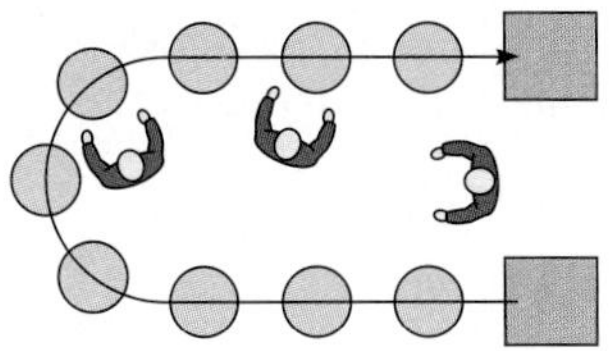

Improved layout—in U shape, workers have better access. Four cross-trained workers were reduced to three.

balanced; and (5) communication is enhanced. Work cells are sometimes organized in a U shape, as shown on the right side of Figure 9.10.

About half of U.S. plants with fewer than 100 employees use some sort of cellular system, whereas 75% of larger plants have adopted cellular production methods. Bayside Controls in Queens, New York, for example, has in the past decade increased sales from $300,000 per year to $11 million. Much of the gain was attributed to its move to cellular manufacturing. As noted in the *OM in Action* box, Canon has had similar success with work cells.

Staffing and Balancing Work Cells

Once the work cell has the appropriate equipment located in the proper sequence, the next task is to staff and balance the cell. Efficient production in a work cell requires appropriate staffing.

OM in Action ▶ Work Cells Increase Productivity at Canon

Look quickly at Canon's factory near Tokyo, and you might think you stepped back a few decades. Instead of the swiftly moving assembly lines you might expect to see in a high-cost, sophisticated digital camera and photo copier giant, you see workers gathered in small groups called *work cells*. Each cell is responsible for one product or a small family of products. The product focus encourages employees to exchange ideas about how to improve the assembly process. They also accept more responsibility for their work.

Canon's work cells have increased productivity by 30%. But how?

First, conveyor belts and their spare parts take up space, an expensive commodity in Japan. The shift to the cell system has freed 12 miles of conveyor-belt space at 54 plants and allowed Canon to close 29 parts warehouses, saving $280 million in real estate costs. Employees are encouraged to work in ever-tighter cells, with prizes given to those who free up the most space.

Second, the cells enable Canon to change the product mix more quickly to meet market demands for innovative products—a big advantage as product life cycles become shorter and shorter.

Third, staff morale has increased because instead of performing a single task over and over, employees are trained to put together whole machines. Some of Canon's fastest workers are so admired that they have become TV celebrities.

A layout change that improves morale while increasing productivity is a win–win for Canon.

Sources: *The Wall Street Journal* (September 27, 2004): R11; and *Financial Times* (September 23, 2003): 14.

Takt time
Pace of production to meet customer demands.

This involves two steps. First, determine the **takt time**,[2] which is the pace (frequency) of production units necessary to meet customer orders:

$$\text{Takt time} = \text{Total work time available/Units required} \quad (9\text{-}2)$$

Second, determine the number of operators required. This requires dividing the total operation time in the work cell by the takt time:

$$\text{Workers required} = \text{Total operation time required/Takt time} \quad (9\text{-}3)$$

Example 2 considers these two steps when staffing work cells.

EXAMPLE 2 ▶ Staffing work cells

Stephen Hall's company in Dayton makes auto mirrors. The major customer is the Honda plant nearby. Honda expects 600 mirrors delivered daily, and the work cell producing the mirrors is scheduled for 8 hours. Hall wants to determine the takt time and the number of workers required.

APPROACH ▶ Hall uses Equations (9-2) and (9-3) and develops a work balance chart to help determine the time for each operation in the work cell, as well as total time.

SOLUTION ▶

$$\text{Takt time} = (8 \text{ hours} \times 60 \text{ minutes})/600 \text{ units} = 480/600 = .8 \text{ minute} = 48 \text{ seconds}$$

Therefore, the customer requirement is one mirror every 48 seconds.

The *work balance chart* in Figure 9.11 shows that 5 operations are necessary, for a total operation time of 140 seconds:

$$\begin{aligned}\text{Workers required} &= \text{Total operation time required/Takt time}\\ &= (50 + 45 + 10 + 20 + 15)/48\\ &= 140/48 = 2.92\end{aligned}$$

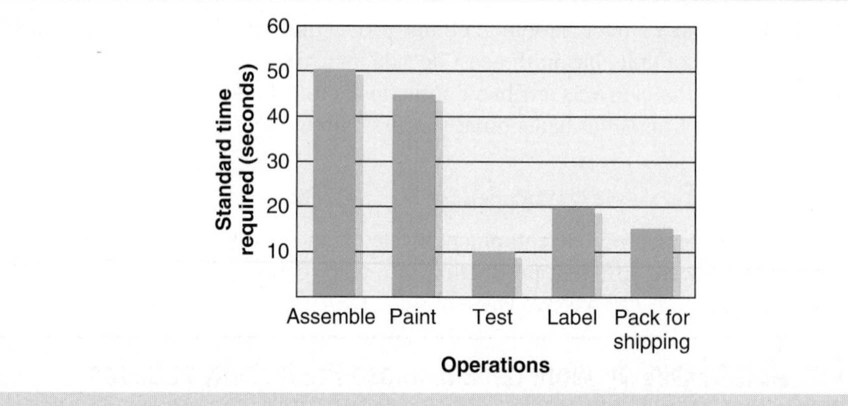

▶ **FIGURE 9.11 Work Balance Chart for Mirror Production**

INSIGHT ▶ To produce one unit every 48 seconds will require 2.92 people. With three operators this work cell will be producing one unit each 46.67 seconds (140 seconds/3 employees = 46.67) and 617 units per day (480 minutes available × 60 seconds)/46.67 seconds for each unit = 617).

LEARNING EXERCISE ▶ If testing time is expanded to 20 seconds, what is the staffing requirement? [Answer: 3.125 employees.]

RELATED PROBLEM ▶ 9.10

A *work balance chart* (like the one in Example 2) is also valuable for evaluating the operation times in work cells. Some consideration must be given to determining the bottleneck operation. Bottleneck operations can constrain the flow through the cell. Imbalance in a work cell is seldom an issue if the operation is manual, as cell members by definition are part of a cross-trained team.

[2] *Takt* is German for "time," "measure," or "beat" and is used in this context as the rate at which completed units must be produced to satisfy customer demand.

Consequently, the inherent flexibility of work cells typically overcome modest imbalance issues within a cell. However, if the imbalance is a machine constraint, then an adjustment in machinery, process, or operations may be necessary. In such situations the use of traditional assembly-line-balancing analysis, the topic of our next section, may be helpful.

In many arrangements, without cells and without cross training, if one operation is halted for whatever reason (reading a drawing, getting a tool, machine maintenance, etc.), the entire flow stops. Multiple-operator cells are therefore preferred. However, we should note that the increasing capability of multitasking machines can complicate work cell design and staffing.

The success of work cells is not limited to manufacturing. Kansas City's Hallmark, which has over half the U.S. greeting card market and produces some 40,000 different cards, has modified the offices into a cellular design. In the past, its 700 creative professionals would take up to 2 years to develop a new card. Hallmark's decision to create work cells consisting of artists, writers, lithographers, merchandisers, and accountants, all located in the same area, has resulted in card preparation in a fraction of the time that the old layout required. Work cells have also yielded higher performance and better service for the American Red Cross blood donation process.[3]

Commercial software, such as ProPlanner and Factory Flow, is available to aid managers in their move to work cells. These programs typically require information that includes AutoCAD layout drawings; part routing data; and cost, times, and speeds of material handling systems.

The Focused Work Center and the Focused Factory

When a firm has *identified a family of similar products that have a large and stable demand*, it may organize a focused work center. A **focused work center** moves production from a general-purpose, process-oriented facility to a large work cell that remains part of the present plant. If the focused work center is in a separate facility, it is often called a **focused factory**. A fast-food restaurant is a focused factory—most are easily reconfigured for adjustments to product mix and volume. Burger King, for example, changes the number of personnel and task assignments rather than moving machines and equipment. In this manner, Burger King balances the assembly line to meet changing production demands. In effect, the "layout" changes numerous times each day.

Focused work center
A permanent or semi-permanent product-oriented arrangement of machines and personnel.

Focused factory
A facility designed to produce similar products or components.

The term *focused factories* may also refer to facilities that are focused in ways other than by product line or layout. For instance, facilities may be focused in regard to meeting quality, new product introduction, or flexibility requirements.

Focused facilities in both manufacturing and services appear to be better able to stay in tune with their customers, to produce quality products, and to operate at higher margins. This is true whether they are steel mills like CMC, Nucor, or Chaparral; restaurants like McDonald's and Burger King; or a hospital like Arnold Palmer.

Table 9.2 summarizes our discussion of work cells, focused work centers, and focused factories.

◄ **TABLE 9.2**
Work Cells, Focused Work Centers, and the Focused Factory

	Work Cell	Focused Work Center	Focused Factory
Description	A work cell is a temporary product-oriented arrangement of machines and personnel in what is ordinarily a process-oriented facility	A focused work center is a permanent product-oriented arrangement of machines and personnel in what is ordinarily a process-oriented facility	A focused factory is a permanent facility to produce a product or component in a product-oriented facility. Many of the focused factories currently being built were originally part of a process-oriented facility
Example	A job shop with machinery and personnel rearranged to produce 300 unique control panels	Pipe bracket manufacturing at a shipyard	A plant to produce window mechanisms or seat belts for automobiles

[3]Mark Pagell and Steven A. Melnyk, "Assessing the Impact of Alternative Manufacturing Layouts in a Service Setting," *Journal of Operations Management* 22 (2004): 413–429.

AUTHOR COMMENT
The traditional assembly line handles repetitive production.

REPETITIVE AND PRODUCT-ORIENTED LAYOUT

Product-oriented layouts are organized around products or families of similar high-volume, low-variety products. Repetitive production and continuous production, which are discussed in Chapter 7, use product layouts. The assumptions are that:

LO7: Define product-oriented layout

1. Volume is adequate for high equipment utilization
2. Product demand is stable enough to justify high investment in specialized equipment
3. Product is standardized or approaching a phase of its life cycle that justifies investment in specialized equipment
4. Supplies of raw materials and components are adequate and of uniform quality (adequately standardized) to ensure that they will work with the specialized equipment

Fabrication line
A machine-paced, product-oriented facility for building components.

Assembly line
An approach that puts fabricated parts together at a series of workstations; used in repetitive processes.

Two types of a product-oriented layout are fabrication and assembly lines. The **fabrication line** builds components, such as automobile tires or metal parts for a refrigerator, on a series of machines, while an **assembly line** puts the fabricated parts together at a series of workstations. However, both are repetitive processes, and in both cases, the line must be "balanced": That is, the time spent to perform work on one machine must equal or "balance" the time spent to perform work on the next machine in the fabrication line, just as the time spent at one workstation by one assembly-line employee must "balance" the time spent at the next workstation by the next employee. The same issues arise when designing the "disassembly lines" of slaughterhouses and automobile makers (see the *OM in Action* box "From Assembly Lines to Green Disassembly Lines").

Fabrication lines tend to be machine-paced and require mechanical and engineering changes to facilitate balancing. Assembly lines, on the other hand, tend to be paced by work tasks assigned to individuals or to workstations. Assembly lines, therefore, can be balanced by moving tasks from one individual to another. The central problem, then, in product-oriented layout planning is to balance the tasks at each workstation on the production line so that it is nearly the same while obtaining the desired amount of output.

Management's goal is to create a smooth, continuing flow along the assembly line with a minimum of idle time at each workstation. A well-balanced assembly line has the advantage of high

OM in Action ► From Assembly Lines to Green Disassembly Lines

Almost 100 years have passed since assembly lines were developed to *make* automobiles—and now we're developing disassembly lines to take them apart. Sprawling graveyards of rusting cars and trucks bear testimony to the need for automotive disassembly lines. But those graveyards are slowly beginning to shrink as we learn the art of automobile disassembly. New *disassembly* lines now take apart so many automobiles that recycling is the 16th-largest industry in the U.S. The motivation for this disassembly comes from many sources, including mandated industry recycling standards and a growing consumer interest in purchasing cars based on how "green" they are.

New car designs have traditionally been unfriendly to recyclers, with little thought given to disassembly. However, manufacturers now design in such a way that materials can be easily reused in the next generation of cars. The 2009 Mercedes S-class is 95% recyclable and already meets the 2015 EU standard. BMW has disassembly plants in Europe and Japan as well as U.S. salvage centers in New York, Los Angeles, and Orlando. A giant 200,000-square-foot facility in Baltimore (called CARS) can disassemble up to 30,000 vehicles per year. At CARS's initial "greening station," special tools puncture tanks and drain fluids, and the battery and gas tank are removed. Then on a semi-automated track, which includes a giant steel vise that can flip a 7,500-pound car upside-down, wheels, doors, hood, and trunk are removed; next come the interior items; then plastic parts are removed and sorted for recycling; then glass and interior and trunk materials. Eventually the chassis is in a bale and sold as a commodity to minimills that use scrap steel.

Disassembly lines are not easy. Some components, like air bags, are hard to handle, dangerous, and take time to disassemble. Reusable parts are bar coded and entered into a database. Various color-coded plastics must be recycled differently to support being remelted and turned into new parts, such as intake manifolds. After the engines, transmissions, radios, and exhausts have been removed, the remaining metal parts of the disassembly line are easier: with shredders and magnets, baseball-sized chunks of metal are sorted. Assembly lines put cars together, and disassembly lines take them apart.

Sources: The Wall Street Journal (April 29, 2008): A1, A9; *The New York Times* (September 19, 2005): D5; and *Automotive Industry Trends* (March 2004).

personnel and facility utilization and equity among employees' work loads. Some union contracts require that work loads be nearly equal among those on the same assembly line. The term most often used to describe this process is **assembly-line balancing**. Indeed, the *objective of the product-oriented layout is to minimize imbalance in the fabrication or assembly line*.

Assembly-line balancing
Obtaining output at each workstation on a production line so delay is minimized.

The main advantages of product-oriented layout are:

1. The low variable cost per unit usually associated with high-volume, standardized products
2. Low material handling costs
3. Reduced work-in-process inventories
4. Easier training and supervision
5. Rapid throughput

The disadvantages of product layout are:

1. The high volume required because of the large investment needed to establish the process
2. Work stoppage at any one point ties up the whole operation
3. A lack of flexibility when handling a variety of products or production rates

Because the problems of fabrication lines and assembly lines are similar, we focus our discussion on assembly lines. On an assembly line, the product typically moves via automated means, such as a conveyor, through a series of workstations until completed. This is the way fast-food hamburgers are made (see Figure 9.12), automobiles and some planes (see the photo of the Boeing 737 on the next page) are assembled, television sets and ovens are produced. Product-oriented layouts use more automated and specially designed equipment than do process layouts.

VIDEO 9.2
Facility Layout at Wheeled Coach Ambulances

Assembly-Line Balancing

LO8: Explain how to balance production flow in a repetitive or product-oriented facility

Line balancing is usually undertaken to minimize imbalance between machines or personnel while meeting a required output from the line. To produce at a specified rate, management must know the tools, equipment, and work methods used. Then the time requirements for each assembly task (e.g., drilling a hole, tightening a nut, or spray-painting a part) must be determined. Management also needs to know the *precedence relationship* among the activities—that is, the sequence in which various tasks must be performed. Example 3 shows how to turn these task data into a precedence diagram.

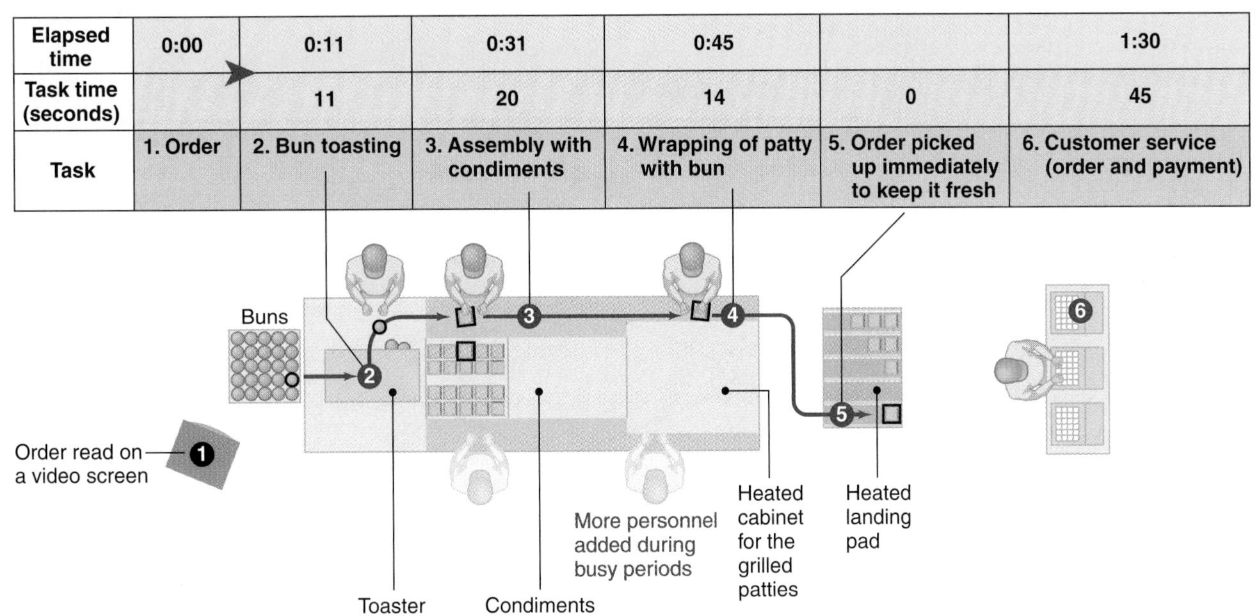

Elapsed time	0:00	0:11	0:31	0:45		1:30
Task time (seconds)		11	20	14	0	45
Task	1. Order	2. Bun toasting	3. Assembly with condiments	4. Wrapping of patty with bun	5. Order picked up immediately to keep it fresh	6. Customer service (order and payment)

▲ FIGURE 9.12 **McDonald's Hamburger Assembly Line**

The Boeing 737, the world's most popular commercial airplane, is produced on a moving production line, traveling at 2 inches a minute through the final assembly process. The moving line, one of several lean manufacturing innovations at the Renton, Washington, facility, has enhanced quality, reduced flow time, slashed inventory levels, and cut space requirements. Final assembly is only 11 days—a time savings of 50%—and inventory is down more than 55%. Boeing has expanded the moving line concept to its 747 jumbo jet.

EXAMPLE 3 ▶

Developing a precedence diagram for an assembly line

Boeing wants to develop a precedence diagram for an electrostatic wing component that requires a total assembly time of 66 minutes.

APPROACH ▶ Staff gather tasks, assembly times, and sequence requirements for the component in Table 9.3.

▶ TABLE 9.3 Precedence Data for Wing Component

Task	Assembly Time (minutes)	Task Must Follow Task Listed Below	
A	10	—	This means that tasks B and E cannot be done until task A has been completed.
B	11	A	
C	5	B	
D	4	B	
E	12	A	
F	3	C, D	
G	7	F	
H	11	E	
I	3	G, H	
	Total time 66		

SOLUTION ▶ Figure 9.13 shows the precedence diagram.

▶ FIGURE 9.13 Precedence Diagram

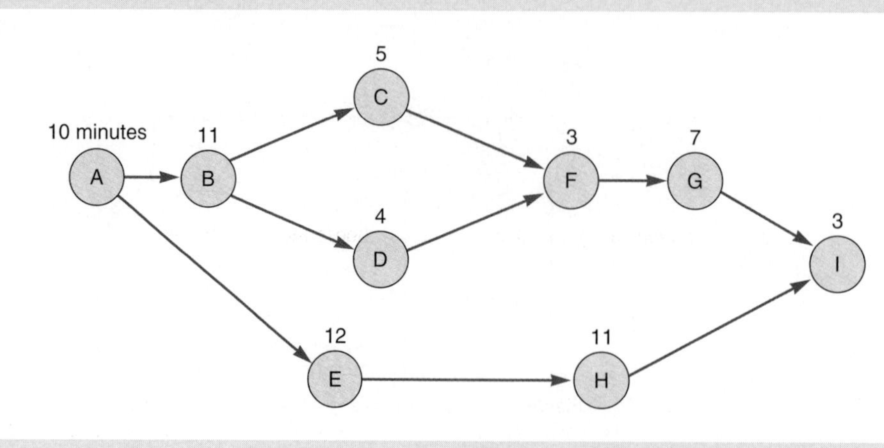

INSIGHT ▶ The diagram helps structure an assembly line and workstations, and it makes it easier to visualize the sequence of tasks.

LEARNING EXERCISE ▶ If task D had a second preceding task (C), how would Figure 9.13 change? [Answer: There would also be an arrow pointing from C to D.]

RELATED PROBLEMS ▶ 9.12a, 9.14a, 9.15a, 9.16a, 9.19a

Once we have constructed a precedence chart summarizing the sequences and performance times, we turn to the job of grouping tasks into job stations so that we can meet the specified production rate. This process involves three steps:

1. Take the units required (demand or production rate) per day and divide it into the productive time available per day (in minutes or seconds). This operation gives us what is called the **cycle time**[4]—namely, the maximum time allowed at each workstation if the production rate is to be achieved:

Cycle time
The maximum time that a product is allowed at each workstation.

$$\text{Cycle time} = \frac{\text{Production time available per day}}{\text{Units required per day}} \quad (9\text{-}4)$$

2. Calculate the theoretical minimum number of workstations. This is the total task-duration time (the time it takes to make the product) divided by the cycle time. Fractions are rounded to the next higher whole number:

$$\text{Minimum number of workstations} = \frac{\sum_{i=1}^{n} \text{Time for task } i}{\text{Cycle time}} \quad (9\text{-}5)$$

where n is the number of assembly tasks.
3. Balance the line by assigning specific assembly tasks to each workstation. An efficient balance is one that will complete the required assembly, follow the specified sequence, and keep the idle time at each workstation to a minimum. A formal procedure for doing this is the following:
   a. Identify a master list of tasks.
   b. Eliminate those tasks that have been assigned.
   c. Eliminate those tasks whose precedence relationship has not been satisfied.
   d. Eliminate those tasks for which inadequate time is available at the workstation.
   e. Use one of the line-balancing "heuristics" described in Table 9.4. The five choices are (1) longest task time, (2) most following tasks, (3) ranked positional weight, (4) shortest

◀ **TABLE 9.4**
Layout Heuristics That May Be Used to Assign Tasks to Workstations in Assembly-Line Balancing

1. *Longest task (operation) time*	From the available tasks, choose the task with the largest (longest) time.
2. *Most following tasks*	From the available tasks, choose the task with the largest number of following tasks.
3. *Ranked positional weight*	From the available tasks, choose the task for which the sum of the times for each following task is longest. (In Example 4 we see that the ranked positional weight of task C = 5(C) + 3(F) + 7(G) + 3(I) = 18, whereas the ranked positional weight of task D = 4(D) + 3(F) + 7(G) + 3(I) =17; therefore, C would be chosen first, using this heuristic.)
4. *Shortest task (operations) time*	From the available tasks, choose the task with the shortest task time.
5. *Least number of following tasks*	From the available tasks, choose the task with the least number of subsequent tasks.

[4]*Cycle time* is the actual time to accomplish a task or process step. Several process steps may be necessary to complete the product. *Takt time*, discussed earlier, is determined by the customer and is the speed at which completed units must be produced to satisfy customer demand.

Heuristic
Problem solving using procedures and rules rather than mathematical optimization.

task time, and (5) least number of following tasks. You may wish to test several of these **heuristics** to see which generates the "best" solution—that is, the smallest number of workstations and highest efficiency. Remember, however, that although heuristics provide solutions, they do not guarantee an optimal solution.

Example 4 illustrates a simple line-balancing procedure.

EXAMPLE 4 ▶ Balancing the assembly line

On the basis of the precedence diagram and activity times given in Example 3, Boeing determines that there are 480 productive minutes of work available per day. Furthermore, the production schedule requires that 40 units of the wing component be completed as output from the assembly line each day. It now wants to group the tasks into workstations.

APPROACH ▶ Following the three steps above, we compute the cycle time using Equation (9-4) and minimum number of workstations using Equation (9-5), and we assign tasks to workstations—in this case using the *most following tasks* heuristic.

SOLUTION ▶

$$\text{Cycle time (in minutes)} = \frac{480 \text{ minutes}}{40 \text{ units}}$$
$$= 12 \text{ minutes/unit}$$

$$\text{Minimum number of workstations} = \frac{\text{Total task time}}{\text{Cycle time}} = \frac{66}{12}$$
$$= 5.5 \text{ or } 6 \text{ stations}$$

Figure 9.14 shows one solution that does not violate the sequence requirements and that groups tasks into six one-person stations. To obtain this solution, activities with the most following tasks were moved into workstations to use as much of the available cycle time of 12 minutes as possible. The first workstation consumes 10 minutes and has an idle time of 2 minutes.

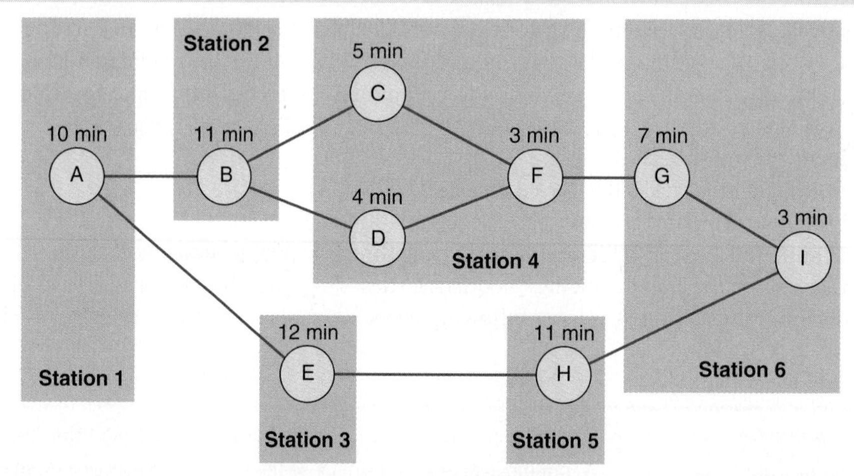

▶ **FIGURE 9.14**
A Six-Station Solution to the Line-Balancing Problem

AUTHOR COMMENT
Tasks C, D, and F can be grouped together in one workstation, provided that the physical facilities and skill levels meet the work requirements.

INSIGHT ▶ This is a reasonably well-balanced assembly line. The second workstation uses 11 minutes, and the third consumes the full 12 minutes. The fourth workstation groups three small tasks and balances perfectly at 12 minutes. The fifth has 1 minute of idle time, and the sixth (consisting of tasks G and I) has 2 minutes of idle time per cycle. Total idle time for this solution is 6 minutes per cycle.

LEARNING EXERCISE ▶ If task I required 6 minutes (instead of 3 minutes), how would this change the solution? [Answer: The cycle time would not change, and the *theoretical* minimum number of workstations would still be 6 (rounded up from 5.75), but it would take 7 stations to balance the line.]

RELATED PROBLEMS ▶ 9.11, 9.12, 9.13, 9.14, 9.15, 9.16, 9.17, 9.18, 9.19, 9.20, 9.21, 9.22, 9.23

We can compute the efficiency of a line balance by dividing the total task time by the product of the number of workstations required times the assigned (actual) cycle time of the longest workstation:

$$\text{Efficiency} = \frac{\Sigma \text{ Task times}}{(\text{Actual number of workstations}) \times (\text{Largest assigned cycle time})} \quad \text{(9-6)}$$

Operations managers compare different levels of efficiency for various numbers of workstations. In this way, a firm can determine the sensitivity of the line to changes in the production rate and workstation assignments.

◀ EXAMPLE 5

Determining line efficiency

Boeing needs to calculate the balance efficiency for Example 4.

APPROACH ▶ Equation (9-6) is applied.

SOLUTION ▶ $\text{Efficiency} = \frac{66 \text{ minutes}}{(6 \text{ stations}) \times (12 \text{ minutes})} = \frac{66}{72} = 91.7\%$

Note that opening a seventh workstation, for whatever reason, would decrease the efficiency of the balance to 78.6% (assuming that at least one of the workstations still required 12 minutes):

$$\text{Efficiency} = \frac{66 \text{ minutes}}{(7 \text{ stations}) \times (12 \text{ minutes})} = 78.6\%$$

INSIGHT ▶ Increasing efficiency may require that some tasks be divided into smaller elements and reassigned to other tasks. This facilitates a better balance between workstations and means higher efficiency.

LEARNING EXERCISE ▶ What is the efficiency if an eighth workstation is opened? [Answer: Efficiency = 68.75%.]

RELATED PROBLEMS ▶ 9.12f, 9.13c, 9.14f, 9.16c, 9.17b, 9.18b, 9.19e,g

Large-scale line-balancing problems, like large process-layout problems, are often solved by computers. Several computer programs are available to handle the assignment of workstations on assembly lines with 100 (or more) individual work activities. Two computer routines, COMSOAL (Computer Method for Sequencing Operations for Assembly Lines) and ASYBL (General Electric's Assembly Line Configuration program), are widely used in larger problems to evaluate the thousands, or even millions, of possible workstation combinations much more efficiently than could ever be done by hand.

In the case of slaughtering operations, the assembly line is actually a disassembly line. The line-balancing procedures described in this chapter are the same as for an assembly line. The chicken-processing plant shown here must balance the work of several hundred employees. The total labor content in each of the chickens processed is a few minutes.

CHAPTER SUMMARY

Layouts make a substantial difference in operating efficiency. The seven layout situations discussed in this chapter are (1) office, (2) retail, (3) warehouse, (4) fixed position, (5) process oriented, (6) work cells, and (7) product oriented. A variety of techniques have been developed to solve these layout problems. Office layouts often seek to maximize information flows, retail firms focus on product exposure, and warehouses attempt to optimize the trade-off between storage space and material handling cost.

The fixed-position layout problem attempts to minimize material handling costs within the constraint of limited space at the site. Process layouts minimize travel distances times the number of trips. Product layouts focus on reducing waste and the imbalance in an assembly line. Work cells are the result of identifying a family of products that justify a special configuration of machinery and equipment that reduces material travel and adjusts imbalances with cross-trained personnel.

Often, the issues in a layout problem are so wide-ranging that finding an optimal solution is not possible. For this reason, layout decisions, although the subject of substantial research effort, remain something of an art.

Key Terms

Office layout (p. 346)
Retail layout (p. 347)
Slotting fees (p. 347)
Servicescape (p. 348)
Warehouse layout (p. 349)
Cross-docking (p. 350)
Random stocking (p. 350)
Customizing (p. 350)
Fixed-position layout (p. 350)
Process-oriented layout (p. 351)
Job lots (p. 352)
Work cell (p. 356)
Takt time (p. 358)
Focused work center (p. 359)
Focused factory (p. 359)
Fabrication line (p. 360)
Assembly line (p. 360)
Assembly-line balancing (p. 361)
Cycle time (p. 363)
Heuristic (p. 364)

Ethical Dilemma

Although buried by mass customization and a proliferation of new products of numerous sizes and variations, grocery chains continue to seek to maximize payoff from their layout. Their layout includes a marketable commodity—shelf space—and they charge for it. This charge is known as a *slotting fee*.* Recent estimates are that food manufacturers now spend some 13% of sales on trade promotions, which is paid to grocers to get them to promote and discount the manufacturer's products. A portion of these fees is for slotting; but slotting fees drive up the manufacturer's cost. They also put the small company with a new product at a disadvantage, because small companies with limited resources are squeezed out of the market place. Slotting fees may also mean that customers may no longer be able to find the special local brand. How ethical are slotting fees?

Discussion Questions

1. What are the seven layout strategies presented in this chapter?
2. What are the three factors that complicate a fixed-position layout?
3. What are the advantages and disadvantages of process layout?
4. How would an analyst obtain data and determine the number of trips in:
   (a) a hospital?
   (b) a machine shop?
   (c) an auto-repair shop?
5. What are the advantages and disadvantages of product layout?
6. What are the four assumptions (or preconditions) of establishing layout for high-volume, low-variety products?
7. What are the three forms of work cells discussed in the textbook?
8. What are the advantages and disadvantages of work cells?
9. What are the requirements for a focused work center or focused factory to be appropriate?
10. What are the two major trends influencing office layout?

*For an interesting discussion of slotting fees, see J. G. Kaikati and A. M. Kaikati, "Slotting and Promotional Allowances," *Supply Chain Management* 11, no. 2 (2006): 140–147; or J. L. Stanton and K. C. Herbst, "Slotting Allowances," *International Journal of Retail & Distribution Management* 34, no. 2/3 (2006): 187–197.

11. What layout variables would you consider particularly important in an office layout where computer programs are written?
12. What layout innovations have you noticed recently in retail establishments?
13. What are the variables that a manager can manipulate in a retail layout?
14. Visit a local supermarket and sketch its layout. What are your observations regarding departments and their locations?
15. What is random stocking?
16. What information is necessary for random stocking to work?
17. Explain the concept of cross-docking.
18. What is a heuristic? Name several that can be used in assembly-line balancing.

Using Software to Solve Layout Problems

In addition to the many commercial software packages available for addressing layout problems, Excel OM and POM for Windows, both of which accompany this text, contain modules for the process problem and the assembly-line-balancing problem.

Using Excel OM

Excel OM can assist in evaluating a series of department work assignments like the one we saw for the Walters Company in Example 1. The layout module can generate an optimal solution by enumeration or by computing the "total movement" cost for each layout you wish to examine. As such, it provides a speedy calculator for each flow–distance pairing.

Program 9.1 illustrates our inputs in the top two tables. We first enter department flows, then provide distances between work areas. Entering area assignments on a trial-and-error basis in the upper left of the top table generates movement computations at the bottom of the screen. Total movement is recalculated each time we try a new area assignment. It turns out that the assignment shown is optimal at 430 feet of movement.

▼ PROGRAM 9.1 Using Excel OM's Process Layout Module to Solve the Walters Company Problem in Example 1

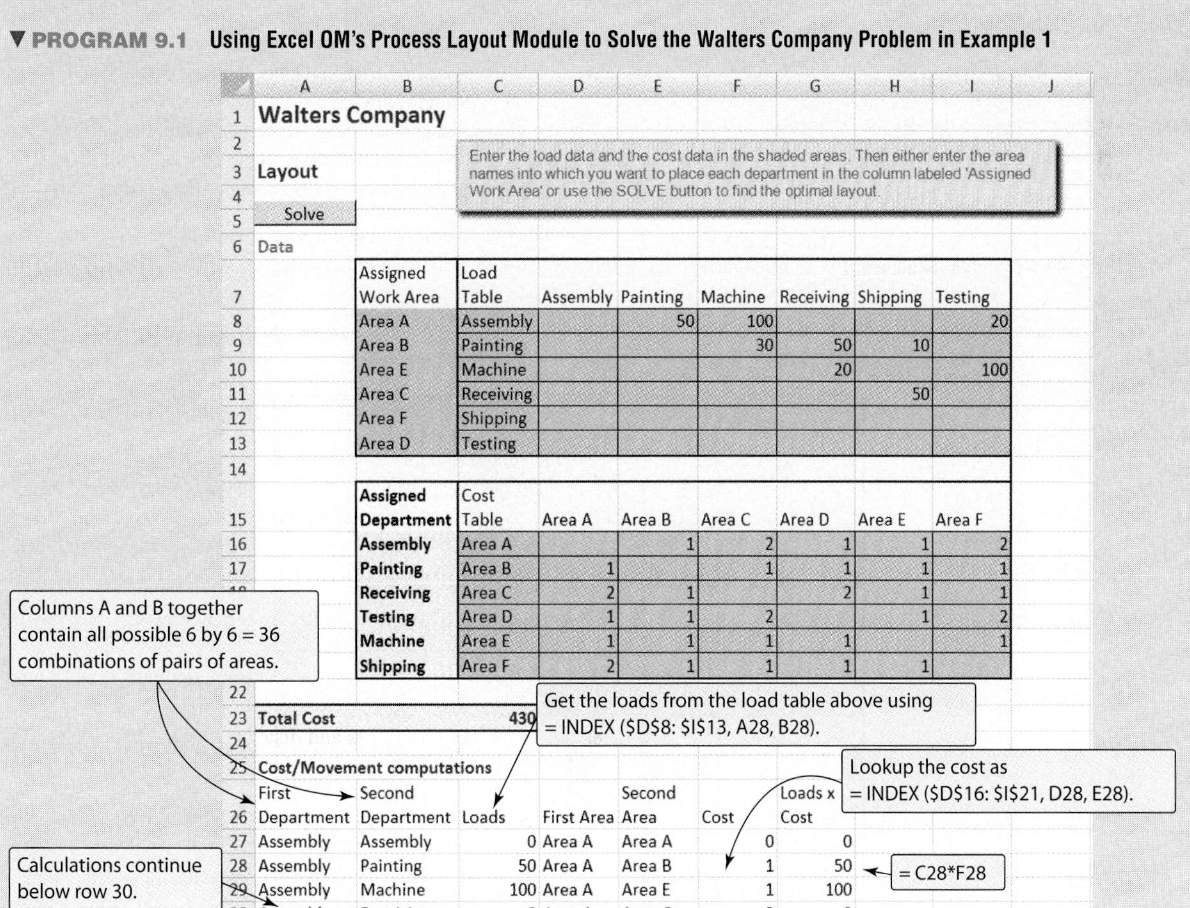

Assigned Work Area	Load Table	Assembly	Painting	Machine	Receiving	Shipping	Testing
Area A	Assembly		50	100			20
Area B	Painting			30	50	10	
Area E	Machine				20		100
Area C	Receiving					50	
Area F	Shipping						
Area D	Testing						

Assigned Department	Cost Table	Area A	Area B	Area C	Area D	Area E	Area F
Assembly	Area A		1	2	1	1	2
Painting	Area B	1		1	1	1	1
Receiving	Area C	2	1		2	1	1
Testing	Area D	1	1	2		1	2
Machine	Area E	1	1	1	1		1
Shipping	Area F	2	1	1	1	1	

First Department	Second Department	Loads	First Area	Second Area	Cost	Loads x Cost
Assembly	Assembly	0	Area A	Area A	0	0
Assembly	Painting	50	Area A	Area B	1	50
Assembly	Machine	100	Area A	Area E	1	100
Assembly	Receiving	0	Area A	Area C	2	0

Using POM for Windows

The POM for Windows facility layout module can be used to place up to 10 departments in 10 rooms to minimize the total distance traveled as a function of the distances between the rooms and the flow between departments. The program exchanges departments until no exchange will reduce the total amount of movement, meaning an optimal solution has been reached.

The POM for Windows and Excel OM modules for line balancing can handle a line with up to 99 tasks, each with up to 6 immediate predecessors. In this program, cycle time can be entered either (1) *given*, if known, or (2) the *demand* rate can be entered with time available as shown. All five "heuristic rules" are used: (1) longest operation (task) time, (2) most following tasks, (3) ranked positional weight, (4) shortest operation (task) time, and (5) least number of following tasks. No one rule can guarantee an optimal solution, but POM for Windows displays the number of stations needed for each rule.

Appendix IV discusses further details regarding POM for Windows.

Solved Problems

Virtual Office Hours help is available at www.myomlab.com.

▼ SOLVED PROBLEM 9.1

Aero Maintenance is a small aircraft engine maintenance facility located in Wichita, Kansas. Its new administrator, Ann Daniel, decides to improve material flow in the facility, using the process-layout method she studied at Wichita State University. The current layout of Aero Maintenance's eight departments is shown in Figure 9.15.

The only physical restriction perceived by Daniel is the need to keep the entrance in its current location. All other departments can be moved to a different work area (each 10 feet square) if layout analysis indicates a move would be beneficial.

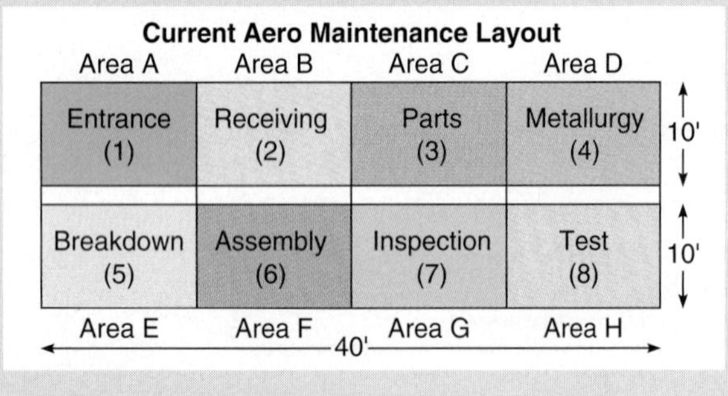

Current Aero Maintenance Layout

Area A	Area B	Area C	Area D	
Entrance (1)	Receiving (2)	Parts (3)	Metallurgy (4)	10'
Breakdown (5)	Assembly (6)	Inspection (7)	Test (8)	10'
Area E	Area F	Area G	Area H	

← 40' →

▲ **FIGURE 9.15 Aero Maintenance Layout**

First, Daniel analyzes records to determine the number of material movements among departments in an average month. These data are shown in Figure 9.16. Her objective, Daniel decides, is to lay out the departments so as to minimize the total movement (distance traveled) of material in the facility. She writes her objective as:

$$\text{Minimize material movement} = \sum_{i=1}^{8} \sum_{j=1}^{8} X_{ij}C_{ij}$$

where X_{ij} = number of material movements per month (loads or trips) moving from department i to department j

C_{ij} = distance in feet between departments i and j (which, in this case, is the equivalent of cost per load to move between departments)

Note that this is only a slight modification of the cost-objective equation shown earlier in the chapter.

► **FIGURE 9.16 Number of Material Movements (Loads) between Departments in One Month**

Department	Entrance (1)	Receiving (2)	Parts (3)	Metallurgy (4)	Breakdown (5)	Assembly (6)	Inspection (7)	Test (8)
Entrance (1)		100	100	0	0	0	0	0
Receiving (2)			0	50	20	0	0	0
Parts (3)				30	30	0	0	0
Metallurgy (4)					20	0	0	20
Breakdown (5)						20	0	10
Assembly (6)							30	0
Inspection (7)								0
Test (8)								

Daniel assumes that adjacent departments, such as entrance (now in work area A) and receiving (now in work area B), have a walking distance of 10 feet. Diagonal departments are also considered adjacent and assigned a distance of 10 feet. Nonadjacent departments, such as the entrance and parts (now in area C) or the entrance and inspection (area G) are 20 feet apart, and nonadjacent rooms, such as entrance and metallurgy (area D), are 30 feet apart. (Hence, 10 feet is considered 10 units of cost, 20 feet is 20 units of cost, and 30 feet is 30 units of cost.)

Given the above information, redesign Aero Maintenance's layout to improve its material flow efficiency.

▼ SOLUTION

First, establish Aero Maintenance's current layout, as shown in Figure 9.17. Then, by analyzing the current layout, compute material movement:

$$\begin{aligned}\text{Total movement} = {} & \underset{1\text{ to }2}{(100\times 10')} + \underset{1\text{ to }3}{(100\times 20')} + \underset{2\text{ to }4}{(50\times 20')} + \underset{2\text{ to }5}{(20\times 10')} \\ & + \underset{3\text{ to }4}{(30\times 10')} + \underset{3\text{ to }5}{(30\times 20')} + \underset{4\text{ to }5}{(20\times 30')} + \underset{4\text{ to }8}{(20\times 10')} \\ & + \underset{5\text{ to }6}{(20\times 10')} + \underset{5\text{ to }8}{(10\times 30')} + \underset{6\text{ to }7}{(30\times 10')} \\ = {} & 1{,}000 + 2{,}000 + 1{,}000 + 200 + 300 + 600 + 600 \\ & + 200 + 200 + 300 + 300 \\ = {} & 6{,}700 \text{ feet}\end{aligned}$$

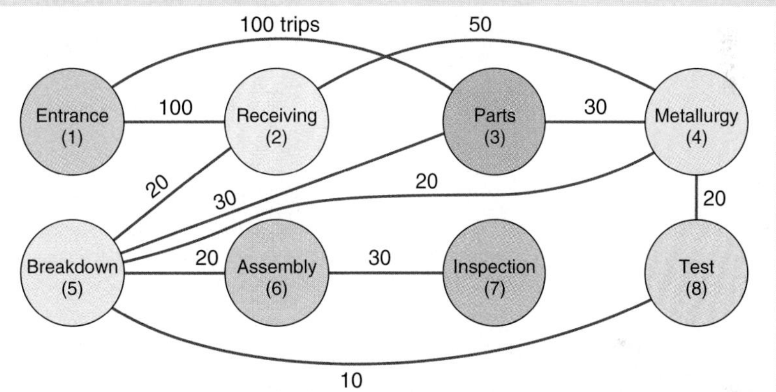

▶ FIGURE 9.17
Current Material Flow

Propose a new layout that will reduce the current figure of 6,700 feet. Two useful changes, for example, are to switch departments 3 and 5 and to interchange departments 4 and 6. This change would result in the schematic shown in Figure 9.18:

$$\begin{aligned}\text{Total movement} = {} & \underset{1\text{ to }2}{(100\times 10')} + \underset{1\text{ to }3}{(100\times 10')} + \underset{2\text{ to }4}{(50\times 10')} + \underset{2\text{ to }5}{(20\times 10')} \\ & + \underset{3\text{ to }4}{(30\times 10')} + \underset{3\text{ to }5}{(30\times 20')} + \underset{4\text{ to }5}{(20\times 10')} + \underset{4\text{ to }8}{(20\times 20')} \\ & + \underset{5\text{ to }6}{(20\times 10')} + \underset{5\text{ to }8}{(10\times 10')} + \underset{6\text{ to }7}{(30\times 10')} \\ = {} & 1{,}000 + 1{,}000 + 500 + 200 + 300 + 600 + 200 \\ & + 400 + 200 + 100 + 300 \\ = {} & 4{,}800 \text{ feet}\end{aligned}$$

Do you see any room for further improvement?

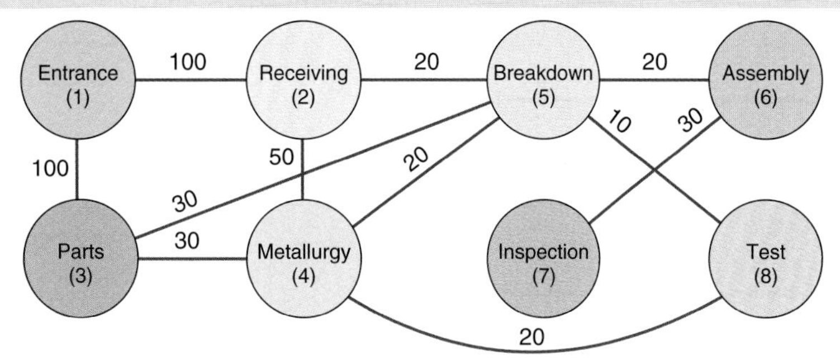

▶ FIGURE 9.18
Improved Layout

▼ SOLVED PROBLEM 9.2

The assembly line whose activities are shown in Figure 9.19 has an 8-minute cycle time. Draw the precedence graph and find the minimum possible number of one-person workstations. Then arrange the work activities into workstations so as to balance the line. What is the efficiency of your line balance?

Task	Performance Time (minutes)	Task Must Follow This Task
A	5	—
B	3	A
C	4	B
D	3	B
E	6	C
F	1	C
G	4	D, E, F
H	2	G
	28	

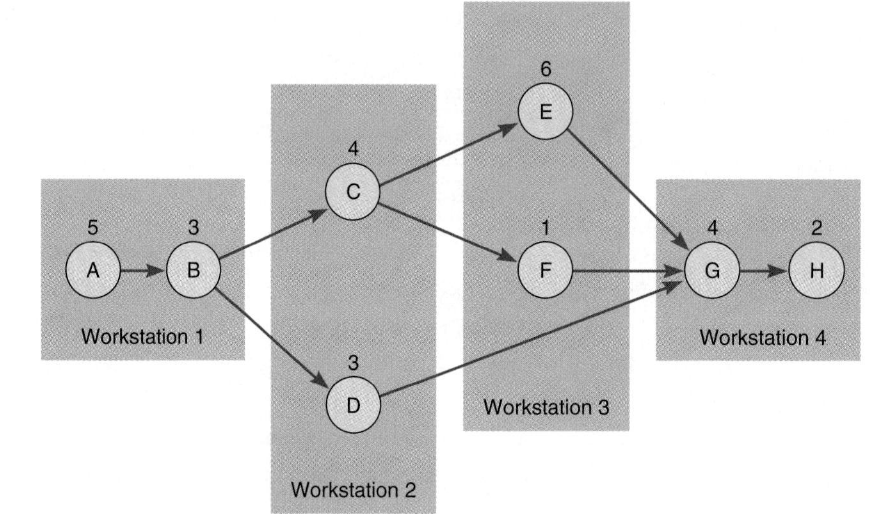

▶ **FIGURE 9.19**
Four-Station Solution to the Line-Balancing Problem

▼ SOLUTION

The theoretical minimum number of workstations is:

$$\frac{\Sigma t_i}{\text{Cycle time}} = \frac{28 \text{ minutes}}{8 \text{ minutes}} = 3.5, \text{ or } 4 \text{ stations}$$

The precedence graph and one good layout are shown in Figure 9.19.

$$\text{Efficiency} = \frac{\text{Total task time}}{(\text{Number of workstations}) \times (\text{Largest cycle time})} = \frac{28}{(4)(8)} = 87.5\%$$

Problems*

•• **9.1** Michael Plumb's job shop has four work areas, A, B, C, and D. Distances in feet between centers of the work areas are:

	A	B	C	D
A	—	4	9	7
B	—	—	6	8
C	—	—	—	10
D	—	—	—	—

Workpieces moved, in 100s of workpieces per week, between pairs of work areas, are:

	A	B	C	D
A	—	8	7	4
B	—	—	3	2
C	—	—	—	6
D	—	—	—	—

It costs Michael $1 to move 1 work piece 1 foot. What is the weekly total material handling cost of the layout? Px

•• **9.2** A Missouri job shop has four departments—machining (M), dipping in a chemical bath (D), finishing (F), and plating (P)—

**Note:* Px means the problem may be solved with POM for Windows and/or Excel OM.

assigned to four work areas. The operations manager, Mary Marrs, has gathered the following data for this job shop as it is currently laid out (Plan A).

100s of Workpieces Moved Between Work Areas Each Year
Plan A

	M	D	F	P
M	—	6	18	2
D	—	—	4	2
F	—	—	—	18
P	—	—	—	—

Distances Between Work Areas (Departments) in Feet

	M	D	F	P
M	—	20	12	8
D	—	—	6	10
F	—	—	—	4
P	—	—	—	—

It costs $0.50 to move 1 workpiece 1 foot in the job shop. Marrs's goal is to find a layout that has the lowest material handling cost.

a) Determine cost of the current layout, Plan A, from the data above.
b) One alternative is to switch those departments with the high loads, namely, finishing (F) and plating (P), which alters the distance between them and machining (M) and dipping (D), as follows:

Distances Between Work Areas (Departments) in Feet
Plan B

	M	D	F	P
M	—	20	8	12
D	—	—	10	6
F	—	—	—	4
P	—	—	—	—

What is the cost of *this* layout?

c) Marrs now wants you to evaluate Plan C, which also switches milling (M) and drilling (D), below.

Distance Between Work Areas (Departments) in Feet
Plan C

	M	D	F	P
M	—	20	10	6
D	—	—	8	12
F	—	—	—	4
P	—	—	—	—

What is the cost of *this* layout?

d) Which layout is best from a cost perspective? PX

• **9.3** Three departments—milling (M), drilling (D), and sawing (S)—are assigned to three work areas in Samuel Smith's machine shop in Baltimore. The number of work pieces moved per day and the distances between the centers of the work areas, in feet, are shown in the next column.

Pieces Moved Between Work Areas Each Day

	M	D	S
M	—	23	32
D	—	—	20
S	—	—	—

Distances Between Centers of Work Areas (Departments) in Feet

	M	D	S
M	—	10	5
D	—	—	8
S	—	—	—

It costs $2 to move 1 workpiece 1 foot.
What is the cost? PX

•• **9.4** Roy Creasey Enterprises, a machine shop, is planning to move to a new, larger location. The new building will be 60 feet long by 40 feet wide. Creasey envisions the building as having six distinct production areas, roughly equal in size. He feels strongly about safety and intends to have marked pathways throughout the building to facilitate the movement of people and materials. See the following building schematic.

Building Schematic (with work areas 1–6)

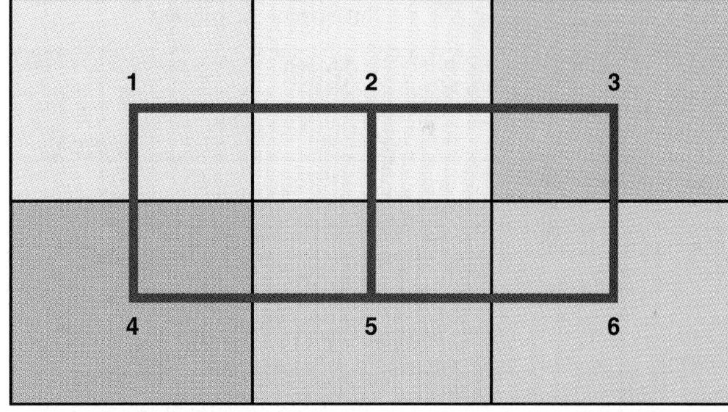

His foreman has completed a month-long study of the number of loads of material that have moved from one process to another in the current building. This information is contained in the following flow matrix.

Flow Matrix between Production Processes

From \ To	Materials	Welding	Drills	Lathes	Grinders	Benders
Materials	0	100	50	0	0	50
Welding	25	0	0	50	0	0
Drills	25	0	0	0	50	0
Lathes	0	25	0	0	20	0
Grinders	50	0	100	0	0	0
Benders	10	0	20	0	0	0

Finally, Creasey has developed the following matrix to indicate distances between the work areas shown in the building schematic.

Distance between Work Areas						
	1	2	3	4	5	6
1		20	40	20	40	60
2			20	40	20	40
3				60	40	20
4					20	40
5						20
6						

What is the appropriate layout of the new building? PX

•• **9.5** Registration at Southern University has always been a time of emotion, commotion, and lines. Students must move among four stations to complete the trying semiannual process. Last semester's registration, held in the fieldhouse, is described in Figure 9.20. You can see, for example, that 450 students moved from the paperwork station (A) to advising (B), and 550 went directly from A to picking up their class cards (C). Graduate students, who for the most part had preregistered, proceeded directly from A to the station where registration is verified and payment collected (D). The layout used last semester is also shown in Figure 9.20. The registrar is preparing to set up this semester's stations and is anticipating similar numbers.

Interstation Activity Mix

	Pick up paperwork and forms (A)	Advising station (B)	Pick up class cards (C)	Verification of status and payment (D)
Paperwork/forms (A)	—	450	550	50
Advising (B)	350	—	200	0
Class cards (C)	0	0	—	750
Verification/payment (D)	0	0	0	—

Existing Layout

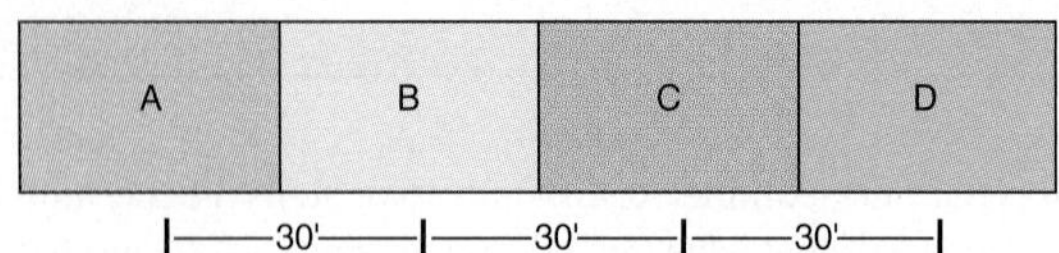

▲ **FIGURE 9.20 Registration Flow of Students**

a) What is the "load × distance," or "movement cost," of the layout shown?

b) Provide an improved layout and compute its movement cost. PX

••• **9.6** You have just been hired as the director of operations for Reid Chocolates, a purveyor of exceptionally fine candies. Reid Chocolates has two kitchen layouts under consideration for its recipe making and testing department. The strategy is to provide the best kitchen layout possible so that food scientists can devote their time and energy to product improvement, not wasted effort in the kitchen. You have been asked to evaluate these two kitchen layouts and to prepare a recommendation for your boss, Mr. Reid, so that he can proceed to place the contract for building the kitchens. (See Figure 9.21(a), and Figure 9.21(b).) PX

▼ **FIGURE 9.21(a) Layout Options**

Number of trips between work centers:

From: \ To:		Refrigerator 1	Counter 2	Sink 3	Storage 4	Stove 5
Refrig.	1	0	8	13	0	0
Counter	2	5	0	3	3	8
Sink	3	3	12	0	4	0
Storage	4	3	0	0	0	5
Stove	5	0	8	4	10	0

▼ **FIGURE 9.21(b)**

Kitchen layout #1

Walking distance in feet

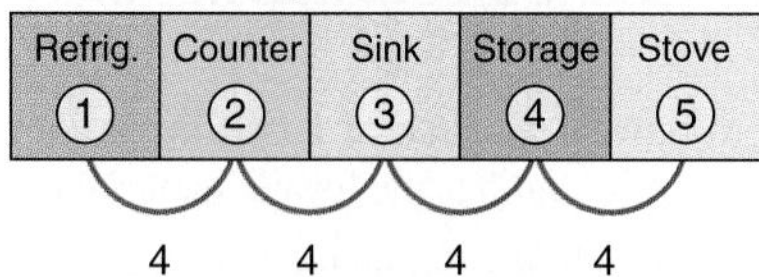

Kitchen layout #2

Walking distance in feet

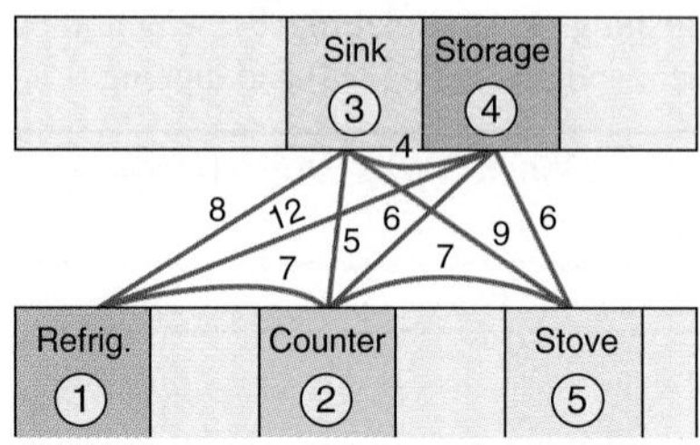

•• **9.7** Reid Chocolates (see Problem 9.6) is considering a third layout, as shown below. Evaluate its effectiveness in trip-distance feet. PX

Kitchen layout #3

Walking distance in feet

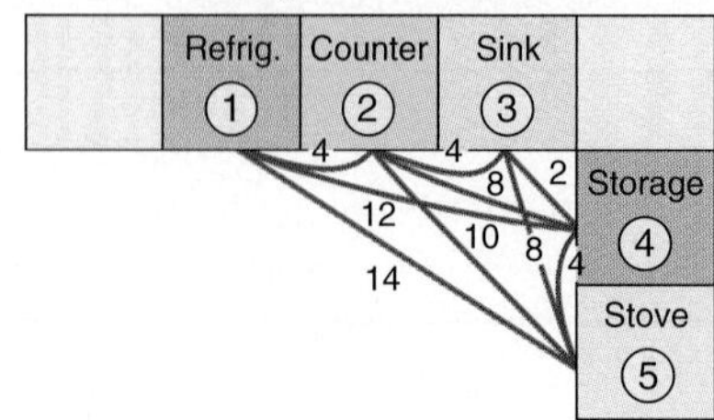

•• **9.8** Reid Chocolates (see Problems 9.6 and 9.7) has yet two more layouts to consider.

a) Layout 4 is shown on the next page. What is the total trip distance?

b) Layout 5, which also follows, has what total trip distance?

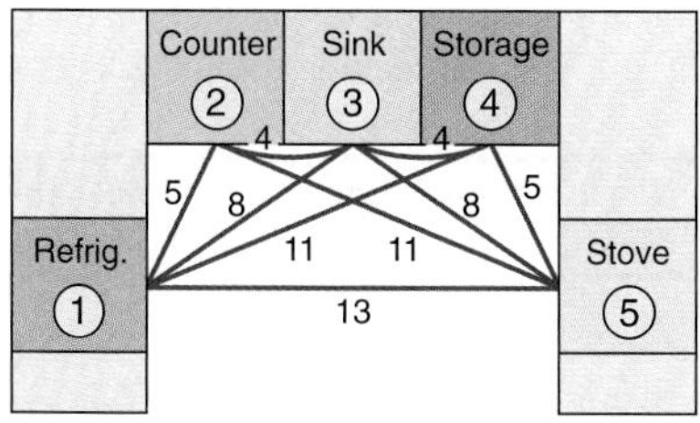

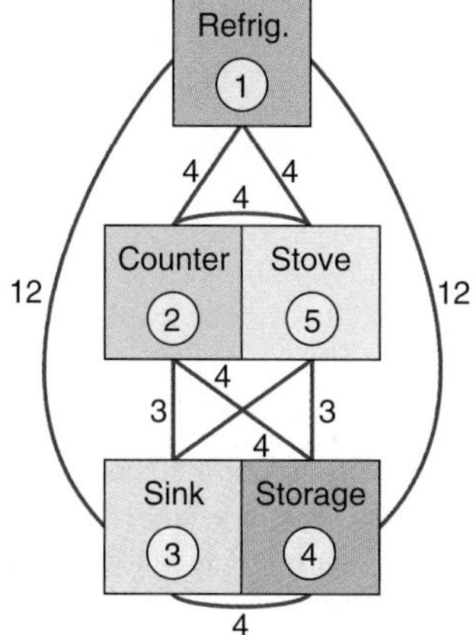

•• **9.9** Six processes are to be laid out in six areas along a long corridor at Linda Babat Accounting Services. The distance between adjacent work centers is 40 feet. The number of trips between work centers is given in the following table:

	Trips between Processes					
	To					
From	**A**	**B**	**C**	**D**	**E**	**F**
A		18	25	73	12	54
B			96	23	31	45
C				41	22	20
D					19	57
E						48
F						

a) Assign the processes to the work areas in a way that minimizes the total flow, using a method that places processes with highest flow adjacent to each other.
b) What assignment minimizes the total traffic flow? PX

•• **9.10** After an extensive product analysis using group technology, Bob Buerlein has identified a product he believes should be pulled out of his process facility and handled in a work cell. Bob has identified the following operations as necessary for the work cell. The customer expects delivery of 250 units per day, and the work day is 420 minutes.
a) What is the takt time?
b) How many employees should be cross-trained for the cell?
c) Which operations may warrant special consideration?

Operation	Standard time (min)
Shear	1.1
Bend	1.1
Weld	1.7
Clean	3.1
Paint	1.0

•• **9.11** Stanford Rosenberg Electronics wants to establish an assembly line for producing a new product, the Personal Little Assistant (PLA). The tasks, task times, and immediate predecessors for the tasks are as follows:

Task	Time (sec)	Immediate Predecessors
A	12	—
B	15	A
C	8	A
D	5	B, C
E	20	D

Rosenberg's goal is to produce 180 PLAs per hour.
a) What is the cycle time?
b) What is the theoretical minimum for the number of workstations that Rosenberg can achieve in this assembly line?
c) Can the theoretical minimum actually be reached when workstations are assigned? PX

••• **9.12** South Carolina Furniture, Inc., produces all types of office furniture. The "Executive Secretary" is a chair that has been designed using ergonomics to provide comfort during long work hours. The chair sells for \$130. There are 480 minutes available during the day, and the average daily demand has been 50 chairs. There are eight tasks:

Task	Performance Time (min)	Task Must Follow Task Listed Below
A	4	—
B	7	—
C	6	A, B
D	5	C
E	6	D
F	7	E
G	8	E
H	6	F, G

a) Draw a precedence diagram of this operation.
b) What is the cycle time for this operation?
c) What is the *theoretical* minimum number of workstations?
d) Assign tasks to workstations.
e) What is the idle time per cycle?
f) How much total idle time is present each day?
g) What is the overall efficiency of the assembly line? PX

•• **9.13** Rita Gibson Appliances wants to establish an assembly line to manufacture its new product, the Mini-Me Microwave Oven. The goal is to produce five Mini-Me Microwave Ovens per hour. The tasks, task times, and immediate predecessors for producing one Mini-Me Microwave Oven are as follows:

Task	Time (min)	Immediate Predecessors
A	10	—
B	12	A
C	8	A, B
D	6	B, C
E	6	C
F	6	D, E

a) What is the *theoretical* minimum for the smallest number of workstations that Gibson can achieve in this assembly line?
b) Graph the assembly line and assign workers to workstations. Can you assign them with the theoretical minimum?
c) What is the efficiency of *your* assignment? PX

•• **9.14** The Temple Toy Company has decided to manufacture a new toy tractor, the production of which is broken into six steps. The demand for the tractor is 4,800 units per 40-hour workweek:

Task	Performance Time (sec)	Predecessors
A	20	None
B	30	A
C	15	A
D	15	A
E	10	B, C
F	30	D, E

a) Draw a precedence diagram of this operation.
b) Given the demand, what is the cycle time for this operation?
c) What is the *theoretical* minimum number of workstations?
d) Assign tasks to workstations.
e) How much total idle time is present each cycle?
f) What is the overall efficiency of the assembly line with five stations; and with six stations? PX

•• **9.15** The following table details the tasks required for Dallas-based T. Liscio Industries to manufacture a fully portable industrial vacuum cleaner. The times in the table are in minutes. Demand forecasts indicate a need to operate with a cycle time of 10 minutes.

Activity	Activity Description	Immediate Predecessors	Time
A	Attach wheels to tub	—	5
B	Attach motor to lid	—	1.5
C	Attach battery pack	B	3
D	Attach safety cutoff	C	4
E	Attach filters	B	3
F	Attach lid to tub	A, E	2
G	Assemble attachments	—	3
H	Function test	D, F, G	3.5
I	Final inspection	H	2
J	Packing	I	2

a) Draw the appropriate precedence diagram for this production line.
b) Assign tasks to workstations and determine how much idle time is present each cycle?
c) Discuss how this balance could be improved to 100%.
d) What is the *theoretical* minimum number of workstations? PX

•• **9.16** Tailwind, Inc., produces high-quality but expensive training shoes for runners. The Tailwind shoe, which sells for $210, contains both gas- and liquid-filled compartments to provide more stability and better protection against knee, foot, and back injuries. Manufacturing the shoes requires 10 separate tasks. There are 400 minutes available for manufacturing the shoes in the plant each day. Daily demand is 60. The information for the tasks is as follows:

Task	Performance Time (min)	Task Must Follow Task Listed Below
A	1	—
B	3	A
C	2	B
D	4	B
E	1	C, D
F	3	A
G	2	F
H	5	G
I	1	E, H
J	3	I

a) Draw the precedence diagram.
b) Assign tasks to the minimum feasible number of workstations according to the "ranked positioned weight" decision rule.
c) What is the efficiency of the process?
d) What is the idle time per cycle? PX

•• **9.17** The Mach 10 is a one-person sailboat manufactured by Creative Leisure. The final assembly plant is in Cupertino, California. The assembly area is available for production of the Mach 10 for 200 minutes per day. (The rest of the time it is busy making other products.) The daily demand is 60 boats. Given the following information,

a) Draw the precedence diagram and assign tasks using five workstations.
b) What is the efficiency of the assembly line, using your answer to (a)?
c) What is the *theoretical* minimum number of workstations?
d) What is the idle time per boat produced? PX

Task	Performance Time (min)	Task Must Follow Task Listed Below
A	1	—
B	1	A
C	2	A
D	1	C
E	3	C
F	1	C
G	1	D, E, F
H	2	B
I	1	G, H

•• **9.18** Because of the expected high demand for Mach 10, Creative Leisure has decided to increase manufacturing time available to produce the Mach 10 (see Problem 9.17).

a) If demand remained the same but 300 minutes were available each day on the assembly line, how many workstations would be needed?
b) What would be the efficiency of the new system?
c) What would be the impact on the system if 400 minutes were available? PX

••• **9.19** Dr. Lori Baker, operations manager at Nesa Electronics, prides herself on excellent assembly-line balancing. She has been told that the firm needs to complete 96 instruments per 24-hour day. The assembly-line activities are:

Task	Time (min)	Predecessors
A	3	—
B	6	—
C	7	A
D	5	A, B
E	2	B
F	4	C
G	5	F
H	7	D, E
I	1	H
J	6	E
K	4	G, I, J
	50	

a) Draw the precedence diagram.
b) If the daily (24-hour) production rate is 96 units, what is the highest allowable cycle time?
c) If the cycle time after allowances is given as 10 minutes, what is the daily (24-hour) production rate?
d) With a 10-minute cycle time, what is the theoretical minimum number of stations with which the line can be balanced?
e) With a 10-minute cycle time and six workstations, what is the efficiency?
f) What is the total idle time per cycle with a 10-minute cycle time and six workstations?
g) What is the best work station assignment you can make without exceeding a 10-minute cycle time and what is its efficiency? PX

•• **9.20** Suppose production requirements in Solved Problem 9.2 (see page 370) increase and require a reduction in cycle time from 8 minutes to 7 minutes. Balance the line once again, using the new cycle time. Note that it is not possible to combine task times so as to group tasks into the minimum number of workstations. This condition occurs in actual balancing problems fairly often. PX

•• **9.21** The preinduction physical examination given by the U.S. Army involves the following seven activities:

Activity	Average Time (min)
Medical history	10
Blood tests	8
Eye examination	5
Measurements (i.e., weight, height, blood pressure)	7
Medical examination	16
Psychological interview	12
Exit medical evaluation	10

These activities can be performed in any order, with two exceptions: Medical history must be taken first, and Exit medical evaluation is last. At present, there are three paramedics and two physicians on duty during each shift. Only physicians can perform exit evaluations and conduct psychological interviews. Other activities can be carried out by either physicians or paramedics.
a) Develop a layout and balance the line.
b) How many people can be processed per hour?
c) Which activity accounts for the current bottleneck?
d) What is the total idle time per cycle?
e) If one more physician and one more paramedic can be placed on duty, how would you redraw the layout? What is the new throughput?

••• **9.22** Frank Pianki's company wants to establish an assembly line to manufacture its new product, the iScan phone. Frank's goal is to produce 60 iScans per hour. Tasks, task times, and immediate predecessors are as follows:

Task	Time (sec)	Immediate Predecessors	Task	Time (sec)	Immediate Predecessors
A	40	—	F	25	C
B	30	A	G	15	C
C	50	A	H	20	D, E
D	40	B	I	18	F, G
E	6	B	J	30	H, I

a) What is the theoretical minimum for the number of workstations that Frank can achieve in this assembly line?
b) Use the *most following tasks* heuristic to balance an assembly line for the iScan phone.
c) How many workstations are in your answer to (b)?
d) What is the efficiency of your answer to (b)? PX

•••• **9.23** As the Cottrell Bicycle Co. of St. Louis completes plans for its new assembly line, it identifies 25 different tasks in the production process. VP of Operations Jonathan Cottrell now faces the job of balancing the line. He lists precedences and provides time estimates for each step based on work-sampling techniques. His goal is to produce 1,000 bicycles per standard 40-hour workweek.

Task	Time (sec)	Precedence Tasks	Task	Time (sec)	Precedence Tasks
K3	60	—	E3	109	F3
K4	24	K3	D6	53	F4
K9	27	K3	D7	72	F9, E2, E3
J1	66	K3	D8	78	E3, D6
J2	22	K3	D9	37	D6
J3	3	—	C1	78	F7
G4	79	K4, K9	B3	72	D7, D8, D9, C1
G5	29	K9, J1	B5	108	C1
F3	32	J2	B7	18	B3
F4	92	J2	A1	52	B5
F7	21	J3	A2	72	B5
F9	126	G4	A3	114	B7, A1, A2
E2	18	G5, F3			

a) Balance this operation, using various heuristics. Which is best and why?
b) What happens if the firm can change to a 41-hour workweek? PX

▶ **Refer to myomlab for these additional homework problems: 9.24–9.27**

Case Studies

▶ State Automobile License Renewals

Henry Coupe, the manager of a metropolitan branch office of the state department of motor vehicles, attempted to analyze the driver's license–renewal operations. He had to perform several steps. After examining the license-renewal process, he identified those steps and associated times required to perform each step, as shown in the following table:

State Automobile License–Renewal Process Times

Step	Average Time to Perform (seconds)
1. Review renewal application for correctness	15
2. Process and record payment	30
3. Check file for violations and restrictions	60
4. Conduct eye test	40
5. Photograph applicant	20
6. Issue temporary license	30

Coupe found that each step was assigned to a different person. Each application was a separate process in the sequence shown. He determined that his office should be prepared to accommodate a maximum demand of processing 120 renewal applicants per hour.

He observed that work was unevenly divided among clerks and that the clerk responsible for checking violations tended to shortcut her task to keep up with the others. Long lines built up during the maximum-demand periods.

Coupe also found that Steps 1 to 4 were handled by general clerks who were each paid \$12 per hour. Step 5 was performed by a photographer paid \$16 per hour. (Branch offices were charged \$10 per hour for each camera to perform photography.) Step 6, issuing temporary licenses, was required by state policy to be handled by uniformed motor vehicle officers. Officers were paid \$18 per hour but could be assigned to any job except photography.

A review of the jobs indicated that Step 1, reviewing applications for correctness, had to be performed before any other step could be taken. Similarly, Step 6, issuing temporary licenses, could not be performed until all the other steps were completed.

Henry Coupe was under severe pressure to increase productivity and reduce costs, but he was also told by the regional director that he must accommodate the demand for renewals. Otherwise, "heads would roll."

Discussion Questions

1. What is the maximum number of applications per hour that can be handled by the present configuration of the process?
2. How many applications can be processed per hour if a second clerk is added to check for violations?
3. If the second clerk could be added *anywhere* you choose (and not necessarily to check for violations, as in question 2), what is the maximum number of applications the process can handle? What is the new configuration?
4. How would you suggest modifying the process to accommodate 120 applications per hour? What is the cost per application of this new configuration?

Source: Modified from a case by W. Earl Sasser, Paul R. Olson, and D. Daryl Wyckoff, *Management of Services Operations: Text, Cases, and Readings* (Boston: Allyn & Bacon).

▶ Laying Out Arnold Palmer Hospital's New Facility

Video Case

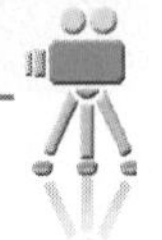

When Orlando's Arnold Palmer Hospital began plans to create a new 273-bed, 11-story hospital across the street from its existing facility, which was bursting at the seams in terms of capacity, a massive planning process began. The \$100 million building, opened in 2006, was long overdue, according to Executive Director Kathy Swanson: "We started Arnold Palmer Hospital in 1989, with a mission to provide quality services for children and women in a comforting, family-friendly environment. Since then we have served well over 1.5 million women and children and now deliver more than 12,000 babies a year. By 2001, we simply ran out of room, and it was time for us to grow."

The new hospital's unique, circular pod design provides a maximally efficient layout in all areas of the hospital, creating a patient-centered environment. *Servicescape* design features include a serene environment created through the use of warm colors, private rooms with pull-down Murphy beds for family members, 14-foot ceilings, and natural lighting with oversized windows in patient rooms. But these radical new features did not come easily. "This pod concept with a central nursing area and pie-shaped rooms resulted from over 1,000 planning meetings of 35 user groups, extensive motion and time studies, and computer simulations of the daily movements of nurses," says Swanson.

In a traditional linear hospital layout, called the *racetrack* design, patient rooms line long hallways, and a nurse might walk 2.7 miles per day serving patient needs at Arnold Palmer. "Some nurses spent 30% of their time simply walking. With the nursing shortage and the high cost of health care professionals, efficiency is a major concern," added Swanson. With the nursing station in the center of 10- or 12-bed circular pods, no patient room is more than 14 feet from a station. The time savings are in the 20% range. Swanson pointed to Figures 9.22 and 9.23 as examples of the old and new walking and trip distances.*

"We have also totally redesigned our neonatal rooms," says Swanson. "In the old system, there were 16 neonatal beds in a large and often noisy rectangular room. The new building features

*Layout and walking distances, including some of the numbers in Figures 9.22 and 9.23, have been simplified for purposes of this case.

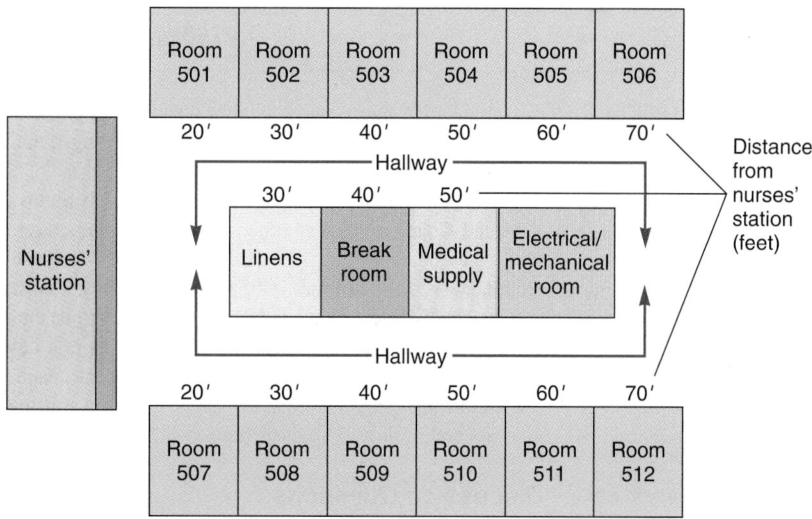

◄ **FIGURE 9.22**
Traditional Hospital Layout
Patient rooms are on two linear hallways with exterior windows. Supply rooms are on interior corridors. This layout is called a "racetrack" design.

semiprivate rooms for these tiny babies. The rooms are much improved, with added privacy and a quiet, simulated night atmosphere, in addition to pull-down beds for parents to use. Our research shows that babies improve and develop much more quickly with this layout design. Layout and environment indeed impact patient care!"

Discussion Questions*

1. Identify the many variables that a hospital needs to consider in layout design.
2. What are the advantages of the circular pod design over the traditional linear hallway layout found in most hospitals?
3. Figure 9.22 illustrates a sample linear hallway layout. During a period of random observation, nurse Thomas Smith's day includes 6 trips from the nursing station to each of the 12 patient rooms (back and forth), 20 trips to the medical supply room, 5 trips to the break room, and 12 trips to the linen supply room. What is his total distance traveled in miles?
4. Figure 9.23 illustrates an architect's drawing of Arnold Palmer Hospital's new circular pod system. If nurse Susan Jones's day includes 7 trips from the nursing pod to each of the 12 rooms (back and forth), 20 trips to central medical supply, 6 trips to the break room, and 12 trips to the pod linen supply, how many miles does she walk during her shift? What are the differences in the travel times between the two nurses for this random day?
5. The concept of *servicescapes* is discussed in this chapter. Describe why this is so important at Arnold Palmer Hospital and give examples of its use in layout design.

*You may wish to view the video that accompanies this case before addressing these questions.

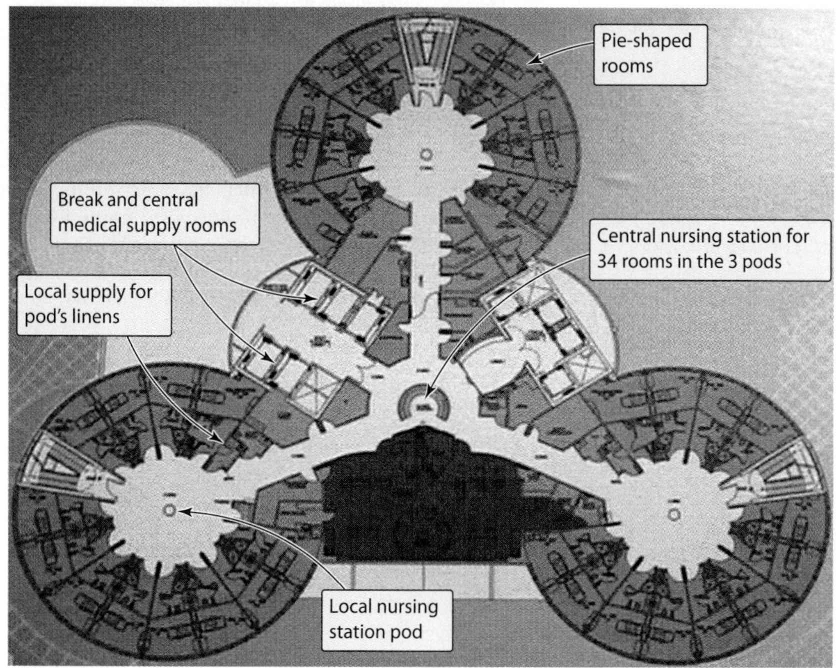

◄ **FIGURE 9.23**
New Pod Design for Hospital Layout
Note that each room is 14 feet from the pod's *local* nursing station. The *break rooms* and the *central medical station* are each about 60 feet from the local nursing pod. Pod *linen supply* rooms are also 14 feet from the local nursing station.

▶ Facility Layout at Wheeled Coach

Video Case

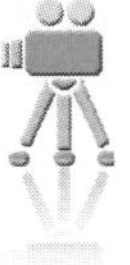

When President Bob Collins began his career at Wheeled Coach, the world's largest manufacturer of ambulances, there were only a handful of employees. Now the firm's Florida plant has a workforce of 350. The physical plant has also expanded, with offices, R&D, final assembly, and wiring, cabinetry, and upholstery work cells in one large building. Growth has forced the painting work cell into a separate building, aluminum fabrication and body installation into another, inspection and shipping into a fourth, and warehousing into yet another.

Like many other growing companies, Wheeled Coach was not able to design its facility from scratch. And although management realizes that material handling costs are a little higher than an ideal layout would provide, Collins is pleased with the way the facility has evolved and employees have adapted. The aluminum cutting work cell lies adjacent to body fabrication, which, in turn, is located next to the body-installation work cell. And while the vehicle must be driven across a street to one building for painting and then to another for final assembly, at least the ambulance is on wheels. Collins is also satisfied with the flexibility shown in design of the work cells. Cell construction is flexible and can accommodate changes in product mix and volume. In addition, work cells are typically small and movable, with many work benches and staging racks borne on wheels so that they can be easily rearranged and products transported to the assembly line.

Assembly-line balancing is one key problem facing Wheeled Coach and every other repetitive manufacturer. Produced on a schedule calling for four 10-hour work days per week, once an ambulance is on one of the six final assembly lines, it *must* move forward each day to the next workstation. Balancing just enough workers and tasks at each of the seven workstations is a never-ending challenge. Too many workers end up running into each other; too few can't finish an ambulance in 7 days. Constant shifting of design and mix and improved analysis has led to frequent changes.

Discussion Questions*

1. What analytical techniques are available to help a company like Wheeled Coach deal with layout problems?
2. What suggestions would you make to Bob Collins about his layout?
3. How would you measure the "efficiency" of this layout?

*You may wish to view the video that accompanies this case before addressing these questions.

▶**Additional Case Study:** Visit **www.myomlab.com** or **www.pearsonhighered.com/heizer** *for this free case study:*
Microfix, Inc.: This company needs to balance its PC manufacturing assembly line and deal with sensitivity analysis of time estimates.

Bibliography

Birchfield, J. C., and J. Birchfield. *Design and Layout of Foodservice Facilities*, 3rd ed. New York, Wiley & Sons, 2007.

Francis, R. L., L. F. McGinnis, and J. A. White. *Facility Layout and Location*, 3rd ed. Upper Saddle River, NJ: Prentice Hall, 1998.

Gultekin, H., O. Y. Karasan, and M. S. Akturk. "Pure Cycles in Flexible Robotic Cells." *Computers & Operations Research* 36, no. 2 (February 2009): 329.

Heragu, S. S. *Facilities Design,* 3rd ed. New York: CRC Press, 2008.

Heyer, N., and U. Wemmerlöv. *Reorganizing the Factory: Competing through Cellular Manufacturing.* Portland, OR: Productivity Press, 2002.

Johnson, Alan. "Getting the Right Factory Layout." *Manufacturer's Monthly* (July 2008): 16.

Kator, C. "Crossdocking on the Rise." *Modern Materials Handling* 63, no. 6 (June 2008): 15.

Kee, Micah R. "The Well-Ordered Warehouse." *APICS: The Performance Advantage* (March 2003): 20–24.

Keeps, David A. "Out-of-the-Box Offices." *Fortune* 159, no.1 (January 19, 2009): 45.

Larson, S. "Extreme Makover—OR Edition." *Nursing Management* (November 2005): 26.

Panchalavarapu, P. R., and V. Chankong. "Design of Cellular Manufacturing System with Assembly Considerations." *Computers & Industrial Engineering* 48, no. 3 (May 2005): 448.

Roodbergen, K. J., and I. F. A. Vis. "A Model for Warehouse Layout." *IIE Transactions* 38, no. 10 (October 2006): 799–811.

Stanowy, A. "Evolutionary Strategy for Manufacturing Cell Design." *Omega* 34, no. 1 (January 2006): 1.

Tompkins, James A. *Facility Planning*, 4th ed. New York: Wiley, 2009.

Upton, David. "What Really Makes Factories Flexible?" *Harvard Business Review* 73, no. 4 (July–August 1995): 74–84.

Zeng, A. Z., M. Mahan, and N. Fleut. "Designing an Efficient Warehouse Layout to Facilitate the Order-Filling Process." *Production and Inventory Management Journal* 43, no. 3–4 (3rd/4th Quarter 2002): 83–88.

Zhao, T., and C. L. Tseng. "Flexible Facility Interior Layout." *The Journal of the Operational Research Society* 58, no. 6 (June 2007): 729–740.

Chapter 9 ***Rapid* Review**

PEARSON myomlab

Main Heading	Review Material	
THE STRATEGIC IMPORTANCE OF LAYOUT DECISIONS (p. 344)	Layout has numerous strategic implications because it establishes an organization's competitive priorities in regard to capacity, processes, flexibility, and cost, as well as quality of work life, customer contact, and image. *The objective of layout strategy is to develop an effective and efficient layout that will meet the firm's competitive requirements.*	
TYPES OF LAYOUT (pp. 344–346)	Types of layout and examples of their typical objectives include: 1. *Office layout:* Locate workers requiring frequent contact close to one another. 2. *Retail layout:* Expose customers to high-margin items. 3. *Warehouse layout:* Balance low-cost storage with low-cost material handling. 4. *Fixed-position layout:* Move material to the limited storage areas around the site. 5. *Process-oriented layout:* Manage varied material flow for each product. 6. *Work-cell layout:* Identify a product family, build teams, and cross-train team members. 7. *Product-oriented layout:* Equalize the task time at each workstation.	
OFFICE LAYOUT (pp. 346–347)	■ **Office layout**—The grouping of workers, their equipment, and spaces/offices to provide for comfort, safety, and movement of information. A *relationship chart* displays a "closeness value" between each pair of people and/or departments that need to be placed in the office layout.	
RETAIL LAYOUT (pp. 347–349)	■ **Retail layout**—An approach that addresses flow, allocates space, and responds to customer behavior. Retail layouts are based on the idea that sales and profitability vary directly with customer exposure to products. The main *objective of retail layout is to maximize profitability per square foot of floor space* (or, in some stores, per linear foot of shelf space). ■ **Slotting fees**—Fees manufacturers pay to get shelf space for their products. ■ **Servicescape**—The physical surroundings in which a service takes place and how they affect customers and employees.	
WAREHOUSING AND STORAGE LAYOUT (pp. 349–350)	■ **Warehouse layout**—A design that attempts to minimize total cost by addressing trade-offs between space and material handling. The variety of items stored and the number of items "picked" has direct bearing on the optimal layout. Modern warehouse management is often an automated procedure using *automated storage and retrieval systems* (ASRSs). ■ **Cross-docking**—Avoiding the placement of materials or supplies in storage by processing them as they are received for shipment. Cross-docking requires both tight scheduling and accurate inbound product identification. ■ **Random stocking**—Used in warehousing to locate stock wherever there is an open location. ■ **Customizing**—Using warehousing to add value to a product through component modification, repair, labeling, and packaging.	
FIXED-POSITION LAYOUT (pp. 350–351)	■ **Fixed-position layout**—A system that addresses the layout requirements of stationary projects. Fixed-position layouts involve three complications: (1) There is limited space at virtually all sites, (2) different materials are needed at different stages of a project, and (3) the volume of materials needed is dynamic.	
PROCESS-ORIENTED LAYOUT (pp. 351–355)	■ **Process-oriented layout**—A layout that deals with low-volume, high-variety production in which like machines and equipment are grouped together. ■ **Job lots**—Groups or batches of parts processed together. Material handling cost minimization $= \sum_{i=1}^{n}\sum_{j=1}^{n} X_{ij} C_{ij}$ (9-1)	Problems: 9.1–9.9 Virtual Office Hours for Solved Problem: 9.1 **VIDEO 9.1** Arnold Palmer Hospital **ACTIVE MODEL 9.1**

Chapter 9 **Rapid Review** *continued*

PEARSON myomlab

Main Heading	Review Material	
WORK CELLS (pp. 356–359)	■ **Work cell**—An arrangement of machines and personnel that focuses on making a single product or family of related products. ■ **Takt time**—Pace of production to meet customer demands. Takt time = Total work time available/Units required (9-2) Workers required = Total operation time required/Takt time (9-3) ■ **Focused work center**—A permanent or semi-permanent product-oriented arrangement of machines and personnel. ■ **Focused factory**—A facility designed to produce similar products or components.	Problem: 9.10
REPETITIVE AND PRODUCT-ORIENTED LAYOUT (pp. 360–365)	■ **Fabrication line**—A machine-paced, product-oriented facility for building components. ■ **Assembly line**—An approach that puts fabricated parts together at a series of workstations; a repetitive process. ■ **Assembly-line balancing**—Obtaining output at each workstation on a production line in order to minimize delay. Cycle time = Production time available per day ÷ Units required per day (9-4) Minimum number of workstations = $\sum_{i=1}^{n}$ Time for task i ÷ Cycle time (9-5) ■ **Heuristic**—Problem solving using procedures and rules rather than mathematical optimization. Line balancing heuristics include *longest task (operation) time, most following tasks, ranked positional weight, shortest task (operation) time, and least number of following tasks.* $\text{Efficiency} = \dfrac{\sum \text{Task times}}{(\text{Actual number of workstations}) \times (\text{Largest assigned cycle time})}$ (9-6)	Problems: 9.11–9.22 **VIDEO 9.2** Facility Layout at Wheeled Coach Ambulances Virtual Office Hours for Solved Problem: 9.2

Self Test

■ **Before taking the self-test,** refer to the learning objectives listed at the beginning of the chapter and the key terms listed at the end of the chapter.

LO1. Which of the statements below best describes *office layout*?
- **a)** Groups workers, their equipment, and spaces/offices to provide for movement of information.
- **b)** Addresses the layout requirements of large, bulky projects such as ships and buildings.
- **c)** Seeks the best personnel and machine utilization in repetitive or continuous production.
- **d)** Allocates shelf space and responds to customer behavior.
- **e)** Deals with low-volume, high-variety production.

LO2. Which of the following does *not* support the retail layout objective of maximizing customer exposure to products?
- **a)** Locate high-draw items around the periphery of the store.
- **b)** Use prominent locations for high-impulse and high-margin items.
- **c)** Maximize exposure to expensive items.
- **d)** Use end-aisle locations.
- **e)** Convey the store's mission with the careful positioning of the lead-off department.

LO3. The major problem addressed by the warehouse layout strategy is:
- **a)** minimizing difficulties caused by material flow varying with each product.
- **b)** requiring frequent contact close to one another.
- **c)** addressing trade-offs between space and material handling.
- **d)** balancing product flow from one workstation to the next.
- **e)** none of the above.

LO4. A fixed-position layout:
- **a)** groups workers to provide for movement of information.
- **b)** addresses the layout requirements of large, bulky projects such as ships and buildings.
- **c)** seeks the best machine utilization in continuous production.
- **d)** allocates shelf space based on customer behavior.
- **e)** deals with low-volume, high-variety production.

LO5. A process-oriented layout:
- **a)** groups workers to provide for movement of information.
- **b)** addresses the layout requirements of large, bulky projects such as ships and buildings.
- **c)** seeks the best machine utilization in continuous production.
- **d)** allocates shelf space based on customer behavior.
- **e)** deals with low-volume, high-variety production.

LO6. For a focused work center or focused factory to be appropriate, the following three factors are required:
- **a)** ______________________
- **b)** ______________________
- **c)** ______________________

LO7. Before considering a product-oriented layout, it is important to be certain that:
- **a)** ______________________
- **b)** ______________________
- **c)** ______________________
- **d)** ______________________

LO8. An assembly line is to be designed for a product whose completion requires 21 minutes of work. The factory works 400 minutes per day. Can a production line with five workstations make 100 units per day?
- **a)** Yes, with exactly 100 minutes to spare.
- **b)** No, but four workstations would be sufficient.
- **c)** No, it will fall short even with a perfectly balanced line.
- **d)** Yes, but the line's efficiency is very low.
- **e)** Cannot be determined from the information given.

Answers: LO1. a; LO2. c; LO3. c; LO4. b; LO5. e; LO6. family of products, stable forecast (demand), volume; LO7. adequate volume, stable demand, standardized product, adequate/quality supplies; LO8. c.

10 Human Resources, Job Design, and Work Measurement

Chapter Outline

10

OM Strategy Decisions

- Ten OM Strategy Decisions
- Design of Goods and Services
- Managing Quality
- Process Strategy
- Location Strategies
- Layout Strategies
- **Human Resources**
- Supply-Chain Management
- Inventory Management
- Scheduling
- Maintenance

HIGH-PERFORMANCE TEAMWORK FROM THE PIT CREW MAKES THE DIFFERENCE BETWEEN WINNING AND LOSING

In the 1990s, the popularity of NASCAR (National Association for Stock Car Auto Racing) exploded, bringing hundreds of millions of TV and sponsorship dollars into the sport. With more money, competition increased, as did the rewards for winning on Sunday. The teams, headed by such names as Rusty Wallace, Jeff Gordon, Dale Earnhardt, Jr., and Tony Stewart, are as famous as the New York Yankees, Atlanta Hawks, or Chicago Bears.

The race car drivers may be famous, but it's the pit crews who often determine the outcome of a race. Twenty years ago, crews were auto mechanics during the week who simply did double duty on Sundays in the pits. They did pretty well to change four tires in less than 30 seconds. Today, because NASCAR teams find competitive advantage wherever they can, taking more than 16 seconds can be disastrous. A botched pit stop is the equivalent of ramming your car against the wall—crushing all hopes for the day.

▲ This Goodyear tire comes off Rusty Wallace's car and is no longer needed after going around the track for more than 40 laps in a June 19 Michigan International Speedway race.

On Rusty Wallace's team, as on all the top NASCAR squads, the crewmen who go "over the wall" are now athletes, usually ex-college football or basketball players with proven agility and strength. The Evernham team, for example, includes a former defensive back from Fairleigh Dickinson (who is now a professional tire carrier) and a 300-pound lineman from East Carolina University (who handles the jack). The Chip Ganassi racing team includes baseball players from Wake Forest, football players from University of Kentucky and North Carolina, and a hockey player from Dartmouth.

Tire changers—the guys who wrench lug nuts off and on—are a scarce human resource and average $100,000 a year in salary. Jeff Gordon was reminded of the importance of coordinated teamwork when five of his "over-the-wall" guys jumped to Dale Jarrett's organization a few years ago; it was believed to be a $500,000 per year deal.

A pit crew consists of seven men: a front-tire changer; a rear-tire changer; front- and rear-tire carriers; a man who jacks the car up; and two gas men with an 11-gallon can.

Every sport has its core competencies and key metrics—for example, the speed of a pitcher's fastball,

▲ Jamie Rolewicz takes tires from a pile of used tires and puts them onto a cart.

▲ Lap 91—Tire is removed from Rusty Wallace's car.

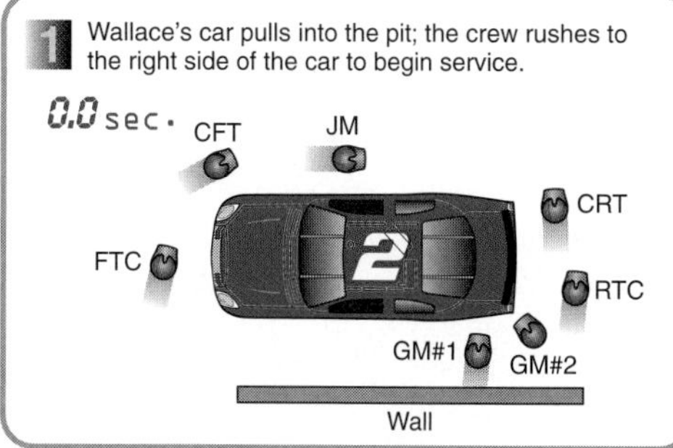

1 Wallace's car pulls into the pit; the crew rushes to the right side of the car to begin service.

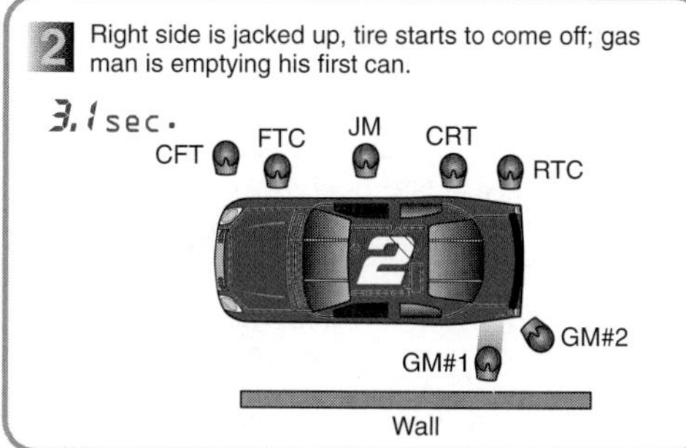

2 Right side is jacked up, tire starts to come off; gas man is emptying his first can.

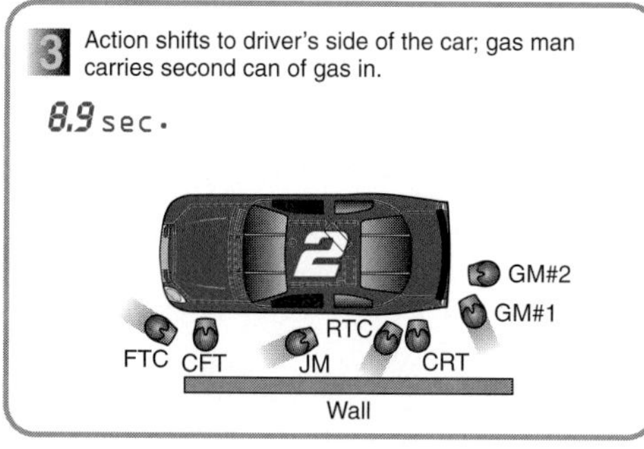

3 Action shifts to driver's side of the car; gas man carries second can of gas in.

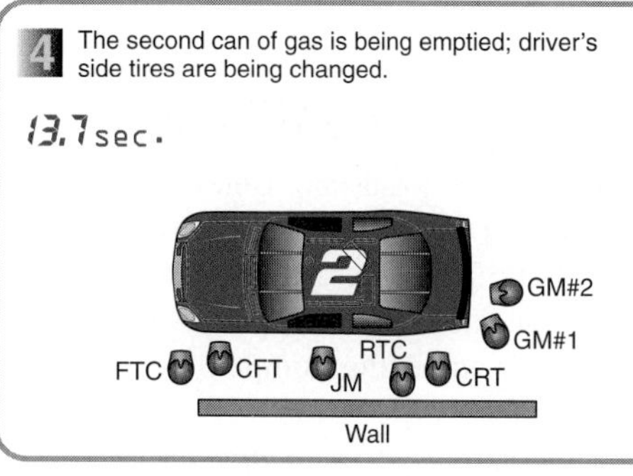

4 The second can of gas is being emptied; driver's side tires are being changed.

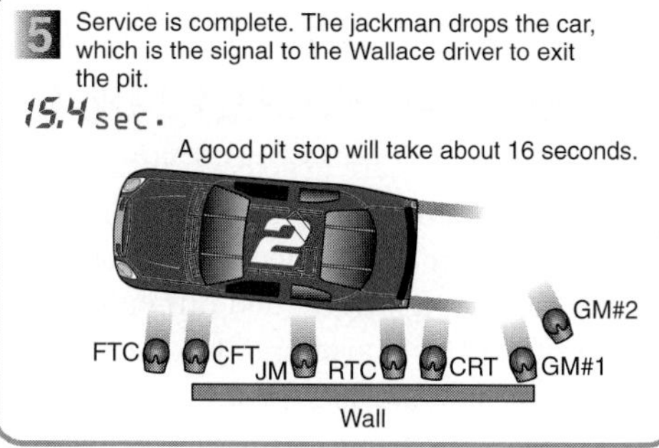

5 Service is complete. The jackman drops the car, which is the signal to the Wallace driver to exit the pit.

Movement of the pit crew members who go over the wall...

JM = Jackman
FTC = Front tire carrier
CFT = Changer front tire
RTC = Rear tire carrier
CRT = Changer rear tire
GM#1 = Gas man #1
GM#2 = Gas man #2

▲ ***JM (Jackman)*** The jackman carries the hydraulic jack from the pit wall to raise the car's right side. After new tires are bolted on, he drops the car to the ground and repeats the process on the left side. His timing is crucial during this left side change, because when he drops the car again, it's the signal for the driver to go. The jackman has the most dangerous job of all the crew members; during the right-side change, he is exposed to oncoming traffic down pit row. **FTC (Front tire carrier)** Each tire carrier hauls a new 75-pound tire to the car's right side, places it on the wheel studs and removes the old tire after the tire change. They repeat this process on the left side of the car with a new tire rolled to them by crew members behind the pit wall. **CFT (Changer front tire)** Tire changers run to the car's right side and using an air impact wrench, they remove five lug nuts off the old tire and bolt on a new tire. They repeat the process on the left side. **RTC (Rear tire carrier)** Same as front tire carrier, except RTC may also adjust the rear jack bolt to alter the car's handling. **CRT (Changer rear tire)** Same as FT but on two rear tires. **Gas man #1** This gas man is usually the biggest and strongest person on the team. He goes over the wall carrying a 75-pound, 11-gallon "dump can" whose nozzle he jams into the car's fuel cell receptacle. He is then handed (or tossed) another can, and the process is repeated. **Gas man #2** Gets second gas can to Gas man #1 and catches excess fuel that spills out.

a running back's time on the 40-yard dash. In NASCAR, a tire changer should get 5 lug nuts off in 1.2 seconds. The jackman should haul his 25-pound aluminum jack from the car's right side to left in 3.8 seconds. For tire carriers, it should take .7 seconds to get a tire from the ground to mounted on the car.

The seven men who go over the wall are coached and orchestrated. Coaches use the tools of OM and watch "game tape" of pit stops and make intricate adjustments to the choreography.

"There's a lot of pressure," says D. J. Richardson, a Rusty Wallace team tire changer—and one of the best in the business. Richardson trains daily with the rest of the crew in the shop of the team owner. They focus on cardiovascular work and two muscle groups daily. Twice a week, they simulate pit stops—there can be from 12 to 14 variations—to work on their timing.

In a recent race in Michigan, Richardson and the rest of the Rusty Wallace team, with ergonomically designed gas cans, tools, and special safety gear, were ready. On lap 43, the split-second frenzy began, with Richardson—air gun in hand—jumping over a 2-foot white wall and sprinting to the right side of the team's Dodge. A teammate grabbed the tire and set it in place while Richardson secured it to the car. The process was repeated on the left side while the front crew followed the same procedure. Coupled with refueling, the pit stop took 12.734 seconds.

After catching their breath for a minute, Richardson and the other pit crew guys reviewed a videotape, looking for split-second flaws.

The same process was repeated on lap 91. The Wallace driver made a late charge on Jeff Burton and Kurt Busch on the last lap and went from 14th place to a 10th place finish.

Sources: The Wall Street Journal (June 15, 2005): A1; and Orlando Sentinel (June 26, 2005): C10–C12 and (February 11, 2001): M10–M11.

Chapter 10 **Learning Objectives**

AUTHOR COMMENT
Mutual trust and commitment are key to a successful human resource strategy.

HUMAN RESOURCE STRATEGY FOR COMPETITIVE ADVANTAGE

Good human resource strategies are expensive, difficult to achieve, and hard to sustain. But, like a NASCAR team, many organizations, from Hard Rock Cafe to Frito-Lay to Southwest Airlines, have demonstrated that sustainable competitive advantage can be built through a human resource strategy. The payoff can be significant and difficult for others to duplicate. In this chapter, we will examine some of the tools available to operations managers for achieving competitive advantage via human resource management.

The objective of a human resource strategy is to manage labor and design jobs so people are effectively and efficiently utilized. As we focus on a human resource strategy, we want to ensure that people:

VIDEO 10.1
Human Resources at Hard Rock Cafe

1. Are efficiently utilized within the constraints of other operations management decisions.
2. Have a reasonable quality of work life in an atmosphere of mutual commitment and trust.

By reasonable *quality of work life* we mean a job that is not only reasonably safe and for which the pay is equitable but that also achieves an appropriate level of both physical and psychological requirements. *Mutual commitment* means that both management and employee strive to meet common objectives. *Mutual trust* is reflected in reasonable, documented employment policies that are honestly and equitably implemented to the satisfaction of both management and employee.[1] When management has a genuine respect for its employees and their contributions to the firm, establishing a reasonable quality of work life and mutual trust is not particularly difficult.

This chapter is devoted to showing how operations managers can achieve an effective human resource strategy, which, as we have suggested in our opening profile of NASCAR racing teams, may provide a competitive advantage.

Constraints on Human Resource Strategy

As Figure 10.1 suggests, many decisions made about people are constrained by other decisions. First, the product mix may determine seasonality and stability of employment. Second, technology, equipment, and processes may have implications for safety and job content. Third, the location decision may have an impact on the ambient environment in which the employees work. Finally, layout decisions, such as assembly line versus work cell, influence job content.

Technology decisions impose substantial constraints. For instance, some of the jobs in steel mills are dirty, noisy, and dangerous; slaughterhouse jobs may be stressful and subject workers to stomach-crunching stench; assembly-line jobs are often boring and mind numbing; and high capital investments such as those required for manufacturing semiconductor chips may require 24-hour, 7-day-a-week operation in restrictive clothing.

We are not going to change these jobs without making changes in our other strategic decisions. So, the trade-offs necessary to reach a tolerable quality of work life are difficult. Effective managers consider such decisions simultaneously. The result: an effective, efficient system in which both individual and team performance are enhanced through optimum job design.

Acknowledging the constraints imposed on human resource strategy, we now look at three distinct decision areas of human resource strategy: *labor planning*, *job design*, and *labor standards*.

[1]We find many companies calling their employees *associates*, *individual contributors*, or members of a particular team.

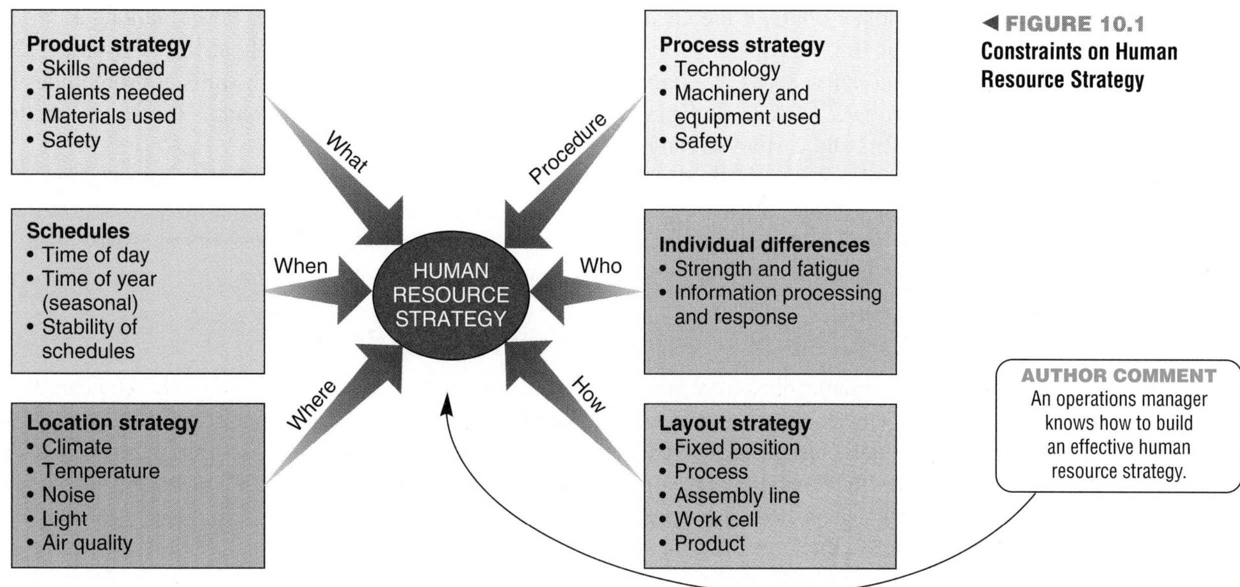

◀ **FIGURE 10.1 Constraints on Human Resource Strategy**

AUTHOR COMMENT An operations manager knows how to build an effective human resource strategy.

LABOR PLANNING

AUTHOR COMMENT Achieving employment stability, favorable work schedules, and acceptable work rules can be challenging.

Labor planning is determining staffing policies that deal with (1) employment stability, (2) work schedules, and (3) work rules.

Employment-Stability Policies

Labor planning
A means of determining staffing policies dealing with employment stability, work schedules, and work rules.

Employment stability deals with the number of employees maintained by an organization at any given time. There are two very basic policies for dealing with stability:

1. *Follow demand exactly:* Following demand exactly keeps direct labor costs tied to production but incurs other costs. These other costs include (a) hiring and layoff costs, (b) unemployment insurance, and (c) premium wages to entice personnel to accept unstable employment. This policy tends to treat labor as a variable cost.
2. *Hold employment constant:* Holding employment levels constant maintains a trained workforce and keeps hiring, layoff, and unemployment costs to a minimum. However, with employment held constant, employees may not be utilized fully when demand is low, and the firm may not have the human resources it needs when demand is high. This policy tends to treat labor as a fixed cost.

LO1: Describe labor planning policies

The above policies are only two of many that can be efficient *and* provide a reasonable quality of work life. Firms must determine policies about employment stability.

Work Schedules

Although the standard work schedule in the U.S. is still five 8-hour days, many variations exist. A currently popular variation is a work schedule called flextime. *Flextime* allows employees, within limits, to determine their own schedules. A flextime policy might allow an employee (with proper notification) to be at work at 8 A.M. plus or minus 2 hours. This policy allows more autonomy and independence on the part of the employee. Some firms have found flextime a low-cost fringe benefit that enhances job satisfaction. The problem from the OM perspective is that much production work requires full staffing for efficient operations. A machine that requires three people cannot run at all if only two show up. Having a waiter show up to serve lunch at 1:30 P.M. rather than 11:30 A.M. is not much help either.

Similarly, some industries find that their process strategies severely constrain their human resource scheduling options. For instance, paper manufacturing, petroleum refining, and power stations require around-the-clock staffing except for maintenance and repair shutdown.

Another option is the *flexible workweek*. This plan often calls for fewer but longer days, such as four 10-hour days or, as in the case of light-assembly plants, 12-hour shifts. Working 12-hour shifts usually means working 3 days one week and 4 the next. Such shifts are sometimes called *compressed workweeks*. These schedules are viable for many operations functions—as long as suppliers and customers can be accommodated.

Another option is shorter days rather than longer days. This plan often moves employees to *part-time status*. Such an option is particularly attractive in service industries, where staffing for peak loads is necessary. Banks and restaurants often hire part-time workers. Also, many firms reduce labor costs by reducing fringe benefits for part-time employees.

Job Classifications and Work Rules

Many organizations have strict job classifications and work rules that specify who can do what, when they can do it, and under what conditions they can do it, often as a result of union pressure. These job classifications and work rules restrict employee flexibility on the job, which in turn reduces the flexibility of the operations function. Yet part of an operations manager's task is to manage the unexpected. Therefore, the more flexibility a firm has when staffing and establishing work schedules, the more efficient and responsive it *can* be. This is particularly true in service organizations, where extra capacity often resides in extra or flexible staff. Building morale and meeting staffing requirements that result in an efficient, responsive operation are easier if managers have fewer job classifications and work-rule constraints. If the strategy is to achieve a competitive advantage by responding rapidly to the customer, a flexible workforce may be a prerequisite.

AUTHOR COMMENT Job design is a key ingredient of a motivated workforce.

JOB DESIGN

Job design
An approach that specifies the tasks that constitute a job for an individual or a group.

Job design specifies the tasks that constitute a job for an individual or a group. We examine five components of job design: (1) job specialization, (2) job expansion, (3) psychological components, (4) self-directed teams, and (5) motivation and incentive systems.

Labor Specialization

Labor specialization (or job specialization)
The division of labor into unique ("special") tasks.

The importance of job design as a management variable is credited to the 18th-century economist Adam Smith. Smith suggested that a division of labor, also known as **labor specialization** (or **job specialization**), would assist in reducing labor costs of multiskilled artisans. This is accomplished in several ways:

1. *Development of dexterity* and faster learning by the employee because of repetition
2. *Less loss of time* because the employee would not be changing jobs or tools
3. *Development of specialized tools* and the reduction of investment because each employee has only a few tools needed for a particular task

LO2: Identify the major issues in job design

The 19th-century British mathematician Charles Babbage determined that a fourth consideration was also important for labor efficiency. Because pay tends to follow skill with a rather high correlation, Babbage suggested *paying exactly the wage needed for the particular skill required.* If the entire job consists of only one skill, then we would pay for only that skill. Otherwise, we would tend to pay for the highest skill contributed by the employee. These four advantages of labor specialization are still valid today.

A classic example of labor specialization is the assembly line. Such a system is often very efficient, although it may require employees to do short, repetitive, mind-numbing jobs. The wage rate for many of these jobs, however, is very good. Given the relatively high wage rate for the modest skills required in many of these jobs, there is often a large pool of employees from which to choose.

From the manager's point of view, a major limitation of specialized jobs is their failure to bring the whole person to the job. Job specialization tends to bring only the employee's manual skills to work. In an increasingly sophisticated knowledge-based society, managers may want employees to bring their mind to work as well.

Job Expansion

Moving from labor specialization toward more varied job design may improve the quality of work life. The theory is that variety makes the job "better" and that the employee therefore enjoys a higher quality of work life. This flexibility thus benefits the employee and the organization.

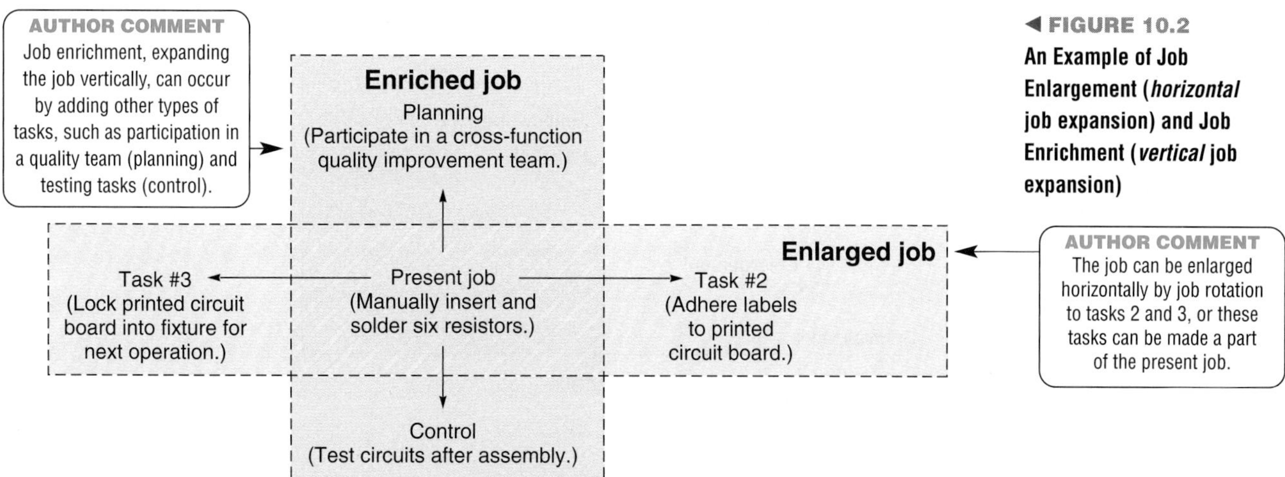

◄ **FIGURE 10.2**
An Example of Job Enlargement (*horizontal* job expansion) and Job Enrichment (*vertical* job expansion)

We modify jobs in a variety of ways. The first approach is **job enlargement**, which occurs when we add tasks requiring similar skill to an existing job. **Job rotation** is a version of job enlargement that occurs when the employee is allowed to move from one specialized job to another. Variety has been added to the employee's perspective of the job. Another approach is **job enrichment**, which adds planning and control to the job. An example is to have department store salespeople responsible for ordering, as well as selling, their goods. Job enrichment can be thought of as *vertical expansion*, as opposed to job enlargement, which is *horizontal*. These ideas are shown in Figure 10.2.

A popular extension of job enrichment, **employee empowerment** is the practice of enriching jobs so employees accept responsibility for a variety of decisions normally associated with staff specialists. Empowering employees helps them take "ownership" of their jobs so they have a personal interest in improving performance.

Job enlargement
The grouping of a variety of tasks about the same skill level; horizontal enlargement.

Job rotation
A system in which an employee is moved from one specialized job to another.

Job enrichment
A method of giving an employee more responsibility that includes some of the planning and control necessary for job accomplishment; vertical expansion.

Employee empowerment
Enlarging employee jobs so that the added responsibility and authority is moved to the lowest level possible.

Psychological Components of Job Design

An effective human resources strategy also requires consideration of the psychological components of job design. These components focus on how to design jobs that meet some minimum psychological requirements.

Hawthorne Studies The Hawthorne studies introduced psychology to the workplace. They were conducted in the late 1920s at Western Electric's Hawthorne plant near Chicago. These studies were initiated to determine the impact of lighting on productivity. Instead, they found the dynamic social system and distinct roles played by employees to be more important than the intensity of the lighting. They also found that individual differences may be dominant in what an employee expects from the job and what the employee thinks her or his contribution to the job should be.

Core Job Characteristics In the decades since the Hawthorne studies, substantial research regarding the psychological components of job design has taken place. Hackman and Oldham have incorporated much of that work into five desirable characteristics of job design.[2] They suggest that jobs should include the following characteristics:

1. *Skill variety*, requiring the worker to use a variety of skills and talents
2. *Job identity*, allowing the worker to perceive the job as a whole and recognize a start and a finish
3. *Job significance*, providing a sense that the job has an impact on the organization and society
4. *Autonomy*, offering freedom, independence, and discretion
5. *Feedback*, providing clear, timely information about performance

Including these five ingredients in job design is consistent with job enlargement, job enrichment, and employee empowerment. We now want to look at some of the ways in which teams can be used to expand jobs and achieve these five job characteristics.

[2]See "Motivation Through the Design of Work," in Jay Richard Hackman and Greg R. Oldham, eds., *Work Redesign* (Reading, MA: Addison-Wesley, 1980), and A. Thomas, W. C. Buboltz, and C. Winkelspecht, "Job Characteristics and Personality as Predictors of Job Satisfaction," *Organizational Analysis*, 12, no. 2 (2004): 205–219.

▶ FIGURE 10.3
Job Design Continuum

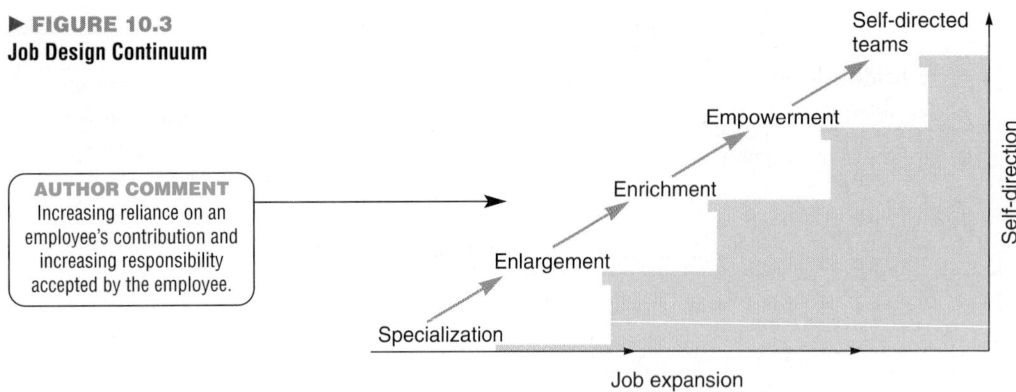

Self-Directed Teams

Self-directed team
A group of empowered individuals working together to reach a common goal.

Many world-class organizations have adopted teams to foster mutual trust and commitment, and provide the core job characteristics. One team concept of particular note is the **self-directed team**: a group of empowered individuals working together to reach a common goal. These teams may be organized for long- or short-term objectives. Teams are effective primarily because they can easily provide employee empowerment, ensure core job characteristics, and satisfy many of the psychological needs of individual team members. A job design continuum is shown in Figure 10.3.

Limitations of Job Expansion If job designs that enlarge, enrich, empower, and use teams are so good, why are they not universally used? Mostly it is because of costs. Here are a few limitations of expanded job designs:

- *Higher capital cost:* Job expansion may require additional equipment and facilities.
- *Individual differences:* Some employees opt for the less complex jobs.
- *Higher wage rates:* Expanded jobs may well require a higher average wage.
- *Smaller labor pool:* Because expanded jobs require more skill and acceptance of more responsibility, job requirements have increased.
- *Higher training costs:* Job expansion requires training and cross-training. Therefore, training budgets need to increase.

Despite these limitations, firms are finding a substantial payoff in job expansion.

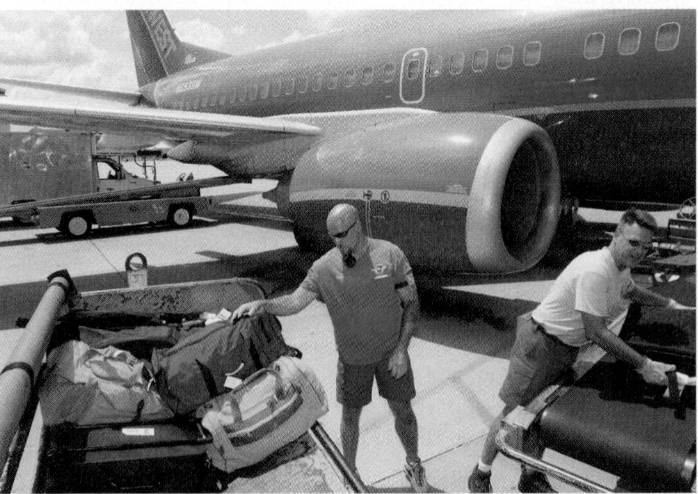

Southwest Airlines—consistently at the top of the airline pack in travel surveys, fewest lost bags and complaints, and highest profits—hires people with enthusiasm and empowers them to excel. A barefoot chairman of the board, Herb Kelleher, clings to the tail of a jet (left photo). Says Kelleher, "I've tried to create a culture of caring for people in the totality of their lives, not just at work. Someone can go out and buy airplanes and ticket counters, but they can't buy our culture, our *esprit de corps.*"

Motivation and Incentive Systems

Our discussion of the psychological components of job design provides insight into the factors that contribute to job satisfaction and motivation. In addition to these psychological factors, there are monetary factors. Money often serves as a psychological as well as financial motivator. Monetary rewards take the form of bonuses, profit and gain sharing, and incentive systems.

Bonuses, typically in cash or stock options, are often used at executive levels to reward management. Profit-sharing systems provide some part of the profit for distribution to employees. A variation of profit sharing is gain sharing, which rewards employees for improvements made in an organization's performance. The most popular of these is the Scanlon plan, in which any reduction in the cost of labor is shared between management and labor.

Incentive systems based on individual or group productivity are used throughout the world in a wide variety of applications, including nearly half of the manufacturing firms in America. Production incentives often require employees or crews to produce at or above a predetermined standard. The standard can be based on a "standard time" per task or number of pieces made. Both systems typically guarantee the employee at least a base rate. Incentives, of course, need not be monetary. Awards, recognition, and other kinds of preferences such as a preferred work schedule can be effective. (See the *OM in Action* box "Using Incentives to Unsnarl Traffic Jams in the OR.") Hard Rock Cafe has successfully reduced its turnover by giving every employee—from the CEO to the busboys—a $10,000 gold Rolex watch on their 10th anniversary with the firm.

With the increasing use of teams, various forms of team-based pay are also being developed. Many are based on traditional pay systems supplemented with some form of bonus or incentive system. However, because many team environments require cross training of enlarged jobs, *knowledge-based* pay systems have also been developed. Under knowledge-based (or skill-based) pay systems, a portion of the employee's pay depends on demonstrated knowledge or skills possessed. At Wisconsin's Johnsonville Sausage Co., employees receive pay raises *only* by mastering new skills such as scheduling, budgeting, and quality control.

ERGONOMICS AND THE WORK ENVIRONMENT

AUTHOR COMMENT Ergonomics becomes more critical as technologies become more complex.

With the foundation provided by Frederick W. Taylor, the father of the era of scientific management, we have developed a body of knowledge about people's capabilities and limitations. This knowledge is necessary because humans are hand/eye animals possessing exceptional capabilities and some limitations. Because managers must design jobs that can be done, we now introduce a few of the issues related to people's capabilities and limitations.

Ergonomics The operations manager is interested in building a good interface between humans, the environment, and machines. Studies of this interface are known as **ergonomics**. Ergonomics means "the study of work." (*Ergon* is the Greek word for "work.") The term *human*

Ergonomics
The study of the human interface with the environment and machines.

OM in Action ► Using Incentives to Unsnarl Traffic Jams in the OR

Hospitals have long offered surgeons a precious perk: scheduling the bulk of their elective surgeries in the middle of the week so they can attend conferences, teach, or relax during long weekends. But at Boston Medical Center, St. John's Health Center (in Missouri), and Elliot Health System (in New Hampshire), this practice, one of the biggest impediments to a smooth-running hospital, is changing. "Block scheduling" jams up operating rooms, overloads nurses at peak times, and bumps scheduled patients for hours and even days.

Boston Medical Center's delays and cancellations of elective surgeries were nearly eliminated after surgeons agreed to stop block scheduling and to dedicate one OR for emergency cases. Cancellations dropped to 3, from 334, in just one 6-month period. In general, hospitals changing to the new system of spreading out elective surgeries during the week increase their surgery capacity by 10%, move patients through the operating room faster, and reduce nursing overtime.

To get doctors on board at St. John's, the hospital offered a carrot and two sticks: Doctors who were more than 10 minutes late 10% of the time lost their coveted 7:30 A.M. start times *and* were fined a portion of their fee—with proceeds going to a kitty that rewarded the best on-time performers. Surgeons' late start times quickly dropped from 16% to 5% and then to less than 1% within a year.

Sources: International Journal of Production Economics (January–February 2006): 52; *The Wall Street Journal* (August 10, 2005): D1, D3; and *Hospitals & Health Networks* (September 2005): 24–25.

Ergonomic issues occur in the office as well as in the factory. Here an ergonomics consultant is measuring the angle of a computer operator's neck. Posture, which is related to desk height, chair height and position, keyboard placement, and computer screen, is an important factor in reducing back and neck pain that can be caused by extended hours at a computer.

factors is often substituted for the word *ergonomics*. Understanding ergonomic issues helps to improve human performance.

Male and female adults come in limited configurations. Therefore, design of tools and the workplace depends on the study of people to determine what they can and cannot do. Substantial data have been collected that provide basic strength and measurement data needed to design tools and the workplace. The design of the workplace can make the job easier or impossible. Additionally, we now have the ability, through the use of computer modeling, to analyze human motions and efforts.

LO3: Identify major ergonomic and work environment issues

Operator Input to Machines Operator response to machines, be they hand tools, pedals, levers, or buttons, needs to be evaluated. Operations managers need to be sure that operators have the strength, reflexes, perception, and mental capacity to provide necessary control. Such problems as *carpal tunnel syndrome* may result when a tool as simple as a keyboard is poorly designed. The photo of the Champ race car steering wheel below shows one innovative approach to critical operator input.

Feedback to Operators Feedback to operators is provided by sight, sound, and feel; it should not be left to chance. The mishap at the Three Mile Island nuclear facility, America's worst nuclear experience, was in large part the result of poor feedback to the operators about reactor performance. Nonfunctional groups of large, unclear instruments and inaccessible controls, combined with hundreds of confusing warning lights, contributed to that failure. Such relatively simple issues make a difference in operator response and, therefore, performance. The photos showing changes in aircraft cockpits indicate recent efforts to improve feedback to operators.

The Work Environment The physical environment in which employees work affects their performance, safety, and quality of work life. Illumination, noise and vibration, temperature, humidity, and air quality are work-environment factors under the control of the organization and the operations manager. The manager must approach them as controllable.

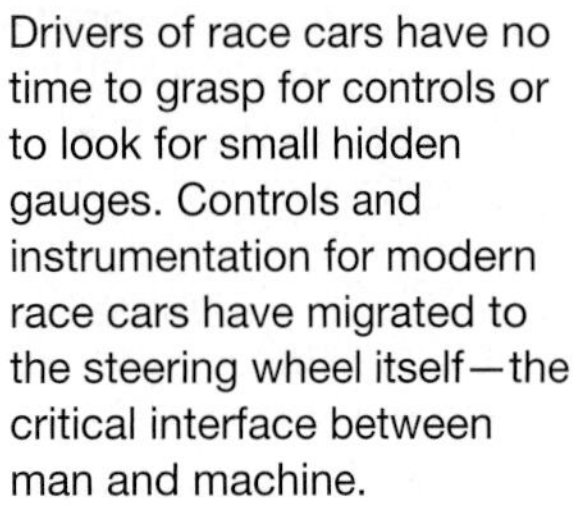

Drivers of race cars have no time to grasp for controls or to look for small hidden gauges. Controls and instrumentation for modern race cars have migrated to the steering wheel itself—the critical interface between man and machine.

An important human factor/ergonomic issue in the aircraft industry is cockpit design. Newer "glass cockpits" (on the right) display information in more concise form than the traditional rows of round analog dials and gauges (on the left). New displays reduce the chance of human error, which is a factor in about two-thirds of commercial air accidents. Fractions of a second in the cockpit can literally mean the difference between life and death.

▼ **FIGURE 10.4a Recommended Levels of Illumination (using foot-candles (ft-c) as the measure of illumination)**

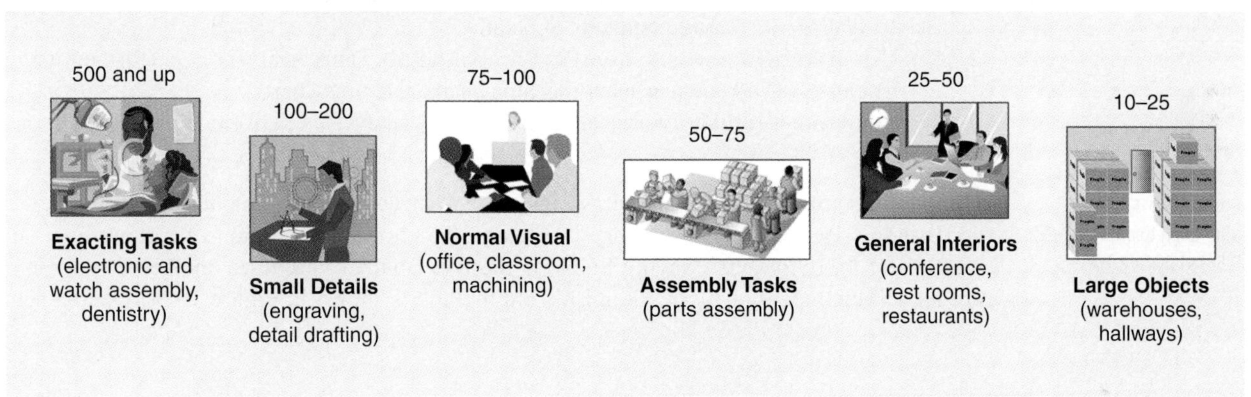

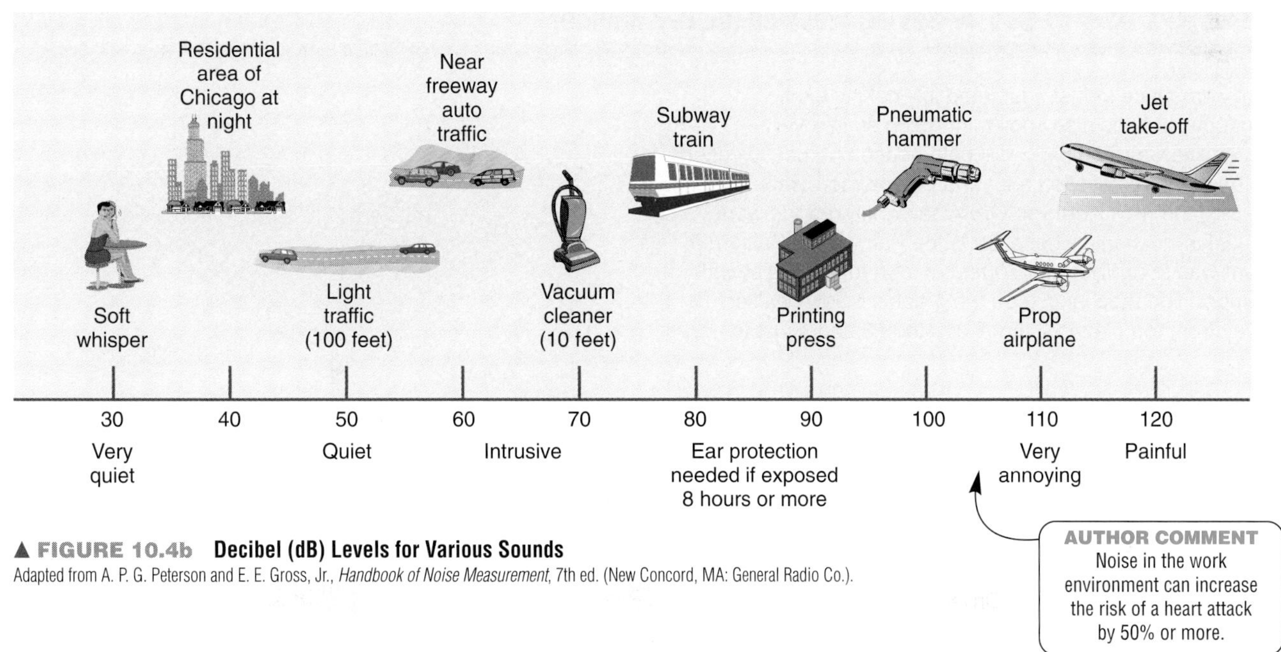

▲ **FIGURE 10.4b Decibel (dB) Levels for Various Sounds**

Adapted from A. P. G. Peterson and E. E. Gross, Jr., *Handbook of Noise Measurement*, 7th ed. (New Concord, MA: General Radio Co.).

AUTHOR COMMENT
Noise in the work environment can increase the risk of a heart attack by 50% or more.

Illumination is necessary, but the proper level depends on the work being performed. Figure 10.4a provides some guidelines. However, other lighting factors are important. These include reflective ability, contrast of the work surface with surroundings, glare, and shadows.

Noise of some form is usually present in the work area, and most employees seem to adjust well. However, high levels of sound will damage hearing. Figure 10.4b provides indications of the sound generated by various activities. Extended periods of exposure to decibel levels above 85 dB are permanently damaging. The Occupational Safety and Health Administration (OSHA) requires ear protection above this level if exposure equals or exceeds 8 hours. Even at low levels, noise and vibration can be distracting and can raise a person's blood pressure, so managers make substantial effort to reduce noise and vibration through good machine design, enclosures, or insulation.

Temperature and humidity parameters have also been well established. Managers with activities operating outside the established comfort zone should expect adverse effect on performance.

AUTHOR COMMENT
Methods analysis provides the tools for understanding systems.

METHODS ANALYSIS

Methods analysis
A system that involves developing work procedures that are safe and produce quality products efficiently.

LO4: Use the tools of methods analysis

Methods analysis focuses on *how* a task is accomplished. Whether controlling a machine or making or assembling components, how a task is done makes a difference in performance, safety, and quality. Using knowledge from ergonomics and methods analysis, methods engineers are charged with ensuring that quality and quantity standards are achieved efficiently and safely. Methods analysis and related techniques are useful in office environments as well as in the factory. Methods techniques are used to analyze:

1. Movement of individuals or material. The analysis is performed using *flow diagrams* and *process charts* with varying amounts of detail.
2. Activity of human and machine and crew activity. This analysis is performed using *activity charts* (also known as man–machine charts and crew charts).
3. Body movement (primarily arms and hands). This analysis is performed using *operations charts*.

Flow diagram
A drawing used to analyze movement of people or material.

Flow diagrams are schematics (drawings) used to investigate movement of people or material. Britain's Paddy Hopkirk Factory in Figure 10.5 shows one version of a flow diagram, and the *OM in Action* box "Saving Steps on the B-2 Bomber" provides another way to analyze long-cycle repetitive tasks. Hopkirk's old method is shown in Figure 10.5(a), and a new

OM in Action ▶ Saving Steps on the B-2 Bomber

The aerospace industry is noted for making exotic products, but it is also known for doing so in a very expensive way. The historical batch-based processes used in the industry have left a lot of room for improvement. In leading the way, Northrop Grumman analyzed the work flow of a mechanic whose job in the Palmsdale, California, plant was to apply about 70 feet of tape to the B-2 stealth bomber. The mechanic (see the graphic below) walked away from the plane 26 times and took 3 hours just to

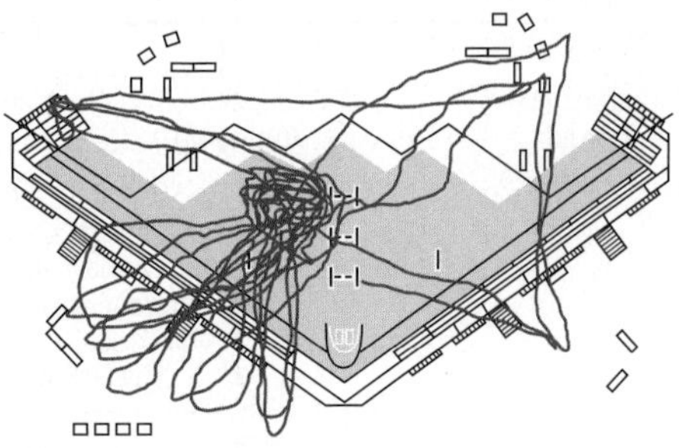

The 26 trips to various workstations to gather the tools and equipment to apply tape to the B-2 bomber are shown as blue lines above.

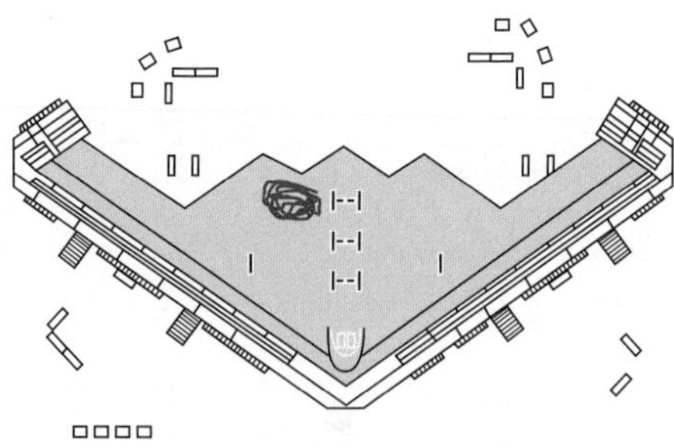

The mechanic's work path is reduced to the small area of blue lines shown here.

gather chemicals, hose, gauges, and other material needed just to get ready for the job. By making prepackaged kits for the job, Northrop Grumman cut preparation time to zero and the time to complete the job dropped from 8.4 hours to 1.6 hours (as seen above).

Sources: *BusinessWeek* (May 28, 2001): 14; *Aviation Week & Space Technology* (January 17, 2000): 44; and *New York Times* (March 9, 1999): C1, C9.

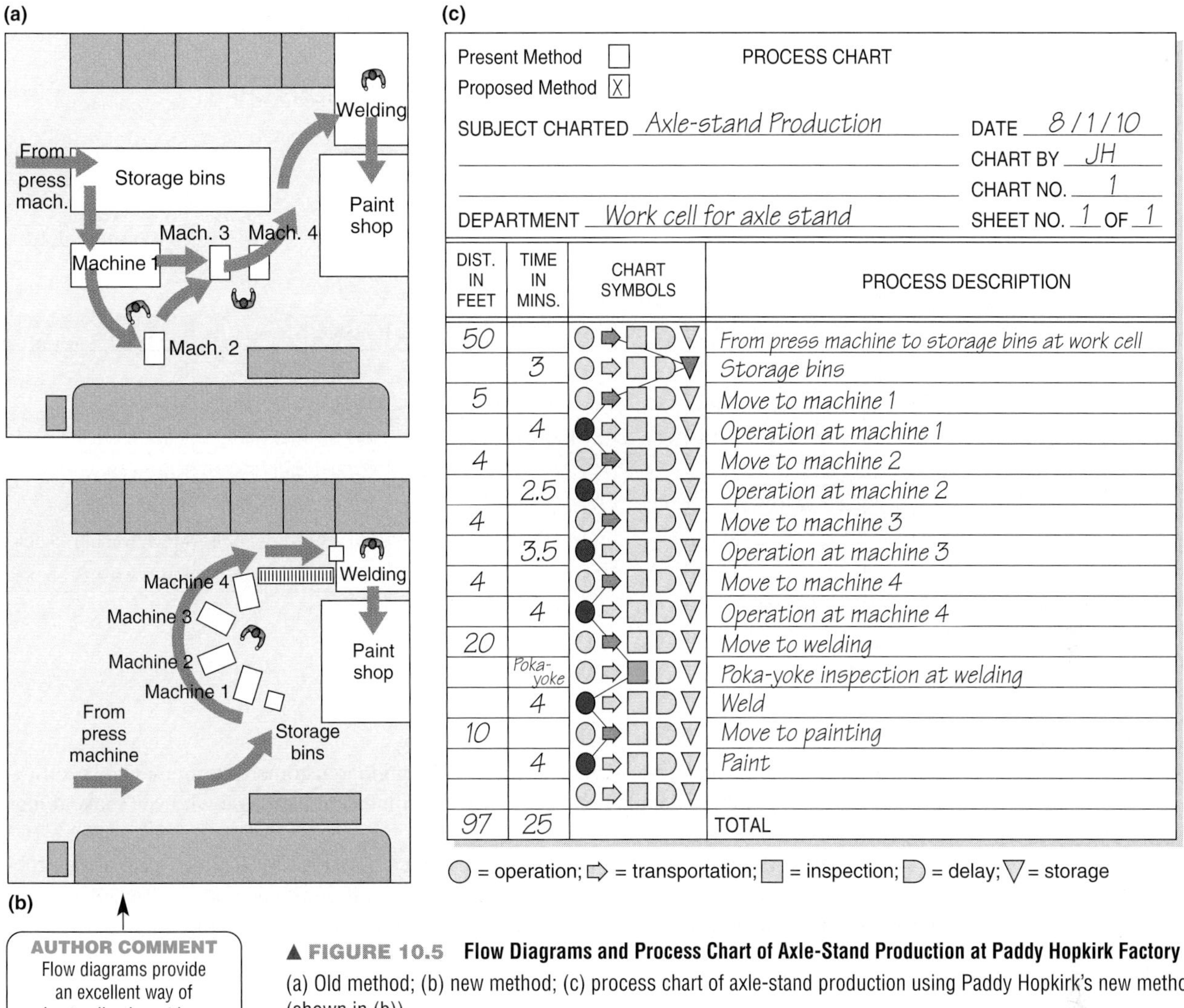

Present Method ☐	PROCESS CHART	
Proposed Method ☒		
SUBJECT CHARTED Axle-stand Production		DATE 8/1/10
		CHART BY JH
		CHART NO. 1
DEPARTMENT Work cell for axle stand		SHEET NO. 1 OF 1

DIST. IN FEET	TIME IN MINS.	CHART SYMBOLS	PROCESS DESCRIPTION
50		○➡☐D▽	From press machine to storage bins at work cell
	3	○⇨☐D▼	Storage bins
5		○➡☐D▽	Move to machine 1
	4	●⇨☐D▽	Operation at machine 1
4		○➡☐D▽	Move to machine 2
	2.5	●⇨☐D▽	Operation at machine 2
4		○➡☐D▽	Move to machine 3
	3.5	●⇨☐D▽	Operation at machine 3
4		○➡☐D▽	Move to machine 4
	4	●⇨☐D▽	Operation at machine 4
20		○➡☐D▽	Move to welding
	Poka-yoke	○⇨■D▽	Poka-yoke inspection at welding
	4	●⇨☐D▽	Weld
10		○➡☐D▽	Move to painting
	4	●⇨☐D▽	Paint
		○⇨☐D▽	
97	25		TOTAL

○ = operation; ⇨ = transportation; ☐ = inspection; D = delay; ▽ = storage

AUTHOR COMMENT
Flow diagrams provide an excellent way of understanding layout issues.

▲ **FIGURE 10.5 Flow Diagrams and Process Chart of Axle-Stand Production at Paddy Hopkirk Factory**
(a) Old method; (b) new method; (c) process chart of axle-stand production using Paddy Hopkirk's new method (shown in (b)).

method, with improved work flow and requiring less storage and space, is shown in Figure 10.5(b). **Process charts** use symbols, as in Figure 10.5(c), to help us understand the movement of people or material. In this way non-value-added activities can be recognized and operations made more efficient. Figure 10.5(c) is a process chart used to supplement the flow diagrams shown in Figure 10.5(b).

Process chart
Graphic representations that depict a sequence of steps for a process.

Activity charts are used to study and improve the utilization of an operator and a machine or some combination of operators (a "crew") and machines. The typical approach is for the analyst to record the present method through direct observation and then propose the improvement on a second chart. Figure 10.6 is an activity chart to show a proposed improvement for a two-person crew at Quick Car Lube.

Activity chart
A way of improving utilization of an operator and a machine or some combination of operators (a crew) and machines.

Body movement is analyzed by an **operations chart**. It is designed to show economy of motion by pointing out wasted motion and idle time (delay). The operations chart (also known as a *right-hand/left-hand chart*) is shown in Figure 10.7.

Operations chart
A chart depicting right- and left-hand motions.

THE VISUAL WORKPLACE

A **visual workplace** uses low-cost visual devices to share information quickly and accurately. Well-designed displays and graphs root out confusion and replace difficult-to-understand printouts and paperwork. Because workplace data change quickly and often, operations managers

Visual workplace
Uses a variety of visual communication techniques to rapidly communicate information to stakeholders.

▼ FIGURE 10.6 Activity Chart for Two-Person Crew Doing an Oil Change in 12 Minutes at Quick Car Lube

ACTIVITY CHART

	OPERATOR #1		OPERATOR #2	
	TIME	%	TIME	%
WORK	12	100	12	100
IDLE	0	0	0	0

OPERATION: Oil change & fluid check
EQUIPMENT: One bay/pit
OPERATOR: Two-person crew
STUDY NO.: ______ ANALYST: NG

SUBJECT *Quick Car Lube* DATE *8-1-10*
PRESENT / PROPOSED DEPT. SHEET *1* OF *1* CHART BY *LSA*

TIME	Operator #1	Operator #2
	Take order	Move car to pit
2	Vacuum car	Drain oil
4	Clean windows	Check transmission
6	Check under hood	Change oil filter
8	Fill with oil	Replace oil plug
10	Complete bill	Move car to front for customer
12	Greet next customer	Move next car to pit
14	Vacuum car	Drain oil
16	Clean windows	Check transmission
18	↓	↓

Repeat cycle

AUTHOR COMMENT
Activity charts are helpful for understanding crew or man–machine interaction.

▼ FIGURE 10.7 Operations Chart (right-hand/left-hand chart) for Bolt-Washer Assembly

OPERATIONS CHART

SYMBOLS	PRESENT LH	PRESENT RH	PROPOSED LH	PROPOSED RH
○ OPERATION	2	3		
⇨ TRANSPORT.	1	1		
□ INSPECTION				
D DELAY	4	3		
▽ STORAGE				

PROCESS: Bolt–washer assembly
EQUIPMENT:
OPERATOR: KJH
STUDY NO: ______ ANALYST: ______
DATE: 8 / 1 / 10 SHEET NO. 1 of 1
METHOD (PRESENT / PROPOSED)
REMARKS:

LEFT-HAND ACTIVITY Present METHOD	DIST.	SYMBOLS	SYMBOLS	DIST.	RIGHT-HAND ACTIVITY Present METHOD
1 Reach for bolt		●⇨□D▽	○⇨□**D**▽		Idle
2 Grasp bolt		●⇨□D▽	○⇨□**D**▽		Idle
3 Move bolt	6″	○➡□D▽	○⇨□**D**▽		Idle
4 Hold bolt		○⇨□**D**▽	●⇨□D▽		Reach for washer
5 Hold bolt		○⇨□**D**▽	●⇨□D▽		Grasp washer
6 Hold bolt		○⇨□**D**▽	○➡□D▽	8″	Move washer to bolt
7 Hold bolt		○⇨□**D**▽	●⇨□D▽		Place washer on bolt

need to share accurate and up-to-date information. Changing customer requirements, specifications, schedules, and other details must be rapidly communicated to those who can make things happen.

The visual workplace can eliminate non-value-added activities by making standards, problems, and abnormalities visual (see Figure 10.8). The visual workplace needs less supervision because employees understand the standard, see the results, and know what to do.

▼ FIGURE 10.8 The Visual Workplace

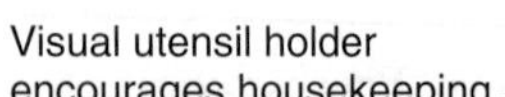

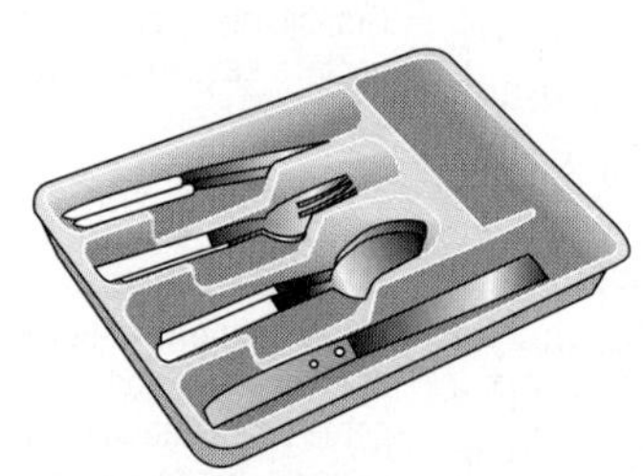

A "3-minute service" clock reminds employees of the goal.

Visual signals at the machine notify support personnel.

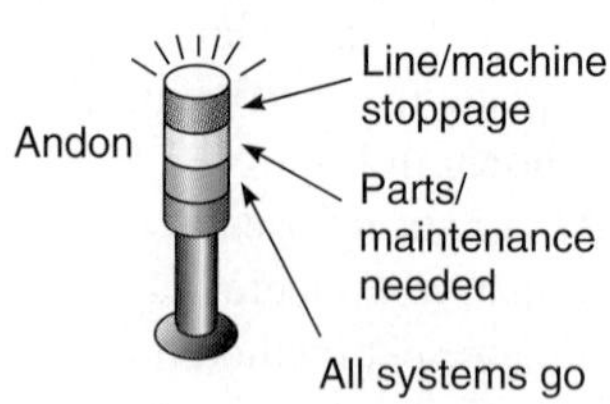

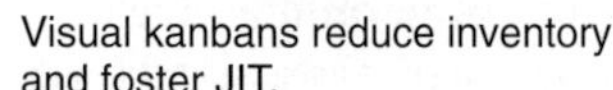

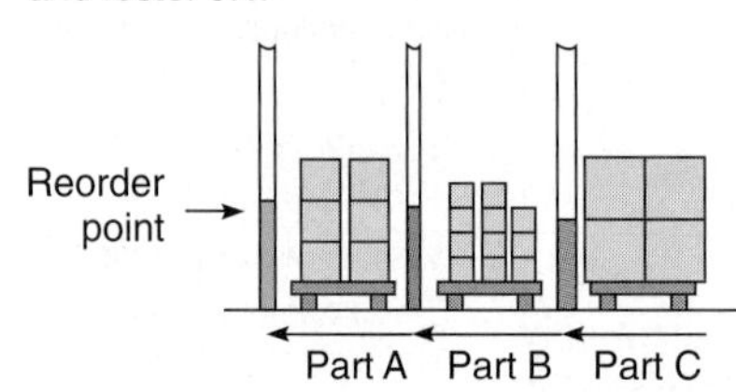

Quantities in bins indicate ongoing daily requirements and clipboards provide information on schedule changes.

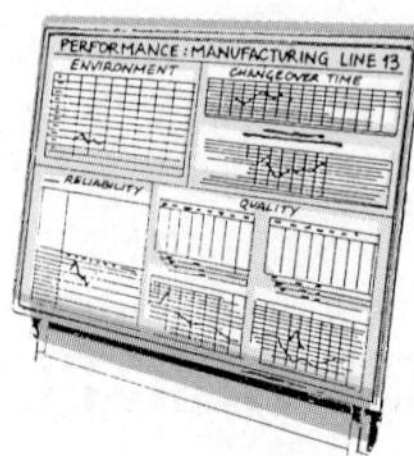

Process specifications and operating procedures are posted in each work area.

LABOR STANDARDS

AUTHOR COMMENT
Labor standards exist for check-out clerks, mechanics, UPS drivers, and many factory workers.

So far in this chapter, we have discussed labor planning and job design. The third requirement of an effective human resource strategy is the establishment of labor standards. **Labor standards** are the amount of time required to perform a job or part of a job. Effective manpower planning is dependent on a knowledge of the labor required.

Labor standards
The amount of time required to perform a job or part of a job.

Modern labor standards originated with the works of Frederick W. Taylor and Frank and Lillian Gilbreth at the beginning of the 20th century. At that time, a large proportion of work was manual, and the resulting labor content of products was high. Little was known about what constituted a fair day's work, so managers initiated studies to improve work methods and understand human effort. These efforts continue to this day. Although labor costs are often less than 10% of sales, labor standards remain important and continue to play a major role in both service and manufacturing organizations. They are often a beginning point for determining staffing requirements. With over half of the manufacturing plants in America using some form of labor incentive system, good labor standards are a requirement.

Effective operations management requires meaningful standards that help a firm determine:

1. Labor content of items produced (the labor cost)
2. Staffing needs (how many people it will take to meet required production)
3. Cost and time estimates prior to production (to assist in a variety of decisions, from cost estimates to make-or-buy decisions)
4. Crew size and work balance (who does what in a group activity or on an assembly line)
5. Expected production (so that both manager and worker know what constitutes a fair day's work)
6. Basis of wage-incentive plans (what provides a reasonable incentive)
7. Efficiency of employees and supervision (a standard is necessary against which to determine efficiency)

LO5: Identify four ways of establishing labor standards

Properly set labor standards represent the amount of time that it should take an average employee to perform specific job activities under normal working conditions. Labor standards are set in four ways:

1. Historical experience
2. Time studies
3. Predetermined time standards
4. Work sampling

Historical Experience

Labor standards can be estimated based on *historical experience*—that is, how many labor-hours were required to do a task the last time it was performed. Historical standards have the advantage of being relatively easy and inexpensive to obtain. They are usually available from employee time cards or production records. However, they are not objective, and we do not know their accuracy, whether they represent a reasonable or a poor work pace, and whether unusual occurrences are included. Because these variables are unknown, their use is not recommended. Instead, time studies, predetermined time standards, and work sampling are preferred.

Time Studies

AUTHOR COMMENT
Stopwatch studies are the most widely used labor standard method.

The classical stopwatch study, or **time study**, originally proposed by Frederick W. Taylor in 1881, involves timing a sample of a worker's performance and using it to set a standard. (See the *OM In Action* box, "Saving Seconds at Retail Boosts Productivity.") A trained and experienced person can establish a standard by following these eight steps:

Time study
Timing a sample of a worker's performance and using it as a basis for setting a standard time.

1. Define the task to be studied (after methods analysis has been conducted).
2. Divide the task into precise elements (parts of a task that often take no more than a few seconds).
3. Decide how many times to measure the task (the number of job cycles or samples needed).
4. Time and record elemental times and ratings of performance.

Each day—in fact, 130 times each day—Tim Nelson leans back into a La-Z-Boy recliner, sofa section, or love seat at the company's Dayton factory. He inspects for overall comfort; he must sink slightly into the chair, but not too far. As in the fable "Goldilocks and the Three Bears," the chair must not be too firm or too soft; it must be just right—or it is sent back for restuffing. If it passes the "firm" test, he then rocks back and forth, making certain the chair is properly balanced and moves smoothly. Then Tim checks the footrest, arches his back, and holds the position. Hopping to his feet, he does a walk-around visual check; then it is on to the next chair. One down, and 129 to go.

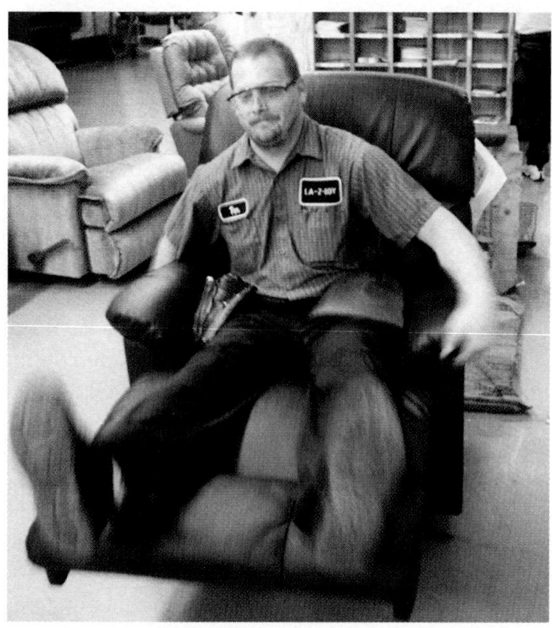

Average observed time
The arithmetic mean of the times for each element measured, adjusted for unusual influence for each element.

Normal time
The average observed time, adjusted for pace.

5. Compute the average observed (actual) time. The **average observed time** is the arithmetic mean of the times for *each* element measured, adjusted for unusual influence for each element:

$$\text{Average observed time} = \frac{(\text{Sum of the times recorded to perform each element})}{\text{Number of observations}} \quad \text{(10-1)}$$

6. Determine performance rating (work pace) and then compute the **normal time** for each element.

$$\text{Normal time} = (\text{Average observed time}) \times (\text{Performance rating factor}) \quad \text{(10-2)}$$

The performance rating adjusts the average observed time to what a trained worker could expect to accomplish working at a normal pace. For example, a worker should be able to walk 3 miles per hour. He or she should also be able to deal a deck of 52 cards into 4 equal piles in 30 seconds. A performance rating of 1.05 would indicate that the observed worker performs the task slightly *faster* than average. Numerous videos specify work pace on

OM in Action ► Saving Seconds at Retail Boosts Productivity

Retail services, like factory assembly lines, need labor standards. And the Gap, Office Depot, Toys "R" Us, and Meijer are among the many firms that use them. Labor is usually the largest single expense after purchases in retailing, meaning it gets special attention. Labor standards are set for everything from greeting customers, to number of cases loaded onto shelves, to scanning merchandise at the cash register.

Meijer, a Midwestern chain of 190 "big box" stores, includes cashiers in its labor standards. Since Meijer sells everything from groceries to clothes to automotive goods, cashier labor standards include adjustments of allowances for the vast variety of merchandise being purchased. This includes clothes with hard-to-find bar codes and bulky items that are not usually removed from the shopping cart. Allowances are also made for how customers pay, the number of customers returning to an aisle for a forgotten item, and elderly and handicapped customers.

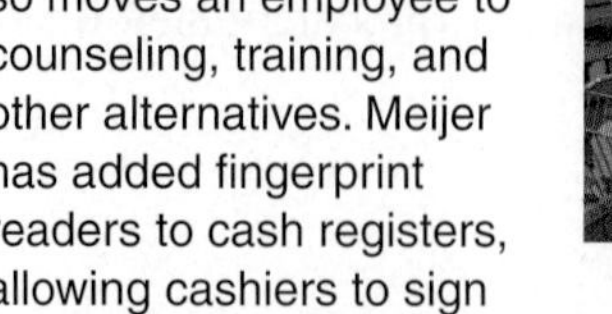

Employees are expected to meet 95% of the standard. Failure to do so moves an employee to counseling, training, and other alternatives. Meijer has added fingerprint readers to cash registers, allowing cashiers to sign in directly at their register. This saves time and boosts productivity by avoiding a stop at the time clock.

The bottom line: as retail firms seek competitive advantage via lower prices, they are finding that good labor standards are not only shaving personnel costs by 5% to 15% but also contributing to more accurate data for improved scheduling.

Sources: The Wall Street Journal, (November 17, 2008): A1, A15; **www.Meijer.com**; and *Labor Talk,* (Summer 2007).

▼ **TABLE 10.1 Allowance Factors (in percentage) for Various Classes of Work**

1. Constant allowances:	
(A) Personal allowance	5
(B) Basic fatigue allowance	4
2. Variable allowances:	
(A) Standing allowance	2
(B) Abnormal position allowance:	
(i) Awkward (bending)	2
(ii) Very awkward (lying, stretching)	7
(C) Use of force or muscular energy in lifting, pulling, pushing	
Weight lifted (pounds):	
20	3
40	9
60	17
(D) Bad light:	
(i) Well below recommended	2
(ii) Quite inadequate	5
(E) Atmospheric conditions (heat and humidity): Variable	0–10
(F) Close attention:	
(i) Fine or exacting	2
(ii) Very fine or very exacting	5
(G) Noise level:	
(i) Intermittent—loud	2
(ii) Intermittent—very loud or high pitched	5
(H) Mental strain:	
(i) Complex or wide span of attention	4
(ii) Very complex	8
(I) Tediousness:	
(i) Tedious	2
(ii) Very tedious	5

which professionals agree, and benchmarks have been established by the Society for the Advancement of Management. Performance rating, however, is still something of an art.

7. Add the normal times for each element to develop a total normal time for the task.
8. Compute the **standard time**. This adjustment to the total normal time provides for allowances such as *personal* needs, unavoidable work *delays*, and worker *fatigue*:

Standard time
An adjustment to the total normal time; the adjustment provides allowances for personal needs, unavoidable work delays, and fatigue.

$$\text{Standard time} = \frac{\text{Total normal time}}{1 - \text{Allowance factor}} \tag{10-3}$$

Personal time allowances are often established in the range of 4% to 7% of total time, depending on nearness to rest rooms, water fountains, and other facilities. *Delay allowances* are often set as a result of the actual studies of the delay that occurs. *Fatigue allowances* are based on our growing knowledge of human energy expenditure under various physical and environmental conditions. A sample set of personal and fatigue allowances is shown in Table 10.1. Example 1 illustrates the computation of standard time.

EXAMPLE 1
Determining normal and standard time

The time study of a work operation at a Red Lobster restaurant yielded an average observed time of 4.0 minutes. The analyst rated the observed worker at 85%. This means the worker performed at 85% of normal when the study was made. The firm uses a 13% allowance factor. Red Lobster wants to compute the normal time and the standard time for this operation.

APPROACH ▶ The firm needs to apply Equations (10–2) and (10–3).

SOLUTION

▶ Average observed time = 4.0 min

$$\text{Normal time} = (\text{Average observed time}) \times (\text{Performance rating factor})$$
$$= (4.0)(.85)$$
$$= 3.4 \text{ min}$$

$$\text{Standard time} = \frac{\text{Normal time}}{1 - \text{Allowance factor}} = \frac{3.4}{1 - .13} = \frac{3.4}{.87}$$
$$= 3.9 \text{ min}$$

INSIGHT ▶ Because the observed worker was rated at 85% (slower than average), the normal time is less than the worker's 4.0-minute average time.

LEARNING EXERCISE ▶ If the observed worker is rated at 115% (faster than average), what are the new normal and standard times? [Answer: 4.6 min, 5.287 min.]

RELATED PROBLEMS ▶ 10.13, 10.14, 10.15, 10.16, 10.17, 10.18, 10.19, 10.20, 10.21, 10.33

LO6: Compute the normal and standard times in a time study

Example 2 uses a series of actual stopwatch times for each element.

EXAMPLE 2

Using time studies to compute standard time

Management Science Associates promotes its management development seminars by mailing thousands of individually composed and typed letters to various firms. A time study has been conducted on the task of preparing letters for mailing. On the basis of the following observations, Management Science Associates wants to develop a time standard for this task. The firm's personal, delay, and fatigue allowance factor is 15%.

	Observations (minutes)					
Job Element	**1**	**2**	**3**	**4**	**5**	**Performance Rating**
(A) Compose and type letter	8	10	9	21*	11	120%
(B) Type envelope address	2	3	2	1	3	105%
(C) Stuff, stamp, seal, and sort envelopes	2	1	5*	2	1	110%

APPROACH ▶ Once the data have been collected, the procedure is to:

1. Delete unusual or nonrecurring observations.
2. Compute the *average time* for each element, using Equation (10-1).
3. Compute the *normal time* for each element, using Equation (10-2).
4. Find the total normal time.
5. Compute the *standard time*, using Equation (10-3).

SOLUTION ▶

1. Delete observations such as those marked with an asterisk (*). (These may be due to business interruptions, conferences with the boss, or mistakes of an unusual nature; they are not part of the job element, but may be personal or delay time.)
2. Average time for each job element:

$$\text{Average time for A} = \frac{8 + 10 + 9 + 11}{4}$$
$$= 9.5 \text{ min}$$
$$\text{Average time for B} = \frac{2 + 3 + 2 + 1 + 3}{5}$$
$$= 2.2 \text{ min}$$
$$\text{Average time for C} = \frac{2 + 1 + 2 + 1}{4}$$
$$= 1.5 \text{ min}$$

3. Normal time for each job element:

$$\text{Normal time for A} = (\text{Average observed time}) \times (\text{Performance rating})$$
$$= (9.5)(1.2)$$
$$= 11.4 \text{ min}$$
$$\text{Normal time for B} = (2.2)(1.05)$$
$$= 2.31 \text{ min}$$
$$\text{Normal time for C} = (1.5)(1.10)$$
$$= 1.65 \text{ min}$$

Note: Normal times are computed for each element because the performance rating factor (work pace) may vary for each element, as it did in this case.

4. Add the normal times for each element to find the total normal time (the normal time for the whole job):

$$\text{Total normal time} = 11.40 + 2.31 + 1.65$$
$$= 15.36 \text{ min}$$

5. Standard time for the job:

$$\text{Standard time} = \frac{\text{Total normal time}}{1 - \text{Allowance factor}} = \frac{15.36}{1 - .15}$$
$$= 18.07 \text{ min}$$

Thus, 18.07 minutes is the time standard for this job.

INSIGHT ▶ When observed times are not consistent they need to be reviewed. Abnormally short times may be the result of an observational error and are usually discarded. Abnormally long times need to be analyzed to determine if they, too, are an error. However, they may *include* a seldom occurring but legitimate activity for the element (such as a machine adjustment) or may be personal, delay, or fatigue time.

LEARNING EXERCISE ▶ If the two observations marked with an asterisk were *not* deleted, what would be the total normal time and the standard time? [Answer: 18.89 min, 22.22 min.]

RELATED PROBLEMS ▶ 10.22, 10.23, 10.24, 10.25, 10.28a,b, 10.29a, 10.30a

Time study requires a sampling process; so the question of sampling error in the average observed time naturally arises. In statistics, error varies inversely with sample size. Thus, to determine just how many cycles we should time, we must consider the variability of each element in the study.

To determine an adequate sample size, three items must be considered:

1. How accurate we want to be (e.g., is ±5% of observed time close enough?).
2. The desired level of confidence (e.g., the z-value; is 95% adequate or is 99% required?).
3. How much variation exists within the job elements (e.g., if the variation is large, a larger sample will be required).

The formula for finding the appropriate sample size, given these three variables, is:

$$\text{Required sample size} = n = \left(\frac{zs}{h\bar{x}}\right)^2 \quad \text{(10-4)}$$

where h = accuracy level (acceptable error) desired in percent of the job element, expressed as a decimal (5% =.05)
z = number of standard deviations required for desired level of confidence (90% confidence = 1.65; see Table 10.2 or Appendix I for more z-values)
s = standard deviation of the initial sample
$\bar{x}$ = mean of the initial sample
n = required sample size

▼ TABLE 10.2
Common z-Values

Desired Confidence (%)	z-Value (standard deviation required for desired level of confidence)
90.0	1.65
95.0	1.96
95.45	2.00
99.0	2.58
99.73	3.00

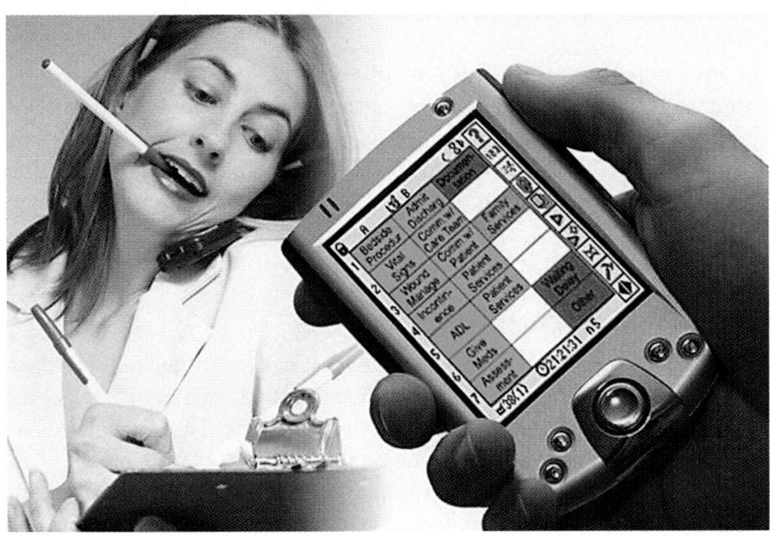

Since the days of F. W. Taylor, time studies have been performed by using a stopwatch. However, with the development of PDA software, such as the program shown here, study elements, time, performance rate, and statistical confidence intervals can be created, edited, managed, and logged with a PDA. Handheld technology eliminates the need for data entry and sends the data directly to a program to be analyzed. The software shown here is available from Laubrass Inc. **(www.laubrass.com).**

We demonstrate with Example 3.

EXAMPLE 3 ▶

Computing sample size

Thomas W. Jones Manufacturing Co. has asked you to check a labor standard prepared by a recently terminated analyst. Your first task is to determine the correct sample size. Your accuracy is to be within 5% and your confidence level at 95%. The standard deviation of the sample is 1.0 and the mean 3.00.

APPROACH ▶ You apply Equation (10-4).

SOLUTION ▶

$$h = .05 \qquad \bar{x} = 3.00 \qquad s = 1.0$$

$z = 1.96$ (from Table 10.2 or Appendix I)

$$n = \left(\frac{zs}{h\bar{x}}\right)^2$$

$$n = \left(\frac{1.96 \times 1.0}{.05 \times 3}\right)^2 = 170.74 \approx 171$$

Therefore, you recommend a sample size of 171.

INSIGHT ▶ Notice that as the confidence level required increases, the sample size also increases. Similarly, as the desired accuracy level increases (say, from 5% to 1%), the sample size increases.

LEARNING EXERCISE ▶ The confidence level for Jones Manufacturing Co. can be set lower, at 90%, while retaining the same ±5% accuracy levels. What sample size is needed now? [Answer: $n = 121$.]

RELATED PROBLEMS ▶ 10.26, 10.27, 10.28c, 10.29b, 10.30b

LO7: Find the proper sample size for a time study

Now let's look at two variations of Example 3.

First, if h, the desired accuracy, is expressed as an absolute amount of error (say, 1 minute of error is acceptable), then substitute e for $h\bar{x}$, and the appropriate formula is:

$$n = \left(\frac{zs}{e}\right)^2 \qquad \text{(10-5)}$$

where e is the absolute time amount of acceptable error.

Second, for those cases when s, the standard deviation of the sample, is not provided (which is typically the case outside the classroom), it must be computed. The formula for doing so is given in Equation (10-6):

$$s = \sqrt{\frac{\sum(x_i - \bar{x})^2}{n-1}} = \sqrt{\frac{\sum(\text{Each sample observation} - \bar{x})^2}{\text{Number in sample} - 1}} \qquad \text{(10-6)}$$

where x_i = value of each observation
$\bar{x}$ = mean of the observations
n = number of observations in the sample

An example of this computation is provided in Solved Problem 10.4 on page 408.

Although time studies provide accuracy in setting labor standards (see the *OM in Action* box "UPS: The Tightest Ship in the Shipping Business"), they have two disadvantages. First, they require a trained staff of analysts. Second, these standards cannot be set before tasks are actually performed. This leads us to two alternative work-measurement techniques that we discuss next.

AUTHOR COMMENT Families of predetermined time standards have been developed for many occupations.

Predetermined Time Standards

Predetermined time standards
A division of manual work into small basic elements that have established and widely accepted times.

In addition to historical experience and time studies, we can set production standards by using predetermined time standards. **Predetermined time standards** divide manual work into small basic elements that already have established times (based on very large samples of workers). To estimate the time for a particular task, the time factors for each basic element of that task are added together. Developing a comprehensive system of predetermined time standards would be prohibitively expensive for any given firm. Consequently, a number of systems are commercially

OM in Action ▶UPS: The Tightest Ship in the Shipping Business

United Parcel Service (UPS) employs 425,000 people and delivers an average of 16 million packages a day to locations throughout the U.S. and 200 other countries. To achieve its claim of "running the tightest ship in the shipping business," UPS methodically trains its delivery drivers in how to do their jobs as efficiently as possible.

Industrial engineers at UPS have time-studied each driver's route and set standards for each delivery, stop, and pickup. These engineers have recorded every second taken up by stoplights, traffic volume, detours, doorbells, walkways, stairways, and coffee breaks. Even bathroom stops are factored into the standards. All this information is then fed into company computers to provide detailed time standards for every driver, every day.

To meet their objective of 200 deliveries and pickups each day (versus only 80 at FedEx), UPS drivers must follow procedures exactly. As they approach a delivery stop, drivers unbuckle their seat belts, honk their horns, and cut their engines. In one seamless motion, they are required to yank up their emergency brakes and push their gearshifts into first. Then they slide to the ground with their electronic clipboards under their right arm and their packages in their left hand. Ignition keys, teeth up, are in their right hand. They walk to the customer's door at the prescribed 3 feet per second and knock first to avoid lost seconds searching for the doorbell. After making the delivery, they do the paperwork on the way back to the truck.

Productivity experts describe UPS as one of the most efficient companies anywhere in applying effective labor standards.

Sources: G.Niemann *Big Brown*: 1; *The Untold Story of UPS* NewYork: Wiley, 2007; and *IIE Solutions* (March 2002): 16.

available. The most common predetermined time standard is *methods time measurement* (MTM), which is a product of the MTM Association.[3]

Predetermined time standards are an outgrowth of basic motions called therbligs. The term *therblig* was coined by Frank Gilbreth (*Gilbreth* spelled backwards, with the *t* and *h* reversed). **Therbligs** include such activities as select, grasp, position, assemble, reach, hold, rest, and inspect. These activities are stated in terms of **time measurement units (TMUs)**, which are equal to only .00001 hour, or .0006 minute each. MTM values for various therbligs are specified in very detailed tables. Figure 10.9, for example, provides the set of time standards for the motion GET and PLACE. To use GET and PLACE, one must know what is "gotten," its approximate weight, and where and how far it is supposed to be placed.

Therbligs
Basic physical elements of motion.

Time measurement units (TMUs)
Units for very basic micromotions in which 1 TMU = .0006 min or 100,000 TMUs = 1 hr.

Example 4 shows a use of predetermined time standards in setting service labor standards.

Before an assembly line, like this one in China, is set up, the company establishes labor standards to assist in layout and staff planning.

[3]MTM is really a family of products available from the Methods Time Measurement Association. For example, MTM-HC deals with the health care industry, MTM-C handles clerical activities, MTM-M involves microscope activities, MTM-V deals with machine shop tasks, and so on.

▶ **FIGURE 10.9**
Sample MTM Table for GET and PLACE Motion
Time values are in TMUs.

Source: Copyrighted by the MTM Association for Standards and Research. No reprint permission without consent from the MTM Association, 16–01 Broadway, Fair Lawn, NJ 07410. Used with permission of MTM Association for Standards & Research.

GET and PLACE			DISTANCE RANGE IN IN.	<8	>8 <20	>20 <32
WEIGHT	CONDITIONS OF GET	PLACE ACCURACY	MTM CODE	1	2	3
<2 LB	EASY	APPROXIMATE	AA	20	35	50
		LOOSE	AB	30	45	60
		TIGHT	AC	40	55	70
	DIFFICULT	APPROXIMATE	AD	20	45	60
		LOOSE	AE	30	55	70
		TIGHT	AF	40	65	80
	HANDFUL	APPROXIMATE	AG	40	65	80
>2 LB <18 LB		APPROXIMATE	AH	25	45	55
		LOOSE	AJ	40	65	75
		TIGHT	AK	50	75	85
>18 LB <45 LB		APPROXIMATE	AL	90	106	115
		LOOSE	AM	95	120	130
		TIGHT	AN	120	145	160

EXAMPLE 4 ▶

Using predetermined time (MTM analysis) to determine standard time

General Hospital wants to set the standard time for lab technicians to pour a tube specimen using MTM.[4]

APPROACH ▶ This is a repetitive task for which the MTM data in Table 10.3 may be used to develop standard times. The sample tube is in a rack and the centrifuge tubes in a nearby box. A technician removes the sample tube from the rack, uncaps it, gets the centrifuge tube, pours, and places both tubes in the rack.

TABLE 10.3 ▶
MTM-HC Analysis: Pouring Tube Specimen

Element Description	Element	Time
Get tube from rack	AA2	35
Uncap, place on counter	AA2	35
Get centrifuge tube, place at sample tube	AD2	45
Pour (3 sec)	PT	83
Place tubes in rack (simo)	PC2	40
		Total TMU 238

$.0006 \times 238 =$ Total standard minutes $= .143$ or about 8.6 seconds

SOLUTION ▶ The first work element involves getting the tube from the rack. The conditions for GETTING the tube and PLACING it in front of the technician are:

- *Weight:* (less than 2 pounds)
- *Conditions of GET:* (easy)
- *Place accuracy:* (approximate)
- *Distance range:* (8 to 20 inches)

Then the MTM element for this activity is AA2 (as seen in Figure 10.9). The rest of Table 10.3 is developed from similar MTM tables.

INSIGHT ▶ Most MTM calculations are computerized, so the user need only key in the appropriate MTM codes, such as AA2 in this example.

LEARNING EXERCISE ▶ General Hospital decides that the first step in this process really involves a distance range of 4 inches (getting the tube from the rack). The other work elements are unchanged. What is the new standard time? [Answer: .134 min. or just over 8 seconds]

RELATED PROBLEM ▶ 10.36

[4] A. S. Helms, B. W. Shaw, and C. A. Lindner, "The Development of Laboratory Workload Standards through Computer-Based Work Measurement Technique, Part I," *Journal of Methods-Time Measurement* 12: 43. Used with permission of MTM Association for Standards and Research.

Predetermined time standards have several advantages over direct time studies. First, they may be established in a laboratory environment, where the procedure will not upset actual production activities (which time studies tend to do). Second, because the standard can be set *before* a task is actually performed, it can be used for planning. Third, no performance ratings are necessary. Fourth, unions tend to accept this method as a fair means of setting standards. Finally, predetermined time standards are particularly effective in firms that do substantial numbers of studies of similar tasks. To ensure accurate labor standards, some firms use both time studies and predetermined time standards.

Work Sampling

The fourth method of developing labor or production standards, work sampling, was developed in England by L. Tippet in the 1930s. **Work sampling** estimates the percent of the time that a worker spends on various tasks. Random observations are used to record the activity that a worker is performing. The results are primarily used to determine how employees allocate their time among various activities. Knowledge of this allocation may lead to staffing changes, reassignment of duties, estimates of activity cost, and the setting of delay allowances for labor standards. When work sampling is done to establish delay allowances, it is sometimes called a *ratio delay study*.

Work sampling
An estimate, via sampling, of the percent of the time that a worker spends on various tasks.

The work-sampling procedure can be summarized in five steps:

1. Take a preliminary sample to obtain an estimate of the parameter value (e.g., percent of time a worker is busy).
2. Compute the sample size required.
3. Prepare a schedule for observing the worker at appropriate times. The concept of random numbers is used to provide for random observation. For example, let's say we draw the following five random numbers from a table: 07, 12, 22, 25, and 49. These can then be used to create an observation schedule of 9:07 A.M., 9:12, 9:22, 9:25, 9:49.
4. Observe and record worker activities.
5. Determine how workers spend their time (usually as a percentage).

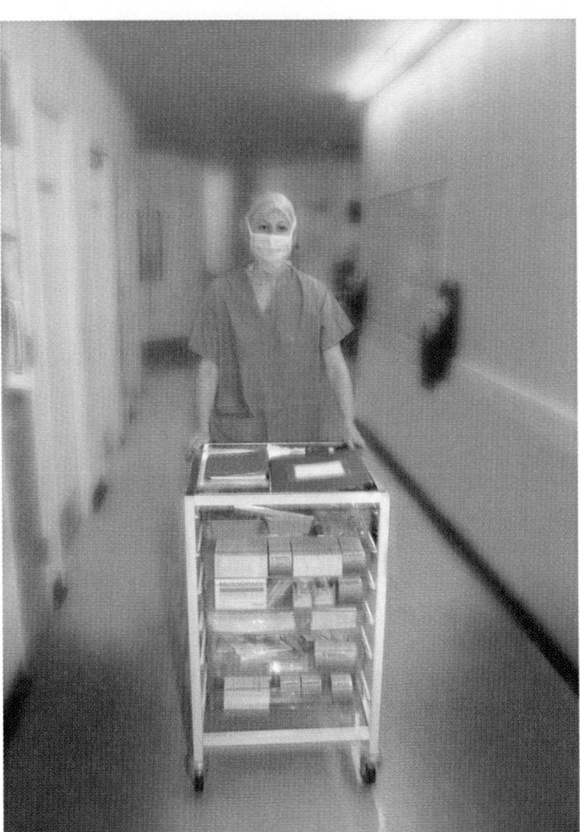

Using the techniques of this chapter to develop labor standards, operations managers at Orlando's Arnold Palmer Hospital determined that nurses walked an average of 2.7 miles per day. This constitutes up to 30% of the nurse's time, a terrible waste of critical talent. Analysis resulted in a new layout design that has reduced walking distances by 20%.

To determine the number of observations required, management must decide on the desired confidence level and accuracy. First, however, the analyst must select a preliminary value for the parameter under study (Step 1 above). The choice is usually based on a small sample of perhaps 50 observations. The following formula then gives the sample size for a desired confidence and accuracy:

$$n = \frac{z^2 p(1 - p)}{h^2} \tag{10-7}$$

where n = required sample size
z = number of standard deviations for the desired confidence level ($z = 1$ for 68% confidence, $z = 2$ for 95.45% confidence, and $z = 3$ for 99.73% confidence—these values are obtained from Table 10.2 or the normal table in Appendix I)
p = estimated value of sample proportion (of time worker is observed busy or idle)
h = acceptable error level, in percent

Example 5 shows how to apply this formula.

EXAMPLE 5 ▶

Determining the number of work sample observations needed

The manager of Michigan County's welfare office, Dana Johnson, estimates that her employees are idle 25% of the time. She would like to take a work sample that is accurate within 3% and wants to have 95.45% confidence in the results.

APPROACH ▶ Dana applies Equation (10-7) to determine how many observations should be taken.

SOLUTION ▶ Dana computes n:

$$n = \frac{z^2 p(1 - p)}{h^2}$$

where n = required sample size
p = 2 for 95.45% confidence level
p = estimate of idle proportion = 25% =.25
h = acceptable error of 3% = .03

She finds that

$$n = \frac{(2)^2(.25)(.75)}{(.03)^2} = 833 \text{ observations}$$

INSIGHT ▶ Thus, 833 observations should be taken. If the percent of idle time observed is not close to 25% as the study progresses, then the number of observations may have to be recalculated and increased or decreased as appropriate.

LEARNING EXERCISE ▶ If the confidence level increases to 99.73%, how does the sample size change? [Answer: n = 1,875.]

RELATED PROBLEMS ▶ 10.31, 10.32, 10.35, 10.37

ACTIVE MODEL 10.1 This example is further illustrated in Active Model 10.1 at **www.pearsonhighered.com/heizer**.

The focus of work sampling is to determine how workers allocate their time among various activities. This is accomplished by establishing the percent of time individuals spend on these activities rather than the exact amount of time spent on specific tasks. The analyst simply records in a random, nonbiased way the occurrence of each activity. Example 6 shows the procedure for evaluating employees at the state welfare office introduced in Example 5.

EXAMPLE 6 ▶

Determining employee time allocation with work sampling

Dana Johnson, the manager of Michigan County's welfare office, wants to be sure her employees have adequate time to provide prompt, helpful service. She believes that service to welfare clients who phone or walk in without an appointment deteriorates rapidly when employees are busy more than 75% of the time. Consequently, she does not want her employees to be occupied with client service activities more than 75% of the time.

APPROACH ▶ The study requires several things: First, based on the calculations in Example 5, 833 observations are needed. Second, observations are to be made in a random, nonbiased way over a period of 2 weeks to ensure a true sample. Third, the analyst must define the activities that are "work." In this case, work is defined as all the activities necessary to take care of the client (filing, meetings, data entry, discussions with the supervisor, etc.). Fourth, personal time is to be included in the 25% of nonwork time. Fifth, the observations are made in a nonintrusive way so as not to distort the normal work patterns. At the end of the 2 weeks, the 833 observations yield the following results:

No. of Observations	Activity
485	On the phone or meeting with a welfare client
126	Idle
62	Personal time
23	Discussions with supervisor
137	Filing, meeting, and computer data entry
833	

SOLUTION ▶ The analyst concludes that all but 188 observations (126 idle and 62 personal) are work related. Since 22.6% (= 188/833) is less idle time than Dana believes necessary to ensure a high client service level, she needs to find a way to reduce current workloads. This could be done through a reassignment of duties or the hiring of additional personnel.

INSIGHT ▶ Work sampling is particularly helpful when determining staffing needs or the reallocation of duties (see Figure 10.10).

LEARNING EXERCISE ▶ The analyst working for Dana recategorizes several observations. There are now 450 "on the phone/meeting with client" observations, 156 "idle," and 67 "personal time" observations. The last two categories saw no changes. Do the conclusions change? [Answer: Yes; now about 27% of employee time is not work related—over the 25% Dana desires.]

RELATED PROBLEM ▶ 10.34

The results of similar studies of salespeople and assembly-line employees are shown in Figure 10.10.

Work sampling offers several advantages over time-study methods. First, because a single observer can observe several workers simultaneously, it is less expensive. Second, observers usually do not require much training, and no timing devices are needed. Third, the study can be temporarily delayed at any time with little impact on the results. Fourth, because work sampling uses instantaneous observations over a long period, the worker has little chance of affecting the study's outcome. Fifth, the procedure is less intrusive and therefore less likely to generate objections.

The disadvantages of work sampling are (1) it does not divide work elements as completely as time studies, (2) it can yield biased or incorrect results if the observer does not follow random

▼ **FIGURE 10.10 Work-Sampling Time Studies**

These two work-sampling time studies were done to determine what salespeople do at a wholesale electronics distributor (left) and a composite of several auto assembly-line employees (right).

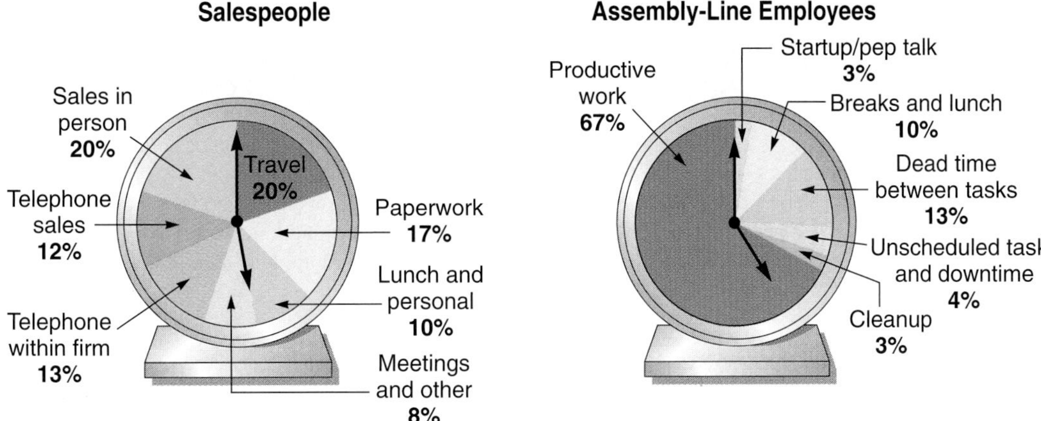

routes of travel and observation, and (3) because it is less intrusive, it tends to be less accurate; this is particularly true when job content times are short.

AUTHOR COMMENT Mutual trust and commitment cannot be acheived without ethical behavior.

ETHICS

Ethics in the workplace presents some interesting challenges. As we have suggested in this chapter, many constraints influence job design. The issues of fairness, equity, and ethics are pervasive. Whether the issue is equal opportunity or safe working conditions, an operations manager is often the one responsible. Managers do have some guidelines. By knowing the law, working with OSHA,[5] MSDS,[6] state agencies, unions, trade associations, insurers, and employees, managers can often determine the parameters of their decisions. Human resource and legal departments are also available for help and guidance through the labyrinth of laws and regulations.

Management's role is to educate employees; specify the necessary equipment, work rules, and work environment; and then enforce those requirements, even when employees think it is not necessary to wear safety equipment. We began this chapter with a discussion of mutual trust and commitment, and that is the environment that managers should foster. Ethical management requires no less.

CHAPTER SUMMARY

Outstanding firms know that their human resource strategy can yield a competitive advantage. Often a large percentage of employees and a large part of labor costs are under the direction of OM. Consequently, an operations manager usually has a major role to play in achieving human resource objectives. A requirement is to build an environment with mutual respect and commitment and a reasonable quality of work life. Successful organizations have designed jobs that use both the mental and physical capabilities of their employees. Regardless of the strategy chosen, the skill with which a firm manages its human resources ultimately determines its success.

Labor standards are required for an efficient operations system. They are needed for production planning, labor planning, costing, and evaluating performance. They are used throughout industry—from the factory to finance, sales, and the office. They can also be used as a basis for incentive systems. Standards may be established via historical data, time studies, predetermined time standards, and work sampling.

Key Terms

Labor planning (p. 385)
Job design (p. 386)
Labor specialization (or job specialization) (p. 386)
Job enlargement (p. 387)
Job rotation (p. 387)
Job enrichment (p. 387)
Employee empowerment (p. 387)
Self-directed team (p. 388)
Ergonomics (p. 389)
Methods analysis (p. 392)
Flow diagram (p. 392)
Process chart (p. 393)
Activity chart (p. 393)
Operations chart (p. 393)
Visual workplace (p. 393)
Labor standards (p. 395)
Time study (p. 395)
Average observed time (p. 396)
Normal time (p. 396)
Standard time (p. 397)
Predetermined time standards (p. 400)
Therbligs (p. 401)
Time measurement units (TMUs) (p. 401)
Work sampling (p. 403)

Ethical Dilemma

Birmingham's McWane Inc., with 10 major foundries, is one of the world's largest makers of cast-iron water and sewer pipes. In one of the nation's most dangerous industries, McWane is perhaps the most unsafe, with four times the injury rate of its six competitors combined. Its worker death rate is six times that of its industry's. McWane plants were also found in violation of pollution and emission limits 450 times in a recent 7-year period.

Workers who protest dangerous work conditions claim they are "bull's-eyed"—marked for termination. Supervisors have bullied injured workers and intimidated union leaders. Line workers who

[5]The Occupational Safety and Health Administration (OSHA) is a federal government agency whose task is to ensure the safety and health of U.S. workers.
[6]Material safety data sheets (MSDS) contain details of hazards associated with chemicals and give information on their safe use.

fail to make daily quotas get disciplinary actions. Managers have put up safety signs *after* a worker was injured to make it appear the worker ignored posted policies. They alter safety records and doctor machines to cover up hazards. When the government investigated one worker's death in 2000, inspectors found the McWane policy "was not to correct anything until OSHA found it."

McWane plants have also been repeatedly fined for failing to stop production to repair broken pollution controls. Five plants have been designated "high priority" violators by the EPA. Inside the plants, workers have repeatedly complained of blurred vision, severe headaches, and respiratory problems after being exposed, without training or protection, to chemicals used to make pipes. Near one plant in Phillipsburg, New Jersey, school crossing guards have had to wear gas masks—that location alone received 150 violations between 1995 and 2002. McWane's "standard procedure" (according to a former plant manager) is to illegally dump industrial contaminants into local rivers and creeks. Workers wait for night or heavy rainstorms before flushing thousands of gallons from their sump pumps.

Given the following fictional scenarios: What is your position, and what action should you take?

a. On your spouse's recent move to Birmingham, you accepted a job, perhaps somewhat naively, as a company nurse in one of the McWane plants. After 2 weeks on the job you became aware of the work environment noted above.
b. You are a contractor who has traditionally used McWane's products, which meet specifications. McWane is consistently the low bidder. Your customers are happy with the product.
c. You are McWane's banker.
d. You are a supplier to McWane.

Sources: *The New York Times* (January 9, 2003: E5, (May 26, 2004): A19, and (August 30, 2005): A16; and *The Wall Street Journal* (May 27, 2004): A8.

Discussion Questions

1. How would you define a good quality of work life?
2. What are some of the worst jobs you know about? Why are they bad jobs? Why do people want these jobs?
3. If you were redesigning the jobs described in Question 2, what changes would you make? Are your changes realistic? Would they improve productivity (not just *production* but *productivity*)?
4. Can you think of any jobs that push the man–machine interface to the limits of human capabilities?
5. What are the five core characteristics of a good job design?
6. What are the differences among job enrichment, job enlargement, job rotation, job specialization, and employee empowerment?
7. Define ergonomics. Discuss the role of ergonomics in job design.
8. List the techniques available for carrying out methods analysis.
9. Identify four ways in which labor standards are set.
10. What are some of the uses to which labor standards are put?
11. How would you classify the following job elements? Are they personal, fatigue, or delay?
    a) The operator stops to talk to you.
    b) The operator lights up a cigarette.
    c) The operator opens his luch pail (it is not lunch time), removes an apple, and takes an occasional bite.
12. How do you classify the time for a drill press operator who is idle for a few minutes at the beginning of every job waiting for the setup person to complete the setup? Some of the setup time is used in going for stock, but the operator typically returns with stock before the setup person is finished with the setup.
13. How do you classify the time for a machine operator who, between every job and sometimes in the middle of jobs, turns off the machine and goes for stock?
14. The operator drops a part, which you pick up and hand to him. Does this make any difference in a time study? If so, how?

Solved Problems

Virtual Office Hours help is available at www.myomlab.com.

▼ SOLVED PROBLEM 10.1

As pit crew manager for Rusty Wallace's NASCAR team (see the *Global Company Profile* that opens this chapter), you would like to evaluate how your "Jackman" (JM) and "Gas Man #1" (GM #1) are utilized. Recent stopwatch studies have verified the following times:

Pit crew	Activity	Time (seconds)
JM	Move to right side of car and raise car	4.0
GM #1	Move to rear gas filler	2.5
JM	Move to left side of car and raise car	3.8
JM	Wait for tire	1.0
GM #1	Load fuel (per gallon)	0.5
JM	Wait for tire	1.2
JM	Move back over wall from left side	2.5
GM #1	Move back over the wall from gas filler	2.5

Use an activity chart similar to the one in Figure 10.6 as an aid.

▼ **SOLUTION**

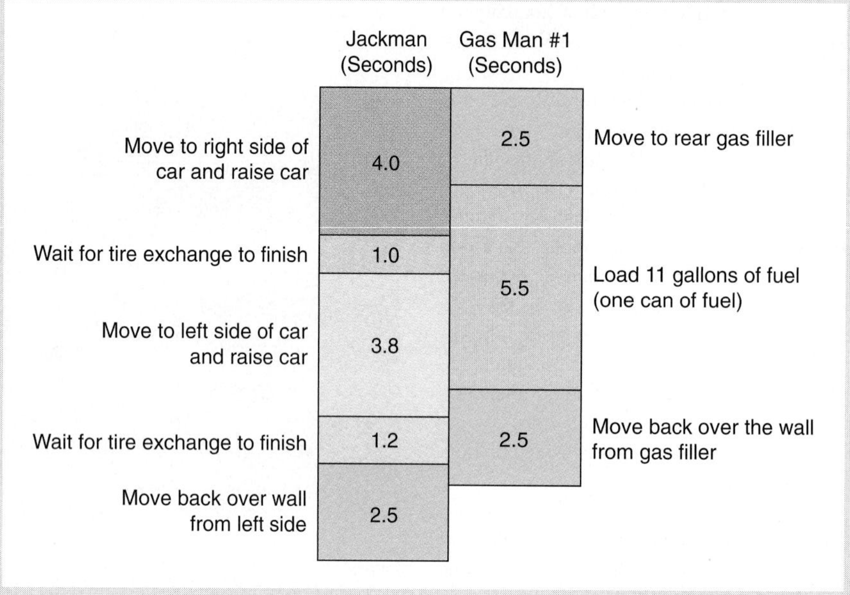

	Jackman (Seconds)	Gas Man #1 (Seconds)	
Move to right side of car and raise car	4.0	2.5	Move to rear gas filler
Wait for tire exchange to finish	1.0	5.5	Load 11 gallons of fuel (one can of fuel)
Move to left side of car and raise car	3.8		
Wait for tire exchange to finish	1.2	2.5	Move back over the wall from gas filler
Move back over wall from left side	2.5		

▼ **SOLVED PROBLEM 10.2**

A work operation consisting of three elements has been subjected to a stopwatch time study. The recorded observations are shown in the following table. By union contract, the allowance time for the operation is personal time 5%, delay 5%, and fatigue 10%. Determine the standard time for the work operation.

Job Element	Observations (minutes) 1	2	3	4	5	6	Performance Rating (%)
A	.1	.3	.2	.9	.2	.1	90
B	.8	.6	.8	.5	3.2	.7	110
C	.5	.5	.4	.5	.6	.5	80

▼ **SOLUTION**

First, delete the two observations that appear to be very unusual (.9 minute for job element A and 3.2 minutes for job element B). Then:

$$\text{A's average observed time} = \frac{.1 + .3 + .2 + .2 + .1}{5} = .18 \text{ min}$$

$$\text{B's average observed time} = \frac{.8 + .6 + .8 + .5 + .7}{5} = .68 \text{ min}$$

$$\text{C's average observed time} = \frac{.5 + .5 + .4 + .5 + .6 + .5}{6} = .50 \text{ min}$$

$$\text{A's normal time} = (.18)(.90) = .16 \text{ min}$$

$$\text{B's normal time} = (.68)(1.10) = .75 \text{ min}$$

$$\text{C's normal time} = (.50)(.80) = .40 \text{ min}$$

$$\text{Normal time for job} = .16 + .75 + .40 = 1.31 \text{ min}$$

$$\text{Note, the total allowance factor} = .05 + .05 + .10 = .20$$

$$\text{Then: Standard time} = \frac{1.31}{1 - .20} = 1.64 \text{ min}$$

▼ **SOLVED PROBLEM 10.3**

The preliminary work sample of an operation indicate the following:

Number of times operator working	60
Number of times operator idle	40
Total number of preliminary observations	100

What is the required sample size for a 99.73% confidence level with ±4% precision?

▼ **SOLUTION**

$z = 3$ for 99.73% confidence; $p = \frac{60}{100} = .6$; $h = .04$

So:

$$n = \frac{z^2 p(1 - p)}{h^2} = \frac{(3)^2(.6)(.4)}{(.04)^2} = 1{,}350 \text{ sample size}$$

▼ **SOLVED PROBLEM 10.4**

Amor Manufacturing Co. of Geneva, Switzerland, has just observed a job in its laboratory in anticipation of releasing the job to the factory for production. The firm wants rather good accuracy for costing and labor forecasting. Specifically, it wants to provide a 99% confidence level and a cycle time that is within 3% of the true value. How many observations should it make? The data collected so far are as follows:

Observation	Time
1	1.7
2	1.6
3	1.4
4	1.4
5	1.4

▼ **SOLUTION**

First, solve for the mean, $\bar{x}$, and the sample standard deviation, s:

$$s = \sqrt{\frac{\sum(\text{Each sample observation} - \bar{x})^2}{\text{Number in sample} - 1}}$$

Observation	x_i	$\bar{x}$	$x_i - \bar{x}$	$(x_i - \bar{x})^2$
1	1.7	1.5	.2	0.04
2	1.6	1.5	.1	0.01
3	1.4	1.5	−.1	0.01
4	1.4	1.5	−.1	0.01
5	1.4	1.5	−.1	0.01
	$\bar{x} = 1.5$			$0.08 = \sum(x_i - \bar{x})^2$

$$s = \sqrt{\frac{.08}{n-1}} = \sqrt{\frac{.08}{4}} = .141$$

Then, solve for $n = \left(\frac{zs}{h\bar{x}}\right)^2 = \left[\frac{(2.58)(.141)}{(.03)(1.5)}\right]^2 = 65.3$

where $\bar{x} = 1.5$
$s = .141$
$z = 2.58$ (from Table 10.2)
$h = .03$

Therefore, you round up to 66 observations.

▼ **SOLVED PROBLEM 10.5**

At Maggard Micro Manufacturing, Inc., workers press semiconductors into predrilled slots on printed circuit boards. The elemental motions for normal time used by the company are as follows:

Reach 6 inches for semiconductors	40 TMU
Grasp the semiconductor	10 TMU
Move semiconductor to printed circuit board	30 TMU
Position semiconductor	35 TMU
Press semiconductor into slots	65 TMU
Move board aside	20 TMU

(Each time measurement unit is equal to .0006 min.) Determine the normal time for this operation in minutes and in seconds.

▼ **SOLUTION**

Add the time measurement units:

$$40 + 10 + 30 + 35 + 65 + 20 = 200$$
$$\text{Time in minutes} = (200)(.0006 \text{ min.}) = .12 \text{ min}$$
$$\text{Time in seconds} = (.12)(60 \text{ sec}) = 7.2 \text{ sec}$$

▼ **SOLVED PROBLEM 10.6**

To obtain the estimate of time a worker is busy for a work sampling study, a manager divides a typical workday into 480 minutes. Using a random-number table to decide what time to go to an area to sample work occurrences, the manager records observations on a tally sheet like the following:

Status	Tally
Productively working	卌 卌 卌 |
Idle	||||

▼ **SOLUTION**

In this case, the supervisor made 20 observations and found that employees were working 80% of the time. So, out of 480 minutes in an office workday, 20%, or 96 minutes, was idle time, and 384 minutes was productive. Note that this procedure describes that a worker is busy, not necessarily what he or she *should* be doing.

Problems*

• **10.1** Make a process chart for changing the right rear tire on an automobile.

• **10.2** Draw an activity chart for a machine operator with the following operation. The relevant times are as follows:

Prepare mill for loading (cleaning, oiling, and so on)	.50 min
Load mill	1.75 min
Mill operating (cutting material)	2.25 min
Unload mill	.75 min

••• **10.3** Draw an activity chart (a crew chart similar to Figure 10.6) for a concert (for example, Nickelback, Linkin Park, Lil'

*Note: PX means the problem may be solved with POM for Windows and/or Excel.

Wayne, or Bruce Springsteen) and determine how to put together the concert so the star has reasonable breaks. For instance, at what point is there an instrumental number, a visual effect, a duet, a dance moment, that allows the star to pause and rest physically or at least rest his or her voice? Do other members of the show have moments of pause or rest?

•• **10.4** Make an operations chart of one of the following:
a) Putting a new eraser in (or on) a pencil
b) Putting a paper clip on two pieces of paper
c) Putting paper in a printer

• **10.5** Develop a process chart for installing a new memory board in your personal computer.

• **10.6** Rate a job you have had using Hackman and Oldham's core job characteristics (see page 387) on a scale from 1 to 10. What is your total score? What about the job could have been changed to make you give it a higher score?

•• **10.7** Using the data in Solved Problem 10.1, prepare an activity chart like the one in the Solved Problem, but a second Gas Man also delivers 11 gallons.

•• **10.8** Prepare a process chart for the Jackman in Solved Problem 10.1.

•• **10.9** Draw an activity chart for changing the right rear tire on an automobile with:
a) Only one person working
b) Two people working

••• **10.10** Draw an activity chart for washing the dishes in a double-sided sink. Two people participate, one washing, the other rinsing and drying. The rinser dries a batch of dishes from the drip rack as the washer fills the right sink with clean but unrinsed dishes. Then the rinser rinses the clean batch and places them on the drip rack. All dishes are stacked before being placed in the cabinets.

••• **10.11** Your campus club is hosting a car wash. Due to demand, three people are going to be scheduled per wash line. (Three people have to wash each vehicle.) Design an activity chart for washing and drying a typical sedan. You must wash the wheels but ignore the cleaning of the interior, because this part of the operation will be done at a separate vacuum station.

•••• **10.12** Design a process chart for printing a short document on a laser printer at an office. Unknown to you, the printer in the hallway is out of paper. The paper is located in a supply room at the other end of the hall. You wish to make five stapled copies of the document once it is printed. The copier, located next to the printer, has a sorter but no stapler. How could you make the task more efficient with the existing equipment?

• **10.13** If Charlene Brewster has times of 8.4, 8.6, 8.3, 8.5, 8.7, and 8.5 and a performance rating of 110%, what is the normal time for this operation? Is she faster or slower than normal? Px

• **10.14** If Charlene, the worker in Problem 10.13, has a performance rating of 90%, what is the normal time for the operation? Is she faster or slower than normal? Px

•• **10.15** Refer to Problem 10.13.
a) If the allowance factor is 15%, what is the standard time for this operation?
b) If the allowance factor is 18% and the performance rating is now 90%, what is the standard time for this operation? Px

•• **10.16** Maurice Browne recorded the following times assembling a watch. Determine (a) the average time, (b) the normal time, and (c) the standard time taken by him, using a performance rating of 95% and a personal allowance of 8%.

Assembly Times Recorded

Observation No.	Time (minutes)	Observation No.	Time Minutes
1	0.11	9	0.12
2	0.10	10	0.09
3	0.11	11	0.12
4	0.10	12	0.11
5	0.14	13	0.10
6	0.10	14	0.12
7	0.10	15	0.14
8	0.09	16	0.09

• **10.17** A Northeast Airlines gate agent, Chip Gilliken, gives out seat assignments to ticketed passengers. He takes an average of 50 seconds per passenger and is rated 110% in performance. How long should a *typical* agent be expected to take to make seat assignments? Px

• **10.18** After being observed many times, Marilyn Jones, a hospital lab analyst, had an average observed time for blood tests of 12 minutes. Marilyn's performance rating is 105%. The hospital has a personal, fatigue, and delay allowance of 16%.
a) Find the normal time for this process.
b) Find the standard time for this blood test. Px

• **10.19** Jell Lee Beans is famous for its boxed candies, which are sold primarily to businesses. One operator had the following observed times for gift wrapping in minutes: 2.2, 2.6, 2.3, 2.5, 2.4. The operator has a performance rating of 105% and an allowance factor of 10%. What is the standard time for gift wrapping? Px

• **10.20** After training, Mary Fernandez, a computer technician, had an average observed time for memory-chip tests of 12 seconds. Mary's performance rating is 100%. The firm has a personal fatigue and delay allowance of 15%.
a) Find the normal time for this process.
b) Find the standard time for this process. Px

•• **10.21** Susan Cottenden clocked the observed time for welding a part onto truck doors at 5.3 minutes. The performance rating of the worker timed was estimated at 105%. Find the normal time for this operation.
Note: According to the local union contract, each welder is allowed 3 minutes of personal time per hour and 2 minutes of fatigue time per hour. Further, there should be an average delay allowance of 1 minute per hour. Compute the allowance factor and then find the standard time for the welding activity. Px

•• **10.22** A hotel housekeeper, Alison Harvey, was observed five times on each of four task elements, as shown in the following table. On the basis of these observations, find the standard time for the process. Assume a 10% allowance factor.

Element	Performance Rating (%)	*Observations (minutes per cycle)* 1	2	3	4	5
Check minibar	100	1.5	1.6	1.4	1.5	1.5
Make one bed	90	2.3	2.5	2.1	2.2	2.4
Vacuum floor	120	1.7	1.9	1.9	1.4	1.6
Clean bath	100	3.5	3.6	3.6	3.6	3.2

PX

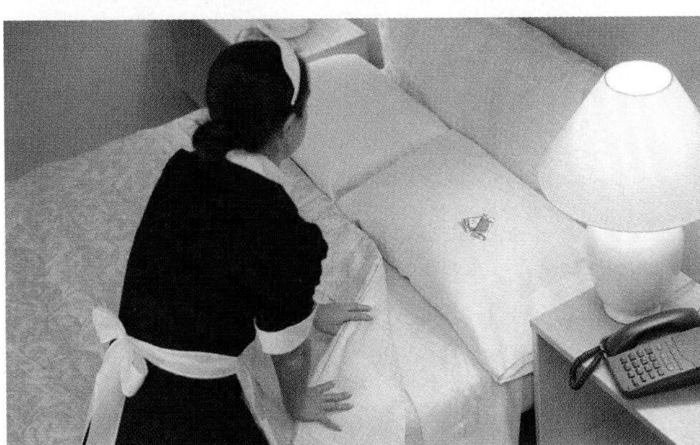

•• **10.23** Virginia College promotes a wide variety of executive-training courses for firms in the Arlington, Virginia, region. Director Marilyn Helms believes that individually typed letters add a personal touch to marketing. To prepare letters for mailing, she conducts a time study of her secretaries. On the basis of the observations shown in the following table, she wishes to develop a time standard for the whole job.

The college uses a total allowance factor of 12%. Helms decides to delete all unusual observations from the time study. What is the standard time?

Element	*Observations (minutes)* 1	2	3	4	5	6	Performance Rating (%)
Typing letter	2.5	3.5	2.8	2.1	2.6	3.3	85
Typing envelope	.8	.8	.6	.8	3.1[a]	.7	100
Stuffing envelope	.4	.5	1.9[a]	.3	.6	.5	95
Sealing, sorting	1.0	2.9[b]	.9	1.0	4.4[b]	.9	125

[a]Disregard—secretary stopped to answer the phone.
[b]Disregard—interruption by supervisor. PX

• **10.24** The results of a time study to perform a quality control test are shown in the following table. On the basis of these observations, determine the normal and standard time for the test, assuming a 23% allowance factor. PX

Task Element	Performance Rating (%)	*Observations (minutes)* 1	2	3	4	5
1	97	1.5	1.8	2.0	1.7	1.5
2	105	.6	.4	.7	3.7[a]	.5
3	86	.5	.4	.6	.4	.4
4	90	.6	.8	.7	.6	.7

[a]Disregard—employee is smoking a cigarette (included in personal time).

•• **10.25** Peter Rourke, a loan processor at Wentworth Bank, has been timed performing four work elements, with the results shown in the following table. The allowances for tasks such as this are personal, 7%; fatigue, 10%; and delay, 3%.

Task Element	Performance Rating (%)	*Observations (minutes)* 1	2	3	4	5
1	110	.5	.4	.6	.4	.4
2	95	.6	.8	.7	.6	.7
3	90	.6	.4	.7	.5	.5
4	85	1.5	1.8	2.0	1.7	1.5

a) What is the normal time?
b) What is the standard time? PX

•• **10.26** Each year, Lord & Taylor, Ltd., sets up a gift-wrapping station to assist its customers with holiday shopping. Preliminary observations of one worker at the station produced the following sample time (in minutes per package): 3.5, 3.2, 4.1, 3.6, 3.9. Based on this small sample, what number of observations would be necessary to determine the true cycle time with a 95% confidence level and an accuracy of 5%? PX

•• **10.27** A time study of a factory worker has revealed an average observed time of 3.20 minutes, with a standard deviation of 1.28 minutes. These figures were based on a sample of 45 observations. Is this sample adequate in size for the firm to be 99% confident that the standard time is within 5% of the true value? If not, what should be the proper number of observations? PX

•• **10.28** Based on a careful work study in the Richard Dulski Corp., the results shown in the following table have been observed:

Element	*Observations (minutes)* 1	2	3	4	5	Performance Rating (%)
Prepare daily reports	35	40	33	42	39	120
Photocopy results	12	10	36[a]	15	13	110
Label and package reports	3	3	5	5	4	90
Distribute reports	15	18	21	17	45[b]	85

[a]Photocopying machine broken; included as delay in the allowance factor.
[b]Power outage; included as delay in the allowance factor.

a) Compute the normal time for each work element.
b) If the allowance for this type of work is 15%, what is the standard time?
c) How many observations are needed for a 95% confidence level within 5% accuracy? (*Hint:* Calculate the sample size of each element.)

•• **10.29** The Dubuque Cement Company packs 80-pound bags of concrete mix. Time-study data for the filling activity are shown in the following table. Because of the high physical demands of the job, the company's policy is a 23% allowance for workers.
a) Compute the standard time for the bag-packing task.
b) How many observations are necessary for 99% confidence, within 5% accuracy?

Element	*Observations (seconds)* 1	2	3	4	5	Performance Rating (%)
Grasp and place bag	8	9	8	11	7	110
Fill bag	36	41	39	35	112[a]	85
Seal bag	15	17	13	20	18	105
Place bag on conveyor	8	6	9	30[b]	35[b]	90

[a]Bag breaks open; included as delay in the allowance factor.
[b]Conveyor jams; included as delay in the allowance factor.

•• **10.30** Installing mufflers at the Stanley Garage in Golden, Colorado, involves five work elements. Linda Stanley has timed workers performing these tasks seven times, with the results shown in the following table.

Job Element	Observations (minutes) 1	2	3	4	5	6	7	Performance Rating (%)
1. Select correct mufflers	4	5	4	6	4	15[a]	4	110
2. Remove old muffler	6	8	7	6	7	6	7	90
3. Weld/install new muffler	15	14	14	12	15	16	13	105
4. Check/inspect work	3	4	24[a]	5	4	3	18[a]	100
5. Complete paperwork	5	6	8	—	7	6	7	130

[a]Employee has lengthy conversations with boss (not job related).

By agreement with her workers, Stanley allows a 10% fatigue factor, a 10% personal-time factor but no time for delay. To compute standard time for the work operation, Stanley excludes all observations that appear to be unusual or nonrecurring. She does not want an error of more than 5%.

a) What is the standard time for the task?
b) How many observations are needed to assure a 95% confidence level? PX

• **10.31** Bank manager Art Hill wants to determine the percent of time that tellers are working and idle. He decides to use work sampling, and his initial estimate is that the tellers are idle 15% of the time. How many observations should Hill take to be 95.45% confident that the results will not be more than 4% from the true result? PX

•• **10.32** Supervisor Robert Hall wants to determine the percent of time a machine in his area is idle. He decides to use work sampling, and his initial estimate is that the machine is idle 20% of the time. How many observations should Hall take to be 98% confident that the results will be less than 5% from the true results?

••• **10.33** In the photo on page 396, Tim Nelson's job as an inspector for La-Z-Boy is discussed. Tim is expected to inspect 130 chairs per day.

a) If he works an 8-hour day, how many minutes is he allowed for each inspection (i.e., what is his "standard time")?
b) If he is allowed a 6% fatigue allowance, a 6% delay allowance, and 6% for personal time, what is the normal time that he is assumed to take to perform each inspection?

••• **10.34** A random work sample of operators taken over a 160-hour work month at Tele-Marketing, Inc., has produced the following results. What is the percent of time spent working?

On phone with customer	858
Idle time	220
Personal time	85

•• **10.35** A total of 300 observations of Bob Ramos, an assembly-line worker, were made over a 40-hour work week. The sample also showed that Bob was busy working (assembling the parts) during 250 observations.

a) Find the percentage of time Bob was working.
b) If you want a confidence level of 95%, and if 3% is an acceptable error, what size should the sample be?
c) Was the sample size adequate? PX

• **10.36** Sharpening your pencil is an operation that may be divided into eight small elemental motions. In MTM terms, each element may be assigned a certain number of TMUs:

Reach 4 inches for the pencil	6 TMU
Grasp the pencil	2 TMU
Move the pencil 6 inches	10 TMU
Position the pencil	20 TMU
Insert the pencil into the sharpener	4 TMU
Sharpen the pencil	120 TMU
Disengage the pencil	10 TMU
Move the pencil 6 inches	10 TMU

What is the total normal time for sharpening one pencil? Convert your answer into minutes and seconds.

•• **10.37** Supervisor Vic Sower at Huntsville Equipment Company is concerned that material is not arriving as promptly as needed at work cells. A new kanban system has been installed, but there seems to be some delay in getting the material moved to the work cells so that the job can begin promptly. Sower is interested in determining how much delay there is on the part of his highly paid machinists. Ideally, the delay would be close to zero. He has asked his assistant to determine the delay factor among his 10 work cells. The assistant collects the data on a random basis over the next 2 weeks and determines that of the 1,200 observations, 105 were made while the operators were waiting for materials. Use a 95% confidence level and a 3% acceptable error. What report does he give to Sower? PX

•••• **10.38** The Winter Garden Hotel has 400 rooms. Every day, the housekeepers clean any room that was occupied the night before. If a guest is checking out of the hotel, the housekeepers give the room a thorough cleaning to get it ready for the next guest. This takes about 30 minutes. If a guest is staying another night, the housekeeper only "refreshes" the room, which takes 15 minutes.

Each day, each housekeeper reports for her 6-hour shift, then prepares her cart. She pushes the cart to her floor and begins work. She usually has to restock the cart once per day; then she pushes it back to the storeroom at the end of the day and puts the things away. Here is a timetable:

1) Arrive at work and stock cart (10 minutes).
2) Push cart to floor (10 minutes).
3) Take morning break (15 minutes).
4) Stop for lunch (30 minutes).
5) Restock cart (20 minutes).
6) Take afternoon break (15 minutes).
7) Push cart back to laundry and store items (20 minutes).

Last night, the hotel was full (all 400 rooms were occupied). People are checking out of 200 rooms. Their rooms will need to be thoroughly cleaned. The other 200 rooms will need to be refreshed.

a) How many minutes per day of actual room cleaning can each housekeeper do?
b) How many minutes of room cleaning will the Winter Garden Hotel need today?
c) How many housekeepers will be needed to clean the hotel today?
d) If *all* the guests checked out this morning, how many housekeepers would be needed to clean the 400 rooms?

▶ **Refer to myomlab for these additional homework problems: 10.39–10.46**

Case Studies

▶ Jackson Manufacturing Company

Kathleen McFadden, vice president of operations at Jackson Manufacturing Company, has just received a request for quote (RFQ) from DeKalb Electric Supply for 400 units per week of a motor armature. The components are standard and either easy to work into the existing production schedule or readily available from established suppliers on a JIT basis. But there is some difference in assembly. Ms. McFadden has identified eight tasks that Jackson must perform to assemble the armature. Seven of these tasks are very similar to ones performed by Jackson in the past; therefore, the average time and resulting labor standard of those tasks is known.

The eighth task, an *overload* test, requires performing a task that is very different from any performed previously, however. Kathleen has asked you to conduct a time study on the task to determine the standard time. Then an estimate can be made of the cost to assemble the armature. This information, combined with other cost data, will allow the firm to put together the information needed for the RFQ.

To determine a standard time for the task, an employee from an existing assembly station was trained in the new assembly process. Once proficient, the employee was then asked to perform the task 17 times so a standard could be determined. The actual times observed (in minutes) were as follows:

The worker had a 115% performance rating. The task can be performed in a sitting position at a well-designed ergonomic workstation in an air-conditioned facility. Although the armature itself weighs 10.5 pounds, there is a carrier that holds it so that the operator need only rotate the armature. But the detail work remains high; therefore, the fatigue allowance should be 8%. The company has an established personal allowance of 6%. Delay should be very low. Previous studies of delay in this department average 2%. This standard is to use the same figure.

The workday is 7.5 hours, but operators are paid for 8 hours at an average of $12.50 per hour.

Discussion Questions

In your report to Ms. McFadden, you realize you will want to address several factors:

1. How big should the sample be for a statistically accurate standard (at, say, the 99.73% confidence level and accuracy of 5%)?
2. Is the sample size adequate?
3. How many units should be produced at this workstation per day?
4. What is the cost per unit for this task in direct labor cost?

1	2	3	4	5	6	7	8	9	10	11	12	13	14	15	16	17
2.05	1.92	2.01	1.89	1.77	1.80	1.86	1.83	1.93	1.96	1.95	2.05	1.79	1.82	1.85	1.85	1.99

Source: Professor Hank Maddux, Sam Houston State University.

▶ Hard Rock's Human Resource Strategy

Video Case

Everyone—managers and hourly employees alike—who goes to work for Hard Rock Cafe takes Rock 101, an initial 2-day training class. There they receive their wallet-sized "Hard Rock Values" card which they carry at all times. The Hard Rock value system is to bring a fun, healthy, nurturing environment into the Hard Rock Cafe culture.* This initial course and many other courses help employees develop both personally and professionally. The human resource department plays a critical role in any service organization, but at Hard Rock, with its "experience strategy," the human resource department takes on added importance.

Long before Jim Knight, manager of corporate training, begins the class, the human resource strategy of Hard Rock has had an impact. Hard Rock's strategic plan includes building a culture that allows for acceptance of substantial diversity and individuality. From a human resource perspective, this has the benefit of enlarging the pool of applicants as well as contributing to the Hard Rock culture.

Creating a work environment above and beyond a paycheck is a unique challenge. Outstanding pay and benefits are a start, but the key is to provide an environment that works for the employees. This includes benefits that start for part-timers who work at least 19 hours per week (while others in the industry start at 35 hours per week); a unique respect for individuality; continuing training; and a high level of internal promotions—some 60% of the managers are promoted from hourly employee ranks. The company's training is very specific, with job-oriented interactive CDs covering kitchen, retail, and front-of-the-house service. Outside volunteer work is especially encouraged to foster a bond between the workers, their community, and issues of importance to them.

Applicants also are screened on their interest in music and their ability to tell a story. Hard Rock builds on a hiring criterion of bright, positive-attitude, self-motivated individuals with an employee bill of rights and substantial employee empowerment. The result is a unique culture and work environment which, no doubt, contributes to the low turnover of hourly people—one-half the industry average.

The layout, memorabilia, music, and videos are important elements in the Hard Rock "experience," but it falls on the waiters and waitresses to make the experience come alive. They are particularly focused on providing an authentic and memorable dining experience. Like Southwest Airlines, Hard Rock is looking for people with a cause—people who like to serve. By succeeding with its human resource strategy, Hard Rock obtains a competitive advantage.

* Hard Rock Cafe's mission, mottos, and operating values are available at **www.hardrock.com/corporate/careers**.

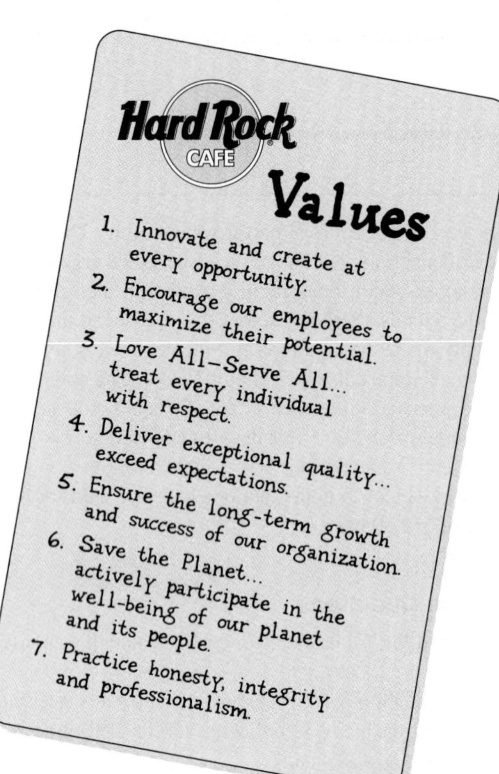

Discussion Questions†

1. What has Hard Rock done to lower employee turnover to half the industry average?
2. How does Hard Rock's human resource department support the company's overall strategy?
3. How would Hard Rock's value system work for automobile assembly line workers? (*Hint:* Consider Hackman and Oldham's core job characteristics.)
4. How might you adjust a traditional assembly line to address more "core job characteristics"?

†Before answering these questions, you may wish to view the video that accompanies this case.

▶**Additional Case Studies:** Visit **www.myomlab.com** or **www.pearsonhighered.com/heizer** for these free case studies:
Chicago Southern Hospital: Examines the requirements for a work-sampling plan for nurses.
Karstadt versus JCPenney: Compares the work culture in retailing in the U.S. to Germany.
The Fleet That Wanders: Requires a look at ergonomic issues for truck drivers.

Bibliography

Aft, Larry, and Neil Schmeidler. "Work Measurement Practices." *Industrial Engineer* 35, no. 11 (November 2003): 44.

Barber, Felix, and Rainer Strack. "The Surprising Economics of a People Business." *Harvard Business Review* 83, no. 6 (June 2005): 81–90.

Barnes, R. M. *Motion and Time Study, Design and Measurement of Work*, 7th ed. New York: Wiley, 1980.

Bridger, R. S. *Introduction to Ergonomics*, 3rd ed. New York: CRC Press, 2008.

De Jong, A., K. De Ruyter, and J. Lemmink. "Service Climate in Self-Managing Teams." *The Journal of Management Studies* 42, no. 8 (December 2005): 1593.

Elnekave, M., and I. Gilad. "Rapid Video-Based Analysis System for Advanced Work Measurement." *International Journal of Production Research* 44, no. 2 (January 2006): 271.

Freivalds, Andris, and B. W. Niebel. *Methods, Standards, and Work Design*, 12th ed. New York: Irwin/McGraw-Hill, 2009.

Huselid, Mark A., Richard W. Beatty, and Brian E. Becker. " 'A Players' or 'A Positions'? The Strategic Logic of Workforce Management." *Harvard Business Review* (December 2005): 110–117.

Konz, S., and Steven Johnson. *Work Design: Industrial Ergonomics*, 6th ed. Scottsdale, AZ: Holcomb Hathaway, 2004.

Muthusamy, S. K., J. V. Wheeler, and B. L. Simmons. "Self-Managing Work Teams." *Organization Development Journal* 23, no. 3 (Fall 2005): 53–66.

Pfeffer, Jeffrey. "Producing Sustainable Competitive Advantage Through the Effective Management of People." *Academy of Management Executive* 19, no. 4 (2005): 95.

Sadikoglu, E. "Integration of Work Measurement and Total Quality Management." *Total Quality Management and Business Excellence* 16, no. 5 (July 2005): 597.

Salvendy, G., ed. *Handbook of Human Factors and Ergonomics*, 3rd ed. New York: Wiley, 2006.

Tolo, B. "21st-Century Stopwatch." *Industrial Engineer* 37, no. 7 (July 2005): 34–37.

Walsh, Ellen. "Get Results with Workload Management." *Nursing Management* (October 2003): 16.

Chapter 10 **Rapid Review**

Main Heading	Review Material	myomlab
HUMAN RESOURCE STRATEGY FOR COMPETITIVE ADVANTAGE (pp. 384–385)	*The objective of a human resource strategy is to manage labor and design jobs so people are effectively and efficiently utilized.* *Quality of work life* refers to a job that is not only reasonably safe with equitable pay but that also achieves an appropriate level of both physical and psychological requirements. *Mutual commitment* means that both management and employees strive to meet common objectives. *Mutual trust* is reflected in reasonable, documented employment policies that are honestly and equitably implemented to the satisfaction of both management and employees.	**VIDEO 10.1** Human Resources at Hard Rock Cafe
LABOR PLANNING (pp. 385–386)	▪ **Labor planning**—A means of determining staffing policies dealing with employment stability, work schedules, and work rules. *Flextime* allows employees, within limits, to determine their own schedules. *Flexible* (or *compressed*) *workweeks* often call for fewer but longer workdays. *Part-time status* is particularly attractive in service industries with fluctuating demand loads.	
JOB DESIGN (pp. 386–389)	▪ **Job design**—Specifies the tasks that constitute a job for an individual or group. ▪ **Labor specialization** (or **job specialization**)—The division of labor into unique ("special") tasks. ▪ **Job enlargement**—The grouping of a variety of tasks about the same skill level; horizontal enlargement. ▪ **Job rotation**—A system in which an employee is moved from one specialized job to another. ▪ **Job enrichment**—A method of giving an employee more responsibility that includes some of the planning and control necessary for job accomplishment; vertical expansion. ▪ **Employee empowerment**—Enlarging employee jobs so that the added responsibility and authority is moved to the lowest level possible. ▪ **Self-directed team**—A group of empowered individuals working together to reach a common goal.	
ERGONOMICS AND THE WORK ENVIRONMENT (pp. 389–392)	▪ **Ergonomics**—The study of the human interface with the environment and machines. The physical environment affects performance, safety, and quality of work life. Illumination, noise and vibration, temperature, humidity, and air quality are controllable by management.	
METHODS ANALYSIS (pp. 392–393)	▪ **Methods analysis**—A system that involves developing work procedures that are safe and produce quality products efficiently. ▪ **Flow diagram**—A drawing used to analyze movement of people or material. ▪ **Process chart**—A graphic representation that depicts a sequence of steps for a process. ▪ **Activity chart**—A way of improving utilization of an operator and a machine or some combination of operators (a crew) and machines. ▪ **Operations chart**—A chart depicting right- and left-hand motions.	Virtual Office Hours for Solved Problems: 10.1
THE VISUAL WORKPLACE (pp. 393–394)	▪ **Visual workplace**—Uses a variety of visual communication techniques to rapidly communicate information to stakeholders.	
LABOR STANDARDS (pp. 395–396)	▪ **Labor standards**—The amount of time required to perform a job or part of a job. Labor standards are set in four ways: (1) historical experience, (2) time studies, (3) predetermined time standards, and (4) work sampling. ▪ **Time study**—Timing a sample of a worker's performance and using it as a basis for setting a standard time. ▪ **Average observed time**—The arithmetic mean of the times for each element measured, adjusted for unusual influence for each element: $\text{Average observed time} = \frac{\text{Sum of the times recorded to perform each element}}{\text{Number of observations}}$ **(10-1)** ▪ **Normal time**—The average observed time, adjusted for pace: $\text{Normal time} = (\text{Average observed time}) \times (\text{Performance rating factor})$ **(10-2)**	Virtual Office Hours for Solved Problems: 10.2–10.6 Problems 10.13–10.37

Main Heading	Review Material
	■ **Standard time**—An adjustment to the total normal time; the adjustment provides allowances for personal needs, unavoidable work delays, and fatigue:

$$\text{Standard time} = \frac{\text{Total normal time}}{1 - \text{Allowance factor}} \quad \textbf{(10-3)}$$

Personal time allowances are often established in the range of 4% to 7% of total time.

$$\text{Required sample size} = n = \left(\frac{zs}{h\bar{x}}\right)^2 \quad \textbf{(10-4)}$$

$$n = \left(\frac{zs}{e}\right)^2 \quad \textbf{(10-5)}$$

$$s = \sqrt{\frac{\sum(x_i - \bar{x})^2}{n-1}} = \sqrt{\frac{(\text{Each sample observation} - \bar{x})^2}{\text{Number in sample} - 1}} \quad \textbf{(10-6)}$$

■ **Predetermined time standards**—A division of manual work into small basic elements that have established and widely accepted times.

The most common predetermined time standard is *methods time measurement* (MTM).

■ **Therbligs**—Basic physical elements of motion.

■ **Time measurement units (TMUs)**—Units for very basic micromotions in which 1 TMU = 0.0006 min or 100,000 TMUs = 1 hr.

■ **Work sampling**—An estimate, via sampling, of the percent of the time that a worker spends on various tasks.

Work sampling sample size for a desired confidence and accuracy:

$$n = \frac{z^2 p(1-p)}{h^2} \quad \textbf{(10-7)}$$

ETHICS (p. 406)

Management's role is to educate the employee; specify the necessary equipment, work rules, and work environment; and then enforce those requirements.

Self Test

■ **Before taking the self-test,** refer to the learning objectives listed at the beginning of the chapter and the key terms listed at the end of the chapter.

LO1. When product demand fluctuates and yet you maintain a constant level of employment, some of your cost savings might include:
- **a)** reduction in hiring costs.
- **b)** reduction in layoff costs and unemployment insurance costs.
- **c)** lack of need to pay a premium wage to get workers to accept unstable employment.
- **d)** having a trained workforce rather than having to retrain new employees each time you hire for an upswing in demand.
- **e)** all of the above.

LO2. The difference between *job enrichment* and *job enlargement* is that:
- **a)** enlarged jobs contain a larger number of similar tasks, while enriched jobs include some of the planning and control necessary for job accomplishment.
- **b)** enriched jobs contain a larger number of similar tasks, while enlarged jobs include some of the planning and control necessary for job accomplishment.
- **c)** enriched jobs enable an employee to do a number of boring jobs instead of just one.
- **d)** all of the above.

LO3. The work environment includes these factors:
- **a)** Lighting, noise, temperature, and air quality
- **b)** Illumination, carpeting, and high ceilings
- **c)** Enough space for meetings and videoconferencing
- **d)** Noise, humidity, and number of coworkers
- **e)** Job enlargement and space analysis

LO4. *Methods analysis* focuses on:
- **a)** the design of the machines used to perform a task.
- **b)** how a task is accomplished.
- **c)** the raw materials that are consumed in performing a task.
- **d)** reducing the number of steps required to perform a task.

LO5. The least preferred method of establishing labor standards is:
- **a)** time studies.
- **b)** work sampling.
- **c)** historical experience.
- **d)** predetermined time standards.

LO6. The allowance factor in a time study:
- **a)** adjusts normal time for errors and rework.
- b adjusts standard time for lunch breaks.
- **c)** adjusts normal time for personal needs, unavoidable delays, and fatigue
- **d)** allows workers to rest every 20 minutes.

LO7. To set the required sample size in a time study, you must know:
- **a)** the number of employees.
- **b)** the number of parts produced per day.
- **c)** the desired accuracy and confidence levels.
- **d)** management's philosophy toward sampling.

Answers: LO1. e; LO2. a; LO3. a; LO4. b; LO5. c; LO6. c; LO7. c.

11 Supply-Chain Management

PART THREE
Managing Operations
(Chapters 11–17)

Chapter Outline

OM Strategy Decisions

- ► Design of Goods and Services
- ► Managing Quality
- ► Process Strategy
- ► Location Strategies
- ► Layout Strategies
- ► Human Resources
- ► **Supply-Chain Management**
- ► Inventory Management
- ► Scheduling
- ► Maintenance

DARDEN'S SUPPLY CHAIN YIELDS A COMPETITIVE EDGE

Darden Restaurants, Inc., is the largest publicly traded casual dining restaurant company in the world. It serves over 400 million meals annually from more than 1,700 restaurants in the U.S. and Canada. Each of its well-known flagship brands—Olive Garden and Red Lobster—generates sales of $2 billion annually. Darden's other brands include Bahama Breeze, Seasons 52, Capital Grille, and LongHorn Steakhouse. The firm employs more than 150,000 people and is the 29th largest employer in the U.S.

"Operations is typically thought of as an execution of strategy. For us it is the strategy," Darden's former chairman, Joe R. Lee, stated.

In the restaurant business, a winning strategy requires a winning supply chain. Nothing is more important than sourcing and delivering healthy, high-quality food; and there are very few other industries where supplier performance is so closely tied to the customer.

Darden sources its food from five continents and thousands of suppliers. To meet Darden's needs for fresh ingredients, the company has developed four distinct supply chains: one for seafood; one for dairy/produce/other refrigerated foods; a third for other food items, like baked goods; and a fourth for restaurant supplies (everything from dishes to ovens to uniforms). Over $1.5 billion is spent in these supply chains annually. (See the *Video Case Study* at the end of this chapter for details.)

Darden's four supply channels have some common characteristics. They all require *supplier qualification*, have *product tracking*, are subject to *independent audits*, and employ *just-in-time delivery*. With best-in-class techniques and processes, Darden creates worldwide supply-chain partnerships and alliances that are rapid, transparent, and efficient. Darden achieves competitive advantage through its superior supply chain.

▲ **Qualifying Worldwide Sources:** Part of Darden's supply chain begins with a crab harvest in the frigid waters off the coast of Alaska. But long before a supplier is qualified to sell to Darden, a total quality team is appointed. The team provides guidance, assistance, support, and training to the suppliers to ensure that overall objectives are understood and desired results accomplished.

▲ **Aquaculture Certification:** Shrimp in this Asian plant are certified to ensure traceability. The focus is on quality control certified by the Aquaculture Certification Council, of which Darden is a member. Farming and inspection practices yield safe and wholesome shrimp.

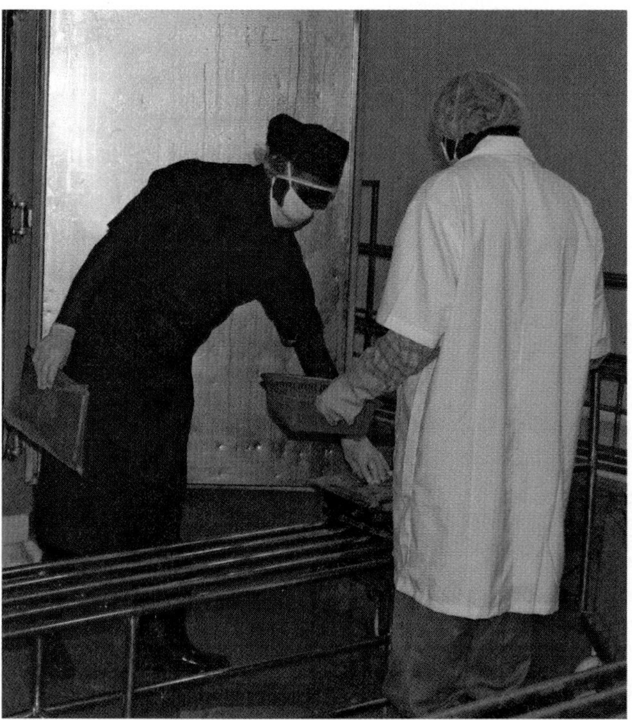

▲ **Independent audits of suppliers:** To provide fair and accurate assessment, Darden's Total Quality Supplier Program includes an independent verification program. Each supplier is evaluated regularly by independent auditors on a risk-based schedule to determine the supplier's effectiveness.

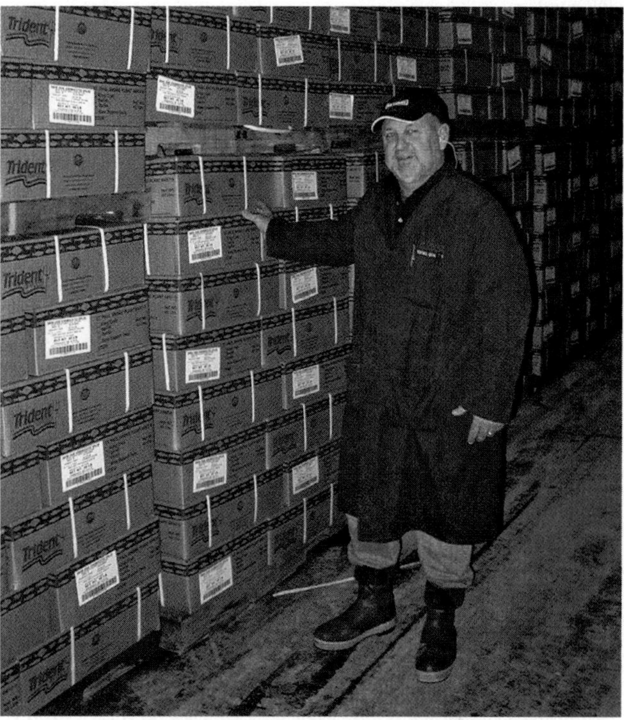

▲ **Product tracking:** Darden's seafood inspection team developed an integral system that uses a lot ID to track seafood from its origin through shipping and receipt. Darden uses a modified atmosphere packaging (MAP) process to extend the shelf life and preserve the quality of its fresh fish. The tracking includes time temperature monitoring.

▲ **JIT Delivery:** For many products, temperature monitoring begins immediately and is tracked through the entire supply chain, to the kitchen at each of Darden's 1,700 restaurants and ultimately to the guest.

Chapter 11 **Learning Objectives**

AUTHOR COMMENT Competition today is not between companies; it is between supply chains.

THE SUPPLY CHAIN'S STRATEGIC IMPORTANCE

Most firms, like Darden, spend a huge portion of their sales dollars on purchases. Because an increasing percentage of an organization's costs are determined by purchasing, relationships with suppliers are increasingly integrated and long term. Joint efforts that improve innovation, speed design, and reduce costs are common. Such efforts, when part of a corporate-wide strategy, can dramatically improve both partners' competitiveness. This integrated focus places added emphasis on managing supplier relationships.

Supply-chain management
Management of activities that procure materials and services, transform them into intermediate goods and final products, and deliver them through a distribution system.

Supply-chain management is the integration of the activities that procure materials and services, transform them into intermediate goods and final products, and deliver them to customers. These activities include purchasing and outsourcing activities, plus many other functions that are important to the relationship with suppliers and distributors. As Figure 11.1 suggests, supply-chain management includes determining (1) transportation vendors, (2) credit and cash transfers, (3) suppliers, (4) distributors, (5) accounts payable and receivable, (6) warehousing and

▼ FIGURE 11.1 A Supply Chain for Beer

The supply chain includes all the interactions among suppliers, manufacturers, distributors, and customers. The chain includes transportation, scheduling information, cash and credit transfers, as well as ideas, designs, and material transfers. Even can and bottle manufacturers have their own tiers of suppliers providing components such as lids, labels, packing containers, etc. (Costs are approximate and include substantial taxes.)

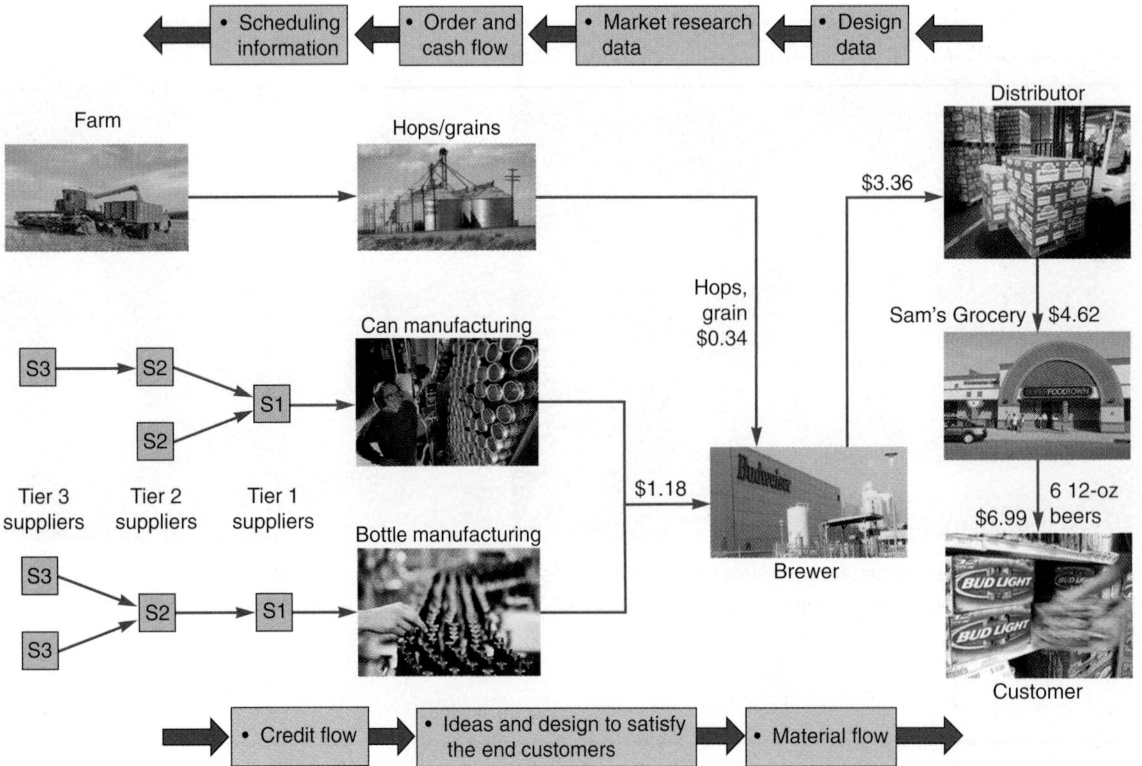

▼ **TABLE 11.1 How Supply-Chain Decisions Affect Strategy***

	Low-Cost Strategy	Response Strategy	Differentiation Strategy
Supplier's goal	Supply demand at lowest possible cost (e.g., Emerson Electric, Taco Bell)	Respond quickly to changing requirements and demand to minimize stockouts (e.g., Dell Computer)	Share market research; jointly develop products and options (e.g., Benetton)
Primary selection criteria	Select primarily for cost	Select primarily for capacity, speed, and flexibility	Select primarily for product development skills
Process characteristics	Maintain high average utilization	Invest in excess capacity and flexible processes	Use modular processes that lend themselves to mass customization
Inventory characteristics	Minimize inventory throughout the chain to hold down costs	Develop responsive system, with buffer stocks positioned to ensure supply	Minimize inventory in the chain to avoid obsolescence
Lead-time characteristics	Shorten lead time as long as it does not increase costs	Invest aggressively to reduce production lead time	Invest aggressively to reduce development lead time
Product-design characteristics	Maximize performance and minimize cost	Use product designs that lead to low setup time and rapid production ramp-up	Use modular design to postpone product differentiation for as long as possible

*See related table and discussion in Marshall L. Fisher, "What Is the Right Supply Chain for Your Product?" *Harvard Business Review* (March–April 1997): 105.

inventory, (7) order fulfillment, and (8) sharing customer, forecasting, and production information. The *objective is to build a chain of suppliers that focuses on maximizing value to the ultimate customer.*

As firms strive to increase their competitiveness via product customization, high quality, cost reductions, and speed to market, added emphasis is placed on the supply chain. Effective supply chain management makes suppliers "partners" in the firm's strategy to satisfy an ever-changing marketplace. A competitive advantage may depend on a close long-term strategic relationship with a few suppliers.

To ensure that the supply chain supports the firm's strategy, managers need to consider the supply chain issues shown in Table 11.1. Activities of supply chain managers cut across accounting, finance, marketing, and the operations discipline. Just as the OM function supports the firm's overall strategy, the supply chain must support the OM strategy. Strategies of low cost or rapid response demand different things from a supply chain than a strategy of differentiation. For instance, a low-cost strategy, as Table 11.1 indicates, requires suppliers be selected based primarily on cost. Such suppliers should have the ability to design low-cost products that meet the functional requirements, minimize inventory, and drive down lead times. However, if you want roses that are fresh, build a supply chain that focuses on response (see the *OM in Action* box "A Rose Is a Rose, but Only if It Is Fresh").

LO1: Explain the strategic importance of the supply chain

Firms must achieve integration of strategy up and down the supply chain, and must expect that strategy to be different for different products and to change as products move through their life cycle. Darden Restaurants, as noted in the opening *Global Company Profile*, has mastered worldwide product and service complexity by segmenting its supply chain and at the same time integrating four unique supply chains into its overall strategy.

VIDEO 11.1
Darden's Global Supply Chain

Supply-Chain Risk

AUTHOR COMMENT
The environment, controls, and process performance all affect supply-chain risk.

In this age of increasing specialization, low communication cost, and fast transportation, companies are making less and buying more. This means more reliance on supply chains and more risk. Managing the new integrated supply chain is a strategic challenge. Having fewer suppliers makes the supplier and customer more dependent on each other, increasing risk for both. This risk is compounded by globalization and logistical complexity. In any supply chain, vendor reliability and quality may be challenging, but the new paradigm of a tight, fast, low-inventory supply chain, operating across political and cultural boundaries, adds a new dimension to risk. As organizations go global, shipping time may increase, logistics may be less reliable, and tariffs

OM in Action ► A Rose Is a Rose, but Only if It Is Fresh

Supply chains for food and flowers must be fast, and they must be good. When the food supply chain has a problem, the best that can happen is the customer does not get fed on time; the worst that happens is the customer gets food poisoning and dies. In the floral industry, the timing and temperature are also critical. Indeed, flowers are the most perishable agricultural item—even more so than fish. Flowers not only need to move fast, but they must also be kept cool, at a constant temperature of 33 to 37 degrees. And they must be provided preservative-treated water while in transit. Roses are especially delicate, fragile, and perishable.

Seventy percent of the roses sold in the U.S. market arrive by air from rural Colombia and Ecuador. Roses move through this supply chain via an intricate but fast transportation network. This network stretches from growers who cut, grade, bundle, pack and ship, to importers who make the deal, to the U.S. Department of Agriculture personnel who quarantine and inspect for insects, diseases, and parasites, to U.S. Customs agents who inspect and approve, to facilitators who provide clearance and labeling, to wholesalers who distribute, to retailers who arrange and sell, and finally to the customer. Each and every minute the product is deteriorating. The time and temperature sensitivity of perishables like roses requires sophistication and refined standards in the supply chain.

Success yields quality and low losses. After all, when it's Valentine's Day, what good is a shipment of roses that arrives wilted or late? This is a difficult supply chain; only an excellent one will get the job done.

Sources: IIE Solutions (February 2002): 26–32; and *World Trade* (June 2004): 22–25.

and quotas may block companies from doing business. In addition, international supply chains complicate information flows and increase political and currency risks.

Thus, the development of a successful strategic plan for supply-chain management requires careful research, an understanding of the risk involved, and innovative planning. Reducing risk in this increasingly global environment suggests that management must be able to mitigate and react to disruptions in:

1. *Processes* (raw material and component availability, quality, and logistics)
2. *Controls* (management metrics and reliable secure communication for financial transactions, product designs, and logistics scheduling)
3. *Environment* (customs duties, tariffs, security screening, natural disaster, currency fluctuations, terrorist attacks, and political issues)

Let's look at how several organizations address these risks in their supply chains:

- To reduce *process risk*, McDonald's planned its supply chain 6 years in advance of its opening in Russia. Creating a $60 million "food town," it developed independently owned supply plants in Moscow to keep its transportation costs and handling times low and its quality and customer-service levels high. Every component in this food chain—meat plant, chicken plant, bakery, fish plant, and lettuce plant—is closely monitored to make sure that all the system's links are strong.
- Ford's *process risk* reduction strategy is to develop a global network of *few but exceptional* suppliers who will provide the lowest cost and highest quality. This has driven one division's supplier base down to only 227 suppliers worldwide, compared with 700 previously.
- Darden Restaurants has placed extensive *controls*, including third-party audits, on supplier processes and logistics to ensure constant monitoring and reduction of risk.
- Boeing is reducing *control* risk through its state-of-the-art international communication system that transmits engineering, scheduling, and logistics data not only to Boeing facilities but to the suppliers of the 75% to 80% of the 787 Dreamliner that is built by non-Boeing companies.
- Hard Rock Cafe is reducing *environmental* (political) risk by franchising and licensing, rather than owning, when the political and cultural barriers seem significant.
- Toyota, after its experience with both fire and earthquakes, has moved to reduce *environmental* (natural disaster) risk with a policy of having at least two suppliers for each component.

Tight integration of the supply chain can have significant benefits, but the risks can and must be managed.

ETHICS AND SUSTAINABILITY

Let's look at three aspects of ethics in the supply chain: personal ethics, ethics within the supply chain, and ethical behavior regarding the environment.

AUTHOR COMMENT
Because so much money passes through the supply chain, the opportunity for ethical lapses is significant.

Personal Ethics Ethical decisions are critical to the long-term success of any organization. However, the supply chain is particularly susceptible to ethical lapses, as the opportunities for unethical behavior are enormous. With sales personnel anxious to sell and purchasing agents spending huge sums, temptations abound. Many salespeople become friends with customers, do favors for them, take them to lunch, or present small (or large) gifts. Determining when tokens of friendship become bribes can be challenging. Many companies have strict rules and codes of conduct that limit what is acceptable. Recognizing these issues, the Institute for Supply Management has developed principles and standards to be used as guidelines for ethical behavior (as shown in Table 11.2). As the supply chain becomes international, operations managers need to expect an additional set of ethical issues to manifest themselves as they deal with new cultural values.

Ethics within the Supply Chain In this age of hyper-specialization, much of any organization's resources are purchased, putting great stress on ethics in the supply chain. Managers may be tempted to ignore ethical lapses by suppliers or offload pollution to suppliers. But firms must establish standards for their suppliers, just as they have established standards for themselves. Society expects ethical performance throughout the supply chain. For instance, Gap Inc. reported that of its 3,000-plus factories worldwide, about 90% failed their initial evaluation.[1] The report indicated that 10% to 25% of its Chinese factories engaged in psychological or verbal abuse, and more than 50% of the factories visited in sub-Saharan Africa operate without proper safety devices. The challenge of enforcing ethical standards is significant, but responsible firms such as Gap are finding ways to deal with this difficult issue.

Ethical Behavior Regarding the Environment While ethics on both a personal basis and in the supply chain are important, so is ethical behavior in regard to the environment. Good ethics extends to doing business in a way that supports conservation and renewal of resources. This requires evaluation of the entire environmental impact, from raw material, to manufacture, through use, and final disposal. For instance, Darden and Walmart require their shrimp and fish suppliers in Southeast Asia to abide by the standards of the Global Aquaculture Alliance. These standards must be met if suppliers want to maintain the business relationship. Operations

▼ TABLE 11.2 Principles and Standards of Ethical Supply Management Conduct

INTEGRITY IN YOUR DECISIONS AND ACTIONS; VALUE FOR YOUR EMPLOYER; LOYALTY TO YOUR PROFESSION

1. **PERCEIVED IMPROPRIETY** Prevent the intent and appearance of unethical or compromising conduct in relationships, actions and communications.
2. **CONFLICTS OF INTEREST** Ensure that any personal, business or other activity does not conflict with the lawful interests of your employer.
3. **ISSUES OF INFLUENCE** Avoid behaviors or actions that may negatively influence, or appear to influence, supply management decisions.
4. **RESPONSIBILITIES TO YOUR EMPLOYER** Uphold fiduciary and other responsibilities using reasonable care and granted authority to deliver value to your employer.
5. **SUPPLIER AND CUSTOMER RELATIONSHIPS** Promote positive supplier and customer relationships.
6. **SUSTAINABILITY AND SOCIAL RESPONSIBILITY** Champion social responsibility and sustainability practices in supply management.
7. **CONFIDENTIAL AND PROPRIETARY INFORMATION** Protect confidential and proprietary information.
8. **RECIPROCITY** Avoid improper reciprocal agreements.
9. **APPLICABLE LAWS, REGULATIONS AND TRADE AGREEMENTS** Know and obey the letter and spirit of laws, regulations and trade agreements applicable to supply management.
10. **PROFESSIONAL COMPETENCE** Develop skills, expand knowledge and conduct business that demonstrates competence and promotes the supply management profession.

Source: www.ism.ws

[1]Amy Merrick, "Gap Offers Unusual Look at Factory Conditions," *The Wall Street Journal* (May 12, 2004): A1, A12.

managers also ensure that sustainability is reflected in the performance of second- and third-tier suppliers. Enforcement can be done by in-house inspectors, third-party auditors, governmental agencies, or nongovernmental watchdog organizations. All four approaches are used.

AUTHOR COMMENT
A huge part of a firm's revenue is typically spent on purchases, so this is a good place to look for savings.

The incoming supply chain garners most of the attention, but it is only part of the ethical challenge of sustainability. The "return" supply chain is also significant. Returned products can only be burned, buried, or reused. And the first two options have adverse consequences. Once viewed in this manner, the need for operations managers to evaluate the entire product life cycle is apparent.

While 84% of an automobile and 90% of an airplane are recycled, these levels are not easily achieved. Recycling efforts began at product and process design. Then special end-of-product-life processes were developed. Oil, lead, gasoline, explosives in air bags, acid in batteries, and the many components (axles, differentials, jet engines, hydraulic valves) that still have many years of service all demand their own unique recovery, remanufacturing, or recycling process. This complexity places significant demands on the producer as well as return and reuse supply chains in the quest for sustainability. But pursuing this quest is the ethical thing to do. Saving the earth is a challenging task.

▼ **TABLE 11.3**
Supply-Chain Costs as a Percentage of Sales

Industry	% Purchased
Automobile	67
Beverages	52
Chemical	62
Food	60
Lumber	61
Metals	65
Paper	55
Petroleum	79
Transportation	62

SUPPLY-CHAIN ECONOMICS

The supply chain receives such attention because it is an integral part of a firm's strategy and the most costly activity in most firms. For both goods and services, supply chain costs as a percent of sales are often substantial (see Table 11.3). Because such a huge portion of revenue is devoted to the supply chain, an effective strategy is vital. The supply chain provides a major opportunity to reduce costs and increase contribution margins.

Table 11.4 and Example 1 illustrate the amount of leverage available to the operations manager through the supply chain.

These numbers indicate the strong role that supply chains play in profitability.

EXAMPLE 1 ▶
Profit potential in the supply chain

Hau Lee Furniture Inc. spends 50% of its sales dollar in the supply chain and has a net profit of 4%. Hau wants to know how many dollars of sales is equivalent to supply-chain savings of $1.

APPROACH ▶ Table 11.4 (given Hau's assumptions) can be used to make the analysis.

SOLUTION ▶ Table 11.4 indicates that every $1 Hau can save in the supply chain results in the same profit that would be generated by $3.70 in sales.

▶ **TABLE 11.4**
Dollars of Additional Sales Needed to Equal $1 Saved through the Supply Chain[a]

Percentage Net Profit of Firm	*Percentage of Sales Spent in the Supply Chain* 30%	40%	50%	60%	70%	80%	90%
2	$2.78	$3.23	$3.85	$4.76	$6.25	$9.09	$16.67
4	$2.70	$3.13	$3.70	$4.55	$5.88	$8.33	$14.29
6	$2.63	$3.03	$3.57	$4.35	$5.56	$7.69	$12.50
8	$2.56	$2.94	$3.45	$4.17	$5.26	$7.14	$11.11
10	$2.50	$2.86	$3.33	$4.00	$5.00	$6.67	$10.00

[a]The required increase in sales assumes that 50% of the costs other than purchases are variable and that half the remaining costs (less profit) are fixed. Therefore, at sales of $100 (50% purchases and 2% margin), $50 are purchases, $24 are other variable costs, $24 are fixed costs, and $2 profit. Increasing sales by $3.85 yields the following:

Purchases at 50%	$ 51.93 (50% of $103.85)
Other Variable Costs	24.92 (24% of $103.85)
Fixed Cost	24.00 (fixed)
Profit	3.00 (from $2 to $3 profit)
	$103.85

Through $3.85 of additional sales, we have increased profit by $1, from $2 to $3. The same increase in margin could have been obtained by reducing supply-chain costs by $1.

INSIGHT ▶ Effective management of the supply chain can generate substantial benefits.

LEARNING EXERCISE ▶ If Hau increases his profit to 6%, how much of an increase in sales is necessary to equal $1 savings? [Answer: $3.57.]

RELATED PROBLEMS ▶ 11.6, 11.7

Make-or-Buy Decisions

A wholesaler or retailer buys everything that it sells; a manufacturing operation hardly ever does. Manufacturers, restaurants, and assemblers of products buy components and subassemblies that go into final products. As we saw in Chapter 5, choosing products and services that can be advantageously obtained *externally* as opposed to produced *internally* is known as the **make-or-buy decision**. Supply-chain personnel evaluate alternative suppliers and provide current, accurate, and complete data relevant to the buy alternative. Increasingly, firms focus not on an analytical make-or-buy decision but on identifying their core competencies.

Make-or-buy decision
A choice between producing a component or service in-house or purchasing it from an outside source.

Outsourcing

Outsourcing transfers some of what are traditional internal activities and resources of a firm to outside vendors, making it slightly different from the traditional make-or-buy decision. Outsourcing is part of the continuing trend toward utilizing the efficiency that comes with specialization. The vendor performing the outsourced service is an expert in that particular specialty. This leaves the outsourcing firm to focus on its critical success factors, that is, its core competencies that yield a competitive advantage. Outsourcing is the focus of the supplement to this chapter.

Outsourcing
Transferring a firm's activities that have traditionally been internal to external suppliers.

SUPPLY-CHAIN STRATEGIES

AUTHOR COMMENT
Supply-chain strategies come in many varieties; choosing the correct one is the trick.

For goods and services to be obtained from outside sources, the firm must decide on a supply chain strategy. One such strategy is the approach of *negotiating with many suppliers* and playing one supplier against another. A second strategy is to develop *long-term "partnering"* relationships with a few suppliers to satisfy the end customer. A third strategy is *vertical integration*, in which a firm decides to use vertical backward integration by actually buying the supplier. A fourth approach is some type of collaboration that allows two or more firms to combine resources—typically in what is called a *joint venture*—to produce a component. A fifth variation is a combination of few suppliers and vertical integration, known as a *keiretsu*. In a *keiretsu, suppliers become part of a company coalition*. Finally, a sixth strategy is to develop *virtual companies that use suppliers on an as-needed basis*. We will now discuss each of these strategies.

LO2: Identify six supply-chain strategies

Many Suppliers

With the many-suppliers strategy, a supplier responds to the demands and specifications of a "request for quotation," with the order usually going to the low bidder. This is a common strategy when products are commodities. This strategy plays one supplier against another and places the burden of meeting the buyer's demands on the supplier. Suppliers aggressively compete with one another. Although many approaches to negotiations can be used with this strategy, long-term "partnering" relationships are not the goal. This approach holds the supplier responsible for maintaining the necessary technology, expertise, and forecasting abilities, as well as cost, quality, and delivery competencies.

Few Suppliers

A strategy of few suppliers implies that rather than looking for short-term attributes, such as low cost, a buyer is better off forming a long-term relationship with a few dedicated suppliers. Long-term suppliers are more likely to understand the broad objectives of the procuring firm and the end customer. Using few suppliers can create value by allowing suppliers to have economies of scale and a learning curve that yields both lower transaction costs and lower production costs.

Few suppliers, each with a large commitment to the buyer, may also be more willing to participate in JIT systems as well as provide design innovations and technological expertise. Many firms have moved aggressively to incorporate suppliers into their supply systems. Ford, for one, now seeks to choose suppliers even before parts are designed. Motorola also evaluates suppliers on rigorous criteria, but in many instances has eliminated traditional supplier bidding, placing added emphasis on quality and reliability. On occasion these relationships yield contracts that extend through the product's life cycle. The expectation is that both the purchaser and

VIDEO 11.2
Supply-Chain Management at Regal Marine

supplier collaborate, becoming more efficient and reducing prices over time. The natural outcome of such relationships is fewer suppliers, but those that remain have long-term relationships.

Service companies like Marks & Spencer, a British retailer, have also demonstrated that cooperation with suppliers can yield cost savings for customers and suppliers alike. This strategy has resulted in suppliers that develop new products, winning customers for Marks & Spencer and the supplier. The move toward tight integration of the suppliers and purchasers is occurring in both manufacturing and services.

Like all strategies, a downside exists. With few suppliers, the cost of changing partners is huge, so both buyer and supplier run the risk of becoming captives of the other. Poor supplier performance is only one risk the purchaser faces. The purchaser must also be concerned about trade secrets and suppliers that make other alliances or venture out on their own. This happened when the U.S. Schwinn Bicycle Co., needing additional capacity, taught Taiwan's Giant Manufacturing Company to make and sell bicycles. Giant Manufacturing is now the largest bicycle manufacturer in the world, and Schwinn was acquired out of bankruptcy by Pacific Cycle LLC.

Vertical Integration

Vertical integration
Developing the ability to produce goods or services previously purchased or actually buying a supplier or a distributor.

Purchasing can be extended to take the form of vertical integration. By **vertical integration**, we mean developing the ability to produce goods or services previously purchased or to actually buy a supplier or a distributor. As shown in Figure 11.2, vertical integration can take the form of *forward* or *backward integration*.

Backward integration suggests a firm purchase its suppliers, as in the case of Ford Motor Company deciding to manufacture its own car radios. Forward integration, on the other hand, suggests that a manufacturer of components make the finished product. An example is Texas Instruments, a manufacturer of integrated circuits that also makes calculators and flat-screens containing integrated circuits for TVs.

Vertical integration can offer a strategic opportunity for the operations manager. For firms with the capital, managerial talent, and required demand, vertical integration may provide substantial opportunities for cost reduction, quality adherence, and timely delivery. Other advantages, such as inventory reduction and scheduling, can accrue to the company that effectively manages vertical integration or close, mutually beneficial relationships with suppliers.

Because purchased items represent such a large part of the costs of sales, it is obvious why so many organizations find interest in vertical integration. Vertical integration appears to work best when the organization has large market share and the management talent to operate an acquired vendor successfully.

The relentless march of specialization continues, meaning that a model of "doing everything" or "vertical integration" is increasingly difficult. Backward integration may be particularly dangerous for firms in industries undergoing technological change if management cannot keep abreast of those changes or invest the financial resources necessary for the next wave of technology. The alternative, particularly in high-tech industries, is to establish close-relationship suppliers. This allows partners to focus on their specific contribution. Research and development costs are too high and technology changes too rapid for one company to sustain leadership in every component. Most organizations are better served concentrating on their specialty and leveraging

▶ **FIGURE 11.2**
Vertical Integration Can Be Forward or Backward

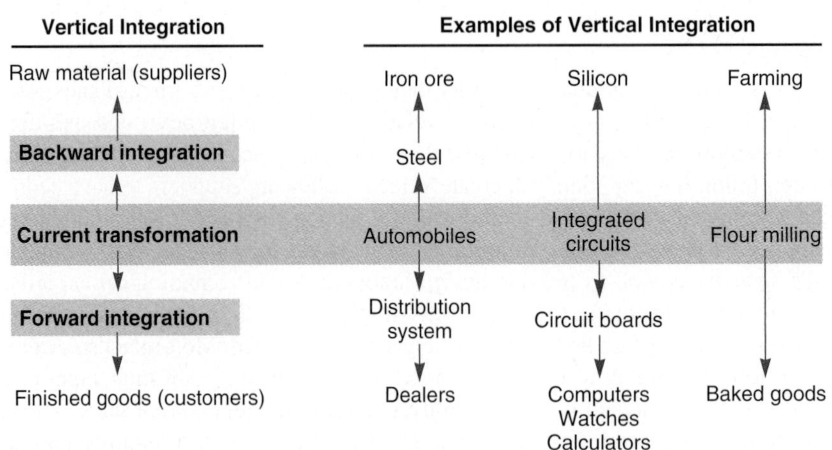

the partners' contributions. Exceptions do exist. Where capital, management talent, and technology are available and the components are also highly integrated, vertical integration may make sense. On the other hand, it made no sense for Jaguar to make commodity components for its autos as it did until recently.

Joint Ventures

Because vertical integration is so dangerous, firms may opt for some form of formal collaboration. As we noted in Chapter 5, firms may engage in collaboration to enhance their new product prowess or technological skills. But firms also engage in collaboration to secure supply or reduce costs. One version of a joint venture is the current Daimler–BMW effort to develop and produce standard automobile components. Given the global consolidation of the auto industry, these two rivals in the luxury segment of the automobile market are at a disadvantage in volume. Their relatively low volume means fewer units over which to spread fixed costs, hence the interest in consolidating to cut development and production costs. As in all other such collaborations, the trick is to cooperate without diluting the brand or conceding a competitive advantage.

Keiretsu Networks

Many large Japanese manufacturers have found another strategy; it is part collaboration, part purchasing from few suppliers, and part vertical integration. These manufacturers are often financial supporters of suppliers through ownership or loans. The supplier becomes part of a company coalition known as a ***keiretsu***. Members of the *keiretsu* are assured long-term relationships and are therefore expected to collaborate as partners, providing technical expertise and stable quality production to the manufacturer. Members of the *keiretsu* can also have suppliers farther down the chain, making second- and even third-tier suppliers part of the coalition.

Keiretsu
A Japanese term that describes suppliers who become part of a company coalition.

Virtual Companies

The limitations to vertical integration are severe. Our technological society continually demands more specialization, which complicates vertical integration. Moreover, a firm that has a department or division of its own for everything may be too bureaucratic to be world class. So rather than letting vertical integration lock an organization into businesses that it may not understand or be able to manage, another approach is to find good flexible suppliers. **Virtual companies** rely on a variety of supplier relationships to provide services on demand. Virtual companies have fluid, moving organizational boundaries that allow them to create a unique enterprise to meet changing market demands. Suppliers may provide a variety of services that include doing the payroll, hiring personnel, designing products, providing consulting services, manufacturing components, conducting tests, or distributing products. The relationships may be short or long term and may include true partners, collaborators, or simply able suppliers and subcontractors. Whatever the formal relationship, the result can be exceptionally lean performance. The advantages of virtual companies include specialized management expertise, low capital investment, flexibility, and speed. The result is efficiency.

Virtual companies
Companies that rely on a variety of supplier relationships to provide services on demand. Also known as hollow corporations or network companies.

The apparel business provides a *traditional* example of virtual organizations. The designers of clothes seldom manufacture their designs; rather, they license the manufacture. The manufacturer may then rent space, lease sewing machines, and contract for labor. The result is an organization that has low overhead, remains flexible, and can respond rapidly to the market.

A *contemporary* example is exemplified by Vizio, Inc., a California-based producer of LCD TVs that has only 85 employees but huge sales. Vizio uses modules to assemble its own brand of TVs. Because the key components of TVs are now readily available and sold almost as commodities, innovative firms such as Vizio can specify the components, hire a contract manufacturer, and market the TVs with very little startup cost. In a virtual company, the supply chain is the company. Managing it is dynamic and demanding.

MANAGING THE SUPPLY CHAIN

AUTHOR COMMENT
Trust, agreed-upon goals, and compatible cultures make supply-chain management easier.

As managers move toward integration of the supply chain, substantial efficiencies are possible. The cycle of materials—as they flow from suppliers, to production, to warehousing, to distribution, to the customer—takes place among separate and often very independent organizations. Therefore, there are significant management issues that may result in serious inefficiencies.

VIDEO 11.3
Arnold Palmer Hospital's Supply Chain

Success begins with mutual agreement on goals, followed by mutual trust, and continues with compatible organizational cultures.

Mutual Agreement on Goals An integrated supply chain requires more than just agreement on the contractual terms of a buy/sell relationship. Partners in the chain must appreciate that the only entity that puts money into a supply chain is the end customer. Therefore, establishing a mutual understanding of the mission, strategy, and goals of participating organizations is essential. The integrated supply chain is about adding economic value and maximizing the total content of the product.

Trust Trust is critical to an effective and efficient supply chain. Members of the chain must enter into a relationship that shares information. Visibility throughout the supply chain—what Darden Restaurants calls a transparent supply chain—is a requirement. Supplier relationships are more likely to be successful if risk and cost savings are shared—and activities such as end-customer research, sales analysis, forecasting, and production planning are joint activities. Such relationships are built on mutual trust.

Compatible Organizational Cultures A positive relationship between the purchasing and supplying organizations that comes with compatible organizational cultures can be a real advantage when making a supply chain hum. A champion within one of the two firms promotes both formal and informal contacts, and those contacts contribute to the alignment of the organizational cultures, further strengthening the relationship.

The operations manager is dealing with a supply chain that is made up of independent specialists, each trying to satisfy its own customers at a profit. This leads to actions that may not optimize the entire chain. On the other hand, the supply chain is replete with opportunities to reduce waste and enhance value. We now look at some of the significant issues and opportunities.

Issues in an Integrated Supply Chain

LO3: Explain issues and opportunities in the supply chain

Three issues complicate development of an efficient, integrated supply chain: local optimization, incentives, and large lots.

Local Optimization Members of the chain are inclined to focus on maximizing local profit or minimizing immediate cost based on their limited knowledge. Slight upturns in demand are overcompensated for because no one wants to be caught short. Similarly, slight downturns are overcompensated for because no one wants to be caught holding excess inventory. So fluctuations are magnified. For instance, a pasta distributor does not want to run out of pasta for its retail customers; the natural response to an extra large order from the retailer is to compensate with an even larger order to the manufacturer on the assumption that retail sales are picking up. Neither the distributor nor the manufacturer knows that the retailer had a major one-time promotion that moved a lot of pasta. This is exactly the issue that complicated the implementation of efficient distribution at the Italian pasta maker Barilla.

Incentives (Sales Incentives, Quantity Discounts, Quotas, and Promotions) Incentives push merchandise into the chain for sales that have not occurred. This generates fluctuations that are ultimately expensive to all members of the chain.

Large Lots There is often a bias toward large lots because large lots tend to reduce unit costs. A logistics manager wants to ship large lots, preferably in full trucks, and a production manager wants long production runs. Both actions drive down unit shipping and production costs, but fail to reflect actual sales and increased holding costs.

These three common occurrences—local optimization, incentives, and large lots—contribute to distortions of information about what is really occurring in the supply chain. A well-running supply system needs to be based on accurate information about how many products are truly being pulled through the chain. The inaccurate information is unintentional, but it results in distortions and fluctuations in the supply chain and causes what is known as the bullwhip effect.

Bullwhip effect
The increasing fluctuation in orders that often occurs as orders move through the supply chain.

The **bullwhip effect** occurs as orders are relayed from retailers, to distributors, to wholesalers, to manufacturers, with fluctuations increasing at each step in the sequence. The "bullwhip" fluctuations in the supply chain increase the costs associated with inventory, transportation, shipping, and receiving, while decreasing customer service and profitability. Procter & Gamble found that although the use of Pampers diapers was steady and the retail-store orders had little fluctuation, as orders moved through the supply chain, fluctuations increased. By the time orders were initiated for raw material, the variability was substantial. Similar behavior has been observed and documented at many companies, including Campbell Soup, Hewlett-Packard, and Applied Materials.

The bullwhip effect can occur when orders decrease as well as when they increase. A number of opportunities exist for reducing the bullwhip effect and improving opportunities in the supply chain. These are discussed in the following section.

Opportunities in an Integrated Supply Chain

Opportunities for effective management in the supply chain include the following 11 items.

Accurate "Pull" Data Accurate **pull data** are generated by sharing (1) point-of-sales (POS) information so that each member of the chain can schedule effectively and (2) computer-assisted ordering (CAO). This implies using POS systems that collect sales data and then adjusting that data for market factors, inventory on hand, and outstanding orders. Then a net order is sent directly to the supplier who is responsible for maintaining the finished-goods inventory.

Pull data
Accurate sales data that initiate transactions to "pull" product through the supply chain.

Lot Size Reduction Lot sizes are reduced through aggressive management. This may include (1) developing economical shipments of less than truckload lots; (2) providing discounts based on total annual volume rather than size of individual shipments; and (3) reducing the cost of ordering through techniques such as standing orders and various forms of electronic purchasing.

Single-Stage Control of Replenishment **Single-stage control of replenishment** means designating a member in the chain as responsible for monitoring and managing inventory in the supply chain based on the "pull" from the end user. This approach removes distorted information and multiple forecasts that create the bullwhip effect. Control may be in the hands of:

Single-stage control of replenishment
Fixing responsibility for monitoring and managing inventory for the retailer.

- A sophisticated retailer who understands demand patterns. Walmart does this for some of its inventory with radio frequency ID (RFID) tags as shown in the *OM in Action* box "Radio Frequency Tags: Keeping the Shelves Stocked."

OM in Action ►Radio Frequency Tags: Keeping the Shelves Stocked

Supply chains work smoothly when sales are steady, but often break down when confronted by a sudden surge or rapid drop in demand. Radio frequency ID (or RFID) tags can change that by providing real-time information about what's happening on store shelves. Here's how the system works for Procter & Gamble's (P&G's) Pampers.

1. A special promotion causes Walmart shoppers to snap up boxes of Pampers Baby-Dry.

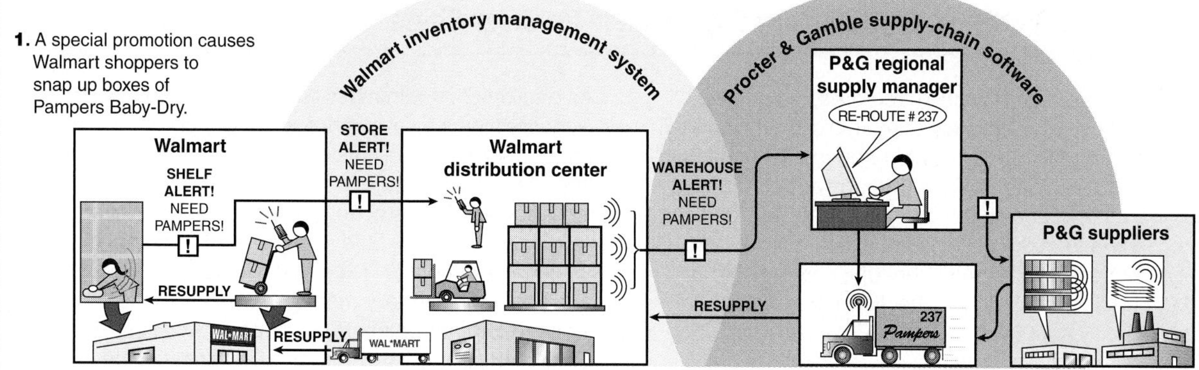

2. Each box of Pampers has an RFID tag. Shelf-mounted scanners alert the stockroom of urgent need for restock.

3. Walmart's inventory management system tracks and links its in-store stock and its warehouse stock, prompting quicker replenishment and providing accurate real-time data.

4. Walmart's systems are linked to the P&G supply-chain management system. Demand spikes reported by RFID tags are immediately visible throughout the supply chain.

5. P&G's logistics software tracks its trucks with GPS locators, and tracks their contents with RFID tag readers. Regional managers can reroute trucks to fill urgent needs.

6. P&G suppliers also use RFID tags and readers on their raw materials, giving P&G visibility several tiers down the supply chain, and giving suppliers the ability to accurately forecast demand and production.

Sources: *Financial Times* (August 22, 2008): 12; *Business 2.0* (May 2002): 86; and *Knight Ridder Tribune Business News* (August 6, 2006): 1.

- A distributor who manages the inventory for a particular distribution area. Distributors who handle grocery items, beer, and soft drinks may do this. Anheuser-Busch manages beer inventory and delivery for many of its customers.
- A manufacturer who has a well-managed forecasting, manufacturing, and distribution system. TAL Apparel Ltd., discussed in the *OM in Action* box, "The JCPenney Supply Chain for Dress Shirts," does this for JCPenney.

Vendor-managed inventory (VMI)
A system in which a supplier maintains material for the buyer, often delivering directly to the buyer's using department.

Vendor-Managed Inventory **Vendor-managed inventory (VMI)** means the use of a local supplier (usually a distributor) to maintain inventory for the manufacturer or retailer. The supplier delivers directly to the purchaser's using department rather than to a receiving dock or stockroom. If the supplier can maintain the stock of inventory for a variety of customers who use the same product or whose differences are very minor (say, at the packaging stage), then there should be a net savings. These systems work without the immediate direction of the purchaser.

Collaborative planning, forecasting, and replenishment (CPFR)
A joint effort of members of a supply chain to share information in order to reduce supply-chain costs.

Collaborative Planning, Forecasting, and Replenishment (CPFR) Like single-stage control and vendor-managed inventory, **CPFR** is another effort to manage inventory in the supply chain. With CPFR, members of the supply chain share planning, forecasting, and inventory information. Partners in a CPFR effort begin with collaboration on product definition and a joint marketing plan. Promotion, advertising, forecasts, and timing of shipments are all included in the plan in a concerted effort to drive down inventory and related costs.

Blanket order
A long-term purchase commitment to a supplier for items that are to be delivered against short-term releases to ship.

Blanket Orders Blanket orders are unfilled orders with a vendor.[2] A **blanket order** is a contract to purchase certain items from a vendor. It is not an authorization to ship anything. Shipment is made only on receipt of an agreed-on document, perhaps a shipping requisition or shipment release.

Standardization The purchasing department should make special efforts to increase levels of standardization. That is, rather than obtaining a variety of similar components with labeling, coloring, packaging, or perhaps even slightly different engineering specifications, the purchasing agent should try to have those components standardized.

Postponement
Delaying any modifications or customization to a product as long as possible in the production process.

Postponement **Postponement** withholds any modification or customization to the product (keeping it generic) as long as possible. The concept is to minimize internal variety while maximizing external variety. For instance, after analyzing the supply chain for its printers, Hewlett-Packard (HP) determined that if the printer's power supply was moved out of the printer itself and into a power cord, HP could ship the basic printer anywhere in the world. HP modified the printer, its power cord, its packaging, and its documentation so that only the power cord and documentation needed to be added at the final distribution point. This modification allowed the

OM in Action ► The JCPenney Supply Chain for Dress Shirts

Purchase a white Stafford wrinkle-free dress shirt, size 17 neck, 34/35 sleeve at JCPenney at Atlanta's Northlake Mall on a Tuesday, and the supply chain responds. Within a day, TAL Apparel Ltd. in Hong Kong downloads a record of the sale. After a run through its forecasting model, TAL decides how many shirts to make and in what styles, colors, and sizes. By Wednesday afternoon, the replacement shirt is packed to be shipped directly to the JCPenney Northlake Mall store. The system bypasses the JCPenney warehouse—indeed all warehouses—as well as the JCPenney corporate decision makers.

In a second instance, two shirts are sold, leaving none in stock. TAL, after downloading the data, runs its forecasting model but comes to the decision that this store needs to have two in stock. Without consulting JCPenney, a TAL factory in Taiwan makes two new shirts. It sends one by ship, but because of the outage, the other goes by air.

As retailers deal with mass customization, fads, and seasonal swings they also strive to cut costs—making a responsive supply chain critical. Before globalization of the supply chain, JCPenney would have had thousands of shirts warehoused across the country. Now JCPenney stores, like those of many retailers, hold a very limited inventory of shirts.

JCPenney's supplier, TAL, is providing both sales forecasting and inventory management, a situation not acceptable to many retailers. But what is most startling is that TAL also places its own orders! A supply chain like this works only when there is trust between partners. The rapid changes in supply-chain management not only place increasing technical demands on suppliers but also increase demands for trust between the parties.

Sources: Apparel (April 2006): 14–18; *The Wall Street Journal* (September 11, 2003): A1, A9; and *International Trade Forum* (Issue 3, 2005): 12–13.

[2]Unfilled orders are also referred to as "open" orders, or "incomplete" orders.

firm to manufacture and hold centralized inventories of the generic printer for shipment as demand changed. Only the unique power system and documentation had to be held in each country. This understanding of the entire supply chain reduced both risk and investment in inventory.

Drop Shipping and Special Packaging **Drop shipping** means the supplier will ship directly to the end consumer, rather than to the seller, saving both time and reshipping costs. Other cost-saving measures include the use of special packaging, labels, and optimal placement of labels and bar codes on containers. The final location down to the department and number of units in each shipping container can also be indicated. Substantial savings can be obtained through management techniques such as these. Some of these techniques can be of particular benefit to wholesalers and retailers by reducing shrinkage (lost, damaged, or stolen merchandise) and handling cost.

Drop shipping
Shipping directly from the supplier to the end consumer rather than from the seller, saving both time and reshipping costs.

For instance, Dell Computer has decided that its core competence is not in stocking peripherals, but in assembling PCs. So if you order a PC from Dell, with a printer and perhaps other components, the computer comes from Dell, but the printer and many of the other components will be drop shipped from the manufacturer.

Pass-through Facility A **pass-through facility** is a distribution center where merchandise is held, but it functions less as a holding area and more as a shipping hub. These facilities, often run by logistics vendors, use the latest technology and automated systems to expedite orders. For instance, UPS works with Nike at such a facility in Louisville, Kentucky, to immediately handle orders. Similarly, FedEx's warehouse next to the airport in Memphis can receive an order after a store closes for the evening and can locate, package, and ship the merchandise that night. Delivery is guaranteed by 10 A.M. the next day.

Pass-through facility
Expedites shipment by holding merchandise and delivering from shipping hubs.

Channel Assembly Channel assembly is an extension of the pass-through facility. **Channel assembly** sends individual components and modules, rather than finished products, to the distributor. The distributor then assembles, tests, and ships. Channel assembly treats distributors more as manufacturing partners than as distributors. This technique has proven successful in industries where products are undergoing rapid change, such as personal computers. With this strategy, finished-goods inventory is reduced because units are built to a shorter, more accurate forecast. Consequently, market response is better, with lower investment—a nice combination.

Channel assembly
Postpones final assembly of a product so the distribution channel can assemble it.

E-PROCUREMENT

AUTHOR COMMENT
The Internet has revolutionized procurement.

E-procurement uses the Internet to facilitate purchasing. E-procurement speeds purchasing, reduces costs, and integrates the supply chain, enhancing an organization's competitive advantage. The traditional supply chain is full of paper transactions, such as requisitions, requests for bids, bid evaluations, purchase orders, order releases, receiving documents, invoices, and the issuance of checks. E-procurement reduces this barrage of paperwork and at the same time provides purchasing personnel with an extensive database of vendor, delivery, and quality data. With this history, vendor selection has improved.

E-procurement
Purchasing facilitated through the Internet.

In this section, we discuss traditional techniques of electronic ordering and funds transfer and then move on to online catalogs, auctions, RFQs, and real-time inventory tracking.

Electronic Ordering and Funds Transfer Electronic ordering and bank transfers are traditional approaches to speeding transactions and reducing paperwork. Transactions between firms often use **electronic data interchange (EDI)**, which is a standardized data-transmittal format for computerized communications between organizations. EDI provides data transfer for virtually any business application, including purchasing. Under EDI, data for a purchase order, such as order date, due date, quantity, part number, purchase order number, address, and so forth, are fitted into the standard EDI format. EDI also provides for the use of **advanced shipping notice (ASN)**, which notifies the purchaser that the vendor is ready to ship. Although some firms are still moving to EDI and ASN, the Internet's ease of use and lower cost is proving more popular.

Electronic data interchange (EDI)
A standardized data-transmittal format for computerized communications between organizations.

Advanced shipping notice (ASN)
A shipping notice delivered directly from vendor to purchaser.

Online Catalogs

Purchase of standard items is often accomplished via online catalogs. Such catalogs provide current information about products in electronic form. Online catalogs support cost comparisons and incorporate voice and video clips, making the process efficient for both buyers and sellers. Online catalogs are available in three versions:

1. Typical of *catalogs provided by vendors* are those of W. W. Grainger and Office Depot. W. W. Grainger is probably the world's largest seller of MRO items (items for maintenance, repair, and operations), while Office Depot provides the same service for office supplies.
2. *Catalogs provided by intermediaries* are Internet sites where business buyers and sellers can meet. These intermediaries typically create industry specific catalogs with content from many suppliers.
3. One of the first online *exchanges provided by buyers* was Avendra (**www.avendra.com**). Avendra was created by Marriott and Hyatt (and subsequently joined by other large hotel firms) to economically purchase the huge range of goods needed by the 2,800 hotels now in the exchange.

Such exchanges—and there are many—move companies from a multitude of individual phone calls, faxes, and e-mails to a centralized online system, and drive billions of dollars of waste out of the supply chain.

Auctions

Online auction sites can be maintained by sellers, buyers, or intermediaries. Operations managers find online auctions a fertile area for disposing of excess raw material and discontinued or excess inventory. Online auctions lower entry barriers, encouraging sellers to join and simultaneously increase the potential number of buyers.

The key for auction firms, such as Ariba of Sunnyvale, California (see the photo), is to find and build a huge base of potential bidders, improve client buying procedures, and qualify new suppliers.

RFQs

When purchasing requirements are nonstandard, time spent preparing requests for quotes (RFQs) and the related bid package can be substantial. Consequently, e-procurement has now moved these often expensive parts of the purchasing process online, allowing purchasing agents to inexpensively attach electronic copies of the necessary drawings to RFQs.

Real-Time Inventory Tracking

FedEx's pioneering efforts at tracking packages from pickup to delivery has shown the way for operations managers to do the same for their shipments and inventory. Because tracking cars and trucks has been a chronic and embarrassingly inexact science, Ford has hired UPS to track millions of vehicles as they move from factory to dealers. Using bar codes and the Internet, Ford dealers are now able to log onto a Web site and find out exactly where the ordered vehicles are in the distribution system. As operations managers move to an era of mass customization, with customers ordering exactly the cars they want, customers will expect to know where their cars are and

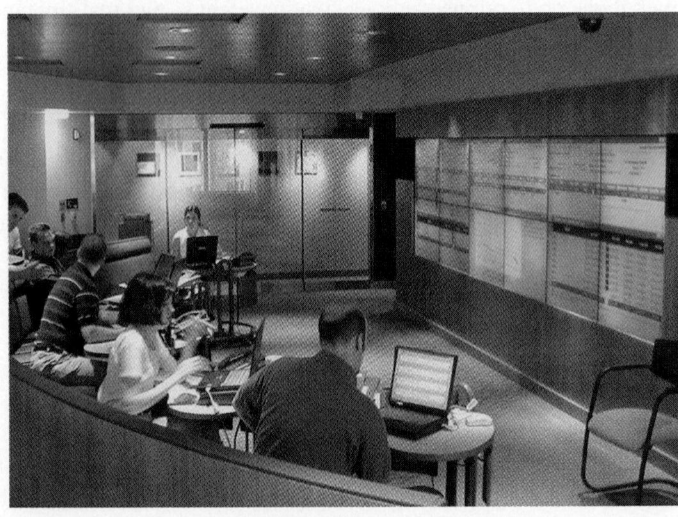

Here an Ariba team monitors an online market from the firm's Global Market Operations Center. Ariba provides support for the entire global sourcing process, including software, supplier development, competitive negotiations, and savings implementation. Online bidding leads to greater cost savings than more traditional procurement.

exactly when they can be picked up. E-procurement, supported by bar codes and RFID, can provide economical inventory tracking on the shop floor, in warehouses, and in logistics.

VENDOR SELECTION

LO4: Describe the steps in vendor selection

For those goods and services a firm buys, vendors must be selected. Vendor selection considers numerous factors, such as strategic fit, vendor competence, delivery, and quality performance. Because a firm may have some competence in all areas and may have exceptional competence in only a few, selection can be challenging. Procurement policies also need to be established. Those might address issues such as percent of business done with any one supplier or with minority businesses. We now examine vendor selection as a three-stage process: (1) vendor evaluation, (2) vendor development, and (3) negotiations.

Vendor Evaluation

The first stage of vendor selection, *vendor evaluation*, involves finding potential vendors and determining the likelihood of their becoming good suppliers. This phase requires the development of evaluation criteria such as criteria shown in Example 2. However, both the criteria and the weights selected vary depending on the supply-chain strategy being implemented. (Refer to Table 11.1, on page 421.)

EXAMPLE 2

Weighted approach to vendor evaluation

Erin Davis, president of Creative Toys in Palo Alto, is interested in evaluating suppliers who will work with him to make nontoxic, environmentally friendly paints and dyes for his line of children's toys. This is a critical strategic element of his supply chain, and he desires a firm that will contribute to his product.

APPROACH ▶ Erin begins his analysis of one potential supplier, Faber Paint and Dye, by using the weighted approach to vendor evaluation.

SOLUTION ▶ Erin first reviews the supplier differentiation attributes in Table 11.1 and develops the following list of selection criteria. He then assigns the weights shown to help him perform an objective review of potential vendors. His staff assigns the scores shown and computes the total weighted score.

Criteria	Weights	Scores (1–5) (5 highest)	Weight × Score
Engineering/research/innovation skills	.20	5	1.0
Production process capability (flexibility/technical assistance)	.15	4	.6
Distribution/delivery capability	.05	4	.2
Quality systems and performance	.10	2	.2
Facilities/location	.05	2	.1
Financial and managerial strength (stability and cost structure)	.15	4	.6
Information systems capability (e-procurement, ERP)	.10	2	.2
Integrity (environmental compliance/ethics)	.20	5	1.0
	1.00		3.9 Total

Faber Paint and Dye receives an overall score of 3.9.

INSIGHT ▶ Erin now has a basis for comparison with other potential vendors, selecting the one with the highest overall rating.

LEARNING EXERCISE ▶ If Erin believes that the weight for "engineering/research/innovation skills" should be increased to .25 and the weight for "financial and managerial strength" reduced to .10, what is the new score? [Answer: Faber Paint and Dye now goes to 3.95.]

RELATED PROBLEMS ▶ 11.2, 11.3, 11.4

The selection of competent suppliers is critical. If good suppliers are not selected, then all other supply-chain efforts are wasted. As firms move toward using fewer longer-term suppliers, the issues of financial strength, quality, management, research, technical ability, and potential for a close long-term relationship play an increasingly important role. These attributes should be noted in the evaluation process.

Vendor Development

The second stage of vendor selection is *vendor development*. Assuming that a firm wants to proceed with a particular vendor, how does it integrate this supplier into its system? The buyer makes sure the vendor has an appreciation of quality requirements, product specifications, schedules and delivery, the purchaser's payment system, and procurement policies. *Vendor development* may include everything from training, to engineering and production help, to procedures for information transfer.

Negotiations

Regardless of the supply chain strategy adopted, negotiations regarding the critical elements of the contractual relationship must take place. These negotiations often focus on quality, delivery, payment, and cost. We will look at three classic types of **negotiation strategies**: the cost-based model, the market-based price model, and competitive bidding.

Negotiation strategies
Approaches taken by supply chain personnel to develop contractual relationships with suppliers.

Cost-Based Price Model The *cost-based price model* requires that the supplier open its books to the purchaser. The contract price is then based on time and materials or on a fixed cost with an escalation clause to accommodate changes in the vendor's labor and materials cost.

Market-Based Price Model In the market-based price model, price is based on a published, auction, or index price. Many commodities (agriculture products, paper, metal, etc.) are priced this way. Paperboard prices, for instance, are available via the *Official Board Markets* weekly publication (**www.advanstar.com**). Nonferrous metal prices are quoted in *Platt's Metals Week* (**www.platts.com/plattsmetals/**), and prices of other metals are quoted at **www.metalworld.com**.

Competitive Bidding When suppliers are not willing to discuss costs or where near-perfect markets do not exist, competitive bidding is often appropriate. Infrequent work (such as construction, tooling, and dies) is usually purchased based on a bid. Bidding may take place via mail, fax, or an Internet auction. Competitive bidding is the typical policy in many firms for the majority of their purchases. Bidding policies usually require that the purchasing agent have several potential suppliers of the product (or its equivalent) and quotations from each. The major disadvantage of this method, as mentioned earlier, is that the development of long-term relations between buyer and seller is hindered. Competitive bidding may effectively determine initial cost. However, it may also make difficult the communication and performance that are vital for engineering changes, quality, and delivery.

Yet a fourth approach is *to combine one or more* of the preceding negotiation techniques. The supplier and purchaser may agree on review of certain cost data, accept some form of market data for raw material costs, or agree that the supplier will "remain competitive." In any case, a good supplier relationship is one in which both partners have established a degree of mutual trust and a belief in each other's competence, honesty, and fair dealing.

AUTHOR COMMENT
Time, cost, and reliability variables make logistic decisions demanding.

LOGISTICS MANAGEMENT

Procurement activities may be combined with various shipping, warehousing, and inventory activities to form a logistics system. The purpose of **logistics management** is to obtain efficiency of operations through the integration of all material acquisition, movement, and storage activities. When transportation and inventory costs are substantial on both the input and output sides of the production process, an emphasis on logistics may be appropriate. When logistics issues are significant or expensive, many firms opt for outsourcing the logistics function. Logistics specialists can often bring expertise not available in-house. For instance, logistics companies often have tracking technology that reduces transportation losses and supports delivery schedules that adhere to precise delivery windows. The potential for competitive advantage is found via both reduced costs and improved customer service.

Logistics management
An approach that seeks efficiency of operations through the integration of all material acquisition, movement, and storage activities.

Firms recognize that the distribution of goods to and from their facilities can represent as much as 25% of the cost of products. In addition, the total distribution cost in the U.S. is over 10% of the gross national product (GNP). Because of this high cost, firms constantly evaluate their means of distribution. Five major means of distribution are trucking, railroads, airfreight, waterways, and pipelines.

Distribution Systems

Trucking The vast majority of manufactured goods moves by truck. The flexibility of shipping by truck is only one of its many advantages. Companies that have adopted JIT programs in recent years have put increased pressure on truckers to pick up and deliver on time, with no damage, with paperwork in order, and at low cost. Trucking firms are using computers to monitor weather, find the most effective route, reduce fuel cost, and analyze the most efficient way to unload. In spite of these advances, the motor carrier industry averages a capacity utilization of only 50%. That underutilized space costs the U.S. economy over $31 billion per year. To improve logistics efficiency, the industry is establishing Web sites such as Schneider National's connection (**www.schneider.com**), which lets shippers and truckers find each other to use some of this idle capacity. Shippers may pick from thousands of approved North American carriers that have registered with Schneider logistics.

LO5: Explain major issues in logistics management

Railroads Railroads in the U.S. employ 187,000 people and ship 90% of all coal, 67% of autos, 68% of paper products, and about half of all food, lumber, and chemicals. Containerization has made intermodal shipping of truck trailers on railroad flat cars, often piggybacked as double-deckers, a popular means of distribution. More than 36 million trailer loads are moved in the U.S. each year by rail. With the growth of JIT, however, rail transport has been the biggest loser because small-batch manufacture requires frequent, smaller shipments that are likely to move via truck or air.

Airfreight Airfreight represents only about 1% of tonnage shipped in the U.S. However, the recent proliferation of airfreight carriers such as FedEx, UPS, and DHL makes it the fastest-growing mode of shipping. Clearly, for national and international movement of lightweight items, such as medical and emergency supplies, flowers, fruits, and electronic components, airfreight offers speed and reliability.

Waterways Waterways are one of the nation's oldest means of freight transportation, dating back to construction of the Erie Canal in 1817. Included in U.S. waterways are the nation's rivers, canals, the Great Lakes, coastlines, and oceans connecting to other countries. The usual cargo on waterways is bulky, low-value cargo such as iron ore, grains, cement, coal, chemicals, limestone, and petroleum products. Internationally, millions of containers are shipped at very low cost via huge oceangoing ships each year. Water transportation is important when shipping cost is more important than speed.

Pipelines Pipelines are an important form of transporting crude oil, natural gas, and other petroleum and chemical products. An amazing 90% of the state of Alaska's budget is derived from the 1.5 million barrels of oil pumped daily through the pipeline at Prudhoe Bay.

Third-Party Logistics

Supply-chain managers may find that outsourcing logistics is advantageous in driving down inventory investment and costs while improving delivery reliability and speed. Specialized logistics firms support this goal by coordinating the supplier's inventory system with the service

As this photo of the port of Charleston suggests, with 16 million containers entering the U.S. annually, tracking location, content, and condition of trucks and containers is a challenge. But new technology may improve both security and JIT shipments.

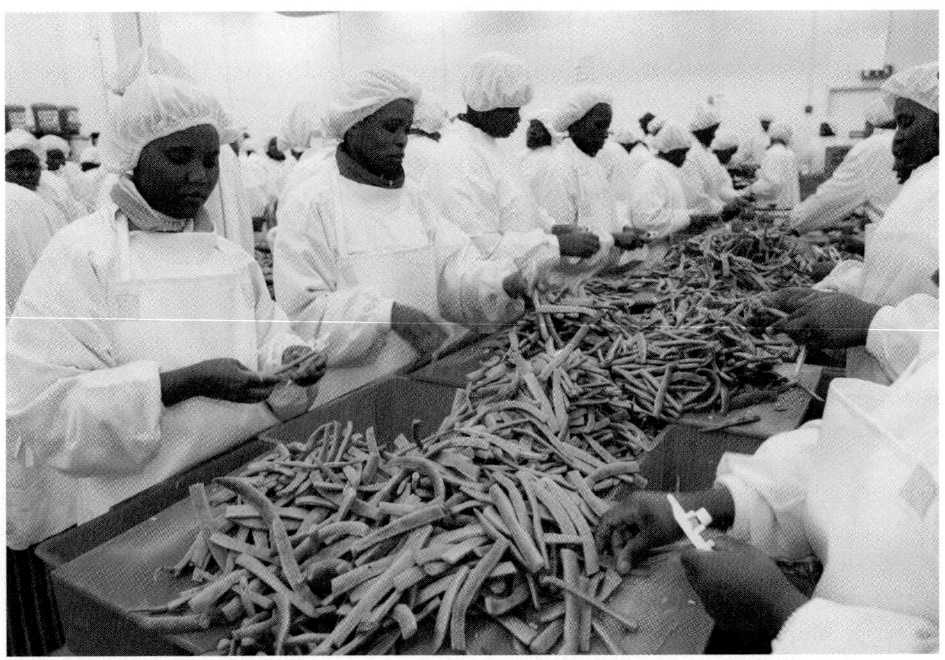

Seven farms within a 2-hour drive of Kenya's Nairobi Airport supply 300 tons of fresh beans, bok choy, okra, and other produce that is packaged at the airport and shipped overnight to Europe. The time between harvest and arrival in Europe is 2 days. When a good supply chain and good logistics work together, the results can be startling—and fresh food.

capabilities of the delivery firm. FedEx, for example, has a successful history of using the Internet for online tracking. At **FedEx.com**, a customer can compute shipping costs, print labels, adjust invoices, and track package status all on the same Web site. FedEx, UPS, and DHL play a core role in other firms' logistics processes. In some cases, they even run the server for retailer Web sites. In other cases, such as for Dell Computer, FedEx operates warehouses that pick, pack, test, and assemble products, then it handles delivery and customs clearance when necessary. The *OM in Action* box "DHL's Role in the Supply Chain" provides another example of how outsourcing logistics can reduce costs while shrinking inventory and delivery times.

Cost of Shipping Alternatives

The longer a product is in transit, the longer the firm has its money invested. But faster shipping is usually more expensive than slow shipping. A simple way to obtain some insight into this trade-off is to evaluate holding cost against shipping options. We do this in Example 3.

OM in Action ► DHL's Role in the Supply Chain

It's the dead of night at DHL International's air express hub in Brussels, yet the massive building is alive with busy forklifts and sorting workers. The boxes going on and off the DHL plane range from Dell computers and Cisco routers to Caterpillar mufflers and Komatsu hydraulic pumps. Sun Microsystems computers from California are earmarked for Finland; DVDs from Teac's plant in Malaysia are destined for Bulgaria.

The door-to-door movement of time-sensitive packages is key to the global supply chain. JIT, short product life cycles, mass customization, and reduced inventories depend on logistics firms such as DHL, FedEx, and UPS. These powerhouses are in continuous motion.

With a decentralized network covering 225 countries and territories (more than are in the UN), DHL is a true multinational. The Brussels headquarters has only 450 of the company's 124,000 employees but includes 26 nationalities.

DHL has assembled an extensive global network of express logistics centers for strategic goods. In its Brussels logistics center, for instance, DHL upgrades, repairs, and configures Fijitsu computers, InFocus projectors, and Johnson & Johnson medical equipment. It stores and provides parts for EMC and Hewlett-Packard and replaces Nokia and Philips phones. "If something breaks down on a Thursday at 4 o'clock, the relevant warehouse knows at 4:05, and the part is on a DHL plane at 7 or 8 that evening," says Robert Kuijpers, DHL International's CEO.

Sources: Journal of Commerce (August 15, 2005): 1; *Hoover's Company Records* (May 1, 2009): 40126; and *Forbes* (October 18, 1999): 120–124.

EXAMPLE 3

Determining daily cost of holding

A shipment of new connectors for semiconductors needs to go from San Jose to Singapore for assembly. The value of the connectors is $1,750 and holding cost is 40% per year. One airfreight carrier can ship the connectors 1 day faster than its competitor, at an extra cost of $20.00. Which carrier should be selected?

APPROACH ▶ First we determine the daily holding cost and then compare the daily holding cost with the cost of faster shipment.

SOLUTION ▶ Daily cost of holding the product = (Annual holding cost × Product value)/365

= (.40 × $1,750)/365

= $1.92

Since the cost of saving one day is $20.00, which is much more than the daily holding cost of $1.92, we decide on the less costly of the carriers and take the extra day to make the shipment. This saves $18.08 ($20.00 – $1.92).

INSIGHT ▶ The solution becomes radically different if the 1-day delay in getting the connectors to Singapore delays delivery (making a customer angry) or delays payment of a $150,000 final product. (Even 1 day's interest on $150,000 or an angry customer makes a savings of $18.08 insignificant.)

LEARNING EXERCISE ▶ If the holding cost is 100% per year, what is the decision? [Answer: Even with a holding cost of $4.79 per day, the less costly carrier is selected.]

RELATED PROBLEMS ▶ 11.8, 11.9, 11.10

Example 3 looks only at holding costs versus shipping cost. For the operations or logistics manager there are many other considerations, including coordinating shipments to maintain a schedule, getting a new product to market, and keeping a customer happy. Estimates of these other costs can be added to the estimate of daily holding cost. Determining the impact and cost of these many other considerations makes the evaluation of shipping alternatives interesting.

Security and JIT

There is probably no society more open than the U.S. This includes its borders and ports—but they are swamped. About 7 million containers enter U.S. ports each year, along with thousands of planes, cars, and trucks each day. Even under the best of conditions, some 5% of the container movements are misrouted, stolen, damaged, or excessively delayed.

Since the September 11, 2001, terrorist attacks, supply chains have become more complex. Technological innovations, though, in the supply chain are improving security and JIT, making logistics more reliable. Technology is now capable of knowing truck and container location, content, and condition. New devices can detect whether someone has broken into a sealed container

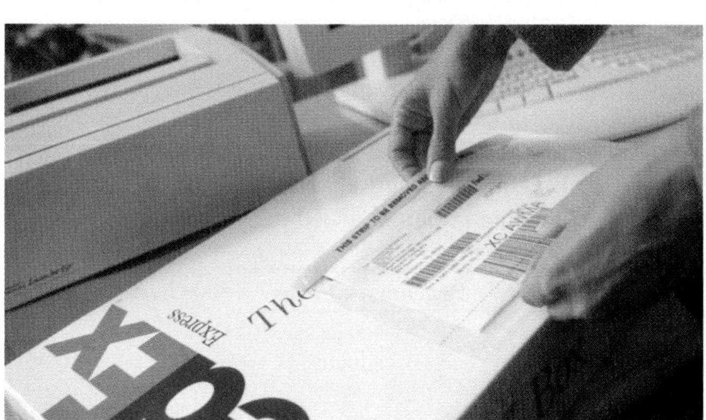

Speed and accuracy in the supply chain are supported by bar-code tracking of shipments. At each step of a journey, from initial pickup to final destination, bar codes (left) are read and stored. Within seconds, this tracking information is available online to customers worldwide (right).

and can communicate that information to the shipper or receiver via satellite or radio. Motion detectors can also be installed inside containers. Other sensors can record interior data including temperature, shock, radioactivity, and whether a container is moving. Tracking lost containers, identifying delays, or just reminding individuals in the supply chain that a shipment is on its way will help expedite shipments. Improvements in security may aid JIT, and improvements in JIT may aid security—both of which can improve supply-chain logistics.

AUTHOR COMMENT
If you can't measure it, you can't control it.

MEASURING SUPPLY-CHAIN PERFORMANCE

LO6: Compute the percentage of assets committed to inventory and inventory turnover

Like all other managers, supply-chain managers require standards (or *metrics*, as they are often called) to evaluate performance. Evaluation of the supply chain is particularly critical for these managers because they spend most of the organization's money. In addition, they make scheduling and quantity decisions that determine the assets committed to inventory. Only with effective metrics can managers determine: (1) how well the *supply chain is performing* and (2) *the assets committed to inventory.* We will now discuss these two metrics.

Supply-Chain Performance The benchmark metrics shown in Table 11.5 focus on procurement and vendor performance issues. World-class benchmarks are the result of well-managed supply chains that drive down costs, lead times, late deliveries, and shortages while improving quality.

Assets Committed to Inventory Three specific measures can be helpful here. The first is the amount of money invested in inventory, usually expressed as a percentage of assets, as shown in Equation (11-1) and Example 4:

$$\text{Percentage invested in inventory} = (\text{Total inventory investment}/\text{Total assets}) \times 100 \quad \textbf{(11-1)}$$

EXAMPLE 4 ▶

Tracking Home Depot's inventory investment

Home Depot's management wishes to track its investment in inventory as one of its performance measures. Home Depot had $11.4 billion invested in inventory and total assets of $44.4 billion in 2006.

APPROACH ▶ Determine the investment in inventory and total assets and then use Equation (11-1).

SOLUTION ▶ Percent invested in inventory $= (11.4/44.4) \times 100 = 25.7\%$

INSIGHT ▶ Over one-fourth of Home Depot assets are committed to inventory.

LEARNING EXERCISE ▶ If Home Depot can drive its investment down to 20% of assets, how much money will it free up for other uses? [Answer: $11.4 - (44.4 \times .2) = \$2.52$ billion.]

RELATED PROBLEMS ▶ 11.11b, 11.12b

Specific comparisons with competitors may assist evaluation. Total assets committed to inventory in manufacturing approach 15%, in wholesale 34%, and retail 27%—with wide variations, depending on the specific business model, the business cycle, and management (see Table 11.6).

The second common measure of supply chain performance is *inventory turnover* (see Table 11.7). Its reciprocal, *weeks of supply,* is the third. **Inventory turnover** is computed on an annual basis, using Equation (11-2):

Inventory turnover
Cost of goods sold divided by average inventory.

$$\text{Inventory turnover} = \text{Cost of goods sold}/\text{Inventory investment} \quad \textbf{(11-2)}$$

Cost of goods sold is the cost to produce the goods or services sold for a given period. Inventory investment is the average inventory value for the same period. This may be the average of several periods of inventory or beginning and ending inventory added together and divided by 2.

▶TABLE 11.5
Metrics for Supply-Chain Performance

	Typical Firms	Benchmark Firms
Lead time (weeks)	15	8
Time spent placing an order	42 minutes	15 minutes
Percent of late deliveries	33%	2%
Percent of rejected material	1.5%	.0001%
Number of shortages per year	400	4

Source: Adapted from a McKinsey & Company report.

▼ **TABLE 11.6**
Inventory as Percentage of Total Assets (with examples of exceptional performance)

Manufacturer (Toyota 5%)	15%
Wholesale (Coca-Cola 2.9%)	34%
Restaurants (McDonald's .05%)	2.9%
Retail (Home Depot 25.7%)	27%

▼ **TABLE 11.7**
Examples of Annual Inventory Turnover

Food, Beverage, Retail	
Anheuser Busch	15
Coca-Cola	14
Home Depot	5
McDonald's	112
Manufacturing	
Dell Computer	90
Johnson Controls	22
Toyota (overall)	13
Nissan (assembly)	150

Often, average inventory investment is based on nothing more than the inventory investment at the end of the period—typically at year-end.[3]

In Example 5, we look at inventory turnover applied to PepsiCo.

EXAMPLE 5
Inventory turnover at PepsiCo, Inc.

PepsiCo, Inc., manufacturer and distributor of drinks, Frito-Lay, and Quaker Foods, provides the following in its 2005 annual report (shown here in $ billions). Determine PepsiCo's turnover.

Net revenue		$32.5
Cost of goods sold		$14.2
Inventory:		
Raw material inventory	$.74	
Work-in-process inventory	$.11	
Finished goods inventory	$.84	
Total inventory investment		$1.69

APPROACH ▶ Use the inventory turnover computation in Equation (11-2) to measure inventory performance. Cost of goods sold is $14.2 billion. Total inventory is the sum of raw material at $.74 billion, work-in-process at $.11 billion, and finished goods at $.84 billion, for total inventory investment of $1.69 billion.

SOLUTION ▶

$$\text{Inventory Turnover} = \text{Cost of goods sold}/\text{Inventory investment}$$
$$= 14.2/1.69$$
$$= 8.4$$

INSIGHT ▶ We now have a standard, popular measure by which to evaluate performance.

LEARNING EXERCISE ▶ If Coca-Cola's cost of goods sold is $10.8 billion and inventory investment is $.76 billion, what is its inventory turnover? [Answer: 14.2.]

RELATED PROBLEMS ▶ 11.11a, 11.12c, 11.13

Weeks of supply, as shown in Example 6, may have more meaning in the wholesale and retail portions of the service sector than in manufacturing. It is computed below as the reciprocal of inventory turnover:

$$\text{Weeks of supply} = \text{Inventory investment}/(\text{Annual cost of goods sold}/52 \text{ weeks}) \quad \textbf{(11-3)}$$

[3]Inventory quantities often fluctuate wildly, and various types of inventory exist (e.g., raw material, work-in-process, finished goods, and maintenance, repair, and operating supplies [MRO]). Therefore, care must be taken when using inventory values; they may reflect more than just supply-chain performance.

EXAMPLE 6 ▶

Determining weeks of supply at PepsiCo

Using the PepsiCo data in Example 5, management wants to know the weeks of supply.

APPROACH ▶ We know that inventory investment is \$1.69 billion and that weekly sales equal annual cost of goods sold (\$14.2 billion) divided by 52 = \$14.2/52 = \$.273 billion.

SOLUTION ▶ Using Equation (11-3), we compute weeks of supply as:

$$\text{Weeks of supply} = (\text{Inventory investment}/\text{Average weekly cost of goods sold})$$

$$= 1.69/.273 = 6.19 \text{ weeks}$$

INSIGHT ▶ We now have a standard measurement by which to evaluate a company's continuing performance or by which to compare companies.

LEARNING EXERCISE ▶ If Coca-Cola's average inventory investment is \$.76 billion and its average weekly cost of goods sold is \$.207 billion, what is the firm's weeks of supply? [Answer: 3.67 weeks.]

RELATED PROBLEMS ▶ 11.12a, 11.14

Supply-chain management is critical in driving down inventory investment. The rapid movement of goods is key. Walmart, for example, has set the pace in the retailing sector with its world-renowned supply-chain management. By doing so, it has established a competitive advantage. With its own truck fleet, distribution centers, and a state-of-the-art communication system, Walmart (with the help of its suppliers) replenishes store shelves an average of twice per week. Competitors resupply every other week. Economical and speedy resupply means both rapid response to product changes and customer preferences, as well as lower inventory investment. Similarly, while many manufacturers struggle to move inventory turnover up to 10 times per year, Dell Computer has inventory turns exceeding 90 and supply measured in *days*—not weeks. Supply-chain management provides a competitive advantage when firms effectively respond to the demands of global markets and global sources.

The SCOR Model

In addition to the metrics presented above, the Supply-Chain Council (SCC) has developed 200 process elements, 550 metrics, and 500 best practices. The SCC (www.supply-chain.org) is a 900-member not-for-profit association for the improvement of supply-chain effectiveness. The council has developed the five-part **Supply-Chain Operations Reference (SCOR) model.** The five parts are Plan, Source, Make, Deliver, and Return, as shown in Figure 11.3.

Supply-Chain Operations Reference (SCOR) model
A set of processes, metrics, and best practices developed by the Supply-Chain Council.

The council believes the model provides a structure for its processes, metrics, and best practices to be (1) implemented for competitive advantage; (2) defined and communicated precisely; (3) measured, managed, and controlled; and (4) fine-tuned as necessary to a specific application.

▶ FIGURE 11.3
The Supply-Chain Operations Reference (SCOR) Model

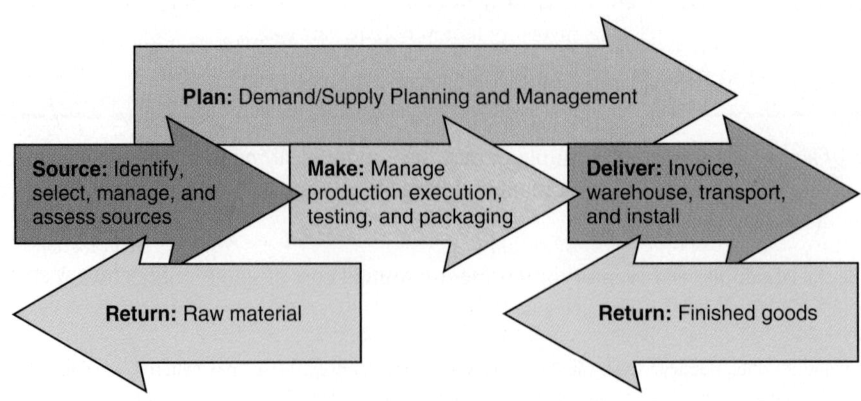

CHAPTER SUMMARY

Competition is no longer between companies but between supply chains. For many firms, the supply chain determines a substantial portion of product cost and quality, as well as opportunities for responsiveness and differentiation. Six supply-chain strategies have been identified: (1) many suppliers, (2) few suppliers, (3) vertical integration, (4) joint ventures, (5) *keiretsu* networks, and (6) virtual companies. Skillful supply-chain management provides a great strategic opportunity for competitive advantage.

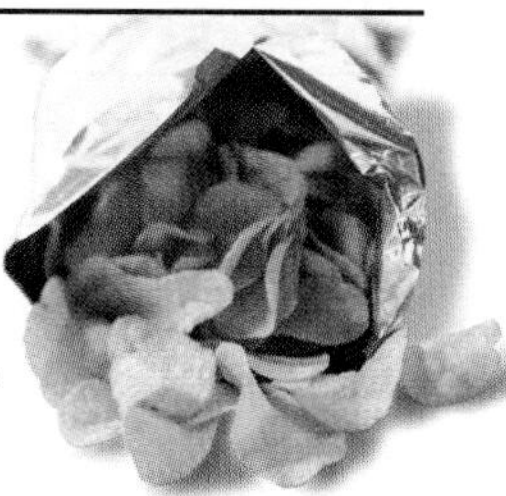

Key Terms

Supply-chain management (p. 420)
Make-or-buy decision (p. 425)
Outsourcing (p. 425)
Vertical integration (p. 426)
Keiretsu (p. 427)
Virtual companies (p. 427)
Bullwhip effect (p. 428)
Pull data (p. 429)
Single-stage control of replenishment (p. 429)
Vendor-managed inventory (VMI) (p. 430)
Collaborative planning, forecasting, and replenishment (CPFR) (p. 430)
Blanket order (p. 430)
Postponement (p. 430)
Drop shipping (p. 431)
Pass-through facility (p. 431)
Channel assembly (p. 431)
E-procurement (p. 431)
Electronic data interchange (EDI) (p. 431)
Advanced shipping notice (ASN) (p. 431)
Negotiation strategies (p. 434)
Logistics management (p. 434)
Inventory turnover (p. 438)
Supply-Chain Operations Reference (SCOR) model (p. 440)

Ethical Dilemma

For generations, the policy of Sears Roebuck and Company, the granddaddy of retailers, was not to purchase more than 50% of any of its suppliers' output. The rationale of this policy was that it allowed Sears to move to other suppliers, as the market dictated, without destroying the supplier's ability to stay in business. In contrast, Walmart purchases more and more of a supplier's output. Eventually, Walmart can be expected to sit down with that supplier and explain why the supplier no longer needs a sales force and that the supplier should eliminate the sales force, passing the cost savings on to Walmart.

Sears is losing market share, has been acquired by K-Mart, and is eliminating jobs; Walmart is gaining market share and hiring. What are the ethical issues involved, and which firm has a more ethical position?

Discussion Questions

1. Define *supply-chain management.*
2. What are the objectives of supply-chain management?
3. What is the objective of logistics management?
4. How do we distinguish between the types of risk in the supply chain?
5. What is vertical integration? Give examples of backward and forward integration.
6. What are three basic approaches to negotiations?
7. How does a traditional adversarial relationship with suppliers change when a firm makes a decision to move to a few suppliers?
8. What is the difference between postponement and channel assembly?
9. What is CPFR?
10. What is the value of online auctions in e-commerce?
11. Explain how FedEx uses the Internet to meet requirements for quick and accurate delivery.
12. How does Walmart use drop shipping?
13. What are blanket orders? How do they differ from invoiceless purchasing?
14. What can purchasing do to implement just-in-time deliveries?
15. What is e-procurement?
16. How does Darden Restaurants, described in the *Global Company Profile*, find competitive advantage in its supply chain?
17. What is SCOR, and what purpose does it serve?

Solved Problems

Virtual Office Hours help is available at www.myomlab.com

▼ SOLVED PROBLEM 11.1

Jack's Pottery Outlet has total end-of-year assets of $5 million. The first-of-the-year inventory was $375,000, with a year-end inventory of $325,000. The annual cost of goods sold was $7 million. The owner, Eric Jack, wants to evaluate his supply chain performance by measuring his percent of assets in inventory, his inventory turnover, and his weeks of supply. We use Equations (11-1), (11-2), and (11-3) to provide these measures.

▼ SOLUTION

First, determine *average inventory*:

$$(\$375{,}000 + \$325{,}000)/2 = \$350{,}000$$

Then, use Equation (11-1) to determine percent invested in inventory:

$$\begin{aligned}\text{Percent invested in inventory} &= (\text{Total inventory investment}/\text{Total assets}) \times 100\\ &= (350{,}000/5{,}000{,}000) \times 100\\ &= 7\%\end{aligned}$$

Third, determine inventory turnover, using Equation (11-2):

$$\begin{aligned}\text{Inventory turnover} &= \text{Cost of goods sold}/\text{Inventory investment}\\ &= 7{,}000{,}000/350{,}000\\ &= 20\end{aligned}$$

Finally, to determine weeks of inventory, use Equation (11-3), adjusted to weeks:

$$\begin{aligned}\text{Weeks of inventory} &= \text{Inventory investment}/\text{Weekly cost of goods sold}\\ &= 350{,}000/(7{,}000{,}000/52)\\ &= 350{,}000/134{,}615\\ &= 2.6\end{aligned}$$

We conclude that Jack's Pottery Outlet has 7% of its assets invested in inventory, that the inventory turnover is 20, and that weeks of supply is 2.6.

Problems

•• **11.1** Choose a local establishment that is a member of a relatively large chain. From interviews with workers and information from the Internet, identify the elements of the supply chain. Determine whether the supply chain represents a low-cost, rapid response, or differentiation strategy (refer to Chapter 2). Are the supply-chain characteristics significantly different from one product to another?

•• **11.2** As purchasing agent for Woolsey Enterprises in Golden, Colorado, you ask your buyer to provide you with a ranking of "excellent," "good," "fair," or "poor" for a variety of characteristics for two potential vendors. You suggest that "Products" total be weighted 40% and the other three categories' totals be weighted 20% each. The buyer has returned the following ranking:

VENDOR RATING

Company	Excellent (4)	Good (3)	Fair (2)	Poor (1)
Financial Strength			K	D
Manufacturing Range			KD	
Research Facilities	K		D	
Geographical Locations		K	D	
Management		K	D	
Labor Relations			K	D
Trade Relations			KD	

Service				
Deliveries on Time		KD		
Handling of Problems		KD		
Technical Assistance		K	D	

Products	Excellent (4)	Good (3)	Fair (2)	Poor (1)
Quality	KD			
Price			KD	
Packaging			KD	

Sales				
Product Knowledge			D	K
Sales Calls			K	D
Sales Service		K	D	

DONNA INC. = D
KAY CORP. = K

Which of the two vendors would you select?

•• **11.3** Using the data in Problem 11.2, assume that both Donna, Inc. and Kay Corp. are able to move all their "poor" ratings to "fair." How would you then rank the two firms?

•• **11.4** Develop a vendor-rating form that represents your comparison of the education offered by universities in which you considered (or are considering) enrolling. Fill in the necessary data, and identify the "best" choice. Are you attending that "best" choice? If not, why not?

•• **11.5** Using sources from the Internet, identify some of the problems faced by a company of your choosing as it moves toward, or operates as, a virtual organization. Does its operating as a virtual organization simply exacerbate old problems, or does it create new ones?

• **11.6** Using Table 11.4, determine the sales necessary to equal a dollar of savings on purchases for a company that has:
a) A net profit of 4% and spends 40% of its revenue on purchases.
b) A net profit of 6% and spends 80% of its revenue on purchases.

• **11.7** Using Table 11.4, determine the sales necessary to equal a dollar of savings on purchases for a company that has:
a) A net profit of 6% and spends 60% of its revenue on purchases.
b) A net profit of 8% and spends 80% of its revenue on purchases.

•• **11.8** Your options for shipping $100,000 of machine parts from Baltimore to Kuala Lumpur, Malaysia, are (1) use a ship that will take 30 days at a cost of $3,800, or (2) truck the parts to Los Angeles and then ship at a total cost of $4,800. The second option will take only 20 days. You are paid via a letter of credit the day the parts arrive. Your holding cost is estimated at 30% of the value per year.

a) Which option is more economical?
b) What customer issues are not included in the data presented?

•• **11.9** If you have a third option for the data in Problem 11.8, and it costs only $4,000 and also takes 20 days, what is your most economical plan?

•• **11.10** Monczka-Trent Shipping is the logistics vendor for Handfield Manufacturing Co. in Ohio. Handfield has daily shipments of a power-steering pump from its Ohio plant to an auto assembly line in Alabama. The value of the standard shipment is $250,000. Monczka-Trent has two options: (1) its standard 2-day shipment or (2) a subcontractor who will team drive overnight with an effective delivery of 1 day. The extra driver costs $175. Handfield's holding cost is 35% annually for this kind of inventory.
a) Which option is more economical?
b) What production issues are not included in the data presented?

•• **11.11** Baker Mfg Inc. (see Table 11.8) wishes to compare its inventory turnover to those of industry leaders, who have turnover of about 13 times per year and 8% of their assets invested in inventory.
a) What is Baker's inventory turnover?
b) What is Baker's percent of assets committed to inventory?
c) How does Baker's performance compare to the industry leaders?

▼ TABLE 11.8 For Problems 11.11 and 11.12

Arrow Distributing Corp.	
Net revenue	$16,500
Cost of sales	$13,500
Inventory	$ 1,000
Total assets	$ 8,600
Baker Mfg. Inc.	
Net revenue	$27,500
Cost of sales	$21,500
Inventory	$ 1,250
Total assets	$16,600

•• **11.12** Arrow Distributing Corp. (see Table 11.8) likes to track inventory by using weeks of supply as well as by inventory turnover.
a) What is its weeks of supply?
b) What percent of Arrow's assets are committed to inventory?
c) What is Arrow's inventory turnover?
d) Is Arrow's supply-chain performance, as measured by these inventory metrics, better than that of Baker, in Problem 11.11?

• **11.13** The grocery industry has an annual inventory turnover of about 14 times. Organic Grocers, Inc., had a cost of goods sold last year of $10.5 million; its average inventory was $1.0 million. What was Organic Grocers's inventory turnover, and how does that performance compare with that of the industry?

•• **11.14** Mattress Wholesalers, Inc. is constantly trying to reduce inventory in its supply chain. Last year, cost of goods sold was $7.5 million and inventory was $1.5 million. This year, costs of goods sold is $8.6 million and inventory investment is $1.6 million.
a) What were the weeks of supply last year?
b) What are the weeks of supply this year?
c) Is Mattress Wholesalers making progress in its inventory-reduction effort?

▶ **Refer to myomlab for this additional homework problem: 11.15**

Case Studies

► Dell's Value Chain

Dell Computer, with close supplier relationships, encourages suppliers to focus on their individual technological capabilities to sustain leadership in their components. Research and development costs are too high and technological changes are too rapid for any one company to sustain leadership in every component. Suppliers are also pressed to drive down lead times, lot sizes, and inventories. Dell, in turn, keeps its research customer-focused and leverages that research to help itself and suppliers. Dell also constructs special Web pages for suppliers, allowing them to view orders for components they produce as well as current levels of inventory at Dell. This allows suppliers to plan based on actual end customer demand; as a result, it reduces the bullwhip effect. The intent is to work with suppliers to keep the supply chain moving rapidly, products current, and the customer order queue short. Then, with supplier collaboration, Dell can offer the latest options, can build-to-order, and can achieve rapid throughput. The payoff is a competitive advantage, growing market share, and low capital investment.

On the distribution side, Dell uses direct sales, primarily via the Internet, to increase revenues by offering a virtually unlimited variety of desktops, notebooks, and enterprise products. Options displayed over the Internet allow Dell to attract customers that value choice. Customers select recommended product configurations or customize them. Dell's customers place orders at any time of the day from anywhere in the world. And Dell's price is cheaper; retail stores have additional costs because of their brick-and-mortar model. Dell has also customized Web pages that enable large business customers to track past purchases and place orders consistent with their purchase history and current needs. Assembly begins immediately after receipt of a customer order. Competing firms have previously assembled products filling the distribution channels (including shelves at retailers) before a product reaches the customer. Dell, in contrast, introduces a new product to customers over the Internet as soon as the first of that model is ready. In an industry where products have life cycles measured in months, Dell enjoys a huge early-to-market advantage.

Dell's model also has cash flow advantages. Direct sales allow Dell to eliminate distributor and retailer margins and increase its own margin. Dell collects payment in a matter of days after products are sold. But Dell pays its suppliers according to the more traditional billing schedules. Given its low levels of inventory, Dell is able to operate its business with negative working capital because it manages to receive payment before it pays its suppliers for components. These more traditional supply chains often require 60 or more days for the cash to flow from customer to supplier—a huge demand on working capital.

Dell has designed its order processing, products, and assembly lines so that customized products can be assembled in a matter of hours. This allows Dell to postpone assembly until after a customer order has been placed. In addition, any inventory is often in the form of components that are common across a wide variety of finished products. Postponement, component modularity, and tight scheduling allow low inventory and support mass customization. Dell maximizes the benefit of postponement by focusing on new products for which demand is difficult to forecast. Manufacturers who sell via distributors and retailers find postponement virtually impossible. Therefore, traditional manufacturers are often stuck with product configurations that are not selling while simultaneously being out of the configurations that *are* selling. Dell is better able to match supply and demand.

One of the few negatives for Dell's model is that it results in higher outbound shipping costs than selling through distributors and retailers. Dell sends individual products directly to customers from its factories. But many of these shipments are small (often one or a few products), while manufacturers selling through distributors and retailers ship with some economy of scale, using large shipments via truck to warehouses and retailers, with the end user providing the final portion of delivery. As a result, Dell's outbound transportation costs are higher, but the relative cost is low (typically 2% to 3%), and thus the impact on the overall cost is low.

What Dell has done is build a collaborative supply chain and an innovative ordering and production system. The result is what Dell likes to refer to as its *value chain*—a chain that brings value from supplier to the customer and provides Dell with a competitive advantage.

Discussion Questions

1. How has Dell used its direct sales and build-to-order model to develop an exceptional supply chain?
2. How has Dell exploited the direct sales model to improve operations performance?
3. What are the main disadvantages of Dell's direct sales model?
4. How does Dell compete with a retailer who already has a stock?
5. How does Dell's supply chain deal with the bullwhip effect?

Sources: Adapted from S. Chopra and P. Meindl, *Supply Chain Management*, 3rd ed. (Upper Saddle River, NJ: Prentice Hall, 2007); R. Kapuscinski, et al., "Inventory Decisions in Dell's Supply Chain," *Interfaces* 34, no. 3 (May–June 2004): 191–205; and A. A. Thompson, A. J. Strickland, and J. E. Gamble, "Dell, Inc. in 2006: Can Rivals Beat Its Strategy?" *Crafting and Executing Strategy*, 15th ed. (New York: McGraw-Hill, 2007).

► Darden's Global Supply Chains

Video Case

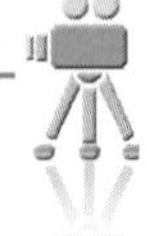

Darden Restaurants (subject of the *Global Company Profile* at the beginning of this chapter), owner of popular brands such as Olive Garden and Red Lobster, requires unique supply chains to serve more than 300 million meals annually. Darden's strategy is operations excellence, and Senior VP Jim Lawrence's task is to ensure competitive advantage via Darden's supply chains. For a firm with purchases exceeding $1.5 billion, managing the supply chains is a complex and challenging task.

Darden, like other casual dining restaurants, has unique supply chains that reflect its menu options. Darden's supply chains are rather shallow, often having just one tier of suppliers. But it has four distinct supply chains.

First, "smallware" is a restaurant industry term for items such as linens, dishes, tableware and kitchenware, and silverware. These are purchased, with Darden taking title as they are received at the Darden Direct Distribution (DDD) warehouse in Orlando, Florida. From this single warehouse, smallware items are shipped via common carrier (trucking companies) to Olive Garden, Red Lobster, Bahama Breeze, and Seasons 52 restaurants.

Second, frozen, dry, and canned food products are handled economically by Darden's 11 distribution centers in North America, which are managed by major U.S. food distributors, such as MBM, Maines, and Sygma. This is Darden's second supply line.

Third, the fresh food supply chain (not frozen and not canned), where life is measured in days, includes dairy products, produce, and meat. This supply chain is B2B, where restaurant managers directly place orders with a preselected group of independent suppliers.

Fourth, Darden's worldwide seafood supply chain is the final link. Here Darden has developed independent suppliers of salmon, shrimp, tilapia, scallops, and other fresh fish that are source inspected by Darden's overseas representatives to ensure quality. These fresh products are flown to the U.S. and shipped to 16 distributors, with 22 locations, for quick delivery to the restaurants. With suppliers in 35 countries, Darden must be on the cutting edge when it comes to collaboration, partnering, communication, and food safety. It does this with heavy travel schedules for purchasing and quality control personnel, native-speaking employees onsite, and aggressive communication. Communication is a critical element; Darden tries to develop as much forecasting transparency as possible. "Point of sale (POS) terminals," says Lawrence, "feed actual sales every night to suppliers."

Discussion Questions*

1. What are the advantages of each of Darden's four supply chains?
2. What are the complications of having four supply chains?
3. Where would you expect ownership/title to change in each of Darden's four supply chains?
4. How do Darden's four supply chains compare with those of other firms, such as Dell or an automobile manufacturer? Why do the differences exist, and how are they addressed?

*You may wish to view the video that accompanies this case before answering these questions.

► Arnold Palmer Hospital's Supply Chain

Video Case

Arnold Palmer Hospital, one of the nation's top hospitals dedicated to serving women and children, is a large business with over 2,000 employees working in a 431-bed facility totaling 676,000 square feet in Orlando, Florida. Like many other hospitals, and other companies, Arnold Palmer Hospital had been a long-time member of a large buying group, one servicing 900 members. But the group did have a few limitations. For example, it might change suppliers for a particular product every year (based on a new lower-cost bidder) or stock only a product that was not familiar to the physicians at Arnold Palmer Hospital. The buying group was also not able to negotiate contracts with local manufacturers to secure the best pricing.

So in 2003, Arnold Palmer Hospital, together with seven other partner hospitals in central Florida, formed its own much smaller, but still powerful (with $200 million in annual purchases) Healthcare Purchasing Alliance (HPA) corporation. The new alliance saved the HPA members $7 million in its first year with two main changes. First, it was structured and staffed to assure that the bulk of the savings associated with its contracting efforts went to its eight members. Second, it struck even better deals with vendors by guaranteeing a *committed* volume and signing not 1-year deals but 3- to 5-year contracts. "Even with a new internal cost of $400,000 to run HPA, the savings and ability to contract for what our member hospitals really want makes the deal a winner," says George DeLong, head of HPA.

Effective supply chain management in manufacturing often focuses on development of new product innovations and efficiency through buyer–vendor collaboration. However, the approach in a service industry has a slightly different emphasis. At Arnold Palmer Hospital, supply-chain opportunities often manifest themselves through the Medical Economic Outcomes Committee. This committee (and its subcommittees) consists of users (including the medical and nursing staff) who evaluate purchase options with a goal of better medicine while achieving economic targets. For instance, the heart pacemaker negotiation by the cardiology subcommittee allowed for the standardization to two manufacturers, with annual savings of $2 million for just this one product.

Arnold Palmer Hospital is also able to develop custom products that require collaboration down to the third tier of the supply chain. This is the case with custom packs that are used in the operating room. The custom packs are delivered by a distributor, McKesson General Medical, but assembled by a pack company that uses materials the hospital wanted purchased from specific manufacturers. The HPA allows Arnold Palmer Hospital to be creative in this way. With major cost savings, standardization, blanket purchase orders, long-term contracts, and more control of product development, the benefits to the hospital are substantial.

Discussion Questions*

1. How does this supply chain differ from that in a manufacturing firm?
2. What are the constraints on making decisions based on economics alone at Arnold Palmer Hospital?
3. What role do doctors and nurses play in supply-chain decisions in a hospital? How is this participation handled at Arnold Palmer Hospital?
4. Doctor Smith just returned from the Annual Physician's Orthopedic Conference, where she saw a new hip joint replacement demonstrated. She decides she wants to start using the replacement joint at Arnold Palmer Hospital. What process will Dr. Smith have to go through at the hospital to introduce this new product into the supply chain for future surgical use?

*You may wish to view the video that accompanies this case before answering the questions.

▶ Supply-Chain Management at Regal Marine

Video Case

Like most other manufacturers, Regal Marine finds that it must spend a huge portion of its revenue on purchases. Regal has also found that the better its suppliers understand its end users, the better are both the supplier's product and Regal's final product. As one of the 10 largest U.S. power boat manufacturers, Regal is trying to differentiate its products from the vast number of boats supplied by 300 other companies. Thus, the firm works closely with suppliers to ensure innovation, quality, and timely delivery.

Regal has done a number of things to drive down costs while driving up quality, responsiveness, and innovation. First, working on partnering relationships with suppliers ranging from providers of windshields to providers of instrument panel controls, Regal has brought timely innovation at reasonable cost to its product. Key vendors are so tightly linked with the company that they meet with designers to discuss material changes to be incorporated into new product designs.

Second, the company has joined about 15 other boat manufacturers in a purchasing group, known as American Boat Builders Association, to work with suppliers on reducing the costs of large purchases. Third, Regal is working with a number of local vendors to supply hardware and fasteners directly to the assembly line on a just-in-time basis. In some of these cases, Regal has worked out an arrangement with the vendor so that title does not transfer until parts are used by Regal. In other cases, title transfers when items are delivered to the property. This practice drives down total inventory and the costs associated with large-lot delivery.

Finally, Regal works with a personnel agency to outsource part of the recruiting and screening process for employees. In all these cases, Regal is demonstrating innovative approaches to supply-chain management that help the firm and, ultimately, the end user. The *Global Company Profile* featuring Regal Marine (which opens Chapter 5) provides further background on Regal's operations.

Discussion Questions*

1. What other techniques might Regal use to improve supply-chain management?
2. What kind of response might members of the supply chain expect from Regal in response to their "partnering" in the supply chain?
3. Why is supply-chain management important to Regal?

*You may wish to view the video that accompanies this case before answering the questions.

▶**Additional Case Study:** Visit **www.myomlab.com** or **www.pearsonhighered.com/heizer** for this free case study:
Amazon.com: Discusses opportunities and issues in an innovative business model for the Internet.

Bibliography

Blackburn, Joseph, and Gary Scudder. "Supply Chain Strategies for Perishable Products." *Production and Operations Management* 18, no. 2 (March–April 2009): 129–137.

Boyer, Kenneth K., and G. Tomas M. Hult. "Extending the Supply Chain: Integrating Operations and Marketing in the Online Grocery Industry." *Journal of Operations Management* 23, no. 6 (September 2005): 642–661.

Chopra, Sunil, and Peter Meindl. *Supply Chain Management*, 4th ed. Upper Saddle River, NJ: Prentice Hall (2010).

Crook, T. Russell, and James G. Combs. "Sources and Consequences of Bargaining Power in Supply Chains." *Journal of Operations Management* 25, no. 2 (March 2007): 546–555.

Hu, J., and C. L. Munson. "Speed versus Reliability Trade-offs in Supplier Selection." *International Journal Procurement Management* 1, no. 1/2 (2007): 238–259.

Kersten, Wolfgang, and Thorsten Blecker (eds.). *Managing Risk in Supply Chains*. Berlin: Erich Schmidt Verlag GmbH & Co. (2006).

Kreipl, Stephan, and Michael Pinedo. "Planning and Scheduling in Supply Chains." *Production and Operations Management* 13, no. 1 (Spring 2004): 77–92.

Linton, J. D., R. Klassen, and V. Jayaraman. "Sustainable Supply Chains: An Introduction." *Journal of Operations Management* 25, no. 6 (November, 2007): 1075–1082.

Monczka, R. M., R. B. Handfield, L. C. Gianipero, and J. L. Patterson. *Purchasing and Supply Chain Management*, 4th ed. Mason, OH: Cengage (2009).

Narayanan, Sriram, Ann S. Marucheck, and Robert B. Handfield. "Electronic Data Interchange: Research Review and Future Directions." *Decisions Sciences* 40, no. 1 (February 2009): 121–163.

Pisano, Gary P., and Roberto Verganti. "Which Kind of Collaboration Is Right for You?" *Harvard Business Review* 86, no. 12 (December, 2008): 78–86.

Sinha, K. K., and E. J. Kohnke. "Health Care Supply Chain Design." *Decision Sciences* 40, no. 2 (May 2009): 197–212.

Stanley, L. L., and V. R. Singhal. "Service Quality Along the Supply Chain." *Journal of Operations Management* 19, no. 3 (May 2001): 287–306.

Wisner, Joel, K. Tan, and G. Keong Leong. *Principles of Supply Chain Management,* 3rd ed., Mason, OH: Cengage (2009).

Chapter 11 *Rapid* Review

Main Heading	Review Material	PEARSON myomlab
THE SUPPLY CHAIN'S STRATEGIC IMPORTANCE (pp. 420–422)	Most firms spend a huge portion of their sales dollars on purchases. ▪ **Supply-chain management**—Management of activities related to procuring materials and services, transforming them into intermediate goods and final products, and delivering them through a distribution system. The *objective is to build a chain of suppliers that focuses on maximizing value to the ultimate customer.* Competition is no longer between companies; it is between supply chains.	**VIDEO 11.1** Darden's Global Supply Chain
ETHICS AND SUSTAINABILITY (pp. 423–424)	Ethics includes personal ethics, ethics within the supply chain, and ethical behavior regarding the environment. The Institute for Supply Management has developed a set of Principles and Standards for ethical conduct.	
SUPPLY-CHAIN ECONOMICS (pp. 424–425)	▪ **Make-or-buy decision**—A choice between producing a component or service in-house or purchasing it from an outside source. ▪ **Outsourcing**—Transferring to external suppliers a firm's activities that have traditionally been internal.	Problems: 11.6, 11.7
SUPPLY-CHAIN STRATEGIES (pp. 425–427)	Six supply-chain strategies for goods and services to be obtained from outside sources are: 1. Negotiating with many suppliers and playing one supplier against another 2. Developing long-term partnering relationships with a few suppliers 3. Vertical integration 4. Joint ventures 5. Developing *keiretsu* networks 6. Developing virtual companies that use suppliers on an as-needed basis ▪ **Vertical integration**—Developing the ability to produce goods or services previously purchased or actually buying a supplier or a distributor. ▪ ***Keiretsu***—A Japanese term that describes suppliers who become part of a company coalition. ▪ **Virtual companies**—Companies that rely on a variety of supplier relationships to provide services on demand. Also known as hollow corporations or network companies.	**VIDEO 11.2** Supply-Chain Management at Regal Marine
MANAGING THE SUPPLY CHAIN (pp. 427–431)	Supply-chain integration success begins with mutual agreement on goals, followed by mutual trust, and continues with compatible organizational cultures. Three issues complicate the development of an efficient, integrated supply chain: local optimization, incentives, and large lots. ▪ **Bullwhip effect**—Increasing fluctuation in orders or cancellations that often occurs as orders move through the supply chain. ▪ **Pull data**—Accurate sales data that initiate transactions to "pull" product through the supply chain. ▪ **Single stage control of replenishment**—Fixing responsibility for monitoring and managing inventory for the retailer. ▪ **Vendor-managed inventory (VMI)**—A system in which a supplier maintains material for the buyer, often delivering directly to the buyer's using department. ▪ **Collaborative planning, forecasting, and replenishment (CPFR)**—A system in which members of a supply chain share information in a joint effort to reduce supply-chain costs. ▪ **Blanket order**—A long-term purchase commitment to a supplier for items that are to be delivered against short-term releases to ship. The purchasing department should make special efforts to increase levels of standardization. ▪ **Postponement**—Delaying any modifications or customization to a product as long as possible in the production process. Postponement strives to minimize internal variety while maximizing external variety. ▪ **Drop shipping**—Shipping directly from the supplier to the end consumer rather than from the seller, saving both time and reshipping costs. ▪ **Pass-through facility**—A facility that expedites shipment by holding merchandise and delivering from shipping hubs. ▪ **Channel assembly**—A system that postpones final assembly of a product so the distribution channel can assemble it.	**VIDEO 11.3** Arnold Palmer Hospital's Supply Chain

Main Heading	Review Material	myomlab
E-PROCUREMENT (pp. 431–433)	■ **E-procurement**—Purchasing facilitated through the Internet. ■ **Electronic data interchange (EDI)**—A standardized data-transmittal format for computerized communications between organizations. ■ **Advanced shipping notice (ASN)**—A shipping notice delivered directly from vendor to purchaser. Online catalogs move companies from a multitude of individual phone calls, faxes, and e-mails to a centralized online system and drive billions of dollars of waste out of the supply chain.	
VENDOR SELECTION (pp. 433–434)	Vendor selection is a three-stage process: (1) vendor evaluation, (2) vendor development, and (3) negotiations. *Vendor evaluation* involves finding potential vendors and determining the likelihood of their becoming good suppliers. *Vendor development* may include everything from training, to engineering and production help, to procedures for information transfer. ■ **Negotiation strategies**—Approaches taken by supply-chain personnel to develop contractual relationships with suppliers. Three classic types of negotiation strategies are (1) the cost-based price model, (2) the market-based price model, and (3) competitive bidding.	Problems: 11.2, 11.3
LOGISTICS MANAGEMENT (pp. 434–438)	■ **Logistics management**—An approach that seeks efficiency of operations through the integration of all material acquisition, movement, and storage activities. The total distribution cost in the United States is over 10% of the gross national product (GNP). Five major means of distribution are trucking, railroads, airfreight, waterways, and pipelines. The vast majority of manufactured goods move by truck.	Problems: 11.8–11.10
MEASURING SUPPLY-CHAIN PERFORMANCE (pp. 438–440)	Typical supply-chain benchmark metrics include lead time, time spent placing an order, percent of late deliveries, percent of rejected material, and number of shortages per year: Percent invested in inventory = (Total inventory investment/Total assets) × 100 **(11-1)** ■ **Inventory turnover**—Cost of goods sold divided by average inventory: Inventory turnover = Cost of goods sold ÷ Inventory investment **(11-2)** Weeks of supply = Inventory investment ÷ (Annual cost of goods sold/52 weeks) **(11-3)** ■ **Supply Chain Operations Reference (SCOR) Model**—A set of processes, metrics, and best practices developed by the Supply Chain Council. The five parts of the SCOR model are Plan, Source, Make, Deliver, and Return.	Problems: 11.11–11.15 Virtual Office Hours for Solved Problem: 11.1

Self Test

■ **Before taking the self-test,** refer to the learning objectives listed at the beginning of the chapter and the key terms listed at the end of the chapter.

LO1. The objective of supply-chain management is to _______.

LO2. The term *vertical integration* means to:
- **a)** develop the ability to produce products that complement or supplement the original product.
- **b)** produce goods or services previously purchased.
- **c)** develop the ability to produce the specified good more efficiently.
- **d)** all of the above.

LO3. The bullwhip effect can be aggravated by:
- **a)** local optimization.
- **b)** sales incentives.
- **c)** quantity discounts.
- **d)** promotions.
- **e)** all of the above.

LO4. Vendor selection requires:
- **a)** vendor evaluation and effective third-party logistics.
- **b)** vendor development and logistics.
- **c)** negotiations, vendor evaluation, and vendor development.
- **d)** an integrated supply chain.
- **e)** inventory and supply-chain management.

LO5. A major issue in logistics is:
- **a)** cost of purchases.
- **b)** vendor evaluation.
- **c)** product customization.
- **d)** cost of shipping alternatives.
- **e)** excellent suppliers.

LO6. Inventory turnover =
- **a)** Cost of goods sold ÷ Weeks of supply.
- **b)** Weeks of supply ÷ Annual cost of goods sold.
- **c)** Annual cost of goods sold ÷ 52 weeks.
- **d)** Inventory investment ÷ Cost of goods sold.
- **e)** Cost of goods sold ÷ Inventory investment.

Answers: LO1. build a chain of suppliers that focuses on maximizing value to the ultimate customer; LO2. b; LO3. e; LO4. c; LO5. d; LO6. e.

Supplement 11: Outsourcing as a Supply-Chain Strategy

Supplement Outline

Contract manufacturers such as Flextronics provide outsourcing service to IBM, Cisco Systems, HP, Microsoft, Motorola, Sony, Nortel, Ericsson, and Sun, among many others. Flextronics is a high-quality producer that has won over 450 awards, including the Malcolm Baldrige Award. One of the side benefits of outsourcing is that client firms such as IBM can actually improve their performance by using the competencies of an outstanding firm like Flextronics. But there are risks involved in outsourcing. Outsourcing decisions, as part of the supply-chain strategy, are explored in this supplement.

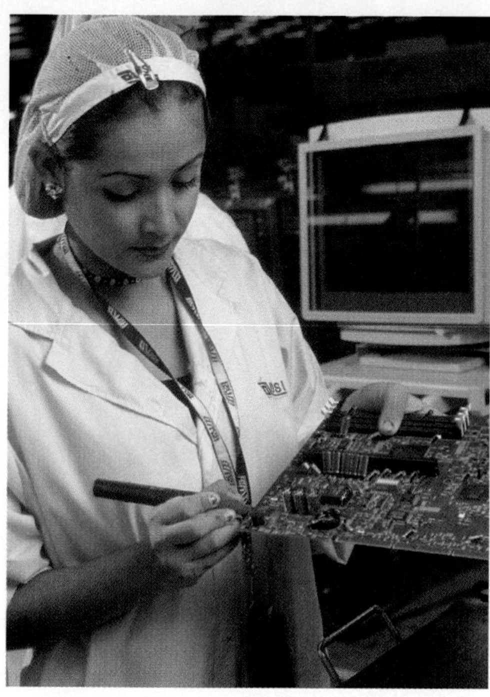

Supplement 11 **Learning Objectives**

AUTHOR COMMENT
Outsourcing is a supply-chain strategy that can deliver tremendous value to an organization.

WHAT IS OUTSOURCING?

Outsourcing is a creative management strategy. Indeed, some organizations use outsourcing to replace entire purchasing, information systems, marketing, finance, and operations departments. Outsourcing is applicable to firms throughout the world. And because outsourcing decisions are risky and many are not successful, making the right decision may mean the difference between success and failure.[1]

Because outsourcing grows by double digits every year, students and managers need to understand the issues, concepts, models, philosophies, procedures, and practices of outsourcing. This supplement describes current concepts, methodologies, and outsourcing strategies.

Outsourcing
Procuring from external sources services or products that are normally part of an organization.

Offshoring
Moving a business process to a foreign country but retaining control of it.

Outsourcing means procuring from external suppliers services or products that are normally a part of an organization. In other words, a firm takes functions it was performing in-house (such as accounting, janitorial, or call center functions) and has another company do the same job. If a company owns two plants and reallocates production from the first to the second, this is not considered outsourcing. If a company moves some of its business processes to a foreign country but retains control, we define this move as **offshoring**, not outsourcing. For example, China's Haier Group recently offshored a $40 million refrigerator factory to South Carolina (with huge savings in transportation costs). Or, as Thomas Friedman wrote in his book *The World is Flat*, "Offshoring is when a company takes one of its factories that it is operating in Canton, Ohio and moves the whole factory to Canton, China."

[1]The authors wish to thank Professor Marc J. Schneiderjans, of the University of Nebraska–Lincoln, for help with the development of this supplement. His book *Outsourcing and Insourcing in an International Context*, with Ashlyn Schniederjans and Dara Schniederjans (Armonk, NY: M.E. Sharpe, 2005), provided insight, content, and references that shaped our approach to the topic.

Early in their lives, many businesses handle their activities internally. As businesses mature and grow, however, they often find competitive advantage in the specialization provided by outside firms. They may also find limitations on locally available labor, services, materials, or other resources. So organizations balance the potential benefits of outsourcing with its potential risks. Outsourcing the wrong activities can cause major problems.

Outsourcing is not a new concept; it is simply an extension of the long-standing practice of *subcontracting* production activities. Indeed, the classic make-or-buy decision concerning products (which we discussed in Chapter 11) is an example of outsourcing.

So why has outsourcing expanded to become a major strategy in business the world over? From an economic perspective, it is due to the continuing move toward specialization in an increasingly technological society. More specifically, outsourcing's continuing growth is due to (1) increasing expertise, (2) reduced costs of more reliable transportation, and (3) the rapid development and deployment of advancements in telecommunications and computers. Low-cost communication, including the Internet, permits firms anywhere in the world to provide previously limited information services.

Examples of outsourcing include:

- Call centers for Brazil in Angola (a former Portuguese colony in Africa) and for the U.S. and England in India
- DuPont's legal services routed to the Philippines
- IBM handling travel services and payroll, and Hewlett-Packard providing IT services to P&G
- ADP providing payroll services for thousands of firms
- Production of the Audi A4 convertible and Mercedes CLK convertible by Wilheim Karmann in Osnabruck, Germany
- Blue Cross sending hip resurfacing surgery patients to India

VIDEO S11.1
Outsourcing Offshore at Darden

Outsourced manufacturing, also known as *contract manufacturing*, is becoming standard practice in many industries, from computers to automobiles.

Paralleling the growth of outsourcing is the growth of international trade. With the passage of landmark trade agreements like the North American Free Trade Agreement (NAFTA), the work of the World Trade Organization and the European Union, and other international trade zones established throughout the world, we are witnessing the greatest expansion of international commerce in history.

Table S11.1 provides a ranking of the top five and bottom five outsourcing locations (out of 50 countries) in the annual A.T. Kearney Global Options survey. Scores are based on a Global Services Location Index tallying financial attractiveness, workforce availability, employee skill set, and business environment.

▼ TABLE S11.1 Desirable Outsourcing Destinations

Rank	Country	Score
1	India	6.9
2	China	6.6
3	Malaysia	6.1
4	Thailand	6.0
5	Brazil	5.9
⋮		
46	Ukraine	4.9
47	France	4.9
48	Turkey	4.8
49	Portugal	4.8
50	Ireland	4.2

Source: Based on A. T. Kearney, 2009.

Types of Outsourcing Nearly any business activity can be outsourced. A general contractor in the building industry, who subcontracts various construction activities needed to build a home, is a perfect example of an outsourcer. Every component of the building process, including the architect's design, a consultant's site location analysis, a lawyer's work to obtain the building permits, plumbing, electrical work, dry walling, painting, furnace installation, landscaping, and sales, is usually outsourced. Outsourcing implies an agreement (typically a legally binding contract) with an external organization.

Among the business processes outsourced are (1) purchasing, (2) logistics, (3) R&D, (4) operation of facilities, (5) management of services, (6) human resources, (7) finance/accounting, (8) customer relations, (9) sales/marketing, (10) training, and (11) legal processes. Note that the first six of these are OM functions that we discuss in this text.

STRATEGIC PLANNING AND CORE COMPETENCIES

AUTHOR COMMENT Ford Motor used to mine its own ore, make and ship its own steel, and sell cars directly, but those days are long gone.

As we saw in Chapter 2, organizations develop missions, long-term goals, and strategies as general guides for operating their businesses. The strategic planning process begins with a basic mission statement and establishing goals. Given the mission and goals, strategic planners next undertake an internal analysis of the organization to identify how much or little each business activity contributes to the achievement of the mission.

During such an analysis, firms identify their strengths—what they do well or better than their competitors. These unique skills, talents, and capabilities are called **core competencies**. Core

Core competencies
An organization's unique skills, talents, and capabilities.

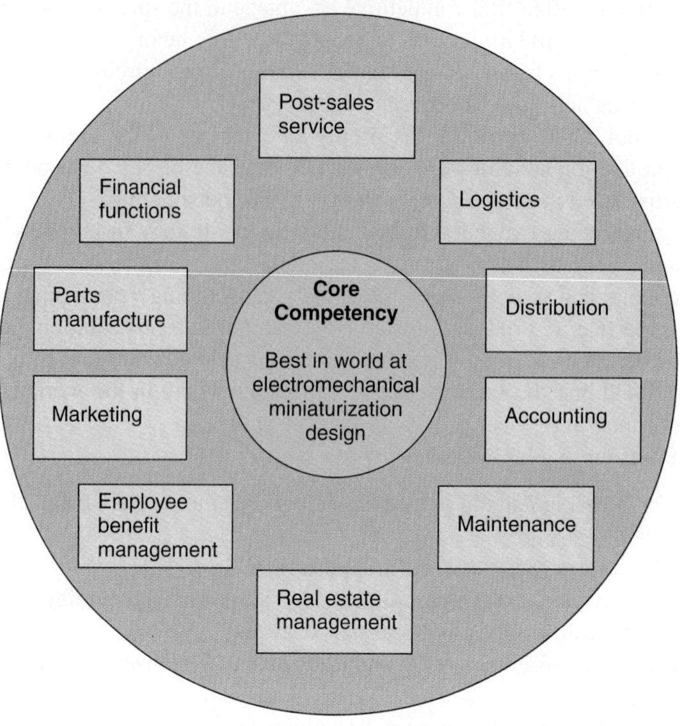

▶ **FIGURE S11.1 Sony, an Outsourcing Company**

Based on J. B. Quinn. "Outsourcing Innovation." *Sloan Management Review* (Summer 2000): 20.

LO1: Explain how core competencies relate to outsourcing

competencies may include specialized knowledge, proprietary technology or information, and unique production methods. The trick is to identify what the organization does better than anyone else. Common sense dictates that core competencies are the activities that a firm should perform. By contrast, *non-core activities*, which can be a sizable portion of an organization's total business, are good candidates for outsourcing.

Sony's core competency, for example, is electromechanical design of chips. This is its core, and Sony is one of the best in the world when it comes to rapid response and specialized production of these chips. But, as Figure S11.1 suggests, outsourcing could offer Sony continuous innovation and flexibility. Leading specialized outsource providers are likely to come up with major innovations in such areas as software, human resources, and distribution. That is their business, not Sony's.

Managers evaluate their strategies and core competencies and ask themselves how to use the assets entrusted to them. Do they want to be the offshore company that does low-margin work at 3%–4% or the innovative firm that makes a 30%–40% margin? PC or iPod assemblers in China and Taiwan earn 3%–4%, but Apple, which innovates, designs, and sells, has a margin 10 times as large.

To summarize, management must be cautious in outsourcing those elements of the product or service that provide a competitive advantage.

AUTHOR COMMENT
Author James Champy writes, "Although you may be good at something tactically, someone else may do it better and at lower cost."

The Theory of Comparative Advantage

The motivation for international outsourcing comes from the **theory of comparative advantage**. This theory focuses on the basic economics of outsourcing internationally. According to the theory, if an external provider, regardless of its geographic location, can perform activities more productively than the purchasing firm, then the external provider should do the work. This allows the purchasing firm to focus on what it does best, its core competencies.

Theory of comparative advantage
A theory which states that countries benefit from specializing in (and exporting) products and services in which they have relative advantage, and importing goods in which they have a relative disadvantage.

However, comparative advantage is not static. Companies, and indeed countries, strive to find comparative advantage. Countries such as India, China, and Russia have made it a government priority and set up agencies to support the easy transition of foreign firms into their outsourcing markets. Work and jobs go to countries that reduce risk through the necessary legal structures, effective infrastructure, and an educated workforce.

The dynamics of comparative advantage are evident from a recent study of five manufactured products. In an effort to meet "optimal" prices on auto parts in 2005, companies were moving work from Mexico to China. At that time China had a 22% price advantage on these parts over the U.S. But by 2009 that gap had dropped to 5.5%—and in some instances manufacturing in China was

In the ultimate risk in outsourcing, NASA has awarded contracts of $3.5 billion to a team, led by Orbital Sciences Corp., to ship cargo to the International Space Station starting in 2011. The company will be solely responsible for designing, building, and launching rockets on a regular basis. NASA hopes to save time and money by outsourcing.

20% more expensive than Mexico. As a result, some manufacturing began migrating back to Mexico and the U.S.; the price gap wasn't large enough to merit the hassle of manufacturing halfway around the world.[2]

Nonetheless, consistent with the theory of comparative advantage, the trend toward outsourcing continues to grow. This does not mean all existing outsourcing decisions are perfect. The term **backsourcing** has been used to describe the return of business activity to the original firm. We will now discuss the risks associated with outsourcing.

Backsourcing
The return of business activity to the original firm.

RISKS OF OUTSOURCING

AUTHOR COMMENT
The substantial risk in outsourcing requires managers to invest the effort to make sure they do it right.

Risk management starts with a realistic analysis of risks and results in a strategy that minimizes the impact of these uncertainties. Indeed, outsourcing can look very risky. And it is. Perhaps half of all outsourcing agreements fail because of inappropriate planning and analysis. For one thing, few promoters of international outsourcing mention the erratic power grids in some foreign countries or the difficulties with local government officials, inexperienced managers, and unmotivated employees. On the other hand, when managers set an outsourcing goal of 75% cost reduction and receive only a 30%–40% cost reduction, they view the outsourcing as a failure, when, in fact, it may be a success.

Quality can also be at risk. A recent survey of 150 North American companies found that, as a group, those that outsourced customer service saw a drop in their score on the American Consumer Satisfaction Index. We should point out that the declines were roughly the same whether companies outsourced domestically or overseas.[3]

LO2: Describe the risks of outsourcing

Another risk is the political backlash that results from outsourcing to foreign countries. The perceived loss of U.S. jobs (as well as the loss of jobs in European countries) has fueled anti-outsourcing rhetoric and action from government officials. (See the *OM in Action* box "Backsourcing to Small-Town U.S.A.").

Despite the negative impression created by government actions, the press, and public opinion, data suggest that foreigners outsource far more services to the U.S. than U.S. companies send abroad. And while U.S. jobs are outsourced, a minuscule few are outsourced offshore. A recent Organization for Economic Cooperation and Development (OECD) report on the subject shows that outsourcing is not as big a cause in job losses as, say, improved technology, and has an overall positive effect.[4] It is also a two-way street. India's cartoon producer Jadoo Works, for example, outsources projects to U.S. animators.

[2]"China's Eroding Advantage" *Business Week* (June 15, 2009): 54:55. The report dealt with five categories of machined products, ranging from large engine parts requiring significant labor to small plastic components that need little.

[3]J. Whitaker, M. S. Krishnan, and C. Fornell. "How Offshore Outsourcing Affects Customer Satisfaction." *The Wall Street Journal* (July 7, 2008): R4.

[4]"Outsourcing: Old Assumptions Are Being Challenged as the Outsourcing Industry Matures," *The Economist* (July 28, 2007): 65–66.

OM in Action ▶ Backsourcing to Small-Town U.S.A.

U.S. companies continue their global search for efficiency by outsourcing call centers and back-office operations, but many find they need to look no farther than a place like Dubuque, Iowa.

To U.S. firms facing quality problems with their outsourcing operations overseas and bad publicity at home, small-town America is emerging as a pleasant alternative. Dubuque (pop'n 57,313), Nacogdoches, Texas (pop'n 29,914), or Twin Falls, Idaho (pop'n 34,469), may be the perfect call center location. Even though the pay is only $8 an hour, the jobs are some of the best available to small-town residents.

By moving out of big cities to the cheaper labor and real estate of small towns, companies can save millions and still increase productivity. A call center in a town that just lost its major manufacturing plant finds the jobs easy to fill.

IBM, which has been criticized in the past for moving jobs to India and other offshore locations, picked Dubuque for its new remote computer-services center that opened in 2010 with 1,300 jobs.

Taking advantage of even cheaper wages in other countries will not stop soon, though. Is India the unstoppable overseas call center capital that people think it is? Not at all. Despite its population of 1.2 billion, only a small percent of its workers have the language skills and technical education to work in Western-style industries. Already, India has been warned that if call centers can't recruit at reasonable wages, its jobs will move to the Philippines, South Africa, and Ghana. And indeed, Dell, Apple, and Britain's Powergen have backsourced from Indian call centers, claiming their costs had become too high.

Sources: The Wall Street Journal (January 15, 2009): B2; (April 18–19, 2009): B1, B5; and (May 30/31, 2009): A14

Table S11.2 lists some of the risks inherent in outsourcing.

In addition to the external risks, operations managers must deal with other issues that outsourcing brings. These include (1) changes in employment levels, (2) changes in facilities and processes needed to receive components in a different state of assembly, and (3) vastly expanded logistics issues, including insurance, customs, and timing.

What can be done to mitigate the risks of outsourcing? Research indicates that of all the reasons given for outsourcing failure, the most common is that the decision was made without sufficient understanding and analysis. The next section provides a methodology that helps analyze the outsourcing decision process.

▶ TABLE S11.2
The Outsourcing Process and Related Risks

Outsourcing Process	Examples of Possible Risks
Identify non-core competencies	Can be incorrectly identified as a non-core competency.
Identify non-core activities that should be outsourced	Just because the activity is not a core competency for your firm does not mean an outsource provider is more competent and efficient.
Identify impact on existing facilities, capacity, and logistics	Failing to understand the change in resources and talents needed internally.
Establish goals and draft outsourcing agreement specifications	Setting goals so high that failure is certain.
Identify and select outsource provider	Selecting the wrong outsource provider.
Negotiate goals and measures of outsourcing performance	Misinterpreting measures and goals, how they are measured, and what they mean.
Monitor and control current outsourcing program	Being unable to control product development, schedules, and quality.
Evaluate and give feedback to outsource provider	Having a non-responsive provider (i.e., one that ignores feedback).
Evaluate international political and currency risks	Country's currency may be unstable, a country may be politically unstable, or cultural and language differences may inhibit successful operations.
Evaluate coordination needed for shipping and distribution	Understanding of the timing necessary to manage flows to different facilities and markets.

AUTHOR COMMENT
Cultural differences may indeed be why companies are less frequently outsourcing their call centers.

EVALUATING OUTSOURCING RISK WITH FACTOR RATING

The factor-rating method, first introduced in Chapter 8, is an excellent tool for dealing with both country risk assessment and provider selection problems.

AUTHOR COMMENT
The factor-rating model adds objectivity to decision making.

Rating International Risk Factors

Suppose a company has identified for outsourcing an area of production that is a non-core competency. Example S1 shows how to rate several international risk factors using an *unweighted* factor-rating approach.

EXAMPLE S1

Establishing risk factors for four countries

Toronto Airbags produces auto and truck airbags for Nissan, Chrysler, Mercedes, and BMW. It wants to conduct a risk assessment of outsourcing manufacturing. Four countries—England, Mexico, Spain, and Canada (the current home nation)—are being considered. Only English- or Spanish-speaking countries are included because they "fit" with organizational capabilities.

APPROACH: ▶ Toronto's management identifies nine factors, listed in Table S11.3, and rates each country on a 0–3 scale, where 0 is no risk and 3 is high risk. Risk ratings are added to find the lowest-risk location.

TABLE S11.3
Toronto Airbag's International Risk Factors, by Country (an unweighted approach)*

Risk Factor	England	Mexico	Spain	Canada (home country)
Economic: Labor cost/laws	1	0	2	1
Economic: Capital availability	0	2	1	0
Economic: Infrastructure	0	2	2	0
Culture: Language	0	0	0	0
Culture: Social norms	2	0	1	2
Migration: Uncontrolled	0	2	0	0
Politics: Ideology	2	0	1	2
Politics: Instability	0	1	2	2
Politics: Legalities	3	0	2	3
Total risk rating scores	8	7	11	10

*Risk rating scale: 0 = no risk, 1 = minor risk, 2 = average risk, 3 = high risk

SOLUTION ▶ Based on these ratings, Mexico is the least risky of the four locations being considered.

INSIGHT ▶ As with many other quantitative methods, assessing risk factors is not easy and may require considerable research, but the technique adds objectivity to a decision.

LEARNING EXERCISE ▶ Social norms in England have just been rescored by an economist, and the new rating is "no risk." How does this affect Toronto's decision? [Answer: England now has the lowest rating, at 6, for risk.]

RELATED PROBLEMS ▶ S11.1, S11.3

In Example S1, Toronto Airbags considered only English- and Spanish-speaking countries. But it is worth mentioning that countries like China, India, and Russia have millions of English-speaking personnel. This may have an impact on the final decision.

LO3: Use factor rating to evaluate both country and provider outsourcers

Example S1 considered the home country of the outsourcing firm. This inclusion helps document the risks that a domestic outsourcing provider poses compared to the risks posed by international providers. Including the home country in the analysis also helps justify final strategy selection to stakeholders who might question it.

Indeed, **nearshoring** (i.e., choosing an outsource provider located in the home country or in a nearby country) can be a good strategy for businesses and governments seeking both control and cost advantages. U.S. firms are interested in nearshoring to Canada because of Canada's cultural similarity and geographic nearness to the U.S. This allows the company wanting to outsource to exert more control than would be possible when outsourcing to most other countries. Nearshoring represents a compromise in which some cost savings are sacrificed for greater control because Canada's smaller wage differential limits the labor cost reduction advantage.

Nearshoring
Choosing an outsource provider in the home country or in a nearby country.

Rating Outsource Providers

In Chapter 8 (see Example 1) we illustrated the factor-rating method's computations when each factor has its own importance weight. We now apply that concept in Example S2 to compare outsourcing providers being considered by a firm.

EXAMPLE S2

Rating provider selection criteria

National Architects, Inc., a San Francisco–based designer of high-rise buildings, has decided to outsource its information technology (IT) function. Three outsourcing providers are being actively considered: one in the U.S., one in India, and one in Israel.

APPROACH: ▶ National's VP–Operations, Susan Cholette, has made a list of seven criteria she considers critical. After putting together a committee of four other VPs, she has rated each firm (on a 1–5 scale, with 5 being highest) and has also placed an importance weight on each of the factors, as shown in Table S11.4.

▶TABLE S11.4
Factor Ratings Applied to National Architects's Potential IT Outsourcing Providers

		Outsource Providers		
Factor (criterion)*	**Importance Weight**	**BIM (U.S.)**	**S.P.C. (India)**	**Telco (Israel)**
1. Can reduce operating costs	.2	3	3	5
2. Can reduce capital investment	.2	4	3	3
3. Skilled personnel	.2	5	4	3
4. Can improve quality	.1	4	5	2
5. Can gain access to technology not in company	.1	5	3	5
6. Can create additional capacity	.1	4	2	4
7. Aligns with policy/ philosophy/culture	.1	2	3	5
Totals	1.0	3.9	3.3	3.8

* These seven major criteria are based on a survey of 165 procurement executives, as reported in J. Schildhouse, "Outsourcing Ins and Outs," *Inside Supply Management* (December 2005): 22–29.

SOLUTION: ▶ Susan multiplies each rating by the weight and sums the products in each column to generate a total score for each outsourcing provider. She selects BIM, which has the highest overall rating.

INSIGHT: ▶ When the total scores are as close (3.9 vs. 3.8) as they are in this case, it is important to examine the sensitivity of the results to inputs. For example, if one of the importance weights or factor scores changes even marginally, the final selection may change. Management preference may also play a role here.

LEARNING EXERCISE: ▶ Susan decides that "Skilled personnel" should instead get a weight of 0.1 and "Aligns with policy/philosophy/culture" should increase to 0.2. How do the total scores change? [Answer: BIM = 3.6, S.P.C. = 3.2, and Telco = 4.0, so Telco is selected.]

RELATED PROBLEMS: ▶ S11.2, S11.4, S11.5, S11.6, S11.7

Most U.S. toy companies now outsource their production to Chinese manufacturers. Cost savings are significant, but there are several downsides, including loss of control over such issues as quality. In 2007 alone, Mattel had to recall 10.5 million Elmos, Big Birds, and SpongeBobs. These made-in-China toys contained excessive levels of lead in their paint. In 2008 the quality headlines dealt with poisonous pet food from China, and in 2009 it was tainted milk products.

ADVANTAGES AND DISADVANTAGES OF OUTSOURCING

Advantages of Outsourcing

LO4: List the advantages and disadvantages of outsourcing

As mentioned earlier, companies outsource for five main reasons. They are, in order of importance: (1) cost savings, (2) gaining outside expertise, (3) improving operations and service, (4) focusing on core competencies, and (5) gaining outside technology.

Cost Savings The number-one reason driving outsourcing for many firms is the possibility of significant cost savings, particularly for labor. (See the *OM in Action* box "Walmart's Link to China.")

Gaining Outside Expertise In addition to gaining access to a broad base of skills that are unavailable in-house, an outsourcing provider may be a source of innovation for improving products, processes, and services.

Improving Operations and Service An outsourcing provider may have production flexibility. This may allow the firm outsourcing its work to win orders by more quickly introducing new products and services.

Focusing on Core Competencies An outsourcing provider brings *its* core competencies to the supply chain. This frees up a firm's human, physical, and financial resources to reallocate to core competencies.

Gaining Outside Technology Firms can outsource to state-of-the-art providers instead of retaining old (legacy) systems. This means they do not have to invest in new technology, thereby cutting risks.

Other Advantages There are additional advantages in outsourcing. For example, a firm may improve its performance and image by associating with an outstanding supplier. Outsourcing can also be used as a strategy for downsizing, or "reengineering," a firm.

Disadvantages of Outsourcing

There are a number of potential disadvantages in outsourcing. Here are just a few.

Increased Transportation Costs Delivery costs may rise substantially if distance increases from an outsourcing provider to a firm using that provider.

Loss of Control This disadvantage can permeate and link to all other problems with outsourcing. When managers lose control of some operations, costs may increase because it's harder to assess and control them. For example, production of most of the world's laptops is now outsourced. This means that companies like Dell and HP find themselves using the same contractor (Quanta) to make their machines in China. This can leave them struggling to maintain control over the supplier.

OM in Action ► Walmart's Link to China

No other company has a more efficient supply chain, and no other company has embraced outsourcing to China more vigorously than Walmart. Perhaps as much as 85% of Walmart's merchandise is made abroad, and Chinese factories are by far the most important and fastest growing of these sources.

A whopping 10%–13% of everything China sends to the U.S. ends up on Walmart's shelves—over $15 billion worth of goods a year. Walmart has almost 600 people on the ground in China just to negotiate and make purchases.

As much as Walmart has been demonized for its part in offshoring jobs, its critical mass allows Chinese firms to build assembly lines that are so huge that they drive prices down through economies of scale.

Walmart's Chinese suppliers achieve startling, market-shaking price cuts. For example, the price of portable DVDs with 7″ LCD screens dropped in half when Walmart found a Chinese factory to build in giant quantities. Walmart's success in going abroad and pressing suppliers for price breaks has forced both retailers and manufacturers to reevaluate their supply chains.

The company has also led the way to sustainability and product safety through its "Responsible Sourcing" program, announced in 2008. Because Chinese products have been riddled with safety issues, Walmart in 2009 required "an identifiable trail" from raw materials to suppliers.

It also told its top 200 Chinese suppliers that they have until 2012 to become energy and resource efficient, cutting energy use by 20%.

Sources: *The Wall Street Journal* (October 22, 2008): B1; **About.com**: Logistics/Supply Chain (November 26, 2008); and *Financial Times* (December 12, 2008): 9.

Creating Future Competition Intel, for example, outsourced a core competency, chip production, to AMD when it could not keep up with early demands. Within a few years, AMD became a leading competitor, manufacturing its own chips.

Negative Impact on Employees Employee morale may drop when functions are outsourced, particularly when friends lose their jobs. Employees believe they may be next, and indeed they may be. Productivity, loyalty, and trust—all of which are needed for a healthy, growing business—may suffer.

Longer-Term Impact Some disadvantages of outsourcing tend to be longer term than the advantages of outsourcing. In other words, many of the risks firms run by outsourcing may not show up on the bottom line until some time in the future. This permits CEOs who prefer short-term planning and are interested only in bottom-line improvements to use the outsourcing strategy to make quick gains at the expense of longer-term objectives.

The advantages and disadvantages of outsourcing may or may not occur but should be thought of as possibilities to be managed effectively.

AUDITS AND METRICS TO EVALUATE PERFORMANCE

Regardless of the techniques and success in selection of outsourcing providers, agreements must specify results and outcomes. Whatever the outsourced component or service, management needs an evaluation process to ensure satisfactory continuing performance. At a minimum, the product or service must be defined in terms of quality, customer satisfaction, delivery, cost, and improvement. The mix and detail of the performance measures will depend on the nature of the product.

In situations where the outsourced product or service plays a major role in strategy and winning orders, the relationship needs to be more than after-the-fact audits and reports. It needs to be based on continuing communication, understanding, trust, and performance. The relationship should manifest itself in the mutual belief that "we are in this together" and go well beyond the written agreement.

However, when outsourcing is for less critical components, agreements that include the traditional mix of audits and metrics (such as cost, logistics, quality, and delivery) may be reported weekly or monthly. When a *service* has been outsourced, more imaginative metrics may be necessary. For instance, in an outsourced call center, these metrics may deal with personnel evaluation and training, call volume, call type, and response time, as well as tracking complaints. In this dynamic environment, reporting of such metrics may be required daily.

AUTHOR COMMENT Because outsourcing is rife with potential abuse, companies have to be careful not to harm individuals, societies, or nature.

ETHICAL ISSUES IN OUTSOURCING

Laws, trade agreements, and business practices are contributing to a growing set of international, ethical practices for the outsourcing industry. Table S11.5 presents several tenets of conduct that have fairly universal acceptance.

In the electronics industry, HP, Dell, IBM, Intel and twelve other companies have created the Electronics Industry Code of Conduct (EICC). The EICC sets environmental standards, bans child labor and excessive overtime, and audits outsourcing producers to ensure compliance.

TABLE S11.5 Ethical Principles and Related Outsourcing Linkages

Ethics Principle	Outsourcing Linkage
Do no harm to indigenous cultures	Avoid outsourcing in a way that violates religious holidays (e.g., making employees work during religious holidays).
Do no harm to the ecological systems	Don't use outsourcing to move pollution from one country to another.
Uphold universal labor standards	Don't use outsourcing to take advantage of cheap labor that leads to employee abuse.
Uphold basic human rights	Don't accept outsourcing that violates basic human rights.
Pursue long-term involvement	Don't use outsourcing as a short-term arrangement to reduce costs; view it as a long-term partnership.
Share knowledge and technology	Don't think outsourcing agreements will prevent loss of technology, but use the inevitable sharing to build good relationships.

SUPPLEMENT SUMMARY

Companies can give many different reasons why they outsource, but the reality is that outsourcing's most attractive feature is that it helps firms cut costs. Workers in low-cost countries simply work much more cheaply, with fewer fringe benefits, work rules, and legal restrictions, than their U.S. and European counterparts. For example, a comparable hourly wage of $20 in the U.S. and $30 in Europe is well above the $1.26 per hour in China. Yet China often achieves quality levels equivalent to (or even higher than) plants in the West.

There is a growing economic pressure to outsource. But there is also a need for planning outsourcing to make it acceptable to all participants. When outsourcing is done in the right way, it creates a win–win situation.

Key Terms

Outsourcing (p. 450)
Offshoring (p. 450)
Core competencies (p. 451)
Theory of comparative advantage (p. 452)
Backsourcing (p. 453)
Nearshoring (p. 455)

Discussion Questions

1. How would you summarize outsourcing trends?
2. What potential cost saving advantages might firms experience by using outsourcing?
3. What internal issues must managers address when outsourcing?
4. How should a company select an outsourcing provider?
5. What are international risk factors in the outsourcing decision?
6. How can ethics be beneficial in an outsourcing organization?
7. What are some of the possible consequences of poor outsourcing?

Using Software to Solve Outsourcing Problems

Excel, Excel OM, and POM for Windows may be used to solve most of the problems in this supplement.

Excel OM and POM for Windows both contain Factor Rating modules that can address issues such as the ones we saw in Examples S1 and S2. The Factor-Rating module was illustrated earlier in Program 8.1 in Chapter 8.

Problems*

• **S11.1** Claudia Program Technologies, Inc., has narrowed its choice of outsourcing provider to two firms located in different countries. Program wants to decide which one of the two countries is the better choice, based on risk-avoidance criteria. She has polled her executives and established four criteria. The resulting ratings for the two countries are presented in the table below, where 1 is a lower risk and 3 is a higher risk.

a) Using the unweighted factor-rating method, which country would you select?
b) If the first two factors (price and nearness) are given a weight of 2, and the last two factors (technology and history) are given a weight of 1, how does your answer change? PX

Selection Criterion	England	Canada
Price of service from outsourcer	2	3
Nearness of facilities to client	3	1
Level of technology	1	3
History of successful outsourcing	1	2

*Note: PX means the problem may be solved with POM for Windows and/or Excel OM.

• **S11.2** Using the same ratings given in Problem S11.1, assume that the executives have determined four criteria weightings: Price, with a weight of 0.1; Nearness, with 0.6; Technology, with 0.2; and History, with 0.1.

a) Using the weighted factor-rating method, which country would you select?
b) Double each of the weights used in part (a) (to 0.2, 1.2, 0.4, and 0.2, respectively). What effect does this have on your answer? Why? PX

• **S11.3** Ranga Ramasesh is the operations manager for a firm that is trying to decide which one of four countries it should research for possible outsourcing providers. The first step is to select a country based on cultural risk factors, which are critical to eventual business success with the provider. Ranga has reviewed outsourcing provider directories and found that the four countries in the table that follows have an ample number of providers from which they can choose. To aid in the country selection step, he has enlisted the aid of a cultural expert, John Wang, who has provided ratings of the various criteria in the table that follows. The resulting ratings are on a 1 to 10 scale, where 1 is a low risk and 10 is a high risk.

a) Using the unweighted factor-rating method, which country should Ranga select based on risk avoidance?

b) If Peru's ratings for "Society value of quality work" and "Individualism attitudes" are each lowered by 50%, how does your answer to part (a) change? PX

Culture Selection Criterion	Mexico	Panama	Costa Rica	Peru
Trust	1	2	2	1
Society value of quality work	7	10	9	10
Religious attitudes	3	3	3	5
Individualism attitudes	5	2	4	8
Time orientation attitudes	4	6	7	3
Uncertainty avoidance attitudes	3	2	4	2

•• **S11.4** Using the same ratings given in Problem S11.3(a), assume that John Wang has determined six criteria weightings: Trust, with a weight of 0.4; Quality, with 0.2; Religious, with 0.1; Individualism, with 0.1; Time, with 0.1; and Uncertainty, with 0.1. Using the weighted factor-rating method, which country should Ranga select? PX

•• **S11.5** Charles Teplitz's firm wishes to use factor rating to help select an outsourcing provider of logistics services.

a) With weights from 1–5 (5 highest) and ratings 1–100 (100 highest), use the following table to help Teplitz make his decision:

		Rating of Logistics Providers		
Criterion	**Weight**	**Atlanta Shipping**	**Seattle Delivery**	**Utah Freight**
Quality	5	90	80	75
Delivery	3	70	85	70
Cost	2	70	80	95

b) Teplitz decides to increase the weights for quality, delivery, and cost to 10, 6, and 4, respectively. How does this change your conclusions? Why?

c) If Atlanta Shipping's ratings for each of the factors increase by 10%, what are the new results? PX

• **S11.6** Walker Accounting Software is marketed to small accounting firms throughout the U.S. and Canada. Owner George Walker has decided to outsource the company's help desk and is considering three providers: Manila Call Center (Philippines), Delhi Services (India), and Moscow Bell (Russia). The following table summarizes the data Walker has assembled. Which outsourcing firm has the best rating? (Higher weights imply higher importance and higher ratings imply more desirable providers.) PX

		Provider Ratings		
Criterion	**Importance Weight**	**Manila**	**Delhi**	**Moscow**
Flexibility	0.5	5	1	9
Trustworthiness	0.1	5	5	2
Price	0.2	4	3	6
Delivery	0.2	5	6	6

•••• **S11.7** Price Technologies, a California-based high-tech manufacturer, is considering outsourcing some of its electronics production. Four firms have responded to its request for bids, and CEO Willard Price has started to perform an analysis on the scores his OM team has entered in the table below.

		Ratings of Outsource Providers			
Factor	**Weight**	**A**	**B**	**C**	**D**
Labor	w	5	4	3	5
Quality procedures	30	2	3	5	1
Logistics system	5	3	4	3	5
Price	25	5	3	4	4
Trustworthiness	5	3	2	3	5
Technology in place	15	2	5	4	4
Management team	15	5	4	2	1

Weights are on a scale from 1 through 30, and the outsourcing provider scores are on a scale of 1 through 5. The weight for the labor factor is shown as a w because Price's OM team cannot agree on a value for this weight. For what range of values of w, if any, is company C a recommended outsourcing provider, according to the factor-rating method?

Case Studies

▶ Outsourcing to Tata

While some states, such as Tennessee, have been quick to ban or limit international outsourcing of government activities, other state governments have sought to take advantage of low-cost opportunities that international outsourcing can offer.

The state of New Mexico's Labor Department hired Tata Consultancy Services, an Indian outsourcing firm, to redo New Mexico's unemployment compensation computer system. While Tata had completed work for other states, including Pennsylvania and New York, it had never worked on an unemployment compensation system. Also, New Mexico agreed to allow Tata to do all computer software work in India, apparently with insufficient monitoring of progress by New Mexico officials responsible for the outsourcing project.

The new system should have been completed in 6 months, which put the due date in December 2001. Unfortunately, things did not work out well. The initial system was delivered 1 year later. But in late 2004 it was still not working. Also, the outsourcing project went way over the budget of $3.6 million, up to $13 million. The warranty for the system ended in 2003, leaving New Mexico with a situation of either suing Tata to complete the project (it was estimated at 80% complete) or hiring someone to fix it. Tata's position was that it had complied with the outsourcing agreement and was willing to continue fixing the system if it could receive additional compensation to justify additional work.

Discussion Questions

1. Use the process in Table S11.2 to analyze what New Mexico could have done to achieve a more successful outcome.
2. Is this a case of cultural misunderstanding, or could the same result have occurred if a U.S. firm, such as IBM, had been selected?
3. Conduct your own research to assess the risks of outsourcing any information technology project. (*Computerworld* is one good source.)

▶ Outsourcing Offshore at Darden

Video Case

Darden Restaurants, owner of popular brands such as Olive Garden and Red Lobster, serves more than 300 million meals annually in over 1,700 restaurants across the U.S. and Canada. To achieve competitive advantage via its supply chain, Darden must achieve excellence at each step. With purchases from 35 countries, and seafood products with a shelf life as short as 4 days, this is a complex and challenging task.

Those 300 million meals annually mean 40 million pounds of shrimp and huge quantities of tilapia, swordfish, and other fresh purchases. Fresh seafood is typically flown to the U.S. and monitored each step of the way to ensure that 34°F is maintained.

Darden's purchasing agents travel the world to find competitive advantage in the supply chain. Darden personnel from supply chain and development, quality assurance, and environmental relations contribute to developing, evaluating, and checking suppliers. Darden also has seven native-speaking representatives living on other continents to provide continuing support and evaluation of suppliers. All suppliers must abide by Darden's food standards, which typically exceed FDA and other industry standards. Darden expects continuous improvement in durable relationships that increase quality and reduce cost.

Darden's aggressiveness and development of a sophisticated supply chain provides an opportunity for outsourcing. Much food preparation is labor intensive and is often more efficient when handled in bulk. This is particularly true where large volumes may justify capital investment. For instance, Tyson and Iowa Beef prepare meats to Darden's specifications much more economically than can individual restaurants. Similarly, Darden has found that it can outsource both the cutting of salmon to the proper portion size and the cracking/peeling of shrimp more cost-effectively offshore than in U.S. distribution centers or individual restaurants.

Discussion Questions*

1. What are some outsourcing opportunities in a restaurant?
2. What supply-chain issues are unique to a firm sourcing from 35 countries?
3. Examine how other firms or industries develop international supply chains as compared to Darden.
4. Why does Darden outsource harvesting and preparation of much of its seafood?

*You may wish to view the video that accompanies this case study before answering these questions.

Bibliography

Aron, R., and J. V. Singh. "Getting Offshoring Right." *Harvard Business Review* (December 2005): 135–143.

Bravard, J., and R. Morgan. *Smarter Outsourcing.* Upper Saddle River, NJ: Pearson (2006).

Champy, James. *Avoiding the Seven Deadly Sins of Outsourcing Relationships.* Plano, TX: Perot Systems (2005).

Friedman, Thomas. *The World Is Flat: A Brief History of the 21st Century.* New York: Farrar, Straus, and Giroux (2005).

Greenwald, Bruce C., and Judd Kahn. *Globalization: The Irrational Fear That Someone in China Will Take Your Job.* New York: Wiley (2009).

Halvey, J. K., and B. M. Melby. *Business Process Outsourcing,* 2nd ed. New York: Wiley (2007).

Hirschheim, R., A. Heinzl, and J. Dibbern. *Information Systems Outsourcing.* Secaucus, NJ: Springer (2009).

Lee, Hau L., and Chung-Yee Lee. *Building Supply Chain Excellence in Emerging Economies.* Secaucus, NJ: Springer (2007).

Messner, W. *Working with India*, Secaucus, NJ: Springer (2009).

Midler, Paul. *Poorly Made in China: An Insider's Account of the Tactics behind China's Production Game.* New York: Wiley (2009).

Thomas, A. R., and T. J. Wilkinson. "The Outsourcing Compulsion." *MIT Sloan Management Review* 48, no. 1 (Fall 2006): 10.

Webb, L., and J. Laborde. "Crafting a Successful Outsourcing Vendor/Client Relationship." *Business Process Management Journal* 11, no. 5 (2005): 437–443.

Whitten, Dwayne, and Dorothy Leidner. "Bringing IT Back: An Analysis of the Decision to Backsource or Switch Vendors." *Decision Sciences* 37, no. 4 (November 2006): 605–621.

Yourdon, Edward. *Outsource: Competing in the Global Productivity Race.* Upper Saddle River, NJ: Prentice Hall (2005).

Supplement 11 *Rapid* Review

Main Heading	Review Material	myomlab
WHAT IS OUTSOURCING? (pp. 450–451)	■ **Outsourcing**—Procuring from external sources services or products that are normally part of an organization. Some organizations use outsourcing to replace entire purchasing, information systems, marketing, finance, and operations departments. ■ **Offshoring**—Moving a business process to a foreign country but retaining control of it. Outsourcing is not a new concept; it is simply an extension of the long-standing practice of *subcontracting* production activities. Outsourced manufacturing, also known as contract manufacturing, is becoming standard practice in many industries. Outsourcing implies an agreement (typically a legally binding contract) with an external organization.	**VIDEO S11.1** Outsourcing offshore at Darden
STRATEGIC PLANNING AND CORE COMPETENCIES (pp. 451–453)	■ **Core competencies**—An organization's unique skills, talents, and capabilities. Core competencies may include specialized knowledge, proprietary technology or information, and unique production methods. *Non-core activities*, which can be a sizable portion of an organization's total business, are good candidates for outsourcing. ■ **Theory of comparative advantage**—A theory which states that countries benefit from specializing in (and exporting) products and services in which they have relative advantage and importing goods in which they have a relative disadvantage. ■ **Backsourcing**—The return of business activity to the original firm.	
RISKS OF OUTSOURCING (pp. 453–454)	Perhaps half of all outsourcing agreements fail because of inappropriate planning and analysis. Potential risks of outsourcing include: • In some countries, erratic power grids, difficult local government officials, inexperienced managers, or unmotivated employees • A drop in quality or customer service • Political backlash that results from outsourcing to foreign countries • Changes in employment levels • Changes in facilities and processes needed to receive components in a different state of assembly • Vastly expanded logistics issues, including insurance, customs, and timing The most common reason given for outsourcing failure is that the decision was made without sufficient understanding and analysis.	
EVALUATING OUTSOURCING RISK WITH FACTOR RATING (pp. 455–456)	The factor-rating method is an excellent tool for dealing with both country risk assessment and provider selection problems. Including the home country of the outsourcing firm in a factor-rating analysis helps document the risks that a domestic outsourcing provider poses compared to the risks posed by international providers. Including the home country in the analysis also helps justify final strategy selection to stakeholders who might question it. ■ **Nearshoring**—Choosing an outsource provider in the home country or in a nearby country. Nearshoring can be a good strategy for businesses and governments seeking both control and cost advantages.	 Problems: S11.1–S11.7
ADVANTAGES AND DISADVANTAGES OF OUTSOURCING (pp. 457–458)	Advantages of outsourcing include: • *Cost savings*: The number-one reason driving outsourcing for many firms is the possibility of significant cost savings, particularly for labor. • *Gaining outside expertise*: In addition to gaining access to a broad base of skills that are unavailable in-house, an outsourcing provider may be a source of innovation for improving products, processes, and services. • *Improving operations and service*: An outsourcing provider may have production flexibility. This may allow the client firm to win orders by more quickly introducing new products and services. • *Focusing on core competencies*: An outsourcing provider brings *its* core competencies to the supply chain. This frees up the firm's human, physical, and financial resources to reallocate to the firm's own core competencies.	

Main Heading	Review Material
	• *Gaining outside technology*: Firms can outsource to state-of-the-art providers instead of retaining old (legacy) systems. These firms do not have to invest in new technology, thereby cutting risks. • *Other advantages*: The client firm may improve its performance and image by associating with an outstanding supplier. Outsourcing can also be used as a strategy for downsizing, or "reengineering," a firm. Potential disadvantages of outsourcing include: • *Increased transportation costs*: Delivery costs may rise substantially if distance increases from an outsourcing provider to a client firm. • *Loss of control*: This disadvantage can permeate and link to all other problems with outsourcing. When managers lose control of some operations, costs may increase because it's harder to assess and control them. • *Creating future competitors* • *Negative impact on employees*: Employee morale may drop when functions are outsourced, particularly when friends lose their jobs. • *Longer-term impact*: Some disadvantages of outsourcing tend to be longer term than the advantages of outsourcing. In other words, many of the risks firms run by outsourcing may not show up on the bottom line until some time in the future.
AUDITS AND METRICS TO EVALUATE PERFORMANCE (p. 458)	Outsourcing agreements must specify results and outcomes. Management needs an evaluation process to ensure satisfactory continuing performance. At a minimum, the product or service must be defined in terms of quality, customer satisfaction, delivery, cost, and improvement. When the outsourced product or service plays a major role in strategy and winning orders, the relationship needs to be based on continuing communication, understanding, trust, and performance.
ETHICAL ISSUES IN OUTSOURCING (p. 458)	Some outsourcing policies linked to ethical principles include avoid outsourcing in a way that violates religious holidays; don't use outsourcing to move pollution from one country to another; don't use outsourcing to take advantage of cheap labor that leads to employee abuse; don't accept outsourcing that violates basic human rights; don't use outsourcing as a short-term arrangement to reduce costs—view it as a long-term partnership; and don't think an outsourcing agreement will prevent loss of technology, but use the inevitable sharing to build a good relationship with outsourcing firms.

***Self* Test**

■ **Before taking the self-test,** refer to the learning objectives listed at the beginning of the supplement and the key terms listed at the end of the supplement.

LO1. Core competencies are those strengths in a firm that include:
- **a)** specialized skills.
- **b)** unique production methods.
- **c)** proprietary information/knowledge.
- **d)** things a company does better than others.
- **e)** all of the above.

LO2. Outsourcing can be a risky proposition because:
- **a)** about half of all outsourcing agreements fail.
- **b)** it saves only about 30% in labor costs.
- **c)** labor costs are increasing throughout the world.
- **d)** a non-core competency is outsourced.
- **e)** shipping costs are increasing.

LO3. Evaluating outsourcing providers by comparing their weighted average scores involves:
- **a)** factor-rating analysis.
- **b)** cost-volume analysis.
- **c)** transportation model analysis.
- **d)** linear regression analysis.
- **e)** crossover analysis.

LO4. Advantages of outsourcing include:
- **a)** focusing on core competencies and cost savings.
- **b)** gaining outside technology and creating new markets in India for U.S. products.
- **c)** improving operations by closing plants in Malaysia.
- **d)** employees wanting to leave the firm.
- **e)** reduced problems with logistics

Answers: LO1. e; LO2. a; LO3. a; LO4. a.

12 Inventory Management

Chapter Outline

OM Strategy Decisions

- Design of Goods and Services
- Managing Quality
- Process Strategy
- Location Strategies
- Layout Strategies
- Human Resources
- Supply-Chain Management
- **Inventory Management**
  - Independent Demand
  - Dependent Demand
  - JIT & Lean Operations
- Scheduling
- Maintenance

INVENTORY MANAGEMENT PROVIDES COMPETITIVE ADVANTAGE AT AMAZON.COM

When Jeff Bezos opened his revolutionary business in 1995, Amazon.com was intended to be a "virtual" retailer—no inventory, no warehouses, no overhead—just a bunch of computers taking orders and authorizing others to fill them. Things clearly didn't work out that way. Now, Amazon stocks millions of items of inventory, amid hundreds of thousands of bins on metal shelves, in warehouses (seven around the U.S. and three in Europe) that have twice the floor space of the Empire State Building.

Precisely managing this massive inventory has forced Amazon into becoming a world-class leader in warehouse management and automation, with annual sales of over $20 billion to 88 million customers. This profile shows what goes on to accurately fill orders.

When you place an order at Amazon.com, not only are you doing business with an Internet company, you are doing business with a company that obtains competitive advantage through inventory management.

1. You order three items, and a computer in Seattle takes charge. A computer assigns your order—a book, a game, and a digital camera—to one of Amazon's massive U.S. distribution centers, such as the 750,000-square-foot facility in Coffeyville, Kansas.

2. The "flow meister" in Coffeyville receives your order. She determines which workers go where to fill your order.

3. Rows of red lights show which products are ordered. Workers move from bulb to bulb, retrieving an item from the shelf above and pressing a button that resets the light. This is known as a "pick-to-light" system. This system doubles the picking speed of manual operators and drops the error rate to nearly zero.

4. Your items are put into crates on moving belts. Each item goes into a large green crate that contains many customers' orders. When full, the crates ride a series of conveyor belts that wind more than 10 miles through the plant at a constant speed of 2.9 feet per second. The bar code on each item is scanned 15 times, by machines and by many of the 600 workers. The goal is to reduce errors to zero—returns are very expensive.

5. All three items converge in a chute and then inside a box. All the crates arrive at a central point where bar codes are matched with order numbers to determine who gets what. Your three items end up in a 3-foot-wide chute—one of several thousand—and are placed into a cardboard box with a new bar code that identifies your order. Picking is sequenced to reduce operator travel.

6. Any gifts you've chosen are wrapped by hand. Amazon trains an elite group of gift wrappers, each of whom processes 30 packages an hour.

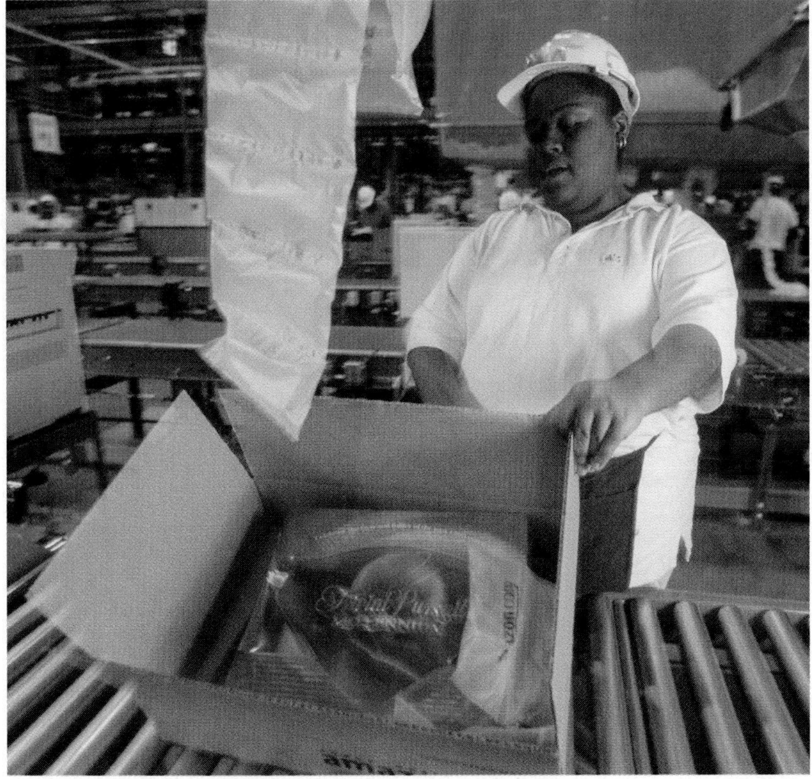

7. The box is packed, taped, weighed, and labeled before leaving the warehouse in a truck. The Coffeyville plant was designed to ship as many as 200,000 pieces a day. About 60% of orders are shipped via the U.S. Postal Service; nearly everything else goes through United Parcel Service.

8. Your order arrives at your doorstep. In one or two days, your order is delivered.

Chapter 12 **Learning Objectives**

THE IMPORTANCE OF INVENTORY

As Amazon.com well knows, inventory is one of the most expensive assets of many companies, representing as much as 50% of total invested capital. Operations managers around the globe have long recognized that good inventory management is crucial. On the one hand, a firm can reduce costs by reducing inventory. On the other hand, production may stop and customers become dissatisfied when an item is out of stock. *The objective of inventory management is to strike a balance between inventory investment and customer service*. You can never achieve a low-cost strategy without good inventory management.

All organizations have some type of inventory planning and control system. A bank has methods to control its inventory of cash. A hospital has methods to control blood supplies and pharmaceuticals. Government agencies, schools, and, of course, virtually every manufacturing and production organization are concerned with inventory planning and control.

In cases of physical products, the organization must determine whether to produce goods or to purchase them. Once this decision has been made, the next step is to forecast demand, as discussed in Chapter 4. Then operations managers determine the inventory necessary to service that demand. In this chapter, we discuss the functions, types, and management of inventory. We then address two basic inventory issues: how much to order and when to order.

Functions of Inventory

VIDEO 12.1
Frito-Lay's Inventory

Inventory can serve several functions that add flexibility to a firm's operations. The four functions of inventory are:

1. To "*decouple*" *or separate various parts of the production process*. For example, if a firm's supplies fluctuate, extra inventory may be necessary to decouple the production process from suppliers.

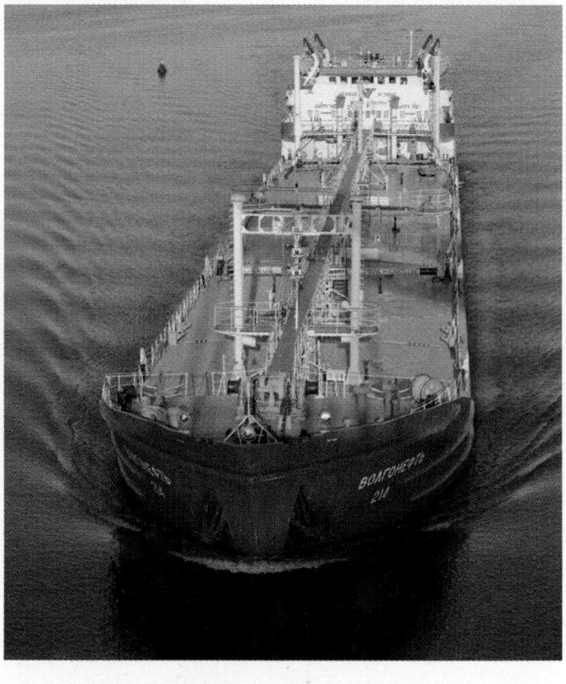

Hedging inventories of oil is complicated when onshore storage units are full. This supertanker is the world's newest kind of inventory warehouse. When oil traders are betting that prices will rise and want to store oil, a supertanker may be used as a warehouse. These huge floating warehouses can stay at sea for months, waiting for a price that makes the hedge successful.

2. To *decouple the firm from fluctuations in demand* and *provide a stock of goods that will provide a selection for customers*. Such inventories are typical in retail establishments.
3. To *take advantage of quantity discounts*, because purchases in larger quantities may reduce the cost of goods or their delivery.
4. To *hedge against inflation* and upward price changes (as shown in the supertanker photo).

Types of Inventory

To accommodate the functions of inventory, firms maintain four types of inventories: (1) raw material inventory, (2) work-in-process inventory, (3) maintenance/repair/operating supply (MRO) inventory, and (4) finished-goods inventory.

Raw material inventory has been purchased but not processed. This inventory can be used to decouple (i.e., separate) suppliers from the production process. However, the preferred approach is to eliminate supplier variability in quality, quantity, or delivery time so that separation is not needed. **Work-in-process (WIP) inventory** is components or raw material that have undergone some change but are not completed. WIP exists because of the time it takes for a product to be made (called *cycle time*). Reducing cycle time reduces inventory. Often this task is not difficult: During most of the time a product is "being made," it is in fact sitting idle. As Figure 12.1. shows, actual work time, or "run" time, is a small portion of the material flow time, perhaps as low as 5%.

MROs are inventories devoted to **maintenance/repair/operating** supplies necessary to keep machinery and processes productive. They exist because the need and timing for maintenance and repair of some equipment are unknown. Although the demand for MRO inventory is often a function of maintenance schedules, other unscheduled MRO demands must be anticipated. **Finished-goods inventory** is completed product awaiting shipment. Finished goods may be inventoried because future customer demands are unknown.

Raw material inventory
Materials that are usually purchased but have yet to enter the manufacturing process.

Work-in-process (WIP) inventory
Products or components that are no longer raw materials but have yet to become finished products.

MRO
Maintenance, repair, and operating materials.

Finished-goods inventory
An end item ready to be sold, but still an asset on the company's books.

MANAGING INVENTORY

Operations managers establish systems for managing inventory. In this section, we briefly examine two ingredients of such systems: (1) how inventory items can be classified (called *ABC analysis*) and (2) how accurate inventory records can be maintained. We will then look at inventory control in the service sector.

AUTHOR COMMENT
Firms must carefully control critical items, keep accurate records, count inventory regularly, and avoid theft and damage.

ABC Analysis

ABC analysis divides on-hand inventory into three classifications on the basis of annual dollar volume. ABC analysis is an inventory application of what is known as the *Pareto principle* (named after Vilfredo Pareto, a 19th century Italian economist). The Pareto principle states that there are a "critical few and trivial many." The idea is to establish inventory policies that focus resources on the *few critical* inventory parts and not the many trivial ones. It is not realistic to monitor inexpensive items with the same intensity as very expensive items.

ABC analysis
A method for dividing on-hand inventory into three classifications based on annual dollar volume.

To determine annual dollar volume for ABC analysis, we measure the *annual demand* of each inventory item times the *cost per unit*. *Class A* items are those on which the annual dollar volume

▼ FIGURE 12.1 **The Material Flow Cycle**
Most of the time that work is in-process (95% of the cycle time) is not productive time.

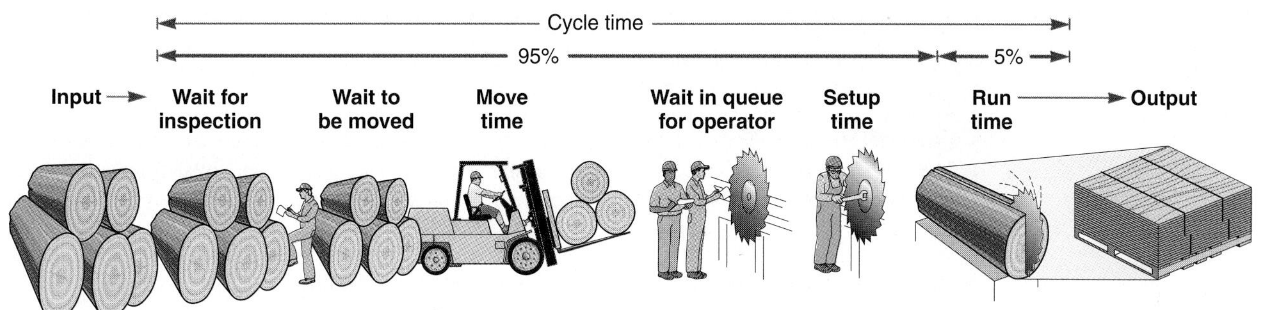

▶ **FIGURE 12.2**
Graphic Representation of ABC Analysis

AUTHOR COMMENT
A, B, and C categories need not be exact. The idea is to recognize that levels of control should match the risk.

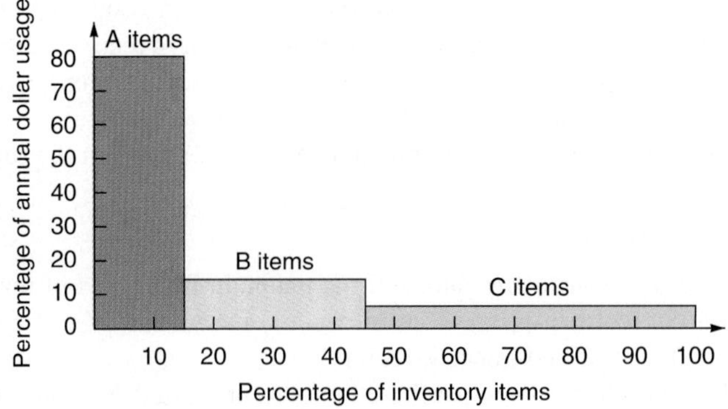

is high. Although such items may represent only about 15% of the total inventory items, they represent 70% to 80% of the total dollar usage. *Class B* items are those inventory items of medium annual dollar volume. These items may represent about 30% of inventory items and 15% to 25% of the total value. Those with low annual dollar volume are *Class C*, which may represent only 5% of the annual dollar volume but about 55% of the total inventory items.

Graphically, the inventory of many organizations would appear as presented in Figure 12.2. An example of the use of ABC analysis is shown in Example 1.

EXAMPLE 1 ▶

ABC analysis for a chip manufacturer

Silicon Chips, Inc., maker of superfast DRAM chips, wants to categorize its 10 major inventory items using ABC analysis.

APPROACH ▶ ABC analysis organizes the items on an annual dollar-volume basis. Shown below (in columns 1–4) are the 10 items (identified by stock numbers), their annual demands, and unit costs.

SOLUTION ▶ Annual dollar volume is computed in column 5, along with the percentage of the total represented by each item in column 6. Column 7 groups the 10 items into A, B, and C categories.

ABC Calculation

(1) Item Stock Number	(2) Percentage of Number of Items Stocked	(3) Annual Volume (units)	×	(4) Unit Cost	=	(5) Annual Dollar Volume	(6) Percentage of Annual Dollar Volume		(7) Class
#10286	20%	1,000		$ 90.00		$ 90,000	38.8%	72%	A
#11526		500		154.00		77,000	33.2%		A
#12760		1,550		17.00		26,350	11.3%		B
#10867	30%	350		42.86		15,001	6.4%	23%	B
#10500		1,000		12.50		12,500	5.4%		B
#12572		600		14.17		8,502	3.7%		C
#14075		2,000		.60		1,200	.5%		C
#01036	50%	100		8.50		850	.4%	5%	C
#01307		1,200		.42		504	.2%		C
#10572		250		.60		150	.1%		C
		8,550				$232,057	100.0%		

LO1: Conduct an ABC analysis

INSIGHT ▶ The breakdown into A, B, and C categories is not hard and fast. The objective is to try to separate the "important" from the "unimportant."

LEARNING EXERCISE ▶ The unit cost for Item #10286 has increased from $90.00 to $120.00. How does this impact the ABC analysis? [Answer: The total annual dollar volume increases by $30,000, to $262,057, and the two A items now comprise 75% of that amount.]

RELATED PROBLEMS ▶ 12.1, 12.2, 12.3

EXCEL OM Data File **Ch12Ex1.xls** can be found at **www.pearsonhighered.com/heizer**.

Criteria other than annual dollar volume can determine item classification. For instance, anticipated engineering changes, delivery problems, quality problems, or high unit cost may dictate upgrading items to a higher classification. The advantage of dividing inventory items into classes allows policies and controls to be established for each class.

Policies that may be based on ABC analysis include the following:

1. Purchasing resources expended on supplier development should be much higher for individual A items than for C items.
2. A items, as opposed to B and C items, should have tighter physical inventory control; perhaps they belong in a more secure area, and perhaps the accuracy of inventory records for A items should be verified more frequently.
3. Forecasting A items may warrant more care than forecasting other items.

Better forecasting, physical control, supplier reliability, and an ultimate reduction in safety stock can all result from appropriate inventory management policies. ABC analysis guides the development of those policies.

Record Accuracy

Good inventory policies are meaningless if management does not know what inventory is on hand. Accuracy of records is a critical ingredient in production and inventory systems. Record accuracy allows organizations to focus on those items that are needed, rather than settling for being sure that "some of everything" is in inventory. Only when an organization can determine accurately what it has on hand can it make precise decisions about ordering, scheduling, and shipping.

To ensure accuracy, incoming and outgoing record keeping must be good, as must be stockroom security. A well-organized stockroom will have limited access, good housekeeping, and storage areas that hold fixed amounts of inventory. Bins, shelf space, and parts will be labeled accurately. The U.S. Marines' approach to improved inventory record accuracy is discussed in the *OM in Action* box "What the Marines Learned about Inventory from Walmart."

Cycle Counting

Even though an organization may have made substantial efforts to record inventory accurately, these records must be verified through a continuing audit. Such audits are known as **cycle counting**. Historically, many firms performed annual physical inventories. This practice often meant shutting down the facility and having inexperienced people count parts and material. Inventory records should instead be verified via cycle counting. Cycle counting uses inventory classifications developed through ABC analysis. With cycle counting procedures, items are counted, records are verified, and inaccuracies are periodically documented. The cause of inaccuracies is then traced and appropriate remedial action taken to ensure integrity of the inventory system.

Cycle counting
A continuing reconciliation of inventory with inventory records.

OM in Action ► What the Marines Learned about Inventory from Walmart

The U.S. Marine Corps knew it had inventory problems. A few years ago, when a soldier at Camp Pendleton, near San Diego, put in an order for a spare part, it took him a week to get it—from the other side of the base. Worse, the Corps had 207 computer systems worldwide. Called the "Rats' Nest" by Marine techies, most systems didn't even talk to each other.

To execute a victory over uncontrolled supplies, the Corps studied Walmart, Caterpillar, Inc., and UPS. "We're in the middle of a revolution," says General Gary McKissock. McKissock aims to reduce inventory for the Corps by half, saving $200 million, and to shift 2,000 Marines from inventory detail to the battlefield.

By replacing inventory with information, the Corps won't have to stockpile tons of supplies near the battlefield, as it did during the Gulf War, only to find it couldn't keep track of what was in containers. Then there was the Marine policy requiring a 60-day supply of everything. McKissock figured out there was no need to overstock commodity items, like office supplies, that can be obtained anywhere. And with advice from the private sector, the Marines have been upgrading warehouses, adding wireless scanners for real-time inventory placement and tracking. Now, if containers need to be sent into a war zone, they will have radio frequency transponders that, when scanned, will link to a database detailing what's inside.

Sources: Modern Materials Handling (August 2005): 24–25; and *BusinessWeek* (December 24, 2001): 24.

At John Deere, two workers fill orders for 3,000 parts from a six-stand carousel system, using a sophisticated computer system. The computer saves time searching for parts and speeds orders in the miles of warehouse shelving. While a worker pulls a part from one carousel, the computer sends the next request to the adjacent carousel.

A items will be counted frequently, perhaps once a month; **B** items will be counted less frequently, perhaps once a quarter; and **C** items will be counted perhaps once every 6 months. Example 2 illustrates how to compute the number of items of each classification to be counted each day.

EXAMPLE 2 ▶

Cycle counting at a truck manufacturer

Cole's Trucks, Inc., a builder of high-quality refuse trucks, has about 5,000 items in its inventory. It wants to determine how many items to cycle count each day.

APPROACH ▶ After hiring Matt Clark, a bright young OM student, for the summer, the firm determined that it has 500 A items, 1,750 B items, and 2,750 C items. Company policy is to count all A items every month (every 20 working days), all B items every quarter (every 60 working days), and all C items every 6 months (every 120 working days). The firm then allocates some items to be counted each day.

SOLUTION ▶

Item Class	*Quantity*	*Cycle Counting Policy*	*Number of Items Counted per Day*
A	500	Each month (20 working days)	500/20 = 25/day
B	1,750	Each quarter (60 working days)	1,750/60 = 29/day
C	2,750	Every 6 months (120 working days)	2,750/120 = 23/day
			77/day

Seventy-seven items are counted each day.

INSIGHT ▶ This daily audit of 77 items is much more efficient and accurate than conducting a massive inventory count once a year.

LEARNING EXERCISE ▶ Cole's reclassifies some B and C items so there are now 1,500 B items and 3,000 C items. How does this change the cycle count? [Answer: B and C both change to 25 items each per day, for a total of 75 items per day.]

RELATED PROBLEM ▶ 12.4

LO 2: Explain and use cycle counting

In Example 2, the particular items to be cycle counted can be sequentially or randomly selected each day. Another option is to cycle count items when they are reordered.

Cycle counting also has the following advantages:

1. Eliminates the shutdown and interruption of production necessary for annual physical inventories.
2. Eliminates annual inventory adjustments.
3. Trained personnel audit the accuracy of inventory.

4. Allows the cause of the errors to be identified and remedial action to be taken.
5. Maintains accurate inventory records.

Control of Service Inventories

Management of service inventories deserves special consideration. Although we may think of the service sector of our economy as not having inventory, that is not always the case. For instance, extensive inventory is held in wholesale and retail businesses, making inventory management crucial and often a factor in a manager's advancement. In the food-service business, for example, control of inventory can make the difference between success and failure. Moreover, inventory that is in transit or idle in a warehouse is lost value. Similarly, inventory damaged or stolen prior to sale is a loss. In retailing, inventory that is unaccounted for between receipt and time of sale is known as **shrinkage**. Shrinkage occurs from damage and theft as well as from sloppy paperwork. Inventory theft is also known as **pilferage**. Retail inventory loss of 1% of sales is considered good, with losses in many stores exceeding 3%. Because the impact on profitability is substantial, inventory accuracy and control are critical. Applicable techniques include the following:

Shrinkage
Retail inventory that is unaccounted for between receipt and sale.

Pilferage
A small amount of theft.

1. *Good personnel selection, training, and discipline:* These are never easy but very necessary in food-service, wholesale, and retail operations, where employees have access to directly consumable merchandise.
2. *Tight control of incoming shipments:* This task is being addressed by many firms through the use of bar-code and radio frequency ID (RFID) systems that read every incoming shipment and automatically check tallies against purchase orders. When properly designed, these systems are very hard to defeat. Each item has its own unique stock keeping unit (SKU; pronounced "skew").
3. *Effective control of all goods leaving the facility:* This job is accomplished with bar codes on items being shipped, magnetic strips on merchandise, or via direct observation. Direct observation can be personnel stationed at exits (as at Costco and Sam's Club wholesale stores) and in potentially high-loss areas or can take the form of one-way mirrors and video surveillance.

A handheld reader can scan RFID tags, aiding control of both incoming and outgoing shipments.

Successful retail operations require very good store-level control with accurate inventory in its proper location. One recent study found that consumers and clerks could not find 16% of the items at one of the U.S.'s largest retailers—not because the items were out of stock but because they were misplaced (in a backroom, a storage area, or on the wrong aisle). By the researcher's estimates, major retailers lose 10% to 25% of overall profits due to poor or inaccurate inventory records.[1]

Pharmaceutical distributor McKesson Corp., which is one of Arnold Palmer Hospital's main suppliers of surgical materials, makes heavy use of bar-code readers to automate inventory control. The device on the warehouse worker's arm combines a scanner, a computer, and a two-way radio to check orders. With rapid and accurate data, items are easily verified, improving inventory and shipment accuracy.

[1]See E. Malykhina, "Retailers Take Stock," *Information Week* (February 7, 2005): 20–22 and A. Raman, N. DeHoratius, and Z. Ton, "Execution: The Missing Link in Retail Operations," *California Management Review* 43, no. 3 (Spring 2001): 136–141.

VIDEO 12.2
Inventory Control at Wheeled Coach Ambulance

INVENTORY MODELS

We now examine a variety of inventory models and the costs associated with them.

Independent vs. Dependent Demand

Inventory control models assume that demand for an item is either independent of or dependent on the demand for other items. For example, the demand for refrigerators is *independent* of the demand for toaster ovens. However, the demand for toaster oven components is *dependent* on the requirements of toaster ovens.

This chapter focuses on managing inventory where demand is *independent*. Chapter 14 presents *dependent* demand management.

Holding, Ordering, and Setup Costs

Holding cost
The cost to keep or carry inventory in stock.

Holding costs are the costs associated with holding or "carrying" inventory over time. Therefore, holding costs also include obsolescence and costs related to storage, such as insurance, extra staffing, and interest payments. Table 12.1 shows the kinds of costs that need to be evaluated to determine holding costs. Many firms fail to include all the inventory holding costs. Consequently, inventory holding costs are often understated.

Ordering cost
The cost of the ordering process.

Setup cost
The cost to prepare a machine or process for production.

Ordering cost includes costs of supplies, forms, order processing, purchasing, clerical support, and so forth. When orders are being manufactured, ordering costs also exist, but they are a part of what is called setup costs. **Setup cost** is the cost to prepare a machine or process for manufacturing an order. This includes time and labor to clean and change tools or holders. Operations managers can lower ordering costs by reducing setup costs and by using such efficient procedures as electronic ordering and payment.

Setup time
The time required to prepare a machine or process for production.

In manufacturing environments, setup cost is highly correlated with **setup time**. Setups usually require a substantial amount of work even before a setup is actually performed at the work center. With proper planning much of the preparation required by a setup can be done prior to shutting down the machine or process. Setup times can thus be reduced substantially. Machines and processes that traditionally have taken hours to set up are now being set up in less than a minute by the more imaginative world-class manufacturers. As we shall see later in this chapter, reducing setup times is an excellent way to reduce inventory investment and to improve productivity.

INVENTORY MODELS FOR INDEPENDENT DEMAND

In this section, we introduce three inventory models that address two important questions: *when to order* and *how much to order*. These *independent* demand models are:

1. Basic economic order quantity (EOQ) model
2. Production order quantity model
3. Quantity discount model

▶TABLE 12.1
Determining Inventory Holding Costs

Category	Cost (and range) as a Percentage of Inventory Value
Housing costs (building rent or depreciation, operating cost, taxes, insurance)	6% (3–10%)
Material handling costs (equipment lease or depreciation, power, operating cost)	3% (1–3.5%)
Labor cost (receiving, warehousing, security)	3% (3–5%)
Investment costs (borrowing costs, taxes, and insurance on inventory)	11% (6–24%)
Pilferage, scrap, and obsolescence (much higher in industries undergoing rapid change like PCs and cell phones)	3%(2–5%)
Overall carrying cost	26%

Note: All numbers are approximate, as they vary substantially depending on the nature of the business, location, and current interest rates.

AUTHOR COMMENT
An overall inventory carrying cost of less than 15% is very unlikely, but this cost can exceed 40%, especially in high-tech and fashion industries.

The Basic Economic Order Quantity (EOQ) Model

The **economic order quantity (EOQ) model** is one of the most commonly used inventory-control techniques. This technique is relatively easy to use but is based on several assumptions:

Economic order quantity (EOQ) model
An inventory-control technique that minimizes the total of ordering and holding costs.

1. Demand for an item is known, reasonably constant, and independent of decisions for other items.
2. Lead time—that is, the time between placement and receipt of the order—is known and consistent.
3. Receipt of inventory is instantaneous and complete. In other words, the inventory from an order arrives in one batch at one time.
4. Quantity discounts are not possible.
5. The only variable costs are the cost of setting up or placing an order (setup or ordering cost) and the cost of holding or storing inventory over time (holding or carrying cost). These costs were discussed in the previous section.
6. Stockouts (shortages) can be completely avoided if orders are placed at the right time.

LO3: Explain and use the EOQ model for independent inventory demand

With these assumptions, the graph of inventory usage over time has a sawtooth shape, as in Figure 12.3. In Figure 12.3, Q represents the amount that is ordered. If this amount is 500 dresses, all 500 dresses arrive at one time (when an order is received). Thus, the inventory level jumps from 0 to 500 dresses. In general, an inventory level increases from 0 to Q units when an order arrives.

Because demand is constant over time, inventory drops at a uniform rate over time. (Refer to the sloped lines in Figure 12.3.) Each time the inventory level reaches 0, the new order is placed and received, and the inventory level again jumps to Q units (represented by the vertical lines). This process continues indefinitely over time.

Minimizing Costs

The objective of most inventory models is to minimize total costs. With the assumptions just given, significant costs are setup (or ordering) cost and holding (or carrying) cost. All other costs, such as the cost of the inventory itself, are constant. Thus, if we minimize the sum of setup and holding costs, we will also be minimizing total costs. To help you visualize this, in Figure 12.4 we graph total costs as a function of the order quantity, Q. The optimal order size, Q^*, will be the quantity that minimizes the total costs. As the quantity ordered increases, the total number of orders placed per year will decrease. Thus, as the quantity ordered increases, the annual setup or ordering cost will decrease (Figure 12.4(a)). But as the order quantity increases, the holding cost will increase due to the larger average inventories that are maintained (Figure 12.4(b)).

As we can see in Figure 12.4(c), a reduction in either holding or setup cost will reduce the total cost curve. A reduction in the setup cost curve also reduces the optimal order quantity (lot size). In addition, smaller lot sizes have a positive impact on quality and production flexibility. At

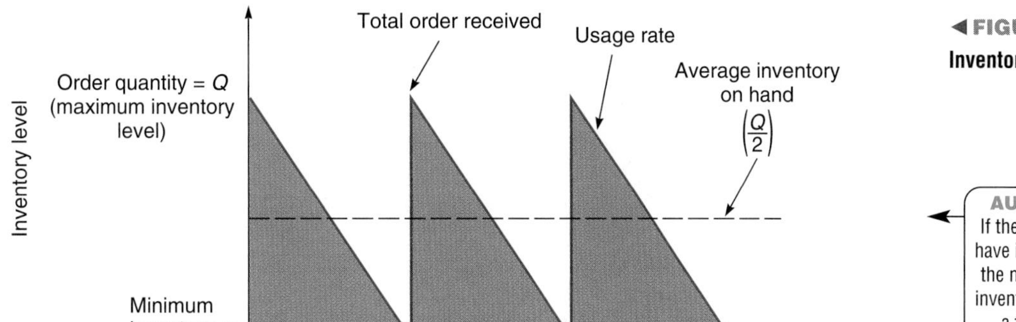

◄ **FIGURE 12.3**
Inventory Usage over Time

AUTHOR COMMENT
If the maximum we can ever have is Q (say, 500 units) and the minimum is zero, then if inventory is used (or sold) on a fairly steady rate, the average = $(Q + 0)/2 = Q/2$.

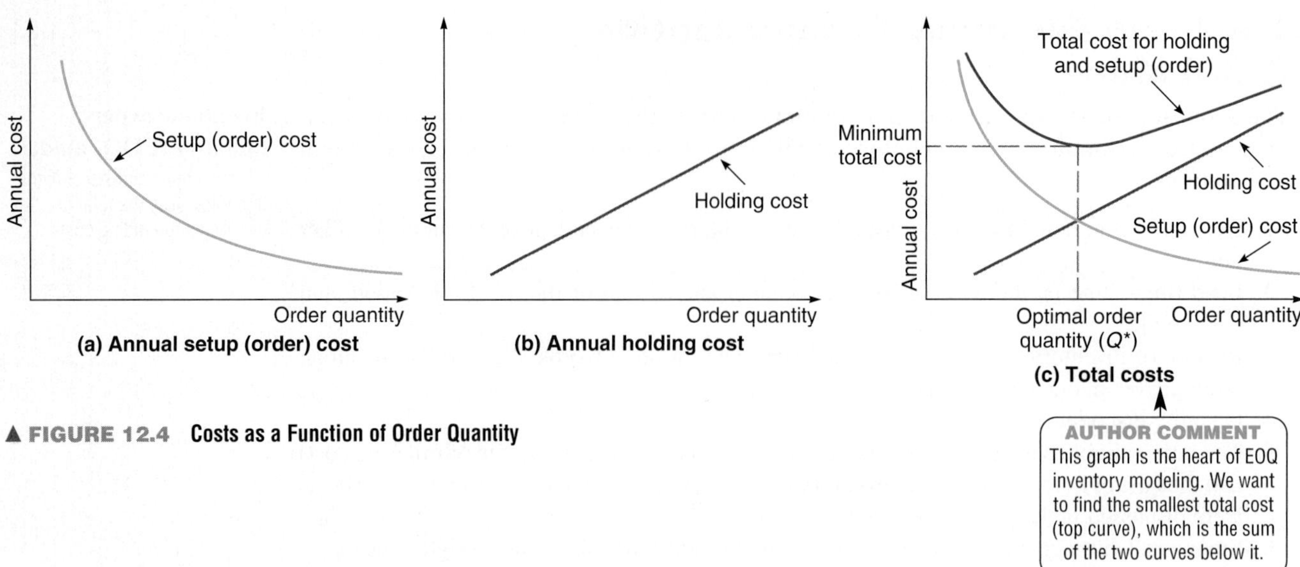

▲ **FIGURE 12.4 Costs as a Function of Order Quantity**

AUTHOR COMMENT This graph is the heart of EOQ inventory modeling. We want to find the smallest total cost (top curve), which is the sum of the two curves below it.

Toshiba, the $40 billion Japanese conglomerate, workers can make as few as 10 laptop computers before changing models. This lot-size flexibility has allowed Toshiba to move toward a "build-to-order" mass customization system, an important ability in an industry that has product life cycles measured in months, not years.

You should note that in Figure 12.4(c), the optimal order quantity occurs at the point where the ordering-cost curve and the carrying-cost curve intersect. This was not by chance. With the EOQ model, the optimal order quantity will occur at a point where the total setup cost is equal to the total holding cost.[2] We use this fact to develop equations that solve directly for Q^*. The necessary steps are:

1. Develop an expression for setup or ordering cost.
2. Develop an expression for holding cost.
3. Set setup (order) cost equal to holding cost.
4. Solve the equation for the optimal order quantity.

Using the following variables, we can determine setup and holding costs and solve for Q^*:

Q = Number of units per order
Q^* = Optimum number of units per order (EOQ)
D = Annual demand in units for the inventory item
S = Setup or ordering cost for each order
H = Holding or carrying cost per unit per year

1. Annual setup cost = (Number of orders placed per year) × (Setup or order cost per order)

$$= \left(\frac{\text{Annual demand}}{\text{Number of units in each order}}\right)(\text{Setup or order cost per order})$$

$$= \left(\frac{D}{Q}\right)(S)$$

$$= \frac{D}{Q}S$$

[2]This is the case when holding costs are linear and begin at the origin—that is, when inventory costs do not decline (or they increase) as inventory volume increases and all holding costs are in small increments. In addition, there is probably some learning each time a setup (or order) is executed—a fact that lowers subsequent setup costs. Consequently, the EOQ model is probably a special case. However, we abide by the conventional wisdom that this model is a reasonable approximation.

2. Annual holding cost = (Average inventory level) × (Holding cost per unit per year)

$$= \left(\frac{\text{Order quantity}}{2}\right)(\text{Holding cost per unit per year})$$

$$= \left(\frac{Q}{2}\right)(H) = \frac{Q}{2}H$$

3. Optimal order quantity is found when annual setup (order) cost equals annual holding cost, namely:

$$\frac{D}{Q}S = \frac{Q}{2}H$$

4. To solve for Q^*, simply cross-multiply terms and isolate Q on the left of the equal sign:

$$2DS = Q^2H$$

$$Q^2 = \frac{2DS}{H}$$

$$Q^* = \sqrt{\frac{2DS}{H}} \qquad \text{(12-1)}$$

Now that we have derived the equation for the optimal order quantity, Q^*, it is possible to solve inventory problems directly, as in Example 3.

◄ EXAMPLE 3

Finding the optimal order size at Sharp, Inc.

Sharp, Inc., a company that markets painless hypodermic needles to hospitals, would like to reduce its inventory cost by determining the optimal number of hypodermic needles to obtain per order.

APPROACH ▶ The annual demand is 1,000 units; the setup or ordering cost is \$10 per order; and the holding cost per unit per year is \$.50.

SOLUTION ▶ Using these figures, we can calculate the optimal number of units per order:

$$Q^* = \sqrt{\frac{2DS}{H}}$$

$$Q^* = \sqrt{\frac{2(1{,}000)(10)}{0.50}} = \sqrt{40{,}000} = 200 \text{ units}$$

INSIGHT ▶ Sharp, Inc., now knows how many needles to order per order. The firm also has a basis for determining ordering and holding costs for this item, as well as the number of orders to be processed by the receiving and inventory departments.

LEARNING EXERCISE ▶ If D increases to 1,200 units, what is the new Q^*? [Answer: $Q^* = 219$ units.]

RELATED PROBLEMS ▶ 12.5, 12.6, 12.7, 12.8, 12.9, 12.12, 12.13, 12.15, 12.35, 12.37

EXCEL OM Data File **Ch12Ex3.xls** can be found at **www.pearsonhighered.com/heizer**.

ACTIVE MODEL 12.1 This example is further illustrated in Active Model 12.1 at **www.pearsonhighered.com/heizer**.

We can also determine the expected number of orders placed during the year (N) and the expected time between orders (T), as follows:

$$\text{Expected number of orders} = N = \frac{\text{Demand}}{\text{Order quantity}} = \frac{D}{Q^*} \qquad \text{(12-2)}$$

$$\text{Expected time between orders} = T = \frac{\text{Number of working days per year}}{N} \qquad \text{(12-3)}$$

Example 4 illustrates this concept.

EXAMPLE 4 ▶

Computing number of orders and time between orders at Sharp, Inc.

Sharp, Inc. (in Example 3), has a 250-day working year and wants to find the number of orders (N) and the expected time between orders (T).

APPROACH ▶ Using Equations (12-2) and (12-3), Sharp enters the data given in Example 3.

SOLUTION ▶

$$N = \frac{\text{Demand}}{\text{Order quantity}}$$
$$= \frac{1{,}000}{200} = 5 \text{ orders per year}$$

$$T = \frac{\text{Number of working days per year}}{\text{Expected number of orders}}$$
$$= \frac{250 \text{ working days per year}}{5 \text{ orders}} = 50 \text{ days between orders}$$

INSIGHT ▶ The company now knows not only how many needles to order per order but that the time between orders is 50 days and that there are five orders per year.

LEARNING EXERCISE ▶ If D = 1,200 units instead of 1,000, find N and T. [Answer: $N \cong 5.48, T = 45.62$.]

RELATED PROBLEMS ▶ 12.12, 12.13, 12.15

As mentioned earlier in this section, the total annual variable inventory cost is the sum of setup and holding costs:

$$\text{Total annual cost} = \text{Setup (order) cost} + \text{Holding cost} \quad \textbf{(12-4)}$$

In terms of the variables in the model, we can express the total cost TC as:

$$TC = \frac{D}{Q}S + \frac{Q}{2}H \quad \textbf{(12-5)}$$

Example 5 shows how to use this formula.

EXAMPLE 5 ▶

Computing combined cost of ordering and holding

Sharp, Inc. (from Examples 3 and 4), wants to determine the combined annual ordering and holding costs.

APPROACH ▶ Apply Equation (12-5), using the data in Example 3.

SOLUTION ▶

$$TC = \frac{D}{Q}S + \frac{Q}{2}H$$
$$= \frac{1{,}000}{200}(\$10) + \frac{200}{2}(\$.50)$$
$$= (5)(\$10) + (100)(\$.50)$$
$$= \$50 + \$50 = \$100$$

INSIGHT ▶ These are the annual setup and holding costs. The \$100 total does not include the actual cost of goods. Notice that in the EOQ model, holding costs always equal setup (order) costs.

LEARNING EXERCISE ▶ Find the total annual cost if D = 1,200 units in Example 3. [Answer: \$109.54.]

RELATED PROBLEMS ▶ 12.9, 12.12, 12.13, 12.14, 12.37b,c

Inventory costs may also be expressed to include the actual cost of the material purchased. If we assume that the annual demand and the price per hypodermic needle are known values (e.g., 1,000 hypodermics per year at P = \$10) and total annual cost should include purchase cost, then Equation (12-5) becomes:

$$TC = \frac{D}{Q}S + \frac{Q}{2}H + PD$$

This store takes 4 weeks to get an order for Levis 501 jeans filled by the manufacturer. If the store sells 10 pairs of size 30–32 Levis a week, the store manager could set up two containers, keep 40 pairs of jeans in the second container, and place an order whenever the first container is empty. This would be a fixed-quantity reordering system. It is also called a "two-bin" system and is an example of a very elementary, but effective, approach to inventory management

Because material cost does not depend on the particular order policy, we still incur an annual material cost of $D \times P = (1{,}000)(\$10) = \$10{,}000$. (Later in this chapter we will discuss the case in which this may not be true—namely, when a quantity discount is available.)[3]

Robust Model A benefit of the EOQ model is that it is robust. By **robust** we mean that it gives satisfactory answers even with substantial variation in its parameters. As we have observed, determining accurate ordering costs and holding costs for inventory is often difficult. Consequently, a robust model is advantageous. Total cost of the EOQ changes little in the neighborhood of the minimum. The curve is very shallow. This means that variations in setup costs, holding costs, demand, or even EOQ make relatively modest differences in total cost. Example 6 shows the robustness of EOQ.

Robust
Giving satisfactory answers even with substantial variation in the parameters.

EXAMPLE 6
EOQ is a robust model

Management in the Sharp, Inc., examples underestimates total annual demand by 50% (say demand is actually 1,500 needles rather than 1,000 needles) while using the same Q. How will the annual inventory cost be impacted?

APPROACH ▶ We will solve for annual costs twice. First, we will apply the wrong EOQ; then we will recompute costs with the correct EOQ.

SOLUTION ▶ If demand in Example 5 is actually 1,500 needles rather than 1,000, but management uses an order quantity of $Q = 200$ (when it should be $Q = 244.9$ based on $D = 1{,}500$), the sum of holding and ordering cost increases to \$125:

$$\begin{aligned}\text{Annual cost} &= \frac{D}{Q}S + \frac{Q}{2}H \\ &= \frac{1{,}500}{200}(\$10) + \frac{200}{2}(\$.50) \\ &= \$75 + \$50 = \$125\end{aligned}$$

[3]The formula for the economic order quantity (Q^*) can also be determined by finding where the total cost curve is at a minimum (i.e., where the slope of the total cost curve is zero). Using calculus, we set the derivative of the total cost with respect to Q^* equal to 0.

The calculations for finding the minimum of $TC = \frac{D}{Q}S + \frac{Q}{2}H + PD$

are $\frac{d(TC)}{dQ} = \left(\frac{-DS}{Q^2}\right) + \frac{H}{2} + 0 = 0$

Thus, $Q^* = \sqrt{\frac{2DS}{H}}$.

However, had we known that the demand was for 1,500 with an EOQ of 244.9 units, we would have spent $122.47, as shown:

$$\text{Annual cost} = \frac{1{,}500}{244.9}(\$10) + \frac{244.9}{2}(\$.50)$$

$$= 6.125(\$10) + 122.45(\$.50)$$

$$= \$61.25 + \$61.22 = \$122.47$$

INSIGHT ▶ Note that the expenditure of $125.00, made with an estimate of demand that was substantially wrong, is only 2% ($2.52/$122.47) higher than we would have paid had we known the actual demand and ordered accordingly. Note also that were it not due to rounding, the annual holding costs and ordering costs would be exactly equal.

LEARNING EXERCISE ▶ Demand at Sharp remains at 1,000, H is still $.50, and we order 200 needles at a time (as in Example 5). But if the true order cost = S = $15 (rather than $10), what is the annual cost? [Answer: Annual order cost increases to $75, and annual holding cost stays at $50. So the total cost = $125.]

RELATED PROBLEMS ▶ 12.8b, 12.14

We may conclude that the EOQ is indeed robust and that significant errors do not cost us very much. This attribute of the EOQ model is most convenient because our ability to accurately determine demand, holding cost, and ordering cost is limited.

Reorder Points

Lead time

In purchasing systems, the time between placing an order and receiving it; in production systems, the wait, move, queue, setup, and run times for each component produced.

Reorder point (ROP)

The inventory level (point) at which action is taken to replenish the stocked item.

Now that we have decided *how much* to order, we will look at the second inventory question, *when* to order. Simple inventory models assume that receipt of an order is instantaneous. In other words, they assume (1) that a firm will place an order when the inventory level for that particular item reaches zero and (2) that it will receive the ordered items immediately. However, the time between placement and receipt of an order, called **lead time**, or delivery time, can be as short as a few hours or as long as months. Thus, the when-to-order decision is usually expressed in terms of a **reorder point (ROP)**—the inventory level at which an order should be placed (see Figure 12.5).

The reorder point (ROP) is given as:

$$\text{ROP} = (\text{Demand per day}) \times (\text{Lead time for a new order in days})$$
$$= d \times L \qquad \textbf{(12-6)}$$

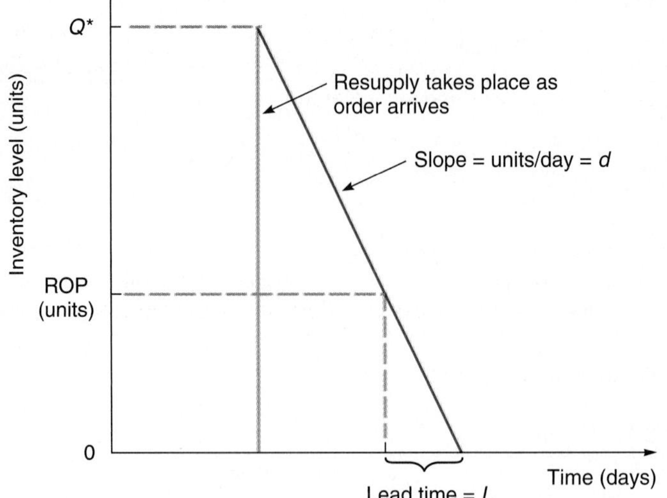

▶ FIGURE 12.5
The Reorder Point (ROP)

Q^* is the optimum order quantity, and lead time represents the time between placing and receiving an order.

This equation for ROP *assumes that demand during lead time and lead time itself are constant.* When this is not the case, extra stock, often called **safety stock**, should be added.

Safety stock
Extra stock to allow for uneven demand; a buffer.

The demand per day, d, is found by dividing the annual demand, D, by the number of working days in a year:

$$d = \frac{D}{\text{Number of working days in a year}}$$

Computing the reorder point is demonstrated in Example 7.

EXAMPLE 7

Computing reorder points (ROP) for iPods

An Apple distributor has a demand for 8,000 iPods per year. The firm operates a 250-day working year. On average, delivery of an order takes 3 working days. It wants to calculate the reorder point.

APPROACH ▶ Compute the daily demand and then apply Equation (12-6).

SOLUTION ▶

$$d = \frac{D}{\text{Number of working days in a year}} = \frac{8{,}000}{250}$$
$$= 32 \text{ units}$$
$$ROP = \text{Reorder point} = d \times L = 32 \text{ units per day} \times 3 \text{ days}$$
$$= 96 \text{ units}$$

INSIGHT ▶ Thus, when iPod inventory stock drops to 96 units, an order should be placed. The order will arrive 3 days later, just as the distributor's stock is depleted.

LEARNING EXERCISE ▶ If there are only 200 working days per year, what is the correct ROP? [Answer: 120 iPods.]

RELATED PROBLEMS ▶ 12.9d, 12.10, 12.11, 12.13f

LO4: Compute a reorder point and explain safety stock

Safety stock is especially important in firms whose raw material deliveries may be uniquely unreliable. For example, San Miguel Corp. in the Philippines uses cheese curd imported from Europe. Because the normal mode of delivery is highly variable, safety stock may be substantial.

Production Order Quantity Model

In the previous inventory model, we assumed that the entire inventory order was received at one time. There are times, however, when the firm may receive its inventory over a period of time. Such cases require a different model, one that does not require the instantaneous-receipt assumption. This model is applicable under two situations: (1) when inventory continuously flows or builds up over a period of time after an order has been placed or (2) when units are produced and sold simultaneously. Under these circumstances, we take into account daily production (or inventory-flow) rate and daily demand rate. Figure 12.6 shows inventory levels as a function of time (and inventory dropping to zero between orders).

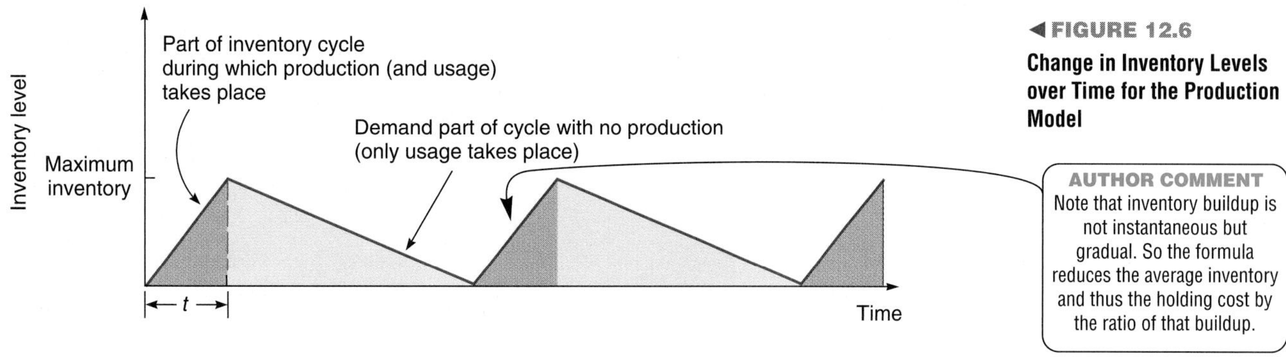

◀ FIGURE 12.6
Change in Inventory Levels over Time for the Production Model

AUTHOR COMMENT
Note that inventory buildup is not instantaneous but gradual. So the formula reduces the average inventory and thus the holding cost by the ratio of that buildup.

Production order quantity model
An economic order quantity technique applied to production orders.

Because this model is especially suitable for the production environment, it is commonly called the **production order quantity model**. It is useful when inventory continuously builds up over time, and traditional economic order quantity assumptions are valid. We derive this model by setting ordering or setup costs equal to holding costs and solving for optimal order size, Q^*. Using the following symbols, we can determine the expression for annual inventory holding cost for the production order quantity model:

$$
\begin{aligned}
Q &= \text{Number of units per order} \\
H &= \text{Holding cost per unit per year} \\
p &= \text{Daily production rate} \\
d &= \text{Daily demand rate, or usage rate} \\
t &= \text{Length of the production run in days}
\end{aligned}
$$

LO5: Apply the production order quantity model

1. $\begin{pmatrix}\text{Annual inventory} \\ \text{holding cost}\end{pmatrix} = (\text{Average inventory level}) \times \begin{pmatrix}\text{Holding cost} \\ \text{per unit per year}\end{pmatrix}$

2. $(\text{Average inventory level}) = (\text{Maximum inventory level})/2$

3. $\begin{pmatrix}\text{Maximum} \\ \text{inventory level}\end{pmatrix} = \begin{pmatrix}\text{Total production during} \\ \text{the production run}\end{pmatrix} - \begin{pmatrix}\text{Total used during} \\ \text{the production run}\end{pmatrix}$

$$= pt - dt$$

However, Q = total produced = pt, and thus $t = Q/P$. Therefore:

$$\text{Maximum inventory level} = p\left(\frac{Q}{p}\right) - d\left(\frac{Q}{p}\right) = Q - \frac{d}{p}Q$$

$$= Q\left(1 - \frac{d}{p}\right)$$

4. Annual inventory holding cost (or simply holding cost) =

$$\frac{\text{Maximum inventory level}}{2}(H) = \frac{Q}{2}\left[1 - \left(\frac{d}{p}\right)\right]H$$

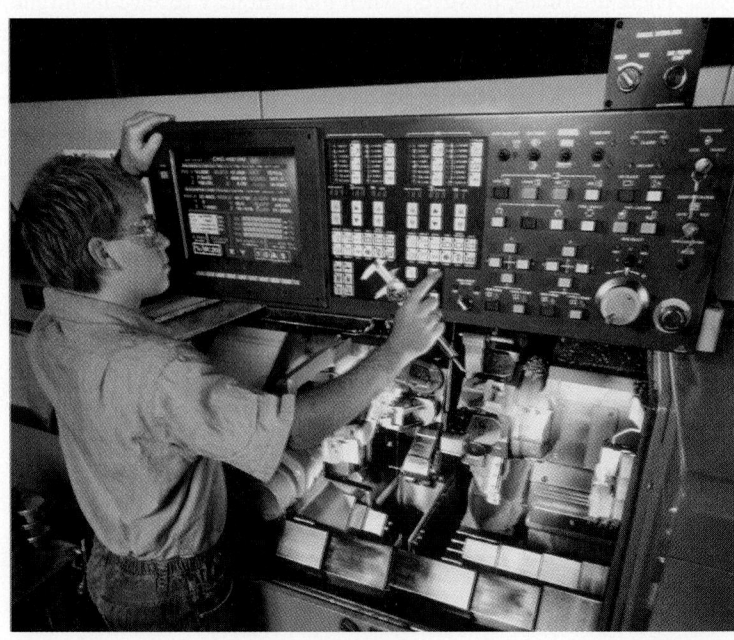

Each order may require a change in the way a machine or process is set up. Reducing setup time usually means a reduction in setup cost; and reductions in setup costs make smaller batches (lots) economical to produce. Increasingly, set up (and operation) is performed by computer-controlled machines, such as this one, operating from previously written programs.

Using this expression for holding cost and the expression for setup cost developed in the basic EOQ model, we solve for the optimal number of pieces per order by equating setup cost and holding cost:

$$\text{Setup cost} = (D/Q)S$$

$$\text{Holding cost} = \tfrac{1}{2}HQ[1 - (d/p)]$$

Set ordering cost equal to holding cost to obtain Q_p^*:

$$\frac{D}{Q}S = \tfrac{1}{2}HQ[1 - (d/p)]$$

$$Q^2 = \frac{2DS}{H[1 - (d/p)]}$$

$$Q_p^* = \sqrt{\frac{2DS}{H[1 - (d/p)]}} \qquad \textbf{(12-7)}$$

In Example 8, we use the above equation, Q_p^*, to solve for the optimum order or production quantity when inventory is consumed as it is produced.

EXAMPLE 8

A production order quantity model

Nathan Manufacturing, Inc., makes and sells specialty hubcaps for the retail automobile aftermarket. Nathan's forecast for its wire-wheel hubcap is 1,000 units next year, with an average daily demand of 4 units. However, the production process is most efficient at 8 units per day. So the company produces 8 per day but uses only 4 per day. The company wants to solve for the optimum number of units per order. (*Note:* This plant schedules production of this hubcap only as needed, during the 250 days per year the shop operates.)

APPROACH ▶ Gather the cost data and apply Equation (12-7):

$$\text{Annual demand} = D = 1{,}000 \text{ units}$$

$$\text{Setup costs} = S = \$10$$

$$\text{Holding cost} = H = \$0.50 \text{ per unit per year}$$

$$\text{Daily production rate} = p = 8 \text{ units daily}$$

$$\text{Daily demand rate} = d = 4 \text{ units daily}$$

SOLUTION ▶

$$Q_p^* = \sqrt{\frac{2DS}{H[1 - (d/p)]}}$$

$$Q_p^* = \sqrt{\frac{2(1{,}000)(10)}{0.50[1 - (4/8)]}}$$

$$= \sqrt{\frac{20{,}000}{0.50(1/2)}} = \sqrt{80{,}000}$$

$$= 282.8 \text{ hubcaps, or } 283 \text{ hubcaps}$$

INSIGHT ▶ The difference between the production order quantity model and the basic EOQ model is the annual holding cost, which is reduced in the production order quantity model.

LEARNING EXERCISE ▶ If Nathan can increase its daily production rate from 8 to 10, how does Q_p^* change? [Answer: $Q_p^* = 258$.]

RELATED PROBLEMS ▶ 12.16, 12.17, 12.18, 12.39

EXCEL OM Data File **Ch12Ex8.xls** can be found at **www.pearsonhighered.com/heizer**.

ACTIVE MODEL 12.2 This example is further illustrated in Active Model 12.2 at **www.pearsonhighered.com/heizer**.

OM in Action ► Inventory Accuracy at Milton Bradley

Milton Bradley, a division of Hasbro, Inc., has been manufacturing toys for 150 years. Founded by Milton Bradley in 1860, the company started by making a lithograph of Abraham Lincoln. Using his printing skills, Bradley developed games, including the Game of Life, Chutes and Ladders, Candy Land, Scrabble, and Lite Brite. Today, the company produces hundreds of games, requiring billions of plastic parts.

Once Milton Bradley has determined the optimal quantities for each production run, it must make them and assemble them as a part of the proper game. Some games require literally hundreds of plastic parts, including spinners, hotels, people, animals, cars, and so on. According to Gary Brennan, director of manufacturing, getting the right number of pieces to the right toys and production lines is the most important issue for the credibility of the company. Some orders can require 20,000 or more perfectly assembled games delivered to their warehouses in a matter of days.

Games with the incorrect number of parts and pieces can result in some very unhappy customers. It is also

time-consuming and expensive for Milton Bradley to supply the extra parts or to have toys or games returned. When shortages are found during the assembly stage, the entire production run is stopped until the problem is corrected. Counting parts by hand or machine is not always accurate. As a result, Milton Bradley now weighs pieces and completed games to determine if the correct number of parts have been included. If the weight is not exact, there is a problem that is resolved before shipment. Using highly accurate digital scales, Milton Bradley is now able to get the right parts in the right game at the right time. Without this simple innovation, the most sophisticated production schedule is meaningless.

Sources: The Wall Street Journal (April 15, 1999): B1; *Plastics World* (March 1997): 22–26; and *Modern Materials Handling* (September 1997): 55–57.

You may want to compare this solution with the answer in Example 3, which had identical D, S, and H values. Eliminating the instantaneous-receipt assumption, where $p = 8$ and $d = 4$, resulted in an increase in Q^* from 200 in Example 3 to 283 in Example 8. This increase in Q^* occurred because holding cost dropped from \$.50 to [\$.50 × $(1 - d/p)$], making a larger order quantity optimal. Also note that:

$$d = 4 = \frac{D}{\text{Number of days the plant is in operation}} = \frac{1{,}000}{250}$$

We can also calculate Q_p^* when *annual* data are available. When annual data are used, we can express Q_p^* as:

$$Q_p^* = \sqrt{\frac{2DS}{H\left(1 - \dfrac{\text{Annual demand rate}}{\text{Annual production rate}}\right)}} \tag{12-8}$$

AUTHOR COMMENT
Think of the discount model as the EOQ model run once for *each* of the discount price levels offered.

Quantity Discount Models

Quantity discount
A reduced price for items purchased in large quantities.

To increase sales, many companies offer quantity discounts to their customers. A **quantity discount** is simply a reduced price (P) for an item when it is purchased in larger quantities. Discount schedules with several discounts for large orders are common. A typical quantity discount schedule appears in Table 12.2. As can be seen in the table, the normal price of the item is \$5. When 1,000 to 1,999 units are ordered at one time, the price per unit drops to \$4.80; when the quantity ordered at one time is 2,000 units or more, the price is \$4.75 per unit. As always, management must decide when and how much to order. However, with an opportunity to save money on quantity discounts, how does the operations manager make these decisions?

► TABLE 12.2
A Quantity Discount Schedule

Discount Number	Discount Quantity	Discount (%)	Discount Price (P)
1	0 to 999	no discount	\$5.00
2	1,000 to 1,999	4	\$4.80
3	2,000 and over	5	\$4.75

As with other inventory models discussed so far, the overall objective is to minimize total cost. Because the unit cost for the third discount in Table 12.2 is the lowest, you may be tempted to order 2,000 units or more merely to take advantage of the lower product cost. Placing an order for that quantity, however, even with the greatest discount price, may not minimize total inventory cost. Granted, as discount quantity goes up, the product cost goes down. However, holding cost increases because orders are larger. Thus the major trade-off when considering quantity discounts is between *reduced product cost* and *increased holding cost*. When we include the cost of the product, the equation for the total annual inventory cost can be calculated as follows:

Total cost = Ordering (setup) cost + Holding cost + Product cost

LO6: Explain and use the quantity discount model

or

$$TC = \frac{D}{Q}S + \frac{Q}{2}H + PD \tag{12-9}$$

where Q = Quantity ordered
D = Annual demand in units
S = Ordering or setup cost per order
P = Price per unit
H = Holding cost per unit per year

Now, we have to determine the quantity that will minimize the total annual inventory cost. Because there are several discounts, this process involves four steps:

STEP 1: For each discount, calculate a value for optimal order size Q^*, using the following equation:

$$Q^* = \sqrt{\frac{2DS}{IP}} \tag{12-10}$$

Note that the holding cost is IP instead of H. Because the price of the item is a factor in annual holding cost, we cannot assume that the holding cost is a constant when the price per unit changes for each quantity discount. Thus, it is common to express the holding cost as a percent (I) of unit price (P) instead of as a constant cost per unit per year, H.

STEP 2: For any discount, if the order quantity is too low to qualify for the discount, adjust the order quantity upward to the *lowest* quantity that will qualify for the discount. For example, if Q^* for discount 2 in Table 12.2 were 500 units, you would adjust this value up to 1,000 units. Look at the second discount in Table 12.2. Order quantities between 1,000 and 1,999 will qualify for the 4% discount. Thus, if Q^* is below 1,000 units, we will adjust the order quantity up to 1,000 units.

The reasoning for Step 2 may not be obvious. If the order quantity, Q^*, is below the range that will qualify for a discount, a quantity within this range may still result in the lowest total cost.

As shown in Figure 12.7, the total cost curve is broken into three different total cost curves. There is a total cost curve for the first ($0 \le Q \le 999$), second ($1{,}000 \le Q \le 1{,}999$), and third ($Q \ge 2{,}000$) discount. Look at the total cost (TC) curve for discount 2. Q^* for discount 2 is less than the allowable discount range, which is from 1,000 to 1,999 units. As the figure shows, the lowest allowable quantity in this range, which is 1,000 units, is the quantity that minimizes total cost. Thus, the second step is needed to ensure that we do not discard an order quantity that may indeed produce the minimum cost. Note that an order quantity computed in step 1 that is *greater* than the range that would qualify it for a discount may be discarded.

STEP 3: Using the preceding total cost equation, compute a total cost for every Q^* determined in Steps 1 and 2. If you had to adjust Q^* upward because it was below the allowable quantity range, be sure to use the adjusted value for Q^*.

STEP 4: Select the Q^* that has the lowest total cost, as computed in Step 3. It will be the quantity that will minimize the total inventory cost.

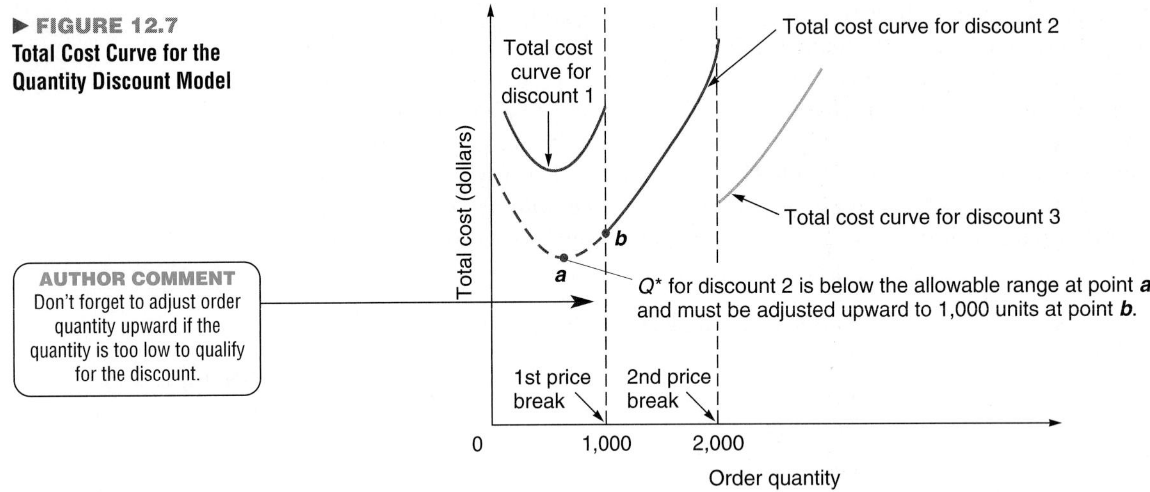

▶ **FIGURE 12.7**
Total Cost Curve for the Quantity Discount Model

AUTHOR COMMENT
Don't forget to adjust order quantity upward if the quantity is too low to qualify for the discount.

Let us see how this procedure can be applied with an example.

EXAMPLE 9 ▶ Quantity discount model

Wohl's Discount Store stocks toy race cars. Recently, the store has been given a quantity discount schedule for these cars. This quantity schedule was shown in Table 12.2. Thus, the normal cost for the toy race cars is $5.00. For orders between 1,000 and 1,999 units, the unit cost drops to $4.80; for orders of 2,000 or more units, the unit cost is only $4.75. Furthermore, ordering cost is $49.00 per order, annual demand is 5,000 race cars, and inventory carrying charge, as a percent of cost, I, is 20%, or .2. What order quantity will minimize the total inventory cost?

APPROACH ▶ We will follow the four steps just outlined for a quantity discount model.

SOLUTION ▶ The first step is to compute Q^* for every discount in Table 12.2. This is done as follows:

$$Q_1^* = \sqrt{\frac{2(5{,}000)(49)}{(.2)(5.00)}} = 700 \text{ cars per order}$$

$$Q_2^* = \sqrt{\frac{2(5{,}000)(49)}{(.2)(4.80)}} = 714 \text{ cars per order}$$

$$Q_3^* = \sqrt{\frac{2(5{,}000)(49)}{(.2)(4.75)}} = 718 \text{ cars per order}$$

The second step is to adjust upward those values of Q^* that are below the allowable discount range. Since Q_1^* is between 0 and 999, it need not be adjusted. Because Q_2^* is below the allowable range of 1,000 to 1,999, it must be adjusted to 1,000 units. The same is true for Q_3^*: It must be adjusted to 2,000 units. After this step, the following order quantities must be tested in the total cost equation:

$$Q_1^* = 700$$
$$Q_2^* = 1{,}000\text{—adjusted}$$
$$Q_3^* = 2{,}000\text{—adjusted}$$

The third step is to use Equation (12-9) and compute a total cost for each order quantity. This step is taken with the aid of Table 12.3, which presents the computations for each level of discount introduced in Table 12.2.

▶**TABLE 12.3**
Total Cost Computations for Wohl's Discount Store

Discount Number	Unit Price	Order Quantity	Annual Product Cost	Annual Ordering Cost	Annual Holding Cost	Total
1	$5.00	700	$25,000	$350	$350	$25,700
2	$4.80	1,000	$24,000	$245	$480	$24,725
3	$4.75	2,000	$23,750	$122.50	$950	$24,822.50

The fourth step is to select that order quantity with the lowest total cost. Looking at Table 12.3, you can see that an order quantity of 1,000 toy race cars will minimize the total cost. You should see, however, that the total cost for ordering 2,000 cars is only slightly greater than the total cost for ordering 1,000 cars. Thus, if the third discount cost is lowered to \$4.65, for example, then this quantity might be the one that minimizes total inventory cost.

INSIGHT ▶ The quantity discount model's third cost factor, annual product cost, is now a major variable with impact on the final cost and decision. It takes substantial increases in order and holding costs to compensate for a large quantity price break.

LEARNING EXERCISE ▶ Wohl's has just been offered a third price break. If it orders 2,500 or more cars at a time, the unit cost drops to \$4.60. What is the optimal order quantity now? [Answer: $Q_4^* = 2{,}500$, for a total cost of \$24,248.]

RELATED PROBLEMS ▶ 12.19, 12.20, 12.21, 12.22, 12.23, 12.24, 12.25

EXCEL OM Data File **Ch12Ex9.xls** can be found at **www.pearsonhighered.com/heizer**.

PROBABILISTIC MODELS AND SAFETY STOCK

AUTHOR COMMENT
Probabilistic models are a real-world adjustment because demand and lead time won't always be known and constant.

All the inventory models we have discussed so far make the assumption that demand for a product is constant and certain. We now relax this assumption. The following inventory models apply when product demand is not known but can be specified by means of a probability distribution. These types of models are called **probabilistic models**.

Probabilistic model
A statistical model applicable when product demand or any other variable is not known but can be specified by means of a probability distribution.

An important concern of management is maintaining an adequate service level in the face of uncertain demand. The **service level** is the *complement* of the probability of a stockout. For instance, if the probability of a stockout is 0.05, then the service level is .95. Uncertain demand raises the possibility of a stockout. One method of reducing stockouts is to hold extra units in inventory. As we noted, such inventory is usually referred to as safety stock. It involves adding a number of units as a buffer to the reorder point. As you recall from our previous discussion:

Service level
The complement of the probability of a stockout.

$$\text{Reorder point} = \text{ROP} = d \times L$$

where d = Daily demand
L = Order lead time, or number of working days it takes to deliver an order

The inclusion of safety stock (ss) changes the expression to:

$$\text{ROP} = d \times L + ss \tag{12-11}$$

The amount of safety stock maintained depends on the cost of incurring a stockout and the cost of holding the extra inventory. Annual stockout cost is computed as follows:

$$\begin{aligned}\text{Annual stockout costs} &= \text{The sum of the units short for each demand level}\\ &\times \text{The probability of that demand level} \times \text{The stockout cost/unit}\\ &\times \text{The number of orders per year}\end{aligned} \tag{12-12}$$

Example 10 illustrates this concept.

EXAMPLE 10
Determining safety stock with probabilistic demand and constant lead time

David Rivera Optical has determined that its reorder point for eyeglass frames is 50 ($d \times L$) units. Its carrying cost per frame per year is \$5, and stockout (or lost sale) cost is \$40 per frame. The store has experienced the following probability distribution for inventory demand during the lead time (reorder period). The optimum number of orders per year is six.

	Number of Units	Probability
	30	.2
	40	.2
ROP →	50	.3
	60	.2
	70	.1
		1.0

How much safety stock should David Rivera keep on hand?

APPROACH ▶ The objective is to find the amount of safety stock that minimizes the sum of the additional inventory holding costs and stockout costs. The annual holding cost is simply the holding cost per unit multiplied by the units added to the ROP. For example, a safety stock of 20 frames, which implies that the new ROP, with safety stock, is $70(= 50 + 20)$, raises the annual carrying cost by $5(20) = $100.

However, computing annual stockout cost is more interesting. For any level of safety stock, stockout cost is the expected cost of stocking out. We can compute it, as in Equation (12-12), by multiplying the number of frames short (Demand − ROP) by the probability of demand at that level, by the stockout cost, by the number of times per year the stockout can occur (which in our case is the number of orders per year). Then we add stockout costs for each possible stockout level for a given ROP.

SOLUTION ▶ We begin by looking at zero safety stock. For this safety stock, a shortage of 10 frames will occur if demand is 60, and a shortage of 20 frames will occur if the demand is 70. Thus the stockout costs for zero safety stock are:

$$(10 \text{ frames short})(.2)(\$40 \text{ per stockout})(6 \text{ possible stockouts per year}) + (20 \text{ frames short})(.1)(\$40)(6) = \$960$$

The following table summarizes the total costs for each of the three alternatives:

Safety Stock	Additional Holding Cost	Stockout Cost	Total Cost
20	(20) ($5) = $100	$ 0	$100
10	(10) ($5) = $ 50	(10) (.1) ($40) (6) = $240	$290
0	$ 0	(10) (.2) ($40) (6) + (20) (.1) ($40) (6) = $960	$960

The safety stock with the lowest total cost is 20 frames. Therefore, this safety stock changes the reorder point to $50 + 20 = 70$ frames.

INSIGHT ▶ The optical company now knows that a safety stock of 20 frames will be the most economical decision.

LEARNING EXERCISE ▶ David Rivera's holding cost per frame is now estimated to be $20, while the stockout cost is $30 per frame. Does the reorder point change? [Answer: Safety stock = 10 now, with a total cost of $380, which is the lowest of the three. ROP = 60 frames.]

RELATED PROBLEMS ▶ 12.29, 12.30, 12.31

When it is difficult or impossible to determine the cost of being out of stock, a manager may decide to follow a policy of keeping enough safety stock on hand to meet a prescribed customer service level. For instance, Figure 12.8 shows the use of safety stock when demand (for hospital resuscitation kits) is probabilistic. We see that the safety stock in Figure 12.8 is 16.5 units, and the reorder point is also increased by 16.5.

The manager may want to define the service level as meeting 95% of the demand (or, conversely, having stockouts only 5% of the time). Assuming that demand during lead time (the reorder period) follows a normal curve, only the mean and standard deviation are needed to define the inventory requirements for any given service level. Sales data are usually adequate for computing the mean and standard deviation. In the following example we use a normal curve with a known mean (μ) and standard deviation (σ) to determine the reorder point and safety stock necessary for a 95% service level. We use the following formula:

$$\text{ROP} = \text{Expected demand during lead time} + Z\sigma_{dLT} \qquad \textbf{(12-13)}$$

where Z = Number of standard deviations

σ_{dLT} = Standard deviation of demand during lead time

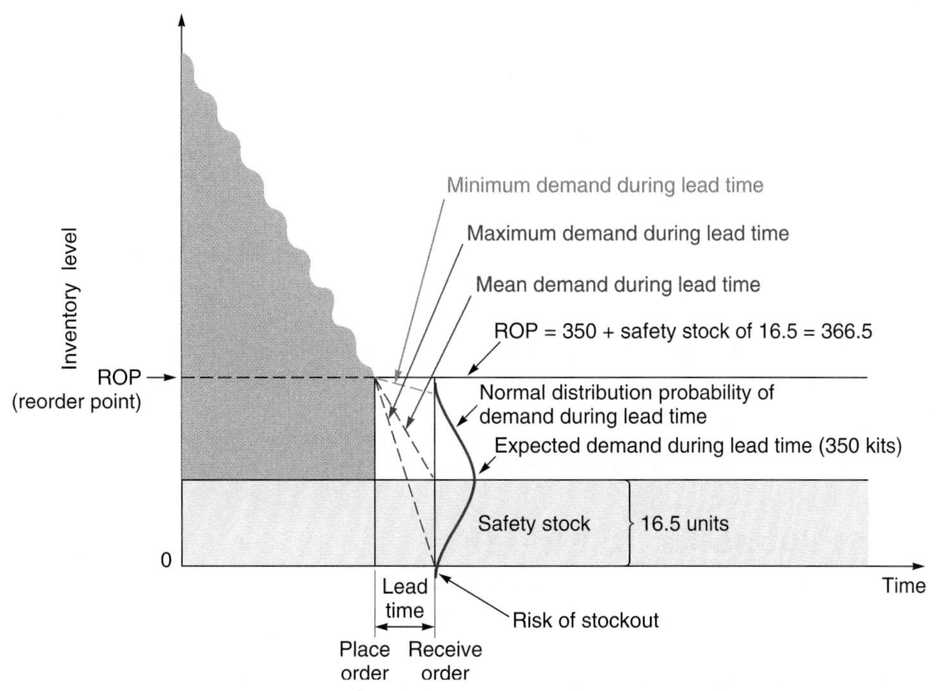

◀ **FIGURE 12.8**
Probabilistic Demand for a Hospital Item

Expected number of kits needed during lead time is 350, but for a 95% service level, the reorder point should be raised to 366.5.

◀ **EXAMPLE 11**

Safety stock with probabilistic demand

Memphis Regional Hospital stocks a "code blue" resuscitation kit that has a normally distributed demand during the reorder period. The mean (average) demand during the reorder period is 350 kits, and the standard deviation is 10 kits. The hospital administrator wants to follow a policy that results in stockouts only 5% of the time.

(a) What is the appropriate value of Z? (b) How much safety stock should the hospital maintain? (c) What reorder point should be used?

APPROACH ▶ The hospital determines how much inventory is needed to meet the demand 95% of the time. The figure in this example may help you visualize the approach. The data are as follows:

$$\mu = \text{Mean demand} = 350 \text{ kits}$$

$$\sigma_{dLT} = \text{Standard deviation of demand during lead time} = 10 \text{ kits}$$

$$Z = \text{Number of standard normal deviations}$$

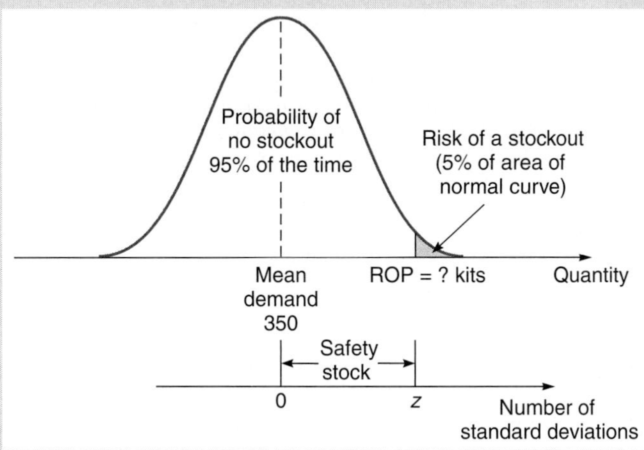

AUTHOR COMMENT
Recall that the service level is 1 minus the risk of a stockout.

SOLUTION ▶

a. We use the properties of a standardized normal curve to get a Z-value for an area under the normal curve of .95 (or 1 − .05). Using a normal table (see Appendix I), we find a Z-value of 1.65 standard deviations from the mean.

b. Because: $\text{Safety stock} = x - \mu$

and: $$Z = \frac{x - \mu}{\sigma_{dLT}}$$

then: $$\text{Safety stock} = Z\sigma_{dLT} \quad \text{(12-14)}$$

Solving for safety stock, as in Equation (12-14), gives:

$$\text{Safety stock} = 1.65(10) = 16.5 \text{ kits}$$

This is the situation illustrated in Figure 12.8.

c. The reorder point is:

$$\begin{aligned}\text{ROP} &= \text{Expected demand during lead time} + \text{Safety stock}\\ &= 350 \text{ kits} + 16.5 \text{ kits of safety stock} = 366.5, \text{ or } 367 \text{ kits}\end{aligned}$$

INSIGHT ▶ The cost of the inventory policy increases dramatically (exponentially) with an increase in service levels.

LEARNING EXERCISE ▶ What policy results in stockouts 10% of the time? [Answer: $Z = 1.28$; safety stock = 12.8; ROP = 363 kits.]

RELATED PROBLEMS ▶ 12.27, 12.28, 12.40

Other Probabilistic Models

Equations (12-13) and (12-14) assume that both an estimate of expected demand during lead times and its standard deviation are available. When data on lead time demand are *not* at hand, these formulas cannot be applied. However, three other models are available. We need to determine which model to use for three situations:

1. Demand is variable and lead time is constant
2. Lead time is variable, and demand is constant
3. Both demand and lead time are variable

LO7: Understand service levels and probabilistic inventory models

All three models assume that demand and lead time are independent variables. Note that our examples use days, but weeks can also be used. Let us examine these three situations separately, because a different formula for the ROP is needed for each.

Demand Is Variable and Lead Time Is Constant When *only the demand is variable*, then:

$$\text{ROP} = (\textit{Average} \text{ daily demand} \times \text{Lead time in days}) + Z\sigma_{dLT} \quad \textbf{(12-15)}$$

where σ_{dLT} = Standard deviation of demand during lead time = $\sigma_d\sqrt{\text{Lead time}}$

and σ_d = Standard deviation of demand per day

EXAMPLE 12 ▶

ROP for variable demand and constant lead time

The *average* daily demand for Apple iPods at a Circuit Town store is 15, with a standard deviation of 5 units. The lead time is constant at 2 days. Find the reorder point if management wants a 90% service level (i.e., risk stockouts only 10% of the time). How much of this is safety stock?

APPROACH ▶ Apply Equation (12-15) to the following data:
Average daily demand (normally distributed) = 15
Lead time in days (constant) = 2
Standard deviation of daily demand = $\sigma_d = 5$
Service level = 90%

SOLUTION ▶ From the normal table (Appendix I), we derive a Z-value for 90% of 1.28. Then:

$$\begin{aligned}\text{ROP} &= (15 \text{ units} \times 2 \text{ days}) + Z\sigma_d\sqrt{\text{Lead time}}\\ &= 30 + 1.28(5)(\sqrt{2})\\ &= 30 + 1.28(5)(1.41) = 30 + 9.02 = 39.02 \cong 39\end{aligned}$$

Thus, safety stock is about 9 iPods.

INSIGHT ▶ The value of Z depends on the manager's stockout risk level. The smaller the risk, the higher the Z.

LEARNING EXERCISE ▶ If the Circuit Town manager wants a 95% service level, what is the new ROP? [Answer: ROP = 41.63, or 42.]

RELATED PROBLEM ▶ 12.32

Lead Time Is Variable and Demand Is Constant When the demand is constant and *only the lead time is variable*, then:

$$\text{ROP} = (\text{Daily demand} \times \textit{Average} \text{ lead time in days}) + Z(\text{Daily demand}) \times \sigma_{LT} \quad \text{(12-16)}$$

where σ_{LT} = Standard deviation of lead time in days

◄ EXAMPLE 13

ROP for constant demand and variable lead time

The Circuit Town store in Example 12 sells about 10 digital cameras a day (almost a constant quantity). Lead time for camera delivery is normally distributed with a mean time of 6 days and a standard deviation of 3 days. A 98% service level is set. Find the ROP.

APPROACH ▶ Apply Equation (12-16) to the following data:
Daily demand = 10
Average lead time = 6 days
Standard deviation of lead time = σ_{LT} = 3 days
Service level = 98%, so Z (from Appendix I) = 2.055

SOLUTION ▶ From the equation we get:

$$\text{ROP} = (10 \text{ units} \times 6 \text{ days}) + 2.055(10 \text{ units})(3)$$
$$= 60 + 61.65 = 121.65$$

The reorder point is about 122 cameras.

INSIGHT ▶ Note how the very high service level of 98% drives the ROP up.

LEARNING EXERCISE ▶ If a 90% service level is applied, what does the ROP drop to? [Answer: ROP = 60 + (1.28)(10)(3) = 60 + 38.4 = 98.4, since the Z-value is only 1.28.]

RELATED PROBLEM ▶ 12.33

Both Demand and Lead Time Are Variable When both the demand and lead time are variable, the formula for reorder point becomes more complex[4]:

$$\text{ROP} = (\text{Average daily demand} \times \text{Average lead time}) + Z\sigma_{dLT} \quad \text{(12-17)}$$

where σ_d = Standard deviation of demand per day
σ_{LT} = Standard deviation of lead time in days
and $\sigma_{dLT} = \sqrt{(\text{Average lead time} \times \sigma_d^2) + (\text{Average daily demand})^2\sigma_{LT}^2}$

◄ EXAMPLE 14

ROP for variable demand and variable lead time

The Circuit Town store's most popular item is six-packs of 9-volt batteries. About 150 packs are sold per day, following a normal distribution with a standard deviation of 16 packs. Batteries are ordered from an out-of-state distributor; lead time is normally distributed with an average of 5 days and a standard deviation of 1 day. To maintain a 95% service level, what ROP is appropriate?

APPROACH ▶ Determine a quantity at which to reorder by applying Equation (12-17) to the following data:

Average daily demand = 150 packs
Standard deviation of demand = σ_d = 16 packs
Average lead time = 5 days
Standard deviation of lead time = σ_{LT} = 1 day
Service level = 95%, so Z = 1.65 (from Appendix I)

SOLUTION ▶ From the equation we compute:

$$\text{ROP} = (150 \text{ packs} \times 5 \text{ days}) + 1.65\,\sigma_{dLT}$$

[4]Refer to S. Narasimhan, D. W. McLeavey, and P. Billington, *Production Planning and Inventory Control*, 2nd ed. (Upper Saddle River, NJ: Prentice Hall, 1995), Chap. 6, for details. Note that Equation (12-17) can also be expressed as ROP = Average daily demand × Average lead time + $Z\sqrt{(\text{Average lead time} \times \sigma_d^2) + \bar{d}^2\sigma_{LT}^2}$.

where $\sigma_{dLT} = \sqrt{(5 \text{ days} \times 16^2) + (150^2 \times 1^2)}$

$$= \sqrt{(5 \times 256) + (22{,}500 \times 1)}$$

$$= \sqrt{1{,}280 + 22{,}500} = \sqrt{23{,}780} \cong 154$$

So ROP $= (150 \times 5) + 1.65(154) \cong 750 + 254 = 1{,}004$ packs

INSIGHT ▶ When both demand and lead time are variable, the formula looks quite complex. But it is just the result of squaring the standard deviations in Equations (12-15) and (12-16) to get their variances, then summing them, and finally taking the square root.

LEARNING EXERCISE ▶ For an 80% service level, what is the ROP? [Answer: $Z = .84$ and ROP = 879 packs.]

RELATED PROBLEM ▶ 12.34

SINGLE-PERIOD MODEL

Single-period inventory model
A system for ordering items that have little or no value at the end of a sales period.

A **single-period inventory model** describes a situation in which *one* order is placed for a product. At the end of the sales period, any remaining product has little or no value. This is a typical problem for Christmas trees, seasonal goods, bakery goods, newspapers, and magazines. (Indeed, this inventory issue is often called the "newsstand problem.") In other words, even though items at a newsstand are ordered weekly or daily, they cannot be held over and used as inventory in the next sales period. So our decision is how much to order at the beginning of the period.

Because the exact demand for such seasonal products is never known, we consider a probability distribution related to demand. If the normal distribution is assumed, and we stocked and sold an average (mean) of 100 Christmas trees each season, then there is a 50% chance we would stock out and a 50% chance we would have trees left over. To determine the optimal stocking policy for trees before the season begins, we also need to know the standard deviation and consider these two marginal costs:

C_s = Cost of shortage (we underestimated) = Sales price/unit − Cost/unit

C_o = Cost of overage (we overestimated) = Cost/unit − Salvage value/unit (if there is any)

The service level, that is, the probability of *not* stocking out, is set at:

$$\text{Service level} = \frac{C_s}{C_s + C_o} \qquad (12\text{-}18)$$

Therefore, we should consider increasing our order quantity until the service level is less than or equal to the ratio of $[C_s/(C_s + C_o).]$

This model, illustrated in Example 15, is used in many service industries, from hotels to airlines to bakeries to clothing retailers.

EXAMPLE 15 ▶

Single-period inventory decision

Chris Ellis's newsstand, just outside the Smithsonian subway station in Washington, DC, usually sells 120 copies of the *Washington Post* each day. Chris believes the sale of the *Post* is normally distributed, with a standard deviation of 15 papers. He pays 70 cents for each paper, which sells for $1.25. The *Post* gives him a 30-cent credit for each unsold paper. He wants to determine how many papers he should order each day and the stockout risk for that quantity.

APPROACH ▶ Chris's data are as follows:

C_s = cost of shortage = \$1.25 − \$.70 = \$.55

C_o = cost of overage = \$.70 − \$.30 (salvage value) = \$.40

Chris will apply Equation (12-18) and the normal table, using $\mu = 120$ and $\sigma = 15$.

SOLUTION ▶

a) $\text{Service level} = \dfrac{C_s}{C_s + C_o} = \dfrac{.55}{.55 + .40} = \dfrac{.55}{.95} = .578$

b) Chris needs to find the Z score for his normal distribution that yields a probability of .578.

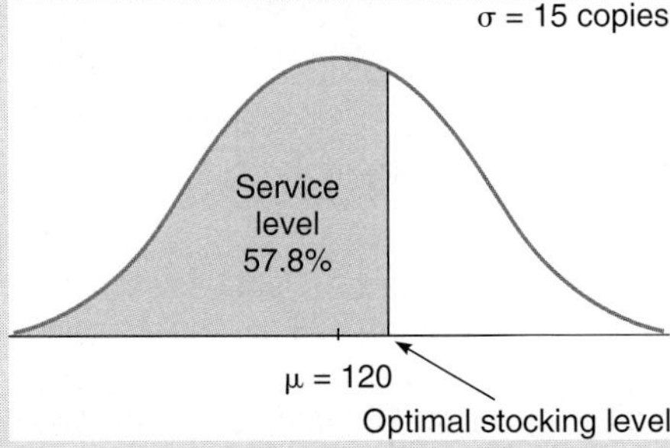

So 57.8% of the area under the normal curve must be to the left of the optimal stocking level.

c) Using Appendix I[5], for an area of .578, the Z value $\cong$ .20.

$$\text{Then, the optimal stocking level} = 120 \text{ copies} + (.20)(\sigma)$$
$$= 120 + (.20)(15) = 120 + 3 = 123 \text{ papers}$$

The stockout risk if Chris orders 123 copies of the *Post* each day is 1 – service level = 1 – .578 = .422 = 42.2%.

INSIGHT ▶ If the service level is ever under .50, Chris should order fewer than 120 copies per day.

LEARNING EXERCISE ▶ How does Chris's decision change if the *Post* changes its policy and offers *no credit* for unsold papers, a policy many publishers are adopting?
[Answer: Service level $= .44$, $Z = -.15$. Therefore, stock $120 + (-.15)(15) = 117.75$ or 118 papers].

RELATED PROBLEMS ▶ 12.36, 12.37 12.38

AUTHOR COMMENT A fixed-period model orders a different quantity each time.

FIXED-PERIOD (P) SYSTEMS

The inventory models that we have considered so far are **fixed-quantity**, or **Q, systems**. That is, the same fixed amount is added to inventory every time an order for an item is placed. We saw that orders are event triggered. When inventory decreases to the reorder point (ROP), a new order for Q units is placed.

Fixed-quantity (*Q*) system
An ordering system with the same order amount each time.

To use the fixed-quantity model, inventory must be continuously monitored.[6] This requires a **perpetual inventory system**. Every time an item is added to or withdrawn from inventory, records must be updated to determine whether the ROP has been reached.

Perpetual inventory system
A system that keeps track of each withdrawal or addition to inventory continuously, so records are always current.

In a **fixed-period system** (also called a periodic review, or **P system**), on the other hand, inventory is ordered at the end of a given period. Then, and only then, is on-hand inventory counted. Only the amount necessary to bring total inventory up to a prespecified target level (T) is ordered. Figure 12.9 illustrates this concept.

Fixed-period (*P*) system
A system in which inventory orders are made at regular time intervals.

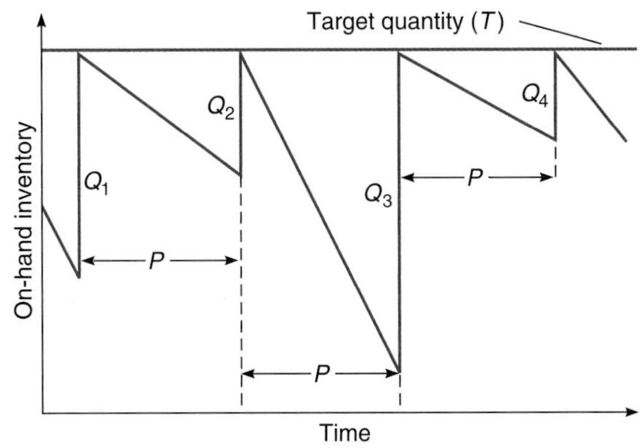

◀ **FIGURE 12.9**
Inventory Level in a Fixed-Period (P) System
Various amounts (Q_1, Q_2, Q_3, etc.) are ordered at regular time intervals (P) based on the quantity necessary to bring inventory up to the target quantity (T).

[5]Alternatively, Microsoft Excel's NORMSINV (probability) function can be applied.
[6]Some in OM call these continuous review systems.

OM in Action ▶ 66,207,896 Bottles of Beer on the Wall

When Dereck Gurden pulls up at one of his customers' stores—7-Eleven, Buy N Save, or one of dozens of liquor marts and restaurants in the 800-square-mile territory he covers in California's Central Valley—managers usually stop what they're doing and grab a note pad. This is because, as Gurden claims, "I know more about these guys' businesses than they do . . . at least in the beer section."

What makes Gurden and other sales reps for Anheuser-Busch distributors so smart? It's BudNet, the King of Beer's top-secret crown jewel—a nationwide data network through which drivers and reps report, in excruciating detail, on sales, shelf space, inventory, and displays at thousands of stores. How does it work? As Gurden walks a store, he inputs what he sees to his handheld PC, then plugs into a cell phone and fires off new orders, along with the data he has gathered. Anheuser has made a deadly accurate science of finding out what beer lovers are buying, as well as when, where, and why.

Matching these data with U.S. census figures of neighborhoods, Anheuser mines data down to the sales at individual stores. The company can pinpoint age, ethnicity, education, political, and sexual orientation of customers at your local 7-Eleven. BudNet is the primary reason Anheuser's share of the $75 billion U.S. beer market continues to increase, and the company has posted double-digit profit gains for 20 straight quarters while its competitors have flat-lined.

Sources: Business 2.0 (January/February 2004): 47–49; *Beverage Industry* (May 2004): 20–23; and *The Wall Street Journal* (March 23, 2004): C3.

Fixed-period systems have several of the same assumptions as the basic EOQ fixed-quantity system:

- The only relevant costs are the ordering and holding costs.
- Lead times are known and constant.
- Items are independent of one another.

The downward-sloped lines in Figure 12.9 again represent on-hand inventory levels. But now, when the time between orders (P) passes, we place an order to raise inventory up to the target quantity (T). The amount ordered during the first period may be Q_1, the second period Q_2, and so on. The Q_i value is the difference between current on-hand inventory and the target inventory level.

The advantage of the fixed-period system is that there is no physical count of inventory items after an item is withdrawn—this occurs only when the time for the next review comes up. This procedure is also convenient administratively.

A fixed-period system is appropriate when vendors make routine (i.e., at fixed-time interval) visits to customers to take fresh orders or when purchasers want to combine orders to save ordering and transportation costs (therefore, they will have the same review period for similar inventory items). For example, a vending machine company may come to refill its machines every Tuesday. This is also the case at Anheuser-Busch, whose sales reps may visit a store every 5 days (see the *OM in Action* box "66,207,896 Bottles of Beer on the Wall").

The disadvantage of the P system is that because there is no tally of inventory during the review period, there is the possibility of a stockout during this time. This scenario is possible if a large order draws the inventory level down to zero right after an order is placed. Therefore, a higher level of safety stock (as compared to a fixed-quantity system) needs to be maintained to provide protection against stockout during both the time between reviews and the lead time.

CHAPTER SUMMARY

Inventory represents a major investment for many firms. This investment is often larger than it should be because firms find it easier to have "just-in-case" inventory rather than "just-in-time" inventory. Inventories are of four types:

1. Raw material and purchased components
2. Work-in-process
3. Maintenance, repair, and operating (MRO)
4. Finished goods

In this chapter, we discussed independent inventory, ABC analysis, record accuracy, cycle counting, and inventory models used to control independent demands. The EOQ model, production order quantity model, and quantity discount model can all be solved using Excel, Excel OM, or POM for Windows software.

Key Terms

Raw material inventory (p. 469)
Work-in-process (WIP) inventory (p. 469)
MRO (p. 469)
Finished-goods inventory (p. 469)
ABC analysis (p. 469)
Cycle counting (p. 471)
Shrinkage (p. 473)
Pilferage (p. 473)
Holding cost (p. 474)
Ordering cost (p. 474)
Setup cost (p. 474)
Setup time (p. 474)
Economic order quantity (EOQ) model (p. 475)
Robust (p. 479)
Lead time (p. 480)
Reorder point (ROP) (p. 480)
Safety stock (p. 481)
Production order quantity model (p. 482)
Quantity discount (p. 484)
Probabilistic model (p. 487)
Service level (p. 487)
Single-period inventory model (p. 492)
Fixed-quantity (Q) system (p. 493)
Perpetual inventory system (p. 493)
Fixed-period (P) system (p. 493)

Ethical Dilemma

Wayne Hills Hospital in tiny Wayne, Nebraska, faces a problem common to large, urban hospitals as well as to small, remote ones like itself. That problem is deciding how much of each type of whole blood to keep in stock. Because blood is expensive and has a limited shelf life (up to 5 weeks under 1–6°C refrigeration), Wayne Hills naturally wants to keep its stock as low as possible. Unfortunately, past disasters such as a major tornado and a train wreck demonstrated that lives would be lost when not enough blood was available to handle massive needs. The hospital administrator wants to set an 85% service level based on demand over the past decade. Discuss the implications of this decision. What is the hospital's responsibility with regard to stocking lifesaving medicines with short shelf lives? How would you set the inventory level for a commodity such as blood?

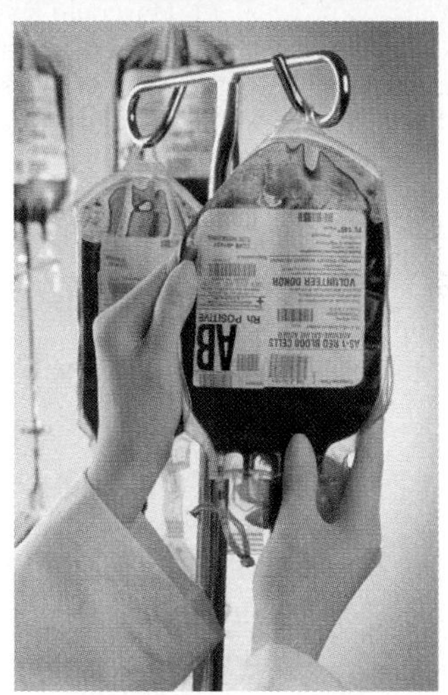

Discussion Questions

1. Describe the four types of inventory.
2. With the advent of low-cost computing, do you see alternatives to the popular ABC classifications?
3. What is the purpose of the ABC classification system?
4. Identify and explain the types of costs that are involved in an inventory system.
5. Explain the major assumptions of the basic EOQ model.
6. What is the relationship of the economic order quantity to demand? to the holding cost? to the setup cost?
7. Explain why it is not necessary to include product cost (price or price times quantity) in the EOQ model, but the quantity discount model requires this information.
8. What are the advantages of cycle counting?
9. What impact does a decrease in setup time have on EOQ?
10. When quantity discounts are offered, why is it not necessary to check discount points that are below the EOQ or points above the EOQ that are not discount points?
11. What is meant by *service level*?
12. Explain the following: All things being equal, the production inventory quantity will be larger than the economic order quantity.
13. Describe the difference between a fixed-quantity (Q) and a fixed-period (P) inventory system.
14. Explain what is meant by the expression "robust model." Specifically, what would you tell a manager who exclaimed, "Uh-oh, we're in trouble! The calculated EOQ is wrong; actual demand is 10% greater than estimated."
15. What is "safety stock"? What does safety stock provide safety against?
16. When demand is not constant, the reorder point is a function of what four parameters?
17. How are inventory levels monitored in retail stores?
18. State a major advantage, and a major disadvantage, of a fixed-period (P) system.

Using Software to Solve Inventory Problems

This section presents three ways to solve inventory problems with computer software. First, you can create your own Excel spreadsheets. Second, you can use the Excel OM software that comes with this text and is found on our website. Third, POM for Windows, also on our website at **www.pearsonhighered.com/heizer**, can solve all problems marked with a P.

Creating Your Own Excel Spreadsheets

Program 12.1 illustrates how you can make an Excel model to solve Example 8 (p. 483). This is a production order quantity model. A listing of the formulas needed to create the spreadsheet is shown.

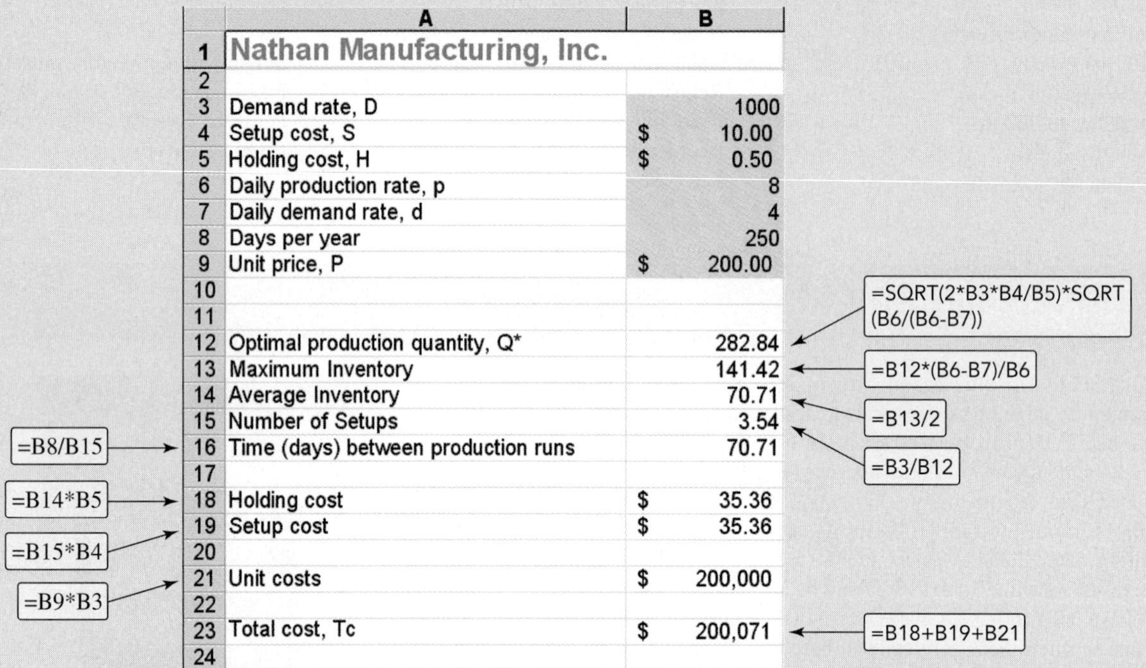

	A	B
1	Nathan Manufacturing, Inc.	
2		
3	Demand rate, D	1000
4	Setup cost, S	$ 10.00
5	Holding cost, H	$ 0.50
6	Daily production rate, p	8
7	Daily demand rate, d	4
8	Days per year	250
9	Unit price, P	$ 200.00
10		
11		
12	Optimal production quantity, Q*	282.84
13	Maximum Inventory	141.42
14	Average Inventory	70.71
15	Number of Setups	3.54
16	Time (days) between production runs	70.71
17		
18	Holding cost	$ 35.36
19	Setup cost	$ 35.36
20		
21	Unit costs	$ 200,000
22		
23	Total cost, Tc	$ 200,071
24		

▲ PROGRAM 12.1 **Using Excel for a Production Model, with Data from Example 8**

Using Excel OM

Excel OM allows us to easily model inventory problems ranging from ABC analysis, to the basic EOQ model, to the production model, to quantity discount situations.

Program 12.2 shows the input data, selected formulas, and results for an ABC analysis, using data from Example 1 (on p. 470). After the data are entered, we use the *Data* and *Sort* Excel commands to rank the items from largest to smallest dollar volumes.

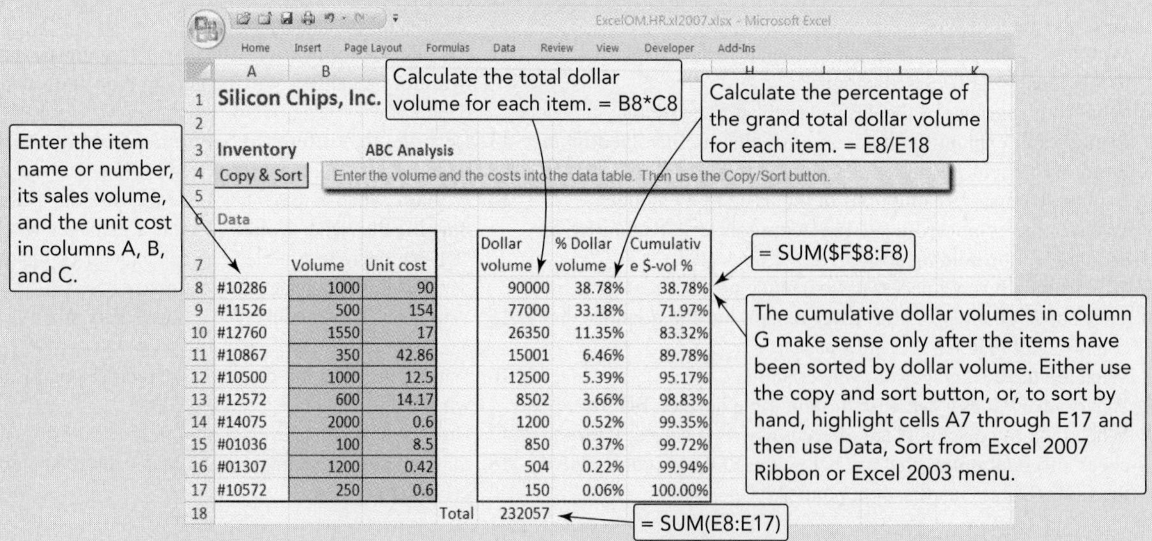

	A	B	C	D	E	F	G
1	Silicon Chips, Inc.						
3	Inventory		ABC Analysis				
6	Data						
7		Volume	Unit cost		Dollar volume	% Dollar volume	Cumulative $-vol %
8	#10286	1000	90		90000	38.78%	38.78%
9	#11526	500	154		77000	33.18%	71.97%
10	#12760	1550	17		26350	11.35%	83.32%
11	#10867	350	42.86		15001	6.46%	89.78%
12	#10500	1000	12.5		12500	5.39%	95.17%
13	#12572	600	14.17		8502	3.66%	98.83%
14	#14075	2000	0.6		1200	0.52%	99.35%
15	#01036	100	8.5		850	0.37%	99.72%
16	#01307	1200	0.42		504	0.22%	99.94%
17	#10572	250	0.6		150	0.06%	100.00%
18				Total	232057		

▲ PROGRAM 12.2 **Using Excel OM for an ABC Analysis, with Data from Example 1**

Using POM for Windows

The POM for Windows Inventory module can also solve the entire EOQ family of problems. Please refer to Appendix IV for further details.

Solved Problems

Virtual Office help is available at www.myomlab.com

▼ SOLVED PROBLEM 12.1

David Alexander has compiled the following table of six items in inventory at Angelo Products, along with the unit cost and the annual demand in units:

Identification Code	Unit Cost ($)	Annual Demand (units)
XX1	5.84	1,200
B66	5.40	1,110
3CPO	1.12	896
33CP	74.54	1,104
R2D2	2.00	1,110
RMS	2.08	961

Use ABC analysis to determine which item(s) should be carefully controlled using a quantitative inventory technique and which item(s) should not be closely controlled.

▼ SOLUTION

The item that needs strict control is 33CP, so it is an A item. Items that do not need to be strictly controlled are 3CPO, R2D2, and RMS; these are C items. The B items will be XX1 and B66.

Code	Annual dollar volume = Unit Cost × Demand
XX1	$ 7,008.00
B66	$ 5,994.00
3CPO	$ 1,003.52
33CP	$ 82,292.16
R2D2	$ 2,220.00
RMS	$ 1,998.88

Total cost = $100,516.56

70% of total cost = $70,347.92

▼ SOLVED PROBLEM 12.2

The Warren W. Fisher Computer Corporation purchases 8,000 transistors each year as components in minicomputers. The unit cost of each transistor is $10, and the cost of carrying one transistor in inventory for a year is $3. Ordering cost is $30 per order.

What are (a) the optimal order quantity, (b) the expected number of orders placed each year, and (c) the expected time between orders? Assume that Fisher operates on a 200-day working year.

▼ SOLUTION

a) $Q^* = \sqrt{\dfrac{2DS}{H}} = \sqrt{\dfrac{2(8{,}000)(30)}{3}} = 400 \text{ units}$

b) $N = \dfrac{D}{Q^*} = \dfrac{8{,}000}{400} = 20 \text{ orders}$

c) $\text{Time between orders} = T = \dfrac{\text{Number of working days}}{N} = \dfrac{200}{20} = 10 \text{ working days}$

With 20 orders placed each year, an order for 400 transistors is placed every 10 working days.

▼ SOLVED PROBLEM 12.3

Annual demand for notebook binders at Meyer's Stationery Shop is 10,000 units. Brad Meyer operates his business 300 days per year and finds that deliveries from his supplier generally take 5 working days. Calculate the reorder point for the notebook binders.

▼ SOLUTION

$$L = 5 \text{ days}$$

$$d = \frac{10{,}000}{300} = 33.3 \text{ units per day}$$

$$\text{ROP} = d \times L = (33.3 \text{ units per day})(5 \text{ days}) = 166.7 \text{ units}$$

Thus, Brad should reorder when his stock reaches 167 units.

▼ SOLVED PROBLEM 12.4

Leonard Presby, Inc., has an annual demand rate of 1,000 units but can produce at an average production rate of 2,000 units. Setup cost is $10; carrying cost is $1. What is the optimal number of units to be produced each time?

▼ SOLUTION

$$Q_p^* = \sqrt{\frac{2DS}{H\left(1 - \dfrac{\text{Annual demand rate}}{\text{Annual production rate}}\right)}} = \sqrt{\frac{2(1{,}000)(10)}{1[1 - (1{,}000/2{,}000)]}}$$

$$= \sqrt{\frac{20{,}000}{1/2}} = \sqrt{40{,}000} = 200 \text{ units}$$

▼ SOLVED PROBLEM 12.5

Whole Nature Foods sells a gluten-free product for which the annual demand is 5,000 boxes. At the moment, it is paying \$6.40 for each box; carrying cost is 25% of the unit cost; ordering costs are \$25. A new supplier has offered to sell the same item for \$6.00 if Whole Nature Foods buys at least 3,000 boxes per order. Should the firm stick with the old supplier, or take advantage of the new quantity discount?

▼ SOLUTION

Under present price of \$6.40 per box:

Economic order quantity, using Equation (12-10):

$$Q^* = \sqrt{\frac{2DS}{IP}}$$

$$Q^* = \sqrt{\frac{2(5{,}000)(25)}{(0.25)(6.40)}}$$

$$= 395.3, \text{ or } 395 \text{ boxes}$$

where D = period demand
S = ordering cost
P = price per box
I = holding cost as percent
H = holding cost = IP

$$\text{Total cost} = \text{Order cost} + \text{Holding cost} + \text{Purchase cost}$$

$$= \frac{DS}{Q} + \frac{Q}{2}H + PD$$

$$= \frac{(5{,}000)(25)}{395} + \frac{(395)(0.25)(6.40)}{2} + (6.40)(5{,}000)$$

$$= 316 + 316 + 32{,}000$$

$$= \$32{,}632$$

Note: Order and carrying costs are rounded.

Under the quantity discount price of \$6.00 per box:

We compute $Q^* = 408.25$, which is below the required order level of 3,000 boxes. So Q^* is adjusted to 3,000.

$$\text{Total cost} = \text{Ordering cost} + \text{Holding cost} + \text{Purchase cost}$$

$$= \frac{DS}{Q} + \frac{Q}{2}H + PD$$

$$= \frac{(5{,}000)(25)}{3{,}000} + \frac{(3{,}000)(0.25)(6.00)}{2} + (6.00)(5{,}000)$$

$$= 42 + 2{,}250 + 30{,}000$$

$$= \$32{,}292$$

Therefore, the new supplier with which Whole Nature Foods would incur a total cost of \$32,292 is preferable, but not by a large amount. If buying 3,000 boxes at a time raises problems of storage or freshness, the company may very well wish to stay with the current supplier.

▼ SOLVED PROBLEM 12.6

Children's art sets are ordered once each year by Ashok Kumar, Inc., and the reorder point, without safety stock (dL) is 100 art sets. Inventory carrying cost is \$10 per set per year, and the cost of a stockout is \$50 per set per year. Given the following demand probabilities during the lead time, how much safety stock should be carried?

Demand during Lead Time	Probability
0	.1
50	.2
ROP → 100	.4
150	.2
200	.1
	1.0

▼ SOLUTION

	Incremental Costs		
Safety Stock	**Carrying Cost**	**Stockout Cost**	**Total Cost**
0	0	$50 \times (50 \times 0.2 + 100 \times 0.1) = 1{,}000$	\$1,000
50	$50 \times 10 = 500$	$50 \times (0.1 \times 50) = 250$	750
100	$100 \times 10 = 1{,}000$	0	1,000

The safety stock that minimizes total incremental cost is 50 sets. The reorder point then becomes 100 sets + 50 sets, or 150 sets.

▼ SOLVED PROBLEM 12.7

What safety stock should Ron Satterfield Corporation maintain if mean sales are 80 during the reorder period, the standard deviation is 7, and Ron can tolerate stockouts 10% of the time?

▼ SOLUTION

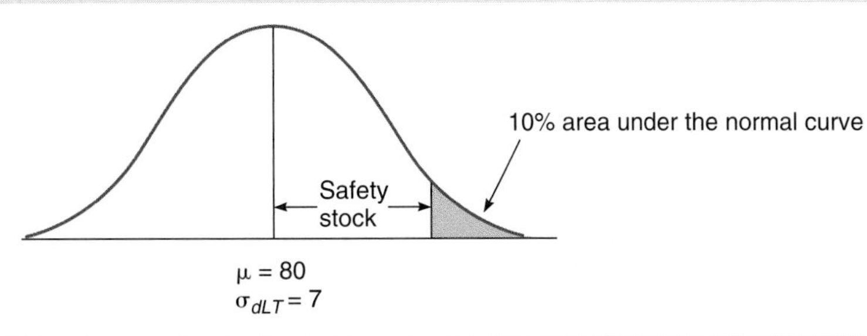

From Appendix I, Z at an area of .9 (or 1 – .10) = 1.28, and Equation (12-14):

$$\begin{aligned}\text{Safety stock} &= Z\sigma_{dLT} \\ &= 1.28(7) = 8.96 \text{ units, or } 9 \text{ units}\end{aligned}$$

▼ SOLVED PROBLEM 12.8

The daily demand for 52″ plasma TVs at Sarah's Discount Emporium is normally distributed, with an average of 5 and a standard deviation of 2 units. The lead time for receiving a shipment of new TVs is 10 days and is fairly constant. Determine the reorder point and safety stock for a 95% service level.

▼ SOLUTION

The ROP for this variable demand and constant lead time model uses Equation (12-15):

$$\text{ROP} = (\text{Average daily demand} \times \text{Lead time in days}) + Z\sigma_{dLT}$$

where $\sigma_{dLT} = \sigma_d \sqrt{\text{Lead time}}$

So, with $Z = 1.65$,

$$\begin{aligned}\text{ROP} &= (5 \times 10) + 1.65(2)\sqrt{10} \\ &= 50 + 10.4 = 60.4 \cong 60 \text{ TVs}\end{aligned}$$

The safety stock is 10.4, or about 10 TVs.

▼ SOLVED PROBLEM 12.9

The demand at Arnold Palmer Hospital for a specialized surgery pack is 60 per week, virtually every week. The lead time from McKesson, its main supplier, is normally distributed, with a mean of 6 weeks for this product and a standard deviation of 2 weeks. A 90% weekly service level is desired. Find the ROP.

▼ SOLUTION

Here the demand is constant and lead time is variable, with data given in weeks, not days. We apply Equation (12-16):

$$\text{ROP} = (\text{Weekly demand} \times \text{Average lead time in weeks}) + Z\,(\text{Weekly demand})\,\sigma_{LT}$$

where σ_{LT} = standard deviation of lead time in weeks = 2

So, with $Z = 1.28$, for a 90% service level:

$$\begin{aligned}\text{ROP} &= (60 \times 6) + 1.28(60)(2) \\ &= 360 + 153.6 = 513.6 \cong 514 \text{ surgery packs}\end{aligned}$$

Problems*

•• **12.1** L. Houts Plastics is a large manufacturer of injection-molded plastics in North Carolina. An investigation of the company's manufacturing facility in Charlotte yields the information presented in the table below. How would the plant classify these items according to an ABC classification system? PX

L. Houts Plastics Charlotte Inventory Levels

Item Code #	Average Inventory (units)	Value ($/unit)
1289	400	3.75
2347	300	4.00
2349	120	2.50
2363	75	1.50
2394	60	1.75
2395	30	2.00
6782	20	1.15
7844	12	2.05
8210	8	1.80
8310	7	2.00
9111	6	3.00

•• **12.2** Boreki Enterprise has the following 10 items in inventory. Theodore Boreki asks you, a recent OM graduate, to divide these items into ABC classifications.

Item	Annual Demand	Cost/Unit
A2	3,000	$ 50
B8	4,000	12
C7	1,500	45
D1	6,000	10
E9	1,000	20
F3	500	500
G2	300	1,500
H2	600	20
I5	1,750	10
J8	2,500	5

a) Develop an ABC classification system for the 10 items.
b) How can Boreki use this information?
c) Boreki reviews the classification and then places item A2 into the A category. Why might he do so? PX

•• **12.3** Jean-Marie Bourjolly's restaurant has the following inventory items that it orders on a weekly basis:

Inventory Item	$ Value/Case	# Ordered/Week
Rib eye steak	135	3
Lobster tail	245	3
Pasta	23	12
Salt	3	2
Napkins	12	2
Tomato sauce	23	11
French fries	43	32
Pepper	3	3
Garlic powder	11	3
Trash can liners	12	3
Table cloths	32	5
Fish filets	143	10
Prime rib roasts	166	6
Oil	28	2
Lettuce (case)	35	24
Chickens	75	14
Order pads	12	2
Eggs (case)	22	7
Bacon	56	5
Sugar	4	2

a) Which is the most expensive item, using annual dollar volume?
b) Which are C items?
c) What is the annual dollar volume for all 20 items? PX

• **12.4** Howard Electronics, a small manufacturer of electronic research equipment, has approximately 7,000 items in its inventory and has hired Joan Blasco-Paul to manage its inventory. Joan has determined that 10% of the items in inventory are A items, 35% are B items, and 55% are C items. She would like to set up a system in which all A items are counted monthly (every 20 working days), all B items are counted quarterly (every 60 working days), and all C items are counted semiannually (every 120 working days). How many items need to be counted each day?

• **12.5** William Beville's computer training school, in Richmond, stocks workbooks with the following characteristics:

$$\text{Demand } D = 19{,}500 \text{ units/year}$$
$$\text{Ordering cost } S = \$25/\text{order}$$
$$\text{Holding cost } H = \$4/\text{unit/year}$$

a) Calculate the EOQ for the workbooks.
b) What are the annual holding costs for the workbooks?
c) What are the annual ordering costs? PX

• **12.6** If $D = 8{,}000$ per month, $S = \$45$ per order, and $H = \$2$ per unit per month,
a) What is the economic order quantity?
b) How does your answer change if the holding cost doubles?
c) What if the holding cost drops in half? PX

•• **12.7** Henry Crouch's law office has traditionally ordered ink refills 60 units at a time. The firm estimates that carrying cost is 40% of the $10 unit cost and that annual demand is about 240 units per year. The assumptions of the basic EOQ model are thought to apply.
a) For what value of ordering cost would its action be optimal?
b) If the true ordering cost turns out to be much greater than your answer to part a, what is the impact on the firm's ordering policy?

• **12.8** Madeline Thimmes's Dream Store sells water beds and assorted supplies. Her best-selling bed has an annual demand of 400 units. Ordering cost is $40; holding cost is $5 per unit per year.
a) To minimize the total cost, how many units should be ordered each time an order is placed?
b) If the holding cost per unit was $6 instead of $5, what would be the optimal order quantity? PX

• **12.9** Southeastern Bell stocks a certain switch connector at its central warehouse for supplying field service offices. The yearly demand for these connectors is 15,000 units. Southeastern estimates its annual holding cost for this item to be $25 per unit. The cost to place and process an order from the supplier is $75. The company operates 300 days per year, and the lead time to receive an order from the supplier is 2 working days.
a) Find the economic order quantity.
b) Find the annual holding costs.
c) Find the annual ordering costs.
d) What is the reorder point? PX

*Note: PX means the problem may be solved with POM for Windows and/or Excel OM.

• **12.10** Lead time for one of your fastest-moving products is 21 days. Demand during this period averages 100 units per day.

a) What would be an appropriate reorder point?
b) How does your answer change if demand during lead time doubles?
c) How does your answer change if demand during lead time drops in half?

• **12.11** Annual demand for the notebook binders at Duncan's Stationery Shop is 10,000 units. Dana Duncan operates her business 300 days per year and finds that deliveries from her supplier generally take 5 working days.

a) Calculate the reorder point for the notebook binders that she stocks.
b) Why is this number important to Duncan?

•• **12.12** Thomas Kratzer is the purchasing manager for the headquarters of a large insurance company chain with a central inventory operation. Thomas's fastest-moving inventory item has a demand of 6,000 units per year. The cost of each unit is $100, and the inventory carrying cost is $10 per unit per year. The average ordering cost is $30 per order. It takes about 5 days for an order to arrive, and the demand for 1 week is 120 units. (This is a corporate operation, and there are 250 working days per year.)

a) What is the EOQ?
b) What is the average inventory if the EOQ is used?
c) What is the optimal number of orders per year?
d) What is the optimal number of days in between any two orders?
e) What is the annual cost of ordering and holding inventory?
f) What is the total annual inventory cost, including cost of the 6,000 units? PX

•• **12.13** Joe Henry's machine shop uses 2,500 brackets during the course of a year. These brackets are purchased from a supplier 90 miles away. The following information is known about the brackets:

Annual demand:	2,500
Holding cost per bracket per year:	$1.50
Order cost per order:	$18.75
Lead time:	2 days
Working days per year:	250

a) Given the above information, what would be the economic order quantity (EOQ)?
b) Given the EOQ, what would be the average inventory? What would be the annual inventory holding cost?
c) Given the EOQ, how many orders would be made each year? What would be the annual order cost?
d) Given the EOQ, what is the total annual cost of managing the inventory?
e) What is the time between orders?
f) What is the reorder point (ROP)? PX

•• **12.14** Myriah Fitzgibbon, of L.A. Plumbing, uses 1,200 of a certain spare part that costs $25 for each order, with an annual holding cost of $24.

a) Calculate the total cost for order sizes of 25, 40, 50, 60, and 100.
b) Identify the economic order quantity and consider the implications for making an error in calculating economic order quantity. PX

••• **12.15** M. Cotteleer Electronics supplies microcomputer circuitry to a company that incorporates microprocessors into refrigerators and other home appliances. One of the components has an annual demand of 250 units, and this is constant throughout the year. Carrying cost is estimated to be $1 per unit per year, and the ordering cost is $20 per order.

a) To minimize cost, how many units should be ordered each time an order is placed?
b) How many orders per year are needed with the optimal policy?
c) What is the average inventory if costs are minimized?
d) Suppose that the ordering cost is not $20, and Cotteleer has been ordering 150 units each time an order is placed. For this order policy (of $Q = 150$) to be optimal, determine what the ordering cost would have to be. PX

•• **12.16** Race One Motors is an Indonesian car manufacturer. At its largest manufacturing facility, in Jakarta, the company produces subcomponents at a rate of 300 per day, and it uses these subcomponents at a rate of 12,500 per year (of 250 working days). Holding costs are $2 per item per year, and ordering costs are $30 per order.

a) What is the economic production quantity?
b) How many production runs per year will be made?
c) What will be the maximum inventory level?
d) What percentage of time will the facility be producing components?
e) What is the annual cost of ordering and holding inventory? PX

•• **12.17** Radovilsky Manufacturing Company, in Hayward, California, makes flashing lights for toys. The company operates its production facility 300 days per year. It has orders for about 12,000 flashing lights per year and has the capability of producing 100 per day. Setting up the light production costs $50. The cost of each light is $1. The holding cost is $0.10 per light per year.

a) What is the optimal size of the production run?
b) What is the average holding cost per year?
c) What is the average setup cost per year?
d) What is the total cost per year, including the cost of the lights? PX

•• **12.18** Arthur Meiners is the production manager of Wheel-Rite, a small producer of metal parts. Wheel-Rite supplies Cal-Tex, a larger assembly company, with 10,000 wheel bearings each year. This order has been stable for some time. Setup cost for Wheel-Rite is $40, and holding cost is $.60 per wheel bearing per year. Wheel-Rite can produce 500 wheel bearings per day. Cal-Tex is a just-in-time manufacturer and requires that 50 bearings be shipped to it each business day.

a) What is the optimum production quantity?
b) What is the maximum number of wheel bearings that will be in inventory at Wheel-Rite?
c) How many production runs of wheel bearings will Wheel-Rite have in a year?
d) What is the total setup + holding cost for Wheel-Rite? PX

•• **12.19** Cesar Rego Computers, a Mississippi chain of computer hardware and software retail outlets, supplies both educational and commercial customers with memory and storage devices. It currently faces the following ordering decision relating to purchases of high-density disks:

$$D = 36{,}000 \text{ disks}$$
$$S = \$25$$
$$H = \$0.45$$
$$\text{Purchase price} = \$.85$$
$$\text{Discount price} = \$0.82$$
$$\text{Quantity needed to qualify for the discount} = 6{,}000 \text{ disks}$$

Should the discount be taken? PX

•• **12.20** Bell Computers purchases integrated chips at $350 per chip. The holding cost is $35 per unit per year, the ordering cost is $120 per order, and sales are steady, at 400 per month. The company's supplier, Rich Blue Chip Manufacturing, Inc., decides to offer price concessions in order to attract larger orders. The price structure is shown below.

a) What is the optimal order quantity and the minimum cost for Bell Computers to order, purchase, and hold these integrated chips?

Rich Blue Chip's Price Structure

Quantity Purchased	Price/Unit
1–99 units	$350
100–199 units	$325
200 or more units	$300

b) Bell Computers wishes to use a 10% holding cost rather than the fixed $35 holding cost in part a. What is the optimal order quantity, and what is the optimal cost? PX

•• **12.21** Wang Distributors has an annual demand for an airport metal detector of 1,400 units. The cost of a typical detector to Wang is $400. Carrying cost is estimated to be 20% of the unit cost, and the ordering cost is $25 per order. If Ping Wang, the owner, orders in quantities of 300 or more, he can get a 5% discount on the cost of the detectors. Should Wang take the quantity discount? PX

•• **12.22** The catering manager of LaVista Hotel, Lisa Ferguson, is disturbed by the amount of silverware she is losing every week. Last Friday night, when her crew tried to set up for a banquet for 500 people, they did not have enough knives. She decides she needs to order some more silverware, but wants to take advantage of any quantity discounts her vendor will offer.

For a small order (2,000 or fewer pieces), her vendor quotes a price of $1.80/piece.

If she orders 2,001–5,000 pieces, the price drops to $1.60/piece. 5,001–10,000 pieces brings the price to $1.40/piece, and 10,001 and above reduces the price to $1.25.

Lisa's order costs are $200 per order, her annual holding costs are 5%, and the annual demand is 45,000 pieces. For the best option:

a) What is the optimal order quantity?
b) What is the annual holding cost?
c) What is the annual ordering (setup) cost?
d) What are the annual costs of the silverware itself with an optimal order quantity?
e) What is the total annual cost, including ordering, holding, and purchasing the silverware? PX

•• **12.23** Rocky Mountain Tire Center sells 20,000 go-cart tires per year. The ordering cost for each order is $40, and the holding cost is 20% of the purchase price of the tires per year. The purchase price is $20 per tire if fewer than 500 tires are ordered, $18 per tire if 500 or more—but fewer than 1,000—tires are ordered, and $17 per tire if 1,000 or more tires are ordered.

a) How many tires should Rocky Mountain order each time it places an order?
b) What is the total cost of this policy? PX

•• **12.24** M. P. VanOyen Manufacturing has gone out on bid for a regulator component. Expected demand is 700 units per month. The item can be purchased from either Allen Manufacturing or Baker Manufacturing. Their price lists are shown in the table. Ordering cost is $50, and annual holding cost per unit is $5.

Allen Mfg.		*Baker Mfg.*	
Quantity	**Unit Price**	**Quantity**	**Unit Price**
1–499	$16.00	1–399	$16.10
500–999	15.50	400–799	15.60
1,000+	15.00	800+	15.10

a) What is the economic order quantity?
b) Which supplier should be used? Why?
c) What is the optimal order quantity and total annual cost of ordering, purchasing, and holding the component? PX

••• **12.25** Chris Sandvig Irrigation, Inc., has summarized the price list from four potential suppliers of an underground control valve. See the table below. Annual usage is 2,400 valves; order cost is $10 per order; and annual inventory holding costs are $3.33 per unit.

Which vendor should be selected and what order quantity is best if Sandvig Irrigation wants to minimize total cost? PX

Vendor A		*Vendor B*	
Quantity	**Price**	**Quantity**	**Price**
1–49	$35.00	1–74	$34.75
50–74	34.75	75–149	34.00
75–149	33.55	150–299	32.80
150–299	32.35	300–499	31.60
300–499	31.15	500+	30.50
500+	30.75		
Vendor C		*Vendor D*	
Quantity	**Price**	**Quantity**	**Price**
1–99	$34.50	1–199	$34.25
100–199	33.75	200–399	33.00
200–399	32.50	400+	31.00
400+	31.10		

••• **12.26** Emery Pharmaceutical uses an unstable chemical compound that must be kept in an environment where both temperature and humidity can be controlled. Emery uses 800 pounds per month of the chemical, estimates the holding cost to be 50% of the purchase price (because of spoilage), and estimates order costs to be $50 per order. The cost schedules of two suppliers are as follows:

Vendor 1		*Vendor 2*	
Quantity	**Price/lb**	**Quantity**	**Price/lb**
1–499	$17.00	1–399	$17.10
500–999	16.75	400–799	16.85
1,000+	16.50	800–1,199	16.60
		1,200+	16.25

a) What is the economic order quantity for each supplier?
b) What quantity should be ordered, and which supplier should be used?
c) What is the total cost for the most economic order size?
d) What factor(s) should be considered besides total cost? PX

•• **12.27** Barbara Flynn is in charge of maintaining hospital supplies at General Hospital. During the past year, the mean lead time demand for bandage BX-5 was 60 (and was normally distributed). Furthermore, the standard deviation for BX-5 was 7. Ms. Flynn would like to maintain a 90% service level.

a) What safety stock level do you recommend for BX-5?
b) What is the appropriate reorder point? PX

•• **12.28** Based on available information, lead time demand for PC jump drives averages 50 units (normally distributed), with a standard deviation of 5 drives. Management wants a 97% service level.

a) What value of Z should be applied?
b) How many drives should be carried as safety stock?
c) What is the appropriate reorder point? PX

••• **12.29** Authentic Thai rattan chairs (shown in the photo) are delivered to Gary Schwartz's chain of retail stores, called The Kathmandu Shop, once a year. The reorder point, without safety stock, is 200 chairs. Carrying cost is \$30 per unit per year, and the cost of a stockout is \$70 per chair per year. Given the following demand probabilities during the lead time, how much safety stock should be carried?

Demand During Lead Time	Probability
0	0.2
100	0.2
200	0.2
300	0.2
400	0.2

•• **12.30** Tobacco is shipped from North Carolina to a cigarette manufacturer in Cambodia once a year. The reorder point, without safety stock, is 200 kilos. The carrying cost is \$15 per kilo per year, and the cost of a stockout is \$70 per kilo per year. Given the following demand probabilities during the lead time, how much safety stock should be carried?

Demand During Lead Time (kilos)	Probability
0	0.1
100	0.1
200	0.2
300	0.4
400	0.2

••• **12.31** Mr. Beautiful, an organization that sells weight training sets, has an ordering cost of \$40 for the BB-1 set. (BB-1 stands for Body Beautiful Number 1.) The carrying cost for BB-1 is \$5 per set per year. To meet demand, Mr. Beautiful orders large quantities of BB-1 seven times a year. The stockout cost for BB-1 is estimated to be \$50 per set. Over the past several years, Mr. Beautiful has observed the following demand during the lead time for BB-1:

Demand During Lead Time	Probability
40	.1
50	.2
60	.2
70	.2
80	.2
90	.1
	1.0

The reorder point for BB-1 is 60 sets. What level of safety stock should be maintained for BB-1?

•• **12.32** Chicago's Hard Rock Hotel distributes a mean of 1,000 bath towels per day to guests at the pool and in their rooms. This demand is normally distributed with a standard deviation of 100 towels per day, based on occupancy. The laundry firm that has the linen contract requires a 2-day lead time. The hotel expects a 98% service level to satisfy high guest expectations.

a) What is the ROP?
b) What is the safety stock?

•• **12.33** First Printing has contracts with legal firms in San Francisco to copy their court documents. Daily demand is almost constant at 12,500 pages of documents. The lead time for paper delivery is normally distributed with a mean of 4 days and a standard deviation of 1 day. A 97% service level is expected. Compute First's ROP.

••• **12.34** Gainesville Cigar stocks Cuban cigars that have variable lead times because of the difficulty in importing the product: Lead time is normally distributed with an average of 6 weeks and a standard deviation of 2 weeks. Demand is also a variable and normally distributed with a mean of 200 cigars per week and a standard deviation of 25 cigars.

a) For a 90% service level, what is the ROP?
b) What is the ROP for a 95% service level?
c) Explain what these two service levels mean. Which is preferable?

••• **12.35** Kim Clark has asked you to help him determine the best ordering policy for a new product. The demand for the new product has been forecasted to be about 1,000 units annually. To help you get a handle on the carrying and ordering costs, Kim has given you the list of last year's costs. He thought that these costs might be appropriate for the new product.

Cost Factor	Cost (\$)	Cost Factor	Cost (\$)
Taxes for the warehouse	2,000	Warehouse supplies	280
Receiving and incoming inspection	1,500	Research and development	2,750
New product development	2,500	Purchasing salaries & wages	30,000
Acct. Dept. costs to pay invoices	500	Warehouse salaries & wages	12,800
Inventory insurance	600	Pilferage of inventory	800
Product advertising	800	Purchase order supplies	500
Spoilage	750	Inventory obsolescence	300
Sending purchasing orders	800	Purchasing Dept. overhead	1,000

He also told you that these data were compiled for 10,000 inventory items that were carried or held during the year. You have also determined that 200 orders were placed last year. Your job as a new operations management graduate is to help Kim determine the economic order quantity for the new product.

•• **12.36** Cynthia Knott's oyster bar buys fresh Louisiana oysters for $5 per pound and sells them for $9 per pound. Any oysters not sold that day are sold to her cousin, who has a nearby grocery store, for $2 per pound. Cynthia believes that demand follows the normal distribution, with a mean of 100 pounds and a standard deviation of 15 pounds. How many pounds should she order each day?

•• **12.37** Henrique Correa's bakery prepares all its cakes between 4 A.M. and 6 A.M. so they will be fresh when customers arrive. Day-old cakes are virtually always sold, but at a 50% discount off the regular $10 price. The cost of baking a cake is $6, and demand is estimated to be normally distributed, with a mean of 25 and a standard deviation of 4. What is the optimal stocking level?

••• **12.38** University of Florida football programs are printed 1 week prior to each home game. Attendance averages 90,000 screaming and loyal Gators fans, of whom two-thirds usually buy the program, following a normal distribution, for $4 each. Unsold programs are sent to a recycling center that pays only 10 cents per program. The standard deviation is 5,000 programs, and the cost to print each program is $1.

a) What is the cost of underestimating demand for each program?
b) What is the overage cost per program?
c) How many programs should be ordered per game?
d) What is the stockout risk for this order size?

•••• **12.39** Emarpy Appliance is a company that produces all kinds of major appliances. Bud Banis, the president of Emarpy, is concerned about the production policy for the company's best-selling refrigerator. The annual demand for this has been about 8,000 units each year, and this demand has been constant throughout the year. The production capacity is 200 units per day. Each time production starts, it costs the company $120 to move materials into place, reset the assembly line, and clean the equipment. The holding cost of a refrigerator is $50 per year. The current production plan calls for 400 refrigerators to be produced in each production run. Assume there are 250 working days per year.

a) What is the daily demand of this product?
b) If the company were to continue to produce 400 units each time production starts, how many days would production continue?
c) Under the current policy, how many production runs per year would be required? What would the annual setup cost be?
d) If the current policy continues, how many refrigerators would be in inventory when production stops? What would the average inventory level be?
e) If the company produces 400 refrigerators at a time, what would the total annual setup cost and holding cost be?
f) If Bud Banis wants to minimize the total annual inventory cost, how many refrigerators should be produced in each production run? How much would this save the company in inventory costs compared to the current policy of producing 400 in each production run? Px

•••• **12.40** A gourmet coffee shop in downtown San Francisco is open 200 days a year and sells an average of 75 pounds of Kona coffee beans a day. (Demand can be assumed to be distributed normally with a standard deviation of 15 pounds per day). After ordering (fixed cost = $16 per order), beans are always shipped from Hawaii within exactly 4 days. Per-pound annual holding costs for the beans are $3.

a) What is the economic order quantity (EOQ) for Kona coffee beans?
b) What are the total annual holding costs of stock for Kona coffee beans?
c) What are the total annual ordering costs for Kona coffee beans?
d) Assume that management has specified that no more than a 1% risk during stockout is acceptable. What should the reorder point (ROP) be?
e) What is the safety stock needed to attain a 1% risk of stockout during lead time?
f) What is the annual holding cost of maintaining the level of safety stock needed to support a 1% risk?
g) If management specified that a 2% risk of stockout during lead time would be acceptable, would the safety stock holding costs decrease or increase?

Refer to myomlab for these additional homework problems: 12.41–12.53

Case Studies

Zhou Bicycle Company

Zhou Bicycle Company (ZBC), located in Seattle, is a wholesale distributor of bicycles and bicycle parts. Formed in 1981 by University of Washington Professor Yong-Pin Zhou, the firm's primary retail outlets are located within a 400-mile radius of the distribution center. These retail outlets receive the order from ZBC within 2 days after notifying the distribution center, provided that the stock is available. However, if an order is not fulfilled by the company, no backorder is placed; the retailers arrange to get their shipment from other distributors, and ZBC loses that amount of business.

The company distributes a wide variety of bicycles. The most popular model, and the major source of revenue to the company, is the AirWing. ZBC receives all the models from a single manufacturer in China, and shipment takes as long as 4 weeks from the time an order is placed. With the cost of communication, paperwork, and customs clearance included, ZBC estimates that each time an order

Demands for AirWing Model

Month	2008	2009	Forecast for 2010
January	6	7	8
February	12	14	15
March	24	27	31
April	46	53	59
May	75	86	97
June	47	54	60
July	30	34	39
August	18	21	24
September	13	15	16
October	12	13	15
November	22	25	28
December	38	42	47
Total	343	391	439

is placed, it incurs a cost of $65. The purchase price paid by ZBC, per bicycle, is roughly 60% of the suggested retail price for all the styles available, and the inventory carrying cost is 1% per month (12% per year) of the purchase price paid by ZBC. The retail price (paid by the customers) for the AirWing is $170 per bicycle.

ZBC is interested in making an inventory plan for 2010. The firm wants to maintain a 95% service level with its customers to minimize the losses on the lost orders. The data collected for the past 2 years are summarized in the preceding table. A forecast for AirWing model sales in 2010 has been developed and will be used to make an inventory plan for ZBC.

Discussion Questions

1. Develop an inventory plan to help ZBC.
2. Discuss ROPs and total costs.
3. How can you address demand that is not at the level of the planning horizon?

Source: Professor Kala Chand Seal, Loyola Marymount University.

▶ Sturdivant Sound Systems

Sturdivant Sound Systems manufactures and sells sound systems for both home and auto. All parts of the sound systems, with the exception of DVD players, are produced in the Rochester, New York, plant. DVD players used in the assembly of Sturdivant systems are purchased from Morris Electronics of Concord, New Hampshire.

Sturdivant purchasing agent Mary Kim submits a purchase requisition for DVD players once every 4 weeks. The company's annual requirements total 5,000 units (20 per working day), and the cost per unit is $60. (Sturdivant does not purchase in greater quantities because Morris Electronics does not offer quantity discounts.) Because Morris promises delivery within 1 week following receipt of a purchase requisition, rarely is there a shortage of DVD players. (Total time between date of order and date of receipt is 5 days.)

Associated with the purchase of each shipment are procurement costs. These costs, which amount to $20 per order, include the costs of preparing the requisition, inspecting and storing the delivered goods, updating inventory records, and issuing a voucher and a check for payment. In addition to procurement costs, Sturdivant incurs inventory carrying costs that include insurance, storage, handling, taxes, and so forth. These costs equal $6 per unit per year.

Beginning in August of this year, Sturdivant management will embark on a companywide cost-control program in an attempt to improve its profits. One area to be closely scrutinized for possible cost savings is inventory procurement.

Discussion Questions

1. Compute the optimal order quantity of DVD players.
2. Determine the appropriate reorder point (in units).
3. Compute the cost savings that the company will realize if it implements the optimal inventory procurement decision.
4. Should procurement costs be considered a linear function of the number of orders?

Source: Reprinted by permission of Professor Jerry Kinard, Western Carolina University.

▶ Managing Inventory at Frito-Lay

Video Case

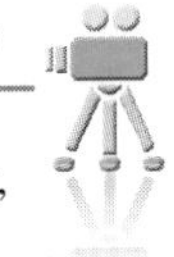

Frito-Lay has flourished since its origin—the 1931 purchase of a small San Antonio firm for $100 that included a recipe, 19 retail accounts, and a hand-operated potato ricer. The multi-billion-dollar company, headquartered in Dallas, now has 41 products—15 with sales of over $100 million per year and 7 at over $1 billion in sales. Production takes place in 36 product-focused plants in the U.S. and Canada, with 48,000 employees.

Inventory is a major investment and an expensive asset in most firms. Holding costs often exceed 25% of product value, but in Frito-Lay's prepared food industry, holding cost can be much higher because the raw materials are perishable. In the food industry, inventory spoils. So poor inventory management is not only expensive but can also yield an unsatisfactory product that in the extreme can also ruin market acceptance.

Major ingredients at Frito-Lay are corn meal, corn, potatoes, oil, and seasoning. Using potato chips to illustrate rapid inventory flow: potatoes are moved via truck from farm, to regional plants for processing, to warehouse, to the retail store. This happens in a matter of hours—not days or weeks. This keeps freshness high and holding costs low.

Frequent deliveries of main ingredients at the Florida plant, for example, take several forms:

- Potatoes are delivered in 10 truckloads per day, with 150,000 lbs consumed in one shift: the entire potato storage area will only hold 7½ hours' worth of potatoes.
- Oil inventory arrives by rail car, which lasts only 4½ days.
- Corn meal arrives from various farms in the Midwest, and inventory typically averages 4 days' production.
- Seasoning inventory averages 7 days.
- Packaging inventory averages 8 to 10 days.

Frito-Lay's product-focused facility is expensive. It represents a major capital investment that must achieve high utilization to be efficient. The capital cost must be spread over a substantial volume to drive down total cost of the snack foods produced. This demand for high utilization requires reliable equipment and tight schedules. Reliable machinery requires an inventory of critical components: this is known as MRO, or maintenance, repair, and operating supplies. MRO inventory of motors, switches, gears, bearings, and other critical specialized components can be costly but is necessary.

Frito-Lay's non-MRO inventory moves rapidly. Raw material quickly becomes work-in-process, moving through the system and out the door as a bag of chips in about 1 1/2 shifts. Packaged finished products move from production to the distribution chain in less than 1.4 days.

Discussion Questions*

1. How does the mix of Frito-Lay's inventory differ from those at a machine or cabinet shop (a process-focused facility)?
2. What are the major inventory items at Frito-Lay, and how rapidly do they move through the process?
3. What are the four types of inventory? Give an example of each at Frito-Lay.
4. How would you rank the dollar investment in each of the four types (from the most investment to the least investment)?
5. Why does inventory flow so quickly through a Frito-Lay plant?
6. Why does the company keep so many plants open?
7. Why doesn't Frito-Lay make all its 41 products at each of its plants?

*You may wish to view the video that accompanies this case before answering these questions.

Source: Professors Jay Heizer, Texas Lutheran University; Barry Render, Rollins College; and Bev Amer, Northern Arizona University.

▶Inventory Control at Wheeled Coach

Video Case

Controlling inventory is one of Wheeled Coach's toughest problems. Operating according to a strategy of mass customization and responsiveness, management knows that success is dependent on tight inventory control. Anything else results in an inability to deliver promptly, chaos on the assembly line, and a huge inventory investment. Wheeled Coach finds that almost 50% of the $40,000 to $100,000 cost of every ambulance it manufactures is purchased materials. A large proportion of that 50% is in chassis (purchased from Ford), aluminum (from Reynolds Metal), and plywood used for flooring and cabinetry construction (from local suppliers). Wheeled Coach tracks these A inventory items quite carefully, maintaining tight security/control and ordering carefully so as to maximize quantity discounts while minimizing on-hand stock. Because of long lead times and scheduling needs at Reynolds, aluminum must actually be ordered as much as 8 months in advance.

In a crowded ambulance industry in which it is the only giant, its 45 competitors don't have the purchasing power to draw the same discounts as Wheeled Coach. But this competitive cost advantage cannot be taken lightly, according to President Bob Collins. "Cycle counting in our stockrooms is critical. No part can leave the locked stockrooms without appearing on a bill of materials."

Accurate bills of material (BOM) are a requirement if products are going to be built on time. Additionally, because of the custom nature of each vehicle, most orders are won only after a bidding process. Accurate BOMs are critical to cost estimation and the resulting bid. For these reasons, Collins was emphatic that Wheeled Coach maintain outstanding inventory control. The *Global Company Profile* featuring Wheeled Coach (which opens Chapter 14) provides further details about the ambulance inventory control and production process.

Discussion Questions*

1. Explain how Wheeled Coach implements ABC analysis.
2. If you were to take over as inventory control manager at Wheeled Coach, what additional policies and techniques would you initiate to ensure accurate inventory records?
3. How would you go about implementing these suggestions?

*You may wish to view the video that accompanies this case before answering these questions.

▶**Additional Case Studies:** Visit **www.myomlab.com** or **www.pearsonhighered.com/heizer** *for these free case studies:*
Southwestern University (F): The university must decide how many football day programs to order, and from whom.
LaPlace Power and Light: This utility company is evaluating its current inventory policies.

Bibliography

Abernathy, Frederick H., et al. "Control Your Inventory in a World of Lean Retailing." *Harvard Business Review* 78, no. 6 (November–December 2000): 169–176.

Arnold, J. R., S. N. Chapman, and L. M. Clive. *Introduction to Materials Management*, 6th ed. Upper Saddle River, NJ: Prentice Hall (2008).

Bradley, James R., and Richard W. Conway. "Managing Cyclic Inventories." *Production and Operations Management* 12, no. 4 (Winter 2003): 464–479.

Burt, D. N., S. Petcavage, and R. Pinkerton. *Supply Management*, 8th ed. Burr Ridge, IL: Irwin/McGraw (2010).

Chapman, Stephen. *Fundamentals of Production Planning and Control*. Upper Saddle River, NJ: Prentice Hall (2006).

Chopra, Sunil, Gilles Reinhardt, and Maqbool Dada. "The Effect of Lead Time Uncertainty on Safety Stocks." *Decision Sciences* 35, no. 1 (Winter 2004): 1–24.

Keren, Baruch. "The Single Period Inventory Model." *Omega* 37, no. 4 (August 2009): 801.

Liu, X., and Z. Lian. "Cost-effective Inventory Control in a Value-added Manufacturing System." *European Journal of Operational Research* 196, no. 2 (July 2009): 534.

McDonald, Stan C. *Materials Management*. New York: Wiley (2009).

Noblitt, James M. "The Economic Order Quantity Model: Panacea or Plague?" *APICS—The Performance Advantage* (February 2001): 53–57.

Render, B., R. M. Stair, and M. Hanna. *Quantitative Analysis for Management*, 11th ed. Upper Saddle River, NJ: Prentice Hall (2011).

Rubin, Paul A., and W. C. Benton. "A Generalized Framework for Quantity Discount Pricing Schedules." *Decision Sciences* 34, no. 1 (Winter 2003): 173–188.

Vollmann, T. E., W. L. Berry, D. C. Whybark, and F. R. Jacobs. *Manufacturing Planning and Control for Supply Chain Management*, 5th ed. Burr Ridge, IL: Irwin/McGraw (2005).

Witt, Clyde E. "Mobile Warehouse Supplies U.S. Marines in Iraq." *Material Handling Management* 60, no. 8 (August 2005): 24–25.

Chapter 12 **Rapid** Review

Main Heading	Review Material	myomlab

THE IMPORTANCE OF INVENTORY
(pp. 468–469)

Inventory is one of the most expensive assets of many companies.
The objective of inventory management is to strike a balance between inventory investment and customer service.
The two basic inventory issues are how much to order and when to order.

- **Raw material inventory**—Materials that are usually purchased but have yet to enter the manufacturing process.
- **Work-in-process (WIP) inventory**—Products or components that are no longer raw materials but have yet to become finished products.
- **MRO**—Maintenance, repair, and operating materials.
- **Finished-goods inventory**—An end item ready to be sold but still an asset on the company's books.

VIDEO 12.1
Managing Inventory at Frito-Lay

MANAGING INVENTORY
(pp. 469–473)

- **ABC analysis**—A method for dividing on-hand inventory into three classifications based on annual dollar volume.
- **Cycle counting**—A continuing reconciliation of inventory with inventory records.
- **Shrinkage**—Retail inventory that is unaccounted for between receipt and sale.
- **Pilferage**—A small amount of theft.

Problems: 12.1–12.4

Virtual Office Hours for Solved Problem: 12.1

INVENTORY MODELS
(p. 474)

- **Holding cost**—The cost to keep or carry inventory in stock.
- **Ordering cost**—The cost of the ordering process.
- **Setup cost**—The cost to prepare a machine or process for production.
- **Setup time**—The time required to prepare a machine or process for production.

INVENTORY MODELS FOR INDEPENDENT DEMAND
(pp. 474–487)

- **Economic order quantity (EOQ) model**—An inventory-control technique that minimizes the total of ordering and holding costs:

$$Q^* = \sqrt{\frac{2DS}{H}} \quad (12\text{-}1)$$

$$\text{Expected number of orders} = N = \frac{\text{Demand}}{\text{Order quantity}} = \frac{D}{Q^*} \quad (12\text{-}2)$$

$$\text{Expected time between orders} = T = \frac{\text{Number of working days per year}}{N} \quad (12\text{-}3)$$

$$\text{Total annual cost} = \text{Setup (order) cost} + \text{Holding cost} \quad (12\text{-}4)$$

$$TC = \frac{D}{Q}S + \frac{Q}{2}H \quad (12\text{-}5)$$

- **Robust**—Giving satisfactory answers even with substantial variation in the parameters.
- **Lead time**—In purchasing systems, the time between placing an order and receiving it; in production systems, the wait, move, queue, setup, and run times for each component produced.
- **Reorder point (ROP)**—The inventory level (point) at which action is taken to replenish the stocked item.

ROP for known demand:

$$\text{ROP} = (\text{Demand per day}) \times (\text{Lead time for a new order in days}) = d \times L \quad (12\text{-}6)$$

- **Safety stock**—Extra stock to allow for uneven demand; a buffer.
- **Production order quantity model**—An economic order quantity technique applied to production orders:

$$Q_p^* = \sqrt{\frac{2DS}{H[1 - (d/p)]}} \quad (12\text{-}7)$$

$$Q_p^* = \sqrt{\frac{2DS}{H\left(1 - \frac{\text{Annual demand rate}}{\text{Annual production rate}}\right)}} \quad (12\text{-}8)$$

- **Quantity discount**—A reduced price for items purchased in large quantities:

$$TC - \frac{D}{Q}S + \frac{Q}{2}H + PD \quad (12\text{-}9)$$

$$Q^* = \sqrt{\frac{2DS}{IP}} \quad (12\text{-}10)$$

Problems: 12.5–12.26, 12.35, 12.39

Virtual Office Hours for Solved Problems: 12.2–12.5

ACTIVE MODELS 12.1, 12.2

VIDEO 12.2
Inventory Control at Wheeled Coach Ambulance

Main Heading	Review Material	myomlab
PROBABILISTIC MODELS AND SAFETY STOCK (pp. 487–492)	■ **Probabilistic model**—A statistical model applicable when product demand or any other variable is not known but can be specified by means of a probability distribution. ■ **Service level**—The complement of the probability of a stockout. *ROP for unknown demand:* $\text{ROP} = d \times L + ss$ (12-11) Annual stockout costs = The sum of the units short for each demand level × The probability of that demand level × The stockout cost/unit × The number of orders per year (12-12) *ROP for unknown demand and given service level:* $\text{ROP} = \text{Expected demand during lead time} + Z\sigma_{dLT}$ (12-13) $\text{Safety stock} = Z\sigma_{dLT}$ (12-14) *ROP for variable demand and constant lead time:* ROP = (*Average* daily demand × Lead time in days) + $Z\sigma_{dLT}$ (12-15) *ROP for constant demand and variable lead time:* ROP = (Daily demand × *Average* lead time in days) + Z(Daily demand) × σ_{LT} (12-16) *ROP for variable demand and variable lead time:* ROP = (Average daily demand × Average lead time) + $Z\sigma_{dLT}$ (12-17) In each case, $\sigma_{dLT} = \sqrt{(\text{Average lead time} \times \sigma_d^2) + \bar{d}^2\sigma_{LT}^2}$ but under constant demand: $\sigma_d^2 = 0$, and while under constant lead time: $\sigma_{LT}^2 = 0$.	Problems: 12.27–12.34 Virtual Office Hours for Solved Problems: 12.6–12.9
SINGLE-PERIOD MODEL (pp. 492–493)	■ **Single-period inventory model**—A system for ordering items that have little or no value at the end of the sales period: $\text{Service Level} = \dfrac{C_s}{C_s + C_o}$ (12-18)	Problems: 12.36–12.38
FIXED-PERIOD (*P*) SYSTEMS (pp. 493–494)	■ **Fixed-quantity (Q) system**—An ordering system with the same order amount each time. ■ **Perpetual inventory system**—A system that keeps track of each withdrawal or addition to inventory continuously, so records are always current. ■ **Fixed-period (*P*) system**—A system in which inventory orders are made at regular time intervals.	

Self Test

■ **Before taking the self-test,** refer to the learning objectives listed at the beginning of the chapter and the key terms listed at the end of the chapter.

LO1. ABC analysis divides on-hand inventory into three classes, based on:
a) unit price. **b)** the number of units on hand.
c) annual demand. **d)** annual dollar values.

LO2. Cycle counting:
a) provides a measure of inventory turnover.
b) assumes that all inventory records must be verified with the same frequency.
c) is a process by which inventory records are periodically verified.
d) all of the above.

LO3. The two most important inventory-based questions answered by the typical inventory model are:
a) when to place an order and the cost of the order.
b) when to place an order and how much of an item to order.
c) how much of an item to order and the cost of the order.
d) how much of an item to order and with whom the order should be placed.

LO4. Extra units in inventory to help reduce stockouts are called:
a) reorder point. **b)** safety stock.
c) just-in-time inventory. **d)** all of the above.

LO5. The difference(s) between the basic EOQ model and the production order quantity model is(are) that:
a) the production order quantity model does not require the assumption of known, constant demand.
b) the EOQ model does not require the assumption of negligible lead time.
c) the production order quantity model does not require the assumption of instantaneous delivery.
d) all of the above.

LO6. The EOQ model with quantity discounts attempts to determine:
a) the lowest amount of inventory necessary to satisfy a certain service level.
b) the lowest purchase price.
c) whether to use a fixed-quantity or fixed-period order policy.
d) how many units should be ordered.
e) the shortest lead time.

LO7. The appropriate level of safety stock is typically determined by:
a) minimizing an expected stockout cost.
b) choosing the level of safety stock that assures a given service level.
c) carrying sufficient safety stock so as to eliminate all stockouts.
d) annual demand.

Answers: LO1. d; LO2. c; LO3. b; LO4. b; LO5. c; LO6. d; LO7. b.

13 Aggregate Planning

Chapter Outline

OM Strategy Decisions

- Design of Goods and Services
- Managing Quality
- Process Strategy
- Location Strategies
- Layout Strategies
- Human Resources
- Supply-Chain Management
- Inventory Management
- Scheduling
  - Aggregate
  - Short-Term
- Maintenance

AGGREGATE PLANNING PROVIDES A COMPETITIVE ADVANTAGE AT FRITO-LAY

Like other organizations throughout the world, Frito-Lay relies on effective aggregate planning to match fluctuating multi-billion-dollar demand to capacity in its 36 North American plants. Planning for the intermediate term (3 to 18 months) is the heart of aggregate planning. Effective aggregate planning combined with tight scheduling, effective maintenance, and efficient employee and facility scheduling are the keys to high plant utilization. High utilization is a critical factor in facilities such as Frito-Lay where capital investment is substantial.

Frito-Lay has more than three dozen brands of snacks and chips, 15 of which sell more than $100 million annually and 7 of which sell over $1 billion. Its brands include such well-known names as Fritos, Lay's, Doritos, Sun Chips, Cheetos, Tostitos, Flat Earth, and Ruffles. Unique processes using specially designed equipment are required to produce each of these products. Because these specialized processes generate high fixed cost, they must operate at very high volume. But such product-focused facilities benefit by having low variable costs. High utilization and performance above the break-even point require a good match between demand and capacity. Idle equipment is disastrous.

At Frito-Lay's headquarters near Dallas, planners create a total demand profile. They use historical product sales, forecasts of new products, product innovations, product promotions, and dynamic local demand data from account managers to forecast demand. Planners then match the total demand profile to existing capacity, capacity expansion plans, and cost. This becomes the aggregate plan. The aggregate plan is communicated to each of the firm's 17 regions and to the 36 plants. Every quarter, headquarters and each plant modify the respective plans to incorporate changing market conditions and plant performance.

Each plant uses its quarterly plan to develop a 4-week plan, which in turn assigns specific products to specific product lines for production runs. Finally, each week raw materials and labor are assigned to each process. Effective aggregate planning is a major factor in high utilization and low cost. As the company's 60% market share indicates, excellent aggregate planning yields a competitive advantage at Frito-Lay.

The aggregate plan adjusts for farm location, yield, and quantities for timely delivery of Frito-Lay's unique varieties of potatoes. During harvest times, potatoes go directly to the plant. During non-harvest months, potatoes are stored in climate-controlled environments to maintain quality, texture, and taste.

As potatoes arrive at the plant, they are promptly washed and peeled to ensure freshness and taste.

After peeling, potatoes are cut into thin slices, rinsed of excess starch, and cooked in sunflower and/or corn oil.

After cooking is complete, inspection, bagging, weighing, and packing operations prepare Lay's potato chips for shipment to customers—all in a matter of hours.

Chapter 13 **Learning Objectives**

AUTHOR COMMENT Idle capacity is expensive, and inadequate capacity loses customers.

THE PLANNING PROCESS

Manufacturers such as Frito-Lay, Anheuser-Busch, GE, and Yamaha face tough decisions when trying to schedule products such as snack foods, beer, air conditioners, and jet skis, the demand for which is heavily dependent on seasonal variation. Developing plans that minimize costs connected with such forecasts is *aggregate planning,* one of the main functions of an operations manager. **Aggregate planning** (also known as **aggregate scheduling**) is concerned with determining the quantity and timing of production for the intermediate future, often from 3 to 18 months ahead. Operations managers try to determine the best way to meet forecasted demand by adjusting production rates, labor levels, inventory levels, overtime work, subcontracting rates, and other controllable variables. Usually, *the objective of aggregate planning is to meet forecasted demand while minimizing cost over the planning period.* However, other strategic issues may be more important than low cost. These strategies may be to smooth employment levels, to drive down inventory levels, or to meet a high level of service.

Aggregate planning (or **aggregate scheduling)**
An approach to determine the quantity and timing of production for the intermediate future (usually 3 to 18 months ahead).

For manufacturers, the aggregate schedule ties the firm's strategic goals to production plans, but for service organizations, the aggregate schedule ties strategic goals to workforce schedules.

LO1: Define aggregate planning

Four things are needed for aggregate planning:

- A logical overall unit for measuring sales and output, such as pounds of Doritos at Frito-Lay, air-conditioning units at GE, or cases of beer at Anheuser-Busch
- A forecast of demand for a reasonable intermediate planning period in these aggregate terms
- A method for determining the relevant costs
- A model that combines forecasts and costs so that scheduling decisions can be made for the planning period

In this chapter we describe the aggregate planning decision, show how the aggregate plan fits into the overall planning process, and describe several techniques that managers use when developing an aggregate plan. We stress both manufacturing and service-sector firms.

Planning Horizons

In Chapter 4, we saw that demand forecasting can address short-, medium-, and long-range problems. Long-range forecasts help managers deal with capacity and strategic issues and are the responsibility of top management (see Figure 13.1). Top management formulates policy-related questions, such as facility location and expansion, new product development, research funding, and investment over a period of several years.

Medium-range planning begins once long-term capacity decisions are made. This is the job of the operations manager. **Scheduling decisions** address the problem of matching productivity to fluctuating demands. These plans need to be consistent with top management's long-range strategy and work within the resources allocated by earlier strategic decisions. Medium- (or "intermediate-") range planning is accomplished by building an aggregate production plan.

Scheduling decisions
Plans that match production to changes in demand.

Short-range planning may extend up to a year but is usually less than 3 months. This plan is also the responsibility of operations personnel, who work with supervisors and foremen to "disaggregate" the intermediate plan into weekly, daily, and hourly schedules. Tactics for dealing with short-term planning involve loading, sequencing, expediting, and dispatching, which are discussed in Chapter 15.

Figure 13.1 illustrates the time horizons and features for short-, intermediate-, and long-range planning.

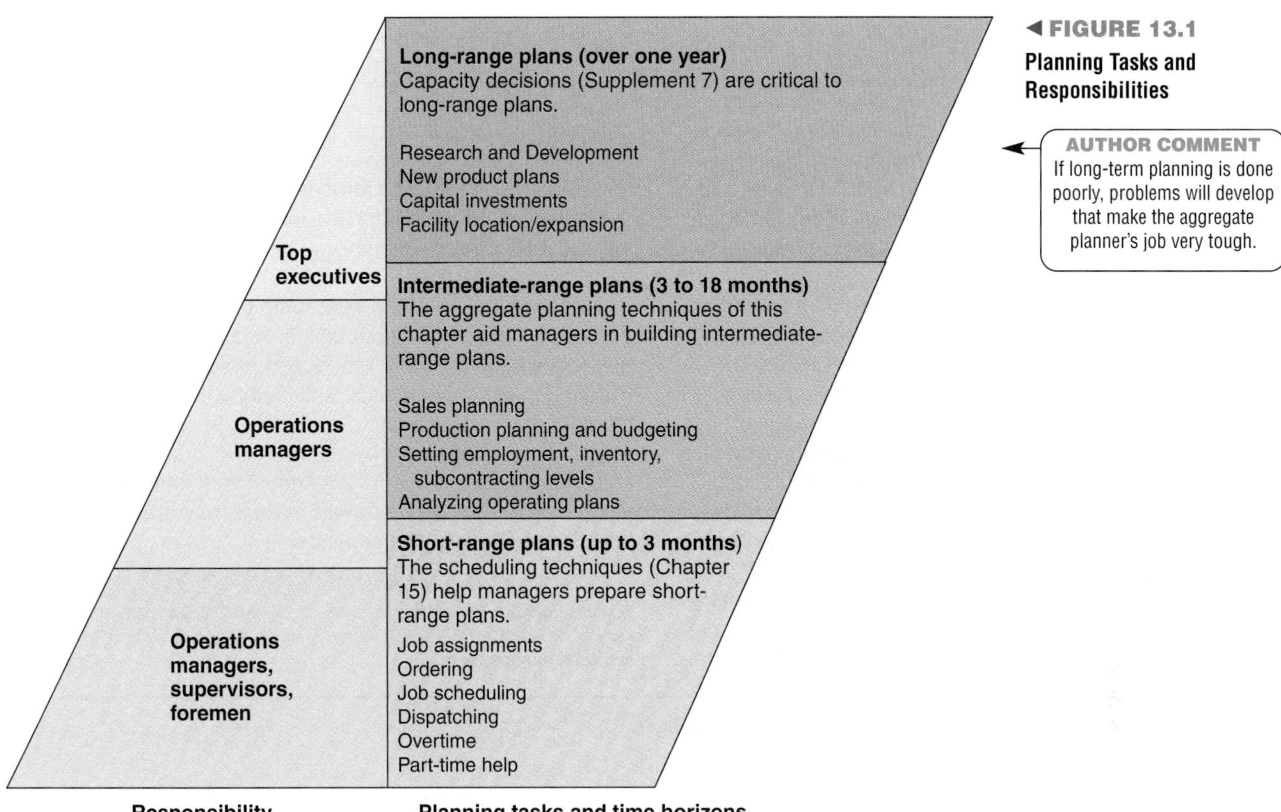

◄ **FIGURE 13.1**
Planning Tasks and Responsibilities

AUTHOR COMMENT
If long-term planning is done poorly, problems will develop that make the aggregate planner's job very tough.

THE NATURE OF AGGREGATE PLANNING

AUTHOR COMMENT
Aggregate plans are formulated in a variety of units, such as pounds of Fritos, tons of steel, or number of students.

As the term *aggregate* implies, an aggregate plan means combining appropriate resources into general, or overall, terms. Given demand forecast, facility capacity, inventory levels, workforce size, and related inputs, the planner has to select the rate of output for a facility over the next 3 to 18 months. The plan can be for firms such as Frito-Lay and Whirlpool, hospitals, colleges, or Prentice Hall, the company that published this textbook.

Take, for a manufacturing example, Snapper, which produces many different models of lawn mowers. It makes walk-behind mowers, rear-engine riding mowers, garden tractors, and many more, for a total of 145 models. For each month in the upcoming 3 quarters, the aggregate plan for Snapper might have the following output (in units of production) for Snapper's "family" of mowers:

Quarter 1			Quarter 2			Quarter 3		
Jan.	Feb.	March	April	May	June	July	Aug.	Sept.
150,000	120,000	110,000	100,000	130,000	150,000	180,000	150,000	140,000

Operations personnel build an aggregate plan using the total expected demand for all of the family products, such as 145 models at Snapper (a few of which are shown above). Only when the forecasts are assembled in the aggregate plan does the company decide how to meet the total requirement with the available resources. These resource constraints include facility capacity, workforce size, supply-chain limitations, inventory issues, and financial resources.

OM in Action ► Building the Plan at Snapper

Every bright red Snapper lawn mower sold anywhere in the world comes from a factory in McDonough, Georgia. Ten years ago, the Snapper line had about 40 models of mowers, leaf blowers, and snow blowers. Today, reflecting the demands of mass customization, the product line is much more complex. Snapper designs, manufactures, and sells 145 models. This means that aggregate planning and the related short-term scheduling have become more complex, too.

In the past, Snapper met demand by carrying a huge inventory for 52 regional distributors and thousands of independent dealerships. It manufactured and shipped tens of thousands of lawn mowers, worth tens of millions of dollars, without quite knowing when they would be sold—a very expensive approach to meeting demand. Some changes were necessary. The new plan's goal is for each distribution center to receive only the minimum inventory necessary to meet demand. Today, operations managers at Snapper evaluate production capacity and use frequent data from the field as inputs to sophisticated software to forecast sales. The new system tracks customer demand and aggregates forecasts for every model in every region of the country. It even adjusts for holidays and weather. And the number of distribution centers has been cut from 52 to 4.

Once evaluation of the aggregate plan against capacity determines the plan to be feasible, Snapper's planners break down the plan into production needs for each model. Production by model is accomplished by building rolling monthly and weekly plans. These plans track the pace at which various units are selling. Then, the final step requires juggling work assignments to various work centers for each shift, such as 265 lawn mowers in an 8-hour shift. That's a new Snapper every 109 seconds.

Sources: Fair Disclosure Wire (January 17, 2008); *The Wall Street Journal* (July 14, 2006): B1, B6; *Fast Company* (January/February 2006): 67–71; and **www.snapper.com.**

Note that the plan looks at production *in the aggregate* (the family of mowers), not as a product-by-product breakdown. Likewise, an aggregate plan for BMW tells the auto manufacturer how many cars to make but not how many should be two-door vs. four-door or red vs. green. It tells Nucor Steel how many tons of steel to produce but does not differentiate grades of steel. (We extend the discussion of planning at Snapper in the *OM in Action* box "Building the Plan at Snapper.")

Aggregate planning is part of a larger production planning system. Therefore, understanding the interfaces between the plan and several internal and external factors is useful. Figure 13.2 shows that the operations manager not only receives input from the marketing department's demand forecast, but must also deal with financial data, personnel, capacity, and availability of raw materials. In a manufacturing environment, the process of breaking the aggregate plan down into greater detail is called **disaggregation**. Disaggregation results in a **master production schedule**, which provides input to material requirements planning (MRP) systems. The master production schedule addresses the purchasing or production of parts or components needed to make final products (see Chapter 14). Detailed work schedules for people and priority scheduling for products result as the final step of the production planning system (and are discussed in Chapter 15).

Disaggregation
The process of breaking an aggregate plan into greater detail.

Master production schedule
A timetable that specifies what is to be made and when.

AUTHOR COMMENT
Managers can meet aggregate plans by adjusting either capacity or demand.

AGGREGATE PLANNING STRATEGIES

When generating an aggregate plan, the operations manager must answer several questions:

1. Should inventories be used to absorb changes in demand during the planning period?
2. Should changes be accommodated by varying the size of the workforce?
3. Should part-timers be used, or should overtime and idle time absorb fluctuations?
4. Should subcontractors be used on fluctuating orders so a stable workforce can be maintained?
5. Should prices or other factors be changed to influence demand?

All of these are legitimate planning strategies. They involve the manipulation of inventory, production rates, labor levels, capacity, and other controllable variables. We will now examine eight options in more detail. The first five are called *capacity options* because they do not try to change demand but attempt to absorb demand fluctuations. The last three are *demand options* through which firms try to smooth out changes in the demand pattern over the planning period.

LO2: Identify optional strategies for developing an aggregate plan

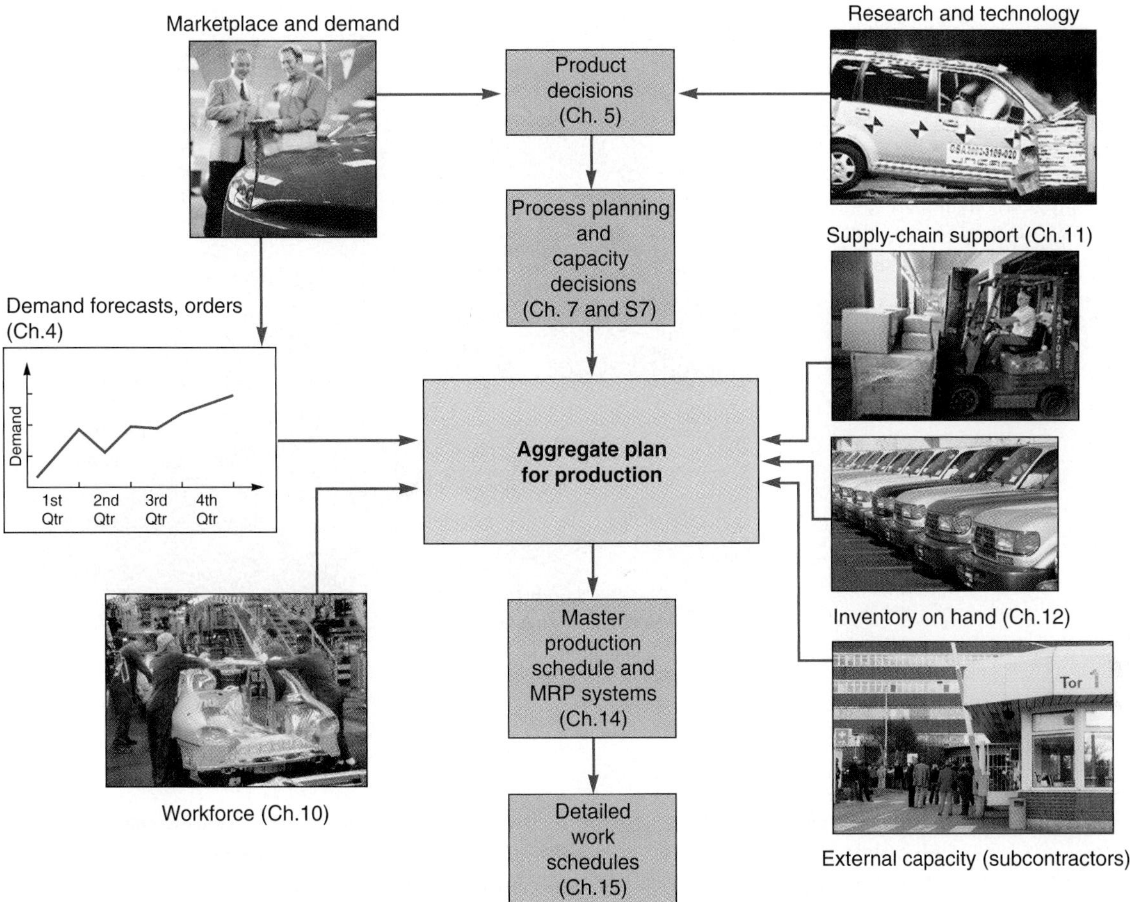

▲ **FIGURE 13.2** **Relationships of an Aggregate Plan**

Capacity Options

A firm can choose from the following basic capacity (production) options:

1. *Changing inventory levels:* Managers can increase inventory during periods of low demand to meet high demand in future periods. If this strategy is selected, costs associated with storage, insurance, handling, obsolescence, pilferage, and capital invested will increase. On the other hand, with low inventory on hand and increasing demand, shortages can occur, resulting in longer lead times and poor customer service.
2. *Varying workforce size by hiring or layoffs:* One way to meet demand is to hire or lay off production workers to match production rates. However, new employees need to be trained, and productivity drops temporarily as they are absorbed into the workforce. Layoffs or terminations, of course, lower the morale of all workers and also lead to lower productivity.
3. *Varying production rates through overtime or idle time:* Keeping a constant workforce while varying working hours may be possible. Yet when demand is on a large upswing, there is a limit on how much overtime is realistic. Overtime pay increases costs and too much overtime can result in worker fatigue and a drop in productivity. Overtime also implies added overhead costs to keep a facility open. On the other hand, when there is a period of decreased demand, the company must somehow absorb workers' idle time—often a difficult and expensive process.
4. *Subcontracting:* A firm can acquire temporary capacity by subcontracting work during peak demand periods. Subcontracting, however, has several pitfalls. First, it may be costly; second, it risks opening the door to a competitor. Third, developing the perfect subcontract supplier can be a challenge.
5. *Using part-time workers:* Especially in the service sector, part-time workers can fill labor needs. This practice is common in restaurants, retail stores, and supermarkets.

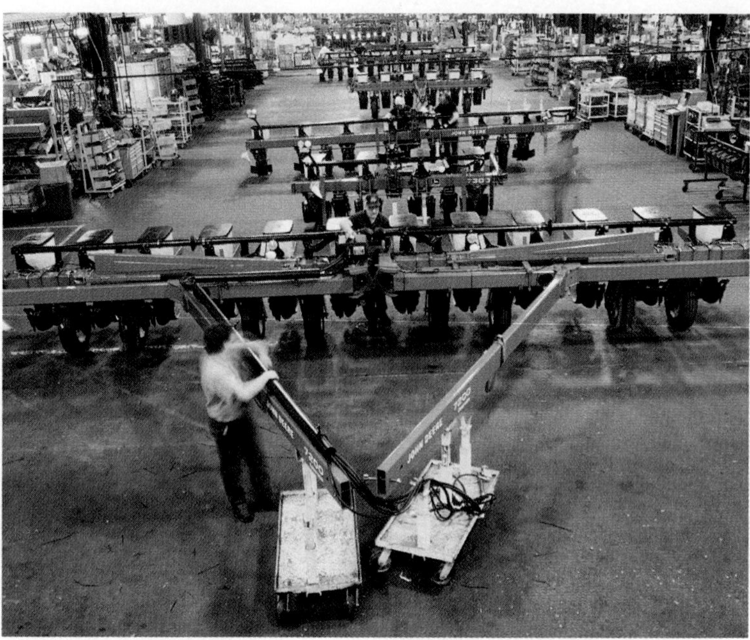

John Deere and Company, the "granddaddy" of farm equipment manufacturers, uses sales incentives to smooth demand. During the fall and winter off-seasons, sales are boosted with price cuts and other incentives. About 70% of Deere's big machines are ordered in advance of seasonal use—about double the industry rate. Incentives hurt margins, but Deere keeps its market share and controls costs by producing more steadily all year long. Similarly, in service businesses like L.L. Bean, some customers are offered free shipping on orders placed before the Christmas rush.

Demand Options

The basic demand options are:

1. *Influencing demand:* When demand is low, a company can try to increase demand through advertising, promotion, personal selling, and price cuts. Airlines and hotels have long offered weekend discounts and off-season rates; telephone companies charge less at night; some colleges give discounts to senior citizens; and air conditioners are least expensive in winter. However, even special advertising, promotions, selling, and pricing are not always able to balance demand with production capacity.
2. *Back ordering during high-demand periods:* Back orders are orders for goods or services that a firm accepts but is unable (either on purpose or by chance) to fill at the moment. If customers are willing to wait without loss of their goodwill or order, back ordering is a possible strategy. Many firms back order, but the approach often results in lost sales.
3. *Counterseasonal product and service mixing:* A widely used active smoothing technique among manufacturers is to develop a product mix of counterseasonal items. Examples include companies that make both furnaces and air conditioners or lawn mowers and snowblowers. However, companies that follow this approach may find themselves involved in products or services beyond their area of expertise or beyond their target market.

These eight options, along with their advantages and disadvantages, are summarized in Table 13.1.

Mixing Options to Develop a Plan

Although each of the five capacity options and three demand options discussed above may produce an effective aggregate schedule, some combination of capacity options and demand options may be better.

Many manufacturers assume that the use of the demand options has been fully explored by the marketing department and those reasonable options incorporated into the demand forecast. The operations manager then builds the aggregate plan based on that forecast. However, using the five capacity options at his command, the operations manager still has a multitude of possible plans. These plans can embody, at one extreme, a *chase strategy* and, at the other, a *level-scheduling strategy*. They may, of course, fall somewhere in between.

Chase strategy
A planning strategy that sets production equal to forecasted demand.

Chase Strategy **A chase strategy** typically attempts to achieve output rates for each period that match the demand forecast for that period. This strategy can be accomplished in a variety of ways. For example, the operations manager can vary workforce levels by hiring or laying off or

▼ **TABLE 13.1 Aggregate Planning Options: Advantages and Disadvantages**

Option	Advantages	Disadvantages	Comments
Changing inventory levels	Changes in human resources are gradual or none; no abrupt production changes.	Inventory holding costs may increase. Shortages may result in lost sales.	Applies mainly to production, not service, operations.
Varying workforce size by hiring or layoffs	Avoids the costs of other alternatives.	Hiring, layoff, and training costs may be significant.	Used where size of labor pool is large.
Varying production rates through overtime or idle time	Matches seasonal fluctuations without hiring/training costs.	Overtime premiums; tired workers; may not meet demand.	Allows flexibility within the aggregate plan.
Subcontracting	Permits flexibility and smoothing of the firm's output.	Loss of quality control; reduced profits; loss of future business.	Applies mainly in production settings.
Using part-time workers	Is less costly and more flexible than full-time workers.	High turnover/training costs; quality suffers; scheduling difficult.	Good for unskilled jobs in areas with large temporary labor pools.
Influencing demand	Tries to use excess capacity. Discounts draw new customers.	Uncertainty in demand. Hard to match demand to supply exactly.	Creates marketing ideas. Overbooking used in some businesses.
Back ordering during high-demand periods	May avoid overtime. Keeps capacity constant.	Customer must be willing to wait, but goodwill is lost.	Many companies back order.
Counterseasonal product and service mixing	Fully utilizes resources; allows stable workforce.	May require skills or equipment outside firm's areas of expertise.	Risky finding products or services with opposite demand patterns.

can vary production by means of overtime, idle time, part-time employees, or subcontracting. Many service organizations favor the chase strategy because the changing inventory levels option is difficult or impossible to adopt. Industries that have moved toward a chase strategy include education, hospitality, and construction.

Level Strategy A level strategy (or **level scheduling**) is an aggregate plan in which production is uniform from period to period. Firms like Toyota and Nissan attempt to keep production at uniform levels and may (1) let the finished-goods inventory vary to buffer the difference between demand and production or (2) find alternative work for employees. Their philosophy is that a stable workforce leads to a better-quality product, less turnover and absenteeism, and more employee commitment to corporate goals. Other hidden savings include employees who are more experienced, easier scheduling and supervision, and fewer dramatic startups and shutdowns. Level scheduling works well when demand is reasonably stable.

Level scheduling
Maintaining a constant output rate, production rate, or workforce level over the planning horizon.

For most firms, neither a chase strategy nor a level strategy is likely to prove ideal, so a combination of the eight options (called a **mixed strategy**) must be investigated to achieve minimum cost. However, because there are a huge number of possible mixed strategies, managers find that aggregate planning can be a challenging task. Finding the one "optimal" plan is not always possible, but as we will see in the next section, a number of techniques have been developed to aid the aggregate planning process.

Mixed strategy
A planning strategy that uses two or more controllable variables to set a feasible production plan.

METHODS FOR AGGREGATE PLANNING

AUTHOR COMMENT
Managers must commit to employment levels, material purchases, and inventory levels; aggregate plans help managers do that.

In this section, we introduce several techniques that operations managers use to develop aggregate plans. They range from the widely used graphical method to a series of more formal mathematical approaches, including the transportation method of linear programming.

Graphical Methods

Graphical techniques are popular because they are easy to understand and use. These plans work with a few variables at a time to allow planners to compare projected demand with existing capacity. They are trial-and-error approaches that do not guarantee an optimal production plan,

Graphical techniques
Aggregate planning techniques that work with a few variables at a time to allow planners to compare projected demand with existing capacity.

LO3: Prepare a graphical aggregate plan

but they require only limited computations and can be performed by clerical staff. Following are the five steps in the graphical method:

1. Determine the demand in each period.
2. Determine capacity for regular time, overtime, and subcontracting each period.
3. Find labor costs, hiring and layoff costs, and inventory holding costs.
4. Consider company policy that may apply to the workers or to stock levels.
5. Develop alternative plans and examine their total costs.

These steps are illustrated in Examples 1 through 4.

EXAMPLE 1 ▶

Graphical approach to aggregate planning for a roofing supplier

A Juarez, Mexico, manufacturer of roofing supplies has developed monthly forecasts for a family of products. Data for the 6-month period January to June are presented in Table 13.2. The firm would like to begin development of an aggregate plan.

▶**TABLE 13.2**
Monthly Forecasts

Month	Expected Demand	Production Days	Demand per Day (computed)
Jan.	900	22	41
Feb.	700	18	39
Mar.	800	21	38
Apr.	1,200	21	57
May	1,500	22	68
June	1,100	20	55
	6,200	124	

APPROACH ▶ Plot daily and average demand to illustrate the nature of the aggregate planning problem.

SOLUTION ▶ First, compute demand per day by dividing the expected monthly demand by the number of production days (working days) each month and drawing a graph of those forecasted demands (Figure 13.3). Second, draw a dotted line across the chart that represents the production rate required to meet average demand over the 6-month period. The chart is computed as follows:

$$\text{Average requirement} = \frac{\text{Total expected demand}}{\text{Number of production days}} = \frac{6{,}200}{124} = 50 \text{ units per day}$$

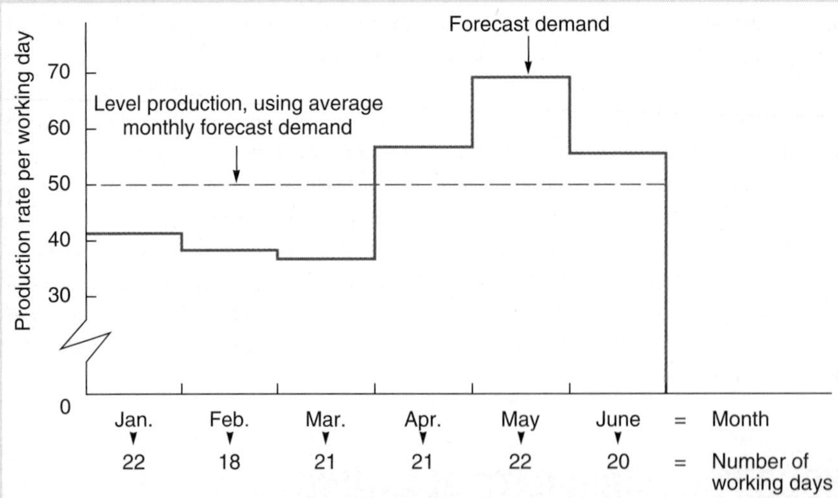

▶ **FIGURE 13.3**
Graph of Forecast and Average Forecast Demand

INSIGHT ▶ Changes in the production rate become obvious when the data are graphed. Note that in the first 3 months, expected demand is lower than average, while expected demand in April, May, and June is above average.

LEARNING EXERCISE ▶ If demand for June increases to 1,200 (from 1,100), what is the impact on Figure 13.3? [Answer: The daily rate for June will go up to 60, and average production will increase to 50.8 (6,300/124).]

RELATED PROBLEM ▶ 13.1

The graph in Figure 13.3 illustrates how the forecast differs from the average demand. Some strategies for meeting the forecast were listed earlier. The firm, for example, might staff in order to yield a production rate that meets *average* demand (as indicated by the dashed line). Or it might produce a steady rate of, say, 30 units and then subcontract excess demand to other roofing suppliers. Other plans might combine overtime work with subcontracting to absorb demand. Examples 2 to 4 illustrate three possible strategies.

EXAMPLE 2

Plan 1 for the roofing supplier—a constant workforce

One possible strategy (call it plan 1) for the manufacturer described in Example 1 is to maintain a constant workforce throughout the 6-month period. A second (plan 2) is to maintain a constant workforce at a level necessary to meet the lowest demand month (March) and to meet all demand above this level by subcontracting. Both plan 1 and plan 2 have level production and are, therefore, called *level strategies*. Plan 3 is to hire and lay off workers as needed to produce exact monthly requirements—*a chase strategy*. Table 13.3 provides cost information necessary for analyzing these three alternatives:

TABLE 13.3 Cost Information

Inventory carrying cost	\$ 5 per unit per month
Subcontracting cost per unit	\$ 20 per unit
Average pay rate	\$ 10 per hour (\$80 per day)
Overtime pay rate	\$ 17 per hour (above 8 hours per day)
Labor-hours to produce a unit	1.6 hours per unit
Cost of increasing daily production rate (hiring and training)	\$300 per unit
Cost of decreasing daily production rate (layoffs)	\$600 per unit

ANALYSIS OF PLAN 1. APPROACH ▶ Here we assume that 50 units are produced per day and that we have a constant workforce, no overtime or idle time, no safety stock, and no subcontractors. The firm accumulates inventory during the slack period of demand, January through March, and depletes it during the higher-demand warm season, April through June. We assume beginning inventory = 0 and planned ending inventory = 0.

SOLUTION ▶ We construct the table below and accumulate the costs:

Month	Production Days	Production at 50 Units per Day	Demand Forecast	Monthly Inventory Change	Ending Inventory
Jan.	22	1,100	900	+200	200
Feb.	18	900	700	+200	400
Mar.	21	1,050	800	+250	650
Apr.	21	1,050	1,200	−150	500
May	22	1,100	1,500	−400	100
June	20	1,000	1,100	−100	0
					1,850

Total units of inventory carried over from one month to the next month = 1,850 units

Workforce required to produce 50 units per day = 10 workers

Because each unit requires 1.6 labor-hours to produce, each worker can make 5 units in an 8-hour day. Therefore, to produce 50 units, 10 workers are needed.

Finally, the costs of plan 1 are computed as follows:

Cost		Calculations
Inventory carrying	\$ 9,250	(= 1,850 units carried × \$5 per unit)
Regular-time labor	99,200	(= 10 workers × \$80 per day × 124 days)
Other costs (overtime, hiring, layoffs, subcontracting)	0	
Total cost	\$108,450	

INSIGHT ▶ Note the significant cost of carrying the inventory.

LEARNING EXERCISE ▶ If demand for June decreases to 1,000 (from 1,100), what is the change in cost? [Answer: Total inventory carried will increase to 1,950 at $5, for an inventory cost of $9,750 and total cost of $108,950]

RELATED PROBLEMS ▶ 13.2, 13.3, 13.4, 13.5, 13.6, 13.7, 13.8, 13.9, 13.10, 13.11, 13.12, 13.19

EXCEL OM Data File **Ch13Ex2.xls** can be found at **www.pearsonhighered.com/heizer**.

ACTIVE MODEL 13.1 This example is further illustrated in Active Model 13.1 at **www.pearsonhighered.com/heizer**.

The graph for Example 2 was shown in Figure 13.3. Some planners prefer a *cumulative* graph to display visually how the forecast deviates from the average requirements. Such a graph is provided in Figure 13.4. Note that both the level production line and the forecast line produce the same total production.

▶ FIGURE 13.4
Cumulative Graph for Plan 1

AUTHOR COMMENT
We saw another way to graph this data in Figure 13.3.

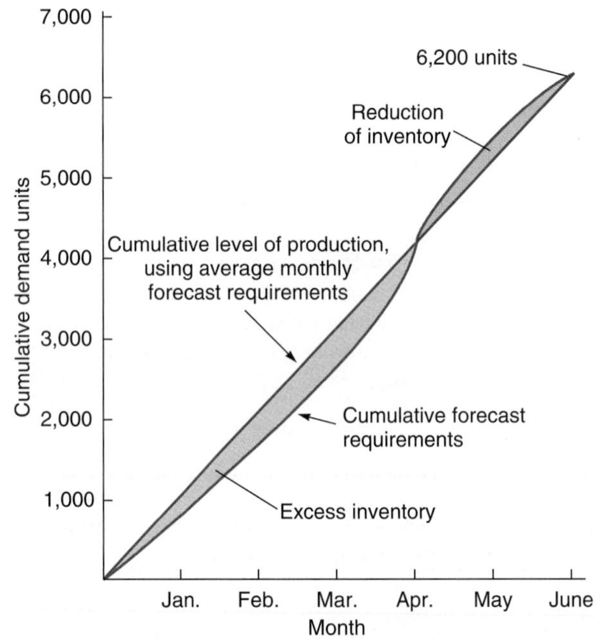

EXAMPLE 3 ▶
Plan 2 for the roofing supplier—use of subcontractors within a constant workforce

ANALYSIS OF PLAN 2. APPROACH ▶ Although a constant workforce is also maintained in plan 2, it is set low enough to meet demand only in March, the lowest demand-per-day month. To produce 38 units per day (800/21) in-house, 7.6 workers are needed. (You can think of this as 7 full-time workers and 1 part-timer.) *All* other demand is met by subcontracting. Subcontracting is thus required in every other month. No inventory holding costs are incurred in plan 2.

SOLUTION ▶ Because 6,200 units are required during the aggregate plan period, we must compute how many can be made by the firm and how many must be subcontracted:

$$\text{In-house production} = 38 \text{ units per day} \times 124 \text{ production days} = 4{,}712 \text{ units}$$

$$\text{Subcontract units} = 6{,}200 - 4{,}712 = 1{,}488 \text{ units}$$

The costs of plan 2 are computed as follows:

Cost		Calculations
Regular-time labor	$ 75,392	(= 7.6 workers × $80 per day × 124 days)
Subcontracting	29,760	(= 1,488 units × $20 per unit)
Total cost	$105,152	

INSIGHT ▶ Note the lower cost of regular labor but the added subcontracting cost.

LEARNING EXERCISE ▶ If demand for June increases to 1,200 (from 1,100), what is the change in cost? [Answer: Subcontracting requirements increase to 1,588 at $20 per unit, for a subcontracting cost of $31,760 and a total cost of $107,152.]

RELATED PROBLEMS ▶ 13.2, 13.3, 13.4, 13.5, 13.6, 13.7, 13.8, 13.9, 13.10, 13.11, 13.12, 13.19

EXAMPLE 4

Plan 3 for the roofing supplier—hiring and layoffs

ANALYSIS OF PLAN 3. APPROACH ▶ The final strategy, plan 3, involves varying the workforce size by hiring and layoffs as necessary. The production rate will equal the demand, and there is no change in production from the previous month, December.

SOLUTION ▶ Table 13.4 shows the calculations and the total cost of plan 3. Recall that it costs $600 per unit produced to reduce production from the previous month's daily level and $300 per unit change to increase the daily rate of production through hirings.

◀ TABLE 13.4 Cost Computations for Plan 3

Month	Forecast (units)	Daily Production Rate	Basic Production Cost (demand × 1.6 hr per unit × $10 per hr)	Extra Cost of Increasing Production (hiring cost)	Extra Cost of Decreasing Production (layoff cost)	Total Cost
Jan.	900	41	$14,400	—	—	$ 14,400
Feb.	700	39	11,200	—	$1,200 (= 2 × $600)	12,400
Mar.	800	38	12,800	—	$ 600 (= 1 × $600)	13,400
Apr.	1,200	57	19,200	$5,700 (= 19 × $300)	—	24,900
May	1,500	68	24,000	$3,300 (= 11 × $300)	—	27,300
June	1,100	55	17,600	—	$7,800 (= 13 × $600)	$ 25,400
			$99,200	$9,000	$9,600	$117,800

Thus, the total cost, including production, hiring, and layoff, for plan 3 is $117,800.

INSIGHT ▶ Note the substantial cost associated with changing (both increasing and decreasing) the production levels.

LEARNING EXERCISE ▶ If demand for June increases to 1,200 (from 1,100), what is the change in cost? [Answer: Daily production for June is 60 units, which is a decrease of 8 units in the daily production rate from May's 68 units, so the new June layoff cost is $4,800 (= 8 × $600), with a total plan 3 cost of $114,800.]

RELATED PROBLEMS ▶ 13.2, 13.3, 13.4, 13.5, 13.6, 13.7, 13.8, 13.9, 13.10, 13.11, 13.12, 13.19

The final step in the graphical method is to compare the costs of each proposed plan and to select the approach with the least total cost. A summary analysis is provided in Table 13.5. We see that because plan 2 has the lowest cost, it is the best of the three options.

◀ TABLE 13.5 Comparison of the Three Plans

Cost	Plan 1 (constant workforce of 10 workers)	Plan 2 (workforce of 7.6 workers plus subcontract)	Plan 3 (hiring and layoffs to meet demand)
Inventory carrying	$ 9,250	$ 0	$ 0
Regular labor	99,200	75,392	99,200
Overtime labor	0	0	0
Hiring	0	0	9,000
Layoffs	0	0	9,600
Subcontracting	0	29,760	0
Total cost	$108,450	$105,152	$117,800

Of course, many other feasible strategies can be considered in a problem like this, including combinations that use some overtime. Although graphing is a popular management tool, its help is in evaluating strategies, not generating them. To generate strategies, a systematic approach that considers all costs and produces an effective solution is needed.

Mathematical Approaches

This section briefly describes some of the mathematical approaches to aggregate planning.

The Transportation Method of Linear Programming When an aggregate planning problem is viewed as one of allocating operating capacity to meet forecasted demand, it can be formulated in a linear programming format. The **transportation method of linear programming** is not a trial-and-error approach like graphing but rather produces an optimal plan for minimizing costs. It is also flexible in that it can specify regular and overtime production in each time period, the number of units to be subcontracted, extra shifts, and the inventory carryover from period to period.

Transportation method of linear programming
A way of solving for the optimal solution to an aggregate planning problem.

In Example 5, the supply consists of on-hand inventory and units produced by regular time, overtime, and subcontracting. Costs per unit, in the upper-right corner of each cell of the matrix in Table 13.7, relate to units produced in a given period or units carried in inventory from an earlier period.

EXAMPLE 5 ▶

Aggregate planning with the transportation method

Farnsworth Tire Company would like to develop an aggregate plan via the transportation method. Data that relate to production, demand, capacity, and cost at its West Virginia plant are shown in Table 13.6.

▶ TABLE 13.6
Farnsworth's Production, Demand, Capacity, and Cost Data

	Sales Period		
	Mar.	**Apr.**	**May**
Demand	800	1,000	750
Capacity:			
Regular	700	700	700
Overtime	50	50	50
Subcontracting	150	150	130
Beginning inventory	100 tires		

Costs	
Regular time	$40 per tire
Overtime	$50 per tire
Subcontract	$70 per tire
Carrying cost	$ 2 per tire per month

APPROACH ▶ Solve the aggregate planning problem by minimizing the costs of matching production in various periods to future demands.

SOLUTION ▶ Table 13.7 illustrates the structure of the transportation table and an initial feasible solution.

SUPPLY FROM		DEMAND FOR *Period 1 (Mar.)*	*Period 2 (Apr.)*	*Period 3 (May)*	*Unused Capacity (dummy)*	TOTAL CAPACITY AVAILABLE (supply)
Beginning inventory		0	2	4	0	
		100				**100**
Period 1	*Regular time*	40	42	44	0	
		700				**700**
	Overtime	50	52	54	0	
			50			**50**
	Subcontract	70	72	74	0	
			150			**150**
Period 2	*Regular time*		40	42	0	
		×	**700**			**700**
	Overtime		50	52	0	
		×	**50**			**50**
	Subcontract		70	72	0	
		×	**50**		**100**	**150**
Period 3	*Regular time*			40	0	
		×	×	**700**		**700**
	Overtime			50	0	
		×	×	**50**		**50**
	Subcontract			70	0	
		×	×		**130**	**130**
TOTAL DEMAND		**800**	**1,000**	**750**	**230**	**2,780**

[a]Cells with an *x* indicate that back orders are not used at Farnsworth. When using Excel OM or POM for Windows to solve, you must insert a *very* high cost (e.g., 9999) in each cell that is not used for production.

◀ **TABLE 13.7**
Farnsworth's Transportation Table[a]

LO4: Solve an aggregate plan via the transportation method of linear programming

When setting up and analyzing this table, you should note the following:

1. Carrying costs are $2/tire per month. Tires produced in 1 period and held for 1 month will have a $2 higher cost. Because holding cost is linear, 2 months' holdover costs $4. So when you move across a row from left to right, regular time, overtime, and subcontracting costs are lowest when output is used the same period it is produced. If goods are made in one period and carried over to the next, holding costs are incurred. Beginning inventory, however, is generally given a unit cost of 0 if it is used to satisfy demand in period 1.
2. Transportation problems require that supply equals demand; so, a dummy column called "unused capacity" has been added. Costs of not using capacity are zero.
3. Because back ordering is not a viable alternative for this particular company, no production is possible in those cells that represent production in a period to satisfy demand in a past period (i.e., those periods with an "X"). If back ordering is allowed, costs of expediting, loss of goodwill, and loss of sales revenues are summed to estimate backorder cost.
4. Quantities in red in each column of Table 13.7 designate the levels of inventory needed to meet demand requirements (shown in the bottom row of the table). Demand of 800 tires in March is met by using 100 tires from beginning inventory and 700 tires from regular time.
5. In general, to complete the table, allocate as much production as you can to a cell with the smallest cost without exceeding the unused capacity in that row or demand in that column. If there is still some demand left in that row, allocate as much as you can to the next-lowest-cost cell. You then repeat this process for periods 2 and 3 (and beyond, if necessary). When you are finished, the sum of all your entries in a row must equal the total row capacity, and the sum of all entries in a column must equal the demand for that period. (This step can be accomplished by the transportation method or by using POM for Windows or Excel OM software.)

Try to confirm that the cost of this initial solution is $105,900. The initial solution is not optimal, however. See if you can find the production schedule that yields the least cost (which turns out to be $105,700) using software or by hand.

INSIGHT ▶ The transportation method is flexible when costs are linear but does not work when costs are nonlinear.

LEARNING EXAMPLE ▶ What is the impact on this problem if there is no beginning inventory? [Answer: Total capacity (units) available is reduced by 100 units and the need to subcontract increases by 100 units.]

RELATED PROBLEMS ▶ 13.13, 13.14, 13.15, 13.16, 13.17, 13.18

EXCEL OM Data File **Ch13Ex5.xls** can be found at **www.pearsonhighered.com/heizer**.

The transportation method of linear programming described in the above example was originally formulated by E. H. Bowman in 1956. Although it works well in analyzing the effects of holding inventories, using overtime, and subcontracting, it does not work when nonlinear or negative factors are introduced. Thus, when other factors such as hiring and layoffs are introduced, the more general method of linear programming must be used.

Management coefficients model
A formal planning model built around a manager's experience and performance.

Management Coefficients Model Bowman's **management coefficients model**[1] builds a formal decision model around a manager's experience and performance. The assumption is that the manager's past performance is pretty good; therefore, it can be used as a basis for future decisions. The technique uses a regression analysis of past production decisions made by managers. The regression line provides the relationship between variables (such as demand and labor) for future decisions. According to Bowman, managers' deficiencies are mostly inconsistencies in decision making.

Other Models Two additional aggregate planning models are the linear decision rule and simulation. The *linear decision rule (LDR)* attempts to specify an optimum production rate and workforce level over a specific period. It minimizes the total costs of payroll, hiring, layoffs, overtime, and inventory through a series of quadratic cost curves.[2]

A computer model called *scheduling by simulation* uses a search procedure to look for the minimum-cost combination of values for workforce size and production rate.

Comparison of Aggregate Planning Methods

Although these mathematical models have been found by researchers to work well under certain conditions, and linear programming has found some acceptance in industry, the fact is that most sophisticated planning models are not widely used. Why? Perhaps it reflects the average manager's attitude about what he or she views as overly complex models. Like all of us, planners like to understand how and why the models on which they are basing important decisions work. Additionally, operations managers need to make decisions quickly based on the changing dynamics of the competitive environment—and building good models is time-consuming. This may explain why the simpler graphical approach is more generally accepted.

Table 13.8 highlights some of the main features of graphing, transportation, management coefficients, and simulation planning models.

AUTHOR COMMENT
The major variable in capacity management for services is labor.

AGGREGATE PLANNING IN SERVICES

Some service organizations conduct aggregate planning in exactly the same way as we did in Examples 1 through 5 in this chapter, but with demand management taking a more active role. Because most services pursue *combinations* of the eight capacity and demand options discussed

[1]E. H. Bowman, "Consistency and Optimality in Managerial Decision Making," *Management Science* 9, no. 2 (January 1963): 310–321.

[2]Because LDR was developed by Charles C. Holt, Franco Modigliani, John F. Muth, and Herbert Simon, it is popularly known as the HMMS rule. For details, see Martin K. Starr, *Production and Operations Management* (Cincinnati, OH: Atomic Dog Publishing, 2004): 490–493.

◀ **TABLE 13.8**
Summary of Four Major Aggregate Planning Methods

Technique	Solution Approaches	Important Aspects
Graphical methods	Trial and error	Simple to understand and easy to use. Many solutions; one chosen may not be optimal.
Transportation method of linear programming	Optimization	LP software available; permits sensitivity analysis and new constraints; linear functions may not be realistic.
Management coefficients model	Heuristic	Simple, easy to implement; tries to mimic manager's decision process; uses regression.
Simulation	Change parameters	Complex; model may be difficult to build and for managers to understand.

earlier, they usually formulate mixed aggregate planning strategies. In industries such as banking, trucking, and fast foods, aggregate planning may be easier than in manufacturing.

Controlling the cost of labor in service firms is critical. Successful techniques include:

1. Accurate scheduling of labor-hours to assure quick response to customer demand
2. An on-call labor resource that can be added or deleted to meet unexpected demand
3. Flexibility of individual worker skills that permits reallocation of available labor
4. Flexibility in rate of output or hours of work to meet changing demand

These options may seem demanding, but they are not unusual in service industries, in which labor is the primary aggregate planning vehicle. For instance:

- Excess capacity is used to provide study and planning time by real estate and auto salespersons.
- Police and fire departments have provisions for calling in off-duty personnel for major emergencies. Where the emergency is extended, police or fire personnel may work longer hours and extra shifts.
- When business is unexpectedly light, restaurants and retail stores send personnel home early.
- Supermarket stock clerks work cash registers when checkout lines become too lengthy.
- Experienced waitresses increase their pace and efficiency of service as crowds of customers arrive.

Approaches to aggregate planning differ by the type of service provided. Here we discuss five service scenarios.

The heavy demands of the December holiday season place a special burden on aggregate planning at UPS. UPS maximizes truck and plane resource availability for the season, as well as overtime and temporary workers to match capacity to demand.

Restaurants

In a business with a highly variable demand, such as a restaurant, aggregate scheduling is directed toward (1) smoothing the production rate and (2) finding the optimal size of the workforce. The general approach usually requires building very modest levels of inventory during slack periods and depleting inventory during peak periods, but using labor to accommodate most of the changes in demand. Because this situation is very similar to those found in manufacturing, traditional aggregate planning methods may be applied to services as well. One difference that should be noted is that even modest amounts of inventory may be perishable. In addition, the relevant units of time may be much smaller than in manufacturing. For example, in fast-food restaurants, peak and slack periods may be measured in fractions of an hour and the "product" may be inventoried for as little as 10 minutes.

Hospitals

Hospitals face aggregate planning problems in allocating money, staff, and supplies to meet the demands of patients. Michigan's Henry Ford Hospital, for example, plans for bed capacity and personnel needs in light of a patient-load forecast developed by moving averages. The necessary labor focus of its aggregate plan has led to the creation of a new floating staff pool serving each nursing pod.

National Chains of Small Service Firms

With the advent of national chains of small service businesses such as funeral homes, oil change outlets, and photocopy/printing centers, the question of aggregate planning versus independent planning at each business establishment becomes an issue. Both purchases and production capacity may be centrally planned when demand can be influenced through special promotions. This approach to aggregate scheduling is often advantageous because it reduces costs and helps manage cash flow at independent sites.

Miscellaneous Services

Most "miscellaneous" services—financial, transportation, and many communication and recreation services—provide intangible output. Aggregate planning for these services deals mainly with planning for human resource requirements and managing demand. The twofold goal is to level demand peaks and to design methods for fully utilizing labor resources during low-demand periods. Example 6 illustrates such a plan for a legal firm.

EXAMPLE 6 ▶

Aggregate planning in a law firm

Klasson and Avalon, a medium-size Tampa law firm of 32 legal professionals, wants to develop an aggregate plan for the next quarter. The firm has developed 3 forecasts of billable hours for the next quarter for each of 5 categories of legal business it performs (column 1, Table 13.9). The 3 forecasts (best, likely, and worst) are shown in columns 2, 3, and 4 of Table 13.9.

▶ TABLE 13.9 Labor Allocation at Klasson and Avalon, Forecasts for Coming Quarter (1 lawyer = 500 hours of labor)

	Labor-Hours Required			*Capacity Constraints*	
(1)	(2)	(3) *Forecasts*	(4)	(5)	(6)
Category of Legal Business	**Best (hours)**	**Likely (hours)**	**Worst (hours)**	**Maximum Demand in People**	**Number of Qualified Personnel**
Trial work	1,800	1,500	1,200	3.6	4
Legal research	4,500	4,000	3,500	9.0	32
Corporate law	8,000	7,000	6,500	16.0	15
Real estate law	1,700	1,500	1,300	3.4	6
Criminal law	3,500	3,000	2,500	7.0	12
Total hours	19,500	17,000	15,000		
Lawyers needed	39	34	30		

APPROACH ▶ If we make some assumptions about the workweek and skills, we can provide an aggregate plan for the firm. Assuming a 40-hour workweek and that 100% of each lawyer's hours are billed, about 500 billable hours are available from each lawyer this fiscal quarter.

SOLUTION ▶ We divide hours of billable time (which is the demand) by 500 to provide a count of lawyers needed (lawyers represent the capacity) to cover the estimated demand. Capacity then is shown to be 39, 34, and 30 for the three forecasts, best, likely, and worst, respectively. For example, the best-case scenario of 19,500 total hours, divided by 500 hours per lawyer, equals 39 lawyers needed. Because all 32 lawyers at Klasson and Avalon are qualified to perform basic legal research, this skill has maximum scheduling flexibility (column 6). The most highly skilled (and capacity-constrained) categories are trial work and corporate law. The firm's best-case forecast just barely covers trial work, with 3.6 lawyers needed (see column 5) and 4 qualified (column 6). And corporate law is short 1 full person.

Overtime may be used to cover the excess this quarter, but as business expands, it may be necessary to hire or develop talent in both of these areas. Available staff adequately covers real estate and criminal practice, as long as other needs do not use their excess capacity. With its current legal staff of 32, Klasson and Avalon's best-case forecast will increase the workload by $[(39 - 32)/32 =]$ 21.8% (assuming no new hires). This represents 1 extra day of work per lawyer per week. The worst-case scenario will result in about a 6% underutilization of talent. For both of these scenarios, the firm has determined that available staff will provide adequate service.

INSIGHT ▶ While our definitions of demand and capacity are different than for a manufacturing firm, aggregate planning is as appropriate, useful, and necessary in a service environment as in manufacturing.

LEARNING EXERCISE ▶ If the criminal law best-case forecast increases to 4,500 hours, what happens to the number of lawyers needed? [Answer: The demand for lawyers increases to 41.]

RELATED PROBLEMS ▶ 13.20, 13.21

Source: Based on Glenn Bassett, *Operations Management for Service Industries* (Westport, CT: Quorum Books, 1992): 110.

Airline Industry

Airlines and auto-rental firms also have unique aggregate scheduling problems. Consider an airline that has its headquarters in New York, two hub sites in cities such as Atlanta and Dallas, and 150 offices in airports throughout the country. This planning is considerably more complex than aggregate planning for a single site or even for a number of independent sites.

Aggregate planning consists of tables or schedules for (1) number of flights in and out of each hub; (2) number of flights on all routes; (3) number of passengers to be serviced on all flights; (4) number of air personnel and ground personnel required at each hub and airport; and (5) determining the seats to be allocated to various fare classes. Techniques for determining seat allocation are called yield, or revenue, management, our next topic.

YIELD MANAGEMENT

AUTHOR COMMENT Yield management changes the focus of aggregate planning from capacity management to demand management.

Most operations models, like most business models, assume that firms charge all customers the same price for a product. In fact, many firms work hard at charging different prices. The idea is to match the demand curve by charging based on differences in the customer's willingness to pay. The management challenge is to identify those differences and price accordingly. The technique for multiple price points is called yield management.

Yield (or revenue) management
Capacity decisions that determine the allocation of resources to maximize profit or yield.

Yield (or **revenue) management** is the aggregate planning process of allocating the company's scarce resources to customers at prices that will maximize yield or revenue. Popular use of the technique dates to the 1980s, when American Airlines's reservation system (called SABRE) allowed the airline to alter ticket prices, in real time and on any route, based on demand information. If it looked like demand for expensive seats was low, more discounted seats were offered. If demand for full-fare seats was high, the number of discounted seats was reduced.

OM in Action ▶ Yield Management at Hertz

For over 90 years, Hertz has been renting standard cars for a fixed amount per day. During the past two decades, however, a significant increase in demand has derived from airline travelers flying for business purposes. As the auto-rental market has changed and matured, Hertz has offered more options, including allowing customers to pick up and drop off in different locations. This option has resulted in excess capacity in some cities and shortages in others.

These shortages and overages alerted Hertz to the need for a yield management system similar to those used in the airline industry. The system is used to set prices, regulate the movement, and ultimately determine the availability of cars at each location. Through research, Hertz found that different city locations peak on different days of the week. So cars are moved to peak-demand locations from locations where the demand is low. By altering both the price and quantity of cars at various locations, Hertz has been able to increase "yield" and boost revenue.

The yield management system is primarily used by regional and local managers to better deal with changes in demand in the U.S. market. Hertz's plan to go global with the system, however, faces major challenges in foreign countries, where restrictions against moving empty cars across national borders are common.

Sources: The Wall Street Journal (December 30, 2003): D1 and (March 3, 2000): W-4; and *Cornell Hotel and Restaurant Quarterly* (December 2001): 33–46.

American Airlines's success in yield management spawned many other companies and industries to adopt the concept. Yield management in the hotel industry began in the late 1980s at Marriott International, which now claims an additional $400 million a year in profit from its management of revenue. The competing Omni hotel chain uses software that performs more than 100,000 calculations every night at each facility. The Dallas Omni, for example, charges its highest rates on weekdays but heavily discounts on weekends. Its sister hotel in San Antonio, which is in a more tourist-oriented destination, reverses this rating scheme, with better deals for its consumers on weekdays. Similarly, Walt Disney World has multiple prices: an annual admission pass for an adult was recently quoted at $421; but for a Florida resident, $318; for a member of the AAA, $307; and for active-duty military, $385. The *OM in Action* box "Yield Management at Hertz" describes this practice in the rental car industry.

LO5: Understand and solve a yield management problem

Organizations that have *perishable inventory*, such as airlines, hotels, car rental agencies, cruise lines, and even electrical utilities, have the following shared characteristics that make yield management of interest[3]:

1. Service or product can be sold in advance of consumption.
2. Demand fluctuates.
3. The resource (capacity) is relatively fixed.
4. Demand can be segmented.
5. Variable costs are low and fixed costs are high.

Example 7 illustrates how yield management works in a hotel.

EXAMPLE 7 ▶
Yield management

The Cleveland Downtown Inn is a 100-room hotel that has historically charged one set price for its rooms, $150 per night. The variable cost of a room being occupied is low. Management believes the cleaning, air-conditioning, and incidental costs of soap, shampoo, and so forth, are $15 per room per night. Sales average 50 rooms per night. Figure 13.5 illustrates the current pricing scheme. Net sales are $6,750 per night with a single price point.

APPROACH ▶ Analyze pricing from the perspective of yield management. We note in Figure 13.5 that some guests would have been willing to spend more than $150 per room—"money left on the table." Others would be willing to pay more than the variable cost of $15 but less than $150—"passed-up contribution."

[3]R. Oberwetter, "Revenue Management," *OR/MS Today* (June 2001): 41–44.

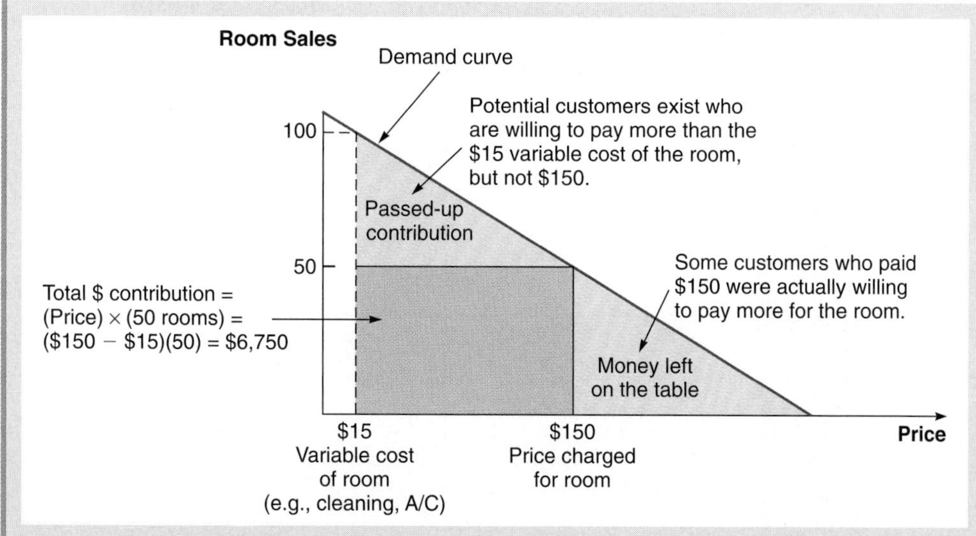

◀ FIGURE 13.5 Hotel Sets Only One Price Level

SOLUTION ▶ In Figure 13.6, the inn decides to set *two* price levels. It estimates that 30 rooms per night can be sold at $100 and another 30 rooms at $200, using yield management software that is widely available.

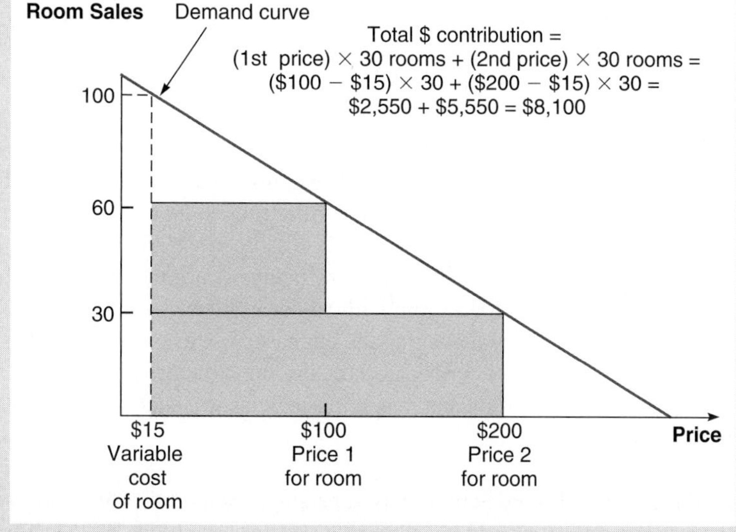

◀ FIGURE 13.6 Hotel with Two Price Levels

INSIGHT ▶ Yield management has increased total contribution to $8,100 ($2,550 from $100 rooms and $5,550 from $200 rooms). It may be that even more price levels are called for at Cleveland Downtown Inn.

LEARNING EXERCISE ▶ If the hotel develops a third price of $150 and can sell half of the $100 rooms at the increased rate, what is the contribution? [Answer: $8,850 = (15 × $85) + (15 × $135) + 30 × $185).]

RELATED PROBLEM ▶ 13.22

Industries traditionally associated with revenue management operate in quadrant 2 of Figure 13.7. They are able to apply variable pricing for their product and control product use or availability (number of airline seats or hotel rooms sold at economy rate). On the other hand, movie theaters, arenas, or performing arts centers (quadrant 1) have less pricing flexibility but still use time (evening or matinee) and location (orchestra, side, or balcony) to manage revenue. In both cases, management has control over the amount of the resource used—both the quantity and the duration of the resource.

▶ **FIGURE 13.7**
Yield Management Matrix
Industries in quadrant 2 are traditionally associated with revenue management.

Source: Adapted from S. Kimes and K. McGuire, "Function Space Revenue Management," *Cornell Hotel and Restaurant Administration Quarterly* 42, no. 6 (December 2001): 33–46.

Use		Price: Tend to be fixed	Price: Tend to be variable
Use	Tend to be predictable	Quadrant 1: Movies Stadiums/arenas Convention centers Hotel meeting space	Quadrant 2: Hotels Airlines Rental cars Cruise lines
Use	Tend to be uncertain	Quadrant 3: Restaurants Golf courses Internet service providers	Quadrant 4: Hospitals Continuing care

In the lower half of Figure 13.7, the manager's job is more difficult because the duration of the use of the resource is less controllable. However, with imagination, managers are using excess capacity even for these industries. For instance, the golf course may sell less desirable tee times at a reduced rate, and the restaurant may have an "early bird" special to generate business before the usual dinner hour.

To make yield management work, the company needs to manage three issues:

1. *Multiple pricing structures:* These structures must be feasible and appear logical (and preferably fair) to the customer. Such justification may take various forms, for example, first-class seats on an airline or the preferred starting time at a golf course. (See the Ethical Dilemma at the end of this chapter).
2. *Forecasts of the use and duration of the use:* How many economy seats should be available? How much will customers pay for a room with an ocean view?
3. *Changes in demand:* This means managing the increased use as more capacity is sold. It also means dealing with issues that occur because the pricing structure may not seem logical and fair to all customers. Finally, it means managing new issues, such as overbooking because the forecast was not perfect.

Precise pricing through yield management has substantial potential. Therefore, several firms now have software available to address the issue. These include NCR's Teradata, SPS, DemandTec, and Oracle with Profit Logic.

CHAPTER SUMMARY

Aggregate planning provides companies with a necessary weapon to help capture market shares in the global economy. The aggregate plan provides both manufacturing and service firms the ability to respond to changing customer demands while still producing at low-cost and high-quality levels.

Aggregate schedules set levels of inventory, production, subcontracting, and employment over an intermediate time range, usually 3 to 18 months. This chapter describes several aggregate planning techniques, ranging from the popular graphical approach to a variety of mathematical models such as linear programming.

The aggregate plan is an important responsibility of an operations manager and a key to efficient use of existing capital investment. Output from the aggregate schedule leads to a more detailed master production schedule, which is the basis for disaggregation, job scheduling, and MRP systems.

Aggregate plans for manufacturing firms and service systems are similar. Restaurants, airlines, and hotels are all service systems that employ aggregate plans, and have an opportunity to implement yield management. But regardless of the industry or planning method, the most important issue is the implementation of the plan. In this respect, managers appear to be more comfortable with faster, less complex, and less mathematical approaches to planning.

Key Terms

Aggregate planning (or aggregate scheduling) (p. 512)
Scheduling decisions (p. 512)
Disaggregation (p. 514)
Master production schedule (p. 514)
Chase strategy (p. 516)
Level scheduling (p. 517)
Mixed strategy (p. 517)
Graphical techniques (p. 517)
Transportation method of linear programming (p. 522)
Management coefficients model (p. 524)
Yield (or revenue) management (p. 527)

Ethical Dilemma

Airline passengers today stand in numerous lines, are crowded into small seats on mostly full airplanes, and often spend time on taxiways because of air-traffic problems or lack of open gates. But what gripes travelers almost as much as these annoyances is finding out that the person sitting next to them paid a much lower fare than they did for their seat. This concept of "yield management" or "revenue management" results in ticket pricing that can range from free to thousands of dollars on the same plane. Figure 13.8 illustrates what passengers recently paid for various seats on an 11:35 A.M. flight from Minneapolis to Anaheim, California, on an Airbus A320.

Make the case for, and then against, this pricing system. Does the general public seem to accept yield management? What would happen if you overheard the person in front of you in line getting a better room rate at a Hilton Hotel? How do customers manipulate the airline systems to get better fares?

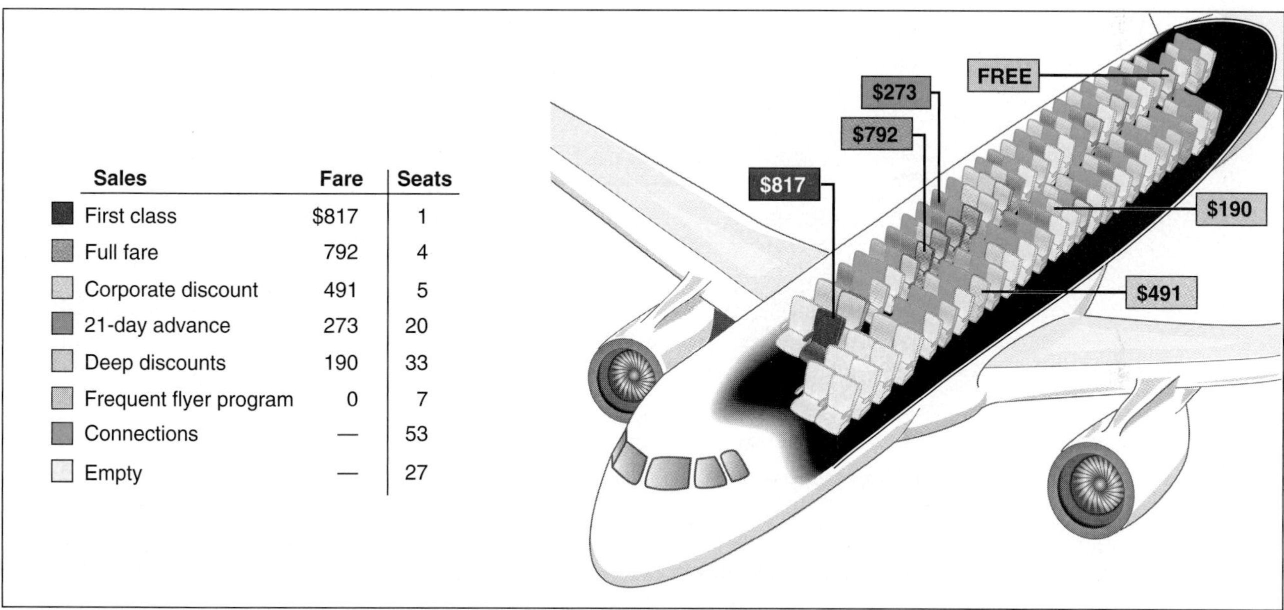

Sales	Fare	Seats
First class	$817	1
Full fare	792	4
Corporate discount	491	5
21-day advance	273	20
Deep discounts	190	33
Frequent flyer program	0	7
Connections	—	53
Empty	—	27

▲ **FIGURE 13.8 Yield Management Seat Costs on a Typical Flight**

Discussion Questions

1. Define *aggregate planning*.
2. Explain what the term *aggregate* in "aggregate planning" means.
3. List the strategic objectives of aggregate planning. Which one of these is most often addressed by the quantitative techniques of aggregate planning? Which one of these is generally the most important?
4. Define *chase strategy*.
5. What is a pure strategy? Provide a few examples.
6. What is level scheduling? What is the basic philosophy underlying it?
7. Define *mixed strategy*. Why would a firm use a mixed strategy instead of a simple pure strategy?
8. What are the advantages and disadvantages of varying the size of the workforce to meet demand requirements each period?
9. Why are mathematical models not more widely used in aggregate planning?
10. How does aggregate planning in service differ from aggregate planning in manufacturing?
11. What is the relationship between the aggregate plan and the master production schedule?
12. Why are graphical aggregate planning methods useful?
13. What are major limitations of using the transportation method for aggregate planning?
14. How does yield management impact an aggregate plan?

Using Software for Aggregate Planning

This section illustrates the use of Excel OM and POM for Windows in aggregate planning.

Using Excel OM

Excel OM's Aggregate Planning module is demonstrated in Program 13.1. Again using data from Example 2, Program 13.1 provides input and some of the formulas used to compute the costs of regular time, overtime, subcontracting, holding, shortage, and increase or decrease in production. The user must provide the production plan for Excel OM to analyze.

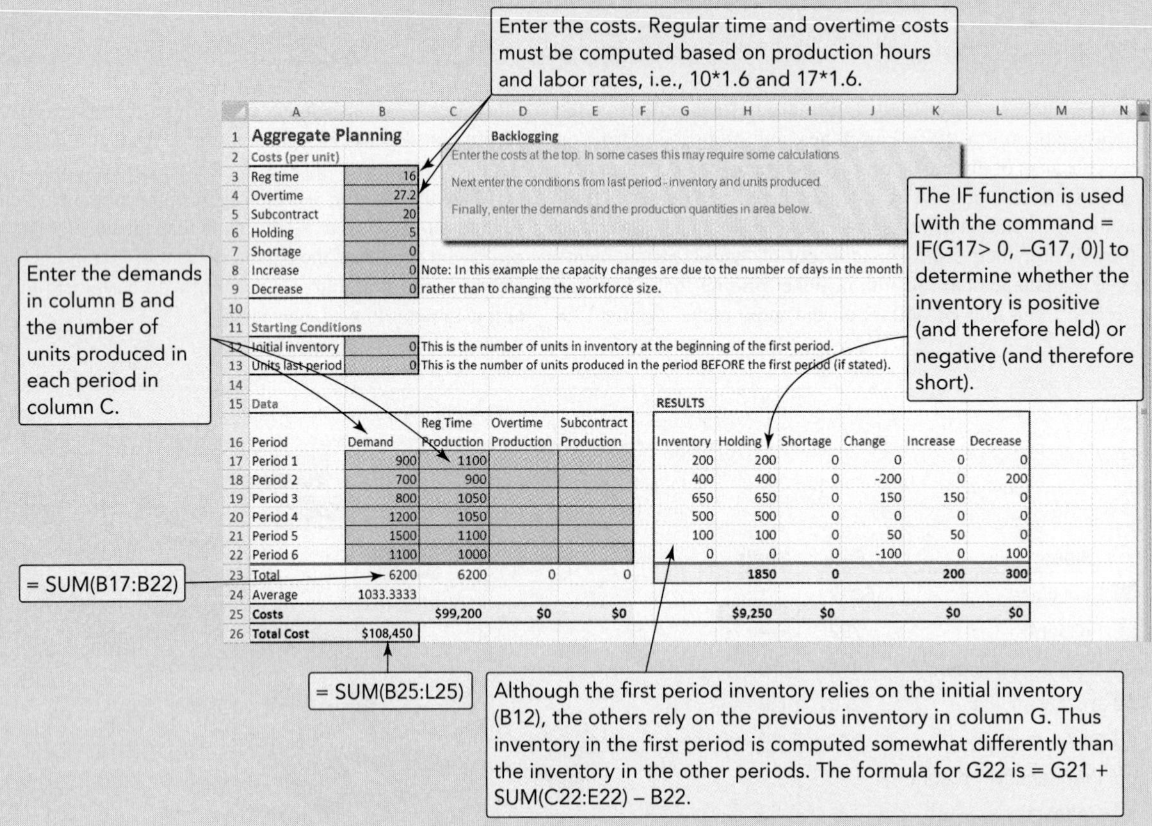

Data					RESULTS					
Period	Demand	Reg Time Production	Overtime Production	Subcontract Production	Inventory	Holding	Shortage	Change	Increase	Decrease
Period 1	900	1100			200	200	0	0	0	0
Period 2	700	900			400	400	0	-200	0	200
Period 3	800	1050			650	650	0	150	150	0
Period 4	1200	1050			500	500	0	0	0	0
Period 5	1500	1100			100	100	0	50	50	0
Period 6	1100	1000			0	0	0	-100	0	100
Total	6200	6200	0	0		1850	0		200	300
Average	1033.3333									
Costs		$99,200	$0	$0		$9,250	$0		$0	$0
Total Cost	$108,450									

▲ **PROGRAM 13.1 Using Excel OM for Aggregate Planning, with Example 2 Data**

Using POM for Windows

The POM for Windows Aggregate Planning module performs aggregate or production planning for up to 90 time periods. Given a set of demands for future periods, you can try various plans to determine the lowest-cost plan based on holding, shortage, production, and changeover costs. Four methods are available for planning. More help is available on each after you choose the method. See Appendix IV for further details.

Solved Problems

Virtual Office Hours help is available at www.myomlab.com

▼ SOLVED PROBLEM 13.1

The roofing manufacturer described in Examples 1 to 4 of this chapter wishes to consider yet a fourth planning strategy (plan 4). This one maintains a constant workforce of eight people and uses overtime whenever necessary to meet demand. Use the information found in Table 13.3 on page 519. Again, assume beginning and ending inventories are equal to zero.

▼ SOLUTION

Employ eight workers and use overtime when necessary. Note that carrying costs will be encountered in this plan.

Month	Production Days	Production at 40 Units per Day	Beginning-of-Month Inventory	Forecast Demand This Month	Overtime Production Needed	Ending Inventory
Jan.	22	880	—	900	20 units	0 units
Feb.	18	720	0	700	0 units	20 units
Mar.	21	840	20	800	0 units	60 units
Apr.	21	840	60	1,200	300 units	0 units
May	22	880	0	1,500	620 units	0 units
June	20	800	0	1,100	300 units	0 units
					1,240 units	80 units

$$\text{Carrying cost totals} = 80 \text{ units} \times \$5/\text{unit}/\text{month} = \$400$$

Regular pay:

$$8 \text{ workers} \times \$80/\text{day} \times 124 \text{ days} = \$79{,}360$$

Overtime pay:
To produce 1,240 units at overtime rate requires 1,240 × 1.6 hours/unit = 1,984 hours.

$$\text{Overtime cost} = \$17/\text{hour} \times 1{,}984 \text{ hours} = \$33{,}728$$

Plan 4

Costs (workforce of 8 plus overtime)		
Carrying cost	$ 400	(80 units carried × $5/unit)
Regular labor	79,360	(8 workers × $80/day × 124 days)
Overtime	33,728	(1,984 hours × $17/hour)
Hiring or firing	0	
Subcontracting	0	
Total costs	$113,488	

Plan 2 is still preferable at $105,152.

▼ SOLVED PROBLEM 13.2

A Dover, Delaware, plant has developed the accompanying supply, demand, cost, and inventory data. The firm has a constant workforce and meets all its demand. Allocate production capacity to satisfy demand at a minimum cost. What is the cost of this plan?

Demand Forecast

Period	Demand (units)
1	450
2	550
3	750

Supply Capacity Available (units)

Period	Regular Time	Overtime	Subcontract
1	300	50	200
2	400	50	200
3	450	50	200

Other Data

Initial inventory	50 units
Regular-time cost per unit	$50
Overtime cost per unit	$65
Subcontract cost per unit	$80
Carrying cost per unit per period	$ 1
Back order cost per unit per period	$ 4

▼ SOLUTION

SUPPLY FROM		DEMAND FOR *Period 1*	*Period 2*	*Period 3*	*Unused Capacity (dummy)*	TOTAL CAPACITY AVAILABLE (supply)
Beginning inventory		0 50	1	2	0	50
Period 1	*Regular time*	50 300	51	52	0	300
	Overtime	65 50	66	67	0	50
	Subcontract	80 50	81	82	0 150	200
Period 2	*Regular time*	54	50 400	51	0	400
	Overtime	69	65 50	66	0	50
	Subcontract	84	80 100	81 50	0 50	200
Period 3	*Regular time*	58	54	50 450	0	450
	Overtime	73	69	65 50	0	50
	Subcontract	88	84	80 200	0	200
TOTAL DEMAND		450	550	750	200	1,950

Cost of plan:

Period 1:	50($0) + 300($50) + 50($65) + 50($80) =	$22,250
Period 2:	400($50) + 50($65) + 100($80) =	$31,250
Period 3:	50($81) + 450($50) + 50($65) + 200($80) =	$45,800*
	Total cost	$99,300

*Includes 50 units of subcontract and carrying cost.

Problems*

• **13.1** Prepare a graph of the monthly forecasts and average forecasted demand for Industrial Air Corp., a manufacturer of a variety of large air conditioners for commercial applications.

Month	Production Days	Demand Forecast
January	22	1,000
February	18	1,100
March	22	1,200
April	21	1,300
May	22	1,350
June	21	1,350
July	21	1,300
August	22	1,200
September	21	1,100
October	22	1,100
November	20	1,050
December	20	900

•• 13.2 a) Develop another plan for the Mexican roofing manufacturer described in Examples 1 to 4 (pages 518–521) and Solved Problem 13.1 (pages 532–533). For this plan, plan 5, the firm wants to maintain a constant workforce of six, using subcontracting to meet remaining demand. Is this plan preferable?

b) The same roofing manufacturer in Examples 1 to 4 and Solved Problem 13.1 has yet a sixth plan. A constant workforce of seven is selected, with the remainder of demand filled by subcontracting.

c) Is this better than plans 1–5? PX

••• 13.3 The president of Hill Enterprises, Terri Hill, projects the firm's aggregate demand requirements over the next 8 months as follows:

Jan.	1,400	May	2,200
Feb.	1,600	June	2,200
Mar.	1,800	July	1,800
Apr.	1,800	Aug.	1,400

**Note:* PX means the problem may be solved with POM for Windows and/or Excel OM.

Her operations manager is considering a new plan, which begins in January with 200 units on hand. Stockout cost of lost sales is $100 per unit. Inventory holding cost is $20 per unit per month. Ignore any idle-time costs. The plan is called plan A.

Plan A: Vary the workforce level to execute a "chase" strategy by producing the quantity demanded in the *prior* month. The December demand and rate of production are both 1,600 units per month. The cost of hiring additional workers is $5,000 per 100 units. The cost of laying off workers is $7,500 per 100 units. Evaluate this plan. PX

•• **13.4** Using the information in Problem 13.3, develop plan B. Produce at a constant rate of 1,400 units per month, which will meet minimum demands. Then use subcontracting, with additional units at a premium price of $75 per unit. Evaluate this plan by computing the costs for January through August. PX

•• **13.5** Hill is now considering plan C. Beginning inventory, stockout costs, and holding costs are provided in Problem 13.3:

a) Plan C: Keep a stable workforce by maintaining a constant production rate equal to the average requirements and allow varying inventory levels.
b) Plot the demand with a graph that also shows average requirements. Conduct your analysis for January through August. PX

••• **13.6** Hill's operations manager (see Problems 13.3 through 13.5) is also considering two mixed strategies for January–August:

a) Plan D: Keep the current workforce stable at producing 1,600 units per month. Permit a maximum of 20% overtime at an additional cost of $50 per unit. A warehouse now constrains the maximum allowable inventory on hand to 400 units or less.
b) Plan E: Keep the current workforce, which is producing 1,600 units per month, and subcontract to meet the rest of the demand.
c) Evaluate plans D and E and make a recommendation. PX

••• **13.7** Michael Carrigg, Inc., is a disk manufacturer in need of an aggregate plan for July through December. The company has gathered the following data:

Costs	
Holding cost	$8/disk/month
Subcontracting	$80/disk
Regular-time labor	$12/hour
Overtime labor	$18/hour for hours above 8 hours/worker/day
Hiring cost	$40/worker
Layoff cost	$80/worker

Demand*	
July	400
Aug.	500
Sept.	550
Oct.	700
Nov.	800
Dec.	700

*No costs are incurred for unmet demand.

Other Data	
Current workforce (June)	8 people
Labor-hours/disk	4 hours
Workdays/month	20 days
Beginning inventory	150 disks**
Ending inventory	0 disks

**Note that there is no holding cost for June.

What will each of the two following strategies cost?

a) Vary the workforce so that production meets demand. Carrigg had eight workers on board in June.
b) Vary overtime only and use a constant workforce of eight. PX

•• **13.8** You manage a consulting firm down the street from Michael Carrigg, Inc., and to get your foot in the door, you have told Mr. Carrigg (see Problem 13.7) that you can do a better job at aggregate planning than his current staff. He said, "Fine. You do that, and you have a 1-year contract." You now have to make good on your boast using the data in Problem 13.7. You decide to hire 5 workers in August and 5 more in October.

••• **13.9** Mary Rhodes, operations manager at Kansas Furniture, has received the following estimates of demand requirements:

July	Aug.	Sept.	Oct.	Nov.	Dec.
1,000	1,200	1,400	1,800	1,800	1,600

a) Assuming stockout costs for lost sales of $100 per unit, inventory carrying costs of $25 per unit per month, and zero beginning and ending inventory, evaluate these two plans on an *incremental* cost basis:
   - Plan A: Produce at a steady rate (equal to minimum requirements) of 1,000 units per month and subcontract additional units at a $60 per unit premium cost.
   - Plan B: Vary the workforce, which performs at a current production level of 1,300 units per month. The cost of hiring additional workers is $3,000 per 100 units produced. The cost of layoffs is $6,000 per 100 units cut back. PX
b) Which plan is best and why?

••• **13.10** Mary Rhodes (see Problem 13.9) is considering two more mixed strategies. Using the data in Problem 13.9, compare plans C and D with plans A and B and make a recommendation.

- Plan C: Keep the current workforce steady at a level producing 1,300 units per month. Subcontract the remainder to meet demand. Assume that 300 units remaining from June are available in July.
- Plan D: Keep the current workforce at a level capable of producing 1,300 units per month. Permit a maximum of 20%

overtime at a premium of $40 per unit. Assume that warehouse limitations permit no more than a 180-unit carryover from month to month. This plan means that any time inventories reach 180, the plant is kept idle. Idle time per unit is $60. Any additional needs are subcontracted at a cost of $60 per incremental unit.

••• **13.11** Liz Perry Health and Beauty Products has developed a new shampoo and you need to develop its aggregate schedule. The cost accounting department has supplied you the cost relevant to the aggregate plan and the marketing department has provided a four-quarter forecast. All are shown as follows:

Quarter	Forecast
1	1,400
2	1,200
3	1,500
4	1,300

Costs	
Previous quarter's output	1,500 units
Beginning inventory	0 units
Stockout cost for backorders	$50 per unit
Inventory holding cost	$10 per unit for every unit held at the end of the quarter
Hiring workers	$40 per unit
Layoff workers	$80 per unit
Unit cost	$30 per unit
Overtime	$15 extra per unit
Subcontracting	Not available

Your job is to develop an aggregate plan for the next four quarters.

a) First, try a chase plan by hiring and layoffs (to meet the forecast) as necessary.
b) Then try a plan that holds employment steady.
c) Which is the more economical plan for Liz Perry Health and Beauty Products? PX

••• **13.12** Missouri's Soda Pop, Inc., has a new fruit drink for which it has high hopes. Steve Allen, the production planner, has assembled the following cost data and demand forecast:

Quarter	Forecast
1	1,800
2	1,100
3	1,600
4	900

Costs/Other Data
Previous quarter's output = 1,300 cases
Beginning inventory = 0 cases
Stockout cost = $150 per case
Inventory holding cost = $40 per case at end of quarter
Hiring employees = $40 per case
Terminating employees = $80 per case
Subcontracting cost = $60 per case
Unit cost on regular time = $30 per case
Overtime cost = $15 extra per case
Capacity on regular time = 1,800 cases per quarter

Steve's job is to develop an aggregate plan. The three initial options he wants to evaluate are:

- Plan A: a chase strategy that hires and fires personnel as necessary to meet the forecast.
- Plan B: a level strategy.
- Plan C: a level strategy that produces 1,200 cases per quarter and meets the forecasted demand with inventory and subcontracting.

a) Which strategy is the lowest-cost plan?
b) If you are Steve's boss, the VP for operations, which plan do you implement and why? PX

•• **13.13** Josie Gall's firm has developed the following supply, demand, cost, and inventory data. Allocate production capacity to meet demand at a minimum cost using the transportation method. What is the cost? Assume that the initial inventory has no holding cost in the first period and backorders are not permitted.

Supply Available

Period	Regular Time	Overtime	Subcontract	Demand Forecast
1	30	10	5	40
2	35	12	5	50
3	30	10	5	40

Initial inventory	20 units
Regular-time cost per unit	$100
Overtime cost per unit	$150
Subcontract cost per unit	$200
Carrying cost per unit per month	$ 4

PX

•• **13.14** Haifa Instruments, an Israeli producer of portable kidney dialysis units and other medical products, develops a 4-month aggregate plan. Demand and capacity (in units) are forecast as follows:

Capacity Source	Month 1	Month 2	Month 3	Month 4
Labor				
Regular time	235	255	290	300
Overtime	20	24	26	24
Subcontract	12	15	15	17
Demand	255	294	321	301

The cost of producing each dialysis unit is $985 on regular time, $1,310 on overtime, and $1,500 on a subcontract. Inventory carrying cost is $100 per unit per month. There is to be no beginning or ending inventory in stock and backorders are not permitted. Set up a production plan that minimizes cost using the transportation method. PX

•• **13.15** The production planning period for flat-screen monitors at Georgia's Fernandez Electronics, Inc., is 4 months. Cost data are as follows:

Regular-time cost per monitor	$ 70
Overtime cost per monitor	$110
Subcontract cost per monitor	$120
Carrying cost per monitor per month	$ 4

For each of the next 4 months, capacity and demand for flat-screen monitors are as follows:

	Period			
	Month 1	Month 2	Month 3[a]	Month 4
Demand	2,000	2,500	1,500	2,100
Capacity				
Regular time	1,500	1,600	750	1,600
Overtime	400	400	200	400
Subcontract	600	600	600	600

[a]Factory closes for 2 weeks of vacation.

Fernandez Electronics expects to enter the planning period with 500 monitors in stock. Back ordering is not permitted (meaning, for example, that monitors produced in the second month cannot be used in the first month to cover first month's demand). Develop a production plan that minimizes costs using the transportation method. PX

••• **13.16** A large Omaha feed mill, B. Swart Processing, prepares its 6-month aggregate plan by forecasting demand for 50-pound bags of cattle feed as follows: January, 1,000 bags; February, 1,200; March, 1,250; April, 1,450; May, 1,400; and June, 1,400. The feed mill plans to begin the new year with no inventory left over from the previous year and backorders are not permitted. It projects that capacity (during regular hours) for producing bags of feed will remain constant at 800 until the end of April, and then increase to 1,100 bags per month when a planned expansion is completed on May 1. Overtime capacity is set at 300 bags per month until the expansion, at which time it will increase to 400 bags per month. A friendly competitor in Sioux City, Iowa, is also available as a backup source to meet demand—but can provide only 500 bags total during the 6-month period. Develop a 6-month production plan for the feed mill using the transportation method.

Cost data are as follows:

Regular-time cost per bag (until April 30)	\$12.00
Regular-time cost per bag (after May 1)	\$11.00
Overtime cost per bag (during entire period)	\$16.00
Cost of outside purchase per bag	\$18.50
Carrying cost per bag per month	\$ 1.00

PX

•• **13.17** Lon Min has developed a specialized airtight vacuum bag to extend the freshness of seafood shipped to restaurants. He has put together the following demand cost data:

Quarter	Forecast (units)	Regular time	Over-time	Sub-contract
1	500	400	80	100
2	750	400	80	100
3	900	800	160	100
4	450	400	80	100

Initial inventory = 250 units
Regular time cost = \$1.00/unit
Overtime cost = \$1.50/unit
Subcontracting cost = \$2.00/unit
Carrying cost = \$0.50/unit/quarter
Back-order cost = \$0.50/unit/quarter

Min decides that the initial inventory of 250 units will incur the 20¢/unit cost from each prior quarter (unlike the situation in most companies, where a 0 unit cost is assigned).

a) Find the optimal plan using the transportation method.
b) What is the cost of the plan?
c) Does any regular time capacity go unused? If so, how much in which periods?
d) What is the extent of backordering in units and dollars? PX

••• **13.18** José Martinez of El Paso has developed a polished stainless steel tortilla machine that makes it a "showpiece" for display in Mexican restaurants. He needs to develop a 5-month aggregate plan. His forecast of capacity and demand follows:

	Month				
	1	2	3	4	5
Demand	150	160	130	200	210
Capacity					
Regular	150	150	150	150	150
Overtime	20	20	10	10	10

Subcontracting: 100 units available over the 5-month period
Beginning inventory: 0 units
Ending inventory required: 20 units

Costs	
Regular-time cost per unit	\$100
Overtime cost per unit	\$125
Subcontract cost per unit	\$135
Inventory holding cost per unit per month	\$ 3

Assume that backorders are not permitted. Using the transportation method, what is the total cost of the optimal plan? PX

•••• **13.19** Chris Fisher, owner of an Ohio firm that manufactures display cabinets, develops an 8-month aggregate plan. Demand and capacity (in units) are forecast as follows:

Capacity Source (units)	Jan.	Feb.	Mar.	Apr.	May	June	July	Aug.
Regular time	235	255	290	300	300	290	300	290
Overtime	20	24	26	24	30	28	30	30
Subcontract	12	16	15	17	17	19	19	20
Demand	255	294	321	301	330	320	345	340

The cost of producing each unit is $1,000 on regular time, $1,300 on overtime, and $1,800 on a subcontract. Inventory carrying cost is $200 per unit per month. There is no beginning or ending inventory in stock, and no backorders are permitted from period to period.

a) Set up a production plan that minimizes cost by producing exactly what the demand is each month. Let the workforce vary by using regular time first, then overtime, and then subcontracting. This plan allows no backorders or inventory. What is this plan's cost?
b) Through better planning, regular-time production can be set at exactly the same amount, 275 units, per month. Does this alter the solution?
c) If overtime costs rise from $1,300 to $1,400, will your answer to part (a) change? What if overtime costs then fall to $1,200? Px

••• **13.20** Forrester and Cohen is a small accounting firm, managed by Joseph Cohen since the retirement in December of his partner Brad Forrester. Cohen and his 3 CPAs can together bill 640 hours per month. When Cohen or another accountant bills more than 160 hours per month, he or she gets an additional "overtime" pay of $62.50 for each of the extra hours: This is above and beyond the $5,000 salary each draws during the month. (Cohen draws the same base pay as his employees.) Cohen strongly discourages any CPA from working (billing) more than 240 hours in any given month. The demand for billable hours for the firm over the next 6 months is estimated below:

Month	Estimate of Billable Hours
Jan.	600
Feb.	500
Mar.	1,000
Apr.	1,200
May	650
June	590

Cohen has an agreement with Forrester, his former partner, to help out during the busy tax season, if needed, for an hourly fee of $125. Cohen will not even consider laying off one of his colleagues in the case of a slow economy. He could, however, hire another CPA at the same salary, as business dictates.

a) Develop an aggregate plan for the 6-month period.
b) Compute the cost of Cohen's plan of using overtime and Forrester.
c) Should the firm remain as is, with a total of 4 CPAs?

•• **13.21** Refer to the CPA firm in Problem 13.20. In planning for next year, Cohen estimates that billable hours will increase by 10% in each of the 6 months. He therefore proceeds to hire a fifth CPA. The same regular time, overtime, and outside consultant (i.e., Forrester) costs still apply.

a) Develop the new aggregate plan and compute its costs.
b) Comment on the staffing level with five accountants. Was it a good decision to hire the additional accountant?

•• **13.22** Southeastern Airlines's daily flight from Atlanta to Charlotte uses a Boeing 737, with all-coach seating for 120 people. In the past, the airline has priced every seat at $140 for the one-way flight. An average of 80 passengers are on each flight. The variable cost of a filled seat is $25. Katie Morgan, the new operations manager, has decided to try a yield revenue approach, with seats priced at $80 for early bookings and at $190 for bookings within 1 week of the flight. She estimates that the airline will sell 65 seats at the lower price and 35 at the higher price. Variable cost will not change. Which approach is preferable to Ms. Morgan?

► **Refer to myomlab for these additional homework problems: 13.23–13.26**

Case Studies

► Southwestern University: (G)*

With the rising demands of a successful football program, the campus police chief at Southwestern University, Greg Frazier wants to develop a 2-year plan that involves a request for additional resources.

The SWU department currently has 26 sworn officers. The size of the force has not changed over the past 15 years, but the following changes have prompted the chief to seek more resources:

- The size of the athletic program, especially football, has increased.
- The college has expanded geographically, with some new research facilities and laboratories now miles away from the main campus.
- Traffic and parking problems have increased.
- More portable, expensive computers with high theft potential are dispersed across the campus.
- Alcohol and drug problems have increased.
- The size of the surrounding community has doubled.
- The police need to spend more time on education and prevention programs.

The college is located in Stephenville, Texas, a small town about 30 miles southwest of the Dallas/Forth Worth metroplex. During the summer months, the student population is around 5,000. This number swells to 20,000 during fall and spring semesters. Thus demand for police and other services is significantly lower during the summer months. Demand for police services also varies by:

- Time of day (peak time is between 10 P.M. and 2 A.M.).
- Day of the week (weekends are the busiest).
- Weekend of the year (on football weekends, 50,000 extra people come to campus).
- Special events (check-in, checkout, commencement).

Football weekends are especially difficult to staff. Extra police services are typically needed from 8 A.M. to 5 P.M. on five football Saturdays. All 26 officers are called in to work double shifts. More than 40 law enforcement officers from surrounding locations are paid to come in on their own time, and a dozen state police lend a hand free of charge (when available). Twenty-five students and local residents are paid to work traffic and parking. During the last academic year (a 9-month period), overtime payments to campus police officers totaled over $120,000.

Other relevant data include the following:

- The average starting salary for a police officer is $28,000.
- Work-study and part-time students and local residents who help with traffic and parking are paid $9.00 an hour.

- Overtime is paid to police officers who work over 40 hours a week at the rate of $18.00 an hour. Extra officers who are hired part time from outside agencies also earn $18.00 an hour.
- There seems to be an unlimited supply of officers who will work for the college when needed for special events.
- With days off, vacations, and average sick leave considered, it takes five persons to cover one 24-hour, 7-day-a-week position.

The schedule of officers during fall and spring semesters is:

	Weekdays	Weekend
First shift (7 A.M.–3 P.M.)	5	4
Second shift (3 P.M.–11 P.M.)	5	6
Third shift (11 P.M.–7 A.M.)	6	8

Staffing for football weekends and special events is *in addition to* the preceding schedule. Summer staffing is, on average, half that shown.

Frazier thinks that his present staff is stretched to the limit. Fatigued officers are potential problems for the department and the community. In addition, neither time nor personnel has been set aside for crime prevention, safety, or health programs. Interactions of police officers with students, faculty, and staff are minimal and usually negative in nature. In light of these problems, the chief would like to request funding for four additional officers, two assigned to new programs and two to alleviate the overload on his current staff. He would also like to begin limiting overtime to 10 hours per week for each officer.

Discussion Questions

1. Which variations in demand for police services should be considered in an aggregate plan for resources? Which variations can be accomplished with short-term scheduling adjustments?
2. Evaluate the current staffing plan. What does it cost? Are 26 officers sufficient to handle the normal workload?
3. What would be the additional cost of the chief's proposal? How would you suggest that he justify his request?
4. How much does it currently cost the college to provide police services for football games? What would be the pros and cons of completely subcontracting this work to outside law enforcement agencies?
5. Propose other alternatives.

*This integrated case study runs throughout the text. Other issues facing Southwestern's football expansion include: (A) managing the stadium project (Chapter 3); (B) forecasting game attendance (Chapter 4); (C) quality of facilities (Chapter 6); (D) break-even analysis for food services (Supplement 7 Web site); (E) where to locate the new stadium (Chapter 8 Web site); (F) inventory planning of football programs (Chapter 12 Web site).

Source: Adapted from C. Haksever, B. Render, and R. Russell, *Service Management and Operations*, 2nd ed. (Upper Saddle River, NJ: Prentice Hall, 2000), 308–309. Reprinted by permission of Prentice Hall, Inc.

▶ Andrew-Carter, Inc.

Andrew-Carter, Inc. (A-C), is a major Canadian producer and distributor of outdoor lighting fixtures. Its products are distributed throughout South and North America and have been in high demand for several years. The company operates three plants to manufacture fixtures and distribute them to five distribution centers (warehouses).

During the present global slowdown, A-C has seen a major drop in demand for its products, largely because the housing market has declined. Based on the forecast of interest rates, the head of operations feels that demand for housing and thus for A-C's products will remain depressed for the foreseeable future. A-C is considering closing one of its plants, as it is now operating with a forecast excess capacity of 34,000 units per week. The forecast weekly demands for the coming year are as follows:

Warehouse 1	9,000 units
Warehouse 2	13,000
Warehouse 3	11,000
Warehouse 4	15,000
Warehouse 5	8,000

Plant capacities, in units per week, are as follows:

Plant 1, regular time	27,000 units
Plant 1, on overtime	7,000
Plant 2, regular time	20,000
Plant 2, on overtime	5,000
Plant 3, regular time	25,000
Plant 3, on overtime	6,000

If A-C shuts down any plants, its weekly costs will change, because fixed costs will be lower for a nonoperating plant. Table 1 shows production costs at each plant, both variable at regular time and overtime, and fixed when operating and shut down. Table 2 shows distribution costs from each plant to each distribution center.

▼ **TABLE 1 Andrew-Carter, Inc., Variable Costs and Fixed Production Costs per Week**

Plant	Variable Cost (per unit)	*Fixed Cost per Week* Operating	Not Operating
1, regular time	$2.80	$14,000	$6,000
1, overtime	3.52		
2, regular time	2.78	12,000	5,000
2, overtime	3.48		
3, regular time	2.72	15,000	7,500
3, overtime	3.42		

▼ **TABLE 2 Andrew-Carter, Inc., Distribution Costs per Unit**

	To Distribution Centers				
From Plants	W1	W2	W3	W4	W5
1	$.50	$.44	$.49	$.46	$.56
2	.40	.52	.50	.56	.57
3	.56	.53	.51	.54	.35

Discussion Questions

1. Evaluate the various configurations of operating and closed plants that will meet weekly demand. Determine which configuration minimizes total costs.
2. Discuss the implications of closing a plant.

Source: Reprinted by permission of Professor Michael Ballot, University of the Pacific, Stockton, CA.

▶**Additional Case Study:** Visit **www.myomlab.com** or **www.pearsonhighered.com/heizer** for this free case study:
Cornwell Glass: Involves setting a production schedule for an auto glass producer.

Bibliography

Chen, Fangruo. "Salesforce Initiative, Market Information, and Production/Inventory Planning." *Management Science* 51, no. 1 (January 2005): 60–75.

Hopp, Wallace J., and Mark L. Spearman. *Factory Physics*, 3rd ed. New York: Irwin/McGraw-Hill (2008).

Kimes, S. E., and G. M. Thompson. "Restaurant Revenue Management at Chevy's." *Decision Sciences* 35, no. 3 (Summer 2004): 371–393.

Metters, R., K. King-Metters, M. Pullman, and S. Walton. *Successful Service Operations Management*. 2nd ed. Mason, OH: Thompson-South-Western (2006).

Metters, Richard, et al. "The 'Killer Application' of Revenue Management: Harrah's Cherokee Casino and Hotel." *Interfaces* 38, no. 3 (May–June 2008): 161–178.

Mukhopadhyay, S., S. Samaddar, and G. Colville. "Improving Revenue Management Decision Making for Airlines." *Decision Science* 38, no. 2 (May 2007): 309–327.

Plambeck, Erica L., and Terry A. Taylor. "Sell the Plant? The Impact of Contract Manufacturing on Innovation, Capacity, and Profitability." *Management Science* 51, no. 1 (January 2005): 133–150.

Silver, E. A., D. F. Pyke, and R. Peterson. *Inventory Management and Production Planning and Scheduling*. New York: Wiley (1998).

Vollmann, T. E., W. L. Berry, D. C. Whybark, and F. R. Jacobs. *Manufacturing Planning and Control for Supply Chain Management*, 5th ed. Burr Ridge, IL: Irwin (2005).

Chapter 13 *Rapid* Review

Main Heading	Review Material	myomlab
THE PLANNING PROCESS (pp. 512–513)	■ **Aggregate planning** (or **aggregate scheduling**)—An approach to determine the quantity and timing of production for the intermediate future (usually 3 to 18 months ahead) Usually, *the objective of aggregate planning is to meet forecasted demand while minimizing cost over the planning period.* Four things are needed for aggregate planning: 1. A logical overall unit for measuring sales and output 2. A forecast of demand for a reasonable intermediate planning period in these aggregate terms 3. A method for determining the relevant costs 4. A model that combines forecasts and costs so that scheduling decisions can be made for the planning period ■ **Scheduling decisions**—Plans that match production to changes in demand.	
THE NATURE OF AGGREGATE PLANNING (pp. 513–514)	An aggregate plan looks at production *in the aggregate* (a family of products), not as a product-by-product breakdown. ■ **Disaggregation**—The process of breaking an aggregate plan into greater detail. ■ **Master production schedule**—A timetable that specifies what is to be made and when.	
AGGREGATE PLANNING STRATEGIES (pp. 514–517)	The basic aggregate planning capacity (production) options are: • *Changing inventory levels* • *Varying workforce size by hiring or layoffs* • *Varying production rates through overtime or idle time* • *Subcontracting* • *Using part-time workers* The basic aggregate planning demand options are: • *Influencing demand* • *Back ordering during high-demand periods* • *Counterseasonal product and service mixing* ■ **Chase strategy**—A planning strategy that sets production equal to forecasted demand. Many service organizations favor the chase strategy because the inventory option is difficult or impossible to adopt. ■ **Level scheduling**—Maintaining a constant output rate, production rate, or work-force level over the planning horizon. Level scheduling works well when demand is reasonably stable. ■ **Mixed strategy**—A planning strategy that uses two or more controllable variables to set a feasible production plan.	
METHODS FOR AGGREGATE PLANNING (pp. 517–524)	■ **Graphical techniques**—Aggregate planning techniques that work with a few variables at a time to allow planners to compare projected demand with existing capacity. Graphical techniques are trial-and-error approaches that do not guarantee an optimal production plan, but they require only limited computations. The five steps of the graphical method are: 1. Determine the demand in each period. 2. Determine capacity for regular time, overtime, and subcontracting each period. 3. Find labor costs, hiring and layoff costs, and inventory-holding costs. 4. Consider company policy that may apply to the workers or to stock levels. 5. Develop alternative plans and examine their total costs. A *cumulative* graph displays visually how the forecast deviates from the average requirements. ■ **Transportation method of linear programming**—A way of solving for the optimal solution to an aggregate planning problem. The transportation method of linear programming is flexible in that it can specify regular and overtime production in each time period, the number of units to be subcontracted, extra shifts, and the inventory carryover from period to period. Transportation problems require that supply equals demand, so when it does not, a dummy column called "unused capacity" may be added. Costs of not using capacity are zero.	Problems: 13.2–13.19 Virtual Office Hours for Solved Problems: 13.1, 13.2 **ACTIVE MODEL 13.1**

Main Heading	Review Material
	Demand requirements are shown in the bottom row of a transportation table. Total capacity available (supply) is shown in the far right column. In general, to complete a transportation table, allocate as much production as you can to a cell with the smallest cost, without exceeding the unused capacity in that row or demand in that column. If there is still some demand left in that row, allocate as much as you can to the next-lowest-cost cell. You then repeat this process for periods 2 and 3 (and beyond, if necessary). When you are finished, the sum of all your entries in a row must equal total row capacity, and the sum of all entries in a column must equal the demand for that period. The transportation method was originally formulated by E. H. Bowman in 1956. The transportation method does not work when nonlinear or negative factors are introduced. ■ **Management coefficients model**—A formal planning model built around a manager's experience and performance.
AGGREGATE PLANNING IN SERVICES (pp. 524–527)	Successful techniques for controlling the cost of labor in service firms include: 1. Accurate scheduling of labor-hours to ensure quick response to customer demand. 2. An on-call labor resource that can be added or deleted to meet unexpected demand. 3. Flexibility of individual worker skills that permits reallocation of available labor. 4. Flexibility in rate of output or hours of work to meet changing demand.
YIELD MANAGEMENT (pp. 527–530)	■ **Yield** (or **revenue) management**—Capacity decisions that determine the allocation of resources to maximize profit or yield. Organizations that have *perishable inventory*, such as airlines, hotels, car rental agencies, and cruise lines, have the following shared characteristics that make yield management of interest: 1. Service or product can be sold in advance of consumption. 2. Demand fluctuates. 3. The resource (capacity) is relatively fixed. 4. Demand can be segmented. 5. Variable costs are low, and fixed costs are high. To make yield management work, the company needs to manage three issues: 1. *Multiple pricing structures.* 2. *Forecasts of the use and duration of the use.* 3. *Changes in demand.*

Self Test

■ **Before taking the self-test,** refer to the learning objectives listed at the beginning of the chapter and the key terms listed at the end of the chapter.

LO1. Aggregate planning is concerned with determining the quantity and timing of production in the:
- **a)** short term.
- **b)** intermediate term.
- **c)** long term.
- **d)** all of the above.

LO2. Aggregate planning deals with a number of constraints. These typically are:
- **a)** job assignments, job ordering, dispatching, and overtime help.
- **b)** part-time help, weekly scheduling, and SKU production scheduling.
- **c)** subcontracting, employment levels, inventory levels, and capacity.
- **d)** capital investment, expansion or contracting capacity, and R&D.
- **e)** facility location, production budgeting, overtime, and R&D.

LO3. Which of the following is not one of the graphical method steps?
- **a)** Determine the demand in each period.
- **b)** Determine capacity for regular time, overtime, and subcontracting each period.
- **c)** Find labor costs, hiring and layoff costs, and inventory holding costs.
- **d)** Construct the transportation table.
- **e)** Consider company policy that may apply to the workers or stock levels.
- **f)** Develop alternative plans and examine their total costs.

LO4. When might a dummy column be added to a transportation table?
- **a)** When supply does not equal demand
- **b)** When overtime is greater than regular time
- **c)** When subcontracting is greater than regular time
- **d)** When subcontracting is greater than regular time plus overtime
- **e)** When production needs to spill over into a new period

LO5. Yield management requires management to deal with:
- **a)** multiple pricing structures.
- **b)** changes in demand.
- **c)** forecasts of use.
- **d)** forecasts of duration of use.
- **e)** all of the above.

Answers: LO1. b; LO2. c; LO3. d; LO4. a; LO5. e.

14 Material Requirements Planning (MRP) and ERP

Chapter Outline

10 OM Strategy Decisions

- Design of Goods and Services
- Managing Quality
- Process Strategy
- Location Strategies
- Layout Strategies
- Human Resources
- Supply-Chain Management
- Inventory Management
  - Independent Demand
  - Dependent Demand
  - JIT and Lean Operations
- Scheduling
- Maintenance

MRP PROVIDES A COMPETITIVE ADVANTAGE FOR WHEELED COACH

Wheeled Coach, headquartered in Winter Park, Florida, is the largest manufacturer of ambulances in the world. The $200 million firm is an international competitor that sells more than 25% of its vehicles to markets outside the U.S. Twelve major ambulance designs are produced on assembly lines (i.e., a repetitive process) at the Florida plant, using 18,000 different inventory items, of which 6,000 are manufactured and 12,000 purchased. Most of the product line is custom designed and assembled to meet the specific and often unique requirements

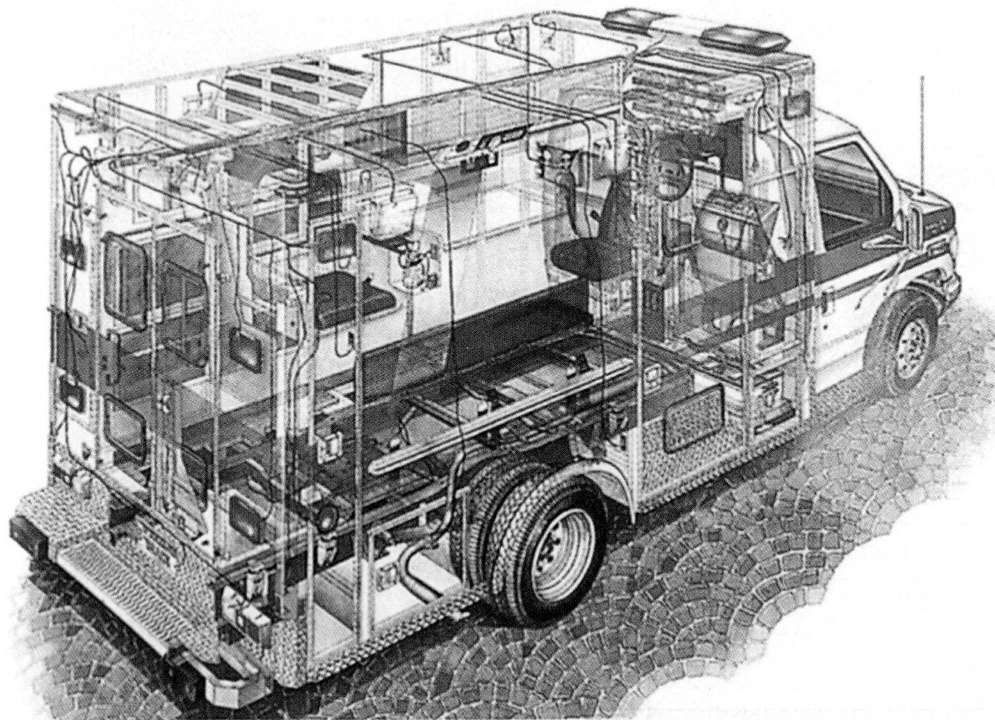

This cutaway of one ambulance interior indicates the complexity of the product, which for some rural locations may be the equivalent of a hospital emergency room in miniature. To complicate production, virtually every ambulance is custom ordered. This customization necessitates precise orders, excellent bills of materials, exceptional inventory control from supplier to assembly, and an MRP system that works.

Wheeled Coach uses work cells to feed the assembly line. It maintains a complete carpentry shop (to provide interior cabinetry), a paint shop (to prepare, paint, and detail each vehicle), an electrical shop (to provide for the complex electronics in a modern ambulance), an upholstery shop (to make interior seats and benches), and as shown here, a metal fabrication shop (to construct the shell of the ambulance).

demanded by the ambulance's application and customer preferences.

This variety of products and the nature of the process demand good material requirements planning. Effective use of an MRP system requires accurate bills of material and inventory records. The Wheeled Coach system, which uses MAPICS DB software, provides daily updates and has reduced inventory by more than 30% in just 2 years.

Wheeled Coach insists that four key tasks be performed properly. First, the material plan must meet both the requirements of the master schedule and the capabilities of the production facility. Second, the plan must be executed as designed. Third, inventory investment must be minimized through effective "time-phased" material deliveries, consignment inventories, and a constant review of purchase methods. Finally, excellent record integrity must be maintained. Record accuracy is recognized as a fundamental ingredient of Wheeled Coach's successful MRP program. Its cycle counters are charged with material audits that not only correct errors but also investigate and correct problems.

Wheeled Coach Industries uses MRP as the catalyst for low inventory, high quality, tight schedules, and accurate records. Wheeled Coach has found competitive advantage via MRP.

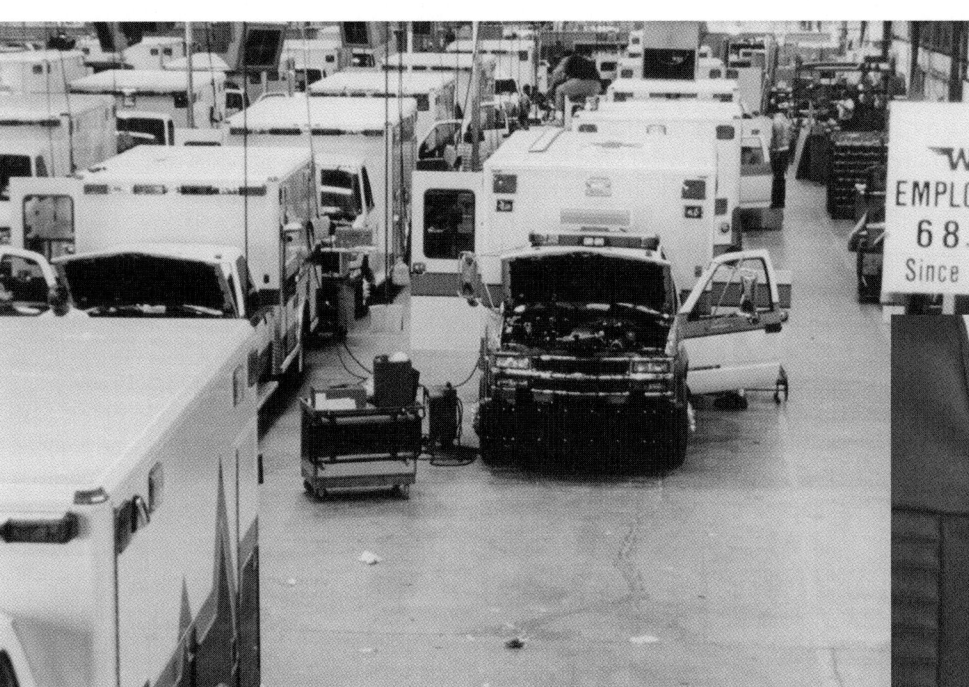

On six parallel lines, ambulances move forward each day to the next workstation. The MRP system makes certain that just the materials needed at each station arrive overnight for assembly the next day.

VIDEO 14.1
MRP at Wheeled Coach Ambulances

Here an employee is installing the wiring for an ambulance. There are an average of 15 miles of wire in a Wheeled Coach vehicle. This compares to 17 miles of wire in a sophisticated F-16 fighter jet.

Chapter 14 **Learning Objectives**

AUTHOR COMMENT
"Dependent demand" means the demand for one item is related to the demand for another item.

DEPENDENT DEMAND

Wheeled Coach, the subject of the *Global Company Profile*, and many other firms have found important benefits in MRP. These benefits include (1) better response to customer orders as the result of improved adherence to schedules, (2) faster response to market changes, (3) improved utilization of facilities and labor, and (4) reduced inventory levels. Better response to customer orders and to the market wins orders and market share. Better utilization of facilities and labor yields higher productivity and return on investment. Less inventory frees up capital and floor space for other uses. These benefits are the result of a strategic decision to use a *dependent* inventory scheduling system. Demand for every component of an ambulance is dependent.

Demand for items is dependent when the relationship between the items can be determined. Therefore, once management receives an order or makes a forecast for the final product, quantities for all components can be computed. All components are dependent items. The Boeing Aircraft operations manager who schedules production of one plane per week, for example, knows the requirements down to the last rivet. For any product, all components of that product are dependent demand items. *More generally, for any product for which a schedule can be established, dependent techniques should be used.*

Material requirements planning (MRP)
A dependent demand technique that uses a bill-of-material, inventory, expected receipts, and a master production schedule to determine material requirements.

When the requirements of MRP are met, dependent models are preferable to the EOQ models described in Chapter 12.[1] Dependent models are better not only for manufacturers and distributors but also for a wide variety of firms from restaurants to hospitals. The dependent technique used in a production environment is called **material requirements planning (MRP)**.

Because MRP provides such a clean structure for dependent demand, it has evolved as the basis for Enterprise Resource Planning (ERP). ERP is an information system for identifying and planning the enterprise-wide resources needed to take, make, ship, and account for customer orders. We will discuss ERP in the latter part of this chapter.

DEPENDENT INVENTORY MODEL REQUIREMENTS

Effective use of dependent inventory models requires that the operations manager know the following:

1. Master production schedule (what is to be made and when)
2. Specifications or bill of material (materials and parts required to make the product)
3. Inventory availability (what is in stock)
4. Purchase orders outstanding (what is on order, also called expected receipts)
5. Lead times (how long it takes to get various components)

We now discuss each of these requirements in the context of material requirements planning.

Master Production Schedule

Master production schedule (MPS)
A timetable that specifies what is to be made and when.

A **master production schedule (MPS)** specifies what is to be made (i.e., the number of finished products or items) and when. The schedule must be in accordance with a production plan. The production plan sets the overall level of output in broad terms (e.g., product families, standard

[1]The inventory models (EOQ) discussed in Chapter 12 assumed that the demand for one item was independent of the demand for another item. For example, EOQ assumes the demand for refrigerator parts is *independent* of the demand for refrigerators and that demand for parts is constant.

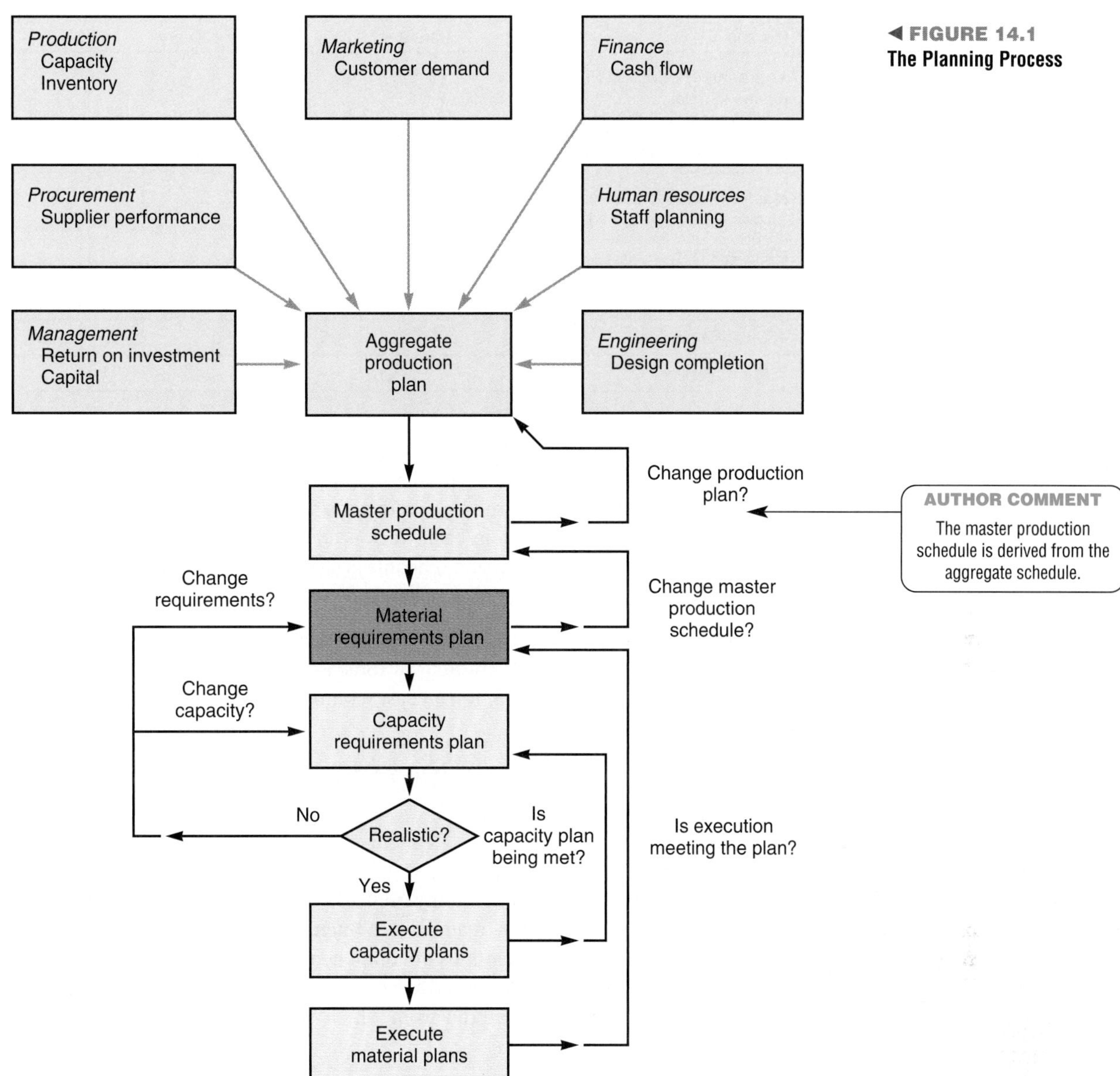

◀ **FIGURE 14.1**
The Planning Process

AUTHOR COMMENT
The master production schedule is derived from the aggregate schedule.

hours, or dollar volume). The plan also includes a variety of inputs, including financial plans, customer demand, engineering capabilities, labor availability, inventory fluctuations, supplier performance, and other considerations. Each of these inputs contributes in its own way to the production plan, as shown in Figure 14.1

As the planning process moves from the production plan to execution, each of the lower-level plans must be feasible. When one is not, feedback to the next higher level is used to make the necessary adjustment. One of the major strengths of MRP is its ability to determine precisely the feasibility of a schedule within aggregate capacity constraints. This planning process can yield excellent results. The production plan sets the upper and lower bounds on the master production schedule. The result of this production planning process is the master production schedule.

The master production schedule tells us what is required to satisfy demand and meet the production plan. This schedule establishes what items to make and when: It *disaggregates* the aggregate production plan. While the *aggregate production plan* (as discussed in Chapter 13) is established in gross terms such as families of products or tons of steel, the *master production schedule* is established in terms of specific products. Figure 14.2 shows the master production schedules for three stereo models that flow from the aggregate production plan for a family of stereo amplifiers.

Managers must adhere to the schedule for a reasonable length of time (usually a major portion of the production cycle—the time it takes to produce a product). Many organizations establish a master production schedule and establish a policy of not changing ("fixing") the near-term portion of the plan. This near-term portion of the plan is then referred to as the "fixed," "firm," or "frozen"

▶ **FIGURE 14.2**
The Aggregate Production Plan Is the Basis for Development of the Detailed Master Production Schedule

Months	January				February			
Aggregate Production Plan (Shows the total quantity of amplifiers)	1,500				1,200			
Weeks	1	2	3	4	5	6	7	8
Master Production Schedule (Shows the specific type and quantity of amplifier to be produced)								
240-watt amplifier	100		100		100		100	
150-watt amplifier		500		500		450		450
75-watt amplifier			300				100	

schedule. Wheeled Coach, the subject of the *Global Company Profile* for this chapter, fixes the last 14 days of its schedule. Only changes farther out, beyond the fixed schedule, are permitted. The master production schedule is a "rolling" production schedule. For example, a fixed 7-week plan has an additional week added to it as each week is completed, so a 7-week fixed schedule is maintained. Note that the master production schedule is a statement of *what is to be produced*, not a forecast of demand. The master schedule can be expressed in any of the following terms:

1. A *customer order in a job shop* (make-to-order) company
2. *Modules in a repetitive* (assemble-to-order or forecast) company
3. An *end item in a continuous* (stock-to-forecast) company

This relationship of the master production schedule to the processes is shown in Figure 14.3.

A master production schedule for two of Nancy's Specialty Foods' products, crabmeat quiche and spinach quiche, might look like Table 14.1.

Bills of Material

Bill of material (BOM)
A listing of the components, their description, and the quantity of each required to make one unit of a product.

Defining what goes into a product may seem simple, but it can be difficult in practice. As we noted in Chapter 5, to aid this process, manufactured items are defined via a bill of material. A **bill of material (BOM)** is a list of quantities of components, ingredients, and materials required to make a product. Individual drawings describe not only physical dimensions but also any special processing as well as the raw material from which each part is made. Nancy's Specialty

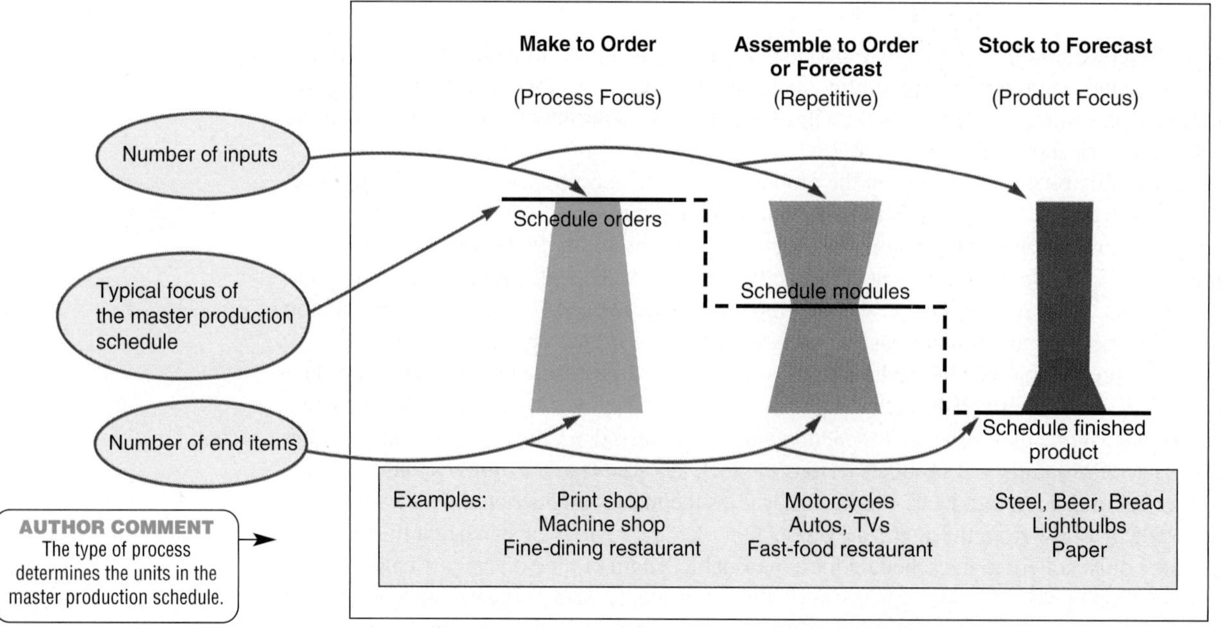

▲ **FIGURE 14.3** **Typical Focus of the Master Production Schedule in Three Process Strategies**

◀ **TABLE 14.1 Master Production Schedule for Crabmeat Quiche and Spinach Quiche at Nancy's Specialty Foods**

Gross Requirements for Crabmeat Quiche										
Day	6	7	8	9	10	11	12	13	14	and so on
Amount	50		100	47	60		110	75		

Gross Requirements for Spinach Quiche										
Day	7	8	9	10	11	12	13	14	15	16	and so on
Amount	100	200	150			60	75		100		

Foods has a recipe for quiche, specifying ingredients and quantities, just as Wheeled Coach has a full set of drawings for an ambulance. Both are bills of material (although we call one a recipe, and they do vary somewhat in scope).

Because there is often a rush to get a new product to market, however, drawings and bills of material may be incomplete or even nonexistent. Moreover, complete drawings and BOMs (as well as other forms of specifications) often contain errors in dimensions, quantities, or countless other areas. When errors are identified, engineering change notices (ECNs) are created, further complicating the process. An *engineering change notice* is a change or correction to an engineering drawing or bill of material.

One way a bill of material defines a product is by providing a product structure. Example 1 shows how to develop the product structure and "explode" it to reveal the requirements for each component. A bill of material for item A in Example 1 consists of items B and C. Items above any level are called *parents*; items below any level are called *components* or *children*. By convention, the top level in a BOM is the 0 level.

◀ **EXAMPLE 1**

Developing a product structure and gross requirements

Speaker Kits, Inc., packages high-fidelity components for mail order. Components for the top-of-the-line speaker kit, "Awesome" (A), include 2 standard 12-inch speaker kits (Bs) and 3 speaker kits with amp-boosters (Cs).

Each B consists of 2 speakers (Ds) and 2 shipping boxes each with an installation kit (E). Each of the three 300-watt speaker kits (Cs) has 2 speaker boosters (Fs) and 2 installation kits (Es). Each speaker booster (F) includes 2 speakers (Ds) and 1 amp-booster (G). The total for each Awesome is 4 standard 12-inch speakers and twelve 12-inch speakers with the amp-booster. (Most purchasers require hearing aids within 3 years, and at least one court case is pending because of structural damage to a men's dormitory.) As we can see, the demand for B, C, D, E, F, and G is completely dependent on the master production schedule for A—the Awesome speaker kits.

APPROACH ▶ Given the above information, we construct a product structure and "explode" the requirements.

LO1: Develop a product structure.

SOLUTION ▶ This structure has four levels: 0, 1, 2, and 3. There are four parents: A, B, C, and F. Each parent item has at least one level below it. Items B, C, D, E, F, and G are components because each item has at least one level above it. In this structure, B, C, and F are both parents and components. The number in parentheses indicates how many units of that particular item are needed to make the item immediately above it. Thus, $B_{(2)}$ means that it takes two units of B for every unit of A, and $F_{(2)}$ means that it takes two units of F for every unit of C.

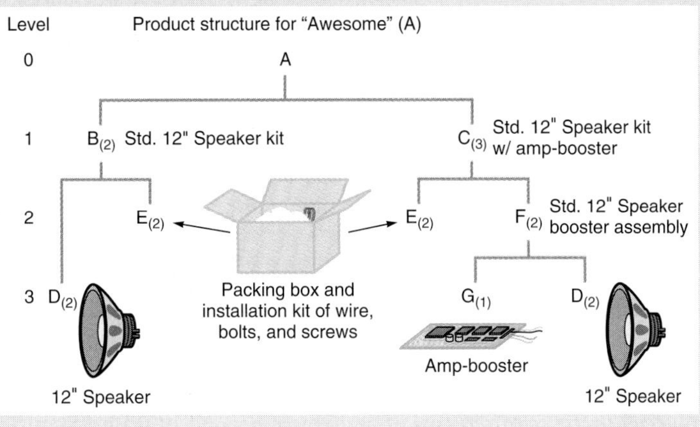

Once we have developed the product structure, we can determine the number of units of each item required to satisfy demand for a new order of 50 Awesome speaker kits. We "explode" the requirements as shown:

Part B:	$2 \times$ number of As =	$(2)(50) =$	100
Part C:	$3 \times$ number of As =	$(3)(50) =$	150
Part D:	$2 \times$ number of Bs + $2 \times$ number of Fs =	$(2)(100) + (2)(300) =$	800
Part E:	$2 \times$ number of Bs + $2 \times$ number of Cs =	$(2)(100) + (2)(150) =$	500
Part F:	$2 \times$ number of Cs =	$(2)(150) =$	300
Part G:	$1 \times$ number of Fs =	$(1)(300) =$	300

INSIGHT ▶ We now have a visual picture of the Awesome speaker kit requirements and knowledge of the quantities required. Thus, for 50 units of A, we will need 100 units of B, 150 units of C, 800 units of D, 500 units of E, 300 units of F, and 300 units of G.

LEARNING EXERCISE ▶ If there are 100 Fs in stock, how many Ds do you need? [Answer: 600.]

RELATED PROBLEMS ▶ 14.1, 14.3a, 14.13a, 14.25a

EXCEL OM Data File **Ch14Ex1.xls** can be found at **www.pearsonhighered.com/heizer**.

Bills of material not only specify requirements but also are useful for costing, and they can serve as a list of items to be issued to production or assembly personnel. When bills of material are used in this way, they are usually called *pick lists*.

Modular bills
Bills of material organized by major subassemblies or by product options.

Modular Bills Bills of material may be organized around product modules (see Chapter 5). *Modules* are not final products to be sold but are components that can be produced and assembled into units. They are often major components of the final product or product options. Bills of material for modules are called **modular bills**. Bills of material are sometimes organized as modules (rather than as part of a final product) because production scheduling and production are often facilitated by organizing around relatively few modules rather than a multitude of final assemblies. For instance, a firm may make 138,000 different final products but may have only 40 modules that are mixed and matched to produce those 138,000 final products. The firm builds an aggregate production plan and prepares its master production schedule for the 40 modules, not the 138,000 configurations of the final product. This approach allows the MPS to be prepared for a reasonable number of items (the narrow portion of the middle graphic in Figure 14.3) and to postpone assembly. The 40 modules can then be configured for specific orders at final assembly.

Planning bills (or **kits**)
A material grouping created in order to assign an artificial parent to a bill of material; also called "pseudo" bills.

Phantom bills of material
Bills of material for components, usually assemblies, that exist only temporarily; they are never inventoried.

Planning Bills and Phantom Bills Two other special kinds of bills of material are planning bills and phantom bills. **Planning bills** (sometimes called "pseudo" bills or super bills) are created in order to assign an artificial parent to the bill of material. Such bills are used (1) when we want to group subassemblies so the number of items to be scheduled is reduced and (2) when we want to issue "kits" to the production department. For instance, it may not be efficient to issue inexpensive items such as washers and cotter pins with each of numerous subassemblies, so we call this a *kit* and generate a planning bill. The planning bill specifies the *kit* to be issued. Consequently, a planning bill may also be known as **kitted material**, or **kit**. **Phantom bills of material** are bills of material for components, usually subassemblies, that exist only temporarily. These components go directly into another assembly and are never inventoried. Therefore, components of phantom bills of material are coded to receive special treatment; lead times are zero, and they are handled as an integral part of their parent item. An example is a transmission shaft with gears and bearings assembly that is placed directly into a transmission.

Low-level coding
A number that identifies items at the lowest level at which they occur.

Low-Level Coding Low-level coding of an item in a BOM is necessary when identical items exist at various levels in the BOM. **Low-level coding** means that the item is coded at the lowest level at which it occurs. For example, item D in Example 1 is coded at the lowest level at which it is used. Item D could be coded as part of B and occur at level 2. However, because D is also part of F, and F is level 2, item D becomes a level-3 item. Low-level coding is a convention to allow easy computing of the requirements of an item. When the BOM has thousands of items or when requirements are frequently recomputed, the ease and speed of computation become a major concern.

Accurate Inventory Records

As we saw in Chapter 12, knowledge of what is in stock is the result of good inventory management. Good inventory management is an absolute necessity for an MRP system to work. If the firm does not exceed 99% record accuracy, then material requirements planning will not work.[2]

Purchase Orders Outstanding

Knowledge of outstanding orders exists as a by-product of well-managed purchasing and inventory-control departments. When purchase orders are executed, records of those orders and their scheduled delivery dates must be available to production personnel. Only with good purchasing data can managers prepare meaningful production plans and effectively execute an MRP system.

Lead time
In purchasing systems, the time between recognition of the need for an order and receiving it; in production systems, it is the order, wait, move, queue, setup, and run times for each component.

Lead Times for Components

Once managers determine when products are needed, they determine when to acquire them. The time required to acquire (that is, purchase, produce, or assemble) an item is known as **lead time**. Lead time for a manufactured item consists of *move*, *setup*, and *assembly* or *run times* for each component. For a purchased item, the lead time includes the time between recognition of need for an order and when it is available for production.

When the bill of material for Awesome speaker kits (As), in Example 1, is turned on its side and modified by adding lead times for each component (see Table 14.2), we then have a *time-phased product structure*. Time in this structure is shown on the horizontal axis of Figure 14.4 with item A due for completion in week 8. Each component is then offset to accommodate lead times.

▼ **TABLE 14.2**
Lead Times for Awesome Speaker Kits (As)

Component	Lead Time
A	1 week
B	2 weeks
C	1 week
D	1 week
E	2 weeks
F	3 weeks
G	2 weeks

MRP STRUCTURE

Although most MRP systems are computerized, the MRP procedure is straightforward and we can illustrate a small one by hand. A master production schedule, a bill of material, inventory and purchase records, and lead times for each item are the ingredients of a material requirements planning system (see Figure 14.5).

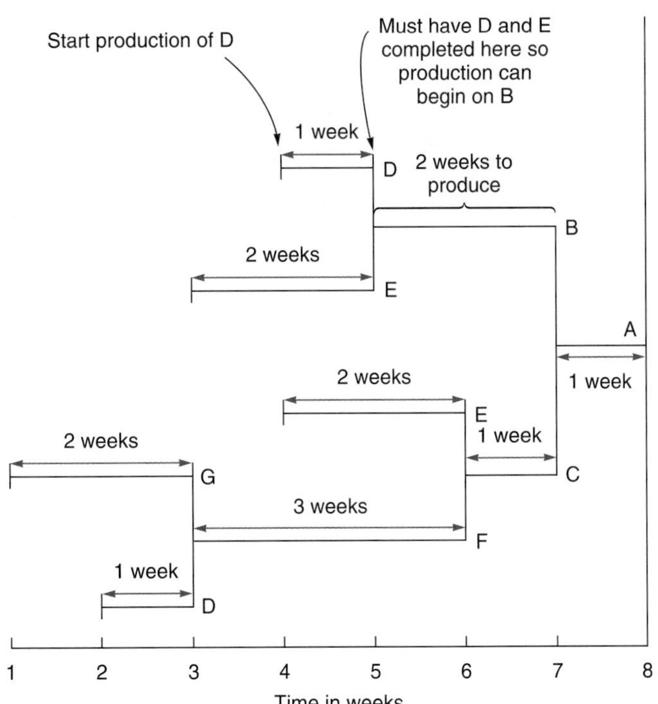

◀ **FIGURE 14.4**
Time-Phased Product Structure

AUTHOR COMMENT
This is a product structure on its side, with lead times.

[2]Record accuracy of 99% may sound good, but note that even when each component has an availability of 99% and a product has only seven components, the likelihood of a product being completed is only .932 (because $.99^7 = .932$).

▶ **FIGURE 14.5**
Structure of the MRP System

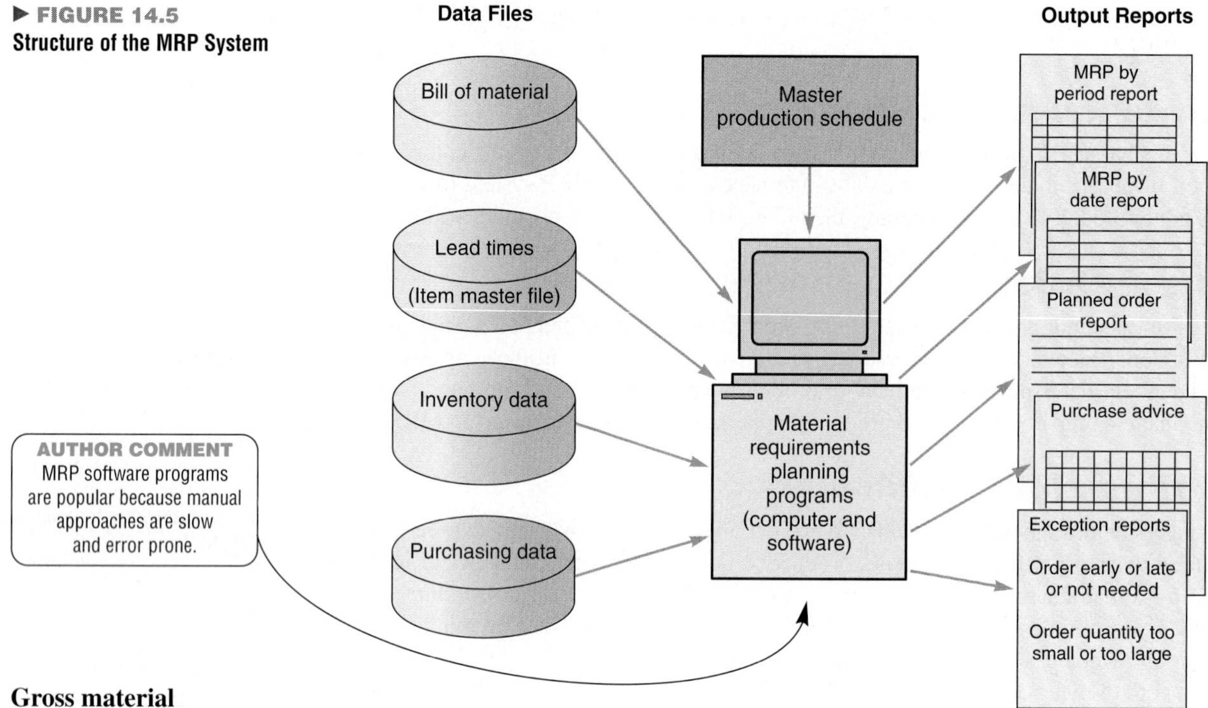

AUTHOR COMMENT
MRP software programs are popular because manual approaches are slow and error prone.

Gross material requirements plan
A schedule that shows the total demand for an item (prior to subtraction of on-hand inventory and scheduled receipts) and (1) when it must be ordered from suppliers, or (2) when production must be started to meet its demand by a particular date.

Once these ingredients are available and accurate, the next step is to construct a gross material requirements plan. The **gross material requirements plan** is a schedule, as shown in Example 2. It combines a master production schedule (that requires one unit of A in week 8) and the time-phased schedule (Figure 14.4). It shows when an item must be ordered from suppliers if there is no inventory on hand or when the production of an item must be started to satisfy demand for the finished product by a particular date.

EXAMPLE 2 ▶
Building a gross requirements plan

Each Awesome speaker kit (item A of Example 1) requires all the items in the product structure for A. Lead times are shown in Table 14.2.

APPROACH ▶ Using the information in Example 1 and Table 14.2, we construct the gross material requirements plan with a production schedule that will satisfy the demand of 50 units of A by week 8.

SOLUTION ▶ We prepare a schedule as shown in Table 14.3.

▶ **TABLE 14.3**
Gross Material Requirements Plan for 50 Awesome Speaker Kits (As)

	Week								
	1	2	3	4	5	6	7	8	Lead Time
A. Required date								50	
Order release date							50		1 week
B. Required date							100		
Order release date					100				2 weeks
C. Required date							150		
Order release date						150			1 week
E. Required date					200	300			
Order release date			200	300					2 weeks
F. Required date						300			
Order release date			300						3 weeks
D. Required date			600		200				
Order release date		600		200					1 week
G. Required date			300						
Order release date	300								2 weeks

LO2: Build a gross requirements plan

You can interpret the gross material requirements shown in Table 14.3 as follows: If you want 50 units of A at week 8, you must start assembling A in week 7. Thus, in week 7, you will need 100 units of B and 150 units of C. These two items take 2 weeks and 1 week, respectively, to produce. Production of B, therefore, should start in week 5, and production of C should start in week 6 (lead time subtracted from the required date for these items). Working backward, we can perform the same computations for all of the other items. Because D and E are used in two different places in Awesome speaker kits, there are two entries in each data record.

INSIGHT ▶ The gross material requirements plan shows when production of each item should begin and end in order to have 50 units of A at week 8. Management now has an initial plan.

LEARNING EXERCISE ▶ If the lead time for G decreases from 2 weeks to 1 week, what is the new order release date for G? [Answer: 300 in week 2.]

RELATED PROBLEMS ▶ 14.2, 14.4, 14.6, 14.8b, 14.9, 14.10a, 14.11a, 14.13b, 14.25b

So far, we have considered *gross material requirements*, which assumes that there is no inventory on hand. When there is inventory on hand, we prepare a **net requirements plan**. When considering on-hand inventory, we must realize that many items in inventory contain subassemblies or parts. If the gross requirement for Awesome speaker kits (As) is 100 and there are 20 of those speakers on hand, the net requirement for Awesome speaker kits (As) is 80 (that is, 100 – 20). However, each Awesome speaker kit on hand contains 2 Bs. As a result, the requirement for Bs drops by 40 Bs (20 A kits on hand × 2 Bs per A). Therefore, if inventory is on hand for a parent item, the requirements for the parent item and all its components decrease because each Awesome kit contains the components for lower-level items. Example 3 shows how to create a net requirements plan.

Net material requirements
The result of adjusting gross requirements for inventory on hand and scheduled receipts.

EXAMPLE 3

Determining net requirements

Speaker Kits, Inc., developed a product structure from a bill of material in Example 1. Example 2 developed a gross requirements plan. Given the following on-hand inventory, Speaker Kits, Inc., now wants to construct a net requirements plan.

Item	On Hand	Item	On Hand
A	10	E	10
B	15	F	5
C	20	G	0
D	10		

APPROACH ▶ A net material requirements plan includes gross requirements, on-hand inventory, net requirements, planned order receipt, and planned order release for each item. We begin with A and work backward through the components.

SOLUTION ▶ Shown in the chart on the next page is the net material requirements plan for product A.

Constructing a net requirements plan is similar to constructing a gross requirements plan. Starting with item A, we work backward to determine net requirements for all items. To do these computations, we refer to the product structure, on-hand inventory, and lead times. The gross requirement for A is 50 units in week 8. Ten items are on hand; therefore, the net requirements and the scheduled **planned order receipt** are both 40 items in week 8. Because of the 1-week lead time, the **planned order release** is 40 items in week 7 (see the arrow connecting the order receipt and order release). Referring to week 7 and the product structure in Example 1, we can see that 80 (2 × 40) items of B and 120 (3 × 40) items of C are required in week 7 to have a total for 50 items of A in week 8. The letter superscripted A to the right of the gross figure for items B and C was generated as a result of the demand for the parent, A. Performing the same type of analysis for B and C yields the net requirements for D, E, F, and G. Note the on-hand inventory in row E in week 6 is zero. It is zero because the on-hand inventory (10 units) was used to make B in week 5. By the same token, the inventory for D was used to make F in week 3.

Planned order receipt
The quantity planned to be received at a future date.

Planned order release
The scheduled date for an order to be released.

INSIGHT ▶ Once a net requirement plan is completed, management knows the quantities needed, an ordering schedule, and a production schedule for each component.

▼ Net Material Requirements Plan for Product A *(the superscript is the source of the demand)*

Lot Size	Lead Time (weeks)	On Hand	Safety Stock	Allocated	Low-Level Code	Item Identification			Week 1	2	3	4	5	6	7	8
Lot-for-Lot	1	10	—	—	0	A	Gross Requirements									50
							Scheduled Receipts									
							Projected On Hand	10	10	10	10	10	10	10	10	10
							Net Requirements									40
							Planned Order Receipts									40
							Planned Order Releases								40	
Lot-for-Lot	2	15	—	—	1	B	Gross Requirements								80^{A}	
							Scheduled Receipts									
							Projected On Hand	15	15	15	15	15	15	15	15	
							Net Requirements								65	
							Planned Order Receipts								65	
							Planned Order Releases						65			
Lot-for-Lot	1	20	—	—	1	C	Gross Requirements								120^{A}	
							Scheduled Receipts									
							Projected On Hand	20	20	20	20	20	20	20	20	
							Net Requirements								100	
							Planned Order Receipts								100	
							Planned Order Releases							100		
Lot-for-Lot	2	10	—	—	2	E	Gross Requirements						130^{B}	200^{C}		
							Scheduled Receipts									
							Projected On Hand	10	10	10	10	10	10			
							Net Requirements						120	200		
							Planned Order Receipts						120	200		
							Planned Order Releases				120	200				
Lot-for-Lot	3	5	—	—	2	F	Gross Requirements							200^{C}		
							Scheduled Receipts									
							Projected On Hand	5	5	5	5	5	5	5		
							Net Requirements							195		
							Planned Order Receipts							195		
							Planned Order Releases				195					
Lot-for-Lot	1	10	—	—	3	D	Gross Requirements				390^{F}		130^{B}			
							Scheduled Receipts									
							Projected On Hand	10	10	10	10					
							Net Requirements				380		130			
							Planned Order Receipts				380		130			
							Planned Order Releases			380		130				
Lot-for-Lot	2	0	—	—	3	G	Gross Requirements				195^{F}					
							Scheduled Receipts									
							Projected On Hand				0					
							Net Requirements				195					
							Planned Order Receipts				195					
							Planned Order Releases		195							

LEARNING EXERCISE ▶ If the on-hand inventory quantity of component F is 95 rather than 5, how many units of G will need to be ordered in week 1? [Answer: 105 units.]

RELATED PROBLEMS ▶ 14.5, 14.7, 14.8c, 14.10b, 14.11b, 14.12, 14.13c, 14.14b, 14.15a,b,c, 14.16a, 14.25c, 14.27

ACTIVE MODEL 14.1 This example is further illustrated in Active Model 14.1 at **www.pearsonhighered.com/heizer**.

Examples 2 and 3 considered only product A, the Awesome speaker kit, and its completion only in week 8. Fifty units of A were required in week 8. Normally, however, there is a demand for many products over time. For each product, management must prepare a master production schedule (as we saw earlier in Table 14.1). Scheduled production of each product is added to the

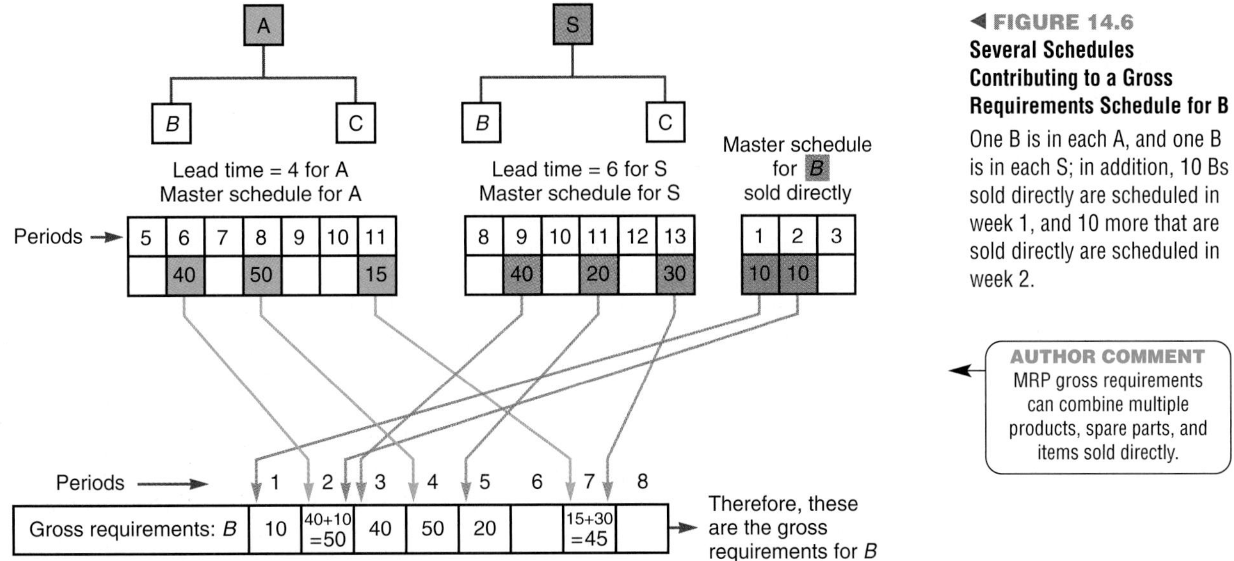

◄ **FIGURE 14.6 Several Schedules Contributing to a Gross Requirements Schedule for B**

One B is in each A, and one B is in each S; in addition, 10 Bs sold directly are scheduled in week 1, and 10 more that are sold directly are scheduled in week 2.

AUTHOR COMMENT MRP gross requirements can combine multiple products, spare parts, and items sold directly.

master schedule and ultimately to the net material requirements plan. Figure 14.6 shows how several product schedules, including requirements for components sold directly, can contribute to one gross material requirements plan.

Most inventory systems also note the number of units in inventory that have been assigned to specific future production but not yet used or issued from the stockroom. Such items are often referred to as *allocated* items. Allocated items increase requirements and may then be included in an MRP planning sheet, as shown in Figure 14.7.

The allocated quantity has the effect of increasing the requirements (or, alternatively, reducing the quantity on hand). The logic, then, of a net requirements MRP is:

LO3: Build a net requirements plan

$$\underbrace{[(\text{Gross requirements}) + (\text{Allocations})]}_{\text{Total requirements}} - \underbrace{[(\text{On hand}) + (\text{Scheduled receipts})]}_{\text{Available inventory}} = \text{Net requirements}$$

Safety Stock The continuing task of operations managers is to remove variability. This is the case in MRP systems as in other operations systems. Realistically, however, managers need to realize that bills of material and inventory records, like purchase and production quantities, as well as lead times, may not be perfect. This means that some consideration of safety stock may be prudent. Because of the significant domino effect of any change in requirements, safety stock should be minimized, with a goal of ultimate elimination. When safety stock is deemed absolutely necessary, the usual policy is to build it into the projected on-hand inventory of the MRP logic. Distortion can be minimized when safety stock is held at the finished goods level and at the purchased component or raw material level.

▼ **FIGURE 14.7 Sample MRP Planning Sheet for Item Z**

Lot Size	Lead Time	On Hand	Safety Stock	Allocated	Low-Level Code	Item ID		Period 1	2	3	4	5	6	7	8
Lot FoR Lot	1	0	0	10	0	Z	Gross Requirements								~~80~~ 90
							Scheduled Receipts								0
							Projected On Hand 0	0	0	0	0	0	0	0	0
							Net Requirements								90
							Planned Order Receipts								90
							Planned Order Releases							90	

AUTHOR COMMENT
Using MRP to the utmost is serious work.

MRP MANAGEMENT

The material requirements plan is not static. And since MRP systems increasingly are integrated with just-in-time (JIT) techniques, we now discuss these two issues.

MRP Dynamics

Bills of material and material requirements plans are altered as changes in design, schedules, and production processes occur. In addition, changes occur in material requirements whenever the master production schedule is modified. Regardless of the cause of any changes, the MRP model can be manipulated to reflect them. In this manner, an up-to-date requirements schedule is possible.

The inputs to MRP (the master schedule, BOM, lead times, purchasing, and inventory) frequently change. Conveniently, a central strength of MRP systems is timely and accurate replanning. This occurs in one of two ways: by recomputing (also known as "regenerating") the requirement and schedule periodically, often weekly, or via a "net change" calculation. Net change in an MRP system means the MRP system creates new requirements in response to transactions. However, many firms find they do not want to respond to minor scheduling or quantity changes even if they are aware of them. These frequent changes generate what is called **system nervousness** and can create havoc in purchasing and production departments if implemented. Consequently, OM personnel reduce such nervousness by evaluating the need and impact of changes prior to disseminating requests to other departments. Two tools are particularly helpful when trying to reduce MRP system nervousness.

System nervousness
Frequent changes in an MRP system.

The first is time fences. **Time fences** allow a segment of the master schedule to be designated as "not to be rescheduled." This segment of the master schedule is therefore not changed during the periodic regeneration of schedules. The second tool is pegging. **Pegging** means tracing upward in the BOM from the component to the parent item. By pegging upward, the production planner can determine the cause for the requirement and make a judgment about the necessity for a change in the schedule.

Time fences
A means for allowing a segment of the master schedule to be designated as "not to be rescheduled."

Pegging
In material requirements planning systems, tracing upward in the bill of material from the component to the parent item.

With MRP, the operations manager *can* react to the dynamics of the real world. How frequently the manager wishes to impose those changes on the firm requires professional judgment. Moreover, if the nervousness is caused by legitimate changes, then the proper response may be to investigate the production environment—not adjust via MRP.

MRP and JIT

MRP does not do detailed scheduling—it plans. MRP will tell you that a job needs to be completed on a certain week or day but does not tell you that Job X needs to run on Machine A at 10:30 A.M. and be completed by 11:30 A.M. so that Job X can then run on machine B. MRP is also a planning technique with *fixed* lead times. Fixed lead times can be a limitation. For instance, the lead time to produce 50 units may vary substantially from the lead time to produce 5 units. These limitations complicate the marriage of MRP and just-in-time (JIT). What is needed is a way to make MRP more responsive to moving material rapidly in small batches. An MRP system combined with JIT can provide the best of both worlds. MRP provides the plan and an accurate picture of requirements; then JIT rapidly moves material in small batches, reducing work-in-process inventory. Let's look at four approaches for integrating MRP and JIT: finite capacity scheduling, small buckets, balanced flow, and supermarkets.

Finite Capacity Scheduling (FCS) Most MRP software loads work into infinite size "buckets." The **buckets** are time units, usually one week. Traditionally, when work is to be done in a given week, MRP puts the work there without regard to capacity. Consequently, MRP is considered an *infinite* scheduling technique. Frequently, as you might suspect, this is not realistic. Finite capacity scheduling (FCS), which we discuss in Chapter 15, considers department and machine capacity, which is *finite*, hence the name. FCS provides the precise scheduling needed for rapid material movement. We are now witnessing a convergence of FCS and MRP. Sophisticated FCS systems modify the output from MRP systems to provide a finite schedule.

Buckets
Time units in a material requirements planning system.

Small Bucket Approach MRP is an excellent tool for resource and scheduling management in process-focused facilities, that is, in job shops. Such facilities include machine shops, hospitals, and restaurants, where lead times are relatively stable and poor balance between work centers is expected. Schedules are often driven by work orders, and lot sizes are the exploded bill-of-material size. In these enterprises, MRP can be integrated with JIT through the following steps.

STEP 1: Reduce MRP "buckets" from weekly to daily to perhaps hourly. Buckets are time units in an MRP system. Although the examples in this chapter have used weekly *time buckets*, many firms now use daily or even fraction-of-a-day time buckets. Some systems use a **bucketless system** in which all time-phased data have dates attached rather than defined time periods or buckets.

Bucketless system
Time-phased data are referenced using dated records rather than defined time periods, or buckets.

STEP 2: The planned receipts that are part of a firm's planned orders in an MRP system are communicated to the work areas for production purposes and used to sequence production.

STEP 3: Inventory is moved through the plant on a JIT basis.

STEP 4: As products are completed, they are moved into inventory (typically finished-goods inventory) in the normal way. Receipt of these products into inventory reduces the quantities required for subsequent planned orders in the MRP system.

STEP 5: A system known as *back flush* is used to reduce inventory balances. **Back flushing** uses the bill of material to deduct component quantities from inventory as each unit is completed.

Back flush
A system to reduce inventory balances by deducting everything in the bill of material on completion of the unit.

The focus in these facilities becomes one of maintaining schedules. Nissan achieves success with this approach by computer communication links to suppliers. These schedules are confirmed, updated, or changed every 15 to 20 minutes. Suppliers provide deliveries 4 to 16 times per day. Master schedule performance is 99% on time, as measured every hour. On-time delivery from suppliers is 99.9% and for manufactured piece parts, 99.5%.

Balanced Flow Approach MRP supports the planning and scheduling necessary for repetitive operations, such as the assembly lines at Harley-Davidson, Whirlpool, and a thousand other places. In these environments, the planning portion of MRP is combined with JIT execution. The JIT portion uses kanbans, visual signals, and reliable suppliers to pull the material through the facility. In these systems, execution is achieved by maintaining a carefully balanced flow of material to assembly areas with small lot sizes.

Supermarket Another technique that joins MRP and JIT is the use of a "supermarket." In many firms, subassemblies, their components, and hardware items are common to a variety of products. In such cases, releasing orders for these common items with traditional lead-time offset, as is done in an MRP system, is not necessary. The subassemblies, components, and hardware items can be maintained in a common area, sometimes called a **supermarket**, adjacent to the production areas where they are used. For instance, Ducati, Italy's high-performance motorcycle manufacturer, pulls "kits" with the materials needed for one engine or vehicle from the supermarket and delivers them to the assembly line on a JIT basis. Items in the supermarket are replenished by a JIT/kanban system.

Supermarket
An inventory area that holds common items that are replenished by a kanban system.

LOT-SIZING TECHNIQUES

AUTHOR COMMENT
Managers need to know how to group/order the "planned order releases."

An MRP system is an excellent way to determine production schedules and net requirements. However, whenever we have a net requirement, a decision must be made about *how much* to order. This decision is called a **lot-sizing decision**. There are a variety of ways to determine lot sizes in an MRP system; commercial MRP software usually includes the choice of several lot-sizing techniques. We now review a few of them.

Lot-sizing decision
The process of, or techniques used in, determining lot size.

Lot-for-Lot In Example 3, we used a lot-sizing technique known as **lot-for-lot**, which produced exactly what was required. This decision is consistent with the objective of an MRP system, which is to meet the requirements of *dependent* demand. Thus, an MRP system should produce units only as needed, with no safety stock and no anticipation of further orders. When frequent orders are economical and just-in-time inventory techniques implemented, lot-for-lot can be very efficient. However, when setup costs are significant or management has been unable to implement JIT, lot-for-lot can be expensive. Example 4 uses the lot-for-lot criteria and determines cost for 10 weeks of demand.

Lot-for-lot
A lot-sizing technique that generates exactly what is required to meet the plan.

EXAMPLE 4

Lot sizing with lot-for-lot

Speaker Kits, Inc., wants to compute its ordering and carrying cost of inventory on lot-for-lot criteria.

APPROACH ▶ With lot-for-lot, we order material only as it is needed. Once we have the cost of ordering (setting up), the cost of holding each unit for a given time period, and the production schedule, we can assign orders to our net requirements plan.

SOLUTION ▶ Speaker Kits has determined that, for the 12-inch speaker unit, setup cost is $100 and holding cost is $1 per period. The production schedule, as reflected in net requirements for assemblies, is as follows:

MRP Lot Sizing: Lot-for-Lot Technique*

		1	2	3	4	5	6	7	8	9	10
Gross requirements		35	30	40	0	10	40	30	0	30	55
Scheduled receipts											
Projected on hand	35	35	0	0	0	0	0	0	0	0	0
Net requirements		0	30	40	0	10	40	30	0	30	55
Planned order receipts			30	40		10	40	30		30	55
Planned order releases		30	40		10	40	30		30	55	

*Holding costs = $1/unit/week; setup cost = $100; gross requirements average per week = 27; lead time = 1 week.

The lot-sizing solution using the lot-for-lot technique is shown in the table. The holding cost is zero as there is never any inventory. (Inventory in the first period is used immediately and therefore has no holding cost.) But seven separate setups (one associated with each order) yield a total cost of $700. (Holding cost $= 0 \times 1 = 0$; ordering cost $= 7 \times 100 = 700$.)

INSIGHT ▶ When supply is reliable and frequent orders are inexpensive, but holding cost or obsolescence is high, lot-for-lot ordering can be very efficient.

LEARNING EXERCISE ▶ What is the impact on total cost if holding cost is $2 per period rather than $1? [Answer: Total holding cost remains zero, as no units are held from one period to the next with lot-for-lot.]

RELATED PROBLEMS ▶ 14.17, 14.20, 14.21, 14.22

LO4: Determine lot sizes for lot-for-lot, EOQ, and PPB

Economic Order Quantity As discussed in Chapter 12, EOQ can be used as a lot-sizing technique. But as we indicated there, EOQ is preferable when *relatively constant* independent demand exists, not when we *know* the demand. EOQ is a statistical technique using averages (such as average demand for a year), whereas the MRP procedure assumes *known* (dependent)

This Nissan line in Smyrna, Tennessee, has little inventory because Nissan schedules to a razor's edge. At Nissan, MRP helps reduce inventory to world-class standards. World-class automobile assembly requires that purchased parts have a turnover of slightly more than once a day and that overall turnover approaches 150 times per year.

demand reflected in a master production schedule. Operations managers should take advantage of demand information when it is known, rather than assuming a constant demand. EOQ is examined in Example 5.

◀ **EXAMPLE 5**

Lot sizing with EOQ

With a setup cost of $100 and a holding cost per week of $1, Speaker Kits, Inc., wants to examine its cost with lot sizes based on an EOQ criteria.

APPROACH ▶ Using the same cost and production schedule as in Example 4, we determine net requirements and EOQ lot sizes.

SOLUTION ▶ Ten-week usage equals a gross requirement of 270 units; therefore, weekly usage equals 27, and 52 weeks (annual usage) equals 1,404 units. From Chapter 12, the EOQ model is:

$$Q^* = \sqrt{\frac{2DS}{H}}$$

where D = annual usage = 1,404
S = setup cost = $100
H = holding (carrying) cost, on an annual basis per unit
= $1 × 52 weeks = $52

$$Q^* = 73 \text{ units}$$

MRP Lot Sizing: EOQ Technique*

		1	2	3	4	5	6	7	8	9	10
Gross requirements		35	30	40	0	10	40	30	0	30	55
Scheduled receipts											
Projected on hand	35	35	0	43	3	3	66	26	69	69	39
Net requirements		0	30	0	0	7	0	4	0	0	16
Planned order receipts			73			73		73			73
Planned order releases		73			73		73			73	

*Holding costs = $1/unit/week; setup cost = $100; gross requirements average per week = 27; lead time = 1 week.

$$\text{Setups} = 1{,}404/73 = 19 \text{ per year}$$
$$\text{Annual Setup cost} = 19 \times \$100 = \$1{,}900$$
$$\text{Annual Holding cost} = \tfrac{73}{2} \times (\$1 \times 52 \text{ weeks}) = \$1{,}898$$
$$\text{Annual Setup cost} + \text{Holding cost} = \$1{,}900 + 1{,}898 = \$3{,}798$$

The EOQ solution yields a computed 10-week cost of $730 [$3,798 × (10 weeks/52 weeks) = $730].

INSIGHT ▶ EOQ can be an effective lot-sizing technique when demand is relatively constant. However, notice that actual holding cost will vary from the computed $730, depending on the rate of actual usage. From the preceding table, we can see that in our 10-week example, costs really are $400 for four setups, plus a holding cost of 375 units (includes 57 remaining at the end of the period) at $1 per week for a total of $775. Because usage was not constant, the actual computed cost was in fact more than the theoretical EOQ ($730) and the lot-for-lot rule ($700). If any stockouts had occurred, these costs too would need to be added to our actual EOQ cost of $775.

LEARNING EXERCISE ▶ What is the impact on total cost if holding cost is $2 per period rather than $1? [Answer: The EOQ quantity becomes 52, the theoretical annual total cost becomes $5,404, and the 10-week cost is $1,039 ($5,404 × (10/52).]

RELATED PROBLEMS ▶ 14.18, 14.20, 14.21, 14.22

Part Period Balancing **Part period balancing (PPB)** is a more dynamic approach to balance setup and holding cost.[3] PPB uses additional information by changing the lot size to reflect requirements of the next lot size in the future. PPB attempts to balance setup and holding cost for

Part period balancing (PPB)
An inventory ordering technique that balances setup and holding costs by changing the lot size to reflect requirements of the next lot size in the future.

[3]J. J. DeMatteis, "An Economic Lot-Sizing Technique: The Part-Period Algorithms," *IBM Systems Journal* 7 (1968): 30–38.

Economic part period (EPP)

A period of time when the ratio of setup cost to holding cost is equal.

known demands. Part period balancing develops an **economic part period (EPP)**, which is the ratio of setup cost to holding cost. For our Speaker Kits example, EPP = \$100/\$1 = 100 units. Therefore, holding 100 units for one period would cost \$100, exactly the cost of one setup. Similarly, holding 50 units for two periods also costs \$100 (2 periods × \$1 × 50 units). PPB merely adds requirements until the number of part periods approximates the EPP—in this case, 100. Example 6 shows the application of part period balancing.

EXAMPLE 6 ▶ Lot sizing with part period balancing

Speaker Kits, Inc., wants to compute the costs associated with lot sizing using part period balancing. It will use a setup cost of \$100 and a \$1 holding cost.

APPROACH ▶ Using the same costs and production schedule as Examples 3 and 4, we develop a format that helps us compute the PPB quantity and apply that to our net requirements plan.

SOLUTION ▶ The procedure for computing the order releases of 80, 100, and 55 is shown in the following PPB calculation. In the second table, we apply the PPB order quantities to the net requirements plan.

PPB Calculations

Periods Combined	Trial Lot Size (cumulative net requirements)	Part Periods	Costs: Setup	Costs: Holding	Costs: Total
2	30	0			
2, 3	70	40 = 40 × 1			
2, 3, 4	70	40			
2, 3, 4, 5	80	70 = 40 × 1 + 10 × 3	100 +	70	= 170
2, 3, 4, 5, 6	120	230 = 40 × 1 + 10 × 3 + 40 × 4			
(Therefore, combine periods 2 through 5; 70 is as close to our EPP of 100 as we are going to get.)					
6	40	0			
6, 7	70	30 = 30 ×1			
6, 7, 8	70	30 = 30 × 1 + 0 × 2			
6, 7, 8, 9	100	120 = 30 × 1 + 30 × 3	100 +	120	= 220
(Therefore, combine periods 6 through 9; 120 is as close to our EPP of 100 as we are going to get.)					
10	55	0	100 +	0	= 100
			300 +	190	= 490

40 units held for 1 period = \$40
10 units held for 3 periods = \$30

MRP Lot Sizing: PPB Technique*

		1	2	3	4	5	6	7	8	9	10
Gross requirements		35	30	40	0	10	40	30	0	30	55
Scheduled receipts											
Projected on hand	35	35	0	50	10	10	0	60	30	30	0
Net requirements		0	30	0	0	0	40	0	0	0	55
Planned order receipts			80				100				55
Planned order releases		80				100				55	

*Holding costs = \$1/unit/week; setup cost = \$100; gross requirements average per week = 27; lead time = 1 week.

EPP is 100 (setup cost divided by holding cost = \$100/\$1). The first lot is to cover periods 2, 3, 4, and 5 and is 80.

The total costs are \$490, with setup costs totaling \$300 and holding costs totaling \$190.

INSIGHT ▶ Both the EOQ and PPB approaches to lot sizing balance holding cost and ordering cost. But PPB places an order each time holding cost equals ordering cost, while EOQ takes a longer averaging approach.

LEARNING EXERCISE ▶ What is the impact on total cost if holding cost is \$2 per period rather than \$1? [Answer: With higher holding costs [PPB becomes 100/2 = 50], reorder points become more frequent, with orders now being placed for 70 units in period 1, 50 in period 4, 60 in period 6, and 55 in period 9.]

RELATED PROBLEMS ▶ 14.19, 14.20, 14.21, 14.22

Wagner-Whitin Algorithm The **Wagner-Whitin procedure** is a dynamic programming model that adds some complexity to the lot-size computation. It assumes a finite time horizon beyond which there are no additional net requirements. It does, however, provide good results.[4]

Wagner-Whitin procedure
A technique for lot-size computation that assumes a finite time horizon beyond which there are no additional net requirements to arrive at an ordering strategy.

Lot-Sizing Summary In the three Speaker Kits lot-sizing examples, we found the following costs:

Lot-for-lot	$700
EOQ	$730
Part period balancing	$490

These examples should not, however, lead operations personnel to hasty conclusions about the preferred lot-sizing technique. In theory, new lot sizes should be computed whenever there is a schedule or lot-size change anywhere in the MRP hierarchy. However, in practice, such changes cause the instability and system nervousness referred to earlier in this chapter. Consequently, such frequent changes are not made. This means that all lot sizes are wrong because the production system cannot respond to frequent changes.

In general, the lot-for-lot approach should be used whenever low-cost deliveries can be achieved. Lot-for-lot is the goal. Lots can be modified as necessary for scrap allowances, process constraints (for example, a heat-treating process may require a lot of a given size), or raw material purchase lots (for example, a truckload of chemicals may be available in only one lot size). However, caution should be exercised prior to any modification of lot size because the modification can cause substantial distortion of actual requirements at lower levels in the MRP hierarchy. When setup costs are significant and demand is reasonably smooth, part period balancing (PPB), Wagner-Whitin, or even EOQ should provide satisfactory results. Too much concern with lot sizing yields false accuracy because of MRP dynamics. A correct lot size can be determined only after the fact, based on what actually happened in terms of requirements.

EXTENSIONS OF MRP

In this section, we review three extensions of MRP.

Material Requirements Planning II (MRP II)

Material requirements planning II is an extremely powerful technique. Once a firm has MRP in place, requirements data can be enriched by resources other than just components. When MRP is used this way, *resource* is usually substituted for *requirements,* and MRP becomes **MRP II**. It then stands for material *resource* planning.

Material requirements planning II (MRP II)
A system that allows, with MRP in place, inventory data to be augmented by other resource variables; in this case, MRP becomes *material resource planning.*

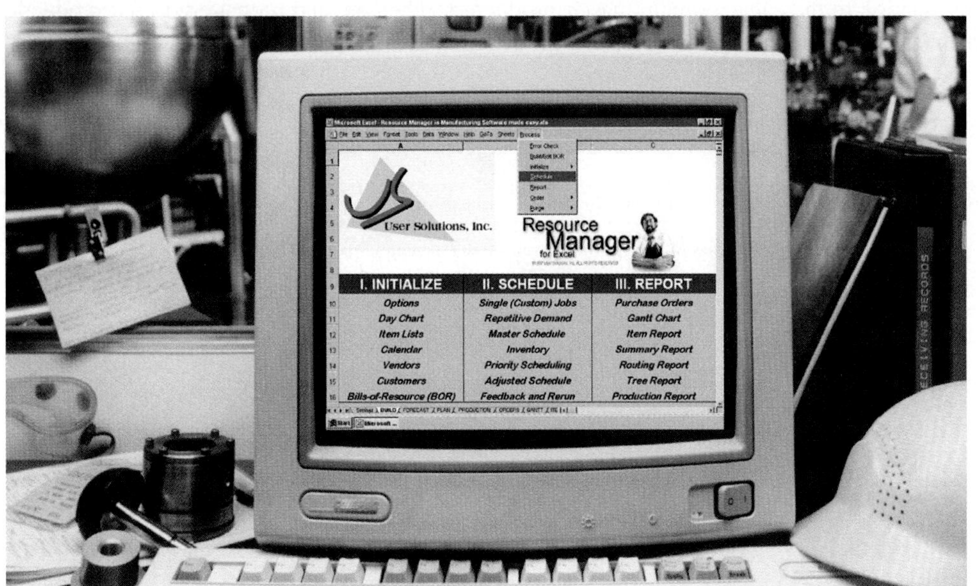

Many MRP programs, such as *Resource Manager for Excel* and *DB*, are commercially available. *Resource Manager's* initial menu screen is shown here.

A demo program is available for student use at **www.usersolutions.com**.

[4]We leave discussion of the algorithm to mathematical programming texts. The Wagner-Whitin algorithm yields a cost of $455 for the data in Examples 4, 5, and 6.

▶ TABLE 14.4 Material Resource Planning (MRP II)

By utilizing the logic of MRP, resources such as labor, machine-hours, scrap, and cost can be accurately determined and scheduled. Weekly demand for labor, machine-hours, scrap, and payables for 100 computers are shown.

	Lead Time	WEEKS 5	6	7	8
Computer	1				100
Labor-hours: .2 each					20
Machine-hours: .2 each					20
Scrap: 1 ounce fiberglass each					6.25 lbs
Payables: $0					$0
PC board (1 each)	2			100	
Labor-hours: .15 each				15	
Machine-hours: .1 each				10	
Scrap: .5 ounces copper each				3.125 lb	
Payables: raw material at $5 each				$500	
Processors (5 each)	4	500			
Labor-hours: .2 each		100			
Machine-hours: .2 each		100			
Scrap: .01 ounces of acid waste each		0.3125 lb			
Payables: processors at $10 each		$5,000			

So far in our discussion of MRP, we have scheduled products and their components. However, products require many resources, such as energy and money, beyond the product's tangible components. In addition to these resource inputs, *outputs* can be generated as well. Outputs can include such things as scrap, packaging waste, effluent, and carbon emissions. As OM becomes increasingly sensitive to the environmental and sustainability issues, identifying and managing byproducts becomes increasingly important. MRP II provides a vehicle for doing so. Table 14.4 provides an example of labor-hours, machine-hours, pounds of scrap, and cash, in the format of a gross requirements plan. With MRP II, management can identify both the inputs and outputs as well as the relevant schedule. MRP II provides another tool in OM's battle for sustainable operations.

LO5: Describe MRP II

MRP II systems are seldom stand-alone programs. Most are tied into other computer software that provide data to the MRP system or receive data from the MRP system. Purchasing, production scheduling, capacity planning, inventory, and warehouse management are a few examples of this data integration.

Closed-loop MRP system
A system that provides feedback to the capacity plan, master production schedule, and production plan so planning can be kept valid at all times.

Closed-Loop MRP

Closed-loop material requirements planning implies an MRP system that provides feedback to scheduling from the inventory control system. Specifically, a **closed-loop MRP system** provides information to the capacity plan, master production schedule, and ultimately to the production plan (as shown in Figure 14.8). Virtually all commercial MRP systems are closed-loop.

LO6: Describe closed-loop MRP

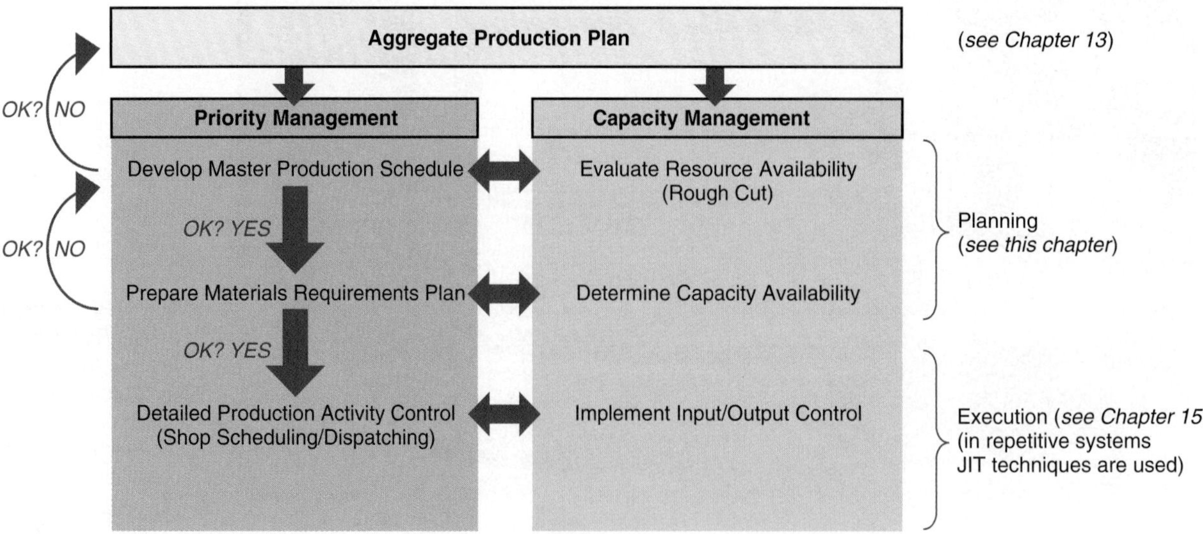

▲ **FIGURE 14.8 Closed-Loop Material Requirements Planning**

Capacity Planning

In keeping with the definition of closed-loop MRP, feedback about workload is obtained from each work center. **Load reports** show the resource requirements in a work center for all work currently assigned to the work center, all work planned, and expected orders. Figure 14.9(a) shows that the initial load in the milling center exceeds capacity on days 2, 3, and 5. Closed-loop MRP systems allow production planners to move the work between time periods to smooth the load or at least bring it within capacity. (This is the "capacity planning" part of Figure 14.8.) The closed-loop MRP system can then reschedule all items in the net requirements plan (see Figure 14.9[b]).

Load report
A report for showing the resource requirements in a work center for all work currently assigned there as well as all planned and expected orders.

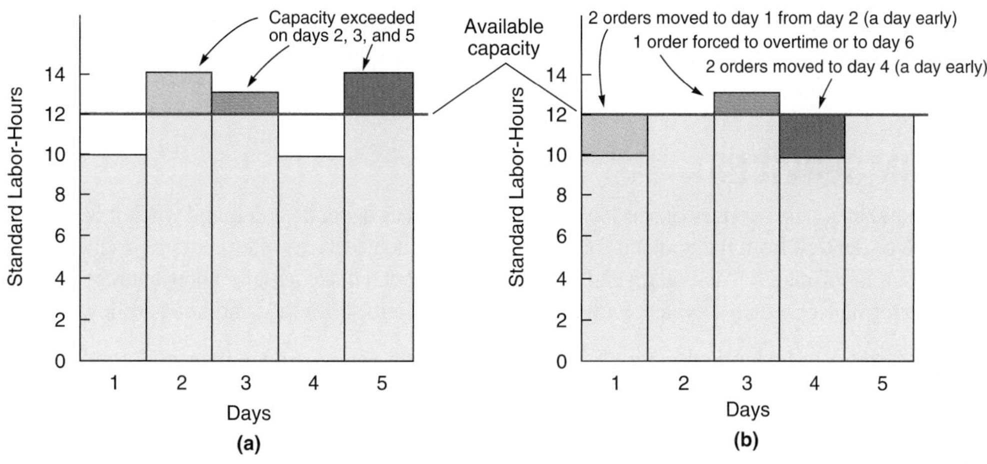

◀ **FIGURE 14.9**
(a) Initial Resource Requirements Profile for a Work Center (b) Smoothed Resource Requirements Profile for a Work Center

Tactics for smoothing the load and minimizing the impact of changed lead time include the following:

1. *Overlapping,* which reduces the lead time, sends pieces to the second operation before the entire lot is completed on the first operation.
2. *Operations splitting* sends the lot to two different machines for the same operation. This involves an additional setup, but results in shorter throughput times, because only part of the lot is processed on each machine.
3. *Order* or, *lot splitting,* involves breaking up the order and running part of it earlier (or later) in the schedule.

Example 7 shows a brief detailed capacity scheduling example using order splitting to improve utilization.

◀ **EXAMPLE 7**
Order splitting

Kevin Watson, the production planner at Wiz Products, needs to develop a capacity plan for a work center. He has the production orders shown below for the next 5 days. There are 12 hours available in the work cell each day. The parts being produced require 1 hour each.

Day	1	2	3	4	5
Orders	10	14	13	10	14

APPROACH ▶ Compute the time available in the work center and the time necessary to complete the production requirements.

SOLUTION ▶

Day	Units Ordered	Capacity Required (hours)	Capacity Available (hours)	Utilization: Over/ (Under) (hours)	Production Planner's Action	New Production Schedule
1	10	10	12	(2)		12
2	14	14	12	2	Split order: move 2 units to day 1	12
3	13	13	12	1	Split order: move 1 unit to day 6 or request overtime	13
4	10	10	12	(2)		12
5	14	14	12	2	Split order: move 2 units to day 4	12
	61					

INSIGHT ▶ By moving orders, the production planner is able to utilize capacity more effectively and still meet the order requirements, with only 1 order produced on overtime in day 3.

LEARNING EXERCISE ▶ If the units ordered for day 5 increase to 16, what are the production planner's options? [Answer: In addition to moving 2 units to day 4, move 2 units of production to day 6, or request overtime.]

RELATED PROBLEMS ▶ 14.23, 14.24

When the workload consistently exceeds work-center capacity, the tactics just discussed are not adequate. This may mean adding capacity. Options include adding capacity via personnel, machinery, overtime, or subcontracting.

MRP IN SERVICES

The demand for many services or service items is classified as dependent demand when it is directly related to or derived from the demand for other services. Such services often require product-structure trees, bills-of-material and labor, and scheduling. MRP can make a major contribution to operational performance in such services. Examples from restaurants, hospitals, and hotels follow.

Restaurants In restaurants, ingredients and side dishes (bread, vegetables, and condiments) are typically meal components. These components are dependent on the demand for meals. The meal is an end item in the master schedule. Figure 14.10 shows (a) a product-structure tree and (b) a bill of material for veal picante, a top-selling entrée in a New Orleans restaurant. Note that the various components of veal picante (that is, veal, sauce, spinach, and linguini) are prepared by different kitchen personnel (see part [a] of Figure 14.10). These preparations also require different amounts of time to complete. Figure 14.10(c) shows a bill-of-labor for the veal dish. It lists the operations to be performed, the order of operations, and the labor requirements for each operation (types of labor and labor-hours).

Hospitals MRP is also applied in hospitals, especially when dealing with surgeries that require known equipment, materials, and supplies. Houston's Park Plaza Hospital and many hospital suppliers, for example, use the technique to improve the scheduling and management of expensive surgical inventory.

Hotels Marriott develops a bill of material (BOM) and a bill of labor when it renovates each of its hotel rooms. Marriott managers explode the BOM to compute requirements for materials, furniture, and decorations. MRP then provides net requirements and a schedule for use by purchasing and contractors.

Distribution Resource Planning (DRP)

Distribution resource planning (DRP)
A time-phased stock-replenishment plan for all levels of a distribution network.

When dependent techniques are used in the supply chain, they are called distribution resource planning (DRP). **Distribution resource planning (DRP)** is a time-phased stock-replenishment plan for all levels of the supply chain.

DRP procedures and logic are analogous to MRP. With DRP, expected demand becomes gross requirements. Net requirements are determined by allocating available inventory to gross requirements. The DRP procedure starts with the forecast at the retail level (or the most distant point of the distribution network being supplied). All other levels are computed. As is the case with MRP, inventory is then reviewed with an aim to satisfying demand. So that stock will arrive when it is needed, net requirements are offset by the necessary lead time. A planned order release quantity becomes the gross requirement at the next level down the distribution chain.

DRP *pulls* inventory through the system. Pulls are initiated when the retail level orders more stock. Allocations are made to the retail level from available inventory and production after being adjusted to obtain shipping economies. Effective use of DRP requires an integrated information system to rapidly convey planned order releases from one level to the next. The goal of the DRP system is small and frequent replenishment within the bounds of economical ordering and shipping.[5]

[5]For an expanded discussion of time-phased stock-replenishment plans, see the section "Opportunities in an Integrated Supply Chain" in Chapter 11 of this text.

(a) PRODUCT STRUCTURE TREE

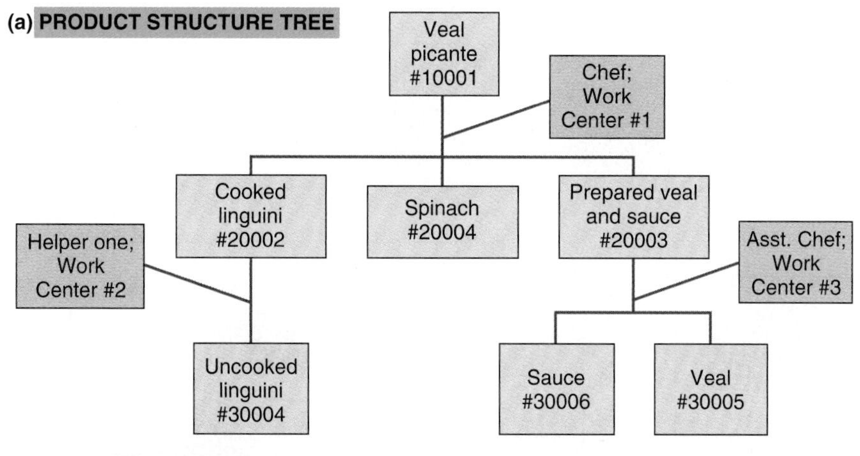

(b) BILL OF MATERIALS

Part Number	Description	Quantity	Unit of Measure	Unit Cost
10001	Veal picante	1	Serving	—
20002	Cooked linguini	1	Serving	—
20003	Prepared veal and sauce	1	Serving	—
20004	Spinach	0.1	Bag	0.94
30004	Uncooked linguini	0.5	Pound	—
30005	Veal	1	Serving	2.15
30006	Sauce	1	Serving	0.80

(c) BILL OF LABOR FOR VEAL PICANTE

			Labor-Hours	
Work Center	Operation	Labor Type	Setup Time	Run Time
1	Assemble dish	Chef	.0069	.0041
2	Cook linguini	Helper one	.0005	.0022
3	Cook veal and sauce	Assistant chef	.0125	.0500

◄ FIGURE 14.10 **Product Structure Tree, Bill-of-Material, and Bill-of-Labor for Veal Picante**

Source: Adapted from John G. Wacker, "Effective Planning and Cost Control for Restaurants," *Production and Inventory Management* (Vol. 26, no. 1): 60. Reprinted by permission of American Production and Inventory Control Society.

ENTERPRISE RESOURCE PLANNING (ERP)

AUTHOR COMMENT ERP tries to integrate all of a firm's information.

Advances in MRP II systems that tie customers and suppliers to MRP II have led to the development of enterprise resource planning (ERP) systems. **Enterprise resource planning (ERP)** is software that allows companies to (1) automate and integrate many of their business processes, (2) share a common database and business practices throughout the enterprise, and (3) produce information in real time. A schematic showing some of these relationships for a manufacturing firm appears in Figure 14.11.

Enterprise resource planning (ERP)
An information system for identifying and planning the enterprise-wide resources needed to take, make, ship, and account for customer orders.

The objective of an ERP system is to coordinate a firm's whole business, from supplier evaluation to customer invoicing. This objective is seldom achieved, but ERP systems are evolving as umbrella systems that tie together a variety of specialized systems. This is accomplished by using a centralized database to assist the flow of information among business functions. Exactly what is tied together, and how, varies on a case-by-case basis. In addition to the traditional components of MRP, ERP systems usually provide financial and human resource (HR) management information. ERP systems also include:

LO7: Describe ERP

- *Supply chain management (SCM)* software to support sophisticated vendor communication, e-commerce, and those activities necessary for efficient warehousing and logistics. The idea is to tie operations (MRP) to procurement, to materials management, and to suppliers, providing the tools necessary for effective management of all four areas.
- *Customer relationship management (CRM)* software for the incoming side of the business. CRM is designed to aid analysis of sales, target the most profitable customers, and manage the sales force.

In addition to data integration, ERP software promises reduced transaction costs and fast, accurate information. A strategic emphasis on just-in-time systems and supply chain integration

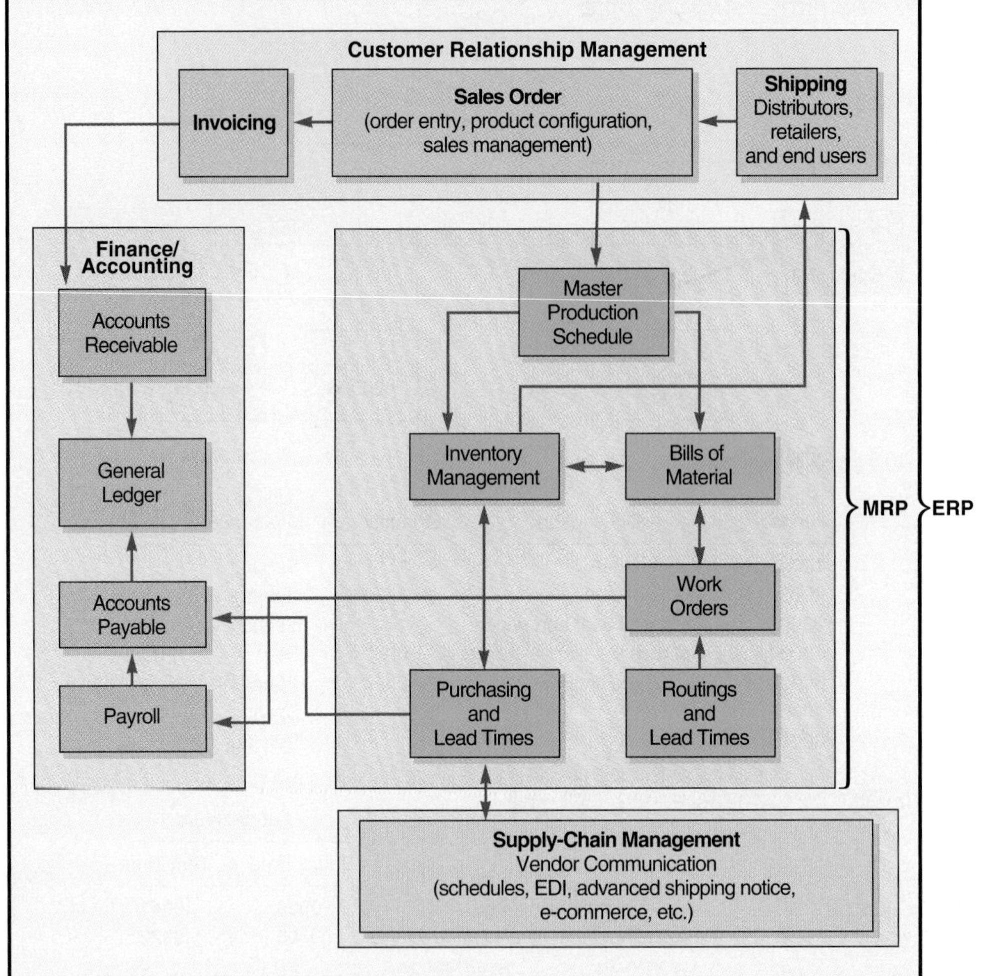

▶ **FIGURE 14.11**
MRP and ERP Information Flows, Showing Customer Relationship Management (CRM), Supply-Chain Management (SCM), and Finance/Accounting
Other functions such as human resources are often also included in ERP systems.

drives the desire for enterprise-wide software. The *OM in Action* box "Managing Benetton with ERP Software" provides an example of how ERP software helps integrate company operations.

OM in Action ▶ Managing Benetton with ERP Software

Thanks to ERP, the Italian sportswear company Benetton can probably claim to have the world's fastest factory and the most efficient distribution in the garment industry. Located in Ponzano, Italy, Benetton makes and ships 50 million pieces of clothing each year. That is 30,000 boxes every day—boxes that must be filled with exactly the items ordered going to the correct store of the 5,000 Benetton outlets in 60 countries. This highly automated distribution center uses only 19 people. Without ERP, hundreds of people would be needed.

Here is how ERP software works:

1. *Ordering:* A salesperson in the south Boston store finds that she is running out of a best-selling blue sweater. Using a laptop PC, her local Benetton sales agent taps into the ERP sales module.
2. *Availability:* ERP's inventory software simultaneously forwards the order to the mainframe in Italy and finds that half the order can be filled immediately from the Italian warehouse. The rest will be manufactured and shipped in 4 weeks.
3. *Production:* Because the blue sweater was originally created by computer-aided design (CAD), ERP manufacturing software passes the specifications to a knitting machine. The knitting machine makes the sweaters.
4. *Warehousing:* The blue sweaters are boxed with a radio frequency ID (RFID) tag addressed to the Boston store and placed in one of the 300,000 slots in the Italian warehouse. A robot flies by, reading RFID tags, picks out any and all boxes ready for the Boston store, and loads them for shipment.
5. *Order tracking:* The Boston salesperson logs onto the ERP system through the Internet and sees that the sweater (and other items) are completed and being shipped.
6. *Planning:* Based on data from ERP's forecasting and financial modules, Benetton's chief buyer decides that blue sweaters are in high demand and quite profitable. She decides to add three new hues.

Sources: The Wall Street Journal (April 10, 2007): B1; *Frontline Solutions* (April 2003): 54; and *MIT Sloan Management Review* (Fall 2001): 46–53.

In an ERP system, data are entered only once into a common, complete, and consistent database shared by all applications. For example, when a Nike salesperson enters an order into his ERP system for 20,000 pairs of sneakers for Foot Locker, the data are instantly available on the manufacturing floor. Production crews start filling the order if it is not in stock, accounting prints Foot Locker's invoice, and shipping notifies the Foot Locker of the future delivery date. The salesperson, or even the customer, can check the progress of the order at any point. This is all accomplished using the same data and common applications. To reach this consistency, however, the data fields must be defined identically across the entire enterprise. In Nike's case, this means integrating operations at production sites from Vietnam to China to Mexico, at business units across the globe, in many currencies, and with reports in a variety of languages.

Each ERP vendor produces unique products. The major vendors, SAP AG (a German firm), BEA (Canada), SSAGlobal, American Software, PeopleSoft/Oracle, CMS Software (all of the U.S.), sell software or modules designed for specific industries (a set of SAP's modules is shown in Figure 14.12). However, companies must determine if their way of doing business will fit the standard ERP module. If they determine that the product will not fit the standard ERP product, they can change the way they do business to accommodate the software. But such a change can have an adverse impact on their business process, reducing a competitive advantage. Alternatively, ERP software can be customized to meet their specific process requirements. Although the vendors build the software to keep the customization process simple, many companies spend up to five times the cost of the software to customize it. In addition to the expense, the major downside of customization is that when ERP vendors provide an upgrade or enhancement to the software, the customized part of the code must be rewritten to fit into the new version. ERP programs cost from a minimum of $300,000 for a small company to hundreds of millions of dollars for global giants like Ford and Coca-Cola. It is easy to see, then, that ERP systems are expensive, full of hidden issues, and time-consuming to install.

▼ **FIGURE 14.12 SAP's Modules for ERP**

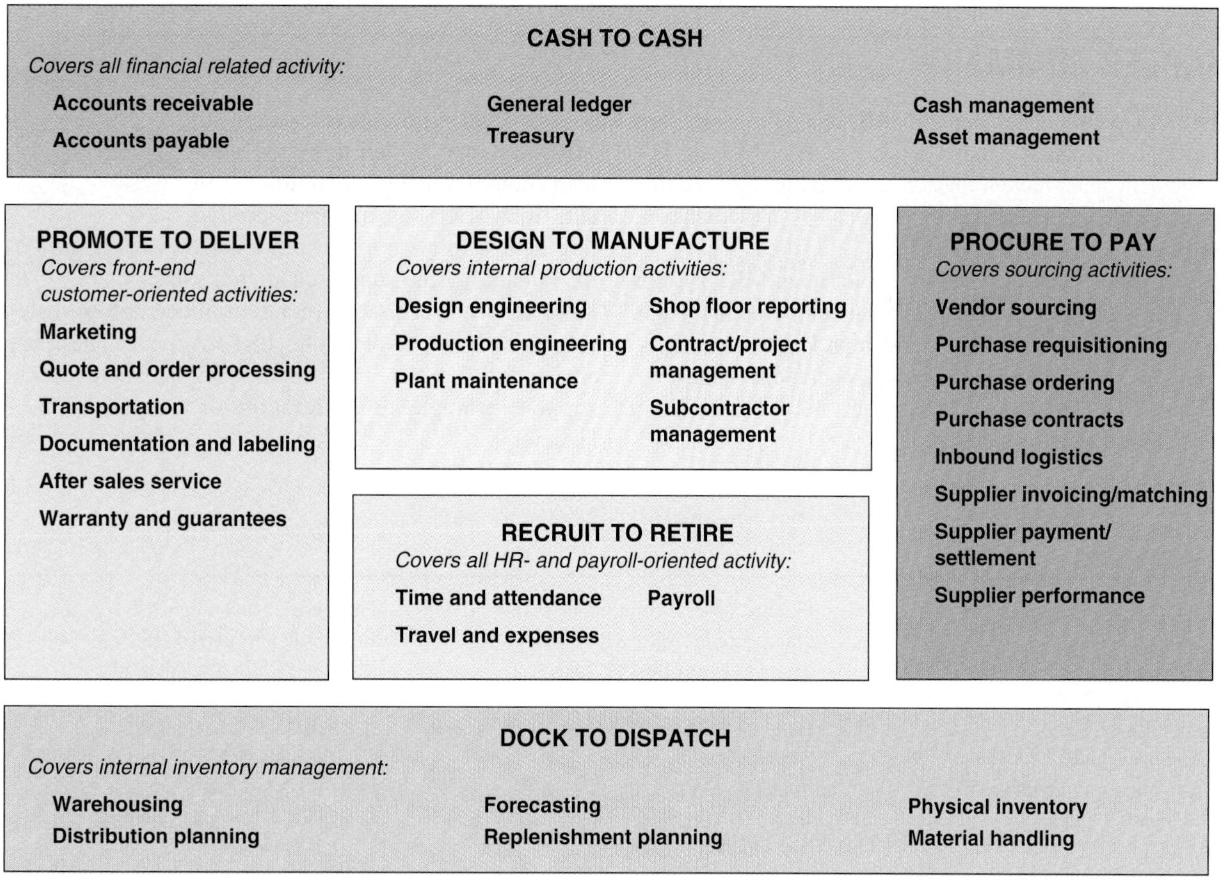

CASH TO CASH
Covers all financial related activity:
- Accounts receivable
- Accounts payable
- General ledger
- Treasury
- Cash management
- Asset management

PROMOTE TO DELIVER
Covers front-end customer-oriented activities:
- Marketing
- Quote and order processing
- Transportation
- Documentation and labeling
- After sales service
- Warranty and guarantees

DESIGN TO MANUFACTURE
Covers internal production activities:
- Design engineering
- Production engineering
- Plant maintenance
- Shop floor reporting
- Contract/project management
- Subcontractor management

RECRUIT TO RETIRE
Covers all HR- and payroll-oriented activity:
- Time and attendance
- Travel and expenses
- Payroll

PROCURE TO PAY
Covers sourcing activities:
- Vendor sourcing
- Purchase requisitioning
- Purchase ordering
- Purchase contracts
- Inbound logistics
- Supplier invoicing/matching
- Supplier payment/settlement
- Supplier performance

DOCK TO DISPATCH
Covers internal inventory management:
- Warehousing
- Distribution planning
- Forecasting
- Replenishment planning
- Physical inventory
- Material handling

Source: www.sap.com.

Advantages and Disadvantages of ERP Systems

We have alluded to some of the pluses and minuses of ERP. Here is a more complete list of both.

Advantages:

1. Provides integration of the supply chain, production, and administrative process.
2. Creates commonality of databases.
3. Can incorporate improved, reengineered, "best processes."
4. Increases communication and collaboration among business units and sites.
5. Has a software database that is off-the-shelf coding.
6. May provide a strategic advantage over competitors.

Disadvantages:

1. Is very expensive to purchase, and even more costly to customize.
2. Implementation may require major changes in the company and its processes.
3. Is so complex that many companies cannot adjust to it.
4. Involves an ongoing process for implementation, which may never be completed.
5. Expertise in ERP is limited, with staffing an ongoing problem.

ERP in the Service Sector

ERP vendors have developed a series of service modules for such markets as health care, government, retail stores, and financial services. Springer-Miller Systems, for example, has created an ERP package for the hotel market with software that handles all front- and back-office functions. This system integrates tasks such as maintaining guest histories, booking room and dinner reservations, scheduling golf tee times, and managing multiple properties in a chain. PeopleSoft/Oracle combines ERP with supply chain management to coordinate airline meal preparation. In the grocery industry, these supply chain systems are known as *efficient consumer response* (ECR) systems. As is the case in manufacturing, **efficient consumer response** systems tie sales to buying, to inventory, to logistics, and to production.

Efficient consumer response (ECR)
Supply chain management systems in the grocery industry that tie sales to buying, to inventory, to logistics, and to production.

CHAPTER SUMMARY

Material requirements planning (MRP) schedules production and inventory when demand is dependent. For MRP to work, management must have a master schedule, precise requirements for all components, accurate inventory and purchasing records, and accurate lead times.

Production should often be lot-for-lot in an MRP system. When properly implemented, MRP can contribute in a major way to reduction in inventory while improving customer service levels. MRP techniques allow the operations manager to schedule and replenish stock on a "need-to-order" basis rather than simply a "time-to-order" basis.

The continuing development of MRP systems has led to its use with lean manufacturing techniques. In addition, MRP can integrate production data with a variety of other activities, including the supply chain and sales. As a result, we now have integrated database-oriented enterprise resource planning (ERP) systems. These expensive and difficult-to-install ERP systems, when successful, support strategies of differentiation, response, and cost leadership.

Key Terms

Material requirements planning (MRP) (p. 546)
Master production schedule (MPS) (p. 546)
Bill of material (BOM) (p. 548)
Modular bills (p. 550)
Planning bills (or kits) (p. 550)
Phantom bills of material (p. 550)
Low-level coding (p. 550)
Lead time (p. 551)
Gross material requirements plan (p. 552)
Net material requirements (p. 553)
Planned order receipt (p. 553)
Planned order release (p. 553)
System nervousness (p. 556)
Time fences (p. 556)
Pegging (p. 556)
Buckets (p. 556)
Bucketless system (p. 557)
Back flush (p. 557)
Supermarket (p. 557)
Lot-sizing decision (p. 557)
Lot-for-lot (p. 557)
Part period balancing (PPB) (p. 559)
Economic part period (EPP) (p. 560)
Wagner-Whitin procedure (p. 561)
Material requirements planning II (MRP II) (p. 561)
Closed-loop MRP system (p. 562)
Load report (p. 563)
Distribution resource planning (DRP) (p. 564)
Enterprise resource planning (ERP) (p. 565)
Efficient consumer response (ECR) (p. 568)

Ethical Dilemma

For many months your prospective ERP customer has been analyzing the hundreds of assumptions built into the $900,000 ERP software you are selling. So far, you have knocked yourself out to try to make this sale. If the sale goes through, you will reach your yearly quota and get a nice bonus. On the other hand, loss of this sale may mean you start looking for other employment.

The accounting, human resource, supply chain, and marketing teams put together by the client have reviewed the specifications and finally recommended purchase of the software. However, as you looked over their shoulders and helped them through the evaluation process, you began to realize that their purchasing procedures—with much of the purchasing being done at hundreds of regional stores—were not a good fit for the software. At the very least, the customizing will add $250,000 to the implementation and training cost. The team is not aware of the issue, and you know that the necessary $250,000 is not in the budget.

What do you do?

Discussion Questions

1. What is the difference between a *gross* requirements plan and a *net* requirements plan?
2. Once a material requirements plan (MRP) has been established, what other managerial applications might be found for the technique?
3. What are the similarities between MRP and DRP?
4. How does MRP II differ from MRP?
5. Which is the best lot-sizing policy for manufacturing organizations?
6. What impact does ignoring carrying cost in the allocation of stock in a DRP system have on lot sizes?
7. MRP is more than an inventory system; what additional capabilities does MRP possess?
8. What are the options for the production planner who has: (a) scheduled more than capacity in a work center next week? (b) a consistent lack of capacity in that work center?
9. Master schedules are expressed in three different ways depending on whether the process is continuous, a job shop, or repetitive. What are these three ways?
10. What functions of the firm affect an MRP system? How?
11. What is the rationale for (a) a phantom bill of material, (b) a planning bill of material, and (c) a pseudo bill of material?
12. Identify five specific requirements of an effective MRP system.
13. What are the typical benefits of ERP?
14. What are the distinctions between MRP, DRP, and ERP?
15. As an approach to inventory management, how does MRP differ from the approach taken in Chapter 12, dealing with economic order quantities (EOQ)?
16. What are the disadvantages of ERP?
17. Use the Web or other sources to:
    (a) Find stories that highlight the advantages of an ERP system.
    (b) Find stories that highlight the difficulties of purchasing, installing, or failure of an ERP system.
18. Use the Web or other sources to identify what an ERP vendor (SAP, PeopleSoft/Oracle, American Software, etc.) includes in these software modules:
    (a) Customer relationship management.
    (b) Supply-chain management.
    (c) Product life cycle management.
19. The very structure of MRP systems suggests fixed lead times. However, many firms have moved toward JIT and kanban techniques. What are the techniques, issues, and impact of adding JIT inventory and purchasing techniques to an organization that has MRP?

Using Software to Solve MRP Problems

There are many commercial MRP software packages, for companies of all sizes. MRP software for small and medium-size companies includes User Solutions, Inc., a demo of which is available at **www.usersolutions.com,** and MAX, from Exact Software North America, Inc. Software for larger systems is available from SAP, CMS, BEA, Oracle, i2 Technologies, and many others. The Excel OM software that accompanies this text includes an MRP module, as does POM for Windows. The use of both is explained in the following sections.

Using Excel OM

Using Excel OM's MRP module requires the careful entry of several pieces of data. The initial MRP screen is where we enter (1) the total number of occurrences of items in the BOM (including the top item), (2) what we want the BOM items to be called (i.e., Item no., Part), (3) total number of periods to be scheduled, and (4) what we want the periods called (i.e., days, weeks).

Excel OM's second MRP screen provides the data entry for an indented bill of material. Here we enter (1) the name of each item in the BOM, (2) the quantity of that item in the assembly, and (3) the correct indent (i.e., parent/child relationship) for each item. The indentations are critical as they provide the logic for the BOM explosion. The indentations should follow the logic of the product structure tree with indents for each assembly item in that assembly.

Excel OM's third MRP screen repeats the indented BOM and provides the standard MRP tableau for entries. This is shown in Program 14.1 using the data from Examples 1, 2, and 3.

▶ **PROGRAM 14.1**
Using Excel OM's MRP Module to Solve Examples 1, 2, and 3

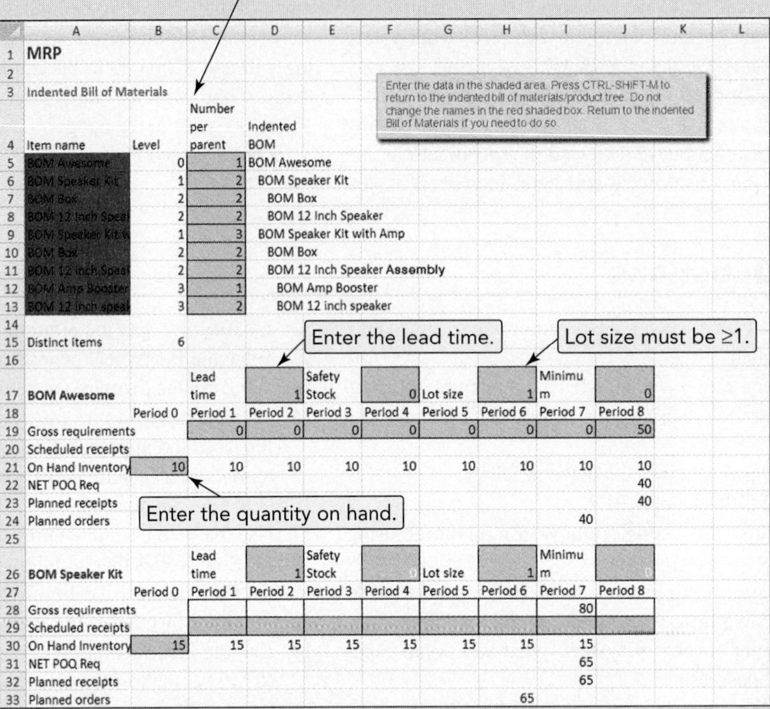

Using POM for Windows

The POM for Windows MRP module can also solve Examples 1 to 3. Up to 18 periods can be analyzed. Here are the inputs required:

1. *Item names:* The item names are entered in the left column. The same item name will appear in more than one row if the item is used by two parent items. Each item must follow its parents.
2. *Item level:* The level in the indented BOM must be given here. The item *cannot* be placed at a level more than one below the item immediately above.
3. *Lead-time:* The lead time for an item is entered here. The default is 1 week.
4. *Number per parent:* The number of units of this subassembly needed for its parent is entered here. The default is 1.
5. *On hand:* List current inventory on hand once, even if the subassembly is listed twice.
6. *Lot size:* The lot size can be specified here. A 0 or 1 will perform lot-for-lot ordering. If another number is placed here, then all orders for that item will be in integer multiples of that number.
7. *Demands:* The demands are entered in the end item row in the period in which the items are demanded.
8. *Scheduled receipts:* If units are scheduled to be received in the future, they should be listed in the appropriate time period (column) and item (row). (An entry here in level 1 is a demand; all other levels are receipts.)

Further details regarding POM for Windows are seen in Appendix IV.

Solved Problems

Virtual Office Hours help is available at www.myomlab.com

▶ **SOLVED PROBLEM 14.1**

Determine the low-level coding and the quantity of each component necessary to produce 10 units of an assembly we will call Alpha. The product structure and quantities of each component needed for each assembly are noted in parentheses.

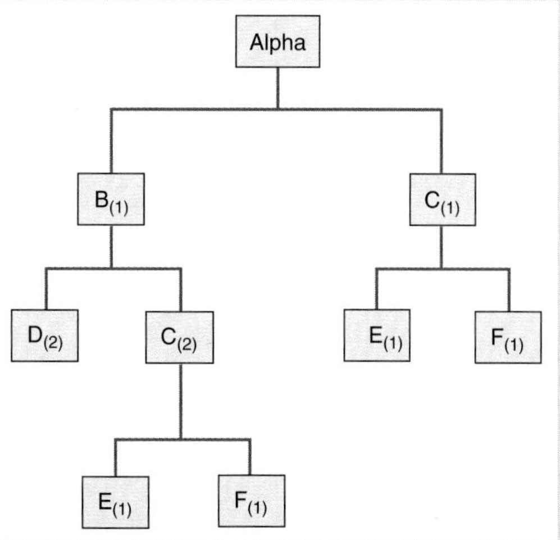

▶ SOLUTION

Redraw the product structure with low-level coding. Then multiply down the structure until the requirements of each branch are determined. Then add across the structure until the total for each is determined.

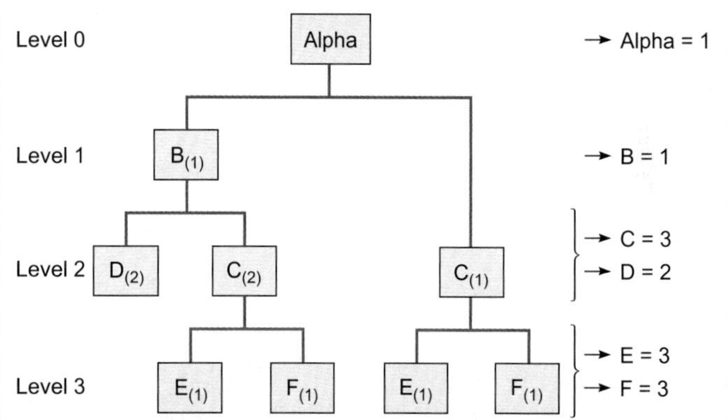

Es required for left branch:

$$(1_{\text{alpha}} \times 1_{\text{B}} \times 2_{\text{C}} \times 1_{\text{E}}) = 2 \text{ Es}$$

and Es required for right branch:

$$(1_{\text{alpha}} \times 1_{\text{C}} \times 1_{\text{E}}) = \underline{1 \text{ E}}$$

3 Es required in total

Then "explode" the requirement by multiplying each by 10, as shown in the table to the right:

Level	Item	Quantity per Unit	Total Requirements for 10 Alpha
0	Alpha	1	10
1	B	1	10
2	C	3	30
2	D	2	20
3	E	3	30
3	F	3	30

▶ SOLVED PROBLEM 14.2

Using the product structure for Alpha in Solved Problem 14.1, and the following lead times, quantity on hand, and master production schedule, prepare a net MRP table for Alphas.

Item	Lead Time	Quantity on Hand
Alpha	1	10
B	2	20
C	3	0
D	1	100
E	1	10
F	1	50

Master Production Schedule for Alpha

Period	6	7	8	9	10	11	12	13
Gross requirements			50			50		100

▼ SOLUTION

See the chart on following page.

Lot Size	Lead Time (# of Periods)	On Hand	Safety Stock	Allo-cated	Low-Level Code	Item ID			1	2	3	4	5	6	7	8	9	10	11	12	13
Lot-for-Lot	1	10	—	—	0	Alpha (A)	Gross Requirements									50			50		100
							Scheduled Receipts														
							Projected On Hand	10								10					
							Net Requirements									40			50		100
							Planned Order Receipts									40			50		
							Planned Order Releases								40			50		100	100
Lot-for-Lot	2	20	—	—	1	B	Gross Requirements								40(A)			50(A)		100(A)	
							Scheduled Receipts														
							Projected On Hand	20							20						
							Net Requirements								20			50		100	
							Planned Order Receipts								20			50		100	
							Planned Order Releases						20			50		100			
Lot-for-Lot	3	0	—	—	2	C	Gross Requirements						40(B)		40(A)	100(B)		200(B) + 50(A)		100(A)	
							Scheduled Receipts														
							Projected On Hand	0													
							Net Requirements						40		40	100		250		100	
							Planned Order Receipts						40		40	100		250		100	
							Planned Order Releases			40		40	100		250		100				
Lot-for-Lot	1	100	—	—	2	D	Gross Requirements						40(B)			100(B)		200(B)			
							Scheduled Receipts														
							Projected On Hand	100					100			60					
							Net Requirements						0			40		200			
							Planned Order Receipts						0			40		200			
							Planned Order Releases					0			40		200				
Lot-for-Lot	1	10	—	—	3	E	Gross Requirements			40(C)		40(C)	100(C)		250(C)		100(C)				
							Scheduled Receipts														
							Projected On Hand	10		10											
							Net Requirements			30		40	100		250		100				
							Planned Order Receipts			30		40	100		250		100				
							Planned Order Releases		30		40	100		250		100					
Lot-for-Lot	1	50	—	—	3	F	Gross Requirements			40(C)		40(C)	100(C)		250(C)		100(C)				
							Scheduled Receipts														
							Projected On Hand	50		50		10					—				
							Net Requirements			0		30	100		250		100				
							Planned Order Receipts					30	100		250		100				
							Planned Order Releases				30	100		250		100					

Net Material Requirements Planning Sheet for Alpha

The letter in parentheses (A) is the source of the demand.

Problems*

• **14.1** You have developed the following simple product structure of items needed for your gift bag for a rush party for prospective pledges in your organization. You forecast 200 attendees. Assume that there is no inventory on hand of any of the items. Explode the bill of material. (Subscripts indicate the number of units required.)

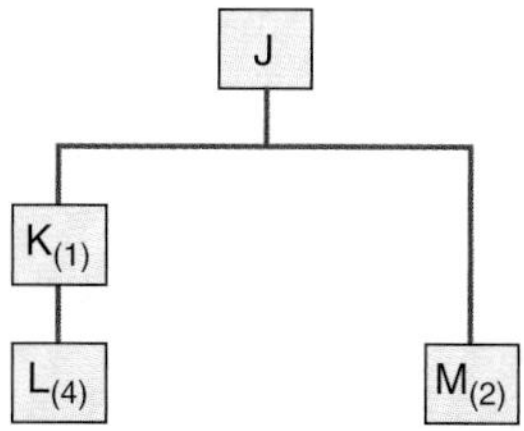

•• **14.2** You are expected to have the gift bags in Problem 14.1 ready at 5 P.M.. However, you need to personalize the items (monogrammed pens, note pads, literature from the printer, etc.). The lead time is 1 hour to assemble 200 Js once the other items are prepared. The other items will take a while as well. Given the volunteers you have, the other time estimates are item K (2 hours), item L (1 hour), and item M (4 hours). Develop a time-phased assembly plan to prepare the gift bags.

•• **14.3** The demand for subassembly S is 100 units in week 7. Each unit of S requires 1 unit of T and 2 units of U. Each unit of T requires 1 unit of V, 2 units of W, and 1 unit of X. Finally, each unit of U requires 2 units of Y and 3 units of Z. One firm manufactures all items. It takes 2 weeks to make S, 1 week to make T, 2 weeks to make U, 2 weeks to make V, 3 weeks to make W, 1 week to make X, 2 weeks to make Y, and 1 week to make Z.

a) Construct a product structure. Identify all levels, parents, and components.
b) Prepare a time-phased product structure.

•• **14.4** Using the information in Problem 14.3, construct a gross material requirements plan. Px

•• **14.5** Using the information in Problem 14.3, construct a net material requirements plan using the following on-hand inventory.

*Note: Px means the problem may be solved with POM for Windows and/or Excel OM. Many of the exercises in this chapter (14.1 through 14.16 and 14.23 through 14.27) can be done on *Resource Manager for Excel*, a commercial system made available by User Solutions, Inc. Access to a trial version of the software and a set of notes for the user is available at **www.usersolutions.com.**

Lot Size	Lead Time (# of periods)	On Hand	Safety Stock	Allo-cated	Low-Level Code	Item ID		Period (week, day)							
								1	2	3	4	5	6	7	8
							Gross Requirements								
							Scheduled Receipts								
							Projected On Hand								
							Net Requirements								
							Planned Order Receipts								
							Planned Order Releases								
							Gross Requirements								
							Scheduled Receipts								
							Projected On Hand								
							Net Requirements								
							Planned Order Receipts								
							Planned Order Releases								
							Gross Requirements								
							Scheduled Receipts								
							Projected On Hand								
							Net Requirements								
							Planned Order Receipts								
							Planned Order Releases								
							Gross Requirements								
							Scheduled Receipts								
							Projected On Hand								
							Net Requirements								
							Planned Order Receipts								
							Planned Order Releases								
							Gross Requirements								
							Scheduled Receipts								
							Projected On Hand								
							Net Requirements								
							Planned Order Receipts								
							Planned Order Releases								

▲ **FIGURE 14.13 MRP Form for Homework Problems in Chapter 14**
For several problems in this chapter, a copy of this form may be helpful.

Item	On-Hand Inventory	Item	On-Hand Inventory
S	20	W	30
T	20	X	25
U	40	Y	240
V	30	Z	40

•• **14.6** Refer again to Problems 14.3 and 14.4. In addition to 100 units of S, there is also a demand for 20 units of U, which is a component of S. The 20 units of U are needed for maintenance purposes. These units are needed in week 6. Modify the *gross material requirements plan* to reflect this change. PX

•• **14.7** Refer again to Problems 14.3 and 14.5. In addition to 100 units of S, there is also a demand for 20 units of U, which is a component of S. The 20 units of U are needed for maintenance purposes. These units are needed in week 6. Modify the *net material requirements plan* to reflect this change. PX

•• **14.8** As the production planner for Gerry Cook Products, Inc., you have been given a bill of material for a bracket that is made up of a base, two springs, and four clamps. The base is assembled from one clamp and two housings. Each clamp has one handle and one casting. Each housing has two bearings and one shaft. There is no inventory on hand.

a) Design a product structure noting the quantities for each item and show the low-level coding.
b) Determine the gross quantities needed of each item if you are to assemble 50 brackets.
c) Compute the net quantities needed if there are 25 of the base and 100 of the clamp in stock. PX

•• **14.9** Your boss at Gerry Cook Products, Inc., has just provided you with the schedule and lead times for the bracket in Problem 14.8. The unit is to be prepared in week 10. The lead times for the components are bracket (1 week), base (1 week), spring (1 week), clamp (1 week), housing (2 weeks), handle (1 week), casting (3 weeks), bearing (1 week), and shaft (1 week).

a) Prepare the time-phased product structure for the bracket.
b) In what week do you need to start the castings? PX

•• **14.10**

a) Given the product structure and master production schedule (Figure 14.14 below), develop a gross requirements plan for all items.
b) Given the preceding product structure, master production schedule, and inventory status (Figure 14.14), develop a net materials requirements (planned order release) for all items. PX

••• **14.11** Given the following product structure, master production schedule, and inventory status (Figure 14.15 on the next page) and assuming the requirements for each BOM item is 1: (a) develop a gross requirements plan for Item C; (b) develop a net requirements plan for Item C. PX

•••• **14.12** Based on the data in Figure 14.15, complete a net material requirements schedule for:

a) All items (10 schedules in all), assuming the requirement for each BOM item is 1.
b) All 10 items, assuming the requirement for all items is 1, except B, C, and F, which require *2 each*. PX

••• **14.13** Electro Fans has just received an order for one thousand 20-inch fans due week 7. Each fan consists of a housing assembly, two grills, a fan assembly, and an electrical unit. The housing assembly consists of a frame, two supports, and a handle. The fan assembly consists of a hub and five blades. The electrical unit consists of a motor, a switch, and a knob. The following table gives lead times, on-hand inventory, and scheduled receipts.

a) Construct a product structure.
b) Construct a time-phased product structure.
c) Prepare a net material requirements plan. PX

Data Table for Problem 14.13

Component	Lead Time	On Hand Inventory	Lot Size*	Scheduled Receipt
20″ Fan	1	100	—	
Housing	1	100	—	
Frame	2	—	—	
Supports (2)	1	50	100	
Handle	1	400	500	
Grills (2)	2	200	500	
Fan Assembly	3	150	—	
Hub	1	—	—	
Blades (5)	2	—	100	
Electrical Unit	1	—	—	
Motor	1	—	—	
Switch	1	20	12	
Knob	1	—	25	200 knobs in week 2

*Lot-for-lot unless otherwise noted

••• **14.14** A part structure, lead time (weeks), and on-hand quantities for product A are shown in Figure 14.16. From the information shown, generate

▼ **FIGURE 14.14 Information for Problem 14.10**

Master Production Schedule for X1

PERIOD	7	8	9	10	11	12
Gross requirements		50		20		100

ITEM	LEAD TIME	ON HAND	ITEM	LEAD TIME	ON HAND
X1	1	50	C	1	0
B1	2	20	D	1	0
B2	2	20	E	3	10
A1	1	5			

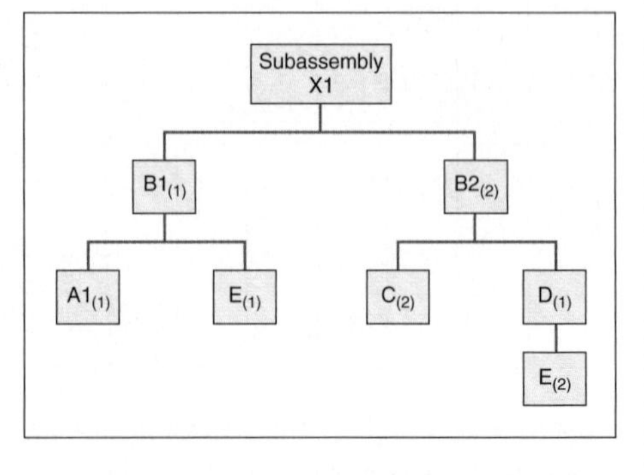

► **FIGURE 14.15**
Information for Problems 14.11 and 14.12

Period	8	9	10	11	12
Gross requirements: A	100		50		150
Gross requirements: H		100		50	

Item	On Hand	Lead Time	Item	On Hand	Lead Time
A	0	1	F	75	2
B	100	2	G	75	1
C	50	2	H	0	1
D	50	1	J	100	2
E	75	2	K	100	2

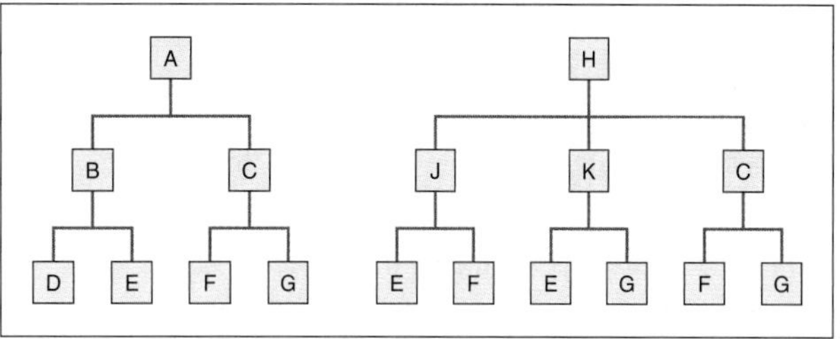

a) An indented bill of material for product A (see Figure 5.9 in Chapter 5 as an example of a BOM).
b) Net requirements for each part to produce 10 As in week 8 using lot-for-lot. Px

••• **14.15** You are product planner for product A (in Problem 14.14 and Figure 14.16). The field service manager, Al Trostel, has just called and told you that the requirements for B and F should each be increased by 10 units for his repair requirements in the field.

a) Prepare a list showing the quantity of each part required to produce the requirements for the service manager *and* the production request of 10 Bs and Fs.
b) Prepare a net requirement plan by date for the new requirements (for both production and field service), assuming that the field service manager wants his 10 units of B and F in week 6 and the 10 production units of A in week 8. Px

••• **14.16** You have just been notified via fax that the lead time for component G of product A (Problem 14.15 and Figure 14.16) has been increased to 4 weeks.

a) Which items have changed and why?
b) What are the implications for the production plan?
c) As production planner, what can you do? Px

Data Table for Problems 14.17 through 14.19*

Period	1	2	3	4	5	6	7	8	9	10	11	12
Gross requirements	30		40		30	70	20		10	80		50

*Holding cost = \$2.50/unit/week; setup cost = \$150; lead time = 1 week; beginning inventory = 40.

••• **14.17** Develop a lot-for-lot solution and calculate total relevant costs for the data in the preceding table. Px

••• **14.18** Develop an EOQ solution and calculate total relevant costs for the data in the preceding table. Stockout costs equal \$10 per unit. Px

••• **14.19** Develop a PPB solution and calculate total relevant costs for the data in the preceding table. Px

••• **14.20** Using the gross requirements schedule in Examples 4, 5, and 6 in the text, prepare an alternative ordering system that always orders 100 units the week prior to a shortage (a fixed order quantity of 100) with the same costs as in the example (setup at \$100 each, holding at \$1 per unit per period). What is the cost of this ordering system? Px

► **FIGURE 14.16**
Information for Problems 14.14, 14.15 and 14.16

Part	Inventory On Hand
A	0
B	2
C	10
D	5
E	4
F	5
G	1
H	10

PART STRUCTURE TREE

A LT = 1
LT = lead time in weeks
(1) = All quantities = 1
B(1) LT = 1
F(1) LT = 1
C(1) LT = 2
D(1) LT = 1
G(1) LT = 3
H(1) LT = 1
E(1) LT = 1
E(1) LT = 1
C(1) LT = 2

••• **14.21** Using the gross requirements schedule in Examples 4, 5, and 6 in the text, prepare an alternative ordering system that orders every 3 weeks for 3 weeks ahead (a periodic order quantity). Use the same costs as in the example (setup at $100 each, holding at $1 per unit per period). What is the cost of this ordering system? PX

••• **14.22** Using the gross requirements schedule in Examples 4, 5, and 6 in the text, prepare an alternative ordering system of your own design that uses the same cost as in the example (setup at $100 each, holding at $1 per unit per period). Can you do better than the costs shown in the text? What is the cost of your ordering system? PX

••• **14.23** Katharine Hepburn, Inc., has received the following orders:

Period	1	2	3	4	5	6	7	8	9	10
Order size	0	40	30	40	10	70	40	10	30	60

The entire fabrication for these units is scheduled on one machine. There are 2,250 usable minutes in a week, and each unit will take 65 minutes to complete. Develop a capacity plan, using lot splitting, for the 10-week time period.

••• **14.24** David Jurman, Ltd., has received the following orders:

Period	1	2	3	4	5	6	7	8	9	10
Order size	60	30	10	40	70	10	40	30	40	0

The entire fabrication for these units is scheduled on one machine. There are 2,250 usable minutes in a week, and each unit will take 65 minutes to complete. Develop a capacity plan, using lot splitting, for the 10-week time period.

•• **14.25** Heather Adams, production manager for a Colorado exercise equipment manufacturer, needs to schedule an order for 50 UltimaSteppers, which are to be shipped in week 8. Subscripts indicate quantity required for each parent. Assume lot-for-lot ordering. Below is information about the steppers:

Item	Lead time	On-Hand Inventory	Components
Stepper	2	20	$A_{(1)}, B_{(3)}, C_{(2)}$
A	1	10	$D_{(1)}, F_{(2)}$
B	2	30	$E_{(1)}, F_{(3)}$
C	3	10	$D_{(2)}, E_{(3)}$
D	1	15	
E	2	5	
F	2	20	

a) Develop a product structure for Heather.
b) Develop a time-phased structure.
c) Develop a net material requirements plan for F. PX

•••• **14.26** You are scheduling production of your popular Rustic Coffee Table. The table requires a top, four legs, $\frac{1}{8}$ gallon of stain, $\frac{1}{16}$ gallon of glue, 2 short braces between the legs and 2 long braces between the legs, and a brass cap that goes on the bottom of each leg. You have 100 gallons of glue in inventory, but none of the other components. All items except the brass caps, stain, and glue are ordered on a lot-for-lot basis. The caps are purchased in quantities of 1,000, stain and glue by the gallon. Lead time is 1 day for each item. Schedule the order releases necessary to produce 640 coffee tables on days 5 and 6, and 128 on days 7 and 8. PX

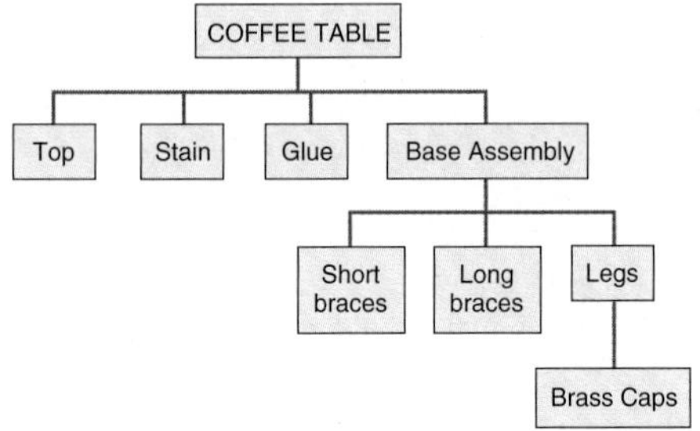

•••• **14.27** Using the data for the coffee table in Problem 14.26, build a labor schedule when the labor standard for each top is 2 labor hours; each leg including brass cap installation requires $\frac{1}{4}$ hour, as does each pair of braces. Base assembly requires 1 labor-hour, and final assembly requires 2 labor-hours. What is the total number of labor-hours required each day, and how many employees are needed each day at 8 hours per day?

▶ **Refer to myomlab for these additional homework problems: 14.28–14.32**

Case Studies

▶ Hill's Automotive, Inc.

Hill's Automotive, Inc., is an aftermarket producer and distributor of automotive replacement parts. Art Hill has slowly expanded the business, which began as a supplier of hard-to-get auto air-conditioning units for classic cars and hot rods. The firm has limited manufacturing capability, but a state-of-the-art MRP system and extensive inventory and assembly facilities. Components are purchased, assembled, and repackaged. Among its products are private-label air-conditioning, carburetors, and ignition kits. The downturn in the economy, particularly the company's discretionary segment, has put downward pressure on volume and margins. Profits have fallen considerably. In addition, customer service levels have declined, with late deliveries now exceeding 25% of orders. And to make matters worse, customer returns have been rising at a rate of 3% per month.

Wally Hopp, vice president of sales, claims that most of the problem lies with the assembly department. He says that although the firm has accurate bills of materials, indicating what goes into each product, it is not producing the proper mix of the product. He also believes the firm has poor quality control and low productivity, and as a result its costs are too high.

Melanie Thompson, treasurer, believes that problems are due to investing in the wrong inventories. She thinks that marketing has too many options and products. Melanie also thinks that purchasing department buyers have been hedging their inventories and requirements with excess purchasing commitments.

The assembly manager, Kalinga Jagoda, says, "The symptom is that we have a lot of parts in inventory, but no place to assemble them in the production schedule. When we have the right part, it is not very good, but we use it anyway to meet the schedule."

Marshall Fisher, manager of purchasing, has taken the stance that purchasing has not let Hill's Automotive down. He has stuck by his old suppliers, used historical data to determine requirements, maintained what he views as excellent prices from suppliers, and evaluated new sources of supply with a view toward lowering cost. Where possible, Marshall reacted to the increased pressure for profitability by emphasizing low cost and early delivery.

Discussion Question

1. Prepare a plan for Art Hill that gets the firm back on a course toward improved profitability. Be sure to identify the symptoms, the problems, and the specific changes you would implement.
2. Explain how MRP plays a role in this plan.

▶ MRP at Wheeled Coach

Video Case

Wheeled Coach, the world's largest manufacturer of ambulances, builds thousands of different and constantly changing configurations of its products. The custom nature of its business means lots of options and special designs—and a potential scheduling and inventory nightmare. Wheeled Coach addressed such problems, and succeeded in solving a lot of them, with an MRP system (described in the *Global Company Profile* that opens this chapter). As with most MRP installations, however, solving one set of problems uncovers a new set.

One of the new issues that had to be addressed by plant manager Lynn Whalen was newly discovered excess inventory. Managers discovered a substantial amount of inventory that was not called for in any finished products. Excess inventory was evident because of the new level of inventory accuracy required by the MRP system. The other reason was a new series of inventory reports generated by the IBM MAPICS MRP system purchased by Wheeled Coach. One of those reports indicates where items are used and is known as the "Where Used" report. Interestingly, many inventory items were not called out on bills-of-material (BOMs) for any current products. In some cases, the reason some parts were in the stockroom remained a mystery.

The discovery of this excess inventory led to renewed efforts to ensure that the BOMs were accurate. With substantial work, BOM accuracy increased and the number of engineering change notices (ECNs) decreased. Similarly, purchase-order accuracy, with regard to both part numbers and quantities ordered, was improved. Additionally, receiving department and stockroom accuracy went up, all helping to maintain schedule, costs, and ultimately, shipping dates and quality.

Eventually, Lynn Whalen concluded that the residual amounts of excess inventory were the result, at least in part, of rapid changes in ambulance design and technology. Another source was customer changes made after specifications had been determined and materials ordered. This latter excess occurs because, even though Wheeled Coach's own throughput time is only 17 days, many of the items that it purchases require much longer lead times.

Discussion Questions*

1. Why is accurate inventory such an important issue at Wheeled Coach?
2. Why does Wheeled Coach have excess inventory, and what kind of a plan would you suggest for dealing with it?
3. Be specific in your suggestions for reducing inventory and how to implement them.

*You may wish to view the video that accompanies this case before answering the questions.

▶**Additional Case Study:** Visit **www.myomlab.com** or **www.pearsonhighered.com/heizer** for this free case study:
Ikon's attempt at ERP: The giant office technology firm faces hurdles with ERP implementation.

Bibliography

Barba-Gutierrez, Y., B. Adenso-Diaz, and S. M. Gupta. "Lot Sizing in Reverse MRP for Scheduling Disassembly." *International Journal of Production Economics* 111, no. 2 (February 2008): 741.

Bell, Steve. "Time Fence Secrets." *APICS* 16, no. 4 (April 2006): 44–48.

Bolander, Steven, and Sam G. Taylor. "Scheduling Techniques: A Comparison of Logic." *Production and Inventory Management Journal* 41, no. 1 (1st Quarter 2000): 1–5.

Crandall, Richard E. "The Epic Life of ERP." *APICS* 16, no. 2 (February 2006): 17–19.

Gattiker, Thomas "Anatomy of an ERP Implementation Gone Awry." *Production and Inventory Management* 43, nos. 3–4 (3rd/4th Quarter 2002): 96–105.

Kanet, J., and V. Sridharan. "The Value of Using Scheduling Information in Planning Material Requirements." *Decision Sciences* 29, no. 2 (Spring 1998): 479–498.

Koh, S. C. L., and S. M. Saad. "Managing Uncertainty in ERP-controlled Manufacturing Environments." *International Journal of Production Economics* 101, no. 1 (May 2006): 109.

Krupp, James A. G. "Integrating Kanban and MRP to Reduce Lead Time." *Production and Inventory Management Journal* 43, no. 3–4 (3rd/4th quarter 2002): 78–82.

Lawrence, Barry F., Daniel F. Jennings, and Brian E. Reynolds. *ERP in Distribution.* Florence, KY: Thomson South-Western, (2005).

Moncrief, Stephen. "Push and Pull." *APICS—The Performance Advantage* (June 2003): 46–51.

Norris, G. *E-Business & ERP.* New York: Wiley (2005).

O' Sullivan, Jill, and Gene Caiola. *Enterprise Resource Planning,* 2nd ed. New York: McGraw-Hill (2008).

Segerstedt, A. "Master Production Scheduling and a Comparison of MRP and Cover-Time Planning." *International Journal of Production Research* 44, no. 18–19 (September 2006): 3585.

Summer, M. *Enterprise Resource Planning.* Upper Saddle River, NJ: Prentice Hall (2005).

Wagner, H. M., and T. M. Whitin. "Dynamic Version of the Economic Lot Size Model." *Management Science* 5, no. 1 (1958): 89–96.

Wu, Jen-Hur, et al. "Using Multiple Variables Decision-Making Analysis for ERP Selection." *International Journal of Manufacturing Technology and Management* 18, no. 2 (2009): 228.

Chapter 14 *Rapid* Review

Main Heading	Review Material	PEARSON myomlab
DEPENDENT DEMAND (p. 546)	Demand for items is *dependent* when the relationship between the items can be determined. For any product, all components of that product are dependent demand items. ■ **Material requirements planning (MRP)**—A dependent demand technique that uses a bill-of-material, inventory, expected receipts, and a master production schedule to determine material requirements.	**VIDEO 14.1** MRP at Wheeled Coach Ambulances
DEPENDENT INVENTORY MODEL REQUIREMENTS (pp. 546–551)	Dependent inventory models require that the operations manager know the: (1) Master production schedule; (2) Specifications or bill of material; (3) Inventory availability; (4) Purchase orders outstanding; and (5) Lead times ■ **Master production schedule (MPS)**—A timetable that specifies what is to be made and when. The MPS is a statement of *what is to be produced*, not a forecast of demand. ■ **Bill of material (BOM)**—A listing of the components, their description, and the quantity of each required to make one unit of a product. Items above any level in a BOM are called *parents*; items below any level are called *components*, or *children*. The top level in a BOM is the 0 level. ■ **Modular bills**—Bills of material organized by major subassemblies or by product options. ■ **Planning bills (or kits)**—A material grouping created in order to assign an artificial parent to a bill of material; also called "pseudo" bills. ■ **Phantom bills of material**—Bills of material for components, usually subassemblies, that exist only temporarily; they are never inventoried. ■ **Low-level coding**—A number that identifies items at the lowest level at which they occur. ■ **Lead time**—In purchasing systems, the time between recognition of the need for an order and receiving it; in production systems, it is the order, wait, move, queue, setup, and run times for each component. When a bill of material is turned on its side and modified by adding lead times for each component, it is called a *time-phased product structure*.	Problems: 14.1, 14.3 Virtual Office Hours for Solved Problem: 14.1
MRP STRUCTURE (pp. 551–555)	■ **Gross material requirements plan**—A schedule that shows the total demand for an item (prior to subtraction of on-hand inventory and scheduled receipts) and (1) when it must be ordered from suppliers, or (2) when production must be started to meet its demand by a particular date. ■ **Net material requirements**—The result of adjusting gross requirements for inventory on hand and scheduled receipts. ■ **Planned order receipt**—The quantity planned to be received at a future date. ■ **Planned order release**—The scheduled date for an order to be released. Net requirements = Gross requirements + Allocations − (On hand + Scheduled receipts)	Problems: 14.2, 14.4–14.8 Virtual Office Hours for Solved Problem: 14.2 **ACTIVE MODEL 14.1**
MRP MANAGEMENT (pp. 556–557)	■ **System nervousness**—Frequent changes in an MRP system. ■ **Time fences**—A means for allowing a segment of the master schedule to be designated as "not to be rescheduled." ■ **Pegging**—In material requirements planning systems, tracing upward the bill of material from the component to the parent item. Four approaches for integrating MRP and JIT are (1) finite capacity scheduling, (2) small buckets, (3) balanced flow, and (4) supermarkets. ■ **Buckets**—Time units in a material requirements planning system. Finite capacity scheduling (FCS) considers department and machine capacity. FCS provides the precise scheduling needed for rapid material movement. ■ **Bucketless system**—Time-phased data are referenced using dated records rather than defined time periods, or buckets. ■ **Back flush**—A system to reduce inventory balances by deducting everything in the bill of material on completion of the unit. ■ **Supermarket**—An inventory area that holds common items that are replenished by a kanban system.	
LOT-SIZING TECHNIQUES (pp. 557–561)	■ **Lot-sizing decision**—The process of, or techniques used in, determining lot size. ■ **Lot-for-lot**—A lot-sizing technique that generates exactly what is required to meet the plan. ■ **Part period balancing (PPB)**—An inventory ordering technique that balances setup and holding costs by changing the lot size to reflect requirements of the next lot size in the future.	Problems: 14.17–14.22

Main Heading	Review Material
	■ **Economic part period (EPP)**—A period of time when the ratio of setup cost to holding cost is equal. ■ **Wagner-Whitin procedure**—A technique for lot-size computation that assumes a finite time horizon beyond which there are no additional net requirements to arrive at an ordering strategy. In general, the lot-for-lot approach should be used whenever low-cost deliveries can be achieved.
EXTENSIONS OF MRP (pp. 561–564)	■ **Material requirements planning II (MRP II)**—A system that allows, with MRP in place, inventory data to be augmented by other resource variables; in this case, MRP becomes *material resource planning*. ■ **Closed-loop MRP system**—A system that provides feedback to the capacity plan, master production schedule, and production plan so planning can be kept valid at all times. ■ **Load report**—A report for showing the resource requirements in a work center for all work currently assigned there as well as all planned and expected orders. Tactics for smoothing the load and minimizing the impact of changed lead time include: *Overlapping*, *Operations splitting*, and *Order*, or, *lot splitting*.
MRP IN SERVICES (pp. 565–568)	■ **Distribution resource planning (DRP)**—A time-phased stock-replenishment plan for all levels of a distribution network.
ENTERPRISE RESOURCE PLANNING (ERP) (p. 568)	■ **Enterprise resource planning (ERP)**—An information system for identifying and planning the enterprise-wide resources needed to take, make, ship, and account for customer orders. In an ERP system, data are entered only once into a common, complete, and consistent database shared by all applications. ■ **Efficient consumer response (ECR)**—Supply-chain management systems in the grocery industry that tie sales to buying, to inventory, to logistics, and to production.

Self Test

■ **Before taking the self-test,** refer to the learning objectives listed at the beginning of the chapter and the key terms listed at the end of the chapter.

LO1. In a product structure diagram:
- **a)** parents are found only at the top level of the diagram.
- **b)** parents are found at every level in the diagram.
- **c)** children are found at every level of the diagram except the top level.
- **d)** all items in the diagrams are both parents and children.
- **e)** all of the above.

LO2. The difference between a gross material requirements plan (gross MRP) and a net material requirements plan (net MRP) is:
- **a)** the gross MRP may not be computerized, but the net MRP must be computerized.
- **b)** the gross MRP includes consideration of the inventory on hand, whereas the net MRP doesn't include the inventory consideration.
- **c)** the net MRP includes consideration of the inventory on hand, whereas the gross MRP doesn't include the inventory consideration.
- **d)** the gross MRP doesn't take taxes into account, whereas the net MRP includes the tax considerations.
- **e)** the net MRP is only an estimate, whereas the gross MRP is used for actual production scheduling.

LO3. Net requirements =
- **a)** Gross requirements + Allocations − On-hand inventory + Scheduled receipts.
- **b)** Gross requirements − Allocations − On-hand inventory − Scheduled receipts.
- **c)** Gross requirements − Allocations − On-hand inventory + Scheduled receipts.
- **d)** Gross requirements + Allocations − On-hand inventory − Scheduled receipts.

LO4. A lot-sizing procedure that assumes a finite time horizon beyond which there are no additional net requirements is:
- **a)** Wagner-Whitin algorithm.
- **b)** part period balancing.
- **c)** economic order quantity.
- **d)** all of the above.

LO5. MRP II stands for:
- **a)** material resource planning.
- **b)** management requirements planning.
- **c)** management resource planning.
- **d)** material revenue planning.
- **e)** material risk planning.

LO6. A(n) ________ MRP system provides information to the capacity plan, to the master production schedule, and ultimately to the production plan.
- **a)** dynamic
- **b)** closed-loop
- **c)** continuous
- **d)** retrospective
- **e)** introspective

LO7. Which system extends MRP II to tie in customers and suppliers?
- **a)** MRP III
- **b)** JIT
- **c)** IRP
- **d)** ERP
- **e)** Enhanced MRP II

Answers: LO1. c; LO2. c; LO3. d; LO4. a; LO5. a; LO6. b; LO7. d.

15 Short-Term Scheduling

Chapter Outline

OM Strategy Decisions

- Design of Goods and Services
- Managing Quality
- Process Strategy
- Location Strategies
- Layout Strategies
- Human Resources
- Supply-Chain Management
- Inventory Management
- **Scheduling**
  - Aggregate
  - Short-Term
- Maintenance

GLOBAL COMPANY PROFILE: DELTA AIR LINES

SCHEDULING AIRPLANES WHEN WEATHER IS THE ENEMY

Operations managers at airlines learn to expect the unexpected. Events that require rapid rescheduling are a regular part of life. Throughout the ordeals of tornadoes, ice storms, and snowstorms, airlines across the globe struggle to cope with delays, cancellations, and furious passengers. The inevitable changes to the schedule often create a ripple effect that impacts passengers at dozens of airports in the network. Close to 10% of Delta Air Lines's flights are disrupted in a typical year, half because of weather; the cost is $440 million in lost revenue, overtime pay, and food and lodging vouchers.

Now Delta is taking the sting out of the scheduling nightmares that come from weather-related problems with its $33-million high-tech nerve center adjacent to the Hartsfield-Jackson Atlanta International Airport. From computers to telecommunications systems to deicers, Delta's Operations Control Center more quickly

4 A.M.	**10 A.M.**	**1:30 P.M.**	**5 P.M.**	**10 P.M.**
FORECAST: Rain with a chance of light snow for Atlanta.	FORECAST: Freezing rain after 5 P.M.	FORECAST: Rain changing to snow.	FORECAST: Less snow than expected.	FORECAST: Snow tapering off.
ACTION: Discuss status of planes and possible need for cancellations.	ACTION: Ready deicing trucks; develop plans to cancel 50% to 80% of flights after 6 P.M.	ACTION: Cancel half the flights from 6 P.M. to 10 A.M.; notify passengers and reroute planes.	ACTION: Continue calling passengers and arrange alternate flights.	ACTION: Find hotels for 1,600 passengers stranded by the storm.

Here is what Delta officials had to do one December day when a storm bore down on Atlanta.

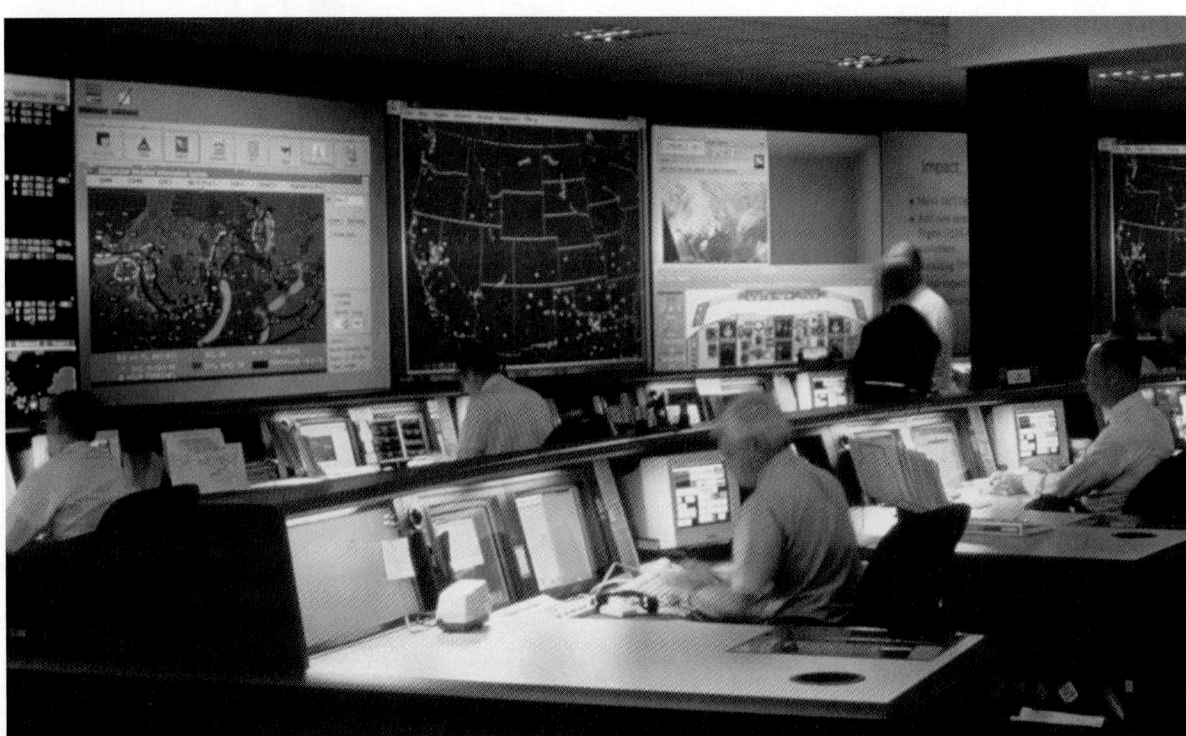

To improve flight rescheduling efforts, Delta employees monitor giant screens that display meteorological charts, weather patterns, and maps of Delta flights at its Operations Control Center in Atlanta.

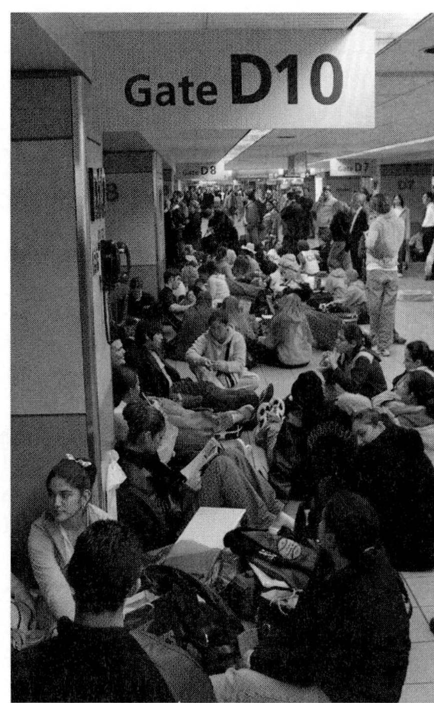

Weather-related disruptions can create major scheduling and expensive snow removal issues for airlines (left), just as they create major inconveniences for passengers (right).

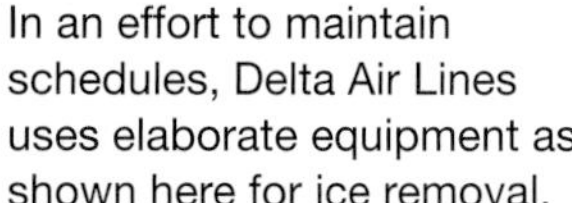
In an effort to maintain schedules, Delta Air Lines uses elaborate equipment as shown here for ice removal.

notifies customers of schedule changes, reroutes flights, and gets jets into the air. The Operations Control Center's job is to keep flights flowing as smoothly as possible in spite of the disruptions.

With earlier access to information, the center's staff of 18 pores over streams of data transmitted by computers and adjusts to changes quickly. Using mathematical scheduling models described in this chapter, Delta decides on schedule and route changes. This means coordinating incoming and outgoing aircraft, ensuring that the right crews are on hand, rescheduling connections to coordinate arrival times, and making sure information gets to passengers as soon as possible.

Delta's software, called the Inconvenienced Passenger Rebooking System, notifies passengers of cancellations or delays, and even books them onto rival airlines if necessary. With 150,000 passengers flying into and out of Atlanta every day, Delta estimates its scheduling efforts save $35 million a year.

Chapter 15 **Learning Objectives**

AUTHOR COMMENT Good scheduling means lower costs and faster and more dependable delivery.

THE IMPORTANCE OF SHORT-TERM SCHEDULING

Delta Air Lines doesn't schedule just its 753 aircraft every day. It also schedules over 10,000 pilots and flight attendants to accommodate passengers who wish to reach their destinations. This schedule, based on huge computer programs, plays a major role in satisfying customers. Delta finds competitive advantage with its flexibility for last-minute adjustments to demand and weather disruptions.

Manufacturing firms also make schedules that match production to customer demands. Lockheed Martin's Dallas plant schedules machines, tools, and people to make aircraft parts. Lockheed's mainframe computer downloads schedules for parts production into a flexible machining system (FMS) in which a manager makes the final scheduling decision. The FMS allows parts of many sizes or shapes to be made, in any order. This scheduling versatility results in parts produced on a just-in-time basis, with low setup times, little work-in-process, and high machine utilization. Efficient scheduling is how companies like Lockheed Martin meet due dates promised to customers and face time-based competition.

The strategic importance of scheduling is clear:

- Effective scheduling means faster movement of goods and services through a facility. This means greater use of assets and hence greater capacity per dollar invested, which, in turn, *lowers cost.*
- Added capacity, faster throughput, and the related flexibility mean better customer service through *faster delivery.*
- Good scheduling also contributes to realistic commitments and hence *dependable delivery.*

AUTHOR COMMENT Scheduling decisions range from years, for capacity planning, to minutes/hours/days, called short-term scheduling. This chapter focuses on the latter.

SCHEDULING ISSUES

Scheduling deals with the timing of operations. The types of scheduling decisions made in five organizations—a hospital, a college, a manufacturer, a restaurant, and an airline—are shown in Table 15.1. As you can see from Figure 15.1, a sequence of decisions affects scheduling. Schedule decisions begin with *capacity* planning, which involves *total facility and equipment resources available* (discussed in Chapter 7 and Supplement 7). **Capacity plans** are usually annual or quarterly as new equipment and facilities are purchased or discarded. **Aggregate planning** (Chapter 13) makes decisions regarding the use of facilities, inventory, people, and outside contractors. Aggregate plans are typically monthly, and *resources are allocated in terms of an aggregate measure such as total units, tons, or shop hours.* However, the **master schedule** breaks down the aggregate plan and develops a *schedule for specific products or product lines for each week.* **Short-term schedules** then translate capacity decisions, aggregate (intermediate) planning, and master schedules into job sequences and *specific assignments of personnel, materials, and machinery.* In this chapter, we describe the narrow issue of scheduling goods and services in the *short run* (that is, matching daily or hourly requirements to specific personnel and equipment).

LO1: Explain the relationship between short-term scheduling, capacity planning, aggregate planning, and a master schedule

The objective of scheduling is to allocate and prioritize demand (generated by either forecasts or customer orders) to available facilities. Two significant factors in achieving this allocation and prioritizing are (1) the type of scheduling, forward or backward, and (2) the criteria for priorities. We discuss these two topics next.

◀ **TABLE 15.1 Scheduling Decisions**

Organization	Managers Schedule the Following:
Arnold Palmer Hospital	Operating room use Patient admissions Nursing, security, maintenance staffs Outpatient treatments
University of Missouri	Classrooms and audiovisual equipment Student and instructor schedules Graduate and undergraduate courses
Lockheed Martin factory	Production of goods Purchases of materials Workers
Hard Rock Cafe	Chef, waiters, bartenders Delivery of fresh foods Entertainers Opening of dining areas
Delta Air Lines	Maintenance of aircraft Departure timetables Flight crews, catering, gate, and ticketing personnel

VIDEO 15.1 Scheduling at Hard Rock

▼ **FIGURE 15.1 The Relationship between Capacity Planning, Aggregate Planning, Master Schedule, and Short-Term Scheduling for a Bike Co.**

Capacity Planning
(Long term; years)
Changes in Facilities
Changes in Equipment
See Chapter 7 and Supplement 7

Capacity Plan for New Facilities
Adjust capacity to the demand suggested by strategic plan

Aggregate Planning
(Intermediate term; quarterly or monthly)
Facility utilization
Personnel changes
Subcontracting
See Chapter 13

Aggregate Production Plan for All Bikes
(Determine personnel or subcontracting necessary to match aggregate demand to existing facilities/capacity)

Month	1	2
Bike Production	800	850

Master Schedule
(Intermediate term; weekly)
Material requirements planning
Disaggregate the aggregate plan
See Chapters 13 and 14

Master Production Schedule for Bike Models
(Determine weekly capacity schedule)

	Month 1				Month 2			
Week	1	2	3	4	5	6	7	8
Model 22		200		200		200		200
Model 24	100		100		150		100	
Model 26	100		100		100		100	

Short-Term Scheduling
(Short term; days, hours, minutes)
Work center loading
Job sequencing/dispatching
See this chapter

Work Assigned to Specific Personnel and Work Centers
Make finite capacity schedule by matching specific tasks to specific people and machines

Assemble Model 22 in work center 6

Forward and Backward Scheduling

Scheduling involves assigning due dates to specific jobs, but many jobs compete simultaneously for the same resources. To help address the difficulties inherent in scheduling, we can categorize scheduling techniques as (1) forward scheduling and (2) backward scheduling.

Forward scheduling
Scheduling that begins the schedule as soon as the requirements are known.

Forward scheduling starts the schedule as soon as the job requirements are known. Forward scheduling is used in a variety of organizations such as hospitals, clinics, fine-dining restaurants, and machine tool manufacturers. In these facilities, jobs are performed to customer order, and delivery is often requested as soon as possible. Forward scheduling is usually designed to produce a schedule that can be accomplished even if it means not meeting the due date. In many instances, forward scheduling causes a buildup of work-in-process inventory.

Backward scheduling
Scheduling that begins with the due date and schedules the final operation first and the other job steps in reverse order.

Backward scheduling begins with the due date, scheduling the *final* operation first. Steps in the job are then scheduled, one at a time, in reverse order. By subtracting the lead time for each item, the start time is obtained. However, the resources necessary to accomplish the schedule may not exist. Backward scheduling is used in many manufacturing environments, as well as service environments such as catering a banquet or scheduling surgery. In practice, a combination of forward and backward scheduling is often used to find a reasonable trade-off between what can be achieved and customer due dates.

Machine breakdowns, absenteeism, quality problems, shortages, and other factors further complicate scheduling. (See the *OM in Action* box "Scheduling Workers Who Fall Asleep Is a Killer—Literally.") Consequently, assignment of a date does not ensure that the work will be performed according to the schedule. Many specialized techniques have been developed to aid in preparing reliable schedules.

Scheduling Criteria

The correct scheduling technique depends on the volume of orders, the nature of operations, and the overall complexity of jobs, as well as the importance placed on each of four criteria. These four criteria are:

1. *Minimize completion time:* This criterion is evaluated by determining the average completion time per job.
2. *Maximize utilization:* This is evaluated by determining the percent of the time the facility is utilized.
3. *Minimize work-in-process (WIP) inventory:* This is evaluated by determining the average number of jobs in the system. The relationship between the number of jobs in the system and WIP inventory will be high. Therefore, the fewer the number of jobs that are in the system, the lower the inventory.
4. *Minimize customer waiting time:* This is evaluated by determining the average number of late days.

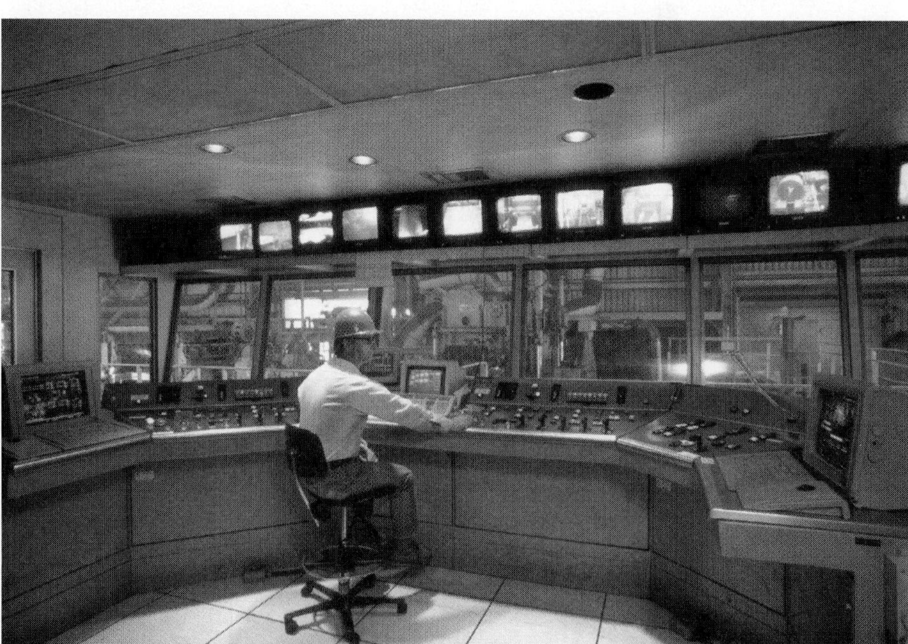

U.S. Steel maintains its world-class operation by automating the scheduling of people, machines, and tools through its cold-reduction-mill control room. Computerized scheduling software helps managers monitor production.

OM in Action ▶ Scheduling Workers Who Fall Asleep Is a Killer—Literally

The accidents at the nuclear plants at Three Mile Island, Pennsylvania, and Chernobyl, Russia, and the disaster at Bhopal, India, all had one thing in common: they occurred between midnight and 4:00 A.M. These facilities had other problems, but the need for sleep simply results in unreliable workplace performance. In some cases, unable to cope with a constantly changing work schedule, workers just plain fall asleep.

The same is true for pilots. Their inconsistent schedules and long flights often force them to snooze in the cockpit to get enough sleep. (Delta's flight from Atlanta to Mumbai, India, for example, takes about 18 hours.) The Bombardier regional jet flying from Honolulu to Hilo, Hawaii, encountered a serious problem in 2008 as it flew over Maui: both pilots were so fast asleep that they failed to respond to frantic calls from air-traffic controllers for 18 minutes. (The plane, with 40 passengers, overshot its destination as it flew 26 miles over the Pacific.) One FedEx pilot even complained of falling asleep while taxiing to take off.

Millions of people work in industries that maintain round-the-clock schedules. Employees from graveyard shifts report tales of seeing sleeping assembly-line workers fall off their stools, batches of defective parts sliding past dozing inspectors, and exhausted forklift operators crashing into walls. Virtually all shift workers are sleep deprived. And the National Highway Traffic Safety Administration indicates that drowsiness may be a factor in as many as 100,000 crashes annually.

Scheduling is a major problem in firms with 24/7 shifts, but some managers are taking steps to deal with schedule-related sleep problems among workers. Motorola, Dow Chemical, Detroit Edison, Pennzoil, and Exxon, for instance, all give workers several days off between shift changes.

Operations managers can make shift work less dangerous with shifts that do not exceed 12 hours, that encourage 8 hours of sleep each day, and that have extended time off between shift changes. As more is learned about the economic toll of non-daytime schedules and changing schedules, companies are learning to improve scheduling.

Sources: The Wall Street Journal (September 12, 2008): A1, A14 and (October 25, 2009): A:1; and *Air Safety and Health* (January 2004): 14.

These four criteria are used in this chapter, as they are in industry, to evaluate scheduling performance. In addition, good scheduling approaches should be simple, clear, easily understood, easy to carry out, flexible, and realistic.

Table 15.2 provides an overview of different processes and approaches to scheduling.

We now examine scheduling in process-focused facilities, in repetitive facilities, and in the service sector.

SCHEDULING PROCESS-FOCUSED FACILITIES

AUTHOR COMMENT The facilities discussed here are built around processes.

Process-focused facilities (also known as *intermittent* or *job-shop facilities*),[1] as we see in Table 15.2, are high-variety, low-volume systems commonly found in manufacturing and service organizations. These are production systems in which products are made to order. Items made under this system usually differ considerably in terms of materials used, order of processing, processing requirements, time of processing, and setup requirements. Because of these differences, scheduling can be complex. To run a facility in a balanced and efficient manner, the manager needs a production planning and control system. This system should:

- Schedule incoming orders without violating capacity constraints of individual work centers.
- Check the availability of tools and materials before releasing an order to a department.
- Establish due dates for each job and check progress against need dates and order lead times.
- Check work in progress as jobs move through the shop.
- Provide feedback on plant and production activities.
- Provide work efficiency statistics and monitor operator times for payroll and labor distribution analyses.

[1]Much of the literature on scheduling is about manufacturing; therefore, the traditional term *job-shop scheduling* is often used.

▶ TABLE 15.2 Different Processes Suggest Different Approaches to Scheduling

Process-focused facilities (job shops)
- Focus is on generating a forward-looking schedule.
- MRP generates due dates that are refined with finite capacity scheduling techniques.
- *Examples:* foundries, machine shops, cabinet shops, print shops, many restaurants, and the fashion industry.

Work cells (focused facilities that process families of similar components)
- Focus is on generating a forward-looking schedule.
- MRP generates due dates, and subsequent detail scheduling/dispatching is done at the work cell with kanbans and priority rules.
- *Examples:* work cells at ambulance manufacturer Wheeled Coach, aircraft engine rebuilder Standard Aero, greeting-card maker Hallmark.

Repetitive facilities (assembly lines)
- Focus is on generating a forward-looking schedule that is achieved by balancing the line with traditional assembly-line techniques.
- Pull techniques, such as JIT and kanban, signal component scheduling to support the assembly line.
- Challenging scheduling problems typically occur only when the process is new or when products or models change.
- *Examples:* assembly lines for a wide variety of products from autos to home appliances and computers.

Product-focused facilities (continuous)
- Focus is on generating a forward-looking schedule that can meet a reasonably stable demand with the existing fixed capacity.
- Capacity in such facilities is usually limited by long-term capital investment.
- Capacity is usually known, as is the setup and run time for the limited range of products.
- *Examples:* facilities with very high volume production and limited-variety products such as paper on huge machines at International Paper, beer in a brewery at Anheuser-Busch, or rolled steel in a Nucor plant.

Whether the scheduling system is manual or automated, it must be accurate and relevant. This means it requires a production database with both planning and control files. Three types of **planning files** are:

1. An *item master file*, which contains information about each component the firm produces or purchases.
2. A *routing file*, which indicates each component's flow through the shop.
3. A *work-center master file*, which contains information about the work center, such as capacity and efficiency.

Control files track the actual progress made against the plan for each work order.

LOADING JOBS

Loading
The assigning of jobs to work or processing centers.

Loading means the assignment of jobs to work or processing centers. Operations managers assign jobs to work centers so that costs, idle time, or completion times are kept to a minimum. Loading work centers takes two forms.[2] One is oriented to capacity; the second is related to assigning specific jobs to work centers.

First, we examine loading from the perspective of capacity via a technique known as *input–output* control. Then, we present two approaches used for loading: *Gantt charts* and the *assignment method* of linear programming.

Input–Output Control

Many firms have difficulty scheduling (that is, achieving effective throughput) because they overload the production processes. This often occurs because they do not know actual performance in the work centers. Effective scheduling depends on matching the schedule to performance. Lack of knowledge about capacity and performance causes reduced throughput.

Input–output control
A system that allows operations personnel to manage facility work flows by tracking work added to a work center and its work completed.

Input–output control is a technique that allows operations personnel to manage facility work flows. If the work is arriving faster than it is being processed, the facility is overloaded, and a backlog develops. Overloading causes crowding in the facility, leading to inefficiencies and quality problems. If the work is arriving at a slower rate than jobs are being performed, the facility is

[2]Note that this discussion can apply to facilities that might be called a "shop" in a manufacturing firm, a "unit" in a hospital, or a "department" in an office or a large kitchen.

underloaded, and the work center may run out of work. Underloading the facility results in idle capacity and wasted resources. Example 1 shows the use of input–output controls.

◄ EXAMPLE 1

Input-output control

DNC Machining, Inc., manufactures driveway security fences and gates. It wants to develop an input–output control report for the aluminum machining work center for 5 weeks (weeks 6/6 through 7/4). The planned input is 280 standard hours per week. The actual input is close to this figure, varying between 250 and 285. Output is scheduled at 320 standard hours, which is the assumed capacity. A backlog exists in the work center.

APPROACH ► DNC uses schedule information to create Figure 15.2, which monitors the workload-capacity relationship at the work center.

SOLUTION ► The deviations between scheduled input and actual output are shown in Figure 15.2. Actual output (270 hours) is substantially less than planned. Therefore, neither the input plan nor the output plan is being achieved.

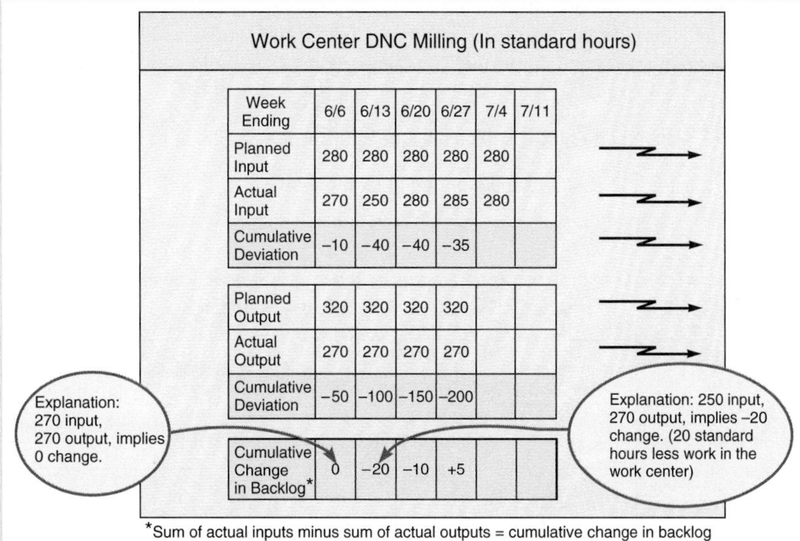

Work Center DNC Milling (In standard hours)

Week Ending	6/6	6/13	6/20	6/27	7/4	7/11
Planned Input	280	280	280	280	280	
Actual Input	270	250	280	285	280	
Cumulative Deviation	–10	–40	–40	–35		
Planned Output	320	320	320	320		
Actual Output	270	270	270	270		
Cumulative Deviation	–50	–100	–150	–200		
Cumulative Change in Backlog*	0	–20	–10	+5		

Explanation: 270 input, 270 output, implies 0 change.
Explanation: 250 input, 270 output, implies –20 change. (20 standard hours less work in the work center)

*Sum of actual inputs minus sum of actual outputs = cumulative change in backlog

◄ FIGURE 15.2
Input–Output Control

INSIGHT ► The backlog of work in this work center has actually increased by 5 hours by week 6/27. This increases work-in-process inventory, complicating the scheduling task and indicating the need for manager action.

LEARNING EXERCISE ► If actual output for the week of 6/27 was 275 (instead of 270), what changes? [Answer: Output cumulative deviation now is –195, and cumulative change in backlog is 0.]

RELATED PROBLEM ► 15.21

Input–output control can be maintained by a system of **ConWIP cards**, which control the amount of work in a work center. ConWIP is an acronym for *constant work-in-process*. The ConWIP card travels with a job (or batch) through the work center. When the job is finished, the card is released and returned to the initial workstation, authorizing the entry of a new batch into the work center. The ConWIP card effectively limits the amount of work in the work center, controls lead time, and monitors the backlog.

ConWIP cards
Cards that control the amount of work in a work center, aiding input–output control.

The options available to operations personnel to manage facility work flow include the following:

1. Correcting performances
2. Increasing capacity
3. Increasing or reducing input to the work center by (a) routing work to or from other work centers, (b) increasing or decreasing subcontracting, (c) producing less (or producing more)

Producing less is not a popular solution, but the advantages can be substantial. First, customer-service levels may improve because units may be produced on time. Second, efficiency may actually improve because there is less work in process cluttering the work center and adding to overhead costs. Third, quality may improve because less work-in-process hides fewer problems.

Gantt Charts

Gantt charts
Planning charts used to schedule resources and allocate time.

Gantt charts are visual aids that are useful in loading and scheduling. The name is derived from Henry Gantt, who developed them in the late 1800s. The charts show the use of resources, such as work centers and labor.

When used in *loading*, Gantt charts show the loading and idle times of several departments, machines, or facilities. They display the relative workloads in the system so that the manager knows what adjustments are appropriate. For example, when one work center becomes overloaded, employees from a low-load center can be transferred temporarily to increase the workforce. Or if waiting jobs can be processed at different work centers, some jobs at high-load centers can be transferred to low-load centers. Versatile equipment may also be transferred among centers. Example 2 illustrates a simple Gantt load chart.

EXAMPLE 2 ▶

Gantt load chart

A New Orleans washing machine manufacturer accepts special orders for machines to be used in such unique facilities as submarines, hospitals, and large industrial laundries. The production of each machine requires varying tasks and durations. The company wants to build a load chart for the week of March 8.

APPROACH ▶ The Gantt chart is selected as the appropriate graphical tool.

SOLUTION ▶ Figure 15.3 shows the completed Gantt chart.

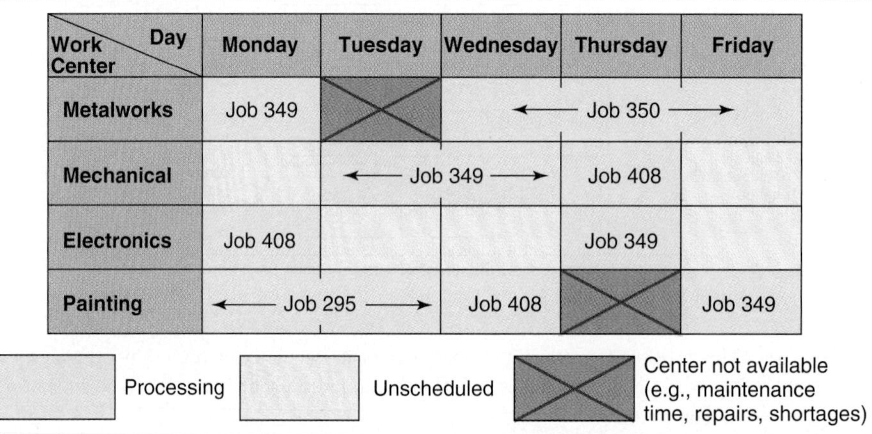

Work Center
Day
Monday
Tuesday
Wednesday
Thursday
Friday
Metalworks
Job 349
Job 350
Mechanical
Job 349
Job 408
Electronics
Job 408
Job 349
Painting
Job 295
Job 408
Job 349
Processing
Unscheduled
Center not available (e.g., maintenance time, repairs, shortages)

▶ FIGURE 15.3
Gantt Load Chart for the Week of March 8

INSIGHT ▶ The four work centers process several jobs during the week. This particular chart indicates that the metalworks and painting centers are completely loaded for the entire week. The mechanical and electronic centers have some idle time scattered during the week. We also note that the metalworks center is unavailable on Tuesday, and the painting center is unavailable on Thursday, perhaps for preventive maintenance.

LEARNING EXERCISE ▶ What impact results from the electronics work center closing on Tuesday for preventive maintenance? [Answer: none.]

RELATED PROBLEM ▶ 15.1b

LO2: Draw Gantt loading and scheduling charts

The Gantt *load chart* has a major limitation: It does not account for production variability such as unexpected breakdowns or human errors that require reworking a job. Consequently, the chart must also be updated regularly to account for new jobs and revised time estimates.

A Gantt *schedule chart* is used to monitor jobs in progress (and is also used for project scheduling). It indicates which jobs are on schedule and which are ahead of or behind schedule. In practice, many versions of the chart are found. The schedule chart in Example 3 places jobs in progress on the vertical axis and time on the horizontal axis.

EXAMPLE 3
Gantt scheduling chart

First Printing in Winter Park, Florida, wants to use a Gantt chart to show the scheduling of three orders, jobs A, B, and C.

APPROACH ▶ In Figure 15.4, each pair of brackets on the time axis denotes the estimated starting and finishing of a job enclosed within it. The solid bars reflect the actual status or progress of the job. We are just finishing day 5.

SOLUTION ▶

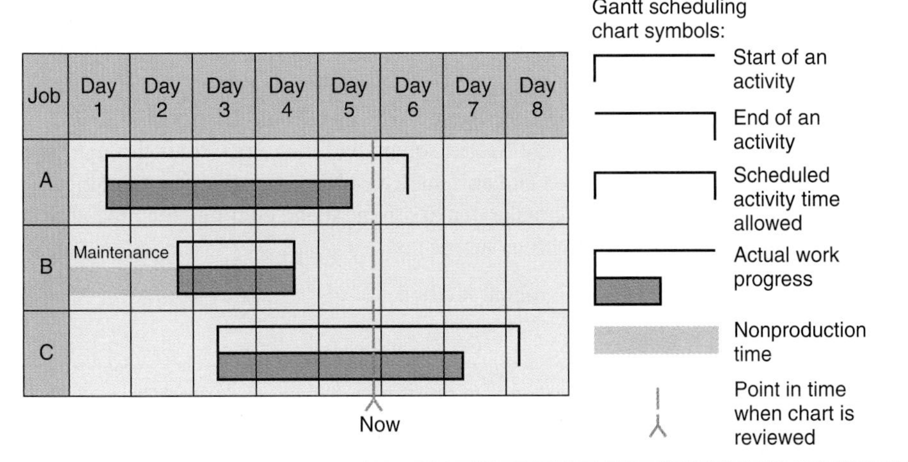

◀ **FIGURE 15.4**
Gantt Scheduling Chart for Jobs A, B, and C at a Printing Firm

INSIGHT ▶ Figure 15.4 illustrates that job A is about a half-day behind schedule at the end of day 5. Job B was completed after equipment maintenance. We also see that job C is ahead of schedule.

LEARNING EXERCISE ▶ Redraw the Gantt chart to show that job A is a half-day *ahead* of schedule. [Answer: The orangish bar now extends all the way to the end of the activity.]

RELATED PROBLEMS ▶ 15.1a, 15.2

Assignment Method

The **assignment method** involves assigning tasks or jobs to resources. Examples include assigning jobs to machines, contracts to bidders, people to projects, and salespeople to territories. The objective is most often to minimize total costs or time required to perform the tasks at hand. One important characteristic of assignment problems is that only one job (or worker) is assigned to one machine (or project).

Assignment method
A special class of linear programming models that involves assigning tasks or jobs to resources.

Each assignment problem uses a table. The numbers in the table will be the costs or times associated with each particular assignment. For example, if First Printing has three available typesetters (A, B, and C) and three new jobs to be completed, its table might appear as follows. The dollar entries represent the firm's estimate of what it will cost for each job to be completed by each typesetter.

LO3: Apply the assignment method for loading jobs

	Typesetter		
Job	**A**	**B**	**C**
R-34	\$11	\$14	\$ 6
S-66	\$ 8	\$10	\$11
T-50	\$ 9	\$12	\$ 7

The assignment method involves adding and subtracting appropriate numbers in the table to find the lowest *opportunity cost*[3] for each assignment. There are four steps to follow:

1. Subtract the smallest number in each row from every number in that row and then, from the resulting matrix, subtract the smallest number in each column from every number in that

[3]Opportunity costs are those profits forgone or not obtained.

column. This step has the effect of reducing the numbers in the table until a series of zeros, meaning *zero opportunity costs*, appear. Even though the numbers change, this reduced problem is equivalent to the original one, and the same solution will be optimal.

2. Draw the minimum number of vertical and horizontal straight lines necessary to cover all zeros in the table. If the number of lines equals either the number of rows or the number of columns in the table, then we can make an optimal assignment (see step 4). If the number of lines is less than the number of rows or columns, we proceed to step 3.
3. Subtract the smallest number not covered by a line from every other uncovered number. Add the same number to any number(s) lying at the intersection of any two lines. Do not change the value of the numbers that are covered by only one line. Return to step 2 and continue until an optimal assignment is possible.
4. Optimal assignments will always be at zero locations in the table. One systematic way of making a valid assignment is first to select a row or column that contains only one zero square. We can make an assignment to that square and then draw lines through its row and column. From the uncovered rows and columns, we choose another row or column in which there is only one zero square. We make that assignment and continue the procedure until we have assigned each person or machine to one task.

Example 4 shows how to use the assignment method.

EXAMPLE 4 ▶

Assignment method

AUTHOR COMMENT
You can also tackle assignment problems with our Excel OM or POM software or with Excel's Solver add-in.

First Printing wants to find the minimum total cost assignment of 3 jobs to 3 typesetters.

APPROACH ▶ The cost table shown earlier in this section is repeated here, and steps 1 through 4 are applied.

JOB \ TYPESETTER	A	B	C
R-34	$11	$14	$ 6
S-66	$ 8	$10	$11
T-50	$ 9	$12	$ 7

SOLUTION ▶

STEP 1A: Using the previous table, subtract the smallest number in each row from every number in the row. The result is shown in the table on the left.

JOB \ TYPESETTER	A	B	C
R-34	5	8	0
S-66	0	2	3
T-50	2	5	0

JOB \ TYPESETTER	A	B	C
R-34	5	6	0
S-66	0	0	3
T-50	2	3	0

STEP 1B: Using the above left table, subtract the smallest number in each column from every number in the column. The result is shown in the table on the right.

STEP 2: Draw the minimum number of vertical and horizontal straight lines needed to cover all zeros. Because two lines suffice, the solution is not optimal.

JOB \ TYPESETTER	A	B	C
R-34	5	6	0
S-66	0	0	3
T-50	(2)	3	0

Smallest uncovered number

STEP 3: Subtract the smallest uncovered number (2 in this table) from every other uncovered number and add it to numbers at the intersection of two lines.

JOB \ TYPESETTER	A	B	C
R-34	3	4	0
S-66	0	0	5
T-50	0	1	0

Return to step 2. Cover the zeros with straight lines again.

JOB \ TYPESETTER	A	B	C
R-34	3	4	0
S-66	0	0	
T-50	0	1	0

Because three lines are necessary, an optimal assignment can be made (see step 4). Assign R-34 to person C, S-66 to person B, and T-50 to person A. Referring to the original cost table, we see that:

$$\text{Minimum cost} = \$6 + \$10 + \$9 = \$25$$

INSIGHT ▶ If we had assigned S-66 to typesetter A, we could not assign T-50 to a zero location.

LEARNING EXERCISE ▶ If it costs $10 for Typesetter C to complete Job R-34 (instead of $6), how does the solution change? [Answer: R-34 to A, S-66 to B, T-50 to C: cost = $28.]

RELATED PROBLEMS ▶ 15.3, 15.4, 15.5, 15.6, 15.7, 15.8, 15.9

EXCEL OM Data File **Ch15Ex4.xls** can be found at **www.pearsonhighered.com/heizer**.

Some assignment problems entail *maximizing* profit, effectiveness, or payoff of an assignment of people to tasks or of jobs to machines. An equivalent minimization problem can be obtained by converting every number in the table to an *opportunity loss*. To convert a maximizing problem to an equivalent minimization problem, we create a minimizing table by subtracting every number in the original payoff table from the largest single number in that table. We then proceed to step 1 of the four-step assignment method. Minimizing the opportunity loss produces the same assignment solution as the original maximization problem.

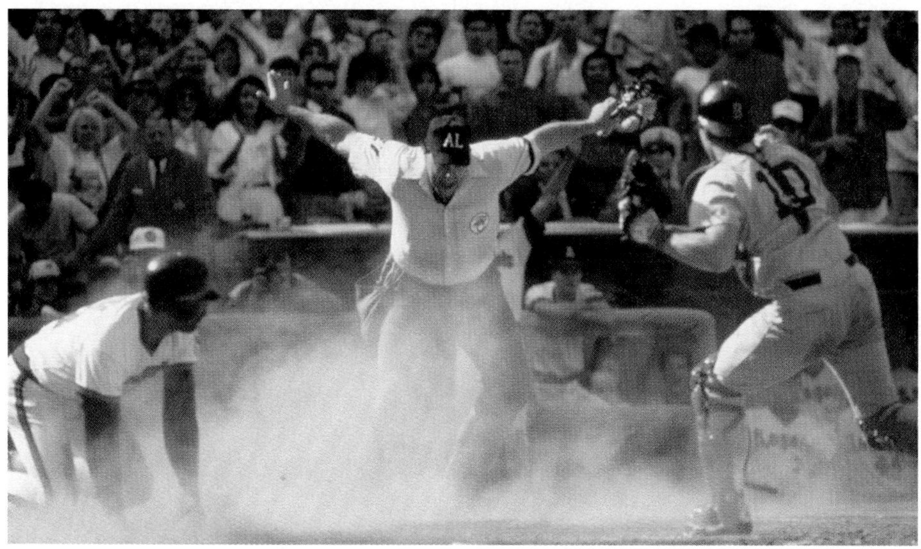

The problem of scheduling major league baseball umpiring crews from one series of games to the next is complicated by many restrictions on travel, ranging from coast-to-coast time changes, airline flight schedules, and night games running late. The league strives to achieve these two conflicting objectives: (1) balance crew assignments relatively evenly among all teams over the course of a season and (2) minimize travel costs. Using the assignment problem formulation, the time it takes the league to generate a schedule has been significantly decreased, and the quality of the schedule has improved.

AUTHOR COMMENT
Once jobs are loaded, managers must decide the sequence in which they are to be completed.

Sequencing
Determining the order in which jobs should be done at each work center.

Priority rules
Rules used to determine the sequence of jobs in process-oriented facilities.

First come, first served (FCFS)
Jobs are completed in the order they arrived.

Shortest processing time (SPT)
Jobs with the shortest processing times are assigned first.

Earliest due date (EDD)
Earliest due date jobs are performed first.

Longest processing time (LPT)
Jobs with the longest processing time are completed first.

SEQUENCING JOBS

Scheduling provides a basis for assigning jobs to work centers. *Loading* is a capacity-control technique that highlights overloads and underloads. **Sequencing** (also referred to as dispatching) specifies the order in which jobs should be done at each center. For example, suppose that 10 patients are assigned to a medical clinic for treatment. In what order should they be treated? Should the first patient to be served be the one who arrived first or the one who needs emergency treatment? Sequencing methods provide such guidelines. These methods are referred to as priority rules for sequencing or dispatching jobs to work centers.

Priority Rules for Dispatching Jobs

Priority rules provide guidelines for the sequence in which jobs should be worked. The rules are especially applicable for process-focused facilities such as clinics, print shops, and manufacturing job shops. We will examine a few of the most popular priority rules. Priority rules try to minimize completion time, number of jobs in the system, and job lateness while maximizing facility utilization.

The most popular priority rules are:

- **FCFS: first come, first served.** The first job to arrive at a work center is processed first.
- **SPT: shortest processing time.** The shortest jobs are handled first and completed.
- **EDD: earliest due date.** The job with the earliest due date is selected first.
- **LPT: longest processing time.** The longer, bigger jobs are often very important and are selected first.

Example 5 compares these rules.

EXAMPLE 5 ▶
Priority rules for dispatching

Five architectural rendering jobs are waiting to be assigned at Avanti Sethi Architects. Their work (processing) times and due dates are given in the following table. The firm wants to determine the sequence of processing according to (1) FCFS, (2) SPT, (3) EDD, and (4) LPT rules. Jobs were assigned a letter in the order they arrived.

Job	Job Work (Processing) Time (Days)	Job Due Date (Days)
A	6	8
B	2	6
C	8	18
D	3	15
E	9	23

APPROACH ▶ Each of the four priority rules is examined in turn. Four measures of effectiveness can be computed for each rule and then compared to see which rule is best for the company.

SOLUTION ▶

1. The *FCFS* sequence shown in the next table is simply A–B–C–D–E. The "flow time" in the system for this sequence measures the time each job spends waiting plus time being processed. Job B, for example, waits 6 days while job A is being processed, then takes 2 more days of operation time itself; so it will be completed in 8 days—which is 2 days later than its due date.

Job Sequence	Job Work (Processing) Time	Flow Time	Job Due Date	Job Lateness
A	6	6	8	0
B	2	8	6	2
C	8	16	18	0
D	3	19	15	4
E	9	28	23	5
	28	77		11

The first-come, first-served rule results in the following measures of effectiveness:

a. Average completion time $= \dfrac{\text{Sum of total flow time}}{\text{Number of jobs}}$

$= \dfrac{77 \text{ days}}{5} = 15.4 \text{ days}$

b. Utilization metric $= \dfrac{\text{Total job work (processing) time}}{\text{Sum of total flow time}}$

$= \dfrac{28}{77} = 36.4\%$

c. Average number of jobs in the system $= \dfrac{\text{Sum of total flow time}}{\text{Total job work (processing) time}}$

$= \dfrac{77 \text{ days}}{28 \text{ days}} = 2.75 \text{ jobs}$

d. Average job lateness $= \dfrac{\text{Total late days}}{\text{Number of jobs}} = \dfrac{11}{5} = 2.2 \text{ days}$

2. The *SPT* rule shown in the next table results in the sequence B–D–A–C–E. Orders are sequenced according to processing time, with the highest priority given to the shortest job.

Job Sequence	Job Work (Processing) Time	Flow Time	Job Due Date	Job Lateness
B	2	2	6	0
D	3	5	15	0
A	6	11	8	3
C	8	19	18	1
E	9	28	23	5
	28	65		9

Measurements of effectiveness for SPT are:

a. Average completion time $= \dfrac{65}{3} = 13 \text{ days}$

b. Utilization metric $= \dfrac{28}{65} = 43.1\%$

c. Average number of jobs in the system $= \dfrac{65}{28} = 2.32 \text{ jobs}$

d. Average job lateness $= \dfrac{9}{5} = 1.8 \text{ days}$

3. The *EDD* rule shown in the next table gives the sequence B–A–D–C–E. Note that jobs are ordered by earliest due date first.

Job Sequence	Job Work (Processing) Time	Flow Time	Job Due Date	Job Lateness
B	2	2	6	0
A	6	8	8	0
D	3	11	15	0
C	8	19	18	1
E	9	28	23	5
	28	68		6

LO4: Name and describe each of the priority sequencing rules

Measurements of effectiveness for EDD are:

a. Average completion time $= \dfrac{68}{5} = 13.6 \text{ days}$

b. Utilization metric $= \dfrac{28}{68} = 41.2\%$

c. Average number of jobs in the system $= \dfrac{68}{28} = 2.43 \text{ jobs}$

d. Average job lateness $= \dfrac{6}{5} = 1.2 \text{ days}$

4. The *LPT* rule shown in the next table results in the order E–C–A–D–B.

Job Sequence	Job Work (Processing) Time	Flow Time	Job Due Date	Job Lateness
E	9	9	23	0
C	8	17	18	0
A	6	23	8	15
D	3	26	15	11
B	2	28	6	22
	28	103		48

Measures of effectiveness for LPT are:

a. Average completion time $= \frac{103}{5} = 20.6$ days

b. Utilization metric $= \frac{28}{103} = 27.2\%$

c. Average number of jobs in the system $= \frac{103}{28} = 3.68$ jobs

d. Average job lateness $= \frac{48}{5} = 9.6$ days

The results of these four rules are summarized in the following table:

Rule	Average Completion Time (Days)	Utilization Metric (%)	Average Number of Jobs in System	Average Lateness (Days)
FCFS	15.4	36.4	2.75	2.2
SPT	13.0	43.1	2.32	1.8
EDD	13.6	41.2	2.43	1.2
LPT	20.6	27.2	3.68	9.6

INSIGHT ▶ LPT is the least effective measurement for sequencing for the Avanti Sethi firm. SPT is superior in 3 measures, and EDD is superior in the fourth (average lateness).

LEARNING EXERCISE ▶ If job A takes 7 days (instead of 6), how do the 4 measures of effectiveness change under the FCFS rule? [Answer: 16.4 days, 35.4%, 2.83 jobs, 2.8 days late.]

RELATED PROBLEMS ▶ 15.10, 15.12a–d, 15.13, 15.14

EXCEL OM Data File **Ch15Ex5.xls** can be found at **www.pearsonhighered.com/heizer.**

ACTIVE MODEL 15.1 This example is further illustrated in Active Model 15.1 at **www.pearsonhighered.com/heizer.**

The results in Example 5 are typically true in the real world also. No one sequencing rule always excels on all criteria. Experience indicates the following:

1. **Shortest processing time** is generally the best technique for minimizing job flow and minimizing the average number of jobs in the system. Its chief disadvantage is that long-duration jobs may be continuously pushed back in priority in favor of short-duration jobs. Customers may view this dimly, and a periodic adjustment for longer jobs must be made.
2. **First come, first served** does not score well on most criteria (but neither does it score particularly poorly). It has the advantage, however, of appearing fair to customers, which is important in service systems.
3. **Earliest due date** minimizes maximum tardiness, which may be necessary for jobs that have a very heavy penalty after a certain date. In general, EDD works well when lateness is an issue.

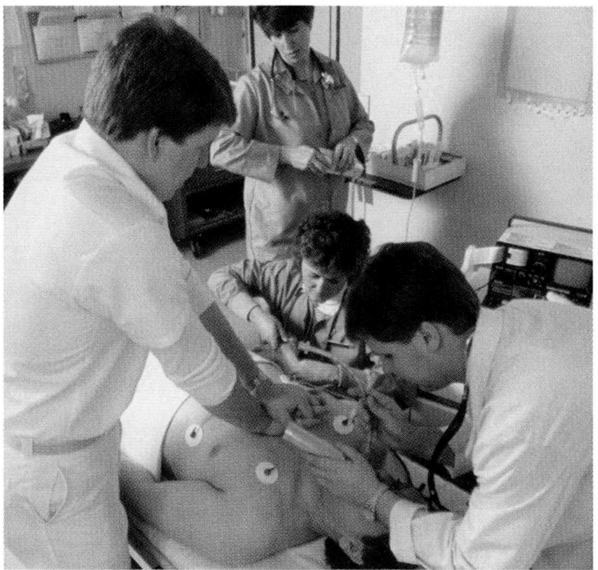

Your doctor may use a first-come, first-served priority rule satisfactorily. However, such a rule may be less than optimal for this emergency room. What priority rule might be best, and why? What priority rule is often used on TV hospital dramas?

Critical Ratio

Another type of sequencing rule is the critical ratio. The **critical ratio (CR)** is an index number computed by dividing the time remaining until due date by the work time remaining. As opposed to the priority rules, critical ratio is dynamic and easily updated. It tends to perform better than FCFS, SPT, EDD, or LPT on the average job-lateness criterion.

Critical ratio (CR)
A sequencing rule that is an index number computed by dividing the time remaining until due date by the work time remaining.

The critical ratio gives priority to jobs that must be done to keep shipping on schedule. A job with a low critical ratio (less than 1.0) is one that is falling behind schedule. If CR is exactly 1.0, the job is on schedule. A CR greater than 1.0 means the job is ahead of schedule and has some slack.

The formula for critical ratio is:

$$CR = \frac{\text{Time remaining}}{\text{Workdays remaining}} = \frac{\text{Due date} - \text{Today's date}}{\text{Work (lead) time remaining}}$$

Example 6 shows how to use the critical ratio.

EXAMPLE 6
Critical ratio

Today is day 25 on Zyco Medical Testing Laboratories' production schedule. Three jobs are on order, as indicated here:

Job	Due Date	Workdays Remaining
A	30	4
B	28	5
C	27	2

APPROACH ▶ Zyco wants to compute the critical ratios, using the formula for CR.

SOLUTION ▶

Job	Critical Ratio	Priority Order
A	$(30 - 25)/4 = 1.25$	3
B	$(28 - 25)/5 = .60$	1
C	$(27 - 25)/2 = 1.00$	2

INSIGHT ▶ Job B has a critical ratio of less than 1, meaning it will be late unless expedited. Thus, it has the highest priority. Job C is on time and job A has some slack. Once job B has been completed, we would recompute the critical ratios for jobs A and C to determine whether their priorities have changed.

LEARNING EXERCISE ▶ Today is day 24 (a day earlier) on Zyco's schedule. Recompute the CRs and determine the priorities. [Answer: 1.5, 0.8, 1.5; B is still number 1, but now jobs A and C are tied for second.]

RELATED PROBLEMS ▶ 15.11, 15.12e, 15.16

In most production scheduling systems, the critical-ratio rule can help do the following:

1. Determine the status of a specific job.
2. Establish relative priority among jobs on a common basis.
3. Relate both make-to-stock and make-to-order jobs on a common basis.
4. Adjust priorities (and revise schedules) automatically for changes in both demand and job progress.
5. Dynamically track job progress.

Sequencing *N* Jobs on Two Machines: Johnson's Rule

The next step in complexity is the case in which *N* jobs (where *N* is 2 or more) must go through two different machines or work centers in the same order. This is called the *N*/2 problem.

Johnson's rule
An approach that minimizes processing time for sequencing a group of jobs through two work centers while minimizing total idle time in the work centers.

Johnson's rule can be used to minimize the processing time for sequencing a group of jobs through two work centers. It also minimizes total idle time on the machines. *Johnson's rule* involves four steps:

1. All jobs are to be listed, and the time that each requires on a machine is to be shown.
2. Select the job with the shortest activity time. If the shortest time lies with the first machine, the job is scheduled first. If the shortest time lies with the second machine, schedule the job last. Ties in activity times can be broken arbitrarily.
3. Once a job is scheduled, eliminate it.
4. Apply Steps 2 and 3 to the remaining jobs, working toward the center of the sequence.

Example 7 shows how to apply Johnson's rule.

EXAMPLE 7 ▶
Johnson's rule

Five specialty jobs at a La Crosse, Wisconsin, tool and die shop must be processed through two work centers (drill press and lathe). The time for processing each job follows:

Work (processing) Time for Jobs (hours)

Job	Work Center 1 (drill press)	Work Center 2 (lathe)
A	5	2
B	3	6
C	8	4
D	10	7
E	7	12

The owner, Niranjan Pati, wants to set the sequence to minimize his total processing time for the five jobs.

APPROACH ▶ Pati applies the four steps of Johnson's rule.

SOLUTION ▶

1. The job with the shortest processing time is A, in work center 2 (with a time of 2 hours). Because it is at the second center, schedule A last. Eliminate it from consideration.

				A

2. Job B has the next shortest time (3 hours). Because that time is at the first work center, we schedule it first and eliminate it from consideration.

B				A

3. The next shortest time is job C (4 hours) on the second machine. Therefore, it is placed as late as possible.

LO5: Use Johnson's rule

B			C	A

4. There is a tie (at 7 hours) for the shortest remaining job. We can place E, which was on the first work center, first. Then D is placed in the last sequencing position.

B	E	D	C	A

The sequential times are:

Work center 1	3	7	10	8	5
Work center 2	6	12	7	4	2

The time-phased flow of this job sequence is best illustrated graphically:

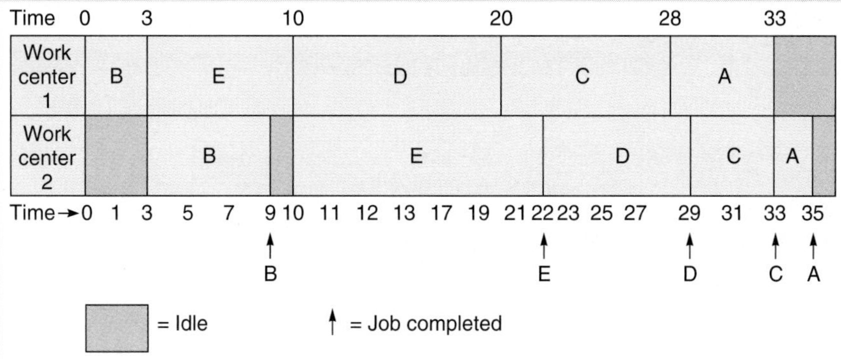

Thus, the five jobs are completed in 35 hours.

INSIGHT ▶ The second work center will wait 3 hours for its first job, and it will also wait 1 hour after completing job B.

LEARNING EXERCISE ▶ If job C takes 8 hours in work center 2 (instead of 4 hours), what sequence is best? [Answer: B–E–C–D–A.]

RELATED PROBLEMS ▶ 15.15, 15.17, 15.18

Limitations of Rule-Based Dispatching Systems

The scheduling techniques just discussed are rule-based techniques, but rule-based systems have a number of limitations. Among these are the following:

1. Scheduling is dynamic; therefore, rules need to be revised to adjust to changes in orders, process, equipment, product mix, and so forth.

2. Rules do not look upstream or downstream; idle resources and bottleneck resources in other departments may not be recognized.
3. Rules do not look beyond due dates. For instance, two orders may have the same due date. One order involves restocking a distributor and the other is a custom order that will shut down the customer's factory if not completed. Both may have the same due date, but clearly the custom order is more important.

Despite these limitations, schedulers often use sequencing rules such as SPT, EDD, or critical ratio. They apply these methods at each work center and then modify the sequence to deal with a multitude of real-world variables. They may do this manually or with finite capacity scheduling software.

FINITE CAPACITY SCHEDULING (FCS)

Finite capacity scheduling (FCS)
Computerized short-term scheduling that overcomes the disadvantage of rule-based systems by providing the user with graphical interactive computing.

LO6: Define finite capacity scheduling

Short-term scheduling is also called finite capacity scheduling.[4] **Finite capacity scheduling (FCS)** overcomes the disadvantages of systems based exclusively on rules by providing the scheduler with interactive computing and graphic output. In dynamic scheduling environments such as job shops (with a high variety, low volume, and shared resources) we expect changes—but changes disrupt schedules. Therefore, operations managers are moving toward FCS systems that allow virtually instantaneous change by the operator. Improvements in communication on the shop floor are also enhancing the accuracy and speed of information necessary for effective control in job shops. Computer-controlled machines can monitor events and collect information in near real-time. This means the scheduler can make schedule changes based on up-to-the-minute information. These schedules are often displayed in Gantt chart form. In addition to including priority rule options, many of the current FCS systems also combine an "expert system" or simulation techniques and allow the scheduler to assign costs to various options. The scheduler has the flexibility to handle any situation, including order, labor, or machine changes.

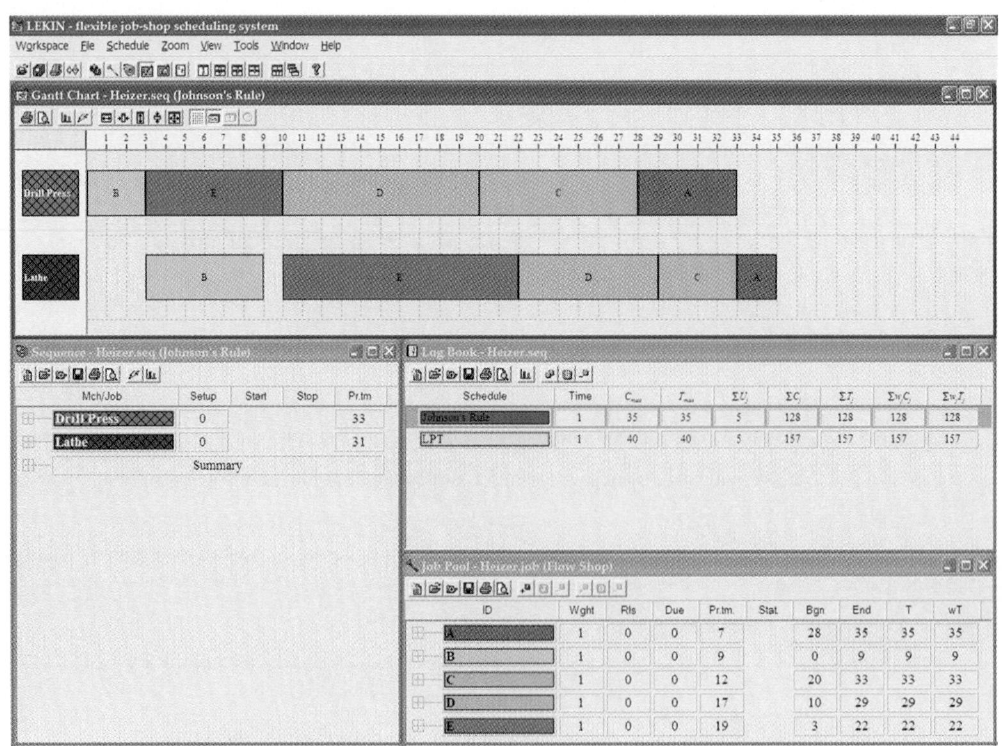

This Lekin® finite capacity scheduling software presents a schedule of the five jobs and the two work centers shown in Example 7 (pages 598–599) in Gantt chart form. The software is capable of using a variety of priority rules, several shop types, up to 50 jobs, 20 work centers, and 100 machines to generate a schedule. The Lekin software is available for free at **www.stern.nyc.edu/om/software/lekin/download/html** and can solve many of the problems at the end of this chapter.

[4]Finite capacity scheduling (FCS) systems go by a number of names, including finite scheduling and advance planning systems (APS). The name manufacturing execution systems (MES) may also be used, but MES tends to suggest an emphasis on the reporting system from shop operations back to the scheduling activity.

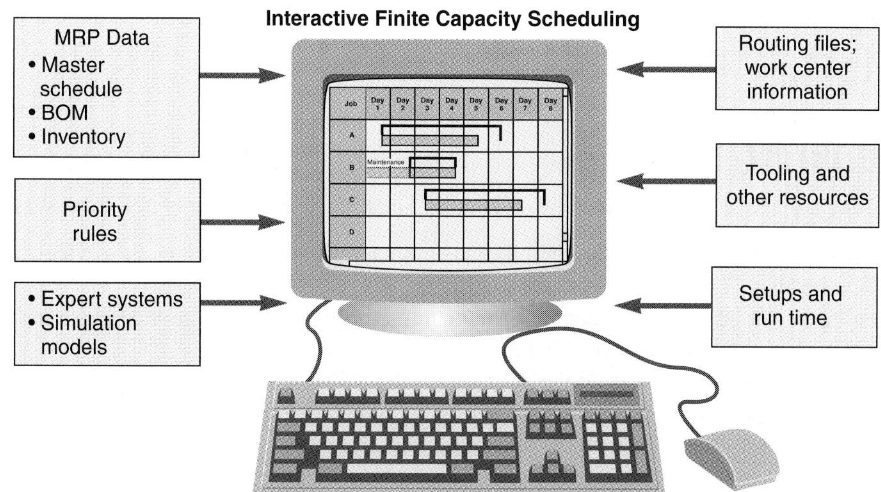

◄ **FIGURE 15.5**
Finite Capacity Scheduling Systems Combine MRP and Shop Floor Production Data to Generate a Gantt Chart That Can Be Manipulated by the User on a Computer Screen

The initial data for finite scheduling systems is often the output from an MRP system. The output from MRP systems is traditionally in weekly "buckets" that have no capacity constraint. These systems just tell the planner when the material is needed, ignoring the capacity issue. Because *infinite*-size buckets are unrealistic and inadequate for detail scheduling, MRP data require refinement. MRP output is combined with routing files, due dates, capacity of work centers, tooling, and other resource availability to provide the data needed for effective FCS. These are the same data needed in any manual system, but FCS software formalizes them, speeds analysis, and makes changes easier. The combining of MRP and FCS data, priority rules, models to assist analysis, and Gantt chart output is shown in Figure 15.5.

Finite capacity scheduling allows delivery requirements to be based on today's conditions and today's orders, not according to some predefined rule. The scheduler determines what constitutes a "good" schedule. FCS software packages such as Lekin, ProPlanner, Preactor, Asprova, Tactic, and Jobplan are currently used at over 60% of U.S. plants.

SCHEDULING REPETITIVE FACILITIES

AUTHOR COMMENT Repetitive producers create forward-looking schedules with level material use.

The scheduling goals defined at the beginning of this chapter are also appropriate for repetitive production. You may recall from Chapter 7 that repetitive producers make standard products from modules. The usual approach is to develop a forward-looking schedule on a balanced assembly line. (Refer to Table 15.2 on page 588).

Repetitive producers want to satisfy customer demands, lower inventory investment, and reduce the batch (or lot) size, with existing equipment and processes. A technique to move toward these goals is to use a level-material-use schedule. **Level material use** means frequent, high-quality, small lot sizes that contribute to just-in-time production. This is exactly what world-class producers such as Harley-Davidson, John Deere, and Johnson Controls do. The advantages of level material use are:

Level material use
The use of frequent, high-quality, small lot sizes that contribute to just-in-time production.

1. Lower inventory levels, which releases capital for other uses
2. Faster product throughput (that is, shorter lead times)
3. Improved component quality and hence improved product quality
4. Reduced floor-space requirements
5. Improved communication among employees because they are closer together (which can result in improved teamwork and *esprit de corps*)
6. Smoother production process because large lots have not "hidden" the problems

Suppose a repetitive producer runs large monthly batches: With a level-material-use schedule, management would move toward shortening this monthly cycle to a weekly, daily, or even hourly cycle.

One way to develop a level-material-use schedule is to first determine the minimum lot size that will keep the production process moving. This is illustrated in the next chapter, "JIT and Lean Operations."

AUTHOR COMMENT Scheduling people to perform services can be even more complex than scheduling machines.

SCHEDULING SERVICES

Scheduling service systems differs from scheduling manufacturing systems in several ways:

- In manufacturing, the scheduling emphasis is on machines and materials; in services, it is on staffing levels.
- Inventories can help smooth demand for manufacturers, but many service systems do not maintain inventories.
- Services are labor intensive, and the demand for this labor can be highly variable.
- Legal considerations, such as wage and hour laws and union contracts that limit hours worked per shift, week, or month, constrain scheduling decisions.
- Because services usually schedule people rather than material, behavioral, social, seniority, and status issues complicate scheduling.

The following examples note the complexity of scheduling services.

Hospitals A hospital is an example of a service facility that may use a scheduling system every bit as complex as one found in a job shop. Hospitals seldom use a machine shop priority system such as first-come, first-served (FCFS) for treating emergency patients. However, they do schedule products (such as surgeries) just like a factory, and capacities must meet wide variations in demand.

Banks Cross training of the workforce in a bank allows loan officers and other managers to provide short-term help for tellers if there is a surge in demand. Banks also employ part-time personnel to provide a variable capacity.

Retail Stores Scheduling optimization systems, such as Workbrain, Cybershift, and Kronos, are used at retailers including Walmart, Payless Shoes, Target, and Radio Shack. These systems track individual store sales, transactions, units sold, and customer traffic in 15-minute increments to create work schedules. Walmart's 1.3 million and Target's 350,000 employees used to take thousands of managers' hours to schedule; now staffing is drawn up nationwide in a few hours, and customer checkout experience has improved dramatically.

Airlines Airlines face two constraints when scheduling flight crews: (1) a complex set of FAA work-time limitations and (2) union contracts that guarantee crew pay for some number of hours each day or each trip. Airline planners must build crew schedules that meet or exceed crews' pay guarantees. Planners must also make efficient use of their other expensive resource: aircraft. These schedules are typically built using linear programming models. The *OM in Action* box "Scheduling Aircraft Turnaround" details how very short-term schedules (20 minutes) can help an airline become more efficient.

Good scheduling in the health care industry can help keep nurses happy and costs contained. Here, nurses in Boston protest nurse-staffing levels in Massachusetts hospitals. Shortages of qualified nurses is a chronic problem.

OM in Action ► Scheduling Aircraft Turnaround

Airlines that face increasingly difficult financial futures have recently discovered the importance of efficient scheduling of ground turnaround activities for flights. For some low-cost, point-to-point carriers like Southwest Airlines, scheduling turnarounds in 20 minutes has been standard policy for years. Yet for others, like Continental, United, and US Airways, the approach is new. This figure illustrates how US Airways deals with speedier schedules. Now its planes average seven trips a day, instead of six, meaning the carrier can sell tens of thousands more seats a day. And with this improved scheduling, its punctuality moved from near the bottom in 2007 to virtually tie Southwest for first place 2 years later.

► US Airways has cut the turnaround time on commercial flights from the current 45 minutes to 20 minutes for Boeing 737s. To the right is a list of procedures that must be completed before the flight can depart:

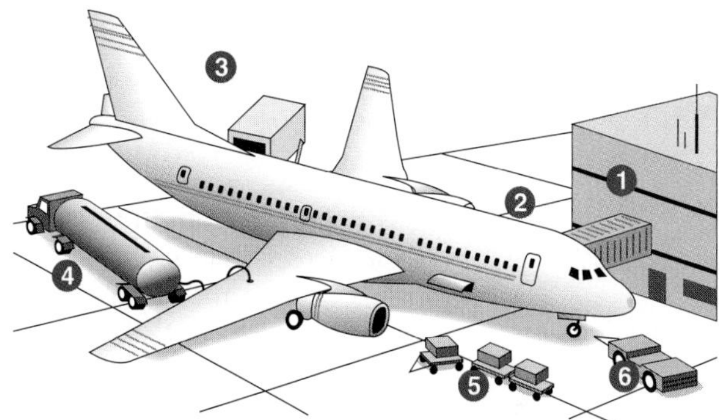

1. Ticket agent takes flight plan to pilot, who loads information into aircraft computer. About 130 passengers disembark from the plane.
2. Workers clean trash cans, seat pockets, lavatories, etc.
3. Catering personnel board plane and replenish supply of drinks and ice.
4. A fuel truck loads up to 5,300 gallons of fuel into aircraft's wings.
5. Baggage crews unload up to 4,000 pounds of luggage and 2,000 pounds of freight. "Runners" rush the luggage to baggage claim area in terminal.
6. Ramp agents, who help park aircraft upon arrival, "push" plane back away from gate.

Sources: US Airways, Boeing, *The Wall Street Journal* (January 6, 2009): D8; and *Aviation Week & Space Technology* (January 29, 2001): 50.

24/7 Operations Emergency hotlines, police/fire departments, telephone operations, and mail-order businesses (such as L.L. Bean) schedule employees 24 hours a day, 7 days a week. To allow management flexibility in staffing, sometimes part-time workers can be employed. This provides both benefits (in using odd shift lengths or matching anticipated workloads) and difficulties (from the large number of possible alternatives in terms of days off, lunch hour times, rest periods, starting times). Most companies use computerized scheduling systems to cope with these complexities. The *OM in Action* box "Scheduling for Peaks by Swapping Employees" provides yet another example of flexibility in scheduling.

OM in Action ► Scheduling for Peaks by Swapping Employees

When calls to Choice Hotel International's reservation line surged after a recent ad campaign, Choice V.P. Don Brockwell found his call center short-staffed. So he quickly arranged to add 20 agents per shift—but not by hiring or calling a temp service. Instead, the additional workers were employees of 1-800-Flowers.com. Choice and Flowers's unusual deal helps both reduce reliance on outsourcers. It also bolsters recruiting and retention because call center workers have more varied work and are less subject to a seasonal business cycle.

The deal works in part because Choice's high season is mid-May through early October, while Flowers's call volume increases between October and May, with surges at Christmas, Valentine's Day, and Mother's Day. The companies typically lend each other as many as 100 employees, for weeks at a time, in the three call centers they share. But some workers might even change assignments in the middle of a shift. Most employees like the variety. "When you sit down and sell hotel rooms for 8 hours a day, selling flowers is a nice break," says Rick Hilliner, a former teacher, now at the Grand Junction, Colorado, center.

Sources: The Wall Street Journal (April 10, 2006): B3; and *Call Center Magazine* (March 2005): 18–24.

Scheduling Service Employees with Cyclical Scheduling

A number of techniques and algorithms exist for scheduling service-sector employees such as police officers, nurses, restaurant staff, tellers, and retail sales clerks. Managers, trying to set a timely and efficient schedule that keeps personnel happy, can spend substantial time each month developing employee schedules. Such schedules often consider a fairly long planning period (say, 6 weeks). One approach that is workable yet simple is *cyclical scheduling*.

LO7: Use the cyclical scheduling technique

Cyclical Scheduling Cyclical scheduling with inconsistent staffing needs is often the case in services such as restaurants and police work. Here the objective focuses on developing a schedule with the minimum number of workers. In these cases, each employee is assigned to a shift and has time off. Let's look at Example 8.

EXAMPLE 8 ▶

Cyclical scheduling

Hospital administrator Doris Laughlin wants to staff the oncology ward using a standard 5-day workweek with two consecutive days off, but also wants to minimize the staff. However, as in most hospitals, she faces an inconsistent demand. Weekends have low usage. Doctors tend to work early in the week, and patients peak on Wednesday then taper off.

APPROACH ▶ Doris must first establish staffing requirements. Then the following five-step process is applied.

SOLUTION ▶

1. Determine the necessary daily staffing requirements. Doris has done this:

Day	Monday	Tuesday	Wednesday	Thursday	Friday	Saturday	Sunday
Staff required	5	5	6	5	4	3	3

2. Identify the two consecutive days that have the *lowest total requirement* and circle these. Assign these two days off to the first employee. In this case, the first employee has Saturday and Sunday off because 3 plus 3 is the *lowest sum* of any 2 days. In the case of a tie, choose the days with the lowest adjacent requirement, or by first assigning Saturday and Sunday as an "off" day. If there are more than one, make an arbitrary decision.
3. We now have an employee working each of the uncircled days; therefore, make a new row for the next employee by subtracting 1 from the first row (because one day has been worked)—except for the circled days (which represent the days not worked) and any day that has a zero. That is, do not subtract from a circled day or a day that has a value of zero.
4. In the new row, identify the two consecutive days that have the lowest total requirement and circle them. Assign the next employee to the remaining days.
5. Repeat the process (steps 3 and 4) until all staffing requirements are met.

	MONDAY	TUESDAY	WEDNESDAY	THURSDAY	FRIDAY	SATURDAY	SUNDAY
Employee 1	5	5	6	5	4	(3)	(3)
Employee 2	4	4	5	4	3	(3)	(3)
Employee 3	3	3	4	3	(2)	(3)	3
Employee 4	2	2	3	(2)	(2)	3	2
Employee 5	(1)	(1)	2	2	2	2	1
Employee 6	1	1	1	1	1	(1)	(0)
Employee 7						1	
Capacity (measured in number of employees)	5	5	6	5	4	3	3
Excess capacity	0	0	0	0	0	1	0

Doris needs six full-time employees to meet the staffing needs and one employee to work Saturday.

Notice that capacity (number of employees) equals requirements, provided an employee works overtime on Saturday, or a part-time employee is hired for Saturday.

INSIGHT ▶ Doris has implemented an efficient scheduling system that accommodates 2 consecutive days off for every employee.

LEARNING EXERCISE ▶ If Doris meets the staffing requirement for Saturday with a full-time employee, how does she schedule that employee? [Answer: That employee can have any 2 days off, except Saturday, and capacity will exceed requirements by 1 person each day the employee works (except Saturday).]

RELATED PROBLEMS ▶ 15.19, 15.20

Using the approach in Example 8, Colorado General Hospital saved an average of 10 to 15 hours a month and found these added advantages: (1) no computer was needed, (2) the nurses were happy with the schedule, (3) the cycles could be changed seasonally to accommodate avid skiers, and (4) recruiting was easier because of predictability and flexibility. This approach yields an optimum, although there may be multiple optimal solutions.

Other cyclical scheduling techniques have been developed to aid service scheduling. Some approaches use linear programming: This is how Hard Rock Cafe schedules its services (see the Video Case Study at the end of this chapter). There is a natural bias in scheduling to use tools that are understood and yield solutions that are accepted.

CHAPTER SUMMARY

Scheduling involves the timing of operations to achieve the efficient movement of units through a system. This chapter addressed the issues of short-term scheduling in process-focused, repetitive, and service environments. We saw that process-focused facilities are production systems in which products are made to order and that scheduling tasks in them can become complex. Several aspects and approaches to scheduling, loading, and sequencing of jobs were introduced. These ranged from Gantt charts and the assignment method of scheduling to a series of priority rules, the critical-ratio rule, Johnson's rule for sequencing, and finite capacity scheduling.

Service systems generally differ from manufacturing systems. This leads to the use of first-come, first-served rules and appointment and reservation systems, as well as to heuristics and linear programming approaches for matching capacity to demand in service environments.

Key Terms

Forward scheduling (p. 586)
Backward scheduling (p. 586)
Loading (p. 588)
Input–output control (p. 588)
ConWIP cards (p. 589)
Gantt charts (p. 590)
Assignment method (p. 591)
Sequencing (p. 594)
Priority rules (p. 594)
First come, first served (FCFS) (p. 594)
Shortest processing time (SPT) (p. 594)
Earliest due date (EDD) (p. 594)
Longest processing time (LPT) (p. 594)
Critical ratio (CR) (p. 597)
Johnson's rule (p. 598)
Finite capacity scheduling (FCS) (p. 600)
Level material use (p. 601)

Ethical Dilemma

Scheduling people to work second and third shifts (evening and "graveyard") is a problem in almost every 24-hour company. The *OM in Action* box "Scheduling Workers Who Fall Asleep Is a Killer—Literally," on page 587, describes potentially dangerous issues on the night shift at FedEx and a nuclear power plant. Perhaps even more significantly, ergonomic data indicate the body does not respond well to significant shifts in its natural circadian rhythm of sleep. There are also significant long-run health issues with frequent changes in work and sleep cycles.

Consider yourself the manager of a nonunion steel mill that must operate 24-hour days, and where the physical demands are such that 8-hour days are preferable to 10- or 12-hour days. Your empowered employees have decided that they want to work weekly rotating shifts. That is, they want a repeating work cycle of 1 week, 7 A.M. to 3 P.M., followed by a second week from 3 P.M. to 11 P.M., and the third week from 11 P.M. to 7 A.M. You are sure this is not a good idea in terms of both productivity and the long-term health of the employees. If you do not accept their decision, you undermine the work empowerment program, generate a morale issue, and perhaps, more significantly, generate few more votes for a union. What is the ethical position and what do you do?

Discussion Questions

1. What is the overall objective of scheduling?
2. List the four criteria for determining the effectiveness of a *scheduling* decision. How do these criteria relate to the four criteria for *sequencing* decisions?
3. Describe what is meant by "loading" work centers. What are the two ways work centers can be loaded? What are two techniques used in loading?
4. Name five priority sequencing rules. Explain how each works to assign jobs.
5. What are the advantages and disadvantages of the shortest processing time (SPT) rule?
6. What is a due date?
7. Explain the terms *flow time* and *lateness*.
8. Which shop-floor scheduling rule would you prefer to apply if you were the leader of the only team of experts charged with defusing several time bombs scattered throughout your building? You can see the bombs; they are of different types. You can tell how long each one will take to defuse. Discuss.
9. When is Johnson's rule best applied in job-shop scheduling?
10. State the four effectiveness measures for dispatching rules.
11. What are the steps of the assignment method of linear programming?
12. What are the advantages of level material flow?
13. What is input–output control?

Using Software for Short-Term Scheduling

In addition to the commercial software we noted in this chapter, short-term scheduling problems can be solved with the Excel OM software that comes free at our website **www.pearsonhighered.com/heizer**. POM for Windows also includes a scheduling module. The use of each of these programs is explained next.

Using Excel OM

Excel OM has two modules that help solve short-term scheduling problems: Assignment and Job Shop Scheduling. The Assignment module is illustrated in Programs 15.1 and 15.2. The input screen, using the Example 4 data, appears first, as Program 15.1. Once the data are all entered, we choose the Tools command, followed by the Solver command. Excel's Solver uses linear programming to optimize assignment problems. The constraints are also shown in Program 15.1. We then select the Solve command and the solution appears in Program 15.2.

Excel OM's Job Shop Scheduling module is illustrated in Program 15.3. Program 15.3 uses Example 5's data. Because jobs are listed in the sequence in which they arrived (see column A), the results are for the FCFS rule. Program 15.3 also shows some of the formulas (columns F, G, H, I, J) used in the calculations.

To solve with the SPT rule, we need four intermediate steps: (1) Select (that is, highlight) the data in columns A, B, C for all jobs; (2) invoke the Data command; (3) invoke the Sort command; and (4) sort by Time (column C) in *ascending* order. To solve for EDD, step 4 changes to sort by Due Date (column D) in *ascending* order. Finally, for an LPT solution, step 4 becomes sort by Due Date (column D) in *descending* order.

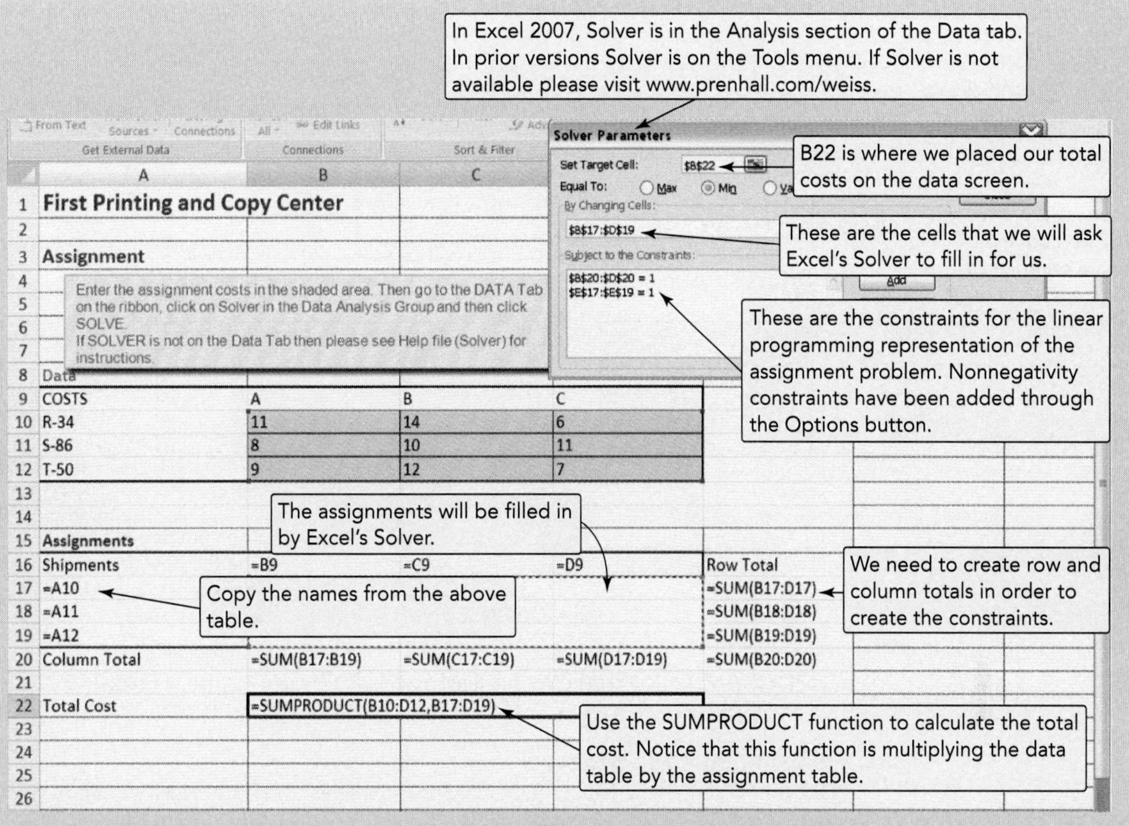

Data	A	B	C	
COSTS	A	B	C	
R-34	11	14	6	
S-86	8	10	11	
T-50	9	12	7	
Assignments				
Shipments	=B9	=C9	=D9	Row Total
=A10				=SUM(B17:D17)
=A11				=SUM(B18:D18)
=A12				=SUM(B19:D19)
Column Total	=SUM(B17:B19)	=SUM(C17:C19)	=SUM(D17:D19)	=SUM(B20:D20)
Total Cost	=SUMPRODUCT(B10:D12,B17:D19)			

▲ **PROGRAM 15.1 Excel OM's Assignment Module Using Example 4's Data**
After entering the problem data in the yellow area, select Tools, then Solver.

▼ **PROGRAM 15.2 Excel OM Output Screen for Assignment Problem Described in Program 15.1**

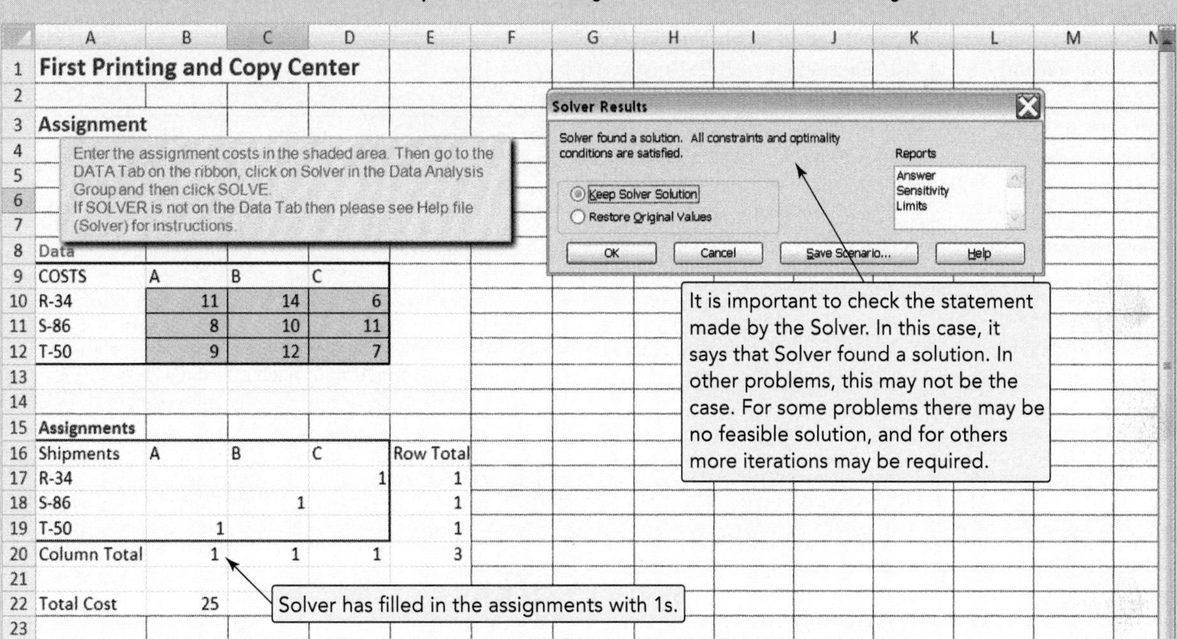

COSTS	A	B	C	
R-34	11	14	6	
S-86	8	10	11	
T-50	9	12	7	
Assignments				
Shipments	A	B	C	Row Total
R-34			1	1
S-86		1		1
T-50	1			1
Column Total	1	1	1	3
Total Cost	25			

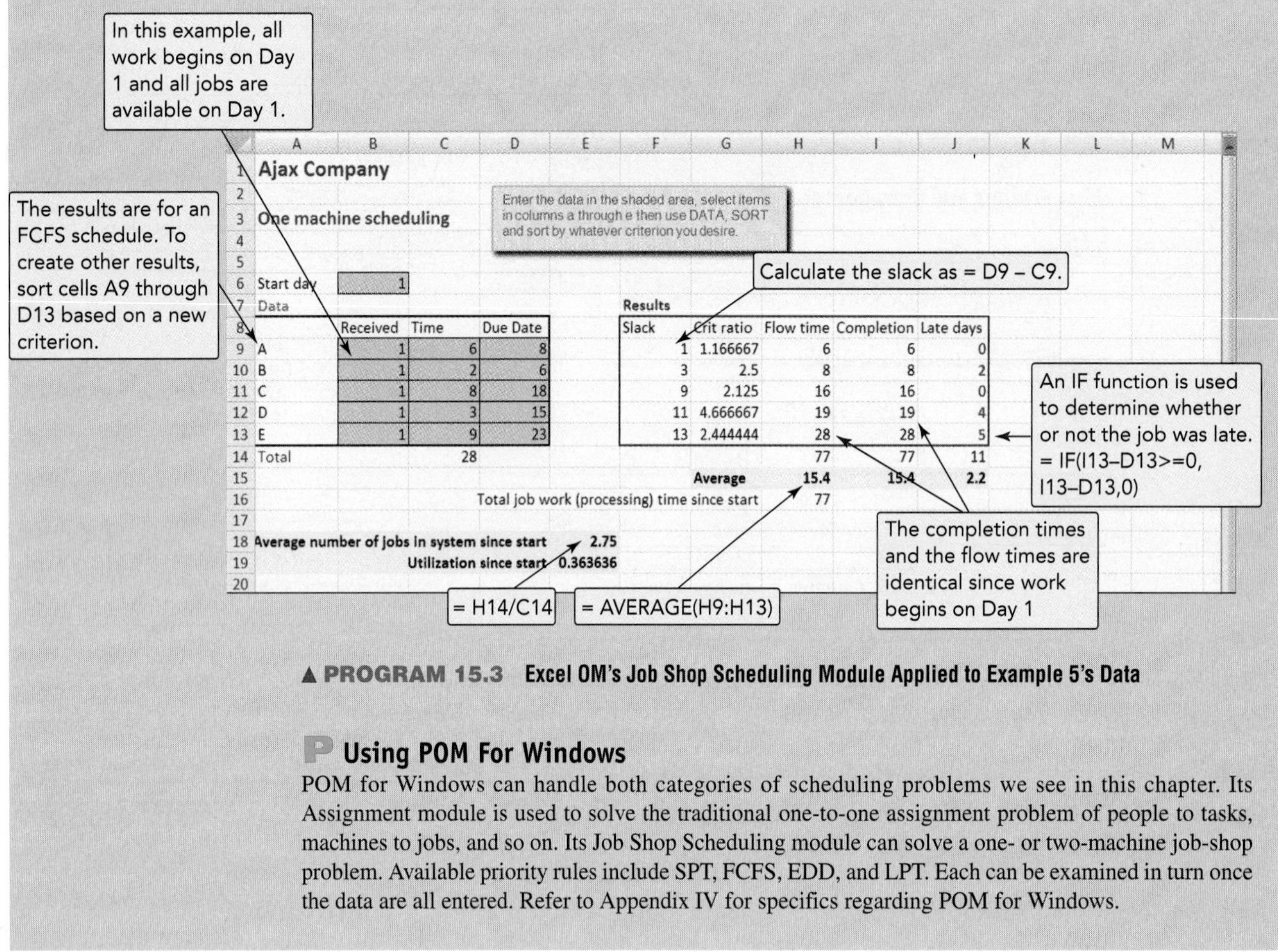

▲ **PROGRAM 15.3** **Excel OM's Job Shop Scheduling Module Applied to Example 5's Data**

Using POM For Windows

POM for Windows can handle both categories of scheduling problems we see in this chapter. Its Assignment module is used to solve the traditional one-to-one assignment problem of people to tasks, machines to jobs, and so on. Its Job Shop Scheduling module can solve a one- or two-machine job-shop problem. Available priority rules include SPT, FCFS, EDD, and LPT. Each can be examined in turn once the data are all entered. Refer to Appendix IV for specifics regarding POM for Windows.

Solved Problems

Virtual Office Hours help is available at www.myomlab.com

▼ SOLVED PROBLEM 15.1

King Finance Corporation, headquartered in New York, wants to assign three recently hired college graduates, Julie Jones, Al Smith, and Pat Wilson, to regional offices. However, the firm also has an opening in New York and would send one of the three there if it were more economical than a move to Omaha, Dallas, or Miami. It will cost $1,000 to relocate Jones to New York, $800 to relocate Smith there, and $1,500 to move Wilson. What is the optimal assignment of personnel to offices?

HIREE \ OFFICE	OMAHA	MIAMI	DALLAS
Jones	$800	$1,100	$1,200
Smith	$500	$1,600	$1,300
Wilson	$500	$1,000	$2,300

▼ SOLUTION

(a) The cost table has a fourth column to represent New York. To "balance" the problem, we add a "dummy" row (person) with a zero relocation cost to each city.

HIREE \ OFFICE	OMAHA	MIAMI	DALLAS	NEW YORK
Jones	$800	$1,100	$1,200	$1,000
Smith	$500	$1,600	$1,300	$ 800
Wilson	$500	$1,000	$2,300	$1,500
Dummy	0	0	0	0

(b) Subtract the smallest number in each row and cover all zeros (column subtraction of each column's zero will give the same numbers and therefore is not necessary):

HIREE \ OFFICE	OMAHA	MIAMI	DALLAS	NEW YORK
Jones	0	300	400	200
Smith	0	1,100	800	300
Wilson	0	500	1,800	1,000
Dummy	0	0	0	0

(c) Only 2 lines cover, so subtract the smallest uncovered number (200) from all uncovered numbers, and add it to each square where two lines intersect. Then cover all zeros:

OFFICE / HIREE	OMAHA	MIAMI	DALLAS	NEW YORK
Jones	0	100	200	0
Smith	0	900	600	100
Wilson	0	300	1,600	800
Dummy	200	0	0	0

(d) Only 3 lines cover, so subtract the smallest uncovered number (100) from all uncovered numbers, and add it to each square where two lines intersect. Then cover all zeros:

OFFICE / HIREE	OMAHA	MIAMI	DALLAS	NEW YORK
Jones	0	0	100	0
Smith	0	800	500	100
Wilson	0	200	1,500	800
Dummy	300	0	0	100

(e) Still only 3 lines cover, so subtract the smallest uncovered number (100) from all uncovered numbers, add it to squares where two lines intersect, and cover all zeros:

OFFICE / HIREE	OMAHA	MIAMI	DALLAS	NEW YORK
Jones	100	0	100	0
Smith	0	700	400	0
Wilson	0	100	1,400	700
Dummy	400	0	0	100

(f) Because it takes four lines to cover all zeros, an optimal assignment can be made at zero squares. We assign:

Wilson to Omaha
Jones to Miami
Dummy (no one) to Dallas
Smith to New York

$$\text{Cost} = \$500 + \$1{,}100 + \$0 + \$800 = \$2{,}400$$

▼ SOLVED PROBLEM 15.2

A defense contractor in Dallas has six jobs awaiting processing. Processing time and due dates are given in the table. Assume that jobs arrive in the order shown. Set the processing sequence according to FCFS and evaluate.

JOB	JOB PROCESSING TIME (DAYS)	JOB DUE DATE (DAYS)
A	6	22
B	12	14
C	14	30
D	2	18
E	10	25
F	4	34

▼ SOLUTION

FCFS has the sequence A–B–C–D–E–F.

JOB SEQUENCE	JOB PROCESSING TIME	FLOW TIME	DUE DATE	JOB LATENESS
A	6	6	22	0
B	12	18	14	4
C	14	32	30	2
D	2	34	18	16
E	10	44	25	19
F	4	48	34	14
	48	182		55

1. Average completion time $= 182/6 = 30.33$ days
2. Average number of jobs in system $= 182/48 = 3.79$ jobs
3. Average job lateness $= 55/6 = 9.16$ days
4. Utilization $= 48/182 = 26.4\%$

▼ SOLVED PROBLEM 15.3

The Dallas firm in Solved Problem 15.2 also wants to consider job sequencing by the SPT priority rule. Apply SPT to the same data and provide a recommendation.

▼ SOLUTION

SPT has the sequence D–F–A–E–B–C.

Job Sequence	Job Processing Time	Flow Time	Due Date	Job Lateness
D	2	2	18	0
F	4	6	34	0
A	6	12	22	0
E	10	22	25	0
B	12	34	14	20
C	14	48	30	18
	48	124		38

1. Average completion time = 124/6 = 20.67 days
2. Average number of jobs in system = 124/48 = 2.58 jobs
3. Average job lateness = 38/6 = 6.33 days
4. Utilization = 48/124 = 38.7%

SPT is superior to FCFS in this case on all four measures. If we were to also analyze EDD, we would, however, find its average job lateness to be lowest at 5.5 days. SPT is a good recommendation. SPT's major disadvantage is that it makes long jobs wait, sometimes for a long time.

▼ SOLVED PROBLEM 15.4

Use Johnson's rule to find the optimum sequence for processing the jobs shown through two work centers. Times at each center are in hours.

Job	Work Center 1	Work Center 2
A	6	12
B	3	7
C	18	9
D	15	14
E	16	8
F	10	15

▼ SOLUTION

B	A	F	D	C	E

The sequential times are:

Work center 1	3	6	10	15	18	16
Work center 2	7	12	15	14	9	8

▼ SOLVED PROBLEM 15.5

Illustrate the throughput time and idle time at the two work centers in Solved Problem 15.4 by constructing a time-phased chart.

▼ SOLUTION

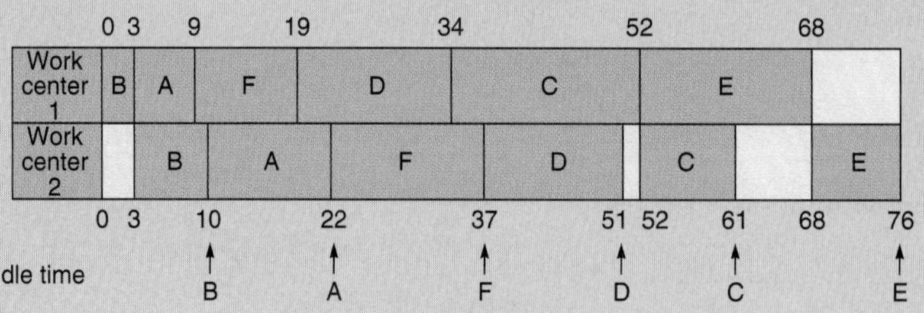

Problems*

•• **15.1** Ron Satterfield's excavation company uses both Gantt scheduling charts and Gantt load charts.

a) Today, which is the end of day 7, Ron is reviewing the Gantt chart depicting these schedules:
   - Job #151 was scheduled to begin on day 3 and to take 6 days. As of now, it is 1 day ahead of schedule.
   - Job #177 was scheduled to begin on day 1 and take 4 days. It is currently on time.
   - Job #179 was scheduled to start on day 7 and take 2 days. It actually got started on day 6 and is progressing according to plan.
   - Job #211 was scheduled to begin on day 5, but missing equipment delayed it until day 6. It is progressing as expected and should take 3 days.
   - Job #215 was scheduled to begin on day 4 and take 5 days. It got started on time but has since fallen behind 2 days.

Draw the Gantt scheduling chart for the activities above.

b) Ron now wants to use a Gantt load chart to see how much work is scheduled in each of his three work teams: Able, Baker, and Charlie. Five jobs constitute the current work load for these three work teams: Job #250, requiring 48 hours and #275 requiring 32 hours for Work Team Able; Jobs #210, and #280 requiring 16 and 24 hours, respectively, for Team Baker; and Job #225, requiring 40 hours, for Team Charlie.

Prepare the Gantt load chart for these activities.

•• **15.2** First Printing and Copy Center has 4 more jobs to be scheduled, in addition to those shown in Example 3 in the chapter. Production scheduling personnel are reviewing the Gantt chart at the end of day 4.

- Job D was scheduled to begin early on day 2 and to end on the middle of day 9. As of now (the review point after day 4), it is 2 days ahead of schedule.
- Job E should begin on day 1 and end on day 3. It was on time.
- Job F was to begin on day 3, but maintenance forced a delay of 1½ days. The job should now take 5 full days. It is now on schedule.
- Job G is a day behind schedule. It started at the beginning of day 2 and should require 6 days to complete.

Develop a Gantt schedule chart for First Printing and Copy Center.

• **15.3** The Orange Top Cab Company has a taxi waiting at each of four cabstands in Evanston, Illinois. Four customers have called and requested service. The distances, in miles, from the waiting taxis to the customers are given in the following table. Find the optimal assignment of taxis to customers so as to minimize total driving distances to the customers.

	Customer			
Cab Site	A	B	C	D
Stand 1	7	3	4	8
Stand 2	5	4	6	5
Stand 3	6	7	9	6
Stand 4	8	6	7	4

PX

Note: PX means the problem may be solved with POM for Windows and/or Excel OM.

• **15.4** Molly Riggs's medical testing company wishes to assign a set of jobs to a set of machines. The following table provides the production data of each machine when performing the specific job:

	Machine			
Job	A	B	C	D
1	7	9	8	10
2	10	9	7	6
3	11	5	9	6
4	9	11	5	8

a) Determine the assignment of jobs to machines that will *maximize* total production.

b) What is the total production of your assignments? PX

• **15.5** The Johnny Ho Manufacturing Company in Columbus, Ohio, is putting out four new electronic components. Each of Ho's four plants has the capacity to add one more product to its current line of electronic parts. The unit-manufacturing costs for producing the different parts at the four plants are shown in the accompanying table. How should Ho assign the new products to the plants to minimize manufacturing costs?

Electronic Component	*Plant* 1	2	3	4
C53	$0.10	$0.12	$0.13	$0.11
C81	0.05	0.06	0.04	0.08
D5	0.32	0.40	0.31	0.30
D44	0.17	0.14	0.19	0.15

PX

• **15.6** Claire Consultants has been entrusted with the task of evaluating a business plan that has been divided into four sections—marketing, finance, operations and human resources. Chris, Steve, Juana, and Rebecca form the evaluation team. Each of them has expertise in a certain field and tends to finish that section faster. The estimated times taken by each team member for each section have been outlined in the table below. Further information states that each of these individuals is paid $60/hour.

a) Assign each member to a different section such that Claire Consultants's overall cost is minimized.

b) What is the total cost of these assignments?

Times Taken by Team Members for Different Sections (minutes)

	Marketing	Finance	Operations	HR
Chris	80	120	125	140
Steve	20	115	145	160
Juana	40	100	85	45
Rebecca	65	35	25	75

PX

•• **15.7** The Akron Police Department has five detective squads available for assignment to five open crime cases. The chief of detectives, Paul Kuzdrall, wishes to assign the squads so that the total time to conclude the cases is minimized. The average number of days, based on past performance, for each squad to complete each case is as follows:

	Case				
Squad	A	B	C	D	E
1	14	7	3	7	27
2	20	7	12	6	30
3	10	3	4	5	21
4	8	12	7	12	21
5	13	25	24	26	8

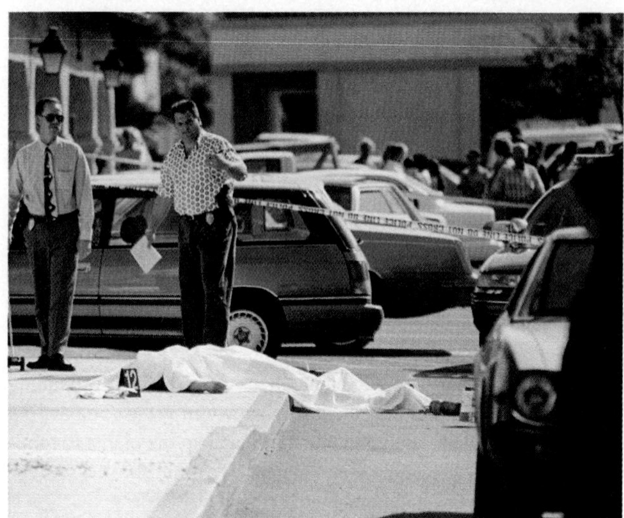

Each squad is composed of different types of specialists, and whereas one squad may be very effective in certain types of cases, it may be almost useless in others.

a) Solve the problem by using the assignment method.
b) Assign the squads to the above cases, but with the constraint that squad 5 cannot work on case E because of a conflict. Px

• **15.8** Tigers Sports Club has to select four separate co-ed doubles teams to participate in an inter-club table tennis tournament. The pre-selection results in the selection of a group of four men—Raul, Jack, Gray, and Ajay—and four women—Barbara, Dona, Stella, and Jackie. Now, the task ahead lies in pairing these men and women in the best fashion. The table below shows a matrix that has been designed for this purpose, indicating how each of the men complements the game of each of the women. A higher score indicates a higher degree of compatibility in the games of the two individuals concerned. Find the best pairs.

Game Compatibility Matrix

	Barbara	Dona	Stella	Jackie
Raul	30	20	10	40
Jack	70	10	60	70
Gray	40	20	50	40
Ajay	60	70	30	90

Px

••• **15.9** James Gross, chairman of the College of Oshkosh's business department, needs to assign professors to courses next semester. As a criterion for judging who should teach each course, Professor Gross reviews the past 2 years' teaching evaluations (which were filled out by students). Since each of the four professors taught each of the four courses at one time or another during the 2-year period, Gross is able to record a course rating for each instructor. These ratings are shown in the following table.

a) Find the assignment of professors to courses to maximize the overall teaching rating.
b) Assign the professors to the courses with the exception that Professor Fisher cannot teach Statistics. Px

	Course			
Professor	**Statistics**	**Management**	**Finance**	**Economics**
W. W. Fisher	90	65	95	40
D. Golhar	70	60	80	75
Z. Hug	85	40	80	60
N. K. Rustagi	55	80	65	55

•• **15.10** The following jobs are waiting to be processed at the same machine center. Jobs are logged as they arrive:

Job	Due Date	Duration (days)
A	313	8
B	312	16
C	325	40
D	314	5
E	314	3

In what sequence would the jobs be ranked according to the following decision rules: (a) FCFS, (b) EDD, (c) SPT, and (d) LPT? All dates are specified as manufacturing planning calendar days. Assume that all jobs arrive on day 275. Which decision is best and why? Px

• **15.11** The following 5 overhaul jobs are waiting to be processed at Avianic's Engine Repair Inc. These jobs were logged as they arrived. All dates are specified as planning calendar days. Assume that all jobs arrived on day 180; today's date is 200.

Job	Due Date	Remaining Time (days)
103	214	10
205	223	7
309	217	11
412	219	5
517	217	15

Using the critical ratio scheduling rule, in what sequence would the jobs be processed? Px

•• **15.12** An Alabama lumberyard has four jobs on order, as shown in the following table. Today is day 205 on the yard's schedule.

Job	Due Date	Remaining Time (days)
A	212	6
B	209	3
C	208	3
D	210	8

Px

In what sequence would the jobs be ranked according to the following decision rules:
a) FCFS
b) SPT
c) LPT
d) EDD
e) Critical ratio
Which is best and why? Which has the minimum lateness?

•• **15.13** The following jobs are waiting to be processed at Rick Carlson's machine center. Carlson's machine center has a relatively long backlog and sets fresh schedules every 2 weeks, which do not disturb earlier schedules. Below are the jobs received during the previous 2 weeks. They are ready to be scheduled today, which is day 241 (day 241 is a work day). Job names refer to names of clients and contract numbers.

Job	Date Job Received	Production Days Needed	Date Job Due
BR-02	228	15	300
CX-01	225	25	270
DE-06	230	35	320
RG-05	235	40	360
SY-11	231	30	310

a) Complete the table below. (Show your supporting calculations.)
b) Which dispatching rule has the best score for flow time?
c) Which dispatching rule has the best score for utilization metric?
d) Which dispatching rule has the best score for lateness?
e) Which dispatching rule would you select? Support your decision.

Dispatching Rule	Job Sequence	Flow Time	Utilization Metric	Average Number of Jobs	Average Lateness
EDD					
SPT					
LPT					
FCFS					

PX

•• **15.14** The following jobs are waiting to be processed at Julie Morel's machine center:

Job	Date Order Received	Production Days Needed	Date Order Due
A	110	20	180
B	120	30	200
C	122	10	175
D	125	16	230
E	130	18	210

In what sequence would the jobs be ranked according to the following rules: (a) FCFS, (b) EDD, (c) SPT, and (d) LPT? All dates are according to shop calendar days. Today on the planning calendar is day 130, and none of the jobs have been started or scheduled. Which rule is best? PX

•• **15.15** Sunny Park Tailors has been asked to make three different types of wedding suits for separate customers. The table below highlights the time taken in hours for (1) cutting and sewing and (2) delivery of each of the suits. Which schedule finishes sooner: First-come, first-served (123) or a schedule using Johnson's rule?

Times Taken for Different Activities (hours)

Suit	Cut and Sew	Deliver
1	4	2
2	7	7
3	6	5

PX

•• **15.16** The following jobs are waiting to be processed at Jeremy LaMontagne's machine center. Today is day 250.

Job	Date Job Received	Production Days Needed	Date Job Due
1	215	30	260
2	220	20	290
3	225	40	300
4	240	50	320
5	250	20	340

Using the critical ratio scheduling rule, in what sequence would the jobs be processed? PX

•••• **15.17** The following set of seven jobs is to be processed through two work centers at George Heinrich's printing company. The sequence is first printing, then binding. Processing time at each of the work centers is shown in the following table:

Job	Printing (hours)	Binding (hours)
T	15	3
U	7	9
V	4	10
W	7	6
X	10	9
Y	4	5
Z	7	8

a) What is the optimal sequence for these jobs to be scheduled?
b) Chart these jobs through the two work centers.

c) What is the total length of time of this optimal solution?
d) What is the idle time in the binding shop, given the optimal solution?
e) How much would the binding machine's idle time be cut by splitting Job Z in half? Px

••• **15.18** Six jobs are to be processed through a two-step operation. The first operation involves sanding, and the second involves painting. Processing times are as follows:

Job	Operation 1 (hours)	Operation 2 (hours)
A	10	5
B	7	4
C	5	7
D	3	8
E	2	6
F	4	3

Determine a sequence that will minimize the total completion time for these jobs. Illustrate graphically. Px

•• **15.19** Jesse's Barber Shop at O'Hare Airport is open 7 days a week but has fluctuating demand. Jesse is interested in treating his barbers as well as he can with steady work and preferably 5 days of work with two consecutive days off. His analysis of his staffing needs resulted in the following plan. Schedule Jesse's staff with the minimum number of barbers.

	Day						
	Mon.	**Tue.**	**Wed.**	**Thu.**	**Fri.**	**Sat.**	**Sun.**
Barbers needed	6	5	5	5	6	4	3

•• **15.20** Given the following demand for waiters and waitresses at S. Ghosh Bar and Grill, determine the minimum wait staff needed with a policy of 2 consecutive days off.

	Day						
	Mon.	**Tue.**	**Wed.**	**Thu.**	**Fri.**	**Sat.**	**Sun.**
Wait staff needed	3	4	4	5	6	7	4

•• **15.21** Lifang Wu owns an automated machine shop that makes precision auto parts. He has just compiled an input–output report for the grinding work center. Complete this report and analyze the results.

Input–Output Report

Period	**1**	**2**	**3**	**4**	**Total**
Planned input	80	80	100	100	
Actual input	85	85	85	85	
Deviation					
Planned output	90	90	90	90	
Actual output	85	85	80	80	
Deviation					
Initial backlog: 30					

► **Refer to myomlab for these additional homework problems: 15.22–15.27**

Case Studies

► Old Oregon Wood Store

In 2010, George Wright started the Old Oregon Wood Store to manufacture Old Oregon tables. Each table is carefully constructed by hand using the highest-quality oak. Old Oregon tables can support more than 500 pounds, and since the start of the Old Oregon Wood Store, not one table has been returned because of faulty workmanship or structural problems. In addition to being rugged, each table is beautifully finished using a urethane varnish that George developed over 20 years of working with wood-finishing materials.

The manufacturing process consists of four steps: preparation, assembly, finishing, and packaging. Each step is performed by one person. In addition to overseeing the entire operation, George does all of the finishing. Tom Surowski performs the preparation step, which involves cutting and forming the basic components of the tables. Leon Davis is in charge of the assembly, and Cathy Stark performs the packaging.

Although each person is responsible for only one step in the manufacturing process, everyone can perform any one of the steps. It is George's policy that occasionally everyone should complete several tables on his or her own without any help or assistance. A small competition is used to see who can complete an entire table in the least amount of time. George maintains average total and intermediate completion times. The data are shown in Figure 15.6.

It takes Cathy longer than the other employees to construct an Old Oregon table. In addition to being slower than the other employees, Cathy is also unhappy about her current responsibility of packaging, which leaves her idle most of the day. Her first preference is finishing, and her second preference is preparation.

In addition to quality, George is concerned with costs and efficiency. When one of the employees misses a day, it causes major scheduling problems. In some cases, George assigns another employee overtime to complete the necessary work. At other times, George simply waits until the employee returns to work to complete his or her step in the manufacturing process. Both solutions cause problems. Overtime is expensive, and waiting causes delays and sometimes stops the entire manufacturing process.

To overcome some of these problems, Randy Lane was hired. Randy's major duties are to perform miscellaneous jobs and to help out if one of the employees is absent. George has given Randy training in all phases of the manufacturing process, and he is pleased with the speed at which Randy has been able to learn how to completely assemble Old Oregon tables. Randy's average total and intermediate completion times are given in Figure 15.7.

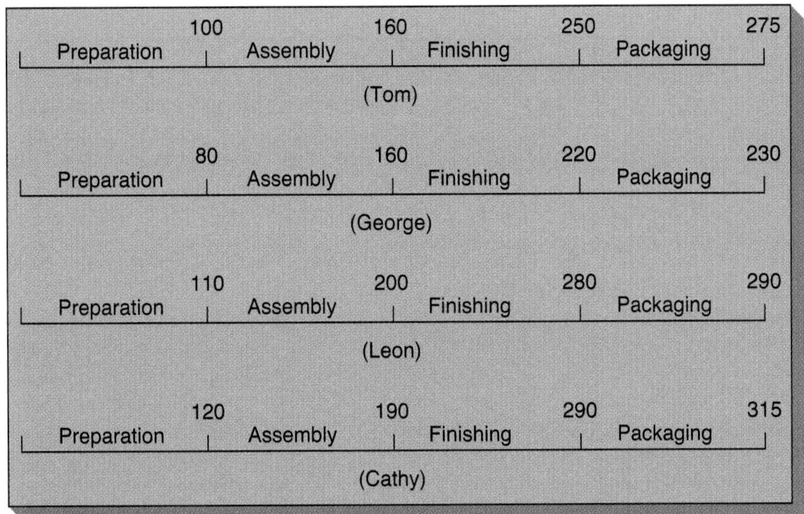

◀ **FIGURE 15.6**
Manufacturing Time in Minutes

110 190 290 300
Preparation | Assembly | Finishing | Packaging

◀ **FIGURE 15.7**
Randy's Completion Times in Minutes

Discussion Questions

1. What is the fastest way to manufacture Old Oregon tables using the original crew? How many could be made per day?
2. Would production rates and quantities change significantly if George would allow Randy to perform one of the four functions and make one of the original crew the backup person?
3. What is the fastest time to manufacture a table with the original crew if Cathy is moved to either preparation or finishing?
4. Whoever performs the packaging function is severely underutilized. Can you find a better way of utilizing the four- or five-person crew than either giving each a single job or allowing each to manufacture an entire table? How many tables could be manufactured per day with this scheme?

▶Scheduling at Hard Rock Cafe

Video Case

Whether it's scheduling nurses at Mayo Clinic, pilots at Southwest Airlines, classrooms at UCLA, or servers at a Hard Rock Cafe, it's clear that good scheduling is important. Proper schedules use an organization's assets (1) more effectively, by serving customers promptly, and (2) more efficiently, by lowering costs.

Hard Rock Cafe at Universal Studios, Orlando, is the world's largest restaurant, with 1,100 seats on two main levels. With typical turnover of employees in the restaurant industry at 80% to 100% per year, Hard Rock General Manager Ken Hoffman takes scheduling very seriously. Hoffman wants his 160 servers to be effective, but he also wants to treat them fairly. He has done so with scheduling software and flexibility that has increased productivity while contributing to turnover that is half the industry average. His goal is to find the fine balance that gives employees financially productive daily work shifts while setting the schedule tight enough so as to not overstaff between lunch and dinner.

The weekly schedule begins with a sales forecast. "First, we examine last year's sales at the cafe for the same day of the week," says Hoffman. "Then we adjust our forecast for this year based on a variety of closely watched factors. For example, we call the Orlando Convention Bureau every week to see what major groups will be in town. Then we send two researchers out to check on the occupancy of nearby hotels. We watch closely to see what concerts are scheduled at Hard Rock Live—the 3,000-seat concert stage next door. From the forecast, we calculate how many people we need to have on duty each day for the kitchen, the bar, as hosts, and for table service."

Once Hard Rock determines the number of staff needed, servers submit request forms, which are fed into the software's linear programming mathematical model. Individuals are given priority rankings from 1 to 9, based on their seniority and how important they are to fill each day's schedule. Schedules are then posted by day and by workstation. Trades are handled between employees, who understand the value of each specific shift and station.

Hard Rock employees like the system, as does the general manager, since sales per labor-hour are rising and turnover is dropping.

Discussion Questions*

1. Name and justify several factors that Hoffman could use in forecasting weekly sales.
2. What can be done to lower turnover in large restaurants?
3. Why is seniority important in scheduling servers?
4. How does the schedule impact on productivity?

*You may wish to view the video that accompanies this case before answering the questions.

▶**Additional Case Study:** Visit **www.myomlab.com** or **www.pearsonhighered.com/heizer** for this free case study:
Payroll Planning, Inc.: Describes setting a schedule for handling the accounting for dozens of client firms.

Bibliography

Baker, Kenneth A., and Dan Trietsch. *Principles of Sequencing and Scheduling*. New York: Wiley (2009).

Bard, Jonathan F. "Staff Scheduling in High Volume Service Facilities with Downgrading." *IIE Transactions* 36 (2004): 985–997.

Bolander, Steven, and Sam G. Taylor. "Scheduling Techniques: A Comparison of Logic." *Production and Inventory Management Journal* (1st Quarter 2000): 1–5.

Cayirli, Tugba, and Emre Veral. "Outpatient Scheduling in Health Care: A Review of Literature." *Production and Operations Management* 12, no. 4 (Winter 2003): 519–549.

Chapman, Stephen. *Fundamentals of Production Planning and Control*. Upper Saddle River, NJ: Prentice Hall (2006).

Deng, Honghui, Q. Wang, G. K. Leong, and S. X. Sun. "Usage of Opportunity Cost to Maximize Performance in Revenue Management." *Decision Sciences* 38, no. 4 (November 2008): 737–758.

Dietrich, Brenda, G. A. Paleologo, and L. Wynter. "Revenue Management in Business Services." *Production and Operations Management* 17, no. 4 (July–August 2008): 475–480.

Farmer, Adam, Jeffrey S. Smith, and Luke T. Miller. "Scheduling Umpire Crews for Professional Tennis Tournaments." *Interfaces* 37, no. 2 (March–April 2007): 187–196.

Geraghty, Kevin. "Revenue Management and Digital Marketing." *OR/MS Today* 35, no. 6 (December 2008): 22–28.

Kellogg, Deborah L., and Steven Walczak. "Nurse Scheduling." *Interfaces* 37, no. 4 (July–August 2007): 355–369.

Lopez, P., and F. Roubellat. *Production Scheduling*. New York: Wiley (2008).

Mondschein, S. V., and G. Y. Weintraub. "Appointment Policies in Service Operations." *Production and Operations Management* 12, no. 2 (Summer 2003): 266–286.

Morton, Thomas E., and David W. Pentico. *Heuristic Scheduling Systems*. New York: Wiley (1993).

Pinedo, M. *Scheduling: Theory, Algorithms, and Systems*, 2nd ed. Upper Saddle River, N.J.: Prentice Hall (2002).

Plenert, Gerhard, and Bill Kirchmier. *Finite Capacity Scheduling*. New York: Wiley (2000).

Render, B., R. M. Stair, and M. Hanna. *Quantitative Analysis for Management*, 10th ed. Upper Saddle River, NJ: Prentice Hall (2009).

Chapter 15 *Rapid* Review

Main Heading	Review Material	myomlab
THE IMPORTANCE OF SHORT-TERM SCHEDULING (p. 584)	The strategic importance of scheduling is clear: • Effective scheduling means *faster movement* of goods and services through a facility. This means greater use of assets and hence greater capacity per dollar invested, which, in turn, *lowers cost*. • Added capacity, faster throughput, and the related flexibility mean better customer service through *faster delivery*. • Good scheduling contributes to realistic commitments, hence *dependable delivery*.	
SCHEDULING ISSUES (pp. 584–587)	*The objective of scheduling is to allocate and prioritize demand (generated by either forecasts or customer orders) to available facilities.* ■ **Forward scheduling**—Begins the schedule as soon as the requirements are known. ■ **Backward scheduling**—Begins with the due date by scheduling the final operation first and the other job steps in reverse order. The four scheduling criteria are (1) *minimize completion time*, (2) *maximize utilization*, (3) *minimize work-in-process (WIP) inventory*, and (4) *minimize customer waiting time*.	**VIDEO 15.1** Scheduling at Hard Rock
SCHEDULING PROCESS-FOCUSED FACILITIES (pp. 587–588)	A process-focused facility is a high-variety, low-volume system commonly found in manufacturing and services. It is also called an intermittent, or job shop, facility. Control files track the actual progress made against the plan for each work order.	
LOADING JOBS (pp. 588–593)	■ **Loading**—The assigning of jobs to work or processing centers. ■ **Input/output control**—Allows operations personnel to manage facility work flows by tracking work added to a work center and its work completed. ■ **ConWIP cards**—Cards that control the amount of work in a work center, aiding input/output control. ConWIP is an acronym for *constant work-in-process.* A ConWIP card travels with a job (or batch) through the work center. When the job is finished, the card is released and returned to the initial workstation, authorizing the entry of a new batch into the work center. ■ **Gantt charts**—Planning charts used to schedule resources and allocate time. The Gantt *load chart* shows the loading and idle times of several departments, machines, or facilities. It displays the relative workloads in the system so that the manager knows what adjustments are appropriate. The Gantt *schedule chart* is used to monitor jobs in progress (and is also used for project scheduling). It indicates which jobs are on schedule and which are ahead of or behind schedule. ■ **Assignment method**—A special class of linear programming models that involves assigning tasks or jobs to resources. In assignment problems, only one job (or worker) is assigned to one machine (or project). The assignment method involves adding and subtracting appropriate numbers in the table to find the lowest *opportunity cost* for each assignment.	Problems: 15.1–15.9, 15.21 Virtual Office Hours for Solved Problems: 15.1
SEQUENCING JOBS (pp. 594–600)	■ **Sequencing**—Determining the order in which jobs should be done at each work center. ■ **Priority rules**—Rules used to determine the sequence of jobs in process-oriented facilities. ■ **First-come, first-served (FCFS)**—Jobs are completed in the order in which they arrived. ■ **Shortest processing time (SPT)**—Jobs with the shortest processing times are assigned first. ■ **Earliest due date**—Earliest due date jobs are performed first. ■ **Longest processing time (LPT)**—Jobs with the longest processing time are completed first: $\text{Average completion time} = \dfrac{\text{Sum of total flow time}}{\text{Number of jobs}}$ $\text{Utilization metric} = \dfrac{\text{Total job work (processing) time}}{\text{Sum of total flow time}}$	Problems: 15.10–15.18 Virtual Office Hours for Solved Problems: 15.2–15.5 **ACTIVE MODEL 15.1**

Main Heading	Review Material	
	Average number of jobs in the system $= \dfrac{\text{Sum of total flow time}}{\text{Total job work (processing) time}}$ Average job lateness $= \dfrac{\text{Total late days}}{\text{Number of jobs}}$ SPT is the best technique for minimizing job flow and average number of jobs in the system. FCFS performs about average on most criteria, and it appears fair to customers. EDD minimizes maximum tardiness. ■ **Critical ratio (CR)**—A sequencing rule that is an index number computed by dividing the time remaining until due date by the work time remaining: $CR = \dfrac{\text{Time remaining}}{\text{Workdays remaining}} = \dfrac{\text{Due date} - \text{Today's date}}{\text{Work (lead) time remaining}}$ As opposed to the priority rules, the critical ratio is dynamic and easily updated. It tends to perform better than FCFS, SPT, EDD, or LPT on the average job-lateness criterion. ■ **Johnson's rule**—An approach that minimizes processing time for sequencing a group of jobs through two work centers while minimizing total idle time in the work centers. Rule-based scheduling systems have the following limitations: (1) Scheduling is dynamic, (2) rules do not look upstream or downstream, and (3) rules do not look beyond due dates.	
FINITE CAPACITY SCHEDULING (FCS) (pp. 600–601)	• **Finite capacity scheduling (FCS)**—Computerized short-term scheduling that overcomes the disadvantage of rule-based systems by providing the user with graphical interactive computing.	
SCHEDULING REPETITIVE FACILITIES (pp. 601–602)	• **Level material use**—The use of frequent, high-quality, small lot sizes that contribute to just-in-time production. Advantages of level material use are (1) lower inventory levels, (2) faster product throughput, (3) improved component and product quality, (4) reduced floor-space requirements, (5) improved communication among employees, and (6) a smoother production process.	
SCHEDULING SERVICES (pp. 602–605)	Cyclical scheduling with inconsistent staffing needs is often the case in services. The objective focuses on developing a schedule with the minimum number of workers. In these cases, each employee is assigned to a shift and has time off.	Problems: 15.19–15.20

Self Test

■ **Before taking the self-test,** refer to the learning objectives listed at the beginning of the chapter and the key terms listed at the end of the chapter.

LO1. Which of the following decisions covers the longest time period?
- **a)** Short-term scheduling
- **b)** Capacity planning
- **c)** Aggregate planning
- **d)** A master schedule

LO2. A visual aid used in loading and scheduling jobs is a:
- **a)** Gantt chart.
- **b)** planning file.
- **c)** bottleneck.
- **d)** load-schedule matrix.
- **e)** level material chart.

LO3. The assignment method involves adding and subtracting appropriate numbers in the table to find the lowest ______ for each assignment.
- **a)** profit
- **b)** number of steps
- **c)** number of allocations
- **d)** range per row
- **e)** opportunity cost

LO4. The most popular priority rules include:
- **a)** FCFS.
- **b)** EDD.
- **c)** SPT.
- **d)** all of the above.

LO5. The job that should be scheduled last when using Johnson's rule is the job with the:
- **a)** largest total processing time on both machines.
- **b)** smallest total processing time on both machines.
- **c)** longest activity time if it lies with the first machine.
- **d)** longest activity time if it lies with the second machine.
- **e)** shortest activity time if it lies with the second machine.

LO6. What is computerized short-term scheduling that overcomes the disadvantage of rule-based systems by providing the user with graphical interactive computing?
- **a)** LPT
- **b)** FCS
- **c)** CSS
- **d)** FCFS
- **e)** GIC

LO7. Cyclical scheduling is used to schedule:
- **a)** jobs.
- **b)** machines.
- **c)** shipments.
- **d)** employees.

Answers: LO1. b; LO2. a; LO3. e; LO4. d; LO5. e; LO6. b; LO7. d.

16 JIT and Lean Operations

Chapter Outline

10

OM Strategy Decisions

- Design of Goods and Services
- Managing Quality
- Process Strategy
- Location Strategies
- Layout Strategies
- Human Resources
- Supply-Chain Management
- Inventory Management
  - Independent Demand
  - Dependent Demand
  - JIT and Lean Operations
- Scheduling
- Maintenance

ACHIEVING COMPETITIVE ADVANTAGE WITH LEAN OPERATIONS AT TOYOTA MOTOR CORPORATION

Toyota Motor Corporation, with annual sales of over 9 million cars and trucks, is the largest vehicle manufacturer in the world. Two techniques, just-in-time (JIT) and the Toyota Production System (TPS), have been instrumental in this post-WWII growth. Toyota, with a wide range of vehicles, competes head-to-head with successful long-established companies in Europe and the U.S. Taiichi Ohno, a former vice president of Toyota, created the basic framework for the world's most discussed systems for improving productivity, JIT and TPS. These two concepts provide much of the foundation for lean operations:

- Central to JIT is a philosophy of continued problem solving. In practice, JIT means making only what is needed, when it is needed. JIT provides an excellent vehicle for finding and eliminating problems because problems are easy to find in a system that has no slack. When excess inventory is eliminated, quality, layout, scheduling, and supplier issues become immediately evident—as does excess production.
- Central to TPS is employee learning and a continuing effort to create and produce products under ideal conditions. Ideal conditions exist only when facilities, machines, and people are brought

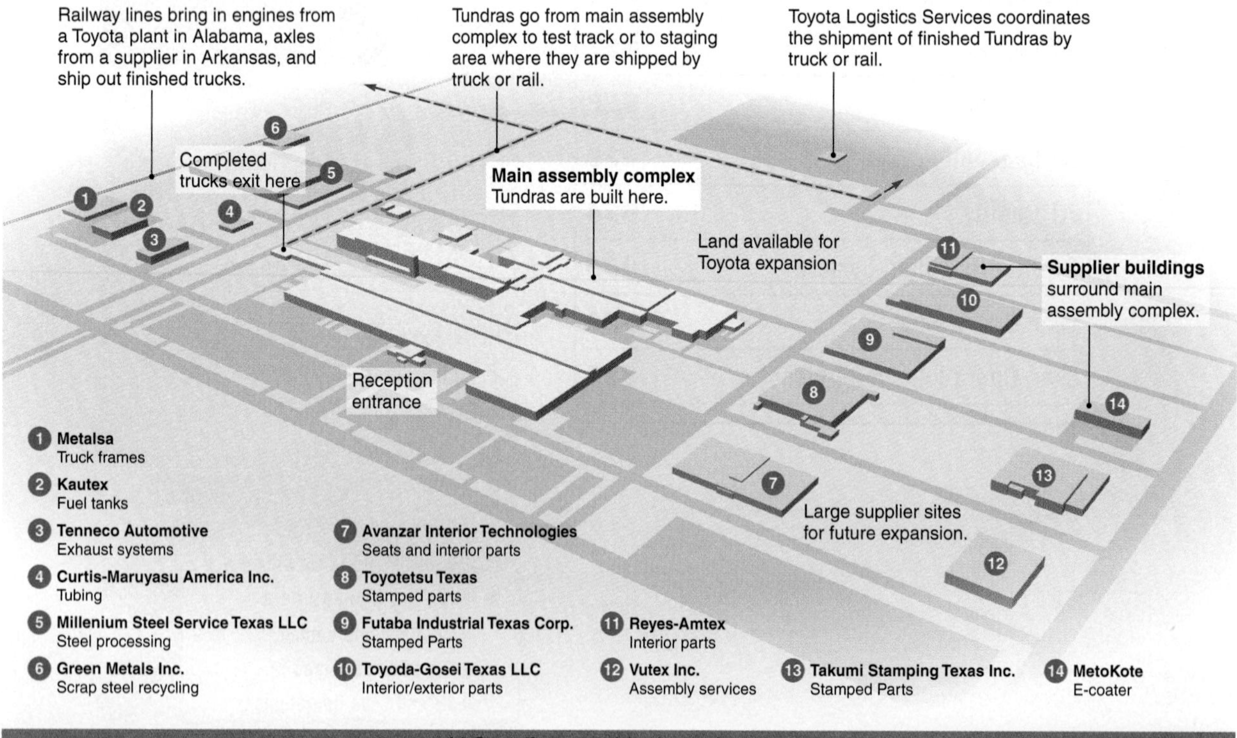
Railway lines bring in engines from a Toyota plant in Alabama, axles from a supplier in Arkansas, and ship out finished trucks.
Tundras go from main assembly complex to test track or to staging area where they are shipped by truck or rail.
Toyota Logistics Services coordinates the shipment of finished Tundras by truck or rail.
Completed trucks exit here
Main assembly complex
Tundras are built here.
Land available for Toyota expansion
Supplier buildings surround main assembly complex.
Reception entrance
Large supplier sites for future expansion.
1 Metalsa
Truck frames
2 Kautex
Fuel tanks
3 Tenneco Automotive
Exhaust systems
4 Curtis-Maruyasu America Inc.
Tubing
5 Millenium Steel Service Texas LLC
Steel processing
6 Green Metals Inc.
Scrap steel recycling
7 Avanzar Interior Technologies
Seats and interior parts
8 Toyotetsu Texas
Stamped parts
9 Futaba Industrial Texas Corp.
Stamped Parts
10 Toyoda-Gosei Texas LLC
Interior/exterior parts
11 Reyes-Amtex
Interior parts
12 Vutex Inc.
Assembly services
13 Takumi Stamping Texas Inc.
Stamped Parts
14 MetoKote
E-coater
14 Suppliers outside the main plant

Outside: Toyota has a 2,000-acre site with 14 of the 21 onsite suppliers, adjacent rail lines, and near-by interstate highway. The site provides expansion space for both Toyota and for its suppliers — and provides an environment for Just-in-time.

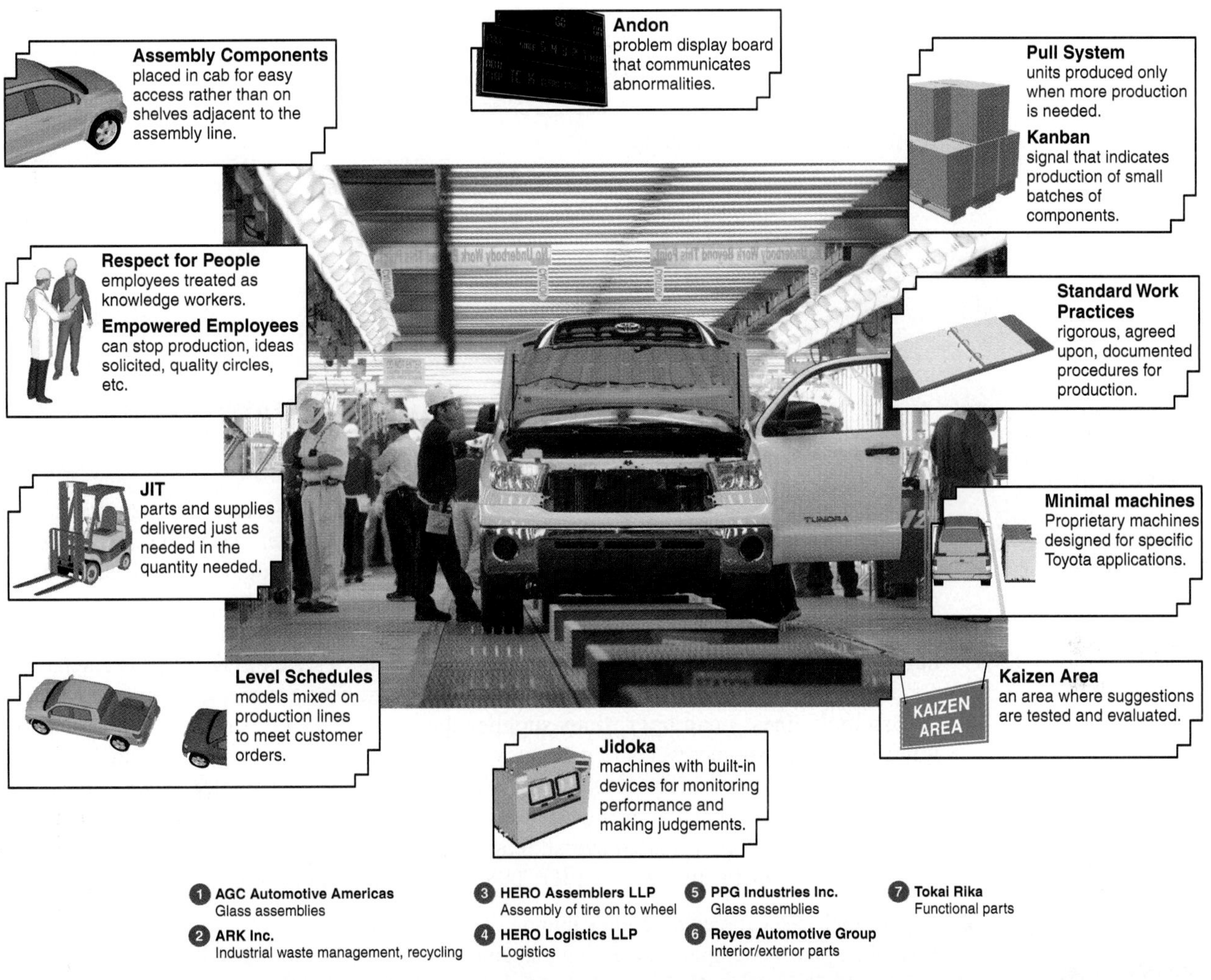

Andon
problem display board that communicates abnormalities.
Assembly Components
placed in cab for easy access rather than on shelves adjacent to the assembly line.
Pull System
units produced only when more production is needed.
Kanban
signal that indicates production of small batches of components.
Respect for People
employees treated as knowledge workers.
Empowered Employees
can stop production, ideas solicited, quality circles, etc.
Standard Work Practices
rigorous, agreed upon, documented procedures for production.
JIT
parts and supplies delivered just as needed in the quantity needed.
Minimal machines
Proprietary machines designed for specific Toyota applications.
Level Schedules
models mixed on production lines to meet customer orders.
KAIZEN AREA
Kaizen Area
an area where suggestions are tested and evaluated.
Jidoka
machines with built-in devices for monitoring performance and making judgements.
1 AGC Automotive Americas
Glass assemblies
2 ARK Inc.
Industrial waste management, recycling
3 HERO Assemblers LLP
Assembly of tire on to wheel
4 HERO Logistics LLP
Logistics
5 PPG Industries Inc.
Glass assemblies
6 Reyes Automotive Group
Interior/exterior parts
7 Tokai Rika
Functional parts

7 Suppliers inside the main plant

Toyota's San Antonio plant has about 2 million interior sq. ft., providing facilities within the final assembly building for 7 of the 21 onsite suppliers, and capacity to build 200,000 pick-up trucks annually. But most importantly, Toyota practices the world-class Toyota Production System and expects its suppliers to do the same thing wherever they are.

together, adding value without waste. Waste undermines productivity by diverting resources to excess inventory, unnecessary processing, and poor quality. Respect for people, extensive training, cross-training, and standard work practices of empowered employees focusing on driving out waste are fundamental to TPS.

Toyota's latest implementation of TPS and JIT is present at its new San Antonio plant, the largest Toyota land site for an automobile assembly plant in the U.S. Interestingly, despite its annual production capability of 200,000 Tundra pick-up trucks, the building itself is one of the smallest in the industry. Modern automobiles have 30,000 parts, but at Toyota, independent suppliers combine many of these parts into sub-assemblies. Twenty-one of these suppliers are on site at the San Antonio facility and transfer components to the assembly line on a JIT basis.

Operations such as these taking place in the new San Antonio plant are why Toyota continues to perform near the top in quality and maintain the lowest labor-hour assembly time in the industry. JIT, TPS, and lean operations work—and they provide a competitive advantage at Toyota Motor Corporation.

Chapter 16 **Learning Objectives**

AUTHOR COMMENT World-class firms everywhere are using these three techniques.

JUST-IN-TIME, THE TOYOTA PRODUCTION SYSTEM, AND LEAN OPERATIONS

LO1: Define just-in-time, TPS, and lean operations

Just-in-time (JIT)
Continuous and forced problem solving via a focus on throughput and reduced inventory.

Toyota Production System (TPS)
Focus on continuous improvement, respect for people, and standard work practices.

Lean operations
Eliminates waste through a focus on exactly what the customer wants.

As shown in the *Global Company Profile*, the Toyota Production System (TPS) contributes to a world-class operation at Toyota Motor Corporation. In this chapter, we discuss JIT, TPS, and lean operations as approaches to continuing improvement that drive out waste and lead to world-class organizations.

Just-in-time (JIT) is an approach of continuous and forced problem solving via a focus on throughput and reduced inventory. The **Toyota Production System (TPS)**, with its emphasis on continuous improvement, respect for people, and standard work practices, is particularly suited for assembly lines. **Lean operations** supplies the customer with exactly what the customer wants when the customer wants it, without waste, through continuous improvement. Lean operations are driven by workflow initiated by the "pull" of the customer's order. When implemented as a comprehensive manufacturing strategy, JIT, TPS, and lean systems sustain competitive advantage and result in increased overall returns.

If there is any distinction between JIT, TPS, and lean operations, it is that:

- JIT emphasizes forced problem solving.
- TPS emphasizes employee learning and empowerment in an assembly-line environment.
- Lean operations emphasize understanding the customer.

However, in practice, there is little difference, and the terms are often used interchangeably. Leading organizations use the approaches and techniques that make sense for them. In this chapter, we use the term *lean operations* to encompass all of the related approaches and techniques.

Regardless of the label put on operations improvement, good production systems require that managers address three issues that are pervasive and fundamental to operations management: eliminate waste, remove variability, and improve throughput. We first introduce these three issues and then discuss the major attributes of JIT, TPS, and lean operations. Finally, we look at lean operations applied to services.

LO2: Define the seven wastes and the 5Ss

Eliminate Waste

Traditional producers have limited goals—accepting, for instance, the production of some defective parts and some inventory. Lean producers set their sights on perfection; no bad parts, no inventory, only value-added activities, and no waste. Any activity that does not add value in the eyes of the customer is a waste. The customer defines product value. If the customer does not want to pay for it, it is a waste. Taiichi Ohno, noted for his work on the Toyota Production System, identified seven categories of waste. These categories have become popular in lean organizations and cover many of the ways organizations waste or lose money. Ohno's **seven wastes** are:

Seven wastes
Overproduction
Queues
Transportation
Inventory
Motion
Overprocessing
Defective product

- *Overproduction:* Producing more than the customer orders or producing early (before it is demanded) is waste. Inventory of any kind is usually a waste.
- *Queues:* Idle time, storage, and waiting are wastes (they add no value).
- *Transportation:* Moving material between plants or between work centers and handling more than once is waste.
- *Inventory:* Unnecessary raw material, work-in-process (WIP), finished goods, and excess operating supplies add no value and are wastes.

- *Motion:* Movement of equipment or people that adds no value is waste.
- *Overprocessing:* Work performed on the product that adds no value is waste.
- *Defective product:* Returns, warranty claims, rework, and scrap are a waste.

A broader perspective—one that goes beyond immediate production—suggests that other resources, such as energy, water, and air, are often wasted but should not be. Efficient, sustainable production minimizes inputs and maximizes outputs, wasting nothing.

For over a century, managers have pursued "housekeeping" for a neat, orderly, and efficient workplace and as a means of reducing waste. Operations managers have embellished "housekeeping" to include a checklist—now known as the 5Ss.[1] The Japanese developed the initial 5Ss. Not only are the 5Ss a good checklist for lean operations, they also provide an easy vehicle with which to assist the culture change that is often necessary to bring about lean operations. The **5Ss** follow:

5Ss
A lean production checklist:
Sort
Simplify
Shine
Standardize
Sustain

- *Sort/segregate:* Keep what is needed and remove everything else from the work area; when in doubt, throw it out. Identify non-value items and remove them. Getting rid of these items makes space available and usually improves work flow.
- *Simplify/straighten:* Arrange and use methods analysis tools (see Chapter 7 and Chapter 10) to improve work flow and reduce wasted motion. Consider long-run and short-run ergonomic issues. Label and display for easy use only what is needed in the immediate work area. For examples of visual displays see Chapter 10, Figure 10.8.
- *Shine/sweep:* Clean daily; eliminate all forms of dirt, contamination, and clutter from the work area.
- *Standardize:* Remove variations from the process by developing standard operating procedures and checklists; good standards make the abnormal obvious. Standardize equipment and tooling so that cross-training time and cost are reduced. Train and retrain the work team so that when deviations occur, they are readily apparent to all.
- *Sustain/self-discipline:* Review periodically to recognize efforts and to motivate to sustain progress. Use visuals wherever possible to communicate and sustain progress.

U.S. managers often add two additional Ss that contribute to establishing and maintaining a lean workplace:

- *Safety:* Build good safety practices into the above five activities.
- *Support/maintenance:* Reduce variability, unplanned downtime, and costs. Integrate daily shine tasks with preventive maintenance.

The Ss provide a vehicle for continuous improvement with which all employees can identify. Operations managers need think only of the examples set by a well-run hospital emergency room or the spit-and-polish of a fire department for a benchmark. Offices and retail stores, as well as manufacturers, have successfully used the 5Ss in their respective efforts to eliminate waste and move to lean operations. A place for everything and everything in its place does make a difference in a well-run office. And retail stores successfully use the Ss to reduce misplaced merchandise and improve customer service. An orderly workplace reduces waste so that assets are released for other, more productive, purposes.

Remove Variability

Managers seek to remove variability caused by both internal and external factors. **Variability** is any deviation from the optimum process that delivers perfect product on time, every time. Variability is a polite word for problems. The less variability in a system, the less waste in the system. Most variability is caused by tolerating waste or by poor management. Among the many sources of variability are:

Variability
Any deviation from the optimum process that delivers perfect product on time, every time.

- Poor production processes that allow employees and suppliers to produce improper quantities or late or non-conforming units
- Unknown customer demands
- Incomplete or inaccurate drawings, specifications, and bills of material

[1]The term 5S comes from the Japanese words seiri (*sort* and clear out), seiton (*straighten* and configure), seiso (*scrub* and cleanup), seiketsu (maintain *sanitation* and cleanliness of self and workplace), and shitsuke (*self-discipline and standardization* of these practices).

Both JIT and inventory reduction are effective tools for identifying causes of variability. The precise timing of JIT makes variability evident, just as reducing inventory exposes variability. The removal of variability allows managers to move good materials on schedule, add value at each step of the production process, drive down costs, and win orders.

Improve Throughput

Throughput
The time required to move orders through the production process, from receipt to delivery.

Manufacturing cycle time
The time between the arrival of raw materials and the shipping of finished products.

Pull system
A concept that results in material being produced only when requested and moved to where it is needed just as it is needed.

Throughput is a measure (in units or time) that it takes to move an order from receipt to delivery. Each minute products remain on the books, costs accumulate and competitive advantage is lost. The time that an order is in the shop is called **manufacturing cycle time**. This is the time between the arrival of raw materials and the shipping of finished product. For example, phone-system manufacturer Northern Telecom now has materials pulled directly from qualified suppliers to the assembly line. This effort has reduced a segment of Northern's manufacturing cycle time from 3 weeks to just 4 hours, the incoming inspection staff from 47 to 24, and problems on the shop floor caused by defective materials by 97%. Driving down manufacturing cycle time can make a major improvement in throughput.

A technique for increasing throughput is a pull system. A **pull system** *pulls* a unit to where it is needed just as it is needed. Pull systems are a standard tool of JIT systems. Pull systems use signals to request production and delivery from supplying stations to stations that have production capacity available. The pull concept is used both within the immediate production process and with suppliers. By *pulling* material through the system in very small lots—just as it is needed—waste and inventory are removed. As inventory is removed, clutter is reduced, problems become evident, and continuous improvement is emphasized. Removing the cushion of inventory also reduces both investment in inventory and manufacturing cycle time. A push system dumps orders on the next downstream workstation, regardless of timeliness and resource availability. Push systems are the antithesis of JIT. Pulling material through a production process as it is needed rather than in a "push" mode typically lowers cost and improves schedule performance, enhancing customer satisfaction.

AUTHOR COMMENT
JIT places added demands on performance, but that is why it pays off.

JUST-IN-TIME (JIT)

With its forced problem solving via a focus on rapid throughput and reduced inventory, JIT provides a powerful strategy for improving operations. With JIT, materials arrive *where* they are needed only *when* they are needed. When good units do not arrive just as needed, a "problem" has been identified. By driving out waste and delay in this manner, JIT reduces costs associated with excess inventory, cuts variability and waste, and improves throughput. JIT is a key ingredient of lean operations and is particularly helpful in supporting strategies of rapid response and low cost.

Many services have adopted JIT techniques as a normal part of their business. Restaurants like Olive Garden and Red Lobster expect and receive JIT deliveries. Both buyer and supplier expect fresh, high-quality produce delivered without fail just when it is needed. The system doesn't work any other way.

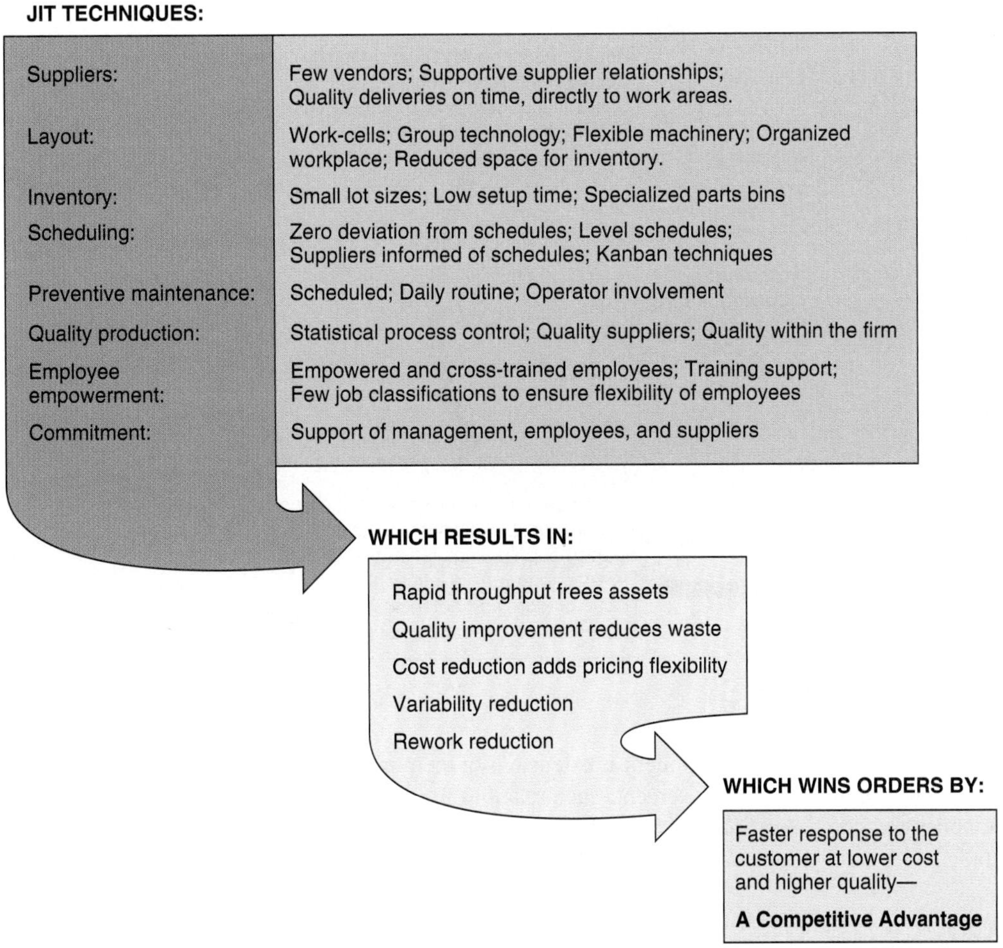

JIT TECHNIQUES:

Suppliers:	Few vendors; Supportive supplier relationships; Quality deliveries on time, directly to work areas.
Layout:	Work-cells; Group technology; Flexible machinery; Organized workplace; Reduced space for inventory.
Inventory:	Small lot sizes; Low setup time; Specialized parts bins
Scheduling:	Zero deviation from schedules; Level schedules; Suppliers informed of schedules; Kanban techniques
Preventive maintenance:	Scheduled; Daily routine; Operator involvement
Quality production:	Statistical process control; Quality suppliers; Quality within the firm
Employee empowerment:	Empowered and cross-trained employees; Training support; Few job classifications to ensure flexibility of employees
Commitment:	Support of management, employees, and suppliers

WHICH RESULTS IN:

Rapid throughput frees assets
Quality improvement reduces waste
Cost reduction adds pricing flexibility
Variability reduction
Rework reduction

WHICH WINS ORDERS BY:

Faster response to the customer at lower cost and higher quality—
A Competitive Advantage

◄ **FIGURE 16.1**
JIT Contributes to Competitive Advantage

Every moment material is held, an activity that adds value should be occurring. Consequently, as Figure 16.1 suggests, JIT often yields a competitive advantage.

Effective JIT requires a meaningful buyer–supplier partnership.

JIT Partnerships

A **JIT partnership** exists when a supplier and a purchaser work together with open communication and a goal of removing waste and driving down costs. Close relationships and trust are critical to the success of JIT. Figure 16.2 shows the characteristics of JIT partnerships. Some specific goals of JIT partnerships are:

JIT partnerships
Partnerships of suppliers and purchasers that remove waste and drive down costs for mutual benefits.

- *Removal of unnecessary activities*, such as receiving, incoming inspection, and paperwork related to bidding, invoicing, and payment.
- *Removal of in-plant inventory* by delivery in small lots directly to the using department as needed.
- *Removal of in-transit inventory* by encouraging suppliers to locate nearby and provide frequent small shipments. The shorter the flow of material in the resource pipeline, the less inventory. Inventory can also be reduced through a technique known as *consignment*. **Consignment inventory** (see the *OM in Action* box "Lean Production at Cessna Aircraft"), a variation of vendor-managed inventory (Chapter 11), means the supplier maintains the title to the inventory until it is used. For instance, an assembly plant may find a hardware supplier that is willing to locate its warehouse where the user currently has its stockroom. In this manner, when hardware is needed, it is no farther than the stockroom. Schedule and production information must be shared with the consignment supplier, or inventory holding costs will just be transferred from the buyer to the supplier, with no net cost reduction. Another option is to have the supplier ship to other, perhaps smaller, purchasers from the "stockroom."
- *Obtain improved quality and reliability* through long-term commitments, communication, and cooperation.

Consignment inventory
An arrangement in which the supplier maintains title to the inventory until it is used.

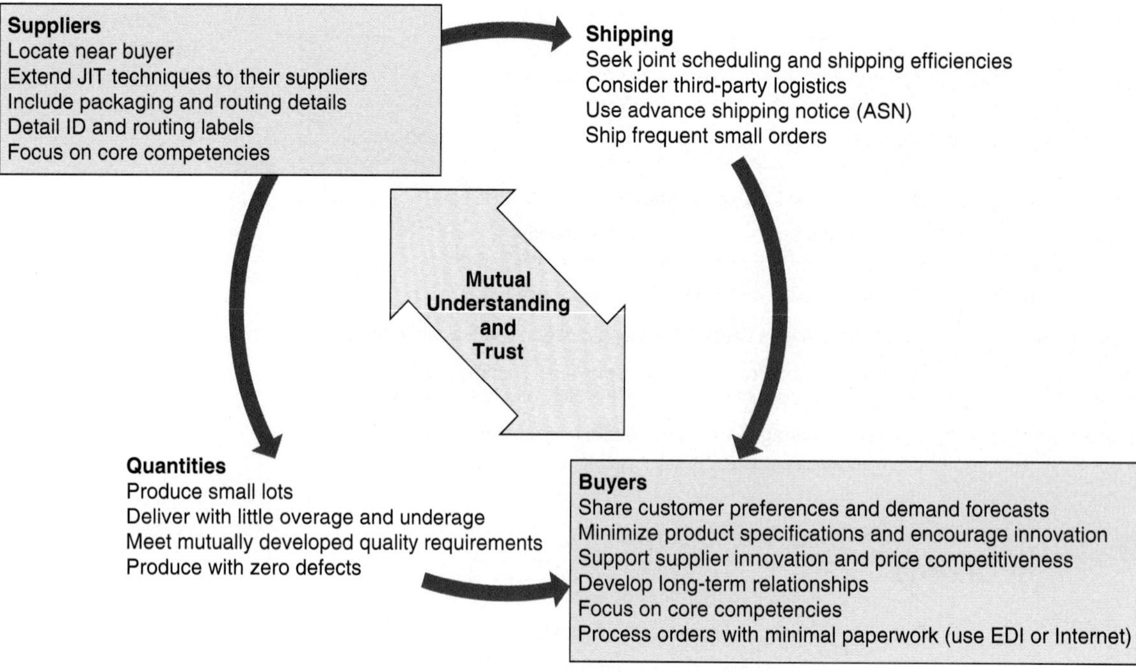

▲ **FIGURE 16.2 Characteristics of JIT Partnerships**

Leading organizations view suppliers as extensions of their own organizations and expect suppliers to be fully committed to improvement. Such relationships require a high degree of respect by both supplier and purchaser. Supplier concerns can be significant; Harley-Davidson, for example, initially had difficulty implementing JIT because supplier issues outweighed the perceived benefits.

LO3: Explain JIT partnerships

Concerns of Suppliers

Successful JIT partnerships require that supplier concerns be addressed. These concerns include:

1. *Diversification:* Suppliers may not want to tie themselves to long-term contracts with one customer. The suppliers' perception is that they reduce their risk if they have a variety of customers.
2. *Scheduling:* Many suppliers have little faith in the purchaser's ability to produce orders to a smooth, coordinated schedule.

OM in Action ▶ Lean Production at Cessna Aircraft

When Cessna Aircraft opened its new plant in Independence, Kansas, it saw the opportunity to switch from a craftwork mentality producing small single-engine planes to a lean manufacturing system. In doing so, Cessna adopted three lean practices.

First, Cessna set up consignment- and vendor-managed inventories with several of its suppliers. Blanket purchase orders allow Honeywell, for example, to maintain a 30-day supply of avionic parts onsite. Other vendors were encouraged to use a nearby warehouse to keep parts that could then be delivered daily to the production line.

Second, Cessna managers committed to cross-training, in which team members learn the duties of other team members and can shift across assembly lines as needed. To develop these technical skills, Cessna brought in 60 retired assembly-line workers to mentor and teach new employees. Employees were taught to work as a team and to assume responsibility for their team's quality.

Third, the company used group technology and manufacturing cells to move away from a batch process that resulted in large inventories and unsold planes. Now, Cessna pulls product through its plant only when a specific order is placed.

These commitments to manufacturing efficiency are part of the lean operations that has made Cessna the world's largest manufacturer of single-engine aircraft.

Sources: **www.cessna.com** (2007); *Strategic Finance* (November 2002): 32; *Purchasing* (September 4, 2003): 25–30; and *Fortune* (May 1, 2000): 1222B.

3. *Lead time:* Engineering or specification changes can play havoc with JIT because of inadequate lead time for suppliers to implement the necessary changes.
4. *Quality:* Suppliers' capital budgets, processes, or technology may limit ability to respond to changes in product and quality.
5. *Lot sizes:* Suppliers may see frequent delivery in small lots as a way to transfer buyers' holding costs to suppliers.

JIT LAYOUT

JIT layouts reduce another kind of waste—movement. The movement of material on a factory floor (or paper in an office) does not add value. Consequently, managers want flexible layouts that reduce the movement of both people and material. JIT layouts place material directly in the location where needed. For instance, an assembly line should be designed with delivery points next to the line so material need not be delivered first to a receiving department and then moved again. This is what VF Corporation's Wrangler Division in Greensboro, North Carolina, did; denim is now delivered directly to the line. Toyota has gone one step farther and places hardware and components in the chassis of each vehicle moving down the assembly line. This is not only convenient, but it allows Toyota to save space and opens areas adjacent to the assembly line previously occupied by shelves. When a layout reduces distance, firms often save labor and space and may have the added bonus of eliminating potential areas for accumulation of unwanted inventory. Table 16.1 provides a list of JIT layout tactics.

▼ TABLE 16.1
JIT Layout Tactics

Build work cells for families of products
Include a large number of operations in a small area
Minimize distance
Design little space for inventory
Improve employee communication
Use poka-yoke devices
Build flexible or movable equipment
Cross-train workers to add flexibility

Distance Reduction

Reducing distance is a major contribution of work cells, work centers, and focused factories (see Chapter 9). The days of long production lines and huge economic lots, with goods passing through monumental, single-operation machines, are gone. Now firms use work cells, often arranged in a U shape, containing several machines performing different operations. These work cells are often based on group technology codes (as discussed in Chapter 5). Group technology codes help identify components with similar characteristics so we can group them into families. Once families are identified, work cells are built for them. The result can be thought of as a small product-oriented facility where the "product" is actually a group of similar products—a family of products. The cells produce one good unit at a time, and ideally they produce the units *only* after a customer orders them.

Increased Flexibility

Modern work cells are designed so they can be easily rearranged to adapt to changes in volume, product improvements, or even new designs. Almost nothing in these new departments is bolted down. This same concept of layout flexibility applies to office environments. Not only is most office furniture and equipment movable, but so are office walls, computer connections, and telecommunications. Equipment is modular. Layout flexibility aids the changes that result from product *and* process improvements that are inevitable with a philosophy of continuous improvement.

Impact on Employees

JIT layouts allow cross-trained employees to bring flexibility and efficiency to the work cell. Employees working together can tell each other about problems and opportunities for improvement. When layouts provide for sequential operations, feedback can be immediate. Defects are waste. When workers produce units one at a time, they test each product or component at each subsequent production stage. Machines in work cells with self-testing poka-yoke functions detect defects and stop automatically when they occur. Before JIT, defective products were replaced from inventory. Because surplus inventory is not kept in JIT facilities, there are no such buffers. Getting it right the first time is critical.

Reduced Space and Inventory

Because JIT layouts reduce travel distance, they also reduce inventory by removing space for inventory. When there is little space, inventory must be moved in very small lots or even single units. Units are always moving because there is no storage. For instance, each month Security

Pacific Corporation's focused facility sorts 7 million checks, processes 5 million statements, and mails 190,000 customer statements. With a JIT layout, mail processing time has been reduced by 33%, salary costs by tens of thousands of dollars per year, floor space by 50%, and in-process waiting lines by 75% to 90%. Storage, including shelves and drawers, has been removed.

AUTHOR COMMENT
Accountants book inventory as an asset, but operations managers know it is costly.

JIT INVENTORY

Just-in-time inventory
The minimum inventory necessary to keep a perfect system running.

"Inventory is evil."
S. Shingo

Inventories in production and distribution systems often exist "just in case" something goes wrong. That is, they are used just in case some variation from the production plan occurs. The "extra" inventory is then used to cover variations or problems. Effective inventory tactics require "just in time," not "just in case." **Just-in-time inventory** is the minimum inventory necessary to keep a perfect system running. With just-in-time inventory, the exact amount of goods arrives at the moment it is needed, not a minute before or a minute after. Some useful JIT inventory tactics are shown in Table 16.2 and discussed in more detail in the following sections.

Reduce Inventory and Variability

Operations managers move toward JIT by first removing inventory. The idea is to eliminate variability in the production system hidden by inventory. Reducing inventory uncovers the "rocks" in Figure 16.3(a) that represent the variability and problems currently being tolerated. With reduced inventory, management chips away at the exposed problems. After the lake is lowered, managers make additional cuts in inventory and continue to chip away at the next level of exposed problems (see Figure 16.3[b,c]). Ultimately, there will be virtually no inventory and no problems (variability).

Dell estimates that the rapid changes in technology costs $\frac{1}{2}$% to 2% of its inventory's value *each week*. Shigeo Shingo, co-developer of the Toyota JIT system, says, "Inventory is evil." He is not far from the truth. If inventory itself is not evil, it hides evil at great cost.

▼ **TABLE 16.2**
JIT Inventory Tactics

Use a pull system to move inventory
Reduce lot size
Develop just-in-time delivery systems with suppliers
Deliver directly to the point of use
Perform to schedule
Reduce setup time
Use group technology

Reduce Lot Sizes

Just-in-time has also come to mean elimination of waste by reducing investment in inventory. The key to JIT is producing good product in small lot sizes. Reducing the size of batches can be a major help in reducing inventory and inventory costs. As we saw in Chapter 12, when inventory usage is constant, the average inventory level is the sum of the maximum inventory plus the minimum inventory divided by 2. Figure 16.4 shows that lowering the order size increases the number of orders but drops inventory levels.

Ideally, in a JIT environment, order size is one and single units are being pulled from one adjacent process to another. More realistically, analysis of the process, transportation time, and containers used for transport are considered when determining lot size. Such analysis typically results in a small lot size but a lot size larger than one. Once a lot size has been determined, the

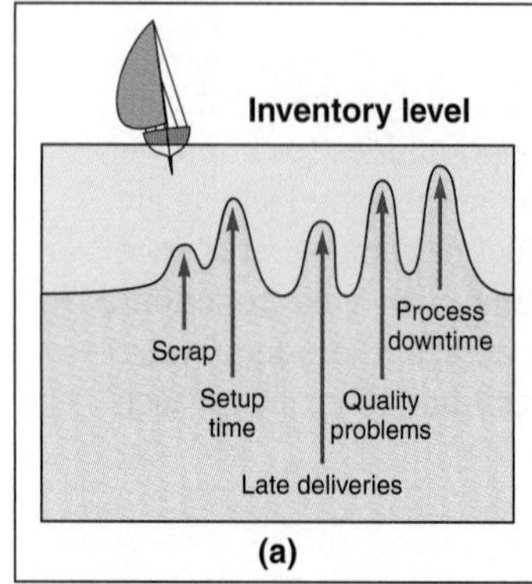

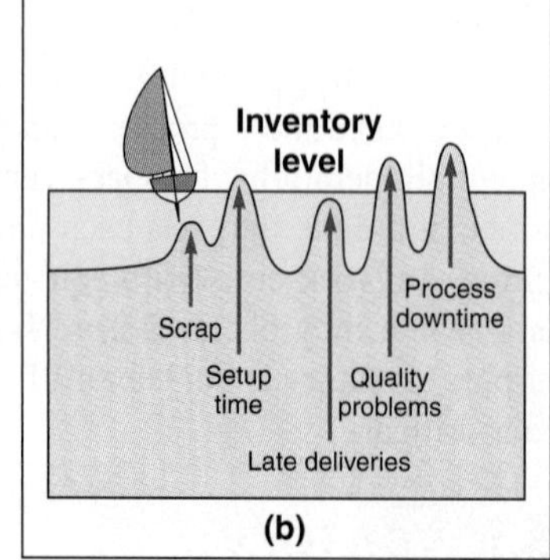

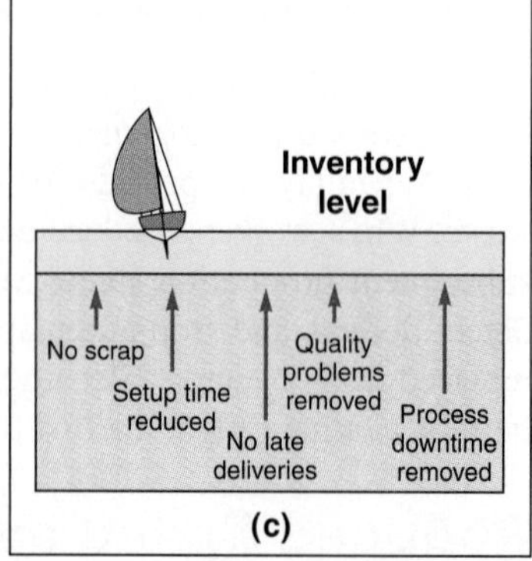

▲ **FIGURE 16.3 High levels of inventory hide problems (a), but as we reduce inventory, problems are exposed (b), and finally after reducing inventory and removing problems we have lower inventory, lower costs, and smooth sailing (c).**

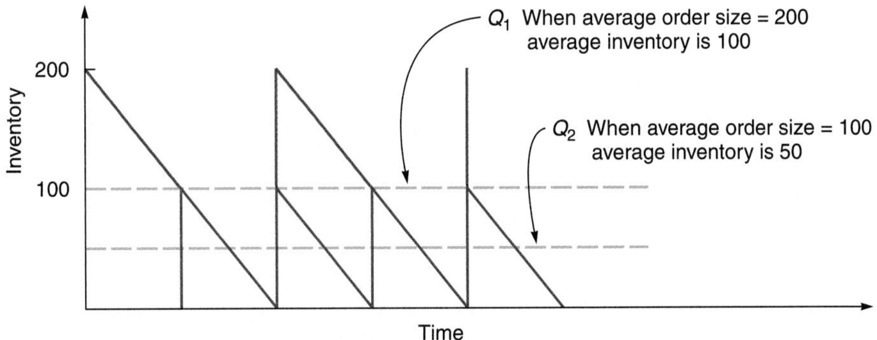

◄ FIGURE 16.4
Frequent Orders Reduce Average Inventory
A lower order size increases the number of orders and total ordering cost but reduces average inventory and total holding cost.

EOQ production order quantity model can be modified to determine the desired setup time. We saw in Chapter 12 that the production order quantity model takes the form:

$$Q^* = \sqrt{\frac{2DS}{H[1 - (d/p)]}} \tag{16-1}$$

where D = Annual demand; d = Daily demand
S = Setup cost; p = Daily production
H = Holding cost

Example 1 shows how to determine the desired setup time.

◄ EXAMPLE 1
Determining optimal setup time

Crate Furniture, Inc., a firm that produces rustic furniture, desires to move toward a reduced lot size. Crate Furniture's production analyst, Aleda Roth, determined that a 2-hour production cycle would be acceptable between two departments. Further, she concluded that a setup time that would accommodate the 2-hour cycle time should be achieved.

APPROACH ► Roth developed the following data and procedure to determine optimum setup time analytically:

D = Annual demand = 400,000 units
d = Daily demand = 400,000 per 250 days = 1,600 units per day
p = Daily production rate = 4,000 units per day
Q = EOQ desired = 400 (which is the 2-hour demand; that is, 1,600 per day per four 2-hour periods)
H = Holding cost = \$20 per unit per year
S = Setup cost (to be determined)

SOLUTION ► Roth determines that the cost, on an hourly basis, of setting up equipment is \$30. Further, she computes that the setup cost per setup should be:

LO4: Determine optimal setup time

$$Q = \sqrt{\frac{2DS}{H(1 - d/p)}}$$

$$Q^2 = \frac{2DS}{H(1 - d/p)}$$

$$S = \frac{(Q^2)(H)(1 - d/p)}{2D} \tag{16-2}$$

$$= \frac{(400)^2(20)(1 - 1{,}600/4{,}000)}{2(400{,}000)}$$

$$= \frac{(3{,}200{,}000)(0.6)}{800{,}000} = \$2.40$$

$$\text{Setup time} = \$2.40/(\text{hourly labor rate})$$
$$= \$2.40/(\$30 \text{ per hour})$$
$$= 0.08 \text{ hour, or } 4.8 \text{ minutes}$$

INSIGHT ▶ Now, rather than produce components in large lots, Crate Furniture can produce in a 2-hour cycle with the advantage of an inventory turnover of four *per day*.

LEARNING EXERCISE ▶ If labor cost goes to $40 per hour, what should be the setup time? [Answer: .06 hour, or 3.6 minutes.]

RELATED PROBLEMS ▶ 16.8, 16.9, 16.10

Only two changes need to be made for small-lot material flow to work. First, material handling and work flow need to be improved. With short production cycles, there can be very little wait time. Improving material handling is usually easy and straightforward. The second change is more challenging, and that is a radical reduction in setup times. We discuss setup reduction next.

AUTHOR COMMENT Reduced lot sizes must be accompanied by reduced setup times.

Reduce Setup Costs

Both inventory and the cost of holding it go down as the inventory-reorder quantity and the maximum inventory level drop. However, because inventory requires incurring an ordering or setup cost that must be applied to the units produced, managers tend to purchase (or produce) large orders. With large orders, each unit purchased or ordered absorbs only a small part of the setup cost. Consequently, the way to drive down lot sizes *and* reduce average inventory is to reduce setup cost, which in turn lowers the optimum order size.

The effect of reduced setup costs on total cost and lot size is shown in Figure 16.5. Moreover, smaller lot sizes hide fewer problems. In many environments, setup cost is highly correlated with setup time. In a manufacturing facility, setups usually require a substantial amount of preparation. Much of the preparation required by a setup can be done prior to shutting down the machine or process. Setup times can be reduced substantially, as shown in Figure 16.6. For instance, in Kodak's Guadalajara, Mexico, plant a team reduced the setup time to change a bearing from 12 hours to 6 minutes! This is the kind of progress that is typical of world-class manufacturers.

Just as setup costs can be reduced at a machine in a factory, setup time can also be reduced during the process of getting the order ready. It does little good to drive down factory setup time from hours to minutes if orders are going to take 2 weeks to process or "set up" in the office. This is exactly what happens in organizations that forget that JIT concepts have applications in offices as well as in the factory. Reducing setup time (and cost) is an excellent way to reduce inventory investment and to improve productivity.

AUTHOR COMMENT Effective scheduling is required for effective use of capital and personnel.

JIT SCHEDULING

Effective schedules, communicated both within the organization and to outside suppliers, support JIT. Better scheduling also improves the ability to meet customer orders, drives down inventory by allowing smaller lot sizes, and reduces work-in-process. For instance, Ford

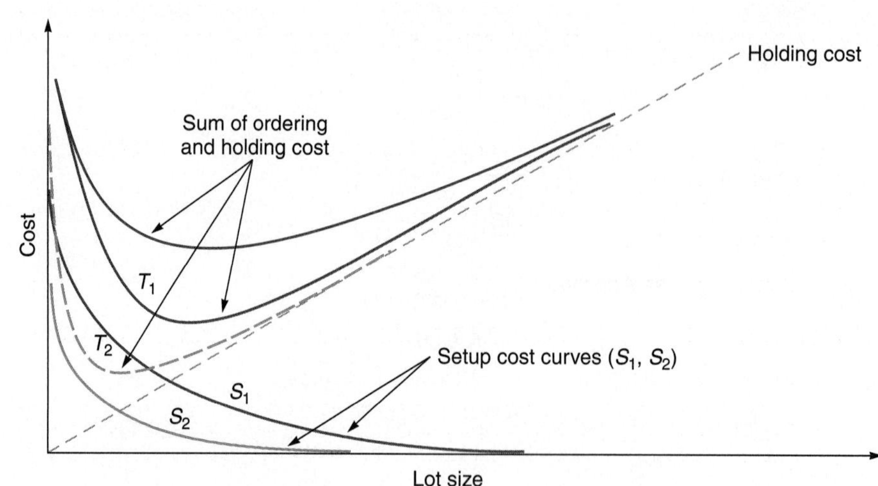

▶ FIGURE 16.5 Lower Setup Costs Will Lower Total Cost

More frequent orders require reducing setup costs; otherwise, inventory costs will rise. As the setup costs are lowered (from S_1 to S_2), total inventory costs also fall (from T_1 to T_2).

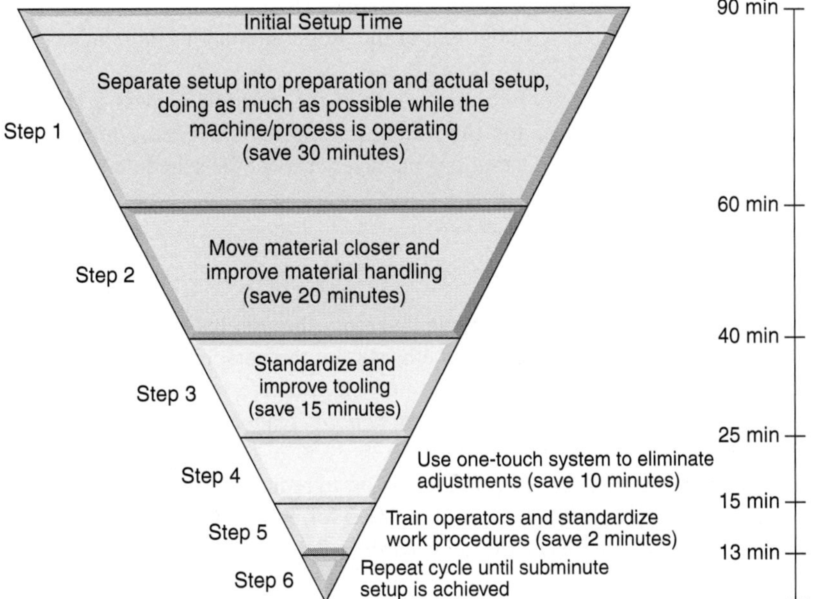

◄ **FIGURE 16.6**
Steps for Reducing Setup Times
Reduced setup times are a major JIT component.

Motor Company now ties some suppliers to its final assembly schedule. Ford communicates its schedules to bumper manufacturer Polycon Industries from the Ford Oakville production control system. The scheduling system describes the style and color of the bumper needed for each vehicle moving down the final assembly line. The scheduling system transmits the information to portable terminals carried by Polycon warehouse personnel who load the bumpers onto conveyors leading to the loading dock. The bumpers are then trucked 50 miles to the Ford plant. Total time is 4 hours. However, as we saw in our opening *Global Company Profile*, Toyota has moved its seat supplier inside the new Tundra plant; this has driven down delivery time even further.

Table 16.3 suggests several items that can contribute to achieving these goals, but two techniques (in addition to communicating schedules) are paramount. They are *level schedules* and *kanban*.

▼ **TABLE 16.3**
JIT Scheduling Tactics

JIT Scheduling Tactics
Communicate schedules to suppliers
Make level schedules
Freeze part of the schedule
Perform to schedule
Seek one-piece-make and one-piece-move
Eliminate waste
Produce in small lots
Use kanbans
Make each operation produce a perfect part

Level Schedules

Level schedules process frequent small batches rather than a few large batches. Because this technique schedules many small lots that are always changing, it has on occasion been called "jelly bean" scheduling. Figure 16.7 contrasts a traditional large-lot approach using large batches with a JIT level schedule using many small batches. The operations manager's task is to make and move small lots so the level schedule is economical. This requires success with the issues discussed in this chapter that allow small lots. As lots get smaller, the constraints may change and become increasingly challenging. At some point, processing a unit or two may not be feasible.

Level schedules
Scheduling products so that each day's production meets the demand for that day.

▼ **FIGURE 16.7 Scheduling Small Lots of Parts A, B, and C Increases Flexibility to Meet Customer Demand and Reduces Inventory**
The JIT approach to scheduling produces just as many of each model per time period as the large-lot approach, provided that setup times are lowered.

JIT Level Material-Use Approach

AA BBB C AA BBB C AA BBB C AA BBB C AA BBB C AA BBB C AA BBB C AA BBB C

Large-Lot Approach

AAAAAA BBBBBBBBB CCC AAAAAA BBBBBBBBB CCC AAAAAA BBBBBBBBB CCC

Time

The constraint may be the way units are sold and shipped (four to a carton), or an expensive paint changeover (on an automobile assembly line), or the proper number of units in a sterilizer (for a food-canning line).

The scheduler may find that *freezing* the portion of the schedule closest to due dates allows the production system to function and the schedule to be met. Freezing means not allowing changes to be part of the schedule. Operations managers expect the schedule to be achieved with no deviations from the schedule.

Kanban

One way to achieve small lot sizes is to move inventory through the shop only as needed rather than *pushing* it on to the next workstation whether or not the personnel there are ready for it. As noted earlier, when inventory is moved only as needed, it is referred to as a *pull* system, and the ideal lot size is one. The Japanese call this system *kanban*. Kanbans allow arrivals at a work center to match (or nearly match) the processing time.

Kanban

The Japanese word for *card*, which has come to mean "signal"; a kanban system moves parts through production via a "pull" from a signal.

Kanban is a Japanese word for *card*. In their effort to reduce inventory, the Japanese use systems that "pull" inventory through work centers. They often use a "card" to signal the need for another container of material—hence the name *kanban*. *The card is the authorization for the next container of material to be produced.* Typically, a kanban signal exists for each container of items to be obtained. An order for the container is then initiated by each kanban and "pulled" from the producing department or supplier. A sequence of kanbans "pulls" the material through the plant.

The system has been modified in many facilities so that even though it is called a *kanban*, the card itself does not exist. In some cases, an empty position on the floor is sufficient indication that the next container is needed. In other cases, some sort of signal, such as a flag or rag (Figure 16.8) alerts that it is time for the next container.

When there is visual contact between producer and user, the process works like this:

LO5: Define kanban

1. The user removes a standard-size container of parts from a small storage area, as shown in Figure 16.8.
2. The signal at the storage area is seen by the producing department as authorization to replenish the using department or storage area. Because there is an optimum lot size, the producing department may make several containers at a time.

Figure 16.9 shows how a kanban works, pulling units as needed from production. This system is similar to the resupply that occurs in your neighborhood supermarket: The customer buys; the stock clerk observes the shelf or receives notice from the end-of-day sales list and restocks. When the limited supply, if any, in the store's storage is depleted, a "pull" signal is sent to the warehouse, distributor, or manufacturer for resupply, usually that night. The complicating factor in a manufacturing firm is the time needed for actual manufacturing (production) to take place.

A kanban need not be as formal as signal lights or empty carts. The cook in a fast-food restaurant knows that when six cars are in line, eight meat patties and six orders of french fries should be cooking.

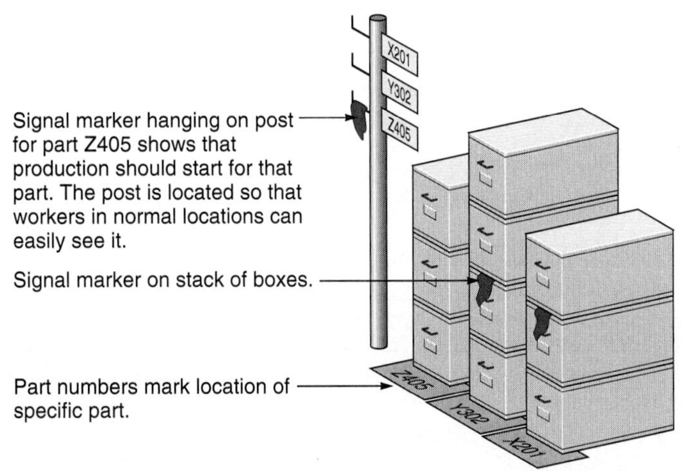

Signal marker hanging on post for part Z405 shows that production should start for that part. The post is located so that workers in normal locations can easily see it.
Signal marker on stack of boxes.
Part numbers mark location of specific part.
X201
Y302
Z405

◄ **FIGURE 16.8 Diagram of Outbound Stockpoint with Warning-Signal Marker**

Several additional points regarding kanbans may be helpful:

- When the producer and user are not in visual contact, a card can be used; otherwise, a light or flag or empty spot on the floor may be adequate.
- Because a pull station may require several resupply components, several kanban pull techniques can be used for different products at the same pull station.
- Usually, each card controls a specific quantity of parts, although multiple card systems are used if the producing work cell produces several components or if the lot size is different from the move size.
- In an MRP system (see Chapter 14), the schedule can be thought of as a "build" authorization and the kanban as a type of "pull" system that initiates the actual production.
- The kanban cards provide a direct control (limit) on the amount of work-in-process between cells.
- If there is an immediate storage area, a two-card system may be used—one card circulates between user and storage area, and the other circulates between the storage area and the producing area.

Determining the Number of Kanban Cards or Containers The number of kanban cards, or containers, in a JIT system sets the amount of authorized inventory. To determine the number of containers moving back and forth between the using area and the producing areas, management first sets the size of each container. This is done by computing the lot size, using a

▼ **FIGURE 16.9 Kanban Signals "Pull" Material Through the Production Process**

As a customer "pulls" an order from finished goods, a signal (kanban card) is sent to the final assembly area. Final assembly produces and resupplies finished goods. When final assembly needs components, it sends a signal to *its* supplier, a work cell. The work cell, in turn, sends a signal to the material/parts supplier.

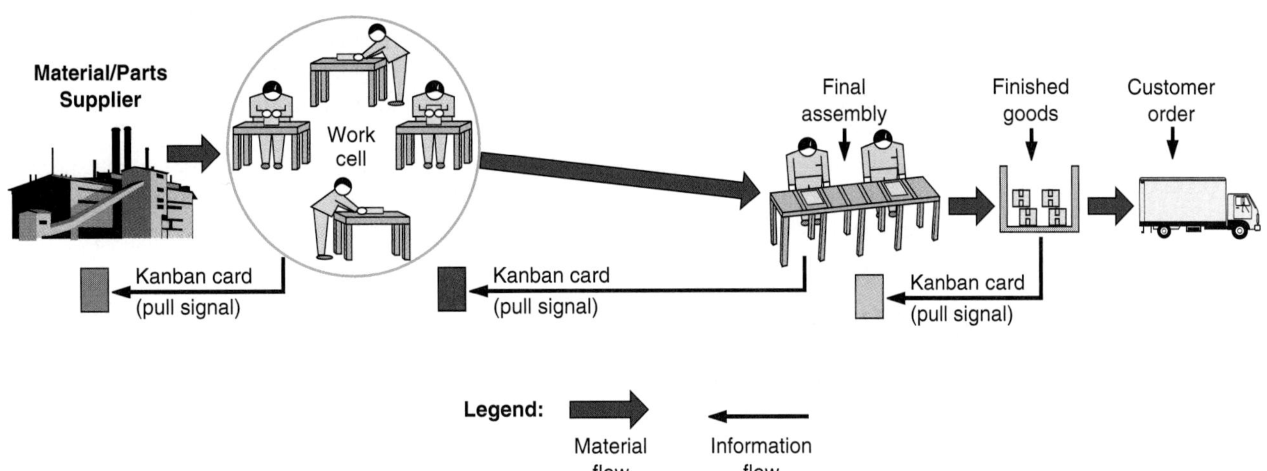

model such as the production order quantity model (discussed in Chapter 12 and shown again on page 629 in Equation [16–1]). Setting the number of containers involves knowing (1) lead time needed to produce a container of parts and (2) the amount of safety stock needed to account for variability or uncertainty in the system. The number of kanban cards is computed as follows:

$$\text{Number of kanbans (containers)} = \frac{\text{Demand during lead time} + \text{Safety stock}}{\text{Size of container}} \quad \text{(16-3)}$$

Example 2 illustrates how to calculate the number of kanbans needed.

EXAMPLE 2 ▶

Determining the number of kanban containers

Hobbs Bakery produces short runs of cakes that are shipped to grocery stores. The owner, Ken Hobbs, wants to try to reduce inventory by changing to a kanban system. He has developed the following data and asked you to finish the project.

$$\text{Daily demand} = 500 \text{ cakes}$$

$$\text{Production lead time} = \text{Wait time} + \text{Material handling time} + \text{Processing time} = 2 \text{ days}$$

$$\text{Safety stock} = \tfrac{1}{2} \text{ day}$$

$$\text{Container size (determined on a production order size EOQ basis)} = 250 \text{ cakes}$$

APPROACH ▶ Having determined that the EOQ size is 250, we then determine the number of kanbans (containers) needed.

SOLUTION ▶ Demand during lead time =

$$\text{Lead time} \times \text{Daily demand} = 2 \text{ days} \times 500 \text{ cakes} = 1{,}000$$

$$\text{Safety stock} = 250$$

LO6: Compute the required number of kanbans

Number of kanbans (containers) needed =

$$\frac{\text{Demand during lead time} + \text{Safety stock}}{\text{Container size}} = \frac{1{,}000 + 250}{250} = 5$$

INSIGHT ▶ Once the reorder point is hit, five containers should be released.

LEARNING EXERCISE ▶ If lead time drops to 1 day, how many containers are needed? [Answer: 3.]

RELATED PROBLEMS ▶ 16.1, 16.2, 16.3, 16.4, 16.5, 16.6

Advantages of Kanban Containers are typically very small, usually a matter of a few hours' worth of production. Such a system requires tight schedules. Small quantities must be produced several times a day. The process must run smoothly with little variability in quality of lead time because any shortage has an almost immediate impact on the entire system. Kanban places added emphasis on meeting schedules, reducing the time and cost required by setups, and economical material handling.

Whether it is called kanban or something else, the advantages of small inventory and *pulling* material through the plant only when needed are significant. For instance, small batches allow only a very limited amount of faulty or delayed material. Problems are immediately evident. Numerous aspects of inventory are bad; only one aspect—availability—is good. Among the bad aspects are poor quality, obsolescence, damage, occupied space, committed assets, increased insurance, increased material handling, and increased accidents. Kanban systems put downward pressure on all these negative aspects of inventory.

In-plant kanban systems often use standardized, reusable containers that protect the specific quantities to be moved. Such containers are also desirable in the supply chain. Standardized containers reduce weight and disposal costs, generate less wasted space in trailers, and require less labor to pack, unpack, and prepare items.

AUTHOR COMMENT Good quality costs less.

JIT QUALITY

The relationship between JIT and quality is a strong one. They are related in three ways. First, JIT cuts the cost of obtaining good quality. This saving occurs because scrap, rework, inventory investment, and damage costs are buried in inventory. JIT forces down inventory; therefore, fewer bad units are produced and fewer units must be reworked. In short, whereas inventory *hides* bad quality, JIT immediately *exposes* it.

This auto plant, like most JIT facilities, empowers employees so they can stop the entire production line by pulling the overhead cord if any quality problems are spotted.

Second, JIT improves quality. As JIT shrinks queues and lead time, it keeps evidence of errors fresh and limits the number of potential sources of error. In effect, JIT creates an early warning system for quality problems so that fewer bad units are produced and feedback is immediate. This advantage can accrue both within the firm and with goods received from outside vendors.

Finally, better quality means fewer buffers are needed and, therefore, a better, easier-to-employ JIT system can exist. Often the purpose of keeping inventory is to protect against unreliable quality. If consistent quality exists, JIT allows firms to reduce all costs associated with inventory. Table 16.4 suggests some requirements for quality in a JIT environment.

▼ **TABLE 16.4**
JIT Quality Tactics

Use statistical process control
Empower employees
Build fail-safe methods (poka-yoke, checklists, etc.)
Expose poor quality with small lot JIT
Provide immediate feedback

TOYOTA PRODUCTION SYSTEM

AUTHOR COMMENT
TPS brings the entire person to work.

Toyota Motor's Eiji Toyoda and Taiichi Ohno are given credit for the Toyota Production System (TPS) (see the *Global Company Profile* that opens this chapter). Three core components of TPS are continuous improvement, respect for people, and standard work practice.

Continuous Improvement

Continuous improvement under TPS means building an organizational culture and instilling in its people a value system stressing that processes can be improved—indeed, that improvement is an integral part of every employee's job. This process is formalized in TPS by **kaizen**, the Japanese word for change for the good, or what is more generally known as *continuous improvement.* In application, it means making a multitude of small or incremental changes as one seeks elusive perfection. (See the *OM in Action Box* "Kaizen at Ducati."). Instilling the mantra of continuous improvement begins at recruiting and continues through extensive and continuing training. One of the reasons continuous improvement works at Toyota, we should note, is because of another core value at Toyota, Toyota's respect for people.

Kaizen
A focus on continuous improvement.

Respect for People

At Toyota, people are recruited, trained, and treated as knowledge workers. Aided by aggressive cross-training and few job classifications, TPS engages the mental as well as physical capacities of employees in the challenging task of improving operations. Employees are empowered. They are empowered to make improvements. They are empowered to stop machines and processes when quality problems exist. Indeed, empowered employees are a necessary part of TPS. This means that those tasks that have traditionally been assigned to staff are moved to employees. Toyota recognizes that employees know more about their jobs than anyone else. TPS respects employees by giving them the opportunity to enrich both their jobs and their lives.

Standard Work Practice

Standard work practice at Toyota includes these underlying principles:

LO7: Explain the principles of the Toyota Production System

- Work is completely specified as to content, sequence, timing, and outcome.
- Internal and external customer–supplier connections are direct, specifying personnel, methods, timing, and quantity.

OM in Action ▶ Kaizen at Ducati

Ducati Motor Holding SpA of Bologna, Italy, is a motorcycle racing company whose engineering department replicates its high-performance racing machines for street use. But the production department is more interested in replicating lean thinking and adapting the Toyota Production System to Ducati's culture. Ducati has trained everyone throughout the plant, not just assembly specialists, in lean thinking. One result is a total productive maintenance effort and improved material flow that has increased machine reliability 12% and cut hourly costs 23%.

Another successful approach to drive out waste was Ducati's 4-week workshop approach to kaizen. This is a longer commitment to kaizen teams than is typical, as kaizens are not designed for perfection on the first pass; progress, not perfection, is the objective. This approach provided an opportunity for incremental but significant changes. The kaizen workshops also provided the added advantage of bringing people together in cross-functional teams, which reinforces a culture of continuous improvement.

The astounding results at Ducati would make Eiji Toyoda and Taiichi Ohno, founders of TPS, proud. Production costs are down by 25%, manufacturing cycle time has been reduced by 50%, and quality before delivery has been increased by 70%.

Sources: The Wall Street Journal (March 26, 2008): D1, D5; *Target* 27, no. 4 (2007): 10–15; and **www.oracle.com**.

- Product and service flows are to be simple and direct. Goods and services are directed to a specific person or machine.
- Improvements in the system must be made in accordance with the "scientific method," at the lowest possible level in the organization.[2]

TPS requires that activities, connections, and flows include built-in tests to automatically signal problems. Any gap between what is expected and what occurs becomes immediately evident. The education and training of Toyota's employees and the responsiveness of the system to problems make the seemingly rigid system flexible and adaptable to changing circumstances. The result is ongoing improvements in reliability, flexibility, safety, and efficiency.

AUTHOR COMMENT Lean drives out non-value-added activities.

LEAN OPERATIONS

Lean production can be thought of as the end result of a well-run OM function. While JIT and TPS tend to have an *internal* focus, lean production begins *externally* with a focus on the customer. Understanding what the customer wants and ensuring customer input and feedback are starting points for lean production. Lean operations means identifying customer value by analyzing all the activities required to produce the product and then optimizing the entire process from the customer's perspective.

Building a Lean Organization

The transition to lean production is difficult. Building an organizational culture where learning, empowerment, and continuous improvement are the norm is a challenge. However, organizations that focus on JIT, quality, and employee empowerment are often lean producers. Such firms drive out activities that do not add value in the eyes of the customer: they include leaders like United Parcel Service, Harley-Davidson, and, of course, Toyota. Even traditionally craft-oriented organizations such as Louis Vuitton (see the *OM in Action* box) find improved productivity with lean operations. Lean operations adopt a philosophy of minimizing waste by striving for perfection through continuous learning, creativity, and teamwork. They tend to share the following attributes:

- *Use JIT techniques* to eliminate virtually all inventory.
- *Build systems that help employees* produce a perfect part every time.
- *Reduce space requirements* by minimizing travel distance.

[2]Adopted from Steven J. Spear, "Learning to Lead at Toyota," *Harvard Business Review* 82, no. 5 (May 2004): 78–86; and Steven Spear and H. Kent Bowen, "Decoding the DNA of the Toyota Production System," *Harvard Business Review* 77, no. 5 (September–October 1999): 97–106.

OM in Action ▶ Going Lean at Louis Vuitton

LVMH Moet Hennessy Louis Vuitton is the world's largest luxury-goods company. Its Louis Vuitton unit, responsible for half of the company's profit, makes very upscale handbags and enjoys a rich markup on sales of about $5 billion. The return-on-investment is excellent, but sales could be even better: the firm often can't match production to the sales pace of a successful new product. In the high fashion business that is all about speed-to-market, this is bad news; a massive overhaul was in order.

Changes on the factory floor were key to the overhaul. The traditional approach to manufacturing at Louis Vuitton was batch production: craftsmen, working on partially completed handbags, performed specialized tasks such as cutting, gluing, sewing, and assembly. Carts moved batches of semi-finished handbags on to the next workstation. It took 20 to 30 workers 8 days to make a handbag. And defects were high. Lean manufacturing looked like the way to go.

Craftsmen were retrained to do multiple tasks in small U-shaped work cells. Each work cell now contains 6 to 12 cross-trained workers and the necessary sewing machines and work tables. Consistent with one-piece flow, the work is passed through the cell from worker to worker. The system reduces inventory and allows workers to detect flaws earlier. Rework under the old system was sometimes as high as 50% and internal losses as high as 4%. Returns are down by two-thirds. The system has not only improved productivity and quality, it also allows Louis Vuitton to respond to the market faster—with daily scheduling as opposed to weekly scheduling.

Sources: The Wall Street Journal (October 9, 2006): A1, A15 and (January 31, 2006): A1, A13.

- *Develop partnerships with suppliers*, helping them to understand the needs of the ultimate customer.
- *Educate suppliers* to accept responsibility for satisfying end customer needs.
- *Eliminate all but value-added activities.* Material handling, inspection, inventory, and rework are the likely targets because these do not add value to the product.
- *Develop employees* by constantly improving job design, training, employee commitment, teamwork, and empowerment.
- *Make jobs challenging*, pushing responsibility to the lowest level possible.
- *Build worker flexibility* through cross-training and reducing job classifications.

Success requires the full commitment and involvement of managers, employees, and suppliers. The rewards that lean producers reap are spectacular. Lean producers often become benchmark performers.

LEAN OPERATIONS IN SERVICES

AUTHOR COMMENT JIT, TPS, and lean began in factories but are now also used in services throughout the world.

The features of lean operations apply to services just as they do in other sectors. (See the *OM in Action* box "Toyota University Teaches Lean Thinking.") Here are some examples applied to suppliers, layout, inventory, and scheduling in the service sector.

Suppliers As we have noted, virtually every restaurant deals with its suppliers on a JIT basis. Those that do not are usually unsuccessful. The waste is too evident—food spoils, and customers complain or get sick.

Layouts Lean layouts are required in restaurant kitchens, where cold food must be served cold and hot food hot. McDonald's, for example, has reconfigured its kitchen layout at great expense to drive seconds out of the production process, thereby speeding delivery to customers. With the new process, McDonald's can produce made-to-order hamburgers in 45 seconds. Layouts also make a difference in airline baggage claim, where customers expect their bags just-in-time.

Inventory Stockbrokers drive inventory down to nearly zero every day. Most sell and buy orders occur on an immediate basis because an unexecuted sell or buy order is not acceptable to the client. A broker may be in serious trouble if left holding an unexecuted trade. Similarly, McDonald's reduces inventory waste by maintaining a finished-goods inventory of only 10 minutes; after that, it is thrown away. Hospitals, such as Arnold Palmer (described in this chapter's

VIDEO 16.1
JIT at Arnold Palmer Hospital

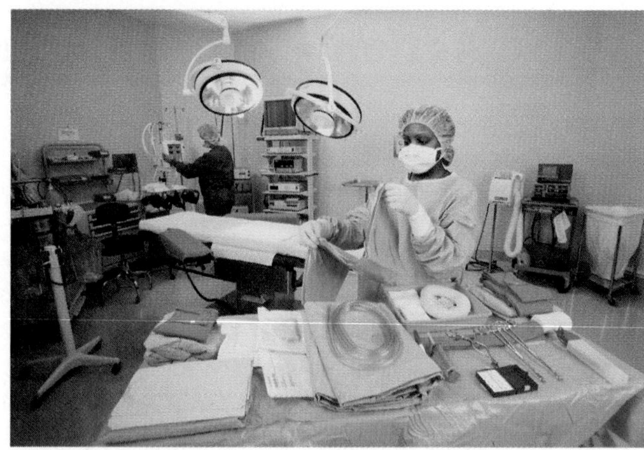

Lean operations take on an unusual form in an operating room. McKesson-General, Baxter International, and many other hospital suppliers provide surgical supplies for hospitals on a JIT basis. (1) They deliver prepackaged surgical supplies based on hospital operating schedules, and (2) the surgical packages themselves are prepared so supplies are available in the sequence in which they will be used during surgery.

Video Case Study), manage JIT inventory and low safety stocks for many items. Even critical supplies such as pharmaceuticals may be held to low levels by developing community networks as backup systems. In this manner, if one pharmacy runs out of a needed drug, another member of the network can supply it until the next day's shipment arrives.

Scheduling At airline ticket counters, the focus of the system is on adjusting to customer demand. But rather than being accommodated by inventory availability, demand is satisfied by personnel. Through elaborate scheduling, ticket counter personnel show up just-in-time to cover peaks in customer demand. In other words, rather than "things" inventoried, personnel are scheduled. At a salon, the focus is only slightly different: the *customer* and the staff are scheduled to assure prompt service. At McDonald's and Walmart, scheduling of personnel is down to 15-minute increments, based on precise forecasting of demand. Additionally, at McDonald's, production is done in small lots to ensure that fresh, hot hamburgers are delivered just-in-time. In short, both personnel and production are scheduled to meet specific demand. Notice that in all three of these lean organizations—the airline ticket counter, the salon, and McDonald's—scheduling is a key ingredient. Excellent forecasts drive those schedules. Those forecasts may be very elaborate, with seasonal, daily, and even hourly components in the case of the airline ticket counter (holiday sales, flight time, etc.), seasonal and weekly components at the salon (holidays and Fridays create special problems), and down to a few minutes (to respond to the daily meal cycle) at McDonald's.

To deliver goods and services to customers under continuously changing demand, suppliers need to be reliable, inventories lean, cycle times short, and schedules nimble. A lean focus engages and empowers employees to create and deliver the customer's perception of value, eliminating whatever does not contribute to this goal. Lean operations are currently being developed with great success in many firms, regardless of their products. Lean techniques are widely used in both goods-producing and service-producing firms; they just look different.

OM in Action ► Toyota University Teaches Lean Thinking

Based in Gardenia, California, Toyota University teaches its employees the Toyota Production System. But Toyota has also opened its door to others. As a public service, Toyota has been teaching lean thinking classes to the Los Angeles Police Department and the U.S. military. Classes begin, as one might expect, with a car-building exercise. Using model cars and desks as workstations and delivery areas, students begin with a focus on fast throughput and high production goals. This results in a "push" system, with lots of work-in-process piling up, lots of defects to be reworked, and too many of the wrong kind of cars on the "dealer's" lot.

The exercise is then revised, and students are taught to respond to orders and to form *kaizen* (continuous improvement) teams. The revised exercise then uses a "pull" system that responds to orders and fixes even the most minor problems immediately. With a focus only on filling orders and "pulling" demand through the production process with no defects, a faster, more efficient production line is formed.

Instructor Matthew May's observation about adapting lean methods beyond the factory: "If you can do it with LAPD, you can do it anywhere."

Sources: The Wall Street Journal (March 5, 2007): B1, B4; and **www.isosupport.com**.

CHAPTER SUMMARY

JIT, TPS, and lean operations are philosophies of continuous improvement. Lean operations focus on customer desires, TPS focuses on respect for people and standard work practices, and JIT focuses on driving out waste by reducing inventory. But all three approaches reduce waste in the production process. And because waste is found in anything that does not add value, organizations that implement these techniques are adding value more efficiently than other firms. The expectation of these systems is that empowered employees work with committed management to build systems that respond to customers with ever-lower cost and higher quality.

Key Terms

Just-in-time (JIT) (p. 622)
Toyota Production System (TPS) (p. 622)
Lean operations (p. 622)
Seven wastes (p. 622)
5Ss (p. 623)
Variability (p. 623)
Throughput (p. 624)
Manufacturing cycle time (p. 624)
Pull system (p. 624)
JIT partnerships (p. 625)
Consignment inventory (p. 625)
Just-in-time inventory (p. 628)
Level schedules (p. 631)
Kanban (p. 632)
Kaizen (p. 635)

Ethical Dilemma

In this lean operations world, in an effort to lower handling costs, speed delivery, and reduce inventory, retailers are forcing their suppliers to do more and more in the way of preparing their merchandise for their cross-docking warehouses, shipment to specific stores, and shelf presentation. Your company, a small manufacturer of aquarium decorations, is in a tough position. First, Mega-Mart wanted you to develop bar-code technology, then special packaging, then small individual shipments bar coded for each store (this way when the merchandise hits the warehouse it is cross-docked immediately to the correct truck and store and is ready for shelf placement). And now Mega-Mart wants you to develop RFID—immediately. Mega-Mart has made it clear that suppliers that cannot keep up with the technology will be dropped.

Earlier, when you didn't have the expertise for bar codes, you had to borrow money and hire an outside firm to do the development, purchase the technology, and train your shipping clerk. Then, meeting the special packaging requirement drove you into a loss for several months, resulting in a loss for last year. Now it appears that the RFID request is impossible. Your business, under the best of conditions, is marginally profitable, and the bank may not be willing to bail you out again. Over the years, Mega-Mart has slowly become your major customer and without them, you are probably out of business. What are the ethical issues and what do you do?

Discussion Questions

1. What is JIT?
2. What is a lean producer?
3. What is TPS?
4. What is level scheduling?
5. JIT attempts to remove delays, which do not add value. How then does JIT cope with weather and its impact on crop harvest and transportation times?
6. What are three ways in which JIT and quality are related?
7. How does TPS contribute to competitive advantage?
8. What are the characteristics of just-in-time partnerships with respect to suppliers?
9. Discuss how the Japanese word for *card* has application in the study of JIT.
10. Standardized, reusable containers have fairly obvious benefits for shipping. What is the purpose of these devices within the plant?
11. Does lean production work in the service sector? Provide an illustration.
12. Which lean techniques work in both the manufacturing *and* service sectors?

Solved Problems **Virtual Office Hours help is available at www.myomlab.com**

▼ SOLVED PROBLEM 16.1

Krupp Refrigeration, Inc., is trying to reduce inventory and wants you to install a kanban system for compressors on one of its assembly lines. Determine the size of the kanban and the number of kanbans (containers) needed.

Setup cost = $10
Annual holding cost per compressor = $100
Daily production = 200 compressors
Annual usage = 25,000 (50 weeks × 5 days each × daily usage of 100 compressors)
Lead time = 3 days
Safety stock = $\frac{1}{2}$ day's production of compressors

▼ **SOLUTION**

First, we must determine kanban container size. To do this, we determine the production order quantity (see discussion in Chapter 12 or Equation [16-1]), which determines the kanban size:

$$Q_p^* = \sqrt{\frac{2DS}{H\left(1 - \frac{d}{p}\right)}} = \sqrt{\frac{2(25{,}000)(10)}{H\left(1 - \frac{d}{p}\right)}} = \sqrt{\frac{500{,}000}{100\left(1 - \frac{100}{200}\right)}} = \sqrt{\frac{500{,}000}{50}}$$

$= \sqrt{10{,}000} = 100$ compressors. So the production order size and the size of the kanban container = 100.

Then we determine the number of kanbans:

$$\text{Demand during lead time} = 300 \; (= 3 \text{ days} \times \text{daily usage of } 100)$$

$$\text{Safety stock} = 100 \; (= \tfrac{1}{2} \times \text{daily production of } 200)$$

$$\text{Number of kanbans} = \frac{\text{Demand during lead time} + \text{Safety stock}}{\text{Size of container}}$$

$$= \frac{300 + 100}{100} = \frac{400}{100} = 4 \text{ containers}$$

Problems*

• **16.1** Leblanc Electronics, Inc., in Nashville, produces short runs of custom airwave scanners for the defense industry. You have been asked by the owner, Larry Leblanc, to reduce inventory by introducing a kanban system. After several hours of analysis, you develop the following data for scanner connectors used in one work cell. How many kanbans do you need for this connector?

Daily demand	1,000 connectors
Lead time	2 days
Safety stock	$\frac{1}{2}$ day
Kanban size	500 connectors

• **16.2** Chip Gillikin's company wants to establish kanbans to feed a newly established work cell. The following data have been provided. How many kanbans are needed?

Daily demand	250 units
Production lead time	$\frac{1}{2}$ day
Safety stock	$\frac{1}{4}$ day
Kanban size	50 units

•• **16.3** Chris Millikan Manufacturing, Inc., is moving to kanbans to support its telephone switching-board assembly lines. Determine the size of the kanban for subassemblies and the number of kanbans needed.

Setup cost = \$30
Annual holding cost = \$120 per subassembly
Daily production = 20 subassemblies
Annual usage = 2,500 (50 weeks × 5 days each × daily usage of 10 subassemblies)
Lead time = 16 days
Safety stock = 4 days' production of subassemblies. PX

•• **16.4** Maggie Moylan Motorcycle Corp. uses kanbans to support its transmission assembly line. Determine the size of the kanban for the mainshaft assembly and the number of kanbans needed.

Setup cost = \$20
Annual holding cost of mainshaft assembly = \$250 per unit
Daily production = 300 mainshafts
Annual usage = 20,000 (= 50 weeks × 5 days each × daily usage of 80 mainshafts)
Lead time = 3 days
Safety stock = $\frac{1}{2}$ day's production of mainshafts PX

• **16.5** Discount-Mart, a major East Coast retailer, wants to determine the economic order quantity (see Chapter 12 for EOQ formulas) for its halogen lamps. It currently buys all halogen lamps

*Note: PX means the problem may be solved with POM for Windows and/or Excel OM.

from Specialty Lighting Manufacturers, in Atlanta. Annual demand is 2,000 lamps, ordering cost per order is $30, annual carrying cost per lamp is $12.

a) What is the EOQ?
b) What are the total annual costs of holding and ordering (managing) this inventory?
c) How many orders should Discount-Mart place with Specialty Lighting per year? PX

••• **16.6** Discount-Mart (see Problem 16.5), as part of its new JIT program, has signed a long-term contract with Specialty Lighting and will place orders electronically for its halogen lamps. Ordering costs will drop to $.50 per order, but Discount-Mart also reassessed its carrying costs and raised them to $20 per lamp.

a) What is the new economic order quantity?
b) How many orders will now be placed?
c) What is the total annual cost of managing the inventory with this policy? PX

•• **16.7** How do your answers to Problems 16.5 and 16.6 provide insight into a JIT purchasing strategy?

••• **16.8** Bill Penny has a repetitive manufacturing plant producing trailer hitches in Arlington, Texas. The plant has an average inventory turnover of only 12 times per year. He has therefore determined that he will reduce his component lot sizes. He has developed the following data for one component, the safety chain clip:

Annual demand = 31,200 units
Daily demand = 120 units
Daily production (in 8 hours) = 960 units
Desired lot size (1 hour of production) = 120 units
Holding cost per unit per year = $12
Setup labor cost per hour = $20

How many minutes of setup time should he have his plant manager aim for regarding this component?

••• **16.9** Given the following information about a product, at Phyllis Simon's firm, what is the appropriate setup time?

Annual demand = 39,000 units
Daily demand = 150 units
Daily production = 1,000 units
Desired lot size = 150 units
Holding cost per unit per year = $10
Setup labor cost per hour = $40

••• **16.10** Rick Wing has a repetitive manufacturing plant producing automobile steering wheels. Use the following data to prepare for a reduced lot size. The firm uses a work year of 305 days.

Annual demand for steering wheels	30,500
Daily demand	100
Daily production (8 hours)	800
Desired lot size (2 hours of production)	200
Holding cost per unit per year	$10

a) What is the setup cost, based on the desired lot size?
b) What is the setup time, based on $40 per hour setup labor?

▶ **Refer to myomlab for these additional homework problems: 16.11–16.12**

Case Studies

▶ Mutual Insurance Company of Iowa

Mutual Insurance Company of Iowa (MICI) has a major insurance office facility located in Des Moines, Iowa. The Des Moines office is responsible for processing all of MICI's insurance claims for the entire nation. The company's sales have experienced rapid growth during the last year, and as expected, record levels in claims followed. Over 2,500 forms for claims a day are now flowing into the office for processing. Unfortunately, fewer than 2,500 forms a day are flowing out. The total time to process a claim, from the time it arrives to the time a check is mailed, has increased from 10 days to 10 weeks. As a result, some customers are threatening legal action. Sally Cook, the manager of Claims Processing, is particularly distressed, as she knows that a claim seldom requires more than 3 hours of actual work. Under the current administrative procedures, human resources limitations, and facility constraints, there appear to be no easy fixes for the problem. But clearly, something must be done, as the workload has overwhelmed the existing system.

MICI management wants aggressive, but economical, action taken to fix the problem. Ms. Cook has decided to try a JIT approach to claim processing. With support from her bosses, and as a temporary fix, Cook has brought in part-time personnel from MICI sales divisions across the country to help. They are to work down the claims backlog while a new JIT system is installed.

Meanwhile, Claims Processing managers and employees are to be trained in JIT principles. With JIT principles firmly in mind, managers will redesign jobs to move responsibilities for quality control activities to each employee, holding them responsible for quality work and any necessary corrections. Cook will also initiate worker-training programs that explain the entire claim processing flow, as well as provide comprehensive training on each step in the process. Data-entry skills will also be taught to both employees and managers in an effort to fix responsibility for data accuracy on the processor rather than on data entry clerks. Additionally, cross-training will be emphasized to enable workers within departments to process a variety of customer claim applications in their entirety.

Cook and her supervisors are also reexamining the insurance and claim forms currently in use. They want to see if standardization of forms will cut processing time, reduce data-entry time, and cut work-in-process.

They hope the changes will also save training time. Making changes in work methods and worker skills leads logically to a need for change in the layout of the Claims Processing Department. This potential change represents a major move from the departmental layout of the past, and will be a costly step. To help ensure the successful implementation of this phase of the

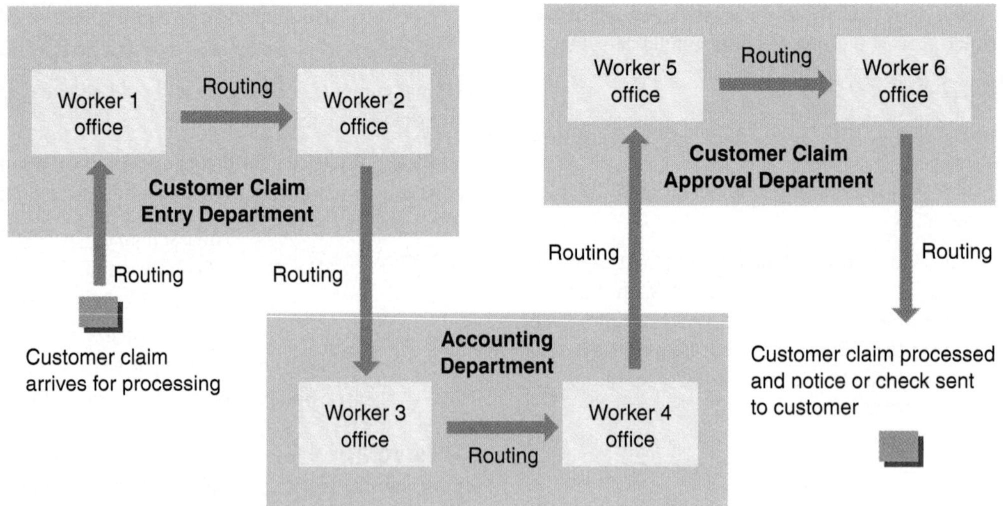

▲ **FIGURE 16.10 Claims Processing Department Layout**

changeover, Cook established a team made up of supervisors, employees, and an outside office layout consultant. She also had the team visit the Kawasaki motorcycle plant in Lincoln, Nebraska, to observe their use of work cells to aid JIT.

The team concluded that a change in the office facilities was necessary to successfully implement and integrate JIT concepts at MICI. The team believes it should revise the layout of the operation and work methods to bring them in line with "group technology cell" layouts. An example of the current departmental layout and claim processing flow pattern is presented in Figure 16.10. As can be seen in this figure, customer claims arrive for processing at the facility and flow through a series of offices and departments to eventually complete the claim process. Although the arrangement of the offices and workers in Figure 16.10 is typical, the entire facility actually operates 20 additional flows, each consisting of the same three departments. However, not all of the 20 flows are configured the same. The number of employees, for example, varies depending on the claim form requirements (larger claims have to be approved by more people). So while all forms must pass through the same three departments (Customer Claim Entry, Accounting, and Customer Claim Approval), the number of workers for each claim may vary from two to four. For this reason, the MICI facility currently maintains a staff of over 180 office workers just to process and route claims. All these people work for Ms. Cook.

Discussion Questions

1. Identify the attributes you would expect the Claims Processing Department at MICI to have once the new JIT system is in place.
2. What will the restructured cell layout for claim processing in Figure 16.10 look like? Draw it.
3. What assumptions are you making about personnel and equipment in the new group technology cell layout?
4. How will the new JIT oriented system benefit the MICI operation? Explain.

Source: Adapted from Marc J. Schniederjans, *Topics in Just-in-Time Management*, pp. 283–285. Reprinted by permission of Pearson Education, Inc., Upper Saddle River, NJ.

▶ JIT after a Catastrophe

You name the catastrophe, and JIT has been through it and survived. Toyota Motor Corporation has had its world-renowned JIT system tested by fire. The massive fire incinerated the main source of crucial brake valves that Toyota buys from the Aisin Seiki plant in Kariya, Japan, and uses in most of its cars. The impact was the loss of 70,000 cars not produced while Toyota got the supply chain repaired. Then an earthquake destroyed Toyota's transmission supplier, Riken, shutting down production in a dozen factories. Chrysler and many others had their JIT systems tested on September 11, 2001, when the terrorists attacks shut down their state-of-the-art air delivery systems. And on February 5, 2008, during the second shift at Caterpillar's high-pressure couplings plant in Oxford, Mississippi, a tornado all but destroyed the facility. Despite these catastrophes, managers at these firms, like other executives all over the world, are still cutting costs by consolidating production, reducing inventory, and implementing JIT.

Consistent with JIT practice, these firms maintain minimal inventory of components and tight supply chains. There are very few components in these closely knit networks that constitute their respective supply chains. Without critical components, production comes to a rapid halt. And in Caterpillar's case, the Oxford plant is the only plant in the world that makes this unique coupling. The couplings link hydraulic hoses on *every* piece of machinery Caterpillar makes. Depending on a single source and holding little inventory is a risk, but it also keeps firms lean and costs low.

The morning after the tornado tore apart the Oxford plant, Greg Folley, who runs Caterpillar's parts division, toured the plant. Much of the roof, including 10-ton heating and air-conditioning units, had fallen onto three critical metal stamping machines. The first piece of equipment was up and running in 2 weeks; getting production back to normal would take 6 months. But the Oxford plant had been making over 1 million of the critical couplings each month; this left a huge hole in Caterpillar's supply line.

Discussion Questions

1. If you are Mr. Folley, looking over the devastation at the Oxford plant, what do you do to keep Caterpillar's worldwide production running?
2. Given the inherent risk in JIT and the trauma that the companies have experienced, why has JIT survived?
3. What do these experiences, and the continuing popularity of JIT, tell you about just-in-time?
4. What actions or changes in policy do you suggest for Caterpillar?

Sources: Case is based on material in: *The Wall Street Journal* (May 19, 2008): B1, B2; (July 20, 2007): B1; **www.USAToday.com/money/world/2007-07-18-toyota-quake**; and *Harvard Business Review* (September–October 1999): 97–106.

► JIT at Arnold Palmer Hospital

Video Case

Orlando's Arnold Palmer Hospital, founded in 1989, specializes in treatment of women and children and is renowned for its high-quality rankings (top 10% of 2000 benchmarked hospitals), its labor and delivery volume (more than 16,000 births per year, and growing), and its neonatal intensive care unit (one of the highest survival rates in the nation). But quality medical practices and high patient satisfaction require costly inventory—some $30 million per year and thousands of SKUs.* With pressure on medical care to manage and reduce costs, Arnold Palmer Hospital has turned toward controlling its inventory with just-in-time (JIT) techniques.

Within the hospital, for example, drugs are now distributed at nursing workstations via dispensing machines (almost like vending machines) that electronically track patient usage and post the related charge to each patient. The dispensing stations are refilled each night, based on patient demand and prescriptions written by doctors.

To address JIT issues externally, Arnold Palmer Hospital turned toward a major distribution partner, McKesson General Medical, which as a first-tier supplier provides the hospital with about one quarter of all its medical/surgical inventory. McKesson supplies sponges, basins, towels, mayo stand covers, syringes, and hundreds of other medical/surgical items. To ensure coordinated daily delivery of inventory purchased from McKesson, an account executive has been assigned to the hospital on a full-time basis, as well as two other individuals who address customer service and product issues. The result has been a drop in Central Supply average daily inventory from $400,000 to $114,000 since JIT.

JIT success has also been achieved in the area of *custom surgical packs*. Custom surgical packs are the sterile coverings, disposable plastic trays, gauze, and the like, specialized to each type of surgical procedure. Arnold Palmer Hospital uses 10 different custom packs for various surgical procedures. "Over 50,000 packs are used each year, for a total cost of about $1.5 million," says George DeLong, head of Supply-Chain Management.

The packs are not only delivered in a JIT manner but packed that way as well. That is, they are packed in the reverse order they are used so each item comes out of the pack in the sequence it is needed. The packs are bulky, expensive, and must remain sterile. Reducing the inventory and handling while maintaining an assured sterile supply for scheduled surgeries presents a challenge to hospitals.

Here is how the supply chain works: Custom packs are *assembled* by a packing company with *components supplied* primarily from manufacturers selected by the hospital, and *delivered* by McKesson from its local warehouse. Arnold Palmer Hospital works with its own surgical staff (through the Medical Economics Outcome Committee) to identify and standardize the custom packs to reduce the number of custom pack SKUs. With this integrated system, pack safety stock inventory has been cut to one day.

The procedure to drive the custom surgical pack JIT system begins with a "pull" from the doctors' daily surgical schedule. Then, Arnold Palmer Hospital initiates an electronic order to McKesson between 1:00 and 2:00 P.M. daily. At 4:00 A.M. the next day, McKesson delivers the packs. Hospital personnel arrive at 7:00 A.M. and stock the shelves for scheduled surgeries. McKesson then reorders from the packing company, which in turn "pulls" necessary inventory for the quantity of packs needed from the manufacturers.

Arnold Palmer Hospital's JIT system reduces inventory investment, expensive traditional ordering, and bulky storage, and supports quality with a sterile delivery.

Discussion Questions**

1. What do you recommend be done when an error is found in a pack as it is opened for an operation?
2. How might the procedure for custom surgical packs described here be improved?
3. When discussing JIT in services, the text notes that suppliers, layout, inventory, and scheduling are all used. Provide an example of each of these at Arnold Palmer Hospital.
4. When a doctor proposes a new surgical procedure, how do you recommend the SKU for a new custom pack be entered into the hospital's supply-chain system?

*SKU = stock keeping unit
**You may wish to view the video that accompanies this case before answering these questions.

Bibliography

Burke, Robert, and Gregg Messel. "From Simulation to Implementation: Cardinal Health's Lean Journey." *Target: Innovation at Work* 19, no. 2 (2nd Quarter 2003): 27–32.

Flinchbauh, Jamie. *The Hitchhiker's Guide to Lean*, Dearborn, MI: Society of Manufacturing Engineers (2006).

Graban, Mark. *Lean Hospitals*. New York: CRC Press (2009).

Hall, Robert W. "'Lean' and the Toyota Production System." *Target* 20, no. 3 (3rd Issue 2004): 22–27.

Keyte, Beau, and Drew Locher. *The Complete Lean Enterprise*. University Park, IL: Productivity Press (2004).

Morgan, James M., and Jeffrey K. Liker. *The Toyota Product Development System*. New York: Productivity Press (2007).

Nelson-Peterson, Dana L., and Carol J. Leppa, "Creating an Environment of Caring Using Lean Principles of the Virginia Mason Production System, "*Journal of Nursing Administration* 37 (2007): 289.

Parks, Charles M. "The Bare Necessities of Lean." *Industrial Engineer* 35, no. 8 (August 2003): 39.

Schonberger, Richard J. "Lean Extended." *Industrial Engineer* (December 2005): 26–31.

van Veen-Dirks, Paula. "Management Control and the Production Environment." *International Journal of Production Economics* 93 (January 8, 2005): 263.

Womack, James P., and Daniel T. Jones. "Lean Consumption." *Harvard Business Review* 83 (March 2005): 58–68.

Womack, James P., and Daniel T. Jones. *Lean Solutions: How Companies and Customers Can Create Value and Wealth Together.* New York: The Free Press (2005).

Chapter 16 ***Rapid*** **Review**

Main Heading	Review Material	myomlab
JUST-IN-TIME, THE TOYOTA PRODUCTION SYSTEM, AND LEAN OPERATIONS (pp. 622–624)	▪ **Just-in-time (JIT)**—Continuous and forced problem solving via a focus on throughput and reduced inventory. ▪ **Toyota Production System (TPS)**—Focus on continuous improvement, respect for people, and standard work practices. ▪ **Lean operations**—Eliminates waste through a focus on exactly what the customer wants. *When implemented as a comprehensive manufacturing strategy, JIT, TPS, and lean systems sustain competitive advantage and result in increased overall returns.* ▪ **Seven wastes**—Overproduction, queues, transportation, inventory, motion, overprocessing, and defective product. ▪ **5Ss**—A lean production checklist: sort, simplify, shine, standardize, and sustain. U.S. managers often add two additional *S*s to the 5 original ones: *safety* and *support/maintenance*. ▪ **Variability**—Any deviation from the optimum process that delivers perfect product on time, every time. Both JIT and inventory reduction are effective tools for identifying causes of variability. ▪ **Throughput**—The time required to move orders through the production process, from receipt to delivery. ▪ **Manufacturing cycle time**—The time between the arrival of raw materials and the shipping of finished products. ▪ **Pull system**—A concept that results in material being produced only when requested and moved to where it is needed just as it is needed. Pull systems use signals to request production and delivery from supplying stations to stations that have production capacity available.	
JUST-IN-TIME (JIT) (pp. 624–627)	▪ **JIT partnerships**—Partnerships of suppliers and purchasers that remove waste and drive down costs for mutual benefits. Some specific goals of JIT partnerships are: *removal of unnecessary activities, removal of in-plant inventory*; *removal of in-transit inventory*; and *obtain improved quality and reliability*. ▪ **Consignment inventory**—An arrangement in which the supplier maintains title to the inventory until it is used. Concerns of suppliers in JIT partnerships include: (1) *diversification*; (2) *scheduling*; (3) *lead time*; (4) *quality*; and (5) *lot sizes*.	
JIT LAYOUT (pp. 627–628)	JIT layout tactics include building work cells for families of products, include a large number of operations in a small area, minimizing distance, designing little space for inventory, improving employee communication, using poka-yoke devices, building flexible or movable equipment, and cross-training workers to add flexibility.	
JIT INVENTORY (pp. 628–630)	▪ **Just-in-time inventory**—The minimum inventory necessary to keep a perfect system running. The idea behind JIT is to eliminate inventory that hides variability in the production system. JIT inventory tactics include using a pull system to move inventory, reducing lot size, developing just-in-time delivery systems with suppliers, delivering directly to the point of use, performing to schedule, reducing setup time, and using group technology. $$Q^* = \sqrt{\frac{2DS}{H[1 - (d/p)]}} \quad (16\text{-}1)$$ Using (16–1), for a given desired lot size, Q, we can solve for the optimal setup cost, S: $$S = \frac{(Q^2)(H)(1 - d/p)}{2D} \quad (16\text{-}2)$$	Problems: 16.8–16.10

Main Heading	Review Material	PEARSON myomlab
JIT SCHEDULING (pp. 630–634)	JIT scheduling tactics include: communicate schedules to suppliers, make level schedules, freeze part of the schedule, perform to schedule, seek one-piece-make and one-piece-move, eliminate waste, produce in small lots, use kanbans, and make each operation produce a perfect part. ▪ **Level schedules**—Scheduling products so that each day's production meets the demand for that day. ▪ **Kanban**—The Japanese word for *card*, which has come to mean "signal"; a kanban system moves parts through production via a "pull" from a signal: $$\text{Number of Kanbans (containers)} = \frac{\text{Demand during lead time} + \text{Safety stock}}{\text{Size of container}} \quad (16\text{-}3)$$	Problems: 16.1–16.6 Virtual Office Hours for Solved Problem: 16.1
JIT QUALITY (pp. 634–635)	Whereas inventory *hides* bad quality, JIT immediately *exposes* it. JIT quality tactics include using statistical process control, empowering employees, building fail-safe methods (poka-yoke, checklists, etc.), exposing poor quality with small lot JIT, and providing immediate feedback.	
TOYOTA PRODUCTION SYSTEM (pp. 635–636)	▪ **Kaizen**—A focus on continuous improvement. At Toyota, people are recruited, trained, and treated as knowledge workers. They are empowered. TPS employs aggressive cross-training and few job classifications.	
LEAN OPERATIONS (pp. 636–637)	Lean operations tend to share the following attributes: *use JIT techniques* to eliminate virtually all inventory; *build systems that help employees* produce a perfect part every time; *reduce space requirements* by minimizing travel distance; *develop partnerships with suppliers*, helping them to understand the needs of the ultimate customer; *educate suppliers* to accept responsibility for satisfying end customer needs; *eliminate all but value-added activities*; *develop employees* by constantly improving job design, training, employee commitment, teamwork, and empowerment; *make jobs challenging*, pushing responsibility to the lowest level possible; and *build worker flexibility* through cross-training and reducing job classifications.	
LEAN OPERATIONS IN SERVICES (pp. 637–638)	The features of lean operations apply to services just as they do in other sectors. Forecasts in services may be very elaborate, with seasonal, daily, hourly, or even shorter components.	**VIDEO 16.1** JIT at Arnold Palmer Hospital

Self Test

▪ **Before taking the self-test,** refer to the learning objectives listed at the beginning of the chapter and the key terms listed at the end of the chapter.

LO1. Continuous improvement and forced problem solving via a focus on throughput and reduced inventory is a reasonable definition of:
- **a)** lean operations.
- **b)** expedited management.
- **c)** the 5*S*s of housekeeping.
- **d)** just-in-time.
- **e)** Toyota Production System.

LO2. The 5*S*s for lean production are _______, _______, _______, _______, and ________.

LO3. Concerns of suppliers when moving to JIT include:
- **a)** small lots sometimes seeming economically prohibitive.
- **b)** realistic quality demands.
- **c)** changes without adequate lead time.
- **d)** erratic schedules.
- **e)** all of the above.

LO4. What is the formula for optimal setup time?
- **a)** $\sqrt{2DQ/[H(1 - d/p)]}$
- **b)** $\sqrt{Q^2H(1 - d/p)/(2D)}$
- **c)** $QH(1 - d/p)/(2D)$
- **d)** $Q^2H(1 - d/p)/(2D)$
- **e)** $H(1 - d/p)$

LO5. Kanban is the Japanese word for:
- **a)** car.
- **b)** pull.
- **c)** card.
- **d)** continuous improvement.
- **e)** level schedule.

LO6. The required number of kanbans equals:
- **a)** 1.
- **b)** Demand during lead time/Q
- **c)** Size of container.
- **d)** Demand during lead time.
- **e)** (Demand during lead time + safety stock)/Size of container.

LO7. TPS's standard work practices include:
- **a)** completely specified work.
- **b)** "pull" systems.
- **c)** level scheduling.
- **d)** kanbans.
- **e)** JIT techniques.

Answers: LO1. d; LO2. sort, simplify, shine, standardize, sustain; LO3. e; LO4. d; LO5. c; LO6. e; LO7. a.

17 Maintenance and Reliability

Chapter Outline

OM Strategy Decisions

- Design of Goods and Services
- Managing Quality
- Process Strategy
- Location Strategies
- Layout Strategies
- Human Resources
- Supply-Chain Management
- Inventory Management
- Scheduling
- **Maintenance**

MAINTENANCE PROVIDES A COMPETITIVE ADVANTAGE FOR ORLANDO UTILITIES COMMISSION

The Orlando Utilities Commission (OUC) owns and operates power plants that supply power to two central Florida counties. Every year, OUC takes each one of its power-generating units off-line for 1 to 3 weeks to perform maintenance work.

Additionally, each unit is also taken off-line every 3 years for a complete overhaul and turbine generator inspection. Overhauls are scheduled for spring and fall, when the weather is mildest and demand for power is low. These overhauls last from 6 to 8 weeks.

Units at OUC's Stanton Energy Center require that maintenance personnel perform approximately 12,000 repair and preventive maintenance tasks a year. To accomplish these tasks efficiently, many of these jobs are scheduled daily via a computerized maintenance management program. The computer generates preventive maintenance work orders and lists of required materials.

Every day that a plant is down for maintenance costs OUC about $110,000 extra for the replacement cost of power that must be generated elsewhere. However, these costs pale beside the costs associated with a forced outage. An unexpected outage could cost OUC an additional $350,000 to $600,000 each day!

Scheduled overhauls are not easy; each one has 1,800 distinct tasks and requires 72,000 labor-hours. But the value of preventive maintenance was illustrated by the first overhaul of a new turbine generator. Workers discovered a cracked rotor blade, which could have destroyed a $27 million piece of equipment. To find such cracks, which are invisible to the naked eye, metals are examined using dye tests, X-rays, and ultrasound.

At OUC, preventive maintenance is worth its weight in gold. As a result, OUC's electric distribution system has been ranked number one in the Southeast U.S. by PA Consulting Group—a leading consulting firm. Effective maintenance provides a competitive advantage for the Orlando Utilities Commission.

The Stanton Energy Center in Orlando.

◀ Two employees are on scaffolding near the top of Stanton Energy Center's 23-story high boiler, checking and repairing super heaters.

▲ This inspector is examining a low-pressure section of turbine. The tips of these turbine blades will travel at supersonic speeds of 1,300 miles per hour when the plant is in operation. A crack in one of the blades can cause catastrophic failure.

▲ Maintenance of capital-intensive facilities requires good planning to minimize downtime. Here, turbine overhaul is under way. Organizing the thousands of parts and pieces necessary for a shutdown is a major effort.

Chapter 17 **Learning Objectives**

AUTHOR COMMENT
If the system is not reliable, everything else is more difficult.

THE STRATEGIC IMPORTANCE OF MAINTENANCE AND RELIABILITY

Managers at Orlando Utilities Commission (OUC), the subject of the chapter-opening *Global Company Profile*, fight for reliability to avoid the undesirable results of equipment failure. At OUC, a generator failure is very expensive for both the company and its customers. Power outages are instantaneous, with potentially devastating consequences. Similarly, managers at Frito-Lay, Walt Disney Company, and United Parcel Service (UPS) are intolerant of failures or breakdowns. Maintenance is critical at Frito-Lay to achieve high plant utilization and excellent sanitation. At Disney, sparkling-clean facilities and safe rides are necessary to retain its standing as one of the most popular vacation destinations in the world. Likewise, UPS's famed maintenance strategy keeps its delivery vehicles operating and looking as good as new for 20 years or more.

VIDEO 17.1
Maintenance Drives Profits at Frito-Lay

These companies, like most others, know that poor maintenance can be disruptive, inconvenient, wasteful, and expensive in dollars and even in lives. As Figure 17.1 illustrates, the interdependency of operator, machine, and mechanic is a hallmark of successful maintenance and reliability. Good maintenance and reliability management enhances a firm's performance and protects its investment.

The objective of maintenance and reliability is to maintain the capability of the system. Good maintenance removes variability. Systems must be designed and maintained to reach expected performance and quality standards. **Maintenance** includes all activities involved in keeping a system's equipment in working order. **Reliability** is the probability that a machine part or product will function properly for a specified time under stated conditions.

Maintenance
The activities involved in keeping a system's equipment in working order.

Reliability
The probability that a machine part or product will function properly for a specified time under stated conditions.

In this chapter, we examine four important tactics for improving the reliability and maintenance not only of products and equipment but also of the systems that produce them. The four tactics are organized around reliability and maintenance.

The reliability tactics are:

1. Improving individual components
2. Providing redundancy

AUTHOR COMMENT
Employee commitment makes a big difference.

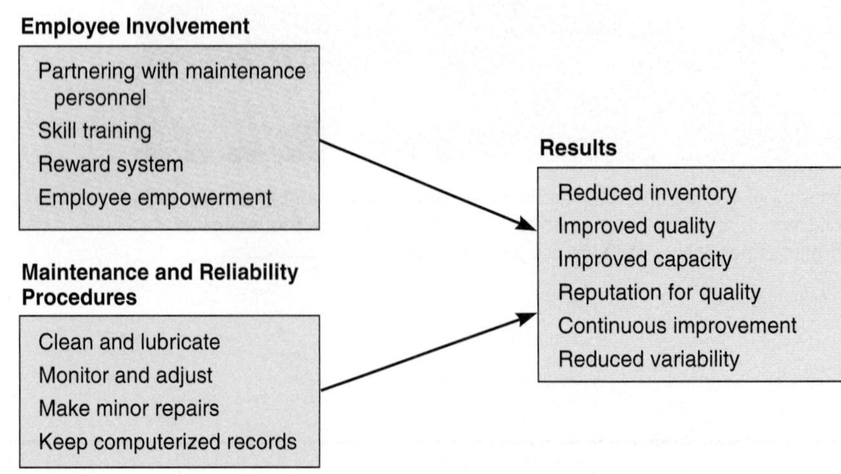

▶ **FIGURE 17.1**
Good Maintenance and Reliability Management Requires Employee Involvement and Good Procedures

The maintenance tactics are:

1. Implementing or improving preventive maintenance
2. Increasing repair capabilities or speed

Variability corrupts processes and creates waste. The operations manager must drive out variability: Designing for reliability and managing for maintenance are crucial ingredients for doing so.

RELIABILITY

AUTHOR COMMENT Designing for reliability is an excellent place to start reducing variability.

Systems are composed of a series of individual interrelated components, each performing a specific job. If any *one* component fails to perform, for whatever reason, the overall system (for example, an airplane or machine) can fail. First, we discuss improving individual components, and then we discuss providing redundancy.

LO1: Describe how to improve system reliability

Improving Individual Components

Because failures do occur in the real world, understanding their occurrence is an important reliability concept. We now examine the impact of failure in a series. Figure 17.2 shows that as the number of components in a *series* increases, the reliability of the whole system declines very quickly. A system of $n = 50$ interacting parts, each of which has a 99.5% reliability, has an overall reliability of 78%. If the system or machine has 100 interacting parts, each with an individual reliability of 99.5%, the overall reliability will be only about 60%!

To measure reliability in a system in which each individual part or component may have its own unique rate of reliability, we cannot use the reliability curve in Figure 17.2. However, the method of computing system reliability (R_s) is simple. It consists of finding the product of individual reliabilities as follows:

$$R_s = R_1 \times R_2 \times R_3 \times \ldots \times R_n \qquad \text{(17-1)}$$

where R_1 = reliability of component 1
R_2 = reliability of component 2

and so on.

Equation (17-1) assumes that the reliability of an individual component does not depend on the reliability of other components (that is, each component is independent). Additionally, in this equation as in most reliability discussions, reliabilities are presented as *probabilities*. Thus, a .90 reliability means that the unit will perform as intended 90% of the time. It also means that it will fail $1 - .90 = .10 = 10\%$ of the time. We can use this method to evaluate the reliability of a service or a product, such as the one we examine in Example 1.

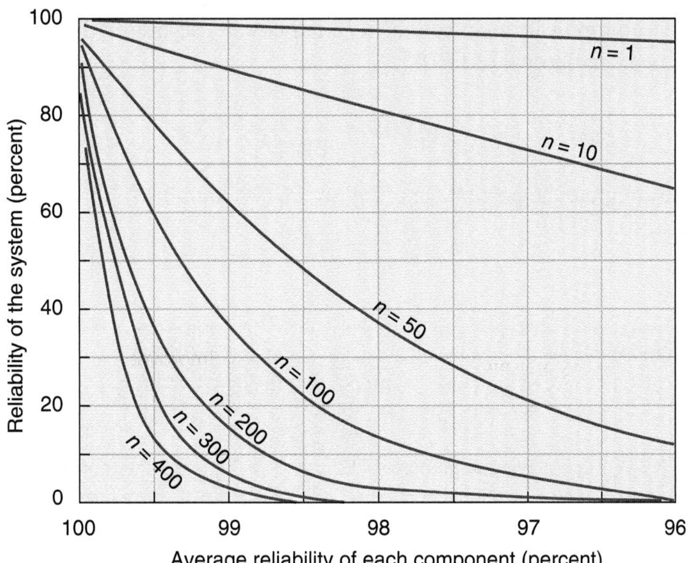

FIGURE 17.2 Overall System Reliability as a Function of Number of *n* Components (Each with the Same Reliability) and Component Reliability with Components in a Series

EXAMPLE 1 ▶

Reliability in a series

The National Bank of Greeley, Colorado, processes loan applications through three clerks set up in series, with reliabilities of .90, .80, and .99. It wants to find the system reliability.

APPROACH ▶ Apply Equation (17-1) to solve for R_s.

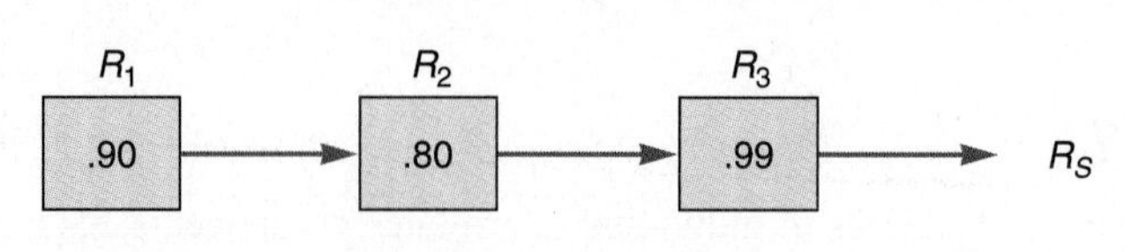

SOLUTION ▶ The reliability of the loan process is:

$$R_s = R_1 \times R_2 \times R_3 = (.90)(.80)(.99) = .713, \text{ or } 71.3\%$$

LO2: Determine system reliability

INSIGHT ▶ Because each clerk in the series is less than perfect, the error probabilities are cumulative and the resulting reliability for this series is .713, which is less than any one clerk.

LEARNING EXERCISE ▶ If the lowest-performing clerk (.80) is replaced by a clerk performing at .95 reliability, what is the new expected reliability? [Answer: .846.]

RELATED PROBLEMS ▶ 17.1, 17.2, 17.5, 17.11

ACTIVE MODEL 17.1 This example is further illustrated in Active Model 17.1 at **www.pearsonhighered.com/heizer**.

Component reliability is often a design or specification issue for which engineering design personnel may be responsible. However, supply-chain personnel may be able to improve components of systems by staying abreast of suppliers' products and research efforts. Supply-chain personnel can also contribute directly to the evaluation of supplier performance.

The basic unit of measure for reliability is the *product failure rate* (FR). Firms producing high-technology equipment often provide failure-rate data on their products. As shown in Equations (17-2) and (17-3), the failure rate measures the percent of failures among the total number of products tested, FR(%), or a number of failures during a period of time, FR(N):

$$\text{FR}(\%) = \frac{\text{Number of failures}}{\text{Number of units tested}} \times 100\% \tag{17-2}$$

$$\text{FR}(N) = \frac{\text{Number of failures}}{\text{Number of unit-hours of operation time}} \tag{17-3}$$

Mean time between failures (MTBF)
The expected time between a repair and the next failure of a component, machine, process, or product.

Perhaps the most common term in reliability analysis is the **mean time between failures (MTBF)**, which is the reciprocal of FR(N):

$$\text{MTBF} = \frac{1}{\text{FR}(N)} \tag{17-4}$$

In Example 2, we compute the percentage of failure FR(%), number of failures FR(N), and mean time between failures (MTBF).

EXAMPLE 2 ▶

Determining mean time between failures

Twenty air-conditioning systems designed for use by astronauts in NASA's space shuttles were operated for 1,000 hours at NASA's Huntsville, Alabama, test facility. Two of the systems failed during the test—one after 200 hours and the other after 600 hours.

APPROACH ▶ To determine the percent of failures [FR(%)], the number of failures per unit of time [FR(N)], and the mean time between failures (MTBF), we use Equations (17–2), (17–3), and (17–4), respectively.

SOLUTION ▶ Percentage of failures:

$$FR(\%) = \frac{\text{Number of failures}}{\text{Number of units tested}} = \frac{2}{20}(100\%) = 10\%$$

Number of failures per operating hour:

$$FR(N) = \frac{\text{Number of failures}}{\text{Operating time}}$$

where

$$\begin{aligned} \text{Total time} &= (1{,}000\text{ hr})(20\text{ units}) \\ &= 20{,}000\text{ unit-hour} \\ \text{Nonoperating time} &= 800\text{ hr for 1st failure} + 400\text{ hr for 2nd failure} \\ &= 1{,}200\text{ unit-hour} \\ \text{Operating time} &= \text{Total time} - \text{Nonoperating time} \end{aligned}$$

$$\begin{aligned} FR(N) &= \frac{2}{20{,}000 - 1{,}200} = \frac{2}{18{,}800} \\ &= .000106\text{ failure/unit-hour} \end{aligned}$$

Because $\text{MTBF} = \dfrac{1}{FR(N)}$

$$\text{MTBF} = \frac{1}{.000106} = 9{,}434\text{ hr}$$

LO3: Determine mean time between failures (MTBF)

If the typical space shuttle trip lasts 6 days, NASA may be interested in the failure rate per trip:

$$\begin{aligned} \text{Failure rate} &= (\text{Failures/unit-hr})(24\text{ hr/day})(6\text{ days/trip}) \\ &= (.000106)(24)(6) \\ &= .0153\text{ failure/trip} \end{aligned}$$

INSIGHT ▶ Mean time between failures (MTBF) is the standard means of stating reliability.

LEARNING EXERCISE ▶ If non-operating time drops to 800, what is the new MTBF? [Answer: 9,606 hr.]

RELATED PROBLEMS ▶ 17.6, 17.7

If the failure rate recorded in Example 2 is too high, NASA will have to either increase the reliability of individual components, and thus of the system, or install several backup air-conditioning units on each space shuttle. Backup units provide redundancy.

Providing Redundancy

To increase the reliability of systems, **redundancy** is added. The technique here is to "back up" components with additional components. This is known as putting units in parallel and is a standard operations management tactic. Redundancy is provided to ensure that if one component fails, the system has recourse to another. For instance, say that reliability of a component is .80 and we back it up with another component with reliability of .80. The resulting reliability is the probability of the first component working plus the probability of the backup (or parallel) component working multiplied by the probability of needing the backup component ($1 - .8 = .2$). Therefore:

Redundancy
The use of components in parallel to raise reliability.

$$\begin{pmatrix}\text{Probability}\\ \text{of first}\\ \text{component}\\ \text{working}\end{pmatrix} + \left[\begin{pmatrix}\text{Probability}\\ \text{of second}\\ \text{component}\\ \text{working}\end{pmatrix} \times \begin{pmatrix}\text{Probability}\\ \text{of needing}\\ \text{second}\\ \text{component}\end{pmatrix}\right] =$$

$$(.8) \quad + \quad [(.8) \quad \times \quad (1 - .8)] \quad = .8 + .16 = .96$$

Example 3 shows how redundancy can improve the reliability of the loan process presented in Example 1.

EXAMPLE 3 ▶

Reliability with a parallel process

The National Bank is disturbed that its loan-application process has a reliability of only .713 (see Example 1) and would like to improve this situation.

APPROACH ▶ The bank decides to provide redundancy for the two least reliable clerks.

SOLUTION ▶ This procedure results in the following system:

$$
\begin{array}{ccc}
R_1 & R_2 & R_3 \\
0.90 & 0.80 & \\
\downarrow & \downarrow & \\
0.90 \rightarrow & 0.80 \rightarrow & 0.99
\end{array}
\begin{aligned}
&= [.9 + .9(1 - .9)] \times [.8 + .8(1 - .8)] \times .99 \\
&= [.9 + (.9)(.1)] \times [.8 + (.8)(.2)] \times .99 \\
&= .99 \times .96 \times .99 = .94
\end{aligned}
$$

INSIGHT ▶ By providing redundancy for two clerks, National Bank has increased reliability of the loan process from .713 to .94.

LEARNING EXERCISE ▶ What happens when the bank replaces both R_2 clerks with one new clerk who has a reliability of .90. [Answer: R_s = .88.]

RELATED PROBLEMS ▶ 17.8, 17.9, 17.10, 17.12, 17.13, 17.14, 17.16, 17.18

ACTIVE MODEL 17.2 This example is further illustrated in Active Model 17.2 at **www.pearsonhighered.com/heizer**.

AUTHOR COMMENT Even the most reliable systems require maintenance.

MAINTENANCE

There are two types of maintenance: preventive maintenance and breakdown maintenance. **Preventive maintenance** involves performing routine inspections and servicing and keeping facilities in good repair. These activities are intended to build a system that will find potential failures and make changes or repairs that will prevent failure. Preventive maintenance is much more than just keeping machinery and equipment running. It also involves designing technical and human systems that will keep the productive process working within tolerance; it allows the system to perform. The emphasis of preventive maintenance is on understanding the process and keeping it working without interruption. **Breakdown maintenance** occurs when equipment fails and must be repaired on an emergency or priority basis.

Preventive maintenance
A plan that involves routine inspections, servicing, and keeping facilities in good repair to prevent failure.

Breakdown maintenance
Remedial maintenance that occurs when equipment fails and must be repaired on an emergency or priority basis.

Implementing Preventive Maintenance

Preventive maintenance implies that we can determine when a system needs service or will need repair. Therefore, to perform preventive maintenance, we must know when a system requires service or when it is likely to fail. Failures occur at different rates during the life of a product. A high initial failure rate, known as **infant mortality**, may exist for many products.[1] This is why many electronic firms "burn in" their products prior to shipment: That is to say, they execute a variety of tests (such as a full wash cycle at Whirlpool) to detect "startup" problems prior to shipment. Firms may also provide 90-day warranties. We should note that many infant mortality failures are not product failures per se, but rather failure due to improper use. This fact points up the importance in many industries of operations management's building an after-sales service system that includes installing and training.

Infant mortality
The failure rate early in the life of a product or process.

Once the product, machine, or process "settles in," a study can be made of the MTBF (mean time between failures) distribution. Such distributions often follow a normal curve. When these distributions exhibit small standard deviations, then we know we have a candidate for preventive maintenance, even if the maintenance is expensive.

LO4: Distinguish between preventive and breakdown maintenance

[1] Infant mortality failures often follow a negative exponential distribution.

Once our firm has a candidate for preventive maintenance, we want to determine *when* preventive maintenance is economical. Typically, the more expensive the maintenance, the narrower must be the MTBF distribution (that is, have a small standard deviation). In addition, if the process is no more expensive to repair when it breaks down than the cost of preventive maintenance, perhaps we should let the process break down and then do the repair. However, the consequence of the breakdown must be fully considered. Even some relatively minor breakdowns have catastrophic consequences. (See the *OM in Action* box "Preventive Maintenance Saves Lives" on the next page). At the other extreme, preventive maintenance costs may be so incidental that preventive maintenance is appropriate even if the MTBF distribution is rather flat (that is, it has a large standard deviation). In any event, consistent with job enrichment practices, machine operators must be held responsible for preventive maintenance of their own equipment and tools.

With good reporting techniques, firms can maintain records of individual processes, machines, or equipment. Such records can provide a profile of both the kinds of maintenance required and the timing of maintenance needed. Maintaining equipment history is an important part of a preventive maintenance system, as is a record of the time and cost to make the repair. Such records can also provide information about the family of equipment and suppliers.

LO5: Describe how to improve maintenance

Reliability and maintenance are of such importance that most systems are now computerized. Figure 17.3 shows the major components of such a system with files to be maintained on the left and reports generated on the right.

Both Boeing and General Motors are pursuing competitive advantage via their reliability and maintenance information systems. Boeing can now monitor the health of an airplane in flight and relay relevant information in real time to the ground, providing a head start on reliability and maintenance issues. Similarly, General Motors, with its On Star wireless satellite service, alerts car owners to 1,600 possible diagnostic failures, such as faulty airbags sensor or even the need for an oil change. For GM, the service provides immediate data that its engineers can use to jump on quality issues before customers even notice a problem. This has saved the firm an estimated $100 million in warranty costs by catching problems early.

Figure 17.4(a) shows a traditional view of the relationship between preventive maintenance and breakdown maintenance. In this view, operations managers consider a *balance* between the two costs. Allocating more resources to preventive maintenance will reduce the number of breakdowns. At some point, however, the decrease in breakdown maintenance costs may be less than the increase in preventive maintenance costs. At this point, the total cost curve begins to rise. Beyond this optimal point, the firm will be better off waiting for breakdowns to occur and repairing them when they do.

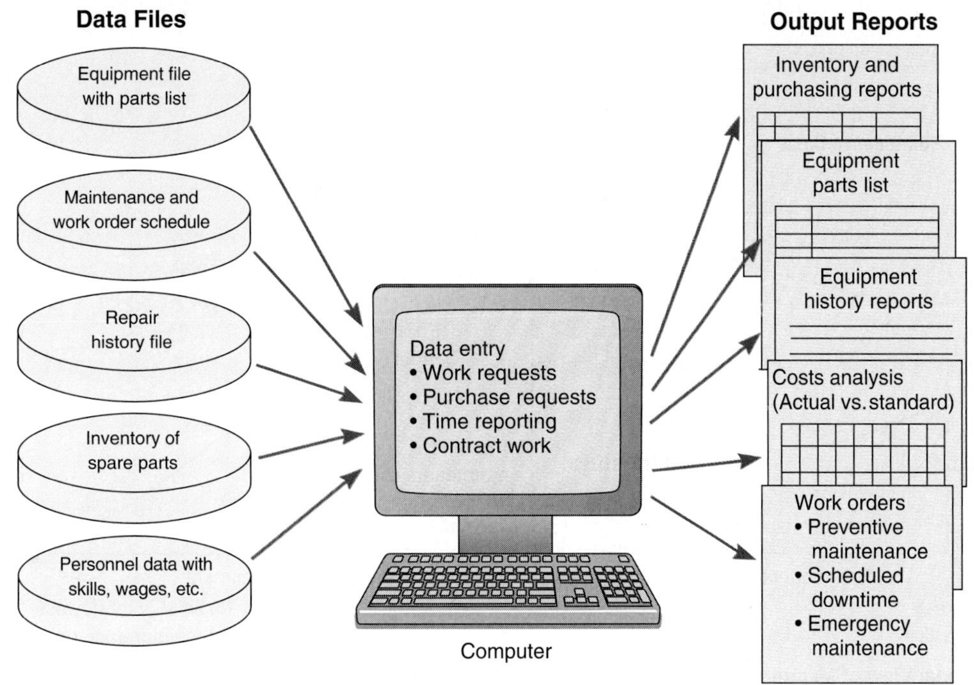

◀ **FIGURE 17.3**
A Computerized Maintenance System

OM in Action ► Preventive Maintenance Saves Lives

Flight 5481's trip was short. It lasted 70 seconds. The flight left the Charlotte Airport, bound for Greenville/Spartanburg, but seconds after lift-off, the nose of the aircraft pitched upward, the plane rolled, and, moments later, slammed into the corner of a maintenance facility at the airport. The Beech 1900D commuter plane carried 21 people to their death. The following are selected comments from the final moments of the flight:

8:47:02—Co-pilot Jonathan Gibbs: "Wuh."
8:47:03—Capt. Katie Leslie: "Help me. . . . You got it?"
8:47:05—Gibbs: "Oh (expletive). Push down."
8:47:12—Leslie: "Push the nose down."
8:47:14—Leslie: "Oh my God."
8:47:16—Leslie (calling to controllers): "We have an emergency for Air Midwest fifty-four eighty-one."
8:47:18—Faint voice from passenger area: "Daddy."
8:47:26—Leslie: "Oh my God, ahh."
8:47:26—Gibbs: "Uh, uh, God, ahh (expletive)."
8:47:28 End of recording

The National Transportation Safety Board's focus in this situation is a preventive maintenance error made two days prior to the crash. The mechanic and a supervisor skipped at least 12 steps required in the maintenance of the tension of the pitch-control cables during the *Detail 6* check that include the pitch of the control cable tension. Data show that the control column position changed during the maintenance and the plane lost about two-thirds down-elevator capability. Investigators believe that the aircraft would have been flyable with fully functioning controls had it been given proper preventive maintenance. Maintenance can improve quality, reduce costs, and win orders. It can also be a matter of life and death.

Sources: Aviation Week and Space Technology (May 26, 2003): 52; *USA Today* (May 21, 2003): 8A; and *The Wall Street Journal* (May 21, 2003): D3 and (May 20, 2003): D1, D3.

Unfortunately, cost curves such as in Figure 17.4(a) seldom consider the *full costs of a breakdown*. Many costs are ignored because they are not *directly* related to the immediate breakdown. For instance, the cost of inventory maintained to compensate for downtime is not typically considered. Moreover, downtime can have a devastating effect on safety and morale. Employees may also begin to believe that performance to standard and maintaining equipment are not important. Finally, downtime adversely affects delivery schedules, destroying customer relations and future sales. When the full impact of breakdowns is considered, Figure 17.4(b) may be a better representation of maintenance costs. In Figure 17.4(b), total costs are at a minimum when the system does not break down.

Assuming that all potential costs associated with downtime have been identified, the operations staff can compute the optimal level of maintenance activity on a theoretical basis. Such analysis, of course, also requires accurate historical data on maintenance costs, breakdown probabilities,

AUTHOR COMMENT When all breakdown costs are considered, much more maintenance may be advantageous.

▼ **FIGURE 17.4 Maintenance Costs**

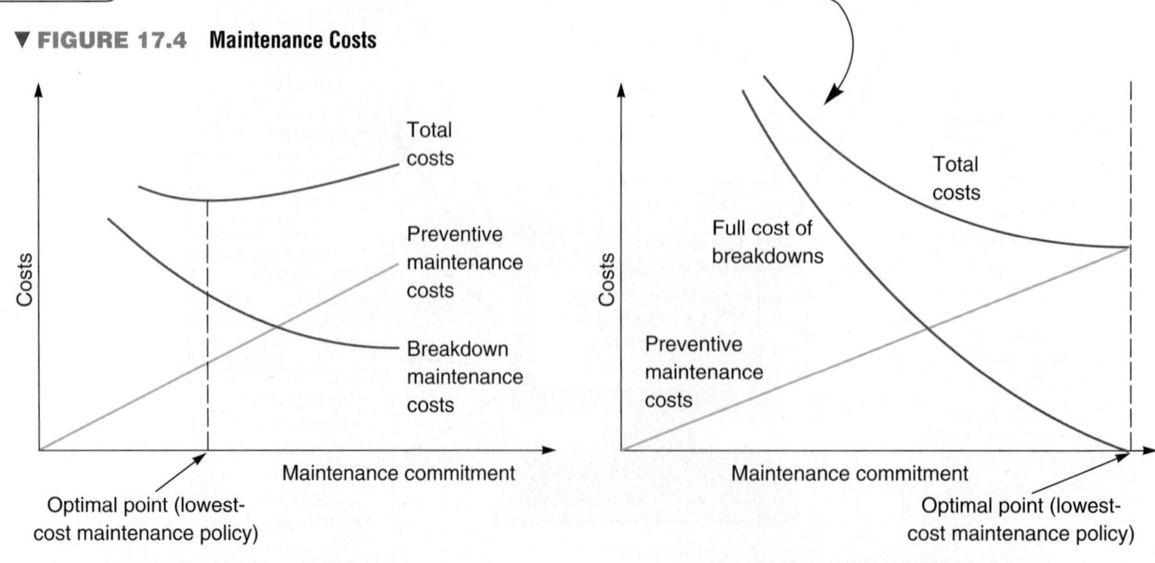

and repair times. Example 4 shows how to compare preventive and breakdown maintenance costs to select the least expensive maintenance policy.

EXAMPLE 4

Comparing preventive and breakdown maintenance costs

Farlen & Halikman is a CPA firm specializing in payroll preparation. The firm has been successful in automating much of its work, using high-speed printers for check processing and report preparation. The computerized approach, however, has problems. Over the past 20 months, the printers have broken down at the rate indicated in the following table:

Number of Breakdowns	Number of Months That Breakdowns Occurred
0	2
1	8
2	6
3	4
	Total: 20

Each time the printers break down, Farlen & Halikman estimates that it loses an average of $300 in production time and service expenses. One alternative is to purchase a service contract for preventive maintenance. Even if Farlen & Halikman contracts for preventive maintenance, there will still be breakdowns, *averaging* one breakdown per month. The price for this service is $150 per month.

APPROACH ▶ To determine if the CPA firm should follow a "run until breakdown" policy or contract for preventive maintenance, we follow a 4-step process:

LO6: Compare preventive and breakdown maintenance costs

STEP 1. Compute the *expected number* of breakdowns (based on past history) if the firm continues as is, without the service contract.
STEP 2. Compute the expected breakdown cost per month with no preventive maintenance contract.
STEP 3. Compute the cost of preventive maintenance.
STEP 4. Compare the two options and select the one that will cost less.

SOLUTION ▶

STEP 1.

Number of Breakdowns	Frequency	Number of Breakdowns	Frequency
0	2/20 = .1	2	6/20 = 0.3
1	8/20 = .4	3	4/20 = 0.2

$$\begin{pmatrix}\text{Expected number}\\ \text{of breakdowns}\end{pmatrix} = \sum\left[\begin{pmatrix}\text{Number of}\\ \text{breakdowns}\end{pmatrix} \times \begin{pmatrix}\text{Corresponding}\\ \text{frequency}\end{pmatrix}\right]$$
$$= (0)(.1) + (1)(.4) + (2)(.3) + (3)(.2)$$
$$= 0 + .4 + .6 + .6$$
$$= 1.6 \text{ breakdowns/month}$$

STEP 2.

$$\text{Expected breakdown cost} = \begin{pmatrix}\text{Expected number}\\ \text{of breakdowns}\end{pmatrix} \times \begin{pmatrix}\text{Cost per}\\ \text{breakdown}\end{pmatrix}$$
$$= (1.6)(\$300)$$
$$= \$480/\text{month}$$

STEP 3.

$$\begin{pmatrix}\text{Preventive}\\ \text{maintenance cost}\end{pmatrix} = \begin{pmatrix}\text{Cost of expected}\\ \text{breakdowns if service}\\ \text{contract signed}\end{pmatrix} + \begin{pmatrix}\text{Cost of}\\ \text{service contract}\end{pmatrix}$$
$$= (1 \text{ breakdown/month})(\$300) + \$150/\text{month}$$
$$= \$450/\text{month}$$

STEP 4. Because it is less expensive overall to hire a maintenance service firm ($450) than to not do so ($480), Farlen & Halikman should hire the service firm.

INSIGHT ▶ Determining the expected number of breakdowns for each option is crucial to making a good decision. This typically requires good maintenance records.

LEARNING EXERCISE ▶ What is the best decision if the preventive maintenance contract cost increases to $195 per month? [Answer: At $495(= $300 + $195) per month, "run until breakdown" becomes less expensive (assuming that all costs are included in the $300 per breakdown cost).]

RELATED PROBLEMS ▶ 17.3, 17.4, 17.17

Using variations of the technique shown in Example 4, operations managers can examine maintenance policies.

Increasing Repair Capabilities

Because reliability and preventive maintenance are seldom perfect, most firms opt for some level of repair capability. Enlarging or improving repair facilities can get the system back in operation faster. A good maintenance facility should have these six features:

1. Well-trained personnel
2. Adequate resources
3. Ability to establish a repair plan and priorities[2]
4. Ability and authority to do material planning
5. Ability to identify the cause of breakdowns
6. Ability to design ways to extend MTBF

However, not all repairs can be done in the firm's facility. Managers must, therefore, decide where repairs are to be performed. Figure 17.5 provides a continuum of options and how they rate in terms of speed, cost, and competence. Moving to the right in Figure 17.5 may improve the competence of the repair work, but at the same time it increases costs and replacement time.

LO7: Define autonomous maintenance

Autonomous Maintenance

Autonomous maintenance
Operators partner with maintenance personnel to observe, check, adjust, clean, and notify.

Preventive maintenance policies and techniques must include an emphasis on employees accepting responsibility for the "observe, check, adjust, clean, and notify" type of equipment maintenance. Such policies are consistent with the advantages of employee empowerment. This approach is known as **autonomous maintenance**. Employees can predict failures, prevent breakdowns, and prolong equipment life. With autonomous maintenance, the manager is making a step toward both employee empowerment and maintaining system performance.

AUTHOR COMMENT
Maintenance improves productivity.

TOTAL PRODUCTIVE MAINTENANCE

Many firms have moved to bring total quality management concepts to the practice of preventive maintenance with an approach known as **total productive maintenance (TPM)**. It involves the concept of reducing variability through autonomous maintenance and excellent maintenance practices. Total productive maintenance includes:

Total productive maintenance (TPM)
Combines total quality management with a strategic view of maintenance from process and equipment design to preventive maintenance.

- Designing machines that are reliable, easy to operate, and easy to maintain
- Emphasizing total cost of ownership when purchasing machines, so that service and maintenance are included in the cost
- Developing preventive maintenance plans that utilize the best practices of operators, maintenance departments, and depot service
- Training for autonomous maintenance so operators maintain their own machines and partner with maintenance personnel

[2]You may recall from our discussion of network planning in Chapter 3 that DuPont developed the critical path method (CPM) to improve the scheduling of maintenance projects.

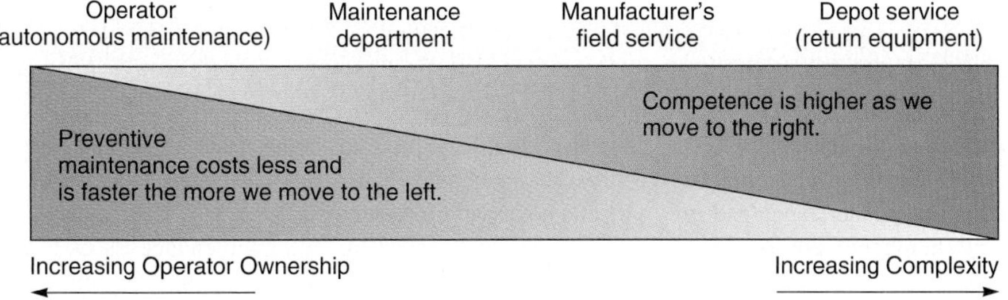

FIGURE 17.5 The Operations Manager Determines How Maintenance Will Be Performed

High utilization of facilities, tight scheduling, low inventory, and consistent quality demand reliability. Total productive maintenance is the key to reducing variability and improving reliability.

TECHNIQUES FOR ENHANCING MAINTENANCE

AUTHOR COMMENT Both OM techniques and the physical sciences can improve maintenance.

Three techniques have proven beneficial to effective maintenance: simulation, expert systems, and sensors.

Simulation Because of the complexity of some maintenance decisions, computer simulation is a good tool for evaluating the impact of various policies. For instance, operations personnel can decide whether to add more staff by determining the trade-offs between machine reliability and the costs of additional labor. Management can also simulate the replacement of parts that have not yet failed as a way of preventing future breakdowns. Simulation via physical models can also be useful. For example, a physical model can vibrate an airplane to simulate thousands of hours of flight time to evaluate maintenance needs.

Expert Systems OM managers use expert systems (that is, computer programs that mimic human logic) to assist staff in isolating and repairing various faults in machinery and equipment. For instance, General Electric's DELTA system asks a series of detailed questions that aid the user in identifying a problem. DuPont uses expert systems to monitor equipment and to train repair personnel.

Automated Sensors Sensors warn when production machinery is about to fail or is becoming damaged by heat, vibration, or fluid leaks. The goal of such procedures is not only to avoid failures but also to perform preventive maintenance before machines are damaged.

CHAPTER SUMMARY

Operations managers focus on design improvements and backup components to improve reliability. Reliability improvements also can be obtained through the use of preventive maintenance and excellent repair facilities.

Firms give employees "ownership" of their equipment. When workers repair or do preventive maintenance on their own machines, breakdowns are less common. Well-trained and empowered employees ensure reliable systems through preventive maintenance. In turn, reliable, well-maintained equipment not only provides higher utilization but also improves quality and performance to schedule. Top firms build and maintain systems that drive out variability so that customers can rely on products and services to be produced to specifications and on time.

Key Terms

Maintenance (p. 650)
Reliability (p. 650)
Mean time between failures (MTBF) (p. 652)
Redundancy (p. 653)
Preventive maintenance (p. 654)
Breakdown maintenance (p. 654)
Infant mortality (p. 654)
Autonomous maintenance (p. 658)
Total productive maintenance (TPM) (p. 658)

Ethical Dilemma

The Space Shuttle *Columbia* disintegrated over Texas on its 2003 return to Earth. The *Challenger* exploded shortly after launch in 1986. An *Apollo 1* spacecraft imploded in fire on the launch pad in 1967. In each case, the lives of all crew members were lost. The hugely complex shuttle may look a bit like an airplane, but it is very different. In reality, its overall statistical reliability is such that about 1 out of every 50 flights will have a major malfunction. In fact, there have been almost 130 shuttle flights to date.

NASA has cut safety inspections by more than 50% since 1989. Employees often face a cumbersome process for bringing safety issues to management. And the agency continues to face pressure to launch the shuttle on missions to the space station and elsewhere. Of course, as one aerospace manager has stated "you can be perfectly safe and never get off the ground."

Given the huge reliability and maintenance issues NASA faces (e.g., seals cracking in cold weather, heat shielding tiles falling off), should astronauts be allowed to fly? (In earlier *Atlas* rockets, men were inserted not out of necessity but because test pilots and politicians thought they should be there.) What are the pros and cons of manned space exploration from an ethical perspective? Should the U.S. spend billions of dollars to return an astronaut to the moon?

Discussion Questions

1. What is the objective of maintenance and reliability?
2. How does one identify a candidate for preventive maintenance?
3. Explain the notion of "infant mortality" in the context of product reliability.
4. Why is simulation often an appropriate technique for maintenance problems?
5. What is the trade-off between operator-performed maintenance versus supplier-performed maintenance?
6. How can a manager evaluate the effectiveness of the maintenance function?
7. How does machine design contribute to either increasing or alleviating the maintenance problem?
8. What roles can information technology play in the maintenance function?
9. During an argument as to the merits of preventive maintenance at Windsor Printers, the company owner asked, "Why fix it before it breaks?" How would you, as the director of maintenance, respond?
10. Will preventive maintenance eliminate *all* breakdowns?

Using Software to Solve Reliability Problems

Excel OM and POM for Windows may be used to solve reliability problems. The reliability module allow us to enter (1) number of systems (components) in the series (1 through 10); (2) number of backup, or parallel, components (1 through 12); and (3) component reliability for both series and parallel data.

Solved Problems

Virtual Office Hours help is available at www.myomlab.com

▼ SOLVED PROBLEM 17.1

The semiconductor used in the Sullivan Wrist Calculator has five circuits, each of which has its own reliability rate. Component 1 has a reliability of .90; component 2, .95; component 3, .98; component 4, .90; and component 5, .99. What is the reliability of one semiconductor?

▼ SOLUTION

$$\begin{aligned}\text{Semiconductor reliability, } R_s &= R_1 \times R_2 \times R_3 \times R_4 \times R_5 \\ &= (.90)(.95)(.98)(.90)(.99) \\ &= .7466\end{aligned}$$

▼ SOLVED PROBLEM 17.2

A recent engineering change at Sullivan Wrist Calculator places a backup component in each of the two least reliable transistor circuits. The new circuits will look like the following:

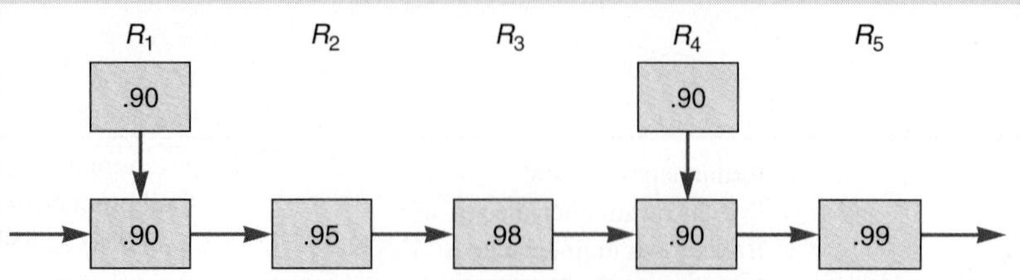

What is the reliability of the new system?

▼ **SOLUTION**

$$\begin{aligned}\text{Reliability} &= [.9 + (1 - .9) \times .9] \times .95 \times .98 \times [.9 + (1 - .9) \times .9] \times .99 \\ &= [.9 + .09] \times .95 \times .98 \times [.9 + .09] \times .99 \\ &= .99 \times .95 \times .98 \times .99 \times .99 \\ &= .903\end{aligned}$$

Problems*

• **17.1** The Beta II computer's electronic processing unit contains 50 components in series. The average reliability of each component is 99.0%. Using Figure 17.2, determine the overall reliability of the processing unit.

• **17.2** A testing process at Boeing Aircraft has 400 components in series. The average reliability of each component is 99.5%. Use Figure 17.2 to find the overall reliability of the whole testing process.

• **17.3** What are the *expected* number of yearly breakdowns for the power generator at Orlando Utilities that has exhibited the following data over the past 20 years? PX

Number of breakdowns	0	1	2	3	4	5	6
Number of years in which breakdown occurred	2	2	5	4	5	2	0

• **17.4** Each breakdown of a graphic plotter table at Airbus Industries costs $50. Find the expected daily breakdown cost, given the following data: PX

Number of breakdowns	0	1	2	3	4
Daily breakdown probability	.1	.2	.4	.2	.1

•• **17.5** A new aircraft control system is being designed that must be 98% reliable. This system consists of three components in series. If all three of the components are to have the same level of reliability, what level of reliability is required? PX

•• **17.6** Robert Klassan Manufacturing, a medical equipment manufacturer, subjected 100 heart pacemakers to 5,000 hours of testing. Halfway through the testing, 5 pacemakers failed. What was the failure rate in terms of the following:

a) Percentage of failures?
b) Number of failures per unit-hour?
c) Number of failures per unit-year?
d) If 1,100 people receive pacemaker implants, how many units can we expect to fail during the following year?

**Note:* PX means the problem may be solved with POM for Windows and/or Excel OM.

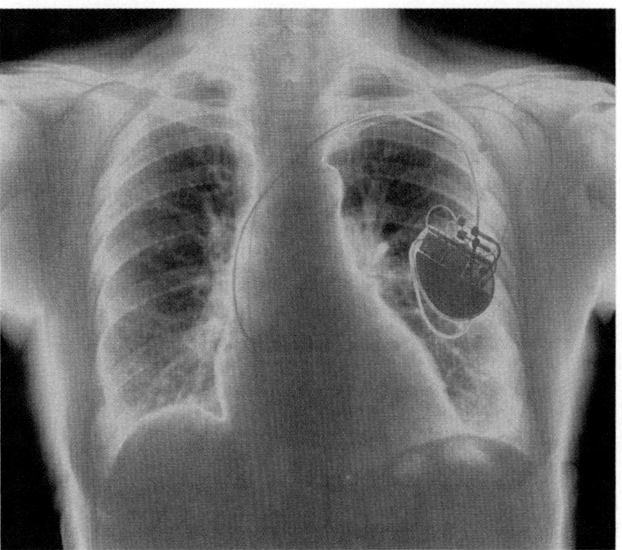

•• **17.7** A manufacturer of disk drives for notebook computers wants a MTBF of at least 50,000 hours. Recent test results for 10 units were one failure at 10,000 hrs, another at 25,000 hrs, and two more at 45,000 hrs. The remaining units were still running at 60,000 hours. Determine the following:

a) Percent of failures.
b) Number of failures per unit-hour
c) MTBF at this point in the testing

•• **17.8** What is the reliability of the following production process? $R_1 = 0.95$, $R_2 = 0.90$, $R_3 = 0.98$.

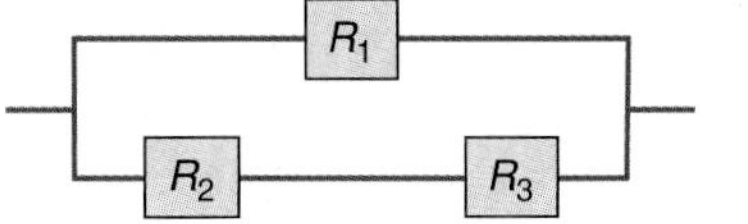

PX

•• **17.9** What is the reliability that bank loans will be processed accurately if each of the 5 clerks shown in the chart has the reliability shown?

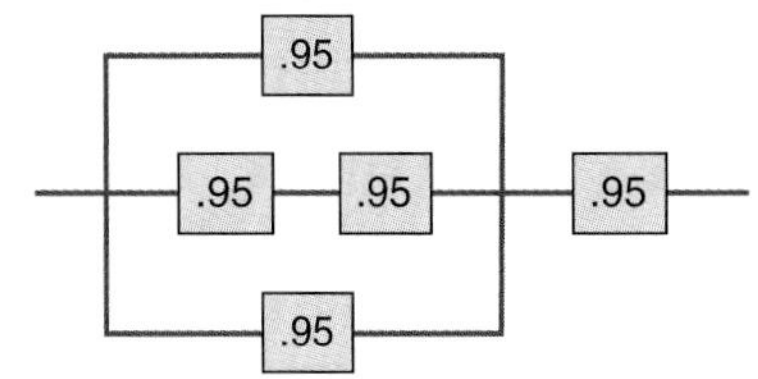

•• **17.10** Merrill Kim Sharp has a system composed of three components in parallel. The components have the following reliabilities:

$$R_1 = 0.90, \quad R_2 = 0.95, \quad R_3 = 0.85$$

What is the reliability of the system? (*Hint:* See Example 3.) PX

• **17.11** A medical control system has three components in series with individual reliabilities (R_1, R_2, R_3) as shown:

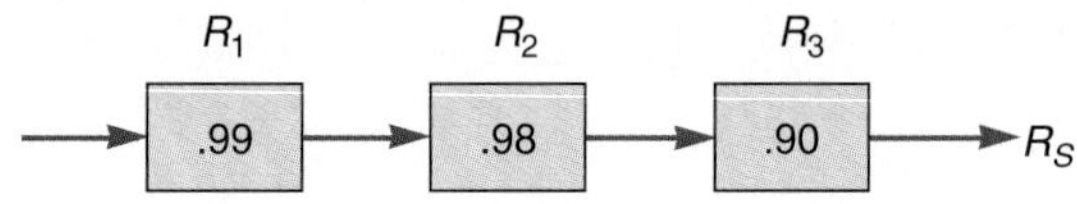

What is the reliability of the system? PX

•• **17.12** a) What is the reliability of the system shown?

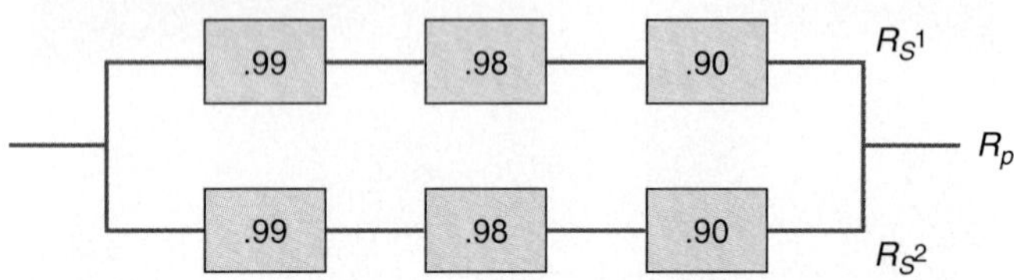

b) How much did reliability improve if the medical control system shown in Problem 17.11 changed to the redundant parallel system shown here? PX

••• **17.13** Assume that for cardiac bypass surgery, 85% of patients survive the surgery, 95% survive the recovery period after surgery, 80% are able to make the lifestyle changes needed to extend their survival to 1 year or more, and only 10% of those who do not make the lifestyle changes survive more than a year. What is the likelihood that a given patient will survive more than a year? PX

•• **17.14** Elizabeth Irwin's design team has proposed the following system with component reliabilities as indicated:

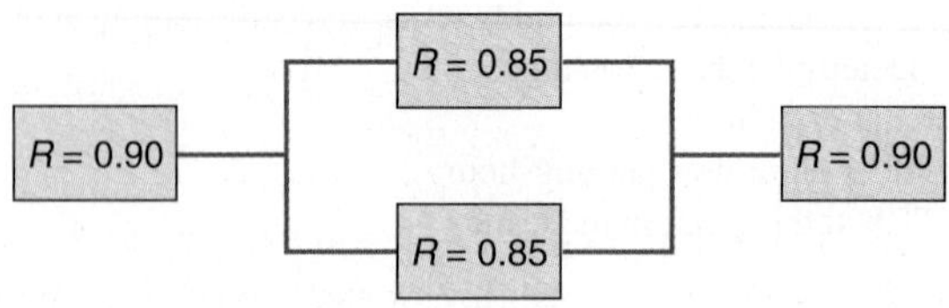

What is the reliability of the system? PX

•• **17.15** The maintenance department at Mechanical Dynamics has presented you with the following failure curve. What does it suggest?

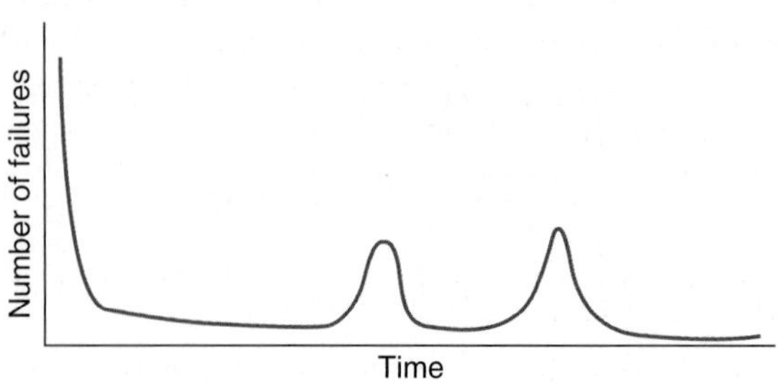

•• **17.16** Rick Wing, salesperson for Wave Soldering Systems, Inc. (WSSI), has provided you with a proposal for improving the temperature control on your present machine. The machine uses a hot-air knife to cleanly remove excess solder from printed circuit boards; this is a great concept, but the hot-air temperature control lacks reliability. According to Wing, engineers at WSSI have improved the reliability of the critical temperature controls. The new system still has the four sensitive integrated circuits controlling the temperature, but the new machine has a backup for each. The four integrated circuits have reliabilities of .90, .92, .94, and .96. The four backup circuits all have a reliability of .90.

a) What is the reliability of the new temperature controller?
b) If you pay a premium, Wing says he can improve all four of the backup units to .93. What is the reliability of this option? PX

••• **17.17** The fire department has a number of failures with its oxygen masks and is evaluating the possibility of outsourcing preventive maintenance to the manufacturer. Because of the risk associated with a failure, the cost of each failure is estimated at $2,000. The current maintenance policy (with station employees performing maintenance) has yielded the following history:

Number of breakdowns	0	1	2	3	4	5
Number of years in which breakdowns occurred	4	3	1	5	5	0

This manufacturer will guarantee repairs on any and all failures as part of a service contract. The cost of this service is $5,000 per year.

a) What is the expected number of breakdowns per year with station employees performing maintenance?
b) What is the cost of the current maintenance policy?
c) What is the more economical policy?

••• **17.18** As VP for operations at Brian Normoyle Engineering, you must decide which product design, A or B, has the higher reliability. B is designed with backup units for components R_3 and R_4. What is the reliability of each design?

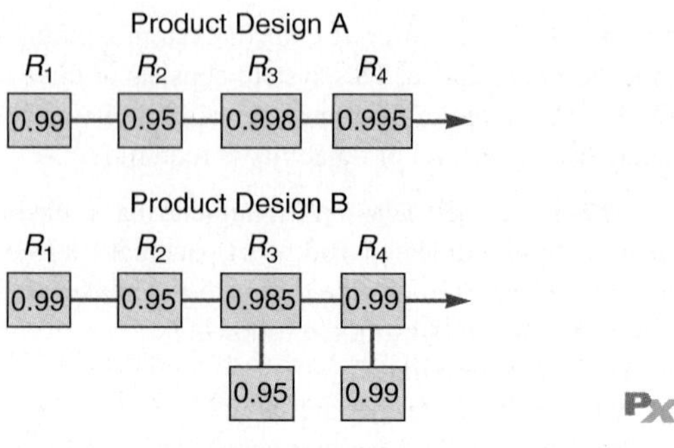

PX

•••• **17.19** A typical retail transaction consists of several smaller steps, which can be considered components subject to failure. A list of such components might include:

Component	Description	Definition of Failure
1	Find product in proper size, color, etc.	Can't find product
2	Enter cashier line	No lines open; lines too long; line experiencing difficulty
3	Scan product UPC for name, price, etc.	Won't scan; item not on file; scans incorrect name or price
4	Calculate purchase total	Wrong weight; wrong extension; wrong data entry; wrong tax
5	Make payment	Customer lacks cash; check not acceptable; credit card refused
6	Make change	Makes change incorrectly
7	Bag merchandise	Damages merchandise while bagging; bag splits
8	Conclude transaction and exit	No receipt; unfriendly, rude, or aloof clerk

Let the eight probabilities of success be .92, .94, .99, .99, .98, .97, .95, and .96. What is the reliability of the system, that is, the probability that there will be a satisfied customer? If you were the store manager, what do you think should be an acceptable value for this probability? Which components would be good candidates for backup, which for redesign?

Refer to myomlab for these additional homework problems: 17.20–17.24

Case Studies

Maintenance Drives Profits at Frito-Lay

Video Case Study

Frito-Lay, the multi-billion-dollar subsidiary of food and beverage giant PepsiCo, maintains 36 plants in the U.S. and Canada. These facilities produce dozen of snacks, including the well-known Lay's, Fritos, Cheetos, Doritos, Ruffles, and Tostitos brands, each of which sells over $1 billion per year.

Frito-Lay plants produce in the high-volume, low-variety process model common to commercial baked goods, steel, glass, and beer industries. In this environment, preventive maintenance of equipment takes a major role by avoiding costly downtime. Tom Rao, Vice President for Florida operations, estimates that each 1% of downtime has a negative annual profit impact of $200,000. He is proud of the $1\frac{1}{2}$% unscheduled downtime his plant is able to reach—well below the 2% that is considered the "world-class" benchmark. This excellent performance is possible because the maintenance department takes an active role in setting the parameters for preventive maintenance. This is done with weekly input to the production schedule.

Maintenance policy impacts energy use as well. The Florida plant's technical manager, Jim Wentzel, states, "By reducing production interruptions, we create an opportunity to bring energy and utility use under control. Equipment maintenance and a solid production schedule are keys to utility efficiency. With every production interruption, there is substantial waste."

As a part of its total productive maintenance (TPM) program,* Frito-Lay empowers employees with what it calls the "Run Right" system. Run Right teaches employees to "identify and do." This means each shift is responsible for identifying problems and making the necessary corrections, when possible. This is accomplished through (1) a "power walk" at the beginning of the shift to ensure that equipment and process settings are performing to standard, (2) mid-shift and post-shift reviews of standards and performance, and (3) posting of any issues on a large whiteboard in the shift office. Items remain on the whiteboard until corrected, which is seldom more than a shift or two.

With good manpower scheduling and tight labor control to hold down variable costs, making time for training is challenging. But supervisors, including the plant manager, are available to fill in on the production line when that is necessary to free an employee for training.

The 30 maintenance personnel hired to cover 24/7 operations at the Florida plant all come with multi-craft skills (e.g., welding, electrical, plumbing). "Multi-craft maintenance personnel are harder to find and cost more," says Wentzel, "but they more than pay for themselves."

Discussion Questions**

1. What might be done to help take Frito-Lay to the next level of outstanding maintenance? Consider factors such as sophisticated software.
2. What are the advantages and disadvantages of giving more responsibility for machine maintenance to the operator?
3. Discuss the pros and cons of hiring multi-craft maintenance personnel.

*At Frito-Lay preventive maintenance, autonomous maintenance, and total productive maintenance are part of a Frito-Lay program known as total productive manufacturing.

**You may wish to view the video that accompanies this case before answering these questions.

Source: Professors Barry Render (Rollins College), Jay Heizer (Texas Lutheran University), and Beverly Amer (Northern Arizona University).

▶**Additional Case Studies:** Visit **www.myomlab.com** or **www.pearsonhighered.com/heizer** for these free case studies:
Cartak's Department Store: Requires the evaluation of the impact of an additional invoice verifier.
Worldwide Chemical Company: The maintenance department in this company is in turmoil.

Bibliography

Bauer, Eric, X. Zhang, and D. A. Kimber. *Practical System Reliability.* New York: Wiley (2009).

Blank, Ronald. *The Basics of Reliability*. University Park, IL: Productivity Press (2004).

Cua, K. O., K. E. McKone, and R. G. Schroeder. "Relationships between Implementation of TQM, JIT, and TPM and Manufacturing Performance." *Journal of Operations Management* 19, no. 6 (November 2001): 675–694.

Finigen, Tim, and Jim Humphries. "Maintenance Gets Lean." *IE Industrial Systems* 38, no. 10 (October 2006): 26–31.

Sova, Roger, and Lea A. P. Tonkin. "Total Productive Maintenance at Crown International." *Target: Innovation at Work* 19, no. 1 (1st Quarter 2003): 41–44.

Stephens, M. P. *Productivity and Reliability-Based Maintenance Management.* Upper Saddle River, NJ: Prentice Hall (2004).

Weil, Marty. "Beyond Preventive Maintenance." *APICS* 16, no. 4 (April 2006): 40–43.

Chapter 17 *Rapid* Review

Main Heading	Review Material	myomlab

THE STRATEGIC IMPORTANCE OF MAINTENANCE AND RELIABILITY (pp. 650–651)

Poor maintenance can be disruptive, inconvenient, wasteful, and expensive in dollars and even in lives. The interdependency of operator, machine, and mechanic is a hallmark of successful maintenance and reliability.

Good maintenance and reliability management requires employee involvement and good procedures; it enhances a firm's performance and protects its investment.

The objective of maintenance and reliability is to maintain the capability of the system.

- **Maintenance**—All activities involved in keeping a system's equipment in working order.
- **Reliability**—The probability that a machine part or product will function properly for a specified time under stated conditions.

The two main tactics for improving reliability are:

1. Improving individual components
2. Providing redundancy

The two main tactics for improving maintenance are:

1. Implementing or improving preventive maintenance
2. Increasing repair capabilities or speed

VIDEO 17.1
Maintenance Drives Profits at Frito-Lay

RELIABILITY (pp. 651–654)

A system is composed of a series of individual interrelated components, each performing a specific job. If any *one* component fails to perform, the overall system can fail.

As the number of components in a *series* increases, the reliability of the whole system declines very quickly:

$$R_s = R_1 \times R_2 \times R_3 \times \ldots \times R_n \quad (17\text{-}1)$$

where R_1 = reliability of component 1, R_2 = reliability of component 2, and so on

Equation (17-1) assumes that the reliability of an individual component does not depend on the reliability of other components.

A .90 reliability means that the unit will perform as intended 90% of the time, and it will fail 10% of the time.

The basic unit of measure for reliability is the *product failure rate* (FR). FR(N) is the number of failures during a period of time:

$$\text{FR}(\%) = \frac{\text{Number of failures}}{\text{Number of units tested}} \times 100\% \quad (17\text{-}2)$$

$$\text{FR}(N) = \frac{\text{Number of failures}}{\text{Number of unit-hours of operation time}} \quad (17\text{-}3)$$

- **Mean time between failures (MTBF)**—The expected time between a repair and the next failure of a component, machine, process, or product.

$$\text{MTBF} = \frac{1}{\text{FR}(N)} \quad (17\text{-}4)$$

- **Redundancy**—The use of components in parallel to raise reliability.

The reliability of a component along with its backup equals:

(Probability that 1st component works) + [(Prob. that backup works) × (Prob. that 1st fails)]

Problems: 17.1–17.2, 17.5–17.14, 17.16, 17.18, 17.19

Virtual Office Hours for Solved Problems: 17.1, 17.2

ACTIVE MODEL 17.1

MAINTENANCE (pp. 654–658)

- **Preventive maintenance**—Involves routine inspections, servicing, and keeping facilities in good repair to prevent failure.
- **Breakdown maintenance**—Remedial maintenance that occurs when equipment fails and must be repaired on an emergency or priority basis.
- **Infant mortality**—The failure rate early in the life of a product or process.

Consistent with job enrichment practices, machine operators must be held responsible for preventive maintenance of their own equipment and tools.

Problems: 17.3, 17.4, 17.15, 17.17

Main Heading	Review Material
	Reliability and maintenance are of such importance that most maintenance systems are now computerized. Costs of a breakdown that may get ignored include: • The cost of inventory maintained to compensate for downtime • Downtime, which can have a devastating effect on safety and morale and which adversely affects delivery schedules, destroying customer relations and future sales ■ **Autonomous maintenance**—Partners operators with maintenance personnel to observe, check, adjust, clean, and notify. Employees can predict failures, prevent breakdowns, and prolong equipment life. With autonomous maintenance, the manager is making a step toward both employee empowerment and maintaining system performance.
TOTAL PRODUCTIVE MAINTENANCE (pp. 658–659)	■ **Total productive maintenance (TPM)**—Combines total quality management with a strategic view of maintenance from process and equipment design to preventive maintenance. Total productive maintenance includes: • Designing machines that are reliable, easy to operate, and easy to maintain • Emphasizing total cost of ownership when purchasing machines, so that service and maintenance are included in the cost • Developing preventive maintenance plans that utilize the best practices of operators, maintenance departments, and depot service • Training for autonomous maintenance so operators maintain their own machines and partner with maintenance personnel
TECHNIQUES FOR ENHANCING MAINTENANCE (p. 659)	Three techniques that have proven beneficial to effective maintenance are simulation, expert systems, and sensors. Computer simulation is a good tool for evaluating the impact of various policies. Expert systems are computer programs that mimic human logic. Automatic sensors warn when production machinery is about to fail or is becoming damaged by heat, vibration, or fluid leaks.

Self **Test**

■ **Before taking the self-test,** refer to the learning objectives listed at the beginning of the chapter and the key terms listed at the end of the chapter.

LO1. The two main tactics for improving reliability are ________ and ________.

LO2. The reliability of a system with n independent components equals:
- **a)** the sum of the individual reliabilities.
- **b)** the minimum reliability among all components.
- **c)** the maximum reliability among all components.
- **d)** the product of the individual reliabilities.
- **e)** the average of the individual reliabilities.

LO3. What is the formula for the mean time between failures?
- **a)** Number of failures ÷ Number of unit-hours of operation time
- **b)** Number of unit-hours of operation time ÷ Number of failures
- **c)** (Number of failures ÷ Number of units tested) × 100%
- **d)** (Number of units tested ÷ Number of failures) × 100%
- **e)** 1 ÷ FR(%)

LO4. The process that is intended to find potential failures and make changes or repairs is known as:
- **a)** breakdown maintenance.
- **b)** failure maintenance.
- **c)** preventive maintenance.
- **d)** all of the above.

LO5. The two main tactics for improving maintenance are ________ and ________.

LO6. The appropriate maintenance policy is developed by balancing preventive maintenance costs with breakdown maintenance costs. The problem is that:
- **a)** preventive maintenance costs are very difficult to identify.
- **b)** full breakdown costs are seldom considered.
- **c)** preventive maintenance should be performed, regardless of the cost.
- **d)** breakdown maintenance must be performed, regardless of the cost.

LO7. ________ maintenance partners operators with maintenance personnel to observe, check, adjust, clean, and notify.
- **a)** Partnering
- **b)** Operator
- **c)** Breakdown
- **d)** Six Sigma
- **e)** Autonomous

Answers: LO1. improving individual components, providing redundancy; LO2. d; LO3. b; LO4. c; LO5. implementing or improving preventive maintenance, increasing repair capabilities or speed; LO6. b; LO7. e.

Appendices

APPENDIX I
Normal Curve Areas

APPENDIX II
Values of $e^{-\lambda}$ for Use in the Poisson Distribution

APPENDIX III
Table of Random Numbers

APPENDIX IV
Using Excel OM and POM for Windows

APPENDIX V
Solutions to Even-Numbered Problems

APPENDIX I NORMAL CURVE AREAS

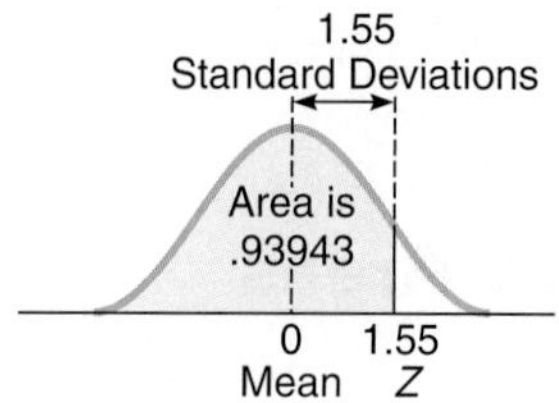

To find the area under the normal curve, you can apply either Table I.1 or Table I.2. In Table I.1, you must know how many standard deviations that point is to the right of the mean. Then, the area under the normal curve can be read directly from the normal table. For example, the total area under the normal curve for a point that is 1.55 standard deviations to the right of the mean is .93943.

Table I.1

Z	.00	.01	.02	.03	.04	.05	.06	.07	.08	.09
.0	.50000	.50399	.50798	.51197	.51595	.51994	.52392	.52790	.53188	.53586
.1	.53983	.54380	.54776	.55172	.55567	.55962	.56356	.56749	.57142	.57535
.2	.57926	.58317	.58706	.59095	.59483	.59871	.60257	.60642	.61026	.61409
.3	.61791	.62172	.62552	.62930	.63307	.63683	.64058	.64431	.64803	.65173
.4	.65542	.65910	.66276	.66640	.67003	.67364	.67724	.68082	.68439	.68793
.5	.69146	.69497	.69847	.70194	.70540	.70884	.71226	.71566	.71904	.72240
.6	.72575	.72907	.73237	.73565	.73891	.74215	.74537	.74857	.75175	.75490
.7	.75804	.76115	.76424	.76730	.77035	.77337	.77637	.77935	.78230	.78524
.8	.78814	.79103	.79389	.79673	.79955	.80234	.80511	.80785	.81057	.81327
.9	.81594	.81859	.82121	.82381	.82639	.82894	.83147	.83398	.83646	.83891
1.0	.84134	.84375	.84614	.84849	.85083	.85314	.85543	.85769	.85993	.86214
1.1	.86433	.86650	.86864	.87076	.87286	.87493	.87698	.87900	.88100	.88298
1.2	.88493	.88686	.88877	.89065	.89251	.89435	.89617	.89796	.89973	.90147
1.3	.90320	.90490	.90658	.90824	.90988	.91149	.91309	.91466	.91621	.91774
1.4	.91924	.92073	.92220	.92364	.92507	.92647	.92785	.92922	.93056	.93189
1.5	.93319	.93448	.93574	.93699	.93822	.93943	.94062	.94179	.94295	.94408
1.6	.94520	.94630	.94738	.94845	.94950	.95053	.95154	.95254	.95352	.95449
1.7	.95543	.95637	.95728	.95818	.95907	.95994	.96080	.96164	.96246	.96327
1.8	.96407	.96485	.96562	.96638	.96712	.96784	.96856	.96926	.96995	.97062
1.9	.97128	.97193	.97257	.97320	.97381	.97441	.97500	.97558	.97615	.97670
2.0	.97725	.97784	.97831	.97882	.97932	.97982	.98030	.98077	.98124	.98169
2.1	.98214	.98257	.98300	.98341	.98382	.98422	.98461	.98500	.98537	.98574
2.2	.98610	.98645	.98679	.98713	.98745	.98778	.98809	.98840	.98870	.98899
2.3	.98928	.98956	.98983	.99010	.99036	.99061	.99086	.99111	.99134	.99158
2.4	.99180	.99202	.99224	.99245	.99266	.99286	.99305	.99324	.99343	.99361
2.5	.99379	.99396	.99413	.99430	.99446	.99461	.99477	.99492	.99506	.99520
2.6	.99534	.99547	.99560	.99573	.99585	.99598	.99609	.99621	.99632	.99643
2.7	.99653	.99664	.99674	.99683	.99693	.99702	.99711	.99720	.99728	.99736
2.8	.99744	.99752	.99760	.99767	.99774	.99781	.99788	.99795	.99801	.99807
2.9	.99813	.99819	.99825	.99831	.99836	.99841	.99846	.99851	.99856	.99861
3.0	.99865	.99869	.99874	.99878	.99882	.99886	.99899	.99893	.99896	.99900
3.1	.99903	.99906	.99910	.99913	.99916	.99918	.99921	.99924	.99926	.99929
3.2	.99931	.99934	.99936	.99938	.99940	.99942	.99944	.99946	.99948	.99950
3.3	.99952	.99953	.99955	.99957	.99958	.99960	.99961	.99962	.99964	.99965
3.4	.99966	.99968	.99969	.99970	.99971	.99972	.99973	.99974	.99975	.99976
3.5	.99977	.99978	.99978	.99979	.99980	.99981	.99981	.99982	.99983	.99983
3.6	.99984	.99985	.99985	.99986	.99986	.99987	.99987	.99988	.99988	.99989
3.7	.99989	.99990	.99990	.99990	.99991	.99991	.99992	.99992	.99992	.99992
3.8	.99993	.99993	.99993	.99994	.99994	.99994	.99994	.99995	.99995	.99995
3.9	.99995	.99995	.99996	.99996	.99996	.99996	.99996	.99996	.99997	.99997

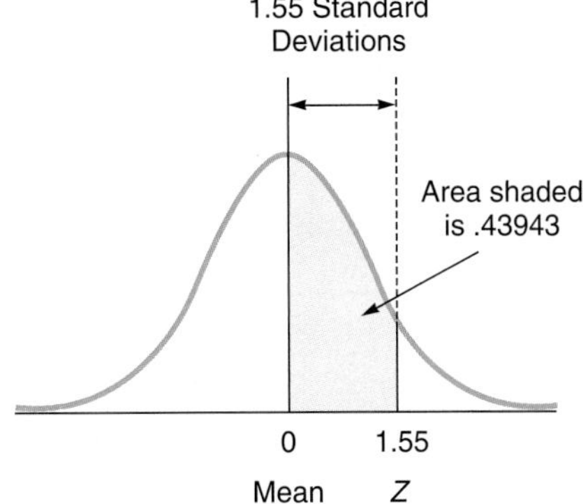

As an alternative to Table I.1, the numbers in Table I.2 represent the proportion of the total area away from the mean, μ, to one side. For example, the area between the mean and a point that is 1.55 standard deviations to its right is .43943.

TABLE I.2

Z	.00	.01	.02	.03	.04	.05	.06	.07	.08	.09
0.0	.00000	.00399	.00798	.01197	.01595	.01994	.02392	.02790	.03188	.03586
0.1	.03983	.04380	.04776	.05172	.05567	.05962	.06356	.06749	.07142	.07535
0.2	.07926	.08317	.08706	.09095	.09483	.09871	.10257	.10642	.11026	.11409
0.3	.11791	.12172	.12552	.12930	.13307	.13683	.14058	.14431	.14803	.15173
0.4	.15542	.15910	.16276	.16640	.17003	.17364	.17724	.18082	.18439	.18793
0.5	.19146	.19497	.19847	.20194	.20540	.20884	.21226	.21566	.21904	.22240
0.6	.22575	.22907	.23237	.23565	.23891	.24215	.24537	.24857	.25175	.25490
0.7	.25804	.26115	.26424	.26730	.27035	.27337	.27637	.27935	.28230	.28524
0.8	.28814	.29103	.29389	.29673	.29955	.30234	.30511	.30785	.31057	.31327
0.9	.31594	.31859	.32121	.32381	.32639	.32894	.33147	.33398	.33646	.33891
1.0	.34134	.34375	.34614	.34850	.35083	.35314	.35543	.35769	.35993	.36214
1.1	.36433	.36650	.36864	.37076	.37286	.37493	.37698	.37900	.38100	.38298
1.2	.38493	.38686	.38877	.39065	.39251	.39435	.39617	.39796	.39973	.40147
1.3	.40320	.40490	.40658	.40824	.40988	.41149	.41309	.41466	.41621	.41174
1.4	.41924	.42073	.42220	.42364	.42507	.42647	.42786	.42922	.43056	.43189
1.5	.43319	.43448	.43574	.43699	.43822	.43943	.44062	.44179	.44295	.44408
1.6	.44520	.44630	.44738	.44845	.44950	.45053	.45154	.45254	.45352	.45449
1.7	.45543	.45637	.45728	.45818	.45907	.45994	.46080	.46164	.46246	.46327
1.8	.46407	.46485	.46562	.46638	.46712	.46784	.46856	.46926	.46995	.47062
1.9	.47128	.47193	.47257	.47320	.47381	.47441	.47500	.47558	.47615	.47670
2.0	.47725	.47778	.47831	.47882	.47932	.47982	.48030	.48077	.48124	.48169
2.1	.48214	.48257	.48300	.48341	.48382	.48422	.48461	.48500	.48537	.48574
2.2	.48610	.48645	.48679	.48713	.48745	.48778	.48809	.48840	.48870	.48899
2.3	.48928	.48956	.48983	.49010	.49036	.49061	.49086	.49111	.49134	.49158
2.4	.49180	.49202	.49224	.49245	.49266	.49286	.49305	.49324	.49343	.49361
2.5	.49379	.49396	.49413	.49430	.49446	.49461	.49477	.49492	.49506	.49520
2.6	.49534	.49547	.49560	.49573	.49585	.49598	.49609	.49621	.49632	.49643
2.7	.49653	.49664	.49674	.49683	.49693	.49702	.49711	.49720	.49728	.49736
2.8	.49744	.49752	.49760	.49767	.49774	.49781	.49788	.49795	.49801	.49807
2.9	.49813	.49819	.49825	.49831	.49836	.49841	.49846	.49851	.49856	.49861
3.0	.49865	.49869	.49874	.49878	.49882	.49886	.49889	.49893	.49897	.49900
3.1	.49903	.49906	.49910	.49913	.49916	.49918	.49921	.49924	.49926	.49929

APPENDIX II VALUES OF $e^{-\lambda}$ FOR USE IN THE POISSON DISTRIBUTION

Values of $e^{-\lambda}$

λ	$e^{-\lambda}$	λ	$e^{-\lambda}$	λ	$e^{-\lambda}$	λ	$e^{-\lambda}$
.0	1.0000	1.6	.2019	3.1	.0450	4.6	.0101
.1	.9048	1.7	.1827	3.2	.0408	4.7	.0091
.2	.8187	1.8	.1653	3.3	.0369	4.8	.0082
.3	.7408	1.9	.1496	3.4	.0334	4.9	.0074
.4	.6703	2.0	.1353	3.5	.0302	5.0	.0067
.5	.6065	2.1	.1225	3.6	.0273	5.1	.0061
.6	.5488	2.2	.1108	3.7	.0247	5.2	.0055
.7	.4966	2.3	.1003	3.8	.0224	5.3	.0050
.8	.4493	2.4	.0907	3.9	.0202	5.4	.0045
.9	.4066	2.5	.0821	4.0	.0183	5.5	.0041
1.0	.3679	2.6	.0743	4.1	.0166	5.6	.0037
1.1	.3329	2.7	.0672	4.2	.0150	5.7	.0033
1.2	.3012	2.8	.0608	4.3	.0136	5.8	.0030
1.3	.2725	2.9	.0550	4.4	.0123	5.9	.0027
1.4	.2466	3.0	.0498	4.5	.0111	6.0	.0025
1.5	.2231						

APPENDIX III TABLE OF RANDOM NUMBERS

52	06	50	88	53	30	10	47	99	37	66	91	35	32	00	84	57	07
37	63	28	02	74	35	24	03	29	60	74	85	90	73	59	55	17	60
82	57	68	28	05	94	03	11	27	79	90	87	92	41	09	25	36	77
69	02	36	49	71	99	32	10	75	21	95	90	94	38	97	71	72	49
98	94	90	36	06	78	23	67	89	85	29	21	25	73	69	34	85	76
96	52	62	87	49	56	59	23	78	71	72	90	57	01	98	57	31	95
33	69	27	21	11	60	95	89	68	48	17	89	34	09	93	50	44	51
50	33	50	95	13	44	34	62	64	39	55	29	30	64	49	44	30	16
88	32	18	50	62	57	34	56	62	31	15	40	90	34	51	95	26	14
90	30	36	24	69	82	51	74	30	35	36	85	01	55	92	64	09	85
50	48	61	18	85	23	08	54	17	12	80	69	24	84	92	16	49	59
27	88	21	62	69	64	48	31	12	73	02	68	00	16	16	46	13	85
45	14	46	32	13	49	66	62	74	41	86	98	92	98	84	54	33	40
81	02	01	78	82	74	97	37	45	31	94	99	42	49	27	64	89	42
66	83	14	74	27	76	03	33	11	97	59	81	72	00	64	61	13	52
74	05	81	82	93	09	96	33	52	78	13	06	28	30	94	23	37	39
30	34	87	01	74	11	46	82	59	94	25	34	32	23	17	01	58	73
59	55	72	33	62	13	74	68	22	44	42	09	32	46	71	79	45	89
67	09	80	98	99	25	77	50	03	32	36	63	65	75	94	19	95	88
60	77	46	63	71	69	44	22	03	85	14	48	69	13	30	50	33	24
60	08	19	29	36	72	30	27	50	64	85	72	75	29	87	05	75	01
80	45	86	99	02	34	87	08	86	84	49	76	24	08	01	86	29	11
53	84	49	63	26	65	72	84	85	63	26	02	75	26	92	62	40	67
69	84	12	94	51	36	17	02	15	29	16	52	56	43	26	22	08	62
37	77	13	10	02	18	31	19	32	85	31	94	81	43	31	58	33	51

Source: Excerpted from *A Million Random Digits with 100,000 Normal Deviates*, The Free Press (1955): 7, with permission of the RAND Corporation.

APPENDIX IV USING EXCEL OM AND POM FOR WINDOWS

Two approaches to computer-aided decision making are provided with this text: **Excel OM** and **POM** (Production and Operations Management) **for Windows**. These are the two most user-friendly software packages available to help you learn and understand operations management. Both programs can be used either to solve homework problems identified with a computer logo or to check answers you have developed by hand. Both software packages use the standard Windows interface and run on any IBM-compatible PC operating Windows XP or better.

EXCEL OM

Excel OM has also been designed to help you to better learn and understand both OM and Excel. Even though the software contains 24 modules and more than 50 submodules, the screens for every module are consistent and easy to use. Modules can be accessed through either of two menus that are added to Excel. The Heizer menu lists the modules in *chapter* order as illustrated for Excel 2007 in Program IV.1a. The Excel OM menu lists the modules in alphabetical order, as illustrated for earlier versions of Excel in Program IV.1b. This software is provided at no cost to purchasers of this textbook at our Web sites, www.pearsonhighered.com/heizer and www.myomlab.com. Excel 2000 or better must be on your PC.

To install Excel OM, after the web page opens, click on the Software option on the left hand side, click on Excel OM (version 3) and follow the instructions. Default values have been assigned in the setup program, but you may change them if you like. The default folder into which the program will be installed is named C:\ProgramFiles\ExcelOM3, and the default name

▼ PROGRAM IV.1A Excel OM Modules Menu in Add-Ins Tab in Excel 2007

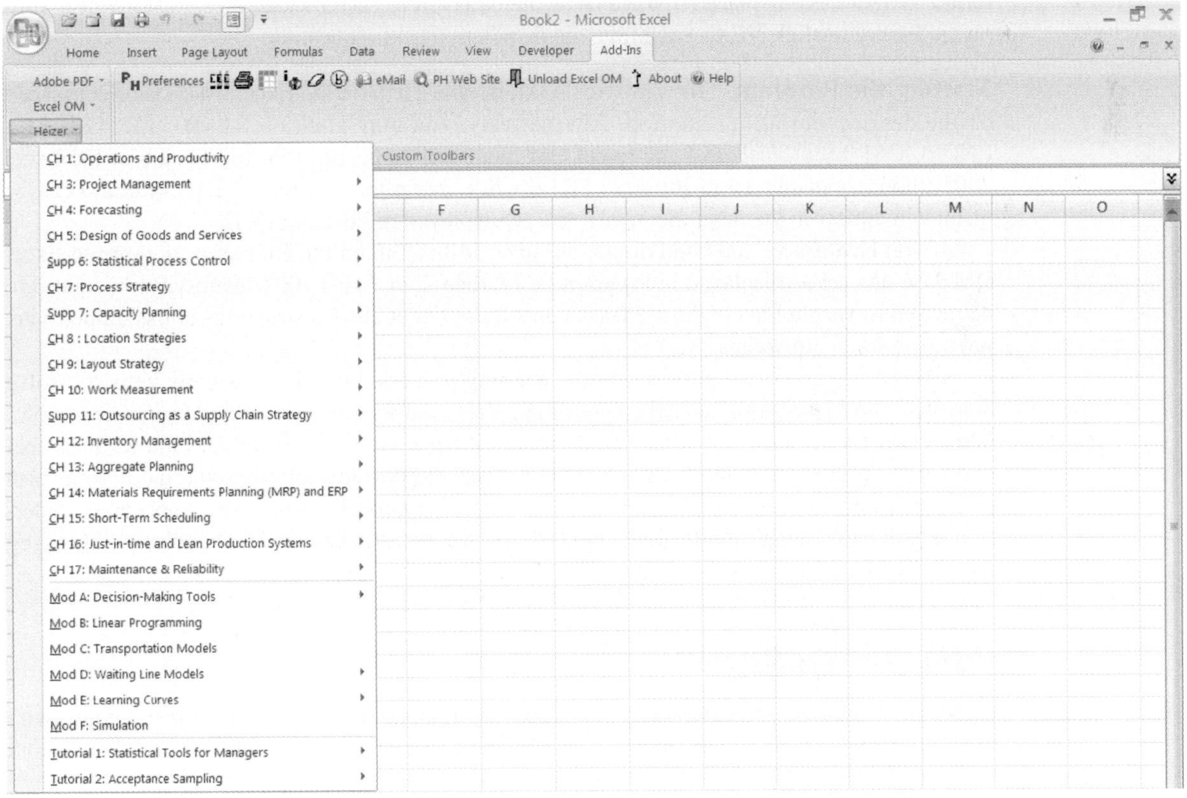

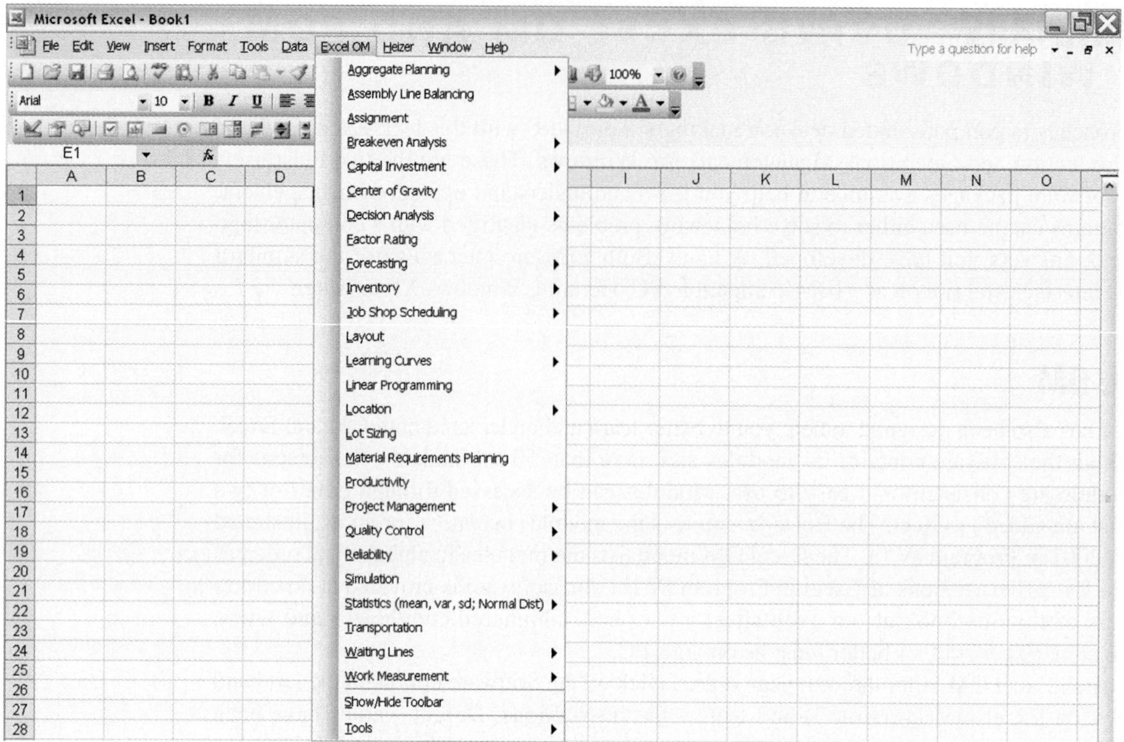

▲ **PROGRAM IV.1B Excel OM Modules Menu in Main Excel Menu for Versions of Excel Prior to Excel 2007**

for the program group placed in the START menu is Excel OM 3. Generally speaking, it is simply necessary to click NEXT each time the installation asks a question.

Starting the Program To start Excel OM, double-click on the Excel OM 3 shortcut placed on the desktop during installation. Alternatively, you may click on START, PROGRAMS, EXCEL OM 3. In Excel 2007 the Excel OM menu will appear in the Add-Ins tab of the Excel 2007 ribbon as displayed in Program IV.1a, while in earlier versions of Excel the Excel OM menu will appear in the main menu of Excel as displayed in Program IV.1b.

If you have Excel 2007 and do not see an Add-Ins Tab on the Ribbon or do not see Excel OM 3 on this tab as displayed in Program IV.1a, then your Excel 2007 security settings need to be revised to enable Excel OM 3. Please consult the Excel 2007 instructions at the support site, **www.prenhall.com/weiss**.

Excel OM serves two purposes in the learning process. First, it can simply help you solve homework problems. You enter the appropriate data, and the program provides numerical solutions. POM for Windows operates on the same principle. However, Excel OM allows for a second approach; that is, noting the Excel *formulas* used to develop solutions and modifying them to deal with a wider variety of problems. This "open" approach enables you to observe, understand, and even change the formulas underlying the Excel calculations, hopefully conveying Excel's power as an OM analysis tool.

POM FOR WINDOWS

POM for Windows is decision support software that is also offered free to students who purchased this text and is available at our Web sites www.pearsonhighered.com/heizer and

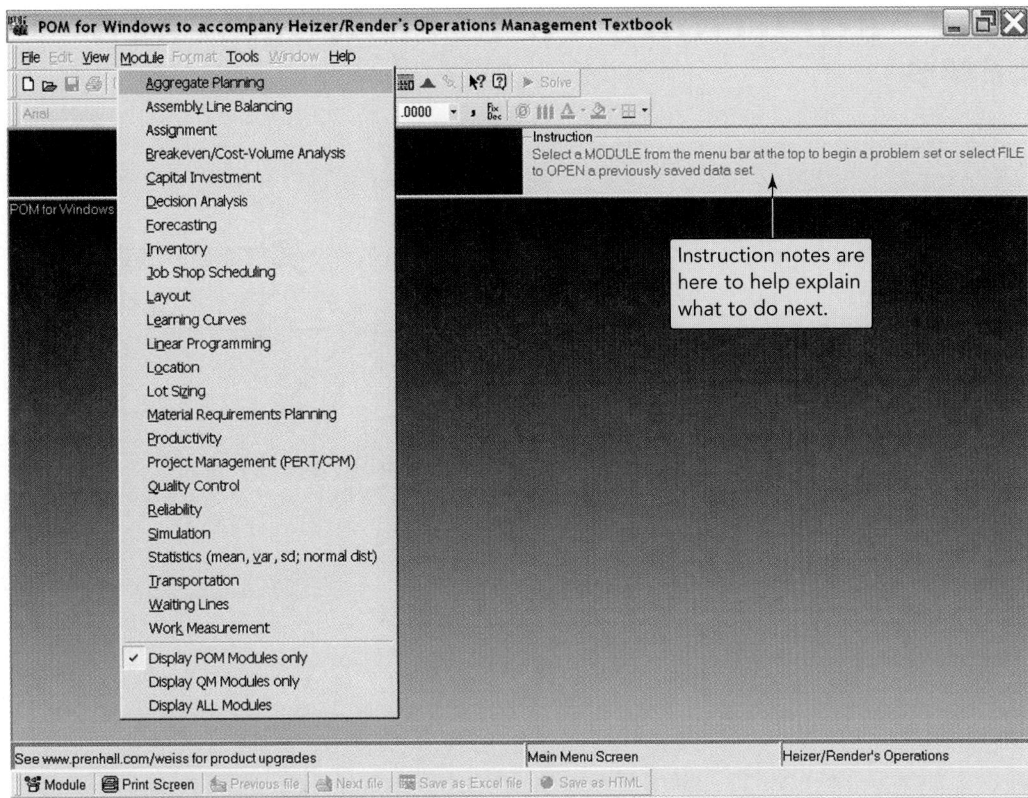

▲ **PROGRAM IV.2** **POM for Windows Module List**

www.myomlab.com. Program IV.2 shows a list of 24 OM modules on the Web site that will be installed on your hard drive. Once you follow the standard setup instructions, a POM for Windows program icon will be added to your start menu and desktop. The program may be accessed by double-clicking on the icon. Updates to POM for Windows are available on the Internet through the Pearson download library, found at **www.prenhall.com/weiss**.

APPENDIX V SOLUTIONS TO EVEN-NUMBERED PROBLEMS

Chapter 1

1.2 **(a)** 2 valves/hr.
(b) 2.25 valves/hr.
(c) 12.5%

1.4 Varies by site and source.

1.6 Productivity of labor: 9.3%
Productivity of resin: 11.1%
Productivity of capital: –10.0%
Productivity of energy: 6.1%

1.8 **(a)** .0096 rugs/labor-dollar
(b) .00787 rugs/dollar

1.10 Productivity of capital dropped; labor and energy productivity increased.

1.12 **(a)** Before: 25 boxes/hr.
After: 27.08 boxes/hr.
(b) Increase: 8.3%
(c) 29.167 boxes/hr.

1.14 **(a)** .293 loaves/dollar
(b) .359 loaves/dollar
(c) Labor change: 0%; Investment change: 22.5%

1.16 **(a)** 220 hours per laborer; 66,000 labor hours
(b) 200 hours per laborer

Chapter 2

2.2 Cost leadership: Sodexho
Response: a catering firm
Differentiation: a fine-dining restaurant

2.4 The first few:
Arrow; Bidermann International, France
Braun; Procter & Gamble, U.S.
Lotus Autos; Proton, Malaysia
Firestone; Bridgestone, Japan
Godiva; Campbell Soup, U.S.

2.6 Some general thoughts to get you going:
(a) Energy costs change the cost structure of airlines.
(b) Environmental constraints force changes in process technology (paint manufacturing and application) and product design (autos).

2.8 Look at current ranking at **www.weforum.org**.

Chapter 3

3.2 Here are some detailed activities for the first two activities for Mefford's WBS:
1.11 Set initial goals for fundraising.
1.12 Set strategy, including identifying sources and solicitation.
1.13 Raise the funds.
1.21 Identify voters' concerns.
1.22 Analyze competitor's voting record.
1.23 Establish position on issues.

3.4

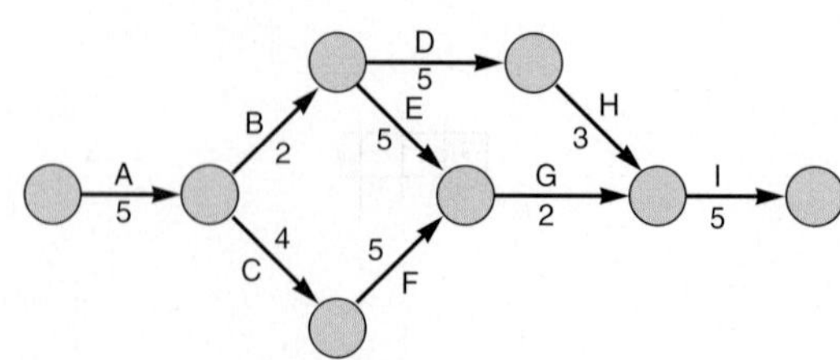

A–C–F–G–I is critical path; 21 days.
This is an AOA network.

3.6 **(a)**

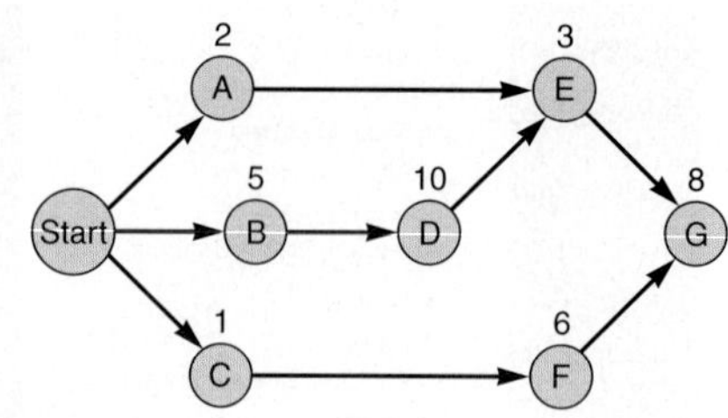

(b) B–D–E–G
(c) 26 days
(d)

Activity	Slack
A	13
B	0
C	11
D	0
E	0
F	11
G	0

3.8

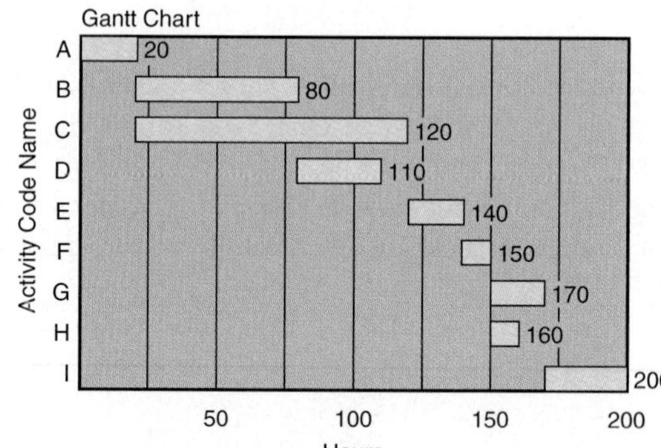

3.10

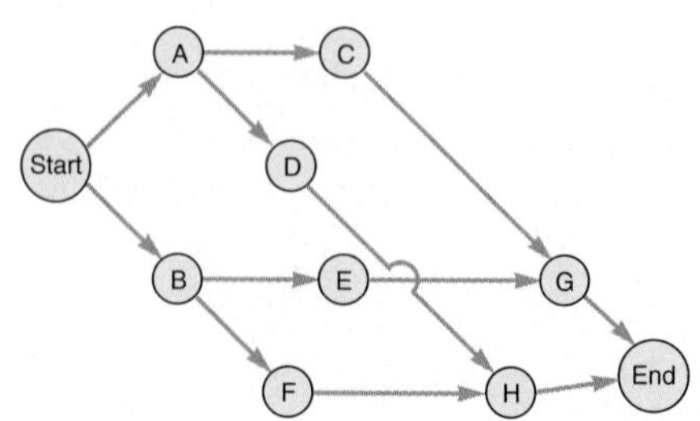

3.12 **(a)**

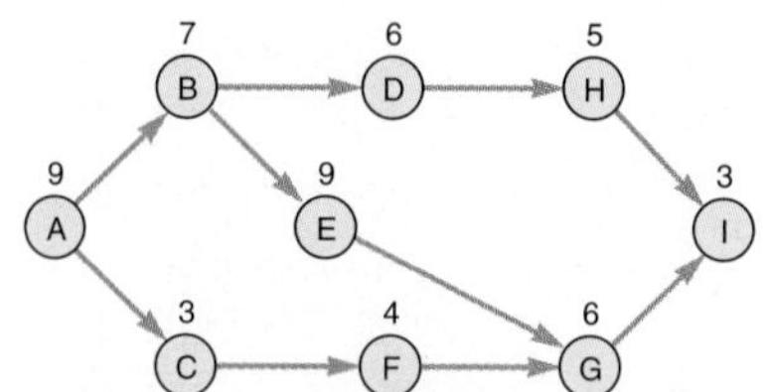

(b) A–B–E–G–I, is critical path.
(c) 34

3.14 **(a)** A, 5.83, 0.69 G, 2.17, 0.25
B, 3.67, 0.11 H, 6.00, 1.00
C, 2.00, 0.11 I, 11.00, 0.11
D, 7.00, 0.11 J, 16.33, 1.00
E, 4.00, 0.44 K, 7.33, 1.78
F, 10.00, 1.78
(b) C.P. is C–D–E–F–H–K. Time = 36.33 days.
(c) Slacks are 7.17, 5.33, 0, 0, 0, 0, 2.83, 0, 2.83, 18, and 0, respectively, for A through K.
(d) $P = .946$

3.16 Crash C to 3 weeks at $200 total for one week. Now both paths are critical. Not worth it to crash further.

3.18 Critical path currently is C–E for 12 days. $1,100 to crash by 4 days. Watch for parallel critical paths as you crash.

3.20 **(a)** 16 (A–D–G)
(b) $12,300
(c) D; 1 wk. for $75
(d) 7 wk.; $1,600

3.22 **(a)** A–C–E–H–I–K–M–N; 50 days
(b) 82.1%
(c) 58 days

3.24 **(a)** .0228
(b) .3085
(c) .8413
(d) .97725
(e) 24 mo.

3.26 **(a)**

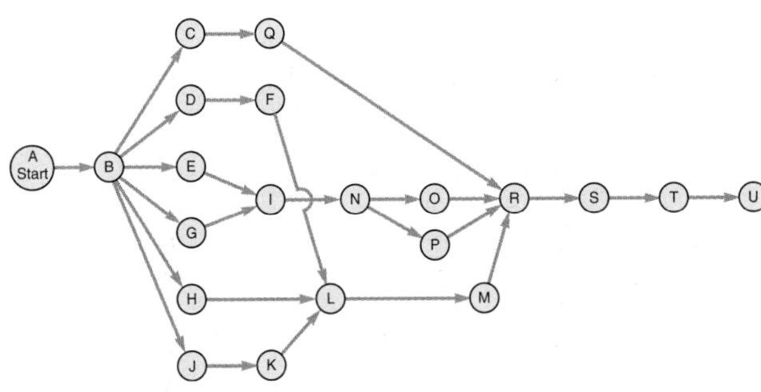

(b) Critical path is A–B–J–K–L–M–R–S–T–U for 18 days.
(c) **i.** No, transmissions and drivetrains are not on the critical path.
ii. No, halving engine-building time will reduce the critical path by only 1 day.
iii. No, it is not on the critical path.
(d) Reallocating workers not involved with critical-path activities to activities along the critical path will reduce the critical path length.

Chapter 4

4.2 **(a)** None obvious.
(b) 7, 7.67, 9, 10, 11, 11, 11.33, 11, 9
(c) 6.4, 7.8, 11, 9.6, 10.9, 12.2, 10.5, 10.6, 8.4
(d) The 3-yr. moving average.

4.4 **(a)** 41.6
(b) 42.3
(c) Banking industry's seasonality.

4.6 **(b)** Naive = 23; 3-mo. moving = 21.33; 6-mo. weighted = 20.6; trend = 20.67
(c) Trend projection.

4.8 **(a)** 91.3
(b) 89
(c) MAD = 2.7
(d) MSE = 13.35
(e) MAPE = 2.99%

4.10 **(a)** 4.67, 5.00, 6.33, 7.67, 8.33, 8.00, 9.33, 11.67, 13.7
(b) 4.50, 5.00, 7.25, 7.75, 8.00, 8.25, 10.00, 12.25, 14.0
(c) Forecasts are about the same.

4.12 72

4.14 Method 1: MAD = .125; MSE = .021
Method 2: MAD = .1275; MSE = .018

4.16 $y = 421 + 33.6x$. When $x = 6$, $y = 622.8$.

4.18 49

4.20 $\alpha = .1$, $\beta = .8$, August forecast = $71,303; MSE = 12.7 for $\beta = .8$ vs. MSE = 18.87 for $\beta = .2$ in Problem 4.19.

4.22 Confirm that you match the numbers in Table 4.1.

4.24 **(a)** Observations do not form a straight line but do cluster about one.
(b) $y = .676 + 1.03x$
(c) 10 drums
(d) $r^2 = .68$; $r = .825$

4.26 270, 390, 189, 351 for fall, winter, spring, and summer, respectively.

4.28 Index is 0.709, winter; 1.037, spring; 1.553, summer; 0.700, fall.

4.30 **(a)** 337
(b) 380
(c) 423

4.32 **(a)** $y = 50 + 18x$
(b) $410

4.34 **(a)** 28
(b) 43
(c) 58

4.36 **(a)** $452.50
(b) Request is higher than predicted, so seek additional documentation.
(c) Include other variables (such as a destination cost index) to try to increase r and r^2.

4.38 **(a)** $y = -.158 + .1308x$
(b) 2.719
(c) $r = .966$; $r^2 = .934$

4.40 131.2 → 72.7 patients; 90.6 → 50.6 patients

4.42 **(a)** They need more data and must be able to address seasonal *and* trend factors.
(b) Try to create your own naive model because seasonality is strong.
(c) Compute and graph your forecast.

4.44 Trend adjustment does not appear to give any significant improvement.

4.46 **(a)** $y = 1.03 + .0034x$, $r^2 = .479$
(b) For $x = 350$; $y = 2.22$
(c) For $x = 800$; $y = 3.75$
(Some rounding may occur, depending on software.)

4.48 **(a)** Sales $(y) = -9.349 + .1121$ (contracts)
(b) $r = .8963$; $S_{xy} = 1.3408$

Chapter 5

5.2 House of quality for a lunch:

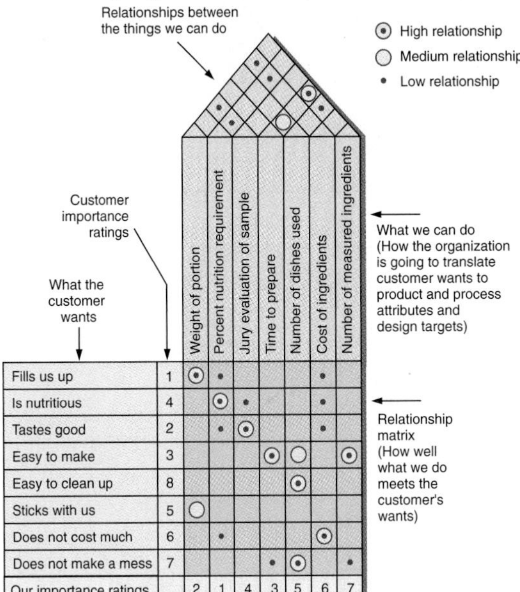

5.4 Individual answer. Build a house of quality similar to the one shown in Problem 5.2, entering the *wants* on the left and entering the *hows* at the top.

5.6 An assembly chart for the eyeglasses is shown below:

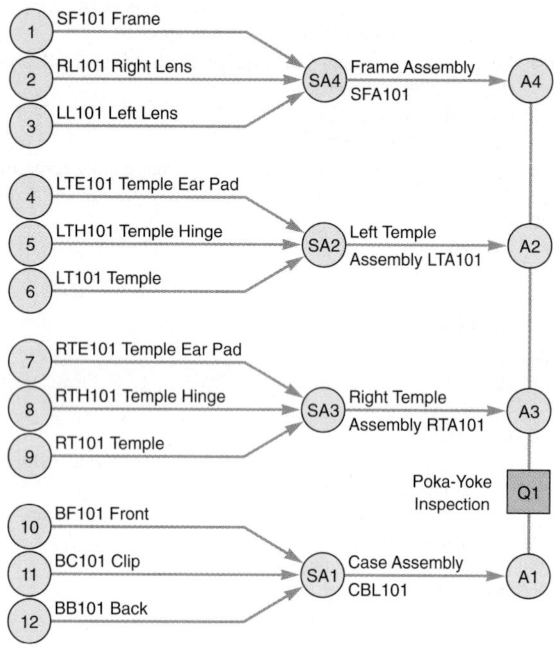

5.8 Assembly chart for a table lamp:

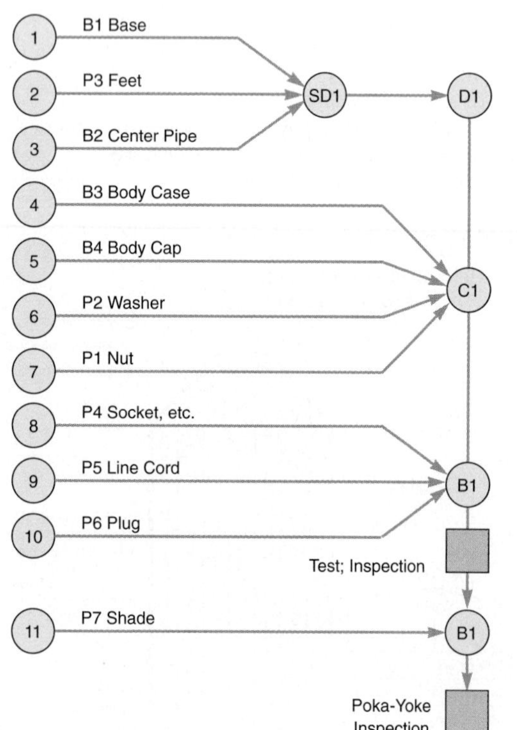

5.10 *Possible strategies:*

Kindle 2 (growth phase):

Increase capacity and improve balance of production system.
Attempt to make production facilities more efficient.

Netbook (introductory phase):

Increase R&D to better define required product characteristics.
Modify and improve production process.
Develop supplier and distribution systems.

Hand calculator (decline phase):

Concentrate on production and distribution cost reduction.

5.12 EMV of Proceed = $49,500,000
EMV of Do Value Analysis = $55,025,000
Therefore, do value analysis.

5.14

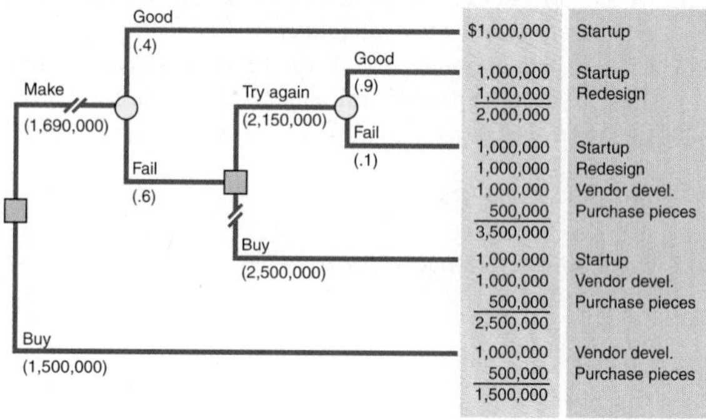

(a) The best decision would be to buy the semiconductors. This decision has an expected payoff of $1,500,000.

(b) Expected monetary value, minimum cost.

(c) The worst that can happen is that Ritz ends up buying the semiconductors and spending $3,500,000.
The best that can happen is that they make the semiconductors and spend only $1,000,000.

5.16 EMV (Design A) = $875,000
EMV (Design B) = $700,000

5.18 Use K1 with EMV = $27,500

Chapter 6

6.2 Individual answer, in the style of Figure 6.6(b).

6.4 Individual answer, in the style of Figure 6.6(f).

6.6 Partial flowchart for planning a party:

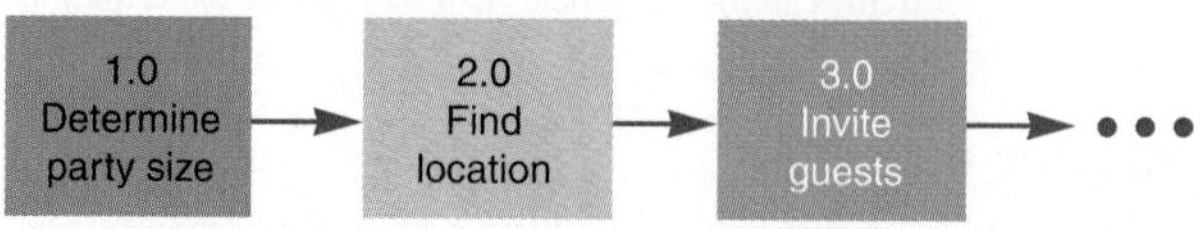

6.8 See figure on next page.

6.10 Individual answer, in the style of Figure 6.7 in the chapter.

6.12 Pareto chart, in the style of Example 1 with parking/drives most frequent, pool second, etc.

6.14 See figure on next page.
Materials: 4, 12, 14; Methods: 3, 7, 15, 16; Manpower: 1, 5, 6, 11; Machines: 2, 8, 9, 10, 13.

6.16 **(a)** A scatter diagram in the style of Figure 6.6(b) that shows a strong positive relationship between shipments and defects

(b) A scatter diagram in the style of Figure 6.6(b) that shows a mild relationship between shipments and turnover

(c) A Pareto chart in the style of Figure 6.6(d) that shows frequency of each type of defect

(d) A fishbone chart in the style of Figure 6.6(c) with the 4 *M*s showing possible causes of increasing defects in shipments

▼ *Figure for Problem 6.8.*

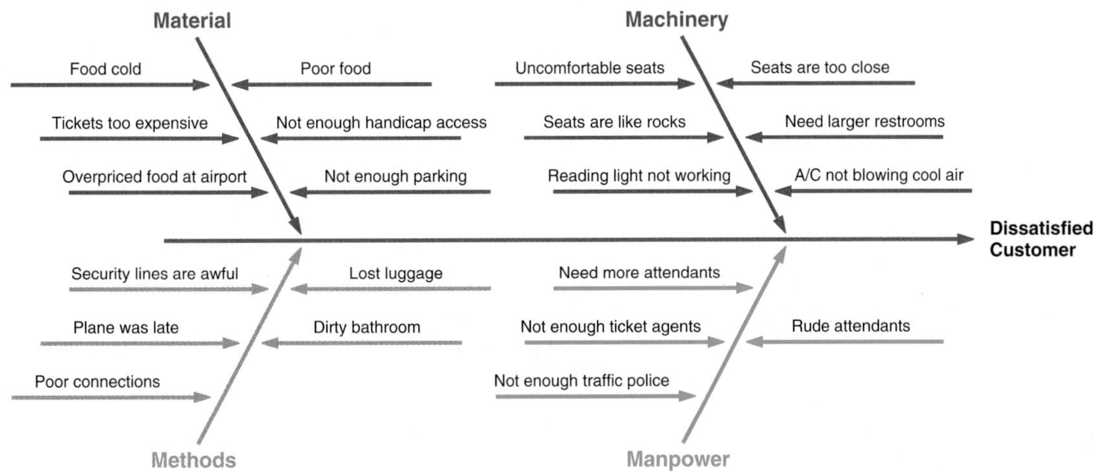

▼ *Figure for Problem 6.14*

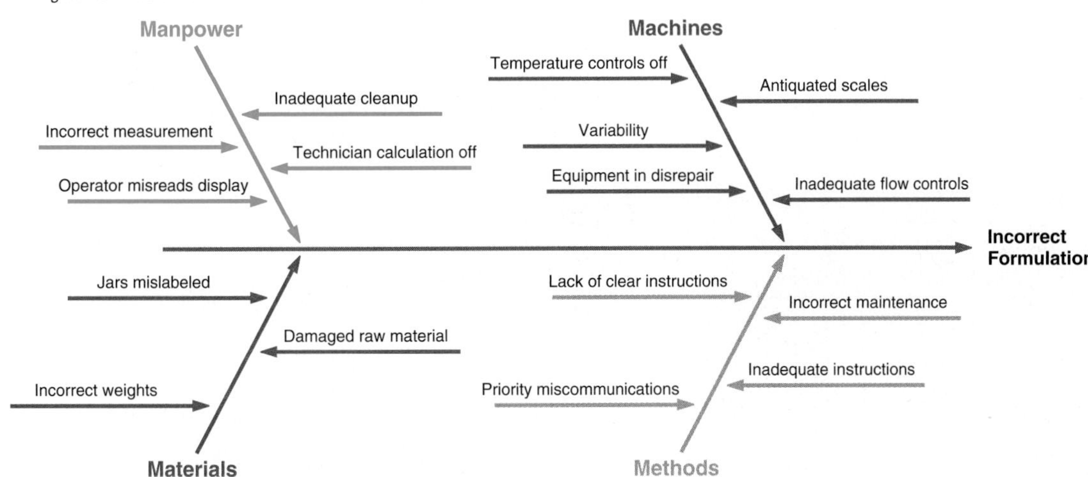

Chapter 6 Supplement

S6.2 **(a)** $UCL_{\bar{x}} = 52.31$
$LCL_{\bar{x}} = 47.69$
(b) $UCL_{\bar{x}} = 51.54$
$LCL_{\bar{x}} = 48.46$

S6.4 **(a)** $UCL_{\bar{x}} = 440$ calories
$LCL_{\bar{x}} = 400$ calories
(b) $UCL_{\bar{x}} = 435$ calories
$LCL_{\bar{x}} = 405$ calories

S6.6 $UCL_{\bar{x}} = 3.728$
$LCL_{\bar{x}} = 2.236$
$UCL_R = 2.336$
$LCL_R = 0.0$
The process is in control.

S6.8 **(a)** $UCL_{\bar{x}} = 16.08$
$LCL_{\bar{x}} = 15.92$
(b) $UCL_{\bar{x}} = 16.12$
$LCL_{\bar{x}} = 15.88$

S6.10 **(a)** 1.36, 0.61
(b) Using $\sigma_{\bar{x}}$, $UCL_{\bar{x}} = 11.83$, and $LCL_{\bar{x}} = 8.17$.
(c) Using A_2, $UCL_{\bar{x}} = 11.90$, and $LCL_{\bar{x}} = 8.10$.
(c) $UCL_R = 6.98$; $LCL_R = 0$
(d) Yes

S6.12 $UCL_R = 6.058$; $LCL_R = 0.442$
Averages are increasing.

S6.14

UCL	LCL
.062	0
.099	0
.132	0
.161	0
.190	.01

S6.16 $UCL_p = .0313$; $LCL_p = 0$

S6.18 **(a)** $UCL_p = 0.077$; $LCL_p = 0.003$

S6.20 **(a)** $UCL_p = .0581$
$LCL_p = 0$
(b) in control
(c) $UCL_p = .1154$
$LCL_p = 0$

S6.22 **(a)** *c*-chart
(b) $UCL_c = 13.35$
$LCL_c = 0$
(c) in control
(d) not in control

S6.24 **(a)** $UCL_c = 26.063$
$LCL_c = 3.137$
(b) No point out of control.
S6.26 $C_p = 1.0$. The process is barely capable.
S6.28 $C_{pk} = 1.125$. Process *is* centered and will produce within tolerance.
S6.30 $C_{pk} = .1667$
S6.32 AOQ = 2.2%
S6.34 **(a)** $UCL_{\bar{x}} = 61.131, LCL_{\bar{x}} = 38.421, UCL_R = 41.62, LCL_R = 0$
(b) Yes, the process is in control for both $\bar{x}$- and R-charts.
(c) They support West's claim. But variance from the mean needs to be reduced and controlled.

Chapter 7

7.2

Present Method ☒ — PROCESS CHART — Proposed Method ☐
SUBJECT CHARTED Shoe Shine — DATE 1/15/10
CHART BY J.C.
DEPARTMENT — SHEET NO. 1 OF 1

DIST. IN FEET	TIME IN MINS.	CHART SYMBOLS	PROCESS DESCRIPTION
	.67	○⇨□D▽	Clean/Brush Shoes
1.	.05	○⇨□D▽	Obtain Polish
	.5	○⇨□D▽	Open and Apply Polish
	.75	○⇨□D▽	Buff
	.05	○⇨□D▽	Inspect
	.25	○⇨□D▽	Collect Payment
1.	2.27	4 1 1	Totals

7.4

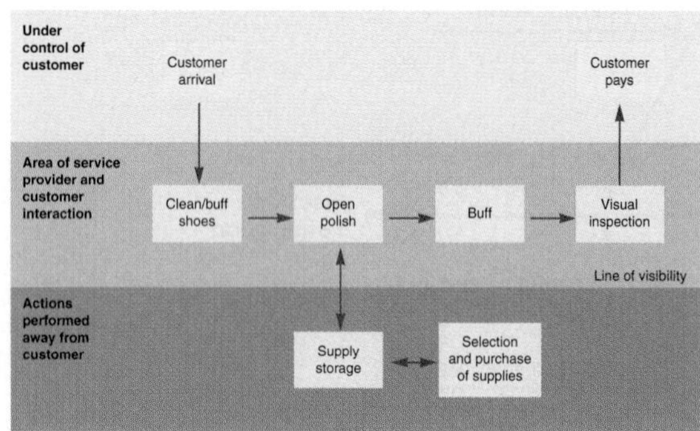

7.6 GPE is best below 100,000.
FMS is best between 100,000 and 300,000.
DM is best over 300,000.
7.8 Optimal process will change at 100,000 and 300,000.
7.10 **(a)**

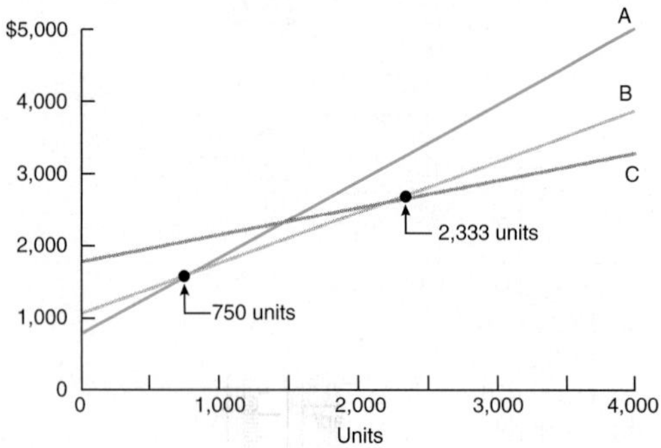

(b) Plan c
(c) Plan b
7.12 Rent HP software since projected volume of 80 is above the crossover point of 75.
7.14 **(a)** Intermittent
(b) $200,000

Chapter 7 Supplement

S7.2 69.2%
S7.4 88.9%
S7.6 Design = 88,920
Fabrication = 160,680
Finishing = 65,520
S7.8 5.17 (or 6) bays
S7.10 15 min./unit
S7.12 **(a)** Process cycle time = 40 min.
(b) System process time = 12 min.
(c) Weekly capacity = 240 units
S7.14 **(a)** Work station C at 20 min./unit
(b) 3 units/hr.
S7.16 **(a)** 2,000 units
(b) $1,500
S7.18 **(a)** $150,000
(b) $160,000
S7.20 **(a)** $BEP_A = 1{,}667$;
$BEP_B = 2{,}353$
(b, c) Oven A slightly more profitable
(d) 13,333 pizzas
S7.22 **(a)** $18,750
(b) 375,000
S7.24 Yes, purchase new equipment and raise price. Profit = $2,500
S7.26 $BEP_\$ = \$7{,}584.83$ per mo.
Daily meals = 9
S7.28 Option B; $74,000
S7.30 $4,590
S7.32 NPV = $1,764
S7.34 **(a)** Purchase two large ovens.
(b) Equal quality, equal capacity.
(c) Payments are made at end of each time period. And future interest rates are known.

Chapter 8

8.2 China, $1.44
8.4 India is $.05 less than elsewhere.
8.6 **(a)** Atlanta = 53; Charlotte = 60; select Charlotte.
(b) Charlotte now = 66.
8.8 **(a)** Hyde Park, with 54.5 points.
(b) Present location = 51 points.
8.10 **(a)** Location C, with a total *weighted* score of 1,530.
(b) Location B = 1,360
(c) B can never be in first place.
8.12 **(a)** Great Britain, at 36;
(b) Great Britain is now 31; Holland is 30.
8.14 **(a)** Italy is highest.
(b) Spain always lowest.
8.16 **(a)** Site 1 up to 125, site 2 from 125 to 233, site 3 above 233
(b) Site 2
8.18 **(a)** Above 10,000 cars, site C is lowest cost
(b) Site A optimal from 0–10,000 cars.
(c) Site B is never optimal.
8.20 **(a)** (5.15, 7.31)
(b) (5.13, 7.67)
8.22 **(a)** (6.23, 6.08); **(b)** safety, etc.
8.24 **(a)** Site C is best, with a score of 374
(b) For all positive values of w_7 such that $w_7 \leq 14$

Chapter 9

9.2 **(a)** $23,400
(b) $20,600
(c) $22,000
(d) Plan B
9.4 Benders to area 1; Materials to 2; Welders to 3; Drills to 4; Grinder to 5; and Lathes to 6; Trips × Distance = 13,000 ft.
9.6 Layout #1, distance = 600 with areas fixed
Layout #2, distance = 602 with areas fixed

9.8 Layout #4, distance = 609
Layout #5, distance = 478

9.10 **(a)** 1.68 minutes
(b) 4.76 ≈ 5
(c) cleaning

9.12 **(b)** Cycle time = 9.6 min.;
(e) Idle time/cycle = 15 min.
(f) 15 hours/day idle.
(g) 8 workstations with 76.6% efficiency is possible.

9.14 **(a)**

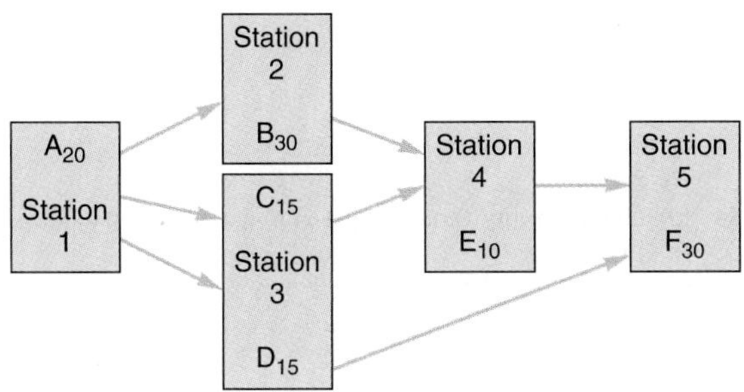

(b) cycle time = 30 sec./unit
(c) 4 stations = *theoretical* minimum, but 5 are needed
(d) Station 1–Task A; 2–B; 3–C, D; 4–E; 5–F
(e) Total idle = 30 sec.
(f) E = 80% with 5 stations; E = 66.6% with 6 stations

9.16 **(a, b)** Cycle time = 6.67 min./unit. Multiple solutions with 5 stations. Here is a sample: A, F, G to station 1; B, C to station 2; D, E to station 3; H to station 4; and I, J to station 5. **(c)** Actual efficiency with 5 stations = 83% **(d)** Idle time = 5 min./cycle.

9.18 **(a)** Minimum no. of workstations = 2.6 (or 3).
(b) Efficiency = 86.7%.
(c) Cycle time = 6.67 min./unit with 400 min./day; minimum no. of workstations = 1.95 (or 2).

9.20 Minimum (theoretical) = 4 stations. Efficiency = 93.3% with 5 stations and 6 min. cycle time. Several assignments with 5 are possible.

9.22 **(a)** Theoretical min. no. workstations = 5
(b) There are several possibilities. For example; Station 1–Task A; 2–C; 3–B and F; 4–D and G; 5–E, H, and I; 6–J. Or 1–A; 2–C; 3–B and F; 4–D and G; 5–E, H and I; 6–J.
(c) $n = 6$
(d) Efficiency = .7611

Chapter 10

10.2

Time	Operator	Time	Machine	Time
0–0.5	Prepare Mill	0–2	Idle	
0.5–2	Load Mill			1, 2
2–4.5	Idle	2–4.5	Mill Operating (Cutting Material)	3, 4
4.5–5.2	Unload Mill	4.5–5.2	Idle	5
6		6		6

10.4 The first 10 steps of 10.4(a) are shown below. The remaining 10 steps are similar.

OPERATIONS CHART	SUMMARY						
PROCESS: CHANGE ERASER	SYMBOL	PRESENT LH	PRESENT RH	PROPOSED LH	PROPOSED RH	DIFF. LH	DIFF. RH
ANALYST:	○ OPERATIONS	1	8				
DATE:	⇨ TRANSPORTS	3	8				
SHEET: 1 of 2	□ INSPECTIONS	1					
METHOD: (PRESENT) PROPOSED	D DELAYS	15	4				
REMARKS:	▽ STORAGE						
	TOTALS	20	20				

LEFT HAND	DIST.	SYMBOL	SYMBOL	DIST.	RIGHT HAND
1 Reach for pencil		⇨	D		Idle
2 Grasp pencil		○	D		Idle
3 Move to work area		⇨	⇨		Move to pencil top
4 Hold pencil		D	○		Grasp pencil top
5 Hold pencil		D	○		Remove pencil top
6 Hold pencil		D	⇨		Set top aside
7 Hold pencil		D	⇨		Reach for old eraser
8 Hold pencil		D	○		Grasp old eraser
9 Hold pencil		D	○		Remove old eraser
10 Hold pencil		D	⇨		Set aside old eraser

10.6 Individual solution.

10.8

Process Chart	Summary	
Charted by H. Molano	○ Operation	2
Date ______ Sheet 1 of 1	⇨ Transport	3
Problem Pit crew jack man	□ Inspect	
	D Delay	2
	▽ Store	
	Vert. Dist.	
	Hor. Dist.	
	Time (seconds)	12.5

Distance (feet)	Time (seconds)	Chart Symbols	Process Description
15	2.0	⇨	Move to right side of car
	2.0	○	Raise car
	1.0	D	Wait for tire exchange to finish
10	1.8	⇨	Move to left side of car
	2.0	○	Raise car
	1.2	D	Wait for tire exchange to finish
5	2.5	⇨	Move back over wall from left side

10.10 The first portion of the activity chart is shown below.

ACTIVITY CHART

	OPERATOR #1 TIME	OPERATOR #1 %	OPERATOR #2 TIME	OPERATOR #2 %
WORK	11.75	84	11.75	84
IDLE	2.25	16	2.25	16

OPERATIONS: Wash and Dry Dishes
EQUIPMENT: Sink, Drip Rack, Towels, Soap
OPERATOR:
STUDY NO.: 1 ANALYST: HSM

SUBJECT: PRESENT (PROPOSED) DEPT. HOUSECLEANING — DATE — SHEET 1 OF 1 — CHART BY Hank

TIME	Operator #1	TIME	Operator #2	TIME
	Fill sink w/dishes		Idle	
	Fill sink w/soap/water		Idle	
	Wash dishes (2 min.)		Idle	
			Rinse (1 min.)	
	Fill sink w/dishes (1 min.)		Dry dishes (3 min.)	

10.12 The first portion of the process chart is shown below.

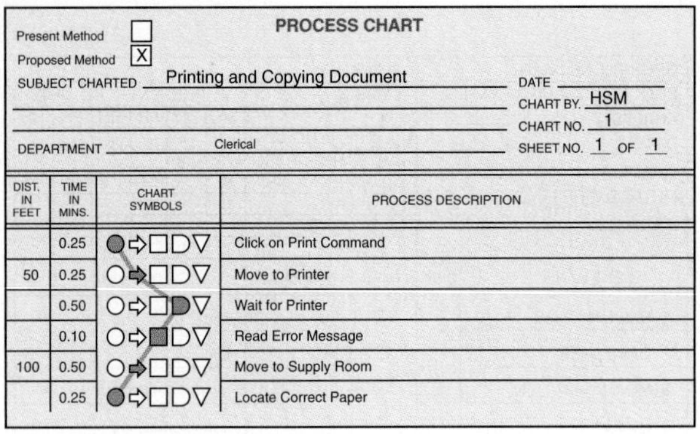

PROCESS CHART	
Present Method ☐	
Proposed Method ☒	
SUBJECT CHARTED Printing and Copying Document	DATE
	CHART BY HSM
	CHART NO. 1
DEPARTMENT Clerical	SHEET NO. 1 OF 1

DIST. IN FEET	TIME IN MINS.	CHART SYMBOLS	PROCESS DESCRIPTION
	0.25	●⇨□D▽	Click on Print Command
50	0.25	○➡□D▽	Move to Printer
	0.50	○⇨□◗▽	Wait for Printer
	0.10	○⇨■D▽	Read Error Message
100	0.50	○➡□D▽	Move to Supply Room
	0.25	●⇨□D▽	Locate Correct Paper

10.14 NT = 7.65 sec.; slower than normal
10.16 **(a)** 6.525 sec.
(b) 6.2 sec.
(c) 6.739 sec.
10.18 **(a)** 12.6 min.
(b) 15 min.
10.20 **(a)** 12.0 sec.
(b) 14.12 sec.
10.22 10.12 min.
10.24 **(a)** 3.24 min.
(b) 4.208 min.
10.26 n = 14.13, or 15 observations
10.28 **(a)** 45.36, 13.75, 3.6, 15.09
(b) 91.53 min.
(c) 96 samples
10.30 **(a)** 47.6 min.
(b) 75 samples
10.32 n = 348
10.34 73.8%
10.36 6.55 sec.
10.38 **(a)** 240 min.
(b) 150 hr.
(c) Clean 8 rooms; refresh 16 rooms; 38 housekeepers
(d) 50 employees

Chapter 11

11.2 Donna Inc, 8.2; Kay Corp., 9.8
11.4 Individual responses. Issues might include: academics, location, financial support, size, facilities, etc.
11.6 **(a)** \$3.13
(b) \$7.69
11.8 **(a)** Option a is most economical.
(b) The customer requirements may demand a faster schedule.
11.10 **(a)** Go with faster subcontractor.
(b) Internal production or testing may require a faster schedule.
11.12 **(a)** Weeks of supply = 3.85
(b) % of assets in inventory = 11.63%
(c) Turnover = 13.5
(d) No, but note they are in different industries
11.14 **(a)** Last year = 10.4
(b) This year = 9.67
(c) Yes

Chapter 11 Supplement

S11.2 **(a)** Canada, 1.7
(b) No change
S11.4 Mexico, 3.3
S11.6 Moscow Bell, 7.1

Chapter 12

12.2 **(a)** A items are G2 and F3; B items are A2, C7, and D1; all others are C.
12.4 108 items
12.6 **(a)** 600 units
(b) 424.26 units
(c) 848.53 units
12.8 **(a)** 80 units
(b) 73 units
12.10 **(a)** 2,100 units
(b) 4,200 units
(c) 1,050 units
12.12 **(a)** 189.74 units
(b) 94.87
(c) 31.62
(d) 7.91
(e) \$1,897.30
(f) \$601,897
12.14 **(a)** Order quantity variations have limited impact on total cost.
(b) EOQ = 50
12.16 **(a)** 671 units
(b) 18.63
(c) 559 = max. inventory
(d) 16.7%
(e) \$1,117.90
12.18 **(a)** 1,217 units
(b) 1,095 = max. inventory
(c) 8.22 production runs
(e) \$657.30
12.20 **(a)** EOQ = 200, total cost = \$1,446,380
(b) EOQ = 200, total cost = \$1,445,880
12.22 **(a)** 16,971 units
(b) \$530.33
(c) \$530.33
(d) \$56,250
(e) \$57,310.66
12.24 **(a)** EOQ = 410
(b) Vendor Allen has slightly lower cost.
(c) Optimal order quantity = 1,000 @ total cost of \$128,920
12.26 **(a)** EOQ (1) = 336; EOQ (2) = 335
(b) Order 1,200 from Vendor 2.
(c) At 1,200 lb., total cost = \$161,275.
(d) Storage space and perishability.
12.28 **(a)** Z = 1.88
(b) Safety stock $= Z\sigma = 1.88(5) = 9.4$ drives
(c) ROP = 59.4 drives
12.30 100 kilos of safety stock
12.32 **(a)** 2,291 towels
(b) 291 towels
12.34 **(a)** ROP = 1,718 cigars
(b) 1,868 cigars
(c) A higher service level means a lower probability of stocking out.
12.36 103 pounds
12.38 **(a)** \$3
(b) \$.90
(c) 63,675 programs
(d) 23.1%
12.40 **(a)** Q = 400 lb.
(b) \$600
(c) \$600
(d) ROP = 369.99
(e) 69.99
(f) \$209.97
(g) Safety stock = 61.61

Chapter 13

13.2 **(a)** \$109,120 = total cost
(b) \$106,640 = total cost
(c) No, plan 2 is better at \$105,152.

13.4 Cost = $214,000 for plan B

13.6 **(a)** Plan D, $122,000;
(b) plan E is $129,000

13.8 Extra total cost = $2,960.

13.10 **(a)** Plan C, $92,000; **(b)** plan D, $81,800, assuming initial inventory = 0

13.12 **(a)** Cost is $314,000.
(b) Cost is $329,000 (but an alternative approach yields $259,500).
(c) Cost is $222,000.
(d) Plan C.
(e) Plan C, with lowest cost and steady employment.

13.14 $1,186,810

13.16 $100,750

13.18 $90,850

13.20 **(a)** Cost using O.T. and Forrester = $195,625.
(b) A case could be made for either position.

13.22 Current model = $9,200 in sales; proposed model yields $9,350, which is only slightly better.

Chapter 14

14.2 The time-phased plan for the gift bags is:

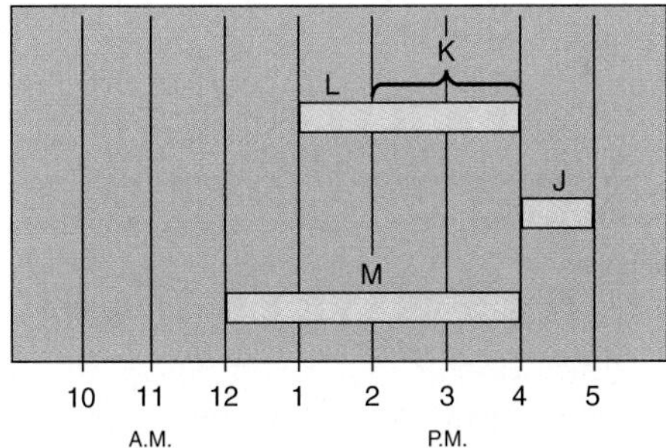

Someone should start on item M by noon.

14.4 Gross material requirements plan:

Item		Week 1	2	3	4	5	6	7	8	Lead Time (wk.)
S	Gross req.							100		
	Order release					100				2
T	Gross req.					100				
	Order release				100					1
U	Gross req.					200				
	Order release			200						2
V	Gross req.				100					
	Order release		100							2
W	Gross req.				200					
	Order release	200								3
X	Gross req.				100					
	Order release			100						1
Y	Gross req.			400						
	Order release	400								2
Z	Gross req.			600						
	Order release		600							1

14.6 Gross material requirements plan, modified to include the 20 units of U required for maintenance purposes:

Item		Week 1	2	3	4	5	6	7	8	Lead Time (wk.)
S	Gross req.							100		
	Order release					100				2
T	Gross req.					100				
	Order release				100					1
U	Gross req.					200	20			
	Order release			200	20					2
V	Gross req.				100					
	Order release		100							2
W	Gross req.				200					
	Order release	200								3
X	Gross req.				100					
	Order release			100						1
Y	Gross req.			400	40					
	Order release	400	40							2
Z	Gross req.			600	60					
	Order release		600	60						1

14.8 **(a)**

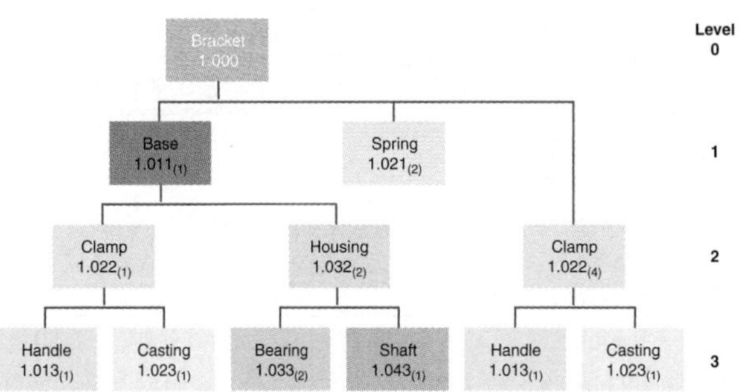

(b) For 50 brackets, the gross requirements are for 50 bases, 100 springs, 250 clamps, 250 handles, 250 castings, 100 housings, 200 bearings, and 100 shafts.

(c) For 50 brackets, net requirements are 25 bases, 100 springs, 125 clamps, 125 handles, 125 castings, 50 housings, 100 bearings, and 50 shafts.

14.10 **(a)** Gross material requirements plan for the first three items:

Item		Week 1	2	3	4	5	6	7	8	9	10	11	12
X1	Gross req.								50		20		100
	Order release							50		20		100	
B1	Gross req.							50		20		100	
	Order release					50		20		100			
B2	Gross req.							100		40		200	
	Order release					100		40		200			

(b) The net materials requirement plan for the first two items:

Level: 0 Item: X1	Parent: Lead Time:							Quantity: Lot Size: L4L				
Week No.	1	2	3	4	5	6	7	8	9	10	11	12
Gross Requirement								50		20		100
Scheduled Receipt												
On-hand Inventory								50		0		0
Net Requirement								0		20		100
Planned Order Receipt										20		100
Planned Order Release									20		100	

Level: 1 Item: B1	Parent: X1 Lead Time: 2							Quantity: 1X Lot Size: L4L				
Week No.	1	2	3	4	5	6	7	8	9	10	11	12
Gross Requirement									20		100	
Scheduled Receipt												
On-hand Inventory									20		0	
Net Requirement									0		100	
Planned Order Receipt											100	
Planned Order Release									100			

14.12 **(a)** Net material requirements schedule (only items A and H are shown):

	Week											
	1	2	3	4	5	6	7	8	9	10	11	12
A Gross Required								100		50		150
On Hand								0		0		0
Net Required								100		50		150
Order Receipt								100		50		150
Order Release							100		50		150	
H Gross Required									100		50	
On Hand									0		0	
Net Required									100		50	
Order Receipt									100		50	
Order Release								100		50		

(b) Net material requirements schedule (only items B and C are shown; schedule for items A and H remains the same as in part a.)

		Week												
		1	2	3	4	5	6	7	8	9	10	11	12	13
B Gross Requirements								200		100		300		
Scheduled Receipts														
Projected On Hand	100							100		0		0		
Net Requirements								100		100		300		
Planned Order Receipts								100		100		300		
Planned Order Releases						100		100		300				
C Gross Requirements								200	200	100	100	300		
Scheduled Receipts														
Projected On Hand	50							50		0		0		
Net Requirements								150	200	100	100	300		
Planned Order Receipts								150	200	100	100	300		
Planned Order Releases						150	200	100	100	300				

14.14 **(a)**

Level	Description	Qty
0	A	1
1	B	1
2	C	1
2	D	1
3	E	1
1	F	1
2	G	1
2	H	1
3	E	1
3	C	1

Note: with low-level coding "C" would be a level-3 code

(b) Solution for Items A, B, F (on next page):

14.14 (b)

Lot Size	Lead Time	On Hand	Safety Stock	Allo-cated	Low-Level Code	Item ID		Period (week) 1	2	3	4	5	6	7	8
Lot	1	0	—	—	0	A	Gross Requirement								10
for							Scheduled Receipt								
Lot							Projected On Hand								0
							Net Requirement								10
							Planned Receipt								10
							Planned Release							10	
Lot	1	2	—	—	1	B	Gross Requirement							10	
for							Scheduled Receipt								
Lot							Projected On Hand	2	2	2	2	2	2	2	0
							Net Requirement							8	
							Planned Receipt							8	
							Planned Release						8		
Lot	1	5	—	—	1	F	Gross Requirement							10	
for							Scheduled Receipt								
Lot							Projected On Hand	5	5	5	5	5	5	5	0
							Net Requirement							5	
							Planned Receipt							5	
							Planned Release						5		

14.16 (a) Only item G changes.
(b) Component F and 4 units of A will be delayed one week.
(c) Options include: delaying 4 units of A for 1 week; asking supplier of G to expedite production.

14.18 EOQ = 57; Total cost \$ = \$1,630

14.20 \$650

14.22 \$455

14.24 Selection for first 5 weeks:

Week	Units	Capacity Required (time)	Capacity Available (time)	Over/ (Under)	Production Scheduler's Action
1	60	3,900	2,250	1650	Lot split. Move 300 minutes (4.3 units) to week 2 and 1,350 minutes to week 3.
2	30	1,950	2,250	(300)	
3	10	650	2,250	(1,600)	
4	40	2,600	2,250	350	Lot split. Move 250 minutes to week 3. Operations split. Move 100 minutes to another machine, overtime, or subcontract.
5	70	4,550	2,250	2,300	Lot split. Move 1,600 minutes to week 6. Overlap operations to get product out door. Operations split. Move 700 minutes to another machine, overtime, or subcontract.

14.26 Here are the order releases for the table and the top:

Lot Size	Lead Time (# of periods)	On Hand	Safety Stock	Allo-cated	Low-Level Code	Item ID		Period (day) 1	2	3	4	5	6	7	8
Lot for Lot	1	—	—	—	0	Table	Gross Requirements					640	640	128	128
							Scheduled Receipts								
							Projected on Hand								
							Net Requirements					640	640	128	128
							Planned Order Receipts					640	640	128	128
							Planned Order Releases				640	640	128	128	
Lot for Lot	1	—	—	—	1	Top	Gross Requirements				640	640	128	128	
							Scheduled Receipts								
							Projected on Hand								
							Net Requirements				640	640	128	128	
							Planned Order Receipts				640	640	128	128	
							Planned Order Releases			640	640	128	128		

Chapter 15

15.2

Job	Day 1	Day 2	Day 3	Day 4	Day 5	Day 6	Day 7	Day 8	Day 9
D									
E									
F									
G									

Now

15.4 **(a)** 1–D, 2–A, 3–C, 4–B
(b) 40
15.6 Chris–Finance, Steve–Marketing, Juana–H.R., Rebecca–Operations, $210
15.8 Ajay–Jackie, Jack–Barbara, Gray–Stella, Raul–Dona, 230.
15.10 **(a)** A, B, C, D, E
(b) B, A, D, E, C
(c) E, D, A, B, C
(d) C, B, A, D, E
(e) SPT is best.
15.12 **(a)** A, B, C, D
(b) B, C, A, D
(c) D, A, C, B
(d) C, B, D, A
(e) D, C, A, B
SPT is best on all measures.
15.14 **(a)** A, B, C, D, E
(b) C, A, B, E, D
(c) C, D, E, A, B
(d) B, A, E, D, C
EDD, then FCFS are best on lateness; SPT on other two measures.
15.16 1, 3, 4, 2, 5
15.18 E, D, C, A, B, F
15.20 7 employees needed; 6 have two consecutive days off. The 7th works only 3 days/week.

Chapter 16

16.2 3.75, or 4 kanbans
16.4 Size of kanban = 66; number of kanbans = 5.9, or 6
16.6 **(a)** EOQ = 10 lamps
(b) 200 orders/yr.
(c) $200
16.8 7.26 min.
16.10 **(a)** Setup cost = $5.74
(b) Setup time = 8.61 min.

Chapter 17

17.2 From Figure 17.2, about 13% overall reliability.
17.4 Expected daily breakdowns = 2.0
Expected cost = $100 daily
17.6 **(a)** 5.0%
(b) .00001026 failures/unit-hr.
(c) .08985
(d) 98.83
17.8 $R_s = .9941$
17.10 $R_p = .99925$
17.12 **(a)** $R_p = .984$
(b) Increase by 11.1%.
17.14 $R = .7918$
17.16 **(a)** .972
(b) .980
17.18 System B is slightly higher, at .9397.

Online Tutorial 1

T1.2 5.45; 4.06
T1.4 **(a)** .2743;
(b) 0.5
T1.6 .1587; .2347; .1587
T1.8 **(a)** .0548;
(b) .6554;
(c) .6554;
(d) .2119

Online Tutorial 2

T2.2 (selected values)

Fraction Defective	Mean of Poisson	$P(x \le 1)$
.01	.05	.999
.05	.25	.974
.10	.50	.910
.30	1.50	.558
.60	3.00	.199
1.00	5.00	.040

T2.4 The plan meets neither the producer's nor the consumer's requirement.

Online Tutorial 3

T3.2 **(a)** $x_1 + 4x_2 + s_1 = 24$
$x_1 + 2x_2 + s_2 = 16$
(b) See the steps in the tutorial.
(c) Second tableau:

c_j	Mix	x_1	x_2	s_1	s_2	Qty.
9	x_2	.25	1	.25	0	6
0	s_2	.50	0	−.50	1	4
	z_j	2.25	9	2.25	0	54
	$c_j - z_j$	.75	0	−2.25	0	

(d) $x_1 = 8$, $x_2 = 4$, Profit = $60
T3.4 Basis for 1st tableau:
$A_1 = 80$
$A_2 = 75$
Basis for 2nd tableau:
$A_1 = 55$
$X_1 = 25$
Basis for 3rd tableau:
$X_1 = 14$
$X_2 = 33$
Cost = $221 at optimal solution
T3.6 **(a)** x_1
(b) A_1

Online Tutorial 4

T4.2 Cost = $980; 1–A = 20; 1–B = 50; 2–C = 20; 2–Dummy = 30; 3–A = 20; 3–C = 40
T4.4 Total = 3,100 mi.; Morgantown–Coaltown = 35; Youngstown–Coal Valley = 30; Youngstown–Coaltown = 5; Youngstown–Coal Junction = 25; Pittsburgh–Coaltown = 5; Pittsburgh–Coalsburg = 20

T4.6 **(a)** Using VAM, cost = 635; A–Y = 35; A–Z = 20; B–W = 10; B–X = 20; B–Y = 15; C–W = 30.
(b) Using MODI, cost is also 635 (i.e., initial solution was optimal). An alternative optimal solution is A–X = 20; A–Y = 15; A–Z = 20; B–W = 10; B–Y = 35; C–W = 30.

Online Tutorial 5

T5.2 **(a)** $I_{13} = 12$
(b) $I_{35} = 7$
(c) $I_{51} = 4$

T5.4 **(a)** Tour: 1–2–4–5–7–6–8–3–1; 37.9 mi.
(b) Tour: 4–5–7–1–2–3–6–8–4; 39.1 mi.

T5.6 **(a)** Vehicle 1: Tour 1–2–4–3–5–1 = $134
(b) Vehicle 2: Tour 1–6–10–9–8–7–1 = $188

T5.8 The cost matrix is shown below:

	1	2	3	4	5	6	7	8
1	—	107.26	118.11	113.20	116.50	123.50	111.88	111.88
2		—	113.53	111.88	118.10	125.30	116.50	118.10
3			—	110.56	118.70	120.50	119.90	124.90
4				—	109.90	119.10	111.88	117.90
5					—	111.88	106.60	118.50
6						—	111.88	123.50
7							—	113.20
8								—

Name Index

Note: Page numbers beginning with a T refer to the Online Tutorial chapters that appear on our website **www.pearsonhighered.com/heizer**.

General Index

Note: Page numbers beginning with a T refer to the Online Tutorial chapters that appear on our website **www.pearsonhighered.com/heizer**.

Photo Credits

CHAPTER 1: p. 2 (top): Andre Jenny/Alamy Images; p. 2 (bottom): Hard Rock Café; p. 3: Hard Rock Café; p. 9: From the Collections of Henry Ford Museum & Greenfield Village; p. 14: © Marc Asnin/CORBIS, all rights reserved; p. 17 (left): TEK Image/Photo Researchers, Inc.; p. 17 (right): John McLean/Photo Researchers, Inc.; p. 18: Siemens press picture, Courtesy of Siemens AG, Munich/Berlin; p. 22: Taras Vyshnya/Shutterstock.
CHAPTER 2: p. 28: Boeing Commerical Airplane Group; p. 29: Boeing Commercial Airplane Group; p. 31: © Disney Enterprises, Inc.; p. 33: Kraipit Phanvut/SIPA Press; p. 37: AP Wide World Photos; p. 44: Courtesy of American Honda Motor Co., Inc.; p. 44 (top middle): Julie Lucht/Shutterstock; p. 44 (bottom middle): Courtesy of www.HondaNews.com; p. 47 (left): Copyright © 1997 Komatsu Ltd. All rights reserved; p. 47 (right): Reprinted courtesy of Caterpillar Inc.; p. 48: © Michael Yamashita/CORBIS.
CHAPTER 3: p. 56 (left): © Bechtel Corporation; p. 56 (right): Q&A Photos, Ltd., www.qaphotos.com; p. 57: Bill Pogue/Getty Images Inc. —Stone Allstock; p. 57 (bottom right): Joe Cavaretta/AP Wide World Photos; p. 57 (bottom left): Thomas Hartwell/U.S. Agency for International Development (USAID); p. 62 (top): Getty Images, Inc.; p. 62 (bottom left): Jonathan Bailey Associates; p. 62 (bottom right): Courtesy of Jonathan Bailey Associates; p. 66: Jeffrey Allan Salter/Redux Pictures; p. 73: Hard Rock Café; p. 75: Paul Chesley/Getty Images Inc. —Stone Allstock; p. 82: Mai/Mai/Getty Images/Time Life Pictures; p. 84: David Young-Wolff/PhotoEdit Inc.; p. 93 (left): Markus Dlouhy/Peter Arnold, Inc.; p. 93 (right): Paramount/Dreamworks/Picture Desk, Inc./Kobal Collection.
CHAPTER 4: p. 102 (top): Kelly-Mooney Photography/CORBIS/© Disney Enterprises, Inc.; p. 102 (bottom): Jeff Greenberg/PhotoEdit, Inc./© Disney Enterprises, Inc.; p. 103: Peter Cosgrove/AP Wide World Photos/Disney characters © Disney Enterprises, Inc. Used by permission from Disney Enterprises, Inc.; p. 103 (top right): © Kevin Fleming/CORBIS, all rights reserved/Used by permission from Disney Enterprises, Inc.; p. 103 (bottom): Getty Images, Inc./Disney characters © Disney Enterprise, Inc. Used by permission from Disney Enterprises, Inc.; p. 106: Wikipedia, The Free Encyclopedia; p. 109: Fred Prouser/CORBIS-NY; p. 122: Courtesy of Yamaha Motor media; p. 129: ICI Paints; p. 135: Anton Vengo/SuperStock, Inc.; p. 136: Getty Images — Photodisc-Royalty Free; p. 141: Condor 36/Shutterstock; p. 144: Alan Copson/Photolibrary.com.
CHAPTER 5: p. 152: Regal Marine Industries, Inc.; p. 153: Regal Marine Industries, Inc.; p. 155 (left): John Acurso. NIKE and the Swoosh Design logo are trademarks of Nike, Inc. and its affiliates. Used by permission; p. 155 (middle): © FranAois Grelet/Michelin/Newscom; p. 155 (right): Dutch Boy Paints/Sherwin Williams; p. 164 (left): Maximilian Stock LTD/Phototake NYC; p. 164 (middle): Courtesy of Silicon Graphics, Inc.; p. 164 (right): Maximilian Stock LTD/Phototake NYC; p. 165: Courtesy 3D Systems; p. 166: BMW of North America, LLC; p. 168 (left): Dainis Derics/Shutterstock; p. 168 (right): Eugene Hoshiko/AP Wide World Photos; p. 171: David Murray © Dorling Kindersley; p. 174 (left): J.R. Simplot Company; p. 174 (right): David R. Frazier/David R. Frazier Photolibrary, Inc.; p. 179: Nikolay Stefanvo Dimitrov/Shutterstock; p. 181: Maximillian Stock LTD/Phototake NYC.
CHAPTER 6: p. 188: Jonathan Bailey Associates; p. 189 (top): Courtesy of Cardinal Health; p. 189 (middle and bottom): Jonathan Bailey Associates; p. 194: Courtesy of Subaru of Indiana Automotive, Inc. p. 197: TRW Automotive; p. 198: Clive Mason/Allsport Concepts/Getty Images; p. 205: Ralf-Finn Hestoft/CORBIS-NY; p. 206 (left): Jonathan Nourok/PhotoEdit, Inc.; p. 206 (right): © David Joel/Getty Images; p. 207: Ann States Photography; p. 211: Christophe Testi/Shutterstock.
SUPPLEMENT 6: p. 218: Courtesy of BetzDearborn, A Division of Hercules Incorporated; p. 227 (left): Donna McWilliam/AP Wide World Photos; p. 227 (right): Richard Pasley Photography; p. 229: © Charles O'Rear/CORBIS, all rights reserved; p. 233: Georgia Institute of Technology; p. 241: Corbis RF.
CHAPTER 7: p. 250: © Igor Lubnevskiy/Alamy; p. 251 (top left): Courtesy of Harley-Davidson; page 251 (bottom right): Catherine Karnow/Woodfin Camp & Associates, Inc.; p. 251 (top right): Dave Bartruff/Stock Boston; p. 251 (bottom left): Steven Rubin/The Image Works; p. 253 (left): Brasiliao/Shutterstock; p. 253 (middle, left): 300 dpi/Shutterstock; p. 253 (middle, right): Tund/Shutterstock; p. 253: (right): Archman/Shutterstock; p. 264: Courtesy of aligntech.com; p. 267: Courtesy of Anheuser-Busch, Inc.; p. 269 (top left): Getty Images, Inc. — Stone Allstock; p. 269 (top right): G2 Classic, Gensym Corporation; p. 269 (middle left): Ron Sully/Omnica Corporation; p. 269 (bottom middle): Tate Carlson/Stockphoto.com; p. 269 (bottom right): iStockphoto.com; p. 269 (bottom left): Courtesy of Diamond Phoenix Corporation; p. 271 (left): Kruell/laif/Redux Pictures; p. 271 (right): Courtesy of RF Technologies, Inc.; p. 273: © John Rodriguez/iStockphoto.com; p. 275: Eric Limon/Shutterstock.
SUPPLEMENT 7: p. 282: John Garrett/Getty Images, Inc.-Stone Allstock; p. 286: Chitose Suzuki/AP Wide World Photos; p. 287 (left): © Bob Krist/CORBIS; p. 287 (right): Michelangelo Gisone/AP Wide World Photos; p. 288: © Lester Lefkowitz/CORBIS, all rights reserved; p. 294: Getty Images; p. 295: Jupiter Images Royalty Free; p. 305: Corbis RF.
CHAPTER 8: p. 312 (top): Chris Sorensen Photography; p. 312 (bottom): AP Wide World Photos; p. 313 (top): Jon Riley/Southern Stock/Photolibrary.com; p. 313 (middle): Matt York/AP Wide World Photos; p. 313 (bottom): Shi Li/shzq/ImagineChina.com; p. 317: Allen Tannenbaum; p. 325 (left): Monica Lewis/True Bethel Baptist Church; p. 325 (right): Courtesy of Jay Heizer; p. 327: MayInfo Corporation; p. 332: Andrea Catenaro Doherty/Shutterstock; p. 335: David Buffington/Getty Images, Inc.-Photodisc/Royalty Free.
CHAPTER 9: p. 342: Rick Wiliking/CORBIS-NY; p. 343: Callie Lipkin Photography, Inc. p. 343 (top): Nancy Siesel/NYT Pictures; p. 345: Chuck Keeler/Getty Images, Inc. —Stone Allstock; p. 348 (top): Courtesy of walmartfacts.com/www.walmartfacts.com/articles/4939.aspx; p. 348 (bottom): Courtesy of Hard Rock Café; p. 349: Fabian Bimmer/AP Wide World Photos; p. 351 (top): Craig Ruttle/AP Wide World Photos; p. 351 (middle): Dick Blume/The Image Works; p. 351 (bottom): CORBIS-NY; p. 356: UGS; p. 362: Boeing Commercial Airplane Group; p. 365: Cary Wolinsky/Stock Boston; p. 366: David Young-Wolff/PhotoEdit, Inc.; p. 375: T. Matsumoto/CORBIS-NY; p. 377: Jonathan Bailey Associates.
CHAPTER 10: p. 382: John Raoux/The Orlando Sentinel; p. 388 (left): Pam Francis/Southwest Airlines Co.: p. 388 (right): Courtesy of Southwest Airlines; p. 390 (top): Andy Freeberg Photography; p. 390 (bottom): Scott Hirko/iStockphoto.com; p. 391 (left): Chad Ehlers/Stock Connection; page 391 (right): © NUFEA/Boeing; p. 396 (top): AP Wide World Photos; p. 396 (bottom): Tony Freeman/PhotoEdit Inc.; p. 399: Laubrass, Inc.; p. 401: F. Hoffmann/The Images Works; p. 403: Samuel Ashfield/Photo Researchers, Inc.; p. 407: Mark Winfrey/Shutterstock; p. 410: Lynn Goldsmith/CORBIS-NY; p. 411: www.comstock.com.
CHAPTER 11: p. 418: Courtesy of Darden Corporation: p. 419: Courtesy of Darden Corporation; pp. 420 and 494 (top left): Bill Stormont/CORBIS-NY; p. 420 (top middle): Susan Van Etten/PhotoEdit Inc.; p. 420 (middle bottom): David de Lossy, Ghislain & Marie/Getty Images Inc. —Image Bank; p. 420 (middle): Getty Images/Digial Vision; p. 420 (middle): Michael Newman/PhotoEdit Inc.; p. 420 (top right): Jose Manuel Riberio, REUTERS/CORBIS-NY; p. 420 (middle right): Peter Byron/PhotoEdit Inc.; p. 420 (bottom right): Richard Levine/Alamy.com; p. 422: Courtesy of Jackson & Perkins; p. 432: Courtesy of Ariba, Inc.; p. 435: South Carolina State Port Authority; p. 436: Francesco Broli; p. 437: Courtesy of Federal Express Corporation; p. 441: Spencer Tirey/AP Wide World Photos; p. 443: Thomas Raupach/Peter Arnold, Inc.
SUPPLEMENT 11: p. 450: Keith Dannemiller/Alamy Images; p. 453: NASA/Associated Press; p. 454: © Sherwin Crasto/Reuters/CORBIS, all rights reserved; p. 456: A. Ramey/PhotoEdit Inc.
CHAPTER 12: p. 466 (top): Marilyn Newton; p. 466 (middle and bottom): David Burnett/Contact Press Images, Inc.; p. 467 (top): David Burnett/Contact Press Images, Inc.; p. 467 (bottom): Contact Press Images, Inc.; p. 468: Anna Sheveleva/Shutterstock; p. 472: Courtesy of Deere & Company, Moline, IL, USA; p. 473: McKesson Corporation; p. 479: AP Wide World Photos; p. 482: Telegraph Colour Library/Lester Lefkowitz/Getty Images, Inc. —Taxi; p. 484: Anthony Labbe Photography; p. 494: Richard Levine/Alamy.com; p. 495: Steve Dunwell/Getty Images Inc. —Image Bank.
CHAPTER 13: p. 513: Courtesy of Simplicity Manufacturing, Inc.; p. 515 (top left) Getty Images —Stockbyte, Royalty Free; p. 515 (top right): Courtesy of OSA (National Organization for Automotive Safety and Victim's Aid). Copyright 2003. All rights reserved. Reprinted with permission; p. 515 (left bottom): Ron Sherman/Creative Eye/MIRA.com; p. 515 (middle right): Mark Richards/PhotoEdit Inc.; p. 515 (middle right): Michael Newman/PhotoEdit Inc.; p. 515 (bottom right): GmbH & Co. KG/Alamy Images; p. 516: John Deere & Company; p. 525: Greg Foster/Gregory Foster, Inc.; p. 528: Getty Images; p. 535: Bobby Deal/Shutterstock; p. 537: Fernando Sanchez.
CHAPTER 14: p. 544 (left): Collins Industries, Inc.; p. 544 (right): Wheeled Coach Industries Incorporated; p. 545 (left): Wheeled Coach Industries Incorporated; p. 545 (right): Collins Industries, Inc.; p. 558: John Russell/AP Wide World Photos: p. 561: Courtesy of User Solutions, Inc.

CHAPTER 15: p. 582: Courtesy of Delta Air Lines; p. 583 (top left): Mike Segar/CORBIS-NY; p. 583 (bottom): Etienne de Malglaive/ZUMA Press-Gamma; p. 583 (top right): AP Wide World Photos; p. 585 (top): Michael Newman/Photo Edit Inc.; p. 585 (bottom): Peter Endig/Landov Media; p. 586: Tom Carroll/Phototake NYC; p. 593: PCN Photography; p. 597: Charles Gupton/Charles Gupton Photography; p. 602: Patricia McDonnell/AP Wide World Photos; p. 603: (c) Courtesy of Choice Hotels International; p. 606: Marcel Mooij/Shutterstock; p. 612: Dana Fisher/AP Wide World Photos; p. 613: Ann Prival/Omni-Photo Communications, Inc.

CHAPTER 16: p. 621: © Bob Daemmrich/CORBIS, all rights reserved; p. 624: © Culinary Institute of America; p. 626: Cessna Aircraft Company; p. 632: Donna Shader; p. 635: New United Motor Manufacturing, Inc. (NUMMI); p. 636: Gerardo Burgos Galindo/Shutterstock; p. 637: Colin Young-Wolff/PhotoEdit Inc.; p. 638: Courtesy of Cardinal Health, Inc.; p. 640: Green Gear Cycling, Inc.

CHAPTER 17: p. 648: Orlando Utilities Commission; p. 649: Orlando Utilities Commission; p. 661: PHT/Photo Researchers, Inc.